MACMILLAN
COMPENDIUM

The Supreme Court

MACMILLAN
COMPENDIUM

The Supreme Court

SELECTIONS FROM THE FOUR-VOLUME

Encyclopedia of the American Constitution and Supplement

Philip Weinberg

Editor in Chief

MACMILLAN LIBRARY REFERENCE USA

New York

Interior Design by Kevin Hanek
Jacket Design by Judy Kahn

Macmillan Library Reference USA
1633 Broadway, 7th Floor
New York, NY 10019

Manufactured in the United States of America

Printing number
1 2 3 4 5 6 7 8 9 10

ISBN: 0-02-865369-6
LC #: 99-22507

Library of Congress Cataloging-in-Publication Data

The Supreme Court : selections from the four-volume Encyclopedia
    of the American Constitution and supplement.
      Encyclopedia of the American Constitution.   Selections.
        p.   cm. — (Macmillan compendium)
      Includes bibliographical references and index.
      ISBN 0-02-865369-6 (hardcover : alk. paper)
      1. United States.   Supreme Court—Encyclopedias.
    2. Constitutional law—United States—Encyclopedias.   I. Title.
    II. Series.
      KF8742.E53   1999
    347.73'26—dc21   99-22507
                                                            CIP

This paper meets the requirements of ANSI/NISO Z39.48-1992 (Permanence of Paper).

Table of Contents

Table of Contents

Table of Contents

Table of Contents

Preface

ORIGINS

The Judicial Power of the United States shall be vested in one supreme Court.

Article III, section 1
United States Constitution

To commemorate the bicentennial of the Constitutional Convention in 1987, Macmillan Reference published the prestigious *Encyclopedia of the American Constitution* to tremendous critical success. It was enhanced and updated by a supplementary volume in 1991. The *Encyclopedia* encompasses five general categories: doctrinal concepts of constitutional law, public acts such as statutes, treaties, and executive orders, historical periods, and people and judicial decisions of the Supreme Court. For years, students, library patrons, attorneys, and historians have indicated a need for a single-volume version of the award-winning *Encyclopedia of the American Constitution*, especially one that concentrates on the cases and personnel of the Supreme Court. *The Supreme Court Compendium* is designed to fulfill that need

The Supreme Court retains the alphabetical structure and chronological sweep of the classic selected cases and articles that represent the essential decisions of the Supreme Court in order to meet the needs of most students, library patrons, and researchers.

FEATURES

To add visual appeal and enhance the usefulness of the volume, the page format was designed to include the following helpful features.

- **Call-out Quotations:** These relevant, often provocative quotations are highlighted in the margins to promote exploration and add visual appeal to the page.

- **Cross-references:** Appearing at the base of many margins, "See also" cross-references cite related articles to encourage further research.
- **Definitions:** Brief definitions of important terms in the main text can also be found the margins.
- **Sidebars:** Appearing in a gray box, these provocative asides relate to the text and amplify topics or highlight short but important cases.
- **Index:** A thorough index provides thousands of additional points of entry into the work.

ACKNOWLEDGMENTS

The Supreme Court contains over one hundred illustrations. Acknowledgments of sources for illustrations can be found within the illustration captions.

The articles herein, selected by Philip Weinberg of St. John's University, were written for *The Encyclopedia of the American Constitution* and its one-volume Supplement by leading authorities at work in history, law, and political science. The opinions expressed therein are the contributors' own. *The Encyclopedia of the American Constitution* was edited by Leonard W. Levy of the Claremont Graduate School, Kenneth L. Karst of the University of California, Los Angeles, and Dennis J. Mahoney and John G. West also of Claremont Graduate School.

We are grateful to all of these scholars and experts for their contributions to these important reference works. We would also like to thank the in-house staff whose hard work and creativity made this book possible.

Editorial Staff
Macmillan Library Reference

A

ABINGTON TOWNSHIP SCHOOL DISTRICT v. SCHEMPP

374 U.S. 203 (1963)

A Pennsylvania statute required that at least ten verses from the Holy Bible be read, without comment, at the opening of each public school day. A child might be excused from this exercise upon the written request of his parents or guardian.

In *Engel* v. *Vitale* (1962) the school prayer held unconstitutional had been written by state officials. The question in *Schempp* was whether this made a difference—there being no claim that Pennsylvania was implicated in the authorship of the holy scripture.

Justice Tom C. Clark concluded that the Pennsylvania exercise suffered from an establishment-clause infirmity every bit as grave as that afflicting New York's prayer. Clark's opinion in *Schempp* was the first strict separationist opinion of the Court not written by Justice Hugo L. Black, and Clark formulated a test for establishment clause validity with a precision that had eluded Black. A state program touching upon religion or religious institutions must have a valid secular purpose and must not have the primary effect of advancing or inhibiting religion. The Pennsylvania Bible reading program failed the test on both counts.

Justices William O. Douglas and William J. Brennan concurred separately in opinions reflecting an even stricter separationism than Clark's. Justice Arthur J. Goldberg also filed a brief concurring opinion.

Justice Potter Stewart dissented, as he had in *Engel,* arguing that religious exercises as part of public ceremonies were permissible so long as children were not coerced to participate.

Schempp, along with *Murray* v. *Curlett* (decided the same day), settled whatever lingering question there may have been about the constitutionality of religion in public schools.

—RICHARD E. MORGAN

ABLEMAN v. BOOTH

21 Howard 506 (1859)

Ableman v. *Booth,* Chief Justice Roger B. Taney's last major opinion, was part of the dramatic confrontation between the Wisconsin Supreme Court, intent on judicial nullification of the Fugitive Slave Acts, and the Supreme Court of the United States, seeking to protect the reach of that statute into the free states.

For his role in organizing a mob that freed Joshua Glover, an alleged fugitive, Sherman Booth was charged with violation of the Fugitive Slave Act of 1850. After trial and conviction, he was released by a writ of habeas corpus from the Wisconsin Supreme Court, which held the Fugitive Slave Act unconstitutional, the first instance in which a state court did so. The Wisconsin court instructed its clerk to make no return to a writ of error from the United States Supreme Court and no entry on the records of the court concerning that writ, thus defying the United States Supreme Court.

The Court took jurisdiction despite the procedural irregularity. In a magisterial opinion for a unanimous Court, Taney condemned the obstruction of the Wisconsin court and reaffirmed federal judicial supremacy under

> Schempp *settled whatever lingering question there may have been about the constitutionality of religion in public schools.*

See also

Engel v. *Vitale*

Establishment Clause

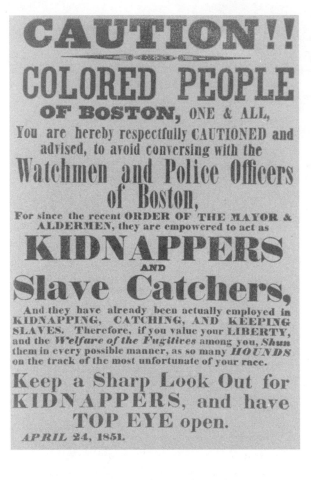

ON THE RUN

An 1851 poster warns fugitive slaves of the dangers of kidnappers and slave catchers. (Corbis)

For his role in organizing a mob that freed alleged fugitive Joshua Glover, Sherman Booth was charged with violation of the Fugitive Slave Act of 1850.

See also

Judicial Supremacy

section 25 of the Judiciary Act of 1789. Because the state's sovereignty "is limited and restricted by the Constitution of the United States," no state court process, including habeas corpus, could interfere with the enforcement of federal law. Taney also delivered two significant dicta. He anticipated the later doctrine of dual sovereignty, which was to hamper state and federal regulatory authority in the early twentieth century, when he wrote that though the powers of the state and federal governments are exercised within the same territorial limits, they "are yet separate and distinct sovereignties, acting separately and independently of each other, within their respective spheres." Taney concluded his opinion by declaring the Fugitive Slave Act of 1850 to be "in all of its provisions, fully authorized by the Constitution."

A reconstituted Wisconsin Supreme Court later conceded the validity of Taney's interpretation of section 25 and apologized to the United States Supreme Court, conceding that its earlier actions were "a breach of that comity, or good behavior, which should be maintained between the courts of the two governments."

—WILLIAM M. WIECEK

ABOOD v. DETROIT BOARD OF EDUCATION

431 U.S. 209 (1977)

Abood is one of the cases where union or agency shop agreements create speech and association problems, because individuals must join unions in order to hold jobs and then must pay dues to support union activities with which the individuals may not agree. Here the union represented public employees. The Supreme Court has consistently held that there is no right *not* to associate in a labor union for the purposes of collective bargaining but that a union must develop methods of relieving a member of those portions of union dues devoted to union ideological activities to which he objects.

—MARTIN SHAPIRO

ABORTION AND THE CONSTITUTION

With President Ronald Reagan's elevation of Justice William H. Rehnquist to Chief Justice and his appointment of Justices Antonin Scalia and Anthony M. Kennedy, many expected the Supreme Court to revisit its decision in *Roe* v. *Wade* (1973), which struck down laws against abortion. Tension mounted when the Supreme Court noted probable jurisdiction in *Webster* v. *Reproductive Health Services* (1989). Relying on *Roe*, the lower court in *Webster* had held unconstitutional several provisions of a Missouri statute regulating abortions, including a statement from its preamble that human life begins at conception, a requirement that the aborting physician perform a viability test when he or she has reason to believe the woman is at least twenty weeks' pregnant, and a prohibition on the use of public employees or public facilities to perform an abortion that is not necessary to save the mother's life. In its appeal, Missouri, joined by the Department of Justice as amicus curiae, argued not only that the invalidated provisions should be upheld under *Roe* and the Court's subsequent abortion cases but, more significantly, that *Roe* itself should be overruled.

Without passing on the constitutional validity of all the statutory provisions that had been challenged, the Court, in a 5–4 decision, reversed the lower court and gave the pro-life movement its first major legal victory since *Roe* was decided. Whether *Webster* will prove a truly significant victory for this movement, however, remains to be seen. First and most encouraging for pro-choice advocates, the Court once again found no occasion to revisit *Roe*'s controversial conclusion that the right to an abortion is protected by the Constitution's due process clauses. Second, although the Court's judgment of reversal garnered majority support, portions of Chief Justice Rehnquist's opinion did not obtain five votes. Particularly noteworthy was Justice Sandra Day O'Connor's refusal to join important sections of the opinion. Third, the extraordinary media publicity surrounding *Webster* may have contributed to exaggerated perceptions by both sides of what the Court actually held.

In upholding Missouri's restriction on the use of public employees or facilities to perform abortions, the *Webster* majority relied on the Court's previous abortion-funding cases. The Court emphasized, as it had done before, that as long as the states do not actually restrict the abortion decision, the Constitution allows them to make the value judgment that childbirth is preferable to abortion. In denying the use of public employees and facilities for abortions, Missouri did not place

any obstacles in the path of women who choose to have an abortion; that is, Missouri's restriction left pregnant women with the same choices they would have had if the state had not chosen to operate public hospitals at all. In short, although the Constitution, as interpreted by *Roe,* may not allow the states to prohibit abortions, it does not give either doctors or women a right of access to public facilities for the performance of abortions.

Many pro-choice commentators have criticized this aspect of the Court's holding in *Webster* because of its alleged effect on the availability of abortions for certain women. The Court's task, however, was to decide not whether Missouri made a wise or good policy choice but whether anything in the Constitution invalidated the choice that Missouri made through its democratic process. Viewed in this light, *Webster* and the previous abortion-funding cases are consistent with prevailing constitutional doctrine. Few would argue, for example, that because the state may not prohibit parents from sending their children to private schools, the state must fund private education for those parents who cannot afford it.

The statute's viability-testing requirement gave the Court more difficulty. The section of Chief Justice Rehnquist's opinion regarding this requirement, which was joined by only two other Justices, said that the constitutionality of the viability-testing requirement was called into doubt by the rigid trimester system established in *Roe* and followed in the Court's other abortion cases. The Chief Justice reached this conclusion because mandatory testing when the physician reasonably believes the pregnancy is at least in the twentieth week may impose burdens on second-trimester abortions involving fetuses who have not yet become viable. Taking the position that stare decisis has less force in constitutional law than elsewhere, the plurality then abandoned *Roe*'s trimester framework as unsound in principle and unworkable in practice.

See also

Freedom of Speech

Labor and Employment Law

The plurality emphasized that the concepts of trimesters and viability are not found in the Constitution's text or in any other place one might expect to find a constitutional principle, thus describing the Court's previous holdings as resembling an intricate code of regulations more than a body of constitutional doctrine. The plurality also questioned why the state's interest in protecting potential human life should come into existence only at the point of viability. Finally, eschewing strict scrutiny, the plurality upheld Missouri's testing requirement by concluding that it permissibly furthers the state's legitimate interest in protecting potential life. Without otherwise purporting to disturb *Roe,* the plurality thus modified and narrowed it.

Justice Harry A. Blackmun, the author of *Roe,* wrote a stinging dissent contending that *Roe* could not survive the plurality's analysis. Justice Scalia wrote a concurring opinion agreeing with Justice Blackmun that the plurality's analysis effectively would overrule *Roe,* something he was prepared to do explicitly. Nevertheless, a majority of the Court did not accept Justice Scalia's invitation.

Three years after *Webster* the Court, in *Planned Parenthood of Southeastern Pennsylvania* v. *Casey* (1992), unequivocally reaffirmed the "essential holding" of *Roe* v. *Wade.* Justices O'Connor, Kennedy, and Souter held it would be inappropriate to overrule *Roe,* citing the reliance on the right enunciated in that decision to "the availability of abortion in the event that contraception should fail." These justices emphasized the importance of adhering to Supreme Court precedent. They distinguished the two prime examples of dramatic reversals of precedent by the Court in recent decades: the rejection of the *Lochner* v. *New York* view that the due process clause circumscribes laws regulating wages, hours of work, prices, and other economic issues, and the overturning of the infamous separate-but-equal doctrine embodied in Plessy v. *Ferguson,* which attempted to rationalize racial segregation. These shifts in direction, they maintained, were plainly warranted by shifts in "facts, or an understanding of facts," and were "applications of constitutional principle to facts as they had not been seen by the Court before." Nothing of the sort, the Justices believed, had occurred that would warrant overruling *Roe.*

However, the Court in *Casey* did hold that the proper test in the abortion area should be whether government had placed an "undue burden" on the ability to obtain an abortion. This somewhat reduced the applicable standard from the strict scrutiny prescribed by *Roe* that required any law restricting abrtion to be narrowly tailored to serve a compelling government interest. This constituted a significant advance for opponents of *Roe* despite the Court's reaffirmation of *Roe*'s holding.

In addition, the Court in *Casey* sustained most of Pennsylvania's statutory limits on abortion. It upheld requirements that women seeking abortions be informed as to the health risks of the procedure and the "probable gestational age of the unborn child," as well as information about medical assistance for childbirth and about adoption. The Court also sustained a twenty-four-hour waiting period before abortions could be performed. Both these provisions excepted "medical emergencies," defined by the courts to encompass situations that "pose a significant threat to the life or health of a woman."

But the Court overturned a state law requiring the husband's consent to the abortion, except in emergencies and in cases where notifying the husband would likely result in bodily injury. It held that the state failed to consider the impact of psychological abuse, threats of financial retaliation, and the like, and that in any event that provision "embodies a view of marriage . . . repugnant to our present understanding of marriage and of the nature of the rights secured by the Constitution."

Finally, the Court rejected the trimester framework of *Roe*, holding that "the State's profound interest in potential life" justifies measures to advance that interest throughout a pregnancy.

Justices Stevens and Blackmun (the author of the *Roe* decision) concurred in the reaffirmance of *Roe* and the overturning of the spousal consent requirement, but dissented from the Court's upholding of the other restrictions. Justice Blackmun in particular defended the trimester framework of *Roe*. Chief Justice Rehnquist and Justices White, Scalia, and Thomas, conversely, concurred in the sustaining of the informational and twenty-four-hour waiting period provisions and dissented from the rest, arguing, as they had in *Webster*, that "*Roe* was wrongly decided."

Thus a narrow majority preserved the essence of the *Roe* decision, although expanding the right of the states to limit abortion in some respects, with the introductory remarks of Justices O'Connor, Kennedy, and Souter providing an explanation for their adherence to *Roe* and reluctance to overrule it.

—JOSEPH D. GRANO

Bibliography

Bopp, James, Jr. (1989). Will There Be a Constitutional Right to Abortion After Reconsideration of *Roe v. Wade? Journal of Contemporary Law* 15:131–173.

Bork, Robert J. (1989). *The Tempting of America,* pages 110–116. New York: Free Press.

Farber, Daniel (1989). Abortion After *Webster. Constitutional Commentary* 6:225–230.

Glendon, Mary Ann (1987). *Abortion and Divorce in Western Law.* Cambridge, Mass.: Harvard University Press.

Grano, Joseph (1981). Judicial Review and a Written Constitution in a Democratic Society. *Wayne Law Review* 28:1–75.

Hirshman, Linda (1988). Bronte, Bloom and Bork: An Essay on the Moral Education

Despite antiabortion protests, the Court has continued to uphold the validity of Roe v. Wade. *(Corbis/Bettmann)*

of Judges. *University of Pennsylvania Law Review* 137:177–231.

Loewy, Arnold (1989). Why *Roe v. Wade* Should Be Overruled. *North Carolina Law Review* 67:939–948.

Noonan, John (1984). The Root and Branch of *Roe v. Wade*. *Nebraska Law Review* 63: 668–679.

ABRAMS v. UNITED STATES

250 U.S. 616 (1919)

In *Schenck* v. *United States* (1919) Justice Oliver Wendell Holmes introduced the clear and present danger test in upholding the conviction under the Espionage Act of a defendant who had mailed circulars opposing military conscription. Only nine months later, in very similar circumstances, the Supreme Court upheld an Espionage Act conviction and Holmes and Louis D. Brandeis offered the danger test in dissent. *Abrams* is famous for Holmes's dissent, which became a classic libertarian pronouncement.

Abrams and three others distributed revolutionary circulars that included calls for a general strike, special appeals to workers in ammunitions factories, and language suggesting armed disturbances as the best means of protecting the Russian revolution against American intervention. These circulars had appeared while the United States was still engaged against the Germans in World War I. Their immediate occasion was the dispatch of an American expeditionary force to Russia at the time of the Russian revolution. The majority reasoned that, whatever their particular occasion, the circulars' purpose was that of hampering the general war effort. Having concluded that "the language of these circulars was obviously intended to provoke and to encourage resistance to the United States in the war" and that they urged munitions workers to strike for the purpose of curtailing

the production of war materials, the opinion upheld the convictions without actually addressing any constitutional question. The majority obviously believed that the Espionage Act might constitutionally be applied to speech intended to obstruct the war effort.

Justice Holmes mixed a number of elements in his dissent, and the mixture has bedeviled subsequent commentary. Although it is not clear whether Holmes was focusing on the specific language of the Espionage Act or arguing a more general constitutional standard, his central argument was that speech may not be punished unless it constitutes an attempt at some unlawful act; an essential element in such an attempt must be a specific intent on the part of the speaker to bring about the unlawful act. He did not read the circulars in evidence or the actions of their publishers as showing the specific intent to interfere with the war effort against Germany that would be required to constitute a violation of the Espionage Act.

His *Abrams* opinion shows the extent to which Holmes's invention of the danger rule was a derivation of his thinking about the role of specific intent and surrounding circumstances in the law of attempts. For in the midst of his discussion of specific intent he wrote, "I do not doubt . . . that by the same reasoning that would justify punishing persuasion to murder, the United States constitutionally may punish speech that produces or is intended to produce a clear and imminent danger that it will bring about forthwith certain substantive evils that the United States constitutionally may seek to prevent. . . . It is only the present danger of immediate evil or an intent to bring it about that warrants Congress in setting a limit to the expression of opinion. . . ."

Over time, however, what has survived from Holmes's opinion is not so much the specific intent argument as the more general impression that the "poor and puny anonymities" of the circulars could not possibly have constituted a clear and present danger to the war effort. At least in contexts such as that presented in *Abrams,* the clear and present danger test seems to be a good means of unmasking and constitutionally invalidating prosecutions because of the ideas we hate, when the precautions are undertaken not because the ideas constitute any real danger to our security but simply because we hate them. Although the specific intent aspect of the *Abrams* opinion has subsequently been invoked in a number of cases, particularly those involving membership in the Communist party, the *Abrams* dissent has typically been cited along with *Schenck* as the basic authority for the more general version of the clear and present danger standard that became the dominant freedom of speech doctrine during the 1940s and has since led a checkered career.

Justice Holmes also argued in *Abrams* that the common law of seditious libel has not survived in the United States; the Supreme Court finally adopted that position in *New York Times* v. *Sullivan* (1964).

The concluding paragraph of the *Abrams* dissent has often been invoked by those who wish to make of Holmes a patron saint of the libertarian movement.

Persecution for the expression of opinions seems to me perfectly logical . . . but when men have realized that time has upset many fighting faiths, they may come to believe even more the very foundations of their own conduct that the ultimate good desired is better reached by free trade in ideas—that the best test of truth is the power of the thought to get itself accepted in the competition of the market, and that truth is the only ground upon which their wishes safely can be carried out. That at any rate is the theory of our Constitution. It is an experiment, as all life is an experiment. Every year if not every day we have

ABRAMS v. UNITED STATES

250 U.S. 616 (1919)

See also

New York Times v. *Sullivan*

Schenck v. *United States*

ADAMSON v. CALIFORNIA

332 U.S. 46 (1947)

By a 5-4 vote the Supreme Court, speaking through Justice Stanley F. Reed, sustained the constitutionality of provisions of California laws permitting the trial court and prosecutor to call the jury's attention to the accused's failure to explain or deny evidence against him. Adamson argued that the Fifth Amendment's right against self-incrimination is a fundamental national privilege protected against state abridgment by the Fourteenth Amendment and that the same amendment's due process clause prevented comment on the accused's silence. Reed, relying on *Twining* v. *New Jersey* (1908) and *Palko* v. *Connecticut* (1937), ruled that the Fifth Amendment does not apply to the states and that even adverse comment on the right to silence does not deny due process.

The case is notable less for Reed's opinion, which *Griffin* v. *California* (1965) overruled, than for the classic debate between Justices Felix Frankfurter, concurring, and Hugo L. Black, in dissent, on the incorporation doctrine. Joined by Justice William O. Douglas, Black read the history of the origins of the Fourteenth Amendment to mean that its framers and ratifiers intended to make the entire Bill of Rights applicable to the states, a position that Justice Frank Murphy, joined by Justice Wiley Rutledge, surpassed by adding that the Fourteenth Amendment also protected unenumerated rights. Frankfurter, seeking to expose the inconsistency of the dissenters, suggested that they did not mean what they said. They would not fasten on the states the requirement of the Seventh Amendment that civil cases involving more than $20 require a trial by jury. They really intended only a "selective incorporation," Frankfurter declared, and consequently they offered "a merely subjective test." Black, in turn, purporting to be quite literal in his interpretation, ridiculed Frankfurter's subjective reliance on "civilized decency" to explain due process. History probably supports Frankfurter's argument on the original intent of the Fourteenth Amendment, but the Justices on both sides mangled the little historical evidence they knew to make it support preconceived positions.

—LEONARD W. LEVY

See also

Palko v. *Connecticut*

to wager our salvation upon some prophecy based upon imperfect knowledge. While that experiment is part of our system I think that we should be eternally vigilant against attempts to check the expression of opinions that we loathe and believe to be fraught with death, unless they so imminently threaten immediate interference with the lawful and pressing purposes of the law that an immediate check is required to save the country. . . . Only the emergency that makes it immediately dangerous to leave the correction of evil counsels to time warrants making any exception to the sweeping command, "Congress shall make no law . . . abridging the freedom of speech."

Sensitized by the destructive powers of such "fighting faiths" as fascism and communism, subsequent commentators have criticized the muscular, relativistic pragmatism of this pronouncement as at best an inadequate philosophic basis for the libertarian position and at worst an invitation to totalitarianism. The ultimate problem is, of course, what is to be done if a political faith that proposes the termination of freedom of speech momentarily wins the competition in the marketplace of ideas and then shuts down the market. Alternatively it has been argued that Holmes's clear and present danger approach in *Abrams* was basically conditioned by his perception of the ineffectualness of leftist revolutionary rhetoric in the American context of his day. In this view, he was saying no more than that deviant ideas must be tolerated until there is a substantial risk that a large number of Americans will listen to them. The clear and present danger test is often criticized for withdrawing protection of political speech at just the point when the speech threatens to become effective. Other commentators have argued that no matter how persuasive Holmes's comments may be in context, the clear and present danger approach ought not to be uncritically accepted as the single free-

dom of speech test, uniformly applied to speech situations quite different from those in *Abrams*. Perhaps the most telling criticism of the Holmes approach is that it vests enormous discretion in the judge, for ultimately it depends on the judge's prediction of what will happen rather than on findings of what has happened. Subsequent decisions such as that in *Feiner* v. *New York* (1951) showed that judges less brave than Holmes or less contemptuously tolerant of dissident ideas, might be quicker to imagine danger. However, in *Brandenburg* v. *Ohio* (1969), the Court unanimously reaffirmed that advocacy of force is protected by the First Amendment except when it amounts to "inciting or producing imminent lawless action and is likely to incite or produce such action."

—MARTIN SHAPIRO

Bibliography

Chafee, Zechariah (1941). *Free Speech in the United States.* Cambridge, Mass.: Harvard University Press.

ADARAND CONSTRUCTORS, INC. v. PENA

515 U.S. 200 (1995)

This major decision definitively holds that affirmative action programs must undergo strict scrutiny in order not to be violative of the Equal Protection Clause. Earlier rulings such as *Regents of University of California* v. *Bakke* had left his question unresolved. In *Richmond (City of)* v. *J. A. Croson Co.* in 1989 the Court ruled that affirmative action requirements by state and local governments must meet this stringent test, which requires the government to show the provision is narrowly tailored to serve a compelling state interest. However, other decisions, such as *Fullilove* v. *Klutznick and Metro Broadcasting, Inc.* v. *Federal Com-*

munications Commission* (1990), had left unclear whether federal (as opposed to state or local) affirmative action provisions had to meet that standard. *Metro*, in fact, held by a 5–4 margin that a lower degree of scrutiny would suffice. *Adarand* reached the opposite conclusion by a similar narrow vote.

Overruling *Metro*, the *Adarand* Court, in an opinion by Justice Sandra Day O'Connor, held federal, like state and local, affirmative action programs, constitute discrimination by government based on race, and therefore require strict scrutiny. The earlier distinction, based on the seemingly broader authority of Congress to legislate based on Section Five of the Fourteenth Amendment (which empowers Congress to enforce the provisions of that amendment), was erased.

Adarand involved a federal statute authorizing companies contracting with the United States Department of Transportation to receive a monetary bonus if they subcontract with firms controlled by "socially and economically disadvantaged" persons, which the statute presumes to include racial minority groups. Adarand, a non-minority subcontractor whose bid was rejected, challenged the statute.

The Court held the reasons advanced in *Croson* for close examination of affirmative action requirements applied equally here. It reaffirmed the holding in *Croson* that "benign" racial classifications are as suspect as the traditional classifications working to the detriment of minorities, long held to be subject to strict scrutiny.

However, the Court made clear that the strict scrutiny requirement does not automatically invalidate an affirmative action mandate. It emphasized that in *United States* v. *Paradise* the Court upheld a requirement that the Alabama Department of Public Safety hire and promote state police based on a formula designed to benefit blacks, since there was proof of "pervasive, systematic, and obstinate discriminatory conduct" that warranted that remedy. Justices Antonin Scalia and

Clarence Thomas concurred, agreeing that affirmative action invariably requires strict scrutiny but arguing, as they did in prior opinions, that "under our Constitution there can be no such thing as either a creditor or a debtor race," so that "government can never have a 'compelling interest' in discriminating on the basis of race in order to 'make up' for past racial discrimination in the opposite direction."

Justice John Paul Stevens, joined by Justice Ruth Bader Ginsburg, dissented, asserting there is "no moral or constitutional equivalence between a policy that is designed to perpetuate a caste system and one that seeks to eradicate" it. Justice David H. Souter, joined by Justices Ginsburg and Stephen G. Breyer, likewise dissented, contending the *Fullilove* decision, holding Section Five of the Fourteenth Amendment accords Congress greater authority than the states to redress racial discrimination, should be adhered to.

In fact the majority in *Adarand* was careful not to overrule *Fullilove*, where the Court had sustained a federal law requiring certain contracts to be set aside for minority business enterprises. It did, however, clarify the applicable degree of scrutiny, which the fragmented decision in *Fullilove* had not conclusively determined. In the end, the *Adarand* Court sent the case back for the trial court to rule on whether the particular provision satisfies the strict scrutiny test. It can be argued that the *Adarand* statute imposes less of a burden on federal contractors than did the mandatory (with limited exceptions) provision upheld in *Fullilove*. In addition, the *Adarand* statute is aimed not at minority businesses as such but at firms controlled by "disadvantaged" persons—presumed to include racial minorities. The Court will doubtless have to decide whether that is a distinction without a difference.

While some have concluded that *Adarand* dealt a severe blow to affirmative action, the Court pointedly left intact its holdings in *Fullilove* and *Paradise*. The difficult issue for the future will be exactly what governmental

While some have concluded that Adarand *dealt a severe blow to affirmative action, the Court pointedly left intact its holdings in* Fullilove *and* Paradise.

interests, other than redressing prior discrimination on the part of the specific entity involved, will be found to meet the strict scrutiny standard. The language in *Bakke* by Justice Lewis F. Powell suggesting that state universities have a compelling interest in maintaining a racially diverse student body still stands, though the unyielding set-aside of a specific tier of seats for minorities was struck down there as not narrowly tailored to achieve that goal.

Adarand makes clear that federal, like state, affirmative action programs must be shown to be narrowly tailored to serve a compelling governmental interest. But it also reminds us that this burden, though stringent, in fact may be met.

—PHILIP WEINBERG

ADKINS v. CHILDREN'S HOSPITAL

261 U.S. 525 (1923)

The *Adkins* case climaxed the assimilation of laissez-faire economics into constitutional law. At issue was the constitutionality of a congressional minimum wage law for women and children in the District of Columbia. The impact of the case was nationwide, affecting all similar state legislation. In the exercise of its police power over the District, Congress in 1918 established an administrative board with investigatory powers over wages and living standards for underprivileged, unorganized workers. After notice and hearing, the board could order wage increases by fixing minima for women and minors. The board followed a general standard set by the legislature: wages had to be reasonably sufficient to keep workers "in good health" and "protect their morals." A corporation maintaining a hospital in the District and a woman who had lost a job paying $35 a month and two meals daily claimed that the statute violated the Fifth Amendment's due process clause, which protected their freedom of contract on terms mutually desirable.

The constitutionality of minimum wage legislation had come before the Court in *Stettler* v. *O'Hara* (1917) but because Justice Louis D. Brandeis had disqualified himself, the Court had split evenly, settling nothing. In the same year, however, Professor Felix Frankfurter won from the Court a decision sustaining the constitutionality of a state maximum hours law in *Bunting* v. *Oregon* (1917). Although the Court sustained that law for men as well as for women and children, it neglected to overrule *Lochner* v. *New York* (1905). In that case the Court had held that minimum wage laws for bakers violated the freedom of contract protected by due process of law. Nevertheless, *Bunting* seemed to supersede *Lochner* and followed Justice Oliver Wendell Holmes's *Lochner* dissent. The Court in *Bunting* presumed the constitutionality of the statute, disavowed examination of the legislature's wisdom in exercising its police power, and asserted that the reasonableness of the legislation need not be proved; the burden of proving unreasonableness fell upon those opposed to the social measure.

Because *Bunting* superseded *Lochner* without overruling it, Frankfurter, who again defended the constitutionality of the statute, took no chances in *Adkins.* He relied on the principles of *Bunting,* the plenary powers of Congress over the District, and the overwhelmingly favorable state court precedents. In the main, however, he sought to show the reasonableness of the minimum wage law for women and children in order to rebut the freedom of contract doctrine. In a Brandeis brief, he proved the relation between the very low wages that had prevailed before the statute and the high incidences of child neglect, disease, broken homes, prostitution, and death.

A recent appointee, Justice George Sutherland, spoke for the *Adkins* majority. Chief Justice William Howard Taft, joined by Justice

Edward Sanford, dissented also, separately. The vote was 5-3. Brandeis disqualified himself from participating because his daughter worked for the minimum wage board. Sutherland dismissed Frankfurter's brief with the comment that his facts were "interesting but only mildly persuasive." Such facts, said Sutherland, were "proper enough for the consideration of lawmaking bodies, since their tendency is to establish the desirability or undesirability of the legislation; but they reflect no legitimate light upon the question of its validity, and that is what we are called upon to decide." The Court then found, on the basis of its own consideration of policy, that the statute was unwise and undesirable. Sutherland assumed that prostitution among the poor was unrelated to income. He claimed that the recently acquired right of women to vote had elevated them to the same status as men, stripping them of any legal protection based on sexual differences. That disposed of the 1908 ruling in *Muller* v. *Oregon.* Consequently, women had the same right of freedom of contract as men, no more or less.

That freedom was not an absolute, Sutherland conceded, but this case did not fall into any of the exceptional categories of cases in which the government might reasonably restrict that freedom. Female elevator operators, scrubwomen, and dishwashers had a constitutional right to work for whatever they pleased, even if for less than a minimum prescribed by an administrative board. Employers had an equal right to pay what they pleased. If the board could fix minimum wages, employers might be forced to pay more than the value of the services rendered and might have to operate at a loss or even go out of business. By comparing the selling of labor with the selling of goods, Sutherland, ironically, supported the claim that capitalism regarded labor as a commodity on the open market. On such reasoning the Court found that the statute conflicted with the freedom of contract incorporated within the Fifth Amendment's due process clause. Paradoxi-

cally the Court distinguished away *Muller* and *Bunting* because they were maximum hours cases irrelevant to a case involving minimum wages, yet it relied heavily on *Lochner* as controlling, though it too was a maximum hours case.

All this was too much for even that stalwart conservative, Chief Justice Taft, who felt bound by precedent to support the statute. Like Holmes, Taft perceived no difference in principle between a maximum hours law, which was valid, and a minimum wages law, which was not. Holmes went further. In addition to showing that both kinds of legislation interfered with freedom of contract to the same extent, he repudiated the freedom of conduct doctrine as he had in his famous *Lochner* dissent. He criticized the Court for expanding an unpretentious assertion of the liberty to follow one's calling into a far-reaching, rigid dogma. Like Taft, Holmes thought that *Bunting* had silently overruled *Lochner.* Both Taft and Holmes took notice of Frankfurter's evidence to make the point that the statute was not unreasonable. Holmes observed that it "does not compel anybody to pay anything. It simply forbids employment at rates below those fixed as the minimum requirement of health and right living." Holmes also remarked that more than a women's suffrage amendment would be required to make him believe that "there are no differences between men and women, or that legislation cannot take those differences into account." Yet, the most caustic line in the dissenting opinions was Taft's: "It is not the function of this court to hold congressional acts invalid simply because they are passed to carry out economic views which the court believes to be unwise or unsound."

By this decision, the Court voided minimum wage laws throughout the country. Per curiam opinions based on *Adkins* disposed of state statutes whose supporters futilely sought to distinguish their administrative standards from the one before the Court in *Adkins.* Samuel Gompers, the leader of

At issue was the constitutionality of a congressional minimum wage law for women and children in the District of Columbia.

American trade unionism, bitterly remarked, "To buy the labor of a woman is not like buying pigs' feet in a butcher shop." A cartoon in the New York *World* showed Sutherland handing a copy of his opinion to a woman wage earner, saying, "This decision affirms your constitutional right to starve." By preventing minimum wage laws, the Court kept labor unprotected when the Depression struck. *Adkins* remained the law of the land controlling decisions as late as 1936; the Court did not overrule it until 1937.

—LEONARD W. LEVY

Bibliography

Berman, Edward. The Supreme Court and the Minimum Wage. *Journal of Political Economy* 31:852–856.

Powell, Thomas Reed (1924). The Judiciality of Minimum Wage Legislation. *Harvard Law Review* 37:545–573.

ADMINISTRATIVE LAW

"Administrative law" describes the legal structure of much of the executive branch of government, particularly the quasi-independent agencies, and the procedural constraints under which they operate. Most of these constraints are statutory; those that do involve the Constitution flow chiefly from the doctrine of separation of powers and the due process clause. To comprehend the effects of either of these on administrative law one must understand the growth of the administrative agency in the modern American state.

The early years of the twentieth century saw both a growth in the executive branch of the federal government and, perhaps more important, increased expectations about tasks it should perform. Some have seen these changes as a natural concomitant of industrialization; some as a growth in the power of a new professional class claiming to possess a nonpolitical expertise; some as the result of political pressure developed by farmers and small-town residents who looked to government to contain corporate juggernauts; some as the consequence of the desire of those very juggernauts to gain government sanction shielding them from the competitive forces of the marketplace. Whatever the causes, federal, state, and municipal governments took on new tasks in the closing decades of the nineteenth and the opening ones of the twentieth centuries.

Agencies such as the Interstate Commerce Commission, the Federal Trade Commission, the Food and Drug Administration, and the Federal Reserve Board bore witness to national perceptions that the existing economic and social mechanisms left something to be desired and that increased government intervention was the solution. At the local level the rise of social welfare agencies and zoning boards bespoke similar concerns.

With the coming of the Great Depression the federal government sought to revive the economy through numerous public programs designed both to coordinate sectors of the nation's industrial and commercial life (the Wagner National Labor Relations Act, the Agricultural Adjustment Act, the National Industrial Recovery Act) and to create public jobs to reduce unemployment and increase consumer demand (the Civilian Conservation Corps, the Works Progress Administration, the Public Works Administration). Such agencies, generating regulations under the statutory umbrella of broad enabling legislation, came to be a standard feature on the American scene.

In a parallel development state governments created a number of agencies to coordinate and regulate everything from barbers to new car dealers, from avocado marketing to the licensing of physicians. Some of these boards appear to function chiefly as means of controlling entry into occupations and thereby shielding current practitioners from competition, but all function as branches of

See also

Lochner v. *New York*

Muller v. *Oregon*

West Coast Hotel Co. v. *Parrish*

the government armed with at least some forms of regulatory power.

In some respects such state and national agencies represent not a new form of governmental power but a transfer to state and national levels of what had once been tasks of city government. The functioning of such municipal bureaucracies was, however, largely idiosyncratic and local—defined by the terms of the cities' charters and thus beyond the reach of national law. The migration of regulatory control from city to state and nation both enabled and necessitated the development of a new "administrative" law, which in America is almost entirely a creature of the twentieth century.

Most of that law is statutory, a function of the legislation that creates the board, agency, or commission and defines its tasks and powers. Citizens and enterprises wishing either to invoke or to challenge such powers use the statutorily specified procedures, which often involve both internal agency and external judicial review of administrative actions. At two points, however, the Constitution does speak to the structure and conduct of the agencies. In the formative years of the administrative state the Supreme Court expressed doubt about the place of the agency in the divided federal system of government. Since the New Deal the constitutional focus has turned to the processes employed by administrative agencies, and the courts have regularly required agencies' procedures to conform to the due process clause.

The Constitution establishes three branches of the national government, and the courts early decided that no branch should exceed its own powers or intrude on areas designated as the province of another branch. This principle, known as the separation of powers, applies to numerous activities of the federal government, but it impinges particularly on the operation of administrative agencies charged with the formation and enforcement of broad federal policy.

Congress could not possibly specify just what tasks it wishes federal agencies to accomplish and also exactly how to perform them. At the opposite extreme it would just as obviously violate the separation of powers if Congress were to throw up its hands at the task of forming policy and instead direct the president to hit on whatever combination of revenue collection and expenditure he deemed best to fulfill the needs of the country. The concern is that Congress, if it asks an administrative agency not just to carry out defined tasks but also to participate in the formation of policy, has impermissibly given—delegated—its legislative power to the agency (a part of the executive branch).

That concern surfaced in a pair of Supreme Court decisions invalidating New Deal legislation. *Panama Refining Co.* v. *Ryan* (1935) struck down a portion of the National Industrial Recovery Act that permitted the president to ban the interstate shipment of petroleum; the Court's ground was that Congress had provided no guidance as to when the president should do so or what aims were to justify the ban. A few months later, in *Schechter Poultry Corp.* v. *United States*, the Court held unconstitutional another section of the same act; its delegation of power permitted the president to create codes of fair competition for various industries. Congress had defined neither the content of such codes nor the conditions for their proclamation, and some members of the Court evinced concern that the absence of standards could pave the way for what amounted to a governmentally sanctioned system of industrial cartels.

Since these two cases the Court has not invalidated a congressional delegation of power, but some have argued that the memory of these cases has induced the legislature to indicate more clearly the goals it intends the agency to accomplish, the means by which they are to be accomplished, and the processes that should accompany their implementation.

Administrative law describes the legal structure of much of the executive branch of government and the procedural constraints under which they operate.

♦ ripeness
The status of a case when circumstances have advanced to the point of sufficient specificity and concreteness to justify decision or review.

Even though an administrative agency does not perform tasks that constitutionally belong only to Congress, it might nevertheless violate the constitutional structure of government by performing tasks belonging to the courts. The problem has several guises.

In some instances Congress in creating the agency has given it jurisdiction that might otherwise have been exercised by the courts (for example, over maritime accidents). Did such congressional action, which could be viewed as a transfer of federal judicial jurisdiction to an agency, violate the constitutional structure of government or the rights of the parties? In *Crowell* v. *Benson* (1932) the Court concluded that if Congress established fair administrative procedures, the agency could hear and determine cases that might otherwise have been heard by the courts—with the saving proviso that the federal courts might review the agency's determination of questions of law.

That proviso pointed to another difficult question: the extent to which the courts might review agency decisions. Summarizing the history of this question, Louis Jaffe has said that we have moved from a nineteenth-century presumption of unreviewability to a twentieth-century presumption of reviewability. Such reviewability, however, flows from statutory interpretation rather than from constitutional compulsion: if Congress is sufficiently explicit, it can make an agency determination final and unreviewable—either because the statute explicitly says so or because it so clearly makes the decision in question a matter of agency discretion that there is no law to apply. For the most part, however, courts routinely scrutinize agency action for legality and at least minimal rationality and are prepared to give the agencies fairly great leeway in performing their tasks.

One measure of this leeway the agencies enjoy is the set of requirements imposed on litigants seeking to invoke federal judicial review of agency action. Such parties must satisfy the courts that they have standing (that is, actual injury caused by the agency action), that the dispute is ripe for judicial review (that is, that the case comes to the courts when it has sufficiently developed to render a judicial decision not merely abstract or hypothetical), and that they have exhausted their administrative remedies (that is, that they have sought such administrative redress as is available). Only the first two of these requirements—standing and ripeness—stem from the Constitution; all of them, however, condition the federal courts' exercise of judicial review.

Courts are prepared to grant such leeway, however, only to the extent that they are assured that the agency has complied with the requirements of due process in making its decisions. Due process plays two roles in administrative law. To the extent that agencies make rules only after extensive public participation in their deliberations, they address some of the concerns lying at the base of the delegation doctrine—ill-considered and hasty action. Due process also plays a second, more traditional role of assuring adjudicatory fairness. To the extent that agencies take action against those violating their rules, courts have often required that the agencies afford the violators various procedural protections.

Because an increasing number of Americans, from defense contractors and television broadcasters to mothers of dependent children and disabled veterans, depend on state and federal government for their livelihood, such protections have become increasingly important. In the second half of the twentieth century the courts have held many of those interests to be property, thus giving their holders the right to due process—sometimes including a fair hearing—before suffering their deprivation. Thus state and federal agencies must give welfare recipients an opportunity to know and to contest factual findings before ending benefits; public schools and colleges have to supply students some form of notice and process before suspending or expelling them; and public employers must grant tenured employees an opportunity to contest their dismissal. Courts have left the agencies some discretion as to the form of such procedures, which need not, for example, always include a hearing, but the process must suit the circumstances.

Because such protections flow from the due process clauses, they apply equally to state and to federal government; indeed, an important consequence of the constitutionalization of administrative process is that it has penetrated to state bureaucracies, some of which were perhaps less than exemplary in their concern for those affected by their actions. As a result both state courts and state legislatures have directed attention to the procedures of their agencies.

In a large sense, to understand the relationship of the administrative state to the Constitution, one has to spell constitution with a small "c," for the difficulties have been less with specific constitutional provisions than with the general picture of how executive action—especially action in new spheres—fits into received understandings of the world. That question is still debatable, but the debates, at least in the last half of the twentieth century, have taken place at the level of desirable policy, not of constitutional legality: so long as the agencies operate fairly, that much, apparently, is assured.

—STEPHEN C. YEAZELL

Bibliography

Davis, Kenneth C. (1978). *Administrative Law Treatise.* San Diego, Calif.: Davis.

Jaffe, Louis (1965). *Judicial Control of Administrative Action.* Boston: Little, Brown.

Kolko, Gabriel (1963). *The Triumph of Conservatism: A Reinterpretation of American History, 1900–1916.* New York: Free Press.

Wiebe, Robert (1967). *The Search for Order, 1877–1920.* New York: Hill & Wang.

ADVICE AND CONSENT TO SUPREME COURT NOMINATIONS

The proper scope of the Senate's role in confirming Supreme Court nominees has been the subject of recurring and often heated debate. The Constitution provides simply that the president "shall nominate, and by and with the advice and consent of the Senate, shall appoint . . . Judges of the Supreme Court." Although the Senate also has the constitutional responsibility of advising on and consenting to presidential appointments of ambassadors, lower federal court judges, and many executive branch officials, debates over the nature of the Senate's role have generally arisen in the context of Supreme Court nominations.

The central issues of controversy have concerned the criteria the Senate should consider in making confirmation decisions and the appropriate range of questions that may be posed to and answered by a nominee. Debated points regarding appropriate criteria for confirmation have included the degree to which the Senate should defer to the president's preferred choice and whether it is appropriate to take a nominee's political views or judicial philosophy into account. The debate about the scope of questioning has centered on whether it is appropriate for senators to ask and nominees to answer questions about the nominee's political views and judicial philosophy and how these views and philosophy would apply to issues that may come before the Court.

Presidents and some members of the Senate have argued that selecting Justices is the president's prerogative and that, although the president may take a judicial prospect's philosophy into account, the Senate must limit its inquiry to whether the nominee has the basic qualifications for the job. These commentators maintain that the Senate should defer to the president's nomination of

See also

Panama Refining Co. v. *Ryan*

Schechter Poultry Corp. v.

United States

any person who is neither corrupt nor professionally incompetent. Others have contested this view and argued that the Senate, when it decides whether to consent to a nomination, is permitted to take into account the same range of considerations open to the president and to make its own independent determination of whether confirmation of a particular nominee is in the best interests of the country.

Presidents have often taken the position that the Senate should defer to the president's choice. President Richard M. Nixon, for example, claimed in 1971 that the president has "the constitutional responsibility to appoint members of the Court," a responsibility that should not be "frustrated by those who wish to substitute their own philosophy for that of the one person entrusted by the Constitution with the power of appointment." This view was echoed by President Ronald Reagan, who asserted that the president has the "right" to "choose federal judges who share his judicial philosophy" and that the Senate should confirm presidents' nominees "so long as they are qualified by character and competence."

Many of those who agree with Presidents Nixon and Reagan believe that the proper standard for Senate review of Supreme Court nominees is the deferential standard that the Senate has typically accorded to presidential nominations of executive officials, whose confirmation is generally expected unless the nominee is found to lack the character or competence necessary for the job. This analogy between executive and judicial appointments is not wholly apt. Whereas the president is entitled to have in the executive branch officials who share the president's philosophy and will carry out the chief executive's policies, judicial nominees are expected to exercise independent judgment. Those favoring a more active Senate role in the judicial confirmation process suggest that the proper analogy is to the Senate's role in ratifying or rejecting treaties or to the president's decision

to sign or veto legislation—instances in which an independent exercise of judgment by each branch is thought appropriate.

The consideration of the Appointments Clause by the Constitutional Convention of 1787 offers some support for the position that senators should exercise their own independent judgment about whether to confirm a nominee. The convention considered the issue of judicial appointments separately from its consideration of the appointment of executive officers. For much of the summer of 1787, the evolving drafts of the Constitution gave the Senate exclusive authority to appoint judges. Suggestions for giving the appointing authority to the president alone rather than to the Senate were soundly defeated.

On May 29, 1787, the convention began its work on the Constitution by taking up the Virginia Plan, which provided "that a National Judiciary be established . . . to be chosen by the National Legislature. . . ." Under this plan, the executive was to have no role at all in the selection of judges. When this provision came before the Convention on June 5, several members expressed concern that the whole legislature might be too numerous a body to select judges. James Wilson's alternative providing that the president be given the power to choose judges found almost no support, however. John Rutledge of South Carolina stated that he "was by no means disposed to grant so great a power to any single person." James Madison agreed that the legislature was too large a body, but stated that "he was not satisfied with referring the appointment to the Executive." He was "rather inclined to give it to the Senatorial branch" as being "sufficiently stable and independent to follow their deliberate judgments."

One week later on June 13, Madison rendered his inclination into a formal motion that the power of appointing judges be given exclusively to the Senate rather than to the legislature as a whole. This motion was adopted without objection. On July 18 the convention reconsidered and reaffirmed its earlier decision to grant the Senate the exclusive power of appointing judges. James Wilson again moved "that the Judges be appointed by the Executive." His motion was defeated, six states to two, after delegates offered, as Gunning Bedford of Delaware said, "solid reasons against leaving the appointment to the Executive." Luther Martin of Maryland, stating that he "was strenuous for an appointment by the 2nd branch," argued that "being taken from all the States [the Senate] would be the best informed of character and most capable of making a fit choice." Roger Sherman of Connecticut concurred, "adding that the Judges ought to be diffused, which would be more likely to be attended to by the 2d branch, than by the Executive." Nathaniel Gorham of Massachusetts argued against exclusive appointment by the Senate, stating that "public bodies feel no personal responsibility, and give full play to intrigue and cabal." He offered what was to be the final compromise: appointment by the Executive "by and with the advice and consent" of the Senate. At this point in the convention, however, his motion failed on a tie vote.

The issue was considered once again on July 21. After a debate in which George Mason attacked the idea of executive appointment as a "dangerous prerogative [because] it might even give him an influence over the Judiciary department itself," the convention once again reaffirmed exclusive Senate appointment of judges of the Supreme Court. Thus the matter stood until the closing days of the convention. On September 4, less than two weeks before the convention's work was done, a committee of five reported out a new draft providing for the first time for a presidential role in the selection of judges: "The President . . . shall nominate and by and with the advice and consent of the Senate shall appoint Judges of the Supreme Court." Giving the president the power to nominate judges was not seen as tantamount to ousting the Senate from a central role. Gouverneur Morris of Pennsylvania, a member of the Committee, paraphrased the new provision as one that retained in the Senate the power "to appoint Judges nominated to them by the President." With little discussion and without dissent, the Convention adopted this as the final language of the provision. Considering that the convention had repeatedly and decisively rejected any proposal to give the president exclusive power to select judges, it is unlikely that the drafters contemplated reducing the Senate's role to a ministerial one.

During the nineteenth century, the Senate took a broad view of the appropriate criteria to govern "advice and consent" decisions. During this period, the Senate rejected more than one of every four Supreme Court nominations. The Senate first rejected President George Washington's nomination of John Rutledge. The Senate went on to reject five of the nominees proposed by President John Tyler and three of the four nominees put forward by President Millard Fillmore. Since 1900, however, the rate of senatorial rejection of Supreme Court nominees has dropped sharply to a twentieth-century rejection rate of a mere one in thirteen.

Virtually all the parties to the twentieth-century debate on appropriate confirmation criteria agree on two threshold issues. The first is that it is appropriate for senators to consider "judicial fitness." No one contests that adequate judicial competence, ethics, and temperament are necessary conditions for confirmation and, therefore, appropriate criteria for senators to consider. The publicly stated bases of opposition to the nominations of Louis D. Brandeis, Judge Clement F. Haynsworth, and Judge George H. Carswell were presented in terms of these threshold, judicial-fitness criteria.

The unsuccessful opposition to Brandeis, nominated in 1916 by President Woodrow Wilson, based its public case against the nominee on alleged breaches of legal ethics. The successful opposition to confirmation of Judge Haynsworth, nominated to the Supreme Court by President Nixon in 1969,

The formula "advice and consent" is an ancient one.

was articulated primarily in terms of charges that Haynsworth had violated canons of judicial ethics by sitting on cases involving corporations in which he had small financial interests. In addition to the ethics charges, some opponents raised objections to Haynsworth's civil rights record. Two judicial-fitness objections formed the basis for the successful opposition to confirmation of Judge Carswell, nominated to the Supreme Court by President Nixon in 1970. The primary objection was that Carswell allegedly allowed racial prejudice to affect his judicial behavior. The second theme in the opposition to Carswell was that, as a matter of basic competence, he was at best a mediocre jurist.

Thus, in the Brandeis, Haynsworth, and Carswell nominations, opposition was presented as based on the judicial-fitness criteria of judicial temperament, ethics, and basic competence. In all three of these twentieth-century confirmation controversies, the acceptability of the judicial-fitness criteria went unchallenged.

The second area of general agreement in the debate on appropriate criteria for confirmation decisions is that senators should not base their decisions on the nominee's predicted vote on a particular case or "single issue" likely to come before the Court. Supporters of the nomination of Judge John Parker, nominated to the Supreme Court by President Herbert Hoover in 1930, alleged that opposition to the nomination was based on a "single issue" of Parker's position on a particular labor-law question. Parker's opponents took pains to deny that their opposition was based on a single issue and argued that Parker's ruling in a previous case involving the question reflected Parker's own anti-union bias. This accusation—that, as a judge, Parker was biased in his rulings on such matters—was a way for the opponents of confirmation to frame their objection as one of judicial temperament and, thus, judicial fitness. The premise underlying the positions of both opponents and supporters of Parker was that a rejection based on a result-oriented single-issue criterion would be inappropriate.

TOO CONSERVATIVE?

The Senate rejected Robert Bork's 1987 nomination to the Supreme Court amid heated debates over his judicial philosophy. (Corbis/Wally McNamee)

Between the margins of agreement that judicial-fitness criteria are appropriate and that single-issue criteria are inappropriate lies the area of controversy. The debated issue is often framed as whether the nominee's "judicial philosophy" should be considered in the decision-making process. The term "judicial philosophy," when used in this context, refers to a range of concerns including the nominee's theory of judging (that is, the degree of judicial interference with legislative and executive decision making the nominee views as appropriate), the nominee's views on the level of generality at which constitutional provisions should be interpreted, and the nominee's interpretation of specific constitutional clauses or doctrines (such as the applicability of the equal protection clause to women or the existence of a constitutional right of privacy.

The bases of opposition to President Lyndon B. Johnson's 1968 nomination of Justice Abe Fortas (to be Chief Justice) and to President Reagan's nomination of Judge Robert Bork to the Supreme Court were framed largely in terms of these controversial "judicial philosophy" criteria. Consequently, the confirmation battles in these cases raged as much around the appropriateness of the criteria applied as around the merits of the nominees themselves.

The attack on Fortas's judicial philosophy was based on charges that he was a "judicial activist" (meaning that his theory of judging envisioned excessive intervention in the discretion of the elected branches) and that his substantive interpretations (of the First, Fifth, Sixth, and Fourteenth Amendments) were flawed. Supporters of the Fortas nomination responded both on the merits—defending Fortas's theory of judging and his substantive interpretations—and by assailing the judicial philosophy criterion as inappropriate considerations for advice and consent decisions. (Although some ethics charges were raised during the confirmation proceedings, the very serious ethics charges that re-

sulted in Fortas's resignation did not arise until the spring of 1969, during the Nixon presidency, many months after President Johnson had withdrawn his nomination of Justice Fortas to become Chief Justice.)

Like the Fortas nomination, the nomination of Judge Robert Bork to the Supreme Court was opposed largely on judicial philosophy grounds. (Although some critics raised ethics issues, including Bork's role in the "Saturday Night Massacre" in which the special prosecutor in the Watergate affair was fired, these issues did not form a primary basis of opposition.) Judge Bork's theory of judging was assailed as an inadequate conception of the proper role of the Supreme Court in protecting individual and "unenumerated" constitutional rights. Objections were also presented in terms of Bork's interpretations of specific constitutional clauses and doctrines, including his position on the existence of a constitutional right to privacy, his previous and contemporaneous interpretations of the equal protection clause as regards the protections afforded to women, his interpretations of the First Amendment's free speech clause, and his positions on civil rights. Much of the defense of Judge Bork took the form of challenging the acceptability of these controversial criteria.

The contours of the areas of agreement and disagreement on appropriate advice-and-consent criteria are not surprising. The debate on appropriate criteria follows from the constitutional provisions that structure the process of appointments to an independent, principle-oriented, countermajoritarian judiciary in a way that requires the consent of an elected, representative, majoritarian body. Senators' views about the proper role of the judiciary inform their positions on the relevance and propriety of each category of advice-and-consent criteria.

A foundational precept of the role of an independent judiciary is that judges must render decisions based on the rigorous appli-

♦ **advisory opinion**
A judicial opinion on a question of law, rendered without deciding the rights of parties to an adversary proceeding. In the federal courts, advisory opinions are barred by the "case or controversy" requirement.

cation of principles, not their personal preferences, much less their biases. The broad agreement about this precept underlies and is reflected in the broad consensus that judicial fitness is an acceptable category of criteria for consent decisions. Competence in legal reasoning, high ethical standards, and unbiased judicious temperament are prerequisites to the consistent rendering of rigorously reasoned and principled decisions of law.

The same precept—that the essence of the judicial function is to render decisions based on principles—underlies the broad consensus that single-issue result-oriented criteria are unacceptable. Because of the principle-based nature of the judicial function, a judicial nominee must be evaluated on the basis of the anticipated process of his or her application of principles, regardless of whether that process will produce a senator's preferred outcome in any particular case. The ability of elected presidents and elected senators to exert some general influence on the future course of the nation's jurisprudence is an appropriate (and appropriately limited) popular check on the exercise of the power of judicial review, without which this institution might not be acceptable in a constitutional democracy. Nonetheless, for presidents or senators to demand that the judiciary not render decisions based on principle but, rather, act as an agent of the legislature furthering particular preferences, and for senators to enforce this demand by the threat or reality of nonconfirmation, would subvert the independence of the judiciary and violate the spirit of the separation of powers.

Rather than a continued focus on the appropriate criteria for advice-and-consent decisions, a different aspect of the debate over the appropriate role of the Senate in the confirmation process came to the fore during consideration of the nomination of Justice David H. Souter. Souter's views on controversial judicial and political issues were little known. The prominent questions during the Souter confirmation, therefore, were (1) where relatively lit-

tle is known about the nominee's thinking, how may the Senate properly learn more about the nominee; and (2) what questions may properly be posed to the nominee during the confirmation hearings? These questions are not merely derivative of the larger question of what decision-making criteria are legitimate. The core objection to direct questions to the nominee—even on issues that might constitute legitimate decision-making criteria, such as substantive interpretation of particular constitutional clauses—is that, by offering an opinion on such issues, the nominee may thereafter feel bound to hold in subsequent cases in a manner consistent with the opinions stated during the confirmation hearings. Thus, the fear is that the nominee who opines on, say, the level of protection afforded to women by the equal protection clause during the confirmation hearing will, in effect, be "committed" to a certain outcome in future cases involving that issue.

But fear of judicial precommitment may be exaggerated. Surely there is no requirement that the individuals nominated to our highest court have never thought about—or reached tentative conclusions on—the important issues of law that face the country. So the only issue is whether sharing those thoughts with the senators during confirmation hearings would constitute a commitment not to change those views or not to be open to the arguments of parties litigating those issues in the future. There is no reason to believe that a statement of opinion during confirmation would constitute such a commitment. It would seem reasonable to suppose that an opinion mentioned during a confirmation hearing would be seen as not binding if it were generally understood that such statements are not binding. It would seem reasonable that a nominee might preface an opinion on such an issue with a statement that "these are my initial views on the issue, but they would certainly be open to change in the context of a case in which persuasive arguments were put forth by the parties." Justices would not be in any way committed to be "consistent" with their confirmation comments if it were understood that confirmation comments constitute nothing more and nothing less than frank statements by nominees of their best thinking on a particular issue to date.

—MADELINE MORRIS
—WALTER DELLINGER

Bibliography

Morris, Madeline (1988–1989). The Grammar of Advice and Consent: Senate Confirmation of Supreme Court Nominees. *Drake Law Review* 38:863–887.

Rees, Grover, III (1983). Questions for Supreme Court Nominees at Confirmation Hearings: Excluding the Constitution. *Georgia Law Review* 17:913–967.

Tribe, Laurence H. (1985). *God Save This Honorable Court*. New York: Mentor.

AFFIRMATIVE ACTION

Do constitutional guarantees of equal protection command that government must be "color-blind" or only that government may not subordinate any group on the basis of race? The Supreme Court's equal protection decisions have long straddled these two different principles. The color-blindness approach deems race morally irrelevant to governmental decision making under all circumstances. The antisubordination approach, by contrast, sees racial distinctions as illegitimate only when used by government as a deliberate basis for disadvantage. The two approaches divide sharply on the permissibility of affirmative action: advocates of color blindness condemn the use of racial distinctions even to benefit previously disadvantaged racial groups, whereas those who view equal protection solely as a ban on racial subordination see affirmative action as constitutionally benign.

Since 1985, the Supreme Court has continued to steer between these two approaches rather than unequivocally embrace either one. In earlier decisions, the Court had upheld a variety of racial preferences, including the use of race as a factor in university admissions (as long as rigid racial quotas were not employed) in *Regents of University of California* v. *Bakke* (1978), the set-aside of places for blacks in an industrial skills-training program in *United Steelworkers of America* v. *Weber* (1979), and the set-aside of public works construction projects for minority business enterprises in *Fullilove* v. *Klutznick* (1980). These cases made clear that affirmative action would not be struck down as readily as laws harming racial minorities, but neither would it be lightly tolerated. Governments could successfully defend affirmative action programs, but only with an especially strong justification.

The affirmative action cases since 1985 have bitterly divided the Court, and their outcomes have signaled a partial retrenchment for affirmative action. With the appointments of Justices Sandra Day O'Connor, Antonin Scalia, and Anthony M. Kennedy, the Court veered off its middle course and more sharply toward the color-blindness pole. Although the Court readily upheld affirmative action as a court-imposed remedy for racial discrimination against minorities, as in *Local 28, Sheet Metal Workers International Association* v. *EEOC* (1986), the Court struck down two municipalities' efforts to impose affirmative action on themselves. In *Wygant* v. *Jackson Board of Education* (1986) the Court invalidated a school district's plan to protect minority teachers against layoffs ahead of more senior white teachers. And in *Richmond (City of)* v. *J. A. Croson Co.* (1989), the Court struck down a city's reservation of a percentage of public works construction for minority business enterprises—a set-aside modeled on the congressional program upheld in *Fullilove*. *Metro Broadcasting* v. *F.C.C.* (1990), which upheld

Depending upon interpretation, one person's "affirmative action" may well constitute another's "reverse discrimination."

federal policies preferring minority broadcasters in the allocation of broadcast licenses, confounded those who thought *Croson* had sounded the death knell for affirmative action. But in *Adarand Constructors* v. *Pena* (1995) the Court finally made clear that federal, as well as state and municipal, affirmative action programs would be subjected to strict scrutiny, and therefore upheld only when narrowly tailored to meet a compelling government interest.

The central conflict in these cases was over what justification for affirmative action would suffice. Up until *Metro,* the Court accepted only narrowly remedial justifications. Affirmative action was upheld only as penance for particularized past sins of discrimination—not as atonement for "societal discrimination" as a whole. The Court treated affirmative action as a matter of corrective rather than distributive justice; minorities might be preferred for jobs, admissions, or contracts not to build a racially integrated future, but only to cure a racially discriminatory past. However, in *Bakke* the Court, as noted, suggested that state universities might consider race as one element in assuring a diverse student body, even where there was no showing of prior discrimination by that school.

The Court's account of affirmative action as a permissible remedy for past discrimination, however, left both sides unsatisfied. Opponents charged that affirmative action was a poor version of corrective justice because (1) unlike standard compensatory justice, affirmative action extends benefits beyond the specific victims of past discrimination; and (2) unlike standard retributive justice, affirmative action demands current sacrifice of persons who were not the actual perpetrators of past discrimination—persons the Court sometimes labels "innocent" whites. In the opponents' view, if affirmative action were truly remedial, neither would nonvictims benefit nor nonsinners pay. In contrast, advocates of affirmative action found the Court's

requirements for proving remedial justification far too stringent. Governments are reluctant to confess to past sins of discrimination, advocates argued, and should be permitted to adopt affirmative action plans without official *mea culpa*s.

Metro Broadcasting departed from the sin-based approach by accepting a nonremedial justification for the Federal Communications Commission's (FCC) minority-ownership preference policies: increased minority ownership would help diversify broadcast program content. A majority of the Court had never endorsed such a justification before, although Justice Lewis F. Powell's crucial *Bakke* opinion had defended racial preferences in university admissions as producing diversity in the classroom and Justice John Paul Stevens had persistently advocated similar diversity-based justifications for affirmative action, for example, in his *Wygant* dissent. Such justifications implicitly adopt the antisubordination rather than the color-blindness approach: using racial distinctions to increase diversity is not a constitutional evil because it does not use race to impose disadvantage. As Justice Stevens wrote in his *Metro* concurrence, "[n]either the favored nor the disfavored class is stigmatized in any way."

Adarand held a federal set-aside for "disadvantaged" highway subcontractors is subject to strict scrutiny. To that extent the Court overruled the conclusion of *Metro* that federal affirmative action programs need not meet that severe test. The Court in *Metro* had based its view on the power given Congress under section 5 of the Fourteenth Amendment to eliminate discrimination. The *Adarand* Court, rejecting that view, held the federal government and states must meet the same standard.

Under the *Adarand* statute, minority-owned businesses were presumed to be disadvantaged, although others also might show themselves to be. The Supreme Court remanded the case for the trial court to decide

The Supreme Court's restrictive view of Congress's power under the commerce clause in the years following adoption of the Sherman Act produced an extremely narrow interpretation of the act in *United States* v. *E. C. Knight Company* (1895). Manufacturing, said the Court, was not commerce; thus the act did not reach the stock transactions that gave one company almost complete control over sugar refining in the United States. Only "direct" restraints of interstate commerce itself were subject to the act, as the Court held in *Addyston Pipe Steel Company* v. *United States* (1899). The "constitutional revolution" of the 1930s broadened not only the Court's conception of the commerce power but also its interpretation of the reach of the antitrust laws. By the time of *South-Eastern Underwriters Association* v. *United States* (1944), both changes were complete.

More recently, courts and commentators have noted a potential conflict between state authority to control alcoholic beverages under the Twenty-First Amendment and claims that state regulatory authorities have participated in price fixing. This issue illustrates a more basic question: does the Sherman Act decree a national free market, or may the states depart from competitive structures for economic activity otherwise within their regulatory power? The issue has arisen in connection with state utility regulation, control of the legal and medical professions, and agricultural marketing programs, all of which operate on a franchise or monopoly regulation model rather than a free market model. In general, the Supreme Court has held that state action regulating a market does not violate federal law and those complying with state law are not in violation of federal law.

The antitrust laws raise other constitutional questions. The vague language of the Sherman Act has given rise to claims of unconstitutionality when that act is the basis of a felony prosecution. The "big case" raises a variety of due process concerns, for it presses the judicial model to the outer limits of its ca-pacity. The meaning of the right to trial by jury, for example, requires clarification in cases presenting the complexity and gargantuan size found in many antitrust suits.

Perhaps the most puzzling set of constitutional concerns involves the connections between the Sherman Act's prohibitions on collective behavior (which it describes as contracts, combinations, and conspiracies in restraint of trade) and the associational rights protected by the First Amendment. An agreement among competitors seeking to exclude other potential competitors from the market is a conspiracy under the Sherman Act, even if the competitors enlist government agencies in their effort. On the other hand, an agreement among members of an industry to petition the government for legal relief from the economic threat of their competitors is constitutionally protected political activity. Supreme Court opinions "distinguishing" between these two kinds of activity have resorted to a pejorative label to explain their results, finding the political activity immune from antitrust claims unless it is a sham.

Comparable tensions exist between the Sherman Act's prohibitions of economic boycotts—which are seen as concerted refusals to deal—and political boycotts. To maintain this distinction requires a worldview in which economics and politics are unconnected spheres. Yet boycotts are per se offenses under the Sherman Act and some courts have held that political boycotts are a protected form of political protest.

A third tension is found in the case of permissible "natural monopolies"—for example, the owners of the railway terminal at the only point on a wide river suitable for a railway crossing. For three quarters of a century the Court has held that such holders of monopoly power are obligated to share it fairly with others. Several of these decisions treat this obligation as one resembling governmental power which carries along with it an obligation of "due process" procedural fairness. These decisions might be said to impose the constitutional obligation of government on those private accumulations of power that are found not to be prohibited outright by the Sherman Act. Together, the Constitution and the Sherman Act thus represent a total response to the problems of concentrated power in modern society: the Constitution controls governmental power, and the antitrust law controls concentrations of private economic power. At the seam between public and private organizations, the two bodies of law combine to limit the excesses of concentrated power.

—ARTHUR ROSETT

Bibliography

Areeda, P., and Turner, D. (1978–1980). *Antitrust Law: An Analysis of Antitrust Principles and their Application.* 5 vols. Boston: Little, Brown.

Neale, A. D., and Goyder, D. G. (1980). *The Antitrust Laws of the USA.* 3rd ed. Cambridge: At the University Press.

Sullivan, L. (1977). *Antitrust.* St. Paul, Minn.: West Publishing Co.

APEX HOSIERY
COMPANY v. LEADER

310 U.S. 469 (1940)

This opinion marked the shift toward a pro-labor sentiment in the Supreme Court.

Destroying the effect of *Coronado Coal Company* v. *United Mine Workers* (1925), although not overruling it, this opinion marked the shift toward a pro-labor sentiment in the Supreme Court. The Court reaffirmed the application of the Sherman Antitrust Act to unions but held that even a strike that effected a reduction of goods in interstate commerce was no Sherman Act violation if it furthered legitimate union objectives. A particularly violent sit-down strike at the Apex plant reduced the volume of goods in commerce and resulted in extensive physical damage. Did the act forbid the union's actions? Justice Harlan Fiske Stone, for a 6-3 Court, condemned the union's conduct, declaring that the company

had a remedy under state law, but held that restraints not outlawed by the Sherman Act when accomplished peacefully could not be brought within the law's scope because they were accompanied by violence. The Court also denied that the resulting restraint of trade fell under the act. The union was not proceeding illegally by acting to eliminate nonunion or commercial competition in the market, even though a production halt must accompany a strike and lead to a temporary restraint. Only if the restraint led to a monopoly, price control, or discrimination among consumers would a violation occur. The Court thus substituted a test of restraint in the marketplace for the test of intent previously announced in *Bedford Cut Stone* v. *Journeymen Stonecutters* (1927). In dissent, Chief Justice Charles Evans Hughes, joined by Justices Owen Roberts and James C. McReynolds, insisted that the earlier decisions governed and that they had not confined the test of restraint to market control. The Court had abandoned its earlier approach; the next year it would supplement *Apex,* excluding both jurisdictional strikes and secondary boycotts from Sherman Act coverage in *United States* v. *Hutcheson* (1941).

—DAVID GORDON

APPOINTMENT OF
SUPREME COURT
JUSTICES

Under Article II, section 2, of the Constitution, Supreme Court Justices, like all other federal judges, are nominated and, with the advice and consent of the Senate, appointed by the president. No other textual mandate, either procedural or substantive, governs the Chief Executive's selection. However, section 1 of Article III—which deals exclusively with the judicial branch of the government—provides good behavior tenure for all federal judges; in effect, that means appointment for

See also

Standard Oil Company v. *United States*

life. As additional security, that provision of the Constitution provides that the compensation of federal judges "shall not be diminished during their Continuance in Office." But neither the Constitution nor any federal statute provides any clue as to qualifications for office; neither a law degree nor any other proof of professional capability is formally required. But in practice none other than lawyers are appointable to the federal judiciary, in general, and the Supreme Court, in particular. All of the 107 individuals who sat on that highest tribunal through 1998 held degrees from a school of law or had been admitted to the bar via examination. Indeed, although all the Justices were members of the professional bar in good standing at the time of their appointment, it was not until 1922 that a majority of sitting Justices was composed of law school graduates, and not until 1957 that every Justice was a law school graduate. Once confirmed by the Senate, a Justice is removable only via impeachment (by simple majority vote by the House of Representatives) and subsequent conviction (by two-thirds vote of the Senate, there being a quorum on the floor). Only one Justice of the Supreme Court has been impeached by the House—Justice Samuel Chase, by a 72-32 vote in 1804—but he was acquitted on all eight charges by the Senate in 1805. To all intents and purposes, once appointed, a Supreme Court Justice serves as long as he or she wishes—typically until illness or death intervenes.

Theoretically, the president has *carte blanche* in selecting his nominees to the Court. In practice, three facts of political life inform and limit his choices. The first is that it is not realistically feasible for the Chief Executive to designate a Justice and obtain confirmation by the Senate without the at least grudging approval by the two home state senators concerned, especially if the latter are members of the president's own political party. The time-honored practice of "Senatorial courtesy" is an omnipresent phenome-

non, because of senatorial camaraderie and the "blue slip" approval system, under which the Judiciary Committee normally will not favorably report a nominee to the floor if an objecting home-state senator has failed to return that slip. (Senator Edward Kennedy, during his two-year tenure as head of the Committee, abandoned the system in 1979, but it was partly restored by his successor, Senator Strom Thurmond, in 1981.) Although nominations to the Supreme Court are regarded as a personal province of presidential choice far more than the appointment of other judges, the Senate's "advice and consent" is neither routine nor perfunctory, to which recent history amply attests. In 1968, despite a favorable Judiciary Committee vote, the Senate refused to consent to President Johnson's promotion of Justice Abe Fortas to the Chief Justiceship; in 1969 it rejected President Richard M. Nixon's nomination of Judge Clement Haynsworth, Jr., by 55 to 45; and in 1970 it turned down that same president's selection of Judge G. Harrold Carswell by 51 to 45. And in 1988 the Senate rejected Robert Bork, who had been nominated by President Reagan, by a vote of 58 to 42. Douglas Ginsburg, the substitute nominee for Bork, withdrew. Justice Thomas was confirmed in 1991 only after a stormy session and by a vote of 52 to 48. Indeed, to date the Senate, for a variety of reasons, has refused to confirm twenty-nine Supreme Court nominees out of the total of 146 sent to it for its "advice and consent" (twenty-one of these during the nineteenth century).

The second major factor to be taken into account by the president is the evaluative role played by the American Bar Association's fourteen-member Committee on the Federal Judiciary, which has been an unofficial part of the judicial appointments process since 1946. The committee scrutinizes the qualifications of all nominees to the federal bench and normally assigns one of four "grades": Exceptionally Well Qualified, Well Qualified, Qualified, and Not Qualified.

See also

Labor and Employment Law

*Theoretically, the
president has carte
blanche in selecting
his nominees to the
Court.*

♦ **in rem**
*[Latin: against the
thing] A manner of
proceeding in a case so
that the decision and
remedy affect the status of
property with reference
to the whole world rather
than to particular
individuals.*

In the rare instances of a vacancy on the Supreme Court, however, the committee has in recent years adopted a different, threefold, categorization: "High Standards of Integrity, Judicial Temperament, and Professional Competence"; "Not Opposed"; and "Not Qualified."

The third consideration incumbent upon the Chief Executive is the subtle but demonstrable one of the influence, however *sub rosa* and *sotto voce,* of sitting and retired jurists. Recent research points convincingly to that phenomenon, personified most prominently by Chief Justice William Howard Taft. If Taft did not exactly "appoint" colleagues to vacancies that occurred during his nine-year tenure (1921–30), he assuredly vetoed those unacceptable to him. Among others also involved in advisory or lobbying roles, although on a lesser scale than Taft, were Chief Justices Charles Evans Hughes, Harlan F. Stone, Fred Vinson, Earl Warren, and Warren E. Burger and Associate Justices John Marshall Harlan I, Samuel F. Miller, Willis Van Devanter, Louis D. Brandeis, and Felix Frankfurter.

A composite portrait of the 105 men and two women who have been Justices of the Supreme Court provides the following cross-section: native-born: 101; male: 105 (the first woman, Sandra Day O'Connor, was appointed by President Ronald Reagan in the summer of 1981 and the second, Ruth Bader Ginsburg, by President Bill Clinton in 1993); white: 105 (the first black Justice, Thurgood Marshall, was appointed by President Lyndon B. Johnson in 1967); predominantly Protestant: 92 (there have been eight Roman Catholic and seven Jewish Justices—the first in each category were Andrew Jackson's appointment of Chief Justice Roger B. Taney in 1836 and Woodrow Wilson's of Louis D. Brandeis in 1916, respectively); 50–55 years of age at time of appointment (the two youngest have been Joseph Story, 33, in 1812 and William O. Douglas, 41, in 1939); of

Anglo-Saxon ethnic stock (all except nineteen); from an upper middle to high social status (all except a handful); reared in a non-rural but not necessarily urban environment; member of a civic-minded, politically aware, economically comfortable family (all except a handful); holders of B.A. and, in this century, LL.B. or J.D. degrees (with one-third from "Ivy League" institutions); and a background of at least some type of public or community service (all except Justice George Shiras). Contemporary recognition of egalitarianism and "representativeness" may alter this profile, but it is not likely to change radically.

Only the president and his close advisers know the actual motivations for the choice of a particular Supreme Court appointee. But a perusal of the records of the thirty-five presidents who nominated Justices (four—W. H. Harrison, Zachary Taylor, Andrew Johnson, and Jimmy Carter—had no opportunity to do so) points to several predominating criteria, most apparent of which have been: (1) objective merit; (2) personal friendship; (3) considerations of "representativeness"; (4) political ideological compatibility, what Theodore Roosevelt referred to as a selectee's "real politics"; and (5) past judicial experience. Appropriate examples of (1) would be Benjamin N. Cardozo (Herbert Hoover) and John Marshall Harlan (Dwight D. Eisenhower); of (2) Harold H. Burton (Harry S Truman) and Abe Fortas (Lyndon Johnson); of (4) Hugo Black (Franklin D. Roosevelt) and William Howard Taft (Warren G. Harding); of (5) Oliver Wendell Holmes (Theodore Roosevelt) and David J. Brewer (Benjamin Harrison). Deservedly most contentious is motivation (3), under which presidents have been moved to weigh such "equitable" factors as geography, religion, gender, race, and perhaps even age in order to provide a "representative" profile of the Court. Of uncertain justification, it is nonetheless a fact of life of the appointive process. Thus geography proved decisive in

Franklin D. Roosevelt's selection of Wiley Rutledge of Iowa ("Wiley, you have geography," Roosevelt told him) and Abraham Lincoln's selection of Stephen J. Field of California. But given the superb qualifications of Judge Cardozo, despite the presence of two other New Yorkers (Hughes and Stone), the former's selection was all but forced upon Hoover. The notion that there should be a "Roman Catholic" and "Jewish" seat has been present ever since the appointments of Taney and Brandeis. Although there have been periods without such "reserved" seats (for example, 1949–56 in the former case and 1965–1993 in the latter), presidents are aware of the insistent pressures for such "representation." These pressures have increased since the "establishment" of a "black" seat (Marshall in 1967, by Johnson) and a "woman's seat" (O'Connor, by Reagan, in 1981). It has become all but unthinkable that future Supreme Court lineups will not henceforth have "representatives" from such categories. That the Founding Fathers neither considered nor addressed any of these "representative" factors does not gainsay their presence and significance in the political process.

Whatever may be the merits of other criteria motivating presidential Supreme Court appointments, the key factor is the Chief Executive's perception of a candidate's "real" politics—for it is the nominee's likely voting pattern as a Justice that matters most to an incumbent president. To a greater or lesser extent, all presidents have thus attempted to "pack" the bench. Court-packing has been most closely associated with Franklin D. Roosevelt. Failing a single opportunity to fill a Court vacancy during his first term (and five months of his second), and seeing his domestic programs consistently battered by "the Nine Old Men," Roosevelt moved to get his way in one fell swoop with his "Court Packing Bill" of 1937; however, it was reported unfavorably by the Senate Judiciary Committee and was interred by a decisive

recommittal vote. Ultimately, the passage of time enabled him to fill nine vacancies between 1937 and 1943. Yet George Washington was able to nominate fourteen, of whom ten chose to serve, and his selectees were measured against a sextet of criteria: (1) support and advocacy of the Constitution; (2) distinguished service in the revolution; (3) active participation in the political life of the new nation; (4) prior judicial experience on lower tribunals; (5) either a "favorable reputation with his fellows" or personal ties with Washington himself; and (6) geographic "suitability." Whatever the specific predispositions may be, concern with a nominee's "real" politics has been and will continue to be crucial in presidential motivations. It even prompted Republican president Taft to award half of his six nominations to the Court to Democrats, who were kindred "real politics" souls (Horace H. Lurton, Edward D. White's promotion to Chief Justice, and Joseph R. Lamar). In ten other instances the appointee came from a formal political affiliation other than that of the appointer, ranging from Whig president John Tyler's appointment of Democrat Samuel Nelson in 1845 to Republican Richard M. Nixon's selection of Democrat Lewis F. Powell Jr. in 1971.

But to predict the ultimate voting pattern or behavior of a nominee is to lean upon a slender reed. In the characteristically blunt words of President Truman: "Packing the Supreme Court simply can't be done.... I've tried and it won't work. . . . Whenever you put a man on the Supreme Court he ceases to be your friend. I'm sure of that." There is indeed a considerable element of unpredictability in the judicial appointment process. To the question whether a judicial robe makes a person any different, Justice Frankfurter's sharp retort was always, "If he is any good, he does!" In Alexander M. Bickel's words, "You shoot an arrow into a far-distant future when you appoint a Justice and not

The Supreme Court declined to strike down a village's refusal to rezone land to allow multiple-family dwellings, despite the refusal's racially discriminatory adverse effects.

See also

Washington v. Davis

the man himself can tell you what he will think about some of the problems that he will face." And late in 1969, reflecting upon his sixteen years as Chief Justice of the United States, Earl Warren pointed out that he, for one, did not "see how a man could be on the Court and not change his views substantially over a period of years . . . for change you must if you are to do your duty on the Supreme Court." It is clear beyond doubt that the Supreme Court appointment process is fraught with imponderables and guesswork, notwithstanding the carefully composed constitutional obligations of president and Senate.

—HENRY J. ABRAHAM

Bibliography

Abraham, Henry J. (1985). *Justices and Presidents: A Political History of Appointments to the Supreme Court.* 2nd ed. New York: Oxford University Press.

———— (1986). *The Judicial Process: An Introductory Analysis of the Courts of the United States, England and France.* 5th ed. New York: Oxford University Press.

Danelski, David J. (1964). *A Supreme Court Justice Is Appointed.* New York: Random House.

Schmidhauser, John R. (1960). *The Supreme Court: Its Politics, Personalities and Procedures.* New York: Holt, Rinehart & Winston.

———— (1979). *Judges and Justices: The Federal Appellate Judiciary.* Boston: Little, Brown.

ARLINGTON HEIGHTS v. METROPOLITAN HOUSING DEVELOPMENT CORP.

429 U.S. 252 (1977)

This decision confirmed in another context the previous term's holding in *Washington* v. *Davis* (1976) that discriminatory purpose must be shown to establish race-based violations of the equal protection clause. The Supreme Court declined to strike down a village's refusal to rezone land to allow multiple-family dwellings, despite the refusal's racially discriminatory adverse effects. Writing for the Court, Justice Lewis F. Powell elaborated on the nature of the showing that must be made to satisfy the purpose requirement announced in *Washington* v. *Davis.* A plaintiff need not prove that challenged action rested solely on racially discriminatory purposes. Instead, proof that a discriminatory purpose was a motivating factor would require the offending party to prove that it would have taken the challenged action even in the absence of a discriminatory purpose. Powell noted the types of evidence that might lead to a finding of discriminatory purpose: egregious discriminatory effects, the historical background of the governmental action, departures from normal procedure, legislative and administrative history, and, in some instances, testimony by the decision makers themselves.

—THEODORE EISENBERG

B

BAKER v. CARR

369 U.S. 186 (1962)

Chief Justice Earl Warren considered *Baker* v. *Carr* the most important case decided by the Warren Court. Its holding was cryptic: "The right [to equal districts in the Tennessee legislature] is within the reach of judicial protection under the Fourteenth Amendment." Many people expected reapportionment under *Baker* to vitalize American democracy. Others feared that it would snare the judiciary in unresolvable questions of political representation, outside the proper bounds of its constitutional authority.

Tennesseans, like others, had moved from countryside to urban and suburban districts, but no redistricting had taken place since 1901. Supporters of reapportionment claimed that the resulting swollen districts made "second-class citizens" of city voters; they blamed "malapportionment" for urban woes and legislative apathy. Finding little legislative sympathy for these claims, they turned to the courts.

But they had several hurdles to clear. The framers of the Fourteenth Amendment had repeatedly denied that it protected the right to vote. Perhaps it protected rights of representation, but the Court had found such rights too cloudy, too sensitive, and too "political" to settle judicially.

The central hurdle was the "standards problem" expounded by Justice Felix Frankfurter in *Colegrove* v. *Green* (1946) and in his *Baker* dissent. How could the Court tell lower courts and legislatures the difference between good representation and bad, lacking clear constitutional guidance? The Con-

stitution was a complex blend of competing and countervailing principles, not a mandate for equal districts. "What is actually asked of the Court . . . is to choose among competing bases of representation—ultimately, really, among competing theories of philosophy—in order to establish an appropriate form of government for . . . the states. . . ." Frankfurter accused the Court of sending the lower courts into a "mathematical quagmire."

Writing for the majority, Justice William J. Brennan argued that the *Colegrove* court had not found apportionment a political question but had declined to hear it using equity discretion. But he did not answer Frankfurter's challenge to lay down workable standards, nor Justice John Marshall Harlan's objection, later reasserted in *Reynolds* v. *Sims* (1964), that nothing in the Constitution conveyed a right to equal districts. Brennan merely claimed that "judicial standards under the equal protection clause are well developed and familiar," and that "the right asserted is within the reach of judicial protection under the Fourteenth Amendment."

The concurring Justices, William O. Douglas and Tom C. Clark, were not so cautious. Clark felt that "rational" departures from equal districts, such as districts approved by popular referendum, should be permitted. Douglas emphasized that the standards would be flexible (though he would later vote for rigid standards).

These opinions, and *Baker*'s place in history, make sense only in the context of Solicitor General Archibald Cox's amicus curiae brief supporting intervention. To take on a cause that could, and later did, jeopardize the seats of most of the legislators in the country, and invite formidable political reprisals, the

Baker has left us two legacies. The good one is equalizing district size. The bad one is rhetorical indirection, constitutional fabrication, and a penchant for overriding the wishes of people and their representatives.

◆ **comity**
The respect owed by one court or governmental agency to the official acts of a court or agency in another jurisdiction.

Justices had to move with caution. Cox's brief reassured them that the John F. Kennedy administration, like its predecessor, favored intervention. The executive support probably swayed the votes of at least two Justices, Clark and Potter Stewart. Had these voted against intervention, the Court would have divided 4–4, leaving intact the lower court's decision not to hear the case.

Moreover, Cox's brief did address Harlan's and Frankfurter's challenges. As with *Brown* v. *Board of Education* (1954), he argued, constitutional authority could be demonstrated from social need, as perceived by social scien-

GERRYMANDER

A gerrymander is a political district drawn to advantage some and disadvantage others: candidates, parties, or interest groups. The name comes from a particularly spectacular partisan apportionment engineered by Elbridge Gerry in 1812. Technically, any winner-take-all district can be called a gerrymander, for district lines inevitably favor some against others. But common usage limits the term to districts deemed unnatural in form or unfair in intent or effect. The Supreme Court boldly and unanimously attacked a blatant racial gerrymander in *Gomillion* v. *Lightfoot* (1960), but it has been almost uniformly acquiescent since then.

Gomillion voided an "uncouth, 28–sided figure" surgically excluding almost all of the blacks in Tuskegee, Alabama, from voting in the city while retaining every white. It cleared the way for *Baker* v. *Carr* (1962) and the reapportionment revolution. But apart from a few cases of municipal expansion challenged under the Voting Rights Act of 1965, the Court has never since been able or willing to find "cognizable discrimination" in gerrymandering cases.

tists, incorporated into a spacious reading of the Fourteenth Amendment. As for standards, there were two possibilities: an absolute, individual right to vote, perhaps grounded on the equal protection clause, and a loose, group right to equal representation, perhaps grounded on the due process clause. Of the two, Cox seemed to favor the looser one, forbidding "egregious cases" of "gross discrimination." He even showed how such a standard might be drawn on a map of Tennessee. Because he was explicit, Brennan could afford to be cryptic and let the Cox brief draw most of Frankfurter's and Harlan's fire.

Within two years the Court announced in *Reynolds* v. *Sims* that equal representation for equal numbers was the "fundamental goal" of the Constitution and laid down standards so strict that every state but one, Oregon, was compelled to reapportion. Compliance with *Baker* was widespread and quick. Opposition was strong but late. By 1967 the states had come within a few votes of the two-thirds needed to call a constitutional convention to strip courts of redistricting power, but by then reapportionment was largely completed, and the movement died.

Reapportionment added many urban and suburban seats to legislatures, replacing rural ones, but there is little evidence that it produced any of the liberalizing, vitalizing policies its proponents had predicted. What it did bring was a plague of gerrymandering, renewed after each census, because it forced legislators to redistrict without forcing them to be nonpartisan. The Court since *Baker* has been powerless to control gerrymanders. Packing or diluting a group in a district can strengthen or weaken the group, or do both at once. There is no way short of commanding proportional representation to equalize everyone's representation. Nor is there a workable way to equalize representation in the Electoral College, the Senate, the national party conventions, party committees, runoff elections, executive appointments, or multimember districts. The Court opened these doors when it announced that representation was the fundamental goal of the Constitution, but it closed them when it found that they raised the standards problem too plainly to permit intervention, exactly as Frankfurter had warned.

Baker has left us two legacies. The good one is equalizing district size. The bad one is rhetorical indirection, constitutional fabrication, and a penchant for overriding the wishes of people and their representatives, as for example, in *Lucas* v. *Forty-fourth General Assembly* (1964). Whether the good legacy is worth the bad, and whether it even added on balance to equal representation, can be told only with reference to the full breadth of representation which was too complicated for the Court to touch.

—WARD E. Y. ELLIOTT

Bibliography

Cox, Archibald (1967). *The Warren Court: Constitutional Decision as an Instrument of Reform.* Cambridge, Mass.: Harvard University Press.

Dixon, Robert G., Jr. (1968). *Democratic Representation: Reapportionment in Law and Politics.* New York: Oxford University Press.

Elliott, Ward E. Y. (1975). *The Rise of Guardian Democracy: The Supreme Court's Role in Voting Rights Disputes, 1845–1969.* Cambridge, Mass.: Harvard University Press.

Navasky, Victor (1971). *Kennedy Justice.* New York: Atheneum.

BANK OF AUGUSTA v. EARLE

13 Peters 519 (1839)

This case was vitally important to corporations because it raised the question whether a corporation chartered in one state could do business in another. Justice John McKinley on circuit duty ruled against corporations, provoking Justice Joseph Story to say that McKinley's opinion frightened "all the corporations of the country out of their proprieties. He has held that a corporation created in one State has no power to contract or even to act in any other State. . . . So, banks, insurance companies, manufacturing companies, etc. have no capacity to take or discount notes in another State, or to underwrite policies, or to buy or sell goods." McKinley's decision seemed a death sentence to all interstate corporate business. On appeal, Daniel Webster, representing corporate interests, argued that corporations were citizens entitled to the same rights, under the comity clause in Article IV, section 2, of the Constitution, as natural persons to do business. With only McKinley dissenting, Chief Justice Roger B. Taney for the Court steered a middle way between the extremes of McKinley and Webster. He ruled that a corporation, acting through its agents, could do business in other states if they did not expressly prohibit it from doing so. In the absence of such a state prohibition, the Court would presume, from the principle of comity, that out-of-state corporations were invited to transact business. Thus a state might exclude such corporations or admit them conditionally; but the Court overruled McKinley's decision, and corporations as well as Whigs, like Webster and Story, rejoiced.

—LEONARD W. LEVY

BARKER v. WINGO

407 U.S. 514 (1972)

The speedy trial right protects a defendant from undue delay between the time charges are filed and trial. When a defendant is deprived of that right, the only remedy is dismissal with prejudice of the charges pending

McKinley's decision seemed a death sentence to all interstate corporate business.

In Barker, *the leading speedy trial decision, the Supreme Court discussed the criteria by which the speedy trial right is to be judged.*

No state shall violate freedom of religion, freedom of press, or trial by jury in criminal cases.

against him. In *Barker,* the leading speedy trial decision, the Supreme Court discussed the criteria by which the speedy trial right is to be judged. The Court adopted a balancing test involving four factors to be weighed in each case where the issue arises. They are: (1) the length of the delay; (2) the reasons for the delay; (3) the defendant's assertion of his right; and (4) prejudice to the defendant, such as pretrial incarceration and inability to prepare a defense. In reaching its decision the Court noted that the speedy trial right is unique inasmuch as it protects societal rights as well as those of the accused. In many instances, delayed trials benefit a defendant because witnesses disappear or memories fade. The balancing takes into consideration the varied interests protected by that right.

—WENDY E. LEVY

BARRON v. CITY OF BALTIMORE

7 Peters 243 (1833)

When James Madison proposed to the First Congress the amendments that became the

Bill of Rights, he included a provision that no state shall violate freedom of religion, freedom of press, or trial by jury in criminal cases; the proposal to restrict the states was defeated. The amendments constituting a Bill of Rights were understood to be a bill of restraints upon the United States only. In *Barron,* Chief Justice John Marshall for a unanimous Supreme Court ruled in conformance with the clear history of the matter. *Barron* invoked against Baltimore the clause of the Fifth Amendment prohibiting the taking of private property without just compensation. The "fifth amendment," the Court held, "must be understood as restraining the power of the general government, not as applicable to the states."

—LEONARD W. LEVY

BARROWS v. JACKSON

346 U.S. 249 (1953)

Following the decision in *Shelley* v. *Kraemer* (1948), state courts could no longer constitutionally enforce racially restrictive covenants by injunction. The question remained whether

See also

Marshall, John

the covenants could be enforced indirectly, in actions for damages. In *Barrows,* white neighbors sued for damages against co-covenantors who had sold a home to black buyers in disregard of a racial covenant. The Supreme Court held that the sellers had standing to raise the equal protection claims on behalf of the black buyers, who were not in court, and went on to hold that the Fourteenth Amendment barred damages as well as injunctive relief to enforce racial covenants. Chief Justice Fred M. Vinson, who had written the *Shelley* opinion, dissented, saying the covenant itself, "standing alone," was valid, in the absence of judicial ejectment of black occupants.

—KENNETH L. KARST

BATSON v. KENTUCKY

476 U.S. 79 (1986)

This decision made a major change in the law of jury discrimination. In *Swain* v. *Alabama* (1965) the Supreme Court had held that systematic exclusions of black people from criminal trial juries in a series of cases would be a prima facie showing of racial discrimination in violation of the equal protection clause of the Fourteenth Amendment. The Court said, however, that a prosecutor's use of peremptory challenges to keep all potential black jurors from serving in a particular case would not be such a showing. In *Batson* the Court, 7–2, overruled *Swain* on the latter point and set out standards for finding an equal protection violation based on a prosecutor's use of peremptory challenges in a single case.

In a Kentucky state court James Batson had been convicted of burglary and receipt of stolen goods. After the trial judge had ruled on challenges of potential jurors for cause, the prosecutor had used peremptory challenges—challenges that need not be justified by a showing of potential bias—to keep all four black members of the jury panel from

serving on the trial jury. The Kentucky courts denied the defendant's claims that this use of peremptory challenges violated his Sixth Amendment right to trial by jury and his right to equal protection of the laws.

In reversing this decision, the Supreme Court's majority spoke through Justice Lewis F. Powell. The equal protection clause barred a prosecutor from challenging potential jurors solely on account of their race. *Swain*'s narrow evidentiary standard would allow deliberate racial discrimination to go unremedied. Accordingly, the majority ruled that a defendant establishes a prima facie case of racial discrimination by showing that the prosecutor has used peremptory challenges to keep potential jurors of the defendant's race from serving and that the circumstances raise an inference that the prosecutor did so on account of the defendant's race. If the trial court makes these findings, the burden shifts to the prosecution to offer a race-neutral explanation for the challenges. The judge must then decide whether the defendant has established purposeful discrimination. Plainly, *Batson*'s evidentiary standard leaves much to the trial judge's discretion.

Justice Thurgood Marshall concurred, but said he would hold all peremptory challenges unconstitutional because of their potential for discriminatory use. Justices Byron R. White and Sandra Day O'Connor concurred separately, stating that the new evidentiary standard should be applied only prospectively. Chief Justice Warren E. Burger dissented, stating that the long-standing practice of peremptory challenges served the state's interest in jury impartiality and arguing that such challenges were typically made for reasons that could not be articulated on nonarbitrary grounds. Justice William H. Rehnquist also dissented, defending the legitimacy of peremptory challenges even when they are based on crude stereotypes.

Peremptory challenges have, indeed, long been based on group stereotypes. If the

Batson *marked a major change in the law of jury discrimination.*

◆ **venue**
The place where a case is to be heard.

See also

Vinson, Fred M.

**PREEMPTORY
CHALLENGES**

*Potential jurors cannot be
disqualified solely on account
of their race.
(Corbis/Bettmann-UPI)*

Supreme Court were to apply the standard to challenges of other groups, the law would be, in practice, much as Justice Marshall said it should be. Even if the new standard is limited to cases of racial discrimination, if trial judges apply it zealously, prosecutors will likely confine their challenges of potential black jurors in cases involving black defendants to challenges for cause.

In *Holland* v. *Illinois* (1990) the Court rejected, 5–4, a white defendant's claim that the prosecutor's use of peremptory challenges to keep blacks off the trial jury violated the Sixth Amendment right to a jury drawn from a fair cross section of the community. A majority of the Justices, however, expressed the view that *Batson*'s equal protection principle, which in this case the defendant had not raised, would extend to such a case. That view

became law in *Powers* v. *Ohio* (1991). Since then, the *Batson* rule barring discrimination in peremptory challenges has been extended to civil suits, *Edmonson* v. *Leesville Concrete Co.* (1991), and to discrimination based on gender, *J.E.B.* v. *Alabama ex rel. T.B.* (1994).

—KENNETH L. KARST

BEAUHARNAIS
v. ILLINOIS

343 U.S. 250 (1952)

The Supreme Court upheld, 5–4, an Illinois group libel statute that forbade publications depicting a racial or religious group as depraved or lacking in virtue. Justice Felix Frankfurter first argued that certain categories of speech including libel had traditionally been excluded from First Amendment protection, and he then deferred to the legislative judgment redefining libel to include defamation of groups as well as individuals. By mixing excluded-categories arguments with arguments for judicial deference to legislative judgments for which there is a rational basis, the opinion moves toward a position in which the relative merits of a particular speech are weighed against the social interests protected by the statute, with the ultimate constitutional balance heavily weighted in favor of whatever balance the legislature has struck. Although *Beauharnais* has not been overruled, its continued validity is doubtful after *New York Times* v. *Sullivan* (1964).

—MARTIN SHAPIRO

BENDER v. WILLIAMSPORT

475 U.S. 534 (1986)

High-school students in Pennsylvania sought permission to meet together at school for prayer and Bible study during extracurricular periods. School authorities refused permission on the basis of the establishment clause, despite the fact that the school allowed a wide variety of other student groups to meet on school premises. The students filed suit, claiming violation of their First Amendment right to freedom of speech.

The district court sided with the students, invoking the doctrine of equal access enunciated by the Court in *Widmar* v. *Vincent* (1981). However, the appeals court reversed, claiming that allowing the students to meet would violate the establishment clause. The Supreme Court granted certiorari to decide the question, which it subsequently declined to do. A bare majority of the Court's Justices sidestepped the constitutional controversy altogether by holding that the party who appealed the district court ruling lacked standing.

The four dissenters would have reached the merits of the case and extended the analysis of *Widmar* to secondary schools. According to the dissenters, not only did the establishment clause not forbid religious student groups from meeting on school premises, but schools had an affirmative duty under the First Amendment to allow such groups access to school facilities on the same basis as other groups.

The decision in *Bender* allowed the Court to put off indefinitely the question of whether the Constitution requires equal access in secondary schools. While *Bender* was still in litigation, Congress guaranteed equal access by statute, thus reducing pressure on the Court to resolve the free-speech question.

—JOHN G. WEST, JR .

BENTON v. MARYLAND

395 U.S. 784 (1969)

This decision, one of the last of the Warren Court, extended the double jeopardy provision of the Fifth Amendment to the states. A Maryland prisoner, having been acquitted on a larceny charge, successfully appealed his burglary conviction, only to be reindicted and convicted on both counts. A 7–2 Supreme Court, speaking through Justice Thurgood Marshall, overruled *Palko* v. *Connecticut* (1937) and, relying on *Duncan* v. *Louisiana* (1968), declared that the Fifth Amendment guarantee "represents a fundamental ideal" which must be applied. Dissenting, Justices John Marshall Harlan and Potter Stewart reiterated their opposition to incorporation, concluding that the writ of certiorari had been improvidently granted. In obiter dictum they added that retrial here violated even the *Palko* standards.

—DAVID GORDON

High-school students in Pennsylvania sought permission to meet together at school for prayer and Bible sudy during extracurricular periods.

♦ **incorporation**
(1) a doctrine according to which certain specific provisions of the Bill of Rights are made applicable against state authority by virtue of the "due process" clause of the Fourteenth Amendment; (2) a doctrine according to which certain territories are made so intimately a part of the United States that certain constitutional protections become applicable to the inhabitants.

See also

Palko v. *Connecticut*

This case is significant as a dimunition of free speech by students; they cannot say what can be said constitutionally outside a school.

♦ **ordinance**
Any statute. In recent times, most commonly used for enactments by cities, counties, or other local governments.

See also

Freedom of Speech

BETHEL SCHOOL DISTRICT v. FRASER

478 U.S. 675 (1986)

The Supreme Court had previously held that the First Amendment's protection of freedom of speech does not stop at school doors. In this case the Court held that a student's freedom of speech is not coextensive with an adult's because school authorities may rightly punish a student for making indecent remarks in a school assembly, which disrupt the educational process. School authorities might constitutionally teach civility and appropriateness of language by disciplining the offensive student. Justice Thurgood Marshall agreed with the majority on the obligation of the school to safeguard its educational mission, but believed that the authorities failed to prove that the speech was offensive. Justice John Paul Stevens, also dissenting, claimed that the speech was not offensive. The case is significant as a diminution of free speech by students; they cannot say what can be said constitutionally outside a school.

—LEONARD W. LEVY

BISHOP v. WOOD

426 U.S. 341 (1976)

Bishop worked a major change in the modern law of procedural due process, enshrining in the law the view Justice William H. Rehnquist had unsuccessfully urged in *Arnett* v. *Kennedy* (1974): the due process right of a holder of a statutory "entitlement" is defined by positive law, not by the Constitution itself.

Here, a city ordinance that classified a police officer as a "permanent employee" was nonetheless interpreted by the lower federal courts to give an officer employment only "at the will and pleasure of the city." The Supreme Court held, 5–4, that this ordinance created no "property" interest in the officer's employment, and that, absent public disclosure of the reasons for his termination, he had suffered no stigma that impaired a "liberty" interest. The key to the majority's decision presumably lay in this sentence: "The federal court is not the appropriate forum in which to review the multitude of personnel decisions that are made daily by public agencies."

In dissent, Justice William J. Brennan accurately commented that the Court had resurrected the "right/privilege" distinction, discredited in *Goldberg* v. *Kelly* (1970), and insisted that there was a federal constitutional dimension to the idea of "property" interests, not limited by state law and offering the protections of due process to legitimate expectations raised by government.

Since *Bishop* the Court has in large measure returned to its earlier, more generous view of procedural due process, holding in *Cleveland Board of Education* v. *Loudermill* (1985) that a civil service employee is entitled to an opportunity to be heard on charges of misconduct even through the employer had denied the employee that right.

—KENNETH L. KARST

BIVENS v. SIX UNKNOWN NAMED AGENTS OF THE FEDERAL BUREAU OF NARCOTICS

403 U.S. 388 (1971)

This is the leading case concerning implied rights of action under the Constitution. Federal agents conducted an unconstitutional search of Webster Bivens's apartment. Bivens brought an action in federal court seeking damages for a Fourth Amendment violation. Although no federal statute supplied Bivens with a cause of action, the Supreme Court, in an opinion by Justice William J. Brennan, held that Bivens could maintain that action.

Two central factors led to the decision. First, violations of constitutional rights ought not go unremedied. The traditional remedy, enjoining unconstitutional behavior, plainly was inadequate for Bivens. And the Court was unwilling to leave Bivens to the uncertainties of state tort law, his principal alternative source of action. Second, the implied constitutional cause of action makes federal officials as vulnerable as state officials for constitutional misbehavior. Prior to *Bivens,* state officials were subject to suits under Section 1983, Title 42, United States Code, for violating individuals' constitutional rights. An action against federal officials had to be inferred in *Bivens* only because section 1983 is inapplicable to federal officials.

Both factors emerged again in later cases. *Davis* v. *Passman* (1979) recognized an implied constitutional cause of action for claims brought under the Fifth Amendment, and *Carlson* v. *Green* (1980) extended *Bivens* to other constitutional rights. *Butz* v. *Economou* (1978) extended to federal officials the good faith defense that state officials enjoy under section 1983.

Bivens raises important questions about the scope of federal judicial power. Chief Justice Warren E. Burger and Justices Hugo L. Black and Harry Blackmun dissented on the ground that Congress alone may authorize damages against federal officials. The majority, and Justice John Marshall Harlan in a concurring opinion, required no congressional authorization. But they left open the possibility that Congress might have the last word in the area through express legislation.
—THEODORE EISENBERG

BLACKMUN, HARRY A.

(1908–1999)

Harry Andrew Blackmun was born in the small town of Nashville, Illinois, on November 12, 1908, but spent most of his childhood in St. Paul, Minnesota. He attended Harvard College on a scholarship, graduating summa cum laude in 1929 with a major in mathematics. Torn between medicine and law, he chose the latter route and attended Harvard Law School, from which he graduated in 1932.

Immediately after graduation Blackmun served as a law clerk to Judge John B. Sanborn of the United States Court of Appeals for the Eighth Circuit. He then joined the Minneapolis law firm of Dorsey, Coleman, Barker, Scott, and Barber, where he specialized in tax, civil litigation, and estates. Blackmun left the firm in 1950 to become resident counsel at the Mayo Clinic in Rochester, Minnesota, where he says he enjoyed "the happiest years of my professional experience," with "a foot in both camps, law and medicine."

In 1959 President Dwight D. Eisenhower nominated Blackmun to replace his former employer, Judge Sanborn, on the Eighth Circuit. Blackmun served on that court for eleven years, and then, after the Senate refused to confirm Clement F. Haynsworth Jr. and G. Harrold Carswell for Abe Fortas's seat on the Supreme Court, President Richard M. Nixon nominated Blackmun, thus accounting for the nickname that Blackmun uses to refer to himself—"Old No. 3." Blackmun was unanimously confirmed by the Senate and was sworn in as the Supreme Court's ninety-ninth Justice on May 12, 1970.

In appointing Blackmun, Nixon was looking for a judge who shared his philosophy of judicial restraint and would work to reverse the liberal, activist rulings of the Warren Court. Nixon's hopes for his new appointee, coupled with Blackmun's long-term friendship with Chief Justice Warren E. Burger, who had known Blackmun since childhood and had asked Blackmun to serve as the best man at his wedding, led the media to refer to Burger and Blackmun as the "Minnesota Twins." The two Justices' similar voting patterns during Blackmun's early years on the Court lent credence to the epithet.

Bivens raises important questions about the scope of federal judicial power.

♦ **bail**
Money deposited with a court to guarantee the appearance of a defendant for trial, permitting his release from jail until trial.

Although Blackmun generally lived up to Nixon's expectations in criminal procedure cases, he increasingly sided with Justice William J. Brennan Jr. in other controversial cases and is now considered part of the Court's liberal wing. For his part, Blackmun puts little stock in such labels, noting shortly after being nominated to the Supreme Court, "I've been called a liberal and a conservative. Labels are deceiving." He claimed that his views did not change over the years, but that "it's the Court that's changed under me."

Whatever the truth on this issue, Blackmun will likely be best remembered for his controversial and ground-breaking opinion in *Roe* v. *Wade* (1973). *Roe* held that the constitutional right of privacy protected a woman's right to an abortion, thereby in effect invalidating abortion statutes in forty-six states.

Blackmun continued to advocate the constitutional right to abortion. He wrote the Court's opinions in *Planned Parenthood of Central Missouri* v. *Danforth* (1976), invalidating requirements of spousal and parental

consent, and in *Akron* v. *Akron Center for Reproductive Health, Inc.* (1983) and *Thornburgh* v. *American College of Obstetricians and Gynecologists* (1986), striking down various efforts to impose procedural restrictions limiting the availability of abortions.

More recently, however, Blackmun found himself in dissent on the abortion issue. In *Webster* v. *Reproductive Health Services* (1989), Chief Justice William H. Rehnquist, joined by Justices Byron R. White and Anthony M. Kennedy, observed that *Roe's* "rigid trimester analysis" had proved "unsound in principle and unworkable in practice." Although they did not believe the case required the Court to reconsider the validity of *Roe's* holding, Justice Antonin Scalia's concurrence indicated that he was ready to overrule *Roe*. Responding in a passionate dissent, Blackmun voiced his "fear for the liberty and equality of the millions of women who have lived and come of age in the 16 years since *Roe* was decided" and concluded that "for today, at least, . . . the women of this Nation still retain the liberty to control their destinies. But the signs are evident and very ominous, and a chill wind blows."

Although Blackmun's position on abortion remained constant, in other areas he demonstrated an admirable willingness to reconsider his views. His open-mindedness reflected his belief that the law is "not a rigid animal or a rigid profession," but rather a "constant search for truth," as well as his perception that a Supreme Court Justice "grows constitutionally" while on the bench.

One illustration of Blackmun's evolution was his increased tolerance of nontraditional lifestyles. Dissenting in *Cohen* v. *California* (1971), Blackmun argued that the "absurd and immature antic" of wearing a jacket in court bearing the words "Fuck the draft" was not constitutionally protected. He likewise dissented in *Smith* v. *Goguen* (1974), concluding that the states may constitutionally prosecute those who "harm[ ] the physical integrity of the flag by wearing it affixed to the

seats of [their] pants." More recently, however, he joined the controversial majority opinions in *Texas* v. *Johnson* (1989) and *United States* v. *Eichman* (1990), which held that the First Amendment prohibited prosecution of defendants who had burned the American flag during political protests.

Blackmun's growing tolerance of diversity was also obvious in his dissent in *Bowers* v. *Hardwick* (1986), which upheld the criminalization of sodomy. His stinging dissent observed that "a necessary corollary of giving individuals freedom to choose how to conduct their lives is acceptance of the fact that different individuals will make different choices" and that "depriving individuals of the right to choose for themselves how to conduct their intimate relationships poses a far greater threat to the values most deeply rooted in our Nation's history than tolerance of nonconformity could ever do."

As he became more accepting of the unconventional, Blackmun also became more suspicious of institutions. During his early years on the Court, he tended to defer to institutional prerogatives, believing that a judicial policy of noninterference would leave institutions free to exercise their discretion in the public interest. In his first majority opinion, *Wyman* v. *James* (1971), Blackmun rejected a welfare recipient's Fourth Amendment challenge to home visits from the welfare department caseworker, whom Blackmun described as "not a sleuth but rather . . . a friend to one in need." He dissented in *Bivens* v. *Six Unknown Named Agents* (1971) because he feared that creating a tort remedy for Fourth Amendment violations by federal agents would "open[ ] the door for another avalanche of new federal cases," thereby tending "to stultify proper law enforcement and to make the day's labor for the honest and conscientious officer even more onerous."

More recently, however, Blackmun became less trusting of public officials and institutions. In *United States* v. *Bailey* (1980), for example, his recognition of the "atrocities

and inhuman conditions of prison life in America" led him to support a broader duress defense in prison escape cases than the majority was willing to recognize. The picture he painted of prison officials was not a sympathetic one: he described them as indifferent to prisoners' health and safety needs and even as active participants in "the brutalization of inmates."

Given his growing distrust of public officials, Blackmun increasingly minimized the concerns about the federal courts' caseload expressed in his *Bivens* dissent and instead has opposed limitations on access to the courts. He believed that statutes authorizing federal civil rights suits represent "the commitment of our society to be governed by law and to protect the rights of those without power against oppression at the hands of the powerful." Accordingly, in *Allen* v. *McCurry* (1980) he dissented from the Court's holding that federal courts must give preclusive effect to prior state court adjudications in civil rights suits; in *Rose* v. *Lundy* (1982) he opposed the strict exhaustion requirement the majority imposed on habeas corpus petitioners; and in *Atascadero State Hospital* v. *Scanlon* (1985) he joined Justice Brennan's dissent, which would have prohibited the states from invoking the Eleventh Amendment to bar federal question suits in federal court.

Another manifestation of Blackmun's increased suspicion of institutions was his endorsement of more rigorous judicial scrutiny of social and economic legislation under the equal protection clause. Such legislation is upheld so long as it meets the rational basis test—that is, so long as the legislative means are rationally related to a legitimate governmental purpose. Over the years, the Court has given conflicting signals as to how deferential the rational basis test is. In *United States Railroad Retirement Board* v. *Fritz* (1980) the Court held that the test was satisfied if a judge could think of some plausible, hypothetical reason for the statutory scheme; whether this hypothetical justification bore

Subjected to criticism after Roe, *Blackmun was forced, according to one view, to confront fundamental questions about his role as Supreme Court Justice.*

any relationship to the legislature's actual purpose was, the Court said, "constitutionally irrelevant." Less than three months later, however, Blackmun's majority opinion in *Schweiker* v. *Wilson* (1981) observed that the rational basis test is "not a toothless one," and upheld the Medicaid provision at issue there only after finding that the statutory classification represented "Congress' deliberate, considered choice." Similarly, in his separate opinion in *Logan* v. *Zimmerman Brush Company* (1982), Blackmun found a legislative classification irrational, explaining that the justification for statutory classifications "must be something more than the exercise of a strained imagination."

The limitations imposed by federalism on the federal government's powers provide a second illustration of Blackmun's willingness to rethink his views. Blackmun represented the decisive fifth vote in *National League of Cities* v. *Usery* (1976), where the Court concluded that the Tenth Amendment prohibited Congress from regulating the wages and hours of state employees. His brief concurring opinion interpreted the majority opinion as adopting a balancing approach that sought to accommodate competing federal and state concerns and that would permit federal regulation in areas where the federal interest was "demonstrably greater." Although this interpretation may have represented wishful thinking on Blackmun's part, he did join the majority opinion in full.

After deserting the other Justices from the *National League of Cities* majority in both *Federal Energy Regulatory Commission* v. *Mississippi* (1982) and *Equal Employment Opportunity Commission* v. *Wyoming* (1983), Blackmun ultimately wrote the opinion overruling *National League of Cities* in *Garcia* v. *San Antonio Metropolitan Transit Authority* (1985). Blackmun explained that the *National League of Cities* approach had proven unworkable because it had been unable to identify a principled way of defining those integral state functions deserving of Tenth Amendment protection. He likewise renounced his own

balancing approach because it, too, had not provided a coherent standard capable of consistent application by the lower courts.

Though he ultimately rejected a balancing approach in the Tenth Amendment context, one of Blackmun's judicial trademarks was his tendency to reach decisions by balancing conflicting interests. He believes that "complex constitutional issues cannot be decided by resort to inflexible rules or predetermined categories." Consequently, he pays close attention to the facts of a case and often makes decisions on a case-by-case basis, rather than a sweeping doctrinal one.

Illustrative of Blackmun's balancing approach are his majority opinions in *Bigelow* v. *Virginia* (1975), *Virginia State Board of Pharmacy* v. *Virginia Consumers Council* (1976), and *Bates* v. *State Bar of Arizona* (1977), which provided the framework for the Court's modern approach to First Amendment cases involving commercial speech. Prior to these decisions, the Court considered commercial speech outside the realm of constitutional protection. In each of these three cases, however, Blackmun balanced the First Amendment interests of the advertisers against the public interests served by regulating commercial speech, because, as he explained in *Virginia State Board of Pharmacy*, "the free flow of commercial information is indispensable . . . to the proper allocation of resources in a free enterprise system, . . . [and] to the formation of intelligent opinions as to how that system ought to be regulated or altered." Applying this balancing test in each case, Blackmun struck down statutes banning advertisements of abortions, prescription drug prices, and legal fees. In each instance, he decided only the narrow issue confronting the Court, expressly declining to consider the extent to which commercial speech might be regulated in other contexts.

Blackmun's commercial speech opinions also illustrate another characteristic of his judicial philosophy—an interest in the real-world impact of the Court's decisions. His opinions often expressed concern that the Supreme Court operates too frequently from an "ivory tower." In his separate opinion in *Regents of University of California* v. *Bakke* (1978), for example, Blackmun urged his colleagues to "get down the road toward accepting and being a part of the real world, and not shutting it out and away from us." The balancing approach Blackmun adopted in the commercial speech cases likewise avoided abstract generalizations and focused the Court's attention on the concrete results of each case—in *Virginia State Board of Pharmacy*, for example, on the fact that "those whom the suppression of prescription price information hits the hardest are the poor, the sick, and particularly the aged."

Blackmun wrote a series of majority opinions in cases discussing the constitutionality of state efforts to tax interstate and foreign commerce that similarly emphasizes the real-world impact of the state tax at issue in each case. In *Complete Auto Transit, Inc.* v. *Brady* (1977) his opinion overruled prior Supreme Court precedent that held state taxes on the privilege of doing business within the state per se unconstitutional as applied to interstate commerce, and instead adopted a four-part test that stressed the practical effect of the state tax. He followed the same approach in *Department of Revenue* v. *Association of Washington Stevedoring Companies* (1978) and then in *Japan Line, Ltd.* v. *County of Los Angeles* (1979), where he adapted the *Complete Auto Transit* test to state taxation of foreign commerce.

Blackmun's emphasis on real-world concerns was often directed more specifically to the effect of the Court's decisions on the powerless, less fortunate members of society. He strived to do justice to the parties in each case, remarking in one interview, "To me, every case involves people. . . . If we forget the humanity of the litigants before us, . . . we're in trouble, no matter how great our supposed legal philosophy can be." This concern is evident in Blackmun's opinions as well. He concurred only in the result in *O'Bannon* v. *Town Court Nursing Center* (1980) because he found the majority's approach "heartless." His dissent in *Ford Motor Company* v. *Equal Employment Opportunity Commission* (1982), an employment discrimination case, criticized the majority's reliance on "abstract and technical concerns" that bore "little resemblance to those that actually motivated" the injured employees or anyone "living in the real world."

Aliens are perhaps the disadvantaged group for whom Blackmun has spoken most forcefully and consistently. In a series of majority opinions during the 1970s beginning with *Graham* v. *Richardson* (1971), which held that welfare benefits could not be conditioned on citizenship or duration of residence in this country, Blackmun urged that alienage be treated as a suspect classification. His more recent statements on behalf of aliens came in dissent. In *Cabell* v. *Chavez-Salido* (1982), which upheld a statute that denied aliens employment in any "peace officer" position, Blackmun's dissent focused on the majority's failure to consider the practical impact of its holding. He objected that the Court's abandonment of strict scrutiny was more than an academic matter; in *Cabell*, for example, the majority's permissive standard of review might permit the state to exlude aliens from more than seventy jobs, including toll takers, furniture and bedding inspectors, and volunteer fire wardens.

Blackmun also focused on the impact of the Court's decisions on the poor. Although one of his early opinions, *United States* v. *Kras* (1973), upheld a fifty-dollar filing fee in bankruptcy cases in part because paying the fee in installments would result in weekly payments "less than the price of a movie and little more than the cost of a pack or two of cigarettes," Blackmun more recently exhibited greater understanding of the plight of the poor. In addition to the concerns articulated in the commercial speech cases, he dissented from the Court's decision in *Beal* v. *Doe*

B

(1977) to approve a ban on the use of Medicaid funds for nontherapeutic abortions, characterizing the majority's assumption that alternative funding sources for abortions are available to indigent women as "disingenuous and alarming, almost reminiscent of: 'Let them eat cake.' Again, he contrasted the actual impact of the Court's ruling with its abstract, formalistic approach: "There is another world 'out there,' the existence of which the Court, I suspect, either chooses to ignore or fears to recognize."

Finally, Blackmun spoke on behalf of racial minorities and the institutionalized. He has consistently voted to uphold affirmative action plans, concluding in his seperate opinion in *Bakke* that " in order to get beyond racism, we must first take account of race." In *Youngburg* v. *Romeo* (1982) his concurring opinion argued that involuntarily committed retarded persons are entitled to treatment as well as care. "For many mentally retarded peope," he reasoned, "the difference between the capacity to do things for themselves within an institution and total dependence on the institution for all their needs is as much liberty as they ever will know." His dissent in *Bailey* criticized the majority's "impeccable exercise in undisputed general principles and technical legalism" and argued that the scope of the duress defense available in prison escape cases must instead be evaluated in light of the "stark truth" of the "shocking" conditions of prison life.

Although history may best remember Blackmun as the author of *Roe* v. *Wade,* his contribution to the Court was in fact much broader. He thoughtfully balanced conflicting policies, conscientiously and thoroughly digesting the details of each case without reaching out to make decisions based on broad, sweeping generalizations. He was concerned about the actual impact of the Court's decisions, refusing to permit his place on the Court to allow him to lose compassion for the "little people." He was receptive to new ideas and exhibited a capacity for growth, in keeping with his recognition that "there is no room in the law for arrogance" and his sense that he, as well as the Supreme Court, has "human limitations and fallibility."

—KIT KINPORTS

Bibliography

Kobylka, Joseph F. (1985). The Court, Justice Blackmun, and Federalism: A Subtle Movement with Potentially Great Ramifications. *Creighton Law Review* 19:9–49.

Note (1983). The Changing Social Vision of Justice Blackmun. *Harvard Law Review* 96:717–736.

Symposium (1985). Dedication to Justice Harry A. Blackmun—Biography; Tributes; Articles. *Hamline Law Review* 8:1–149.

Symposium (1987). Justice Harry A. Blackmun: The Supreme Court and the Limits of Medical Privacy. *American Journal of Law and Medicine* 13:153–525.

Wasby, Stephen L. (1988). Justice Harry A. Blackmun in the Burger Court. *Hamline Law Review* 11:183–245.

BLYEW v. UNITED STATES

80 U.S. 581 (1872)

The Supreme Court first interpreted the Civil Rights Act of 1866 in April 1872 in *Blyew* v. *United States.* That case narrowly construed a jurisdictional provision, in the act's Section 3, that granted jurisdiction to federal trial courts over criminal and civil "causes" that "affect[ed]" persons who "are denied or cannot enforce" in state court the rights of equality secured by the act's Section 1.

The case arose following the ax murder of a black family in rural Kentucky. Because a state statute precluded the testimony by a black person against a white defendant, it appeared probable that a state court would have excluded the dying declaration of the family's teenage son identifying the perpetrators as John Blyew and George Kennard. The federal attorney for Kentucky, Benjamin Bristow

See also

Dred Scott v. *Sandford*

Garcia v. *San Antonio Metropolitan Transportation Authority*

National League of Cities v. *Usery*

Roe v. *Wade*

(who would soon argue this case as the first solicitor general of the United States), obtained a federal indictment for the state-law crime of murder against Blyew and Kennard and prosecuted them in federal court. To establish jurisdiction under the 1866 act, the indictment asserted that the defendants' victims were denied or could not enforce the same right to testify in state court as white persons enjoy. This was only one among many criminal and civil cases brought in the Kentucky federal court on such a theory.

Convicted and sentenced to death, the defendants appealed. Exercised by this federal interference with its state courts, Kentucky hired (and the Supreme Court permitted) Judge Jeremiah Black to represent Kentucky at oral argument.

The Court, through Justice William Strong, held that in a criminal trial only the government and the defendant, but not the victim, are persons "affected" within the meaning of the 1866 act. Because neither of these parties had been denied rights under Section 1, the federal court lacked jurisdiction.

With its narrow construction of the "affecting" jurisdiction, the Court avoided the constitutional question of whether Congress can enforce the Fourteenth Amendment by granting federal court jurisdiction over state-law causes of action to avoid the risk of a biased state forum. The Court partially resolved this question in *Strauder* v. *West Virginia* (1880), which upheld the 1866 act's removal jurisdiction. But by then Congress had eliminated the narrowly interpreted "affecting" jurisdiction in its 1874 codification of United States statutes.

By its holding, the Court eliminated the important civil rights remedial tool of providing a nondiscriminatory federal forum to enforce the common law of crimes and torts (including common law duties of nondiscrimination). Since *Blyew*, the model for federal civil rights criminal enforcement has primarily involved the adoption of a substantive federal criminal statute, with the attendant constitutional and practical difficulties of defining federal rights under both the Slaughterhouse Cases (1873) and the Civil Rights Cases (1883). Effective civil rights enforcement has been hobbled by this limitation, among others, ever since. Moreover, without the counterexample of the "affecting" jurisdiction, the Court has more plausibly developed doctrines restraining federal court intrusion on discriminatory state enforcement of state law.

The *Blyew* decision permits identifying the Supreme Court's hostility to federal civil rights enactments as early as the end of the first administration of Ulysses S. Grant. It also suggests that by the time the Court rendered the *Slaughterhouse* decision, it understood the implications that decision would have for federal civil rights enforcement. This precludes treating the Court's subsequent decisions limiting civil rights legislation as merely expressing a consensus of the political branches reached in the waning days of reconstruction.

Blyew is also noteworthy because Justice Joseph P. Bradley, in dissent, first put forward a theory of a group right to the adequate protection of the law and the "badges and incidents" theory of the Thirteenth Amendment found in the *Civil Rights Cases*.

The Court's failure to appreciate a class's cognizable interest in the effective protection of the law continues to the present. *Blyew*, for example, anticipated *Linda R. S.* v. *Richard D.* (1973) a century later, in which the Court held that a crime victim lacked standing to challenge a prosecutorial decision, because it directly affected only the state and defendant.

—ROBERT D. GOLDSTEIN

Bibliography

Goldstein, Robert D. (1989). *Blyew:* Variations on a Jurisdictional Theme. *Stanford Law Review* 41:469–566.

Kazcorowski, Robert (1985). *The Politics of Judicial Interpretation: The Federal Courts, Department of Justice and Civil Rights, 1866–1876.* New York: Oceana.

The Supreme Court first interpreted the Civil Rights Act of 1866 in Blyew v. *United States.*

See also
Civil Rights
Oral Argument

*New York authorized
the loan of state-
purchased textbooks
to students in
nonpublic schools.*

BOARD OF EDUCATION v. ALLEN

392 U.S. 236 (1968)

New York authorized the loan of state-purchased textbooks to students in nonpublic schools. Justice Byron R. White, speaking for the Supreme Court, relied heavily on the "pupil benefit theory," which he purportedly derived from *Everson* v. *Board of Education* (1947). If the beneficiaries of the governmental program were principally the children, and not the religious institutions, the program could be sustained.

Justice Hugo L. Black, the author of *Everson*, dissented. *Everson*, he recalled, held that transportation of students to church-related schools went "to the very verge" of what was permissible under the establishment clause. Justices William O. Douglas and Abe Fortas also dissented.

Allen stimulated efforts to aid church-related schools in many state legislatures. Later opinions of the Court, invalidating direct aid programs, have limited *Allen*'s precedential force to cases involving textbook loans as well as transportation, remedial teaching, and similar benefits given the student as opposed to the sectarian school itself.

—RICHARD E. MORGAN

BOARD OF TRUSTEES OF STATE UNIVERSITY OF NEW YORK v. FOX

492 U.S. (1989)

This decision significantly altered the doctrinal formula governing commercial speech. In *Central Hudson Gas and Electric Corp.* v. *Public Service Commission* (1980) the Supreme Court had held that a state's regulation of commercial speech must be "no more extensive than necessary" to achieve the regulation's purposes. In *Fox*, a 6–3 majority explicitly disavowed the idea that a state was limited to the least restrictive means in regulating commercial advertising. Justice Antonin Scalia wrote for the Court.

A state-university regulation of on-campus business activity effectively prevented a seller

---

*Although the
decision attracted
national attention,
it did little to solve
the intractable
constitutional puzzle
of government
speech.*

BOARD OF EDUCATION v. PICO

457 U.S. 853 (1982)

Six students sued a school board in federal court, claiming that the board had violated their First Amendment rights by removing certain books from the high school and junior high school libraries. The board had responded to lists of "objectionable" and "inappropriate" books circulated at a conference of conservative parents. A fragmented Supreme Court, voting 5–4, remanded the case for trial.

Four Justices concluded that it would be unconstitutional for the school board to remove the books from the libraries for the purpose of suppressing ideas. Four others argued for wide discretion by local officials in selecting school materials, including library books. One Justice would await the outcome of a trial before addressing the constitutional issues. On remand, the school board surrendered. The decision succeeded in establishing some right to First Amendment review of public school book removals that are improperly motivated, though its contours are not clearly defined. Thus, although the decision attracted national attention, it did little to solve the intractable constitutional puzzle of government speech.

—KENNETH L. KARST

See also

Everson v. *Board of Education*

of household goods from holding "Tupperware parties" in the dormitories. Although the company's representatives not only sold goods but also made presentations on home economics, the Court concluded that the speech was commercial. The transactions proposed were lawful, and the advertising was not misleading; thus, the interest-balancing part of the *Central Hudson Gas* formula came into play. Here the university had important interests in preserving a noncommercial atmosphere on campus and tranquillity in the dormitories. Although the regulation did directly advance these interests, other means, less restrictive on speech, would arguably have served just as well. Justice Scalia noted that previous opinions had suggested that regulations of advertising must pass a "least restrictive means" test, but decided that such a formulation was too burdensome on the states. Rather, what is required is "a fit [between means and ends] that is not necessarily perfect, but reasonable; that represents not necessarily the single best disposition but one whose scope is 'in proportion to the interest served'" (quoting from *In re R.M.J.* [1980], dealing with lawyer advertising).

Justice Harry A. Blackmun, who had written the Court's early opinions admitting commercial speech into the shelter of the First Amendment, wrote for the three dissenters. He argued that the statute was invalid for overbreadth, and said he need not discuss the least-restrictive-means question.

—KENNETH L. KARST

BOERNE (CITY OF) v. FLORES

521 U.S. 507 (1997)

This decision dramatically limited the power of Congress to legislate pursuant to Section Five of the Fourteenth Amendment, which authorizes Congress to "enforce" the provisions of that Amendment. The salient provisions of the Amendment bar the states from

depriving "any person of life, liberty or property without due process of law" or denying any person the equal protection of the laws.

At issue was a law, the Religious Freedom Restoration Act (RFRA), passed by Congress to undo a rule adopted by the Court in *Employment Division, Department of Human Resources of Oregon v. Smith*. *Smith* rejected a claim that an Oregon law criminalizing the use of peyote in a religious ceremony violated the free exercise clause of the First Amendment, made applicable to the states through the due process clause of the Fourteenth Amendment. The question was, in large measure, what test the courts should apply in evaluating a free exercise claim. Earlier decisions like *Sherbert* v. *Verner* had held the states must satisfy a strict scrutiny test to justify a law allegedly infringing on the free exercise of religion. Under that test the state must show the law is narrowly tailored to serve a compelling governmental interest. *Smith* surprisingly overturned that rule and held, in contrast, that a law not specifically targeted at the exercise of religion should be sustained as long as it has a rational basis. On this basis the Court upheld the peyote statute as a rationally based generally applicable law. Though it did not overrule its prior rulings like *Sherbert*, it limited them to their specific facts.

The reaction to *Smith* was swift and widespread. Religious groups expressed great concern that the Court had virtually written a blank check to legislatures empowering them to abridge religious freedom. This concern, understandably, far transcended the facts of the particular case since the Court had painted with so broad a brush. The result was the Religious Freedom Restoration Act, under which Congress barred governments from substantially burdening the exercise of religion unless the law in question is the "least restrictive means" of furthering "a compelling governmental interest." In other words the Act purported to restore the strict scrutiny mandated by *Sherbert* and similar decisions before *Smith*.

A state-university regulation of on-campus business activity effectively prevented a seller of household goods from holding "Tupperware parties" in the dormitories.

See also

*Central Hudson Gas and
Electric Corp.* v. *Public
Service Commission*

B

BOERNE (CITY OF) v. FLORES

521 U.S. 507 (1997)

Religious groups expressed great concern that the Court had virtually written a blank check to legislatures empowering them to abridge religious freedom.

In another relevant series of cases, however, the Court had looked at exactly how much power Section Five of the Fourteenth Amendment gives Congress to determine what conduct violates the due process or equal protection clauses. In *Oregon* v. *Mitchell*, dealing with congressional laws barring states from denying the vote to persons under twenty-one or imposing literacy tests for voting, the Court, limiting some earlier decisions, held Section Five does not empower Congress to decide totally on its own whether a practice is violative of the Fourteenth Amendment based solely on "its own ideas of wise policy."

In *Flores* the Court continued on this tack, holding Section Five authorizes only remedial statutes to "enforce" the provisions of the Fourteenth Amendment, not statutes that "determine what constitutes a constitutional violation." By attempting to so greatly alter the standard for judicial review of asserted free exercise clause violations, Congress exceeded its powers under Section Five. As Justice Anthony M. Kennedy, writing for the Court, pointed out, "[I]f Congress could define its own powers by altering the Fourteenth Amendment's meaning, no longer would the Constitution be 'superior paramount law, unchangeable by ordinary means.'" This view would enable Congress to alter the Constitution at will—a view rejected by the Court as early as *Marbury* v. *Madison* (1803) and consistently since. It would mean, in effect, that the congressional tail would wag the constitutional dog.

The Court went on to distinguish the RFRA from other congressional enactments sustained as valid exercises of its powers under Section Five. For example, in *South Carolina* v. *Katzenbach* (1966) the Court upheld Voting Rights Act provisions restricting literacy tests in Southern states where voting had been made difficult for black citizens for decades. And in *Morgan* v. *Katzenbach* (1966) it sustained another Voting Rights Act section that forbade states from imposing English-literacy requirements on citizens educated in Puerto Rico. Both these statutes, in contrast to the RFRA, were aimed at enforcing the Fourteenth Amendment (and the Fifteenth Amendment, which bars states from denying the vote on the basis of race, and which contains similar language enabling Congress to enforce it through legislation).

Justice John Paul Stevens concurred on the ground that the RFRA violated the Establishment Clause of the First Amendment by unduly benefiting religious institutions. Justices Sandra Day O'Connor and Stephen G. Breyer took the view that *Smith* was wrongly decided and should be overruled, which would finesse the need to consider the validity of the RFRA. However, while Justice O'Connor concurred with the majority as to the Act's invalidity, Justice Breyer did not express that view and therefore dissented. In addition, Justice David H. Souter dissented, contending the correctness of *Smith* was the prime issue and should be fully reargued.

The specific factual context of *Flores* itself sheds light on these concerns. The case involved a church that had been declared a historic landmark and was denied a permit to build an addition it claimed it needed to service an increased number of parishioners. Thus, the church contended, the city's landmark preservation law substantially burdened its parishioners' exercise of religion, so that under the RFRA the city had to prove its law narrowly tailored to serve a compelling government interest. In fact, municipalities and organizations devoted to historic preservation had campaigned against the Act in Congress, voicing these very concerns that it would inhibit protection of religious buildings under local landmark-preservation laws. Others, on the other hand, contended it would be difficult for a religious body to show that denial of a permit to alter or demolish a structure did in fact substantially burden the free exercise of religion. In the wake of *Flores* the lower courts will have to determine whether the city's landmark law, as applied to the plaintiff, lacks a rational basis—a far more arduous burden for the religious body to meet.

As for the broader constitutional issue in *Flores*, the Court has now made crystal clear its reluctance to allow Congress carte blanche to alter constitutional standards under Section Five. It firmly grounded its decision in separation of powers principles regarding the respective roles of Congress and the courts that will likely prove difficult to overturn.

—PHILIP WEINBERG

BOLLMAN, EX PARTE, v. SWARTWOUT

4 Cranch 75 (1807)

The Supreme Court discharged the prisoners, confederates in Aaron Burr's conspiracy, from an indictment for treason. The indictment specified their treason as levying war against the United States. Chief Justice John Marshall, for the Court, distinguished treason from a conspiracy to commit it. He sought to prevent the crime of treason from being "extended by construction to doubtful cases." To complete the crime of treason or levying war, Marshall said, a body of men must be "actually assembled for the purpose of effecting by force a treasonable purpose," in which everyone involved, to any degree and however remote from the scene of action, is guilty of treason. But the levying of war does not exist short of the actual assemblage of armed men. Congress had the power to punish crimes short of treason, but the Constitution protected Americans from a charge of treason for a crime short of it.

Bollman is also an important precedent in the law of federal jurisdiction. In obiter dictum, Marshall stated that a federal court's power to issue a writ of habeas corpus "must be given by written law," denying by inference that the courts have any inherent power

to grant habeas corpus relief, apart from congressional authorization.

—LEONARD W. LEVY

BOOTH v. MARYLAND

482 U.S. 496 (1987)

Conflicting views on capital punishment emerged in this case dealing with the constitutionality of victim impact statements (VIS). In conformance with state law, the prosecution introduced VIS at the sentencing phase of a capital trial. Those statements described the effects of the crime on the victims and their families. Naturally, they were intensely emotional and, according to the majority of the Court, had the effect of prejudicing the sentencing jury. Dividing 5–4, the Court ruled that the VIS provided information irrelevant to a capital-sentencing decision and that the admission of such statements created a constitutionally unacceptable risk that the jury might impose the death penalty arbitrarily or capriciously. Therefore, according to the Court, the VIS conflicted with the Eighth Amendment's cruel and unusual punishment clause. How the murderer could have been exposed to cruel and unusual punishment by the jurors' having listened to statements describing the impact of his crime is mystifying.

Justice Byron R. White, for the dissenters, believed that VIS are appropriate evidence in capital sentencing hearings. Punishment can be increased in noncapital cases on the basis of the harm caused and so might be increased in capital cases. VIS reminded the jurors that just as the murderer ought to be regarded as an individual, so too should the victim whose death constituted a unique loss to his family and the community. Justice Antonin Scalia, for the same dissenters, contended that the Court's opinion wrongly rested on the principle that the death sentence should be inflicted solely on the basis of moral guilt. He thought the harm done was also relevant. Many people believed that criminal trials

◆ **ex parte**
[Latin: from one party; from the part (of)] (1) A hearing or other legal act at which only one side of a case is represented; (2) in the heading of a case, an identification of the party who is applying for judicial relief.

Many people believed that criminal trials favored the accused too much if they did not consider the harm inflicted on the victim and the victim's family.

See also

Capital Punishment

♦ **due process of law**
*The fair and regular
procedures established by
law. Under the Fifth
and Fourteenth
Amendments, the
government may deprive
a person of life, liberty, or
property only after due
process. The due process
clauses of the
Constitution protect both
procedural and
substantive rights.*

favored the accused too much if they did not consider the harm inflicted on the victim and the victim's family. The Court's previous opinions required that all mitigating factors must be placed before the capital-sentencing jury; yet the Court here required the suppression of the suffering caused by the defendant. This muted one side of the debate on the appropriateness of capital punishment.

—LEONARD W. LEVY

BOSTON BEER COMPANY v. MASSACHUSETTS

97 U.S. 25 (1878)

This case introduced the doctrine of inalienable police power, which weakened the contract clause's protections of property. The company's charter authorized it to manufacture beer subject to a reserved power of the legislature to alter, amend, or repeal the charter. The state subsequently enacted a prohibition statute. The reserved police power should have been sufficient ground for the holding by the Court that the prohibition statute did not impair the company's chartered right to do business. However, Justice Joseph P. Bradley, in an opinion for a unanimous Court, found another and "equally decisive" reason for rejecting the argument that the company had a contract to manufacture and sell beer "forever." The company held its rights subject to the police power of the state to promote the public safety and morals. "The Legislature," Bradley declared, "cannot, by any contract, devest itself of the power to provide for these objects." Accordingly the enactment of a statute prohibiting the manufacture and sale of intoxicating liquors did

AMENDMENT VIII

Excessive bail shall not be required, nor excessive fines imposed, nor cruel and unusual punishments inflicted.

The Eighth Amendment's cruel and unusual punishment clause, derived from common law and held to restrain the states as well as the federal government, applies to noncapital as well as capital criminal punishments. The concept of cruel and unusual punishments, while undoubtedly meant to address extremely harsh or painful methods and kinds of punishment, also incorporates ideas of excessiveness, proportionality, and appropriateness. It is therefore relative, and whether a particular punishment is cruel and unusual depends on prevailing societal standards, objectively determined, regarding punishments. The Supreme Court has held that the clause outlaws not only punishments that are barbarous, involving torture or the inten-

tional and unjustifiable infliction of unnecessary pain, but also forbids confinements whose length or conditions are disproportionate to the severity of crimes, serious deprivations of prisoners' basic human needs, loss of citizenship as a punishment, and punishments for status.

In *Weems* v. *United States* (1910) the Court held the Philippine punishment of *cadena temporal* unconstitutional as applied. The imposed punishment for the crime of making a false entry in a public record—not shown to have injured anyone—was fifteen years' imprisonment at hard and painful labor with chains, loss of civil liberties, and governmental surveillance for life. The Court, in *Estelle* v. *Gamble* (1976), also held that deliberate indifference to a

prisoner's serious medical needs constitutes cruel and unusual punishment. In *Hutto* v. *Finney* (1978) it upheld a lower court's conclusion that routine conditions in the Arkansas prison system were so inhuman as to be cruel and unusual. Earlier, the Court had determined in *Trop* v. *Dulles* (1968) that imposing loss of citizenship on a native-born citizen for desertion in wartime was cruel and unusual because it destroyed the person's political existence and made him stateless. In implicit recognition that states may define as crimes only acts, conduct, or behavior, the Court, in *Robinson* v. *California* (1962), held criminal imprisonment for the status of being a drug addict, unaccompanied by any acts, cruel and unusual.

not violate the contract clause. Decisions such as this, by which the police power prevailed over chartered rights, produced a doctrinal response: the development of substantive due process to protect property.

—LEONARD W. LEVY

BOUNDS v. SMITH

430 U.S. 817 (1977)

Several state prisoners sued North Carolina prison authorities in federal court, claiming they had been denied legal research facilities in violation of their Fourteenth Amendment rights. The Supreme Court, 6–3, upheld this claim in an opinion by Justice Thurgood Marshall.

For the first time the Court explicitly recognized a "fundamental constitutional right of access to the courts." This right imposed on prison authorities the affirmative duty to provide either adequate law libraries or the assistance of law-trained persons, so that prisoners might prepare habeas corpus petitions and other legal papers. The three dissenters each wrote an opinion. Justice William H. Rehnquist complained that the majority had neither defined the content of "meaningful" access nor specified the source of the Fourteenth Amendment right; an equal protection right, he pointed out, would conflict with *Ross* v. *Moffitt* (1974).

—KENNETH L. KARST

BOWEN v. KENDRICK

487 U.S. 589 (1988)

In this case the Court sustained the facial constitutionality of Congress's 1981 Adolescent Family Life Act against a claim that it violated the establishment clause of the First Amendment. The statute authorized federal funds for services, publicly or privately ad-

ministered, that related to adolescent sexuality and pregnancy. A federal district court found that the statute, on its face and as administered, advanced religion by subsidizing and allowing sectarian organizations to preach their message to adolescents; the statute also unduly entangled the government with religion, by requiring official monitoring to ensure that religiously affiliated grantees did not promote their religious missions. The Court, by a 5–4 vote, reversed and remanded the case for a determination whether it was unconstitutionally applied.

Chief Justice William H. Rehnquist, for the majority, observed that the statute neither required grantees to be religiously affiliated nor suggested that religious institutions were specially qualified to provide the services subsidized by the government. Congress merely assumed that religious organizations as well as nonreligious ones could influence adolescent behavior. Congress impartially made the monies available to achieve secular objectives, regardless whether the funds went to sectarian or secular institutions. This was not a case in which the federal subsidies flowed primarily to pervasively sectarian institutions; moreover, the services provided to adolescents, such as pregnancy testing or child care, were not religious in nature. The majority also held that the government monitoring required by the statute did not necessarily entangle it excessively with sectarianism. Conceding, however, that the act could be administered in such a way as to violate the establishment clause, the Court returned the case to the district court for a factual finding on that issue.

The four dissenters, speaking through Justice Harry A. Blackmun, may have been influenced by the fact that the statute banned grants to institutions that advocated abortion. Blackmun, as devoid of doubts as was Rehnquist, confidently deplored a decision that breached the Lemon test by providing federal monies to religious organizations, thereby enabling them to promote their religious missions in ways that were pervasively sectar-

♦ **police power**
The general authority of government to regulate the health, safety, morals, and welfare of the public.

The statute authorized federal funds for services, publicly or privately administered, that related to adolescent sexuality and pregnancy.

♦ **habeas corpus**
[Latin: you shall have the body] A form of writ directing a custodial official to appear before a judge with the person of a prisoner and to give a satisfactory legal justification for having the person in custody. The writ of habeas corpus is frequently used by state prisoners to obtain federal court review of their convictions.

ian and, contradictorily, requiring intrusive oversight by the government to prevent that objective. The majority, Blackmun reasoned, distorted the Court's precedents and engaged in doctrinal missteps to reach their conclusion, by treating the case as if it merely subsidized a neutral function such as dispensing food or shelter instead of pedagogical services that impermissibly fostered religious beliefs.

—LEONARD W. LEVY

BOWERS v. HARDWICK

478 U.S. 186 (1986)

Hardwick was charged with engaging in homosexual sodomy in violation of a Georgia statute, but after a preliminary hearing the prosecutor declined to pursue the case. Despite the fact that Hardwick was not going to be prosecuted, he brought suit in federal court to have the Georgia sodomy statute declared unconstitutional. The court of appeals held that the Georgia statute violated Hard-

wick's fundamental rights because homosexual activity is protected by the Ninth Amendment and the due process clause of the Fourteenth Amendment.

The Supreme Court disagreed, holding 5–4 that the statute did not violate any fundamental rights protected by the Constitution—in particular, that the act did not violate the right of privacy announced by the court in previous cases.

Writing for the majority, Justice Byron R. White contended that previous rulings delineating a constitutional right of privacy could not be used to strike down a law against sodomy. Previous precedents in this field focused on "family, marriage or procreation," said White, and neither Hardwick nor the court of appeals had demonstrated a connection between homosexual activity and these areas. In making his argument from precedent, White explicitly denied that the Court had ever announced a general right of private sexual conduct. Precedent aside, White argued that if the Court itself is to remain con-

Writing for the dissenters, Justice Harry A. Blackmun declared what the majority denied— that a general constitutional right of private sexual conduct (or "intimate association") exists.

AMENDMENT IX

The enumeration in the Constitution, of certain rights, shall not be construed to deny or disparage others retained by the people.

Largely ignored throughout most of our history, the Ninth Amendment has emerged in the past twenty years as a possible source for the protection of individual rights not specifically enumerated in the Constitution's text. Although no Supreme Court decision has yet been based squarely on an interpretation of the Ninth Amendment, it has been mentioned in several leading cases in which the Court enlarged the scope of individual rights. Lawyers, scholars, and judges are understandably intrigued by a provision that, on the basis of language, seems ideally suited to provide a constitutional home for newly found rights: "The enumeration of certain rights in the Constitution shall not be con-

strued to deny or disparage others retained by the people."

The historical origins of the Ninth Amendment lay in James Madison's concern that the inclusion of specified rights in the Bill of Rights might leave other rights unprotected. He recognized, moreover, that the inherent limitations of language could thwart the intent of the authors of the Bill of Rights to provide a permanent charter of personal freedom. These concerns, which led Madison originally to question the wisdom of a Bill of Rights, caused him to propose, in the First Congress, a resolution incorporating the present language of the Ninth Amendment. It was adopted with little debate.

See also

Sexual Orientation

stitutionally legitimate, it must be wary of creating new rights that have little or no basis in the text or design of the Constitution. Such rights can be adopted by the Court only if they are so implicit in the concept of ordered liberty or so rooted in the nation's history that they mandate protection; homosexual sodomy meets neither requirement. Given White's framework of analysis, the other arguments marshaled by Harwick also had to fail. The argument that since his conduct took place in the privacy of his home it must be protected fails because one has no right to engage in criminal conduct within one's home. And the argument that the law has no rational basis because it was based solely on the moral views of its supporters fails because "law . . . is constantly based on notions of morality."

Writing for the dissenters, Justice Harry A. Blackmun declared what the majority denied—that a general constitutional right of private sexual conduct (or "intimate association") exists. Blackmun thereby shifted the burden of proof from Hardwick to the government. Because intimate association is generally protected by the Constitution, the government must prove that any regulations in this area are valid. Georgia did not do so; hence, the statute was invalid.

The Court's ruling in *Bowers* engendered a great deal of controversy. Many had wanted the Court to use the case to place discrimination on the basis of sexual orientation in the same category as racial or gender discrimination. Yet it is understandable why the Court did not do so. Gender and race are not clearly analogous to sexual orientation, for neither is defined by conduct in the way that sexual orientation is. Homosexual sodomy has faced public disapproval for centuries because it is *behavior* that society has judged destructive for a variety of reasons, including its effects on public health, safety, and morality. Whether this judgment is correct or not may be debated, but the Court did not wish to resolve the debate by imposition of its own will in the matter.

However, a few years later, in *Romer* v. *Evans* (1996), the Court overturned a Colorado constitutional amendment that purported to bar any governmental agency or court from considering a claim of discrimination based on sexual orientation. Although reaffirming *Bowers*'s holding that sexual orientation is not a suspect classification, the Court held the Colorado amendment lacked a rational basis since it acted to disadvantage homosexuals, "forbidd[ing them] the safeguards that others enjoy."

—JOHN G. WEST, JR.

Bibliography

Weller, Christopher W. (1986). *Bowers v. Hardwick:* Balancing the Interests of the Moral Order and Individual Liberty. *Cumberland Law Review* 16:555–592.

BOWSHER v. SYNAR

478 U.S. 714 (1986)

A 7–2 Supreme Court held that a basic provision of a major act of Congress unconstitutionally violated the principle of separation of powers because Congress had vested executive authority in an official responsible to Congress. The Balanced Budget and Emergency Deficit Control Act of 1985 (Gramm-Rudman-Hollings) empowered the comptroller general, who is appointed by the President but removable by joint resolution of Congress, to perform executive powers in the enforcement of the statute. In the event of a federal budget deficit, the act requires across-the-board cuts in federal spending. The comptroller general made the final recommendations to the President on how to make the budget cuts.

Five members of the Court, speaking through Chief Justice Warren E. Burger, applied a severely formalistic view of separation of powers. They sharply distinguished executive power from legislative power. The comptroller general was removable only at the ini-

The Constitution mixes powers as well as separates them. The three branches are separate, but their powers are not.

♦ **jurisdiction**
*Legitimate authority.
The term is sometimes
limited to the legitimate
authority of courts to
hear and decide cases.*

tiative of Congress for "transgressions of the legislative will." Congress regarded the official as an officer of the legislative branch, and persons holding the office had so regarded themselves. But the powers exercised by the comptroller general were executive in nature, preparing reports on projected federal revenues and expenditures and specifying the reductions necessary to reach target deficit levels. Because the comptroller general was "Congress's man" and was removable by Congress, the assignment of executive powers to the office gave Congress a direct role in the execution of the laws, contrary to the constitutional structure of the government.

Justice John Paul Stevens, joined by Justice Thurgood Marshall, agreed that the Gramm-Rudman-Hollings provision was unconstitutional, but for wholly different reasons. Stevens too described the comptroller general as a legislative officer, but believed that the removal power was irrelevant. Gramm-Rudman-Hollings was defective because by vesting the officer with important legisla-tive

powers over the budget, it subverted the legislative procedures provided by the Constitution. Money matters require consideration and voting by both houses of Congress; this body cannot constitutionally delegate so great a legislative power to an agent.

Justice Byron R. White, dissenting, believed that the threat to separation of powers conjured up by the seven-member majority was "wholly chimerical." He believed that the necessary and proper clause supported vesting some executive authority in the comptroller general. This officer exercised no powers that deprived the president of authority; the official chosen by Congress to implement its policy was nonpartisan and independent. He or she could not be removed by Congress by joint resolution except with the president's approval.

The concurring Justices and the dissenters understood that the Constitution's separation of powers does not make each branch wholly autonomous; each depends on others and exercises the powers of others

**SEPARATION
OF POWERS**

*A provision of the Balanced
Budget and Emergency Deficit
Control Act of 1985, sponsored
in part by Senator Phil
Gramm (R-TX), was declared
unconstitutional.
(Corbis/Robert Maass)*

to a degree. The Constitution mixes powers as well as separates them. The three branches are separate, but their powers are not. Gramm-Rudman-Hollings reflected the modern administrative state. The majority Justices, who could not even agree among themselves whether the comptroller general exercised executive or legislative powers, lacked the flexibility to understand they did not have to choose between labels. The Court, which quoted Montesquieu and misapplied *The Federalist,* ignored #47 and #48, which warned only against "too great a mixture of powers," but approved of a sharing of powers. Currently, money bills originate in the White House and its Bureau of the Budget, despite the provision in Article I, section 7. The First Congress established the president's cabinet and required the secretary of treasury to report to Congress, and all of Alexander Hamilton's great reports on the economy were made to Congress, not the president. No Court that cared a fig for original intent or that understood the realities of policymaking today would have delivered such simplistic textbookish opinions.

—LEONARD W. LEVY

BOYD v. UNITED STATES

116 U.S. 616 (1886)

Justice Louis D. Brandeis believed that *Boyd* will be remembered "as long as civil liberty lives in the United States." The noble sentiments expressed in Joseph P. Bradley's opinion for the Court merit that estimate, but like many another historic opinion, this one was not convincingly reasoned. To this day, however, members of the Court return to *Boyd* to grace their opinions with its authority or with an imperishable line from Bradley's.

Boyd was the first important search and seizure case as well as the first important case on the right against self-incrimination. It arose not from a criminal prosecution but from a civil action by the United States for the forfeiture of goods imported in violation of customs revenue laws. In such cases an 1874 act of Congress required the importer to produce in court all pertinent records tending to prove the charges against him or suffer the penalty of being taken "as confessed." The Court held the act unconstitutional as a violation of both the Fourth and Fifth Amendments. The penalty made the production of the records compulsory. That compulsion, said Bradley, raised "a very grave question of constitutional law, involving the personal security and privileges and immunities of the citizen. . . ." But did the case involve a search or a seizure, and if so was it "unreasonable," and did it force the importer to be a witness against himself in a criminal case?

Bradley conceded that there was no search and seizure as in the forcible entry into a man's house and examination of his papers. Indeed, there was no search here for evidence of crime. The compulsion was to produce records that the government required importers to keep; no private papers were at issue. Moreover, no property was confiscated as in the case of contraband like smuggled goods. The importer, who was not subject to a search, had merely to produce the needed records in court; he kept custody of them. But the Court treated those records as if they were private papers, which could be used as evidence against him, resulting in the forfeiture of his property, or to establish a criminal charge. Though the proceeding was a civil one, a different section of the same statute did provide criminal penalties for fraud.

Bradley made a remarkable linkage between the right against unreasonable search and seizure and the right against self-incrimination. The "fourth and fifth amendments," he declared, "almost run into each other." That they were different amendments, protected different interests, had separate histories, and reflected different policies was of no consequence to Bradley. He was on sound ground when he found that the forcible production of private papers to convict a man of

Boyd was the first important search and seizure case as well as the first important case on the right against self-incrimination.

See also

Search and Seizure

♦ **nolo contendere**
*[Latin: I do not wish to
contest (it)] A plea
entered by a criminal
defendant equivalent in
effect to a plea of guilty
in the criminal case but
not amounting to an
admission of guilt that
might be used in another
case, either civil or
criminal.*

crime or to forfeit his property violated the Fifth Amendment and was "contrary to the principles of a free government." He was on slippery ground when he found that such a compulsory disclosure was "the equivalent of a search and seizure—and an unreasonable search and seizure—within the meaning of the fourth amendment." His reasoning was that though the case did not fall within the "literal terms" of either amendment, each should be broadly construed in terms of the other. Unreasonable searches and seizures "are almost always made for the purpose of compelling a man to give evidence against himself," and compulsion of such evidence "throws light on the question as to what is an 'unreasonable search and seizure.' . . ." In support of his reasoning Bradley quoted at length from Lord Camden's opinion in *Entick* v. *Carrington* (1765). Camden, however, spoke of a fishing expedition under general warrants issued by an executive officer without authorization by Parliament. There was no warrant in this case, and there was authorization by Congress for a court to compel production of the specific records required by law to be kept for government inspection, concerning foreign commerce which Congress may regulate. In this case, however, Bradley thought meticulous analysis was out of place. He feared that unconstitutional practices got their footing in "slight deviations" from proper procedures, and the best remedy was the rule that constitutional protections "for the security of person and property should be liberally construed." Close construction, he declared, deprived these protections of their efficacy.

Justice Samuel F. Miller, joined by Chief Justice Morrison R. Waite, concurred in the judgment that that offensive section of the act of Congress was unconstitutional. Miller found no search and seizure, let alone an unreasonable one. He agreed, however, that Congress had breached the right against self-incrimination, which he thought should be the sole ground of the opinion.

The modern Court no longer assumes that the Fifth Amendment is a source of the Fourth's exclusionary rule or that the Fourth prohibits searches for mere evidence. Moreover, the production of private papers may be compelled in certain cases, as when the Internal Revenue Service subpoenas records in the hands of one's lawyer or accountant.

—LEONARD W. LEVY

Bibliography

Gerstein, Robert S. (1979). The Demise of *Boyd:* Self-Incrimination and Private Papers in the Burger Court. *UCLA Law Review* 27:343–397.

Landynski, Jacob W. (1966). *Search and Seizure and the Supreme Court.* Pages 49–61. Baltimore: Johns Hopkins University Press.

BRADLEY, JOSEPH P.

(1813–1892)

Joseph P. Bradley's appointment to the Supreme Court in 1870 by President Ulysses S. Grant was seen as part of Grant's supposed court-packing scheme. But whatever shadow that event cast on Bradley's reputation rapidly disappeared. For more than two decades on the bench, he commanded almost unrivaled respect from colleagues, lawyers, and legal commentators, and over time he consistently has been ranked as one of the most influential jurists in the Court's history.

When Bradley was appointed he already was a prominent railroad lawyer and Republican activist. Indeed, friends had been advocating his appointment to the Court nearly a year before his appointment. Shortly after Grant's inauguration in 1869, the Republicans increased the size of the court from eight to nine. While Grant and Congress haggled over the selection of a new Justice, the Court decided, 4–3, that the legal tender laws were unconstitutional. Justice Robert C. Grier clearly was senile, and after he cast his vote against the laws his colleagues persuaded him to resign. That gave Grant two appointments and, on February 7, 1870, he nominated William Strong and Bradley—and the Court almost simultaneously announced its legal tender decision.

Within a year, Bradley and Strong led a new majority to sustain the constitutionality of greenbacks (unsecured paper currency). In his concurring opinion, Bradley saw the power to emit bills of credit as the essential issue in the case, and from that he contended that "the incidental power of giving such bills the quality of legal tender follows almost as matter of course." Bradley also emphasized the government's right to maintain its existence. He insisted it would be a "great wrong" to deny Congress the asserted power, "a power to be seldom exercised, certainly; but one, the possession of which is so essential, and as it seems to me, so undoubted."

Three months after his appointment, Bradley conducted circuit court hearings in New Orleans where he encountered the *Slaughterhouse Cases*. He held unconstitutional the Louisiana statute authorizing a monopoly for slaughtering operations. Three years later, when the case reached the Supreme Court on appeal, Bradley dissented as the majority sustained the regulation. With Justice Stephen J. Field, Bradley believed that the creation of the monopoly and the impairment of existing businesses violated the privileges and immunities clause of the Fourteenth Amendment. Such privileges, Bradley had said earlier in his circuit court opinion, included a citizen's right to "lawful industrial pursuit—not injurious to the community—as he may see fit, without unreasonable regulation or molestation."

The antiregulatory views that Bradley advanced in *Slaughterhouse* did not persist as the major theme of his judicial career, as they did for Justice Field. Judicial review and judicial superintendence of due process of law could be maintained, he said, in *Davidson* v. *New Orleans* (1878), "without interfering with that large discretion which every legislative power has of making wide modifications in the forms of procedure." A year earlier, Bradley had vividly demonstrated his differences with Field when he provided Chief Justice Morrison R. Waite with the key historical sources and principles for the public interest doctrine laid down in *Munn* v. *Illinois* (1877).

The Court largely gutted the *Munn* ruling when it held in *Wabash, St. Louis, and Pacific Railway* v. *Illinois* (1886) that states could not regulate interstate rates, even in the absence of congressional action. Bradley vigorously dissented, protesting that some form of regulation was necessary and that the Court had wrongly repudiated the public interest doctrine of the Granger Cases. Ironically, Bradley, the old railroad lawyer, found himself almost totally isolated when he dissented from the Court's finding that the judiciary,

BRADLEY, JOSEPH P.

(1813–1892)

REPUBLICAN ACTIVIST

Justice Joseph P. Bradley is regarded as one of the most influential jurists in Supreme Court history. (Corbis-Bettmann)

B

BRADLEY, JOSEPH P.

(1813–1892)

For more than two decades on the bench, he commanded almost unrivaled respect from colleagues, lawyers, and legal commentators, and over time he consistently has been ranked as one of the most influential jurists in the Court's history.

See also

Boyd v. *United States*

Bradwell v. *Illinois*

Wabash, St. Louis, and Pacific Railway v. *Illinois*

not legislatively authorized expert commissions, had the right to decide the reasonableness of railroad rates. That decision, in *Chicago, Milwaukee and St. Paul Railway Co.* v. *Minnesota* (1890), marked the triumph of Field's dissenting views in *Munn;* yet Bradley steadfastly insisted that rate regulation "is a legislative prerogative and not a judicial one."

Bradley insisted on responsibility and accountability from the railroads in numerous ways. In *New York Central R.R.* v. *Lockwood* (1873) he wrote that railroads could not, by contract, exempt themselves from liability for negligence. "The carrier and his customer do not stand on a footing of equality," he said. In *Railroad Company* v. *Maryland* (1875) he agreed that Maryland could compel a railroad to return one-fifth of its revenue in exchange for a right of way without compromising congressional control over commerce. But Bradley found clear lines of distinction between federally chartered and state chartered railroads. When the Court, in *Railroad Company* v. *Peniston* (1873), approved Nebraska's tax of a congressionally chartered railroad, Bradley disagreed, arguing that the carrier was a federal government instrumentality; similarly, he joined Field in dissent in the *Sinking Fund Cases* (1879), arguing that Congress's requirement that the Union Pacific deposit some of its earnings to repay its debt to the federal government was tantamount to the "repudiation of government obligations."

Bradley generally advocated a broad nationalist view of the commerce clause. He wrote, for example, the opinion of the Court in *Robbins* v. *Shelby Taxing District* (1887), one of the most famous of the "drummer" cases of the period, holding that discriminatory state taxation of out-of-state salesmen unduly burdened interstate commerce. He also maintained that states could not tax the gross receipts of steamship companies or telegraph messages sent across state lines. Yet he steadfastly resisted the attempts of business to avoid their fair share of tax burdens,

and he ruled that neither goods destined for another state nor goods that arrived at a final destination after crossing state lines were exempt from state taxing.

Despite Bradley's broad reading of the Fourteenth Amendment in the *Slaughterhouse Cases,* he voted with the Court majority that failed in various cases to sustain national protection of the rights of blacks. He ruled against the constitutionality of the Force Act of 1870 while on circuit, and the Court sustained his ruling in *United States* v. *Cruikshank* (1876). He acquiesced in *United States* v. *Reese* (1876), crippling enforcement of the Fifteenth Amendment, and in *Hall* v. *DeCuir* (1878) he agreed that a Louisiana law prohibiting racial segregation on railroads burdened interstate commerce. Unlike that of most of his colleagues, Bradley's interpretation of the commerce power was consistent, for he dissented with John M. Harlan when the Court in 1890 approved a state law requiring segregated railroad cars.

Bradley's most famous statement on racial matters came in the Civil Rights Cases (1883). Speaking for all his colleagues save Harlan, Bradley held unconstitutional the Civil Rights Act of 1875. He limited the scope of the Fourteenth Amendment when he wrote that it forbade only state action and not private racial discrimination. Bradley eloquently—if unfortunately—captured the national mood when he declared: "When a man has emerged from slavery, and by the aid of beneficient legislation has shaken off the inseparable concomitants of that state, there must be some stage in the progress of his elevation when he takes the rank of a mere citizen and ceases to be the special favorite of the laws. . . ." Bradley concurred in *Bradwell* v. *Illinois* (1873), in which the Court held that Illinois had not violated the equal protection clause of the Fourteenth Amendment when it refused to admit a woman to the bar. He stated that a woman's "natural and proper timidity" left her unprepared for many occupations, and he concluded that "the paramount destiny and mission of woman are to fulfill the noble and benign offices of wife and mother." Clearly, there were limits to the liberty that Bradley had so passionately advocated in the *Slaughterhouse Cases*.

The variety of significant opinions by Bradley demonstrates his enormous range and influence. In *Boyd* v. *United States* (1886) he established the modern Fourth Amendment standard for search and seizure questions, advocating a narrow scope for governmental power: "It is the duty of courts to be watchful for the constitutional rights of the citizen, and against any stealthy encroachments thereon." In *Collector* v. *Day* (1871) he dissented when the Court held that state officials were exempt from federal income taxes, and nearly sixty years later the Court adopted his position. He spoke for the Court in *Church of Jesus Christ of Latter-Day Saints* v. *United States* (1890), stipulating that forfeited Mormon property be applied to charitable uses, including the building of common schools in Utah. Finally, he helped resolve the Court's difficulties over the exercise of recently enacted jurisdiction legislation and sustained the right of federal corporations to remove their causes from state to federal courts. That opinion made possible a staggering number of new tort and corporate cases in the federal courts.

Bradley played a decisive role in the outcome of the disputed election of 1877 as he supported Rutherford B. Hayes's claims. He was the fifteenth member chosen on the Electoral Commission whose other members included seven Democrats and seven Republicans. Thus, Hayes and the Compromise of 1877 owed much to Bradley's vote.

Bradley, Field, Harlan, and Samuel F. Miller are the dominant figures of late nineteenth-century judicial history. Field's reputation rests on his forceful advocacy of a conservative ideology that the Court embraced but eventually repudiated. Harlan's claims center on his civil rights views. Miller's notions of judicial restraint continue to have vi-

tality. But Bradley's range of expertise, his high technical competency, and the continuing relevance of his work arguably place him above those distinguished contemporaries. Indeed, a mere handful of Supreme Court Justices have had a comparable impact.

—STANLEY I. KUTLER

Bibliography

Fairman, Charles (1950). What Makes a Great Justice? *Boston University Law Review* 30:49–102.

Magrath, C. Peter (1963). *Morrison R. Waite: The Triumph of Character.* New York: Macmillan.

BRADWELL v. ILLINOIS

16 Wallace 130 (1873)

Bradwell is the earliest Fourteenth Amendment case in which the Supreme Court endorsed sex discrimination. Mrs. Myra Bradwell, the editor of the *Chicago Legal News*, was certified by a board of legal examiners as qualified to be a member of the state bar. An Illinois statute permitted the state supreme court to make rules for admission to the bar. That court denied Mrs. Bradwell's application for admission solely on the ground of sex, although the fact that the applicant was married also counted against her: a married woman at that time was incapable of making binding contracts without her husband's consent, thus disabling her from performing all the duties of an attorney. She argued that the privileges and immunities clause of the Fourteenth Amendment protected her civil right as a citizen of the United States to be admitted to the bar, if she qualified.

Justice Samuel F. Miller, speaking for the Court, declared that the right to be admitted to the practice of law in a state court was not a privilege of national citizenship protected by the Fourteenth Amendment. Justice Joseph P. Bradley, joined by Justices

Bradwell is the earliest Fourteenth Amendment case in which the Supreme Court endorsed sex discrimination.

See also

Civil Rights

Noah Swayne and Stephen J. Field, concurred in the judgment affirming the state court, but offered additional reasons. History, nature, common law, and the civil law supported the majority's reading of the privileges and immunities clause, according to Bradley. The "spheres and destinies" of the sexes were widely different, man being woman's protector; her "timidity and delicacy" unfit her for many occupations, including the law. Unlike Myra Bradwell, an unmarried woman might make contracts, but such a woman was an exception to the rule. "The paramount destiny and mission of woman are to fulfill the noble and benign offices of wife and mother. This is the law of the Creator." Society's rules, Bradley added, ought not be based on exceptions. Chief Justice Salmon P. Chase dissented alone, without opinion, missing a chance to advocate the cause of sex equality, at least in the legal profession.

—LEONARD W. LEVY

BRANDEIS, LOUIS D.

(1856–1941)

The appointment of Louis D. Brandeis to the United States Supreme Court was not merely the crowning glory of an extraordinary career as a practicing lawyer and social activist. It was also the inauguration of an equally extraordinary career on the bench. In twenty-three years as a Justice, Brandeis acquired a stature and influence that few—before or since—could match. In part, this achievement reflected the fact that he was already a public figure when he ascended to the Court. But his skills as a jurist provided the principal explanation. He mastered details of procedure, remained diligent in researching the facts and law of the case, and, whatever the subject, devoted untold hours to make his opinions clear and logical. Perhaps the high-

est compliment came from colleagues who disagreed with his conclusions. "My, how I detest that man's ideas," Associate Justice George Sutherland once observed. "But he is one of the greatest technical lawyers I have ever known."

Brandeis's opinions and votes on the Court were very much a product of his environment and experience. Born in Louisville, Kentucky, shortly before the Civil War, he grew up in a family that provided him with love and security. That background probably helped him in establishing skills as a tenacious lawyer in Boston, where he opened his office one year after graduating from Harvard Law School first in his class. Brandeis attained local and then national fame when he used his formidable talents to effect reform at the height of the Progressive movement in the early 1900s. He fought the establishment of a privately owned subway monopoly in Boston, was instrumental in developing a savings bank life insurance system to prevent exploitation of industrial workers by large insurance companies, developed the famed Brandeis Brief—a detailed compilation of facts and statistics—in defense of Oregon's maximum hour law for women, and even took on the legendary J. P. Morgan when the corporate magnate tried to monopolize New England's rail and steamship lines. Brandeis's renown as "the people's attorney" spread across the country when, in 1910, he led a team of lawyers in challenging Richard A. Ballinger's stewardship of the nation's natural resources as secretary of the interior in the administration of President William Howard Taft.

Because of Brandeis's well-known credentials as a lawyer who had single-handedly taken on the "trusts," Woodrow Wilson turned to him for advice in the presidential campaign of 1912. The relationship ripened, and after his election to the White House Wilson repeatedly called upon Brandeis for help in solving many difficult problems. Through these interactions Wilson came to appreciate Brandeis's keen intelligence and dedication to the public welfare. In January 1916 he nominated the Boston attorney to the Supreme Court. Brandeis was confirmed by the United States Senate almost six months later after a grueling and bitter fight.

For Brandeis, law was essentially a mechanism to shape man's social, economic, and political relations. In fulfilling that function, he believed, the law had to account for two basic principles: first, that the individual was the key force in society, and second, that individuals—no matter what their talents and aspirations—had only limited capabilities. As he explained to Harold Laski, "Progress must proceed from the aggregate of the performances of individual men" and society should adjust its institutions "to the wee size of man and thus render possible his growth and development." At the same time, Brandeis did not want people coddled because of inherent limitations. Quite the contrary. People had to stretch themselves to fulfill their individual potentials.

In this context Brandeis abhorred what he often called "the curse of bigness." People, he felt, could not fully develop themselves if they did not have control of their lives. Individual control, however, was virtually impossible in a large institutional setting—whether it be a union, a corporation, the government, or even a town. From this perspective, Brandeis remained convinced that democracy could be maintained only if citizens—and especially the most talented—returned to small communities in the hinterland and learned to manage their own affairs.

This commitment to individual development led Brandeis to assume a leadership position in the Zionist movement in 1914 and retain it after he went on the Court. In Palestine, Brandeis believed, an individual could control his life in a way that would not be possible in the United States.

This theme—the need for individuals and local communities to control their own affairs—also threads the vast majority of Brandeis's major opinions on the Court. Some of the most controversial of Brandeis's early opinions concerned labor unions. Long before his appointment to the Court he had viewed unions as a necessary element in the nation's economy. Without them large corporations would be able to exploit workers and prevent them from acquiring the financial independence needed for individual control. Brandeis made his views known on this matter in *Hitchman Coal & Coke Company* v. *Mitchell* (1917). That case concerned the United Mine Workers' efforts to unionize the workers in West Virginia. As a condition of employment the mine owner forced his employees to sign a pledge not to join a union. A majority of the Court held that UMW officials had acted illegally in trying to induce the workers to violate that pledge.

Brandeis dissented. He could not accept the majority's conclusion that a union agreement would deprive the workers and mine

THE PEOPLE'S ATTORNEY

In twenty-three years as a Justice, Brandeis acquired a stature and influence that few could match. (Corbis/Bettmann)

owner of their due process rights under the Fourteenth Amendment to freedom of contract. "Every agreement curtails the liberty of those who enter into it," Brandeis responded. "The test of legality is not whether an agreement curtails liberty, but whether the parties have agreed upon some thing which the law prohibits. . . ." Brandeis also saw no merit in the majority's concern with the UMW's pressure on workers to join the union. The plaintiff company's lawsuit was premised "upon agreements secured under similar pressure of economic necessity or disadvantage," he observed. "If it is coercion to threaten to strike unless plaintiff consents to a closed union shop, it is coercion also to threaten not to give one employment unless the applicant will consent to a closed non-union shop."

Brandeis adhered to these views in other labor cases that came before the Court. Eventually, the Court came around to Brandeis's belief that unions had a right to engage in peaceful efforts to push for a closed shop. Brandeis himself added a finishing touch in an opinion he delivered in *Senn* v. *Tile Layers Union* (1937), where he upheld a state law restricting the use of injunctions against picketing.

While concern for the plight of labor was vital to his vision of society, nothing concerned Brandeis more than the right of a state or community to shape its own environment. For this reason he voted to uphold almost every piece of social legislation that came before the Court. Indeed, he wanted to reduce federal jurisdiction in part because, as he told Felix Frankfurter, "In no case practically should the appellate federal courts have to pass on the construction of state statutes." Therefore, if the state wanted to regulate the practices of employment agencies, expand the disability protection to stevedores who worked the docks, or take other social actions, he would not stand in the way. As he explained for the Court in *O'Gorman & Young* v. *Hartford Insurance Company* (1931), "The presumption of constitutionality must

prevail in the absence of some factual foundation of record for overthrowing the statute." This meant that the Court must abide by the legislature's judgment even if the Court found the law to be of doubtful utility.

Only a few months after *O'Gorman* Brandeis applied this principle in *New State Ice Company* v. *Liebmann* (1932). The Oklahoma Legislature had passed a law that prohibited anyone from entering the ice business without first getting a certificate from a state corporation commission showing that there was a public need for the new business. A majority of the Court struck the law down because the ice business was not so affected with a public interest to justify a measure that would, in effect, restrict competition.

Brandeis was all for competition. He had long believed that large corporations were dangerous because they often eliminated competition and with it the right of individuals to control their lives, a proposition he examined in detail in *Liggett Company* v. *Lee* (1933). Whatever misgivings he had about the merits of the Oklahoma law, Brandeis had no trouble accepting the state's right to make its own decisions, especially at a time when the nation was grappling with the problems of the Depression. "It is one of the happy incidents of the federal system," he wrote in dissent, "that a single courageous State may, if its citizens choose, serve as a laboratory; and try novel social and economic experiments without risk to the rest of the country. This Court has the power to prevent an experiment. . . . But in the exercise of this high power, we must be ever on our guard, lest we erect our prejudices into legal principles."

It was, in a way, an ironic warning. For Brandeis himself sometimes allowed personal prejudice to govern his opinions. There was no better example than *Nashville, Chattanooga & St. Louis Railway* v. *Walters* (1935). A railroad challenged the application of a Tennessee law that required it to pay half the cost of an underpass—not to eliminate existing safety hazards but to help improve the national highway system and thereby facilitate its use by newer, high-speed automobiles. The challenge found a sympathetic listener in Brandeis. He hated cars. To him they represented the extravagance and overcapitalization that contributed to the Depression. Brandeis also opposed the construction of the national highway system because its maintenance would require too much public money. Primarily for these reasons the Justice was willing to uphold the railway's argument and ask the state court to reconsider. Nathaniel Nathanson, Brandeis's law clerk at the time, protested (as Brandeis had in other cases) that the Court had no business second-guessing the state, and here there were many conceivable reasons why Tennessee felt justified in asking railroads to assume half the tab for grade crossings. It was all to no avail. "I apply the test of Oliver Wendell Holmes," Brandeis told his clerk. "Does it make you puke?" This case flunked the test. "It may be shocking to mention them in the same breath," Nathanson wrote to Frankfurter afterward, "but I sometimes wonder whether the Justice or [Associate Justice James C.] McReynolds votes more in accordance with his prejudices. . . ."

The Tennessee case was an exception to Brandeis's general inclination to protect the states' right to legislate. In fact, he was so devoted to states' rights that he once openly disregarded one of his most-oft stated juridical principles—never decide constitutional matters that can be avoided. Brandeis relied on this principle when he refused to join the Court's opinion in *Ashwander* v. *Tennessee Valley Authority* (1936) upholding the constitutionality of federal legislation establishing the TVA. In a concurring opinion he argued that they should have dismissed the case without deciding the constitutional issue because the plaintiffs had no standing to bring the lawsuit.

Brandeis was willing to ignore the teachings of his TVA opinion, however, when Chief Justice Charles Evans Hughes asked the aging Justice to write the Court's opinion in *Erie Railroad* v. *Tompkins* (1938). The Court had voted to overrule *Swift* v. *Tyson* (1842), a decision that concerned cases arising under diversity jurisdiction. Specifically, *Swift* allowed federal courts to ignore the laws of the states in which they were located and instead to apply federal common law. *Swift* thus enabled litigants in certain cases to shop for the best forum in filing a lawsuit, for a federal court under *Swift* could and often did follow substantive law different from that applied by local courts.,

Brandeis had long found *Swift* offensive. Not only did it mean that different courts in the same state could come to different conclusions on the same question; of greater importance, *Swift* undermined the ability of the state to control its own affairs. He was no doubt delighted when Hughes gave him the chance to bury *Swift*; and he wanted to make sure there could be no resurrection by a later Court or Congress. He therefore wrote an opinion holding that *Swift* violated the Constitution because it allowed federal courts to assume powers reserved to the states. The constitutional basis for the opinion was startling for two reasons: first, Brandeis could have just as easily overturned *Swift* through a revised construction of the Judiciary Act of 1789; and second, none of the parties had even raised the constitutional issue, let alone briefed it.

Brandeis would depart from his ready endorsement of state legislation if the law violated fundamental freedoms and individual rights. It was not only a matter of constitutional construction. The Bill of Rights played a significant role in the individual's, and ultimately the community's, right to control the future. Brandeis knew, for example, that, without First Amendment protections, he never could have achieved much success as "the people's attorney" in battling vested interests. In those earlier times he had sloughed off personal attacks of the bitterest kind to pursue his goals. He knew that, in many instances, he would have been silenced if his right of speech had depended on majority

♦ **common law**
The body of legal custom and accumulated precedent inherited from England, sometimes inaccurately described as "judge-made law."

B

BRANDEIS, LOUIS D.

(1856–1941)

See also

Erie Railroad v. *Tompkins*

Olmstead v. *United States*

approval. And he expressed great concern when citizens were punished—even during wartime—for saying or writing things someone found objectionable. "The constitutional right of free speech has been declared to be the same in peace and in war," he wrote in dissent in *Schaeffer* v. *United States* (1920). "In peace, too, men may differ widely as to what loyalty to our country demands; and an intolerant majority, swayed by passion or fear, may be prone in the future, as it has often been in the past, to stamp as disloyal opinions with which it disagrees." This point was later amplified in his concurring opinion in *Whitney* v. *California* (1927). The Founding Fathers, Brandeis wrote, recognized "that fear breeds repression; that repression breeds hate; that hate menaces stable government; that the path of safety lies in the opportunity to discuss freely supposed grievances and proposed remedies; and that the fitting remedy for evil counsels is good ones."

Brandeis, then, often brought clear and deep-seated convictions to the conference table. He was not one, however, to twist arms and engage in the lobbying that other Justices found so successful. "I could have had my views prevail in cases of public importance if I had been willing to play politics," he once told Frankfurter. "But I made up my mind I wouldn't—I would have had to sin against my light, and I would have hated myself. And I decided that the price was too large for the doubtful gain to the country's welfare."

Brandeis therefore tried to use established procedures to persuade his colleagues. To that end he would often anticipate important cases and distribute his views as a "memorandum" even before the majority opinion was written. In *Olmstead* v. *United States* (1928), for example, he tried to convince the Court that the federal government should not be allowed to use evidence in a criminal case that its agents had obtained by wiretapping. The eavesdropping had been done without a judicial warrant and in violation of a state statute. Brandeis circulated a memo-

randum reflecting views that had not been debated at conference. The government should not be able to profit by its own wrongdoing, he said—especially when, as here, it impinged on the individual's right to privacy (a right he had examined as a lawyer in a seminal article in the *Harvard Law Review*). The memorandum could not command a majority, and Brandeis later issued an eloquent dissent that focused on the contention that warrantless wiretaps violated the Fourth Amendment's protection against unreasonable searches and seizures.

At other times Brandeis would use the Saturday conferences to urge a view upon his colleagues. On one occasion—involving *Southwestern Bell Telephone Company* v. *Public Service Commission* (1923)—an entire day was devoted to a seminar conducted by Brandeis to explain why a utility's rate of return should be based on prudent investment and not on the reproduction cost of its facilities. Few, if any, Justices shared Brandeis's grasp of rate-making principles. Hence, it took more than two decades of experience and debate before the Court—without Brandeis—accepted the validity of his position.

Brandeis took his losses philosophically. He knew that progress in a democracy comes slowly, and he was prepared to accept temporary setbacks along the way. But he rarely faded in his determination to correct the result. If his brethren remained impervious to his reasoning, he was willing to use other resources. He peppered Frankfurter and others with suggestions on articles for the *Harvard Law Review*. He also turned to the numerous congressmen and senators who frequently dined with him. Were they interested in introducing legislation to restrict federal jurisdiction or some other objective? If the answer was affirmative, Brandeis often volunteered the services of Frankfurter (whose expenses in public interest matters were generally assumed by Brandeis).

Few of these extrajudicial activities produced concrete results. Brandeis was apparently pleased, consequently, when Hughes became Chief Justice in 1930. Brandeis felt that the former secretary of state had a better command of the law than did Taft, the preceding Chief Justice, and would be able to use that knowledge to expedite the disposition of the Court's growing caseload. Of greater significance, Hughes and some other new members of the Court had views that closely coincided with Brandeis's. In fact, in 1937, Benjamin N. Cardozo, Harlan Fiske Stone, and Brandeis—the so-called liberal Justices—began to caucus in Brandeis's apartment on Friday nights to go over the cases for the Saturday conference.

With this kind of working relationship, plus the change in the times, Brandeis was able to join a majority in upholding New Deal legislation (he voted against only three New Deal measures). He also lived to see many of his earlier dissents become holdings of the Court, particularly in cases concerning labor and the right of states to adopt social legislation. After his death, many other dissents—including his First Amendment views and his contention that warrantless wiretaps were unconstitutional—would also become the law of the land. But Brandeis's overriding ambition—the desire to establish a legal framework in which individuals and communities could control their affairs—was frustrated by developments that would not yield to even the most incisive judicial opinion. Unions, like corporations and even government, continued to grow like Topsy. Almost everyone, it seemed, became dependent on a large organization. Brandeis, a shrewd realist, surely recognized the inexorable social, economic, and political forces that impeded the realization of his dreams for America. None of that, however, would have deterred him from pursuing his goals. As he once explained to his brother, the "future has many good things in store for those who can wait, . . . have patience and exercise good judgment."

—LEWIS J. PAPER

Bibliography

Bickel, Alexander M. (1957). *The Unpublished Opinions of Mr. Justice Brandeis: The Supreme Court at Work.* Cambridge, Mass.: Harvard University Press.

Frankfurter, Felix, ed. (1932). *Mr. Justice Brandeis.* New Haven, Conn.: Yale University Press.

Freund, Paul (1964). Mr. Justice Brandeis. In Allison Dunham and Philip B. Kurland, eds., *Mr. Justice.* Chicago: University of Chicago Press.

Konefsky, Samuel J. (1956). *The Legacy of Holmes and Brandeis: A Study in the Influence of Ideas.* New York: Macmillan.

Mason, Alpheus T. (1946). *Brandeis: A Free Man's Life.* New York: Viking Press.

Paper, Lewis J. (1983). *Brandeis.* Englewood Cliffs, N.J.: Prentice-Hall.

BRANDENBURG v. OHIO

395 U.S. 444 (1969)

Libertarian critics of the clear and present danger test had always contended that it provided insufficient protection for speech because it depended ultimately on judicial guesses about the consequences of speech. Judges inimical to the content of a particular speech could always foresee the worst. Thus, to the extent that the test did protect speech, its crucial element was the imminence requirement, that speech was punishable only when it was so closely brigaded in time with unlawful action as to constitute an attempt to commit, or incitement of, unlawful action. When the Supreme Court converted clear and present danger to clear and probable danger in *Dennis* v. *United States* (1951) it actually converted the clear and present danger test into a balancing test that allowed judges who believed in judicial self-restraint to avoid enforcing the First Amendment by striking

*The decision itself
struck down the
Ohio Criminal
Syndicalism Act,
which proscribed
advocacy of violence
as a means of
accomplishing
social reform.*

♦ **per curiam**
*[Latin: by the court] An
unsigned opinion,
attributable to the whole
court and not to an
individual judge as
author.*

See also

Dennis v. *United States*

Masses Publishing Co. v.

Patten

every balance in favor of the nonspeech interest that the government sought to protect by suppressing speech. The *Dennis* conversion, however, was even more damaging to the clear and present danger rule than a flat rejection and open replacement by the balancing standard would have been. A flat rejection would have left clear and present danger as a temporarily defeated libertarian rival to a temporarily triumphant antilibertarian balancing standard. The conversion to probable danger not only defeated the danger test but also discredited it among libertarians by removing the imminence requirement that had been its strongest protection for dissident speakers. Accordingly commentators, both libertarian and advocates of judicial self-restraint, were pleased to announce that *Dennis* had buried the clear and present danger test.

Some critics of the danger test had supported Learned Hand's approach in *Masses Publishing Co.* v. *Patten* (1917), which had focused on the advocacy content of the speech itself, thus avoiding judicial predictions about what the speech plus the surrounding circumstances would bring. *Masses* left two problems, however: the "Marc Antony" speech which on the surface seems innocuous but in the circumstances really is an incitement, and the speech preaching violence in circumstances in which it is harmless. Oliver Wendell Holmes himself had injected a specific intent standard alongside the danger rule, arguing that government might punish a speaker only if it could prove his specific intent to bring about an unlawful act.

Eighteen years after *Dennis,* carefully avoiding the words of the clear and present danger test itself, the Supreme Court brought together these various strands of thought in *Brandenburg* v. *Ohio,* a per curiam holding that "the constitutional guarantees of free speech . . . do not permit a state to forbid or proscribe advocacy of the use of force or law violation except where such advocacy is directed to inciting or producing imminent lawless action and is likely to incite or produce such action." In a footnote the Court interpreted *Dennis* and *Yates* v. *United States* (1957) as upholding this standard. The decision itself struck down the Ohio Criminal Syndicalism Act, which proscribed advocacy of violence as a means of accomplishing social reform. The Court overruled *Whitney* v. *California* (1927).

—MARTIN SHAPIRO

BRANZBURG
v. HAYES

408 U.S. 665 (1972)

Branzburg v. *Hayes* combined several cases in which reporters claimed a First Amendment privilege either not to appear or not to testify before grand juries, although they had witnessed criminal activity or had information relevant to the commission of crimes. The reporters' chief contention was that they should not be required to testify unless a grand jury showed that a reporter possessed information relevant to criminal activity, that similar information could not be obtained from sources outside the press, and that the need for the information was sufficiently compelling to override the First Amendment interest in preserving confidential news sources.

Justice Byron R. White's opinion for the Court not only rejected these showings but also denied the very existence of a First Amendment testimonial privilege. Despite the asserted lack of any First Amendment privilege, the White opinion allowed that "news gathering" was not "without its First Amendment protections" and suggested that such protections would bar a grand jury from issuing subpoenas to reporters "other than in good faith" or "to disrupt a reporter's relationship with his news sources." White rejected any requirement for a stronger showing of relevance, of alternative sources, or of balancing the need for the information against the First Amendment interest.

Nevertheless, Justice Lewis F. Powell, who signed White's 5–4 opinion of the court, attached an ambiguous concurring opinion stating that a claim to privilege "should be judged on its facts by the striking of a proper balance between freedom of the press" and the government interest. Most lower courts have read the majority opinion through the eyes of Justice Powell. An opinion that emphatically denied a First Amendment privilege at various points seems to have created one after all.

—STEVEN SHIFFRIN

BRENNAN, WILLIAM J., JR.

(1906–1997)

After graduating near the top of his Harvard Law School class, William Brennan returned to his hometown, Newark, New Jersey, where he joined a prominent law firm and specialized in labor law. As his practice grew, Brennan, a devoted family man, resented the demands it made on his time and accepted an appointment to the New Jersey Superior Court in order to lessen his workload. Brennan attracted attention as an efficient and fair-minded judge and was elevated to the New Jersey Supreme Court in 1952. President Dwight D. Eisenhower, appointed him to the Supreme Court of the United States in 1956. The appointment was criticized at the time as "political," on the grounds that the nomination of a Catholic Democrat on the eve of the 1956 presidential election was intended to win votes for the Republican ticket.

Once on the Court, Brennan firmly established himself as a leader of the "liberal" wing. Often credited with providing critical behind-the-scenes leadership during the Warren Court years, Brennan fashioned many of that Court's most important decisions. He continued to play a significant role—although more often as a dissenter, lamenting what he believed to be the evisceration of Warren Court precedents—as the ideological complexion of the Court changed in the 1970s and 1980s.

Brennan was a committed civil libertarian who believed that the Constitution guarantees "freedom and equality of rights and

The reporters' chief contention was that they should not be required to testify unless a grand jury showed that a reporter possessed information relevant to criminal activity.

BRASWELL v. UNITED STATES

487 U.S. 99 (1988)

Because the Fifth Amendment's right against self-incrimination is a personal one that can be exercised only by natural persons, the custodian of a corporation's records may not invoke this right. The contents of corporate records are not privileged either. In this case, however, Braswell, who had been subpoenaed to produce the corporation's records, was its sole shareholder. He claimed that the production of the records, under compulsion, forced him to incriminate himself. Had he been the sole proprietor of a business, the Court would have agreed. But because he had incorporated, he lost the protection of the Fifth Amendment.

Four dissenters strongly maintained that the Court majority, by splitting hairs, had ignored realities. The Court used the fiction that the government did not seek the personal incrimination of Braswell, when it forced him as the head of his solely owned corporation to produce the records. This had the effect of giving the government the evidence needed to convict him. The majority openly conceded that to hold otherwise would hurt the government's efforts to prosecute white collar crime.

—LEONARD W. LEVY

The custodian of a corporation's records may not invoke the Fifth Amendment's right against self-incrimination.

opportunities . . . to all people of this nation." For Brennan, courts were the last resort of the politically disfranchised and the politically powerless, and constitutional litigation was often "the sole practicable avenue open to a minority to petition for redress of grievances." Thus, in Brennan's view, the courts played an indispensable role in the enforcement, interpretation, and implementation of the most cherished guarantees of the United States Constitution. As Brennan observed, the Constitution's "broadly phrased guarantees ensure that [it] need never become an anachronism: The Constitution will endure as a vital charter of human liberty as long as there are those with the courage to defend it, the vision to interpret it, and the fidelity to live by it."

Brennan had an especially influential impact in the areas of equal protection of the laws, due process, freedom of speech, and criminal procedure. In his interpretation of the equal protection clause, Brennan evinced little tolerance for invidious discrimination by the government. When Brennan joined the Court in 1956, the equal protection clause was high on the Court's agenda, for the Court had just handed down its explosive decisions in *Brown* v. *Board of Education of Topeka* (1954, 1955). Despite these decisions, and to the Court's mounting frustration, segregation of southern schools remained largely intact more than a decade after *Brown.* In *Green* v. *County School Board of New Kent* (1968), however, Brennan's opinion for the Court finally dismantled the last serious barriers to desegregation by invalidating the "freedom of choice" plans that had been used to forestall desegregation in the rural South. Putting aside the all deliberate speed formula, Brennan emphatically expressed his own and the Court's impatience at the pace of desegregation: "The burden on a school board today is to come forward with a plan that promises realistically to work, and promises realistically to work *now.*"

When the Court first considered the lawfulness of school segregation in a city that had never expressly mandated racially segregated education by statute, it was again Brennan, writing for a closely divided Court in *Keyes* v. *School District No. 1 of Denver* (1973), who took a strong stand on the issue: "A finding of intentionally segregative school board action in a meaningful portion of a school system . . . creates a presumption that other segregated schooling within the system is not adventitious [and] shifts to school authorities the burden of proving that other segregated schools within the system are not also the result of intentionally segregative actions."

Although Brennan naturally assumed a leadership role in condemning racial discrimination, he sharply distinguished such discrimination from race-conscious affirmative action programs designed to protect racial minorities. Brennan explained the distinction in his separate opinion in *Regents of University of California* v. *Bakke* (1978): "Against the background of our history, claims that law must be 'color-blind' or that the datum of race is no longer relevant to public policy must be seen as aspiration rather than as description of reality. [We] cannot . . . let color blindness become myopia which masks the reality that many 'created equal' have been treated within our lifetimes as inferior both by law and by their fellow citizens." Brennan therefore concluded that the purpose of "remedying the effects of past societal discrimination is . . . sufficiently important to justify the use of race-conscious" affirmative action programs "where there is a sound basis for concluding that minority representation is substantial and chronic and that the handicap of past discrimination is impeding access of minorities to the [field]."

Brennan also played a pivotal role in the evolution of equal protection doctrine in the area of sex discrimination. In *Frontiero* v. *Richardson* (1973) Brennan, writing a plurality opinion for four Justices, argued that classifications based on sex are inherently suspect and, like racial classifications, must be subjected to strict scrutiny. Taking a strong stand on the issue, Brennan explained that "our Nation has had a long and unfortunate history of sex discrimination" and that history has traditionally been "rationalized by an attitude of 'romantic paternalism' which, in practical effect, put women, not on a pedestal, but in a cage." Although Brennan never garnered the crucial fifth vote for this position, he did gain a decisive victory in *Craig* v. *Boren* (1976), in which he wrote for the Court that gender-based classifications must be subjected to intermediate scrutiny and that "to withstand constitutional analysis" such classifications "must serve important governmental objectives and must be substantially related to achievement of those objectives."

Brennan also opened the door to the Court's reapportionment revolution. Prior to 1962, the Court had consistently declined to consider claims that state laws prescribing legislative districts that were not approximately equal in population violated the Constitution. As Justice Frankfurter explained in *Colegrove* v. *Green* (1946), such controversies concern "matters that bring courts into immediate and active relations with party contests," and "courts ought not to enter this political thicket." In *Baker* v. *Carr* (1962) Brennan rejected this reasoning and held that a claim that the apportionment of the Tennessee General Assembly violated the appellants' rights under the equal protection clause "by virtue of the debasement of their votes" stated "a justiciable cause of action." Brennan explained that "the question here is the consistency of state action with the Federal Constitution," and such claims are not nonjusticiable merely "because they touch matters of state governmental organization." Brennan's opinion for the Court in *Baker* led the way to *Reynolds* v. *Sims* (1964), and its progeny, which articulated and enforced the constitutional principle of one person, one vote.

Closely related to the Court's reapportionment decisions was the equal protection doctrine of implied fundamental rights. Prior to 1969, the Court had hinted on several occasions that the rational basis standard of review might not be applicable to classifications that penalize the exercise of such rights. Building upon these intimations, Brennan held in *Shapiro* v. *Thompson* (1969) that a law that denied welfare benefits to residents who had not resided within the jurisdiction for at least one year immediately prior to their application for assistance penalized the right to interstate travel by denying newcomers "welfare aid upon which may depend the ability of families to subsist." Brennan concluded that because the classification penalized an implied fundamental right it amounted to unconstitutional "invidious discrimination" unless it was "necessary to promote a compelling governmental interest." Brennan's opinion in *Shapiro* crystallized the implied fundamental rights doctrine and thus opened the door to a series of subsequent decisions invalidating classifications that unequally affected voting rights, the right to be listed on the ballot, the right to travel, and the right to use contraceptives.

Although Brennan played a central role in shaping equal protection doctrine in the 1960s, by the 1970s and 1980s he often found himself fighting rearguard actions in an effort to protect his earlier equal protection decisions, particularly in the areas of reapportionment and implied fundamental rights. Occasionally, however, he won a hard-earned victory. In *Plyler* v. *Doe* (1982), for example, Brennan mustered a five-Justice majority to invalidate a Texas statute that denied free public education to children who had not been legally admitted into the United States. Although conceding that education is not a fundamental right, Brennan nonetheless persuaded four of his brethren that intermediate scrutiny was appropriate because the statute imposed "a lifetime hardship on the discrete class of children not accountable for their disabling status."

As these decisions suggest, Brennan was consistently ready and willing to assert judicial authority to enforce the Constitution's

Brennan viewed courts as the last resort of the politically disenfranchised and the politically powerless.

guarantee of "the equal protection of the laws." This same activism was evident in Brennan's due process opinions. *Goldberg* v. *Kelly* (1970) is perhaps the best example. Traditionally, the Court had defined the "liberty" and "property" interests protected by the due process clause by reference to the common law. The Court held that if government took someone's property or invaded his bodily integrity, the due process clause required some kind of hearing; but the Court deemed the clause inapplicable if government denied an individual some public benefit to which he had no common law right, such as public employment, a license, or welfare. This doctrine seemed increasingly formalistic with the twentieth-century expansion of governmental benefit programs and governmental participation in the economy, for while more and more individuals grew increasingly dependent upon government, prevailing doctrine gave no constitutional protection against even the most arbitrary withdrawal of governmental benefits.

In *Goldberg*, Brennan dramatically redefined the scope of the interests protected by the due process clause. Brennan explained that "much of the existing wealth in this country takes the form of rights that do not fall within traditional common law concepts of property," and it is "realistic today to regard welfare entitlements as more like property than a 'gratuity.'" This being so, Brennan held, a state could not constitutionally terminate public assistance benefits without affording the recipient the opportunity for an evidential hearing prior to termination. In this opinion, Brennan launched a new era in the extension of due process rights, and in subsequent decisions, the Court, building upon *Goldberg*, held that the suspension of drivers' licenses, the termination of public employment, the revocation of parole, the termination of food stamps, and similar matters must be undertaken in accordance with the demands of due process.

Despite his extraordinary contributions to the governing principles of American equal

protection and due process jurisprudence, Brennan's greatest legacy may be in the area of free expression. When Brennan joined the Court, the country was in the throes of its efforts to suppress communism, and this undoubtedly affected Brennan's views on free expression. Brennan's influence on the Court in this area of the law was felt almost immediately. Two years before Brennan's appointment, the Court, in *Barsky* v. *Board of Regents* (1954), reaffirmed the right/privilege distinction in upholding the suspension of a physician's medical license because of events arising out of his communist affiliations. Four years later, in *Speiser* v. *Randall* (1958), Brennan's opinion for the Court explicitly rejected the right/privilege distinction. *Speiser* involved a California law that established a special property tax exemption for veterans, but denied the exemption to any veteran who advocated the violent overthrow of the government. Brennan rejected the state's argument that the disqualification was lawful because it merely withheld a "privilege": "To deny an exemption to claimants who engage in certain forms of speech is in effect to penalize them for such speech. Its deterrent effect is the same as if the State were to fine them for this speech. The appellees are plainly mistaken in their argument that, because a tax exemption is a 'privilege'. . . , its denial may not infringe speech."

Brennan's rejection of the right/privilege distinction in *Speiser* was a critical step in the evolution of First Amendment doctrine. It did not, however, end the case, and Brennan proceeded to articulate a second—and equally important—principle of First Amendment doctrine. Turning to the procedure mandated by the California law, Brennan held that the law violated the First Amendment because it required the applicant to prove that he had not advocated the violent overthrow of government. Brennan explained that "the vice of the present procedure is that, where particular speech falls close to the line separating the lawful and the unlawful, the possibility of mistaken factfinding—inherent in all litigation—will create the danger that the legitimate utterance will be penalized." Moreover, "the man who knows that he must bring forth proof and persuade another of the lawfulness of his conduct must steer far wider of the unlawful zone than if the State must bear these burdens."

This emphasis on the procedure by which government regulates expression was a hallmark of Brennan's First Amendment jurisprudence. Indeed, Brennan was the principal architect of both the First Amendment vagueness principle and the overbreadth doctrine. Brennan's first full articulation of the vagueness principle came in *Keyishian* v. *Board of Regents* (1967), which invalidated a New York law prohibiting schoolteachers from uttering "seditious" words. Building upon his opinion in *Speiser*, Brennan grounded the vagueness principle in his observation that "when one must guess what conduct or utterance may lose him his position, one necessarily will 'steer far wider of the unlawful zone.'"

Brennan coined the term "overbreadth" in *NAACP* v. *Button* (1963), and he first fully explained the rationale of the doctrine in *Gooding* v. *Wilson* (1972): "The transcendent value to all society of constitutionally protected expression is deemed to justify allowing 'attacks on overly broad statutes with no requirement that the person making the attack demonstrate that his own conduct could not be regulated by a statute drawn with the requisite narrow specificity.' . . . This is deemed necessary because persons whose expression is constitutionally protected may well refrain from exercising their rights for fear of criminal sanctions provided by a statute susceptible of application to protected expression."

Brennan's views on free expression were influenced not only by governmental efforts to suppress communism but by the civil rights movement. In *NAACP* v. *Button* (1963), for example, Brennan held that a Virginia law

prohibiting any organization to retain a lawyer in connection with litigation to which it was not a party was unconstitutional as applied to the activities of the NAACP and the NAACP Legal Defense Educational Fund. Brennan explained that "in the context of NAACP objectives, litigation is not a technique of resolving private differences; it is a means for [achieving] equality of treatment [for] the members of the Negro Community." In such circumstances, litigation "is a form of political expression," and "groups which find themselves unable to achieve their objectives through the ballot frequently turn to the courts." Indeed, for the group the NAACP "assists, litigation may be the most effective form of political association." By bringing litigation within the ambit of First Amendment protection, Brennan's opinion for the Court in *Button* both highlighted the central role of courts as effective instruments of political and social change and empowered organizations like the NAACP to pursue aggressively the vindication of constitutional rights without obstruction from often hostile state governments.

Perhaps Brennan's most important First Amendment opinion, *New York Times* v. *Sullivan* (1964), also grew out of the civil rights movement. At issue in *Sullivan* was the Alabama law of libel, which permitted a public official to recover damages for defamatory statements unless the accuser could prove that the statements were true. The case was brought by a Montgomery city commissioner on the basis of several inaccurate statements contained in an advertisement that described the civil rights movement and concluded with an appeal for funds. An Alabama jury found in favor of the commissioner and awarded him damages in the amount of $500,000.

Prior to *Sullivan* it was settled doctrine that libelous utterances were unprotected by the First Amendment and could be regulated without raising "any constitutional problem." With a sensitivity to the history of

He quickly became, in both an intellectual and statistical sense, the center of gravity of the Warren Court, fashioning many of that Court's most important opinions.

♦ **civil law**
*(1) the body of law
dealing with the private
rights and duties of
individuals,
distinguished from
criminal law; (2) a body
of law derived from the
Roman legal codes that is
in force in continental
Europe and elsewhere,
distinguished from
common law. Civil law,
in the latter sense, is the
basis of much of the
private law of
Louisiana, and it is the
original source of some
aspects of property law in
Texas and in states
formed from the Mexican
Cession.*

seditious libel and an awareness of the dangers even civil libel actions pose to free and open debate in cases like *Sullivan*, Brennan rejected settled doctrine and held that "libel can claim no talismanic immunity from constitutional limitations." To the contrary, libel "must be measured by standards that satisfy the First Amendment." Moreover, considering the case "against the background of a profound national commitment to the principle that debate on public issues should be uninhibited, robust, and wide-open," Brennan maintained that the "advertisement, as an expression of grievance and protest on one of the major public issues of our time, would seem clearly to qualify for constitutional protection." Balancing the competing interests, Brennan concluded that because "erroneous statement is inevitable in free debate" and "must be protected if the freedoms of expression are to have the 'breathing space' that they 'need . . . to survive,' " the First Amendment must be understood to prohibit any public official to recover damages for libel unless "he proves that the statement was made with 'actual malice'—that is, with knowledge that it was false or with reckless disregard of whether it was false or not."

Brennan also played a central role in the evolution of the law of obscenity. In *Roth* v. *United States* (1957), the Court's first confrontation with the obscenity issue, Brennan wrote for the Court that obscenity is "utterly without redeeming social importance" and is thus "not within the area of constitutionally protected speech." Characteristically, however, Brennan emphasized that "sex and obscenity are not synonymous" and that it is "vital that the standards for judging obscenity safeguard the protection of . . . material which does not treat sex in a manner appealing to prurient interest." Sixteen years later, after struggling without success satisfactorily to define "obscenity," Brennan came to the conclusion that the very concept is so inherently vague that it is impossible to "bring stability to this area of the law without jeopardizing fundamental

First Amendment values." Brennan therefore concluded in his dissenting opinion in *Paris Adult Theatre I* v. *Slaton* (1973) that "at least in the absence of distribution to juveniles or obtrusive exposure to unconsenting adults," the First Amendment prohibits the suppression of "sexually oriented materials on the basis of their allegedly 'obscene' contents." Not surprisingly, this analysis once again revealed the essential touchstones of Brennan's First Amendment jurisprudence—a recognition of the need for precision of regulation and a sensitivity to the practical dynamics of governmental efforts to limit expression. As Brennan cautioned in *Paris Adult Theatre*, "In the absence of some very substantial interest" in suppressing even low-value speech, "we can hardly condone the ill effects that seem to flow inevitably from the effort."

As in the equal protection area, and as suggested in *Paris Adult Theatre*, Brennan spent most of his energies in free speech cases in the 1970s and 1980s in dissent. This was especially true in cases involving content-neutral regulations of expression, such as *Heffron* v. *International Society for Krishna Consciousness, Inc.* (1981), and cases involving the regulation of sexually oriented expression, such as *Federal Communications Commission* v. *Pacifica Foundation* (1978). As in the equal protection area, however, Brennan won a few notable victories. In *Elrod* v. *Burns* (1976), for example, Brennan wrote a plurality opinion holding the patronage practice of dismissing public employees on a partisan basis violative of the First Amendment; in *Board of Education* v. *Pico* (1982) he wrote a plurality opinion holding unconstitutional the removal of books from a public school library; and in *Texas* v. *Johnson* (1989) he wrote the opinion of the Court holding that an individual who burned the American flag as a form of political protest had engaged in constitutionally protected conduct that could not be prohibited under a state flag desecration statute.

Brennan's opinions in the realm of criminal procedure followed a similar pattern—

landmark opinions expanding civil liberties during the Warren Court, vigorous and often bitter dissents during the Burger Court and the Rehnquist Court. Brennan's earlier opinions are illustrated by *Fay* v. *Noia* (1963), *Davis* v. *Mississippi* (1969), and *United States* v. *Wade* (1967). In *Fay,* Brennan significantly expanded the availability of federal habeas corpus, holding the writ available not only to persons challenging the jurisdiction of the convicting court but to any individual who was convicted in a proceeding that was "so fundamentally defective as to make imprisonment . . . constitutionally intolerable." In *Davis,* Brennan limited the use of dragnet investigations and invalidated as an unreasonable search and seizure the detention of twenty-five black youths for questioning and fingerprinting in connection with a rape investigation where there were no reasonable grounds to believe that any particular individual was the assailant. And in *Wade,* Brennan held that courtroom identifications of an accused must be excluded from evidence where the accused was exhibited to witnesses before trial at a postindictment lineup without notice to the accused's counsel. The common theme of these and other Brennan opinions in the area of criminal procedure was that judges must be especially vigilant to protect those individuals whose rights to fair, decent, and equal treatment in the criminal justice system might too easily be lost to intolerance, indifference, ignorance, or haste.

Brennan also adopted a consistently firm stand against the constitutionality of capital punishment. In *Furman* v. *Georgia,* Brennan maintained that the cruel and unusual punishment clause "must draw its meaning from the evolving standards of decency that mark the progress of a maturing society" and that a punishment is cruel and unusual "if it does not comport with human dignity." Noting that the "uniqueness" of capital punishment is evident in its "pain, in its finality, and in its enormity," Brennan concluded that the death penalty "stands condemned as fatally offensive to human dignity" because it is "degrading" to the individual, "arbitrarily" inflicted, "excessive," and unacceptable to "contemporary society." Although he did not persuade a majority to this point of view, he adhered to this position as a matter of unshakable principle throughout his career.

At the time of his appointment to the Supreme Court, much was made of Brennan's Catholicism. It was thought by many, for better or worse, that he would narrowly represent the interests of a Catholic constituency. Brennan did not meet those expectations. To the contrary, guided by his constitutional philosophy rather than his religion, Brennan frequently angered Catholics on such controversial issues as school prayer, Bible readings, moments of silence, government aid to religious institutions (including parochial schools), public displays of the crèche, birth control, and abortion. In this way, as in others, Brennan no doubt surprised many of those who were most responsible for his appointment to the Court.

After serving more than three decades as an Associate Justice, Brennan resigned from the Supreme Court in 1990. He passed away seven years later, on July 25, 1997. He will be remembered as one of the most influential Justices in the history of the Court. Throughout his long and distinguished tenure, Brennan unflinchingly championed the rights of the poor, the unrepresented, and the powerless. There were, of course, those who rejected Brennan's vision of the Constitution and who maintained that he too readily mistook his own preferences for the demands of the Constitution, but there can be no doubt that Brennan expressed his unique and powerful vision of the Constitution as "a vital charter of human liberty" with rare eloquence, intelligence, clarity, and courage.

—GEOFFREY R. STONE

Bibliography

Berger, Raoul (1988). Justice Brennan vs. the Constitution. *Boston College Law Review* 29:787–801.

◆ **litigant**
A party to a legal action.

Police played on Williams's religious beliefs and convinced him to show where he had buried a child's body so that the child could have a Christian burial.

Blasi, V. (1982). *The Burger Court: The Counter-Revolution That Wasn't.* New Haven, Conn.: Yale University Press.

Brennan, William J., Jr. (1977). State Constitutions and the Protection of Individual Rights. *Harvard Law Review* 90:489–504.

——— (1988). Reason, Passion, and the Progress of the Law. *Cardozo Law Review* 10:23–24.

Kalven, Harry, Jr. (1988). *A Worthy Tradition: Freedom of Speech in America.* New York: Harper & Row.

Leeds, J. (1986). A Life on the Court. *New York Times Magazine,* October 5, pp. 24–80.

Schwartz, H. (1987). *The Burger Years: Rights and Wrongs in the Supreme Court, 1969–1986.* New York: Viking.

Stone, Geoffrey R.; Seidman, Louis M.; Sunstein, Cass R.; and Tushnet, Mark V. (1986). *Constitutional Law.* Boston: Little, Brown.

BREWER v. WILLIAMS

430 U.S. 378 (1977)

This highly publicized case produced three concurring and three dissenting opinions and Justice Potter Stewart's opinion for a 5–4 majority. Williams, who had kidnapped and murdered a child, was being transported by police who had read the Miranda Rules to him. But the police played on his religious beliefs. Although they had agreed not to interrogate him and he had declared that he wanted the assistance of counsel and would tell his story on seeing his counsel, a detective convinced him to show where he had buried the body so that the child could have a Christian burial. The Court reversed his conviction, ruling that the use of evidence relating to or resulting from his incriminating statements violated his right of counsel once adversary proceedings against him had begun, and he had not waived his right.

—LEONARD W. LEVY

BREYER, STEPHEN G.

(1938–   )

Justice Stephen G. Breyer was a finalist for the 1993 Supreme Court opening for which President Clinton nominated Ruth Bader Ginsburg. When Justice Harry Blackmun announced his retirement in April 1994, Clinton again turned to Breyer, though the president also gave serious consideration to Secretary of the Interior Bruce Babbitt and Richard Arnold of Arkansas, Chief Judge of the Court of Appeals for the Eighth Circuit.

When Clinton nominated Judge Breyer to become the 108th justice of the Supreme Court, Breyer had been Chief Judge of the U.S. Court of Appeals for the First Circuit for four years, and had been a judge on that court since 1980. At the time of his nomination, Stephen Breyer was already well known among senators, having served as special counsel to the Senate Judiciary Committee (1974-75) and later as its chief counsel (1979-81), when the committee was headed by Senator Edward M. Kennedy. In his work on the Senate Judiciary Committee Breyer earned the admiration of senators of both parties for his work on a federal criminal code, the charter of the Federal Bureau of Investigation, fair housing law, and legislation on deregulating the airline and trucking industries. He helped in selecting judges and getting them confirmed, and was responsible for drafting a policy barring federal judges from membership in private clubs that discriminate against women and minorities.

Stephen Gerald Breyer was born in San Francisco on August 15, 1938, to Irving and Anne Breyer. Mr. Breyer was an attorney and administrator in the San Francisco public school system. Mrs. Breyer, the daughter of East Prussian immigrants, was active in the local Democratic party and in the League of Women Voters. Irving Breyer made a point of bringing his son along to the voting booth on election day, and instilling in him, as the Justice has recalled, "a trust in, almost a love for the possibilities of a democracy." About his mother, Breyer has said, "She was the one who made absolutely clear to me that whatever intellectual ability I have means nothing . . . unless I can work with other people and use whatever talents I have to help them."

Though bookish in his interests, Breyer was also active in the Boy Scouts, working as a delivery boy, and mixing salads in the city's summer camp. He was regularly exposed to international cultures and influences as well, not only by growing up in San Francisco but because his mother was active in a United Nations program that brought foreign visitors to their home.

Stephen Breyer attended Lowell High School, the flagship of San Francisco's public school system, where his quick intellect and a gift for seeing into the heart of an issue and explaining complex arguments in plain English made him a star of the debate team. (One of his rivals on the team was a future governor of California, Edmund G. Brown Jr.) Breyer was voted most likely to succeed in Lowell's class of 1955.

Breyer attended Stanford University—his parents sensed that the culture at Harvard would cause him to become more bookish than he already was—and graduated with highest honors (and Phi Beta Kappa) in 1959. He won a Marshall Scholarship to Oxford University, where he studied philosophy, politics, and economics. In 1961 Breyer received a B.A. with first-class honors from Oxford.

During law school at Harvard, Breyer was elected articles editor of the *Harvard Law Review*. He wrote a thesis on the pragmatist philosophies of Charles S. Peirce, William James, and Willard Quine, asserting that in making decisions, judges should carefully weigh the likely social, political, and legal consequences on people's lives. Breyer graduated from Harvard Law School in 1964 with an LL.B. degree, magna cum laude.

He served as a clerk for Supreme Court Justice Arthur J. Goldberg from 1964 to 1965, and wrote the first draft of Goldberg's

famous opinion in *Griswold* v. *Connecticut* (1965), the case that established the constitutional right to privacy. In the Department of Justice from 1965 to 1967 Breyer was a special assistant to Assistant Attorney General Donald F. Turner, a Harvard law professor influential in the development of antitrust regulation.

It was during this period that Breyer met Joanna Freda Hare, also an Oxford graduate and the daughter of Lord John Blakenham, leader of Britain's Conservative Party. They married in 1967. She later earned a doctorate in clinical psychology at Harvard and began working at the Dana Farber Cancer Institute in Boston. They have three children: Chloe, Nell, and Michael.

Also in 1967 Breyer began teaching at Harvard Law School, specializing in federal administrative law; in 1970 he was promoted to full professor. Over the next two decades he would shuttle back and forth between Boston and Washington in a fusion of scholarly interests and real-world solutions and applications.

He returned to Washington in 1973 as an assistant special prosecutor in the Watergate investigation, and from 1974 to 1975 served as special counsel to the Senate Judiciary Committee's Subcommittee on Administrative Practices. During this time Breyer criticized the government's regulation of the airline industry, asserting that it had limited the industry's growth and competitiveness. He would later help design the deregulation of the airline industry in 1978.

After serving as chief counsel to the Senate Judiciary Committee under Senator Kennedy from 1979 to 1980, Breyer was nominated by President Jimmy Carter for a seat on the U.S. Court of Appeals for the First Circuit. Largely because in his regulatory work Breyer had demonstrated a remarkable ability to forge bipartisan consensus on divisive issues, he was easily confirmed to the federal bench, even though Republicans, anticipating Reagan's victory in the 1980

B

campaign, stalled many other Carter nominations.

During his tenure on the First Circuit Court of Appeals in Boston over the next fourteen years, Breyer continued teaching at Harvard Law School. He gave the 1992 Oliver Wendell Holmes lectures that became the foundation for his book on the regulatory system, *Breaking the Vicious Circle: Toward Effective Risk Regulation* (1993). The book dealt with the complex issue of risk assessment, the process through which courts and government agencies decide how extensive workplace safety and environmental requirements should be, weighing cost against risks to health and safety. He also wrote a well-known law school casebook on administrative law.

In 1985 he was appointed to serve on the U.S. Sentencing Commission, an independent body within the judicial branch established to rationalize and reform federal criminal sentencing procedures. Once again, Breyer's rational, pragmatic approach succeeded in pulling together a consensus among interests that could well have been wildly divided over the complexities and political sensitivities inherent in reforming the inconsistent and variable system of penalties. It was a task in which it would be impossible to please everyone, but in 1989 the Supreme Court upheld the constitutionality of the U.S. Sentencing Commission in a landmark separation of powers case, *Mistretta* v. *United States.*

On the First Circuit Court of Appeals, Breyer was building a reputation as one of the finest jurists of his time, not only through his intelligence and knowledge of the cases, but by his rare skill in building coalitions on the First Circuit and in unifying opinions that might have polarized under the influence of a less inclusive or open-minded judge. Judge Bruce M. Selya of Providence, Rhode Island, named to the First Circuit Court of Appeals by President Reagan in 1986, said of Breyer,

"He is close to an ideal colleague: bright, intellectually curious and honest, and an indefatigable worker, respectful of the views of others." While he was on the Court of Appeals, Breyer was offered the deanship of Harvard Law School and was a finalist for the presidency of Harvard University.

Justice Breyer's First Circuit decisions showed a willingness to analyze the issues confronting administrative agencies in great detail. He enjoined a government program that allowed offshore oil drilling near the major Georges Bank fishing area off the New England coast, holding the reduced amount of oil likely to be found necessitated revising the government's environmental impact statement. He ruled that appellate courts should be more loath to reverse trial courts on factual findings relating to the correctness of an agency's decision than on issues of law. And he held courts have an obligation to independently examine an agency's insistence on an injunction requiring landfill owners to clean up hazardous waste. One article has aptly described his "affinity for logical analysis" and "capacity to absorb vast administrative records quickly."

It may well have been Breyer's reputation as a pragmatist whose court rarely produced a dissenting opinion that primarily appealed to President Clinton, for several reasons. The first consideration, naturally, would be the nominee's likelihood of confirmation by the Senate, but the long-term interest would be to add to the Supreme Court a moderate, pragmatic justice who could work well with the others and unify some of the ideological differences that had developed in the Rehnquist Court between conservatives and moderates; after the retirements of Thurgood Marshall, William Brennan, and Harry Blackmun, there was little liberalism left on the Court. In addition, Clinton wanted to appoint a justice with a career in public service rather than primarily judicial experience. Bruce Babbitt may have been a stronger candidate in considerations of public service, but, given the likelihood of strong Republican opposition to Babbitt (too liberal) and Clinton's famous reluctance to fight for his nominees, the choice of Breyer, strong in both public and judicial service, was a convenient compromise.

In his remarks upon nominating Breyer, President Clinton said, "Without dispute he is one of the outstanding jurists of our age. . . . He has proven that he can build an effective consensus and get people of diverse views to work together for justice's sake. . . . His writings, in areas ranging from the interpretation of legislation and analysis of the sentencing guidelines to the underpinnings of regulation and the interplay of economics and the law, reveal a keen and vital mind."

Stephen Breyer was confirmed by the Senate by a vote of 87-9.

In his Senate confirmation hearings, Breyer explained his view of the Constitution as a "practical document" that should be viewed not only in terms of its history or the Framers' original intent but in light of "what life is like in the present." He tries always to consider the consequences of a decision, to keep in mind what a holding will mean for future generations—a view consistent with his law school thesis on the pragmatist philosophy of Peirce, James, and Quine. At one point in his testimony he said a judge should "beware of fixed rules" that may be superficially appealing but which may prove more of a trap than an aid. This philosophy now has to work in the same courtroom with Justice Antonin Scalia, well known for his more formalist jurisprudence and reliance on rules and categories. Breyer and Scalia are friendly about this difference of approach, in which they "agree to disagree."

Breyer, for example, as chief counsel to the Senate Judiciary Committee, was responsible for drafting statutes before he was appointed to a bench where he would have to interpret them. Because he knows how legislation (like sausage) is made, he will study a statute's legislative history or context in an effort to interpret what Congress intended, while Scalia is more likely to hold Congress to the letter of the law. In his testimony before the Senate, Breyer explained, "I don't think a court can know whether an interpretation is correct until it understands both the purpose and how the interpretation is likely, in light of that purpose, to work out in the world. In the actual world."

Breyer holds that a judge needs not only a knowledge of a statute's past and context, but also an understanding of what consequences a ruling is likely to have immediately and in the future. "Law requires both a heart and a head," he told the Senate. "If you don't have a heart, it becomes a sterile set of rules removed from human problems, and it won't help. If you don't have a head, there's the risk that in trying to decide a particular person's problem in a case . . . you cause trouble for a lot of other people, making their lives yet worse. It's a question of balance."

In an indication of how he would bring a respectful and cooperative spirit to the Supreme Court, Breyer explained the importance of judges' giving one another a fair hearing. "You listen to the argument, and even if you say in the opinion, 'It might be argued that, but we reject that,' the other judge is much happier because the point of view is taken into account, and that tends to draw people together."

At the time of Breyer's nomination, Professor Akhil Amar of Yale Law School saw reason to hope that the moderate and agreeable Breyer would have a calming and cohesive effect on the Court; Breyer "understands how conservatives think and can talk their talk. He'll come up with solutions that the liberals will like and conservatives will accept and respect."

In his first term on the Court, Breyer wasted no time in establishing his presence. He broke with Court tradition by joining the

Breyer's rational, pragmatic approach succeeded in pulling together a consensus among interests that could well have been wildly divided over political sensitivities.

questioning at his first oral argument, and his first opinion was a dissent. He did not hesitate to differ with Scalia, taking issue with his senior both on matters of style and substance. Breyer's concurring opinion to Scalia's majority opinion in *Plaut* v. *Spendthrift Farm, Inc.* (1995), in which Scalia invalidated a federal statute based on separation-of-powers concerns, agreed but on considerably narrower grounds.

He also showed himself well able to speak for the liberal side, particularly in some important constitutional cases. In *U.S.* v. *Lopez* (1995), for example, Breyer wrote a strong, biting dissent in defense of Congress's authority to regulate the possession of guns in school zones throughout the United States as being within the federal jurisdiction over interstate commerce. He was joined in this dissent by Justices Ginsburg, Souter, and Stevens. In another dissent, in *Sandin* v. *Conner* (1995), Breyer wrote an opinion disagreeing with what he saw as the majority's narrow reading of a prisoner's due process protections. The prisoner had been held in segregated confinement for misconduct following a hearing at which he had not been allowed to present witnesses, and where the authorities could discipline him upon finding no more than "substantial evidence" of his misconduct, rather than a preponderance of proof.

In *Denver Area Educational Telecommunications Consortium* v. *FCC* (1996) Justice Breyer wrote the majority opinion setting aside Congressional restrictions on "offensive" broadcasting depicting sex shown on cable television. The statute required cable operators to block the showing of such material on leased access channels and required a viewer to ask in writing to see the material. Justice Breyer ruled those sanctions were stricter than needed, and not narrowly tailored to meet the government's objective of protecting children. Requiring a written request, in particular, he viewed as overly severe, noting that a phone call would serve the same purpose. He also ruled Congress could

not authorize cable operators to bar the showing of such material on public access channels, where the cable operator has no editorial control over what is broadcast. However, a similar provision allowing cable operators to restrict offensive material on leased access channels was upheld by Justice Breyer since, in contrast to a ban by Congress, it simply authorized the cable operator to curb the material.

In the 1996–97 term, in which the Court heard an unusually high number of landmark cases, the decisions largely continued the Rehnquist Court's trend of a movement of authority from federal to state governments. In *Printz* v. *United States*, whose majority decision was written by Justice Scalia, the Court ruled that in crafting the "Brady Bill" on gun control, Congress's requirement that state and local law enforcement officers conduct background checks on would-be purchasers of handguns violated principles of state sovereignty. Justice Breyer joined Justice John Paul Stevens's dissent, which would have upheld the provision as a valid interim measure needed to implement gun control until a federal computerized background checking system was in place. He also wrote separately, joined by Justice Stevens, to point out that other federal systems such as Switzerland's and Germany's routinely allow the national government to require states to implement laws enacted by the federal legislature.

Another split decision, *Agostini* v. *Felton*, concerned separation of church and state. In her majority opinion, Justice Sandra Day O'Connor overruled a 1985 ruling (*Aguilar* v. *Felton*) that had barred public school systems from sending teachers into parochial schools to teach federally mandated remedial classes. In *Agostini*, O'Connor wrote that the Constitution was in no danger of violation; there was no need to fear that public school teachers would "inculcate religion simply because they happen to be in a sectarian environment." In most 5-4 split decisions where the conservative bloc was the majority, such as *Printz* and *Agostini*, Breyer voted with Justices Ginsburg, Stevens, and Souter.

Justice Breyer showed his independent streak in *Clinton* v. *Jones*, where Justice John Paul Stevens's majority opinion held a sitting president may be sued with regard to events that occurred before his election. The Court ruled allowing the suit would not "impose an unacceptable burden on the President's time and energy," and that the trial court judge "has broad discretion to stay proceedings" that might unduly interfere with presidential duties. However, Justice Breyer concurred in the judgment but wrote separately to note that a trial judge lacks power to schedule litigation in a way that might interfere with presidential responsibilities. He contended the suit might likely impair the president's ability to perform his duties, so that the trial judge ought to have but "a very limited power to second guess a president's reasonable determination . . . of his scheduling needs." Any order significantly interfering with presidential duties, he maintained, would violate the Constitution.

In *Kansas* v. *Hendricks* (1997) Breyer wrote for the four dissenters. The Court sustained a statute enabling the state to civilly commit violent sex offenders after their prison sentence expired. But Justice Breyer viewed the act, which failed to require the inmate to receive any treatment, as no more than "an effort to inflict further punishment" and therefore an ex post facto law. Interestingly, though, Breyer agreed with the majority that the law did not deprive the prisoner of liberty in violation of the Due Process Clause.

In the 1997-98 term, Justice Breyer wrote for a unanimous Court in *Ohio Forestry Association* v. *Sierra Club* (1998) that a suit to overturn a government plan to manage a forest was not ripe for judicial review. The Sierra Club challenged a Forest Service management plan on the ground that it permitted the extensive clearcutting of lumber from a national forest in violation of a statute allowing clearcutting only when that is the optimum means of harvesting the timber. Although a lower court had agreed to hear the suit, Justice Breyer's opinion reversed that court and found the action not yet ripe for review. No timber could actually be cut, he noted, until a site-specific action plan was adopted for each location. Only then could a court entertain an action to restrain clearcutting.

Justice Breyer dissented vigorously from two 1998 decisions involving claims that government regulation of property amounted to a taking of that property, for which government must compensate the owner. In *Eastern Enterprises* v. *Apfel* (1998) the Court overturned a federal law requiring former coal mine operators to retroactively provide health benefits to retired employees. Justice Sandra Day O'Connor, writing for a four-justice plurality, thought this law violated the Takings Clause because it "reaches back 30 to 50 years to impose liability." Justice Anthony M. Kennedy concurred on the ground that the law deprived the mine owners of their property without due process of law. Justice Breyer wrote a dissent in which Justices Stevens, Souter, and Ginsburg joined. He argued the Takings Clause did not apply to "an ordinary liability to pay money," as opposed to physical property. He also rejected the claim that the statute violated the Due Process Clause since it was not "fundamentally unfair."

Justice Breyer again led the same four dissenters in *Phillips* v. *Washington Legal Foundation* (1998). This time Chief Justice Rehnquist held that interest on clients' money held by an attorney for a short time was the property of the client even though under Texas law the interest was earmarked to fund legal services for indigents. This was the prelude to a claim that the state had taken the interest without paying just compensation as mandated by the Takings Clause. Justice Breyer's dissent took the view that the interest could not be the client's property since under earlier law the client's money would not have earned any interest in the first place. (The funds were held for such a short time the bank charges exceeded any interest due.) Only the statute devoting the money to legal services enabled the funds to earn any interest. Therefore "the client could not have had an expectation of receiving interest without intervention," so the interest was in fact never the client's "property."

A significant criminal decision by Justice Breyer, *Gray* v. *Maryland* (1998), ruled that a confession by one defendant could not be introduced at trial against another defendant even though the second defendant's name had been deleted. A 1968 case, *Bruton* v. *United States*, had held a confession implicating a codefendant could not be introduced under the Sixth Amendment's guarantee of an accused person's right to confront the witnesses against him or her. But in *Gray* the actual name of the implicated defendant was replaced by the word "deleted." However, the testifying detective was then asked, "After he gave you that information, you subsequently were able to arrest Mr. Kevin Gray?" Breyer ruled the "obvious deletion may well call the jurors' attention specially to the removed name."

Justice Breyer dissented with Justices Scalia and O'Connor in the 6-3 decision that struck down the Line Item Veto Act of 1996, which would have given the president the authority to veto particular appropriations items in a bill he had signed. Justice Stevens wrote in *Clinton* v. *City of New York* that the law violated the Constitution's rules for enacting legislation.

Throughout his career, in addition to weighing the potential real-life effects of decisions on people in "the actual world," Stephen Breyer has applied the same pragmatism in his efforts to balance the necessity of governmental regulation with the incentives and market advantages of private enterprise. In the 1978 deregulation of the airline

industry, for example, he not only critiqued the anticompetitive effects of government regulation on the industry, but staged public hearings and argued the virtues of increased competition and advocated greater flexibility in airline fares.

Breyer has been described, both in praise and criticism, as a "technocrat" and nonideological centrist who will not impose a particular vision on his legal judgments. The legal historian and former Harvard colleague Morton Horwitz has said that although Breyer's "basic social instincts are conservative, his legal culture is more liberal, and his very flexible pragmatism will enable him to give things a gentle spin in a liberal direction. But he's a person without deep roots of any kind. He won't develop a vision." Some view Breyer as too concerned with economic efficiency, viewing life through a cost-benefit perspective; perhaps only such a person could take genuine interest in the particulars of airline industry regulation. But however analytical his jurisprudence, Breyer's thinking has remained consistent in its attention to law's effects on people's lives. Further, though he may be more of an intellectual than warm and compassionate in his public image, moderates and liberals may take some comfort in having on the Court an intellect that can hold its own with the forceful mind and manner of Justice Antonin Scalia, generally acknowledged as the intellectual leader of the Rehnquist Court.

—PHILIP WEINBERG AND MARK LAFLAUR

Bibliography

Cushman, Cushman, ed. Stephen G. Breyer. 1994– . *The Supreme Court Justices: Illustrated Biographies, 1789–1995.* 2nd ed. Washington, D.C.: Congressional Quarterly and The Supreme Court Historical Society.

Kass, Stephen L., and Michael B. Gerrard, The Record of Judge Breyer. *New York Law Journal,* May 27, 1994.

BROWN v. BOARD OF EDUCATION

347 U.S. 483 (1954)
349 U.S. 294 (1955)

In the dual perspectives of politics and constitutional development, *Brown* v. *Board of Education* was the Supreme Court's most important decision of the twentieth century. In four cases consolidated for decision, the Court held that racial segregation of public school children, commanded or authorized by state law, violated the Fourteenth Amendment's guarantee of the equal protection of the laws. A companion decision, *Bolling* v. *Sharpe* (1954), held that school segregation in the District of Columbia violated the Fifth Amendment's guarantee of due process of law.

Brown illustrates how pivotal historical events, viewed in retrospect, can take on the look of inevitability. To the actors involved, however, the decision was anything but a foregone conclusion. The principal judicial precedent, after all, was *Plessy* v. *Ferguson* (1896), which had upheld the racial segregation of railroad passengers, partly on the basis of an earlier Massachusetts decision upholding school segregation. More recent Supreme Court decisions had invalidated various forms of segregation in higher education without deciding whether *Plessy* should be overruled. Just a few months before the first *Brown* decision, Robert Leflar and Wylie Davis outlined eleven different courses open to the Supreme Court in the cases before it.

The four cases we now call *Brown* were the culmination of a twenty-year litigation strategy of the NAACP, aimed at the ultimate invalidation of segregation in education. Part of that strategy had already succeeded; the Supreme Court had ordered the admission of black applicants to state university law schools, and had invalidated a state university's segregation of a black graduate student. The opinions in those cases had emphasized intangible elements of educational quality, particularly the opportunity to associate with persons of other races. The doctrinal ground was thus prepared for the Court to strike down the segregation of elementary and secondary schools—if the Court was ready to occupy that ground.

The Justices were sensitive to the political repercussions their decision might have. The cases were argued in December 1952, and in the ordinary course would have been decided by the close of the Court's term in the following June or July. Instead of deciding, however, the Court set the five cases for reargument in the following term and proposed a series of questions to be argued, centering on the history of the adoption of the Fourteenth Amendment and on potential remedies if the Court should rule against segregation. The available evidence suggests that the Court was divided on the principal issue in the cases—the constitutionality of separate but equal public schools—and that Justice Felix Frankfurter played a critical role in persuading his brethren to put the case over so that the incoming administration of President Dwight D. Eisenhower might present its views as amicus curiae. It is clear that the discussion at the Court's conference on the cases had dealt not only with the merits of the black children's claims but also with the possible reaction of the white South to a decision overturning school segregation. Proposing questions for the reargument, Justice Frankfurter touched on the same concern in a memorandum to his colleagues: ". . . for me the ultimate crucial factor in the problem presented by these cases is psychological—the adjustment of men's minds and actions to the unfamiliar and the unpleasant."

When Justice Frankfurter wrote of "the adjustment of men's minds," he had whites in mind. For blacks, Jim Crow was an unpleasant reality that was all too familiar. It is not surprising that the Justices centered their political concerns on the white South; lynchings of blacks would have been a vivid memory for

The four cases we now call Brown *were the culmination of a twenty-year litigation strategy of the NAACP, aimed at the ultimate invalidation of segregation in education.*

B

**BROWN v. BOARD
OF EDUCATION**

347 U.S. 483 (1954)
349 U.S. 294 (1955)

VICTORIOUS

*Thurgood Marshall, center,
and co-counsel outside the
Supreme Court after successfully arguing* Brown.
(Corbis/Bettmann)

any Justice who had come to maturity before 1930. In any event the Court handled the *Brown* cases from beginning to end with an eye on potential disorder and violence among southern whites.

Chief Justice Fred M. Vinson, who had written the opinions invalidating segregation in higher education, appeared to some of his brethren to oppose extending the reasoning of those opinions to segregation in the public schools. Late in the summer of 1953, five weeks before the scheduled reargument of *Brown,* Vinson died suddenly from a heart attack. With *Brown* in mind, Justice Frank-furter said, in a private remark that has since become glaringly public, "This is the first in-dication I have ever had that there is a God."

Vinson's replacement was the governor of California, Earl Warren. At the *Brown* rear-

gument, which was put off until December, he did not say much. In conference, however, Warren made clear his view that the separate but equal doctrine must be abandoned and the cases decided in favor of the black chil-dren's equal protection claim. At the same time, he though the Court should avoid "pre-cipitous action that would inflame more than necessary." The conference disclosed an ap-parent majority for the Chief Justice's posi-tion, but in a case of such political magni-tude, a unanimous decision was devoutly to be wished. The vote was thus postponed, while the Chief Justice and Justice Frank-furter sought for ways to unite the Court. Near unanimity seems to have been achieved by agreement on a gradual enforcement of the Court's decision. A vote of 8–1 emerged late in the winter, with Justice Robert H.

Jackson preparing to file a separate concurrence. When Jackson suffered a heart attack, the likelihood of his pursuing an independent doctrinal course diminished. The Chief Justice circulated a draft opinion in early May, and at last Justice Stanley F. Reed was persuaded of the importance of avoiding division in the Court. On May 17, 1954, the Court announced its decision. Justice Jackson joined his brethren at the bench, to symbolize the Court's unanimity.

The opinion of the Court, by Chief Justice Warren, was calculatedly limited in scope, unilluminating as to doctrinal implications, and bland in tone. The South was not lectured, and no broad pronouncements were made concerning the fate of Jim Crow. *Plessy* was not even overruled—not then. Instead, the opinion highlighted two points of distinction: the change in the status of black persons in the years since *Plessy,* and the present-day importance of public education for the individual and for American society. Borrowing from the opinion of the lower court in the Kansas case (*Brown* itself), the Chief Justice concluded that school segregation produced feelings of inferiority in black children, and thus interfered with their motivation to learn; as in the graduate education cases, such intangibles were critical in evaluating the equality of the educational opportunity offered to blacks. In *Plessy,* the Court had brushed aside the argument that segregation stamped blacks with a mark of inferiority; the *Brown* opinion, on the contrary, stated that modern psychological knowledge verified the argument, and in a supporting footnote cited a number of social science authorities. Segregated education was inherently unequal; the separate but equal doctrine thus had no place in education.

In the ordinary equal protection case, a finding of state-imposed inequality is only part of the inquiry; the Court goes on to examine into justifications offered by the state for treating people unequally. In these cases the southern states had argued that segrega-

tion promoted the quality of education, the health of pupils, and the tranquillity of schools. The *Brown* opinion omitted entirely any reference to these asserted justifications. By looking only to the question of inequality, the Court followed the pattern set in earlier cases applying the separate but equal doctrine. However, in its opinion in the companion case from the District of Columbia, the Court added this remark: "Segregation in public education is not reasonably related to any proper governmental objective...." With those conclusory words, the Court announced that further inquiry into justifications for school segregation was foreclosed.

The *Brown* opinion thus presented a near-minimum political target, one that could have been reduced only by the elimination of its social science citations. Everyone understood the importance of educational opportunity. Nothing was intimated about segregation in public accommodations or state courthouses, hospitals, or prisons. Most important of all, the Court issued no orders to the defendant school boards, but set the cases for yet another argument at the next term on questions of remedy: Should segregation be ended at once, or gradually? Should the Supreme Court itself frame the decrees, or leave that task to the lower courts or a special master?

A full year passed before the Court issued its remedial opinion. *Brown II*, as that opinion is sometimes called, not only declined to order an immediate end to segregation but also failed to set deadlines. Instead, the Court told the lower courts to require the school boards to "make a prompt and reasonable start" toward "compliance at the earliest practicable date," taking into account such factors as buildings, transportation systems, personnel, and redrawing of attendance district lines. The lower courts should issue decrees to the end of admitting the plaintiff children to the schools "on a racially nondiscriminatory basis with all deliberate speed...."

This language looked like—and was—a political compromise; something of the sort

In the dual perspectives of politics and constitutional development, Brown v. Board of Education *was the Supreme Court's most important decision of the twentieth century.*

B

BROWN v. BOARD OF EDUCATION

347 U.S. 483 (1954)
349 U.S. 294 (1955)

♦ **amicus curiae**
[Latin: friend of the court] One who, although not a party to the case, submits a brief suggesting how the case, or certain issues in the case, should be decided.

had been contemplated from the beginning by Chief Justice Warren. Despite the Court's statement that constitutional principles could not yield to disagreement, the white South was told, in effect, that it might go on denying blacks their constitutional rights for an indefinite time, while it got used to the idea of stopping. Unquestionably, whatever the Court determined in 1954 or 1955, it would take time to build the sense of interracial community in the South and elsewhere. But in *Brown II* the Court sacrificed an important part of its one legitimate claim to political and moral authority: the defense of principle. A southern intransigent might say: after all, if *Brown* really did stand for a national principle, surely the principle would not be parceled out for separate negotiation in thousands of school districts over an indefinite time. The chief responses of the white South to the Court's gradualism were defiance and evasion. In 1956 a "Southern Manifesto," signed by nineteen Senators and 82 members of the House of Representatives, denounced *Brown* as resting on "personal political and social ideas" rather than the Constitution. One Mississippi senator, seeking to capitalize on the country's recent anticommunist fervor, called racial integration "a radical, pro-Communist political movement." President Eisenhower gave the decision no political support, promising only to carry out the law of the land.

Criticism of another sort came from Herbert Wechsler, a Columbia law professor with impressive credentials as a civil rights advocate. Wechsler argued that the Supreme Court had not offered a principled explanation of the *Brown* decision—had not supported its repeated assertion that segregation harmed black school children. Charles L. Black, Jr., a Texan and a Yale professor who had worked on the NAACP briefs in *Brown*, replied that all Southerners knew that Jim Crow was designed to maintain white supremacy. School segregation, as part of that system, must fall before a constitutional principle forbidding states deliberately to disad-

vantage a racial group. This defense of the *Brown* decision is irrefutable. But the *Brown* opinion had not tied school segregation to the system of Jim Crow, because Chief Justice Warren's strategy had been to avoid sweeping pronouncements in the interest of obtaining a unanimous Court and minimizing southern defiance and violence.

Within a few years, however, in a series of per curiam orders consisting only of citations to *Brown*, the Court had invalidated state-supported segregation in all its forms. In one case *Plessy* was implicitly overruled. Jim Crow was thus buried without ceremony. Yet the intensity of the southern resistance to *Brown* shows that no one had been deceived into thinking that the decision was limited to education. Not only did the occasion deserve a clear statement of the unconstitutionality of the system of racial segregation; political practicalities also called for such a statement. The Supreme Court's ability to command respect for its decisions depends on its candid enunciation of the principles underlying those decisions.

Both *Brown* opinions, then, were evasions. Even so, *Brown* was a great decision, a personal triumph for a great Chief Justice. For if *Brown* was a culmination, it was also a beginning. The decision was the catalyst for a political movement that permanently altered race relations in America. The success of the civil rights movement encouraged challenges to other systems of domination and dependency: systems affecting women, aliens, illegitimate children, the handicapped, homosexuals. Claims to racial equality forced a reexamination of a wide range of institutional arrangements throughout American society. In constitutional/doctrinal terms, *Brown* was the critical event in the modern development of the equal protection clause as an effective guarantee of equal citizenship, a development that led in turn to the rebirth of substantive due process as a guarantee of fundamental personal liberties. After *Brown*, the federal judiciary saw itself in a new light, and all

Americans could see themselves as members of a national community.

—KENNETH L. KARST

Bibliography

Bell, Derrick (1980). *Brown* v. *Board of Education* and the Interest-Convergence Dilemma. *Harvard Law Review* 93: 518–533.

Black, Charles L., Jr. (1960). The Lawfulness of the Segregation Decisions. *Yale Law Journal* 69:421–430.

Kluger, Richard (1975). *Simple Justice.* New York: Knopf.

Leflar, Robert A., and Davis, Wylie H. (1954). Segregation in the Public Schools—1953. *Harvard Law Review* 67:377–435.

Wechsler, Herbert (1959). Toward Neutral Principles of Constitutional Law. *Harvard Law Review* 73:1–35.

Wilkinson, J. Harvie, III (1979). *From Brown to Bakke.* New York: Oxford University Press.

BROWN v. MISSISSIPPI

297 U.S. 278 (1936)

In this landmark decision, the Court for the first time held unconstitutional on due process grounds the use of a coerced confession in a state criminal proceeding. In a unanimous opinion reflecting outrage at the judicial system of Mississippi as well as at its law enforcement officers, Chief Justice Charles Evans Hughes found difficult to imagine methods "more revolting to the sense of justice" than those used by the state in this case. The record showed that prolonged "physical torture" of black suspects extorted their confessions; they were tried in a rush without adequate defense, were convicted solely on the basis of the confessions which they repudiated, and were quickly sentenced to death. The transcript read "like pages torn from some medieval account. . . ."

Yet the state supreme court, over dissenting opinions, had sustained the convictions on the basis of arguments later used by the state before the Supreme Court: under *Twining* v. *Jersey* (1908) the Constitution did not protect against compulsory self-incrimination in state courts, and counsel for the prisoners had not made a timely motion for exclusion of the confessions after proving coercion. To these arguments, Hughes replied, first, "Compulsion by torture to extort a confession is a different matter. . . . The rack and torture chamber may not be substituted for the witness stand" except by a denial of due process of law. The state could regulate its own criminal procedure only on condition that it observed the fundamental principles of liberty and justice. Second, Hughes regarded counsel's technical error as irrelevant compared to the fact that the wrong committed by the state was so fundamental that it made the whole proceeding a "mere pretense of a trial" and rendered the convictions void.

Brown did not revolutionalize state criminal procedure or abolish third-degree methods. But it proved to be the foundation for thirty years of decisions on police interrogation and confessions, finally resulting in an overruling of *Twining* and a constitutional law intended by the Fourteenth Amendment.

—LEONARD W. LEVY

BUCHANAN v. WARLEY

245 U.S. 60 (1917)

Buchanan was the most important race relations case between *Plessy* v. *Ferguson* (1896) and *Shelley* v. *Kraemer* (1948). A number of southern border cities had adopted residential segregation ordinances. NAACP attorneys constructed a test case challenging the constitutionality of Louisville's ordinance, which forbade a "colored" person to move into a house on a block in which a majority of residences were occupied by whites, and vice

B

BUCHANAN v. WARLEY

245 U.S. 60 (1917)

Chief Justice Charles Evans Hughes found difficult to imagine methods "more revolting to the sense of justice" than those used by the state in this case.

See also

Plessy v. *Ferguson*

Shelley v. *Kraemer*

89

♦ **ratio decidendi**
[Latin: reason for being decided] The reasoning supporting the decision of a court in a particular case, establishing a precedent.

Despite the ground for decision, Buchanan *was seen by the press as a major Civil Rights victory for blacks.*

Although Buck *continues to be cited, its current authority as precedent is doubtful.*

See also

Jacobson v. *Massachusetts*

Skinner v. *Oklahoma*

versa. A black agreed to buy from a white a house on a majority-white block, provided that the buyer had the legal right to occupy the house. The seller sued to compel performance of the contract; the buyer defended on the basis of the ordinance. The Kentucky courts upheld the ordinance. In the Supreme Court, both sides focused the argument on the constitutionality of neighborhood segregation. An unusual number of amicus curiae briefs attested to the case's importance.

A unanimous Supreme Court reversed, holding the ordinance invalid. Justice William R. Day's opinion discussed at length the rights to racial equality and the "dignity of citizenship" established in the Thirteenth and Fourteenth Amendments, as well as the rights to purchase and hold property, established by the Civil Rights Act of 1866. He lamely distinguished *Plessy* as a case in which no one had been denied the use of his property. Ultimately, however, he rested decision on a theory of substantive due process: the ordinance unconstitutionally interfered with property rights.

Day's curious opinion may have aimed at persuading two of his brethren. Justice James C. McReynolds generally attached greater weight to claims of constitutional property rights than to claims to racial equality. And Justice Oliver Wendell Holmes had prepared a draft dissenting opinion that was not delivered, arguing that the white seller lacked standing to assert the constitutional right of blacks.

Despite the ground for decision, *Buchanan* was seen by the press as a major civil rights victory for blacks. And when the Supreme Court faced zoning in a nonracial context, it upheld an ordinance in *Village of Euclid* v. *Ambler Realty Co.* (1926). *Buchanan* plainly was more than a property rights decision.

—KENNETH L. KARST

Bibliography

Schmidt, Benno C., Jr. (1982). Principle and Prejudice: The Supreme Court and Race in the Progressive Era. Part 1: The Heyday

of Jim Crow. *Columbia Law Review* 82: 444, 498–523.

BUCK v. BELL

274 U.S. 200 (1927)

In *Buck* the Supreme Court upheld, 8–1, a Virginia law authorizing the sterilization of institutionalized mental defectives without their consent. Justice Oliver Wendell Holmes, for the Court, wrote an opinion notable for epigram and insensitivity. Virginia's courts had ordered the sterilization of a "feeble minded" woman, whose mother and child were similarly afflicted, finding that she was "the probable potential parent of socially inadequate offspring," and that sterilization would promote both her welfare and society's. Holmes, the Civil War veteran, remarked that public welfare might "call upon the best citizens for their lives"; these "lesser sacrifices" were justified to prevent future crime and starvation. There was no violation of substantive due process. Citing *Jacobson* v. *Massachusetts* (1905), he said, "The principle that sustains compulsory vaccination is broad enough to cover cutting the Fallopian tubes. . . . Three generations of imbeciles are enough."

Turning to equal protection, which he called "the usual last resort of constitutional arguments," Holmes saw no violation in the law's reaching only institutionalized mental defectives and not others: "The law does all that is needed when it does all that it can." Justice Pierce Butler noted his dissent.

Although *Buck* continues to be cited, its current authority as precedent is doubtful.

—KENNETH L. KARST

Bibliography

Cynkar, Robert J. (1981). *Buck* v. *Bell:* "Felt Necessities" v. Fundamental Values? *Columbia Law Review* 81:1418–1461.

Gould, Stephen Jay (1984). Carrie Buck's Daughter. *Natural History* (July):14–18.

Lombardo, Paul A. (1985). Three Generations, No Imbeciles: New Light on *Buck v. Bell*. *New York University Law Review* 60:30–62.

BUCKLEY v. VALEO

424 U.S. 1 (1976)

In *Buckley* the Supreme Court dealt with a number of constitutional challenges to the complex provisions of the Federal Elections Campaign Act. The act provided for a Federal Elections Commission, members of which were to be appointed variously by the president and certain congressional leaders. The Court held the congressional appointment unconstitutional; Article 2, section 2, prescribes a process for appointing all officers who carry out executive and quasi-judicial duties: appointment by the president, with confirmation by the Senate. Congress subsequently amended the statute to meet the Court's objections.

Rejecting both First Amendment and equal protection challenges, the Court upheld, 7–2, the provision of public funds for presidential campaigns in amounts that favored major parties over minor parties.

The Court used a balancing test in considering First Amendment challenges to the provisions limiting expenditures by candidates and contributions to candidates in congressional elections. For both expenditures and contributions the Court defined the government's interest as preventing corruption and appearance of corruption.

The Court placed the interest of the candidate in freedom of speech on the other side of the balance in striking down the expenditure provisions. Limiting expenditure limited the amount of speech a candidate might make. The Court rejected the argument that another legitimate purpose of the statute was to equalize the campaign opportunities of rich and poor candidates. The per curiam opinion said that the government might not seek to equalize speech by leveling down the rights of rich speakers. High expenditures by rich candidates created no risk of corruption. Indeed, the opinion demonstrated that such a candidate was not dependent on others' money.

In upholding the contribution limits, the Court characterized the First Amendment interest of contributors not as freedom of speech but freedom of association. It reasoned that the initial contribution of $1,000 allowed by the statute completed the act of association and that further contributions did not significantly enhance the association. Further contributions did, however, increase the risk of corruption.

The statute's requirement that all contributions over $100 be a matter of public record were challenged as violating the right to anonymous political association previously recognized in *NAACP* v. *Alabama* (1958). The Court upheld the reporting provisions but said that individual applications to contributors to small unpopular parties might be unconstitutional.

—MARTIN SHAPIRO

Bibliography

Polsby, Daniel D. (1976). *Buckley* v. *Valeo: The Special Nature of Political Speech. Supreme Court Review* 1976:1–44.

BURGER, WARREN E.

(1907–1998)

Warren Earl Burger was born in St. Paul, Minnesota. He attended the University of Minnesota and, in 1931, received a law degree from St. Paul College of Law (today known as the William Mitchell College of Law). After practicing law in St. Paul for several years, he became the assistant attorney general in charge of the Civil Division of the Department of Justice during the administration of Dwight D. Eisenhower. In 1955

In Buckley, *the Supreme Court dealt with a number of constitutional challenges to the complex provisions of the Federal Elections Campaign Act.*

See also

Freedom of Speech

Burger was appointed a judge on the United States Court of Appeals for the District of Columbia Circuit. He served in that capacity until 1969, when he became the Chief Justice of the United States, having been nominated for that position by Richard M. Nixon.

In the years of his tenure as Chief Justice, the Supreme Court was marked publicly as having a majority of Justices who held a generally conservative orientation toward constitutional issues. Burger himself was widely viewed as a primary proponent of this conservative judicial posture and, at least during the early years of the Burger Court, he was expected to lead the other conservative Justices in a major, if one-sided, battle to undo as much as could be undone of the pathbreaking work of its predecessor, the quite distinctly liberal Warren Court.

To the surprise of many the record of the Burger Court was extraordinarily complicated, or uneven, when viewed against both of its

COMPLEX AND INCONSISTENT

Perhaps the most important characteristic of Chief Justice Warren Burger's opinions is to be found in the area of individual rights and freedoms. (Corbis/Owen Franken)

commonly assumed objectives of overturning Warren Court decisions and of achieving what is often called a "nonactivist" judicial posture toward new claims for constitutional rights. Although it is true that a few Warren Court innovations have been openly discarded (for example, the recognition of a First Amendment right to speak in the context of privately owned shopping centers was overturned) and several other doctrines significantly curtailed (for example, the well-known 1966 ruling in *Miranda* v. *Arizona* has been narrowed as new cases have arisen), it is also true that many Warren Court holdings have been vigorously applied and even extended (for example, the principle of separation of church and state has been forcefully, if still confusingly, applied). What is perhaps most surprising of all, whole new areas of constitutional jurisprudence were opened up. The foremost example here, of course, is the Court's highly controversial decision in *Roe* v. *Wade* (1973), which recognized a woman's constitutional right to have an abortion—subject to a set of conditions that rivaled in their legislation-like refinement the Warren Court's greatly maligned rules for the *Miranda* warnings. Against this history of overrulings, modifications, extensions, and new creations in the tapestry of decisions of its predecessor Courts, it is difficult to characterize the constitutional course steered by the modern Supreme Court under the stewardship of Warren Burger.

The same difficulty arises if one focuses more specifically on the constitutional thought of Burger himself. Burger may properly be regarded as one of the Court's most conservative members. In the field of criminal justice, he tended to support police and prosecutors. He joined in a large number of decisions limiting would-be litigants' access to the federal courts. Although he played an important role in the Court's recognition of constitutional rights in areas such as sex discrimination, discrimination against aliens, and school busing, in each of these areas he resisted extension of the rights initially recognized.

Nonetheless, he was inclined to accept the validity of congressional civil rights legislation, and to read those laws generously. And he was a strong supporter of claims of religious liberty. Generally, he joined the majority as it pursued this surprisingly labyrinthine constitutional course. The starting point, therefore, for thinking about the constitutional thought of Warren Burger (just as it was for the Court as a whole during his tenure) is the realization that his opinions did not reflect an especially coherent vision of the Constitution and its contemporary significance.

But to say that the decisions and opinions of Burger, taken together, did not add up to a coherent whole does not mean that there were no important themes working their way through them. It is in fact quite possible to locate several distinct threads of thought: for example, a desire to return greater political power to the states in the federal system and to give greater protection to property interests was frequently reflected in Burger's constitutional opinions. But perhaps the most important characteristic of Warren Burger's opinions while Chief Justice was to be found in the area of individual rights and freedoms. It is there that one feels the strongest tension between a commitment to constitutional standards that control and limit the legislative process and a desire to maintain legislative control over the moral and intellectual climate of the community. It is in the resolution of that tension that one is able to determine what was most distinctive about Burger's constitutional jurisprudence.

Burger frequently displayed a willingness to protect individual freedom at the expense of the interests of the state. His opinion for the Court in *Reed* v. *Reed* (1971), for example, was the first to subject gender classifications to more rigorous equal protection scrutiny than had theretofore been the case. But, that said, it is also critical to an understanding of Burger's approach to the Bill of Rights to see that the depth of his commitment to individual liberties was limited by a seemingly equal

reluctance to extend constitutional protection to individuals or groups whose challenged behavior went beyond what may be called the customary norms of good behavior.

Two areas of First Amendment decisions are revealing here. In *Wisconsin* v. *Yoder* (1972), for example, Burger wrote an opinion for the Court upholding the right of members of an Amish religious community to refuse, on religious grounds, to comply with the Wisconsin compulsory school-attendance law. In his opinion Burger repeatedly emphasized the fact that the Amish had adopted a traditional lifestyle, saying at one point how "the Amish communities singularly parallel and reflect many of the virtues of Thomas Jefferson's ideal of the 'sturdy yeoman.' " On the other hand, in every case in which a speaker who used indecent language has sought the protection of the First Amendment, Burger rejected the claim (though in these cases, usually in dissent) and, in doing so, stressed the importance of maintaining community norms about proper and improper behavior.

In Burger's opinions, therefore, the protection of a specific liberty was often tied to his assessment of the respectability of the behavior. Sometimes this underlying attitude for a decision was misinterpreted for other motivations. For example, in *Columbia Broadcasting System, Inc.* v. *Democratic National Committee* (1973), a major decision rejecting the claim that individuals and groups have a constitutional and statutory right to purchase airtime from broadcast stations in order to discuss public issues, Burger emphasized the importance of preserving the "journalistic autonomy" or "editorial discretion" of broadcasters, a theme reported in the press accounts of the case at the time. But this suggestion that the decision rested on a heightened respect for editorial freedom, and a preparedness to live with the consequent risks of bad editorial behavior, was considerably undermined by an additional thought Burger expressed. Freedom for broadcast journalists was to be preferred, he said, because broadcasters were reg-

To the surprise of many the record of the Burger Court was extraordinarily complicated.

ulated and therefore "accountable," while "[n]o such accountability attaches to the private individual, whose only qualifications for using the broadcast facility may be abundant funds and a point of view."

It is a noteworthy feature of Burger's constitutional work that in the area of freedom of the press he wrote many of the Court's most prominent decisions upholding claims of the print media for protection against various forms of government regulation. Burger wrote for the Court in *Miami Herald Publishing Co.* v. *Tornillo* (1974), holding that states could not require a newspaper to provide access to political candidates who had been criticized in the newspaper's columns; in *Nebraska Press Association* v. *Stuart* (1976), holding that courts could not enjoin the media from publishing in advance of trial purported confessions and other evidence "implicative" of an accused individual; and in *Richmond Newspapers, Inc.* v. *Virginia* (1980), holding that courts could not follow a course of generally excluding the media from attending and observing criminal trials.

Yet, despite this strong record of extending constitutional protection to the press, the Burger Court, and especially Burger himself, was strongly criticized by various segments of the press for retreating from earlier precedents and for being generally hostile to press claims. Burger, it is true, sometimes voted along with a majority to reject press claims, as, for example, in *Branzburg* v. *Hayes* (1972), when the press urged the Court to recognize a limited constitutional privilege for journalists against being compelled to give testimony to grand juries, or in *Gertz* v. *Robert Welch, Inc.* (1974), when the press sought to extend the "actual malice" standard in libel actions to all discussions of public issues, not just to those discussions concerning public officials and public figures. But an objective assessment of the holdings of the Burger Court does not seem to warrant the general accusation of its hostility to the press. It is too easy to lose sight of the basic truth that in virtually every case that involved significant issues of press freedom Burger supported the press, and in many of them wrote the majority opinions.

Is it possible to account for this discrepancy between criticism and performance? Here again the best explanation is to be found in Burger's disinclination to extend constitutional protection to activity judged as falling below conventional standards of good behavior. But in the area of freedom of the press this disinclination manifested itself less in the actual results Burger reached in particular cases and more in the craftsmanship and the tone of his judicial opinions.

The contrast between the opinions of the Warren Court and of Burger in the freedom of press area is remarkable. With Warren Court opinions the tone struck is almost uniformly that of praise for the role performed by the press in the American democratic political system. They extol the virtues of an open and free press. Although the same theme is to be found in Burger's judicial work, one often encounters rather sharp criticism of the press as well. Burger actively used the forum of the Supreme Court judicial opinion to ventilate his feelings about the condition of the American press, and not everything he had to say in that forum was complimentary. One should consider in this regard one of the major cases in the free press area just mentioned, *Miami Herald Publishing Co.* v. *Tornillo*. In that case Burger's opinion for the Court begins with a lengthy and detailed description of the argument advanced by the state of Florida in support of its statute, which guaranteed limited access for political candidates to the columns of newspapers. The press has grown monopolized and excessively powerful, the state contended: "Chains of newspapers, national newspapers, national wire and news services, and one-newspaper towns, are the dominant features of a press that has become noncompetitive and enormously powerful and influential in its capacity to manipulate popular opinion and change the course of events. . . .

Such national news organizations provide syndicated 'interpretive reporting' as well as syndicated features and commentary, all of which can serve as part of the new school of 'journalism.' " While ultimately rejecting the legal conclusion that the state sought to draw from this assumed social reality, Burger's opinion nevertheless strongly intimates sympathy with the general portrait of the press which the state's argument had painted. Thus, while the press may have had an ally in the constitutional result, it did not in the battle for public opinion generally.

Although Warren Burger retired from the Supreme Court at the end of the 1985–86 term, what the lasting impact of his constitutional thought will be is of course impossible to tell. For the moment the most appropriate general assessment is that Burger's constitutional work displays a general disunity of character, while suggesting a responsiveness to generally conservative instincts, even when he is on the liberal side.

—LEE C. BOLLINGER

Bibliography

Blasi, Vincent, ed. (1983). *The Burger Court: The Counter-Revolution That Wasn't.* New Haven, Conn.: Yale University Press.

Bollinger, Lee C. (1986). *The Tolerant Society: Freedom of Speech and Extremist Speech in America.* New York: Oxford University Press.

Choper, Jesse (1980). *Judicial Review and the National Political Process.* Chicago: University of Chicago Press.

Symposium (1980). The Burger Court: Reflections on the First Decade. *Law and Contemporary Problems* 43:1.

BURGER COURT

(1969–1986)

The roots of the Burger Court lie in the judicial activism of the Warren Court. The social vision of the Supreme Court under Earl Warren was manifested on many fronts—dismantling racial barriers, requiring that legislative apportionment be based upon population, and vastly expanding the range of rights for criminal defendants, among others. At the height of its activity, during the 1960s, the Warren Court became a forum to which many of the great social issues of the time were taken.

Such activism provoked sharp attacks on the Court. Some of the criticism came from the ranks of the academy, other complaints from political quarters. In the 1968 presidential campaign, Richard M. Nixon objected in particular to the Court's criminal procedure decisions—rulings that, he said, favored the country's "criminal forces" against its "peace forces."

During his first term as president, Nixon put four Justices on the Supreme Court—Warren E. Burger, Harry A. Blackmun, Lewis F. Powell Jr., and William H. Rehnquist. Rarely has a president been given the opportunity to fill so many vacancies on the Court in so short a time. Moreover, Nixon was explicit about the ideological basis for his appointments; he saw himself as redeeming his campaign pledge "to nominate to the Supreme Court individuals who share my judicial philosophy, which is basically a conservative philosophy."

Thus was born the Burger Court, which lasted until President Ronald Reagan's appointment of Justice Rehnquist as Chief Justice in 1986 upon Chief Justice Burger's retirement. For a time, pundits, at least those of liberal persuasion, took to calling it "the Nixon Court." Reviewing the 1971 term, *The New Republic* lamented that the "single-mindedness of the Nixon team threatens the image of the Court as an independent institution."

Inevitably, the work of the Burger Court was compared with that of its predecessor, the Warren Court. During the early Burger years, there was evidence that, with Nixon's four appointees on the bench, a new, and more conservative, majority was indeed in the making on the Court.

◆ **grand jury**
An investigatory body that is usually empowered to issue indictments or presentments charging persons with crimes.

By the summer of 1976, a conservative Burger Court seemed to have come of age. For example, near the end of the 1975 term the Court closed the doors of federal courts to large numbers of state prisoners by holding that a prisoner who has had a full and fair opportunity to raise a Fourth Amendment question in the state courts cannot relitigate that question in a federal habeas corpus proceeding. In other criminal justice decisions, the Court whittled away at the rights of defendants, showing particular disfavor for claims seeking to curb police practices.

Decisions in areas other than criminal justice likewise showed a conservative flavor. For example, in the same term, the Court used the Tenth Amendment to place limits on Congress's commerce power, rejected the argument that claims of age discrimination ought to trigger the higher level of judicial review associated with suspect classifications (such as race), and refused to hold that capital punishment is inherently unconstitutional.

By the mid-1970s a student of the Court might have summarized the Burger Court, in contrast with the Warren Court, as being less egalitarian, more sensitive to federalism, more skeptical about the competence of judges to solve society's problems, more inclined to trust the governmental system, and, in general, more inclined to defer to legislative and political processes. By the end of the 1970s, however, such generalizations might have been thought premature—or, at least, have to be tempered. As the years passed, it became increasingly more difficult to draw clean distinctions between the years of Earl Warren and those of Warren Burger.

Cases involving claims of sex discrimination furnish an example. In 1973 four Justices (William J. Brennan, William O. Douglas, Bryon R. White, and Thurgood Marshall) who had been on the Court in the Warren era sought to have the Court rule that classifications based on sex, like those based on race, should be viewed as "inherently suspect" and hence subject to strict scrutiny. The four Nixon

appointees (together with Justice Potter Stewart) joined in resisting such a standard. Yet, overall, the Burger Court's record in sex discrimination cases proved to be one of relative activism, even though the Court applied an intermediate standard of review in those cases, rather than one of strict scrutiny. In the 1978 term, for example, there were eight cases that in one way or another involved claims of sex discrimination; in six of the eight cases the Justices voted favorably to the claim, either on the merits or on procedural grounds.

In the early 1980s, with the Burger Court in its second decade, there was evidence that a working majority, conservative in bent, was taking hold. Two more Justices from the Warren era (William O. Douglas and Potter Stewart) had retired. Taking their place were appointees of Republican presidents—John Paul Stevens (appointed by President Gerald R. Ford) and Sandra Day O'Connor (named by President Ronald Reagan). While Stevens tended to vote with the more liberal Justices, O'Connor appeared to provide a dependable vote for the more conservative bloc on the Court.

In the 1983 term the conservatives appeared to have firm control. The Court recognized a "public safety" exception to the Miranda rules and a "good faith" exception to the exclusionary rule in Fourth Amendment cases. The Justices upheld a New York law providing for the preventive detention of juveniles and sustained the Reagan administration's curb on travel to Cuba. As one commentator put it, "Whenever the rights of the individual confronted the authority of government this term, government nearly always won." The American Civil Liberties Union's legal director called it "a genuinely appalling term," one in which the Court behaved as a "cheerleader for the government."

No sooner had such dire conclusions been drawn than the Burger Court once again confounded the Court-watchers. The very next term saw the Court return to the mainstream of its jurisprudence of the 1970s. The Court's religion cases are an example. Between 1980 and 1984 the Court appeared to be moving in the direction of allowing government to "accommodate" religion, thus relaxing the barriers the First Amendment erects between church and state. The Court rebuffed challenges to Nebraska's paying a legislative chaplain and Pawtucket, Rhode Island's, displaying a Christmas crèche. Yet in the 1984 term the Court resumed a separationist stance, invalidating major programs (both federal and state) found to channel public aid to church schools, invalidating an Alabama statute providing for a "moment of silence or prayer" in public schools, and striking down a Connecticut law making it illegal for an employer to require an employee to work on the employee's chosen Sabbath. The Reagan administration had filed briefs in support of the challenged laws in all four cases, and in each of the four cases a majority of the Justices ruled against the program.

Even so brief a sketch of the Burger Court's evolution conveys something of the dialectical nature of those years on the Court. In reading Burger Court opinions, one is sometimes struck by their conservative thrust, sometimes by a liberal result. Here the Burger Court is activist, there it defers to other branches or bodies. There is continuity with the Warren years, but discontinuity as well. One is struck, above all, by the way in which the Court in the Burger era has become a battleground on which fundamental jurisprudential issues are fought out.

No simple portrait of the Burger Court is possible. Some measure of the Burger years may be had, however, by touching upon certain themes that characterize the Burger Court—the questions which observers of the Court have tended to ask and the issues around which decision making on the Court has tended to revolve.

At the outset of the Burger era, many observers thought that a more conservative tribunal would undo much of the work of the Warren Court. This prophecy has been unfulfilled. The landmarks of the Warren Court remain essentially intact. Among those landmarks are *Brown* v. *Board of Education* (1954) (school desegregation), *Reynolds* v. *Sims* (1964) (legislative reapportionment), and the decisions applying nearly all of the procedural protection of the Bill of Rights in criminal trials to the states.

In all of these areas, there have been, to be sure, important adjustments to Warren Court doctrine. Sometimes, a majority of the Burger Court's Justices have shown a marked distaste for the ethos underlying those precedents. Thus, while leaving such precedents as *Miranda* v. *Arizona* (1956) and *Mapp* v. *Ohio* (1961) standing, the Burger Court has frequently confined those precedents or carved out exceptions. Yet, despite criticisms, on and off the bench, of the incorporation doctrine, there has been no wholesale attempt to turn the clock back to the pre-Warren era.

In school cases, while the Burger Court has rebuffed efforts to provide remedies for de facto segregation, where de jure segregation is proved the Court has been generous in permitting federal judges to fashion effective remedies (it was an opinion of Chief Justice Burger, in *Swann* v. *Charlotte-Mecklenburg Board of Education* (1971) that first explicitly upheld lower courts' use of busing as a remedy in school cases). In legislative apportionment cases, the Burger Court has permitted some deviation from strict conformity to a population basis in drawing state and local government legislative districts, but the essential requirement remains that representation must be based on population.

A common complaint against the Warren Court was that it was too "activist"—that it was too quick to substitute its judgment for decisions of legislative bodies or other elected officials. In opinions written during the Burger years, it is common to find the rhetoric of judicial restraint, of calls for deference to policy judgments of legislatures and the political process generally.

Some Burger Court decisions reflect a stated preference for leaving difficult social

A student of the Court might have summarized the Burger Court as being less egalitarian, more sensitive to federalism, more skeptical about the competence of judges to solve society's problems, and more inclined to defer legislative and political processes.

issues to other forums than the courts. In rejecting an attack of Texas's system of financing public schools through heavy reliance on local property taxes, Justice Powell argued against judges' being too ready to interfere with "informed judgments made at the state and local levels."

Overall, however, the record of the Burger Court was one of activism. One of the hallmarks of activism is the enunciation by the Court of new rights. By that standard, no judicial decision could be more activist than the Burger Court's decision in *Roe* v. *Wade* (1973). There Justice Blackmun drew upon the vague contours of the Fourteenth Amendment's due process clause to decide that the right to privacy (itself a right not spelled out in the Constitution) implies a woman's right to have an abortion.

In the modern Supreme Court, the Fourteenth Amendment's due process and equal protection clauses have been the most conspicuous vehicles for judicial activism. The Warren Court's favorite was the equal protection clause—the so-called new equal protection which, through strict scrutiny and other such tests, produced such decisions as *Reynolds* v. *Sims.* With the advent of the Burger Court came the renaissance of substantive due process.

An example of the Burger Court's use of substantive due process is Justice Powell's plurality opinion in *Moore* v. *East Cleveland* (1977). There the Court effectively extended strict scrutiny to a local ordinance impinging on the "extended family." Powell sought to confine the ambit of substantive due process by offering the "teachings of history" and the "basic values that underlie our society" as guides for judging. It is interesting to recall that, only a few years before *Roe* and *Moore,* even as activist a Justice as Douglas had been uncomfortable with using substantive due process (hence his peculiar "emanations from a penumbra" opinion in *Griswold* v. *Connecticut,* 1965). The Burger Court, in opinions such as *Roe* and *Moore,* openly reestablished

substantive due process as a means to limit governmental power.

Another index of judicial activism in the Supreme Court is the Court's willingness to declare an act of Congress unconstitutional. Striking down a state or local action in order to enforce the Constitution or federal law is common, but invalidation of congressional actions is rarer. The Warren Court struck down, on average, barely over one federal statute per term; the Burger Court has invalidated provisions of federal law at about twice that rate. More revealing is the significance of the congressional policies overturned in Burger Court decisions. Among them have been campaign finance (*Buckley* v. *Valeo,* 1976), the eighteen-year-old vote in state elections (*Oregon* v. *Mitchell,* 1970), special bankruptcy courts (*Northern Pipeline Construction Co.* v. *Marathon Pipe Line Co.,* 1982), and the legislative veto (*Immigration and Naturalization Service* v. *Chadha,* 1983).

Yet another measure of judicial activism is the Court's oversight of the behavior of coordinate branches of the federal government, apart from the substantive results of legislative or executive actions. The Burger Court thrust itself directly into the Watergate crisis, during Nixon's presidency. Even as the impeachment process was underway in Congress, the Supreme Court, bypassing the Court of Appeals, expedited its hearing of the question whether Nixon must turn over the Watergate tapes. Denying Nixon's claim of executive privilege, the Court set in motion the dénoument of the crisis, resulting in Nixon's resignation. The Burger Court has similarly been willing to pass on the ambit of Congress's proper sphere of conduct. For example, the Court's narrow view of what activity is protected by the Constitution's speech or debate clause would have surprised Woodrow Wilson, who placed great emphasis on Congress's role in informing the nation.

Closely related to the question of judicial activism is the breadth and scope of the Court's business—the range of issues that the Court chooses to address. Justice Felix Frankfurter used to warn against the Court's plunging into "political thickets" and was distressed when the Warren Court chose to treat legislative apportionment as appropriate for judicial resolution.

Reviewing the record of the Burger Court, one is struck by the new ground it plowed. Areas that were rarely entered or went untouched altogether in the Warren years since 1969 became a staple of the Court's docket. In the 1960s Justice Arthur J. Goldberg sought in vain to have the Justices debate the merits of capital punishment, but the Court would not even grant certiorari. By contrast, not only did the Burger Court, in *Furman* v. *Georgia* (1972), rule that capital statutes as then administered were unconstitutional, but also death cases have appeared on the Court's calendar with regularity.

Sex discrimination is another area that, because of Burger Court decisions, became a staple on the Justices' table. In *Hoyt* v. *Florida* (1961) the Warren Court took a quite relaxed view of claims of sex discrimination in a decision upholding a Florida law making jury service for women, but not for men, completely voluntary. By the time Warren Burger became Chief Justice, in 1969, the women's movement had become a visible aspect of the American scene, and since that time the Burger Court fashioned a considerable body of law on women's rights.

The Burger Court carried forward—or was carried along with—the "judicialization" or "constitutionalization" of American life. The victories won by blacks in court in the heyday of the civil rights movement have inspired others to emulate their example. Prisoners, voters victimized by malapportionment, women, juveniles, inmates of mental institutions—virtually any group or individual failing to get results from the legislative or political process or from government bureaucracies has turned to the courts for relief. And federal judges have woven remedies for a variety of ills.

The Burger Court might have been expected to resist the process of constitutionalization. On some fronts, the Justices slowed the process. *San Antonio Independent School District* v. *Rodriguez* (1973) represents a victory for a hands-off approach to school finance (although it is undercut somewhat by the Court's subsequent decision in *Plyler* v. *Doe,* 1982). But such decisions seem to be only pauses in the expansion of areas in which the judiciary is willing to inquire.

The Burger Court sometimes reached a "liberal" result, sometimes a "conservative" one. In some cases the Justices lay a restraining hand on the equity powers of federal judges, and in some they were more permissive. All the while, however, the scope of the Supreme Court's docket expanded to include wider terrain. In constitutional litigation, there seems to be a kind of ratchet effect: once judges enter an area, they rarely depart. This pattern characterized the Burger era as much as it does that of Warren.

Even in areas that seemed well developed in the Warren Court, the Burger Court added new glosses. It was long thought that commercial speech fell outside the protection of the First Amendment; the Burger Court brought it inside. It was Burger Court opinions that enlarged press rights under the First Amendment to include, at least in some circumstances, a right of access to criminal trials. The jurisprudence by which government aid to sectarian schools is tested is almost entirely of Burger Court making. Most of the case law sketching out the contours of personal autonomy in such areas as abortion, birth control, and other intimate sexual and family relations dates from the Burger era. If idle hands are the devil's workshop, the Burger Court was a temple of virtue.

The contour of rights consists not only of substantive doctrine; it also includes jurisdiction and procedure. Who shall have access to the federal forum, when, and for the resolution of what rights—these were battlegrounds

The roots of the Burger Court lay in the judicial activism of the Warren Court.

in the Burger Court. If a case may be made that the Burger Court achieved a retrenchment in rights, it may be that the case is the strongest as regards the Court's shaping of procedural devices.

Warren Court decisions reflected a mistrust in state courts as forums for the vindication of federal rights. Burger Court decisions, by contrast, were more likely to speak of the comity owed to state courts. Thus, in a line of decisions beginning with *Younger* v. *Harris* (1971), the Burger Court put significant limitations on the power of federal judges to interfere with proceedings (especially criminal) in state courts. The Court also sharply curtailed the opportunity for state prisoners to seek federal habeas corpus review of state court decisions.

Technical barriers such as standing were used in a number of cases to prevent plaintiffs' access to federal courts. For example, in *Warth* v. *Selden* (1976) black residents of Rochester were denied standing to challenge exclusionary zoning in the city's suburbs. Similarly, in *Simon* v. *Eastern Kentucky Welfare Rights Organization* (1976) poor residents of Appalachia were held not to have standing to challenge federal tax advantages granted to private hospitals that refused to serve the indigent.

By no means, however, were Burger Court decisions invariable in restricting access to federal courts or in limiting remedies for the violation of federal law. Some of the Court's interpretations of Section 1983, of Title 42, United States Code, (a civil rights statute dating back to 1871) made that statute a veritable font of litigation. The Warren Court had ruled, in 1961, that Congress, in enacting section 1983, had not intended that municipalities be among the "persons" subject to suit under the statute; in 1978, the Burger Court undertook a "fresh analysis" of the statute and concluded that municipalities are subject to suit thereunder.

Going further, the Court ruled, in 1980, that municipalities sued under section 1983 may not plead as a defense that the governmental official who was involved in the alleged wrong had acted in "good faith"; the majority disregarded the four dissenters' complaint that "ruinous judgments under the statute could imperil local governments." And in another 1980 decision the Court held that plaintiffs could use section 1983 to redress claims based on federal law generally, thus overturning a long-standing assumption that section 1983's reference to federal "laws" was to equal rights legislation. The Burger Court's section 1983 rulings were a major factor in the "litigation explosion" that in recent years has been the subject of so much legal and popular commentary.

The reach of federal courts' equity powers was another hotly debated issue in the Burger Court. Class actions seeking to reform practices in schools, prisons, jails, and other public institutions made institutional litigation a commonplace. Such suits go far beyond the judge's declaring that a right has been violated; they draw the judge into ongoing supervision of state or local institutions (recalling the quip that in the 1960s federal district judge Frank Johnson was the real governor of Alabama). Institutional litigation in federal courts raises serious questions about federalism and often blurs the line between adjudication, legislation, and administration.

Some Burger Court decisions attempted to curb federal judges' equity power in institutional cases. For example, in *Rizzo* v. *Goode* (1976) Justice Rehnquist, for the majority, reversed a lower court's order to the Philadelphia police department to institute reforms responding to allegations of police brutality; Rehnquist admonished the judge to refrain from interfering in the affairs of local government. Similarly, in prison cases, the Burger Court emphasized the importance of federal judges' deference to state prison officials' judgment about questions of prison security and administration.

In important respects, however, the Burger Court did little to place notable limits on federal courts' equity powers. Especially was this true in school desegregation cases. A wide range of remedies were approved, including busing, redrawing of attendance zones, and other devices. Although the Court maintained the distinction between de facto and de jure segregation (thus requiring evidence of purposeful segregation as part of a plaintiff's prima facie case), decisions such as those from Columbus and Dayton (both in 1979) show great deference to findings of lower courts used to support remedial orders against local school districts.

Painting a coherent portrait of the Burger Court is no easy task. An effort to describe the Court in terms of general themes, such as the Justices' attitude to judicial activism, founders on conflicting remarks in the Court's opinions. Likewise, an attempt to generalize about the Burger Court's behavior in any given area encounters difficulties.

Consider, for example, the expectation—understandable in light of President Nixon's explicit concern about the Warren Court's rulings in criminal justice cases—that the Burger Court would be a "law and order" tribunal. In the early years of the Burger Court (until about 1976), the Court, especially in its rulings on police practices, seemed bent on undermining the protections accorded in decisions of the Warren years. The majority showed their attitude to the exclusionary rule by referring to it as a "judicially created remedy," one whose benefits were to be balanced against its costs (such as to the functioning of a grand jury). In the late 1970s, the Court seemed more sympathetic to *Miranda* and to other devices meant to limit police practices. But in the early 1980s, especially in search and seizure cases, the Court seemed once again markedly sympathetic to law enforcement.

Or consider the Court's attitudes to federalism. In some decisions, the Burger Court seemed sympathetic to the interests of states and localities. In limiting state prisoners' access to federal writs of habeas corpus, the Court showed respect for state courts. In rebuffing attacks on inequalities in the financing of a state's public schools, the Court gave breathing room to local judgments about running those schools. In limiting federal court intervention in prison affairs, the Court gave scope for state judgments about how to run a prison.

Yet many Burger Court decisions were decidedly adverse to state and local governments' interests. The Court's section 1983 rulings exposed municipalities to expensive damage awards. The Burger Court was more active than the Warren Court in using the dormant commerce clause to restrict state laws and regulations found to impinge upon national interests. And in the highly controversial decision of *Garcia* v. *San Antonio Metropolitan Transit Authority* (1985) the Court said that, if the states have Tenth Amendment concerns about acts of Congress, they should seek relief from Congress, not from the courts (in so ruling, the Court in *Garcia* overturned *National League of Cities* v. *Usery*, 1976, itself a Burger Court decision).

How does one account for such a mixed record, replete with conflicting signals about basic jurisprudential values? The temperament and habits of the Justices of the Burger Court play a part. Pundits often imagine the Justices coming to the Court's conference table with "shopping lists," looking for cases on which to hang doctrinal innovations. For most (although not necessarily all) of the Justices, this picture is not accurate. By and large, the Justices tend to take the cases as they come. This tendency is reinforced by the Court's workload pressures. Far more cases came to the Burger Court than came to the Warren Court. Complaints by the Chief Justice about the burden thus placed on the Court were frequent, and in 1975 it was reported that at least five Justices had gone on record as favoring the concept of a National Court of Appeals to ease the Supreme Court's workload.

B

BURGER COURT

(1969–1986)

The Burger years on the Court lacked the larger-than-life figures of the Warren era, Justices like Hugo L. Black and Felix Frankfurter, around whom issues tended to polarize. Those were judges who framed grand designs, a jurisprudence of judging. Through their fully evolved doctrines, and their armtwisting, they put pressure on their colleagues to think about cases in doctrinal terms. After the departure of the great ideologues, the Justices were under less pressure to fit individual cases into doctrinal tableaux. Ad hoc results became the order of the day.

The Burger Court was a somewhat less ideological bench than was the Warren Court. Many of the Court's most important decisions turned upon the vote of the centrists on the bench. It was not unusual to find, especially in 5–4 decisions, that Justice Powell had cast the deciding vote. Powell came to the bench inclined to think in the pragmatic way of the practicing lawyer; as a Justice he soon came to be identified with "balancing" competing interests to arrive at a decision. The Burger Court's pragmatism, its tendency to gravitate to the center, blurred ideological lines and made its jurisprudence often seem to lack any unifying theme or principle.

A Burger Court decision—more often, a line of decisions—often had something for everyone. In *Roe* v. *Wade* the Court upheld the right of a woman to make and effectuate a decision to have an abortion. Yet, while invalidating state laws found to burden the abortion decision directly, the Court permitted state and federal governments to deny funding for even therapeutic abortions while funding other medical procedures. In *Regents of the University of California* v. *Bakke* (1978) a majority of the Justices ruled against racial quotas in a state university's admissions process, but a university, consistent with *Bakke,* may use race as a factor among other factors in the admissions process.

Burger Court decisions showed a distaste for categorical values. The Warren Court's fondness for prophylactic rules, such as *Miranda* or the Fourth Amendment exclusionary rule, was not echoed in the Burger Court. The Burger bench may not have jettisoned those rules outright, but most Justices of that era showed a preference for fact-oriented adjudication rather than for sweeping formulae.

Burger Court opinions were less likely than those of the Warren Court to ring with moral imperatives. Even when resolving so fundamental a controversy as that over abortion, a Burger Court opinion was apt to resemble a legislative committee report more nearly than a tract in political theory. A comparison of such Warren Court opinions as *Brown* v. *Board of Education* and *Reynolds* v. *Sims* and a Burger Court opinion such as *Roe* v. *Wade* is instructive. Warren Court opinions often read as if their authors intended them to have tutorial value (Justice Goldberg once called the Supreme Court "the nation's schoolmaster"); Burger Court opinions are more likely to read like an exercise in problem solving.

For most of its existence, the Burger Court was characterized by a lack of cohesive voting blocs. For much of its history, the Burger years saw a 2–5–2 voting pattern—Burger and Rehnquist in one wing, Brennan and Marshall in the other wing, the remaining five Justices tending to take more central ground. Justice Stewart's replacement by Justice O'Connor (a more conservative Justice) tended to reinforce the Burger-Rehnquist wing, while Justice Stevens gravitated more and more to the Brennan-Marshall camp. Even so, the Burger Court was a long way from the sharp ideological alignments of the Warren years.

The Court's personalities and dynamics aside, the nature of the issues coming before the Burger Court helps account for the mixed character of the Court's record. The Warren Court is well remembered for decisions laying down broad principles; *Brown, Mapp, Miranda,* and *Reynolds* are examples. The task of implementing much of what the Warren Court began fell to the Burger Court. Implementation, by its nature, draws courts into closer judgment calls. It is one thing to lay down the principle that public schools should not be segregated by race, but quite another to pick one's way through the thicket of de facto-de jure distinctions, inter-district remedies, and shifting demographics. Had the Warren Court survived into the 1970s, it might have found implementation as difficult and splintering as did the Burger Court.

If the Warren Court embodied the heritage of progressivism and the optimistic expectations of post–World War II America, the Burger years paralleled a period of doubt and uncertainty about solutions to social problems in the years after the Great Society, the Vietnam War, and Watergate. In a time when the American people might have had less confidence in government's capacity in other spheres, the Supreme Court might well intuitively be less bold in imposing its own solutions. At the same time, there appeared, in the Burger years, to be no turning back the clock on the expectations of lawyers and laity alike as to the place of an activist judiciary in public life. Debate over the proper role of the judiciary in a democracy is not insulated from debate over the role of government generally in a society aspiring to ordered liberty. Judgments about the record of the Burger Court, therefore, tend to mirror contemporary American ideals and values.

—A. E. DICK HOWARD

Bibliography

Blasi, Vincent, ed. (1983). *The Burger Court: The Counter-Revolution That Wasn't.* New Haven, Conn.: Yale University Press.

Emerson, Thomas I. (1980). First Amendment Doctrine and the Burger Court. *California Law Review* 68:422–481.

Funston, Richard Y. (1977). *Constitutional Counterrevolution?: The Warren Court and the Burger Court: Judicial Policy Making in Modern America.* Cambridge, Mass.: Schenkman.

Howard, A. E. Dick (1972). Mr. Justice Powell and the Emerging Nixon Majority. *Michigan Law Review* 70:445–468.

Levy, Leonard W. (1974). *Against the Law: The Nixon Court and Criminal Justice.* New York: Harper & Row.

Mason, Alpheus T. (1979). *The Supreme Court from Taft to Burger.* 3rd ed. Baton Rouge: Louisiana State University Press.

Rehnquist, William H. (1980). The Notion of a Living Constitution. *Texas Law Review* 54:693–706.

Saltzberg, Stephen A. (1980). Foreword: The Flow and Ebb of Constitutional Criminal Procedure in the Warren and Burger Courts. *Georgetown Law Journal* 69: 151–209.

Woodward, Bob, and Armstrong, Scott (1979). *The Brethren: Inside the Supreme Court.* New York: Simon & Schuster.

BURTON v. WILMINGTON PARKING AUTHORITY

365 U.S. 715 (1961)

Burton exemplifies the interest-balancing approach to the state action limitation of the Fourteenth Amendment used by the Supreme Court during the Chief Justiceship of Earl Warren. A private restaurant, leasing space in a publicly owned parking structure, refused to serve Burton because he was black. In a state court action, Burton sought declaratory and injunctive relief, claiming that the restaurant's refusal amounted to state action denying him the equal protection of the laws. The state courts denied relief, but the Supreme Court reversed, 7–2, holding the Fourteenth Amendment applicable to the restaurant's conduct.

Public agencies owned the land and the building, had floated bonds, were collecting revenues to pay for the building's construction and maintenance, and received rent

See also

Reitman v. Mulkey

*A private restaurant,
leasing space in a
publicly owned
parking structure,
refused to serve
Burton because he
was black.*

payments from the restaurant. The restaurant could expect to draw customers from persons parking in the structure; correspondingly, some might park there because of the restaurant's convenience. Profits earned from the restaurant's racial discrimination, the Court said, were indispensable elements in an integral financial plan. All these interrelated mutual benefits taken together amounted to significant involvement of the state in the private racial discrimination. Justice Tom C. Clark, for the majority, disclaimed any pretensions of establishing a general rule about state aid to private discrimination, or even for the leasing of state property. Under "the peculiar facts or circumstances" here, the state action limitation was satisfied.

Justice Potter Stewart, concurring, said simply that a state statute permitting a restaurant's proprietor to refuse service to persons offensive to a majority of patrons amounted to official authorization of private discrimination—a theme explored later in *Reitman* v. *Mulkey* (1967). Justice John Marshall Harlan dissented, joined by Justice Charles E. Whittaker. Harlan complained that the majority had offered no guidance for determining when the state action limitation would be satisfied. Rather than pursue this inquiry, he urged a remand to the state courts for further illumination of the "authorization" question raised by Justice Stewart.

—KENNETH L. KARST

BUTLER, UNITED STATES v.

297 U.S. 1 (1936)

In this historic and monumentally inept opinion, the Supreme Court ruled that the United States has no power to regulate the agrarian sector of the economy. The Agricultural Adjustment Act of 1933 (AAA) sought to increase the purchasing power and living standards of farmers by subsidizing the cur-

tailment of farm production and thus boosting farm prices. Congress raised the money for the subsidies by levying an excise tax on the primary processors of each crop, in this case a cotton mill, which passed on to the consumer the cost of the tax. AAA was the agricultural equivalent of a protective tariff. By a vote of 6–3 the Court held, in an opinion by Justice Owen Roberts, that the statute unconstitutionally invaded the powers reserved to the states by the Tenth Amendment. "It is a statutory plan," Roberts declared, "to regulate and control agricultural production, a matter beyond the powers delegated to the federal government. The tax, the appropriation of the funds raised, and the direction for their disbursement, are but parts of the plan. They are but means to an unconstitutional end." Roberts reached his doctrine of dual federalism by simplistic mechanical jurisprudence. He sought to match the statute with the Constitution and, finding that they did not square, seriously limited the taxing and spending power.

Roberts did not question the power of Congress to levy an excise tax on the processing of agricultural products; he also conceded that "the power of Congress to authorize expenditures of public moneys for public purposes is not limited by the direct grants of legislative power found in the Constitution." He did not even deny that aiding the agrarian sector of the economy benefited the general welfare, in accord with the first clause of Article I, section 8; rather he reasoned that the Court did not need to decide whether an appropriation in aid of agriculture fell within the clause. He simply found that the Constitution did not vest in the government a power to regulate agricultural production. He ruled, too, that the tax was not really a tax, because Congress had not levied it for the benefit of the government; it expropriated money from processors to give to farmers. The tax power cannot, Roberts declared, be used as an instrument to enforce a regulation of matters belonging to the exclusive realm of the states, nor can the tax power be used to coerce a compliance which Congress has no power to command.

Despite Roberts's insistence on calling the crop curtailment program "coercive," it was in fact voluntary; a minority of farmers elected not to restrict production, foregoing subsidies. But Roberts added that even a voluntary plan would be unconstitutional as a "federal regulation of a subject reserved to the states." He added: "It does not help to declare that local conditions throughout the nation have created a situation of national concern; for that is but to say that whenever there is a widespread similarity of local conditions, Congress may ignore constitutional limitations upon its own powers and usurp those reserved to the states."

Justice Harlan Fiske Stone, joined by Justices Louis D. Brandeis and Benjamin N. Cardozo, wrote a scathing, imperishable dissent, one of the most famous in the Court's history. Strongly defending the constitutionality of the AAA on the basis of the power to tax and spend, Stone lambasted Roberts's opinion as hardly rising "to the dignity of an argument" and as a "tortured construction of the Constitution." Stone's opinion confirmed President Franklin D. Roosevelt's belief that it was the Court, not the Constitution, that stood in the way of recovery. The AAA decision helped provoke the constitutional crisis of 1937.

—LEONARD W. LEVY

Bibliography

Hart, Henry M. (1936). Processing Taxes and Protective Tariffs. *Harvard Law Review* 49:610–618.

Murphy, Paul L. (1955). The New Deal Agricultural Program and the Constitution. *Agricultural History* 29:160–169.

BUTLER v. MICHIGAN

352 U.S. 380 (1957)

Michigan convicted Butler for selling to an adult an "obscene" book that might corrupt the morals of a minor. The Supreme Court unanimously reversed, in an opinion by Justice Felix Frankfurter, who declared that the statute was not restricted to the evil with which it dealt; it reduced adults "to reading only what is fit for children," thereby curtailing their First Amendment rights as protected by the due process clause of the Fourteenth Amendment.

—LEONARD W. LEVY

◆ **de facto**
[Latin: in fact] Existing in fact, whether or not existing in law or by right.

See also

Obscenity

TENTH AMENDMENT

Adopted in 1791 as part of the Bill of Rights, the Tenth Amendment declares that "powers not delegated to the United States by the Constitution . . . are reserved to the States respectively, or to the people." This language was an attempt to satisfy the public that the new constitution would not make a reality of that most repeated of anti-federalist fears: a completely centralized or "consolidated" government. But while the Tenth Amendment reminded Congress that its concerns were limited, the Constitution envisioned the effective exercise of national power, as the necessary and proper clause and the supremacy clause indicated. The inevitable question was to be: What happens when Congress's responsibilities require measures the states say are beyond Congress's powers? John Marshall attempted the Supreme Court's first answer to this question in *McCulloch* v. *Maryland* (1819). *McCulloch* is best interpreted as advancing the following propositions: by granting and enumerating powers, the Constitution envisions the pursuit of a limited number of ends; the framers did not and could not have enumerated all the legislative means appropriate to achieving constitutional ends in changing historical circumstances; Congress can select appropriate means to authorized national ends without regard for state prerogatives; the states, by contrast, cannot enact measures conflicting with lawful congressional policies.

CALDER v. BULL

3 Dallas 386 (1798)

Calder is the leading case on the meaning of the constitutional injunction against ex post facto laws. Connecticut had passed an act setting aside a court decree refusing to probate a will, and the plaintiff argued that the act constituted an ex post facto law. In the Court's main opinion Justice Samuel Chase ruled that although all ex post facto laws are necessarily "retrospective," retrospective laws adversely affecting the citizen in his private right of property or contracts are not ex post facto laws. The prohibition against the latter extended only to criminal, not civil, cases. An ex post facto law comprehends any retrospective penal legislation, such as making criminal an act that was not criminal when committed, or aggravating the act into a greater crime than at the time it was committed, or applying increased penalties for the act, or altering the rules of evidence to increase the chances of conviction.

The case is also significant in constitutional history because by closing the door on the ex post facto route in civil cases, it encouraged the opening of another door and thus influenced the course of the doctrine of vested rights. The contract clause probably would not have attained its importance in our constitutional history, nor perhaps the due process clause substantively construed, if the Court had extended the ex post facto clause to civil cases. In *Calder,* Chase endorsed the judicial doctrine of vested rights drawn from the higher law, as announced by Justice William Paterson in *Van Horne's Lessee* v. *Dorrance* (1795). Drawing on "the very nature of our free Republican governments" and "the great first principles of the social compact," Chase declared that the legislative power, even if not expressly restrained by a

> *Calder is the leading case on the meaning of the constitutional injunction against ex post facto laws.*

♦ **ex post facto**
[Latin: from after the fact] A law that makes criminal, or that increases the criminal penalty for, an act committed before the law was passed.

CALIFORNIA v. GREENWOOD

486 U.S. 35 (1988)

A person's trash if subjected to public scrutiny might reveal intimate matters that could be embarrassing and even expose one to blackmail or criminal prosecution. But anyone throwing away household trash takes the risk of exposure, even if the trash is disposed of in an opaque plastic bag that is sealed. This was the Supreme Court's announcement in this case.

Justice Byron R. White, for a 6–2 Court, held that the Fourth Amendment's prohibition against unreasonable searches and seizures does not apply to those who leave their sealed trash outside their curtilage for collection by the trash collector. In this case, an observant policewoman, suspecting Greenwood of dealing in narcotics, obtained the trash collector's cooperation and found enough incriminating evidence to establish probable cause for a search of the residence. This evidence was used to convict him. The question was whether the initial warrantless search of the trash violated the Fourth Amendment. The Court ruled that those discarding their trash by placing it on the street for collection abandoned any reasonable expectation of privacy they might otherwise have. The two dissenters believed that the warrantless investigation of the trash constituted an appalling invasion of privacy.

—LEONARD W. LEVY

*The Cantwells were
convicted of
violating a
Connecticut statute
that prohibited
persons soliciting
money for any cause
without a certificate
issued by the state
secretary of the
Public Welfare
Council.*

◆ **statute**
*A law enacted by a
legislature; a part of the
formal, written law. Also
called an "act" of
Congress or of the
legislature, a statute is to
be distinguished from a
constitution and also
from customary or
common law and case
law.*

written constitution, could not constitutionally violate the right of an antecedent and lawful private contract or the right of private property. To assert otherwise, he maintained, would "be a political heresy," inadmissible to the genius and spirit of our governmental system.

Justice James Iredell concurred in the judgment as well as the definition of ex post facto laws but maintained that judges should not hold an act void "merely because it is, in their judgment, contrary to the principles of natural justice," which he thought undefinable by fixed standards.

—LEONARD W. LEVY

CANTWELL v. CONNECTICUT

310 U.S. 296 (1940)

Newton Cantwell and his sons, Jesse and Russell, were arrested in New Haven, Connecticut. As Jehovah's Witnesses and, by definition, ordained ministers, they were engaged in street solicitation. They distributed pamphlets, made statements critical of the Roman Catholic Church, and offered to play for passersby a phonograph record including an attack on the Roman Catholic religion. The Cantwells were convicted of violating a Connecticut statute that prohibited persons soliciting money for any cause without a certificate issued by the state secretary of the Public Welfare Council. Jesse Cantwell was also convicted of the common law offense of inciting a breach of the peace.

Justice Owen J. Roberts delivered the opinion of a unanimous Court: although Connecticut had a legitimate interest in regulating the use of its streets for solicitation, the means the state had chosen infringed upon the religious freedom of solicitors. The secretary appeared to have unlimited discretion to determine the legitimacy of a religious applicant and either issue or withhold the certificate. If issuance had been a "matter of

course," the requirement could have been maintained, but so wide an official discretion to restrict activity protected by the free exercise clause was unacceptable.

The conviction of Jesse Cantwell for inciting breach of the peace was also constitutionally defective. Justice Roberts noted that the open-endedness of the common law concept of breach of the peace offered wide discretion to law enforcement officials. When such a criminal provision was applied to persons engaging in First Amendment-protected speech or exercise of religion there must be a showing of a clear and present danger of violence or disorder. Although Cantwell's speech was offensive to his listeners, it had not created such a danger.

As a religious freedom precedent, *Cantwell* is important in two ways: first, it made clear that the free exercise clause of the First Amendment applied to the states through the due process clause of the Fourteenth Amendment; second, it suggested (in contrast to previous case law, for example, *Reynolds* v. *United States,* 1879) that the free exercise clause protected not only beliefs but also some actions. The protection of belief was absolute, Roberts wrote, but the protection of action was not; it must give way in appropriate cases to legitimate government regulation. The implication was that at least some government regulations of religion-based conduct would be impermissible.

—RICHARD E. MORGAN

CAPITAL PUNISHMENT

During the 1980s, a majority of Justices on the Supreme Court struggled without success to disengage the Court from playing an intimate role in the day-to-day administration of capital punishment. As early as 1984, an article on the evolving jurisprudence of capital punishment in the Court could plausibly be titled "Deregulating Death," and the Court continued to reject major challenges to state systems of capital punishment for the rest of the decade. In the wake of *McCleskey* v. *Kemp*, decided in 1987, scholars could conclude that "nothing appears left of the abolitionist campaign in the courts—nothing but the possibility of small-scale tinkering."

Yet conflicts about capital punishment have been a persistent and growing problem for the Court through the 1980s, and there are no indications that the burden will lessen soon. The number of capital cases producing opinions increased during the decade from about five per term in the early 1980s to about ten per term in the late 1980s. Moreover, the level of dispute among the Justices has substantially increased during the course of the decade. In the early 1980s, most challenges to capital punishment were rejected by substantial majorities of the Justices, with a 7–2 vote being the most common outcome during the 1982, 1983, and 1984 terms. Only three of seventeen opinions issued during these three terms were decided by 5–4 margins. Justices William J. Brennan and Thurgood Marshall were the isolated dissenters in most of these early cases.

By contrast, in the four terms after October 1985, the Court has been sharply and closely divided. Of the twenty-seven cases decided over this span, fourteen produced 5–4 divisions, with Justices John Paul Stevens and Harry A. Blackmun usually joining Justices Brennan and Marshall in opposition to the deregulatory thrust of the Court majority. We know of no other body of the Supreme Court doctrine in which the majority of cases divide the Court 5–4.

With the Court divided almost to the point of a mathematical law of maximal disagreement, both jurisprudence and decorum have suffered. Few would suggest that the Court's decisions of the past decade cumulate into a body of doctrine that is even minimally coherent. And close decisions on questions that are literally matters of life and death do not promote good manners among Justices locked in conflict. It is thus no surprise that Court decorum has been put at some risk by the sustained contentiousness of the death penalty cases.

Close and acrimonious division of the Justices may also undermine the degree to which the Supreme Court's decisions confer legitimacy on the practice of execution in the 1990s. Confidence in the fairness of the system is not bolstered when four of nine Justices publicly proclaim that the race of the victim has a discriminatory influence on whether defendants receive death sentences. The result is that the consistent but slim majority support on the Court may not provide much momentum for public acceptance of the equity of capital punishment, much as the Court's leadership toward abolition was undermined by a slim and divided majority on the Court in *Furman* v. *Georgia* (1972). A 5–4 majority may lack the institutional credibility to help make executions an accepted part of a modern American governmental system.

One other pattern is of special significance when discussing capital punishment in the Supreme Court during the 1980s: the transition from theory to practice of executions has not yet occurred in most of the United States. Despite the Court's attempts to withdraw from close supervision of death cases, the backlog of death cases has increased substantially, and the lower federal courts continue to play an important role in stopping executions. Indeed, over half of federal court of appeals decisions in death penalty cases result in overturning the death sentence.

This pattern altered dramatically in the 1990s with the retirement of Justices Brennan, Marshall, and Blackmun. Shortly before his retirement, Justice Blackmun, dissenting from the Court's refusal to review a capital conviction in *Callins* v. *Collins* (1994), argued that "I shall no longer tinker with the machinery of death." He maintained it was impossible to eliminate arbitrariness and discrimination in capital cases without doing away with constitutionally mandated individualized sentencing. And, extrapolating from his dissent in *McCleskey*, he believed the "arbitrariness inherent in the sentencer's discretion to afford mercy is exacerbated by the problem of race."

Executions of murderers and rapists were fairly frequent in the United States until the 1960s.

*An early version of the
modern electric chair used
for capital punishment.
(Corbis/Bettmann)*

Through the 1990s the Court repeatedly rejected attempts to reverse death sentences. Overturning a lawfully obtained conviction through habeas corpus, it held, would require "a truly persuasive demonstration of actual innocence," and even then the federal courts could only intervene if there were "no state avenue opened to process such a claim." After holding the states were not precluded from executing one who was sixteen years of age when he committed the offense, (*Stanford* v. *Kentucky* [1989]), the Court ruled a state's procedures properly allowed the jury to consider the defendant's youth even though the jurors were instructed to weigh his future dangerousness yet not specifically told to consider his youth's relation to his culpability (*Johnson* v. *Texas* [1993]). The Court did draw the line at executing one who was fifteen at the time the murder was committed, in *Thompson* v. *Oklahoma* (1988).

As of 1999, thirty-eight states have legislation authorizing capital punishment, and 499 persons have been executed since the reauthorization of the capital punishment in *Gregg* v. *Georgia,* in 1976. Most of the states with a recent execution are located in the South; of the 499 executions, 145 were in Texas, 46 in Virginia, and 39 in Florida. The number of prisoners under death sentence had increased by the end of 1998 to about 3,300. The long involvement of the federal courts had helped produce a death row population six times as great as that which cast a shadow on the Court when *Furman* v. *Georgia* was decided in 1972.

Against this backdrop, an ad hoc committee chaired by retired Justice Lewis F. Powell diagnosed the problem that generated these numbers as the delay produced by repetitive and multiple federal appeals. The committee suggested the enactment of new statutory procedures for handling death penalty cases in the federal court, which, by and large, would eliminate the filing of successor federal petitions. Under the new procedures, if the state has provided counsel to those sentenced to death through the state appeal and habeas corpus process, absent extraordinary circumstances, a federal court would lack the power to stay an execution of the condemned person upon the filing of a successor federal petition.

This resulted in the Anti-Terrorism and Effective Death Penalty Act of 1996, requiring death row inmates to file federal petitions for post-conviction review of their convictions or sentences within 180 days of affirmation of their conviction in the state courts. The act also limits the scope of federal review of state capital convictions, imposes strict time limits on federal courts in these cases, and limits the ability of state prisoners to bring successive suits.

In 1989 and 1990 the Supreme Court, by the familiar 5–4 vote, responded to the considerations that had moved the Powell committee. Now, with few exceptions, a federal habeas corpus petition must be denied when it rests on a claim of a "new right"—one that had not yet been recognized by the Supreme Court when the appeals ended in the state courts. Not only has the Court specifically applied this new bar to death penalty cases, but it has also read the idea of a "new right" broadly enough to bar all but a very few claims.

What would be the impact of true federal court withdrawal from restrictions on execution? The potential number of executions that could result is quite high, two or three times as many as the 199 executions that were to date the twentieth-century high recorded in 1935. How many state governors or state court systems would compensate and to what degree remains to be seen. Practices like executive clemency that used to be a statistically important factor in restricting executions atrophied during the twenty-five years of primary federal court intervention in the capital-punishment process. Whether these processes would reappear under the pressure of large numbers of pending executions in northern industrial states cannot be predicted, nor is it possible to project a likely national number of executions that could represent a new level of equilibrium.

The one certainty is that the U.S. Supreme Court will play a central day-to-day role in any substantial increase in executions. Whatever its doctrinal intentions or public-relations ambitions, the Supreme Court will be for the mass media and the public the court of last resort for every scheduled execution in the United States for the foreseeable future. If executions, currently at 74 per year (as of 1997), climb to 100 or 150 per year, the continuing role of the Court as the last stop before the gallows will be that element of the Court's work most sharply etched in the public mind. For an institution narrowly divided on fundamental questions, this case-by-case process could increase both the labor and the acrimony of the Court's involvement with capital punishment. To escape this role would call for more than a shift in procedure or court personnel; it would require a different country.

Under these circumstances, will the hands-off doctrine the Court has so recently constructed continue as executions multiply? In the short run, any major shift in doctrine would be regarded as a surprise. This is a matter more of personnel than of precedent. stare decisis has not often been a reliable guide to Supreme Court pronouncements in capital punishment. Instead, doctrine seems more the servant of policy than its master in this field, and this is equally the case for *Gregg* v. *Georgia* as for *Furman* v. *Georgia*. But the current majority is apparently firm and includes the four youngest Justices.

In the long run, if the United States is to join the community of Western nations that have abolished capital punishment, the U.S. Supreme Court is the most likely agency of abolition in the national government. The principal flaws in the system of capital punishment are the same as they have been throughout the twentieth century. The doctrinal foundations for reacting to these matters are easily found in the Court's prior work.

No matter the course of the Court's future pronouncements, capital punishment will remain an area of inevitable judicial activism in one important respect: whatever the substance of American policy toward executions, the U.S. Supreme Court will continue to be the dominant institutional influence of national government on executions in the United States.

—FRANKLIN ZIMRING
—MICHAEL LAURENCE

Bibliography

Ad Hoc Committee on Federal Habeas Corpus in Capital Cases (1989). *Committee Report and Proposal.* Washington, D.C.: Judicial Conference of the United States.

See also

McCleskey v. *Kemp*

Warren Court

Burt, Robert A. (1987). Disorder in the Court: The Death Penalty and the Constitution. *Michigan Law Review* 85:1741–1819.

Weisberg, Robert (1983). Deregulating Death. In Philip J. Kurland, Gerhard Gasper, and Dennis J. Hutchinson, eds., *Supreme Court Review,* pp. 305–396. Chicago: University of Chicago Press.

Zimring, Franklin E., and Hawkins, Gordon (1986). *Capital Punishment and the American Agenda.* New York: Cambridge University Press.

CAREY v. POPULATION SERVICES INTERNATIONAL

431 U.S. 678 (1977)

By a 7–2 vote the Supreme Court in *Carey* invalidated three New York laws restricting the advertisement and sale of birth control devices. Justice William J. Brennan wrote for a majority concerning two of the laws. First, he read *Gris-wold* v. *Connecticut* (1965) and *Roe* v. *Wade* (1973) to require strict scrutiny of laws touching the "fundamental" decision "whether to bear or beget a child." New York had limited the distribution of contraceptives to licensed pharmacists, and had not offered a sufficiently compelling justification. Second, he read the First Amendment to forbid a law prohibiting the advertising or display of contraceptives.

The Court was fragmented in striking down the third law, which forbade distribution of contraceptives to minors under sixteen except under medical prescription. Justice Brennan, for himself and three other Justices, conceded that children's constitutional rights may not be the equivalent of adults' rights. Yet he found insufficient justification for the law in the state's policy of discouraging sexual activity among young people. He doubted that a limit on access to contraceptives would discourage such activity, and in any case the state could not delegate to doctors the right to decide which minors should be discouraged. Three concurring Justices expressed less enthusiasm for

Sale of birth control devices such as Norplant is legal, due in part to the Court's decision in Carey. *(Corbis/Bettmann)*

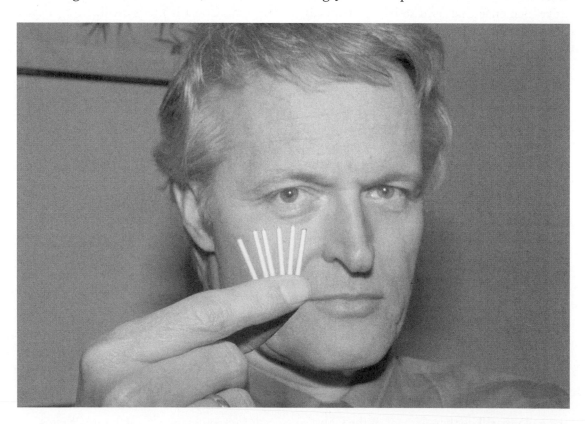

minors' constitutional rights to sexual freedom but found other paths to the conclusion that the New York law as written was invalid.

Chief Justice Warren E. Burger dissented without opinion, and Justice William H. Rehnquist filed a short dissent that was unusually caustic, even by his high standard for the genre.

Carey was not the last word on the troublesome problem of minors' rights concerning reproductive autonomy; the Court has repeatedly returned to the issue in the abortion context. Yet *Carey*'s opinion invalidating the law limiting contraceptives sales to pharmacists was important for its recognition that *Griswold* v. *Connecticut* stood not merely for a right of marital privacy but also for a broad freedom of intimate association.

—KENNETH L. KARST

CAROLENE PRODUCTS COMPANY, UNITED STATES v.

Footnote Four
304 U.S. 144 (1938)

Footnote four to Justice Harlan F. Stone's opinion in *United States* v. *Carolene Products Co.* (1938) undoubtedly is the best known, most controversial footnote in constitutional law. Stone used it to suggest categories in which a general presumption in favor of the constitutionality of legislation might be inappropriate. The issue of if and when particular constitutional claims warrant special judicial scrutiny has been a core concern in constitutional theory for nearly fifty years since Stone's three-paragraph footnote was appended to an otherwise obscure 1938 opinion.

The *Carolene Products* decision, handed down the same day as *Erie Railroad* v. *Tompkins* (1938), itself reflected a new perception of the proper role for federal courts. It articulated a position of great judicial deference in reviewing most legislation. In his majority opinion, Stone sought to consolidate developing restraints on judicial intervention in economic matters, symbolized by *West Coast Hotel Co.* v. *Parrish* (1937). But in footnote four Stone also went on to suggest that legislation, if challenged with certain types of constitutional claims, might not merit the same deference most legislation should enjoy.

Stone's opinion upheld a 1923 federal ban on the interstate shipment of filled milk. The Court thus reversed a lower federal court and, indirectly, the Illinois Supreme Court, in holding that Congress had power to label as adulterated a form of skimmed milk in which butterfat was replaced by coconut milk. Today the decision seems unremarkable; at the time, however, not only was the result in *Carolene Products* controversial but the theory of variable judicial scrutiny suggested by its footnote four was new and perhaps daring.

Actually, only three other Justices joined that part of Stone's opinion which contained the famous footnote, though that illustrious trio consisted of Chief Justice Charles Evans Hughes, Justice Louis D. Brandeis, and Justice Owen J. Roberts. Justice Hugo L. Black refused to agree to the part of Stone's opinion with the footnote because Black wished to go further than Stone in proclaiming deference to legislative judgments. Justice Pierce Butler concurred only in the result; Justice James C. McReynolds dissented; and Justices Benjamin N. Cardozo and Stanley F. Reed did not take part.

In fact, the renowned footnote does no more than tentatively mention the possibility of active review in certain realms. The footnote is nonetheless considered a paradigm for special judicial scrutiny of laws discriminating against certain rights or groups. The first paragraph, added at the suggestion of Chief Justice Hughes, is the least controversial. The paragraph hints at special judicial concern when rights explicitly mentioned in the text of the Constitution are at issue. This rights-oriented, interpretivist position involves less of a judicial leap than the possibility, suggested in the rest of the footnote, of additional grounds for judi-

C

CAROLENE
PRODUCTS
COMPANY, UNITED
STATES V.

Footnote Four
304 U.S. 144 (1938)

Carey *was not the last word on the troublesome problem of minors' rights concerning reproductive autonomy.*

♦ **obiter dictum**
[Latin: said by the way]
Any words in a court's opinion that are not required for the decision of the case, and that are therefore, in theory, not binding as precedent. The term is often misleadingly abbreviated to "dictum" or to its plural, "dicta."

See also

Abortion and the
    Constitution
Griswold v. *Connecticut*
Roe v. *Wade*

C

**CAROLENE
PRODUCTS
COMPANY, UNITED
STATES V.**

*Footnote Four
304 U.S. 144 (1938)*

*Justice Lewis F.
Powell recently
stated that footnote
four contains
"perhaps the most
far-sighted dictum
in our modern
judicial heritage."*

cial refusal or reluctance to defer to judgments of other governmental branches.

The footnote's second paragraph speaks of possible special scrutiny of interference with "those political processes which can ordinarily be expected to bring about repeal of undesirable legislation." To illustrate the ways in which clogged political channels might be grounds for exacting judicial review, Stone cites decisions invalidating restrictions on the right to vote, the dissemination of informa-

FOOTNOTE FOUR
(partial text)

There may be narrower scope for operation of the presumption of constitutionality when legislation appears on its face to be within a specific prohibition of the Constitution, such as those of the first ten Amendments, which are deemed equally specific when held to be embraced within the 14th. [Case citations deleted]

It is unnecessary to consider now whether legislation which restricts those political processes, which can ordinarily be expected to bring about repeal of undesirable legislation, is to be subjected to more exacting judicial scrutiny under the general prohibitions of the 14th Amendment than are most other types of legislation. . . .

Nor need we inquire whether similar considerations enter into the review of statutes directed at particular religious . . . or national . . . or racial minorities; [or] whether prejudice against discrete and insular minorities may be a special condition, which tends seriously to curtail the operation of those political processes ordinarily to be relied upon to protect minorities, and which may call for a correspondingly more searching judicial inquiry. . . .

—Source: 304 U.S. 144 (1938)

tion, freedom of political association, and peaceable assembly.

The footnote's third and final paragraph has been the most vigorously debated. It suggests that prejudice directed against discrete and insular minorities may also call for "more searching judicial inquiry." For this proposition Stone cites two commerce clause decisions, *McCulloch* v. *Maryland* (1819) and *South Carolina State Highway Dept.* v. *Barnwell Bros.* (1938), as well as First Amendment and Fourteenth Amendment decisions invalidating discriminatory laws based on religion, national origin, or race. Judicial and scholarly disagreement since 1938 has focused mainly on two questions. First, even if the category "discrete and insular minorities" seems clearly to include blacks, should any other groups be included? Second, does paragraph three essentially overlap with paragraph two, or does it go beyond protecting groups who suffer particular political disadvantage? The question whether discrimination against particular groups or burdens on certain rights should trigger special judicial sensitivity is a basic problem in constitutional law to this day.

Footnote four thus symbolizes the Court's struggle since the late 1930s to confine an earlier, free-wheeling tradition of judicial intervention premised on freedom of contract and substantive due process, on the one hand, while trying, on the other, to create an acceptable basis for active intervention when judges perceive political disadvantages or racial or other invidious discrimination.

Dozens of Supreme Court decisions and thousands of pages of scholarly commentary since *Carolene Products* have explored this problem. In equal protection analysis, for example, the approach introduced in footnote four helped produce a two-tiered model of judicial review. Within this model, legislation involving social and economic matters would be sustained if any rational basis for the law could be found, or sometimes even conceived of, by a judge. In sharp contrast, strict scrutiny applied to classifications based on race, national origin, and, sometimes, alienage. Similarly, judicial identification of a limited number of fundamental rights, such as voting rights, sometimes seemed to trigger a strict scrutiny described accurately by Gerald Gunther as " 'strict' in theory and fatal in fact."

Though this two-tiered approach prevailed in many decisions of the Warren Court, inevitably the system became more flexible. "Intermediate scrutiny" is now explicitly used in sex discrimination cases, for example. The Court continues to wrestle with the problem suggested in footnote four cases involving constitutional claims of discrimination against whites, discrimination against illegitimate children, and total exclusion of some from important benefits such as public education. Parallel with footnote four, the argument today centers on the question whether it is an appropriate constitutional response to relegate individuals who claim discrimination at the hands of the majority to their remedies within the political process. Yet, as new groups claim discriminatory treatment in new legal realms, the meaning of "discrete and insular minorities" grows more problematic. Undeniably, however, the categories suggested in footnote four still channel the debate. A good example is John Hart Ely's *Democracy and Distrust* (1980), an influential book that expands upon footnote four's theme of political participation.

Justice Lewis H. Powell recently stated that footnote four contains "perhaps the most far-sighted dictum in our modern judicial heritage." Yet Powell also stressed that, in his view, it is important to remember that footnote four was merely obiter dictum and was intended to be no more. Even so, the tentative words of footnote four must be credited with helping to initiate and to define a new era of constitutional development. The questions raised by footnote four remain central to constitutional thought; controversy premised on this famous footnote shows no sign of abating.

—AVIAM SOIFER

Bibliography

Ball, Milner S. (1981). Don't Die Don Quixote: A Response and Alternative to Tushnet, Bobbitt, and the Revised Texas Version of Constitutional Law. *Texas Law Review* 59:787–813.

Ely, John Hart (1980). *Democracy and Distrust.* Cambridge, Mass.: Harvard University Press.

Lusky, Louis (1982). Footnote Redux: A *Carolene Products* Reminiscence. *Columbia Law Review* 82:1093–1105.

Powell, Lewis F., Jr. (1982). *Carolene Products* Revisited. *Columbia Law Review* 82: 1087–1092.

CARROLL v. UNITED STATES

267 U.S. 132 (1925)

In *Carroll* the Supreme Court held that an officer can stop and search an automobile without a warrant if there is probable cause to believe the vehicle contains contraband.

The Court noted that national legislation had routinely authorized warrantless searches of vessels suspected of carrying goods on which duty had been evaded. The analogy was shaky; Congress's complete control over international boundaries would justify searching any imports even without probable cause. The Court also approved this warrantless search on a dubious interpretation of the National Prohibition Act. But the Court had independent grounds beyond history and congressional intent for its decision: the search was justified as an implied exception to the Fourth Amendment's warrant requirement, because the vehicle might be driven away before a warrant could be

♦ **preemption**
A doctrine according to which legislation by the national government explicitly displaces or conflicts with state legislation or has so pervaded a particular area or topic of regulation as to preclude state legislation on the same subject.

See also

Erie Railroad v. *Tompkins*

McCulloch v. *Maryland*

West Coast Hotel Co. v. *Parrish*

NO WARRANT

Officers can stop and search a vehicle without a warrant if there is probable cause. (Corbis/Bettmann-UPI)

The Court noted that national legislation had routinely authorized warrantless searches of vessels suspected of carrying goods on which duty had been evaded.

obtained. Given these exigent circumstances, probable cause rather than a warrant satisfied the constitutional test of reasonableness. Indeed, legislative approval was not considered in the later automobile search cases.

—JACOB W. LANDYNSKI

CARTER v. CARTER COAL CO.

298 U.S. 238 (1936)

This was the New Deal's strongest case yet to come before the Supreme Court, and it lost. At issue was the constitutionality of the Bituminous Coal Act, which regulated the trade practices, prices, and labor relations of the nation's single most important source of energy, the bituminous industry in twenty-seven states. No industry was the subject of greater federal concern or of as many federal investigations. After the Court killed the National Industrial Recovery Act (NIRA) and

with it the bituminous code, Congress enacted a "Little NIRA" for bituminous coal. Although the statute contained no provision limiting the amount of bituminous that could be mined, the Court held it unconstitutional as a regulation of production.

The statute had two basic provisions, wholly separable and administered separately by independent administrative agencies. One agency supervised the price and trade-practices section of the statute; the other the labor section, dealing with maximum hours and minimum wages, and collective bargaining. In *Nebbia* v. *New York* (1934) the Court had sustained against a due process attack the principle of price-fixing in the broadest language. The labor sections seemed constitutional, because strikes had crippled interstate commerce and the national economy on numerous occasions and four times required federal troops to quell disorders. The federal courts had often enjoined the activities of the United Mine Workers as restraining interstate commerce.

The Court voted 6–3 to invalidate the labor provisions and then voted 5–4 to invalidate the entire statute. Justice George Sutherland for the majority did not decide on the merits of the price-fixing provisions. Had he attacked them, he might have lost Justice Owen J. Roberts, who had written the *Nebbia* opinion. The strategy was to hold the price provisions inseparable from the labor provisions, which were unconstitutional, thereby bringing down the whole act, despite the fact that its two sections were separable.

Sutherland relied mainly on the stunted version of the commerce clause that had dominated the Court's opinions in *United States* v. *E. C. Knight Co.* (1895) and more recently in the NIRA and Agricultural Adjustment Act cases: production is local; labor is part of production; therefore the Tenth Amendment reserves all labor matters to the states. That the major coal-producing states, disavowing states' rights, had supported the congressional enactment and emphasized the futility of state regulation of commerce meant nothing to the majority. Sutherland rejected the proposition that "the power of the federal government inherently extends to purposes affecting the nation as a whole with which the states severally cannot deal." In fact the government had relied on the commerce power, not inherent powers. But Sutherland stated that "the local character of mining, of manufacturing, and of crop growing is a fact, whatever may be done with the products." All labor matters—he enumerated them—were part of production. That labor disputes might catastrophically affect interstate commerce was undeniable but irrelevant, Sutherland reasoned, because their effect on interstate commerce must always be indirect and thus beyond congressional control. The effect was indirect because production intervened between a strike and interstate commerce. All the evils, he asserted, "are local evils over which the federal government has no legislative control."

Chief Justice Charles Evans Hughes dissented on the question whether the price-fixing provisions of the statute were separable. Justice Benjamin N. Cardozo, supported by Justices Louis D. Brandeis and Harlan F. Stone, dissented on the same ground, adding a full argument as to the constitutionality of the price-fixing section. He contended too that the issue on the labor section was not ripe for decision, because Carter asked for a decree to restrain the statute's operation before it went into operation. Cardozo's broad view of the commerce power confirmed the Roosevelt administration's belief that the majority's antilabor, anti-New Deal bias, rather than an unconstitutional taint on the statute, explained the decision.

Just a year later the Supreme Court totally reversed its field. In *National Labor Relations Board* v. *Jones & Laughlin Steel Corp.* (1937) the Court upheld the National Labor Relations Act, a Congressional enactment that prohibited unfair labor practices "affecting commerce," as applied to a steel mill. Effectively overruling *Carter*, the Court simply stated it found that decision "not controlling here." Four years later in *United States* v. *Darby* (1941) the Court explicitly overruled *Carter*.

—LEONARD W. LEVY

Bibliography

Stern, Robert L. (1946). The Commerce Clause and the National Economy, 1933–1946. *Harvard Law Review* 49: 664–674.

CASES AND CONTROVERSIES

Article III of the Constitution vests the judicial power of the United States in one constitutionally mandated Supreme Court and such subordinate federal courts as Congress may choose to establish. Federal judges are appointed for life with salaries that cannot be diminished, but they may exercise their independent and politically unaccountable power only to resolve "cases" and "controversies" of

This was the New Deal's strongest case yet to come before the Supreme Court, and it lost.

See also

Nebbia v. *New York*

the kinds designated by Article III, the most important of which are cases arising under the Constitution and other federal law. The scope of the federal judicial power thus depends in large measure on the Supreme Court's interpretations of the "case" and "controversy" limitation applicable to the Court itself and to other Article III tribunals.

That limitation not only inhibits Article III courts from arrogating too much power unto themselves, it also prevents Congress from compelling or authorizing decisions by federal courts in nonjudicial proceedings and precludes Supreme Court review of state court decisions in proceedings that are not considered "cases" or "controversies" under Article III. The limitation thus simultaneously confines federal judges and reinforces their ability to resist nonjudicial tasks pressed on them by others.

The linkage between independence and circumscribed power is a continuously important theme in "case" or "controversy" jurisprudence, as is the connection between "case" or "controversy" jurisprudence and the power of judicial review of government acts for constitutionality—a power that *Marbury* v. *Madison* (1803) justified primarily by the need to apply the Constitution as relevant law to decide a "case." During the Constitutional Convention of 1787, Edmund Randolph, proposed that the President and members of the federal judiciary be joined in a council of revision to veto legislative excesses. The presidential veto power was adopted instead, partly to keep the judiciary out of the legislative process and partly to insure that the judges would decide cases independently, without bias in favor of legislation they had helped to formulate. Similar concerns led the convention to reject Charles Pinckney's proposal to have the Supreme Court provide advisory opinions at the request of Congress or the president. Finally, in response to James Madison's doubts about extending the federal judicial power to expound the Constitution too broadly, the Convention made explicit its

understanding that the power extended only to "cases of a Judiciary nature." The Framers understood that the judicial power of constitutional governance would expand if the concept of "case" or "controversy" did.

What constitutes an Article III "case," of a "judiciary nature," is hardly self-evident. No definition was articulated when the language was adopted, but only an apparent intent to circumscribe the federal judicial function, and to insure that it be performed independently of the other branches. In this century, Justice Felix Frankfurter suggested that Article III precluded federal courts from deciding legal questions except in the kinds of proceedings entertained by the English and colonial courts at the time of the Constitution's adoption. But the willingness of English courts to give advisory opinions then—a practice clearly inconsistent with convention history and the Court's steadfast policy since 1793—refutes the suggestion. Moreover, from the outset the separation of powers aspect of the "case" or "controversy" limitation has differentiated constitutional courts (courts constituted under Article III) from others. Most fundamentally, however, the indeterminate historical contours of "cases" or "controversies" inevitably had to accommodate changes in the forms of litigation authorized by Congress, in the legal and social environment that accompanied the nation's industrial growth and the rise of the regulatory and welfare state, and in the place of the federal judiciary in our national life.

After two centuries of elaboration, the essential characteristics of Article III controversies remain imprecise and subject to change. Yet underlying the various manifestations of "case" or "controversy" doctrine are three core requirements: affected parties standing in an adverse relationship to each other, actual or threatened events that provoke a live legal dispute, and the courts' ability to render final and meaningful judgments. These criteria—concerning, respectively, the litigants, the facts, and judicial efficacy—

have both independent and interrelated significance.

As to litigants, only parties injured by a defendant's behavior have constitutional standing to sue. Collusive suits are barred because the parties' interests are not adverse.

As to extant factual circumstances, advisory opinions are banned. This limitation not only bars direct requests for legal rulings on hypothetical facts but also requires dismissal of unripe or moot cases, because, respectively, they are not yet live, or they once were but have ceased to be by virtue of subsequent events. The parties' future or past adversariness cannot substitute for actual, current adversariness. Disputes that have not yet begun or have already ended are treated as having no more present need for decision than purely hypothetical disputes.

The desire to preserve federal judicial power as an independent, effective, and binding force of legal obligation is reflected both in the finality rule, which bars decision if the judgment rendered would be subject to revision by another branch of government, and in the rule denying standing unless a judgment would likely redress the plaintiff's injury. These two rules are the clearest instances of judicial self-limitation to insure that when the federal courts do act, their judgments will be potent. To exercise judicial power ineffectively or as merely a preliminary gesture would risk undermining compliance with court decrees generally or lessening official and public acceptance of the binding nature of judicial decisions, especially unpopular constitutional judgments. Here the link between the limitations on judicial power and that power's independence and effectiveness is at its strongest.

Historically, congressional attempts to expand the use of Article III judicial power have caused the greatest difficulty, largely because the federal courts are charged simultaneously with enforcing valid federal law as an arm of the national government and with restraining unconstitutional behavior of the co-equal branches of that government. The enforcement role induces judicial receptivity to extensive congressional use of the federal courts, especially in a time of expansion of both the federal government's functions and the use of litigation to resolve public disputes. The courts' checking function, however, cautions judicial resistance to congressional efforts to enlarge the scope of "cases" or "controversies" for fear of losing the strength, independence, or finality needed to resist unconstitutional action by the political branches.

The early emphasis of "case" or "controversy" jurisprudence was on consolidating the judiciary's independence and effective power. The Supreme Court's refusal in 1793 to give President George Washington legal advice on the interpretation of treaties with France—the founding precedent for the ban on advisory opinions—rested largely on the desire to preserve the federal judiciary as a check on Congress and the executive when actual disputes arose. Similarly, Hayburn's Case (1792) established that federal courts would not determine which Revolutionary War veterans were entitled to disability pensions so long as the secretary of war had the final say on their entitlement: Congress could employ the federal judicial power only if the decisions of federal courts had binding effect. In the mid-nineteenth century the concern for maintaining judicial efficacy went beyond finality of substantive judgment to finality of remedy. The Supreme Court refused to accept appeals from the Court of Claims, which Congress had established to hear monetary claims against the United States, because the statutory scheme forbade payment until the Court certified its judgments to the treasury secretary for presentation to Congress, which would then have to appropriate funds. The Court concluded that Congress could not invoke Article III judicial power if the judges lacked independent authority to enforce their judgments as well as render them.

See also
Marbury v. *Madison*
Muskrat v. *United States*

*Historically,
congressional
attempts to expand
the use of Article III
judicial power have
caused the greatest
difficulty.*

Preserving judicial authority remains an important desideratum in the twentieth century, but the growing pervasiveness of federal law as a means of government regulation—often accompanied by litigant and congressional pressure to increase access to the federal courts—inevitably has accentuated the law-declaring enforcement role of the federal judiciary and tended to expand the "case" or "controversy" realm. *Muskrat* v. *United States* (1911) cited the courts' inability to execute a judgment as a reason to reject Congress's authorization of a test case to secure a ruling on the constitutionality of specific statutes it had passed. Similarly, the Court initially doubted the federal courts' power to give declaratory judgments. Yet, by the late 1930s the Supreme Court had upheld both its own power to review state declaratory judgment actions and the federal Declaratory Judgment Act of 1934. The declaratory judgment remedy authorizes federal courts to decide controversies before legal rights are actually violated. The judge normally enters no coercive order, but confines the remedy to a binding declaration of rights. So long as the controversy is a live one, between adverse parties, and the decision to afford a binding remedy rests wholly with the judiciary, the advisory opinion and finality objections pose no obstacles. A controversy brought to court too early may fail Article III ripeness criteria, but the declaratory remedy itself does not preclude the existence of a "case" or "controversy."

Congress has succeeded in expanding the reach of federal judicial power not only by creating new remedies for the federal courts to administer but also by creating new substantive rights for them to enforce. The Supreme Court maintains as a fundamental "case" or "controversy" requirement that a suing party, to have standing, must have suffered some distinctive "injury in fact." The injury must be particularized, not diffuse; citizen or taxpayer frustration with alleged government illegality is insufficient by itself. In theory, Congress cannot dispense with this requirement and authorize suits by individuals who are not in-

jured. Congress may, however, increase the potential for an injury that will satisfy Article III, simply by legislating protection of new rights, the violation of which amounts to a constitutional "injury in fact." For example, *Trafficante* v. *Metropolitan Life Insurance Company* (1972) held that a federal civil rights ban on housing discrimination could be enforced not only by persons refused housing but also by current tenants claiming loss of desired interracial associations; the Court interpreted the statute to create a legally protected interest in integrated housing. To a point, then, Article III "cases" or "controversies" expand correspondingly with the need to enforce new federal legislation. Yet the scope of congressional power to transform diffuse harm into cognizable Article III injury remains uncertain and apparently stops short of providing everyone a judicially enforceable generalized right to be free of illegal governmental behavior, without regard to more individualized effects.

In the 1980s the Court embarked on a series of decisions employing the case or controversy requirement to limit the federal courts' jurisdiction. In *Allen* v. *Wright* (1984) it denied standing to parents of minority public-school students asserting the Internal Revenue Service had failed to deny tax-exempt status to segregated private schools. The Court rejected the plaintiffs' claim that this interfered with their children's ability to receive a desegregated education. In *Valley Forge Christian College* v. *Americans United for Separation of Church and State* (1982) the Court held taxpayers lacked a case or controversy when they alleged the government had donated buildings to a sectarian school in violation of the Establishment Clause of the First Amendment. The 1990s saw this trend gain momentum. The Court held citizens did not allege a case or controversy when they claimed the Agency for International Development had failed to consult with the Interior Department over an overseas project that might harm the habitat of endangered species. *Lujan* v. *Defenders of Wildlife* (1992) so ruled despite a statute allowing "any person" to bring such an action. These and similar decisions evince the Court's determination to use the Constitution's case or controversy requirement to deny standing to those seeking to challenge government actions in a wide variety of settings.

The historically approved image is that federal judges decide politically significant public law issues only to resolve controversies taking the form of private litigation. Over the years, however, this picture has had to accommodate not only congressional creation of enforceable rights and remedies but also the modern realities of public forms of litigation such as the class action, the participation of organized public interest lawyers, and lawsuits aimed at reforming government structures and practices. Public law adjudication, especially constitutional adjudication, is certainly the most important function of the federal courts. The inclination to stretch the boundaries of "cases" or "controversies" to provide desired legal guidance on important social problems, although it has varied among federal judges and courts of different eras, increases in response to congressional authorization and the perception of social need. Offsetting that impulse, however, are two countervailing considerations. First, the judges realize that the more public the issues raised, the more democratically appropriate is a political rather than a judicial resolution. Second, they understand the importance of a litigation context that does not threaten judicial credibility, finality, or independence; that presents a realistic need for decision; and that provides adequate information and legal standards for confident, well-advised decision making. These competing considerations will continue to shape the meaning of "cases" and "controversies," setting the limits of the federal judicial function in ways that preserve the courts' checking and enforcement roles in the face of changes in the forms and objectives of litigation, in the dimensions of federal law, and in the expectations of government officials and members of the public.

—JONATHAN D. VARAT

Bibliography

Brilmayer, Lea (1979). The Jurisprudence of Article III: Perspectives on the "Case or Controversy" Requirement. *Harvard Law Review* 93:297–321.

Monaghan, Henry P. (1973). Constitutional Adjudication: The Who and When. *Yale Law Journal* 82:1363–1397.

Radcliffe, James E. (1978). *The Case-or-Controversy Provision.* University Park: Pennsylvania State University Press.

Tushnet, Mark V. (1980). The Sociology of Article III: A Response to Professor Brilmayer. *Harvard Law Review* 93: 1698–1733.

C

CENTRAL HUDSON
GAS & ELECTRIC
CORP. v. PUBLIC
SERVICE
COMMISSION

447 U.S. 557 (1980)

CENTRAL HUDSON GAS & ELECTRIC CORP. v. PUBLIC SERVICE COMMISSION

447 U.S. 557 (1980)

Central Hudson is the leading decision establishing ground rules for the Supreme Court's modern protection of commercial speech under the First Amendment. New York's Public Service Commission (PSC), in the interest of conserving energy, forbade electrical utilities to engage in promotional advertising. The Supreme Court held, 8–1, that this prohibition was unconstitutional.

Justice Lewis F. Powell, for the Court, used an analytical approach to commercial speech that combined a two-level theory with a balancing test. First, he wrote, it must be determined whether the speech in question is protected by the First Amendment. The answer to that question is affirmative unless the speech is "misleading" or it is "related to illegal activity" (for example, by proposing an unlawful transaction). Second, if the speech falls within the zone of First Amendment protection, the speech can be regulated only if government satisfies all the elements of a three-part interest-balancing

Central Hudson *is the leading decision establishing ground rules for the Supreme Court's modern protection of commercial speech under the First Amendment.*

See also

Equal Protection of the Laws

Freedom of Speech

*Certiorari is today
the chief mode of
the Supreme Court's
exercise of appellate
jurisdiction.*

◆ **certiorari**

*[Latin: to be made more
certain] A form of writ
directing a lower court to
forward the record of a
case to a higher court for
review; it is the primary
form of discretionary
appellate review by the
U.S. Supreme Court.*

formula: the asserted governmental interest must be "substantial"; the regulation must "directly advance" that interest; and the regulation must not be "more extensive than is necessary to serve that interest."

This intermediate standard of review seems loosely patterned after the standard used under the equal protection clause in cases involving sex discrimination. In those cases, the Court typically accepts that the governmental interest is important; when a statute is invalidated, the Court typically regards gender discrimination as an inappropriate means for achieving the governmental interest. The *Central Hudson* opinion followed this pattern: the promotional advertising was protected speech, and the state's interest in conservation was substantial and directly advanced by the PSC's regulation. However, prohibiting all promotional advertising, including statements that would not increase net energy use, was not the least restrictive means for achieving conservation.

Concurring opinions by Justices Harry A. Blackmun and John Paul Stevens, both joined by Justice William J. Brennan, adopted more speech-protective doctrinal positions. Justice William H. Rehnquist, in lone dissent, argued that the PSC's regulation was only an economic regulation of a state-regulated monopoly, raising no important First Amendment issue.

—KENNETH L. KARST

CERTIORARI, WRIT OF

A writ of certiorari is an order from a higher court directing a lower court to transmit the record of a case for review in the higher court. The writ was in use in England and America before the Revolution. Unlike the writ of error, which was used routinely to review final judgments of lower courts, certiorari was a discretionary form of review that might be granted even before the lower court had given judgment.

When Congress established the circuit courts of appeals in 1891, it expressly authorized the Supreme Court to review certain of these courts' decisions, otherwise declared to be "final," by issuing the writ of certiorari, which remained discretionary. In 1925 Congress expanded the Court's certiorari jurisdiction and reduced the availability of the writ of error (renamed appeal). Certiorari is today the chief mode of the Supreme Court's exercise of appellate jurisdiction. Proposals to abolish the Court's theoretically obligatory jurisdiction over appeals would leave appellate review entirely to certiorari, and thus to the Court's discretion.

By statute the Court is authorized to grant certiorari in any case that is "in" a federal court of appeals. Thus in an appropriate case the Court can bypass the court of appeals and directly review the action of the district court, as it did in the celebrated case of *United States v. Nixon* (1974).

The Supreme Court's rules have long stated some considerations governing the Court's discretionary grant or denial of certiorari. Three factors are emphasized: (1) conflicts among the highest courts of the states or the federal courts of appeals; (2) the resolution of important unsettled issues of federal law; and (3) the correction of error. These factors do not exhaust but only illustrate the considerations influencing the Court's certiorari policy.

—KENNETH L. KARST

Bibliography

Linzer, Peter (1979). The Meaning of Certiorari Denials. *Columbia Law Review* 79:1227–1305.

CHAMBERS v. FLORIDA

309 U.S. 227 (1940)

Chambers was the first coerced confession case to come before the Court since the landmark decision in *Brown* v. *Mississippi* (1936). In *Brown,* the physical torture being uncontested, the state had relied mainly on the point that the right against self-incrimination did not apply to state proceedings. In *Chambers,* before the state supreme court finally affirmed the convictions it had twice reversed so that juries could determine whether the confessions had been freely and voluntarily made, and the record showed no physical coercion. Moreover, the state contested the jurisdiction of the Supreme Court to review the judgments, arguing that there was no question of federal law to be denied. However, the Supreme Court, in an eloquent opinion by Justice Hugo L. Black, unanimously asserted jurisdiction and reversed the state court.

Black rejected the state's jurisdictional argument, declaring that the Supreme Court could determine for itself whether the confessions had been obtained by means that violated the constitutional guarantee of due process of law. Reviewing the facts Black found that the black prisoners, having been arrested on suspicion without warrant, had been imprisoned in a mob-dominated environment, held incommunicado, and interrogated over five days and through a night until they abandoned their disclaimers of guilt and "confessed." Police interrogation had continued until the prosecutor got what he wanted. On the basis of these facts Black wrote a stirring explanation of the rela-

tion between due process and free government, concluding that courts in our constitutional system stand "as havens of refuge for those who might otherwise suffer because they are helpless, weak, outnumbered, or because they are non-conforming victims of prejudice...." Applying the exclusionary rule of *Brown,* the Court held that psychological as well as physical torture violated due process.

—LEONARD W. LEVY

CHAMBERS v. MARONEY

399 U.S. 42 (1970)

In this important Fourth Amendment case involving the automobile exception to the search warrant clause, the police had seized a car without a warrant and had searched it later, without a warrant, after having driven it to the police station, where they impounded it. Justice Byron R. White for the Supreme Court acknowledged that the search could not be justified as having been conducted as a search incident to arrest; nor could he find exigent circumstances that justified the warrantless search.

White simply fudged the facts. He declared that there was "no difference between

Applying the exclusionary rule of Brown, *the Court held that psychological as well as physical torture violated due process.*

See also

Brown v. *Mississippi*

THE FOURTH AMENDMENT

(Historical Origins)

Appended to the United States Constitution as part of the Bill of Rights in 1789, the Fourth Amendment declares that "The right of the people to be secure in their persons, houses, papers and effects against unreasonable searches and seizures shall not be violated, and no warrants shall issue but upon probable cause, supported by oath or affirmation, and particularly describing the place to be searched and the persons or things to be seized." In identifying the "specific" warrant as its orthodox method of search, the amendment constitutionally repudiated its antithesis, the general warrant.

The general warrant did not confine its reach to a particular person, place, or object but allowed its bearer to arrest, search, and seize as his suspicions directed. In 1763, a typical warrant by the British secretaries of state commanded "diligent search" for the unidentified author, printer, and publisher of a satirical journal, *The North Briton, No. 45,* and the seizure of their papers. At least five houses were consequently searched, forty-nine (mostly innocent) persons arrested, and thousands of books and papers confiscated. Resentment against such invasions ultimately generated an antidote in the Fourth Amendment and is crucial to its understanding.

Until this case, mere probable cause for a search, as judged only by a police officer, did not by itself justify a warrantless search.

In 1895 Congress forbade interstate transportation of lottery tickets, seeking to safeguard public morals.

See also

Fuller, Melville W.

on the one hand seizing and holding a car before presenting the probable cause issue to a magistrate and on the other hand carrying out an immediate search without a warrant." Either course was "reasonable under the Fourth Amendment," but the police had followed neither course in this case. Probable cause for the search had existed at the time of the search, and White declared without explanation that probable cause still existed later when the police made the search at the station, when the felons were in custody. However, the possibility that they might drive off in the car did not exist; that possibility had alone occasioned the automobile exception in the first place. Absent a risk that the culprits might use the vehicle to escape with the fruits of their crime, the constitutional distinction between houses and cars did not matter. White saw no difference in the practical consequences of choosing between an immediate search without a warrant, when probable cause existed, and "the car's immobilization until a warrant is obtained." That logic was irrefutable and irrelevant, because the failure of the police to obtain the warrant gave rise to the case. Only Justice John Marshall Harlan dissented from this line of reasoning.

Until this case mere probable cause for a search, as judged only by a police officer, did not by itself justify a warrantless search; the case is significant, too, because of its implied rule that exigent circumstances need not justify the warrantless search of a car. Following *Chambers*, the Court almost routinely assumed that if a search might have been made at the time of arrest, any warrantless search conducted later, when the vehicle was impounded, was a valid one.

—LEONARD W. LEVY

CHAMPION v. AMES

188 U.S. 321 (1903)

As the twentieth century opened, the Supreme Court began to sustain use of the commerce clause as an instrument to remedy various social and economic ills. In 1895 Congress forbade interstate transportation of lottery tickets, seeking to safeguard public morals. Opponents challenged the act on three grounds: the tickets themselves were not subjects of commerce, Congress's power to regulate interstate commerce did not extend to outright prohibition, and such a power would violate the Tenth Amendment's reservation of certain powers to the states.

A 5–4 Court sustained the act, emphasizing Congress's plenary power over commerce. Because the tickets indicated a cash prize might be won, they were items liable to be bought or sold—thus, subjects of commerce and so subject to regulation. Citing the complete prohibition on foreign commerce in the Embargo Act of 1807, Justice John Marshall Harlan asserted that the power of regulation necessarily included the power of prohibition. Although he rejected the contention that "Congress may arbitrarily exclude from commerce among the states any article . . . it may choose," Harlan justified the ban on transporting lottery tickets on the ground that Congress alone had power to suppress "an evil of such appalling character," thus propounding the noxious products doctrine. Harlan dismissed the Tenth Amendment objection: that provision was no bar to a power that had been "expressly delegated to Congress."

Chief Justice Melville W. Fuller led Justices David Brewer, Rufus Peckham, and George Shiras in dissent. Fuller noted that the motive underlying the legislation was to suppress gambling, not to regulate commerce. He feared the disruption of distinct spheres of authority and the "creation of a centralized government." He also challenged Harlan's assertion that the commerce power included the right of prohibition. The Court, citing *Champion*, however, would soon uphold the Pure Food and Drug Act (in *Hipolite Egg Company v. United States*, 1911), the Mann Act (in *Hoke v. United States*, 1913), and others, relying on its expansive view of the commerce clause.

—DAVID GORDON

CHANDLER v. FLORIDA

449 U.S. 560 (1981)

The Supreme Court here distinguished away *Estes* v. *Texas* (1965), in which it had held that the televising of a criminal trial violated due process of law because of the inherently prejudicial impact on criminal defendants. In *Chandler* an 8–0 Court ruled that the prejudicial effect must be actually shown by the facts of the particular case; Florida's statute, at issue here, imposed adequate safeguards on the use of electronic media in court, thereby insuring due process of law. Presumably the decision promoted freedom of the press and the principle of a public trial.

—LEONARD W. LEVY

CHAPLINSKY v. NEW HAMPSHIRE

315 U.S. 568 (1941)

In *Chaplinsky*, Justice Frank Murphy, writing for a unanimous Supreme Court, introduced into First Amendment jurisprudence the two-level theory that "There are certain well-defined and narrowly limited classes of speech, the prevention and punishment of which have never been thought to raise any constitutional problem. These include the lewd and obscene, the profane, the libelous, and the insulting or 'fighting words'—those which by their very utterance inflict injury or tend to incite an immediate breach of the peace." *Chaplinsky* itself arose under a "fighting words" statute, which the state court had interpreted to punish "words likely to cause an average addressee to fight." In this narrow context the decision can be seen as an application of the clear and present danger test. *Cohen* v. *California* (1971), emphasizing this rationale, offered protection to an offensive term that created no danger of violence.

In its broader conception of categories of speech excluded from First Amendment protection, the case served as an important doc-

trinal source for many later obscenity and libel decisions.

However, the Supreme Court has in recent decades greatly limited the broad holding of *Chaplinsky*. A statute defining "fighting words" in overbroad terms will not support a conviction, even though the same offensive words might have been punishable under a narrowly drafted law. And the Court has made clear that the fighting words must be likely to cause a violent response by the person actually addressed, as in *Gooding* v. *Wilson* (1972). Most recently, in *R.A.V.* v. *City of St. Paul* (1992), a narrow majority ruled that an ordinance proscribing cross burning and other "symbol[s] arous[ing] anger, alarm or resentment . . . on the basis of race, color, creed, religion or gender" was invalid because it improperly discriminated among various classes of fighting words. The other four justices in *R.A.V.* concurred on the basis of the ordinance's overbreadth. *Chaplinsky* was thus an important point of departure, but the train has moved in unexpected directions.

—MARTIN SHAPIRO

CHARLES RIVER BRIDGE v. WARREN BRIDGE COMPANY

11 Peters 420 (1837)

The Charles River Bridge case reflected the tension within Alexis de Tocqueville's proposition that the American people desired a government that would allow them "to acquire the things they covet and which [would] . . . not debar them from the peaceful enjoyment of those possessions which they have already acquired." A metaphor for the legal strains that accompanied technological change, the case spoke more to the emerging questions of railroad development than to the immediate problem of competing bridges over the Charles River.

Following the Revolution, some investors petitioned the Massachusetts legislature for a

Chaplinsky *itself arose under a "fighting words" statute, which the state court had interpreted to punish "words likely to cause an average addressee to fight."*

See also

Estes v. Texas

Freedom of the Press

charter to build a bridge over the Charles River, linking Boston and Charlestown. Commercial interests in both cities supported the proposal, and the state issued the grant in 1785. The charter authorized the proprietors to charge a variety of tolls for passage, pay an annual fee to Harvard College for the loss of its exclusive ferry service across the river, and then, after forty years, return the bridge to the state in "good repair."

Construction of the bridge began immediately, and in 1786, it was open to traffic, benefiting the proprietors, the communities, and the back country. The land route from Medford to Boston, for example, was cut from thirteen to five miles, and trade dramatically increased as the bridge linked the area-wide market. Success invited imitation, and other communities petitioned the legislature for bridge charters. When the state authorized the West Boston Bridge to Cambridge in 1792, the Charles River Bridge proprietors

asked for compensation for the revenue losses they anticipated, and the state extended their charter from forty to seventy years. Ironically, that extension provided the basis for future political and legal assaults against the Charles River Bridge. Other bridges followed and no compensation was offered. The state specifically refuted any monopoly claims and the Charles River Bridge proprietors refrained from claiming any.

Increasing prosperity and population raised the collection of tolls to nearly $20,000 annually in 1805; the share values had increased over 300 percent in value. The toll rates having remained constant since 1786, profits multiplied. Swollen profits stimulated community criticism and animated a long-standing hostility toward monopolies. Opportunity was the watchword and special privilege its bane.

Beginning in 1823, Charlestown merchants launched a five-year effort to build a competing "free" bridge over the Charles.

**BATTLE OF
THE BRIDGES**

Charles River Bridge, *which involved competing bridges spanning the Charles River in Boston, was the forerunner to cases involving railroad development. (Corbis/Robert Holmes)*

They argued that the existing facility was inadequate, overcrowded, and dangerous; but basically, they appealed for public support on the grounds that the tolls on the Charles River Bridge were "burdensome, vexatious, and odious." The proprietors, defending the bridge's utility, offered to expand and improve it. They consistently maintained that the legislature could not grant a new bridge franchise in the vicinity without compensating them for the loss of tolls. But the political climate persuaded legislators to support the new bridge, and in 1828, after rejecting various schemes for compensation, the legislature approved the Warren Bridge charter. The act established the bridge's termini at 915 feet from the existing bridge on the Boston side, and at 260 feet from it on the Charlestown side. The new bridge was given the same toll schedule as the Charles River Bridge, but the state provided that after the builders recovered their investment and five percent interest, the bridge would revert to the commonwealth. In any event, the term for tolls could not exceed six years. Governor Levi Lincoln had previously vetoed similar legislation, but in 1828 he quietly acquiesced.

The new bridge, completed in six months, was an instant success—but at the expense of the Charles River Bridge. During the first six months of the Warren Bridge's operations, receipts for the old bridge rapidly declined. Net income for the Warren Bridge in the early 1830s consistently was twice that for the Charles River Bridge.

Counsel for the old bridge proprietors wasted little time in carrying their arguments to the courts. After Daniel Webster and Lemuel Shaw failed to gain an injunction to prevent construction of the new bridge, they appeared in the state supreme court to argue the merits of the charter in 1829, nearly one year after the bridge's completion. Shaw and Webster contended that the Charles River Bridge proprietors were successors to the Harvard ferry's exclusive franchise. In addition, they argued that the tolls represented

the substance of the 1785 charter. Although the charter for the new bridge did not take away the plaintiffs' franchise, the 1828 act effectively destroyed the tolls—the essence and only tangible property of the franchise. The lawyers thus contended that the new bridge charter violated the contract clause and the state constitutional prohibition against expropriation of private property without compensation. The Warren Bridge defendants denied the old bridge's monopoly claims and emphasized that the state had not deprived the Charles River Bridge proprietors' continued right to take tolls. They also maintained that the old bridge proprietors had waived exclusivity when they accepted an extension of their franchise in 1792 after the state had chartered the West Boston Bridge.

The state supreme court, dividing equally, dismissed the complaint to facilitate a writ of error to the United States Supreme Court. The Jacksonian Democrats on the state court supported the state and their Whig brethren opposed it. The former rejected monopoly claims and berated the Charles River Bridge proprietors for their failure to secure an explicit monopoly grant. Chief Justice Isaac Parker, acknowledging that the 1785 grant was not exclusive, agreed that the state could damage existing property interests for the community's benefit without compensation. But he insisted that "immutable principles of justice" demanded compensation when the forms of property were indistinguishable. He conceded that canals and railroads might legitimately destroy the value of a turnpike; but when the state chartered a similar franchise, then operators of the existing property could claim an indemnity.

The United States Supreme Court first heard arguments in the case in March 1831. Although absences and disagreements prevented any decision before John Marshall's death in 1835, the Court's records offer good circumstantial evidence that he had supported the new bridge. Following several new appointments and Roger B. Taney's confir-

Taney's opinion sought to balance property rights against community needs by strictly construing the old bridge charter.

♦ writ
A court order.

mation as Chief Justice, the Court heard reargument in January 1837. Webster again appeared for the plaintiffs; defendants engaged Simon Greenleaf of Harvard, a close associate of Joseph Story and James Kent. Both sides essentially continued the arguments advanced in the state court. Finally, in February 1837, after nearly nine years of litigation, the Court decisively ruled in behalf of the state's right to charter the new bridge.

Taney's opinion sought to balance property rights against community needs by strictly construing the old bridge charter. He rejected the proprietors' exclusivity claim, contending that nothing would pass by implication. "The charter . . . is a written instrument which must speak for itself," he wrote, "and be interpreted by its own terms." He confidently asserted that the "rule" of strict construction was well settled and he particularly invoked Marshall's 1830 *Providence Bank* v. *Billings* opinion, rejecting a bank's claim to implied tax immunity. Like Marshall, Taney concluded that the implications of exclusivity constituted a derogation of community rights. He argued that the community's "interests" would be adversely affected if the state surrendered control of a line of travel for profit. Taney neatly combined old Federalist doctrines of governmental power with the leaven of Jacksonian rhetoric: "The continued existence of a government would be of no great value," he believed, "if by implications and presumptions, it was disarmed of the powers necessary to accomplish the ends of its creations; and the functions it was designed to perform, transferred to the hands of privileged corporations."

But the touchstone of Taney's opinion was its practical response to the contemporary reality of public policy needs. Taking note of technological changes and improvements, such as the substitution of railroad traffic for that of turnpikes and canals, Taney argued that the law must be a spur, not an impediment, to change. If the Charles River Bridge proprietors could thwart such change, he feared that the courts would be inundated with suits seeking to protect established property forms. Turnpike companies, for example, "awakening from their sleep," would call upon courts to halt improvements which had taken their place. Railroad and canal properties would be jeopardized and venture capital would be discouraged. The Supreme Court, he concluded, would not "sanction principles" that would prevent states from enjoying the advances of science and technology. Taney thus cast the law with the new entrepreneurs and risk-takers as the preferred agents for material progress.

In his dissent Justice Story rejected Taney's reliance upon strict construction and advanced an imposing line of precedents demonstrating that private grants had been construed in favor of the grantees. "It would be a dishonour of the government," Story said, "that it should pocket a fair consideration, and then quibble as to the obscurities and implications of its own contract." But Story's dissent was not merely a defense of vested rights. Like Taney, he, too, was concerned with progress and public policy. But whereas Taney emphasized opportunity, Story maintained that security of title and the full enjoyment of existing property was a necessary inducement for private investment in public improvements. Story insisted that the proprietors were entitled to compensation. He thus discounted the potentially staggering social and economic costs implicit in a universal principle requiring just compensation when new improvement projects diminished the value of existing franchises.

Story's position reflected immediate reality. Several years earlier, the state's behavior in the bridge controversy had discouraged stock sales for the proposed Boston and Worcester Railroad. Lagging investment finally had forced the legislature to grant the railroad a thirty-year guarantee of exclusive privileges on the line of travel.

Given the materialism of the American people, Taney's arguments had the greater appeal and endurance. He allied the law with broadened entrepreneurial opportunities at the expense of past assets. Nothing threatened the economic aspirations of Americans more than the scarcity of capital; nothing, therefore, required greater legal encouragement than venture capital, subject only to the risks of the marketplace. These were the concerns that took a local dispute over a free bridge out of its provincial setting and thrust it into the larger debate about political economy. In a society that placed a premium on "progress" and on the release of creative human energy to propel that progress, the decision was inevitable. And throughout American economic development, the Charles River Bridge case has fostered the process that Joseph Schumpeter called "creative destruction," whereby new forms of property destroy old ones in the name of progress.

—STANLEY I. KUTLER

Bibliography

Kutler, Stanley I. ([1971]1977). *Privilege and Creative Destruction: The Charles River Bridge Case.* Rev. ed. New York: Norton.

CHASE, SALMON P.

(1808–1873)

Born in New Hampshire, Salmon Portland Chase enjoyed an elite education as a private pupil of his uncle, Episcopal Bishop Philander Chase of Ohio, as a Dartmouth student (graduating in 1826), and as an apprentice lawyer (1827–30) to United States Attorney General William Wirt. Subsequently, Chase rose quickly as a Cincinnati attorney, beginning also his numerous, seemingly opportunistic, successive changes in political party affiliations. Abandoning Whig, then Democratic ties, Chase became in turn a member of the Liberty party and of the Republican organizations, winning elections to the United States Senate (1848–55, 1860–61), and to Ohio's governorship (1856–60). He was an unsuccessful candidate for the Republican presidential nomination in 1860. Abraham Lincoln appointed Chase secretary of the treasury (1861–64), and Chief Justice of the United States (1864–73). Yet in 1864 Chase tried to thwart Lincoln's second term, in 1868 he maneuvered for the Democratic presidential nomination, and in 1872 he participated in the "Liberal Republican" schism against Ulysses S. Grant.

Such oscillations reflected more than Chase's large personal ambitions. Constitutional, legal, and moral concerns gave his public life coherence and purpose. These concerns derived from Chase's early conviction that men and society were easily corrupted, that slavery was America's primary spoiling agent, and that political corruption was a close second. Although Chase, observing Wirt in the *Antelope* litigation (1825), found the doctrine in Somerset's Case (1772) an acceptable reconciliation of slavery and the Constitution as of that year, later events, especially those attending fugitive slave recaptures, unpunished assaults on abolitionists, and increases in slave areas due especially to the Mexican War and the treaties that closed it off, brought him to accept abolitionist constitutional theory. Chase concluded that slavery's expansion beyond existing limits would demoralize white labor.

The first steps on this ultimately abolitionist road came from Chase's association with and brave defenses of Ohio antislavery activists, including James Birney, and of fugitive slaves; such defenses won Chase the nickname "attorney general for runaway negroes." A merely opportunistic Cincinnati lawyer would have had easier routes to success than this. Defending runaways and their abettors, Chase abjured higher law pleadings popular among abolitionists; he focused instead on technical procedures and on a carefully developed restatement of state-centered federalism in which he insisted that nonslave

C

Chase brought a particular sense of urgency to the goal of protecting individual rights.

jurisdictions also enjoyed states' rights. Slave states were able to export their recapture laws into free states via the federal fugitive slavery statutes. Chase argued that residents of free states also deserved to have the laws of their states concerning the status of citizens enjoy reciprocal effect and respect within slavery jurisdictions. Such a traffic of free state laws and customs across the federal system was impossible (and was to remain so until Appomattox). Chase insisted that residents of free states possessed at least the right to protect their co-residents of any race within those states from being reduced to servitude without due process.

Chase's evolving ideas culminated in a "freedom national" position, a general program for resolving the dilemma that slavery posed to a federal society based on assumptions of legal remedies, civil rights, and civil liberties. In his thinking, free labor was more than a marketplace phenomenon. It was a moral imperative, a complex of ethical relationships that the nation, under the Constitution, must nurture. Reformed, corruption-free two-party politics, with even blacks voting, was the way Chase discerned finally to nationalize freedom, a nationalization based upon acceptance of the Declaration of Independence and the Bill of Rights as minimum definitions of the nation's interest in private rights adversely affected by state wrongs or private inequities.

The Civil War and the wartime and post–Appomattox Reconstruction of the southern states were the contexts in which Chase refined his thinking about individuals' rights and the nation's duty to protect them. Lincoln found a place in his cabinet for every one of the major competitors for the Republican presidential nomination in 1860, and Chase became secretary of the treasury. Once the war started, Chase had responsibility to provide an adequate circulating medium for the suddenly ballooning marketplace needs of the government, of the banking and commercial communities of the Union states, and of the millions

of urban and rural entrepreneurs who rushed to expand production. Chase helped key congressmen to shape the historic wartime laws on national banking, income taxation, and legal tender (the legitimacy of the last of which Chase himself was to question as Chief Justice, in the *Legal Tender Cases*).

The most outspoken abolitionist in Lincoln's cabinet, Chase also carved out a role for Treasury officials, who were responsible for administering rebels' confiscated property, in the Army's coastal experiments for abandoned, runaway, or otherwise freed blacks. He applauded the Confiscation Acts, the Emancipation Proclamation, the major elements in Lincoln's Military Reconstruction, the Freedmen's Bureau statute, and the Thirteenth Amendment. Upon Roger B. Taney's death in late 1864, Lincoln, well aware of Chase's antipathy to the decision in *Dred Scott* v. *Sandford* (1857) and his commitment to irreversible emancipation, both of which the president shared, named the Ohioan to be Chief Justice.

After Appomattox, Chase, for his first years as Chief Justice, found that the work of the Court was almost exclusively with white men's rights rather than with the momentous, race-centered public questions that faced the Congress and the new president, Andrew Johnson. On circuit, however, Chase's *In re Turner* opinion sustained broadly, in favor of a black female claimant, the provisions of the 1866 Civil Rights Act for enforcing the Thirteenth Amendment. In his opinion, Chase insisted that federal rights against servitude were defendable in national courts as against both state or private action or inaction, and he emphasized that a state's standard of right could serve as an adequate federal standard so long as the state did not discriminate racially.

Some contemporaries applauded *In re Turner* as an articulation of the new, nationalized federal system of rights that the Thirteenth Amendment appeared to have won. Chase's other circuit opinions did not, therefore, disturb race egalitarians, and generally won favor in professional legal and commercial media. These opinions dealt with numerous litigations concerning private relationships such as marriage licenses, trusts and inheritances, business contracts, and insurance policies made under rebel state dispensation. Chase recognized the validity of these legal arrangements. His decisions helped greatly to stabilize commerce and family relationships in the South.

The course of post–Appomattox Reconstruction as controlled both by President Johnson and by Congress, troubled Chase deeply. He knew, from his work in Lincoln's cabinet, how narrowly the Union had escaped defeat and tended, therefore, to sustain wartime measures. Yet he revered both the checks and balances of the national government and the state-centered qualities of the federal system reflected in the Constitution. Therefore, in *Ex Parte Milligan* (1866), Chase, still new on the Court, joined in the unanimous statement that Milligan, who had been tried by a military court, should preferably have been prosecuted in a civilian court for his offenses. But Chase, with three other Justices, dissented from the majority's sweeping condemnation of any federal military authority over civilians in a nonseceded state. The dissenters insisted instead that Congress possessed adequate war power to authorize military courts.

Chase again dissented from the 5–4 decision in the *Test Oath Cases* (1867). Though privately detesting oath tests, Chase held to a public position that legislators, not judges, bore the responsibility to prescribe professional qualifications and licensing standards. By this time Congress had decided on Military Reconstruction. Mississippi officials, appointed earlier by Johnson, asked the Court for an injunction against the president's enforcing Congress's reconstruction law, and for a ruling that it was unconstitutional. For an unanimous Court, Chase refused to honor the petition (*Mississippi* v. *Johnson*, 1867), re-

lying on the political question doctrine. He agreed with his colleagues also in *Georgia* v. *Stanton* (1867) in refusing to allow the Court to intrude into political questions involving enforcement of the Reconstruction statutes. Mississippians again tried to enlist the Court against Congress. In early 1868 *Ex Parte McCardle* raised *Milligan*-like issues of military trials of civilians, and of the Court's jurisdiction to hear such matters under the Habeas Corpus Act of 1867. Congress thereupon diminished the Court's appellate jurisdiction under that statute. Chase, for the Court, acquiesced in the diminution, though pointing out that all other habeas jurisdiction remained in the Court.

He supported Congress's Military Reconstruction as a statutory base for both state restorations and black suffrage, but he was offended by the Third Reconstruction Act (July 1867), providing that military decisions would control civil judgments in the South. The impeachment of Andrew Johnson, with Chase presiding over the Senate trial, seemed to threaten the destruction of tripartite checks and balances. Chase drifted back toward his old Democratic states' rights position, a drift signaled by his advocacy of universal amnesty for ex-rebels and universal suffrage. He had tried, unsuccessfully, to have the Fourteenth Amendment provide for both. His enhanced or renewed respect for states' rights was evident in *United States* v. *DeWitt* (1869), in which the Court declared a federal law forbidding the transit or sale of dangerous naphtha-adulterated kerosene, to be an excessive diminution of state police powers.

This decision, the first in which the Court denied Congress a capacity to act for regulatory purposes under the commerce clause, like the decisions on Reconstruction issues, suggests how far the Chase Court engaged in judicial activism. Striking in this regard were the *Legal Tender Cases*. The first of these, *Hepburn* v. *Griswold* (1870), resulted in a 4–3 decision that the 1862 law authorizing greenbacks as legal tender was invalid as applied to

See also

Dred Scott v. *Sandford*

Texas v. *White*

contracts made before passage of the statute. Chase, for the thin majority, insisted that the statute violated the Fifth Amendment's due process clause, concluding that the spirit of the contract clause, though by its terms restraining only the states, applied also to the federal government. The trio of dissenters—all, like Chase, Republican appointees—saw the money and war powers as adequate authority for the statute.

Then, later in 1870, President Ulysses S. Grant named two new Justices to the Court: Joseph P. Bradley and William Strong. The new appointees created, in *Knox* v. *Lee* (1871), the second *Legal Tender Case* decision, a majority that overruled *Hepburn.* The new majority now upheld the nation's authority to make paper money legal tender for contracts entered into either before or after enactment of the statute, an authority not pinned necessarily to the war power.

Chase was in the minority in the *Slaughterhouse Cases* (1873) in which the majority found no violation of the Thirteenth or Fourteenth Amendments in a state's assignment of a skilled-trade monopoly to private parties. The doctrine of *Slaughterhouse,* that the privileges of United States citizenship did not protect basic civil rights, signaled a sharp retreat from Chase's own *In re Turner* position, and was a fateful step by the Court toward what was to become a general retreat from Reconstruction.

Slaughterhouse, along with Chase's anti-Grant position in 1872, closed off Chase's long and tumultuous career; he died in 1873. His career was consistent in its anticorruption positions and in its infusions of moral and ethical ideas into constitutional, legal, and political issues. Party-jumping was incidental to Chase's ends of a moral democracy, federally arranged in a perpetual union of perpetual states; he gave this concept effective expression in *Texas* v. *White* (1869).

To be sure, neither Chase nor "his" Court created novel legal doctrines. But he, and it, helped greatly to reclaim for the Court a significant role in determining the limits of certain vital public policies, both national and state. In the tumults of Reconstruction, while avoiding unwinnable clashes with Congress, Chase bravely insisted that effective governmental power and individual rights could coexist. He and his fellow Justices advanced novel constitutional doctrines drawn from the prohibitions against ex post facto laws and bills of attainder, and from the commerce and money powers. In retrospect, such experiments with doctrine take on the quality of interim defenses of judicial authority between prewar reliance on the contract clause, as example, and the post-Chase development of the due process clause of the Fourteenth Amendment.

At the same time, Chase tried to focus the Court's attention on individuals' rights as redefined first by the Thirteenth and then by the Fourteenth Amendment, as against both private and public wrongs. As one who for years had observed at first hand the capacity of nation and states and private persons to wrong individuals, Chase, as Chief Justice, brought a particular sense of urgency to the goal of protecting individual rights. He failed to convert a majority of his brethren to this task. Instead, America deferred its constitutional commitments.

—HAROLD M. HYMAN

Bibliography

Fairman, Charles (1971). *History of the Supreme Court of the United States: Reconstruction and Reunion, 1864–1888.* New York: Macmillan.

Hughes, David (1965). Salmon P. Chase: Chief Justice. *Vanderbilt Law Review* 18: 569–614.

Hyman, Harold M., and Wiecek, William M. (1982). *Equal Justice under Law: Constitutional Development 1835–1875.* Chaps. 11–13. New York: Harper & Row.

Walker, Peter F. (1978). *Moral Choices.* Chaps. 13–14. Baton Rouge: Louisiana State University Press.

CHASE COURT

(1864–1873)

The decade of Salmon P. Chase's tenure as Chief Justice of the United States was one of the more turbulent in the history of the Supreme Court. Laboring under the cloud of hostility engendered by *Dred Scott* v. *Sandford* (1857), hurt by partisan attacks from without and divisions within, staggering under loads of new business, the Chase Court nevertheless managed to absorb and consolidate sweeping new jurisdictional grants to the federal courts and to render some momentous decisions.

The Chase Court displayed an unusual continuity of personnel, which was offset by political and ideological heterogeneity. Of the nine men Chase joined on his accession (the Court in 1864 was composed of ten members), seven served throughout all or nearly all his brief tenure. But this largely continuous body was divided within itself by party and ideological differences. John Catron, who died in 1865, James M. Wayne, who died in 1867, and Robert C. Grier, who suffered a deterioration in his faculties that caused his brethren to force him to resign in 1870, were Democrats. Nathan Clifford, an appointee of President James Buchanan, and Stephen J. Field were also Democrats, the latter a War Democrat. Samuel F. Miller, David Davis, and Joseph P. Bradley were Republicans. Chase himself was an ex-Democrat who had helped form the Republican party in 1854, but he drifted back to the Democratic party after the war and coveted its presidential nomination. William Strong, Grier's replacement, and Noah Swayne were also Democrats who turned Republican before the war. Like the Chief Justice, Davis never successfully shook off political ambitions; he accepted and then rejected the Labor Reform party's nomination for the presidency in 1872. From 1870, Republicans dominated the Court, which had long been controlled by Democrats.

The work of the Supreme Court changed greatly during Chase's tenure. In 1862 and 1866 Congress realigned the federal circuits, so as to reduce the influence of the southern states, which under the Judiciary Act of 1837 had five of the nine circuits. Under the Judiciary Act of 1866 the southern circuits were reduced to two. By the same statute, Congress reduced the size of the Court from ten to seven members, mainly to enhance the efficiency of its work, not to punish the Court or deprive President Andrew Johnson of appointments to it. In 1869 Congress again raised the size of the Court to nine, where it has remained ever since. More significantly, the business of the Court expanded. By 1871 the number of cases docketed had doubled in comparison to the war years. This increase resulted in some measure from an extraordinary string of statutes enacted between 1863 and 1867 expanding the jurisdiction of the federal courts in such matters as removal of cases from state to federal courts, habeas corpus, claims against the United States, and bankruptcy.

The Chase Court was not a mere passive, inert repository of augmented jurisdiction: it expanded its powers of judicial review to an extent unknown to earlier Courts. During Chase's brief tenure, the Court held eight federal statutes unconstitutional (as compared with only two in its entire prior history), and struck down state statutes in thirty-six cases (as compared with thirty-eight in its prior history). The attitude that produced this judicial activism was expressed in private correspondence by Justice Davis, when he noted with satisfaction that the Court in *Ex Parte Milligan* (1866) had not "toadied to the prevalent idea, that the legislative department of the government can override everything." This judicial activism not only presaged the Court's involvement in policy during the coming heyday of substantive due process; it also plunged the Chase Court into some of the most hotly contested matters of its own time, especially those connected with Reconstruction. The Court also attracted the public eye because of the activ-

Nearly all the cases in which the Supreme Court disposed of Reconstruction issues were decided during Chase's tenure.

CHASE COURT

(1864–1873)

♦ **dictum (pl. dicta)**
[Latin: something said] Formerly an authoritative pronouncement. Now commonly used as an abbreviation of "obiter dictum," which means "said by the way."

ities of two of its members: Chase's and Davis's availability as presidential candidates, and Chase's firm, impartial service in presiding over the United States Senate as a court of impeachment in the trial of Andrew Johnson.

The Chase Court is memorable for its decisions in four areas: Reconstruction, federal power (in matters not directly related to Reconstruction), state regulatory and tax power, and the impact of the Fourteenth Amendment.

Nearly all the cases in which the Supreme Court disposed of Reconstruction issues were decided during Chase's tenure. The first issue to come up was the role of military commissions. In *Ex Parte Vallandigham,* decided in February 1864 (ten months before Chase's nomination), the Court refused to review the proceedings of a military commission, because the commission is not a court. But that did not settle the issue of the constitutional authority of military commissions. The matter came up again, at an inopportune time, in *Ex Parte Milligan,* decided in December 1866. Milligan had been arrested, tried, convicted, and sentenced to be hanged by a military commission in Indiana in 1864 for paramilitary activities on behalf of the Confederacy. The Court unanimously ruled that his conviction was illegal because Indiana was not in a theater of war, because the civil courts were functioning and competent to try Milligan for treason, and because he was held in violation of the provisions of the Habeas Corpus Act of 1863. But the Court split, 5–4, over an obiter dictum in Justice Davis's majority opinion stating that the Congress could never authorize military commissions in areas outside the theater of operations where the civil courts were functioning. The Chief Justice, writing for the minority, declared that Congress did have the power to authorize commissions, based on the several war powers clauses of Article I, section 8, but that it had not done so; hence Milligan's trial was unauthorized.

Milligan created a furor in Congress and deeply implicated the Court in the politics of Reconstruction. Assuming that military commissions were essential to the conduct of Reconstruction, Democrats taunted Republicans that *Milligan* implied that they were unconstitutional, and hence that proposed Republican measures providing for military trials in the Civil Rights Act of 1866 and Freedmen's Bureau Act violated the Constitution. Taken together with subsequent decisions, *Milligan* caused Republicans some anxiety. But, as Justice Davis noted in private correspondence and as Illinois Republican Lyman Trumbull stated on the floor of the Senate, the decision in reality had no application to the constitutional anomaly of Reconstruction in the South.

The Court next seemed to challenge congressional Reconstruction in the Test Oath Cases, *Ex Parte Garland* and *Cummings* v. *Missouri,* both 1867. The court, by 5–4 decisions, voided federal and state statutes requiring a candidate for public office or one of the professions to swear that he had never participated or assisted in the rebellion. The Court's holding, that they constituted bills of attainder and ex post facto laws, seemingly threatened programs of disfranchisement and oath qualification, another part of proposed Reconstruction measures. Then, in February 1868, the Court announced that it would hear arguments in *Ex Parte McCardle,* another challenge to military commissions. William McCardle had been convicted by a military commission for publishing inflammatory articles. A federal circuit court denied his petition for a writ of habeas corpus under the Habeas Corpus Act of 1867, a measure that had broadened the scope of the writ, and he appealed the denial to the Supreme Court. Alarmed, congressional Republicans enacted a narrowly drawn statute known as the McCardle repealer, denying the Supreme Court appellate jurisdiction in habeas petitions brought under the 1867 act. In 1869 the Court accepted the constitutionality of the repealer, because Article III, section 2, made the Court's appellate jurisdiction subject to "such Exceptions . . . as the Congress shall make." But Chief Justice Chase pointedly reminded the bar that all the rest of the Court's habeas appellate authority was left intact. This broad hint bore fruit in *Ex parte Yerger* (1869), where the Court accepted jurisdiction of a habeas appeal under the Judiciary Act of 1789. Chief Justice Chase chastised Congress for the McCardle repealer and reaffirmed the scope of the Great Writ.

In the meantime, the Court had turned to other Reconstruction issues. As soon as Congress enacted the Military Reconstruction Acts of 1867, southern attorneys sought to enjoin federal officials, including the president and the secretary of war, from enforcing them. In *Mississippi v. Johnson* (1867), the Court unanimously rejected this petition. Chief Justice Chase drew on a distinction, originally suggested by his predecessor Chief Justice John Marshall in *Marbury v. Madison* (1803), between ministerial and discretionary responsibilities of the president, stating that the latter were not subject to the Court's injunctive powers. In *Georgia v. Stanton* (1867), the Court similarly dismissed a petition directed at the secretary of war and General Ulysses S. Grant, holding that the petition presented political questions resolvable only by the political branches of the government. But the words of Justice Nelson's opinion seemed to suggest that if the petition had alleged a threat to private property (rather than the state's property), there might be a basis for providing relief. In May 1867 Mississippi's attorneys moved to amend their petition to specify such a threat. The Court, in a 4–4 order (Justice Grier being absent), rejected the motion. This minor, unnoticed proceeding was probably the truest index to the attitudes of individual Justices on the substantive policy questions of Reconstruction.

The Court's final involvement with Reconstruction came with *Texas v. White* (1869) and *White v. Hart* (1872). In the former case,

decided on the same day that the Supreme Court acknowledged the validity of the McCardle repealer, the postwar government of Texas sought to recover some bonds that the Confederate state government had sold to defray military costs. Because a state was a party, this was an action within the Original Jurisdiction of the Supreme Court. But one of the defendants challenged the jurisdictional basis of the action, claiming that Texas was not a state in the constitutional sense at the time the action was brought (February 1867). This challenge directly raised important questions about the validity of secession and Reconstruction. Chief Justice Chase, writing for the six-man majority (Grier, Swayne, Miller, dissenting) met the issue head on. He first held that secession had been a nullity. The Union was "indissoluble," "an indestructible Union, composed of indestructible States" in Chase's resonant, memorable phrasing. But, he went on, though the relations of individual Texans to the United States could not be severed, secession had deranged the status of the state within the Union. In language suggestive of the "forfeited-rights" theory of Reconstruction propounded by Ohio congressman Samuel Shellabarger that had provided a conceptual basis for Republican Reconstruction, Chase stated that the rights of the state had been "suspended" by secession and war. Congress was responsible for restoring the proper relationship, in wartime because of its authority under the military and militia clauses of Article I, section 8, and in peacetime under the guarantee of a Republican Form of Government in Article IV, section 4. This was preponderantly a question to be resolved by Congress rather than the president, and hence the Lincoln and Johnson governments in power before enactment of the Military Reconstruction Acts were "provisional." Congress enjoyed wide latitude in working out details of Reconstruction policy. The sweeping language of Chase's opinion strongly implied the constitutionality of mil-

itary Reconstruction. The majority opinion also offered a useful distinction between legitimate acts of the Confederate government of Texas, such as those designed to preserve the peace, and invalid ones in support of the rebellion.

In *White* v. *Hart* (1872) the Court reaffirmed its general position in *Texas* v. *White* and emphasized that the relationship of states in the union was a political question for the political branches to resolve. At the same time, the Court disposed of two lingering issues from the war in ways that reaffirmed the doctrine of *Texas* v. *White.* In *Virginia* v. *West Virginia* (1870) it accepted the creation of the daughter state, shutting its eyes to the obvious irregularities surrounding the Pierpont government's consent to the separation, and insisting that there had been a "valid agreement between the two States." And in *Miller* v. *United States* (1871), echoing the *Prize Cases* (1863), a six-man majority upheld the constitutionality of the confiscation provisions of the Second Confiscation Act of 1862 on the basis of the Union's status as a belligerent.

The Chase Court decisions dealing with secession, war, and Reconstruction have stood well the test of time. *Milligan* and the *Test Oath Cases* remain valuable defenses of individual liberty against arbitrary government. The *McCardle* decision was a realistic and valid recognition of an explicit congressional power, while its sequel, *Yerger,* reaffirmed the libertarian implications of *Milligan.* The Court's position in the cases seeking to enjoin executive officials from enforcing Reconstruction was inevitable: it would have been hopeless for the Court to attempt to thwart congressional Reconstruction, or to accede to the Johnson/Democratic demand for immediate readmission of the seceded states. *Texas* v. *White* and *White* v. *Hart* drew on a sound prewar precedent, *Luther* v. *Borden* (1849), to validate actions by the dominant political branch in what was clearly a pure political question. Taken together, the Reconstruction cases evince a high order of judicial statesmanship.

The Chase Court made only tentative beginnings in issues of federal and state regulatory power, but those beginnings were significant. The first federal regulatory question to come up involved the currency. In *Veazie Bank* v. *Fenno* (1869) the Court sustained the constitutionality of sections of the Internal Revenue Acts of 1865 and 1866 that imposed a 10 percent tax on state bank notes for the purpose of driving them out of circulation. Chase first held that the tax was not a direct tax (which would have had to be apportioned among the states) and then upheld Congress's power to issue paper money and create a uniform national currency by eliminating state paper.

The *Legal Tender Cases* were more controversial. As secretary of the treasury, Chase had reluctantly acquiesced in the issuance of federal paper money. But when the issue came before the Court in the *First Legal Tender Case* (*Hepburn* v. *Griswold,* 1870), Chase, speaking for a 4–3 majority, held the Legal Tender Act of 1862 unconstitutional because it made greenbacks legal tender for preexisting debts. The division on the court was partisan: all the majority Justices were Democrats (Chase by this time had reverted to his Democratic antecedents), all the dissenters Republicans. Chase's reasoning was precipitate and unsatisfactory. He asserted that the act violated the obligation of contracts, but the contract clause limited only the states. To this Chase responded that the act was contrary to the "spirit of the Constitution." He also broadly implied that the statute violated the Fifth Amendment's guarantee of due process.

An enlarged Court in 1871 reversed *Hepburn,* upholding the constitutionality of the 1862 statute in the *Second Legal Tender Cases,* with the two new appointees, Bradley and Strong, joining the three dissenters of the first case. Justice Strong for the majority averred that "every contract for the payment of money, simply, is necessarily subject to the constitutional power of the government over the currency." The Court's turnabout suggested to contemporaries that President Grant had packed the Court to obtain a reversal of the first decision. Grant was opposed to the decision, and he knew that Bradley and Strong were also opposed; but he did not secure from them any commitments on the subject, and he did not base his appointments solely on the single issue of legal tender.

Other Chase Court decisions involving federal power were not so controversial. In *United States* v. *Dewitt* (1870) Chase for the Court invalidated an exercise of what would come to be called the national police power, in this case a provision in a revenue statute prohibiting the mixing of illuminating oil with naphtha (a highly flammable mixture). Chase held that the commerce clause conferred no federal power over the internal affairs of the states, and that the subject matter was remote from the topic of raising revenue. He simply assumed that there was no inherent national police power. In *Collector* v. *Day* (1871) Justice Nelson for a divided Court held that federal revenue acts taxing income could not reach the salary of a state judge. Justice Bradley's dissent, maintaining the necessity of federal power to reach sources of income that included some functions of state government, was vindicated in *Graves* v. *New York ex rel. O'Keefe* (1939), which overruled *Day*. In contrast to the foregoing cases, *The Daniel Ball* (1871) upheld the power of Congress to regulate commerce on navigable waterways, even where these were wholly intrastate.

The Chase Court decisions passing on the regulatory and taxing authority of the states caused less controversy. These cases are significant principally as evidence that the Court continued unabated its prewar responsibility of monitoring the functioning of the federal system, inhibiting incursions by the states on national authority and the national

market, while at the same time preserving their scope of regulation and their sources of revenue intact. The first case of this sort, *Gelpcke* v. *Dubuque* (1864), involved a suit on bonds, issued by a city to encourage railroad building, which the city was trying to repudiate. The state courts had reversed their prior decisions and held that citizens could not be taxed to assist a private enterprise such as a railroad. The Supreme Court, in an opinion by Justice Swayne, reversed the result below, thus upholding the validity of the bonds. Swayne intemperately declared that "we shall never immolate truth, justice, and the law, because a state tribunal has erected the altar and decreed the sacrifice." The decision was welcomed in financial circles, particularly European ones, and presaged a Court attitude sympathetic to investors and hostile to repudiation, especially by a public agency.

The Court displayed less passion in other cases. In *Crandall* v. *Nevada* (1868), it struck down a state capitation tax on passengers of public conveyances leaving the state as an unconstitutional interference with the right of persons to move about the country. The commerce clause aspects of the case were left to be decided later. Another case involving personal liberty, *Tarble's Case* (1872), vindicated the Court's earlier position in *Ableman* v. *Booth* (1859) by holding that a state court in a habeas corpus proceeding could not release an individual held in federal custody (here, an allegedly deserting army volunteer).

But most cases testing the scope of state regulatory power dealt with commerce. In *Paul* v. *Virginia* (1869) the Court, through Chase, held that the negotiation of insurance contracts did not constitute commerce within the meaning of the commerce clause, and hence that a state was free to regulate the conduct of insurance companies as it pleased. This doctrine lasted until 1944. But one aspect of Justice Field's concurring opinion in *Paul* had momentous consequences. He asserted that, for purposes of the privileges and immunities clause of Article IV, Corporations could not be considered "citizens," and were thus not entitled to the privileges and immunities of natural persons. This caused attorneys to look to other sources, such as the due process clause (with its term "person") as a source of protection for corporations. During the same term, in *Woodruff* v. *Parham* (1868), the Chase Court upheld a municipal sales tax applied to goods brought into the state in interstate commerce even though they were still in their original package, thus limiting Marshall's original package doctrine announced in *Brown* v. *Maryland* (1827) to imports from other nations.

Three 1873 cases demonstrated the Court carefully adjusting the federal balance. In the *State Freight Tax Case* the Court struck down a state tax on freight carried out of the state. But in the *Case of the State Tax on Railway Gross Receipts* the Court upheld a state tax on a corporation's gross receipts, even when the taxpayer was a carrier and the tax fell on interstate business. And in the *Case of the State Tax on Foreign-Held Bonds* the Court struck down a tax on interest on bonds as applied to the securities of out-of-state bondholders.

The last category of major Chase Court cases dealt with the scope of the Reconstruction Amendments, and the extent to which they would alter the prewar balances of the federal system. One of Chase's circuit court decisions, *In re Turner* (1867), suggested that this potential might be broad. Chase there held a Maryland Black Code's apprenticeship provision unconstitutional on the ground that it imposed a condition of involuntary servitude in violation of the Thirteenth Amendment. This decision might have been the prelude to extensive federal involvement in matters that before the war would have been considered exclusively within the state police power. But this possibility was drastically narrowed in the *Slaughterhouse Cases* (1873), the last major decision of the Chase Court and one of the enduring monuments of American constitutional law. Justice Miller for the majority held that "the one pervading

purpose" of the Reconstruction Amendments was the liberation of black people, not an extension of the privileges and rights of whites. Miller construed the privileges and immunities, due process, and equal proctection clauses of the Fourteenth Amendment in light of this assumption, holding that none of them had deranged the traditional balance of the federal system. The states still remained the source of most substantive privileges and immunities, and the states remained primarily responsible for securing them to individuals. This ruling effectively relegated the definition and protection of freedmen's rights to precisely those governments—Redeemer-dominated southern states—least likely to provide that protection. Because "we do not see in those [Reconstruction] amendments any purpose to destroy the main features of the general system," Miller rejected a substantive interpretation of the new due process clause and restricted the equal protection clause to cases of "discrimination against the negroes as a class."

The future belonged to the *Slaughterhouse* dissenters, Justices Bradley and Field. Bradley articulated the doctrine of substantive due process, arguing that the right to pursue a lawful occupation is a property right which the state may not interfere with arbitrarily or selectively. Field, in a dissent in which Chase joined (Swayne dissented in a separate opinion) relied on the privileges and immunities clause of the Fourteenth Amendment, seeing in it a guarantee of "the fundamental rights" of free men, which cannot be destroyed by state legislation. His insistence on an "equality of right, with exemption from all disparaging and partial enactments, in the lawful pursuits of life" foreshadowed the doctrine of freedom of contract.

Yet Field's and Bradley's insistence on the right to follow a chosen occupation, free of arbitrary discrimination, did not avail Myra Bradwell in her effort to secure admission to the Illinois bar (*Bradwell* v. *Illinois*, 1873). Justice Miller for the majority (Chase being the lone dissenter) refused to overturn a decision of the Illinois Supreme Court denying her admission to the bar solely on the ground of her gender. "The paramount mission and destiny of woman are to fulfill the noble and benign offices of wife and mother. This is the law of the Creator," Bradley wrote in a concurrence. "And the rules of civil society . . . cannot be based upon exceptional cases." The emergent scope of the due process, equal protection, and privileges and immunities clauses were to have a differential application as a result of the *Slaughterhouse* dissents and *Bradwell* ruling, securing the rights of corporations and men in their economic roles, while proving ineffectual to protect others from discrimination based on race and gender.

During its brief span, the Chase Court made enduring contributions to American constitutional development. It handled the unprecedented issues of Reconstruction with balance and a due recognition of the anomalous nature of issues coming before it. Yet in those decisions, Chase and his colleagues managed to preserve protection for individual rights while at the same time permitting the victorious section, majority, and party to assure a constitutional resolution of the war consonant with its military results. In non-Reconstruction cases, the Chase court continued the traditional function of the Supreme Court in monitoring and adjusting the allocation of powers between nation and states. It was more activist than its predecessors in striking down federal legislation, while it displayed the same nicely balanced concern for state regulatory power and protection of the national market that was a characteristic of the Taney Court.

—WILLIAM M. WIECEK

Bibliography

Fairman, Charles (1939). *Mr. Justice Miller and the Supreme Court, 1862–1890.* Cambridge, Mass.: Harvard University Press.
——— (1971). *Reconstruction and Reunion, 1864–88, Part One.* Vol. 6 of the *Oliver Wendell Holmes Devise History of the Supreme Court of the United States*). New York: Macmillan.
Hyman, Harold M., and Wiecek, William M. (1982). *Equal Justice Under Law: Constitutional Development 1835–1875.* New York: Harper & Row.
Kutler, Stanley I. (1968). *Judicial Power and Reconstruction Politics.* Chicago: University of Chicago Press.
Silver, David M. (1957). *Lincoln's Supreme Court.* Urbana: University of Illinois Press.
Swisher, Carl B. (1930). *Stephen J. Field: Craftsman of the Law.* Washington, D.C.: Brookings Institution.
Warren, Charles (1937). *The Supreme Court in United States History.* Rev. ed. Boston: Little, Brown.

CHEROKEE INDIAN CASES

Cherokee Nation v. Georgia
5 Peters 1 (1831)

Worcester v. Georgia
6 Peters 515 (1832)

The Cherokee Indian Cases prompted a constitutional crisis marked by successful state defiance of the Supreme Court, the Constitution, and federal treaties. The United States had made treaties with the Georgia Cherokee, as if they were a sovereign power, and pledged to secure their lands. Later, in 1802, the United States pledged to Georgia that in return for its relinquishment of the Yazoo lands the United States would extinguish the Cherokee land claims in Georgia. The Cherokee, however, refused to leave Georgia voluntarily in return for wild lands west of the Mississippi. In 1824 Georgia claimed legislative jurisdiction over all the Indian lands within its boundaries. The Cherokee, who had a written language and a plantation economy, then adopted a constitution and declared their sovereign indepen-

C

**CHEROKEE INDIAN
CASES**

Cherokee Nation *v.*
Georgia
5 Peters 1 (1831)

Worcester *v.* Georgia
6 Peters 515 (1832)

dence. Georgia, which denied that the United States had authority to bind the state by an Indian treaty, retaliated against the Cherokee by a series of statutes that nullified all Indian laws and land claims and divided Cherokee lands into counties subject to state governance. President Andrew Jackson supported the state against the Indians, and Congress, too, recognizing that the Indians could not maintain a separate sovereignty within the state, urged them to settle on federally granted land in the west or, if remaining in Georgia, to submit to state laws.

The Cherokee turned next to the Supreme Court. Claiming to be a foreign state within the meaning of Article III, section 2, of the Constitution, the Indians invoked the Court's original jurisdiction in a case to which a state was a party and sought an injunction that would restrain Georgia from enforcing any of its laws within Cherokee territory recognized by federal treaties. By scheduling a hearing the Court exposed itself to Georgia's wrath. Without the support of the political branches of the national govern-

ment, the Court faced the prospect of being unable to enforce its own decree or defend the supremacy of federal treaties against state violation.

The case of Corn Tassel, which suddenly intervened, exposed the Court's vulnerability. He was a Cherokee whom Georgia tried and convicted for the murder of a fellow tribesman, though he objected that a federal treaty recognized the exclusive right of his own nation to try him. On Tassel's application Chief Justice John Marshall issued a writ of error to the state trial court and directed the governor of the state to send its counsel to appear before the Supreme Court. Georgia's governor and legislature contemptuously declared that they would resist execution of the Court's writ with all necessary force, denounced the Court's infringement of state sovereignty, and hanged Corn Tassel. Justice Joseph Story spoke of "practical nullification." Newspapers and politicians throughout the nation took sides in the dispute between the Court and the state, and Congress in 1831 debated a bill to repeal section 25 of the

**FORCED FROM
THEIR LAND**

*A mid-19th-century lithograph
shows the Cherokee nation
bound and maligned by
white explorers, railroads,
oil tycoons, and the courts.
(Corbis/Bettmann)*

Judiciary Act of 1789. Although the House defeated the repeal bill, Whigs despondently predicted that the president would not support the Court if it decided the *Cherokee Nation* case contrary to his view of the matter.

The Court wisely decided, 4–2, to deny jurisdiction on the ground that the Cherokee were not a foreign state in the sense of Article III's use of that term. Although Marshall for the Court declared that the Cherokee were a "distinct political society" capable of self-government and endorsed their right to their lands, he candidly acknowledged that the Court could not restrain the government of Georgia "and its physical force." That, Marshall observed, "savors too much of the exercise of political power" and that was what the bill for an injunction asked of the Court.

A year later, however, the Court switched its strategy. At issue in *Worcester* was the constitutionality of a Georgia statute that prohibited white people from residing in Cherokee territory without a state license. Many missionaries, including Samuel Worcester, defied the act in order to bring a test case before the Supreme Court, in the hope that the Court would endorse Cherokee sovereignty and void the state's Cherokee legislation. Worcester and another, having been sentenced to four years' hard labor, were the only missionaries to decline a pardon; they applied to the Court for a writ of error, which Marshall issued. Georgia sent the records of the case but again refused to appear before a Court that engaged in a "usurpation" of state sovereignty. The state legislature resolved that a reversal of the state court would be deemed "unconstitutional" and empowered the governor to employ all force to resist the "invasion" of the state's administration of its laws. The case was sensationally debated in the nation's press, and nearly sixty members of Congress left their seats to hear the argument before the Supreme Court.

In an opinion by Marshall, with Justice Henry Baldwin dissenting, the Court reaffirmed its jurisdiction under section 25, upheld the exclusive power of the United States in Indian matters, endorsed the authority of the Cherokee Nation within boundaries recognized by federal treaties, declared that the laws of Georgia had no force within these boundaries, and held that the "acts of Georgia are repugnant to the Constitution, laws, and treaties of the United States." The Court also reversed the judgment of the Georgia court and commanded the release of Worcester.

Why did the Court deliberately decide on the broadest possible grounds and challenge Georgia? In a private letter, Justice Story, noting that the state was enraged and violent, expected defiance of the Court's writ and no support from the president. "The Court," he wrote, "has done its duty. Let the nation do theirs. If we have a government let its commands be obeyed; if we have not it is as well to know it. . . ." Georgia did resist and Jackson did nothing. He might have made the famous remark, "John Marshall has made his decision; now let him enforce it." But Jackson knew Marshall's reputation for political craftiness, knew that a majority of Congress resisted all efforts to curb the Court, and knew that public opinion favored the Court and revered its Chief as the nation's preeminent Unionist. Jackson did nothing because he did not yet have to act. The state must first refuse execution of the Court's writ before the Court could order a federal marshal to free Worcester, and it could not issue an order to the marshal without a record of the state court's refusal to obey the writ. Not until the next term of the Court could it decide whether it had a course of action that would force the president either to execute the law of the land or disobey his oath of office. Marshall believed that public opinion would compel Jackson to execute the law. In the fall of 1832, however, Marshall pessimistically wrote that "our Constitution cannot last. . . . The Union has been prolonged thus far by miracles. I fear they cannot continue."

Cherokee Nation *v.* Georgia
5 Peters 1 (1831)

Worcester *v.* Georgia
6 Peters 515 (1832)

The United States had made treaties with the Georgia Cherokee, as if they were a sovereign power, and pledged to secure their lands.

See also

Fletcher v. *Peck*

A miracle did occur, making the Court's cause the president's before the Court's next term; the South Carolina Ordinance of Nullification intervened, forcing Jackson to censure state nullification of federal law. Georgia supported Jackson against South Carolina, and he convinced Georgia's governor that the way to dissociate Georgia from nullification was to free Worcester. The governor pardoned him. Worcester, having won the Supreme Court's invalidation of the Georgia Cherokee legislation, accepted the pardon. The lawyers for the Cherokee persuaded them to desist from further litigation in order to preserve a Unionist coalition against nullificationists. In 1838, long after the crisis had passed, the Cherokees were forcibly removed from their lands. The Court could not save them. It never could. It had, however, saved its integrity ("The Court has done its duty") by defending the supreme law of the land at considerable risk.

—LEONARD W. LEVY

Bibliography

Burke, Joseph C. (1969). The Cherokee Cases: A Study of Law, Politics, and Morality. *Stanford Law Review* 21: 500–531.

Warren, Charles (1923). *The Supreme Court in United States History.* 3 vols. Vol. 2:189–229. Boston: Little, Brown.

CHIEF JUSTICE, ROLE OF THE

The title "Chief Justice" appears only once in the Constitution. That mention occurs not in Article III, the judicial article, but in connection with the Chief Justice's role as presiding officer of the Senate during an impeachment trial of the president. With such a meager delineation of powers and duties in the Constitution, the importance of the office was hardly obvious during the early days of the Republic. Despite President George Washington's great expectations for the post, his first appointee, John Jay, left disillusioned and convinced that neither the Supreme Court nor the chief justiceship would amount to anything. Yet, a little over a century later, President William Howard Taft stated that he would prefer the office to his own. During that intervening century, an office of considerable power and prestige had emerged from the constitutional vacuum. Since then, the Chief Justice's role has continued to evolve. Today, the office is the product of both the personalities and the priorities of its incumbents and of the institutional forces which have become stronger as the Supreme Court's role in our government has expanded and matured.

Like the other Justices of the Supreme Court, the Chief Justice of the United States is appointed by the president with the advice and consent of the Senate. He enjoys, along with all other full members of the federal judiciary, life tenure "during his good behavior." With respect to the judicial work of the Court, he has traditionally been referred to as *primus inter pares*—first among equals. He has the same vote as each Associate Justice of the Court. His judicial duties differ only in that he presides over the sessions of the Court and over the Court's private conference at which the cases are discussed and eventually decided. When in the majority, he assigns the writing of the opinion of the Court. Like an Associate Justice, the Chief Justice also performs the duties of a circuit Justice. A circuit Justice must pass upon various applications for temporary relief and bail from his circuit and participate, at least in a liaison or advisory capacity, in the judicial administration of that circuit. By tradition, the Chief Justice is circuit Justice for the Fourth and District of Columbia Circuits.

In addition to his judicial duties, the Chief Justice has, by statute, responsibility for the general administration of the Supreme Court. While the senior officers of the Court are appointed by the entire Court, they perform their daily duties under his general supervision. Other employees of the Court must be approved by the Chief Justice.

The Chief Justice also serves as presiding officer of the Judicial Conference of the United States. The Conference, composed of the chief judge and a district judge from each circuit, has the statutory responsibility for making comprehensive surveys of the business of the federal courts and for undertaking a continuous study of the rules of practice and procedure. The Chief Justice, as presiding officer, must appoint the various committees of the Conference which undertake the studies necessary for the achievement of those statutory objectives. He must also submit to the Congress an annual report of the proceedings of the Conference and a report as to its legislative recommendations. Other areas of court administration also occupy the Chief Justice's attention regularly. He has the authority to assign, temporarily, judges of the lower federal courts to courts other than their own and for service on the Panel on Multidistrict Litigation. He is also the permanent chairman of the board of the Federal Judicial Center, which develops and recommends improvements in the area of judicial administration to the Judicial Conference.

From time to time, Congress has also assigned by statute other duties to the Chief Justice. Some are related to the judiciary; others are not. For instance, he must appoint some of the members of the Commission on Executive, Legislative, and Judicial Salaries; the Advisory Corrections Council; the Federal Records Council; and the National Study Commission on Records and Documents of Federal Officials. He also serves as chancellor of the Smithsonian Institution and as a member of the board of trustees of both the National Gallery of Art and the Joseph H. Hirshhorn Museum and Sculpture Garden.

In addition to these formal duties, the Chief Justice is considered the titular head of the legal profession in the United States. He traditionally addresses the American Bar Association on the state of the judiciary and delivers the opening address at the annual meeting of the American Law Institute. He is regularly invited to other ceremonial and substantive meetings of the bar. Finally, as head of the judicial branch, he regularly participates in national observances and state ceremonies honoring foreign dignitaries.

The foregoing catalog of duties, while describing a burdensome role, does not fully indicate the impact of the Chief Justice on the Supreme Court's work. For instance, with respect to his judicial duties, the Chief Justice, while nominally only "first among equals," may exercise a significant influence on the Court's decision-making process and, consequently, on its final judicial work product. His most obvious opportunity to influence that process is while presiding at the Court's conference. He presents each case initially and is the first to give his views. Thus, he has the opportunity to take the initiative by directing the Court's inquiry to those aspects of the case he believes are crucial. Moreover, although the Justices discuss cases in descending order of seniority, they vote in the opposite order. Therefore, while speaking first, the "Chief," as he is referred to by his colleagues, votes last and commits himself, even preliminarily, only after all of the associates have explained their positions and cast their votes. If he votes with the majority, he may retain the opinion for himself or assign it to a colleague whose views are most compatible with his own. In cases where there is significant indecision among the Justices, it falls to the "Chief" to take the initiative with respect to the Court's further consideration of the case. He may, for instance, suggest that further discussion be deferred until argument of other related cases or he may request that several Justices set forth their views in writing in the hope that such a memorandum might form the basis of a later opinion.

There are also more indirect but highly significant ways by which the "Chief" can in-

The extrajudicial responsibilities of the Chief Justice can place him at a disadvantage in influencing the Court's jurisprudential direction.

C

CHIEF JUSTICE, ROLE OF THE

♦ **justiciability**
The status of a case or controversy indicating that it may appropriately be heard and decided by a court.

fluence the decision-making process. As presiding officer during open session, he sets a "tone" that can make oral argument either a formal, stilted affair or a disciplined but relaxed, productive dialogue between the Court and counsel. Even the Chief Justice's "administrative" duties within the Court can have a subtle influence on the Court's decision-making processes. The efficient administration of the Court's support services as well as the employment of adequate staff personnel can nurture an ambiance conducive to harmonious decision making.

While occupancy of the Court's center chair no doubt gives the incumbent an enhanced capacity to influence jurisprudential developments, there are clear limitations on the exercise of that power. The Court is a collegial institution; disagreement on important issues is a natural phenomenon. In such a context, as Justice William H. Rehnquist put it in a 1976 article: "The power to calm such naturally troubled waters is usually beyond the capacity of any mortal chief justice. He presides over a conference not of eight subordinates, whom he may direct or instruct, but of eight associates who, like him, have tenure during good behavior, and who are as independent as hogs on ice. He may at most persuade or cajole them." Political acumen is often as important as intellectual brilliance. Whatever the Chief's view of his power, he must remember that, in the eyes of the associates, "the Chief Justice is not entitled to a presumption that he knows more law than other members of the Court . . . ," as Justice Rehnquist said in chambers in *Clements* v. *Logan* (1981). Other institutional concerns further constrain the Chief's ability to guide the Court's decisions. All Chief Justices have recognized, although to varying degrees, a responsibility to see not only that the Court gets its business done but also that it does so in a manner that maintains the country's confidence. Sometimes, those objectives require that the Chief refrain from taking a strong ideological stance and act as a mediator in the

formation of a majority. Similarly, while the assignment power can be a powerful tool, it must be exercised to ensure a majority opinion that advances, not retards, growth in the law. Even the prerogative of presiding over the conference has a price. The Chief Justice must spend significant additional time reviewing all the petitions filed with the Court. As the performance of Chief Justice Charles Evans Hughes demonstrated, perceiving those areas of ambiguity and conflict that are most troublesome in the administration of justice is essential to leading effectively the discussion of the conference. For the same reason, the Chief must take the time to master the intricacies of the Court's procedure.

The extrajudicial responsibilities of the Chief Justice can also place him at a distinct disadvantage in influencing the Court's jurisprudential direction. The internal decision-making process of the Court is essentially competitive. There is nothing so humble as a draft opinion with four votes and nothing so arrogant as one with six. Such a process does not easily take into account that one participant must regularly divert his attention because of other official responsibilities. Moreover, there is a special intellectual and physical cost in shifting constantly between the abstract world of the appellate judge and the pragmatic one of the administrator. A Chief Justice who takes all his responsibilities seriously must experience the fatiguing tension that inevitably results from such bifurcation of responsibilities. Here, however, there may be compensating considerations. Whatever advantage the Chief may lose in the judicial bargaining because of administrative distractions may well be partially recovered by the prestige gained by his accomplishments beyond the Court. The Court has benefited from a strong Chief Justice's defense against specific political threats such as President Franklin D. Roosevelt's court-packing plan. It has also benefited when the Chief's efforts have resulted in legislation making its own workload more manageable.

Chief Justice Taft's support of the Judiciary Act of 1925, for instance, gave the Court more control over its own docket and, consequently, increased capacity to address, selectively, the most pressing issues. In modern times, the tremors of the litigation explosion that has engulfed the lower courts have been felt on the Supreme Court. The accomplishments of a Chief Justice in alleviating these problems cannot be overlooked by his associates.

Certainly, with respect to nonjudicial matters, a Chief Justice's special responsibility for institutional concerns has commanded respect from the associates. Even such greats as Justice Louis D. Brandeis regularly consulted the Chief on matters that might have an impact on the reputation of the Court as an institution. This same identification of the Chief Justice with the Supreme Court as an institution has made some Chief Justices the acknowledged spokesperson for both the Supreme Court and the lower federal courts before the other branches of government and, indeed, before the public.

With no specific constitutional mandate to fulfill, early Chief Justices, most especially John Marshall, molded the office in which they served just as they molded the courts over which they presided. In those formative periods, the dominance of personal factors was understandable. Today, however, significant institutional forces also shape the office. In addition to the extrajudicial duties imposed by Congress, the Court, now a mature institution of American government, exerts through its traditions a powerful influence over every new incumbent of its bench—including the person in the center chair.

—KENNETH F. RIPPLE

Bibliography

Frankfurter, Felix (1953). Chief Justices I Have Known. *Virginia Law Review* 39: 883–905.

Freund, Paul A. (1967). Charles Evans Hughes as Chief Justice. *Harvard Law Review* 81:4–43.

Rehnquist, William H. (1976). Chief Justices I Never Knew. *Hastings Constitutional Law Quarterly* 3:637–655.

Swindler, William F. (1971). The Chief Justice and Law Reform. *The Supreme Court Review* 1971:241–264.

CHILLING EFFECT

Law is carried forward on a stream of language. Metaphor not only reflects the growth of constitutional law but nourishes it as well. Since the 1960s, when the Warren Court widened the domain of the First Amendment, Justices have frequently remarked on laws' "chilling effects" on the freedom of speech. A statute tainted by vagueness or overbreadth, for example, restricts the freedom of expression not only by directly subjecting people to the laws' sanctions but also by threatening others. Because the very existence of such a law may induce self-censorship when the reach of the law is uncertain, the law may be held invalid on its face. The assumed causal connection between vague legislation and self-censorship was made by the Supreme Court as early as *Herndon* v. *Lowry* (1937); half a century later, circulating the coinage of Justice Felix Frankfurter, lawyers and judges express similar assumptions in the language of chilling effects.

The assumption plainly makes more sense in some cases than it does in others. For a law's uncertainty actually to chill speech, the would-be speaker must be conscious of the uncertainty. Yet few of us go about our day-to-day business with the statute book in hand. A statute forbidding insulting language may be vague, but its uncertainty is unlikely to have any actual chilling effect on speech in face-to-face street encounters. Yet a court striking that law down—even in application to one whose insults fit the Supreme Court's narrow definition of fighting words—is apt to speak of the law's chilling effects.

For chilling effects that are real rather than assumed, we must look to institutional

Since the 1960s, when the Warren Court widened the domain of the First Amendment, Justices have frequently remarked on laws' "chilling effects" on the freedom of speech.

See also

New York Times v. *Sullivan*

Warren Court

♦ **case law**
The body of law established in court decisions, as distinct from customary and statutory law. Case law is the most important component of the common law.

The principle that officers executing a valid arrest may simultaneously search the arrestee for concealed weapons or evidence has never been challenged.

See also

Weeks v. United States

speakers—publishers, broadcasters, advertisers, political parties, groups promoting causes—who regularly inquire into the letter of the law and its interpretation by the courts. Magazine editors, for example, routinely seek legal counsel about defamation. Here the uncertainty of the law's reach does not lie in any statutory language, for the law of libel and slander is largely the product of common law judges. It was a concern for chilling effects, however, that led three concurring Justices in *New York Times* v. *Sullivan* (1964) to advocate an absolute rule protecting the press against damages for the libel of a public official. The majority's principle in the case, which would allow damages when a newspaper defames an official knowing that its statement is false, or in reckless disregard of its truth or falsity, may, indeed, chill the press. Even slight doubt about information may make an editor hesitate to publish it, for fear that it may turn out to be false—and that a jury years later will decide it was published recklessly. The concern is not to protect false information, but that doubtful editors will play it safe, suppressing information that is true.

Conversely, when the Justices are persuaded that the law's threat will not have the effect of chilling speech, they are disinclined to use the overbreadth doctrine. A prominent modern example is the treatment of commercial speech. Because advertising is profitable, and advertisers seem unlikely to be chilled by laws regulating advertising, such laws are not subject to challenge for overbreadth.

The worry, when a court discusses chilling effects, is that a law's uncertainty will cause potential speakers to censor themselves. Thus, an overly broad law is subject to constitutional challenge even by one whose own speech would be punishable under a law focused narrowly on speech lying outside First Amendment protection. The defendant in court stands as a surrogate for others whose speech would be constitutionally protected—but who have been afraid to speak, and thus have not been prosecuted, and cannot themselves challenge the law. Whether or not this technique amounts to a dilution of the jurisdictional requirements of standing or ripeness, it allows courts to defend against the chilling effects of unconstitutional statutes that would otherwise elude their scrutiny.

—KENNETH L. KARST

Bibliography

Amsterdam, Anthony G. (1960). The Void-for-Vagueness Doctrine in the Supreme Court. *University of Pennsylvania Law Review* 109:67–116.

Note (1970). The First Amendment Overbreadth Doctrine. *Harvard Law Review* 83:844–927.

Schauer, Frederick (1978). Fear, Risk and the First Amendment: Unraveling the "Chilling Effect." *Boston University Law Review* 5:685–732.

CHIMEL v. CALIFORNIA

395 U.S. 752 (1969)

In *Chimel* the Supreme Court considerably narrowed the prevailing scope of search incident to arrest, by limiting the search to the person of the arrestee and his immediate environs. The Court thus ended a divisive, decades-long debate on the subject.

The principle that officers executing a valid arrest may simultaneously search the arrestee for concealed weapons or evidence has never been challenged; it is rooted in common law, and was recognized by the Court in *Weeks* v. *United States* (1914) as an emergency exception to the Fourth Amendment's warrant requirement. That the search may extend beyond the person to the premises in which the arrest is made was recognized in *Agnello* v. *United States* (1925). The extension, too, has never been challenged; it seems sensible to permit officers to eliminate the possibility of a suspect's seizing a gun or destroying evidence within his reach though not on his person. The permissible scope of a warrantless search of the premises has, however, embroiled the Court in controversy.

Some Justices would have allowed a search of the entire place, arguing that after an arrest, even an extensive search is only a minor additional invasion of privacy. The opposing camp, led by Justice Felix Frankfurter, condemned such wholesale rummaging: to allow a search incident to arrest to extend beyond the need that justified it would swallow up the rule requiring a search warrant save in exigent circumstances. The latter view finally prevailed in *Chimel,* when the Court ruled that the search must be limited to the arrestee's person and "the area from which he might gain possession of a weapon or destructible evidence." It may not extend into any room other than the one in which the arrest is made, and even "desk drawers or other closed or concealed areas in that room itself" are off-limits to the officers if the suspect cannot gain access to them.

—JACOB W. LANDYNSKI

CHISHOLM v. GEORGIA

2 Dallas 419 (1793)

The first constitutional law case decided by the Supreme Court, *Chisholm* provoked opposition so severe that the Eleventh Amendment was adopted to supersede its ruling that a state could be sued without its consent by a citizen of another state. Article III of the Constitution extended the judicial power of the United States to all controversies "between a State and citizens of another State" and provided that the Supreme Court should have original jurisdiction in all cases in which a state should be a party. During the ratification controversy, anti-federalists, jealous of state prerogatives and suspicious about the consolidating effects of the proposed union, had warned that Article III would abolish state sovereignty. Ratificationists, including John Marshall, James Madison, and Alexander Hamilton (e.g., *The Federalist* #81) had argued that the clause intended to cover only suits in which a state had given its sovereign consent to being sued or had instituted the suit. Here, however, with Justice James Iredell alone dissenting, the Justices in seriatim opinions held that the states by ratifying the Constitution had agreed to be amenable to the judicial power of the United States and in that respect had abandoned their sovereignty.

The case arose when Chisholm, a South Carolinian executor of the estate of a Tory whose lands Georgia had confiscated during the Revolution, sued Georgia for restitution. The state remonstrated against the Court's taking jurisdiction of the case and refused to argue on the merits. The Justices, confronted by a question of sovereignty, discoursed on

Chisholm, a South Carolinian executor of the estate of a Tory whose lands Georgia had confiscated during the Revolution, sued that state for restitution.

THE ELEVENTH AMENDMENT

The Eleventh Amendment of the Constitution provides that "the Judicial Power of the United States shall not be construed to extend to any suit in law or equity, commenced or prosecuted against one of the United States by citizens of another State, or by citizens or subjects of a foreign State." Congress submitted this amendment, on votes of twenty-three to two in the Senate and eighty-one to nine in the House of Representatives, for ratification in March 1794. By February 1795, the legislatures of three-fourths of the states had ratified, but because of delays in certification of this action, adoption of the amendment was not proclaimed until 1798.

According to traditional theory the purpose of the amendment was to correct an erroneous interpretation of the Constitution by the Supreme Court. Impetus for the amendment undoubtedly was the unpopular decision in *Chisholm* v. *Georgia* (1793)—one of seven early suits instituted against a state by citizens of other states or by aliens. In *Chisholm* the Court, voting 4–1, held that the judicial power of the United States and the jurisdiction of the Court reached such suits under the provision in Article III extending the federal judicial power to "Controversies between a State and Citizens of another State . . . and between a State . . . and foreign States, Citizens or Subjects."

the nature of the Union, giving the case historical importance. Iredell, stressing the sovereignty of the states respecting reserved powers, believed that no sovereign state could be sued without its consent unless Congress so authorized. Chief Justice John Jay and Justice James Wilson, delivering the most elaborate opinions against Georgia, announced for the first time from the bench the ultranationalistic doctrine that the people of the United States, rather than the states or people thereof, had formed the Union and were the ultimate sovereigns. From this view, the suability of the states was compatible with their reserved sovereignty, and the clause in Article III neither excluded suits by outside citizens nor required state consent.

The decision, which seemed to open the treasuries of the states to suits by Tories and other creditors, stirred widespread indignation that crossed sectional and party lines. A special session of the Massachusetts legislature recommended an amendment that would prevent the states from being answerable in the federal courts to suits by individuals. Virginia, taking

the same action, condemned the Court for a decision dangerous to the sovereignty of the states. The Georgia Assembly would have defied the decision by a bill providing that any United States officer attempting to enforce it should "suffer death, without benefit of clergy, by being hanged." Though the state senate did not pass the bill, Georgia remained defiant. Congress, too, opposed the decision and finally agreed on a remedy for it that took the form of the Eleventh Amendment.

—LEONARD W. LEVY

Bibliography

Mathis, Doyle (1967). *Chisholm* v. *Georgia:* Background and Settlement. *Journal of American History* 54:19–29.

CITY OF RENTON v. PLAYTIME THEATRES

475 U.S. 41 (1986)

Renton, Washington, passed a zoning ordinance that prohibited adult theaters from lo-

cating within 1,000 feet of any residence, church, park, or school. The owners of two adult theaters filed suit, claiming the ordinance violated the First Amendment. The Supreme Court disagreed, holding 7–2 that the ordinance was a constitutional response to the serious social problems created by adult theaters.

Writing for six members of the majority, Justice William H. Rehnquist argued that, even though the ordinance was clearly directed at theaters showing a certain kind of film, the law was properly analyzed as a "content neutral" regulation because it was "aimed not at the *content* of the films shown at 'adult motion picture theatres,' but rather at the *secondary effects* of such theatres on the surrounding community." According to Rehnquist, because the ordinance left 520 acres of land on which adult theaters could still locate, it represented a valid time, place, and manner regulation of the type upheld by the Court in many other "content neutral" cases. Rehnquist did not dispute that the zoning restriction might impose financial hardship on adult theaters, but said the First Amendment does not compel the state "to ensure that adult theaters, or any other kinds of speech-related businesses . . . will be able to obtain sites at bargain prices."

In dissent, Justice William J. Brennan objected to the majority's classification of the ordinance as "content neutral." But even under that standard, the ordinance was still unconstitutional according to Brennan because it was not narrowly tailored to fit a significant governmental interest.

—JOHN G. WEST, JR.

CIVIL LIBERTIES

The significant increase in the constitutional protection of civil rights and civil liberties that has occurred since the late 1950s has brought dramatically renewed focus to the question of the appropriate scope of judicial power. Some

argue that the federal judiciary, especially the Supreme Court, should play an active role in helping to shape public values—pushing a sometimes reluctant populace to make more meaningful the broad constitutional guarantees of liberty and equality. Others warn of the antidemocratic nature of judicial review. Constitutional decision making often invalidates the policy choices of popularly elected officials in favor of the rulings of life-tenured unelected judges. Schools are desegregated, prisons are ordered restructured, abortion regulations are voided, and school prayers are prohibited—regardless of how the majority of Americans feel about these decisions.

This countermajoritarian "difficulty" has led to consistent demands for a more passive judiciary. Only if violations of the Constitution are unambiguous, involving significant deprivations of clearly understood civil liberties, the argument goes, should the independent federal judiciary intervene. Otherwise, American democracy should be allowed a loose rein. The choices of the majority, even in most areas that implicate liberty and equality interests, should be considered determinative. And most fundamentally, they should be respected by courts.

How one comes out on this perennial debate, of course, has a major impact upon how one regards the performance of the judiciary in the post-World War II era. The Vinson Court (1946–53) exercised its authority to invalidate governmental practices relatively rarely. As a result, for example, the criminal prosecution of communists under the Smith Act was upheld and the continued implementation of the separate-but-equal doctrine by the states went largely undisturbed by the Court.

The Warren Court (1954–69), however, took a much different tack. Following *Brown* v. *Board of Education* (1954, 1955), the Court launched a virtual constitutional revolution. In fairly rapid succession the Court handed down decisions not only combating racial discrimination on a number of fronts but also requiring the reapportionment of legislatures,

The continuing defense of civil liberties is indispensable if often thankless.

the application of the bulk of the provisions of the Bill of Rights against the states through the incorporation doctrine, giving more content to the First Amendment's speech and press guarantees, protecting voting rights, prohibiting orchestrated public school prayer, assuring the poor some measure of access to the courts, and bolstering the demands of procedural due process. Other institutions of government, both state and federal, were forced to comply with the Justices' aggressive, and often inspiring, vision of the equal dignity of black and white, rich and poor, high and low.

The almost breathless pace of change wrought by the Warren Court led to significant calls for a judicial counterrevolution. President Richard M. Nixon named jurists to the Court who he believed would strictly construe the Constitution. In his view, this meant that the Court would interfere far less frequently with the political branches of government. In many ways, however, the Burger Court (1970–86) failed to fit the bill of strict construction. Some Warren-era doctrines—criminal procedure guarantees and legal protections for the poor, for example—were pared back. But the Supreme Court, if anything, became even more accustomed to enforcing its vision of constitutional mandate against other government actors. Important women's rights, including a right to choose to have an abortion, were recognized for the first time. Protections for freedom of speech were expanded. More surprisingly, perhaps, the Burger Court aggressively patrolled what it considered the appropriate division and separation of powers among the branches of the federal government. By striking down the legislative veto procedure in *Immigration and Naturalization Service* v. *Chadha* (1983), for example, the Court voided, in one stroke, more federal legislative enactments than it had previously in its entire history. The Burger Court may not have been an inspiring Court; it was, however, a powerful one.

The Rehnquist Court, of course, has yet to sketch fully its vision of judicial authority.

William H. Rehnquist was confirmed as Chief Justice in 1986. Six other new justices have joined the Court since. And significant signs are appearing that suggest that the Rehnquist Court may reject much of the activism of its two immediate predecessors and reduce its role in protecting civil liberties through the interpretation of what Justice William J. Brennan has termed the "majestic generalities" of the Constitution and the Bill of Rights. There is increasing reason to believe that after thirty years of political turmoil over the role of the judiciary in American government, a more conservative Court may be in the making.

Consider a few prominent examples. In 1986 the Supreme Court dramatically announced a halt to the growth of a favorite Burger Court product, the right of privacy. The decision in *Bowers* v. *Hardwick* (1986) refused to afford constitutional protection to the private, consensual homosexual acts of an adult male. Michael Hardwick had been arrested—though the prosecution was subsequently dropped—for violating Georgia's sodomy statute by having sexual relations with another adult man in his own bedroom. Hardwick claimed that the Georgia law violated the right to privacy. Earlier decisions like *Griswold* v. *Connecticut* (1965), which protected the right to use contraceptives, and *Roe* v. *Wade* (1973), recognizing the right to terminate a pregnancy, had characterized the right to privacy as "fundamental" and "deeply rooted in this Nation's history and tradition."

The Court in *Bowers* declared that it was not "incline[d] to take a more expansive view of [its] authority to discover new fundamental rights. . . . The Court is most vulnerable and comes nearest to illegitimacy when it deals with judge-made constitutional law having little or no cognizable roots in the language or design of the Constitution." The majority of the Court claimed that if it were to give credence to claims such as that made by Hardwick, it would be "tak[ing] to itself further authority to govern the country without express constitutional authority." The adjective "further" assumes that the Supreme Court has already moved beyond any supportable role in the constitutional structure. Indeed, the Court followed up with *Washington* v. *Glucksberg* (1997), where it refused to extend the constitutionally protected right to die, delineated in *Cruzan* v. *Director, Missouri Dept. of Health* (1990), to apply to physician-assisted suicide.

Again in 1986, the Supreme Court upheld a municipal zoning ordinance making it illegal to locate an "adult" theater within a thousand feet of a residential area, single-family dwelling, church, park, or school. The opinion in *City of Renton* v. *Playtime Theatres, Inc.* (1986) carried many of the suggestions of the diminished judicial role that appeared in *Bowers*. As a result, the decision allowed the regulation of constitutionally protected (nonobscene) speech in order to "maintain property values . . . and preserve the . . . quality of the city's neighborhoods."

Perhaps even more telling, though, was the crux of the Court's rationale. The fact that the statute "may" have been motivated, at least in part, by the city's desire to restrict "the exercise of First Amendment rights" was ruled beyond the scope of the Court's review: "[T]his Court will not strike down an otherwise constitutional statute on the basis of an alleged illicit legislative motive." Furthermore, the Court declared that it is beyond the judicial function to "appraise the wisdom of the city's decision. . . . The city must be allowed a reasonable opportunity to experiment with solutions to admittedly serious problems." This language is at least somewhat surprising in a case involving the regulation of speech that is, as even the Court admits, protected by the First Amendment. In an earlier time, one can almost imagine Justice Hugo L. Black reminding in dissent that legislatures retain a great deal of leeway for experimentation without violating the Bill of Rights.

In the context of public education, the Supreme Court has taken these declarations of deference to local decision makers considerably farther. In *Bethel School District* v. *Fraser* (1986) the Court sustained a school's suspension of a student for making a sexually suggestive nominating speech at a voluntary assembly, concluding flatly that the "determination of what manner of speech in . . . school assembly is inappropriate properly rests with the school board." And in *Hazelwood School District* v. *Kuhlmeier* (1988), in which the Court upheld the censorship of a high school newspaper, it determined that judicial oversight must be reduced in order to give local school administrators the opportunity to "disassociate" themselves from the messages contained in school-sponsored student publications. Accordingly, principals may constitutionally exercise editorial control over high school newspapers "so long as their actions are reasonably related to legitimate pedagogical concerns."

The Supreme Court's controversial abortion ruling in *Webster* v. *Reproductive Health Services* (1989) reflects a major change in emphasis as well. Although a majority refused to overrule *Roe* v. *Wade,* the Court recognized considerably greater authority in state governments to regulate the abortion process. Thereafter in *Planned Parenthood of Southeastern Pennsylvania* v. *Casey* (1992) the Court made clear its view that *Roe* ought not be overruled. Justices O'Connor, Kennedy, and Souter emphasized the need to adhere to precedent unless dramatic shifts in facts warrant overruling a prior case, as when *Brown* v. *Board of Education* abolished the separate-but-equal attempt to rationalize racial segregation.

Other examples—such as the Supreme Court's rulings that minors and mentally retarded defendants can be subjected to capital punishment—could be mentioned. No doubt, though, these few instances constitute far less than a major cross-sampling of the Court's work. In the past decade the Court has occasionally ventured into new arenas of judicial purview. These areas have primarily involved separation of powers claims rather

♦ **dissenting opinion**
An opinion by a judge of a multimember court who disagrees with the court's decision in a case.

than classic civil liberties issues. But the Justices have also bolstered the protection afforded to some economic rights and, even more surprising, tentatively entered the difficult thicket of the gerrymander.

Still, the likelihood is strong that a significant trend is afoot. The present Supreme Court seems determined to reduce its role as a policymaker in American government. If new and difficult civil liberties claims are pressed, the judiciary may be less inclined to impose its will on the more democratically accountable branches of government. Even the Court's higher-profile constitutional decisions reflect something of this tendency. In the controversial and widely noted flag desecration case, *Texas* v. *Johnson* (1989), a majority of the Court voted to reverse a state conviction based upon the burning of a flag. Justice Kennedy's influential concurring opinion, however, emphasized that the Court "cannot here ask another branch to share responsibility . . . for we are presented with a clear and simple statute to be judged against a pure command of the Constitution." This desire to defer to other government actors—if possible—may be the hallmark of the judiciary in the years to come. As a matter of democratic theory, that choice may be a wise one. For this constitutional democracy, however, the verdict may be significantly more complex.

—GENE R. NICHOL

Bibliography

Dworkin, Ronald (1986). *Law's Empire.* Cambridge, Mass.: Harvard University Press.

Fisher, Louis (1988). *Constitutional Dialogues.* Princeton, N.J.: Princeton University Press.

Garvey, J., and Aleinikoff, Alexander (1989). *Modern Constitutional Theory: A Reader.* St. Paul, Minn.: West Publishing Co.

Greenwalt, Kent (1988). *Religious Convictions and Political Choice.* New York: Oxford University Press.

Levinson, Sanford (1988). *Constitutional Faith.* Princeton, N.J.: Princeton University Press.

Mackinnon, Catherine (1987). *Feminism Unmodified.* Cambridge, Mass.: Harvard University Press.

Nagel, Robert (1989). *Constitutional Cultures.* Berkeley: University of California Press.

Perry, Michael (1988). *Morality, Politics and Law.* New York: Oxford University Press.

Symposium (1987). The Bork Nomination. *Cardozo Law Review* 9:1–530.

Tribe, Laurence (1988). *American Constitutional Law,* 2nd ed. New York: Foundation Press.

CIVIL RIGHTS

In contemporary legal discourse, civil rights refer principally to legislative and judicial proscriptions against racial segregation and racial discrimination—although some branches of civil rights law concern sex discrimination and discrimination based on religion, ethnicity, national origin, physical or mental handicap, and sexual orientation. The primary sources of civil rights are the Civil War amendments to the Constitution and congressional legislation enacted pursuant to these amendments. In common usage, however, the term civil rights includes antidiscrimination legislation enacted under Congress's other constitutional powers, federal regulations, executive orders, and state laws, as well as judicial decisions interpreting all of these sources.

There have been two major periods of civil rights activity. The first, commonly referred to as Reconstruction, began at the end of the Civil War and lasted little more than a decade. The beginning of the second period, sometimes called the Second Reconstruction, is often placed at 1954, with the Supreme Court's decision in *Brown* v. *Board of Education of Topeka* (1954).

Although all three branches of the national government have participated in establishing the scope of civil rights, in recent years the Supreme Court has been the focus of continuing interest and often heated debate. The Court has played a highly visible role in determining the applicability of formal civil rights guarantees to social activity, and since *Brown,* the Court has been widely seen as the institution primarily responsible for articulating the morality of racial equality. This perception is ironic, considering the Court's role in eviscerating civil rights legislation during the first reconstruction—a history that seems especially vivid in light of some of the Court's recent decisions narrowing the substantive content of civil rights.

Civil rights jurisprudence generally involves two broad issues: defining the right that has allegedly been violated and determining the scope of the remedy once a violation has been found. In theory, the latter follows the former because the Supreme Court often says that the nature of the violation determines the scope of the remedy. However, in practice, the relation between the two is not so neatly defined. First, civil rights remedies do not ineluctably follow the finding of a violation. For example, although the Court in *Brown* v. *Board of Education* determined that segregation violated the constitutional rights of black school children, the aggrieved children were forced to await *Brown II* v. *Board of Education* (1955) before the Court issued a remedy. Even this remedy was partial; school boards were not required to eliminate the violation immediately, but "with all deliberate speed." It is also not clear that determining the scope of civil rights remedies actually follows the determination that a violation has occurred. The reverse may occasionally be true: commentators often speculate that the Court's decision to reject a claim of constitutional injury has been influenced by concerns over its ability to administer a manageable and effective remedy. Whatever the exact sequence may be, the narrowed conception of

civil rights that evolved during the midstages of the Second Reconstruction has been accompanied by a correspondingly limited scope for remedial policies.

Recent conflicts over civil rights issues reflect the ongoing effort to derive specific resolutions from general principles set forth in the Constitution—an effort that historically has produced shifting and sometimes contradictory interpretations. The Thirteenth Amendment, for example, renders slavery and its badges and incidents unconstitutional, whereas the Fourteenth Amendment guarantees equal citizenship and equality before the law. The late-nineteenth-century Court determined that neither private discrimination nor state-mandated segregation implicated these civil guarantees. Yet these principles are currently interpreted to permit statutory regulation of private discrimination and to prohibit state-sponsored racial segregation.

Thus, although it seems clear that equality before the law is a basic civil right guaranteed by the Fourteenth Amendment, this ideal has historically offered no clear basis for determining the scope of civil rights because equality is subject to multiple interpretations. In the modern civil rights era, equality has been interpreted to forbid racial discrimination, but even this formula offers no clear basis for determining the scope of civil rights. For example, it is not clear whether the proscription against racial discrimination applies only to explicit racial categories or whether it applies more broadly to policies, practices, and customs that appear, on their face, neutral, but exact similar exclusionary effects. It is also not clear whether race-conscious efforts to remedy the effects of racial discrimination are consistent with or a violation of the prohibition. It is also not clear which background circumstances and conditions are relevant and which are not in determining whether an act or policy is discriminatory. Anatole France's oft-quoted saw that "Law in its majestic equality forbids the rich and poor alike from sleeping under bridges" illustrates the transparency of purely formal conceptions of equality that do not acknowledge the importance of social and economic inequality.

Post-1986 developments manifest a ripening of conflict over the question of whether civil rights law contemplates only formal equality or whether it contemplates something more. Judges, scholars, legislators, and laymen have debated whether racial equality requires only the cessation of practices that explicitly discriminate on the basis of race or whether it also demands a full dismantling of practices, policies, and structures that continue to produce racial inequality. The opposing approaches to these questions derive from competing conceptualizations of civil rights: the antidiscrimination approach and the antidomination approach.

The antidiscrimination approach focuses on achieving formal equality through the eradication of racial classifications and purposeful discrimination. It emphasizes individual-centered harms and colorblind remedies. In contrast, the antidomination view tends to look beyond formally manifested or intentional discrimination to the circumstances and conditions of inequality. Ultimately, this wider perspective envisions the creation of legal remedies and social practices that will foster greater racial balance throughout society.

Many, if not most, civil rights decisions are consistent with either approach. However, rough distinctions between the two are apparent in current debates over the extent to which pervasive conditions of racial inequality implicate civil rights and bear on the scope of civil rights remedies. The doctrinal arenas in which this conflict is most apparent have involved discriminatory intent and affirmative action.

Although the scope of the intent doctrine was largely determined in the 1970s, its full impact has become increasingly apparent in subsequent years. Discriminatory intent was first articulated as the *sine qua non* of an equal protection claim in *Washington* v. *Davis* (1976). In this case, plaintiffs challenged the use of a reading and writing test to screen applicants for employment in Washington, D.C., as police officers. Not shown to measure skills necessary for effective performance

DEMANDING RACIAL EQUALITY

Hundreds of activists make their way to the Lincoln Memorial in Washington during a 1960s civil rights march. (Corbis/Flip Schulke)

as a police officer, the test served as an effective barrier to black recruitment. The Court nevertheless determined that an equal-protection claim could be sustained only if the test had been adopted with the intent to discriminate against minority applicants. This intent standard, as further clarified in later cases, could not be satisfied even where the employer adopting the challenged policy or practice did so with full knowledge of its disproportionate impact. In recent years, the discriminatory-intent doctrine has, in effect, provided a presumption of constitutionality to most racially unequal conditions because it is the unusual case in which some discriminatory intent is manifest in a governmental decision. Thus, racial inequalities that have historically burdened nonwhite communities and that continue to exist today in employment, education, housing, and criminal justice generally do not implicate civil rights. Although the Supreme Court has acknowledged that such disparities often result from societal discrimination, unless a particular discriminatory decision can be identified and isolated, such inequalities are not seen to raise any civil rights issues and thus require no remedy.

Many commentators and some members of the Court have criticized the Court's use of the discriminatory-intent test to distinguish inequalities that violate the Constitution from those that do not. They assert that the presence of explicit intent should not exhaust the definition of constitutional injury. Some point out that the model of discrimination contemplated by the intent requirement is simply anachronistic. In the aftermath of *Brown*'s rejection of formal white supremacy, few decision makers currently adopt policies that explicitly discriminate against blacks.

Even on its own terms, the intent standard is inadequate, for racial animus may play a role in decision making, yet be difficult to prove. Indeed, racial motivation may remain hidden even to the actor. Yet another problem is that the intent standard tends to focus inquiry on a single allegedly discriminatory actor when there are often multiple actors, many of whom have acted without animus, but who, in the aggregate, perpetuate the discriminatory effects of past discrimination.

The principle of purposeful discrimination also fails to address inequality that is reproduced by social practices that have now become ingrained in American society. Critics have argued that the intent standard embodies a superficial conceptualization of formal equality in that its critical scope focuses only on the most external aspects of racial discrimination. This framework virtually excludes consideration of racial categories that are effectively created through apparently neutral practices. Sometimes referred to as "procedural discrimination," practices and policies that do not discriminate on their face, but predictably produce racial disparities throughout society are more common sources of inequity than are formal racial categories. Unvalidated standardized tests, subjective evaluation procedures, nepotism, word-of-mouth hiring practices, and even the high-school diploma requirements can unfairly limit the opportunities of minorities. Whether intentional or unthinking, these practices disadvantage and burden minorities in ways that are closely related to the formal discriminations of the past.

Such criticisms are informed by a view that the moral and political objective of the Fourteenth Amendment is to empower the national government to eliminate the effects of white supremacy. Eliminating intentional discrimination does not fully satisfy this mandate, as purposeful harm is simply one of many means of perpetuating white supremacy.

Despite the effective limits that the intent standard places on the scope of civil rights litigation, defenders marshal several arguments to justify its currency. One is that intentional discrimination prevailed during the period preceding *Brown*, and it is this form of discrimination that is now understood as incompatible with the nation's ideals. Institutionally, the intent standard is justified because intentional racial discrimination is precisely the kind of perversion of democracy that the Court is empowered to correct. Remedying these harms and eliminating these tendencies justify and exhaust the moral and ideological commitment of civil rights. Any other rule, it is argued, would involve judicial overreaching and undue interference with myriad governmental and private practices that sometimes produce racially disproportionate results. Moreover, it would stretch the Court's institutional and symbolic resources to fashion appropriate remedies if a broader standard were used. In sum, there is no ideological, political, or moral justification to move beyond intentional discrimination. Racially disparate results do not themselves speak to civil rights; it is racially unequal treatment that constitutes the crux of the injury. Under this view, the intent standard thus effectively mediates between legitimate and illegitimate conceptions of civil rights.

The intent standard, along with other doctrines in current vogue with the Supreme Court's majority, represents a refusal to extend constitutional protections to preclude institutional and systemic discrimination. Although aggregate views of racial disparities suggest that racial separation and stratification are still common in employment, housing, voting, and the criminal justice system, this view is rendered irrelevant by the Court's current framework that seeks one actor when there are often several and current and demonstrably direct causes when many are historical and cumulative.

Those who support an antidomination view of racial equality note that aggregate views of race paint a picture of society that resembles conditions prevailing during periods in which white supremacy was more openly advocated and racial discrimination more explicitly practiced. They regard these disparities as raising legitimate civil rights issues not only because of their probable connection to the more explicit policies of the not-too-distant past, but also because of the devastating effect on the life chances of minorities and the likelihood that such conditions will reproduce themselves for generations to come.

Earlier decisions suggested that the Court might be receptive to this view. For example, in *Griggs* v. *Duke Power Co.* (1971), the Court ruled that an employment practice that disproportionately harmed minorities constituted employment discrimination under the Civil Rights Act of 1964, whether or not the practice was adopted with the intent to discriminate. The fact that the practice disparately burdened minorities was enough to require the employer to produce evidence that the practice was a business necessity.

In subsequent years, however, the Court increasingly disfavored such systemic views of discrimination. An ominous indication of the full implications of this trend was suggested by *McCleskey* v. *Kemp* (1987) and was reinforced in *Wards Cove Packing Co.* v. *Antonio* (1989).

In *McCleskey* v. *Kemp*, Justice Lewis F. Powell accepted the validity of a study indicating that African-Americans in Georgia who killed whites were significantly more likely to receive the death penalty than were blacks who killed blacks or whites who killed either whites or blacks. Nonetheless, the Court determined that these statistics did not substantiate an equal-protection challenge to the Georgia death penalty. Aggregate statistics could not be used because they could not support an inference that intentional racial discrimination had influenced the disposition of the defendant's particular case. Moreover, other factors, such as the state's interests in imposing the death penalty, in maintaining prosecutorial discretion, and in protecting the integrity of jury deliberations, precluded the defendant from gaining access to information needed to prove that racial discrimination affected the disposition of his case.

Although *McCleskey* v. *Kemp* might have been reconciled as consistent with the distinction that the Court drew between constitutional claims (in which systemic claims were generally disfavored) and statutory claims (in which the Court had adopted a more flexible approach toward such claims), *Wards Cove* demonstrates that the Court's rejection of systemic claims is not limited to constitutional claims. In *Wards Cove,* the Court significantly narrowed *Griggs* to require, in part, that employees challenging employment practices that create racial disparities must specify and isolate each practice and its effects. *Ward's Cove* was largely modified by the Civil Rights Act of 1991, shifting the burden to the employer to show justification for practices causing a disparate impact on minorities and women.

McCleskey and *Wards Cove* are two of several cases that illustrate how the Court in the 1980s has employed various analytical and normative preferences to reject the appeal for systemic relief. Its techniques include viewing causation as isolated rather than interrelated, demanding showings of contemporary rather than historical explanations for racial disparities, and embracing merely formal rather than substantive equality as the objective of civil rights law.

The predominance of the intent standard has significantly affected the development of affirmative action, another area in which the conflict between competing visions of civil rights has been most apparent over the past decade. Affirmative action, while largely referring to race-conscious remedial measures, also encompasses more general efforts to dismantle segregation and to cease the reproduction of racial inequality. *Green* v. *County School Board of New Kent* (1968) best represents this broader conceptualization of affirmative action. In this case, the Supreme Court determined that a "free choice" policy was insufficient to remedy the dual school system created by the defendant school board's previous *de jure* segregation. Equality required not only a cessation of discriminatory practices, but in addition, an affirmative effort to dismantle the racial segregation that had been created through express governmental policy and that would likely be maintained by the practices that were institutionally and societally ingrained.

The current controversy over affirmative action centers on the extent to which this task of dismantling a dual society should be undertaken by governmental and private entities in various contexts. Affirmative efforts have been made to integrate public and private industries, higher education, and professional trades. Affirmative-action plans have been developed as remedies following findings of discrimination; some were included in consent decrees and still others were developed voluntarily, sometimes under the threat of suit, but other times out of genuine commitments to increase the numbers of underrepresented groups in various walks of life.

Critics of affirmative action vigorously assailed the use of race-conscious strategies to benefit minority individuals who had not themselves been shown to be victims of discrimination. Their principal argument is that affirmative action is simply "disease as cure," in that it makes use of race classification to distribute opportunities on the basis of race rather than on individual merits. This is precisely the harm that was imposed on racial minorities and that cannot be justified on nondiscrimination grounds. They argue, moreover, that whites harmed by such efforts are in fact victims of racial discrimination and that the use of race-conscious efforts to correct racial imbalances violates the Fourteenth Amendment.

Affirmative action has been most often justified by supporters as necessary to remedy the effects of past discrimination. Most of the arguments boil down to a view that a full remedy for racial discrimination requires affirmative efforts to restructure racial hierarchy by redistributing educational, economic, and employment opportunities across racial groups. Affirmative action has also been characterized as essential to the nondiscrimination principle. In this view, it is a bottom-line effort to minimize the effects of racial bias that works its way into evaluation sys-

In the 1960s sit-ins, freedom rides, and demonstrations burst upon the national scene, aimed first at racial exclusion from privately owned public accommodations.

tems that have historically favored dominant values and interests. Some argue that affirmative action serves as reparation for past discrimination, whereas others justify affirmative action as essential to creating a future society that is not racially stratified. In the words of one Justice, "to get beyond race, we must first take race into account."

Despite the polarized nature of the ongoing affirmative-action debate, affirmative action is a doctrinal area in which the fluctuating majorities on the Court and its shifting sensibilities since 1986 are best illustrated. Indeed, the Court has only recently reached an apparent consensus on the constitutionality of affirmative action.

The much awaited decision in *Regents of University of California* v. *Bakke* (1978) produced something of a stalemate: state universities were permitted to use race as one factor in admission decisions; but, absent some evidence of past discrimination on their part, they could not set aside seats for which only minorities could compete. After *Bakke*, the constitutional status of affirmative action remained murky. In subsequent cases, a shifting majority upheld affirmative-action plans adopted by the federal government in construction contracts (in *Fullilove* v. *Klutznick* [1980]) and in private industry (in *United Steelworkers of America* v. *Weber* [1979]). However, growing concerns over the rights of whites disadvantaged by these efforts finally came to the fore in *Firefighters' Local #1784* v. *Stotts* (1984), in which the Court precluded federal courts from ordering a city employer subject to an affirmative-action consent decree to protect the jobs of less-senior minorities by laying off more-senior whites.

Foes of affirmative action subsequently interpreted *Stotts* to ban all affirmative-action remedies that benefitted persons other than actual victims of discrimination. The U.S. Justice Department, after urging the Court to make such a ruling, used *Stotts* as a basis for challenging affirmative-action programs operated by hundreds of cities and states pursuant to consent decrees. Yet *Stotts* failed to produce

a clear consensus regarding the constitutionality of affirmative action. Subsequent Court decisions upholding other affirmative-action plans benefitting "non-victims" indicated that *Stotts* was not read as encompassing a broad rejection of race-conscious remedies.

Despite these decisions, however, there remained on the Court a vocal opposition to such race-conscious measures. That slim majorities upheld these measures suggested that the constitutionality of affirmative action remained highly contested and subject to limitation. In 1989 a majority finally coalesced in *Richmond (City of)* v. *J. A. Croson Co.* (1989) to hold that race-conscious affirmative-action programs were subject to strict scrutiny. The city of Richmond adopted a thirty percent set-aside program for minority contractors. Although Richmond was 50 percent black, only one sixty-seventh of one percent of all city contracts had gone to minority contractors. The Court held that the city could not undertake an affirmative-action program to correct such gross disparities without some evidence that black contractors had been discriminated against in the past and that this discrimination had caused the disparities. Particularly striking is the Court's refusal to recognize the relevance of Congress's previous findings of industry-wide discrimination, and its willingness to reduce centuries of white supremacy to the same plane as two decades of affirmative action. Such findings could not be "shared," but had to be proved anew in Richmond.

Croson demonstrates how the combination of the intent requirement and the application of strict scrutiny to affirmative action combine to create the tragic irony that institutional and systemic perpetuation of racial inequality escapes constitutional scrutiny, while efforts to break these patterns and practices are constitutionally prohibited.

Moreover, *Croson* represents a decisive victory of the more formal antidiscrimination approach over the more contextual antisubordination approach, at least where Congress has not adopted the latter approach. And shortly thereafter, in *Adarand Constructors* v. *Pena* (1995), the Court held a federal affirmative action program is to be judged by the same strict scrutiny standard as state and municipal plans like the one in *Croson*. There was no reason not to subject federal statutes in this area to the same "searching examination" as state laws, the Court ruled. It expressly rebuffed the argument that section 5 of the Fourteenth Amendment, empowering Congress to enforce the Amendment's civil rights protections, justified a lesser degree of scrutiny for a federal affirmative action plan.

Critics argue that traditional protections for nonwhites are being eroded while the civil rights laws are being interpreted vigorously to preclude some of the more effective remedies. This claim is not implausible when one compares, for example, the language in *Croson* (explaining how the Court's deep commitment to eliminate all forms of racial discrimination mandates a rejection of even remedial race classifications) with the Court's willingness in *Patterson* v. *McLean Credit Union* (1989) to interpret the Civil Rights Act of 1866 to leave a private employer's racial harassment unremedied under this statute. The 1866 Act was amended in 1991, in the wake of *Patterson,* to specifically apply to conditions of employment. Although the contrasting protections in each of these cases might be reconciled by focusing on the distinctions between the separate doctrinal categories under which these cases arise, it is hard to ignore the apparent trend in which minorities are receiving less protection against traditional forms of race discrimination while the racially privileged are receiving more.

Another area receiving the Court's attention in the past decade is that of legislative district lines drawn to favor electing racial-minority candidates. In *Shaw* v. *Reno* (1993) and subsequent cases the Court ruled that while race may be a factor in drawing voting districts, a plan using race as its primary element will be subject to strict scrutiny.

The Court's recent race jurisprudence also suggests that civil rights litigation no longer occupies the status of "high priority litigation." The Court seems to have rejected the view that civil rights plaintiffs play a special role as private attorneys general seeking to effectuate society's highest interest in eradicating discrimination, root and branch. In technical interpretations, the Court has narrowed the availability of remedies and simultaneously shifted advantages to employers and often to white males. Most troubling are rule 11 cases, in which courts have levied severe penalties against civil rights litigants for bringing suits that were judged to be "frivolous." Although rule 11 of the federal rules of civil procedure lay dormant until it was raised in 1983, nearly half of all rule 11 sanctions have involved civil rights and public-interest cases. Other research also suggests civil rights cases are also disproportionately likely to be dismissed given the heightened pleading threshold placed on such claims. The overall effect of these "technical" opinions has been to raise the risk and cost of litigating civil rights claims at precisely the same time that shifts in substantive rules make it unlikely that a plaintiff will prevail. The probable consequence of such decisions is the chilling of the civil rights bar. The long-term consequence may be that law may cease to serve as a meaningful deterrent to discriminatory behavior.

These recent developments have led many to conclude that the Second Reconstruction is largely a dead letter and that the period is now more aptly described as a post–civil rights era. Indeed, the parallels with the Second Reconstruction seem to confirm the cyclical nature of civil rights protection and, more troubling, the cyclical nature of its decline.

—KIMBERLÉ CRENSHAW

Bibliography

Freeman, Alan (1990). Antidiscrimination Law: The View from 1989. *Tulane Law Review* 64:1407–1441.

Lawrence, Charles (1987). The Id, the Ego, and Equal Protection: Reckoning with Unconscious Racism. *Stanford Law Review* 39:317–387.

See also

Buchanan v. *Warley*

Freedom of Speech

Fullilove v. *Klutznick*

Heart of Atlanta Motel v. *United States*

Marsh v. *Alabama*

Millikin v. *Bradley*

Plessy v. *Ferguson*

Right of Privacy

Shelley v. *Kraemer*

Strauder v. *Graham*

Sweatt v. *Painter*

Yick Wo v. *Hopkins*

Ortiz, Daniel (1989). The Myth of Intent in Equal Protection. *Stanford Law Review* 41:1105–1150.

Schnapper, Eric (1983). Perpetuation of Past Discrimination. *Harvard Law Review* 96: 828–864.

Strauss, David A. (1986). The Myth of Colorblindness. *Supreme Court Review* 1986: 99–134.

Tribe, Laurence H. (1988). *American Constitutional Law*. 2nd ed. New York: Foundation Press.

Williams, Patricia (1989). The Obliging Shell: An Informal Essay on Formal Equal Opportunity. *Michigan Law Review* 87: 2128–2151.

CIVIL RIGHTS CASES

109 U.S. 3 (1883)

In an opinion by Justice Joseph P. Bradley, with only Justice John Marshall Harlan dissenting, the Supreme Court ruled that Congress had no constitutional authority under either the Thirteenth or the Fourteenth Amendment to pass the Civil Rights Act of 1875. Holding that act unconstitutional proved to be one of the most fateful decisions in American history. It had the effect of reinforcing racist attitudes and practices, while emasculating a heroic effort by Congress and the president to prevent the growth of a Jim Crow society. The Court also emasculated the Fourteenth Amendment's enforcement clause, section five. The tragedy is that the Court made the Constitution legitimize public immorality on the basis of specious reasoning.

The *Civil Rights Cases* comprised five cases decided together, in which the act of 1875 had been enforced against innkeepers, theater owners, and a railroad company. In each of the five, a black citizen was denied the same accommodations, guaranteed by the statute, as white citizens enjoyed. The Court saw only an invasion of local law by the national government, contrary to the powers reserved to the states under the Tenth Amendment. Bradley began his analysis with the Fourteenth Amendment, observing that its first section, after declaring who shall be a citizen, was prohibitory: it restrained only state action. "Individual invasion of individual rights is not the subject-matter of the amendment." Its fifth section empowered Congress to enforce the amendment by appropriate legislation. "To enforce what? To enforce the prohibition," Bradley answered. He ignored the fact that the enforcement section applied to the entire amendment, including the citizenship clause, which made all persons born or naturalized in the United States and subject to its jurisdiction citizens of the United States and of the states in which they reside. As Harlan pointed out, citizenship necessarily imports "equality of civil rights among citizens of every race in the same state." Congress could guard and enforce rights, including the rights of citizenship, deriving from the Constitution itself. Harlan reminded the Court of its opinion in *Strauder* v. *West Virginia* (1880), where it had said that "a right or immunity created by the constitution or only guaranteed by it, even without any express delegation of power, may be protected by congress."

But Bradley took the view that the legislative power conferred upon Congress by the Fourteenth Amendment does not authorize enactments on subjects "which are within the domain of state legislation. . . . It does not authorize congress to create a code of municipal law for regulation of private rights." Congress can merely provide relief against state action that violates the amendment's prohibitions on the states. Thus, only when the states acted adversely to the rights of citizenship could Congress pass remedial legislation. But its legislation could not cover the whole domain of civil rights or regulate "all private rights between man and man in society." Otherwise, Congress would "supersede" the state legislatures. In effect the Court was saying that the Reconstruction amendments had not revolutionized the federal system. In effect the Court also warned the states not to discriminate racially, lest Congress intervene, as it had in the Civil Rights Act of 1866, which the Court called "corrective" legislation against state action. In the cases under consideration, however, the discrimination derived from purely private acts unsupported by state authority. "The wrongful act of an individual, unsupported by any such authority, is simply a private wrong" that Congress cannot reach. Congress can, of course, reach and regulate private conduct in the normal course of legislation, penalizing individuals; but, Bradley explained, in every such case Congress possesses under the Constitution a power to act on the subject.

Under the Thirteenth Amendment, however, Congress can enact any legislation necessary and proper to eradicate slavery and "all badges and incidents of slavery," and its legislation may operate directly on individuals, whether their acts have the sanction of state authority or not. The question, then, was whether the Thirteenth Amendment vested in Congress the authority to require that all persons shall have equal accommodations in inns, public conveyances, and places of public amusement. The Court conceded that the amendment established "universal civil and political freedom throughout the United States" by abolishing slavery, but it denied that distinctions based on race or color abridged that freedom. Where, Bradley asked, does slavery, servitude, or badges of either arise from race discrimination by private parties? "The thirteenth amendment," he declared, "has respect, not to distinctions of race, or class, or color, but to slavery." The act of the owner of an inn, or theater, or transportation facility in refusing accommodation might inflict an ordinary civil injury, recognizable by state law, but not slavery or an incident of it. "It would be running the slavery argument into the ground," Bradley insisted, "to make it apply to every act of discrimination which a person may see fit to make" as to his guests, or those he will take in his coach,

or those he will admit to his concert. On the theory that mere discrimination on account of race or color did not impose badges of slavery, the Court held that the Thirteenth Amendment, like the Fourteenth, did not validate the Civil Rights Act of 1875.

The case involved questions of law, history, and public policy. Harlan, dissenting, had the weight of argument as to all three, but Bradley had the weight of numbers. It was an 8–1 decision, and the eight scarcely bothered to answer the dissenter. Ignoring him might have been more discreet than trying to rebut him. He met their contentions head-on, starting with a strenuous objection to their parsimonious interpretation of national powers under the Thirteenth and Fourteenth Amendments, both of which expressly made affirmative grants of power. By contrast, Harlan demonstrated, the Court had generously construed the Constitution to support congressional enactments on behalf of slaveholders. The fugitive slave acts, which operated on private individuals, were based on a clause in the Constitution, Article 4, section 2, paragraph 3, that did not empower Congress to legislate at all. The clause merely provided that a fugitive slave be delivered up upon the claim of his owner, yet the Court sustained the acts of 1793 (*Prigg* v. *Pennsylvania*, 1842) and of 1850 (*Ableman* v. *Booth*, 1859), implying a national power to enforce a right constitutionally recognized. The Thirteenth Amendment, as the majority admitted, established a constitutional right: civil freedom for citizens throughout the nation. And, as the majority admitted, the abolition of slavery reached the badges of servitude, so that the freedmen would have the same rights as white men. Similarly, the act of 1875 reached badges of servitude, because it, like the amendments to the Constitution, aimed at erasing the assumption that blacks were racially inferior. For Harlan, racial discrimination was a badge of servitude. Bradley had distinguished the act of 1866 from the act of 1875 on the ground that the earlier statute aimed at protecting rights that only the states

CIVIL RIGHTS CASES

109 U.S. 3 (1883)

A black citizen was denied the same accommodations, guaranteed by the statue, as white citizens enjoyed.

might deny. Harlan replied that citizens regardless of race were entitled to the same civil rights.

Harlan also demonstrated that the rights allegedly violated by purely private parties were denied by individuals and corporations that exercised public functions and wielded power and authority under the state. Relying on a broad concept of state action, he sought to prove that the parties whom the majority regarded as private were, in contemplation of law, public or quasi-public. A railroad corporation, an innkeeper, and a theater-manager had denied accommodations to black citizens. Railroads and streetcars were common carriers, that is, they were public highways, performing state functions; they were public conveyances which, though privately owned, had been established by state authority for a public use and were subject to control by the state for the public benefit. Free citizens of any race were entitled to use such facilities. Similarly, the common law defined innkeepers as exercising a quasi-public employment that obligated them to take in all travelers, regardless of race. Theaters were places of public amusement, licensed by the public, of which the "colored race is a part," and theaters were clothed with a public interest, in accord with *Munn* v. *Illinois* (1877). Congress had not promiscuously sought to regulate the entire body of civil rights nor had it entered the domain of the states by generally controlling public conveyances, inns, or places of public amusement. Congress had simply declared that in a nation of universal freedom, private parties exercising public authority could not discriminate on ground of race; in effect the statute reached state instrumentalities whose action was tantamount to state action.

Under the Thirteenth Amendment, Congress could reach badges of servitude; under the Fourteenth, it could reach racial discrimination by state agencies. Contrary to the Court's assertion, Congress had not outlawed racial discrimination imposed by purely private action. It had aimed at such discrimination only in public places chartered or licensed by the state, in violation of the rights of citizenship which the Fourteenth Amendment affirmed. The amendment's fifth section empowered Congress to pass legislation enforcing its affirmative as well as its prohibitory clauses. Courts, in the normal exercise of judicial review, could hold unconstitutional state acts that violated the prohibitory clauses. Accordingly, section five was not restricted to merely corrective or remedial national legislation. Congress, not the Court, said Harlan, citing *McCulloch* v. *Maryland* (1819), might choose the means best adopted to implementing the ends of the two amendments. Harlan insisted that Congress

may, without transcending the limits of the constitution, do for human liberty and the fundamentals of American citizenship, what it did, with the sanction of this court, for the protection of slavery and the rights of the masters of fugitive slaves. If fugitive slave laws, providing modes and prescribing penalties whereby the master could seize and recover his fugitive slave, were legitimate exertions of an implied power to protect and enforce a right recognized by the constitution, why shall the hands of congress be tied, so that—under an express power, by appropriate legislation, to enforce a constitutional provision granting citizenship—it may not, by means of direct legislation, bring the whole power of this nation to bear upon states and their officers, and upon such individuals and corporations exercising public functions, assumed to abridge the supreme law of the land.

Some old abolitionists, deploring a ruling that returned the freedmen to a "reign of contempt, injury, and ignominy," denounced the "new Dred Scott decision," but most were resigned to defeat. Racial segregation was common throughout the country. Not surprisingly *The Nation* magazine, which approved of the decision, observed that the public's general

See also

Ableman v. *Booth*

Civil Rights

McCullough v. *Maryland*

Strauder v. *West Virginia*

unconcern about the decision indicated "how completely the extravagant expectations as well as the fierce passions of the war have died out." The Court served "a useful purpose in thus undoing the work of Congress," said the *New York Times,* and *Harper's Weekly* agreed. Public opinion supported the Court, but justice and judicial craftsmanship were on the side of Harlan, dissenting.

—LEONARD W. LEVY

Bibliography

Konvitz, Milton R. (1961). *A Century of Civil Rights.* New York: Columbia University Press.

Westin, Alan F. (1962). The Case of the Prejudiced Doorkeeper. Pages 128–144 in Garraty, John A., *Quarrels That Have Shaped the Constitution.* New York: Harper & Row.

CLASSIC, UNITED STATES v.

313 U.S. 299 (1941)

This became a test case used by the United States Attorney in Louisiana and the newly created Civil Rights Division of the Department of Justice to ascertain the federal government's power to protect voting rights in primary elections. Louisiana election commissioners charged with willfully altering and falsely counting congressional primary election ballots were indicted under what are now sections 241 and 242 of Title 18, United States Code. To analyze the indictment under section 241, the Supreme Court had to determine whether the right to have one's ballot counted in a state primary election was a right or a privilege secured by the Constitution. Relying in part on Article I, section 2, of the Constitution, the Court held, 4–3, that the right to choose a congressman was "established and guaranteed" by the Constitution and hence secured by it. The Court then reaf-

firmed earlier holdings that Congress could protect federally secured voting rights against individual as well as state action and squarely held that those rights included participation in state primary elections for members of Congress, thus overruling *Newberry* v. *United States* (1921).

In articulating those rights "secured by the Constitution" within the meaning of section 241, *Classic* forms a link between early interpretations of the phrase, as in *Ex Parte Yarbrough* (1884), and later consideration of it, as in *United States* v. *Guest* (1966) and *Griffin* v. *Breckenridge* (1971), the latter case decided under the civil counterpart to section 241, section 1985(3) of Title 42, United States Code. *Classic* also constitutes an important link in the chain of precedents specifically pertaining to federal power over elections. Later cases from the 1940s include *Smith* v. *Allwright* (1944) and *United States* v. *Saylor* (1944).

Because the *Classic* indictment also charged a violation of section 242, which requires action "under color of law." the case provides an early modern holding on the question whether action in violation of state law can be action under color of law. With virtually no discussion of the issue, the Court held such action to be under color of law, a holding later used to support similar holdings in *Screws* v. *United States* (1945) and *Monroe* v. *Pape* (1961). Dissenters in *Screws* and *Monroe* would object to reliance on *Classic* because of its abbreviated consideration of the issue.

—THEODORE EISENBERG

CLEAR AND PRESENT DANGER

The clear and present danger rule, announced in *Schenck* v. *United States* (1919), was the earliest freedom of speech doctrine of the Supreme Court. Affirming Schenck's conviction, Justice Oliver Wendell Holmes concluded that a speaker might be punished only when "the words are used in such cir-

To analyze the indictment, the Court had to determine whether the right to have one's ballot counted in a state primary election was a right or a privilege secured by the Constitution.

See also

Smith v. *Allwright*

*The clear and
present danger
doctrine was the
earliest freedom of
speech doctrine of
the Supreme Court.*

cumstances and are of such a nature as to create a clear and present danger that they will bring about the substantive evils that Congress has a right to prevent." Holmes was drawing on his own earlier Massachusetts Supreme Judicial Court opinion on the law of attempts. There he had insisted that the state might punish attempted arson only when the preparations had gone so far that no time was left for the prospective arsonist to change his mind, so that the crime would have been committed but for the intervention of the state. In the free speech context, Holmes and Justice Louis D. Brandeis assimilated this idea to the marketplace of ideas rationale, arguing that the best corrective of dangerous speech was more speech rather than criminal punishment; government should intervene only when the speech would do an immediate harm before there was time for other speech to come into play.

In the context of *Schenck,* the danger rule made particular sense; the federal statute under which the defendant was prosecuted made the *act* of espionage a crime, not the speech itself. The danger rule in effect required that before speech might be punished under a statute that forbade action, a close nexus between the speech and the action be shown. The concentration of the rule on the intent of the speaker and the circumstances surrounding the speech also seem most relevant in those contexts in which speech is being punished as if it constituted an attempt at a criminal act. Opponents of the danger rule have often insisted that Holmes initially intended it not as a general First Amendment test but only for cases in which a statute proscribing action was applied to a speaker.

In *Schenck,* Holmes wrote for the Court. The most extended statement of the danger rule came some months later in *Abrams* v. *United States* (1919), but by then it was to be found in a Holmes dissent, joined by Brandeis. In *Gitlow* v. *New York* (1925) the Court used the bad tendency test which openly rejected the imminence or immediacy element of the danger rule—again over dissents by

Holmes and Brandeis. Brandeis kept the danger rule alive in a concurrence in *Whitney* v. *California* (1927) in which he added to the immediacy requirement that the threatened evil be serious. The danger of minor property damage, for example, would not justify suppression of speech.

In the 1930s and 1940s the Court was confronted with a series of cases involving parades and street corner speakers in which the justification offered for suppressing speech was not concern for the ultimate security of the state but the desire to maintain peaceful, quiet, and orderly streets and parks free of disturbance. Behind the proffered justifications usually lurked a desire to muzzle unpopular speakers while leaving other speakers free. In this context the clear and present danger rule was well designed to protect unpopular speakers from discrimination. It required the community to prove that the particular speaker whom it had punished or denied a license did in fact constitute an immediate threat to peace and good order. In such cases as *Herndon* v. *Lowry* (1937) (subversion), *Thornhill* v. *Alabama* (1941) (labor picketing), *Bridges* v. *California* (1941) (contempt of court), *West Virginia Board of Education* v. *Barnette* (1943) (compulsory flag salute), and *Taylor* v. *Mississippi* (1943) (state sedition law), the clear and present danger rule became the majority constitutional test governing a wide range of circumstances, not only for statutes punishing conduct but also those regulating speech itself.

Even while enjoying majority status the rule came under attack from two directions. The "absolutists" led by Alexander Meiklejohn criticized the rule for allowing too broad an exception to First Amendment protections. The rule made the protection of speech dependent on judicial findings whether clear and present danger existed; judges had notoriously broad discretion in making findings of fact, as *Feiner* v. *New York* (1951) and *Terminiello* v. *Chicago* (1949) illustrated. When applied to radical or subversive speech, the danger test seemed to say that ineffectual speech would be tolerated but that speech might be stifled just when it showed promise of persuading substantial numbers of listeners. On the other hand, those favoring judicial self-restraint, led by Justice Felix Frankfurter, argued that the rule was too rigid in its protection of speech and ought to be replaced by a balancing test that weighed the interests in speech against various state interests and did so without rendering the immediacy of the threat to state interests decisive.

Later commentators have also argued that the distinction between speech and conduct on which the danger rule ultimately rests is not viable, pointing to picketing and such symbolic speech as flag desecration which intermingle speech and action. The danger rule also engenders logically unresolvable hostile audience problems. If Holmes's formula had demanded a showing of the specific intent of the speaker to bring about violence or of specific incitement to crime in the content of the speech, it might have afforded greater protection to some speakers. The independent weight the danger formula gives to surrounding circumstances may permit the stifling of speakers because of the real or imagined act or threats of others. Yet focusing exclusively upon intent or upon the presence of the language of incitement may lead to the punishment of speakers whose fervently revolutionary utterances in reality have little or no chance of bringing about any violent action at all.

In *Dennis* v. *United States* (1951) the clear and *present* danger test was converted overtly into a clear and *probable* danger test and covertly into a balancing test. As its origin in the law of attempts reminds us, the cutting edge of Holmes's test had been the imminence or immediacy requirement. Speech might be punished only if so closely brigaded in time and space with criminal action that no intervening factor might abort the substantive evil. The probable danger test held that if the anticipated evil were serious enough the imminence requirement might be greatly relaxed. In practice this evisceration of the danger test left the Court free to balance the

interests to be protected against the degree of infringement on speech, as the proponents of judicial self-restraint argued the Court had always done anyway under the danger standard.

Since *Dennis* the Court has consistently avoided the precise language of the clear and present danger test and with few exceptions commentators announced its demise. In *Brandenburg* v. *Ohio* (1969), however, the Court announced that "constitutional guarantees of free speech . . . do not permit a State to forbid . . . advocacy of the use of force or of law violation except where such advocacy is directed to inciting or producing imminent lawless action and is likely to incite or produce such action." The text and footnotes surrounding this pronouncement, its careful avoidance of the literal clear and present danger formula itself, plus the separate opinions of several of the Justices indicate that *Brandenburg* did not seek to revive Holmes's danger rule per se. Such earlier proponents of the rule as Hugo L. Black and William O. Douglas, feeling that it had been too corrupted by its *Dennis* conversion to retain any power to protect speech, had moved to the position of Meiklejohnian absolutism and its rejection of the danger standard. On the other hand, those Justices wishing to preserve low levels of protection for subversive speech and the high levels of judicial self-restraint toward legislative efforts to curb such speech that had been established in *Dennis* and *Yates* v. *United States* (1957), shied away from the danger test because they knew that, in its Holmesian formulation, it was antithetical to the results that had been achieved in those cases. Apparently, then, Holmes's formula was avoided in *Brandenburg* because some of the participants in the per curiam opinion thought the danger rule protected speech too little and others thought it protected speech too much.

Yet *Brandenburg* did revive the imminence requirement that was the cutting edge of the danger test, and it did so in the context of subversive speech and of overruling *Whitney* v. *California*, in which the Brandeis and Holmes clear and present danger "concur-

C

CLEAR AND PRESENT DANGER

rence" was in reality a dissent. Even when the danger test was exiled by the Supreme Court it continued to appear in state and lower federal court decisions and in popular discourse. Although the distinction between speech and action—like all distinctions the law seeks to impose—is neither entirely logical nor entirely uncontradicted by real life experience, clear and present danger reasoning survives because most decision makers do believe that the core of the First Amendment is that people may be punished for what they do, not for what they say. Yet even from this basic rule that speech alone must not be punished, we are compelled to make an exception when speech becomes part of the criminal act itself or a direct incitement to the act. Even the most absolute defenders of free speech would not shy from punishing the speaker who shouts at a mob, "I've got the rope and the dynamite. Let's go down to the jail, blow open the cell and lynch the bastard." However imperfectly, the Holmesian formula captures this insight about where the general rule of free speech ends and the exception of punishment begins. It is for this reason that the danger rule keeps reappearing in one form or another even after its reported demise.

The danger rule is most comforting when the speech at issue is an open, particular attack by an individual on some small segment of government or society, such as a street corner speech denouncing the mayor or urging an end to abortion clinics. In such instances the general government and legal system clearly retain the strength to intervene successfully should the danger of a substantive evil actually become clear and present. The emasculation of the danger test came in quite a different context, that of covert speech by an organized group constituting a general attack on the political and legal system as a whole. Unlike the situation in particularized attacks, where the reservoir of systemic power to contain the anticipated danger remains intact, should subversive speech actually create a clear and present danger of revolution the system as a whole might not have the capacity to contain the danger. It is one thing to wait until the arsonist has struck the match and quite another to wait until the revolution is ready to attack the police stations. For this reason the Court in *Dennis* reverted to the *Gitlow*-style reasoning that the government need not wait until the revolutionaries had perfected their campaign of conversion, recruitment, and organization. *Dennis* and *Yates* carve out a Communist party exception to the immediacy requirement of the clear and present danger rule. They say that where the speech is that of a subversive organization, the government need not prove a present danger of revolution but only that the organization intends to bring about the revolution as speedily as circumstances permit. Thus the government is permitted to intervene early enough so that its own strength is still intact and that of the revolutionaries still small. When in defense of the danger rule Holmes argued that time had overthrown many fighting faiths, he did so with a supreme confidence that it was the American, democratic, fighting faith that time favored and that subversive movements would eventually peter out in America's liberal climate. It was a failure of that faith in the face of the communist menace that led to the emasculation of the danger rule during the Cold War of the 1950s. With hindsight we can see that Holmes's confidence remained justified, and that communist subversion could not have created even a probable, let alone a present danger. Nonetheless American self-confidence has eroded sufficiently that the Supreme Court remains careful not to reestablish the full force of the danger rule lest it handicap the political and legal system in dealing with those who organize to destroy it.

—MARTIN SHAPIRO

Bibliography

Antieau, Chester James (1950). "Clear and Present Danger"—Its Meaning and Significance. *Notre Dame Lawyer* 1950:3–45.

———— (1950). The Rule of Clear and Present Danger: Scope of Its Applicability. *Michigan Law Review* 48:811–840.

Mendelson, Wallace (1952). Clear and Present Danger—From *Schenck* to *Dennis*. *Columbia Law Review* 52:313–333.

———— (1953). The Degradation of the Clear and Present Danger Rule. *Journal of Politics* 15:349–355.

———— (1961). Clear and Present Danger—Another Decade. *Texas Law Review* 39: 449–456.

Strong, Frank (1969). Fifty Years of "Clear and Present Danger": From *Schenck* to *Brandenburg*—And Beyond. *Supreme Court Review* 1969:427–480.

CLERKS

Each Justice of the Supreme Court employs two or more law clerks. (In recent years, typically each Justice, other than the Chief Justice, has employed four clerks.) Most of the clerks are not long-term career employees, but honor law school graduates who have previously served for a year as clerk to a lower federal judge. Typically, the term of service for these noncareer clerks is one year.

The practice of employing recent law school graduates as short-term clerks began with Justice Horace Gray. Gray employed a highly ranked Harvard Law School graduate each year at his own expense while serving on the Massachusetts Supreme Judicial Court. He continued to do so when appointed to the United States Supreme Court in 1882. Congress assumed the cost of Justices' law clerks in 1886, but only Gray and his sucessor, Oliver Wendell Holmes, continued the pattern of employing recent law school graduates. The widespread use of the Holmes-Gray practice began in 1919, when Congress authorized each Justice to employ both a "law clerk" and a "stenographic clerk." The use of young law school graduates as judges' law clerks for one- or two-year periods is now the prevailing pattern in most lower federal courts. A clerkship position with a Supreme Court Justice is prestigious, and former clerks have become prominent in the legal profession, government, the judiciary, and academe. Three Justices had themselves served as law clerks to Supreme Court Justices (Byron R. White, William H. Rehnquist, and John Paul Stevens).

The employment of noncareer clerks has been defended as exposing the Justices to fresh ideas and the new theories current in their clerks' law schools. Concern that clerks have too large a role in decisions has been expressed, but this is exaggerated, given the clerks' brief tenure and what is known of the Court's decision process. A distinct concern is that with employment of more clerks, they increasingly play an inappropriately large part in the drafting of opinions. That concern is not so easily rebutted, since each Justice has used clerks' services in a distinct fashion, and there is insufficient reliable public information of the roles played by the Court's current clerks. Court opinions, however, have become longer, more elaborate in their arguments, and studded with citations. The opinions of several Justices appear to be written in a uniform law review style, suggesting that staff plays a large part in their drafting.

—WILLIAM COHEN

Bibliography

Oakley, John B., and Thompson, Robert S. (1980). *Law Clerks and the Judicial Process.* Berkeley: University of California Press.

CLEVELAND BOARD OF EDUCATION v. LAFLEUR

414 U.S. 632 (1974)

The Cleveland school board required a pregnant school teacher to take maternity leave, without pay, for five months before the

The practice of employing recent law school graduates as short-term clerks began with Justice Horace Gray.

See also

Equal Protection of the Laws

The Cleveland school board required a pregnant school teacher to take maternity leave, without pay, for five months before the expected birth of her child.

expected birth of her child. A Virginia county school board imposed a similar four-month leave requirement. The Supreme Court, 7–2, held these rules unconstitutional. Justice Potter Stewart, for the majority, invoked the irrebuttable presumptions doctrine. The school boards, by assuming the unfitness of pregnant teachers during the mandatory leave periods, had denied teachers individualized hearings on the question of their fitness, in violation of the guarantee of procedural due process. Justice William O. Douglas concurred in the result, without opinion. Justice Lewis F. Powell rejected the irrebuttable presumptions ground as an equal protection argument in disguise, but concluded that the boards' rules lacked rationality and denied equal protection. Justice William H. Rehnquist, for the dissenters, aptly characterized the irrebuttable presumptions doctrine as "in the last analysis nothing less than an attack upon the very notion of lawmaking itself."

—KENNETH L. KARST

CLINTON v. JONES

520 U.S. 681 (1997)

The Court made clear in this decision that the president is not immune from civil suits

pertaining to activities unrelated to his official duties. Fifteen years earlier, in *Nixon v. Fitzgerald*, the Court held a president absolutely immune from suit for damages stemming from his official acts. However, the Court observed there that no such immunity existed from suits seeking injunctions to compel, or bar, action by a president. Nor, as the Court held in *United States v. Nixon*, is a president immunized from criminal investigation or subpoena.

Clinton v. Jones, in contrast, dealt with a suit totally unconnected with any official activities. The plaintiff alleged that the defendant made unwanted sexual advances to her years before his becoming president. In an opinion by Justice John Paul Stevens, the Court found no immunity existed in this situation. It unanimously rejected the president's argument that the Constitution's separation of powers precludes suit against a sitting president because it might "impose an unacceptable burden on the president's time and energy, and thereby impair the effective performance of his office." The Court found scant support for that defense in history, noting that only three such actions, all trivial in nature, had ever been brought. Viewing the constitutional separation of powers concern more broadly, the Court noted that if "the Judiciary may severely burden the Executive Branch by reviewing the legality of the President's official conduct," as in *Youngstown*, "it must follow that the federal courts have power to determine the legality of his unofficial conduct."

President Clinton's fallback position, that litigation against him should in any event be stayed during his term of office because of the danger of distraction from his official duties and impositions on his time, was likewise rejected. The Court held that the trial court has "broad discretion to stay proceedings" to avoid, or at least minimize, unwarranted burdens on the president's ability to discharge his duties. Indeed, it added, the trial court should surely consider the "high respect that is owed to the office of the Chief Executive" in deciding the time and scope of pretrial discovery. But the president was clearly not entitled to a blanket stay of litigation against him as a matter of law. Surely influencing the Court's decision was the time-honored concept that justice delayed is justice denied, coupled with the recognition that witnesses' memories fade over time. These factors outweighed in the Court's view any generalized concerns over undue imposition on the president's time, which the trial courts have ample power to address.

Justice Stephen G. Breyer alone concurred separately. Though he shared the majority's view that no constitutional immunity existed from civil suits regarding a president's unofficial acts, he believed the Supreme Court should stay the litigation until the president's term expires since the conduct of the suit would almost inevitably interfere with the president's discharge of his official duties. In addition, he voiced concern that there might be a proliferation of civil actions of this sort. In the end he felt a trial judge, under the Constitution, has only "a very limited power to second guess a president's reasonable determination (announced in open court) of his scheduling needs." Further, in his view the Constitution would not permit a trial scheduling order that "would significantly interfere with the President's discharge of his duties."

Following this decision *Clinton* v. *Jones* was settled, though not before the pretrial discovery in the case resulted in President Clinton's denial under oath of other sexual liaisons. This in turn helped trigger further investigation by Independent Counsel Kenneth Starr and the president's subsequent impeachment by the House of Representatives in 1998. Ironically, the litigation did in fact significantly interfere with President Clinton's discharge of his duties, though in a fashion the Court could hardly have predicted.

—PHILIP WEINBERG

COHENS v. VIRGINIA

6 Wheat. 265 (1821)

In the rancorous aftermath of *McCulloch* v. *Maryland* (1819), several states, led by Virginia and Ohio, denounced and defied the Supreme Court. State officers of Ohio entered the vaults of a branch of the Bank of the United States and forcibly collected over $100,000 in state taxes. Virginia's legislature resolved that the Constitution be amended to create "a tribunal for the decision of all questions, in which the powers and authorities of the general government and those of the States, where they are in conflict, shall be decided." Widespread and vitriolic attacks on the Court, its doctrine of implied powers, and section 25 of the Judiciary Act of 1789 showed that *Martin* v. *Hunter's Lessee* (1816) and *McCulloch* were not enough to settle the matters involved, especially as to the jurisdiction of the Court over state acts and decisions in conflict with the supreme law of the land as construed by the Court. Accordingly a case appears to have been contrived to create for Chief Justice John Marshall an opportunity to reply officially to his critics and to reassert both national supremacy and the supreme appellate powers of his Court.

Two brothers surnamed Cohen sold lottery tickets in Norfolk, Virginia, contrary to a state act prohibiting their sale for a lottery not authorized by Virginia. The Cohens sold tickets for a lottery authorized by an act of Congress to benefit the capital city. In Norfolk the borough court found the defendants guilty and fined them $100. By Virginia law, no appeal could be had to a higher state court. The Cohens, prosperous Baltimore merchants who could easily afford the paltry fine, claimed the protection of the act of Congress and removed the case on writ of error from the local court to the highest court of the land; moreover they employed the greatest lawyer in the nation, William Pinckney, whose usual fee

Virginia "won" its case, just as Madison had in Marbury v. Madison *(1803), but no one was fooled this time either.*

See also

Nixon v. *Fitzgerald*

Nixon, United States v.

Youngstown Sheet & Tube Co. v. *Sawyer*

*The public reaction
to* Cohens *depressed
Marshall, because,
as he wrote to
[Justice Joseph]
Story, the opinion of
the Court "has been
assaulted with a
degree of virulence
transcending what
has appeared on
any former
occasion."*

was $2,000 a case, and another distinguished advocate, David B. Ogden, who commanded a fee of $1,000. More was at stake than appeared. "The very title of the case," said the Richmond *Enquirer,* "is enough to stir one's blood"—a reference to the galling fact that the sovereign state of Virginia was being hauled before the Supreme Court of the United States by private individuals in seeming violation of the Eleventh Amendment. The state governor was so alarmed that he notified the legislature, and its committee, referring to the states as "sovereign and independent nations," declared that the state judiciaries were as independent of the federal courts as the state legislatures were of Congress, the twenty-fifth section of the 1789 notwithstanding. The legislature, having adopted solemn resolutions of protest and repudiating federal judicial review, instructed counsel representing Virginia to argue one point alone: that the Supreme Court had no jurisdiction in the case. Counsel, relying on the Eleventh Amendment to argue that a state cannot be sued without its consent, also contended that not a word in the Constitution "goes to set up the federal judiciary above the state judiciary."

Marshall, for a unanimous Court dominated by Republicans, conceded that the main "subject was fully discussed and exhausted in the case of *Martin* v. *Hunter,*" but that did not stop him from writing a fifty-five-page treatise which concluded that under section 25 the Court had jurisdiction in the case. Marshall said little that was new, but he said it with a majestic eloquence and a forcefulness that surpassed Joseph Story's, and the fact that the Chief Justice was the author of the Court's nationalist exposition, addressed to states rights' advocates throughout the country, added weight and provocation to his utterances. He was sublimely rhapsodic about the Constitution and the Union it created, sarcastic and disparaging in restating Virginia's position. Boldly he piled inference upon inference, overwhelming every particle

of disagreement in the course of his triumphs of logic and excursions into the historical record of state infidelity. And he had a sense of the melodramatic that Story lacked, as when Marshall began his opinion by saying that the question of jurisdiction "may be truly said vitally to affect the Union." The defendant in error—Virginia—did not care whether the Constitution and laws of the United States had been violated by the judgment of guilt that the Cohens sought to have reviewed. Admitting such violation, Virginia contended that the United States had no corrective. Virginia, Marshall continued, maintained that the nation possessed no department capable of restraining, peaceably and by authority of law, attempts against the legitimate powers of the nation. "They maintain," he added, "that the constitution of the United States has provided no tribunal for the final construction of itself, or of the laws or treaties of the nation; but that this power may be exercised in the last resort by the courts of every state of the Union." Virginia even maintained that the supreme law of the land "may receive as many constructions as there are states. . . ." Marshall confronted and conquered every objection.

Quickly turning to Article III, Marshall observed that it authorizes Congress to confer federal jurisdiction in two classes of cases, the first depending on the character of the case and the second on the character of the parties. The first class includes "all" cases involving the Constitution and federal laws and treaties, "whoever may be the parties," and the second includes all cases to which states are parties. By ratifying the Constitution the states consented to judicial review in both classes of cases, thereby making possible the preservation of the Union. That Union is supreme in all cases where it is empowered to act, as Article VI, the supremacy clause, insures by making the Constitution and federal law the supreme law of the land. The Court must decide every case coming within its constitutional jurisdiction to prevent the supreme law of the land from being prostrated "at the feet of every state in the Union" or being vetoed by any member of the Union. Collisions between the United States and the states will doubtless occur, but, said Marshall, "a constitution is framed for ages to come, and is designed to approach immortality as nearly as human institutions can approach it." To prevail, the government of the Union derived from the Constitution the means of self-preservation. The federal courts existed to secure the execution of the laws of the Union. History proved, Marshall declared, that the states and their tribunals could not be trusted with a power to defeat by law the legitimate measures of the Union. Thus the Supreme Court can take appellate jurisdiction even in a case between a state and one of its own citizens who relied on the Constitution or federal law. Otherwise Article III would be mere surplusage, as would Article VI. For the Court to decline the jurisdiction authorized by Article III and commanded by Congress would be "treason to the Constitution."

Although Marshall's rhetoric certainly addressed itself, grandiosely, to the question of jurisdiction, his critics regarded all that he had declared thus far as obiter dicta, for he had not yet faced the Eleventh Amendment, which Virginia thought concluded the case on its behalf. Upon finally reaching the Eleventh Amendment question, Marshall twisted a little history and chopped a little logic. The amendment, he said, was adopted not to preserve state dignity or sovereignty but to prevent creditors from initiating suits against states that would raid their treasuries. The amendment did not, therefore, apply to suits commenced by states and appealed by writ of error to the Supreme Court for the sole purpose of inquiring whether the judgment of a state tribunal violated the Constitution or federal law.

The argument that the state and federal judiciaries were entirely independent of each other considered the Supreme Court as "foreign" to state judiciaries. In a grand peroration, Marshall made his Court the apex of a single judicial system that comprehended the state judiciaries to the extent that they shared a concurrent jurisdiction over cases arising under the supreme law of the land. For most important purposes, Marshall declared, the United States was "a single nation," and for all those purposes, its government is supreme; state constitutions and laws to the contrary are "absolutely void." The states "are members of one great empire—for some purposes sovereign, for some purposes subordinate." The role of the federal judiciary, Marshall concluded, was to void state judgments that might contravene the supreme law; the alternative would be "a hydra in government."

Having sustained the jurisdiction of the Court, Marshall offered a sop to Virginia: whether the congressional lottery act intended to operate outside the District of Columbia, he suggested, depended on the words of that act. The case was then reargued on its merits, and Marshall, again for a unanimous Court, quickly sustained the Cohens' conviction: Congress had not intended to permit the sale of lottery tickets in states where such a sale was illegal.

Virginia "won" its case, just as Madison had in *Marbury* v. *Madison* (1803), but no one was fooled this time either. The governor of Virginia in a special message to his legislature spoke of the state's "humiliation" in having failed to vindicate its sovereign rights. A legislative committee proposed amendments to the Constitution that would cripple not only the judicial power of the United States but also (reacting to *McCulloch*) the powers of Congress in passing laws not "absolutely" necessary and proper for carrying out its enumerated powers. In the United States Senate, enemies of the Court proposed constitutional amendments that would vest in the Senate appellate jurisdiction in cases where the laws of a state were impugned and in all cases involving the federal Constitution, laws, or

◆ **class action**
A legal action brought by one or more litigants in the name of a numerous class of whom the particular litigants claim to be representative, or an action against a numerous class of defendants.

treaties. Intermittently for several years senators introduced a variety of amendments to curb the Court or revoke section 25, but those who shared a common cause did not share a common remedy, though *Green* v. *Biddle* (1823) and *Osborn* v. *Bank of the United States* (1824) inflamed their cause.

In Virginia, where the newspapers published Marshall's long opinion to the accompaniment of scathing denunciations, Spencer Roane and John Taylor returned to a long battle that had begun with the *Martin* case and expanded in the wake of *McCulloch*. Roane, as "Algernon Sydney," published five articles on the theme that *Cohens* "negatives the idea that the American states have a real existence, or are to be considered, in any sense, as sovereign and independent states." He excoriated federal judicial review, implied powers, and the subordination of the states, by judicial construction, to "one great consolidated government" that destroyed the equilibrium of the Constitution, leaving that compact of the states nonexistent except in name. Taylor's new book, *Tyranny Unmasked* (1822), continued the themes of his *Construction Construed* (1820), where he argued that the "federal is not a national government: it is a league of nations. By this league, a limited power only over persons and property was given to the representatives of the united nations." The "tyranny" unmasked by the second book turned out to be nationalist programs, such as the protective tariff, and nationalist powers, including the power of the Supreme Court over the states.

Thomas Jefferson read Roane and Taylor, egged them on, and congratulated them for their orthodox repudiation of the Court's "heresies." To Justice William Johnson, who had joined Marshall's opinion, Jefferson wrote that Roane's articles "appeared to me to pulverize every word which had been delivered by Judge Marshall, of the extra-judicial part of his opinion," and to Jefferson "all was extra-judicial"—and he was not wholly

wrong—except the second *Cohens* opinion on the merits. Jefferson also wrote that the doctrine that courts are the final arbiters of all constitutional questions was "dangerous" and "would place us under the despotism of an oligarchy." Recommending the works of Roane and Taylor to a friend, Jefferson militantly declared that if Congress did not shield the states from the dangers originating with the Court, "the states must shield themselves, and meet the invader foot to foot." To Senator Nathaniel Macon of Virginia, Jefferson wrote that the Supreme Court was "the germ of dissolution of our federal government" and "an irresponsible body," working, he said, "like gravity, by day and night, gaining a little today and a little tomorrow, and advancing its noiseless step, like a thief over the fields of jurisdiction, until all shall be usurped from the States, the government of all becoming a consolidated one."

James Madison deplored some of the Court's tactics, especially its mingling of judgments with "comments and reasoning of a scope beyond them," often at the expense of the states; but Madison told Roane flatly that the judicial power of the United States "over cases arising under the Constitution, must be admitted to be a vital part of the System." He thought Marshall wrong on the Eleventh Amendment and extreme on implied powers, but, he wrote to Roane, on the question "whether the federal or the State decisions ought to prevail, the sounder policy would yield to the claims of the former," or else "the Constitution of the U.S. might become different in every State."

The public reaction to *Cohens* depressed Marshall, because, as he wrote to Story, the opinion of the Court "has been assaulted with a degree of virulence transcending what has appeared on any former occasion." Roane's "Algernon Sydney" letters, Marshall feared, might be believed true by the public, and Roane would be hailed as "the champion of state rights, instead of being what he really is, the champion of dismemberment." Marshall saw "a deep design to convert our government into a mere league of States. . . . The attack upon the Judiciary is in fact an attack upon the Union." The whole attack originated, he believed, with Jefferson, "the grand Lama of the mountains." An effort would be made, predicted Marshall, accurately, "to repeal the 25th section of the Judiciary Act." Doubtless the personal attacks on him proved painful. A bit of anonymous doggerel, which circulated in Virginia after *Cohens,* illuminates public feeling.

> *Old Johnny Marshall what's got in ye*
> *To side with Cohens against Virginny.*
> *To call in Court his "Old Dominion."*
> *To insult her with your foul opinion!!*
> *I'll tell you that it will not do*
> *To call old Spencer in review.*
> *He knows the law as well as you.*
> *And once for all, it will not do.*
> *Alas!! Alas!! that you should be*
> *So much against State Sovereignty!!*
> *You've thrown the whole state in a terror,*
> *By this infernal "Writ of Error."*

The reaction to *Cohens* proves, in part, that the Court's prose was overbroad, but Marshall was reading the Constitution in the only way that would make the federal system operate effectively under one supreme law.

—LEONARD W. LEVY

Bibliography

Beveridge, Albert J. (1916–1919). *The Life of John Marshall.* 4 vols. Vol. 4: 340–375. Boston: Houghton-Mifflin.

Hains, Charles Grove (1944). *The Role of the Supreme Court in American Government and Politics, 1789–1835.* Pages 427–461. Berkeley: University of California Press.

Konefsky, Samuel J. (1964). *John Marshall and Alexander Hamilton.* Pages 93–111. New York: Macmillan.

COLORADO v. CONNELLY

479 U.S. 157 (1986)

Narrowly seen, this case deals with true confessions by mentally deranged people, but it resulted in the major holding that the Fifth Amendment's right against compulsory self-incrimination operates only when the coercion is linked to government. A confession that is involuntary in the sense that it is not the product of a rational intellect or free will may, nevertheless, be introduced in evidence because no government agent misbehaved or was responsible for the involuntary character of the confession. In this case, the murderer confessed in obedience to God's voice. He received his Miranda rights, waived them, and insisted on confessing. The court, in a 7–2 decision, found no violation of due process of law and no involuntary self-incrimination. The dissenters believed that the Court was wrong to think that the only involuntary confessions are those obtained by government misconduct. Justice John Paul Stevens, concurring with the decision, sensibly acknowledged that the confession in this case was involuntary but not of such a character that it had to be excluded from evidence.

—LEONARD W. LEVY

COLUMBIA BROADCASTING SYSTEM v. DEMOCRATIC NATIONAL COMMITTEE

412 U.S. 94 (1973)

The Supreme Court here considered a First Amendment challenge to a broadcaster's refusal to accept editorial advertisements except during political campaigns. Some

C

COLUMBIA BROADCASTING SYSTEM v. DEMOCRATIC NATIONAL COMMITTEE

412 U.S. 94 (1973)

The dissenters in Colorado *believed that the Court was wrong to think that the only involuntary confessions are those obtained by government misconduct.*

Broadcasters, the Court observed, were obligated by the fairness doctrine to cover political issues.

See also

Miranda Rules

**COLUMBUS BOARD
OF EDUCATION v.
PENICK**

433 U.S. 449 (1979)

**DAYTON BOARD OF
EDUCATION v.
BRINKMAN**

*433 U.S. 406 (1977);
443 U.S. 526 (1979)*

*In Ohio, racially
segregated schools
had not been
prescribed by law
since 1888.*

♦ de jure
*[Latin: in law] Existing
in law or by virtue of
official acts;
distinguished from de
facto.*

Justices maintained that the broadcaster's action did not amount to governmental action, but the Court did not reach the question. Even assuming state action, it held that the First Amendment permitted broadcasters to discriminate between commercial and political advertisements. Broadcasters, the Court observed, were obligated by the Fairness Doctrine to cover political issues, and their choice to cover such issues outside of commercials protected captive audiences and avoided a threat that the wealthy would dominate broadcast decisions about political issues.

—STEVEN SHIFFRIN

COLUMBUS BOARD OF EDUCATION v. PENICK

443 U.S. 449 (1979)

DAYTON BOARD OF EDUCATION v. BRINKMAN

**433 U.S. 406 (1977);
443 U.S. 526 (1979)**

These cases demonstrated the artificiality of the de facto/de jure distinction in school desegregation litigation. Both cases arose in cities in Ohio, where racially segregated schools had not been prescribed by law since 1888. In both, however, blacks charged another form of de jure segregation: intentional acts by school boards aimed at promoting segregation.

When the *Dayton* case first reached the Supreme Court, a related doctrinal development was still a fresh memory. *Washington* v. *Davis* (1976) had held that racial discrimination was not to be inferred from the fact that governmental action had a racially disproportionate impact; rather the test was whether

such an impact was intended by the legislative body or other officials whose conduct was challenged. *Dayton I* in 1977 applied this reasoning to school segregation, emphasizing that a constitutional violation was to be found only in cases of established segregative intent. The Court remanded the case for more specific findings on the question of intent, and said that any remedy must be tailored to the scope of the segregation caused by any specific constitutional violations.

Many observers took *Dayton I* to portend the undermining of *Keyes* v. *School District No. 1* (1973). In *Keyes* the Court had held that, once a significant degree of de jure segregation was established, systemwide desegregation remedies (including school busing) were appropriate unless the school board showed that any remaining racially separate schools were the product of something other than the board's segregative intent. When the case returned to the Supreme Court two years later, these predictions were confounded.

Dayton II came to the Court along with the *Columbus* case, and they were decided together. *Columbus,* decided by a 7–2 vote, provided the main opinions. Writing for a majority of five, Justice Byron R. White applied the *Keyes* presumptions approach so vigorously that the dissenters remarked that the de facto/de jure distiction had been drained of most of its meaning. None of the Justices disputed the finding that in 1954–55, when *Brown* v. *Board of Education* was decided, the Columbus school board had deliberately drawn boundary lines and selected school sites to maintain racial segregation in a number of schools. What divided the Court was the question of inferences to be drawn from these undisputed facts.

Justice White reasoned that this de jure segregation placed the school board under an affirmative duty to dismantle its dual system. Its actions since 1954, however, had aggravated rather than reduced segregation; the foreseeability of those results helped prove the board's segregative intent. A district-wide busing remedy was thus appropriate under *Keyes*. Justice William H. Rehnquist, dissenting, pointed out the tension between this decision and *Dayton I*. Here there was no showing of a causal relationship between pre-1954 acts of intentional segregation and current racial imbalance in the schools. Thus present-day de facto segregation was enough to generate district-wide remedies, so long as some significant pre-1954 acts of deliberate segregation could be shown.

It will be a rare big-city school district in which such acts cannot be found—with a consequent presumption of current de jure segregation. A school board cannot overcome the presumption merely by relying on a neighborhood school policy and showing that the city's residencies are racially separated. This analysis obviously blurs the de facto/de jure distinction.

Dayton II made clear that a school board's segregative purpose was secondary to its effectiveness in performing its affirmative duty to terminate a dual system—and that effectiveness was to be measured in the present-day facts of racial separation and integration. Justice White again wrote for the majority, but now there were four dissenters. Justice Potter Stewart, the Court's one Ohioan, concurred in Columbus but dissented in *Dayton II,* deferring in each case to the district court's determination as to a continuing constitutional violation. In *Dayton II*, the district court had found pre-1954 acts of deliberate segregation, but had found no causal connection between those acts and present racial separation in the schools. That separation, the district judge concluded, resulted not from any segregative purpose on the part of the school board but from residential segregation. Justice Stewart would have accepted that judgment, but the majority, following the *Columbus* line of reasoning, held that the board had not fulfilled its affirmative duty to dismantle the dual system that had existed in 1954. Chief Justice Warren E. Burger joined

Justice Stewart in both cases; Justice Rehnquist dissented in *Dayton II* chiefly on the basis of his *Columbus* dissent.

Justice Lewis F. Powell joined Justice Rehnquist's dissents, and also wrote an opinion dissenting in both cases. Justice Powell had argued in *Keyes* for abandoning the de facto/de jure distinction, and he did not defend that distinction here. Rather he repeated his skepticism that court orders could ever end racial imbalance in large urban school districts and his opposition to massive busing as a desegregation remedy. Justice Powell, a former school board president, argued that, twenty-five years after *Brown,* the federal courts should be limiting rather than expanding their control of public school operations.

—KENNETH L. KARST

Bibliography

Kitch, Edmund W. (1979). The Return of Color-Consciousness to the Constitution: *Weber, Dayton,* and *Columbus. Supreme Court Review* 1979:1–15.

NO LONGER SEPARATE

African-American students enter a desegregated school as white students look on. (Corbis/Bettmann)

COMPELLING STATE INTEREST

When the Supreme Court concludes that strict scrutiny is the appropriate standard of review, it often expresses its searching examination of the justification of legislation in a formula: the law is invalid unless it is necessary to achieve a "compelling state interest." The inquiry thus touches not only legislative means but also legislative purposes.

Even the permissive rational basis standard of review demands that legislative ends be legitimate. To say that a governmental purpose must be one of compelling importance is plainly to demand more. How much more, however, is something the Court has been unable to say. What we do know is that, once "strict scrutiny" is invoked, only rarely does a law escape invalidation.

Any judicial examination of the importance of a governmental objective implies that a court is weighing interests, engaging in a kind of cost-benefit analysis as a prelude to deciding on the constitutionality of legislation. Yet one would be mistaken to assume that the inquiry follows such a neat, linear, two-stage progression. Given the close correlation between employing the "strict scrutiny" standard and invalidating laws, the very word "scrutiny" may be misleading. A court that has embarked on a search for compelling state interests very likely knows how it intends to decide.

In many a case a court does find a legislative purpose of compelling importance. That is not the end of the "strict scrutiny" inquiry; there remains the question whether the law is necessary to achieve that end. If, for example, there is another way the legislature might have accomplished its purpose, without imposing so great a burden on the constitutionally protected interest in liberty or equality, the availability of that least restrictive means negates the necessity for the legislature's choice. The meaning of "strict scrutiny" is that even a compelling state interest must be pursued by means that give constitutional values their maximum protection.

The phrase "compelling state interest" originated in Justice Felix Frankfurter's concurring opinion in *Sweezy v. New Hampshire* (1957), a case involving the privacy of political association: "For a citizen to be made to forego even a part of so basic a liberty as his political autonomy, the subordinating interest of the State must be compelling." The Supreme Court uses some variation on this formula not only in First Amendment cases but also in cases calling for "strict scrutiny" under the equal protection clause or under the revived forms of substantive due process. The formula, in short, is much used and little explained. The Court is unable to define "compelling state interest" but knows when it does not see it.

—KENNETH L. KARST

Bibliography

Tribe, Laurence H. (1978). *American Constitutional Law.* Pages 1000–1002. Mineola, N.Y.: Foundation Press.

CONGRESS AND THE SUPREME COURT

The delegates to the Constitutional Convention of 1787 confronted two fundamental problems in their quest to correct the political defects of the Articles of Confederation. First, they needed to bolster the powers of government at the national level so as to transform the "league of friendship" created by the Articles into a government with all the coercive powers requisite to government. Second, the Framers sought to create energetic but limited powers that would enable the new national government to govern, but in ways safe to the rights of the people. As James Madison put it in *The Federalist* #51, the task was to "enable the government to control the governed, but in the next place oblige it to control itself."

> *The Court is unable to define "compelling state interest" but knows when it does not see it.*

Their successful solution to this political problem was to separate the powers of government. Because the primary source of trouble in a popular form of government would be the legislative branch, the object was to bolster the coordinate executive and judicial branches, to offer "some more adequate defence . . . for the more feeble, against the more powerful members of the government." The arrangement of checked and balanced institutions would at once avoid "a tyrannical concentration of all the powers of government in the same hands" while rendering the administration of the national government more efficient.

When the Framers examined the existing federal system under the Articles to determine precisely what it was that rendered it "altogether unfit for the administration of the affairs of the Union," the want of an independent judiciary "crown[ed] the defects of the confederation." As Alexander Hamilton put it in *The Federalist* #22, "Laws are a dead letter without courts to expound and define their true meaning and operation." Thus the improved science of politics offered by the friends of the Constitution prominently included provision for "the institution of courts composed of judges, holding their offices during good behavior."

But to some anti-federalist critics of the federalist-backed Constitution, the judiciary was too independent and too powerful. To the New York anti-federalist "Brutus," the proposed judiciary possessed such independence as to allow the courts to "mould the government into almost any shape they please." The "Federal Farmer" was equally critical: his fellow citizens were "more in danger of sowing the seeds of arbitrary government in this department than in any other." With such unanticipated criticism, the Federalists were forced to defend the judicial power more elaborately than had been done in the early pages of *The Federalist*.

So compelling were the anti-federalist arguments that Hamilton saw fit to explain and defend the proposed judicial power in no fewer than six separate essays (#78–83) in *The Federalist*. His task was to show how an independent judiciary was not only *not* a threat to safe popular government but was absolutely essential to it. In making his now famous argument in *The Federalist* #78 that the judiciary would be that branch of the new government "least dangerous to the political rights of the Constitution," Hamilton made the case that the courts were "designed to be an intermediate body between the people and the legislature, in order, among other things, to keep the latter within the limits assigned to their authority." By exercising neither force nor will but merely judgment, the courts would prove to be the "bulwarks of a limited constitution." Such an institution, Hamilton argued, politically independent yet constitutionally rooted, was essential to resist the overwhelming power of the majority of the community. Only with such a constitutional defense could the rights of individuals and of minor parties be protected against majority tyranny; only an independent judiciary could allow the powers of the national government to be sufficiently enhanced, while simultaneously checking the unhealthy impulses of majority rule that had characterized politics at the state level under the Articles.

To counter the anti-federalist complaint that the courts would be imperiously independent, Hamilton reminded them that the courts would not be simply freewheeling sources of arbitrary judgments and decrees. The Constitution, in giving Congress the power to regulate the appellate jurisdiction of the Supreme Court "with such exceptions, and under such regulations, as the Congress shall make," hedged against too expansive a conception of judicial power. "To avoid an arbitrary discretion in the courts," Hamilton noted, "it is indispensable that they should be bound down by strict rules and precedents, which serve to define and point out their duty in every particular case that comes before them." Thus the stage was set for a history of political confrontation between the Congress and the Court.

"Laws are a dead letter without courts to expound and define their true meaning."

The tension between Congress and the Court has been a constant part of American politics at least since *Chisholm* v. *Georgia* (1793) led to the Eleventh Amendment. Each generation has seen dramatic Supreme Court rulings that have prompted political cries to curb the courts. John Marshall's now celebrated opinions in *Marbury* v. *Madison* (1803) and *McCulloch* v. *Maryland* (1819), for example, caused him a good bit of political grief when he wrote them; the decision in *Dred Scott* v. *Sandford* (1857) soon came to be viewed as a judicially "self-inflicted wound" that weakened the Court and exacerbated the conflict that descended into civil war; and more recently, protests against the rulings in *Brown* v. *Board of Education* (1954) and *Roe* v. *Wade* (1973) have caused not only political demands for retaliation against the Court but social conflict and even violence as well. But through it all the Court has weathered the hostility with its independence intact.

Only once were the critics successful in persuading Congress to act against the Court, and the Court validated that move. In *Ex Parte McCardle* (1869) the Court confirmed Congress's power to withdraw a portion of the Court's appellate jurisdiction. Fearing that the Court would use William McCardle's petition for a writ of habeas corpus under the Habeas Corpus Act of 1867 as a vehicle for invalidating the Reconstruction Acts *in toto*, the Congress repealed that portion of the act under which McCardle had brought his action—and after the Court had heard arguments in the case. The Court upheld the constitutionality of Congress's action in repealing this particular part of the Court's jurisdiction. The extent of Congress's power to withdraw the Court's appellate jurisdiction remains a matter of constitutional controversy.

In recent decades the Court has clashed with Congress over a variety of controversial issues. *Powell* v. *McCormack* (1969) held an elected representative could not be denied his seat in Congress as "unqualified" on the ground that he had been accused of misconduct and held in contempt of court in his home state. The Court noted that the sole qualifications dictated by the Constitution are age, citizenship, and residency, and that Congress may not expand the list. In *Immigration and Naturalization Service* v. *Chadha* (1983) the Court ruled that Congress lacked power to veto the actions of an executive-branch official except by the process of enacting amendatory legislation. A statute that empowered one house of Congress to overturn a decision of the attorney general to stay an alien's deportation on hardship grounds exceeded Congress's authority under the Constitution. Likewise, in *Clinton* v. *New York* (1998) the Court held the line-item veto unconstitutional, finding a law purporting to allow the president to delete spending and tax-exemption items from legislation already enacted and become law violated the authority given Congress in the Constitution.

The constitutional relationship between Congress and the Court is one thing; their political relationship is another matter. Although there are often loud cries for reaction against the Court, the critics usually lack sufficient force to achieve political retribution. The reason is most often explained as a matter of political prudence. The courts by their decisions frequently irritate a portion of the community—but usually only a portion. For most decisions will satisfy certain public constituencies that are as vociferous as the critics. Even the most errant exercises of judicial decision making are rarely sufficient to undermine the public respect for the idea of an independent judiciary.

The reason for this is simple enough: an independent judiciary makes good political sense. To make the judiciary too much dependent upon "popularity" as that popularity may be reflected in Congress would be to lower the constitutional barriers to congressional power, barriers generally agreeable to most people most of the time. The arguments of Hamilton in *The Federalist* still carry considerable weight.

Thus in the constitutional design of separating the powers of government through the device of "partial agency"—mingling the powers enough to give each branch some control over the others—is to be found the inevitable gulf between legitimate power and prudent restraint. For Congress to be persuaded to restrict judicial power, the case must first be made that such restrictions are both necessary and proper.

Despite the dangers of legislative power, it was still considered by the Framers to be the cardinal principle of popular sovereignty. Basic to this principle is the belief that it is legitimate for the people through the instrumentality of law to adjust, check, or enhance certain institutions of the government. This belief embraces the power of the legislature to exert some control over the structure and administration of the executive and judicial branches.

The qualified power of the legislature to tamper with the judiciary is not so grave a danger to the balance of the Constitution as some see it. For even when a judicial decision runs counter to particular—and perhaps pervasive—political interests, the institutional arrangements of the Constitution are such as to slow down the popular outrage and give the people time for "more cool and sedate reflection." And given the distance between the people and legislation afforded by such devices as representation (with its multiplicity of interests), bicameralism, and the executive veto power, an immediate legislative backlash to judicial behavior is unlikely. Experience demonstrates that any backlash at all is likely to be "weak and ineffectual." But if the negative response is not merely transient and is widely and deeply felt, then the Constitution wisely provides well-defined mechanisms for a deliberate political reaction to what the people hold to be intolerable judicial excesses.

But ultimately the history of court-curbing efforts in America, from the failed impeachment of Justice Samuel Chase to the court-packing plan of Franklin D. Roosevelt, teaches one basic lesson: the American political sys-

"LEAGUE OF FRIENDSHIP"?

The tension between Congress and the Supreme Court has historically been a part of American politics. (Corbis/Marc Muench)

tem generally operates to the advantage of the judiciary. Presidential court-packing is ineffective as a means of exerting political influence, and impeachment is too difficult to use as an everyday check against unpopular decisions. Not since John Marshall saw fit pseudonymously to defend his opinion in *McCulloch* v. *Maryland* (1819) in the public press has any Justice or judge felt obliged to respond to public outrage over a decision.

Political responses to perceived excesses of judicial power tend to take one of two forms: either a policy response against a particular decision or an institutional response against the structure and powers of the courts. In either event, the response may be either partisan or principled. Usually a policy response will take the form of a proposed constitutional amendment or statute designed to overrule a decision. An institutional response will generally seek to make jurisdictional exceptions, to create special courts with specific jurisdiction, or to make adjustments regarding the personnel, administration, or procedures of the judicial branch. Whatever the response, court-curbing is difficult. Although a majority of one of the houses of Congress may object to particular cases of "judicial impertinence," as one congressman viewed Justice David Davis's controversial opinion in *Ex Parte Milligan* (1866), a variety of objections will issue in different views of what should be done.

On the whole, there has consistently been a consensus that tampering with judicial independence is a serious matter and that rash reprisals against the Court as an institution may upset the constitutional balance. Underlying the occasional outbursts of angry public sentiment against the Court is that "moral force" of the community of which Alexis de Tocqueville wrote. On the whole, the American people continue to view the judiciary as the "boast of the Constitution."

For any political attempt to adjust or limit the judicial power to be successful it is necessary that it be—and be perceived to be—a principled rather than a merely partisan response. Only then will the issue of judicial

activism be met on a ground high enough to transcend the more common—and generally fruitless—debates over judicial liberalism and conservatism. The deepest issue is not whether a particular decision or even a particular court is too liberal for some and too conservative for others; the point is whether the courts are exercising their powers capably and legitimately. Keeping the courts constitutionally legitimate and institutionally capable benefits both the liberal and the conservative elements in American politics.

The system the Framers devised is so structured that the branch the Framers thought "least dangerous" is not so malleable in the hands of Congress as to be powerless. Yet the threat of congressional restriction of the Court remains, a threat that probably helps to keep an otherwise largely unfettered institution within constitutional bounds.

—GARY L. MCDOWELL

Bibliography

Berger, Raoul (1969). *Congress versus the Supreme Court.* Cambridge, Mass.: Harvard University Press.

Breckenridge, A. C. (1971). *Congress Against the Court.* Lincoln: University of Nebraska Press.

Morgan, Donald L. (1967). *Congress and the Constitution.* Cambridge, Mass.: Harvard University Press.

Murphy, Walter F. (1962). *Congress and the Courts.* Chicago: University of Chicago Press.

CONSTITUTIONAL INTERPRETATION

"Constitutional interpretation" comprehends the methods or strategies available to people attempting to resolve disputes about the meaning or application of the Constitution. The possible sources for interpretation include the text of the Constitution, its "original history," including the general social and political context in which it was adopted as well as the events immediately surrounding its adoption, the governmental structures created and recognized by the Constitution, the "ongoing history" of interpretations of the Constitution, and the social, political, and moral values of the interpreter's society or some subgroup of the society. The term "originalist" refers to interpretation concerned with the first three of these sources.

The extraordinary current interest in constitutional interpretation is partly the result of controversy over the Supreme Court's expansive readings of the Fourteenth Amendment; it also parallels developments in literary theory and more generally the humanities. Received notions about the intrinsic meaning of words or texts, access to an author's intentions, and the very notion of "validity" in interpretation have been forcefully attacked and vehemently defended by philosophers, literary theorists, social scientists, and historians of knowledge. Legal writers have imported scholarship from these disciplines into their own, and some humanists have become interested in legal interpretation.

Issues of interpretive methodology have always been politically charged—certainly so in constitutional law. John Marshall's foundational decisions asserting the power of the central government were met by claims that he had willfully misconstrued the document. In our own time, modernist interpretive theories tend to be invoked by proponents of judicial activism, and more conventional views by its opponents. The controversy within the humanities and the social sciences is itself deeply political, for the modernist assertion that truth or validity is socially constructed and hence contingent is often perceived as destabilizing or delegitimating.

The Constitution is a political document; it serves political ends; its interpretations are political acts. Any theory of constitutional interpretation therefore presupposes a normative theory of the Constitution itself—a theory, for example, about the constraints that the words and intentions of the adopters should impose on those who apply or interpret the Constitu-tion. As Ronald Dworkin observed, "Some parts of any constitutional theory must be independent of the intentions or beliefs or indeed the acts of the people the theory designates as Framers. Some part must stand on its own political or moral theory; otherwise the theory would be wholly circular."

The eclectic practices of interpreters and the continuing debate over the appropriate methods or strategies of constitutional interpretation suggest that we have no unitary, received theory of the Constitution. The American tradition of constitutional interpretation accords considerable authority to the language of the Constitution, its adopters' purposes, and the implications of the structures created and recognized by the Constitution. But our tradition also accords authority to precedents and the judicial exegesis of social values and practices, even when these diverge from plausible readings of the text and original understandings.

Any theory of constitutional interpretation must start from the fact that we have a written Constitution. Why is the written Constitution treated as binding? Because, as Chief Justice Marshall asserted in *Marbury* v. *Madison* (1803), it is law—the supreme law of the land—and because since 1789 public institutions and the citizenry have treated it as an authoritative legal document. It is no exaggeration to say that the written Constitution lies at the core of the American "civil religion."

Doubtless, the most frequently invoked canon of textual interpretation is the "plain meaning rule." Marshall wrote in *Sturges* v. *Crowninshield* (1819):

> *[A]lthough the spirit of an instrument, especially of a constitution, is to be respected not less than its letter, yet the spirit is to be collected chiefly from its words. . . . [I]f, in any case, the plain meaning of a provision, not contradicted by any other provision in the same instrument, is to be disregarded, because we believe the framers of that instrument could not intend what they say, it must be one in which the absurdity and in-*

justice of applying the provision to the case, would be so monstrous that all mankind would, without hesitation, unite in rejecting the application.

Marshall did not equate "plain" meaning with "literal" meaning, but rather (as Justice Oliver Wendell Holmes later put it) the meaning that it would have for "a normal speaker of English" under the circumstances in which it was used. The distinction is nicely illustrated by Chief Justice Marshall's opinion in *McCulloch* v. *Maryland* (1819), decided the same year as *Sturges.* Maryland had argued that the necessary and proper clause of Article I authorized Congress only to enact legislation "indispensable" to executing the enumerated powers. Marshall responded with the observation that the word "necessary," as used "in the common affairs of the world, or in approved authors, . . . frequently imports no more than that one thing is convenient, or useful, or essential to another." He continued:

Such is the character of human language, that no word conveys to the mind, in all situations, one single definite idea; and nothing is more common than to use words in a figurative sense. Almost all compositions contain words, which, taken in their rigorous sense, would convey a meaning different from that which is obviously intended. It is essential to just construction that many words which import something excessive, should be understood in a more mitigated sense—in that sense which common usage justifies. . . . This word, then, like others, is used in various senses; and in its construction, the subject, the context, the intention of the person using them, are all to be taken into view.

To read a provision without regard to its context and likely purposes will yield either unresolvable indeterminacies or plain nonsense. An interpreter could not, for example, decide whether the First Amendment's "freedom of speech" encompassed singing, flag-waving, and criminal solicitation; or whether the "writings" protected by the copyright clause included photographs, sculptures, performances, television broadcasts, and computer programs. She would not know whether the provision in Article II that "No person except a natural born Citizen . . . shall be eligible to the Office of President" disqualified persons born abroad or those born by cesarean section. We can identify interpretations as compelling, plausible, or beyond the pale only because we think we understand the concerns that underlie the provisions.

One's understanding of a provision, including the concerns that underlie it, depends partly on the ideological or political presuppositions one brings to the interpretive enterprise. Marshall could so readily label Maryland's construction of the word "necessary" as excessive because of his antecedent conception of a "constitution" as essentially different from a legal code—as a document "intended to endure for ages to come"—and because of his beliefs about the structure of federalism implicit in the United States Constitution. A judge starting from different premises might have found Maryland's construction more plausible.

A meaning thus is "plain" when it follows from the interpreter's presuppositions and when these presuppositions are shared within the society or at least within the relevant "community of interpretation"—for example, the legal profession. Kenneth Abraham has remarked, "The plain is plain because it is constantly recurring in similar contexts and there is general agreement about the meaning of language that may be applied to it. In short, meaning is a function of agreement. . . ."

When a provision is interpreted roughly contemporaneously with its adoption, an interpreter unconsciously places it in the social and linguistic context of her society. Over the course of several centuries, however, even a relatively stable nation will undergo changes—in social and economic relations, in technology, and ultimately in values—to an extent that a later interpreter cannot readily assume that she has direct access to the contexts in which a constitutional provision was adopted. This poses both a normative and a methodological question for the modern interpreter: Should she attempt to read provisions in their original social and linguistic contexts, or in a modern context, or in some way that mediates between the two? And, to the extent that the original contexts are relevant, how can she ascertain them?

Original history includes "legislative history"—the debates and proceedings in the conventions and legislatures that proposed and adopted constitutional provisions—and the broader social, economic, and political contexts surrounding their adoption. Although it is widely acknowledged that original history should play a role in constitutional interpretation, there is little agreement over the aims and methods of historical inquiry. The controversy centers on the level of generality on which an interpreter should try to apprehend the adopters' intentions. On the highest or broadest level, an interpreter poses the questions: "What was the general problem to which this provision was responsive and how did the provision respond to it?" On the most specific level, she inquires: "How would the adopters have resolved the particular issue that we are now considering?"

The first or "general" question elicits answers such as: "The purpose of the commerce clause was to permit Congress to regulate commerce that affects more than one state, or to regulate where the states are separately incompetent to regulate." Or: "The purpose of the equal protection clause was to prohibit invidious discrimination." These characterizations do not purport to describe the scope of a provision precisely. On the contrary, they are avowedly vague or open-ended: the claim is not that the equal protection clause forbids every conceivable invidious discrimination (it may or may not) but that it is generally concerned with preventing invidious discriminations.

The general question is an indispensable component of any textual interpretation. The interpreter seeks a "purpose" that she can plausibly attribute to everyone who voted for the provision, and that, indeed, must have been understood as their purpose even by those who opposed its adoption. The question is often couched in objective-sounding terms: it seeks the "purpose of the provision" rather than the "intent of the framers." And its answer is typically sought in the text read in the social and linguistic context in which it was adopted. As Marshall wrote in *McCulloch*, "The spirit of an instrument . . . is to be collected chiefly from its words." If the status of the written Constitution as "law" demands textual interpretation, it also entails this general inquiry, without which textual interpretation cannot proceed.

The second inquiry, which can be called "intentionalist," seeks very specific answers, such as: "Did the adopters of the Fourteenth Amendment intend to prohibit school segregation?" or "Did they intend to prohibit 'reverse' discrimination?" One rationale for this focus was asserted by Justice George H. Sutherland, dissenting in *Home Building & Loan Association* v. *Blaisdell* (1934): "[T]he whole aim of construction, as applied to a provision of the Constitution, is . . . to ascertain and give effect to the intent of its framers and the people who adopted it." Another rationale is that recourse to the adopters' intentions constrains the interpreter's discretion and hence the imposition of her own values. Some methodological problems are presented by any interpretive strategy that seeks to specify the adopters' intentions.

The procedures by which the *text* of a proposed constitutional provision is adopted are usually straightforward and clear: a text becomes a law if it is adopted by the constitutionally prescribed procedures and receives the requisite number of votes. For example, an amendment proposed in Congress becomes a part of the Constitution when it is approved by two-thirds of the members of each House and ratified by the legislatures in three-fourths of the states, or by conventions in three-fourths of the states, as Congress may prescribe.

How does an *intention* acquire the status of law? Some interpreters assume, without discussion, that by ratifying the framers' language, the thousands of people whose votes are necessary to adopt a constitutional provision either manifest their intent to adopt, or are somehow bound by, the intentions of certain of the drafters or framers—even if those intentions are not evident from the text itself. This view is not supported by anything in the Constitution, however, or by eighteenth- or nineteenth-century legal theory or practice.

If one analogizes the adoption of "an intention" concerning the text of the Constitution to the adoption of a text, an intention would become binding only when it was held by the number and combination of adopters prescribed by Article V. This poses no particular difficulty for an interpreter who wishes to understand the general aims or purposes of a provision. Statements by framers, proponents, and opponents, together with the social and political background against which the provision was adopted, often indicate a shared understanding. But these sources cannot usually answer specific questions about the adopters' intentions. The intentionalist interpreter thus often engages in a degree of speculation that undermines the very rationale for the enterprise.

The adopters of a provision may intend that it prohibit or permit some activity, or that it *not* prohibit or permit the activity; or they may have no intentions at all regarding the matter. An intentionalist interpreter must often infer the adopters' intentions from opaque sources, and must try to describe their intentions with respect to situations that they probably never thought about.

The effort to determine the adopters' intentions is further complicated by the problem of identifying the intended specificity of a provision. This problem is nicely illustrated by an example of Ronald Dworkin's. Consider the possible intentions of those who adopted the cruel and unusual punishment clause of the Eighth Amendment. They might have intended the language to serve only as a shorthand for the Stuart tortures which were their exemplary applications of the clause. Somewhat more broadly, they might have intended the clause to be understood to incorporate the principle of *ejusdem generis*—to include their exemplary applications and other punishments that they found, or would have found, equally repugnant.

More broadly yet, they might have intended to delegate to future decision makers the authority to apply the clause in light of the general principles underlying it. To use Dworkin's terms, they might have intended future interpreters to develop their own "conceptions" of cruel and unusual punishment within the framework of the adopters' general "concept" of the clause. If so, then the fact that they viewed a certain punishment as tolerable does not imply that they intended the clause "not to prohibit" such punishments. Like parents who instill values in their children both by articulating and applying a moral principle, the adopters may have accepted the eventuality that the principle would be applied in ways that diverged from their own particular views.

Whether or not such a motivation seems likely with respect to applications of the clause in the adopters' contemporary society, it may be more plausible with respect to applications by future interpreters, whose understandings of the clause would be affected by changing knowledge, values, and forms of society. On the other hand, the adopters may have thought of themselves as more virtuous or less corruptible than unknown future generations, and for that reason may have intended this and other clauses to be construed narrowly.

How can an interpreter determine the breadth of construction intended by the adopters of any particular provision? Primarily, if not exclusively, from the language of the provision itself. Justice Felix Frankfurter wrote in *National Mutual Insurance Company v. Tidewater Transfer Company* (1949):

The precision which characterizes [the jurisdictional provisions] . . . of Article III is in striking contrast to the imprecision of so many other provisions of the Constitution dealing with other very vital aspects of government. This was not due to chance or ineptitude on the part of the Framers. The differences in subject-matter account for the drastic difference in treatment. Great concepts like "Commerce among the several states," "due process of law," "liberty," "property," were purposely left to gather meaning from experience. For they relate to the whole domain of social and economic fact, and the statesmen who founded this nation knew too well that only a stagnant society remains unchanged. But when the Constitution in turn gives strict definition of power or specific limitations upon it we cannot extend the definition or remove the translation. Precisely because "it is a constitution we are expounding," M'Culloch v. Maryland, we ought not to take liberties with it.

Charles Curtis put the point more generally: "Words in legal documents are simply delegations to others of authority to give them meaning by applying them to particular things or occasions. . . . And the more imprecise the words are, the greater is the delegation, simply because then they can be applied or not to more particulars. This is the only important feature of words in legal draftsmanship or interpretation."

This observation seems correct. Yet it is worth noting that the relative precision of a word or clause itself depends both on context and on interpretive conventions, and is often uncertain and contestable. For example, in *United States* v. *Lovett* (1946) Justice Frankfurter characterized the bill of attainder clause as among the Constitution's very "specific provisions." Yet he construed that clause to apply to punishments besides death, ignoring the technical eighteenth-century distinction between a bill of attainder, which imposed the death penalty, and a bill of

"pains and penalties," which imposed lesser penalties.

The effort to characterize clauses as relatively open or closed confronts a different sort of historical problem as well. The history of interpretation of written constitutions was not extensive in 1787. Marshall's assertion that it is the nature of a constitution "that only its great outlines should be marked" (*McCulloch*) drew more on theory than on practice. But Marshall and his successors practiced this theory. Whatever assumptions the adopters of the original Constitution might have made about the scope of their delegations of authority, the Reconstruction amendments were adopted in the context of decades of "latitudinarian" constitutional interpretation. What bearing should this context have on the interpretation of provisions adopted since the original Constitution?

The intentionalist interpreter's initial task is to situate the provision and documents bearing on it in their original linguistic and social contexts. She can draw on the accumulated knowledge of American social, political, and intellectual history. Ultimately, however, constitutional interpretation is subject to the same limitations that attend all historical inquiry. Quentin Skinner has described the most pervasive of these:

> *[I]t will never in fact be possible simply to study what any given classic writer has said . . . without bringing to bear some of one's own expectations about what he must have been saying. . . . [T]hese models and preconceptions in terms of which we unavoidably organize and adjust our perceptions and thoughts will themselves tend to act as determinants of what we think or perceive. We must classify in order to understand, and we can only classify the unfamiliar in terms of the familiar. The perpetual danger, in our attempts to enlarge our historical understanding, is thus that our expectations about what someone must be saying or doing will themselves deter-*

*The continuing
debate over the
appropriate methods
or strategies of
constitutional
interpretation
suggests that we
have no unitary,
received theory of
the Constitution.*

mine that we understand the agent to be
doing something which he would not—or
even could not—himself have accepted as
an account of what he was doing.*

Trying to understand how the adopters intended a provision to apply in their own time and place is, in essence, doing history. But the intentionalist interpreter must take the further step of translating the adopters' intentions into the present. She must decide how the commerce power applies to modes of transportation, communication, and economic relations not imagined—perhaps not imaginable—by the adopters; how the cruel and unusual punishment clause applies to the death penalty in a society that likely apprehends death differently from a society in which death was both more commonplace and more firmly integrated into a religious cosmology. The Court invoked difficulties of this sort when it concluded that the history surrounding the adoption of the Fourteenth Amendment was "inconclusive" with respect to the constitutionality of school desegregation almost a century later. Noting the vastly different roles of public education in the mid-nineteenth and mid-twentieth centuries, Chief Justice Earl Warren wrote in *Brown* v. *Board of Education* (1954): "[W]e cannot turn back the clock to 1868 when the Amendment was adopted. . . . We must consider public education in the light of its full development and its present place in American life throughout the Nation. Only in this way can it be determined if segregation in public schools deprives these plaintiffs of the equal protection of the laws." In sum, even the historian who attempts to meet and understand the adopters on their own ground is engaging in a creative enterprise. To project the adopters into a world they could not have envisioned borders on fantasy.

In an important lecture given in 1968, entitled "Structure and Relationship in Constitutional Law," Professor Charles L. Black Jr. described a mode of constitutional interpretation based on "inference from the structure and relationships created by the constitution in all its parts or in some principal part." Professor Black observed that in *McCulloch* v. *Maryland*, "Marshall does not place principal reliance on the [necessary and proper] clause as a ground of decision. . . . [Before] he reaches it he has already decided, on the basis of far more general implications, that Congress possesses the power, not expressly named, of establishing a bank and chartering corporations: . . . [h]e addresses himself to the necessary and proper clause only in response to counsel's arguing its *restrictive* force." Indeed, the second part of *McCulloch*, which held that the Constitution prohibited Maryland from levying a tax on the national bank, rested exclusively on inferences from the structure of the federal system and not at all on the text of the Constitution. Similarly, *Crandall* v. *Nevada* (1868) was not premised on the privileges and immunities clause of either Article IV or the Fourteenth Amendment. Rather, the Court inferred a right of personal mobility among the states from the structure of the federal system: "[The citizen] has the right to come to the seat of government to assert any claim he may have upon that government, or to transact any business he may have with it . . . and this right is in its nature independent of the will of any State over whose soil he must pass to exercise it."

Citing examples like these, Professor Black argued that interpreters too often have engaged in "Humpty-Dumpty textual manipulation" rather than relying "on the sort of political inference which not only underlies the textual manipulation but is, in a well constructed opinion, usually invoked to support the interpretation of the cryptic text."

Institutional relationships are abstractions from the text and the purposes of provisions—themselves read on a high level of abstraction. The implications of the structures of government are usually vague, often even ambiguous. Thus, while structural inference is an important method of interpretation, it shares the limitations intrinsic to other interpretive strategies. It seldom yields unequivocal answers to the specific questions that arise in the course of constitutional debates.

For the most part, the Supreme Court—the institution that most systematically and authoritatively interprets and articulates the meaning of the Constitution—has construed the language, original history, and structure of the Constitution on a high level of abstraction. It has treated most provisions in the spirit suggested by Chief Justice Marshall in *McCulloch* v. *Maryland.* This view of the Constitution is partly a political choice, based on the desire to accommodate a venerated and difficult-to-amend historical monument with changing circumstances, attitudes, and needs. But it is no less a consequence of the nature of language and history, which necessarily leave much of the meaning of the Constitution to be determined by its subsequent applications.

Constitutional disputes typically arise against the background of earlier decisions on similar subjects. A complete theory of constitutional interpretation therefore must deal with the role of precedent. Interpreting a judicial precedent is different from interpreting the constitutional provision itself. A precedent consists of a judgment based on a particular set of facts together with the court's various explanations for the judgment. The precedent must be read, not only in terms of its own social context, but against the background of the precedents it invokes or ignores. Lon Fuller wrote:

In the common law it is not too much to say that the judges are always ready to look behind the words of a precedent to what the previous court was trying to say, or to what it would have said if it could have foreseen the nature of the cases that were later to arise, or if its perception of the relevant factors in the case before it had been more acute. There is, then, a real sense in which the written words of the reported decisions are merely the gateway to something lying behind them that may be called, without any excess of poetic license, "unwritten law."

The American doctrine of stare decisis accords presumptive but not indefeasible authority to precedent. Courts sometimes have overruled earlier decisions to return to what is said to be the original understanding of a provision. They have also overruled precedents that seem inconsistent with contemporary norms. For example, in *Harper* v. *Virginia State Board of Elections* (1966), the Supreme Court overruled a twenty-year-old precedent to invalidate, under the equal protection clause, a state law conditioning the right to vote in state election on payment of an annual poll tax of $1.50. After surveying intervening decisions protecting political participation and other interests, Justice William O. Douglas concluded: "In determining what lines are unconstitutionally discriminatory, we have never been confined to historic notions of equality, any more than we have restricted due process to a fixed catalogue of what was at a given time deemed to be the limits of fundamental rights. . . . Notions of what constitutes equal treatment for purposes of the Equal Protection clause *do* change."

The process of constitutional adjudication thus has a dynamic of its own. It creates an independent force that, as a doctrine evolves, may compete with the text and original history as well as with older precedents. Whether or not, as Justice John Marshall Harlan argued in dissent, *Harper* was inconsistent with the original understanding of the Fourteenth Amendment, the decision would have been inconceivable without the intervening expansion of doctrine beyond applications contemplated by the adopters of the Fourteenth Amendment.

Disagreements about the propriety of this evolutionary process are rooted in differing theories of constitutional law. To a strict intentionalist like Raoul Berger, the process

For the most part, the Supreme Court has construed the language, original history, and structure of the Constitution on a high level of abstraction.

appears to be simply the accretion of errors, which should be corrected to the extent possible. Others hold that the process properly accommodates the Constitution to changing needs and values. As Justice Holmes wrote in *Missouri* v. *Holland* (1920):

> [W]hen we are dealing with words that are also a constituent act, like the Constitution of the United States, we must realize that they have called into life a being the development of which could not have been foreseen completely by the most gifted of its begetters. It was enough for them to realize or to hope that they had created an organism; it has taken a century and cost their successors much sweat and blood to prove that they created a nation. The case before us must be considered in the light of our entire experience and not merely in that of what was said a hundred years ago. . . . We must consider what this country has become in deciding what the Amendment has reserved.

Chief Justice Charles Evans Hughes's opinion in *Home Building & Loan* stands as the Court's most explicit assertion of the independent force of precedents and of the changing values they reflect. The Court upheld a law, enacted during the Depression, that postponed a mortgagor's right to foreclose against a defaulting mortgagee. In dissent, Justice Sutherland argued that the contract clause, which had been adopted in response to state debtor-relief legislation enacted during the depression following the Revolutionary War, was intended to prohibit precisely this sort of law. Given his intentionalist premise this disposed of the case. Hughes did not dispute Sutherland's account of the original history. Rather, he reviewed the precedents interpreting the contract clause to conclude:

> It is manifest . . . that there has been a growing appreciation of public needs and

of the necessity of finding ground for a rational compromise between individual rights and public welfare. The settlement and consequent contraction of the public domain, the pressure of a constantly increasing density of population, the interrelation of the activities of our people, and the complexity of our economic interests, have inevitably led to an increased use of the organization of society in order to protect the very bases of individual opportunity. . . . [T]he question is no longer merely that of one party to a contract as against another, but of the use of reasonable means to safeguard the economic structure upon which the good of all depends.

The views articulated by Holmes, Hughes, and Douglas reflect the Court's actual practice in adjudication under the Bill of Rights, the Fourteenth Amendment, and other provisions deemed relatively open-textured. The process bears more resemblance to common law adjudication than to textual exegesis.

In an influential essay, Thomas Grey observed that the American constitutional tradition included practices of nonoriginalist adjudication purportedly based on principles of natural rights or fundamental law, or on widely shared and deeply held values not readily inferred from the text of the written Constitution. Several of the Supreme Court's contemporary decisions involving procreation and the family have invoked this tradition, and have given rise to a heated controversy over the legitimacy of adjudication based on "fundamental values."

Originalist and nonoriginalist adjudication are not nearly so distinct as many of the disputants assume. Constitutional provisions differ enormously in their closed- or open-texturedness. Indeed, a provision's texture is not merely a feature of its language or its original history, but of the particular situation in which it is applied. One's approach to a text is determined by tradition and by social outlooks that can change over time. Depending on one's political philosophy, one may bemoan this inevitability, or embrace it. For better or for worse, however, Terrance Sandalow described an important feature of our constitutional tradition when he remarked that "[t]he Constitution has . . . not only been read in light of contemporary circumstances and values; it has been read *so that* the circumstances and values of the present generation might be given expression in constitutional law."

Most disputes about constitutional interpretation and fundamental values concern interpretation in particular institutional contexts. Today's disputes center on the judicial power to review and strike down the acts of legislatures and agencies and are motivated by what Alexander M. Bickel dubbed the "counter-majoritarian difficulty" of judicial review. Urgings of "judicial restraint" or of a more expansive approach to constitutional adjudication tend to reflect differing opinions of the role of the judiciary in a democratic polity and, more crudely, differing views about the substantive outcomes that these strategies yield. The question, say, of whether Congress, the Supreme Court, or the states themselves should take primary responsibility for elaborating the equal protection clause is essentially political and cannot be resolved by abstract principles of interpretation. But this observation also cautions against taking interpretive positions based on particular institutional concerns and generalizing them beyond the situations that motivated them.

Constitutional interpretation is as much a process of creation as one of discovery. If this view is commonplace among postrealist academics, it is not often articulated by judges and it probably conflicts with the view of many citizens that constitutional interpretation should reflect the will of the adopters of the Constitution rather than its interpreters.

So-called strict construction is an unsatisfactory response to these concerns. First, the most frequently litigated provisions do not lend themselves to "strict" or unambiguous or literal interpretation. (What are the strict meanings of the privileges or immunities, due process, and equal protection clauses?) Second, attempts to confine provisions to their very narrowest meanings typically produce results so ludicrous that even self-styled strict constructionists unconsciously abandon them in favor of less literal readings of texts and broader conceptualizations of the adopters' intentions. (No interpreter would hold that the First Amendment does not protect posters or songs because they are not "speech," or that the commerce clause does not apply to telecommunications because the adopters could not have foreseen this mode of commerce.) An interpreter must inevitably choose among different levels of abstraction in reading a provision—a choice that cannot itself be guided by any rules. Third, the two modes of strict interpretation—literalism and strict intentionalism—far from being synergistic strategies of interpretation, are often antagonistic. (Although the adopters of the First Amendment surely did not intend to protect obscene speech, the language they adopted does not exclude it.) A strict originalist theory of interpretation must opt either for literalism or for intentionalism, or must have some extraconstitutional principle for mediating between the two.

To reject these strategies is not to shed constraints. The text and history surrounding the adoption of a provision originate a line of doctrine, set its course, and continue to impose limitations. Some interpretations are more plausible than others; some are beyond the pale. And the criteria of plausibility are not merely subjective. Rather, they are intersubjective, constituted by others who are engaged in the same enterprise. Beyond the problem of subjectivity, however, the demographic characteristics of the legal interpretive community gives rise to an equally serious concern: the judiciary and the bar more generally have tended to be white, male, Anglo-Saxon, and well-to-do, and one might well wonder whether their interpretations do not embody parochial views or class interests. The concerns cannot be met by the choice of interpretive strategies, however, but only by addressing the composition and structure of the institutions whose interpretations have the force of law.

—PAUL BREST

Bibliography

Abraham, Kenneth (1981). Three Fallacies of Interpretation: A Comment on Precedent and Judicial Decision. *Arizona Law Review* 23:771–783.

Berger, Raoul (1977). *Government by Judiciary: The Transformation of the Fourteenth Amendment.* Cambridge, Mass.: Harvard University Press.

Black, Charles L., Jr. (1969). *Structure and Relationship in Constitutional Law.* Baton Rouge: Louisiana State University Press.

Curtis, Charles (1950). A Better Theory of Legal Interpretation. *Vanderbilt Law Review* 3:407–437.

Dworkin, Ronald (1981). The Forum of Principle. *New York Law Review* 56: 469–518.

Ely, John Hart (1980). *Democracy and Distrust.* Cambridge, Mass.: Harvard University Press.

Fuller, Lon (1968). *Anatomy of Law.* New York: Praeger.

Grey, Thomas (1975). Do We Have an Unwritten Constitution? *Stanford Law Review* 27:703–718.

Holmes, Oliver W. (1899). The Theory of Interpretation. *Harvard Law Review* 12: 417.

Monaghan, Henry (1981). Our Perfect Constitution. *New York University Law Review* 56:353–376.

Sandalow, Terrance (1981). Constitutional Interpretation. *Michigan Law Review* 79:1033–1072.

Skinner, Quentin (1969). Meaning and Understanding in the History of Ideas. *History & Theory* 8:3–53.

Symposium (1985). Constitutional Interpretation. *University of Southern California Law Review* 58:551–725.

Symposium on Law and Literature (1982). *Texas Law Review* 60:373–586.

ten Broek, Jacobus (1938–1939). Admissibility and Use by the Supreme Court of Extrinsic Aids in Constitutional Construction. *California Law Review* 26:287–308, 437–454, 664–681; 27:157–181, 399–421.

COOLEY v. BOARD OF WARDENS OF PORT OF PHILADELPHIA

12 Howard 299 (1851)

The chaos in judicial interpretation that characterized the Taney Court's commerce clause cases was ended in *Cooley*, the most important decision on the subject between *Gibbons* v. *Ogden* (1824) and *United States* v. *E. C. Knight Co.* (1895). The Taney Court finally found a doctrinal formula that allowed a majority to coalesce around a single line of reasoning for the first time since the days of the Marshall Court. That formula was the doctrine of selective exclusiveness, announced for the majority by Justice Benjamin R. Curtis. The doctrine was a compromise, combining aspects of the doctrines of concurrent powers over commerce and exclusive powers, but three Justices of the eight who participated rejected the compromise. Justices John McLean and James M. Wayne, whom Curtis privately called "high-toned Federalists," persisted in their nationalist view, expressed in dissent, that congressional powers over interstate and foreign commerce were always exclusive, while *Peter* v. *Daniel*, an intransigent states-rightist, concurred in the majority's result on the ground that congressional power over commerce was never exclusive.

At issue in *Cooley* was the constitutionality of a Pennsylvania statute requiring ships of a certain size entering or leaving the port of Philadelphia to employ local pilots in local waters. Cooley, claiming that the state act unconstitutionally regulated foreign commerce, refused to pay the pilotage fee. The fact that the first Congress had provided that the states could enact pilotage laws did not alter Cooley's claim. Curtis for the Court acknowledged that if the grant of commerce powers to Congress had divested the states of a power to legislate, the act of Congress could not confer that power on the states. The problem was whether the power of Congress in this case was exclusive.

Commerce, Curtis declared, embraces a vast field of many different subjects. Some subjects imperatively demand a single uniform rule for the whole nation, while others, like pilotage, demand diverse local rules to cope with varying local situations. The power of Congress was therefore selectively exclusive. If the subject required a single uniform rule, the states could not regulate that subject even in the absence of congressional legislation. In such a case congressional powers would be exclusive. Such was the nationalist half of the doctrine. The other half, by which the Court sustained the state act, maintained that the states did possess concurrent powers over commerce if the subject required diversity of regulation. Thus Congress's power was exclusive or concurrent depending on the nature of the subject to be regulated. "It is the opinion of a majority of the court," Curtis declared, "that the mere grant to Congress of the power to regulate commerce, did not deprive the States of power to regulate pilots, and that although Congress has legislated on this subject, its legislation manifests an intention . . . to leave its regulation to the several States."

The Court's doctrine of selective exclusiveness gave it a point of departure for analyzing commerce clause issues. The doctrine, however, had to be interpreted. It did not even suggest how the Court could determine which subjects required national legislation, thus excluding state action, and which required diverse local regulations. The doctrine could be manipulated by Justices who employed nationalist doctrine to invalidate state enactments.

—LEONARD W. LEVY

Bibliography

Swisher, Carl Brent (1974). *History of the Supreme Court.* Vol. 5:404–407. New York: Macmillan.

COOPER v. AARON

358 U.S. 1 (1958)

For several years after its decision in *Brown* v. *Board of Education* (1954–55), the Supreme Court gave little guidance or support to the lower courts charged with supervising the desegregation of the public schools. In this case, however, the Court was confronted with direct defiance of *Brown* by a state's highest officials, and it met that challenge head-on.

Even before the *Brown* remedial opinion in 1955, the school board of Little Rock, Arkansas, had approved a plan for gradual desegregation of the local schools, and the federal district court had upheld the plan. Just before the opening of the fall 1957 term, the state governor, Orval Faubus, ordered the state's National Guard to keep black children out of Little Rock's Central High School. The attorney general of the United States obtained an injunction against the governor's action, and the children entered the school. A hostile crowd gathered, and the children were removed by the police. President Dwight D. Eisenhower was thus prodded into his first significant act supporting desegregation; he sent Army troops to Central High to protect the children, and eight black students attended the school for the full academic year.

In February 1958 the school board asked the district court, in *Cooper* v. *Aaron*, for a delay of two and one-half years in the implementation of its plan, and in June the court agreed, commenting on the "chaos, bedlam and turmoil" at Central High. In August the federal court of appeals reversed, calling for

Cooley *was the most important commerce clause case between* Gibbons v. Ogden *(1824) and* United States v. E. C. Knight Co. *(1895).*

See also
Gibbons v. *Ogden*
Knight Co., E. C.,
United States v.

Cooper's importance was not so much doctrinal as political.

♦ **political question**
An issue reserved for decision by the legislative and executive branches of government, and so not appropriately decided by a court.

implementation of the plan on schedule. The Supreme Court, in an unusual move, accelerated the hearing to September 11, and the next day it issued a brief order affirming the decision of the court of appeals. Later the Court published its full opinion, signed by all nine Justices to emphasize their continued unanimous support of *Brown.*

The opinion dealt quickly with the uncomplicated merits of the case, saying that law and order were not to be achieved at the expense of the constitutional rights of black children. The Court then added a response to the assertion by the Arkansas governor and legislature that the state was not required to abide by *Brown,* because *Brown* itself was an unconstitutional assumption of judicial power.

The response scored two easy points first: the Constitution, under the Supremacy Clause, is "the supreme Law of the Land," and *Marbury* v. *Madison* (1803) had held that it was the province of the judiciary to "say what the law is." The Court's next step, however, was not self-evident: *Marbury* meant that the federal courts are supreme in expounding the Constitution; thus *Brown* was the supreme law of the land, binding state officers. This view, which carried the assertion of judicial power further than *Marbury* had taken it, has been repeated by the Court several times since the *Cooper* decision.

Cooper's importance, however, was not so much doctrinal as political. It reaffirmed principle at a crucial time. The televised pictures of black children being escorted into school through a crowd of hostile whites galvanized northern opinion. The 1960 election brought to office a president committed to a strong civil rights program—although it took his death to enact that program into law.

—KENNETH L. KARST

COPYRIGHT

The Framers of the Constitution delegated to the national government authority to enact copyright laws. The copyright power, together with the patent power, is found in Article I, section 8, clause 8, which empowers Congress "to promote the progress of science and useful arts, by securing for limited times to authors and inventors the exclusive right to their respective writings and discoveries." Because there is no record of any debate on this clause at the Constitutional Convention of 1787, and mention of it in *The Federalist* is perfunctory, the meaning of the clause must be found in case law.

The phrase "to promote the progress of science" states what the Supreme Court, in *Mazer* v. *Stein* (1954), described as "the economic philosophy behind the clause," which is "the conviction that encouragement of individual effort by personal gain is the best way to advance public welfare through the talents of authors. . . ." Most courts, however, would deny that the introductory phrase permits the denial of copyright to any particular work on the ground that it does not contribute to such "progress." In fact, a United States Court of Appeals held in 1979 that obscene content does not invalidate copyright.

The words "by securing" came into contention in *Wheaton* v. *Peters* (1834), the first important copyright case decided by the Supreme Court, and a case involving two of the Court's own reporters. The plaintiff there argued that the federal copyright statute merely added additional remedies to a right that already existed at common law. To bolster this position, he argued that the word "secure" meant to protect, insure, save, and ascertain, not to create. The Court rejected this contention, holding that the federal statute had created a new right, but that the author had not complied with the act's conditions.

Because the clause contains the words, "for limited times," a federal copyright statute that purported to grant copyright protection in perpetuity would clearly be unconstitutional. So too would a term that is nominally "limited" but is in fact the equivalent of perpetual protection (for example, a one thousand year term). The term currently provided for newly created works, the life of the author plus fifty years, conforms with the "limited times" requirement.

Only "authors" may be granted copyright in the first instance, although, once granted, copyright is transferable by an author to others. The term "authors" in the Constitution gives rise to the "originality" requirement in the law of copyright, which excludes from copyright protection material copied from others. An author is no less an author because others have anticipated his work, as long as he did not copy from such others. This Judge Frank contrasted with an "inventor" under the patent power, who must by definition produce something "novel," that is, not anticipated in the prior art. By reason of the phrase "exclusive right," it is clear that Congress has the power to grant to authors the "exclusive right" to exploit their works. But Congress is under no compulsion to exercise its full powers under the Constitution. If it may withhold copyright protection altogether from a given category of works, it may also grant something less than exclusive rights. The phrase "to their respective writings" means that only "writings" may be the subject of copyright. But the concept of a "writing" for copyright purposes has been liberally construed. The Court has held that photographic portraits and sound recordings constitute a "writing." Indeed, in *Goldstein* v. *California* (1973), the Court defined "writings" as "any physical rendering of the fruits of creative intellectual or aesthetic labor." A work that has not been physically fixed is ineligible for copyright protection.

In *Goldstein* the Court held that the copyright power is not exclusive, so that, subject to the supremacy clause, the states retain concurrent power to enact copyright laws. Until adoption of the current Copyright Act in 1978 this reserved state power was significant, because most unpublished works were protected by so-called common law (or state law) copyright. However, under the current Copyright Act this area of state law has been largely preempted, so that most works, published or unpublished, are protected, if at all, under the federal act.

In recent years the courts have begun to question whether, and to what extent, the copyright laws are subject to the freedom of speech and freedom of the press guarantees of the First Amendment. If the First Amendment were literally applied it would invalidate the Copyright Act, since the act clearly abridges the freedom of speech and press of those who would engage in copyright infringement by copying from others. Nothing in the First Amendment limits the freedom protected thereunder to speech that is original with the speaker. Nor does the fact that the Constitution also grants to Congress the power to enact copyright laws render the First Amendment inapplicable. The First Amendment and the remainder of the Bill of Rights limit only those powers that have otherwise been confided to the federal government. If it did not modify such powers, it would have no meaning at all. The conflict between these two socially useful, yet antithetical, interests is, of course, capable of resolution. The Ninth Circuit held in *Krofft* v. *McDonald's Corp.* (1977), and the Supreme Court implicitly agreed in *Zacchini* v. *Scripps-Howard Broadcasting Co.* (1977), that "ideas" lie in the domain of the First Amendment, so that copyright may not be claimed therein, but that the form of "expression" of ideas may be the subject of copyright, notwithstanding the First Amendment.

—MELVILLE B. NIMMER

Bibliography

Nimmer, Melville B. (1978). *Copyright.* 4 vols. Albany, N.Y.: Matthew Bender Co.

COUNSELMAN v. HITCHCOCK

142 U.S. 547 (1892)

The first Supreme Court decision on immunity statutes, *Counselman* remained the leading case until it was distinguished away in

The Framers of the Constitution delegated to the national government authority to enact copyright laws.

♦ **ultra vires**
[Latin: beyond (its) power] An action by a person, corporation, or public agency that is beyond the actor's legitimate authority.

See also
Freedom of Speech
Freedom of the Press
Goldstein v. *California*

♦ **use immunity**
*Immunity from
prosecution based upon or
using evidence of an
offense given by a
witness in exchange for
the grant of immunity.
Prosecution may occur
only if it is based on
independently acquired
evidence.*

♦ **transactional
immunity**
*Immunity from
prosecution for any
offense mentioned in
testimony given in
exchange for the grant of
immunity, regardless of
other evidence that may
be acquired
independently.*

See also

Kastigar v. *United States*

Kastigar v. *United States* (1972). Appellant refused to testify before a federal grand jury on the ground that he might incriminate himself, though he had been granted use immunity under an 1887 act of Congress guaranteeing that his evidence would not be used against him criminally, except in a prosecution for perjury. *Counselman* thus raised the question whether a grant of use immunity could supplant the Fifth Amendment right of a person not to be a witness against himself in a criminal case. The government contended that an investigation before a grand jury was not a criminal case, which could arise only after an indictment should be returned, but that in any instance, Counselman had received immunity in return for his testimony.

Justice Samuel Blatchford for a unanimous Court declared that it is "impossible" that the clause of the Fifth Amendment could mean only what it says, for it is not limited to situations in which one is compelled to be a witness against himself in a "criminal case." The object of the clause is to insure that no person should be compelled as a witness "in any investigation" to testify to anything that might tend to show he had committed a crime. "The privilege is limited to criminal matters, but it is as broad as the mischief against which it seeks to guard," and therefore it applied to grand jury proceedings that might result in a prosecution. Clearly, said Blatchford, a statute cannot abridge a constitutional privilege nor replace one, "unless it is so broad as to have the same extent in scope and effect." The statute did not even do what it purported to do; it did not bar use of the compelled testimony, for its fruits could be used against the witness by searching out any leads, originating with his testimony, to other evidence that could convict him. No statute leaving the witness subject to prosecution after answering incriminating questions can have the effect of supplanting the constitutional provision. The 1887 act of Congress was unconstitutional because it was not a "full substitute" for that provision.

Thus the Court introduced the extraordinary doctrine that a statute could be a substitute for a provision of the Constitution, after having said that a statute could not "replace" such a provision. But the statute, to be constitutional, must serve "co-extensively" with the right it replaces. The Court laid down the standard for transactional immunity: to be valid the statute "must afford absolute immunity against future prosecution for the offense to which the question relates."

—LEONARD W. LEVY

COUNTY OF ALLEGHENY v. AMERICAN CIVIL LIBERTIES UNION

109 S.Ct. 3086 (1989)

Each year the County of Allegheny set up a variety of exhibits to commemorate the holiday season. Inside the county courthouse, a crèche was displayed on the grand staircase. Outside the courthouse stood a Christmas tree and a menorah, the latter a symbol of Hanukkah. The outside display was accompanied by a sign describing it as part of the city's salute to liberty. A splintered Supreme Court ruled that the crèche violated the establishment clause, but the menorah did not.

Justice Harry A. Blackmun delivered the opinion of the Court with respect to the crèche. He argued that the crèche violated the second prong of the Lemon test because it expressed a patently religious message, as indicated by an accompanying banner with the words "Gloria in Excelsis Deo!!" ("Glory to God in the Highest!!"). However, Blackmun argued that the menorah did not endorse religion because in context it was devoid of religious significance. The menorah and Christmas tree together merely symbolized the different facets of the "same winter-holiday season, which has attained a secular status in our society."

Justice Sandra Day O'Connor rejected Blackmun's reasoning with respect to the menorah, although she concurred in the Court's judgment. Unlike Blackmun, O'Connor readily acknowledged the religious meaning of the menorah, but argued that its display was permissible because in context it "conveyed a message of pluralism and freedom of belief" rather than endorsement. Justices William J. Brennan, John Paul Stevens, and Thurgood Marshall disagreed. They contended that both the Christmas tree and the menorah were religious symbols and that their display effected a dual endorsement of Christianity and Judaism.

Four Justices on the Court—William H. Rehnquist, Antonin Scalia, Byron R. White, and Anthony M. Kennedy—took issue with the Court's ruling on the crèche. Writing for this group, Justice Kennedy argued that the guiding principle in establishment-clause cases should be government neutrality toward religion—but neutrality properly understood. Given the pervasive influence of the "modern administrative state," said Kennedy, complete government nonrecognition of religion would send "a clear message of disapproval." Hence, some government recognition of religion may actually further the goal of neutrality. As applied to this case, for the government to recognize only the secular aspects of a holiday with both secular and religious components would signal not neutrality but "callous indifference" toward the religious beliefs of a great many celebrants. Such hostility is not required by the Constitution according to Kennedy. As long as holiday displays do not directly or indirectly coerce people in the area of religion and the displays do not tend toward the establishment of a state religion, they should be constitutional. Under this standard, the crèche, the Christmas tree, and the menorah were all permissible.

—JOHN G. WEST, JR.

COURT-PACKING PLANS

"Court packing" is an ambiguous phrase. It arises more frequently as an epithet in political disputation than as an analytical term in scholarly discourse. "Packing" connotes a deliberate effort by an executive, especially a president, to appoint one or more (usually

Each year the County of Allegheny set up a variety of exhibits to commemorate the holiday season.

See also

Civil Liberties

Establishment of Religion

Freedom of Religion

more) judges to assure that decisions will accord with the ideological predisposition of that executive. *Webster's New International Dictionary* defines "pack" as "to . . . make up unfairly or fraudulently, to secure a certain result." Yet not everyone agrees on what is unfair, and it is not at all extraordinary for presidents to take pains to ascertain that a prospective nominee is likely to behave in ways that will not be out of harmony with the ends of their administrations.

Furthermore, the word "packing" has been employed with respect to two different situations—when a president is filling vacancies that have arisen in the natural course of events, and when a president seeks legislation to increase the membership of courts to create additional opportunities for appointments that may shape the outcome of pending and future litigation.

Although political antagonists have taken advantage of the elasticity of the word to raise the charge of Court packing through much of our history, scholars have largely concentrated their attention on three particular episodes. The first of these events took place on the night of March 3, 1801, when in his final hours in office, President John Adams sat up very late signing commissions of sixteen appointees to circuit judgeships and forty-two justices of the peace for the District of Columbia, including one William Marbury. All these offices had been created in the last three weeks of his term by an obliging Federalist Congress, and Adams, outraged by the victory of the Democratic Republicans in 1800 and fearful of its consequences for the nation, busied himself filling the posts with faithful partisans to serve as a restraint on his successor, Thomas Jefferson. This melodrama of the "midnight judges" would subsequently lead to the landmark case of *Marbury* v. *Madison* (1803).

Historians long thought they had detected another instance of court packing during reconstruction. In 1870, at a time when the membership of the Court had been reduced, the Supreme Court, in *Hepburn* v. *Griswold*, struck down the Legal Tender Act of 1862 as applied to debts incurred before its enactment. The 4–3 vote strictly followed party lines. A year later, in *Knox* v. *Lee* and *Parker* v. *Davis*, the decision was reversed when the three dissenters in the earlier ruling were joined by two new appointees, both Republicans, of President Ulysses S. Grant. Their appointments followed the action of Congress restoring the Court to nine Justices. This sequence gave credibility to the allegation that the Court had been packed in order to save the Republican administration's monetary policy. In fact, however, scholars now agree that neither the augmentation of the size of the bench nor these appointments resulted from partisan or ideological motivations.

By far the most important court-packing plan in American history emerged out of a conflict between the Supreme Court and the administration of Franklin D. Roosevelt in the Great Depression. In 1935 and 1936, the Court again and again struck down New Deal laws, including those creating the two foundation stones of Roosevelt's recovery program, the National Industrial Recovery Act and the Agricultural Adjustment Act of 1935 (AAA). Most of these rulings came on split decisions, with Owen J. Roberts joining the conservative "Four Horsemen"—Pierce Butler, James C. McReynolds, George Sutherland, and Willis Van Devanter—to form a five-man majority, sometimes augmented by the Chief Justice, Charles Evans Hughes.

The Roosevelt administration responded by exploring a number of possibilities for curbing the powers of the Supreme Court. As early as May 1935, Attorney General Homer S. Cummings directed one of his aides to look into how the Court's authority to pass on constitutional questions could be limited. Rumors had circulated from the beginning of the New Deal era that court packing might someday be attempted, and at a cabinet meeting at the end of 1935, the president mentioned packing the Court as the first of a series of options. A cabinet official noted in his diary, however, that Roosevelt characterized it as "a distasteful idea." Still, Roosevelt more than once alluded to the episode in Great Britain earlier in the century when the threat of creating several hundred new peers had compelled the House of Lords to approve reform legislation.

Initially, critics of the judiciary assumed that redress could be achieved only by amending the Constitution, but the behavior of the Court in 1936 turned the thinking of the administration in new directions. When Justice Harlan F. Stone, in a biting dissent in *Butler* v. *United States* (1936), accused the majority in the 6–3 ruling invalidating the AAA processing tax of a "tortured construction of the Constitution," he fostered the idea that Congress need not alter the Constitution because properly interpreted it could accommodate most of the New Deal. Instead, Congress should concern itself with the composition of the Court.

The replacement of even one Justice could shift 5–4 decisions toward approval of FDR's policies without any modification of the Constitution. Yet, although this Court was the oldest ever, not a single vacancy developed in all of Roosevelt's first term. Increasingly, the administration looked for a solution that would eschew the tortuous process of constitutional amendment and instead, by the much simpler procedure of an act of Congress, overcome obstruction by elderly judges.

Shortly after winning reelection in November 1936, Roosevelt told Cummings that the time to act had come. Not only had the Court struck down fundamental New Deal laws in his first term, but in addition, it was expected to invalidate innovative legislation such as the National Labor Relations Act and the Social Security Act when it ruled on these statutes early in his second term. Moreover, although he had won an overwhelming

endorsement from the people in a contest in which he had carried all but two of the states, he was constrained from taking advantage of this mandate because if he tried to put through measures such as a wages and hours law the Court was likely to wipe out those laws too. He saw little prospect that the Court might change its attitude; in the very last decision of the term, *Morehead* v. *New York ex rel. Tipaldo* (1936), it had shocked the nation by striking down a New York State minimum wage law for women, thereby indicating that it did not merely oppose concentrated power in Washington, but was, in the president's words, creating a 'no-man's land' where no Government—State or Federal—can function." Under these circumstances, FDR was determined not to be like President James Buchanan, who sat passively while his world collapsed about him.

During the month of December, Cummings put together the specific proposal that Roosevelt embraced. Cummings was influenced by the political scientist Edward S. Corwin, who suggested linking an age limit of seventy years for Justices to the appointment of additional members of the bench, but he did not find the precise formula until he came upon a 1913 memorandum by James C. McReynolds, then attorney general, recommending that when a judge of the lower federal courts did not retire at seventy the president be required to appoint an additional judge. Cummings seized McReynolds's idea and applied it to the Supreme Court as well. He also worked out a rationale for the scheme by incorporating it in a package of proposals for relieving congestion in the federal judicial system. Roosevelt, for his part, savored the irony that the original notion had come from McReynolds, now the most hostile Justice on the Court.

Through all these months, the president had given little indication of what he was considering. After the adverse decision in *Schechter Poultry Corporation* v. *United States* (1935), he had said, "We have been relegated

*"Court packing" is
an ambiguous
phrase.*

◆ **ex relatione**
[Latin: from what has been related (by)] Legal actions brought by the state upon information supplied by or at the instigation of a private party are said to be "ex relatione." In reports, it is abbreviated "ex rel."

to the horse-and-buggy definition of interstate commerce," but so loud were objections to this remark that he made almost no public utterance about the Court for the next year and a half and did not raise the issue in the 1936 campaign. No cabinet officer save Cummings knew of the surprise he was about to spring, and he confided nothing to his congressional leaders until the very end.

On February 5, 1937, Roosevelt stunned the nation by sending to Congress a plan to reorganize the federal judiciary. He prefaced the proposal by claiming that aged and infirm judges and insufficient personnel had created overcrowded federal court dockets and by asserting that "a constant and systematic addition of younger blood will vitalize the courts." To achieve this goal, he recommended that when a federal judge who had served at least ten years waited more than six months after his seventieth birthday to resign or retire, a president might add a new judge to the bench. He could appoint as many as six new Justices to the Supreme Court and forty-four new judges to the lower federal tribunals.

The president's message elicited boisterous opposition. From the very first day, opponents characterized his scheme as "court packing" and accused Roosevelt of tampering with the judiciary. Within weeks, they had forced him to back away from his crowded dockets-old age rationale by demonstrating that the Supreme Court was abreast of his work. Especially effective was a letter from Chief Justice Hughes read by Senator Burton K. Wheeler at the opening of hearings before the Senate Judiciary committee. An increase in the size of the Court, Hughes objected, would not promote efficiency, but would mean that "there would be more judges to hear, more judges to confer, more judges to discuss, more judges to be convinced and to decide."

Despite fervent and well-organized protests, commentators concluded that the legislation was likely to be approved because Roosevelt had such huge Democratic majorities in both houses of Congress. After the 1936 elections, the Republicans were reduced to only sixteen members in the Senate. In the House, the Democrats had a 4–1 advantage. Although there were some conspicuous defectors, such as Wheeler, it seemed unlikely that enough Democrats would break with a president who had just won such an emphatic popular verdict of approval to deny him the legislation he sought.

A series of unanticipated decisions by the Court, however, drastically altered this situation. On March 29, the Court, in a 5–4 ruling in *West Coast Hotel Co*. v. *Parrish* (1937), validated a minimum wage act of the state of Washington essentially the same as the New York law it had struck down the previous year. Two weeks later, in a cluster of 5–4 decisions, it upheld the constitutionality of the Wagner (National Labor Relations) Act. In May, by 5–4 and 7–2, it validated the Social Security Act. The critical development in these votes was the switch of Justice Roberts, who for the first time since the spring of 1935 broke away from the Four Horsemen to uphold social legislation. Roberts's turnabout gave Roosevelt a 5–4 advantage, which swelled to a prospective 6–3 when, also in May, one of the Four Horsemen, Willis Van Devanter, announced that he was retiring. On that same day, the Senate Judiciary Committee voted, 10–8, to recommend against passage of the bill, and administration polls of the Senate found that as a consequence of these developments Roosevelt no longer had the votes. "A switch in time," it was said, "saved nine."

Roosevelt, however, persisted in trying to put through a modified court-packing measure, and he almost succeeded. In June, he advanced a compromise raising the suggested retirement age from seventy to seventy-five years and permitting him only one appointment per calendar year. Although watered down, this new version preserved the principle of the original bill and would give him two new Justices by January 1, 1938 (one for the calendar year 1937 and one for 1938), as well as a third Justice for the Van Devanter vacancy. In July, when court-packing legislation finally reached the Senate floor, the opposition found that Roosevelt had a majority for this new proposal if it could be brought to the floor. The president's advantage, however, rested on the influence of the domineering Senate Majority Leader, Joseph T. Robinson, but when shortly after the debate began Robinson died, Roosevelt's expectation went down with him. On July 22 the Senate voted to inter the bill in committee.

Roosevelt had suffered a severe defeat, but he insisted that, although he had lost the battle, he had won the war. To the Van Devanter vacancy, he soon named Hugo L. Black, an ardent New Dealer and supporter of court packing, and within two and a half years of his defeat, he was able to appoint a majority of the nine Justices. This "Roosevelt Court," as it was called, never again struck down a New Deal law. Indeed, it took so expansive a view of the commerce power and the spending power and so circumscribed the due process clause that scholars speak of the "Constitutional Revolution of 1937." Not once since then has the Court stuck down any significant law—federal or state—regulating business. The struggle over court packing, however, cost Roosevelt dearly, for it solidified a bipartisan conservative coalition arrayed against further New Deal reforms.

Although no President since Roosevelt has advocated a Court packing statute, the charge of packing has been raised against three of his successors. When, in his final year in office, Lyndon B. Johnson sought to elevate Associate Justice Abe Fortas to the Chief Justiceship, conservative Republicans charged him with a "midnight judge" kind of maneuver to deny his probable successor, Richard M. Nixon, the opportunity to make the selection, and after revelations about Fortas's comportment, the endeavor failed. So frank was Nixon in turn about stating his desire to reverse the doctrines of the Warren Court that he was accused of trying to pack the Supreme Court with conservative jurists when he made nominations such as those of Clement Haynsworth and G. Harrold Carswell. Both of these nominations were rejected, but Nixon won confirmation of four other choices, including Warren E. Burger as Chief Justice, although they were sometimes to disappoint him by their subsequent behavior. An even louder outcry arose over Ronald Reagan's selections. His attempt to place Robert Bork on the Supreme Court was turned aside, but he secured approval of four other nominees, all

This case took on renewed importance in the context of the Civil Rights demonstrations of the 1960s.

See also
Civil Rights

COX v. NEW HAMPSHIRE
312 U.S. 569 (1941)

In this seminal decision, Chief Justice Charles Evans Hughes, writing for a unanimous Supreme Court, synthesized a series of cases involving speeches, parades, and meetings in parks and on streets. He held that there was a "right of assembly . . . and . . . discussion of public questions immemorially associated with resort to public places," but that such a right was limited by the authority of local government to make reasonable regulations governing "the time, place and manner" of such speech, if the regulations did not involve "unfair discrimination" among speakers. The Court upheld a state law requiring parade licenses issued by local governments on the grounds that, as construed by the state supreme court, it authorized only such reasonable and nondiscriminatory regulations. *Cox* is one of the building blocks in the creation of the doctrine of the public forum.

This case took on renewed importance in the context of the civil rights demonstrations of the 1960s. The crucial problem under the *Cox* test is often whether a law purporting to be a neutral regulation of traffic and noise control is actually a façade behind which local authorities seek to deny a public forum to speakers whose speech they dislike.

—MARTIN SHAPIRO

regarded as sharing his conservative outlook. He had even greater success in the lower federal courts. His efforts were decried as, in the title of one book, *Packing the Courts: The Conservative Campaign to Rewrite the Constitution,* but neither Reagan nor Nixon had acted markedly differently from such twentieth-century predecessors as William Howard Taft, Warren G. Harding, and Franklin D. Roosevelt, although none of the others may have exhibited such sedulous ideological zeal.

—WILLIAM E. LEUCHTENBURG

Bibliography

Alsop, Joseph, and Catledge, Turner (1938). *The 168 Days.* Garden City, N.Y.: Doubleday, Doran.

Leuchtenburg, William E. (1966). The Origins of Franklin D. Roosevelt's "Court Packing" Plan. In Philip B. Kurland, ed. *The Supreme Court Review: 1966.* Pages 347–400. Chicago: University of Chicago Press.

——— (1969). Franklin D. Roosevelt's Supreme Court "Packing" Plan. In Harold M. Hollingsworth and William F. Holmes, eds., *Essays on the New Deal.* Pages 69–115. Austin: University of Texas.

COY v. IOWA

487 U.S. 1012 (1988)

Coy was convicted of sexually assaulting two thirteen-year-old girls. During his trial, the girls gave testimony in front of a screen that blocked Coy from their sight. Coy claimed that use of the screen violated his right to confrontation guaranteed by the Fifth Amendment. The Supreme Court agreed, holding that face-to-face examination of witnesses testifying at trial is a fundamental guarantee of the confrontation clause.

Writing for the majority, Justice Antonin Scalia argued that open accusations seem integral to the very idea of fairness; moreover, face-to-face confrontation serves the end of

truth because it is more difficult for witnesses to lie (or lie convincingly) when they must do so to the face of the person their testimony will harm. Scalia argued that the Court's previously carved out exceptions to the confrontation clause were inapposite because they dealt with out-of-court statements and not testimony given during trial. Whether there may be exceptions to the confrontation clause even at trial, Scalia was unwilling to say. All he would acknowledge is that if such exceptions exist they must be "necessary to further an important public policy."

Justice Sandra Day O'Connor, in one of her characteristically narrow concurrences, claimed that nothing in the ruling should be construed as forbidding state efforts to protect child witnesses, and she listed several types of state action that she thought would not raise a "substantial Confrontation Clause problem." O'Connor also seized on the majority's concession that exceptions to the confrontation clause may exist when "necessary to further an important public policy." The key word, O'Connor pointed out, was "necessary," and this would likely be the focus of future litigation. It was; and in 1990, the Court took up the issue again in *Maryland* v. *Craig.*

—JOHN G. WEST, JR.

CRAIG v. BOREN

429 U.S. 190 (1976)

It is ironic that the leading modern decision setting the standard of review for claims of sex discrimination involved discrimination against men, concerning an interest of supreme triviality. Oklahoma allowed women to buy 3.2 percent beer upon reaching the age of eighteen; men, however, had to be twenty-one. A young male would-be buyer and a female beer seller challenged the law's validity. The young man became twenty-one before the Supreme Court's decision; his challenge was thus rejected for mootness. The Court held that the seller had standing to raise the

Coy was convicted of sexually assaulting two thirteen-year-old girls.

See also

Maryland v. *Craig*

young man's constitutional claims, and further held, 8–1, that the law denied equal protection of the laws. Justice William H. Rehnquist dissented.

Speaking through Justice William J. Brennan, the Court held that classifications based on gender were invalid unless they served "important governmental objectives" and were "substantially related to achievement of those objectives." This intermediate standard was a compromise between the two views of the majority in *Frontiero* v. *Richardson* (1973) as to the level of judicial scrutiny of both legislative objectives and legislative means. Under the rational basis standard of review, the objective need be only legitimate, and the means (in equal protection language, the classification) only rationally related to its achievement. At the opposite end of the continuum of standards of review, strict scrutiny demands a legislative objective that is a compelling state interest, and means that are necessary to achieving that objective. The *Craig* standard appears to have been deliberately designed to fall between these two levels of judicial scrutiny of legislation.

In the years since *Craig,* the Supreme Court has often invalidated classifications based on sex but typically has not challenged the importance of legislative objectives. Instead, the Court generally holds that a sex classification is not "substantially related" to a legislative goal. In *Craig* itself, the Court admitted that traffic safety, the state's objective, was important, but said maleness was an inappropriate "proxy for drinking and driving."

Justice John Paul Stevens, concurring, doubted the utility of multitiered levels of judicial scrutiny in equal protection cases, and commented that men, as a class, have not suffered "pervasive discrimination." The classification was objectionable, however, because it was "based on the accident of birth," and perpetuated "a stereotyped attitude" of young men and women. Because the state's traffic safety justification failed, the law was invalid.

—KENNETH L. KARST

CRUIKSHANK, UNITED STATES v.

92 U.S. 542 (1876)

Cruikshank paralyzed the federal government's attempt to protect black citizens by punishing violators of their civil rights and, in effect, shaped the Constitution to the advantage of the Ku Klux Klan. The case arose out of a federal prosecution of nightriders responsible for the Colfax Massacre of 1873 in Grant Parish, Louisiana. Several hundred armed whites besieged a courthouse where hundreds of blacks were holding a public assembly; the attackers burned down the building and murdered about 100 people. The United States tried Cruikshank and others involved in the massacre and convicted three for violating section 6 of the Force Act of 1870. That act, which survives as section 241 of Title 18 of the United States Code, is a general conspiracy statute making it a federal crime, then punishable by a $5,000 fine and up to ten years in prison, for two or more persons to conspire to injure or intimidate any citizen with the intent of hindering his free exercise of any right or privilege guaranteed him by the Constitution or laws of the United States.

In a unanimous opinion by Chief Justice Morrison R. Waite, the Court ignored the statute and focused on the indictment to ascertain whether the rights Cruikshank and others interfered with were granted or secured by the United States. Reasserting the theory of dual citizenship advanced in the *Slaughterhouse Cases* (1873), Waite concluded that the United States cannot grant or secure rights not under its jurisdiction. Examining in turn each right named in the indictment as having been deprived, Waite found that they were all "left under the protection of the States." None was a federal right. The right to peaceably assemble predated the Constitution and remained "subject to state jurisdiction." The United States could neither infringe it nor protect it, for it was not an

In the years since Craig, *the Supreme Court has often invalidated classifications based on sex but typically has not challenged the importance of legislative objectives.*

See also

Equal Protection of the Laws

Sex Discrimination

*Cruikshank
paralyzed the
federal government's
attempt to protect
black citizens by
punishing violators
of their civil rights.*

See also

Civil Rights

attribute of United States citizenship. So too the right to bear arms. The right to be secure in one's person, life, and liberty was protected by the Fourteenth Amendment against state deprivation, but for protection of that right, sovereignty "rests alone with the States." The amendment, said Waite, "adds nothing to the rights of one citizen as against another." Thus the violence here conducted by private persons could not be reached by Congress, which was limited to assuring that the states do not violate the amendment's prohibitions. As for the right to vote, the Fifteenth Amendment merely protected against discrimination based on race. The Constitution did not confer the right to vote on anyone; that right was not, Waite said, an attribute of national citizenship.

By such reasoning the Court held that the indictment did not show that the conspirators had hindered or prevented the enjoyment of any right granted or secured by the Constitution. Accordingly, no conviction based on the indictment could be sustained, and the Court ordered the defendants discharged. The conspiracy statute remained impotent until revived in recent times by the Department of Justice, but the Court did not sustain a conviction under the statute until 1966 (*United States* v. *Price; United States* v. *Guest*), when the Court vitiated *Cruikshank.*

—LEONARD W. LEVY

Bibliography

Magrath, C. Peter (1963). *Morrison R. Waite.* Pages 120–134. New York: Macmillan.

CURTISS-WRIGHT EXPORT CORPORATION, UNITED STATES v.

299 U.S. 304 (1936)

Nearly two years after Paraguay and Bolivia went to war in 1932, Congress authorized President Franklin D. Roosevelt to embargo American arms shipments to the belligerents if he found that the action might contribute to reestablishing peace. Indicted in January 1936 for conspiring to violate the embargo resolution and Roosevelt's implementing proclamation, Curtiss-Wright Export Corporation demurred on grounds of unconstitutional delegation of power. Recent rulings against New Deal legislation in *Panama Refining Co.* v. *Ryan* (1935) and *Schechter Poultry Corp.* v. *United States* (1935) lent weight to the company's position, and the district court sustained the demurrer. On appeal, however, the Supreme Court approved the embargo resolution and proclamation with a ringing endorsement of independent presidential authority in the area of foreign affairs.

For a 7–1 majority, Justice George Sutherland defended the embargo measures by distinguishing between powers of internal and external sovereignty, a distinction the government had not employed in arguing *Curtiss-Wright.* For him, the federal government's domestic authority derived from states having delegated power via the Constitution. External sovereignty had passed, however, from the British Crown to the United Colonies and then to the United States in their collective capacities, with the states severally never possessing it nor delegating it. "Rulers come and go; governments end and forms of government change; but sovereignty survives." In the realm of foreign relations, the authority of the federal government therefore equaled that of any sovereign nation, and the usual constitutional divisions between the president and Congress were largely irrelevant, as was the normal prohibition on delegation of legislative power. Keenly aware of the need for energy and dispatch in the delicate business of conducting foreign relations, the Framers had endorsed this arrangement, Sutherland claimed, and early statesmen put it into practice. Although dissenting, Justice James C. McReynolds filed no opinion.

Later characterized as dictum-laden, Sutherland's argument made sense within the constitutional climate of the 1930s and in view of his own commitments. The government, for example, had claimed that the 1934 embargo resolution and proclamation met the straited *Panama-Schechter* requirement that delegatory legislation specify the findings of fact the president must make before taking the anticipated action. Such an approach ignored the plausible objection that findings involving diplomatic and military imponderables were no firmer than those already disallowed as "opinion" in *Schechter*. An alternative was simply to rely on judicial precedent and legislative practice regarding delegation in areas cognate to foreign relations. Sutherland did examine earlier embargo, tariff, and kindred measures in which Congress had given latitude to the president, but he did so primarily as a means of showing that his view of external sovereignty had been accepted from the beginning. Neither judicial nor legislative iterations carried the same weight as the original intent and first principles he valued so highly. Perhaps most important, Sutherland himself had broached the external-internal distinction the previous May, in *Carter* v. *Carter Coal Company* (1936), and had earlier explicated his full theory of sovereignty in his book *Constitutional Power and World Affairs* (1919).

The real weakness of Sutherland's opinion was its faulty history. Scant evidence exists that the Framers held the extraconstitutional understanding of the foreign relations power he attributed to them. Sutherland also misconstrued many of the earlier episodes and commentaries that, he argued, were informed by his theories of sovereignty and plenary executive authority. *Curtiss-Wright* nevertheless had timing on its side. It soon provided a base for upholding executive agreements as domestic law in *United States* v. *Belmont* (1937) and *United States* v. *Pink* (1942). More broadly, Sutherland's opinion appealed to proponents of an expanded presidential role as the United States acquired global responsibilities, engaged in nuclear diplomacy, fought undeclared wars, and debated the requirements of internal security.

—CHARLES A. LOFGREN

Bibliography

Levitan, David M. (1946). The Foreign Relations Power: An Analysis of Mr. Justice Sutherland's Theory. *Yale Law Journal* 55:467–497.

Lofgren, Charles A. (1973). *United States* v. *Curtiss-Wright Export Corporation:* An Historical Reassessment. *Yale Law Journal* 83:1–32.

C

CURTISS-WRIGHT EXPORT CORPORATION, UNITED STATES v.

299 U.S. 304 (1936)

The real weakness of Sutherland's opinion was its faulty history.

See also

Carter v. *Carter Coal Co.*

Panama Refining Co. v. *Ryan*

Schecter Poultry Corp. v. *United States*

D

DANDRIDGE v. WILLIAMS

397 U.S. 471 (1970)

Dandridge stifled the infant doctrine, born in cases such as *Griffin* v. *Illinois* (1956) and *Douglas* v. *California* (1963), that governmental wealth discrimination, like racial discrimination, demanded strict judicial scrutiny of its justifications. Maryland provided welfare aid to dependent children on the basis of need, partly determined by the number of children in a family. However, payment to any one family was limited to $250 per month, irrespective of the family's size. A 6–3 Supreme Court, speaking through Justice Potter Stewart, characterized the case as one involving "social and economic" regulation, and applied the rational basis standard of review. Here there were legitimate state interests in encouraging employment and avoiding distinctions between welfare recipients and the working poor. Although some welfare beneficiaries were unemployable, the maximum-grant rule was generally reasonable.

Justice Thurgood Marshall, dissenting, rejected the idea of two separate standards of review, rational basis and strict scrutiny. He argued for a "sliding scale" of judicial supervision that would demand progressively more state justification as the classification in question bore more heavily on the powerless and in proportion to the importance of the interest at stake. Here, where indigent children were being deprived of basic subsistence as defined by the state's own standards of need, the permissive rational basis standard was in-appropriate. Marshall also argued that the maximum-grant rule was invalid even under that permissive standard, given the state's aim of aiding children and the unemployability of a large proportion of welfare recipients.

After *Dandridge*, it became futile to argue to the Supreme Court either that welfare subsistence was a fundamental interest or that wealth discrimination implied a suspect classification. Since 1970 the Court has regularly shied away from decisions that would place the judiciary in the position of allocating state resources.

—KENNETH L. KARST

After Dandridge, *it became futile to argue to the Supreme Court either that welfare subsistence was a fundamental interest or that wealth discrimination implied a suspect classification.*

POWERLESS

States can constitutionally limit the amount of aid to indigent children. (Corbis/Joseph Schwartz Collection)

*This case
established that the
national economic
system is subject to
the control of the
only entity that can
possibly control it,
the federal
government.*

DARBY LUMBER COMPANY, UNITED STATES v.

312 U.S. 100 (1941)

This decision held the Fair Labor Standards Act of 1938 to be a valid exercise of federal power under the commerce clause. That was no surprise after the 1937 decisions upholding the Wagner (National Labor Relations) Act and after the retirement of the four Justices who had voted consistently for a narrow interpretation of the commerce clause. The opinion of Justice Harlan Fiske Stone was nevertheless of great significance. For instead of speaking in terms of such nonconstitutional concepts as "direct" and "indirect," it returned to basic constitutional principles as to the scope of the power of Congress.

The commerce clause itself precluded states with high labor standards from protecting their wage levels by forbidding the entry of goods produced elsewhere at lower wages. This meant that in the absence of federal legislative action, states with the lowest labor standards could drive the standards down throughout the country. In 1916 Congress first sought to meet this problem by barring the interstate transportation of goods produced by children. Although that statute was clearly a regulation of interstate commerce the Supreme Court held it unconstitutional by a vote of 5–4 in *Hammer* v. *Dagenhart* (1918) because the purpose of the act was to control what occurred during the course of intrastate production. Five years later, in *Adkins* v. *Children's Hospital* (1923), the Court ruled, 6–3, that the due process clause forbade the fixing of minimum wages by either federal or state governments.

The downward spiral of prices and wages during the Great Depression of the 1930s forced employers seeking to survive to reduce wages to incredibly low levels. Congress sought to deal with this problem by requiring the codes of fair competition under the National Industrial Recovery Act to prescribe maximum hours and minimum wages. *Schechter Poultry Corp.* v. *United States* (1935), holding the NRA unconstitutional, brought this program to a halt, and *Carter* v. *Carter Coal Company* (1936), holding that Congress lacked power to regulate labor conditions and relations in the coal industry, seemed to create an insurmountable impediment. Unpredictably, this lasted for only a year, when *Carter* was in substance overruled in the Wagner Act Cases (1937) and *Adkins* was overruled in *West Coast Hotel Co.* v. *Parrish* (1937). The result was passage of the Fair Labor Standards Act in June 1938.

That statute prescribed a minimum wage of twenty-five cents per hour for employees engaged in interstate commerce or in producing goods for such commerce. Payment of 50 percent more for overtime was required for all hours over forty-four per week (to be reduced to forty after two years). The act penalized violation of those standards or interstate shipment of goods produced in violation of them.

The lumber industry was typically afflicted with depressed wage rates; wages ranged from ten to twenty-seven and one-half cents per hour. The annual average wage for all lumber industry employees in Georgia in 1937 was $389. Fred Darby was paying his employees twelve and one-half to seventeen cents per hour; he devised a scheme to continue doing so after the Fair Labor Standards Act became effective, and he was indicted.

Although the other federal lower courts had seen the light after the Labor Board cases and sustained the new statute, the Georgia district judge deemed himself bound to follow *Hammer* v. *Dagenhart* and Carter until the Supreme Court explicitly overruled them. Accordingly, he dismissed the indictment as an invalid regulation of manufacture, not interstate commerce, and the government appealed directly to the Supreme Court.

In upholding the statute Justice Stone spoke for a unanimous Court—undoubtedly because Justice James C. McReynolds had retired three days before. The Court first held that the prohibition against the interstate shipment of goods produced under substandard labor conditions was "indubitably a regulation of [interstate] commerce." And this was none the less so because the motive or purpose may have been to control the "wages and hours of persons engaged in manufacture." The commerce power of Congress, as defined in *Gibbons* v. *Ogden* (1824), "may be exercised to its utmost extent, and acknowledges no limitations other than are prescribed in the Constitution." "The motive and purpose of a regulation of interstate commerce are matters for the legislative judgment upon which the courts are given no control." The contrary decision in *Hammer* v. *Dagenhart* "by a bare majority of the Court over the powerful and now classic dissent of Mr. Justice [Oliver Wendell] Holmes" was accordingly overruled.

In determining the validity of the regulation of wages and hours for manufacturers, the Court adopted the approach approved in *McCulloch* v. *Maryland* (1819), the initial pronouncement on the scope of the enumerated powers. The test was whether a regulation of intrastate activities was an "appropriate means to the attainment of a legitimate end, the exercise of the granted power of Congress to regulate interstate commerce." The directness or indirectness of the effect on such commerce was not mentioned, although the substantiality of the effect was. The Court noted that legislation under other powers had often been sustained "when the means chosen, although not themselves within the granted power, were nevertheless deemed appropriate aids to the accomplishment of some purpose within an admitted power. . . ." The policy of excluding from interstate commerce goods produced under substandard labor conditions could reasonably be effectuated by prohibiting such conditions for manufacturers producing for interstate distribution. That would suppress a method of interstate competition Congress deemed unfair.

The opinion flatly rejected the contention that the Tenth Amendment restricted the enumerated powers. That amendment, which provides that "the powers not delegated to the United States by the Constitution nor prohibited by it to the states are reserved to the states respectively or to the people," did not deprive the federal government of "authority to resort to all means for the exercise of a granted power which are appropriate and plainly adapted to the permitted end." "The amendment states but a truism that all is retained which has not been surrendered."

Darby was followed a year later by *Wickard* v. *Filburn* in which the Court alluded to the necessary and proper clause, which *McCulloch* v. *Maryland* had emphasized, as the source of the power of Congress to regulate intrastate transactions. It also identified the cases which *Darby* had disapproved by implication, among others *Hammer, Schechter,* and *Carter. Darby* and *Wickard* together have provided the foundation for commerce clause interpretation thereafter. They firmly establish that the national economic system is subject to the control of the only entity that can possibly control it, the federal government.

—ROBERT L. STERN

Bibliography

Dodd, E. Merrick (1946). The Supreme Court and Fair Labor Standards, 1941–1945. *Harvard Law Review* 59: 321–375.

Stern, Robert L. (1946). The Commerce Clause and the National Economy, 1933–1946. *Harvard Law Review* 59: 645–693, 883–947.

See also
Adkins v. *Children's Hospital*
Carter v. *Carter Coal Co.*
Gibbons v. *Ogden*
Hammer v. *Dagenhart*
McCulloch v. *Maryland*
West Coast Hotel Co. v. *Parrish*
Wickard v. *Filburn*

*The most famous
and influential
contract clause case
in our history,
Dartmouth College
was a boon to
higher education
and to corporate
capitalism.*

DARTMOUTH COLLEGE v. WOODWARD

4 Wheaton 518 (1819)

The most famous and influential contract clause case in our history, *Dartmouth College* was a boon to higher education and to corporate capitalism. The case established the doctrine, never overruled, that a corporation charter or the grant by a state of corporate rights to private interests comes within the protection of the contract clause. Although the case involved a small college in New Hampshire rather than a manufacturing concern, a bank, or a transportation company, the Court seized an opportunity to broaden the contract clause by making all private corporations its beneficiaries. Daniel Webster, counsel for the college, said that the judgment was a "defense of vested rights against Courts and Sovereignties," and his cocounsel, Joseph Hopkinson, asserted that it would "secure corporations . . . from legislative despotism. . . ." Corporations were still a recent innovation; James Kent, in his *Commentaries on American Law* (1826), remarked that their rapid multiplication and the avidity with which they were sought by charter from the states arose as a result of the power that large, consolidated capital gave them over business of every sort. The Court's decision in the *Dartmouth College* case, Kent said, more than any other act proceeding from the authority of the United States, threw "an impregnable barrier around all rights and franchises derived from the grant of government; and [gave] solidity and inviolability to the literary, charitable, religious, and commercial institutions of our country." Actually, *Fletcher* v. *Peck* (1810) had made the crucial and original extension of the contract clause, construing it to cover public and executed contracts as well as private executory ones. The *Dartmouth College* doctrine was a logical implication.

The college case was a strange vehicle for the doctrine that emerged from it. Dartmouth, having been chartered in 1769 in the name of the crown to christianize and educate Indians, had become a Christian college for whites and a stronghold of the Congregationalist Church, which had benefited most from the laws establishing the Protestant religion in New Hampshire. The college had become embroiled in state politics on the side of the Federalists, who supported the establishment. When in 1815 the trustees removed the president of the college, they loosed a controversy that drew to the ousted president a coalition of Jeffersonians and religious denominations demanding separation of church and state. The reformers having swept the state elections in 1816, the legislature sought to democratize the college by a series of statutes that converted it into a state university under public control, rather than a private college as provided by the original charter. The state supreme court sustained the state acts, reasoning that the institution had been established with public aid for public purposes of an educational and religious nature. The state court held that the contract clause did not limit the state's power over its own public corporations.

On appeal, the Supreme Court held that Dartmouth was a private eleemosynary corporation whose vested rights could not be divested without infringing a continuing obligation to respect inviolably the trustees' control of property given to the corporation for the advancement of its objectives. The Court held unconstitutional the state acts subjecting Dartmouth to state control and ordered Woodward, the treasurer of the institution who had sided with the state, to return to the trustees the records, corporate seal, and other corporate property which he held.

At every step of his opinion Chief Justice John Marshall misstated the facts about the history of the original charter in order to prove that it established a purely private corporation. That, perhaps, was a matter primarily of interest to the college, which, contrary to Marshall, had received its charter not from George III but from the governor of the colony; moreover, the private donations, which Marshall said had been given to Dartmouth on condition of receiving the charter, had been given unconditionally to an entirely different institution, Moor's Charity School for Indians, and had been transferred to Dartmouth over the donors' objections. Also, the funds of the college, contrary to Marshall, did not consist "entirely of private donations," because the endowment of the college at the time of the issuance of the chapter derived mainly from grants of public lands. Even if the grant of the charter were a contract, as Marshall said it "plainly" was, Parliament could have repealed it at will. The Chief Justice conceded the fact but added that a repeal would have been morally perfidious. If, however, the charter were subject to revocation at the will of the sovereign authority, or the grantor, the "contract" did not bind that party and created no obligation that could be impaired.

Marshall conceded that at the time of Independence, the state suceeded to the power of Parliament and might have repealed or altered the charter at any time before the adoption of the Constitution. The provision in Article I, section 10, preventing states from impairing the obligation of a contract, altered the situation. That clause, Marshall conceded, was not specifically intended to protect charters of incorporation: "It is," he said boldly, "more than possible that the preservation of rights of this description was not particularly in the view of the framers of the constitution," but the clause admitted no exceptions as far as private rights were concerned. "It is not enough to say that this particular case was not in the mind of the convention when the article was framed, nor of the American people when it was adopted." In the absence of proof that the language of the Constitution would have been altered had charters of incorporation been considered, the case came within its injunction against state acts impairing the obligation of contracts.

Although Marshall can be doubted when he said, "It can require no argument to prove that the circumstances of this case constitute a contract," his general doctrine, that any state charter for a private corporation is a constitutionally protected contract, was not far-fetched. The Court must construe the text, not the minds of its framers, and, as he said, "There is no exception in the constitution, no sentiment delivered by its contemporaneous expounders, which would justify us in making it." If a state granted a charter of incorporation to private interests, the charter has "every ingredient of a complete and legitimate contract," should it be made on a valuable consideration for the security and disposition of the property conveyed to the corporation for management by its trustees in perpetuity. Unless, as Justice Joseph Story stressed in his concurring opinion, the government should reserve, in the grant of the charter, a power to alter, modify, or repeal, the rights vested cannot be divested, except by the consent of the incorporators, assuming they have not defaulted. Whether, however, a modification of the charter, as in this case, impairs an obligation, if the charter be executed and by its terms should not specify a term of years for the corporation's existence, is another question. In *Fletcher* v. *Peck,* however, the Court had brought executed as well as public contracts within the meaning of the contract clause. Marshall construed contract rights sweepingly, state powers narrowly.

Max Lerner's comment on the case, referring to Webster's peroration, is provocative. "Every schoolboy," he wrote, "knows Webster's eloquent plea and how Marshall, whom the Yazoo land scandals had left cold, found his own eyes suffused with tears, as Webster, overcome by the emotion of his words, wept. But few schoolboys know that the case had ultimately less to do with colleges than with business corporations; that sanctity of contract was invoked to give them immunity against legislative control, and that business enterprise in America never had more useful mercenaries than the tears Daniel Webster and John Marshall are reputed to have shed so devotedly that March day in Washington. . . ." In fact, the reserved power to alter or repeal, of which Story spoke, limited corporate immunity from legislative control. Moreover, the protection given by the Court to corporate charters came into play after the legislatures, not the Court, issued these charters, often recklessly and corruptly, without consideration of the public good; Marshall's opinion should have put the legislatures and the public on guard. Finally, the case had a great deal to do with higher education as well as business. *Dartmouth College* is the Magna Carta of private colleges and universities, and, by putting them beyond state control, provided a powerful stimulus, not only to business corporations but also to the chartering of state institutions of higher learning. Unable to make private institutions public ones, the states established state universities.

—LEONARD W. LEVY

Bibliography

Beveridge, Albert J. (1916–1919). *The Life of John Marshall.* 4 vols. Vol. 4:220–281. Boston: Little, Brown.

Haines, Charles Grove (1944). *The Role of the Supreme Court in American Government and Politics, 1789–1835.* Pages 378–419. Berkeley: University of California Press.

Shirley, John M. ([1879] 1971). *The Dartmouth College Causes and the Supreme Court.* New York: Da Capo Press.

Stites, Francis N. (1972). *Private Interest and Public Gain: The Dartmouth College Case, 1819.* Amherst: University of Massachusetts Press.

DELEGATION OF POWER

Early in American constitutional history the Supreme Court announced a rule that Congress could not delegate its power to the president or others. Yet the practical demands of

See also

Fletcher v. *Peck*

an increasingly complex governmental environment have forced Congress to delegate, often quite broadly. The Court has rationalized all but a few delegations without abandoning the rule of nondelegation. This has been accomplished through successively more permissive formulations of the rule. Though the rule is in a state of desuetude, some revival is possible in the aftermath of the Court's invalidation of a legislative veto in *Immigration and Naturalization Service* v. *Chadha* (1983).

A few commentators call the rule against delegations a judge-made doctrine lacking genuine constitutional status. This suggests the untenable proposition that genuine rules of constitutional law must be explicit in the constitutional document. Building on a common law maxim against redelegation of delegated authority and on John Locke's observation that only the sovereign people can determine the legitimate location of legislative authority, most commentators have found nondelegation implicit in the separation of powers and in concepts of representative government and due process of law. The status of the rule thus secured, debate has concentrated on exactly what it prohibits.

As if the rule prohibited all delegations, nineteenth-century judges tried to reconcile it with the practical needs of government by denying that delegations in fact were delegations in law. In *The Brig Aurora* (1813) the Supreme Court held that Congress had not breached the rule by empowering the president to make factual finding on which the application of a previously declared congressional policy—an embargo—was contingent. In *Wayman* v. *Southard* (1825) the Court permitted a delegation to federal judges for "filling up the details" of part of the Federal Process Act of 1792. Though the rules announced in these cases were modest when stated in the abstract, the delegations themselves were the objects of acrimonious political conflict. By the early 1900s power to declare facts and fill up details had become the foundation for the delegation of such discretionary authority to the president and administrative agencies as power to decide which grades of tea to exclude from import, to make rules regulating grazing on lands in national forests, and even to vary tariffs on imported goods.

In *J. W. Hampton & Company* v. *United States* (1928) the Court formulated a more realistic delegation doctrine when it acknowledged that transfers of discretionary authority were essential to the effectiveness of Congress's will in modern conditions. The new rule was that congressional delegation is permissible if governed by adequate "legislative standards," a term that now includes statutory specifications of facts to be declared, preambulatory statements of legislative purpose, and even judicial imputations of legislative purpose inferred from legislative and administrative history.

The Court has rarely taken the standards requirement seriously. Illustrative of a pattern that prevails to the present, *Federal Radio Commission* v. *Nelson Brothers* (1933) found adequate guidance for issuing radio station licenses in what Congress called the "public convenience, interest, and necessity." This pattern was interrupted when the Court unexpectedly used the delegation doctrine against the National Industrial Recovery Act (1933) in *Panama Refining Company* v. *Ryan* (1935) and *Schechter Poultry Corporation* v. *United States* (1935). But the spirit of these decisions was not to survive, and by the middle of World War II the Court had returned to using the delegation doctrine more for rationalizing than for limiting transfers of congressional power.

As if delegations were not broad enough, the Court in *United States* v. *Mazurie* (1975) suggested an even more permissive approach. *United States* v. *Curtiss-Wright Export Corporation* (1936) had seemed to hold that because the president had independent powers in the field of foreign affairs, the standards requirement for congressional delegations to

the president could be relaxed in that area. At a time when *Panama* and *Schechter* had recently limited the scope of delegated power, *Curtiss-Wright* was a reasonable move toward flexibility in foreign affairs. But *Curtiss-Wright* featured an unorthodox theory of extraconstitutional or inherent governmental power, and the need for a special approach to foreign affairs delegations disappeared as the Court returned to its old permissiveness toward delegations generally. During the Vietnam War, however, the nondelegation doctrine was raised in opposition to American policy, and, although the Court successfully avoided the issue, government lawyers invoked *Curtiss-Wright* before congressional committees. One of these lawyers was William H. Rehnquist, who later led the Court to its first reaffirmation of *Curtiss-Wright*'s delegation doctrine in *Mazurie*, a relatively noncontroversial case involving a delegation to the tribal council of an American Indian tribe over liquor sales on a reservation. The tribe's council, said Justice Rehnquist, had "independent authority over tribal life," just as the president had over foreign affairs, and *Curtiss-Wright* was cited for a new rule that the standards requirement is "less stringent in cases where the entity exercising the delegated authority itself possesses independent authority over the subject matter." In light of what "less stringent" can mean today, *Mazurie* has a potential for rationalizing virtual abdications of congressional responsibility, not only to the president but to the states, whose legal claims to "independent authority" are stronger than that of Indian tribal councils.

Since the 1930s and with accelerated frequency after the Vietnam War, Congress used the legislative veto to recapture power lost through broad delegations. To the extent—perhaps modest—that regulatory and political conditions permit, Congress may choose to delegate more narrowly now that the legislative veto is unavailable. And if the Court really has renewed its commitment to

A few commentators call the rule against delegations a judge-made doctrine lacking genuine constitutional status.

♦ **standing**
The legal status of a litigant indicating that he is a proper party to litigate an issue or a case or controversy.

*Defenders of the
clear and present
danger rule criticize
Dennis for
abandoning that
rule's essential
feature, the
immediacy
requirement.*

See also

*Immigration and
    Naturalization Service v.
    Chadha*

*Panama Refining Company v.
    Ryan*

*Schecter Poultry Corporation v.
    United States*

the separation of powers, it may honor the standards requirement with something more than mere lip service.

—SOTIRIOS A. BARBER

Bibliography

Barber, Sotirios A. (1975). *The Constitution and the Delegation of Congressional Power.* Chicago: University of Chicago Press.

Davis, Kenneth C. (1958). *Administrative Law Treatise.* St. Paul, Minn.: West Publishing Co.

DENNIS v. UNITED STATES

341 U.S. 494 (1951)

Eugene Dennis and other high officials of the Communist party had been convicted of violating the Alien Registration Act of 1940 (the Smith Act) by conspiring to advocate overthrow of the government by force and violence. Learned Hand, writing the Court of Appeals opinion upholding the constitutionality of the act and of the conviction, was caught in a dilemma. He was bound by the Supreme Court's clear and present danger rule, and the government had presented no evidence that Dennis's activities had created a present danger of communist revolution in the United States. Hand, however, believed that courts had limited authority to enforce the First Amendment. His solution was to restate the danger test as: "whether the gravity of the evil, discounted by its improbability, justifies such invasion of free speech as is necessary to avoid the danger." Because Dennis's conspiracy to advocate was linked to a grave evil, communist revolution, he could be punished despite the remote danger of communist revolution. Hand's restatement allowed a court to pay lip service to the danger rule while upholding nearly any government infringement on speech. If the ultimate threat

posed by the speech is great enough, the speaker may be punished even though there is little or no immediate threat.

The Supreme Court upheld Dennis's conviction with only Justices Hugo L. Black and William O. Douglas dissenting. Chief Justice Fred M. Vinson's plurality opinion adopted Hand's restatement of the danger rule. At least where an organized subversive group was involved, speakers might be punished so long as they intended to bring about overthrow "as speedily as circumstances would permit."

Justice Felix Frankfurter's concurrence openly substituted a balancing test for the danger rule, arguing that the constitutionality of speech limitations ultimately depended on whether the government had a weighty enough interest. Congress, he said, surely was entitled to conclude that the interest in national security outweighed the speech interests of those advocating violent overthrow.

Decided at the height of the Cold War campaign against communists, *Dennis* allied the Court with anticommunist sentiment. No statute would seem more flatly violative on its face of the First Amendment than one that made "advocacy" a crime. Indeed, in *Yates* v. *United States* (1957) the Court later sought to distinguish between active urging or incitement to revolution, which was constitutionally punishable "advocacy," and abstract teaching of Marxist doctrine, which was constitutionally protected speech.

Defenders of the clear and present danger rule criticize *Dennis* for abandoning that rule's essential feature, the immediacy requirement. Such commentators see the Court as correcting its *Dennis* error in *Brandenburg* v. *Ohio* (1969) in which the Court returned to something like "clear and present danger" and placed heavy emphasis on the immediacy requirement. Justices Black and Douglas subsequently treated *Dennis* as a case applying the clear and present danger rule and thus as an illustration of the failure of the rule to provide sufficient protection for speech and of the need to replace it with the more "absolute" free speech protections urged by Alexander Meiklejohn. Proponents of balancing applaud Hand's "discounting" formula as one of the roots of the balancing doctrine, although only the most ardent proponents of judicial self-restraint support Frankfurter's conclusion that Congress, not the Court, should do the final balancing.

It is possible to read *Dennis, Yates,* and *Brandenburg* together as supporting the following theory. The clear and present danger rule, including a strong immediacy requirement, applies to street-corner speakers; so long as their speech does not trigger immediate serious harms, others will have the opportunity to respond to it in the marketplace of ideas, and the government will be able to prepare protective measures against violence that may follow. However, where organized, subversive groups engage in covert speech aimed at secret preparations that will suddenly burst forth in revolution, the "as speedily as circumstances will permit" test is substituted for the immediacy requirement. Covert speech cannot easily be rebutted in the marketplace of ideas; by the time underground groups pose a threat of immediate revolution, they may be so strong that a democratic government cannot stop them or can do so only at the cost of many lives.

Whether or not the Communist party of Eugene Dennis constituted such a covert, underground group impervious to the speech of others and posing a real threat of eventual revolution, a theory such as this is probably the reason the Smith Act was never declared unconstitutional and *Dennis* was never overruled although both have been drastically narrowed by subsequent judicial interpretation.

—MARTIN SHAPIRO

Bibliography

Corwin, Edward S. (1951). Bowing Out Clear and Present Danger. *Notre Dame Lawyer* 27:325–359.

Mendelson, Wallace (1952). Clear and Present Danger—From *Schenk* to *Dennis*. *Columbia Law Review* 52:313–333.

DESHANEY v. WINNEBAGO COUNTY DEPARTMENT OF SOCIAL SERVICES

488 U.S. 189 (1989)

When Joshua DeShaney was one year old, his parents were divorced; the court awarded custody of Joshua to his father, who moved to Wisconsin and remarried. When Joshua was three, his father's second wife complained to the county department of social services (DSS) that the father was abusing the child, hitting him and leaving marks on him. DSS officials interviewed the father, who denied the charges; DSS did not pursue the matter. A year later Joshua was admitted to a hospital with multiple bruises and abrasions; the examining doctor notified DSS; DSS immediately obtained a court order taking custody over Joshua, but the DSS investigating team decided there was insufficient evidence of child abuse to retain Joshua in the court's custody. The father promised DSS that he would enroll Joshua in a preschool program and undertake counseling for himself. A month later the hospital emergency room notified DSS that Joshua had been treated again for suspicious injuries; the caseworker concluded there was no basis for action. Over the next six months the caseworker visited the home, repeatedly saw injuries on Joshua's head, and noted that he had not been enrolled in the preschool program. She recorded all this in her files and did nothing more. About a month later, the emergency room notified DSS that Joshua had been admitted with injuries they believed caused by child abuse. On the caseworker's next two home visits, she was told Joshua was too ill to see her. DSS

See also

Brandenburg v. *Ohio*

Yates v. *United States*

*DeShaney's father
was tried and
convicted of child
abuse, but the case
that reached the
Supreme Court was
a civil action.*

took no action. Four months later, the father beat four-year-old Joshua, who lapsed into a coma; Joshua suffered severe brain damage, but lived. He is expected to spend the rest of his life in an institution for the profoundly retarded.

The father was tried and convicted of child abuse, but the case that reached the Supreme Court was a civil action, brought by Joshua's mother against DSS and some DSS employees, seeking damages on the ground that DSS had deprived Joshua of substantive due process of law in violation of the Fourteenth Amendment. The lower courts denied relief and the Supreme Court affirmed, 6–3. For the majority, Chief Justice William H. Rehnquist concluded that the due process clause imposed no affirmative duty on the state or its officers to protect a citizen's life or liberty against private persons' invasions. Furthermore, no such constitutional duty arose merely because DSS had known of Joshua's situation and indicated its intention to protect him. The case differed from those in which the Court had recognized a state duty to assure minimal safety and medical treatment for prisoners and institutionalized mental patients, for here the state had done nothing to restrain Joshua or otherwise prevent him from protecting himself or receiving protection from other persons. The harm, in other words, "was inflicted not by the State of Wisconsin, but by Joshua's father."

For the dissenters, Justice William J. Brennan castigated the majority for so limited a view of the prison- and mental-hospital cases. Here the state had set up DSS to protect children in precisely Joshua's situation, thus encouraging citizens generally to rely on DSS to prevent child abuse. One had to ignore this context to conclude, as the majority did, that the state had simply failed to act. Justice Harry A. Blackmun, in a separate dissent, objected to the majority's formalistic distinction between state action and state inaction; the state had assumed responsibility

for protecting Joshua from the very abuse that deprived him of much of what it means to have a life.

In a great many ways the Supreme Court has imposed affirmative duties on the states to compensate for inequalities or other harms not directly of the states' making. Its decisions in these areas recognize, if only partially, the artificiality of insisting that constitutional guarantees be rigidly confined to action that is formally governmental, ignoring the interlacing of public and private action that characterizes much behavior in America's complex society. As *DeShaney* sadly illustrates, a mechanical application of the judge-made state-action limitation on the Fourteenth Amendment can permit the systematic evasion of public responsibility.

—KENNETH L. KARST

Bibliography

Tribe, Laurence H. (1989). The Curvature of Constitutional Space: What Lawyers Can Learn from Modern Physics. *Harvard Law Review* 103:1–39.

DISCRETE AND INSULAR MINORITIES

The idea of the "discrete and insular minority" originated in the now famous footnote four of the opinion in *United States* v. *Carolene Products Company* (1938). Justice Harlan F. Stone, writing for only a plurality of the Court, queried—without answering the question— "whether prejudice against discrete and insular minorities may be a special condition, which tends seriously to curtail those political processes ordinarily to be relied upon to protect minorities, and which may call for a correspondingly more searching judicial inquiry." In the wake of the Court's about-face in 1937, Justice Stone was serving notice that the Court might not accord the same deference to statutes directed at "discrete and insular minorities" that it would to statutes directed at economic regulation.

The Court made little use of the concept until the early 1970s, when it began to delineate the class characteristics of such groups. Included were groups that had been "saddled with such disabilities, or subjected to such a history of purposeful unequal treatment, or relegated to such a position of political powerlessness as to command extraordinary protection from the majoritarian political process." Although race, nationality, and alienage seem to have been firmly established as class characteristics of the "discrete and insular minority," the Court has refused to extend such class status to illegitimates, the poor, or conscientious objectors.

Regents of the University of California v. *Bakke* (1978) presented the question of the "discrete and insular minority" in a new light. The question in *Bakke* was whether the same "solicitude" should be applied to test a governmental action designed to benefit rather than injure a "discrete and insular" minority. The university, citing *Carolene Products,* argued that strict scrutiny was reserved exclusively for "discrete and insular minorities." Four Justices agreed that a white male needed no special protection from the political process that authorized the actions of the university. Justice Lewis F. Powell rejected this argument: "The 'rights created by the . . . Fourteenth Amendment are, by its terms, guaranteed to the individual. The rights established are personal rights. . . .' The guarantee of equal protection cannot mean one thing when applied to one individual and something else when applied to a person of another color."

In *Fullilove* v. *Klutznick* (1980) the Court, for the first time since the *Japanese American Cases* (1943–44), upheld a racial classification that was expressed on the face of a law. *Fullilove* involved a challenge to an act of Congress authorizing federal funds for local public works projects and setting aside ten percent of those funds for employment of businesses owned by Negroes, Hispanics, Orientals, American Indians, and Aleuts. Chief Justice Warren E. Burger, writing for a plurality, called for judicial deference to Congress's power under section 5 of the Fourteenth Amendment, as equivalent to "the broad powers expressed in the Necessary and Proper Clause. . . ." The irony was that the idea of the "discrete and insular minority" in its inception was designed to curtail such deference when racial classifications were involved.

In *Adarand Constructors* v. *Pena* (1995) the Court roundly rejected the deference given Congress in *Fullilove,* and held that federal, like state, affirmative action programs demand strict scrutiny. The Court reached the same result in *Shaw* v. *Reno* (1993), ruling that legislative districts drawn with race as the predominant factor are likewise subject to strict scrutiny.

Benign racial classifications, it is sometimes said, are justified because they do not involve the stigma of invidious discrimination. The recipients of the benefits that accrue from the "benign" classification are not branded as members of an "inferior race" as they would be if the classification were an invidious one. This theory erects "stigma" as the standard for equal protection rights. Absent any such stigma the implication is that the Constitution is not offended, even if individuals must bear burdens created by a classification that otherwise would be disallowed by the equal protection clause. As Burger stated in *Fullilove,* " 'a sharing of the burden' by innocent parties is not impermissible." To use the idea of stigma as a racial class concept is, in effect, to translate equal protection rights into class rights.

But the intrusion of class into the Constitution is a dangerous proposition, one that is at odds with the principles of the constitutional regime—principles ultimately derived from the proposition that "all men are created equal." Class considerations explicitly deny this equality because they necessarily abstract from the individual and ascribe to him class

Regents of the University of California *v.* Bakke *presented the question of the "discrete and insular minority" in a new light.*

characteristics that are different—and necessarily unequal—from those of individuals outside the class. A liberal jurisprudence must disallow all class considerations. When there is a conflict between two different "discrete and insular minorities," which should be accorded preference? No principle can answer this question. And the question is not merely theoretical. The Court has already faced this dilemma in cases such as *United Jewish Organizations* v. *Carey* (1977) and *Castenada* v. *Partida* (1977), and in a pluralistic society it is inevitable that many more such cases will arise. Equal protection can be the foundation of a genuine liberal jurisprudence only if it applies to individuals. As Justice John Marshall Harlan remarked in his powerful dissent in *Plessy* v. *Ferguson* (1896), the case that established the separate-but-equal doctrine, "[O]ur Constitution is color-blind, and neither knows nor tolerates classes among citizens. In respect of civil rights, all citizens are equal before the law." This is undoubtedly still the essential principle of liberal government.

James Madison argued, in *The Federalist* #10, that in a large, diverse republic with a multiplicity of interests it was unlikely that there would ever be permanent majorities and permanent minorities; thus there would be little probability that "a majority of the whole will have a common motive to invade the rights of other citizens." On this assumption, the majorities that do form will be composed of coalitions of minorities that come together for limited self-interested purposes. The majority will thus never have a sense of its own interest as a majority.

By and large, the solution of the Founders has worked remarkably well. There have been no permanent majorities, and certainly none based exclusively on race. Understanding American politics in terms of monolithic majorities and "discrete and insular minorities"—as the Supreme Court appears to do—precludes the creation of a common interest that transcends racial class consid-

erations. By transforming the Fourteenth Amendment into an instrument of class politics, the Court risks either making a majority faction more likely by heightening the majority's awareness of its class status as a majority, or transforming the liberal constitutional regime into one no longer based on majority rule.

—EDWARD J. ERLER

Bibliography

Ely, John H. (1980). *Democracy and Distrust: A Theory of Judicial Review.* Pages 75–77 and 135–179. Cambridge, Mass.: Harvard University Press.

Erler, Edward J. (1982). Equal Protection and Personal Rights: The Regime of the "Discrete and Insular Minority." *Georgia Law Review* 16:407–444.

Karst, Kenneth L., and Horowitz, Harold W. (1974). Affirmative Action and Equal Protection. *Virginia Law Review* 60:955–974.

DISSENTING OPINION

In cases in which the judges of a multijudge court are divided as to the decision, it is customary for those in the minority to file a dissenting opinion. This practice is followed in the Supreme Court of the United States. In recent years, dissenting opinions have been filed in as many as 70 percent of all cases decided by the Court. In a typical term over 150 separate dissenting opinions are filed by Justices who find themselves on the losing side.

The author of a dissenting opinion tries to explain why the Court should have decided the case differently. Often a dissenting Justice will attempt to provide the public with an interpretation of the majority opinion in order to narrow its scope or to restrict its impact. A strong dissenting opinion may go far to weaken the decision and may point the way for future litigation.

The opinion of the court is written by a Justice on the prevailing side designated by the Chief Justice (or the senior Justice in the majority), and must reflect a consensus of the majority. Dissenters have a freer hand: they can make their point more sharply because they do not need to accommodate colleagues who might balk at aspects of their argument. Before the decision of a case is announced, the draft opinions circulate among the Justices. A well-argued dissent can induce the author of the majority opinion to modify its content, either to retain majority support, as in *Everson* v. *Board of Education* (1947), or to respond in kind to a particularly harsh attack, as in *Dred Scott* v. *Sandford* (1857). In an extraordinary case, the dissent may attract enough support actually to become the majority opinion.

Dissents are most common during change in the ideological composition of the Court. For a time the dissents portend an imminent revolution in the tendency of judicial thought and point to the future course of decisions. Once the revolution is perfected there follows a time when the dissents resist the new orientation and recall the old orthodoxy. Two of the Court's great dissenters were Justices John Marshall Harlan (1833–1911) and Oliver Wendell Holmes, each of whom stood against the majority of his day and took positions that much later were adopted by the Court.

Charles Evans Hughes once wrote that "a dissent in the court of last resort is an appeal to the brooding spirit of the law, to the intelligence of a future day. . . ." Contemporaneously, Harlan F. Stone wrote that "dissents seldom aid in the right development of the law. They often do harm."

—DENNIS J. MAHONEY

DOUBLE JEOPARDY

Over the past few years, the Supreme Court has decided a substantial number of cases involving double jeopardy issues. For the most part, these decisions continued a trend noted in the *Encyclopedia* of giving additional flexibility to the doctrine, although several notable exceptions expanded the protection provided by the clause. The most significant developments concerned two topics: multiple crimes arising from the same conduct and sentencing. The most disturbing development occurred under the dual-sovereignty doctrine.

In the area of multiple offenses, the Supreme Court continues to adhere to the position that the legislative branch has virtually unlimited power to define as separate crimes and to punish cumulatively individual steps within a criminal transaction and the completed transaction as well. The well-worn test set out in *Blockberger* v. *United States* (1932) determined whether the offenses are separate by asking if each "requires proof of a fact which the other does not." This has been construed as a rule of statutory construction, which is not controlling within a single prosecution if the legislative intent is clear and that multiple punishments are intended.

However, where individual crimes arising from the same events are adjudicated separately, a sharply divided Court expanded the protection of the double jeopardy clause beyond the confines of the *Blockberger* test. In *Grady* v. *Corbin* (1990), the Court concluded that a prosecution for vehicular manslaughter was barred where the defendant had been convicted previously of driving while intoxicated based on the same automobile accident. The Court reasoned that successive prosecutions present dangers that require protection under the double jeopardy doctrine even in circumstances where the two crimes do not constitute the "same offense" under the *Blockberger* test. It formulated a new and certainly more complicated test: the guarantee against double jeopardy is violated by subsequent criminal prosecution when the government establishes an essential element of that crime by proving conduct that constituted an offense for which the defendant has been previously prosecuted.

The decision in *Grady* v. *Corbin* unsettled the law with regard to the important concept

The author of a dissenting opinion tries to explain why the Court should have decided the case differently.

See also
Dred Scott v. *Sandford*
Everson v. *Board of Education*

The Supreme Court is steadfast in its commitment to a monolithic and absolute dual-sovereignty doctrine in the context of double jeopardy.

of what constitutes the "same offense." Its immediate practical effect will be to encourage, if not require, the government to prosecute in a single case all charges arising from the same transaction because some of those that share a common element will be barred by the double jeopardy clause if they are prosecuted later. How this decision will be reconciled with the body of related doctrine—and even whether it will stand the test of time given the Court's history of dramatically changing course on double jeopardy issues—remains to be seen. Indeed, the conflicting nature of the Court's double jeopardy jurisprudence was apparent from cases decided during the same term. In *Dowling* v. *United States* (1990), the Supreme Court determined that evidence of criminal conduct was not barred by the collateral estoppel concept of double jeopardy, even though the defendant had been found not guilty in an earlier trial of that criminal conduct. *Dowling* and *Grady* v. *Corbin* can be reconciled because the crimes in *Dowling* were not part of the same transaction, but the two cases demonstrate that there is no broad consensus within the Court on basic principles, particularly the application of this "same transaction" concept.

In the area of sentencing, the Court decided a number of significant cases. Although the clause does not apply to civil penalties, the Court concluded that in a very rare case a penalty traditionally considered remedial can be so overwhelmingly disproportionate to the damage caused that it must be considered punishment with a purpose of deterrence or retribution. In this circumstance, presented by a series of penalties in *United States* v. *Halper* (1989), the double jeopardy clause bars imposition of civil penalties subsequent to criminal conviction and punishment.

The Court has determined that the double jeopardy clause does not in general prohibit the government, pursuant to statutory authorization, from appealing a sentence or pro-

hibit a court from increasing that sentence after review. In contrast, the double jeopardy clause does impose some limits on resentencing in capital punishment litigation. In *Bullington* v. *Missouri* (1981) the Court concluded that the clause prohibits imposing a death sentence on resentencing where a jury initially imposed a life sentence. The trial-type proceedings involved in such a determination render a decision not to impose a death penalty the equivalent of an acquittal at trial. The double jeopardy clause does not, however, bar the trial judge, under statutory authorization, from overriding a jury recommendation of life imprisonment and imposing a death sentence.

The Court concluded that the double jeopardy doctrine permits either resentencing or judicial modification of a sentence in two other areas. First, it held in *Morris* v. *Mathews* (1986) that where the defendant is convicted of both a jeopardy-barred greater offense and a lesser offense that is not so barred the error may be corrected without resentencing by simply substituting the lesser-included conviction, unless the defendant can demonstrate a reasonable probability that he or she would not have been convicted of the lesser offense absent the joint trial with the jeopardy-barred offense. Second, the decision in *Jones* v. *Thomas* (1989) held that as long as the resentencing remains within legislatively intended limits an appellate court could modify an initially invalid consecutive sentence by vacating the shorter sentence and crediting the defendant for the time served even after the defendant had fully satisfied the shorter sentence. In reaching this conclusion, the Court dismissed longstanding precedent apparently prohibiting resentencing after the defendant had satisfied one of two alternative sentences.

In a disturbing, although not doctrinally surprising, opinion, the Court extended to prosecutions by separate states its very broad holding that double jeopardy is inapplicable where the same conduct is prosecuted by state and federal governments. Reasoning that this dual-sovereignty doctrine rests on the critical determination that two entities draw authority to punish from separate sources of power, the Court concluded in *Heath* v. *Alabama* (1985) that the doctrine operates between states as it does between state and federal governments.

On first examination, applying the doctrine to two states appears to present no major issues. However, an examination of the facts of the case and the underlying policies presents a different picture. *Heath* involved a kidnapping that began in Alabama and ended in a murder across the nearby state line in Georgia. Pursuant to a plea bargain in Georgia, the defendant avoided the death penalty in exchange for a life sentence. He was then prosecuted in Alabama for the same murder and sentenced to death. The Supreme Court's decision resulted in affirming that death sentence.

At a practical level, the operation of the dual-sovereignty doctrine permitted two states to enjoy all the advantages of multiple prosecutions that the double jeopardy clause was intended to prevent. Admittedly, however, these advantages can accrue to the prosecution whenever the dual-sovereignty doctrine is applied. The major difference in this case is that the two sovereigns were protecting the same policy interest—punishing the taking of human life. When the state and federal government are involved, there has historically been not only a separate source of political power, but also a separate interest protected.

Heath demonstrates that the Supreme Court is steadfast in its commitment to a monolithic and absolute dual-sovereignty doctrine in the context of double jeopardy. Given the expansion of federal jurisdiction to almost every area of state criminal law, this position is understandable, if not defensible. Currently, the different policy interest protected by the federal prosecution is often

imaginary, and the decision in *Heath* makes recognition of this fact unnecessary.

—ROBERT P. MOSTELLER

Bibliography

LaFave, Wayne R., and Israel, Jerold H. (1985). *Criminal Procedure.* St. Paul, Minn.: West Publishing Co.

Thomas, George C. (1988). An Elegant Theory of Double Jeopardy. *University of Illinois Law Review* 1988:827–885.

DRED SCOTT v. SANDFORD

19 Howard 393 (1857)

Closely associated with the coming of the Civil War, *Dred Scott* v. *Sandford* remains one of the most famous decisions of the United States Supreme Court. It is certainly the prime historical example of judicial power exercised in the interest of racial subordination, and, as such, it stands in sharp contrast with *Brown* v. *Board of Education* (1954), handed down almost a century later.

Scott was a Missouri slave owned by an army medical officer named John Emerson, who took him to live at military posts in Illinois and in federal territory north of 36°30' where slavery had been prohibited by the Missouri Compromise. In 1846 Scott brought suit against Emerson's widow in St. Louis, claiming that he had been emancipated by his residence on free soil. Missouri precedent was on his side, and after two trials he won his freedom. In 1852, however, the state supreme court reversed that judgment. By a 2–1 vote and in bitterly sectional language, it declared that the state would no longer enforce the antislavery law of other jurisdictions against Missouri's own citizens. Scott's residence elsewhere, it held, did not change his status as a slave in Missouri.

See also

Benton v. *Maryland*

Capital Punishment

STILL A SLAVE

The Court's infamous decision in Dred Scott *made front-page news. (Corbis)*

Normally, the next step should have been an appeal to the United States Supreme Court, but a recent decision in the somewhat similar case of *Strader* v. *Graham* (1851) may have persuaded Scott's legal advisers that the Court would refuse to accept jurisdiction. They decided instead to initiate a brand new suit for freedom in the federal circuit court for Missouri against Mrs. Emerson's brother, John F. A. Sanford of New York, who had been acting as her agent in the Scott litigation and may even have become the slave's owner. Sanford's New York citizenship provided the foundation for diversity jurisdic-

tion. So began the case of *Dred Scott* v. *Sandford* (with Sanford's name misspelled in the official record).

Up to this point, the principal issue in Scott's suit had been how residence on free soil affected the legal status of a slave. It was a familiar issue that dated back to the noted British case of *Somerset* v. *Stewart* (1772) and had been dealt with in a number of state court decisions. During the early decades of American independence, a tacit sectional accommodation had prevailed. Southerners accompanied by slaves were generally able to travel and sojourn in free states without interference. At the same time, southern courts joined in upholding the rule that a slave domiciled in a free state became forever free. Beginning in the 1830s, however, this arrangement broke down under antislavery pressure. State after state in the North withdrew the privilege of maintaining slaves while sojourning, and there was growing judicial acceptance of the view that any slave other than a fugitive became free the moment he set foot on free soil. To Southerners the change meant not only inconvenience but also insult, and by the 1850s they were retaliating in various ways.

Dred Scott v. *Sandford* raised an additional issue. In order to maintain a suit in federal court, Scott had to aver that he was a citizen of Missouri. Sanford's counsel challenged this assertion with a plea in abatement arguing that Negroes were not citizens and that the Court therefore lacked jurisdiction. The trial judge ruled that any person residing in a state and legally capable of owning property was qualified to bring suit under the diverse-citizenship clauses of the Constitution and the Judiciary Act. On the merits of the case, however, he instructed the jury in favor of the defendant. Like the Missouri Supreme Court in *Scott* v. *Emerson,* he declared that Scott's status, after returning to Missouri, depended entirely upon the law of that state, without regard to his residence in Illinois and free federal territory. The jury accordingly brought in a verdict for Sanford.

The case then proceeded on writ of error to the United States Supreme Court, whose membership at the time consisted of five southern Democrats, two northern Democrats, one northern Whig, and one Republican. Argument before the Court in February 1856 introduced another new issue. For the first time, Sanford's lawyers maintained that Scott had not become free in federal territory because the law forbidding slavery there was unconstitutional. This, of course, was the issue that had inflamed national politics for the past decade and would continue to do so in the final years of the sectional crisis. With a presidential contest about to begin, the Justices prudently ordered the case to be reargued at the next session. On March 6, 1857, two days after the inauguration of James Buchanan, Chief Justice Roger B. Taney finally read the decision of the Court.

Although Taney spoke officially for the Court, every other member had something to say, and only one concurred with him in every particular. The effect of the decision was therefore unclear, except that Dred Scott had certainly lost. Seven Justices concluded that at law he remained a slave. Taney, in reasoning his way to that judgment, also ruled that free blacks were not citizens and that Congress had no power to prohibit slavery in the territories. But were these declarations authoritative parts of the decision?

According to some contemporary critics and later historians, Taney did not speak for a majority of the Court in excluding Negroes from citizenship. Their conclusion rests upon the assumption that only those Justices expressly agreeing with him can be counted on his side. Yet, since Taney's opinion was the authorized opinion of the Court, it seems more reasonable to regard only those Justices expressly disagreeing with him as constituting the opposition. By this measure, the opinion never encountered dissent from more than two Justices at any major point. Furthermore, five Justices in their opinions spoke of the citizenship question as having been

Closely associated with the coming of the Civil War, Dred Scott *remains one of the most famous decisions of the Court.*

D

The citizenship issue concerned the status of free Negroes only, for everyone agreed that slaves were not citizens.

decided by the Court. In other words, the authoritativeness of that part of Taney's opinion was attested to by a majority of the Court itself.

More familiar is the charge that Taney indulged in obiter dictum when he ruled against the constitutionality of the Missouri Compromise restriction after having decided that Scott was not a citizen and so had no right to bring suit in a federal court. "Obiter dictum" was the principal battle cry of the Republicans in their attacks on the decision. By dismissing Taney's ruling against territorial power as illegitimate, they were able to salvage the main plank of their party platform without assuming the role of open rebels against judicial authority. What the argument ignored was Taney's not unreasonable contention that throughout his opinion he was canvassing the question of jurisdiction. Having concluded that Scott could not be a citizen because he was a *Negro*, the Chief Justice elected to fortify the conclusion by demonstrating also that Scott could not be a citizen because he was a *slave.* Such reinforcement was especially appropriate because some of the Justices were convinced that the Court could not properly review the citizenship question.

It therefore appears that none of Taney's major rulings can be pushed aside as unauthoritative. In any case, the long-standing argument over what the Court "really decided" has been largely beside the point; for Taney's opinion was accepted as the opinion of the Court by its critics as well as its defenders. As a matter of historical reality, the *Dred Scott* decision is what he declared it to be.

Taney devoted about 44 percent of his opinion to the question of Negro citizenship, 38 percent to the territorial question, 16 percent to various technical issues, and only 2 percent to the original question of whether residence on free soil had the legal effect of emancipating a slave. Throughout the entire document, he made not a single concession to antislavery feeling but instead committed the

Judicial Power of the United States totally to the defense of slavery. Behind his mask of judicial propriety, the Chief Justice had become privately a fierce southern sectionalist, seething with anger at "Northern insult and Northern aggression." His flat legal prose does not entirely conceal the intensity of emotion that animated his *Dred Scott* opinion.

The citizenship issue concerned the status of free Negroes only, for everyone agreed that slaves were not citizens. Yet Taney persistently lumped free Negroes and slaves together as one degraded class of beings who "had been subjugated by the dominant race, and, whether emancipated or not, yet remained subject to their authority." Thus all blacks, in his view, stood on the same ground. Emancipation made no difference. Negroes could not have been regarded as citizens by the Framers of the Constitution, he declared, because at the time they "had no rights which the white man was bound to respect." These notorious words were not mere historical commentary as defenders of the Chief Justice have often insisted. Taney also held that the constitutional status of Negroes had not changed at all since 1787, which meant that in 1857 they still had no federal rights that white men were bound to respect. His reasoning excluded blacks not only from citizenship but also from every protection given to *persons* by the Constitution.

Much more forceful in its political impact was Taney's ruling against the constitutionality of the antislavery provision in the Missouri Compromise. He began by dismissing as irrelevant the one clause of the Constitution in which the word "territory" appears, preferring instead to derive the territorial power of Congress by implication from the power to admit new states. No less remarkable is the fact that he never said precisely why the antislavery provision was unconstitutional. Historians have inferred from one brief passage that he based his holding on the due process clause of the Fifth Amendment.

Yet there is no explicit statement to that effect, and in the end he did not declare that congressional prohibition of slavery in the territories *violated* any part of the Constitution; he said only that it was "not warranted" by the Constitution, a phrasing that suggests reliance on the principle of strict construction.

Not satisfied with ruling in effect that the Republican party was organized for an illegal purpose, the Chief Justice also struck a hard blow at northern Democrats and the doctrine of popular sovereignty. If Congress could not prohibit slavery in a territory, he said, neither could it authorize a territorial legislature to do so. This statement, being on a subject that did not arise in the case, was *dictum*. It exemplified Taney's determination to cover all ground in providing judicial protection for slavery. The dissenting Justices, John McLean and Benjamin R. Curtis, rejected Taney's blanket exclusion of Negroes from citizenship. Having thus affirmed Scott's capacity to bring suit in a federal court, they proceeded to the merits of the case while denying the right of the Court majority to do so. Both men upheld the constitutionality of the Missouri Compromise restriction by interpreting the territory clause, in Republican style, as an express and plenary delegation of power to Congress. They went on to maintain that antislavery law, state or federal, dissolved the legal relationship between any master and slave coming within its purview, thereby working irrevocable emancipation.

Antislavery critics made good use of the dissenting opinions in launching an angry, abusive attack upon the Court majority and its judgment. The influence of the decision on the sectional conflict is difficult to assess. No doubt it contributed significantly to the general accumulation of sectional animosity that made some kind of national crisis increasingly unavoidable. It also aggravated the split in the Democratic party by eliciting Stephen A. Douglas's Freeport doctrine and inspiring southern demands for a territorial slave code. At the same time, there is reason to doubt that the decision enhanced Republican recruiting or had a critical effect on the election of Abraham Lincoln.

For the two principals in the case, the verdict of the Court made little difference. John Sanford died in an insane asylum two months after the reading of the decision. Dred Scott was soon manumitted, but he lived only sixteen months as a free man before succumbing to tuberculosis. The constitutional effect of the decision likewise proved to be slight, especially after the outbreak of the Civil War. The wartime Union government treated *Dred Scott* v. *Sandford* as though it had never been rendered. In June 1862 Congress abolished slavery in all the federal territories. Later the same year, Lincoln's attorney general issued an official opinion holding that free men of color born in the United States were citizens of the United States. The Thirteenth Amendment (1865) and the Fourteenth Amendment (1868) completed the work of overthrowing Taney's decision.

The *Dred Scott* case damaged Taney's reputation but did not seriously weaken the Supreme Court as an institution. Aside from its immediate political effects, the case is significant as the first instance in which a major federal law was ruled unconstitutional. It is accordingly a landmark in the growth of judicial review and an early assertion of the policymaking authority that the Court would come to exercise more and more.

—DON E. FEHRENBACHER

Bibliography

Ehrlich, Walter (1979). *They Have No Rights: Dred Scott's Struggle for Freedom.* Westport, Conn.: Greenwood Press.

Fehrenbacher, Don E. (1978). *The Dred Scott Case: Its Significance in American Law and Politics.* New York: Oxford University Press.

Swisher, Carl B. (1974). *The Taney Period, 1836–1864.* Vol. 5 of the *Oliver Wendell Holmes Devise History of the Supreme*

See also

Brown v. *Board of Education*

Strader v. *Graham*

Taney, Roger B.

The plurality opinion in Dun & Bradstreet *may portend significant changes in the constitutional doctrine governing libel and the first amendment.*

Duncan *reaffirmed the Court's belief that trial by jury is fundamental to American justice.*

Court of the United States. New York: Macmillan.

DUN & BRADSTREET, INC. v. GREENMOSS BUILDERS, INC.

472 U.S. (1985)

The plurality opinion in this case may portend significant changes in the constitutional doctrine governing libel and the First Amendment. Dun & Bradstreet, a credit reporting business, falsely and negligently reported to five subscribers that Greenmoss had filed a petition in bankruptcy, and also negligently misrepresented Greenmoss's assets and liabilities. In an action for defamation, Greenmoss recovered substantial compensatory and punitive damages. Vermont's highest court held that the principle of *Gertz* v. *Robert Welch, Inc.* (1974) did not apply in actions against defendants who were not part of the press or broadcast media. A fragmented Supreme Court avoided this question but affirmed, 5–4.

Justice Lewis F. Powell, for a three-Justice plurality, concluded that *Gertz*—which had held, among other things, that punitive damages could not be awarded against a magazine without proof of knowing or reckless disregard of the falsity of the statement—was applicable only to "expression on a matter of public concern." Justice Powell spoke only generally about the content of the "matter of public concern" standard, but hinted that "media" speech might qualify automatically for protection under *Gertz*. Dun & Bradstreet's report, however, involved "matters of purely private concern." Although such speech is "not wholly unprotected" by the First Amendment, he concluded, it can be the basis of a punitive damages award even absent a showing of reckless disregard of the truth. Chief Justice Warren E. Burger and Justice Byron R. White, in separate concur-

ring opinions, expressed willingness to abandon *Gertz* altogether, but meanwhile agreed with this radical surgery on *Gertz*.

In a footnote pregnant with meaning, Justice Powell remarked that some kinds of constitutionally protected speech are entitled only to "reduced protection"—commercial speech, for example. But he did not place Dun & Bradstreet's report in the latter category, and thus raised speculation that the majority may be prepared to adopt a "sliding scale" for the freedom of speech, with varying (and, as yet, unspecified) degrees of constitutional protection for each kind of speech, depending on the Justices' determinations about the value of the speech and the context in which it is uttered.

Justice William J. Brennan, for the four dissenters, agreed that credit reports were not central to First Amendment values, but argued nonetheless that the *Gertz* requirements should apply to this case: credit and bankruptcy information was "of public concern." Justice Brennan noted with satisfaction that six Justices (the dissenters and authors of the concurring opinions) had rejected a distinction between the First Amendment rights of "media defendants" and of others sued for defamation.

—KENNETH L. KARST

DUNCAN v. LOUISIANA

391 U.S. 145 (1968)

A 7–2 Supreme Court here overruled several earlier decisions and held that the Fourteenth Amendment incorporated the Sixth Amendment right to trial by jury. Louisiana tried Duncan for battery, a misdemeanor charge punishable by up to two years' imprisonment. The court denied his request for a jury trial and sentenced him, upon conviction, to sixty days and a $150 fine. On appeal to the Supreme Court, the Justices abandoned the approach used in *Palko* v. *Connecticut* (1937) and *Adamson* v. *California* (1947), where the Court had examined the circumstances to determine whether they preserved the implicit due process requirement of "fundamental fairness." In his opinion in *Duncan,* Justice Byron R. White asked instead whether trial by jury was "fundamental to the American scheme of justice" and concluded that history supported an affirmative response. Conceding a court's duty to distinguish between petty and serious offenses to determine which cases warranted this protection, White declined to do so as a general rule. He declared that an offense punishable by more than two years' imprisonment was sufficiently serious to apply the Sixth Amendment guarantee. Penalties involving less than six months' time were not accorded that right. As usual, Justices Hugo L. Black and William O. Douglas, concurring separately, advocated the total incorporation doctrine. Justices John Marshall Harlan and Potter Stewart, dissenting, asserted that "the Court's approach and its reading of history are altogether topsy-turvy." Later decisions in *Williams* v. *Florida* (1970) and *Apodaca* v. *Oregon* (1972) have limited the extent of the right incorporated.

—DAVID GORDON

D

DUNCAN v. LOUISIANA

391 U.S. 145 (1968)

See also

Adamson v. *California*

Palko v. *Connecticut*

Williams v. *Florida*

E

EDELMAN v. JORDAN

415 U.S. 651 (1974)

This decision defines states' Eleventh Amendment immunity from suit in federal court. Plaintiffs, alleging that Illinois welfare officials were unconstitutionally administering a welfare program financed by state and federal funds, sought the payments wrongfully withheld. The Supreme Court, in an opinion by Justice William H. Rehnquist, held the Eleventh Amendment to bar the request for retroactive relief but suggested that, as in *Ex Parte Young* (1908), the Eleventh Amendment would not bar relief requiring the state to pay the costs of future constitutional compliance. In *Milliken* v. *Bradley* (1977), the Court reconfirmed *Edelman* by requiring a state to pay the costs of future constitutional compliance.

Edelman also developed the principles regulating Congress's power to modify the states' Eleventh Amendment immunity. First, limiting earlier holdings such as *Parden* v. *Terminal Railway* (1964), *Edelman* held that mere participation by a state in a federal welfare program does not constitute a waiver of the state's Eleventh Amendment protection. It thus confirmed the narrow approach to waiver signaled by *Employees* v. *Department of Public Health and Welfare* (1973). Second, despite Congress's power to abrogate states' Eleventh Amendment immunity, *Edelman* stated that actions brought under Section 1983, Title 42, United States Code, are limited by the Eleventh Amendment. At the time, the state's protection from section 1983 actions seemed to stem from the Court's holding in *Monroe* v. *Pape* (1961) that Congress had not meant to render cities liable un-

der section 1983. With the overruling of that portion of *Monroe* in *Monell* v. *Department of Social Services* (1978), the question whether section 1983 abrogated the states' Eleventh Amendment immunities reemerged. In *Quern* v. *Jordan* (1979), a sequel to *Edelman,* the Court held that section 1983 was not meant to abrogate the states' Eleventh Amendment protection.

—THEODORE EISENBERG

ELLSWORTH, OLIVER

(1745–1807)

Oliver Ellsworth played a key role in the creation of the United States Constitution in 1787 and the establishment of a national judiciary during the Constitution's first decade.

Born into a well-established Connecticut family, he entered Yale in 1762, but left after two years to attend the College of New Jersey (Princeton) where he was graduated with a B.A. in 1766. Ellsworth returned to Connecticut and studied theology for about a year, but abandoned it for the law and was admitted to the bar in 1771. One of the ablest lawyers of his day, he built up an extremely lucrative practice. He also entered politics and was elected to the state's General Assembly in 1773. A warm supporter of the patriot cause against Great Britain, he helped supervise the state's military expenditures during the war for independence, was appointed state attorney for Hartford in 1777, a member of the Governor's Council in 1780, and a judge of the Connecticut Supreme Court in 1785. He also served as one of the state's representatives to the Continental Congress for six terms (1777–83). While in Congress he

Edelman developed the principles regulating Congress's power to modify the states' Eleventh Amendment immunity.

See also

Milliken v. *Bradley*

E

Oliver Ellsworth played a key role in the creation of the United States Constitution.

became a member of the Committee of Appeals which heard appeals from state admiralty courts, and in this capacity he ruled on the important case of Gideon Olmstead and the British sloop *Active,* which eventually culminated in *United States* v. *Peters* (1809).

In 1787 Connecticut selected him to be one of its three delegates to the federal Constitutional Convention in Philadelphia. He played an active role at the convention and won respect for his orderly mind and his effectiveness as a debater. Ellsworth favored the movement to establish a strong and active federal government with the power to act directly on individuals and to levy taxes, as a substitute for the weak central government created by the Articles of Confederation. But he also thought that the Virginia Plan went too far in a nationalist direction. "The only chance of supporting a general government lies in grafting it on those of the original states," he argued. In particular, he opposed the idea of apportioning representation in both houses of Congress according to population, to the clear advantage of larger states. To resolve the differences between the large and the small states he helped forge the successful Great Compromise, which apportioned representation in the lower house according to population and in the Senate by a rule of equality, with each state having two senators. Ellsworth also played an active role on the Committee on Detail, which produced the basic draft of the United States Constitution.

Following adoption of the Constitution, Connecticut elected Ellsworth to the United States Senate. He recognized that the Constitution as written and ratified was only a basic outline; an actual government had to be created and its powers implemented. He supported Alexander Hamilton's financial program and was opposed to attempts to ally the United States too closely with France, but his most important contribution was the drafting of the Judiciary Act of 1789. This law was in many ways an extension of the Constitution

itself, for it fleshed out the terse third article of that document, which dealt with the nature and powers of the federal judiciary. The Judiciary Act of 1789 specified that the Supreme Court should consist of six Justices, that each state should have a district court, and that there should be three circuit courts consisting of two Supreme Court Justices sitting with a district judge. Under this law the federal courts were given exclusive jurisdiction in a number of important areas and concurrent jurisdiction with the state courts in other matters. The act also provided that decisions of the state courts involving the Constitution or laws or treaties of the United States could be appealed to the Supreme Court.

In 1796 President George Washington appointed Ellsworth Chief Justice of the United States. He held the post for three years but had little impact. The cases he heard were not very significant, illness limited his participation in the duties of the Court, and a diplomatic mission took him out of the country. Perhaps his most important decision came in *Wiscart* v. *Dauchy* (1796) in which he examined the relationship of the Supreme Court to the district and circuit courts, established a series of important rules dealing with writs of error, and extended common law procedures in appeals to equity and admiralty jurisdiction as well. His opinions tended to be brief, to the point, and nationalist in orientation. In *United States* v. *La Vengeance* (1796) he expanded the admiralty jurisdiction of the federal courts to inland navigable rivers, the Great Lakes, and other water routes away from the high seas; and while riding circuit in *United States* v. *Isaac Williams* (1799) he upheld the English common law doctrine that citizens of a country did not have the right to expatriate themselves without their native country's consent.

As Chief Justice, Ellsworth encouraged the practice of the Supreme Court's handing down per curiam opinions, with a single deci-

sion representing the will of the entire court, as opposed to having separate seriatim opinions by the individual Justices. John Marshall, who succeeded Ellsworth as Chief Justice, considered the continuation and further development of this practice all-important in maintaining respect for the authority of the Court when it handed down controversial decisions.

In 1799 Ellsworth, over the protest of some of his closest associates, agreed to a request from President John Adams to be a part of a special diplomatic mission to resolve the undeclared naval war with France. The mission was a success, but Ellsworth became ill while abroad, resigned the chief justiceship in October 1800, and stayed in England to recuperate. By the time he returned to America the Jeffersonians had triumphed and he retired from public life.

—RICHARD E. ELLIS

Bibliography

Brown, William Garrott (1905). *The Life of Oliver Ellsworth*. New York: Macmillan.

Goebel, Julius, Jr. (1971). *History of the Supreme Court of the United States, Vol. 1: Antecedents and Beginnings to 1801*. New York: Macmillan.

EMINENT DOMAIN

In his argument as counsel in *West River Bridge Company* v. *Dix* (1848), the first case in which the Supreme Court ruled directly on the constitutionality of the states' power of eminent domain, Daniel Webster thundered against the whole concept of state discretion in "takings." Only in the past few years, he contended, had this power of eminent domain been recognized in American law. Claims for its legitimacy, moreover, were "adopted from writers on other and arbitrary [civil law] governments," he declared; and eminent domain could easily become an instrument for establishment by the states of "unlimited despotisms over the private citizens." Webster tried, in effect, to get the court to impose Fifth Amendment standards on the states.

Webster was engaged in a failing cause. Besides, his history was inaccurate and his predictions of disaster were simplistic. He was certainly right, however, in seeing the eminent domain power as a formidable threat to vested rights, corporate or individual. He understood that eminent domain condemnations might become a proxy for regulation under the police power, undermining the contract clause as a bulwark of property rights. He was right in raising the alarm when he did; when *West River Bridge* was argued there had been a vast increase in activity by government and private corporations in exercise of eminent domain. The transportation revolution in America was in an expansionary phase; extensive new railroad construction reinforced the effects on property law already felt from canal, turnpike, and bridge enterprises. All these ventures required use of the "taking" power in order to accomplish their purposes.

Contrary to Webster's version of legal history, government's power to expropriate privately owned property for a variety of public purposes had long been an element of Anglo-American law. The power of eminent domain was the power to compel transfers to government or government's assignees. In its constitutional version, even in the 1840s, it was understood as a power that could be exercised legitimately only for a public use or public purpose, and that required the payment of just compensation. In English decisions and statutes going back several centuries, in American colonial law, and in the state law of the early republic, this power of taking by governmental authority had been exercised for such purposes as road-building, fortifications, drainage (including the great Fens projects of England in the seventeenth century), navigational improvement on rivers,

Under the Fourteenth Amendment's due process clause, the door was opened to challenges in federal courts of state eminent domain actions.

and construction of bridges and canals. In colonial Massachusetts, statute had extended a variant of the power into the manufacturing sector by authorizing builders of mills to dam up streams, flooding neighboring lands; these "milldam laws" provided for assessment of damages and payment of compensation in cash.

The Fifth Amendment—which the Supreme Court would rule in *Barron* v. *Baltimore* (1833) was not applicable to the states—expressed the views and used language already embodied in several of the state constitutions adopted during the Revolutionary era. Thus the amendment's requirement that property could be taken "for public use" and on payment of "just compensation" had been foreshadowed by such documents as the 1780 Massachusetts Declaration of Rights, which declared that "whenever the public exigencies require that the property of any individual should be appropriated to public uses, he shall receive reasonable compensation therefor."

Although several early state constitutions lacked such language, uniformly the state courts, in reviewing takings cases, ruled that general principles of justice, the writings of the natural-law jurists, or the constitutional values reflected in the Fifth Amendment justified imposition by judges of both a "public use" and a "just compensation" limitation upon their legislatures' uses of the eminent domain power. It was a singular feature of legal development in the states, however, that despite the widespread formal adoption of such limitations, in fact only slight constraints were placed on the legislatures. In practice, compensation paid to persons suffering from takings was far below market value (and, because of offsetting benefits commonly calculated against damages, often they were paid nothing in cash); hence, eminent domain became an instrument for the subsidization, through cost reduction, of both governmental enterprises and favored private undertakings. "Public convenience" became,

in most states, a legitimate reading of the "public use" requirement; and in practice, the legislatures enjoyed wide discretion in deciding what types of enterprise might be vested with the power to expropriate private property. Ironically, the very bridge and railroad corporations that Webster represented so often were among the greatest beneficiaries of eminent domain devolution in that era.

The Court in *West River Bridge* wholly rejected Webster's contentions, ruling that state eminent domain powers were "paramount to all private rights vested under the government." It left the state courts to decide for themselves whether compensation payments were just in particular cases, or whether due process requirements of state constitutions had been met.

So stood constitutional doctrine until the adoption of the Fourteenth Amendment. Under its due process clause, the door was opened to challenges in federal courts of state eminent domain actions. Increasingly, too, in the late nineteenth century, the Supreme Court was called upon to rule upon the constitutionality of regulatory measures that activist state legislatures were enacting. The issue tended to take the form of defining a "taking," with the constitutional requirement it connoted, as opposed to bona fide use of the police power, which did not require compensation. The Court ruled in a succession of cases that the Fourteenth Amendment embodied the requirements of "public use" and "just compensation." It took a broad view, however, of what types of enterprise the states might aid with devolutions of the eminent domain power; in a series of cases on irrigation districts, drainage companies, individual enterprises and corporation activities in other areas such as logging and mining, and the more traditional areas of state activity, the Court upheld legislative discretion under a permissive "public use" standard.

In *Mugler* v. *Kansas* (1887), the Court attempted to distinguish between a taking, which required compensation, and uses of the police power, which it defined as laws abating nuisances or limiting uses of property that were harmful to "health, morals, or safety of the community," not compensable. But drawing the police power/eminent domain line proved difficult; indeed, it perplexes the Court to the present day. In *Pennsylvania Coal Company* v. *Mahon* (1922), Justice Oliver Wendell Holmes argued that the police power and eminent domain power are on a single continuum; differences are a matter of degree, not qualitative. The Court has continued to struggle with the issue, and in modern land-use zoning cases from *Euclid* v. *Ambler Realty* (1926) to *Agins* v. *Tiburon* (1980) it has sought a firmer ground to replace the distinction Holmes found so appropriate.

The Court has upheld congressional discretion in deciding what purposes of federal eminent domain met the Fifth Amendment's "public use" requirement. In *United States* v. *Gettysburg Electric Railway Company* (1896), the Court declared acceptable any use "which is legitimate and lies within the scope of the Constitution." In *United States ex rel. Tennessee Valley Authority* v. *Welch* (1946) the Court carried the doctrine to an extreme, concluding that a congressional decision to authorize expropriation of property "is entitled to deference until it is shown to involve an impossibility." A few years later, *Berman* v. *Parker* (1954) upheld federal eminent domain takings to conduct an urban redevelopment project in the District of Columbia. Here the end was the public welfare, a "broad and inclusive" concept, the Court declared, that certainly embraced slum clearance and an urban development designed to be "beautiful as well as sanitary." Given the validity of this purpose, it was legitimate to invoke eminent domain, which was only a means. Congress must decide as to the need for the project and its design.

Later, in *Hawaii Housing Authority* v. *Midkiff* (1984), the Court sustained an even broader law authorizing the state to acquire property by eminent domain on petition of the tenants residing on that land, and then to convey it to those tenants. It relied on Hawaii's unusual concentration of land ownership in a small group, which effectively prevented most residents from owning the land on which they lived. The Court found the statute therefore fell within the Constitution's requirement that acquisitions by eminent domain be for a public use.

In its quest to develop standards to distinguish takings from legitimate exercise of the police power, the Court has probed to the heart of property concepts. What rights are "vested," how "reasonable expectations" should be defined, what obligations inhere in the ownership of private property—all are questions that come to the surface repeatedly in continuing litigation. Nearly 150 years ago, Chief Justice Lemuel Shaw of Massachusetts admonished, in *Boston Water Power Company* v. *Railroad* (1839), that the eminent domain power "must be large and liberal, so as to meet the public exigencies, and it must be so limited and constrained, as to secure effectually the rights of the citizen; and it must depend, in some instances, upon the nature of the exigencies as they arise, and the circumstances of individual cases." Shaw's view may have lacked prescriptive potential, but it has proved remarkably accurate in predicting the direction that the law would take—and the perplexities that would beset the best efforts of lawmakers and judges to produce definitive formulae.

—HARRY N. SCHEIBER

Bibliography

Dunham, Allison (1962). *Griggs* v. *Allegheny County* in Perspective: Thirty Years of Supreme Court Expropriation Law. *Supreme Court Review* 1962:63–106.

Grant, J. A. C. (1931). The "Higher Law" Background of the Law of Eminent Domain. *Wisconsin Law Review* 6:67–85.

Hurst, James Willard (1964). *Law and Economic Growth: The Legal History of the*

EMPLOYMENT
DIVISION,
DEPARTMENT OF
HUMAN RESOURCES
OF OREGON v. SMITH

110 S.Ct. 1595 (1990)

Lumber Industry in Wisconsin, 1836–1915. Cambridge, Mass.: Harvard University Press.

Scheiber, Harry N. (1971). The Road to *Munn:* Eminent Domain and the Concept of Public Purpose in the State Courts. *Perspectives in American History* 5:327–402.

Stoebuck, William B. (1972). A General Theory of Eminent Domain. *Washington Law Review* 47:553–608.

——— (1980). Police Power, Takings, and Due Process. *Washington and Lee Law Review* 37:1057–1099.

EMPLOYMENT DIVISION, DEPARTMENT OF HUMAN RESOURCES OF OREGON v. SMITH

110 S.Ct. 1595 (1990)

Two drug and alcohol abuse counselors were fired from their jobs after ingesting the hallucinogenic drug peyote during a religious ceremony of the Native American Church. They were subsequently denied unemployment compensation by the state of Oregon because the state determined they had been discharged for work-related "misconduct." The workers filed suit, alleging that the denial of compensation violated the free exercise clause of the First Amendment. The Supreme Court disagreed by a vote of 6–3.

If the Court had handled *Smith* as it had handled most of its previous cases in the field of religious liberty, it would have first asked whether Oregon had a compelling state interest to deny unemployment compensation to the fired workers. If Oregon could demonstrate such an interest, and the denial of compensation was narrowly tailored to further that end, the denial would have been upheld. But the Court did not treat *Smith* as it had previous cases. Instead, it used *Smith* to abolish the compelling-interest standard for challenges brought under the free exercise clause.

Writing for five members of the Court, Justice Antonin Scalia made the astonishing claim that the Court had never really applied the compelling-interest standard to free exercise claims. According to Scalia, the Court had "never held that an individual's religious beliefs excuse him from compliance with an otherwise valid law prohibiting conduct that the State is free to regulate." Of course, the Court had held precisely that in several cases, most notably *Cantwell* v. *Connecticut* (1943) and *Wisconsin* v. *Yoder* (1972). But Scalia noted that these cases implicated other constitutional rights besides free exercise, and he suggested that those other rights were the decisive factor in the Court's decisions to hold unconstitutional particular applications of certain general laws. In *Cantwell,* the invalidated licensing law impinged on the freedom of speech; in *Yoder,* the compulsory education law infringed on the "right of parents . . . to direct the education of their children." Scalia concluded from this that only when the free-exercise clause is joined with other constitutional protections may it invalidate particular applications of general laws. As a practical matter, this means that the free exercise clause alone means very little. Generally applicable laws that do not implicate other constitutional rights are constitutional, no matter how difficult they make it for certain persons to practice their religion; indeed, it is conceivable that a generally applicable law could destroy certain religious groups entirely and yet survive a free exercise challenge under Scalia's approach. Only laws that expressly seek to regulate religious beliefs or to proscribe certain actions only when they are engaged in for religious reasons violate the free exercise clause according to the Court's new standard.

Concurring in the judgment, but disavowing the Court's reasoning, Justice Sandra Day

O'Connor attacked the majority opinion as "incompatible with our Nation's fundamental commitment to individual religious liberty." Carefully recalling prior precedents, O'Connor showed that the compelling-interest test had been applied much more consistently by the Court in free exercise cases than Scalia had suggested. O'Connor further defended the test as an appropriate method by which to enforce "the First Amendment's command that religious liberty is an independent liberty...." Applied to the case at hand, O'Connor believed that the free exercise claim could not prevail, however, because exempting the two workers from drug laws would significantly impair the government's "overriding interest in preventing the physical harm caused by the use of a Schedule I controlled substance."

Justices Thurgood Marshall, William J. Brennan, and Harry A. Blackmun joined most of Justice O'Connor's concurring opinion, but they disagreed with her ultimate conclusion, arguing that enforcement of drug laws against the religious ingestion of peyote was in no way necessary to fulfill the state's legitimate interest in circumscribing drug use. The state had argued that an exemption of the claimants in *Smith* would invite a flood of other claims for exemption to drug laws based on religious beliefs; but Blackmun pointed out that many states already have statutory exemptions for religious peyote use and have suffered no such difficulty.

The debate on the Court that erupted in *Smith* over what standard to apply to free exercise claims was dramatic; and yet it was not entirely unexpected, having been foreshadowed in several previous cases, including *Goldman* v. *Weinberger* (1986) and *O'Lone* v. *Estate of Shabazz* (1987). It also had been preceded for some years by a vigorous debate among scholars such as Walter Berns and Michael McConnell. Berns had long characterized the Court's decision in *Yoder* as contrary to American republicanism. His view clearly triumphed in *Smith*.

Whether or not the Court's new approach is any better than its old one, however, is open to question.

Congress took up the gauntlet shortly after the *Smith* decision, enacting the Religious Freedom Restoration Act. This statute restored the compelling interest test to statutes, state or federal, that "substantially burden" the free exercise of religion. The statute was itself promptly challenged, and in *City of Boerne* v. *Flores* (1997) the Court ruled that Congress lacked power to adopt a statute "altering the Fourteenth Amendment's meaning." That decision leaves *Smith* in force, although Justice O'Connor, joined by Justice Stephen G. Breyer, dissented on the ground that *Smith* was wrongly decided.

One can certainly understand why the Court might want to restrict challenges under the free exercise clause. When only the members of a particular religious group may use an illegal drug or ignore compulsory education laws, the free exercise clause appears to undermine the equality before the law established by the rest of the Constitution. Scalia's approach seeks to avoid this contradiction by defining free exercise in terms of other constitutional rights, such as freedom of speech, freedom of association, and equal protection. Scalia has a keen theoretical mind, and one can readily see the analytical power of his approach. Under his scheme, religious liberty will be protected by general rights applicable to all, rather than by specific exemptions granted only to those who hold peculiar religious beliefs. The principle of equality before the law will be maintained. That this approach may indeed afford protection to religious liberty is demonstrated by the recent development of the doctrine of equal access, which is premised on free-speech and free-association protections rather than the free-exercise clause.

Yet one can legitimately wonder—as Justice O'Connor did in *Smith*—whether Scalia's approach will actually protect the free exercise of religion to its fullest extent. One

Two drug and alcohol abuse counselors were fired from their jobs after ingesting the hallucinogenic drug peyote during a religious ceremony of the Native American Church.

See also

Cantwell v. *Connecticut*

Compelling State Interest

Freedom of Speech

Goldman v. *Weinberger*

Religious Liberty

Wisconsin v. *Yoder*

Use of a school prayer in New York state schools was challenged as an establishment of religion.

suspects that it could only do so if the Court were willing to give an expansive reading to other constitutional rights in order to make up for its restricted interpretation of free exercise. Indeed, Scalia himself had to resort to an unenumerated right of parental control over a child's education to explain the Court's previous ruling in *Wisconsin* v. *Yoder* within his framework. But the Rehnquist Court appears to be in no mood to give a broad reading to any rights just now, which makes its evisceration of the free exercise clause all the more troubling.

Government today wields a wide array of regulatory powers that the Court no longer even presumes to question; the "compelling state interest" test may be the only practical way to insulate religious groups from the destructive effects of such regulatory powers. The Court's failure to appreciate this fact raises troubling questions about its commitment to religious freedom for all.

—JOHN G. WEST, JR.

Bibliography

Berns, Walter (1976). *The First Amendment and the Future of American Democracy.* Chapter 2. New York: Basic Books.

McConnell, Michael W. (1990). The Origins and Historical Understanding of Free Exercise of Religion. *Harvard Law Review* 103:1409–1517.

ENGEL v. VITALE

370 U.S. 421 (1962)

The Board of Regents of the State of New York authorized a short prayer for recitation in schools. The Regents were seeking to defuse the emotional issue of religious exercises in the classroom. The matter was taken out of the hands of school boards and teachers, and the blandest sort of invocation of the Deity was provided: "Almighty God, we acknowledge our dependence upon Thee, and beg Thy blessings upon us, our teachers, and

our country." School districts in New York did not have to use the prayer, and if they did, no child was required to repeat it. But if there were any prayer in a New York classroom it would have to be this one. The Board of Education of New Hyde Park, New York, chose to use the Regents' Prayer and directed its principals to cause it to be said aloud at the beginning of each school day in every classroom.

Use of the prayer was challenged as an establishment of religion. Justice Hugo L. Black, writing for the Court, concluded that neither the nondenominational nature of the prayer nor the fact that it was voluntary could save it from unconstitutionality under the establishment clause. By providing the prayer, New York officially approved theistic religion. With his usual generous quotations from James Madison and Thomas Jefferson, Black found such state support impermissible.

Justice William O. Douglas concurred separately. He had more trouble than Black concluding that the prayer established religion "in the strictly historic meaning of these words." What Douglas feared was the divisiveness engendered in a community when government sponsored a religious exercise.

Only Justice Potter Stewart dissented, concluding that "the Court has misapplied a great constitutional principle." Stewart could not see how a purely voluntary prayer could be held to constitute state adoption of an official religion. For Stewart, an official religion was the only meaning of "establishment of religion." He noted that invocations of the Deity in public ceremonies of all sorts had been a feature of our national life from its outset. Without quite saying so, Stewart asked his brethren how the Regents' Prayer could be anathematized on establishment clause grounds without scraping "In God We Trust" off the pennies.

Engel v. *Vitale* was the first of a series of cases in which the Court used the establishment clause to extirpate from the public schools the least-common-denominator reli-

See also

Separation of Church
    and State
Establishment Clause
Establishment of Religion

gious invocations that had been a traditional part of public ceremonies—especially school ceremonies—in America.

The decision proved extremely controversial. It has been widely circumvented and there have been repeated attempts to amend the Constitution to undo the effect of *Engel*.

—RICHARD E. MORGAN

Bibliography

Berns, Walter (1976). *The First Amendment and the Future of American Democracy*. Pages 33–76. New York: Basic Books.

Muir, William K., Jr. (1967). *Prayer in the Public Schools*. Chicago: University of Chicago Press.

EQUAL PROTECTION OF THE LAWS

Two questions have dominated the Supreme Court's equal protection opinions since 1985. The first, largely a matter of rhetoric, is the question of the appropriate standard of review. The second and more important question is the relevance of racial groups in determining the existence of discrimination and in providing legislative or judicial remedies for the harms of discrimination.

The uninitiated reader of the Court's opinions surely would think the process of decision in an equal protection case begins with a selection of the appropriate standard of judicial review from among three well-worn formulas: (1) strict scrutiny, which requires the government to offer compelling justification for an inequality it has imposed, and so generally results in the invalidation of governmental action; (2) rational basis, in which the Court pays strong deference to the government's assertions of justification and generally upholds the governmental action; or (3) the "intermediate," "heightened" scrutiny that falls between these two polar extremes, requiring "important" justification.

Then, the same reader might imagine, the Court measures the government's asserted justifications against the proper standard of review, and on that basis reaches judgment.

More skeptical readers know that the order of the decisional process is often quite the reverse, with a judgment on the merits of the case preceding—even dictating—the selection of a standard of review as an opinion's rhetorical structure. The skeptics know, too, how misleading it is to speak of "the" standard of review, given the Court's occasional willingness to require significant justification in the name of "rational basis" review. Justice Thurgood Marshall long (and accurately) insisted that the Court's decisions add up to a sliding scale in which the standard of review varies according to the importance of the interests at stake. Justice John Paul Stevens made a similar point when he said, "There is only one equal protection clause." In equal protection cases, as in other cases, the Court decides by weighing interests.

The Court's post-1985 equal protection decisions are illustrative. A 6–3 majority of the Justices used the traditional, highly deferential, "rational basis" standard to uphold two acts of Congress governing eligibility for welfare benefits and food stamps in *Lyng* v. *Castillo* (1986) and *Lyng* v. *Automobile, Aerospace and Agricultural Implement Workers* (1988). Similarly, in *Kadrmas* v. *Dickinson Public Schools* (1988), the Court upheld, 5–4, a state law authorizing some school districts to impose on unwilling parents user fees for school-bus transportation. The majority specifically rejected the argument of two dissenting Justices that *Plyler* v. *Doe* (1982) demanded heightened judicial scrutiny for wealth classifications governing access to public education. *Plyler*'s opinion had been written in the language of "rational basis" review, but no one among the Justices or the Court's commentators had been deceived into believing that the Court was being deferential to the legislature's judgment. In fact, the Court in *Kadrmas* explicitly called *Plyler* a

*A majority of
Justices agree that
Congress has the
power to remedy
societal
discrimination, both
private and
governmental,
through affirmative-
action programs.*

case of heightened scrutiny. The post-1985 decisions may be less than satisfying, but they are conventional applications of existing doctrine.

The dissenters' invocation of *Plyler* v. *Doe* reminds one, however, that Justices can make "rational basis" into the equivalent of heightened scrutiny when they are so inclined. Two recent cases evoked such responses. *Attorney General of New York* v. *Soto-Lopez* (1986) was a challenge to a state law that gave veterans of the armed forces a preference in civil-service hiring, but only if the veterans were New York residents when they entered the forces. A four-Justice plurality concluded that the law failed to pass the heightened scrutiny demanded by the right to travel. Two other Justices rejected both the "right to travel" argument and the conclusion that heightened scrutiny was appropriate; nonetheless, they concluded that the law lacked a rational basis and so violated the equal protection clause. Plainly, this is not a classical "rational basis" decision, any more than was *Plyler* v. *Doe*.

In *Cleburne* v. *Cleburne Living Center* (1985) the Justices were unanimous in holding unconstitutional a Texas town's refusal to grant a zoning variance to allow the operation of a group home for mentally retarded persons. The court of appeals had concluded that an official classification based on mental retardation required justification at the level of "intermediate" scrutiny, but a majority of the Supreme Court disagreed. Vigorously arguing that the proper standard was "rational basis," the majority proceeded to a meticulous examination of the justifications offered by the town, rejecting each one as insufficient. As Justice Marshall, concurring, pointed out, *Cleburne* has taken its place alongside *Plyler* as a leading modern example of the sliding scale of standards of review in action.

In at least two kinds of cases, the "rational basis" standard, initially given "bite" in the fashion of *Plyler* and *Cleburne*, has been transformed into candid recognition of a more rigorous judicial scrutiny of governmental justifications. The law of sex discrimination

moved from the "rational basis" explanation of *Reed* v. *Reed* (1971) to the explicit "intermediate" scrutiny of *Craig* v. *Boren* (1976). A similar rhetorical change is visible in the law governing classifications based on the legal status of illegitimacy. First came the "rational basis" language of *Levy* v. *Louisiana* (1968); eventually, the open adoption of "intermediate" scrutiny in *Clark* v. *Jeter* (1988). These progressions exemplify the normative power of the factual: the practice of heightened scrutiny eventually leads to its formal recognition as doctrine. It is not extravagant to expect a similar treatment of the claims of the mentally retarded in some future opinion. In the end, the standard of judicial review seems not so much to govern decisions as to provide a rhetorical framework on which lawyers and judges can fasten the substantive considerations that are the heart of argument and decision: the harms of governmental actions to constitutionally protected interests and the government's justifications for those actions.

Another recent instance of a possible fine-tuning of one of the levels of equal protection scrutiny—this time, the intermediate level—occurred in *United States* v. *Virginia* (1996). That decision, by Justice Ruth Bader Ginsburg, held Virginia unconstitutionally discriminated based on gender in denying women admission to Virginia Military Institute. The Court stated, citing two earlier cases, that those "who seek to defend gender-based government action must demonstrate an 'exceedingly persuasive justification.'" This led some to question whether the Court had increased its scrutiny a notch from intermediate scrutiny.

In contrast, arguments about the relevance of group harms and the validity of group remedies are of major importance in deciding cases—and, indeed, in deciding whether the nation will seriously address the continuing harms of racial discrimination. Certainly racial discrimination happens to people one by one, but it happens because they are members of a racial group. The harms of group subordination have multiple causes; actions are harmful because of their contexts. Yet our current constitutional law pays little attention to context and, instead, centers on a principle demanding no more of government than formal racial neutrality. To establish a claim of racial discrimination that violates the equal protection clause, normally one must show that identifiable officers of the government have purposefully acted on a racial ground to produce the harm in question—a proposition typically hard to prove.

A rare case in which the requisite purpose was found was *Hunter* v. *Underwood* (1985). The Supreme Court concluded that a clause in Alabama's 1901 state constitution disenfranchising persons convicted of crimes of "moral turpitude" had been adopted for the purpose of preventing black citizens from voting and continued in the present to have racially disparate effects. Accordingly, the Court held that it was unconstitutional for the state to deny the vote on the basis of a conviction for the misdemeanor of passing a worthless check. The Court based its conclusion about the law's continuing racially disparate effects on statistics showing that blacks in two Alabama counties had been disenfranchised under the law at a rate at least 1.7 times the rate for whites.

Two years later, however, in rejecting an equal protection attack on the constitutionality of the death penalty, a majority of the Justices refused to give similar weight to a statistical demonstration of racial discrimination. A study of some 2,000 Georgia murder cases in the 1970s showed dramatic racial disparities in the likelihood that capital punishment would be imposed. In *McCleskey* v. *Kemp* (1987) the Court decided, 5–4, that those statistics were irrelevant; to prevail on a claim of racial discrimination, a defendant must show some specific acts of purposeful discrimination by the prosecutor, jury, or judge in his or her own case. Surely the majority Justices understood that a contrary decision would have threatened wholesale reversals of death sentences—a course they were unwilling to take.

Both the *Hunter* and *McCleskey* cases raised questions concerning the relevance of group subordination in equal protection analysis. *McCleskey* illustrates the present majority's devotion to the principle of formal racial neutrality and its reluctance to accept a showing of disparity among racial groups as proof of the discrimination that violates the equal protection clause. In interpreting a number of federal civil rights statutes, however, the Court has accepted this sort of statistical proof of discrimination.

The issue of the constitutionality of affirmative action brings together the rhetorical question of the standard of judicial review and the more substantive question of group remedies. Although, since 1985, the Supreme Court has remained fragmented on both these aspects of affirmative action, the practical effects of the decisions show a remarkable stability.

Given the acceptability of statistical proof of violation of a number of major antidiscrimination laws, many an affirmative-action program amounts to the substitution of one group remedy for another. Accordingly, there is broad agreement among the Justices on the validity of affirmative-action programs that are seen to be genuinely remedial. Yet the dominant principle for the Court's current majority is one of formal racial neutrality, and there is some awkwardness in squaring affirmative action with this principle. In two recent affirmative-action cases—*Wygant* v. *Jackson Board of Education* (1986), on public hiring, and *Richmond (City of)* v. *J. A. Croson Co.* (1989), on public contracting—the key opinions were written by Justices Lewis F. Powell and Sandra Day O'Connor. On the surface, these opinions minimize group concerns, but together they make clear how a public institution can constitutionally adopt an affirmative action program. The approved method, explained as a form of remedy for past discrimination, makes judicious use of statistics showing racial disparities. In short, Justices Powell and O'Connor have found a way to use the language of individual justice in the cause of ending group subordination.

♦ **action**

*A court case. Before the
unification of law and
equity, an "action" at law
was distinguished from a
proceeding in equity.*

While the Erie *result
itself still finds
general acceptance,
the years since the
decision have seen
much debate about
its rationale, scope,
and application.*

See also

Craig v. *Boren*
McCleskey v. *Kemp*
Plyler v. *Doe*
Wygant v. *Jackson Board of
Education*

The prevailing opinions in *Wygant* and *Croson* emphasize the "strict scrutiny" standard of review, employing this standard both in evaluating the justifications for affirmative action as a remedy for past discrimination and in requiring "narrow tailoring" of a racially based remedy. In *Metro Broadcasting, Inc.* v. *F.C.C.* (1990), however, a different 5–4 majority announced that the less demanding "intermediate" scrutiny was appropriate in evaluating an affirmative-action program approved by Congress. In an opinion by Justice William J. Brennan, the majority upheld a congressionally approved program of the Federal Communications Commission (FCC) for a limited number of racial preferences in the distribution of broadcast licenses. Here the majority said that Congress was not limited to providing remedies for past discrimination; rather, the affirmative-action program was aimed at achieving a greater diversity in broadcast programming. The four dissenters, in opinions by Justice O'Connor and Justice Anthony M. Kennedy, insisted on "strict scrutiny" for congressional affirmative action as well as for state or local governmental programs and argued that the nonremedial purpose of broadcasting diversity was not a sufficiently compelling governmental purpose to pass the test.

Even after the retirement of Justice Brennan, there remains a majority of Justices who agree that Congress has the power, in enforcing the Fourteenth Amendment, to remedy societal discrimination, both private and governmental, through affirmative-action programs. Presumably, in future cases, that result will be described, as it was in *Croson*, as consistent with "strict scrutiny." Indeed, in *Metro Broadcasting* itself one might have imagined an opinion upholding the FCC's diversity program as broadly "remedial." In the affirmative-action context, as elsewhere in equal protection doctrine, discussions of the standard of review serve purposes that are mainly rhetorical.

—KENNETH L. KARST

Bibliography

Bell, Derrick A. (1987). *And We Are Not Saved: The Elusive Quest for Racial Justice.* New York: Basic Books.

Karst, Kenneth L. (1989). *Belonging to America: Equal Citizenship and the Constitution.* New Haven, Conn.: Yale University Press.

Kennedy, Randall L. (1988). *McCleskey* v. *Kamp*: Race, Capital Punishment, and the Supreme Court. *Harvard Law Review* 101:1388–1433.

Lawrence, Charles R., III (1987). The Id, the Ego, and Equal Protection: Reckoning with Unconscious Racism. *Stanford Law Review* 39:317–388.

Minow, Martha (1987). The Supreme Court, 1986 Term—Foreword: Justice Engendered. *Harvard Law Review* 101:10–95.

ERIE RAILROAD CO. v. TOMPKINS

304 U.S. 64 (1938)

The Supreme Court in *Erie* posed the question whether the "oft-challenged doctrine of *Swift* v. *Tyson* (1842) shall now be disapproved," and answered that it should. The Court rejected its earlier construction of the Rules of Decision Act, originally section 34 of the Judiciary Act of 1789, and held that the "laws of the several states"—which, except as otherwise required by federal law, are to be "regarded as rules of decision" in civil actions in the federal courts "in cases where they apply"—included all of the decisional or common law of the states.

Erie, like *Swift*, involved an exercise of the diversity jurisdiction of the federal courts. In *Erie*, plaintiff Tompkins brought a federal court suit against the railroad for personal injuries, and the court of appeals upheld a substantial jury verdict in the face of the railroad's claim that it had not violated the limited duty owned to plaintiff under the decisional law of the state where the injury occurred. That court concluded that, in the absence of a state statute, the question of the scope of the railroad's duty was one not of "local" but of "general" law, and under the general law the railroad had a duty of care that the jury could properly find to have been broken.

The Supreme Court, in an opinion by Justice Louis D. Brandeis, reversed and remanded for application of state law with respect to the scope of the railroad's duty. The Court concluded that (1) the refusal in *Swift* to read the mandate of the Rules of Decision Act as embracing all of the decisional law of the states was based on an incorrect construction of the purpose of that act; (2) the construction in *Swift* had prevented uniformity in the administration of state law and had permitted "grave discrimination by noncitizens [of a state] against citizens"; and (3) the doctrine of *Swift* represented "an unconstitutional assumption of powers by the Courts of the United States." Justices Pierce Butler and James C. McReynolds dissented; Justice Stanley F. Reed concurred in part, believing it unnecessary to reach the constitutional issue addressed by the Court.

Although the parties in *Erie* had not briefed the question whether *Swift* should be overruled, there had been intimations of the Court's intentions in earlier majority and dissenting opinions. And while the *Erie* result itself still finds general acceptance, the years since the decision have seen much debate about its rationale, scope, and application.

—DAVID L. SHAPIRO

ESTABLISHMENT CLAUSE

Three themes dominate recent Supreme Court decision making under the First Amendment's establishment of religion clause. First, the Court has continued to follow the doctrinal framework of *Everson* v. *Board of Education* (1947) and *Lemon* v. *Kurtzman* (1971), but with increasing emphasis on the "endorsement or disapproval" inquiry advocated by Justice Sandra Day O'-Connor. Second, the Court has steered a selective course in applying this framework, upholding certain governmental practices but invalidating others. Third, and potentially most significant, the Justices stand at the brink of a radical change in doctrine. Although a majority of the Court continues to follow *Everson* and *Lemon*, there is growing support for an alternative interpretation that would dramatically weaken the principle of separation of church and state.

In *Everson*, the Supreme Court adopted a broad interpretation of the establishment clause, one that forbids governmental favoritism for religion over irreligion as well as for one religion over another. Since 1971, this broad interpretation has been implemented through the three-part Lemon test. Under *Lemon*, a statute (or other governmental action) can be upheld only if it satisfies three requirements: "First, the statute must have a secular legislative purpose; second, its principal or primary effect must be one that neither advances nor inhibits religion . . . ; finally, the statute must not foster "an excessive governmental entanglement with religion."

Despite persistent criticism, the Court continues to embrace the *Everson* interpretation and the *Lemon* test. The Court has reformulated the first two parts of *Lemon*, however, by emphasizing the "endorsement or disapproval" inquiry that Justice O'Connor initially proposed in her concurring opinion in *Lynch* v. *Donnelly* (1984). In *Wallace* v. *Jaffree* (1985) and *Edwards* v. *Aguillard* (1987), the Court adopted O'Connor's formulation of the "purpose" inquiry: "The purpose prong of the *Lemon* test asks whether government's actual purpose is to endorse or disapprove of religion." In *County of Allegheny* v. *ACLU* (1989) the Justices likewise relied on O'Connor's formulation to modify *Lemon*'s "primary effect" requirement. Thus, the Court held that regardless of purpose, governmental action has a constitutionally impermissible ef-

*There is growing
support for an
alternative
interpretation that
would dramatically
weaken the principle
of separation of
church and state.*

fect if it *appears* to endorse or disapprove religion. "The Establishment Clause, at the very least," wrote the Court, "prohibits government from appearing to take a position on questions of religious belief."

Justice O'Connor's approach does not eliminate difficult questions of application. As suggested by *Corporation of Presiding Bishop* v. *Amos* (1987), for example, there is no "endorsement" when government merely "accommodates" religion by removing burdens that government itself has created. More generally, the line between partisan "endorsement" and neutral "acknowledgment" may be exceedingly difficult to draw.

With or without the O'Connor reformulation, the *Lemon* test provides no more than a framework for analysis. Its application requires an exercise of judgment, an exercise of judgment that depends on the context of specific cases and on the individual philosophies of the Justices. In its recent cases, the Court's applications of *Lemon* have suggested a relaxation of establishment clause restraints on government aid to religious institutions and activities. At the same time, the Court has applied the clause forcefully to prohibit government from advancing religion through the public school curriculum, and it has adopted a fact-specific approach for cases involving religious symbols.

If government singles out religion for special economic benefits, the Supreme Court continues to find an establishment clause violation. Thus, in *Texas Monthly, Inc.* v. *Bullock* (1989) the Court invalidated a Texas sales tax exemption that was limited to religious periodicals. For governmental programs that include secular as well as religious beneficiaries, however, the Court's decisions in *Witters* v. *Washington Department of Services for the Blind* (1986) and *Bowen* v. *Kendrick* (1988) suggest a relaxation of the Court's prior doctrine. In *Witters,* the question was whether the establishment clause required the state of Washington to deny vocational rehabilitation funds to an individual attending a Christian college in preparation

for a religious career. The Washington State Supreme Court had held that the denial was mandated by *Lemon*'s second prong, but the United States Supreme Court unanimously disagreed. Although the opinion of the Court was narrowly drawn, separate concurring opinions, joined by a majority of the Justices, gave a broad reading to *Mueller* v. *Allen* (1983), one that apparently would support the constitutionality of any neutrally drawn educational assistance program, even if most of the individual beneficiaries used the funds for religious training.

In *Bowen* the Court rejected a facial challenge to a federal statute designed to combat teenage sexual relations and pregnancy. In addressing these religiously sensitive topics, the statute not only permitted but expressly encouraged the involvement of religious organizations. Nonetheless, the Court refused to invalidate the statute either in its entirety or with respect to religiously affiliated grantees. Although the Court remanded for a determination of whether particular grants might render the statute unconstitutional as applied, it refused to presume that religiously affiliated grantees would use their grants "in a way that would have the primary effect of advancing religion."

The Court's permissive treatment of governmental funding programs has not been duplicated in the public school context. In *Edwards* v. *Aguillard* the Court considered a challenge to Louisiana's Balanced Treatment Act, which provided that evolution could not be taught in the public schools unless accompanied by the teaching of creationism. With only two Justices dissenting, the Court concluded that the act violated the first prong of *Lemon* and therefore was unconstitutional. Citing mandatory attendance policies and the impressionability of young students, the Court noted that it was "particularly vigilant in monitoring compliance with the Establishment Clause in elementary and secondary schools." Unpersuaded by the legislature's articulation of a secular purpose, the Court concluded that the act was designed "to alter the science curriculum to reflect endorsement of a religious view that is antagonistic to the theory of evolution." The Court found that this "preeminent religious purpose" was at least the "primary purpose" of the act and that the act therefore "endorses religion in violation of the First Amendment."

The Supreme Court's treatment of governmental displays of religious symbols shows neither the permissiveness of the funding cases nor the "particular vigilance" the Court has exercised in policing the public school curriculum. Instead, the Court has adopted a fact-specific approach that requires case-by-case determinations of whether particular religious displays have the purpose or effect of endorsing religion. In *County of Allegheny* v. *ACLU* the Court considered challenges to two separate holiday displays in downtown Pittsburgh, one of a crèche, the other of a menorah. A sharply divided Court found that the crèche violated the establishment clause but that the menorah did not. The Court emphasized that the crèche stood essentially alone in the Allegheny County Courthouse and included a banner that read "Gloria in Excelsis Deo." By contrast, the menorah was placed beside a large Christmas tree and was accompanied by a sign proclaiming the City of Pittsburgh's "salute to liberty." Focusing on the second prong of *Lemon*, as modified by Justice O'Connor, the Court concluded that the crèche sent an impermissible message of religious endorsement, whereas the menorah, in context, sent a permissible message of cultural diversity and freedom of belief.

The Court's recent applications of its establishment clause doctrine are significant and controversial in their own right. A far more important development, however, may be just around the corner. For years, critics have attacked *Everson* and *Lemon* for their alleged hostility to religion. To date, the Court has resisted these attacks, affirming the basic wisdom of its doctrinal framework and continuing to enforce a meaningful separation of church and state. The Court is changing, however, and it may be within one vote of a dramatic shift in doctrine. Speaking for four Justices in *County of Allegheny*, Justice Anthony M. Kennedy wrote that "substantial revision of our Establishment Clause doctrine may be in order." Suggesting the direction such revision might take, he argued that governmental "support" for religion should be permitted unless it involves coercion, "proselytizing" for a particular religion, or "direct benefits" so substantial as to in fact establish or tend to establish a state religion. It seems clear that the four Justices joining this opinion would support a fundamental retreat from the Court's existing doctrine.

Justice Kennedy's suggested course would seriously threaten the political-moral principles and policies that are furthered by the Court's prevailing approach. Governmental "support" for religion causes harm to the religious and irreligious individuals who are not within the government's favor. This harm creates feelings of resentment and alienation, which in turn cause injury to the political community itself. At the same time, the purported support for religion is often illusory; it may demean religion and work to its long-term detriment. The Supreme Court's establishment clause doctrine works to ensure a proper respect for the religious and irreligious beliefs of individuals, supports the maintenance of a religiously inclusive political community, and does no disservice to the important role of religion in our society. Whatever its weaknesses, this doctrine should not be abandoned.

DANIEL O. CONKLE

Bibliography

Conkle, Daniel O. (1988). Toward a General Theory of the Establishment Clause. *Northwestern University Law Review* 82: 1113–1194.

Note (1987). Developments in the Law: Religion and the State. *Harvard Law Review* 100:1606–1781.

Smith, Steven D. (1987). Symbols, Perceptions, and Doctrinal Illusions: Establishment Neutrality and the "No Endorsement" Test. *Michigan Law Review* 86: 266–332.

ESTABLISHMENT OF RELIGION

The First Amendment begins with the clause, "Congress shall make no law respecting an establishment of religion . . ."

The First Amendment begins with the clause, "Congress shall make no law respecting an establishment of religion. . . ." There are two basic interpretations of what the framers meant by this clause. In *Everson* v. *Board of Education* (1947), the first decision on the clause, the Supreme Court unanimously adopted the broad interpretation, although the Justices then and thereafter disagreed on its application. Justice Hugo L. Black declared that the clause means not only that government cannot set up a church but also that government cannot aid all religions impartially or levy a tax for the support of any religious activities, institutions, or practices. "In the words of [Thomas] Jefferson," Black said, "the clause against establishment of religion by laws was intended to erect "a wall of separation between Church and State."

Edward S. Corwin, a distinguished constitutional scholar who espoused the narrow view of the clause, asserted that the Court's interpretation was "untrue historically." What the clause does, he wrote, "and all that it does, is to forbid Congress to give any religious faith, sect, or denomination preferred status. . . . The historical record shows beyond peradventure that the core idea of "an establishment of religion' comprises the idea of preference; and that any act of public authority favorable to religion in general cannot, without manifest falsification of history, be brought under the ban of that phase" (Corwin, "Supreme Court as National School Board," pp. 10, 20). Justice Potter Stewart, dissenting in *Engel* v. *Vitale* (1962), endorsed the narrow view when he noted that a nondenominational school prayer did not confront the Court with "the establishment of a state church" or an "official religion."

The debate in the First Congress, which proposed the First Amendment, provides support for neither the broad nor the narrow interpretation. The history of the drafting of the clause, however, is revealing. Congress carefully considered and rejected various phrasings that embraced the narrow interpretation. At bottom the amendment was an expression of the intention of the Framers of the Constitution to prevent Congress from acting in the field of religion. The "great object" of the Bill of Rights, James Madison, had said, when introducing his draft of amendments to the House, was to "limit and qualify the powers of Government" for the purpose of making certain that none of the powers granted could be exercised in forbidden fields, including religion. The history of the drafting of the establishment clause does not provide a clear understanding of what was meant by the phrase "an establishment of religion." But the narrow interpretation, which permits government aid to religion in general or on a nonpreferential basis, leads to the impossible conclusion that the First Amendment *added* to Congress's powers. The amendment meant to restrict Congress to the powers that it possessed, and since it had no power to legislate on matters concerning religion, and therefore could not support religion on any basis, Congress would have had no such power even in the absence of the First Amendment. To suppose that an express prohibition on power vests or creates power is capriciously unreasonable. The Bill of Rights, as Madison said, was not framed "to imply powers not meant to be included in the enumeration."

Congress did not define "an establishment of religion" because its members knew from common experience what they meant. At the time of the framing of the amendment, six states maintained or authorized establishments of religion. That amendment denied to Congress the power to do what those states were doing, and since *Everson* the states come under the same ban. An establishment meant to the framers of the amendment what it meant in those states. Thus, reference to the American experience with establishments at the time of the framing of the Bill of Rights is essential to any understanding of what the clause in question meant.

The narrow interpretation is based on European precedents but the European form of an establishment was not the American form, except in the Southern colonies before the American Revolution, and the European meaning of establishment was not the American meaning. The revolution triggered a pent-up movement for separation of church and state in the nine states that had establishments. Of these nine, North Carolina (1776), New York (1777), and Virginia (1786) separated church and state. Each of the remaining six states made concessions to anti-establishment sentiment by broadening their old establishments. After the Revolution, none maintained a single or exclusive establishment. In all six an establishment of religion was not restricted to a state church or a system of public support of one denomination; in all an establishment meant public support of all denominations and sects on a nonpreferential basis.

Three of these six states were in New England. The Massachusetts Constitution (1780) authorized its towns and parishes to levy taxes for the support of Protestant churches, provided that each taxpayer's money go to the support "of his own religious sect or denomination" and added that "no subordination of any one sect or denomination to the other shall ever be established by law." An establishment in Massachusetts meant government support of religion. Congregationalists, for a few decades, benefited the most, because they were the most numerous and resorted to various tricks to fleece non-Congregationalists out of their share of religious taxes. But the fact remains that Massachusetts had a multiple, not a single, establishment under which Baptist, Episcopalian, Methodist, and Unitarian churches were publicly supported until the establishment ended in 1833. In 1784 Connecticut and New Hampshire modeled their multiple establishments after that of Massachusetts, ending them in 1818 and 1819, respectively.

In the South, where the Episcopal Church was the sole established church before the revolution, three states either maintained or permitted establishments of religion, and in each the multiple form was the only legal one. Maryland (1776) permitted its legislature to tax for the support of "the Christian religion," with the proviso that every person had the right to designate the church of his choice, making every Christian church an established church on a nonpreferential basis. The legislature sought to pass an enabling act in 1785, but the nonpreferential system was denounced as an establishment and defeated. The situation in Georgia was the same as in Maryland, and a revised constitution (1789), which was in effect when the First Amendment was adopted, continued the multiple establishment system, allowing each person to support only his own church. South Carolina restricted its multiple nonpreferential establishment to Protestant churches. The last Southern establishment died in 1810. Virginia sought to emulate the Maryland system, but a general assessment bill benefiting all Christian churches failed, thanks to the opposition of most non-Episcopal denominations and to Madison's Memorial and Remonstrance; the Virginia Statute of Religious Freedom (1786) then separated church and state.

In none of the six states maintaining or allowing establishments at the time of the framing of the First Amendment was any church but a Christian one established. The multiple establishments of that time comprehended the churches of every denomination and sect with a sufficient number of adherents to form a church. Where Protestantism was established it was synonymous with religion; there were either no Jews or no Roman Catholics or too few of them to make a difference. Where Christianity was established, as

See also

Engel v. *Vitale*

Circus-like live televison and radio broadcasts of Estes's pretrial hearings were so disruptive that many changes were ordered for coverage of the trial.

MEDIA FRENZY

Although Estes held that televising trials was inherently prejudicial, the Court later ruled that media coverage is at the discretion of the judge. Here, the media swarm the Federal Court in Los Angeles during the famous Pentagon Papers indictment. (Corbis/Tim Page)

See also

Chandler v. Florida

in Maryland, which had a significant Roman Catholic minority, Jews were scarcely known. To contend that exclusive establishments of one religion existed in each of the six states ignores the novel American experiment with multiple establishments on an impartial basis. Europe knew only single-church establishments. An establishment of religion in the United States at the time of the First Amendment included nonpreferential government recognition, aid, or sponsorship of religion. The framers of the amendment looked to their own experience, not Europe's.

LEONARD W. LEVY

Bibliography

Antieau, Chester James, et al. (1964). *Freedom from Federal Establishment: Formation and Early History of the First Amendment Religion Clauses.* Milwaukee, Wisc.: Bruce Publishing Co.

Cobb, Sanford H. (1902). *The Rise of Religious Liberty in America.* New York: Macmillan.

Corwin, Edward S. (1949). The Supreme Court as National School Board. *Law and Contemporary Problems* 14:3–22.

Levy, Leonard W. (1986). *The Establishment Clause: Religion and the First Amendment.* New York: Macmillan.

ESTES v. TEXAS

381 U.S. 532 (1965)

The trial of Billy Sol Estes for swindling involved a free press/fair trial confrontation in which the Supreme Court held that televising trials was inherently prejudicial to a fair trial. Circus-like live television and radio broadcasts of Estes's pretrial hearings involved such extensive disruption of the courtroom that many changes were ordered for coverage of the trial. Although live broadcasts of the actual trial were forbidden, excerpts from the proceedings were broadcast regularly.

The Court split 5–4 on the constitutionality of televising the proceedings. Justices Hugo L. Black, William J. Brennan, Potter Stewart, and Byron R. White called the practice unwise and dangerous, but not constitutionally objectionable. Chief Justice Earl Warren and Justices Arthur J. Goldberg and William O. Douglas joined an opinion by Justice Tom C. Clark seeking to ban television completely from the courts—subject to future developments—as a violation of the right to a fair trial. Both the jury and the witnesses, Clark declared, would be under great pressure and be more self-conscious, aware of a large public audience; prospective witnesses might be influenced by the proceedings. The judge would have additional responsibilities (and temptations), and the defendant would be subject to "a form of mental—if not physical—harassment." Clark said, "A defendant on trial for a specific crime is entitled to his day in court, not in a stadium, or a city or nationwide arena." Justice John Marshall Harlan approved the ban here, but indicated he would do so only in cases of "great notoriety."

—DAVID GORDON

EUCLID v. AMBLER REALTY COMPANY

272 U.S. 365 (1926)

This case established the constitutionality of zoning laws to regulate land use. In *Euclid* a Cleveland suburb sought to preserve an area of single-family dwellings by excluding even two-family dwellings and apartment houses, as well as commercial properties and public buildings. Against claims drawn from supposed deprivations of liberty and property without due process of law and a supposed denial of the equal protection of the laws, a 6–3 Supreme Court, speaking through Justice George Sutherland, sustained the comprehensive zoning ordinance. It was, the Court ruled, a legitimate state police power measure intended to maintain the residential area and thus protect the community's health, peace, and safety. As a result of this leading decision on comprehensive zoning laws, no argument drawn from the Fourteenth Amendment or from the takings clause is likely to survive judicial scrutiny in the absence of an ordinance that is demonstrably unrelated to the improvement of a community.

—LEONARD W. LEVY

EVERSON v. BOARD OF EDUCATION

330 U.S. 1 (1947)

A New Jersey statute authorized local school boards to reimburse parents for the cost of public transportation of students to both public and private schools. Such reimbursement for the cost of transportation to church-related schools was challenged as an unconstitutional establishment of religion.

Justice Hugo L. Black delivered the opinion of a 5–4 Supreme Court. He began with a consideration of the background of the establishment clause, which relied heavily on the writings of James Madison and Thomas Jefferson, but he had little to say about the actual legislative history of the First Amendment's language in the First Congress. Black concluded that the establishment clause "means at least this":

> *Neither a state nor the federal government can set up a church. Neither can pass laws which aid one religion, aid all religions or prefer one religion over another. . . . No tax in any amount, large or small, can be levied to support any religious activities or institutions, whatever they may be called, or whatever form they may adopt to teach and practice religion. . . . In the words of Jefferson, the clause against the establishment of religion by law was intended to erect "a wall of separation between church and State."*

But after this sweeping separationist pronouncement, Justice Black pirouetted neatly and upheld the New Jersey program on the grounds that the state aid in that case was a public safety measure designed to protect students and could in no way be construed as aid to church-related schools.

Four dissenters were convinced that Justice Black had missed the point. Justice Robert H. Jackson likened Black's majority opinion to Byron's Julia who, "whispering I will ne'er consent, consented." What could be more helpful to a school, Jackson asked, than depositing the students at its door? Justice Wiley B. Rutledge, with whom Justices Jackson, Felix Frankfurter, and Harold Burton joined, also filed a lengthy dissent. Justice Rutledge also made lavish use of the writings of Madison and Jefferson, and argued that the New Jersey program could not be justified as a public safety expenditure.

Euclid *established the constitutionality of zoning laws to regulate land use.*

Everson *stands at the entrance to the maze of law and litigation concerning participation by church-related schools in public programs.*

Everson stands at the entrance to the maze of law and litigation concerning participation by church-related schools in public programs. It was the first major utterance by the Supreme Court on the meaning of the establishment clause. Those favoring strict separation between religious institutions and government were pleased by Black's rhetoric and dismayed by his conclusion; those favoring a policy of flexibility or accommodation in church-state relations reacted the opposite way. That *Everson* satisfied no one and enraged many was portentous.

—RICHARD E. MORGAN

Bibliography

Johnson, Richard M. (1967). *The Dynamics of Compliance*. Evanston, Ill.: Northwestern University Press.

Morgan, Richard E. (1972). *The Supreme Court and Religion*. Pages 76–122. New York: Free Press.

EXCLUSIONARY RULE

When the police obtain evidence by violating the Bill of Rights, the victim of their miscon-duct may lack any effective legal remedy. Yet some enforcement mechanism is necessary if several important constitutional guarantees are to be a reality and not merely expressions of hope. The Supreme Court responded to this concern by developing a series of rules that have come to be known in the aggregate as the exclusionary rule. In typical application, the rule is that evidence obtained in violation of a person's constitutional rights cannot be used against that person in his or her trial for a criminal offense. The rule is most frequently applied to exclude evidence produced by searches or seizures made in violation of the Fourth Amendment. However, a coerced confession obtained in violation of the defendant's Fifth Amendment right against self-incrimination, or a statement taken from the defendant in violation of his Sixth Amendment's guarantee of the right to counsel, would also be inadmissible at his trial.

The term "exclusionary rule" is of modern origin, but even at common law a coerced confession was excluded or inadmissible as evidence, because its involuntariness cast serious doubt on its reliability. No one today seriously argues that this long-standing rule of evidence should be abandoned. Other aspects of the exclusionary rule, however, have been the source of major controversy among members of the judiciary, professional commentators, law enforcement officials, and the public.

The controversy did not become intense until the era of the Warren Court. But as far back as *Weeks* v. *United States* (1914) the Supreme Court had unanimously held that evidence seized in violation of the Fourth Amendment was inadmissible in a *federal* criminal prosecution. However, even after the Court had held in *Wolf* v. *Colorado* (1949) that the Fourth Amendment's guarantee against unreasonable searches and seizures was applicable to the states, the Court had continued until 1961 to resist the argument that the exclusionary rule should also be extended to *state* prosecutions. In that year, in *Mapp* v. *Ohio*, the Warren Court held that the Fourteenth Amendment did, indeed, impose on the states the exclusionary rule derived from the Fourth Amendment. Subsequent decisions broadened the Sixth Amendment guarantee of the right to counsel to govern the procedures for police interrogation and for the use of lineups; each of these developments was accompanied by an extension of the exclusionary rule to state-court proceedings. Since the "fruit of the poisonous tree" doctrine requires the exclusion not only of evidence immediately obtained by these various forms of constitutional violation but also of other evidence derived from the initial violations, the exclusionary rule in its modern form results in the suppression of many items of evidence of unquestioned reliability and the acquittal of many persons who are guilty.

The primary purpose of the exclusionary rule, as the Supreme Court said in *Elkins* v. *United States* (1960), "is to deter—to compel respect for the constitutional guaranty in the only effectively available way—by removing the incentive to disregard it." Yet this deterrent function is only part of the exclusionary rule's justification. A court that allows the government to profit from unconstitutional police action sullies the judicial process itself, by becoming an accomplice in an unlawful course of conduct. When the Court first applied the rule in *Mapp* to state-court prosecutions, it said:

> *There are those who say, as did Justice (then Judge) [Benjamin N.] Cardozo, that under our constitutional exclusionary doctrine "the criminal is to go free because the constable has blundered." . . . In some cases this will undoubtedly be the result. But, . . . "there is another consideration—the imperative of judicial integrity." . . . The criminal goes free, if he must, but it is the law that sets him free. Nothing can destroy a government more quickly than its failure to observe its own laws, or worse, its disregard of the charter of its own existence. As Mr. Justice Louis D. Brandeis, dissenting, said: . . . "Our government is the potent, the omnipresent teacher. For good or for ill, it teaches the whole people by its example. . . . If the government becomes a lawbreaker, it breeds contempt for law."*

The evidence seized in an illegal search— a knife, a packet of heroin, counterfeit plates—is as trustworthy and material as if the search had been lawful. The rule's critics argue that to protect the privacy of the search victim by letting a guilty person escape responsibility for his crime is illogical. It would make more sense, they say, to use the evidence (as do the courts in Great Britain, for example) and provide civil or criminal remedies against the errant police officers. If the rule's purpose is to deter police lawlessness, the critics argue, the rule misses the point: prosecutors, not police officers, feel the immediate effects of the rule. If the rule is designed to maintain respect for the courts, they ask how the public can be expected to respect a system that frees criminals by suppressing trustworthy evidence of their guilt.

The rule does not in fact significantly impede the police, despite contentions from the rule's opponents that it handcuffs the police.

How many criminals do go free when the constable blunders? Inadequate studies provide no clear-cut answer, except that opponents of the exclusionary rule grossly exaggerate the number of felons it sets loose, and they tend to dramatize the worst cases. In California, whose supreme court has created the most stringent exclusionary rule in the nation, a study by the National Institute of Justice showed that .78 percent of all accused felons are not prosecuted because of search and seizure problems, and of those released, nearly three-fourths were involved in drug-related cases. The effect of the exclusionary rule is slight in cases involving violent crimes. When the charge is murder, rape, assault, or robbery, prosecutors decide not to proceed in one out of every 2,500 cases. Studies of felony court records in other states reach similar conclusions. Only 0.4 percent of all cases that federal prosecutors decide not to prosecute are rejected because of search problems. At the trial level, motions to suppress illegally seized evidence are rarely granted in cases of violent crime. If the exclusionary rule were abolished, the conviction rate in all felony cases would increase by less than half of one percent. Translated into absolute figures, however, thousands of accused felons are released nationally as a result of the exclusionary rule, most of them in drug and weapons possession cases. Street crime does not flourish, though, because of the exclusionary rule, even though it does protect criminals, as do all constitutional rights. They also protect society and help keep us free.

The rule's effectiveness in deterring illegal searches is hotly debated. The critics point out that some ninety percent of criminal prosecutions do not go to trial but are disposed of by pleas of "guilty." (The figure varies from state to state, and according to the nature of the crime.) Without a trial, there is no evidence for the rule to exclude. In the huge number of cases in which the police make arrests but the persons arrested are not prosecuted, the exclusionary rule has, of course, no immediate application. The rule's proponents reply that the decision whether to prosecute or accept a defendant's "guilty" pleas on a lesser offense may itself be influenced by the prosecutor's estimate of the potential operation of the exclusionary rule if the case should go to trial. (In jurisdictions where separate procedures are established to rule on motions to suppress evidence, the rule normally will have operated in advance of the trial.)

Undeniably, however, the exclusionary rule has no application at all to the cases that cry out most for a remedy: cases of police misconduct against innocent persons, who are never even brought to the prosecutors' attention, and cases of illegal searches and seizures made for purposes other than collecting evidence to support prosecutions. In *Terry* v. *Ohio* (1968) Chief Justice Earl Warren admitted: "Regardless how effective the rule may be where obtaining conviction is an important objective of the police, it is powerless to deter invasions of constitutionally guaranteed rights where the police either have no interest in prosecuting or are willing to forego successful prosecution in the interest of serving some other goal." The police may deliberately engage in illegal searches and seizures for a number of reasons: to control crimes such as gambling or prostitution; to confiscate weapons or contraband or stolen property; or to maintain high visibility either to deter crime or to satisfy a public clamoring for aggressive police action. In none of these cases will the exclusionary rule inhibit police violations of the Bill of Rights.

The rule does not in fact significantly impede the police, despite contentions from the rule's opponents that it handcuffs the police. A 1984 report prepared for the National Center for State Courts concluded that a properly administered search warrant process can protect constitutional rights without hampering effective law enforcement. Nevertheless, police try when possible to conduct search and seizure under some exception to the warrant requirement. The overwhelming number of searches and seizures are warrantless. In 1980, for example, only about 1,000

warrants were issued in Los Angeles in about 300,000 cases. Police usually try to make consent searches or searches under what they claim to be exigent circumstances, or they conduct a search to confiscate contraband or harass criminals, without attempting a prosecution. In the few cases in which they seek warrants, they get them almost as if magistrates rubber-stamp their applications, and almost all warrants survive in court despite motions to suppress. Motions to suppress are made in about five percent of all cases but are successful in only less than one percent of all cases. Still more important is the fact that only slightly over half of one percent of all cases result in acquittals because of the exclusion of evidence.

Even when the rule does operate to exclude evidence in a criminal trial, it has no direct, personal effect on the police officer whose misconduct caused the rule to be invoked. The rule does not require discipline to be imposed by the officer's superiors, nor does either civil or criminal responsibility follow as a matter of course. Police officers are prosecuted only extremely rarely for their official misdeeds. Suits for damages by victims are inhibited not only by the defense of "good faith" and probable cause but also by the realization that most officers are neither wealthy nor insured against liability for their official acts. Unsurprisingly, most victims conclude that a lawsuit is not worth its trouble and expense. In the typical case of an illegal search, neither the judge who excludes the fruits of the search from evidence nor the prosecutor whose case is thereby undermined will explain to the officer the error of his ways. The intended educational effect of judicial decisions is also diminished by the time-lag between the police action and its final evaluation by the courts. Even if an officer should hear that a court has excluded the evidence he found in an illegal search some months ago, he will probably have forgotten the details of the event. Incentives and sanctions that might influence the officer's future behavior are not within the exclusionary rule's

contemplation. On the other hand, advocates of the rule emphasize that it is meant to have an institutional or systemic effect on law enforcement agencies generally, not necessarily on particular officers.

The officer is apt to respond not to judicial decisions (which he may regard as unrealistic if they impede his work) but to departmental policies and the approval of his colleagues and superiors. One whose main job is the apprehension of criminals and the deterrence of crime will have a low tolerance for what he sees as procedural niceties. He may even shade the truth in making out a report on a search or when testifying in court. It is not unheard of for the police to arrange to make a valid arrest at a place where they can conduct a warrantless search incident to the arrest, and thus evade the requirement of a search warrant based on probable cause to believe that evidence of crime is in that place. To the extent that the courts have used the exclusionary rule to educate the police, then, the main things learned seem to have been the techniques for evading the rule.

Summarizing the criticisms of the exclusionary rule, Dallin H. Oaks has said:

The harshest criticism of the rule is that it is ineffective. It is the sole means of enforcing the essential guarantees of freedom from unreasonable arrests and searches and seizures by law enforcement officers, and it is a failure in that vital task.

The use of the exclusionary rule imposes excessive costs on the criminal justice system. It provides no recompense for the innocent and it frees the guilty. It creates the occasion and incentive for large-scale lying by law enforcement officers. It diverts the focus on the criminal prosecution from the guilt or innocence of the defendant to a trial of the police. Only a system with limitless patience with irrationality could tolerate the fact that where there has been one wrong, the defendant's, he will be punished, but where there have been two wrongs, the defendant's and the officer's,

♦ **consent decree**
A court order that makes legally binding an agreement between the parties to a case to settle it without further litigation.

both will go free. This would not be an excessive cost for an effective remedy against police misconduct, but it is a prohibitive price to pay for an illusory one.

Despite the severity of criticisms, the exclusionary rule's chief critics have not proposed its total abolition. However, the Supreme Court has limited the rule's application in significant ways. Thus, for the most part, only the victim of an illegal search has standing to claim the benefits of the exclusionary rule; if A's house is searched in violation of the Fourth Amendment, and evidence is found incriminating B, the evidence can be used in B's trial. (State courts are free to extend the exclusionary rule to such cases; some state courts have done so, concluding that the point of the rule is not to protect people against being convicted but to deter the police.) Similarly, in *United States* v. *Calandra* (1974) the Court held that illegally obtained evidence is admissible in grand jury proceedings, and it ruled in *Harris* v. *New York* (1971) that it can be used for the purpose of impeaching the testimony of the accused at his trial. Some uses of illegally obtained evidence have been tolerated as harmless error. More important, the good faith exception to the exclusionary rule allows the use of evidence obtained with a search warrant if the police reasonably believed the warrant to be valid, even though it later proves to be illegal. The rule has also been held inapplicable to collateral proceedings for postconviction relief such as habeas corpus. The Court's opinions in these cases have repeated the familiar criticisms of the exclusionary rule; their logic would seem to suggest abandonment of the rule altogether.

Yet the exclusionary rule remains, largely because no one has yet suggested an effective alternative means for enforcing the Bill of Rights against police misconduct. A federal statute dating from Reconstruction authorizes the award of damages against state or local officials (including police officers) who violate individuals' constitutional rights. In 1971 the Supreme Court found that the

Fourth Amendment itself implicitly authorized similar damages awards against federal officers who violated the Amendment. The future effectiveness of such remedies will depend in part on the Supreme Court itself, as it spells out the victim's burden of proof in these cases and the measure of damages. Partly, however, the civil-damages alternative depends for its effectiveness on legislation to provide for real compensation to victims when the police officers are judgment-proof, and for real punishment of officers for constitutional violations when the payment of damages is unrealistic.

Meanwhile, the Supreme Court has only the exclusionary rule, which everyone agrees is an imperfect deterrent to police misbehavior. The rule survives, then, for want of better alternatives. But it also stands as a symbol that government itself is not above the law.

—LEONARD W. LEVY

Bibliography

LaFave, Wayne R. (1978). *Search and Seizure: A Treatise on the Fourth Amendment.* 3 vols. St. Paul, Minn.: West Publishing Co.

Oaks, Dallin H. (1970). Studying the Exclusionary Rule. *University of Chicago Law Review* 37:665–757.

Schroeder, William (1981). Deterring Fourth Amendment Violations: Alternatives to the Exclusionary Rule. *Georgetown Law Review* 68:1361–1426.

Stewart, Potter (1983). The Road to *Mapp* v. *Ohio* and Beyond: The Origins, Development and Future of the Exclusionary Rule in Search-and-Seizure Cases. *Columbia Law Review* 83:1365–1404.

EXTRATERRITORIALITY

Around the turn of the century, the Supreme Court placed strict territorial limits on the application of United States constitutional and statutory law. In the case of *In re Ross* (1891) the Court held that a citizen could be tried by an American consular court, without indictment by grand jury and without trial by jury, for crimes aboard an American ship in Japan. The Court flatly declared that "[t]he Constitution can have no operation in another country." And in *American Banana Co. v. United Fruit Co.* (1909) Justice Oliver Wendell Holmes asserted that "[a]ll legislation is prima facie territorial." Although he acknowledged that exceptions could be found in the case of laws applying on the high seas or in "uncivilized" countries, Holmes said "the general and almost universal rule is that the character of an act as lawful or unlawful must be determined wholly by the law of the country where the act is done." No doubt these sweeping statements, even then, were not literally followed. In any event, today doctrines limiting the extraterritorial application of both the Constitution and statutory law have been abandoned.

In *Reid* v. *Covert* (1956) the Court effectively overruled *Ross* and held that Congress could not deprive a citizen of the right to a jury trial in a court-martial abroad where capital punishment was potentially involved. Justice Hugo L. Black said: "When the Government reaches out to punish a citizen who is abroad, the shield which the Bill of rights and other parts of the Constitution provide to protect his life and liberty should not be stripped away just because he happens to be in another land." This decision signaled the end of territorial limitations on the Constitution.

In *United States* v. *Toscanino* (2d Cir. 1974) a lower court applied the Fourth and Fifth Amendments where American officials instigated enforcement activity by foreign officials that included torture and violated United States treaty obligations. Although other courts have declined to apply constitutional remedies in the circumstances of particular cases before them, they agree that the Bill of Rights may apply where the United States government instigates conduct that "shocks the conscience." The just compensation

clause of the Fifth Amendment has also been held applicable to takings of property abroad in several lower court cases. As a general rule, therefore, the Constitution now unquestionably applies to acts of government abroad.

At the same time the special circumstances that are invariably present in these cases influence the scope of constitutional protection afforded. Although the court only occasionally confronts these questions, it seems clear that protection against government action abroad is more difficult to obtain than in similar cases without a foreign element. This is especially true when foreign policy or national security interests are at issue, as was the case in *United States* v. *Curtiss-Wright Export Corp.* (1936). Indeed, in *Haig* v. *Agee* (1981) the Supreme Court questioned whether the First Amendment would apply at all to government suppression of speech abroad, where the speech threatened American intelligence activity.

Perhaps the most accurate description of the modern approach to extraterritorial application of constitutional law was made by Justice John Marshall Harlan in *Reid* v. *Covert*. He took exception to the broad suggestion that "every provision of the Constitution must be deemed automatically applicable to American citizens in every part of the world." He believed that "the question is *which* guarantees of the Constitution *should* apply in view of the particular circumstances, the practical necessities, and the possible alternatives which Congress had before it." The Harlan view seems more likely to prevail in a world of increased American involvement and interdependence than the absolutist approach of Justice Black.

A related issue of historical interest was whether the Constitution applied to territories acquired by the United States. Constitutional guarantees limiting legislative and executive power were applicable only when Congress, expressly or by clear implication, "incorporated" the acquired territory into the United States. In unincorporated territories

A related issue of historical interest was whether the Constitution applied to territories acquired by the United States.

♦ **in re**
[Latin: in the matter (of)] A way of titling the report of a case in which there are no adversary parties.

only undefined "fundamental" liberties were guaranteed.

Finally, the courts have repeatedly applied federal statutes to conduct abroad, assuming other jurisdictional prerequisites were met. Occasionally limitations on the application of a particular statute have been imposed, but those limitations have normally been based on the presumed intent of Congress or on international comity, not the Constitution.

—PHILLIP R. TRIMBLE

Bibliography

Coudert, Frederick R. (1926). The Evolution of the Doctrine of Territorial Incorporation. *Columbia Law Review* 26:823–850; *Iowa State Bar Association Report* 1926: 180–228.

Henkin, Louis (1972). *Foreign Affairs and the Constitution.* Pages 266–269. Mineola, N.Y.: Foundation Press.

Kaplan, Steven M. (1977). The Applicability of the Exclusionary Rule in Federal Court to Evidence Seized and Confessions Obtained in Foreign Countries. *Columbia Journal of Transnational Law* 16:495–520.

Note (1985). Predictability and Comity: Toward Common Principles of Extraterritorial Jurisdiction. *Harvard Law Review* 98:1310–1330.

FAY v. NOIA

372 U.S. 391 (1963)

The great writ of habeas corpus allows state prisoners to seek federal court review of constitutional errors made at their trials, but the Judicial Code requires exhaustion of remedies in state court, in order to preserve comity between state and federal courts. Charles Noia's 1942 murder conviction was based solely on a coerced confession procured in violation of his Fourteenth Amendment rights to due process. He chose not to file a state appeal, however, because he feared that a new trial might end in a death sentence. Years later, he sought review of his due process claim in state courts, but they held that his original failure to appeal was a procedural default that barred further review. In *Fay,* a 6–3 Supreme Court held that his failure was not a "deliberate bypass" of state procedures and thus no bar to habeas corpus relief.

Justice William J. Brennan, speaking for the majority, posited a "manifest federal policy" that liberty rights should not be denied without the fullest opportunity for federal judicial review. The concept of comity could not justify denying habeas corpus relief for failure to exhaust a remedy no longer available. As for the state's interests in insuring finality of criminal judgments, or exacting compliance with its procedures through default rules, these could not outweigh the "ideal of fair procedure" and the historic habeas corpus policy favoring the free exercise of federal judicial power to enforce this ideal. Finally, the state's rejection of Noia's claim could not be treated as an adequate state ground, for this jurisdictional deference would unduly burden the vindication of federal rights. Only when a defendant deliberately evaded state adjudication would federalism concerns justify the denial of habeas corpus review.

As dissenting Justice John Marshall Harlan noted, *Fay* marked a dramatic expansion of federal power to supervise state criminal justice. The concepts of exhaustion and adequate state grounds were modified to make

Fay marked a dramatic expansion of federal power to supervise state criminal justice.

♦ **judicial review**
The power of a court to review legislation or other governmental acts, including the acts of administrative agencies. The term is used especially for court review to determine whether an act is in conformance with the Constitution.

FARETTA v. CALIFORNIA

422 U.S. 806 (1975)

In *Faretta* the Supreme Court reversed the conviction of a defendant forced to accept the services of a public defender in a felony case, holding that the Sixth Amendment guarantees the right to self-representation when a defendant "knowingly and intelligently" requests it.

This is a major decision about the waiver of constitutional rights because the argument of the state and the dissent was that society has an interest in a fair trial, independent of the de-fendant's desires. Recognition of such an interest would necessarily mean that the trial judge must have discretion to reject even a knowing and intelligent waiver of the right to counsel.

Standby counsel may be appointed over the defendant's objection to aid him should he request help at the trial, or to intervene if the termination of self-representation becomes necessary.

—BARBARA ALLEN BABCOCK

Faretta represented a major decision about the waiver of constitutional rights.

room for a generous view that excused defendants from uncalculated waiver of constitutional rights in state proceedings. The "deliberately bypassing" defendant was a rare one, and *Fay*'s scope freed most defendants from forfeiting their rights through procedural defaults of every kind. Simultaneously, the Warren Court's application of the Fourth, Fifth, and Sixth Amendments to the states codified a bill of rights for criminal defendants. *Fay* insured a broad federal path of enforcement for these new guarantees, in an era when the state path of review was not always open or receptive to constitutional claims.

The Burger Court era brought a less hospitable federal climate for criminal defendants and, not surprisingly, also brought a corresponding change in the habeas corpus barometer, emerging clearly in *Wainright* v. *Sykes* (1977). *Fay*'s deliberate bypass rule did not endure as an exclusive measure of federalism interests, because a new "manifest" federal policy came to elevate the state's interest in finality above the ideal of fair procedure. With this new federalism, the whole point of habeas corpus review was transformed from the protection of constitutional rights to the protection of those with a claim to innocence.

—CATHERINE HANCOCK

Bibliography

Cover, Robert M., and Aleinikoff, T. Alexander (1977). Dialectical Federalism: Habeas Corpus and the Court. *Yale Law Journal* 86:1035–1102.

FEDERAL COMMON LAW, CIVIL

In the English legal tradition to which this country is heir, judge-made common law—law developed by courts in the absence of applicable legislation—has played a critical role in the determination of rights, duties, and remedies. But because our federal government is one of limited, delegated powers, the questions whether and under what circumstances the federal courts are empowered to formulate federal common law have been the subject of much debate. Although it is now settled that the federal courts do have such authority in civil matters, the debate continues over the sources of that authority and the proper scope of its exercise.

The Supreme Court's decision in *Erie Railroad Co.* v. *Tompkins* (1938) marks a watershed in the evolution of this problem. Prior to that decision, the federal courts did not strive to develop a federal, or national, common law binding on the states and indeed on occasion denied that it existed (*Wheaton* v. *Peters*, 1834; *Smith* v. *Alabama*, 1888). Yet the Supreme Court, in *Swift* v. *Tyson* (1842), upheld the authority of the federal courts, in cases within the diversity jurisdiction, to determine certain controversies on the basis of "general principles and doctrines" of jurisprudence and without regard to the common law decisions of the state courts. Thus, during the reign of *Swift* v. *Tyson*, the federal courts exercised considerable common law authority over a variety of disputes, ultimately extending well beyond the interstate commercial controversy involved in *Swift* itself and involving matters apparently not subject to federal legislative power. The decisions rendered in these cases, however, did not purport to bind the state courts, and the result was often the parallel existence of two different rules of law applicable to the same controversy, with the governing rule dependent on the forum in which the controversy was adjudicated.

Historians disagree on the justification—statutory and constitutional—of the *Swift* decision. In one view, the decision was not rooted in contemporary understanding of the nature of the common law but instead represented the use of judicial power to aid in the redistribution of wealth to promote commercial and industrial growth. A contrasting position is that the decision was fully consistent with the perception of the time that the common law of commercial transactions was not the command of the sovereign but rather was both the embodiment of prevailing customs and a process of applying them to the case at hand.

There is general agreement, however, that the Court expanded *Swift* well beyond its originally intended scope and that its overruling, in *Erie,* reflected a very different perception of the proper role of the federal courts. The Court in *Erie,* speaking through Justice Louis D. Brandeis, concluded that there was no "general" federal common law—that the Rules of Decision Act, originally section 34 of the Judiciary Act of 1789, required adherence to state decisional or common law in controversies such as *Erie* itself, a case that fell within federal jurisdiction solely on the basis of the parties' diversity of citizenship.

But the *Erie* decision helped bring to the surface the existence of what has been called a "specialized" federal common law, operating in those areas where the application of federal law seems warranted even though no federal constitutional or legislative provision points the way to a governing rule. Indeed, on the very day that *Erie* was decided, the Court in *Hinderlider* v. *La Plata River & Cherry Creek Ditch Co.* (1938), again speaking through Justice Brandeis, said that "whether the water of an interstate stream must be apportioned between the two States is a question of 'federal common law' upon which neither the statutes nor the decisions of either State can be conclusive."

What is the source of the authority to formulate federal common law—law that, unlike decisions rendered pursuant to *Swift,* binds state and federal courts alike? To some extent, the source may be traced to specific constitutional provisions, such as the grant of admiralty and maritime jurisdiction in Article III, or the prohibition of unreasonable searches and seizures in the Fourth Amendment. But the line between constitutional interpretation, on the one hand, and the exercise of common law authority, on the other, is indistinct, and there is often disagreement among both judges and commentators about the function the courts are performing. The significance of this disagreement is more than semantic, for the ability of the legislative branch to modify or reject a Supreme Court ruling is plainly more circumscribed if the ruling is seen to be required by the Constitution than if the ruling is a common law one authorized but not compelled by the fundamental law.

In other instances, the source of judicial authority may be found in a particular federal statute. Infrequently, the congressional command is explicit, as in the mandate in Rule 501 of the Federal Rules of Evidence that in certain cases questions of evidentiary privilege "shall be governed by the principles of the common law as they may be interpreted by the courts of the United States in the light of reason and experience." More often, the legislative direction is, at best, implicit and the judicial role may be viewed as that of implementing federal legislative policy by filling the gaps left by the legislation itself. Once again, the line between statutory construction and the exercise of common law authority is not easily drawn.

In a significant number of cases, the exercise of authority to formulate federal common law is difficult to trace to a specific provision in the Constitution or in a statute. In such cases, the authority may be attributed more broadly to the nature of the judicial process, to the structure of our federal constitutional system, and to the relationships created by it. The authority, in other words, may be rooted in necessity. As Justice Robert H. Jackson put it, concurring in *D'Oench Duhme & Co.* v. *F.D.I.C.* (1942): "Were we bereft of the common law, our federal system would be impotent. This follows from the recognized futility of attempting all-complete statutory codes and is apparent from the terms of the Constitution itself."

F

*In many cases, the
exercise of authority
to formulate federal
common law is
difficult to trace to a
specific provision in
the Constitution.*

See also

*Bivens v. Six Unknown
Named Agents*

Erie Railroad Co. v. Tompkins

Some examples of the exercise of this authority may help to clarify its scope. Perhaps most important is the category of those interstate or international disputes that, in the words of the Supreme Court, "implicate conflicting rights of States or our foreign relations" (*Texas Industries, Inc.* v. *Radcliff Materials, Inc.,* 1981). Such disputes do not always fall within the specific jurisdictional grants of Article III applicable to certain interstate or international controversies. In any event, the existence of a conflict between the interests of two states may make it inappropriate for the law of either to govern of its own force. And controversies affecting our relations as sovereign with foreign nations may require a single federal response rather than a cacophony of responses rooted in varying state laws.

Another leading instance of the exercise of common law authority embraces controversies involving the rights, obligations, or proprietary interests of the United States. In such controversies, especially those arising in the administration of nationwide programs, formulation of federal common law may be warranted by the need for uniform treatment of the activities of the federal government or, more modestly, for some degree of federal supervision of the application of state law to those activities.

The amorphous origins and uncertain scope of the federal common law power underscore the need to recognize certain limitations that are anchored in the concerns of federalism and of separation of powers. The first of these concerns focuses on the interests of the states in preserving a measure of autonomy on matters properly within their sphere—interests reflected in the Tenth Amendment. Because federal law is often interstitial in character—written against a background of state laws governing basic human affairs—the concern for federalism supports a presumption that state law ought not to be displaced in the absence of a clear legislative direction, a sharp conflict between the state law and federal program, or the existence of a uniquely federal interest requiring protection. To some extent, this presumption is supported by and reflected in the provision of the Rules of Decision Act that state laws shall constitute the rules of decision except where otherwise required by the Constitution or by federal treaty or statute. But the last phrase of that act—limiting its command to "cases where they (the rules of decision) apply"—gives the provision a circularity that affords little guidance to the resolution of particular problems of potential conflict between federal and state authority.

Even when the exercise of federal authority is warranted, a careful balancing of state and federal interests may lead to the adoption of state laws rather than to the imposition of a uniform federal rule, so long as the state laws in question are compatible with federal interests. Such results were reached, for example, in *De Sylva* v. *Ballentine* (1955), involving a definition of "children" under the Federal Copyright Act, and *United States* v. *Kimbell Foods, Inc.* (1979), dealing with the priority of federal government liens arising from federal lending programs.

The second concern—that of separation of powers—springs from the belief that the primary responsibility for lawmaking should rest with the democratically elected representatives in the legislative branch. At a time when the common law function was seen in terms primarily of the application of established customs and usages, the concern for the proper separation and allocation of federal powers had less force than it does today, when there is more emphasis on the creative potential of the common law. Moreover, the separation of powers question is not unrelated to the regard for state interests, since the bicameral federal legislature is structured in such a way as to protect the states against action that might be taken by a legislature apportioned solely on the basis of population.

Concern that the courts not usurp a function that is properly legislative has led to an emphasis on legislative intent in many instances in which the federal courts have been asked to articulate new rights or develop new remedies not specifically provided for by statute. Moreover, the Supreme Court has stressed the ability of Congress to displace federal common law with statutory regulations, even in some instances in which the source of authority is the Constitution itself.

The problems inherent in the exercise of common law power have been highlighted in the Supreme Court's struggle with the question of implied remedies for federal constitutional or statutory violations. Since *Bivens* v. *Six Unknown Named Agents* (1971), the Court has generally been willing to allow a person harmed by unconstitutional action to sue for damages, despite the lack of any constitutional or statutory provision for suit. But persons harmed by violations of federal statutes have frequently been held unable to obtain relief in the absence of an express statutory remedy or strong evidence of legislative intent to permit such a remedy.

In both types of cases the Supreme Court has perhaps too readily yielded its authority to exercise a principled discretion in determining whether traditional common law remedies should be available to implement federal policy. The tendency toward formalistic insistence on a remedy for every wrong in cases involving constitutional violations, and toward ritualistic invocation of legislative intent in order to deny a remedy in cases of statutory infractions, suggests a relinquishment of the judicial responsibility that lies at the heart of our common law heritage.

—DAVID L. SHAPIRO

Bibliography

Bator, Paul; Mishkin, Paul J.; Shapiro, David L.; and Wechsler, Herbert ([1953] 1973 and 1981 Supp.). *Hart and Wechsler's The Federal Courts and the Federal System.* Pages 691–832. Mineola, N.Y.: Foundation Press.

Bridwell, Randall, and Whitten, Ralph U. (1977). *The Constitution and the Common Law.* Lexington, Mass.: Lexington Books.

Field, Martha A. (1986). Sources of Law: The Scope of Federal Common Law. *Harvard Law Review* 99:883–984.

Friendly, Henry J. (1964). In Praise of *Erie*—And of the New Federal Common Law. *New York University Law Review* 39: 383–422.

Freyer, Tony Allan (1979). *Forums of Order: The Federal Courts and Business in American History.* Greenwich, Conn.: JAI Press, Inc.

Hill, Alfred (1967). The Law-Making Power of the Federal Courts: Constitutional Preemption. *Columbia Law Review* 67: 1024–1081.

Horwitz, Morton J. (1977). *The Transformation of American Law, 1780–1860.* Pages 211–252. Cambridge, Mass.: Harvard University Press.

Redish, Martin H. (1980). *Federal Jurisdiction: Tensions in the Allocation of Judicial Power.* Pages 79–107. Indianapolis, Ind.: Bobbs-Merrill.

FEDERAL COMMUNICATIONS COMMISSION v. PACIFICA FOUNDATION

438 U.S. 726 (1978)

In *FCC* v. *Pacifica Foundation* the Court held that limited civil sanctions could constitutionally be invoked against a radio broadcast containing many vulgar words. The Court stressed that its holding was limited to the particular context, that is, to civil sanctions applied to indecent speech in an afternoon radio broadcast when, the Court assumed, children were in the audience. The opinion did not address criminal sanctions for televised or closed circuit broadcasts or late

F

FEDERAL
COMMUNICATIONS
COMMISSION v.
PACIFICA
FOUNDATION

438 U.S. 726 (1978)

The Court held that limited civil sanctions could constitutionally be invoked against a radio broadcast containing many vulgar words.

Ferguson is often cited as an example of the Court's permissive attitude toward economic regulation challenged as a violation of substantive due process.

evening presentations, nor did it illuminate the concept of indecent speech except to suggest that occasional expletives and Elizabethan comedies may be decent enough even in the early afternoon.

—STEVEN SHIFFRIN

FERGUSON v. SKRUPA

372 U.S. 726 (1963)

This decision is often cited as a leading modern example of the Supreme Court's permissive attitude toward economic regulation challenged as a violation of substantive due process.

Kansas prohibited "the business of debt adjusting" except as an incident of the practice of law. The Court unanimously upheld this statute against a challenge to its constitutionality. Justice Hugo L. Black wrote for the Court. Any argument that the business of debt adjusting had social utility should be addressed to the legislature, not the courts. "We refuse to sit as a "super legislature to weigh the wisdom of legislation." The Court had given up the practice, common during the years before *West Coast Hotel Co.* v. *Parrish* (1937), of using "the 'vague contours' of the Due Process Clause to nullify laws which a majority of the Court believed to be economically unwise." Justice Black, unlike many of his brethren, carried this same view of the judicial function into other areas of constitutional interpretation; see his dissents in *Griswold* v. *Connecticut* (1965) and *Harper* v. *Virginia Board of Elections* (1966).

In *Ferguson* Justice John Marshall Harlan concurred separately on the ground that the law bore "a rational relation to a constitutionally permissible objective." Apparently Justice Harlan wanted to maintain some level of judicial scrutiny of economic regulations, even if it were only the relaxed rational basis standard, and thought the Black opinion suggested a complete abdication of the judicial role in such cases.

—KENNETH L. KARST

FIGHTING WORDS

In *Chaplinsky* v. *New Hampshire* (1942) the Supreme Court upheld the conviction of a Jehovah's Witness who called a policeman "a God damned racketeer" and "a damned Fascist," holding that "fighting words"—face-to-face words plainly likely to provoke the average addressee to fight—were not protected by constitutional free speech guarantees. Viewed narrowly, the fighting words doctrine can be seen as a per se rule effectuating the clear and present danger principle, relieving the government of proving an actual incitement by taking the words themselves as decisive. Taken broadly, *Chaplinsky* strips "four-letter words" of free speech protection. "It has been well observed," Justice Frank Murphy said, "that such utterances are no essential part of any exposition of ideas, and are of such slight social value as a step to the truth that any benefit that may be derived from them is clearly outweighed by the social interest in order and morality."

The modern tendency of the Court has been to extend partial First Amendment protection to even the "excluded" areas of speech. To the extent that *Chaplinsky* refuses protection to four-letter words because they offend against taste or morality, it has been limited by recent decisions such as *Cohen* v. *California* (1971), *Gooding* v. *Wilson* (1972), and *Rosenfeld* v. *New Jersey* (1972). The Justices appear to have been engaging in ad hoc analysis of what persons in what situations are entitled to a measure of protection from the shock to their sensibilities generated by words that, in the language of *Chaplinsky*, "by their very utterances inflict injury."

In addition, these cases make clear that fighting words are punishable only if likely to lead to an immediate breach of the peace by the particular person who is addressed. Other decisions have narrowed the reach of *Chaplinsky* by declaring statutes unconstitutionally overbroad.

Most recently in *R.A.V.* v. *City of St. Paul* (1992) the Court overturned a law that barred "symbol[s] arous[ing] anger, alarm or resentment" based on race, religion, or gender, as applied to a cross burning in front of a black family's home. Four of the justices would have held the statute overbroad, as it plainly was, since much speech causing anger or resentment is constitutionally protected. But the majority, finessing the overbreadth question, ruled that the law improperly distinguished between fighting words relating to race, religion, or gender and others that might be equally offensive.

The shock aspect of four-letter words is obviously related to the shock element in obscenity. In *FCC* v. *Pacifica Foundation* (1978) the Court upheld FCC regulation of "indecent" broadcasting that involved "patently offensive" four-letter words but was not obscene. While admitting that the words in question would warrant constitutional protection under certain circumstances, the Court held that in view of their capacity to offend, their slight social value in the conveying of ideas, and the intrusive character of speech broadcast into the home, their repeated use might constitutionally be banned at least in time slots and programming contexts when children might be listening.

The recent decisions suggest that outside the direct incitement to violence context the Court is prepared to balance privacy against speech interests where four-letter words are at issue. Where statutes go beyond prohibiting incitement to violence, and also bar cursing or reviling, or using opprobrious, indecent, lascivious, or offensive language, they are likely to be held unconstitutionally vague or overbroad.

—MARTIN SHAPIRO

The modern tendency of the Court has been to extend partial First Amendment protection to even the "excluded" areas of speech.

TITLE VII, CIVIL RIGHTS ACT OF 1964, AS AMENDED

Section 2000e-16, Employment by Federal Government

a) Discriminatory practices prohibited; employees or applicants for employment subject to coverage

All personnel actions affecting employees or applicants for employment (except with regard to aliens employed outside the limits of the United States) in military departments as defined in section 102 of title 5, in executive agencies as defined in section 105 of title 5 (including employees and applicants for employment who are paid from nonappropriated funds), in the United States Postal Service and the Postal Rate Commission, in those units of the Government of the District of Columbia having positions in the competitive service, and in those units of the legislative and judicial branches of the Federal Government having positions in the competitive service, and in the Library of Congress shall be made free from any discrimination based on race, color, religion, sex, or national origin.

b) Equal Employment Opportunity Commission; enforcement powers; issuance of rules, regulations, etc.; annual review and approval of national and regional equal employment opportunity plans; review and evaluation of equal employment opportunity programs and publication of progress reports; consultations with interested parties; compliance with rules, regulations, etc.; contents of national and regional equal employment opportunity plans; authority of Librarian of Congress

Except as otherwise provided in this subsection, the Equal Employment Opportunity Commission shall have authority to enforce the provisions of subsection (a) of this section through appropriate remedies, including reinstatement or hiring of employees with or without back pay, as will effectuate the policies of this section, and shall issue such rules, regulations, orders and instructions as it deems necessary and appropriate to carry out its responsibilities under this section.

See also

Chaplinsky v. *New Hampshire*

Clear and Present Danger

Federal Communications Commission v. *Pacifica Foundation*

This case signals an important move toward the restoration of the principle that rights adhere to the individual, and not to the racial class that one happens to inhabit.

Bibliography

Konvitz, Milton (1978). *Fundamental Liberties of a Free People.* Chap. 17. Westport, Conn.: Greenwood Press.

Shea, Thomas (1975). Fighting Words and the First Amendment. *Kentucky Law Journal* 63:1–22.

FIREFIGHTERS LOCAL UNION NO. 1784 v. STOTTS

467 U.S. 561 (1984)

The City of Memphis, Tennessee, laid off white firefighters with more seniority to protect the positions of less senior blacks who had been employed under a "race conscious" affirmative action plan. The white firefighters sued, alleging that their seniority rights were explicitly protected by the Civil Rights Act of 1964.

Justice Byron R. White, writing for the Supreme Court's majority, agreed, noting that "mere membership in the disadvantaged class is insufficient to warrant a seniority award; each individual must prove that the discriminatory practice had an impact on him." White thus affirmed the proposition, which is explicit from the plain language of Title VII, that rights vest in the individual and not in the racial class, and that this fact demands a close fit between injuries and remedies. White's opinion raises some doubt about the power of courts to fashion class-wide remedies where, as in race-conscious affirmative action plans, benefited individuals are not required to demonstrate individual injury. This case signals an important move toward the restoration of the principle that rests at the core of liberal jurisprudence—that rights adhere to the individual, and not to the racial class that one happens to inhabit.

—EDWARD J. ERLER

See also

Affirmative Action

FLAG DESECRATION

The word "desecration" has religious overtones. It means defiling the sacred. Flag burning is the secular equivalent of the offense of blasphemy, a verbal crime signifying an attack, by ridicule or rejection, against God, the Bible, Jesus Christ, Christianity, or religion itself. Flag burning is comparable to a verbal attack on the United States. Burning the nation's symbol signifies contempt and hatred by the flag burner of the things he or she believes the flag stands for, such as colonialism, imperialism, capitalism, exploitation, racism, or militarism. To the overwhelming majority of Americans, however, the flag embodies in a mystical and emotional way the loyalty and love they feel for the United States. With few exceptions we venerate the flag because it symbolizes both our unity and diversity; our commitment to freedom, equality, and justice; and perhaps above all, our constitutional system and its protection of individual rights.

Like blasphemy, therefore, flag burning tests the outermost limits of tolerance even in a free society. Burning the flag is a most offensive outrage that stretches to the breaking point the capacity of a nation to indulge dissidents. But that same form of desecration is not only an act of vandalism; it is symbolic expression that claims the protection of the free speech clause of the First Amendment. Therein lies the problem and the paradox: Should the flag represent a nation whose people have a right to burn its revered symbol?

Imprisoning flag burners would not mean that book burning and thought control are next. We know how to distinguish vandalism from radical advocacy; we would not regard urinating on the Jefferson Memorial or spray painting graffiti on the Washington Monument as a form of constitutionally protected free speech. Special reasons exist for protecting the flag from the splenetic conduct of extremists. A society should be entitled to safeguard its most fundamental values, but dissenters have a right to express verbal opposition to everything we hold dear. Yet, nothing is solved by saying that it is better to live in a country where people are free to burn the flag if they wish, rather than in a country where they want to burn it but cannot. We know the difference between suppressing a particularly offensive mode of conduct and a particularly offensive message. The problem is, however, that the particular mode of conduct may be the vehicle for communicating that offensive message. To suppress the message by suppressing the conduct involves governmental abridgment of a First Amendment freedom. So the Supreme Court held in *Texas* v. *Johnson* in 1989.

In 1984 in Dallas, Gregory Johnson, a member of the Revolutionary Communist Youth Brigade, a Maoist society, publicly burned a stolen American flag to protest the renomination of Ronald Reagan as the Republican candidate. While the flag burned, the protesters, including Maoists, chanted, "America, the red, white, and blue, we spit on you." That the flag burning communicated an unmistakable political message was contested by no one. The police arrested Johnson not for his message but for his manner of delivering it; he had violated a Texas statute that prohibited the desecration of a venerated object by acts that seriously offended onlookers.

State appellate courts reversed Johnson's conviction on ground that his conduct constituted constitutionally protected symbolic speech. Given its context—the Republican convention; Reagan's foreign policy; the protestors' demonstrations, marches, speeches, and slogans—Johnson's burning the flag was clearly speech of the sort contemplated by the First Amendment. The Texas courts also rejected the state's contention that the conviction could be justified as a means of preventing breach of the public peace. In fact, the state admitted that no breach of the peace occurred as a result of the flag desecration. The Supreme Court, 5–4, affirmed the judgment of the Texas Court of Criminal Appeals.

Justice William J. Brennan, spokesman for the majority, showed his political savvy by emphasizing that the courts of the Lone Star State, where red-blooded John Wayne patriotism flourishes, recognized "that the right to differ is the centerpiece of our First Amendment freedoms." Government cannot mandate a feeling of unity or "carve out a symbol of unity and prescribe a set of approved messages to be associated with that symbol." Brennan added that although the First Amendment literally forbids the abridgment of only "speech," the Court had labeled as speech a variety of conduct that communicated opinions, including the wearing of black arm bands to protest war, a sit-in by blacks to protest racial segregation, picketing, and the display of a red flag. Indeed the state conceded that Johnson's conduct was politically expressive. The question was whether that expression could be constitutionally proscribed, like the use of fighting words calculated to provoke a breach of peace. Apart from the fact that no breach occurred here, Brennan reminded, a prime function of free speech is to invite dispute. The "fighting words" doctrine had no relevance in this case because the message communicated by flag burning did not personally insult anyone in particular.

Whether the state could justify the conviction as a means of preserving the flag as a symbol of nationhood and national unity depended on the communicative impact of the mode of expression. Brennan insisted that the restriction on flag desecration was "content-based." Johnson's political expression, he declared, was restricted because of the content of the message that he conveyed. This point is important and unpersuasive. As Chief Justice William H. Rehnquist for the dissenters said, burning the flag was no essential part of the exposition of ideas, for Johnson was free to make any verbal denunciation of the flag that he wished. He led a march through the streets of Dallas, conducted a rally on the front steps of the city hall, shouted his slogans, and was not arrested for any of this. Only when he burned the flag was he arrested. Texas did not punish

Congress has enacted statutes that prescribe how the flag may be displayed and disposed of, and how and for what purposes it may be used.

him because it or his hearers opposed his message, only because he conveyed it by burning the flag.

Brennan replied that by punishing flag burning the state prohibited expressive conduct. "If there is a bedrock principle underlying the First Amendment," he wrote, "it is that the Government may not prohibit the expression of an idea simply because society finds the idea itself offensive or disagreeable." By making an exception for the flag, Texas sought to immunize the ideas for which it stands. Whatever it stands for should not be insulated against protest. In the context of this case, the act of flag burning constituted a means of political protest. Compulsion is not a constitutionally accepted method of achieving national unity.

Brennan believed that the flag's deservedly cherished place as a symbol would be "strengthened, not weakened, by our holding today. Our decision is a reaffirmation of the principles of freedom and inclusiveness that the flag best reflects, and of the conviction that our toleration of criticism such as Johnson's is a sign and source of our strength." This was the Court's strongest point.

Texas v. *Johnson* provided Court watchers with the pleasure of seeing judicial objectivity at work, for the Court did not divide in a predictable way. The majority included Justices Antonin Scalia and Anthony M. Kennedy, Reagan-appointed conservatives, whereas the dissenters included Justice John Paul Stevens, a liberal moderate. Stevens wrote his own dissent. He believed, oddly, that public desecration of the flag "will tarnish its value." He also thought that the Texas statute that the Court struck down did not compel any conduct or profession of respect for any idea or symbol. The case had nothing to do with disagreeable ideas, he said; it involved offensive conduct that diminishes the value of the national symbol. Texas prosecuted Johnson because of the method he used to express dissatisfaction with national policies. Prosecuting him no more violated the First Amendment than prosecuting someone for spray

painting a message of protest on the Lincoln Memorial.

Rehnquist's dissent was suffused with emotional theatrics about the flag and patriotism. His point was that the flag was special, as two hundred years of history showed. Even if flag burning is expressive conduct, he reasoned, it is not an absolute. But he thought it not to be expressive conduct. Flag burning was no essential part of any exposition of ideas, he claimed, but rather was "the equivalent of an inarticulate grunt" meant to antagonize others. By the same reasoning, however, one might say that flag flying is also a grunt of patriotism. That does not alter the point that flag burning is malicious conduct—vandalism rather than speech.

Zealous politicians, eager to capitalize on their love for the flag and opposition to those who burned it, sought to gain political advantage from the Court's opinion. President George Bush, a war hero, had helped spur a paroxysm of patriotism in 1988 by assaulting his opponent for having vetoed a bill that would have compelled teachers to lead their students in a Pledge of Allegiance every day. Bush, having made a photo opportunity of visiting a flag factory in 1988, made another after the decision in *Texas* v. *Johnson*, by holding a ceremony in the White House rose garden. Accepting a replica of the Iwo Jima Memorial, depicting the marines hoisting the flag on a bloody wartime site, Bush condemned flag burning as a danger to "the fabric of our country" and demanded a constitutional amendment outlawing desecration of the flag.

Cynical observers shouted "cheap politics" and criticized the president and his supporters for trying to cover up problems concerning the savings and loan scandals, the deterioration of the nation's schools, the ballooning national debt, the urban underclass, and the army of homeless beggars in American cities. Bush's opponents declared that he sought to desecrate the Constitution by indulging in escapist politics and seeking the first revision of the Bill of Rights in two centuries. Many conservatives in Congress agreed that tampering with the Bill of Rights was not the way to treat the problem of flag burning. Democrats, who felt obligated to "do something" at the risk of being branded unpatriotic, offered the Flag Protection Act of 1989, and so headed off the amendment movement. The new act of Congress provided that whoever knowingly mutilates, defaces, physically defiles, or burns the flag shall be fined or imprisoned for a year, or both.

Members of the "lunatic left" promptly defied the act of Congress by burning the flag on the Capitol steps for the benefit of the TV cameras. Shawn Eichman and company got the publicity they wanted and were arrested. They quickly filed motions to dismiss, on grounds that the act of Congress was unconstitutional, that is, the flag they burned symbolized their freedom to burn it. The government asked the Supreme Court to reconsider its holding in *Texas* v. *Johnson* by holding that flag burning is a mode of expression, like fighting words, that does not enjoy complete protection of the First Amendment.

The Court, by the same 5–4 split, refused to alter its opinion. Brennan, again the majority spokesman, acknowledged that the government may create national symbols and encourage their respectful treatment, but concluded that it went too far with the Flag Protection Act "by criminally proscribing expressive conduct because of its likely communicative impact." Desecrating the flag was deeply offensive to many people, like virulent racial and religious epithets, vulgar repudiations of conscription, and scurrilous caricatures, all of which came within the First Amendment's protection, notwithstanding their offensiveness.

The government sought to distinguish the Flag Protection Act from the state statute involved in *Johnson,* on the theory that the act of Congress did not target expressive conduct on the basis of the content of its message. The government merely claimed its authority to protect the physical integrity of the flag as the symbol of our nation and its ideals. Brennan replied that destruction of the flag could

in no way affect those ideals or the symbol itself. The invalidity of the statute derived from the fact that its criminal penalties applied to those whose treatment of the flag communicated a message. Thus, *United States* v. *Eichman,* resulting in the voiding of the act of Congress, was a replay of *Johnson.*

Stevens, for the dissenters, recapitulated his previous contentions. He believed that the majority opinion concluded at the point where analysis of the issue ought to begin. No one, he declared, disagreed with the proposition that the government cannot constitutionally punish offensive ideas. But, he argued, certain methods of expression, such as flag burning, might be proscribed if the purpose of the proscription did not relate to the suppression of ideas individuals sought to express, if that proscription did not interfere with the individual's freedom to express those ideas by other means, and if on balance the government's interest in the proscription outweighed the individual's choice of the means of expressing themselves. Stevens expatiated on the flag as a symbol and insisted that the government should protect its symbolic value without regard to the specific content of the flag burner's speech. Moreover, Eichman and the other dissidents were completely free to express their ideas by means other than flag burning. Stevens apparently missed the point that Eichman had a right to choose his own means of communicating his political protest. What disturbed Stevens most was the belief that flag burners actually have damaged the symbolic value of the flag. And he added the following in a veiled allusion to the shenanigans of would-be amenders of the Constitution: "Moreover, the integrity of the symbol has been compromised by those leaders who seem to advocate compulsory worship of the flag even by individuals whom it offends, or who seem to manipulate the symbol of national purpose into a pretext for partisan disputes about meaner ends."

Every nation in the world has a flag, and many of them, including some democracies, have laws against desecrating their flag.

F

FLAG SALUTE CASES

Minersville School
District *v.* Gobitis
310 U.S. 586 (1940)

West Virginia Board of
Education *v.* Barnett
319 U.S. 624 (1943)

No other nation has our Bill of Rights. The year 1991 marked the 200th anniversary of its ratification. It requires no limiting amendment. The American people understand that they are not threatened by flag burners, and the American people prefer the First Amendment undiluted. They understand that imprisoning a few extremists is not what patriotism is about. Forced patriotism is not American. Flag burning is all wrong, but a lot of wrongheaded speech is protected by the Constitution. When the nation celebrated the bicentennial of the Bill of Rights, it celebrated a wonderfully terse, eloquent, and effective summation of individual freedoms. Time has not shown a need to add "except for flag burners." That exception, as the Court majority realized, might show that the nation is so lacking in faith in itself that it permits the Johnsons and Eichmans to diminish the flag's meaning. They are best treated, as Brennan urged, by saluting the flag that they burn or by ignoring them contemptuously.

—LEONARD W. LEVY

Bibliography

Greenawalt, Kent (1990). O'er the Land of the Free: Flag Burning as Speech. *UCLA Law Review* 37:925–947.
Kmiec, Douglas W. (1990). In the Aftermath of *Johnson* and *Eichman*. *Brigham Young University Law Review* 1990:577–638.

FLAG SALUTE CASES

Minersville School District *v.* Gobitis
310 U.S. 586 (1940)

West Virginia Board of Education
v. Barnett
319 U.S. 624 (1943)

The Supreme Court's encounter in the early 1940s with the issue of compulsory flag salute exercises in the public schools was one of the turning points in American constitutional history. It presaged the civil libertarian activism that culminated in the Warren Court of the 1960s.

The flag salute ceremony developed in the latter half of the nineteenth century. In the original ceremony the participants faced the flag and pledged "allegiance to my flag and the republic for which it stands, one nation indivisible, with liberty and justice for all." While repeating the words "to my flag" the right hand was extended palm up toward the flag. Over the years the ceremony evolved slightly, with minor changes of wording and with the extended arm salute dropped in 1942 because of its similarity to the Nazi salute. At this point in its evolution, however, the salute had official standing; Congress had prescribed the form of words and substituted the right hand over the heart for the extended arm.

Beginning in 1898 with New York, some states began requiring the ceremony as part of the opening exercise of the school day. The early state flag salute laws did not make the ceremony compulsory for individual pupils, but many local school boards insisted on participation. Many patriotic and fraternal organizations backed the flag salute; opposition came from civil libertarians and some small religious groups. The principal opponents of the compulsory school flag salute were the Jehovah's Witnesses, a tightly knit evangelical sect whose religious beliefs commanded them not to salute the flag as a "graven image."

The Witnesses were blessed with legal talent. "Judge" Joseph Franklin Rutherford, who had become head of the sect, brought in Hayden Covington, who, as chief counsel for the Witnesses in the *Gobitis* litigation and in many other cases, influenced the development of First Amendment doctrine.

The first flag salute case to reach the Supreme Court came out of Minersville, a small community in northwest Pennsylvania. Because of Rutherford's bitter opposition to required flag salute exercises, Lillian and William Gobitis stopped participating in the ceremony in their school and were expelled.

The argument for the Gobitis children was that requiring them to salute the flag, an act repugnant to them on religious grounds, denied that free exercise of religion protected against state action by the due process clause of the Fourteenth Amendment. Arguments for the Minersville School Board relied on *Reynolds* v. *United States* (1878), *Jacobson* v. *Massachusetts* (1905), and the doctrine that a religious objection did not relieve an individual from the responsibility of complying with an otherwise valid secular regulation. The Gobitis children won in the lower federal courts, but the Supreme Court granted certiorari.

The Court in the spring of 1940 had a very different cast from that which had survived Franklin D. Roosevelt's effort to "pack" it three years before. Of the hard-core, pre-1937 conservatives only Justice James C. McReynolds remained. Chief Justice Charles Evans Hughes and Justices Harlan F. Stone and Owen J. Roberts also remained. With them,

however, were five Roosevelt appointees: Felix Frankfurter, Hugo L. Black, William O. Douglas, Stanley F. Reed, and Frank Murphy. On three previous occasions the Court had sustained compulsory flag salutes against religious objection in per curium opinions. Whether because of the extraordinary persistence of the Jehovah's Witnesses or because of the nonconformance of the lower federal courts in this case, the Justices now gave the matter full dress consideration.

Speaking for the majority Justice Frankfurter concluded that "conscientious scruples have not, in the course of the long struggle for religious toleration, relieved the individual from obedience to a general law not aimed at the persecution or a restriction of religious beliefs."

To Justice Stone, dissenting, the crucial issue was that the Gobitis children were forced to bear false witness to their religion. The flag salute compelled the expression of a belief,

F

FLAG SALUTE CASES

Minersville School
District *v.* Gobitis
310 U.S. 586 (1940)

West Virginia Board of
Education *v.* Barnett
319 U.S. 624 (1943)

**"I PLEDGE
ALLEGIANCE..."**

In Barnett, *the Court overturned* Gobitis *and ruled that flag salute exercises in public schools cannot be compulsory. (Corbis/Bettmann)*

F

FLAG SALUTE CASES

Minersville School
District *v.* Gobitis
310 U.S. 586 (1940)

West Virginia Board of
Education *v.* Barnett
319 U.S. 624 (1943)

*The Court's
encounter in the
early 1940s with the
issue of compulsory
flag salute exercises
in public schools
was one of the
turning points in
American
constitutional
history.*

See also

Certiorari

Freedom of Speech

Jacobson v. *Massachusetts*

Reynolds v. *United States*

and "where that expression violate[d] religious convictions," the free exercise clause provided protection.

The reaction to the decision in the law reviews was negative. In the popular press the reaction was mixed but criticism predominated. Most important, the decision seems to have produced a wave of persecution of Jehovah's Witnesses which swept through the country. *Gobitis* emboldened some school authorities. The State Board of Education of West Virginia in January 1942 made the salute to the flag mandatory in the classrooms of that state.

Meanwhile, new decisions of the Supreme Court, notably the 5–4 division of the Justices in *Jones* v. *Opelika*, raised the hopes of opponents of the mandatory flag salute. Hayden Covington sought an injunction barring enforcement of West Virginia's new rule against Walter Barnett and other Jehovah's Witness plaintiffs. After a three-judge District Court issued an injunction, the State Board of Education appealed to the Supreme Court.

The case was argued on March 11, 1943, and the decision came down on June 14. Justice Robert H. Jackson, who had joined the Court after *Gobitis*, wrote for a 6–3 majority, overruling the prior decision. Chief Justice Stone was with Jackson, as were Justices Douglas, Black, and Murphy, who had changed their minds. Justice Frankfurter, the author of *Gobitis*, wrote a long and impassioned dissent.

For Justice Jackson and the majority the crucial point was that West Virginia's action, while not intended either to impose or to anathematize a particular religious belief, did involve a required affirmation of belief: "If there is any fixed star in our constitutional constellation, it is that no official, high or petty, can prescribe what shall be orthodox in politics, nationalism, religion, or other matters of opinion or force citizens to confess by word or act their faith therein." West Virginia was pursuing the legitimate end of enhancing

patriotism, but had not borne the heavy burden of justifying its use of coercive power.

Justice Frankfurter began his dissent by noting that were the matter one of personal choice he would oppose compulsory flag salutes. But it was not for the Court to decide what was and was not an effective means of inculcating patriotism. West Virginia had neither prohibited nor imposed any religious belief. For Frankfurter this fact was controlling, and he reminded his brethren that a liberal spirit cannot be "enforced by judicial invalidation of illiberal legislation."

Barnett was a landmark decision in the strict sense of that overworked word. By 1943 the Roosevelt Court had largely completed its task of dismantling the edifice of substantive due process erected by its predecessors to protect economic liberty. Now the Court set out on the path to a new form of judicial activism in the service of individual rights. *Barnett* was the first long step on that path.

Barnett had doctrinal significance both for freedom of speech and for religious liberty. Jackson's opinion suggested that there were significant limitations on the kinds of patriotic affirmations that government might require, and the decision also moved away from the "secular regulation" rule that had dominated free exercise doctrine.

Barnett also had a significant effect on the Supreme Court. Justice Frankfurter was deeply offended by the majority's treatment of his *Gobitis* opinion and even more alarmed at what he regarded as a misuse of judicial power. The split between the activist disposition of Justices Black and Douglas and the judicial self-restraint championed by Frankfurter date from *Barnett*.

—RICHARD E. MORGAN

Bibliography

Manwaring, David R. (1962). *Render unto Caesar: The Flag Salute Controversy.* Chicago: University of Chicago Press.

FLAST v. COHEN

392 U.S. 83 (1968)

A Warren Court landmark regarding the judicial power of the United States, *Flast* upheld taxpayer standing to complain that disbursements of federal funds to religious schools violate the First Amendment prohibition of an establishment of religion. The decision carved an exception from, but did not overturn, the rule of *Frothingham* v. *Mellon* (1923) that federal taxpayers lack a sufficiently individual or direct interest in spending programs to be allowed to attack them in federal court. To Justice John Marshall Harlan's dissenting chagrin, the Court so ruled knowing that Congress, cognizant of *Frothingham,* had decided against granting taxpayers a right to judicial review of federal support for religious education.

The Court was unanimous on one fundamental point: the taxpayers in *Flast* presented an Article III "case." For the majority, Chief Justice Earl Warren reaffirmed the traditional Article III requirement of a "personal stake in the outcome of the controversy," but deemed that requirement satisfied whenever a taxpayer claims that Congress exercised its taxing and spending power in derogation of specific constitutional limits on that power. The Court found the establishment clause a specific limit, because, historically, the clause was designed to block taxation to support religion.

Dissenting, Justice Harlan could not agree that taxpayers challenging spending, rather than their tax liability, had a personal stake. They had no financial stake, because victory would only change how the government's general revenues are spent—not their tax bill. Nor was the Court's exception tailored to the requirement of a personal stake. A taxpayer's interests did not vary with the power Congress exercised in appropriating funds or with the constitutional provision ("specific" or not) invoked to oppose the expenditures. For Harlan, the taxpayer's interest in government spending was not personal but public—a citizen's concern that official behavior be constitutional. Nonetheless, he thought the "public action" would satisfy Article III, apparently because the parties were sufficiently adversary. But because "public actions" would press judicial authority vis-à-vis the representative branches to the limit, he concluded the Court should not entertain them without congressional authorization.

The bearing of separation of powers on taxpayer standing was the pivotal dividing point in *Flast.* Justice William O. Douglas, too, thought *Flast* a public action, the attempt to distinguish *Frothingham* a failure, and the requirements of Article III met. But he found *Frothingham* deficient, not *Flast,* for he perceived the judicial role as enforcement of basic rights against majoritarian control without awaiting congressional authorization—even in "public actions." Chief Justice Warren's view fell between the Harlan and Douglas poles by disavowing the connection between standing and the separation of powers. Justiciability requires that a suit be appropriate in form for judicial resolution and implicates separation of powers, said Warren, but standing, with its focus on the party suing, not the issues raised, looks only to form.

Under the Burger Court, separation of powers considerations have resurfaced in taxpayer suits, stunting the potential growth of *Flast* into the mature "public action." Typical of the Burger Court approach was *Valley Forge Christian College* v. *Americans United for Separation of Church and State* (1982). The *Flast* landmark has become a historical marker.

—JONATHAN D. VARAT

FLETCHER v. PECK

6 Cranch 87 (1810)

Fletcher was the Court's point of departure for converting the contract clause into the chief link between the Constitution and

The bearing of separation of powers on taxpayer standing was the pivotal dividing point in Flast.

F

FLETCHER v. PECK

6 Cranch 87 (1810)

Fletcher *was the Court's point of departure for converting the contract clause into the chief link between the Constitution and capitalism.*

capitalism. The case arose from the Yazoo land scandal, the greatest corrupt real estate deal in American history. Georgia claimed the territory within her latitude lines westward to the Mississippi, and in 1795 the state legislature passed a bill selling about two-thirds of that so-called Yazoo territory, some 35,000,000 acres of remote wilderness comprising a good part of the present states of Alabama and Mississippi. Four land companies, having bribed every voting member of the state legislature but one, bought the Yazoo territory at a penny and a half an acre. Speculation in land values was a leading form of capitalist enterprise at that time, provoking an English visitor to characterize the United States as "the land of speculation." Respectable citizens engaged in the practice; the piratical companies that bought the Yazoo included two United States senators, some governors and congressmen, and Justice James Wilson. In a year, one of the four companies sold its Yazoo holdings at a 650 percent profit, and the buyers, in the frenzy of speculation that followed, resold at a profit. But in 1796 the voters of Georgia elected a "clean" legislature that voided the bill of sale and publicly burned all records of it but did not return the $500,000 purchase price. In 1802 Georgia sold its western territories to the United States for $1,250,000. In 1814 a Yazooist lobby finally succeeded in persuading Congress to pass a $5,000,000 compensation bill, indemnifying holders of Yazoo land titles.

Fletcher v. *Peck* was part of a twenty-year process of legal and political shenanigans related to the Yazoo land scandal. Georgia's nullification of the original sale imperiled the entire chain of Yazoo land speculations, but the Eleventh Amendment made Georgia immune to a suit. A feigned case was arranged. Peck of Massachusetts sold 15,000 acres of Yazoo land to Fletcher of New Hampshire. Fletcher promptly sued Peck for recovery of his $3,000, claiming that Georgia's nullification of the sale had destroyed Peck's title: the acreage was not his to sell. Actually, both par-

ties shared the same interest in seeking a judicial decision against Georgia's nullification of the land titles—the repeal act of 1796. Thus, by a collusive suit based on diversity of citizenship, a case involving the repeal act got into the federal courts and ultimately reached the Supreme Court. The Court's opinion, by Chief Justice John Marshall, followed the contours of Justice William Paterson's charge in *Van Horne's Lessee* v. *Dorrance* (1795).

Although the fraud that infected the original land grants was the greatest scandal of the time, the Court refused to make an exception to the principle that the judiciary could not properly investigate the motives of a legislative body. The Court also justifiably held that "innocent" third parties should not suffer an annihilation of their property rights as a result of the original fraud. The importance of the case derives from the Court's resolution of the constitutionality of the repeal act.

Alternating in his reasoning between extraconstitutional or higher law principles and constitutional or textual ones, Marshall said that the repealer was invalid. Before reaching the question whether a contract existed that the Constitution protected, he announced this doctrine: "When, then, a law is in its nature a contract, when absolute rights have been vested under that contract, a repeal of the law cannot devest those rights. . . ." In the next sentence he asserted that "the nature of society and of government" limits legislative power. This higher law doctrine of judicially inferred limitations protecting vested rights was the sole basis of Justice William Johnson's concurring opinion. A state has no power to revoke its grants, he declared, resting his case "on a general principle, on the reason and nature of things: a principle which will impose laws even on the Deity." Explicitly Johnson stated that his opinion was not founded on the Constitution's provision against state impairment of the obligation of contracts. The difficulty, he thought, arose from the word "obligation," which ceased once a grant of lands had been executed.

The difficulty with Marshall's contract clause theory was greater than even Johnson made out. The clause was intended to prevent state impairment of executory contracts between private individuals; it had been modeled on the provision of the Northwest Ordinance, which had referred to "private contracts, or engagements *bona fide,* and without fraud previously formed." What was the contract in this case? If there was one, did its obligation still exist at the time of the repeal bill? Was it a contract protected by the contract clause, given that it was a land grant to which the state was a party? If the land grant was a contract, it was a public executed one, not a private executory one. The duties that the parties had assumed toward each other had been fulfilled, the deal consummated. That is why Johnson could find no continuing obligation. Moreover, the obligation of a contract is a creature of state law, and the state in this instance, sustained by its courts, had recognized no obligation.

Marshall overcame all difficulties by employing slippery reasoning. A contract, he observed, is either executory or executed; if executed, its object has been performed. The contract between the state and the Yazoo land buyers had been executed by the grant. But, he added, an executed contract, as well as an executory one, "contains obligations binding on the parties." The grant had extinguished the right of the grantor in the title to the lands and "implies a contract not to reassert that right." Moreover, the Constitution uses only the term "contract, without distinguishing between those which are executory and those which are executed." Having inferred from the higher law that a grant carried a continuing obligation not to repossess, he declined to make a distinction that, he said, the Constitution had not made. Similarly he concluded that the language of the contract clause, referring generally to "contracts," protected public as well as private contracts. Marshall apparently realized that the disembodied or abstract higher law doc-

trine on which Johnson relied would provide an insecure bastion for property holders and a nebulous precedent for courts to follow. So he found a home for the vested rights doctrine in the text of the Constitution.

Marshall seemed, however, to be unsure of the text, because he flirted with the bans on bills of attainder and ex post facto laws, giving the impression that Georgia's repeal act somehow ran afoul of those bans, too, although the suit was a civil one. Marshall's uncertainty emerged in his conclusion. He had no doubt that the repeal act was invalid, but his ambiguous summation referred to both extraconstitutional principles and the text: Georgia "was restrained, either by general principles which are common to our free institutions, or by the particular provisions of the Constitution. . . ." He did not, in the end, specify the particular provisions.

In the first contract clause decision by the Court, that clause became a repository of the higher law doctrine of vested rights and operated to cover even public, executed contracts. The Court had found a constitutional shield for vested rights. And, by expanding the protection offered by the contract clause, the Court invited more cases to be brought before the judiciary, expanding opportunities for judicial review against state legislation.

—LEONARD W. LEVY

Bibliography

Magrath, C. Peter (1966). *Yazoo: Law and Politics in the New Republic, The Case of Fletcher v. Peck.* Providence, R.I.: Brown University Press.

FORD v. WAINWRIGHT

477 U.S. 399 (1986)

The Supreme Court held, 5–4, that the infliction of capital punishment on an insane prisoner violates the ban on cruel and unusual

♦ **vested rights**
Legally recognized rights, especially property rights, of which a person may not be deprived without due process of law.

**44 LIQUORMART, INC.
v. RHODE ISLAND**

517 U.S. 484 (1996)

*The Supreme Court
held that the
infliction of capital
punishment on an
insane prisoner
violates the ban on
cruel and unusual
punishments.*

punishments imposed by the Eight Amendment and the Fourteenth Amendment. Justice Thurgood Marshall for the majority applied the principle that the Eighth Amendment recognizes the evolving standards of decency of a maturing society. No state today permits the execution of the insane. Even at the time of the adoption of the Bill of Rights, the common law disapproved execution of the insane because it lacked retributive value and had no deterrence value. Marshall ruled that Florida's procedure for determining a condemned prisoner's sanity failed to rely on the judiciary to ensure neutrality in fact-finding.

The dissenting Justices contended that the Eighth Amendment did not mandate a right not to be executed while insane. Justice William H. Rehnquist observed that at common law the executive controlled the procedure by which the sanity of the condemned prisoner was judged. The dissenters refused to endorse a constitutional right to a judicial determination of sanity before the death penalty could be imposed. Justice Lewis F. Powell was the swing vote in this case. He agreed that the Eighth Amendment prohibited the execution of the insane, but declined to endorse Justice Marshall's virtual requirement of a judicial proceeding to determine sanity.

—LEONARD W. LEVY

44 LIQUORMART, INC. v. RHODE ISLAND

517 U.S. 484 (1996)

Continuing to wrestle with the issue as to how much protection the First Amendment accords advertising and other commercial speech, the Court in *44 Liquormart* unanimously struck down a state law that barred advertising the price of alcoholic beverages. The decision was fragmented, however, and no clear approach to government regulation of commercial speech emerged.

The Rhode Island statute prohibited "advertising in any manner whatsoever" the price of alcoholic beverages, except for price tags not visible from the street. It also barred the media from advertising such prices.

Historically, commercial speech was not accorded constitutional protection until the Court's 1973 decision in *Virginia State Board of Pharmacy* v. *Virginia Citizens Consumers Council.* That case overturned a law prohibiting advertising the prices of pharmaceuticals, but the extent to which government could regulate commercial speech was left unresolved. However, *Virginia Pharmacy* and later decisions recognized that false, fraudulent, or unlawful advertising may be regulated or, indeed, forbidden. *In Central Hudson Gas & Electric Corp.* v. *Public Service Commission* the Court devised a four-part test for deciding the validity of restraints on commercial speech. To be constitutionally protected, such speech must be lawful and not misleading. Once that is so, restrictions on that speech must directly advance a substantial governmental interest and not be more extensive than necessary to serve that interest. Later, in the controversial *Posadas de Puerto Rico Associates* v. *Tourism Company of Puerto Rico*, the Court, by a 5–4 majority, upheld a statute that barred much advertising of casino gambling on the theory that since a state may ban gambling entirely, it may take the "lesser" step of banning the advertising of that activity. *Posadas* was much criticized as creating a "vice" exception to the First Amendment's protection of commercial speech, which could justify bans on advertising not just gambling, alcohol, and tobacco but all sorts of goods or services a state might deem harmful —motorcycles, or butter, for example.

Though the logic of *Posadas* might have supported Rhode Island's ban on liquor price advertising, the Court overturned the statute. Justice John Paul Stevens, writing for the Court, first noted that though commercial speech was subject to greater state control than "fully protected" political, religious or similar speech, the Court has consistently shown its reluctance to uphold a blanket ban on truthful advertising, such as the Rhode Island law. As he states, the "First Amendment directs us to be especially skeptical of regulations that seek to keep people in the dark for what the government perceives to be their own good."

Although Rhode Island sought to justify the ban by arguing it would promote temperance, the Court sensibly found it unlikely that the ban would significantly lessen alcoholic beverage consumption. As it noted, alternatives that did not restrict speech were available, such as increasing retail prices, increased taxation of liquor, and limiting purchases. Thus there was no "reasonable fit" between the ban and its professed goal. The Court also rejected the state's reliance on *Posadas*. Four of the Justices, led by Justice Stevens, were prepared to overrule *Posadas*. They were unwilling to accept the "greater-includes-the-lesser" reasoning of that case, noting that "banning speech may sometimes prove far more intrusive than banning conduct." The First Amendment itself, these Justices contended, "presumes that attempts to regulate speech are more dangerous than attempts to regulate conduct." And, they found, the concept of "vice" as an exception to the First Amendment would be impossible to cabin, as critics of *Posadas* had earlier noted.

The Court also rebuffed the state's claim that the Twenty-first Amendment, which repealed Prohibition and allowed the states to control or prohibit commerce in alcoholic beverages, justified the advertising ban. It held that provision simply "does not license the States to ignore their obligations under other provisions of the Constitution."

The remaining Justices concurred, all finding the statute failed to fit its asserted goal, and therefore failed the *Central Hudson* test, but without seeing the need to overrule *Posadas* at this time. Justice Clarence Thomas concurred separately, joining the Justices prepared to overrule *Posadas* and, going further, arguing that the state's alleged interest in keeping consumers "ignorant in order to manipulate their choices in the marketplace" does not warrant restricting commercial speech any more than it would fully protected speech. He therefore regarded the separate *Central Hudson* test for commercial speech as "illegitimate" and declined to use it. That view has not been espoused by the Court, which continues to accord commercial speech a lesser level of protection than traditionally fully protected speech.

This decision seriously undercuts the ability to government to restrict truthful advertising of tobacco, alcoholic beverages, and other goods a legislature might consider harmful, though lawful. Proposals to bar the outdoor advertising of cigarettes, for example, which a broad reading of *Posadas* might have supported, are now likely to find heavy weather in the courts. Indeed, the current law prohibiting radio and television advertising of casino gambling, now under court challenge, may fall as a result of *44 Liquormart*. It might be argued, on the other hand, that total bans on advertising the price of consumer goods, the subject of the statutes overturned in both *Virginia Pharmacy* and *44 Liquormart*, are particularly distasteful to the Court.

—PHILIP WEINBERG

FRANK v. MANGUM

237 U.S. 309 (1915)

Vicious anti-Semitism and bitter resentment against encroaching industrialization joined in Atlanta, Georgia, in the spring of 1913. Leo Frank, a young Jewish businessman from the North, was arrested and convicted of murdering a thirteen-year-old girl in a factory he superintended. Prejudice, disorder, and blatant public hostility characterized the trial and its coverage. The Georgia Supreme

Historically, commercial speech was not accorded constitutional protection until 1973, when the Court overturned a law prohibiting advertising the prices of pharmaceuticals.

F

FRANK v. MANGUM

237 U.S. 309 (1915)

Prejudice, disorder, and blatant public hostility characterized the Frank trial and its coverage.

Court denied Frank a new trial, 4–2, dismissing claims of procedural errors, irregularities, and the trial judge's stated doubts about Frank's guilt.

Justices Joseph R. Lamar and Oliver Wendell Holmes each turned down requests for writs of error on procedural grounds (though Holmes was not convinced that Frank had received due process), as did the entire Supreme Court, without opinion. Frank then petitioned for a writ of habeas corpus because mob domination had effectively denied him procedural due process. The Court likewise denied this relief, 7–2. Justice Mahlon Pitney declared that habeas corpus could not be substituted for a writ of error to review procedural irregularities. Further, when Frank neglected to object during the trial, he effectively waived the right to claim a denial of due process later. Justices Holmes and Charles Evans Hughes dissented, pointing to the lack of a fair trial: "Mob law does not become due process of law by securing the as-sent of a terrorized jury." Less than two months after the Georgia governor commuted his death sentence to life imprisonment, Frank was kidnapped from prison and lynched. That he was innocent of the crime for which he was convicted is no longer doubted.

The Supreme Court subsequently embarked on a series of decisions insuring the observance of the constitutional safeguards of procedural due process. In *Moore* v. *Dempsey* (1923), the turning point, Holmes wrote for the Court, permitting the use of habeas corpus as a means of preserving criminal defendants' rights. *Frank's* rule of forfeiture through failure to object, however, returned with only slight modification in *Wainwright* v. *Sykes* (1977).

In 1982 a witness came forward and stated that shortly after the murder he had seen another man carrying the victim's body. In 1986 the governor of Georgia posthumously pardoned Leo Frank.

—DAVID GORDON

PARDONED TOO LATE

Leo Frank was convicted of murdering a thirteen-year-old girl in a factory he superintended. He was later kidnapped from prison and lynched. (Corbis/Underwood & Underwood)

See also

Moore v. *Dempsey*

272

Bibliography

Dinnerstein, Leonard (1968). *The Leo Frank Case*. New York: Columbia University Press.

FREE PRESS/ FAIR TRIAL

Although press coverage has challenged the fairness and dignity of criminal proceedings throughout American history, intensive consideration of free press/fair trial issues by the Supreme Court has mainly been a product of recent decades. The first free press/fair trial issue to receive significant attention was the extent of press freedom from judges' attempts to hold editors and authors in contempt for criticizing or pressuring judicial conduct in criminal proceedings. The next category of decisions to receive attention, reversals of convictions to protect defendants from pretrial publicity, began rather gingerly in 1959, but in the years following the 1964 Warren Commission Report the Supreme Court reversed convictions more readily and dealt in considerable detail with the appropriate treatment of the interests of both the press and defendants when those interests were potentially in conflict. More recently, the Court has considered whether the press can be enjoined from publishing prejudicial material, and whether the press can be excluded from judicial proceedings.

In view of the large number of free press/ fair trial decisions handed down over the years by the Supreme Court, this particular corner of the law of freedom of the press is probably the best developed of any, and offers a particularly instructive model of how the Supreme Court seeks to accommodate colliding interests of constitutional dimension. Overall, the Court has sought a balance that respects Justice Hugo L. Black's obiter dictum in the seminal case of *Bridges* v. *California* (1941) that "free speech and fair trial are two of the most cherished policies of our civilization, and it would be a trying task to choose between them."

In one of our history's pivotal First Amendment cases, the Supreme Court in 1941 sharply restricted the power of state judges to hold persons in contempt for publishing material that attacked or attempted to influence judicial decisions. By a 5–4 vote in *Bridges* the Supreme Court struck down two contempt citations, one against a newspaper based on an editorial that stated that a judge would "make a serious mistake" if he granted probation to two labor "goons," the second against a union leader who had sent a public telegram to the secretary of labor criticizing a judge's decision against his union and threatening to strike if the decision was enforced. Black's majority opinion held that the First Amendment protected these expressions unless they created a clear and present danger of interfering with judicial impartiality. From the start, this test as applied to contempt by publication has been virtually impossible to satisfy. Black insisted that "the substantive evil must be extremely serious and the degree of imminence extremely high before utterances can be punished," and, in order to remove predictions about the likelihood of interference from the ken of lower courts, the Court reinforced the strictness of this standard by using an apparently irrebuttable presumption that judges would not be swayed by adverse commentary. "[T]he law of contempt," wrote Justice William O. Douglas in *Craig* v. *Harney* (1947), echoing a position taken in *Bridges*, "is not made for the protection of judges who may be sensitive to the winds of public opinion. Judges are supposed to be men of fortitude, able to thrive in a hardy climate." Under these decisions, it seems doubtful that anything short of a direct and credible physical threat against a judge would justify punishment for contempt.

For general First Amendment theory and more specifically for the rights of the press in free press/fair trial contexts, the chief significance of the contempt cases is the emergence of a positive conception of protected expression under the First Amendment. As Black put it in *Bridges,* "It is a prized American privilege to speak one's mind, although not always with perfect good taste, on all public questions." Drawing upon the decisions in *Near* v. *Minnesota* (1931) and *De Jonge* v. *Oregon* (1937), which stressed the Madisonian conception of free expression as essential to political democracy, opinions in the contempt cases shifted the clear and present danger rule toward a promise of constitutional immunity for criticism of government. The contempt cases are thus the primary doctrinal bridge between the Court's unsympathetic approach to political dissent during and after World War I and the grand conception of *New York Times Co.* v. *Sullivan* (1964) that the central meaning of the First Amendment is "the right of free discussion of the stewardship of public officials." Beyond this, the contempt cases make it clear that protecting expressions about judges and courts is itself a core function of the First Amendment. Douglas put it this way in *Craig,* in words that have echoed in later free press/fair trial cases: "A trial is a public event. What transpires in the court room is public property.... There is no special perquisite of the judiciary which enables it, as distinguished from other institutions of democratic government, to suppress, edit, or censor events which transpire in proceedings before it."

Although the contempt cases focused on the rights of the press and others who sought to publicize information about trials, the next set of free press/fair trial cases, without dealing with the right to publish, looked with a sympathetic eye toward defendants who might have been convicted because of prejudice caused by such publications. Although individual Justices had objected bitterly to the prejudicial effects of media coverage on jurors, not until 1959 did the Supreme Court reverse a federal conviction because of prejudicial publicity. The first reversal of a state court conviction followed two years later in *Irvin* v. *Dowd* (1961), where 268 of 430 prospective jurors said during their voir dire examination that they had a fixed belief in the defendant's guilt, and 370 entertained some opinion of guilt. News media had made the trial a "cause célèbre of this small community," the Court noted, as the press had reported the defendant's prior criminal record, offers to plead guilty, confessions, and a flood of other prejudicial items.

In 1963, the special problems of television were introduced into the pretrial publicity fray by *Rideau* v. *Louisiana,* producing another reversal by the Supreme Court of a state conviction. A jailed murder suspect was filmed in the act of answering various questions and of confessing to the local sheriff, and the film was televised repeatedly in the community that tried and convicted him. The Supreme Court held that "[a]ny subsequent court proceedings in a community so pervasively exposed to such a spectacle could be but a hollow formality." Two years later, in *Estes* v. *Texas* (1965), a narrowly divided Court held that, at least in a notorious case, the presence of television in the courtroom could generate pressures that added up to a denial of due process.

In the mid-1960s the Court took a more categorical and more aggressive stance against prejudicial publicity. The shift was consistent with the Warren Court's growing impatience toward ad hoc evaluations of fairness in its review of state criminal cases. This period of heightened concern for the defendant was triggered by the disgraceful media circus that surrounded the murder trial of Dr. Sam Sheppard. Before Sheppard's trial, most of the print and broadcast media in the Cleveland area joined in an intense publicity barrage proclaiming Sheppard's guilt. During the trial, journalists swarmed over the courtroom in a manner that impressed upon everyone the spectacular notoriety of the case. "The fact is," wrote Justice Tom C. Clark in his most memorable opinion for the

Court, "that bedlam reigned at the courthouse during the trial and newsmen took over practically the entire courtroom, hounding most of the participants in the trial, especially Sheppard." The deluge of publicity outside the courtroom, and the disruptive behavior of journalists inside, combined to make the trial a " 'Roman holiday' for the news media" that "inflamed and prejudiced the public."

In *Sheppard* v. *Maxwell* (1966) Clark adumbrated the techniques by which trial judges may control prejudicial publicity and disruptions of the judicial process by the press. The opinion is a virtual manual for trial judges, suggesting proper procedures initially by listing the particular errors in the case: that Sheppard was not granted a continuance or a change of venue, that the jury was not sequestered, that the judge merely requested jurors not to follow media commentary on the case rather than directing them not to, that the judge failed "to insulate" the jurors from reporters and photographers, and that reporters invaded the space within the bar of the courtroom reserved for counsel, created distractions and commotion, and hounded people throughout the courthouse.

But the *Sheppard* opinion went beyond these essentially traditional judicial methods for coping with publicity and the press. The Court identified the trial judge's "fundamental error" as his view that he "lacked power to control the publicity about the trial" and insisted that "the cure lies in those remedial measures that will prevent the prejudice at its inception." Specifically, Clark admonished trial judges to insulate witnesses from press interviews, to "impos[e] control over the statements made to the news media by counsel, witnesses, and especially the Coroner and police officers," and to "proscrib[e] extrajudicial statements by any lawyer, party, witness, or court official which divulged prejudicial matters. . . ."

Sheppard left open the central question whether the courts could impose direct restrictions on the press by injunctions that would bar publications that might prejudice an accused. In *Nebraska Press Association* v. *Stuart* (1976) the Supreme Court, unanimous as to result though divided in rationale, answered this question with a seemingly definitive no. The Nebraska state courts had ordered the press and broadcasters not to publish confessions or other information prejudicial to an accused in a pending murder prosecution. Some of the information covered by the injunction had been revealed in an open, public preliminary hearing, and the Supreme Court made clear that a state could in no event bar the publication of matters disclosed in open judicial proceedings. As to other information barred from publication by the state courts, Chief Justice Warren E. Burger's majority opinion went by a curious and circuitous route to the conclusion that the impact of prejudicial publicity on prospective jurors was "of necessity speculative, dealing . . . with factors unknown and unknowable." Thus, the adverse effect on the fairness of the subsequent criminal proceeding "was not demonstrated with the degree of certainty our cases on prior restraint require." Burger's opinion made much of the fact that the state court had not determined explicitly that the protections against prejudicial publicity set out in *Sheppard* would not suffice to guarantee fairness, as if trial court findings to this effect might make a difference in judging the validity of a prior restraint against publication. And Burger said again and again that he was dealing with a particular case and not laying down a general rule. But because Burger termed the evils of prejudicial publicity "of necessity speculative," and viewed the prior restraint precedents as requiring a degree of certainty about the evils of expression before a prior restraint should be tolerated, his opinion for the Court seems to be, in the guise of a narrow and particularistic holding, a categorical rejection of prior restraints on pretrial publicity. Lower courts have read the decision as an absolute bar to judicial injunctions against the press forbidding the publication of possibly prejudicial matters about pending criminal proceedings.

Beyond its rejection of prior restraints against the press to control pretrial publicity, the *Nebraska Press Association* decision emphatically affirmed all the methods of control set out in *Sheppard,* including the validity of judicial orders of silence directed to parties, lawyers, witnesses, court officers, and the like not to reveal information about pending cases to the press. Such orders, indeed, have flourished in the lower courts since the *Nebraska Press Association* decision.

The free press/fair trial conundrum has also presented the Supreme Court with the only occasion it has accepted to shed light on the very murky question whether the First Amendment protects the right to gather information, as against the right to publish or refuse to publish. No doubt in response to the Supreme Court's rejection of direct controls on press publication, either by injunctions or by the contempt power, several lower courts excluded news reporters and the public from preliminary hearings and even from trials themselves to prevent the press from gathering information whose publication might be prejudicial to current or later judicial proceedings. Initially, in *Gannett Co.* v. *De Pasquale* (1979), reviewing a closing of a preliminary hearing dealing with the suppression of evidence, the Supreme Court found no guarantee in the Sixth Amendment of public and press presence. The decision produced an outcry against secret judicial proceedings, and only a year later, in one of the most precipitous and awkward reversals in its history, the Court held in *Richmond Newspapers* v. *Virginia* (1980) that the First Amendment barred excluding the public and the press from criminal trials except where special considerations calling for secrecy, such as privacy or national security, obtained. The decision marks the first occasion in which the Court recognized a First Amendment right of access to courtrooms for purposes of news

gathering, and the Court was careful to limit its holding by resting on the long tradition of open judicial proceedings in English and American law. One year later, in *Chandler* v. *Florida* (1981), the Court held that televising a criminal trial was not invariably a denial of due process, thus removing *Estes* as an absolute bar to television in the courtroom.

Since *Richmond Newspapers* the Court has continued to expand the First Amendment right of the media of access to the courts. In *Globe Newspaper Co.* v. *Superior Court* (1982) it invalidated a law requiring judges to bar the press when juvenile victims of sex crimes testified. *Press–Enterprise Co.* v. *Superior Court* (1984) extended access to the pretrial questioning of jurors. Other decisions have held the state may not punish the media for publishing the name of a juvenile or a judge accused of criminal activity. Only in the most unusual instances may the press be punished for printing truthful information about an investigation or trial.

The pattern of constitutional law formed by the free press/fair trial decisions has several striking aspects. While direct judicial controls on the right of publication have been firmly rejected, the courts have proclaimed extensive power to gag sources of information. Participants in the process can be restrained from talking, but the press cannot be restrained from publishing. However, the broad power to impose secrecy on sources does not go so far as to justify closing judicial proceedings, absent unusual circumstances. The interests of freedom of expression and control over information to enhance the fairness of criminal trials are accommodated not by creating balanced principles of general application but rather by letting each interest reign supreme in competing aspects of the problem. Moreover, the principles fashioned in the cases tend to be sweeping, as if the Supreme Court were acting with special confidence in fashioning First Amendment standards to govern the familiar ground of the judicial process. And in dealing with its own bailiwick, the judicial process, the Supreme Court has acted not defensively but with a powerful commitment to freedom of expression.

—BENNO C. SCHMIDT, JR.

Bibliography

Friendly, Alfred, and Goldfarb, Ronald (1967). *Crime and Publicity.* New York: Twentieth Century Fund.

Jaffe, Louis (1965). Trial by Newspaper. *New York University Law Review* 40:504–524.

Lewis, Anthony (1980). A Public Right to Know about Public Institutions: The First Amendment as Sword. *Supreme Court Law Review* 1980:1–25.

Schmidt, Benno C., Jr. (1977). Nebraska Press Association: An Expansion of Freedom and Contraction of Theory. *Stanford Law Review* 29:431–476.

Taylor, Telford (1969). *Two Studies in Constitutional Interpretation.* Evanston, Ill.: Northwestern University Press.

FREEDMAN v. MARYLAND

380 U.S. 51 (1965)

Although the Supreme Court often remarks that the First Amendment imposes a heavy presumption against the validity of any system of prior restraint on expression, the Court has tolerated state censorship of motion pictures through advance licensing. Typically, such a law authorizes a censorship board to deny a license to a film on the ground of obscenity. Other substantive standards ("immoral," "tending to corrupt morals") have been held invalid for vagueness. In addition, the Court insists that the licensing system's procedures follow strict guidelines designed to avoid the chief evils of censorship. *Freedman* is the leading decision establishing these guidelines.

In a test case, a Baltimore theater owner showed a concededly innocuous film without submitting it to the state censorship board, and he was convicted of a violation of state law. The Supreme Court unanimously reversed the conviction. The *Freedman* opinion, by Justice William J. Brennan, set three procedural requirements for film censorship. First, the censor must have the burden of proving that the film is "unprotected expression" (for example, obscenity). Second, while the state may insist that all films be submitted for advance screening, the censor's determination cannot be given the effect of finality; a judicial determination is required. Thus the censor must, "within a specified brief period, either issue a license or go to court to restrain showing of the film." Advance restraint, before the issue gets to court, must be of the minimum duration consistent with orderly employment of the judicial machinery. Third, the court's decision itself must be prompt. Maryland's statute failed all three parts of this test and accordingly was an unconstitutional prior restraint. Justices William O. Douglas and Hugo L. Black, concurring, would have held any advance censorship impermissible.

—KENNETH L. KARST

FREEDOM OF SPEECH

Although the Supreme Court decided numerous cases addressing freedom of speech issues, most of these decisions merely reaffirmed or only modestly refined existing doctrine. Perhaps most important, the Court has continued to invoke its content-based/content-neutral distinction as a central precept of First Amendment jurisprudence. For purposes of this distinction, a content-based restriction may be defined as a law that limits speech because of the message it conveys. Laws that prohibit seditious libel, ban the publication of confidential information, or outlaw the display of the swastika in certain neighborhoods are examples of content-based restrictions. To test the constitutional-

In a test case, a Baltimore theater owner showed a concededly innocuous film without submitting it to the state censorship board.

See also

Obscenity

Prior Restraint

*The right to freedom
of speech embodied
in the First
Amendment has
expanded into an
elaborate
constitutional
structure.*

ity of such laws, the Court first determines whether the speech restricted occupies only "a subordinate position on the scale of First Amendment values." If so, the Court engages in a form of categorical balancing, through which it defines the precise circumstances in which each category of low-value speech may be restricted. In this manner, the Court deals with such speech as false statements of fact, commercial advertising, fighting words, and obscenity. If the Court finds that the restricted speech does not occupy "a subordinate position on the scale of First Amendment values," it accords the speech virtually absolute protection. Indeed, outside the realm of low-value speech, the Court has invalidated almost every content-based restriction it has considered in the past thirty years.

Content-neutral restrictions, the other half of the content-based/content-neutral distinction, limit expression without regard to the content of the message conveyed. Laws that restrict noisy speeches near a hospital, ban billboards in residential communities, or limit campaign contributions are examples of content-neutral restrictions. In dealing with such restrictions, the Court engages in a relatively open-ended form of balancing: the greater the restriction's interference with the opportunities for free expression, the greater the government's burden of justification.

It may seem odd that the Court uses a stricter standard of review for content-based restrictions (other than those involving low-value speech) than for content-neutral restrictions, since both types of restrictions reduce the sum total of information or opinion disseminated. The explanation is that the First Amendment is concerned not only with the extent to which a law reduces the total quantity of communication but also—and perhaps even more fundamentally—with at least two additional factors: the extent to which a law distorts the content of public debate, and the likelihood that a law was enacted for the constitutionally impermissible motivation of suppressing or disadvantaging unpopular or "offensive" ideas. These two factors, which are more clearly associated with content-based than with content-neutral restrictions, explain both why the Court strictly scrutinizes content-based restrictions of high-value speech and why it does not apply that same level of scrutiny to all content-neutral restrictions. The Court's decisions about freedom of speech continue to reaffirm this basic analytical structure.

Two important recent Supreme Court decisions in the realm of freedom of speech were *Hustler Magazine* v. *Falwell* (1988) and *Texas* v. *Johnson* (1989). In *Hustler Magazine* the Court held that the First Amendment barred an action by the nationally known minister Jerry Falwell against *Hustler* magazine for a "parody" advertisement. The ad contained a fictitious interview with Falwell in which he allegedly said that he had first engaged in sex during a drunken rendezvous with his mother in an outhouse. The Court held that a public figure may not recover damages for the intentional infliction of emotional harm caused by the publication of even gross, outrageous, and repugnant material. In *Johnson* the Court held that an individual may not constitutionally be prosecuted for burning the American flag as a peaceful political protest. The Court explained that "if there is a bedrock principle underlying the First Amendment, it is that the Government may not prohibit the expression of any idea simply because society finds the idea itself offensive or disagreeable." Justice Anthony M. Kennedy observed in a concurring opinion, "It is poignant but fundamental that the flag protects those who hold it in contempt." In each of these decisions, the Court emphatically reaffirmed the central structure of free speech analysis and declined the invitation significantly to expand the concept of low-value speech.

Although *Hustler Magazine* and *Johnson* involved expansive interpretations of freedom of speech, in some other areas the Court has appreciably narrowed the scope of First

Amendment protection. First, there is the issue of commercial speech. Although the Court once had held that commercial advertising is of such low value that it is entirely outside the protection of the First Amendment, the Court overturned that doctrine in 1974 and held that commercial advertising is entitled to substantial—though not full—First Amendment protection. Specifically, the Court held that government may not constitutionally ban the truthful advertising of lawfully sold goods and services on the "highly paternalistic" ground that potential consumers would be "better off" without such information. Though the Court retreated from this position in *Posadas de Puerto Rico Assocs.* v. *Tourism Company of Puerto Rico* (1986), which involved restrictions on advertising for lawful gambling activities, holding even truthful advertising of lawful goods and services can be extensively regulated or banned in order to discourage "undesirable" patterns of consumption, it more recently held in *44 Liquormart* v. *Rhode Island* (1996) that a state may not ban the advertising of the prices of alcoholic beverages, limiting *Posadas* to its facts.

Second, the Court in recent years has increasingly granted broad authority to local governments to regulate expression that is sexually explicit, but not legally obscene. Although failing to classify sexually explicit expression as low-value speech, the Court has repeatedly sustained restrictions that curtail such expression in a discriminatory manner. In *City of Renton* v. *Playtime Theatres* (1986), for example, the Court upheld a city ordinance prohibiting adult-film theaters from locating within 1,000 feet of any residential zone, church, park, or school, even though this effectively excluded such theaters from more than 95 percent of the entire area of the city.

Third, in dealing with speech in "restricted environments," such as the military, prisons, and schools, which are not structured according to traditional democratic principles, the Court has increasingly deferred to the judgment of administrators in the face of claimed infringements of First Amendment rights. In *Bethel School District* v. *Fraser* (1986), for example, the Court upheld the authority of a public high school to discipline a student for making a campaign speech that contained sexual innuendo; in *Hazelwood School District* v. *Kuhlmeier* (1988) the Court upheld the authority of a public high school principal to exclude from a student-edited school newspaper stories dealing with pregnancy and with the impact of divorce on students; in *Turner* v. *Safley* (1987) the Court upheld a prison regulation generally prohibiting correspondence between inmates at different institutions; and in *Thornburgh* v. *Abbott* (1989) the Court upheld a Federal Bureau of Prisons regulation authorizing wardens to prevent prisoners from receiving any publication found to be detrimental "to the security, good order or discipline of the institution." These decisions are in sharp contrast to earlier decisions that granted considerable protection to the freedom of speech even in such restricted environments. It should be noted that the Court's recent inclination to grant broad deference to administrative authority is evident not only in its restricted environment decisions but also in decisions dealing with public forums and with the speech of public employees.

An unusual but seemingly important decision, *R.A.V.* v. *City of St. Paul* (1992), struck down a law that made criminal the display of any symbol intended to cause "anger, alarm or resentment" on the basis of race, religion, or gender, as applied to an accused who burned a cross in front of a black family's residence. The statute was overbroad; much speech leading to anger or resentment is protected by the First Amendment. However, a narrow majority held the law unconstitutional on a different ground, objecting that it treated "fighting words" relating to race, religion, or gender differently from other fighting words. The remaining four Justices maintained the law was unconstitutionally overbroad.

Although not involving the Supreme Court, there was extensive debate and activity with respect to several other free speech issues between 1985 and 1989. First, there has been considerable controversy concerning the law of libel and the First Amendment. In *New York Times* v. *Sullivan* (1964) the Court held that in order to prevent the chilling of "uninhibited, robust and wide-open" debate, public officials could not recover for libel without proof that the libelous statements were false and that they were published with a knowing or reckless disregard of the truth. In recent years, critics have maintained that *New York Times* not only has prevented injured plaintiffs from obtaining judicial correction of published falsehoods but also has produced excessive damage awards against publishers. These critics argue that *New York Times* has thus effectively sacrificed legitimate dignitary interests of the victims of libel without protecting the "uninhibited, robust, and wide-open" debate the rule was designed to promote. Such criticism has provoked a wide range of proposals at both the state and national levels for either judicial or legislative reform. The most common and most intriguing of these proposals calls for the recognition of a civil action for a declaration of falsity, which would require no showing of fault on the part of the publisher but would authorize no award of damages to the plaintiff.

A second area that has generated increased attention in recent years concerns the advent and expansion of cable television. Regulatory agencies and state and federal courts have confronted a broad range of issues arising out of the cable revolution, including the regulation of sexually explicit programming, the applicability of political "fairness" principles, the constitutionality of mandatory access and "must carry" rules, the regulation of subscription rates and franchise fees, and the constitutionality of government restrictions on the number of cable systems. Most fundamentally, the expansion of cable television may ultimately undermine the "scarcity" rationale for government regulation of radio and television broadcasting.

Perhaps the most interesting and most controversial development in recent years relating to freedom of speech concerns the issues of obscenity and pornography. Sixteen years after the 1970 Report of the Commission on Obscenity and Pornography, which found "no evidence that exposure to explicit sexual materials plays a significant role in the causation of delinquent or criminal behavior," a new government commission, the Attorney General's Commission on Pornography, concluded that there is indeed a causal relationship between exposure to sexually violent material and aggressive behavior toward women. This conclusion, which stirred immediate controversy among social scientists, led the 1986 commission to recommend additional legislation at both the state and federal levels and more aggressive enforcement of existing antiobscenity laws.

In a related development, many feminists in recent years have actively supported a more extensive regulation of pornography. Distinguishing "obscenity," which offends conventional standards of morality, from "pornography," which subordinates women, such feminists as Catharine MacKinnon and Andrea Dworkin have proposed legislation that would restrict the sale, exhibition, and distribution of pornography, which they define as "'the sexually explicit subordination of women, graphically depicted, in which women are presented dehumanized as sexual objects, as sexual objects who enjoy pain, humiliation or rape, as sexual objects tied up, or cut up or mutilated or physically hurt, or as whores by nature."

This type of legislation poses a profound challenge to free speech. Opponents maintain that these laws constitute censorship in its worst form and that they are nothing less than blatant attempts to suppress specific points of view because they offend some citizens. Supporters of such legislation maintain that pornography is of only low First Amendment value, that it causes serious harm by shaping attitudes and behaviors of violence and discrimination toward women, and that it is futile to expect "counter-speech" to be an appropriate and sufficient response to such material. Although the courts that have considered the constitutionality of this kind of legislation have thus far held it incompatible with freedom of speech, the pornography issue will no doubt continue to generate constructive debate about the occasionally competing values of equality, dignity, and freedom of speech for some time to come.

—GEOFFREY R. STONE

Bibliography

Bollinger, Lee C. (1986). *The Tolerant Society: Freedom of Speech and Extremist Speech in America.* Oxford: Clarendon Press.

Kalven, Harry, Jr. (1988). *A Worthy Tradition: Freedom of Speech in America.* New York: Harper & Row.

Stone, Geoffrey R.; Seidman, Louis M.; Sunstein, Cass R.; and Tushnet, Mark V. (1986). *Constitutional Law.* Chap. 7. Boston: Little, Brown.

FREEDOM OF THE PRESS

The First Amendment's guarantee of freedom of the press is vitalized, as is freedom of speech, by the synergy among the justifications for the protection of freedom of expression: (1) the marketplace of ideas is the best way of ascertaining truth; (2) full discussion of options is necessary to maintain a self-governing polity; (3) choice of both the means and the content of conveying one's messages is inherent to the notion of individual self-expression; and (4) free discussion is necessary as a check on governmental power by providing information for a resisting citizenry. The justifications have been translated into a set

RIGHT TO PUBLISH

A free press is essential in a democracy, and the Court has never lost sight of this. (Corbis/Jerry Cooke)

A major issue with respect to operations of the press relates to the right of the press to obtain information from the government.

of doctrines that preclude the following in declining order of absoluteness: government licensing the printed press; prepublication censorship; demands that certain information be published; and with tightly circumscribed exceptions, civil or criminal liability for what is published. The right to publish is thus highly protected, but the right to gather news, although essential to the operation of freedom of the press, has proved difficult to implement by judicial decision.

Licensing the printed media, as Great Britain required before its Glorious Revolution, has never been seriously suggested. Occasionally, Congress has debated a specific wartime or national security preclearance censorship provision, but none has been adopted; and if adopted, it would almost certainly have been successfully challenged. When Minnesota did appear to have enacted a limited preclearance scheme with its so-called gag law, the Supreme Court held it unconstitutional in *Near* v. *Minnesota ex rel. Olson* (1931).

Miami Herald Publishing Company v. *Tornillo* (1974), invalidating a right-to-reply law, suggests that a newspaper may never be required to publish or be punished for not publishing an item it wishes to exclude. Tornillo, a candidate for the Florida legislature, had been savaged by a pair of editorials in the *Miami Herald* just before the election. He demanded that the *Herald* print his responses as required by a state law regulating electoral debates. The Court, however, unanimously held the law unconstitutional, reasoning that it would "chill" the newspaper's willingness to enunciate its views and that it intruded into editorial choice. The latter rationale sweeps broadly enough to assure autonomy in deciding what to exclude. It should be noted that the rules in this and other areas are somewhat more restrictive in the case of the broadcast media.

The contested areas of freedom of the press involve attempts by the press to acquire information and attempts by the state to punish publication of certain sensitive information. Under very limited circumstances,

government may successfully block publication by an injunction remedy. Under broader, but still limited circumstances both civil and criminal remedies may be allowable.

Near analogized the Minnesota gag law, which placed a newspaper under a permanent injunction banning future "malicious, scandalous and defamatory" publication, to the traditional common law prior restraint created by preclearance licensing. Because a barebones guarantee of freedom of the press was a ban on prior restraints, the Minnesota gag law was unconstitutional—the first statute ever found to violate the First Amendment. *Near* did not go all the way and ban all prior restraints. Thus, in *Near*'s most famous passage, the Court implied that national security might well be a ground for a prior restraint: "No one would question but that a government [during actual war] might prevent actual obstruction to its recruiting service or the publication of the sailing dates of troops and transports or the number and location of troops." Subsequently, it has been assumed that if a prior restraint were ever appropriate, national security would be the justification. Nevertheless, in *New York Times* v. *United States* (1971), its most publicized national security case, the Supreme Court concluded that the government had not met its burden of proof to prevent publication of the *Pentagon Papers*, which described top secret decision making involving the Vietnam War. The modern reality of copying machines and computer disks has made injunctive prior restraints obsolete because the materials will always show up somewhere else and any injunction will be futile to prevent disclosure—facts not yet reflected in the doctrine.

Despite upholding the press in every single case involving privacy and the First Amendment and in other noncopyright contexts where the press has published truthful information noncoercively obtained from governmental sources, the Court has avoided sweeping rules and always assumed that somewhere lies a situation where the press ought not publish. Again, national security heads the list, and the Court has recognized the enforceability of contracts that forbid publication without approval of the Central Intelligence Agency; it would undoubtedly sustain the federal prohibition on disclosing the identities of intelligence agents as part of a pattern of activities intended to expose covert action. Beyond national security, the protection of sensitive private information of nonpublic figures is the next most likely candidate for a limitation on publication, although any such limitation will have to be carefully circumscribed. Thus, in *Florida Star* v. *B.J.F.* (1989), a civil privacy case, the Court set aside an award of damages for negligent publication of a rape victim's name because the paper had lawfully obtained the information through governmental disclosure. The Court recognized, as it had previously, that the state is in the best position to protect against disclosure through careful internal procedures.

Florida Star may usefully be contrasted with *Seattle Times* v. *Rhinehart* (1984), where the Court held that a trial court can forbid publication of information acquired by the press in state-mandated discovery, unless the information actually comes out in the litigation. *Rhinehart's* balance demonstrates that there are some circumstances where it is too unfair to allow the press to publish (without sanction) information that it has. One may extrapolate from *Rhinehart* that, if the press were to break into property and pillage files (or plant bugs) and later to publish, then the publication could also be penalized.

But these examples of coercive acquisition of information are a far cry from the issue ducked ever since the *Pentagon Papers Cases* (1971): What if the press should publish information unlawfully taken by a third party (as federal law forbids)? Here, outcomes of the Court's decisions, rather than the reasons offered, appear to preclude sanctions in cases where the press does not coercively acquire the information, while leaving the potential deterrent of criminal penalties hanging as a last resort.

Similarly, in the wake of *Branzburg* v. *Hayes* (1972), the courts have recognized a limited

First Amendment protection for the press when it refuses to divulge confidential sources. The Court recognized the importance of such information to a self-governing citizenry, and held government and other litigants may only obtain confidential information from the press when they can show it to be necessary and that no other source is available.

The Court initially rejected claims of the press of access to prisons and pretrial hearings, but in *Richmond Newspapers* v. *Virginia* (1980), it held that the press and public have a right to watch criminal trials—a right later extended to pretrial proceedings such as the questioning of jurors. Although the press acted as if *Richmond Newspapers* might convert the First Amendment into a freedom of information sunshine law, it is not. This decision opens courtroom doors, but not those of grand juries or the other branches of government.

The least satisfying area of the Court's jurisprudence on freedom of the press is the one where the Court has been the most active: the constitutionalization of the law of libel in the wake of *New York Times* v. *Sullivan* (1964). Despite this decision's promise to balance successfully the interests of reputation against the chilling effect that civil liability imposes on the press, over the years the constitutional law of defamation has become an ever more intricate maze of rules that in operation protect neither reputation, the press, nor the public's interest in knowing accurate information.

Although the best-known feature of current libel law may be its division of defamed plaintiffs into two classes, public figures and private figures, with the former having to meet the *New York Times* actual-malice standard—this distinction has had little impact on litigation. The reason is that private figures also need to show actual malice if they are to recover punitive damages—the financial key to their attorneys' taking their cases on contingent fees. At trial, the current constitutional rules attempt to minimize jury discretion. According to *Milkovich* v. *Lorain Journal* (1990), the plaintiff bears the burden of proving falsity, and those statements that "cannot reasonably be interpreted as stating actual facts" are fully protected. There is also strict appellate supervision of the evidence, something unmatched in any other area of law.

The intricate structure of First Amendment libel law has been widely criticized. In operation, the overwhelming number of libel suits are disposed of before trial; in such a case, the plaintiff is never granted an opportunity to show that the defamatory statements were false. If the case goes to a jury, the odds shift heavily to the plaintiff, although the damage awards are likely to be set aside either by the trial judge or the appellate court. It is the rarest of plaintiffs who successfully hurdles all the rules designed to protect the press. As a result, the rules do not provide the public with an opportunity to know the truth about injured plaintiffs; the law underprotects reputation; and in all likelihood, individuals are deterred from entering the public arena where, rightly or wrongly, they are often perceived as fair game.

Nevertheless, current law also fails to serve the interests of the press. A wholly unanticipated aspect of *New York Times* was the way it turned the libel trial away from what the defendant said about the plaintiff to scrutiny of how the press put the story together. When the trial focuses on the practices, care, motives, and views of the press—especially when, as is likely for a case reaching trial, the story is false—the dynamics of the case invite punishment of the press. A good trial lawyer will be able to paint the dispute as a contest between good and evil, and the evidence necessary to prove reckless disregard of the truth leaves no doubt as to which side is evil. In the 1980s the average jury award in cases where reckless disregard was found exceeded $2 million.

It does not reduce the chill on newspapers to learn that few plaintiffs get to keep their awards and that the average successful plaintiff receives a mere $20,000. There seems to be a damages explosion in tort verdicts gener-

ally, and newspapers know catastrophe can arrive with just one huge verdict. An example was the $9 million judgment against the *Alton* (*Illinois*) *Evening Telegraph,* which sent the paper to bankruptcy court (although a subsequent settlement allowed the 38,000–circulation paper to stay in business). What makes defamation a special tort is that the injury that plaintiffs suffer seems far less severe than that suffered by a physically injured tort plaintiff. Large jury verdicts, both for punitive damages and those for emotional pain and suffering, thus seem designed more to punish than to compensate.

The operation of *New York Times* has thus produced a strange landscape. Issues of truth and falsity rarely surface, and reputations are not cleared for the vast majority of plaintiffs. For those few that get to a jury, however, trying the press can lead to a large, albeit momentary, windfall. The possibility of that windfall, coupled with the necessary legal fees to avoid it, maintains a chilling effect, even though appellate supervision typically cuts the verdicts to size. Libel law, having been wholly remade in the wake of *New York Times,* needs to be rethought again. It is not that the Court has misunderstood what to balance; rather, its balance systematically undermines all the values it attempts to protect.

A free press is essential in a democracy, and the Court's doctrines have never lost sight of this. Typically, press cases parallel speech cases, but one area where the Court has split the two is taxation. To protect the press, the Court has struck down press taxes that are unique to the press or treat different parts of the press differently. Whatever the imperfections of the law of freedom of the press, few areas of constitutional law have achieved a more coherent whole than freedom of the press. Even an "outrageous" parody of the Reverend Jerry Falwell in *Hustler Magazine* v. *Falwell* (1988), found by a jury to have inflicted extreme emotional distress, received the unanimous protection of a Court certain that freewheeling caustic discussion must be a central object of constitutional protection if we are to have a free and therefore secure press.

—L. A. POWE, JR.

Bibliography

Anderson, David A. (1975). The Issue Is Control of Press Power. *Texas Law Review* 54:271–282.

Powe, Lucas A., Jr. (1991). *The Fourth Estate and the Constitution: Freedom of Press in America.* Berkeley: University of California Press.

Smolla, Rodney A. (1986). *Suing the Press.* New York: Oxford University Press.

Symposium (1977). Nebraska Press Association v. Stuart. *Stanford Law Review* 29: 383–624.

FRISBY v. SCHULTZ

487 U.S. 474 (1988)

In response to antiabortion protesters picketing the home of a local abortionist, a Wisconsin town passed an ordinance forbidding picketing "before or about the residence . . . of any individual." The Court held in a 6–3 vote that the ordinance did not on its face violate the First Amendment. Writing for five members of the majority, Justice Sandra Day O'Connor narrowly construed the law as applying only to picketing directed at a particular home. The law served a significant government interest, according to O'Connor, because it sought to protect the sanctity of the home from unwanted—and inescapable—intrusions. O'Connor noted that "[t]he First Amendment permits the government to prohibit offensive speech as intrusive when the 'captive' audience cannot avoid the objectionable speech. . . . [Here] [t]he resident is figuratively, and perhaps literally, trapped within the home, and because of the unique and subtle impact of such picketing is left with no ready means of avoiding the unwanted speech."

The dissenters sympathized with the intent of the law, but found that its language suffered from overbreadth.

—JOHN G. WEST, JR.

FULLER, MELVILLE W.

(1833–1910)

Melville Weston Fuller, eighth Chief Justice of the United States, was appointed by Grover Cleveland in 1888 and presided over the Court until his death on July 4, 1910. Fuller's twenty-two-year tenure as Chief Justice, the longest during the Court's second century, spanned one of the most significant periods of constitutional development in American history. Fuller and his associates circumscribed the rights of state criminal defendants under the Fourteenth Amendment, established an inferior legal status for residents of the new overseas colonies, articulated the infamous separate but equal doctrine, and devised a spate of other juristic

F

FULLER, MELVILLE W.

(1833–1910)

A Wisconsin town passed an ordinance forbidding picketing "before or about the residence . . . of any individual."

"THE NEW JUDICIALISM"

The Fuller era abounds with anomalies. (Corbis)

F

Underlying Fuller's management of the Court was a belief that the Chief Justice's primary duty was to convey to the public the impression that in the Court reason triumphed over partisanship.

strategies for avoiding interventions on behalf of black petitioners in the fields of education and voting rights. At the same time the Fuller Court made so many new departures in decisions affecting the economic order that one scholar has described its work as "the new judicialism." Fuller and his colleagues invalidated the federal income tax, emasculated the Interstate Commerce Commission, put the Court's imprimatur on the labor injunction, construed the commerce clause so that the Sherman Antitrust Act frustrated the activities of labor unions yet failed to impede the fusion of manufacturing corporations, and elaborated the concept of substantive due process as a guarantor of vested rights and liberty of contract.

The vast bulk of the Fuller Court's work in constitutional law reflected the Chief Justice's constitutional understanding, the contours of which had been firmly fixed before Fuller came to the bench. Beginning in 1856, when he left his native Maine and settled in Chicago, Fuller was an active stump speaker and essayist for the Illinois Democratic party; he styled himself a disciple of Thomas Hart Benton and Stephen A. Douglas long after both were dead. Fuller spoke often in favor of free trade, hard money, and equal opportunity in the market. "Paternalism, with its constant intermeddling with individual freedom," he wrote in 1880, "has no place in a system which rests for its strength upon the self-reliant energies of the people." But Fuller's version of the equal rights creed had no place for blacks. An exponent of a conservative naturalism that stressed the importance of homogeneous communities and local autonomy in American public life, Fuller believed that union and republican liberty were possible only if the federal government acquiesced in local racial arrangements on the same ground that it acquiesced in state laws regulating the status of women. He objected to the Emancipation Proclamation on the ground that it was "predicated upon the idea that the President may annul the constitutions and laws of sovereign states." He

claimed that the Thirteenth Amendment and Fourteenth Amendment protected only the "common rights" of individuals against discriminatory classification. And he never ceased to insist that Congress's powers to regulate persons or property were limited, derivable only from specific grants and not from any assumption of an underlying national sovereignty. Fuller's longest, most plaintive dissents came in the Insular Cases (1901), where he denied Congress's power to levy tariffs on the products of colonial possessions, and in *Champion* v. *Ames* (1903), where he contended that Congress could not exercise police powers on the pretense of regulating commerce.

Fuller did not grapple with the Court's role in the American system of government following his appointment as Chief Justice. For Fuller, as for Benton, Douglas, and Cleveland, the Constitution was more than a text that allocated specific powers and secured particular rights against government. The Constitution was significant above all as the repository of values so integral to the existence of republicanism that any public official who failed to protect and defend them was guilty of a breach of trust. Consequently, Fuller conceptualized the judicial function in terms of duty rather than in terms of role; his approach to judging was instinctive rather than ratiocinative. Since he had long associated the Constitution with the Democratic party's mid-nineteenth-century dogmas, Fuller impulsively enforced those dogmas as the law of the land. It was no accident that James Bradley Thayer published his path-breaking assessment of "The Origins and Scope of the American Doctrine of Constitutional Law" five years after Fuller's appointment or that a school of jurisprudence dedicated to "judicial self-restraint" grew increasingly large and vocal during his tenure. Other critics accused his Court of aiding the rich and powerful at the expense of the poor and helpless in the name of judicial neutrality. But Fuller neither replied to them nor sought to persuade others to do so. He simply hoped it would always be said of him, as he said of Cleveland in a 1909 eulogy, that "he trod unswervingly the path of duty, undeterred by doubts, single-minded and straightforward."

The Chief Justice's constitutional understanding may have been "single-minded and straight-forward," but the Fuller era abounds with anomalies all the same. First there is the matter of Fuller's reputation. Until Earl Warren's day, no Court was subjected to more strident criticism for a more sustained period of time than Fuller's. Yet when Fuller died the press concurred that none of his predecessors had been so successful in earning the respect and confidence of the country. Even Theodore Roosevelt's *Outlook* conceded that Fuller was "perhaps the most popular" though "not the strongest or most famous Chief Justice." Perceptions of Fuller's capacity for judicial leadership were equally anomalous. The Chief Justice voted with the majority in virtually every leading case decided during his tenure. If Stephen J. Field is to be believed, moreover, Fuller was effective in setting the tenor of conference discussion. "Field told me on the bench this morning," Fuller informed his wife in 1891, "that in the conference I was almost invariably right. He said I was remarkably quick in seizing the best point." Yet contemporary observers invariably described him as a weak Chief Justice who neither led his Court nor exerted a substantial influence on its outlook.

The greatest anomaly of the Fuller era was the doctrinal structure of "the new judicialism." When Fuller contemplated the future of the republic in a centennial address on George Washington, two fears loomed especially large. One was that "the drift toward the exertion of the national will" might ultimately result in "consolidation," which in turn would impair the "vital importance" of the states and undermine self-government by extending the sphere of legislative authority to such a degree that the people no longer controlled it. The other was "the drift . . . towards increased interference by the State in

the attempt to alleviate inequality of conditions." Fuller admitted that "[s]o long as that interference is . . . protective only," it was not only legitimate but necessary. "But," he added, "the rights to life, to use one's faculties in all lawful ways, and to acquire and enjoy property, are morally fundamental rights antecedent to constitutions, which do not create, but secure and protect them." It was imperative, he said, that Americans never grow "unmindful of the fact that it is the duty of the people to support the government and not of the government to support the people." Each of these concerns soon reappeared as major premises in the Court's construction of Congress's commerce power and in its articulation of the liberty of contract protected by the Fifth and Fourteenth Amendments. But the Chief Justice directed a cacophonous band, not an orchestra. Decisions that, in Fuller's view, were consistent with one another looked antithetical to other observers because different Justices expressed the Court's opinions in different language.

Fuller regarded the liberty of contract doctrine as a juristic device for distinguishing between "paternalism," which he thought was unconstitutional, and legislation that "is protective only." Thus the maximum hours law for miners at issue in *Holden* v. *Hardy* (1898) was valid because it protected the health and safety of workers employed in an inherently dangerous occupation. But the maximum hours law for bakery workers invalidated in *Lochner* v. *New York* (1905) and the Erdman Act of Congress prohibiting discrimination against union members were unconstitutional because neither statute was "protective only." In Fuller's view, government had no authority to redress inequalities in the bargaining relation. "The employer and the employee have equality of right," John Marshall Harlan explained for the Court in *Adair* v. *United States* (1908), "and any legislation that disturbs that equality is an arbitrary interference with liberty of contract, which no government can legally justify in a free land." Yet in *Holden* Henry Brown spoke at length

F

about the inequality of bargaining power between employees and employers; he also implied that the worker's inability to contract for fair terms provided a legitimate rationale for government intervention. Although Brown apparently retreated from that position when he joined the *Lochner* majority seven years later, the language he used in *Holden* was never expressly disapproved.

The disparity between Fuller's constitutional understanding and the language used by colleagues in opinions he assigned was even more pronounced in the commerce field. Speaking for the Court in *United States* v. *E. C. Knight Co.* (1895), Fuller held that the Sherman Act could not be constitutionally construed to require the dissolution of manufacturing corporations when the transactions deemed unlawful in the government's complaint involved neither interstate transportation nor interstate sales. "Commerce succeeds to manufacturing," he explained, "and is not part of it." Underlying this distinction were three assumptions that Fuller elaborated with varying degrees of clarity. Congress could not regulate manufacturing combinations under the commerce clause, he said, for if that were permitted there was nothing to prevent Congress from regulating "every branch of human activity." Fuller also contended that that line between manufacturing and commerce was readily ascertainable. In a spate of recent dormant commerce clause decisions the Court had invalidated state tax laws and police regulations that burdened interstate transactions yet had sustained such legislation when it burdened the production process. With the exception of state laws that burdened commerce "indirectly" and might therefore be sustained under the rule of *Cooley* v. *Board of Wardens* (1851), then, Congress could regulate only what the states could not and vice versa. Finally, Fuller made it clear that when manufacturing firms made "contracts to buy, sell, or exchange goods to be transported among the several states," the federal government had a duty to intervene under the Sherman Act if those contracts, or agreements pursuant to

them, were in restraint of trade. In *Robbins* v. *Shelby County Taxing District* (1887), a leading dormant commerce clause case, the Court had held that "the negotiation of sales of goods which are in another state . . . is interstate commerce."

Fuller believed that his construction of Congress's powers under the Sherman Act had two important virtues. It forestalled "consolidation" and it was easy to apply. Congress could certainly reach the agreement at issue in *Addyston Pipe & Steel Co.* v. *United States* (1899), for there a pool had been devised to allocate the interstate distribution of goods among the cooperating firms. And in *Loewe* v. *Lawlor* (1908) the hatters' union had not only gone on strike, thus disrupting the production process, but had engaged in a secondary boycott to prevent the sale of hats in interstate commerce. *Swift & Co.* v. *United States* (1905) posed equally simple issues for Fuller. Some thirty firms had agreed to refrain from bidding against one another when livestock was auctioned prior to its delivery for slaughter at the Chicago packinghouses. Clearly, as the Court explained, "The subject-matter [was] sales and the very point of the combination . . . to restrain and monopolize commerce among the states in respect to such sales." But Fuller had designated Oliver Wendell Holmes to speak for the Court in *Swift*, and Holmes had a great deal more to say. Holmes remarked that "commerce among the States is not a technical legal conception, but a practical one, drawn from the course of business." He spoke metaphorically about a current of commerce, suggesting that local production and interstate marketing were not distinct processes so much as parts of a single, undifferentiated process. And he cast a pall of doubt on the idea, implicit in Fuller's *Knight* opinion, "that the rule which marks the point at which State taxation or regulation becomes permissible necessarily is beyond the scope of interference by Congress in cases where such interference is deemed necessary for the protection of commerce among the States."

Each of the anomalies of the Fuller years is attributable to the personality of the Chief Justice and his conception of the office. Fuller was a self-effacing, amiable man who was gracious and courteous, even deferential, to his colleagues. He made every effort to secure harmonious relations among the Justices. Fuller inaugurated the custom, still followed today, that each Justice greet and shake hands with every other Justice each morning. And he used his authority to assign opinions when in the majority not to enhance his own reputation or to elaborate favorite doctrines but to cultivate the good will of his associates. The opinion in a leading case ordinarily went to the colleague who, in Fuller's judgment, was most likely to want to speak for the Court. Cases involving questions of jurisdiction and practice or mundane matters of private law Fuller kept to himself. Thus he let Field deliver the Court's opinions in *Georgia Banking & Railroad Co.* v. *Smith* (1889), a rate regulation case, and *Chae Chan Ping* v. *United States* (1889), the *Chinese Exclusion Case*. Both controversies raised issues of enormous importance to Field; for that very reason Fuller's predecessor had been disinclined to permit Field to address them for the Court.

Fuller also assumed that Brown would consider *Holden* a plum, for he had recently addressed the American Bar Association on the labor question. Rufus Peckham had earned the right to speak for the majority in *Lochner* by dissenting without opinion in every previous case involving legislative regulation of the labor contract. The *Adair* decision provided Fuller with an opportunity to elaborate his own liberty of contract views in a systematic fashion, but he gave the opinion to Harlan instead. Harlan had dissented in *Lochner* on the grounds that the Court had no authority to reject the legislature's reasonable claim that long hours affected the health and safety of bakery workers. In *Adair* the government advanced no such claim and Harlan's opinion barely noticed the Court's prior liberty of contract rulings. Holmes was the logical choice for *Swift*, for the opinion

would show Roosevelt that the administration had drawn spurious conclusions about Holmes's antitrust views from *Northern Securities Co.* v. *United States* (1904).

The Chief Justice's obsession with courtesy also accounts for the striking differences between his own views and the Court's language in opinions which he assigned. He stubbornly defended his convictions in conference and, if necessary, in dissent. But once he had voted with the majority and had authorized an associate to speak for the Court, Fuller never criticized the work produced by a colleague. Good will among the Justices might be lost forever because of a single quarrel; incongruities of doctrine could always be repaired later. Fuller let it be known that forthright yet polite concurring opinions were preferable to postconference haggling over doctrine, and silent acquiescence in the opinion of the Court was more preferable still. Fuller's own behavior set high standards for his associates; he wrote only seven concurring opinions in twenty-two years.

Underlying Fuller's management of the Court was a belief that the Chief Justice's primary duty was to convey to the public the impression that in the Court, more than in any other institution of government, reason triumphed over partisanship and statesmanship prevailed over pettiness. Fuller's success in achieving that goal while rarely speaking for the Court in landmark cases accounts for misperceptions of his capacity for intellectual leadership and for his great popularity despite persistent criticism of his Court's work. But Fuller's winning personality and the apparent anomalies it produced should not overshadow the relationship between his convictions and the new principles of law his Court articulated. Not since John Marshall's day had the constitutional understanding of the Chief Justice been more at odds with that of voters and party leaders for such a prolonged period of time. Nevertheless, Fuller presided over a Court that made fundamentally new departures in constitutional interpretation which, in the main, incorporated the values he had imbibed during the party battles of a bygone era in American public life. Although Fuller hoped that eulogists would compare him with Cleveland, it might be more appropriate to analogize his career with that of another charming nineteenth-century Democrat. Like Martin Van Buren, he rowed to his objectives with muffled oars.

—CHARLES W. MCCURDY

Bibliography

Fuller, Melville (1890). *Address in Commemoration of the Inauguration of George Washington as First President of the United States, Delivered Before the Two Houses of Congress, December 11, 1889.* New York: Banks & Brothers.

King, Willard L. (1950). *Melville Weston Fuller: Chief Justice of the United States, 1888–1910.* Chicago: University of Chicago Press.

Paul, Arnold M. (1959). *Conservative Crisis and the Rule of Law: Attitudes of Bar and Bench, 1887–1895.* Ithaca, N.Y.: Cornell University Press.

FULLER COURT

(1888–1910)

Melville W. Fuller was Chief Justice of the United States from 1888 to 1910. Lawyers and historians know the period, and its significance for constitutional law, but do not generally identify it with Fuller's name—and for good reason. He was no leader. Fuller discharged his administrative duties effectively, and in "good humor," to borrow a phrase from Oliver Wendell Holmes, one of his admirers, but he was not an important source of the ideas and vision that shaped the work of the Court.

The year of Fuller's appointment, 1888, was nonetheless an important date in the life of the Court because it marked the beginning

of a period of rapid turnover. From 1888 to 1895 there were a considerable number of vacancies, and the two presidents then in office, Grover Cleveland, a Democrat, and Benjamin Harrison, a Republican—whose politics were conservative and largely indistinguishable—appointed six of the Justices. One was Fuller himself. At the time of his appointment he was a respected Chicago lawyer and, perhaps more significantly, a friend of Cleveland's. The others were David J. Brewer, a federal circuit judge in Kansas; Henry Billings Brown, a federal district judge in Detroit; Rufus Peckham, a judge on the New York Court of Appeals; George Shiras, a lawyer from Pittsburgh; and Edward D. White, a senator from Louisiana. (Lucius Q. C. Lamar and Howell Jackson were also appointed during this period, but served for relatively short periods.) The intellectual leaders of this group of six were Brewer and Peckham. They appeared in their written opinions as the most powerful and most eloquent, and the Chief Justice usually turned to one or the other to write for the Court in the major cases.

In constructing their majorities, Brewer and Peckham could usually count on the support of Stephen J. Field (Brewer's uncle), who earlier had achieved his fame by protesting various forms of government regulation in the *Slaughterhouse Cases* and the *Granger Cases*. In the late 1890s Field was replaced by Joseph McKenna, who was chosen by William McKinley, a president who continued in the conservative tradition of Cleveland and Harrison. Another ally of this Cleveland-Harrison group, though perhaps not so steadfast as Field or McKenna, was Horace Gray. Gray was appointed in 1881 by President Chester A. Arthur and served until 1902.

As a result of these appointments, the Court over which Fuller presided was perhaps one of the most homogeneous in the history of the Supreme Court. Even more striking, its composition did not significantly change for most of Fuller's tenure. Fuller died in July 1910, just months after Brewer and Peckham.

See also

Champion v. *Ames*

Cooley v. *Board of Wardens*

Northern Securities Co. v. *United States*

Lochner v. *New York*

Loewe v. *Lawlor*

Swift & Co. v. *United States*

It was almost as though he could not go on without them. Brown resigned in 1906 and Shiras in 1903, but their replacements—William H. Moody and William R. Day—did not radically alter the balance of power. The only important break with the past came when Theodore Roosevelt appointed Oliver Wendell Holmes Jr. to replace Gray.

At the time of his appointment, Holmes was the Chief Justice of the Supreme Judicial Court of Massachusetts and had already written a number of the classics of American jurisprudence. Brown described Holmes's appointment as a "topping off." On the Court, however, Holmes played a different role, for he had no taste for either the method of analysis or general philosophical outlook of the Cleveland-Harrison appointees. His stance was fully captured by his quip in *Lochner* v. *New York* (1905) that "the Fourteenth Amendment does not enact Mr. Herbert Spencer's Social Statics." In this remark Holmes was finally vindicated in 1937 with the constitutional triumph of the New Deal, but in the early 1900s he spoke mostly for himself, at least on the bench, and had no appreciable impact on the course of decisions. No other Justice joined his *Lochner* dissent.

The other significant presence on the Court at the turn of the century was John Marshall Harlan. He was originally appointed by President Rutherford B. Hayes in 1877 and served until 1911. He is greatly admired today for his views on the rights of the newly freed slaves and on the power of the national government. But, like Holmes, Harlan suffered the fate of a prophet: he was a loner. He had his own agenda, and though he sometimes spoke for the Cleveland-Harrison group, Harlan seemed most comfortable playing the role of "the great dissenter."

At the turn of the century, as in many other periods of our history, the Court was principally concerned with the excesses of democracy and the danger of tyranny of the majority. In one instance, the people in Chicago took to the streets and, through a mass strike, tied up the rail system of the nation and threatened the public order. President Cleveland responded by sending the army, and the judiciary helped by issuing an injunction. In *In re Debs* (1895) Brewer, writing for a unanimous Court, upheld the contempt conviction of the leader of the union, and legitimated the use of the federal injunctive power to prevent forcible obstructions of interstate commerce. For the most part, however, the people fought their battles in the legislative halls, and presented the Court with a number of statutes regulating economic relationships. The question posed time and time again was whether these exercises of state power were consistent with the limitations the Constitution imposed upon popular majorities. Sometimes the question was answered in the affirmative, but the Court over which Fuller presided is largely remembered for its negative responses. It stands as a monument to the idea of limited government.

The most important such response consists of *Pollock* v. *Farmers' Loan & Trust Co.* when, in the spring of 1895, the Court invalidated the first federal income tax enacted in peacetime. The statute imposed a 2 percent tax on all annual incomes above $4,000, and it was estimated that, due to the exemption, the tax actually fell on less than 2 percent of the population, the wealthy few who resided in a few northeastern states. The tax was denounced by Joseph Choate, in arguments before the Supreme Court, as an incident in the "communistic march," but the Court chose not to base its decision on a rule that would protect the wealthy few from redistribution. The Court instead largely relied upon that provision of the Constitution linking representation and taxation and requiring the apportionment among the states according to population of all direct taxes.

The Constitution identified a poll tax as an example of a direct tax. It was also assumed by all that a real estate tax would be another example of a direct tax, and the Court first decided that a tax upon the income from real estate is a direct tax. This ruling resulted in the invalidation of the statute as applied to rents (since the tax was not apportioned according to population), but on all other issues the Court was evenly divided, 4–4. The ninth justice, Howell Jackson, was sick at the time. A second argument was held and then the Court continued along the path it had started. Just as a tax on income from real property was deemed a direct tax, so was the tax on income from personal property (such as dividends). This still left unresolved the question whether a tax on wages was a direct tax, but the majority held that the portions of the statute taxing rents and dividends were not severable and that as a result the whole statute would fall. As Fuller reasoned, writing for the majority, if the provision on wages were severable, and it alone sustained, the statute would be transformed, for "what was intended as a tax on capital would remain in substance a tax on occupations and labors."

A decision of the Court invalidating the work of a coordinate branch of government is always problematic. *Pollock* seemed especially so, however, because the Court was sharply divided (5–4), and even more so because one of the Justices (whose identity is still unknown) seems to have switched sides after the reargument. The Justice who did not participate the first time (Jackson) voted to uphold the statute, yet the side he joined lost. It was no surprise, therefore, that *Pollock*, like *Debs*, became an issue in the presidential campaign of 1896, when William Jennings Bryan—a sponsor of the income tax in Congress—wrested control of the Democratic Party from the traditional, conservative elements and fused it with the emerging populist movement. Bryan lost the election, but remained the leader of the party for the next decade or so, during which the political elements critical of the Court grew in number and persuasiveness. By 1913 a constitutional amendment—the first since Reconstruction—was adopted. The Sixteenth Amendment did not directly confront the egalitarian issue, any more than did the Court, but simply declared that an income tax did not have to be apportioned.

The Court's first encounter with the Sherman Act of 1890 was negative and thus bore some resemblance to *Pollock*. In *United States v. E. C. Knight Company*, also announced in 1895, just months before *Debs* and *Pollock*, the Court refused to read the Sherman Act to bar the acquisition of a sugar refinery even though it resulted in a firm that controlled 98 percent of the market and aptly was described (by Harlan in dissent) as a "stupendous combination." The Court reasoned that manufacturing was not within the reach of Congress's power over "commerce." The difference with *Pollock*, however, lay in the fact that this decision (written by Fuller) was in accord with long-standing interpretations of the commerce clause, which equated "commerce" with the transportation of goods and services across state lines. And this decision was not denounced by the populists; they had no desire whatsoever to have the federal government assume jurisdiction over productive activities such as agriculture. In any event, by the end of Fuller's Chief Justiceship, *E. C. Knight* was in effect eradicated by the Court itself. The Court fully indicated that it was prepared to apply the act to manufacturing enterprises, provided the challenged conduct impeded or affected the flow of goods across state lines.

In the late 1890s, almost immediately after *E. C. Knight*, the Court, speaking through Peckham, applied the Sherman Act to prohibit open price-fixing arrangements by a number of railroads. There was little issue in these cases about the reach of the commerce power, because they involved transportation, but the Court was sharply divided over an issue that was presented by these early antitrust cases, namely, whether such an interference with what was then perceived as ordinary or accepted business practices (supposedly aimed at preventing "ruinous competition") was an abridgment of freedom of contract. At first the argument about freedom of contract was presented as a constitutional defense of the application of the Sherman Act, wholly based on the due process clause, but starting with Brewer's separate concurrence in *United States* v. *Northern Securities Company* (1903) and then again in White's opinions for a near-unanimous Court in the *Standard Oil Company* v. *United States* (1911) and *United States* v. *American Tobacco Company* (1911), the liberty issue dissolved into a question of statutory interpretation. The Sherman Act was read to prohibit not all but only "unreasonable" restraints of trade, and if a business practice was "unreasonable," then it was, almost by definition, the proper subject of government regulation.

In the late 1890s and early 1900s, antitrust sentiments were the principal cause of the growing Progressive movement. While populists extolled cooperative activity, progressives tried to use the legislative power to preserve the market and the liberties that it implied. They condemned activities (such as mergers or price fixing) that stemmed from the ruthless pursuit of self-interest but that, if carried to their logical extreme, would destroy the social mechanism that both legitimates and is supposed to control such self-interested activity. Progressives were also concerned, however, with stopping certain practices that did not threaten the existence of the market, but rather offended some standard of "fairness" or "decency" that had a wholly independent source. And they used the legislative power for this end.

The Justices were not unmoved by the moralistic concerns that fueled the progressives, but they were also determined—as they had been in *Pollock*—to make certain that the majorities were not using the legislative power to redistribute wealth or power in their favor. In some instances the Court allowed redistributive measures that benefited some group that was especially disadvantaged and thus could be deemed a ward of the state. On that theory, the Court, in a unanimous opinion by Brewer, upheld in *Muller* v. *Oregon* (1908) a statute creating a sixty-hour maximum work week for women employed in fac-

tories or laundries. More generally, however, the Court voiced the same fears that had animated *Pollock* and insisted that there be a "direct" connection between the legislative rule and an acceptable (that is, nonredistributive) end such as health. The statute at issue in *Lochner* v. *New York,* for example, was defended on the ground that a work week for bakers in excess of sixty hours would endanger their health. Justice Peckham's opinion for the majority acknowledged that there might be some connection between a maximum work week and health, but suspected redistributive purposes and argued that if, in the case of bakers, this connection with health were deemed sufficient—that is, direct—the same could be said for virtually every occupation or profession: "No trade, no occupation, no mode of earning one's living, could escape this all-pervading power."

Just as it was fearful of state intervention to control the terms of employment, the Court was also wary of legislation regulating consumer prices—a practice initiated by the Granger movement of the 1870s but continued by the populists and progressives in the 1890s and the early 1900s. In this instance the Court feared that the customers would enrich themselves at the expense of the investors. The danger was, as Brewer formulated it, one of legalized theft. In contrast to cases like *Lochner,* however, the Court took up this issue with a viable and highly visible precedent on the books, namely, *Munn* v. *Illinois* (1877). Some consideration was given to overruling the decision (there was no limit to the daring of some of the Justices), but the Court finally settled upon a more modest strategy—of cabining *Munn.*

For one thing, the *Munn* formula for determining which industries would be regulated—a formula that allowed the state to reach "any industry affected with a public interest"—was narrowed. In *Budd* v. *New York* (1892) the Court upheld the power of the legislature to regulate the rates of grain operators, but placed no reliance on the *Munn* public interest formula. Instead, it stressed

the presence of monopoly power and the place of the grain operation in the transportation system. Second, the Court began to surround the rate-settling power with procedural guarantees. Legislatures were now delegating the power of setting prices to administrative bodies, such as railroad commissions, and the Court, in *Chicago, Milwaukee & St. Paul Railway Co.* v. *Minnesota,* (1890), required agencies of that type to afford investors a full, quasi-judicial hearing prior to setting rates. Finally, the Court ended the tradition of judicial deference initiated by *Munn* by authorizing judicial review of the rate actually set. The purpose was to insure against confiscation and to this end Brewer articulated in *Reagan* v. *Farmers' Loan & Trust* (1894) a right of fair return on fair value. In that case the rate was set so low as to deny the investors any return at all. In the next case, *Smyth* v. *Ames* (1898), there was some return to the investors, but the Court simply concluded that the rate was "too low."

Reagan v. *Farmers' Loan & Trust* and *Smyth* v. *Ames* were both unanimous and thrust the federal judiciary into the business of policing state rate regulations. A particularly momentous and divisive exercise of this supervisory jurisdiction occurred when a federal judge in Minnesota enjoined the attorney general of that state from enforcing a state statute that set maximum railroad rates. The attorney general disobeyed the injunction and was held in criminal contempt. Peckham wrote the opinion for the Court in *Ex Parte Young* (1908) affirming the contempt conviction, and in doing so, constructed a theory that, notwithstanding the Eleventh Amendment, provided access to the federal equity courts to test the constitutionality of state statutes—an avenue of recourse that was to become critical for the civil rights movement of the 1960s. Ironically, Harlan, who, by dissenting in the Civil Rights Cases (1883) and in *Plessy* v. *Ferguson* (1896), had already earned for himself an honored place in the history of civil rights, bitterly dissented in *Ex parte Young*, because, he argued,

the Court was opening the doors of federal courts to test the validity of all state statutes.

The confrontations between the Court and political branches in economic matters such as antitrust, maximum hours, and rate regulation were considerable—*Northern Securities, Lochner,* and *Ex Parte Young* were important public events of their day. Some of these decisions were denounced by political forces, particularly by the Progressive movement, which had begun to dominate national politics. Roosevelt made his disappointment with Holmes's performance in *Northern Securities* well known ("I could carve out of a banana a judge with more backbone than that"—a comment that seems only to have either amused or pleased Holmes) and finished his presidency in 1908 with a speech to Congress sharply critical of the Court. By 1912 the Supreme Court and its work were once again the subject of debate in a presidential election, as it had been in the election of 1896. It was as though the body politic was scoring the Court over which Fuller had presided for the past twenty years. Now the critical voices were more respected and covered a wider political spectrum than in 1896, but the results were mixed.

In the 1912 election the Democratic candidate, Woodrow Wilson, beat the incumbent William Howard Taft, who was generally seen as the defender, indeed the embodiment, of the judicial power. On the other hand, Wilson was less critical of the Court than Roosevelt, who ran as a Progressive. The legislation of this period also was two-sided. The Clayton Act of 1914, for example, exempted labor from antitrust legislation (thus reversing the *Danbury Hatters* decision of 1908), and also imposed procedural limits on the use of the labor injunction (thus revising *Debs*), but it did not in fact have as critical an edge as the Sixteenth Amendment of 1913. The Clayton Act did not repudiate the idea of the labor injunction altogether nor did it repudiate the rule of reason in antitrust cases. Similarly, although Congress reacted in

1910 to *Ex Parte Young*, it did so only in a trivial, near-cosmetic way, by requiring three judges (as opposed to one) to issue an injunction against the enforcement of state statutes.

In attempting to construct limits on the power of the political branches, and to guard against the tyranny of the majority as it did in *Pollock*, *Ex Parte Young*, and *Lochner*, the Court assumed an activist posture. The Justices were prepared to use their power to frustrate what appeared popular sentiments. The activist posture was, however, mostly confined to economic reforms—redistributing income, regulating prices, controlling the terms of employment—as though the constitutional conception of liberty were structured by an overriding commitment to capitalism and the market. This characterization of their work, voiced in a critical spirit in their day and in ours, is strengthened when a view is taken of the Justices' overall receptiveness to the antitrust program of the progressives, and even more when account is taken of the pattern of decisions outside the economic domain, respecting human rights as opposed to property rights. The Justices were passive about human rights—by and large willing to let majorities have their way.

A particularly striking instance of this passivity consists of their reaction to the treatment of Chinese residents. Ever since the Civil War the Chinese were by statute denied the right to become naturalized citizens, but in the late 1880s and the early 1900s their situation worsened. The doors of the nation were closed to any further immigration, and Congress (in the Geary Act of 1892) created an oppressive regime for those who had previously been admitted. Chinese residents were required to carry passes, and failure to have the passes subjected them to deportation proceedings that were to be conducted by commissioners (rather than judges or juries) and that put them to the task of producing "at least one credible white witness." *Yick Wo* v. *Hopkins* (1886), which invalidated, on equal protection grounds, a San Francisco laundry ordinance that had disadvantaged the Chinese, was already on the books. But neither it nor the passionate dissent of Brewer ("In view of this enactment of the highest legislative body of the foremost Christian nation, may not the thoughtful Chinese disciple of Confucius fairly ask, why do they send missionaries here?") was of much avail. The Court sustained the Geary Act in *Fong Yue Ting* v. *United States* (1893) in virtually all its particulars.

A few years later the Court held in *United States* v. *Wong Kim Ark* (1898) that Chinese children born here were, by virtue of the Fourteenth Amendment, citizens of the United States. But this decision sharply divided the Court, despite the straightforward language of the amendment ("All persons born . . . in the United States and subject to the jurisdiction thereof are citizens of the United States"), and did not materially improve the quality of the process the Chinese received. There was, by virtue of *Wong Kim Ark*, a chance that a Chinese person whom the government was trying to deport was a natural born citizen, yet the Court did not even require that this claim of citizenship be tried by a judge. Holmes wrote the opinion in these cases, *United States* v. *Sing Tuck* (1904) and *United States* v. *Ju Toy* (1905), and once again Brewer, now joined by Peckham, dissented with an intensity equal to that he had exhibited in *Fong Yue Ting*.

The same spirit of acquiescence was manifest in the cases involving the civil rights of blacks, though here it was Harlan who kept the nation's conscience. In *Plessy* v. *Ferguson* (1896) the Court upheld a Louisiana statute requiring racial segregation of rail cars; Harlan dissented and, borrowing a line from Plessy's lawyer, Albion Tourgee, insisted that "our Constitution is colorblind." In *Hodges* v. *United States* (1906) the Court dismissed a federal indictment against a group of white citizens in Arkansas who forced a mill owner to discharge the blacks who had been hired. Brewer, for the majority, said that the power

of the federal government under the Civil War-Reconstruction amendments (and thus under the criminal statute in question) extended only to acts by state officials. He reaffirmed the principle of the *Civil Rights Cases* of 1883 by which the Court effectively ceded to the states exclusive jurisdiction to govern the treatment of one citizen by another. In *Hodges*, Harlan, the Union general from Kentucky, replayed his dissent in the *Civil Rights Cases*, and denounced this principle as a fundamental distortion of the Thirteenth and Fourteenth Amendments. And in *Berea College* v. *Kentucky* (1908) the Court, over Harlan's dissent, upheld a state law that prohibited a private educational corporation from conducting its educational programs on an integrated basis.

Berea College was also written by Brewer. He was mindful of the contrast with a case such as *Lochner*, where the judicial power had been used to the utmost to protect the contractual freedom of worker and employer. Accordingly, Brewer stressed the fact that this law was applicable only to corporations, which, to pick up a theme he had previously articulated in his concurring opinion in *Northern Securities*, were merely artificial entities created by government, not entitled to the same degree of protection as natural persons. He specifically left open the question of the validity of a similar statute if it regulated the conduct of natural persons. Harlan, in an equally equivocal dissent, said that a different result might follow if the statute regulated public rather than private education. In fact, the distorting impact of public subsidies upon the articulation of civil rights had been implicitly acknowledged some years earlier in *Cumming* v. *Board of Education* (1899). In that case Harlan dismissed a challenge by black parents to a decision of a local county, which ran its schools on a segregated basis, to close the only black high school and to send the black students out of the county for their education.

In the 1890s and early 1900s blacks, through one scheme or another, were disen-franchised on a grand scale. The Fifteenth Amendment was reduced to a nullity, as Jim Crow was becoming more firmly entrenched. On several occasions, the Court was presented with challenges to these electoral practices, yet it was unable to respond with the energy that it had summoned in *Pollock* or *Lochner* or *Reagan* or, even more to the point, *Debs*. Holmes, the spokesman in these early voting rights cases, saw judicial relief as nothing but an "empty form": "[R]elief from a great political wrong, if done, as alleged, by the people of a State and the State itself, must be given by them or by the legislative and political department of the government of the United States." Harlan dissented, as might be expected, but so did Brewer. They realized that, because the disenfranchisement was the work of state officials, something more was at issue than the allocation of power between states and nation approved in the *Civil Rights Cases*. What was at issue, according to Brewer and Harlan, was nothing less than the integrity of the judicial power and the duty of the judiciary, to borrow a line from *Debs*, to do whatever it could to fulfill the promise of the Constitution.

The principal issue before the Court at the turn of the century was democracy and, more specifically, the determination of what limits should be placed on popular majorities. As was evident in the civil rights cases, however, the Court was also asked to allocate power between the states and the national government. The federalism issue arose in many contexts, including antitrust, labor, and rate regulation, but the one in which it proved most troublesome was prohibition. By the late 1880s the prohibition movement was an active force in the states, and Fuller began his Chief Justiceship with a set of constitutional decisions that were unstable. In *Mugler* v. *Kansas* (1887) the Court had held that prohibition was within the state police power, yet, just weeks before Chief Justice Morrison R. Waite's death, the Court in *Bowman* v. *Iowa* (1888) had also held that the states were without power to prohibit the importation of liquor from other states. The Court seemed to take away in one decision what it gave in the other. Fuller confronted this problem early on in *Leisy* v. *Hardin* (1890), and in probably his most lasting contribution to constitutional law, fashioned an odd response. First, he announced that the commerce clause barred the states from prohibiting the sale of imported liquor (as well as its actual importation). Second, he invited Congress to intervene, and to authorize states to pass laws that would prohibit out-of-state liquor. Congress quickly responded to this invitation, and in the Wilson Act of 1890 authorized states to enact measures aimed at erecting walls to out-of-state liquor.

The state laws in question in *Leisy* v. *Hardin* were invalidated on the theory that they sought to regulate a matter that required nationwide uniformity. When it came to judging the congressional response, Fuller found the requisite uniformity since it was Congress that had spoken (even though it did no more than allow the states to choose) and on that theory, in *In re Rahrer* (1891), upheld the Wilson Act. In 1898, however, after some change in the composition of the Court and after the responsibility of speaking on this issue had shifted to one of the new appointees, Edward White, a sharply divided Court cut back on the Wilson Act. *Rhodes* v. *Iowa* (1890) held that the Wilson Act authorized a ban on sales of imported liquor within the state but not a ban on the importation itself. White insisted that any other construction would raise grave constitutional doubts as to the validity of the Wilson Act. Fuller joined White's opinion.

Over the next decade, mail order business in out-of-state liquor grew. The conflict between the Court and the prohibition movement escalated. Then in 1913 Congress, as part of the same era that saw the Sixteenth Amendment and the Clayton Act, passed the Webb-Kenyon Act to remove any ambiguity over what it sought to accomplish in the Wilson Act. Congress allowed states to bar both the sale and the importation of out-of-state liquor. After considerable struggle and deliberation, the Webb-Kenyon Act was upheld in an opinion by White (then Chief Justice) on the theory (if that is what it can be called) that "liquor is different." For all other goods, the common market was deemed a constitutional necessity.

The federalism issue has recurred throughout the entire history of the Supreme Court. The Court over which Fuller presided did, however, confront one issue pertaining to structure of government that was unique to the times: colonialism. The issue arose from the "splendid little war," as Secretary of State John Hay called the Spanish-American War of 1898, which left the United States with two former Spanish colonies, Puerto Rico and the Philippines. (Much earlier the United States had purchased Alaska, and in the late 1890s it had also taken possession of Hawaii.) The assumption was that the United States would hold these territories as territories, for an indefinite period, and perhaps ultimately build a colonial empire along the European model. The question posed for the Supreme Court—not just by the litigants but by the nation at large—was whether colonialism was a constitutionally permissible strategy for the United States. Technically, the case involved a challenge to a statute imposing a tariff on goods (sugar) imported from Puerto Rico into the states. The Constitution bars Congress from imposing duties on the importation of goods from one state to another, and so the issue was whether a territory was to be treated the same as a state, or, as phrased in the language of the day, whether the Constitution followed the flag.

Three positions emerged in a series of decisions beginning in 1901 known as the *Insular Cases*. The first, most in keeping with the position of the Court in *Pollock* and the other economic cases, proclaimed the idea of limited government. The government of the United States was formed and established by the Constitution, and thus it was impossible

F

FULLER COURT

(1888–1910)

to conceive of a separation of Constitution and government. This was the position taken by Brewer, Peckham, Fuller, and Harlan. At the opposite end of the spectrum was the so-called annexation position. It proclaimed the separation of Constitution and flag, and generally left the government unrestricted in its activities in the territories; whatever restrictions there were flowed from natural law or from a small group of provisions of the Constitution deemed essential (the tariff provision was not one). This position was most congenial to the government and yet at odds with the general jurisprudence of the Court. Only Justice Brown subscribed to it.

The remaining four Justices, in an opinion written by White, put forth what was called the incorporation theory. It tried to chart a middle course, as appeared to be White's trade. It made the Constitution fully applicable to a territory, but only after that territory was incorporated into the United States. (Prior to incorporation the government would be subject only to the restraints of natural law.) Justice White's opinion also made it clear that the decision to incorporate a territory resided in Congress. In the case before it the Court decided that the territory was not incorporated, but White also acknowledged that incorporation could be done by implication and, even more to the point, he reserved for the judiciary the power to determine whether that act of incorporation had taken place.

Ultimately incorporation was adopted as the position of the Court. But this did not occur until 1905, after an insurrection in the Phillines and other developments in the world (such as the Boer War) had made the idea of a colonial empire seem less attractive, and the danger of further imperial acquisitions seemed to have waned. In fact, incorporation became majority doctrine in *Rassmussen* v. *United States* (1905) in which the Court held that Alaska had been *implicitly* incorporated and that the United States was bound by the Bill of Rights in its governance of that territory. The outcome in this case affirmed the idea of limited government and judicial supremacy, the hallmarks of this Court, and made it possible for Fuller, and perhaps even more significantly, for Brewer and Peckham, to abandon their absolutist position and to support the middle-of-the-road theory of White—perhaps a sign of what was to come in 1910, when Fuller died and Taft, who had once served as the commissioner in the Philippines, replaced him with White.

—OWEN M. FISS

Bibliography

Duker, William (1980). Mr. Justice Rufus W. Peckham: The Police Power and the Individual in a Changing World. *Brigham Young University Law Review* 1980: 47–67.

——— (1980). Mr. Justice Rufus W. Peckham and the Case of *Ex Parte Young:* Lochnerizing *Munn* v. *Illinois. Brigham Young University Law Review* 1980: 539–558.

Goodwyn, Lawrence (1976). *Democratic Promise: The Populist Movement in America.* New York: Oxford University Press.

King, Willard (1967). *Melville Weston Fuller, Chief Justice of the United States, 1888–1910.* Chicago: University of Chicago Press.

Kolko, Gabriel (1963). *The Triumph of Conservatism: A Reinterpretation of American History 1900–1916.* New York: Free Press.

Paul, Arnold (1960). *Conservative Crisis and the Rule of Law: Attitudes of Bar and Bench 1887–1895.* Ithaca, N.Y.: Cornell University Press.

Pierce, Carl (1972). A Vacancy on the Supreme Court: The Politics of Judicial Appointment, 1893–1894. *Tennessee Law Review* 39:555–612.

Roche, John (1974). *Sentenced to Life.* New York: Macmillan.

Rogat, Yosal (1963). The Judge as Spectator. *University of Chicago Law Review* 31: 231–278.

Thorelli, Hans (1954). *The Federal Antitrust Policy: Origination of an American Tradi-*

tion. Baltimore: Johns Hopkins University Press.

Twiss, Benjamin (1942). *Lawyers and the Constitution: How Laissez Faire Came to the Supreme Court*. Princeton, N.J.: Princeton University Press.

Westin, Alan (1953). The Supreme Court, the Populist Movement and the Campaign of 1896. *Journal of Politics* 15:3–41.

——— (1958). Stephen J. Field and the Headnote to *O'Neil* v. *Vermont:* A Snapshot of the Fuller Court at Work. *Yale Law Journal* 67:363–383.

Woodward, C. Vann (1966). *The Strange Career of Jim Crow*. Rev. ed. New York: Oxford University Press.

FULLILOVE v. KLUTZNICK

448 U.S. 448 (1980)

The Supreme Court's fragmentation in *Regents of University of California* v. *Bakke* (1978) left open the question of the constitutionality of government-imposed racial quotas or preferences. The following year, in *United Steelworkers* v. *Weber*, the Court held that a voluntary affirmative action plan, calling for a racial quota in hiring by a private employer and approved by a union, did not violate Title VII of the Civil Rights of 1964. *Fullilove* reopened *Bakke*'s question: Can government impose a racial quota to remedy the effects of past discrimination?

Congress, in a public works statute aimed at reducing unemployment, provided that 10 percent of the funds distributed to each state should be set aside for contracts with "minority business enterprises" (MBE). An MBE was defined as a business at least half owned by persons who are "Negroes, Spanish-speaking, Orientals, Indians, Eskimos and Aleuts." Nonminority contractors challenged this limitation as a denial of the Fifth Amendment's guarantee of equal pro-

tection, as recognized in *Bolling* v. *Sharpe* (1954) and later cases.

The Supreme Court held, 6–3, that the MBE limitation was valid. Three Justices, speaking through Chief Justice Warren E. Burger, paid great deference to Congress's judgment that the racial quota was a "limited and properly tailored remedy to cure the effects of past racial discrimination." Emphasizing the flexibility provided for the law's administration, they said that the funds could be limited to MBEs that were in fact disadvantaged because of race. The other three majority Justices, speaking through Justice Thurgood Marshall, took the position they had taken in *Bakke*, concluding that the racial quota was "substantially related to . . . the important and congressionally articulated goal of remedying the present effects of past racial discrimination."

Justice Potter Stewart, joined by Justice William H. Rehnquist, dissented; they would forbid any statutory racial classification, allowing race-conscious remedies only in cases of proven illegal discrimination. Justice John Paul Stevens was not prepared to take so absolute a position but dissented here because Congress had not sufficiently articulated the reasons for its racial quota and tailored its program to those reasons.

The degree of judicial scrutiny to be given federal affirmative action programs, left unclear by *Fullilove*, was resolved in *Adarand*

RACE-CONSCIOUS REMEDY

Fullilove held that Congress could enact a racial quota by instructing states to set aside funds for contracts with minority-owned businesses. (Corbis/Paul A. Souders)

Can government impose a racial quota to remedy the effects of past discrimination?

See also

Affirmative Action

Racial Quotas

Regents of University of California v. *Bakke*

United Steelworkers v. *Weber*

*The concept of
written constitutions
as the embodiment
of fundamental law
was central to the
federal Constitution
and to later state
constitutions.*

Constructors v. *Pena* (1995). The Court there firmly held that strict scrutiny was required: in other words the government must show its program to be narrowly tailored to serve a compelling governmental interest. It rejected the view that Congress was entitled to greater deference than state or local governments in devising affirmative action plans.

—KENNETH L. KARST

FUNDAMENTAL LAW AND THE SUPREME COURT

The Declaration of Independence explicitly invoked the concept of natural justice—a higher law, timeless and universal—as a defense against tyranny. By the late eighteenth century there had evolved a conviction that the essence of this fundamental law could at one stroke be captured in a document that would endure for ages to come. Of the original state constitutions several were declared in force without constituent ratification and some made no provision for amendment. By the time of the federal Constitutional Convention of 1787, these extreme forms of immutability had given way. Article V provided a formalized process of constitutional amendment, while Article VII conditioned adoption on ratification by state conventions. But the concept of written constitutions as the embodiment of fundamental law was central to the federal Constitution and to later state constitutions.

The issue of whether fundamental law had other appropriate functions in the American constitutional scheme arose early among Justices of the Supreme Court of the United States, and remains critical at the Constitution's bicentenary. Debate opened in *Calder* v. *Bull* (1798). The Connecticut legislature had set aside a court decree refusing to probate a will, granting a new hearing at which the will was admitted. Denied relief in the state courts,

the disappointed heir appealed to the Supreme Court. Outraged at the destruction of the heir's expectancy, Justice Samuel Chase declared, "It is against all reason and justice, for a people to intrust a legislature with such powers, and therefore, it cannot be presumed that they have done it." In Chase's view, the fundamental law could not tolerate "a law that takes property from A and gives it to B," even in the absence of constitutional prohibition. Justice James Iredell challenged this claim of extra-constitutional power to nullify legislation, insisting that if legislation is within constitutional limits "the Court cannot pronounce it to be void, merely because it is, in their judgment, contrary to the principles of natural justice."

Iredell's logic prevailed in *Calder* but in the long run could not hold the line. Chief Justice John Marshall hedged on the question in *Fletcher* v. *Peck* (1810), declaring that Georgia's attempt to revoke fraudulent land grants was void "either by general principles which are common to our free institutions, or by the particular provisions of the constitution of the United States. . . ." Similarly, Justice Joseph Story rested the Court's opinion in *Terrett* v. *Taylor* (1815) upon several grounds, among them "the principles of natural justice" and "the spirit and letter of the [federal] constitution. . . ." *Loan Association* v. *Topeka* (1874), although decided following ratification of the Fourteenth Amendment, was grounded by Justice Samuel F. Miller on extraconstitutional principles founded in fundamental law. The taking from A (by taxation) in aid of B (bridge manufacturer not a public utility) was stricken as an "unauthorized invasion of private right." In contrast, *Dred Scott* v. *Sandford* (1857) and *Hepburn* v. *Griswold* (1869) invalidated congressional "takings" under the Fifth Amendment's due process clause.

At the turn of the century the issue of extraconstitutional adjudication intensified with an obiter dictum in *Allgeyer* v. *Louisiana* (1897). With *Lochner* v. *New York* (1905) and *Adair* v. *United States* (1908), the majority of the court opened a period in which much economic and social legislation was held unconstitutional, ostensibly under the due process clauses. However, the basis given was violation of freedom of contract, for which there was no constitutional warrant. Justice Oliver Wendell Holmes, in his celebrated *Lochner* dissent, insisted that the Fourteenth Amendment, properly construed, should accord with "fundamental principles as they have been understood by the traditions of our people and our law." Yet to him that amendment correctly embraced condemnation of governmental expropriation of property from A for B's benefit, as he made clear in *Pennsylvania Coal Co. v. Mahon* (1922). Justice Louis D. Brandeis there dissented, but he later invoked the identical principle under both due process clauses: the Fifth Amendment clause in *Wright* v. *Vinton Branch of Mountain Trust Bank* (1937) upholding a revised moratorium law, and the Fourteenth Amendment clause in *Thompson* v. *Consolidated Gas Utilities Corp.* (1937). In the latter he declared, "Our law reports present no more glaring instance of the taking of one man's property and giving it to another."

The *Lochner-Adair* venture into noninterpretive constitutionalism was rejected by a split vote in *Nebbia* v. *New York* (1934), followed by unanimity in *Lincoln Federal Labor Union* v. *Northwestern Iron & Metal Co.* (1949). Yet only two years after categorical repudiation in *Ferguson* v. *Scrupa* (1963), the seductive appeal of the philosophy of *Lochner* and its progeny was back, this time in the service of noneconomic interests. In *Griswold* v. *Connecticut* (1965) the due process clause was used to invalidate an anticontraception law; in *Harper* v. *Virginia Board of Elections* (1966) the equal protection clause provided the basis for invalidating the poll tax as a condition for exercise of voting rights. In both cases the majority sought to ground decision in constitutional provisions, but Justice Hugo L. Black, unpersuaded, accused the Court of invoking "the old 'natural-law-due-process formula'," which, he declared, "is no less dangerous when used to enforce this Court's views about personal rights than those about economic rights." *Roe* v. *Wade* (1973), insulating from governmental intervention a woman's decision to have an abortion during the first trimester of pregnancy, rested upon a doctrine of "personhood" demonstrably beyond the ambit of constitutional text, context, or structure. Reaffirmed in *Akron* v. *Akron Center for Reproductive Health, Inc.* (1983) out of respect for stare decisis, *Roe* highlights the Supreme Court's continuing temptation to give constitutional force to extraconstitutional values it finds lying in the recesses of unwritten fundamental law.

—FRANK R. STRONG

Bibliography

Grey, Thomas (1978). Origins of the Unwritten Constitution: Fundamental Law in American Revolutionary Thought. *Stanford Law Review* 30:843–893.

Hand, Learned (1960). *The Spirit of Liberty.* 3rd ed. New York: Knopf.

Perry, Michael (1982). *The Constitution, the Courts, and Human Rights.* Chap. 4. Columbus: Ohio State University Press.

G

GANNETT CO., INC. v. DEPASQUALE

443 U.S. 368 (1978)

In *Gannett* the trial judge excluded the public, including the press, from a pretrial hearing involving evidence of an involuntary confession in a highly publicized murder case. The Supreme Court rejected arguments that the Sixth Amendment provided a constitutional public right to attend criminal trials. Reasoning that the constitutional guarantee of a public trial is designed to benefit the defendant, not the public, the Court concluded that where the litigants agree to close a pretrial proceeding to protect the defendant's right to a fair trial, the Constitution does not require that it remain open to the public. The Court declined to address the corollary issue whether the First Amendment created a right of access to the press to attend criminal trials—a question later answered affirmatively in *Richmond Newspapers, Inc.* v. *Virginia* (1980).

Justice Lewis F. Powell, concurring, conceded that the press had an interest, protected by the First Amendment, in being present at the pretrial hearing, but said that this interest should be balanced against the defendant's right to a fair trial. The order excluding the press from attending the pretrial hearing in *Gannett* was distinguished from the gag order in *Nebraska Press Association* v. *Stuart* (1976) because the press was merely excluded from one source of information; it was not told what it might or might not publish.

Justice Harry A. Blackmun, joined by Justices William J. Brennan, Byron R. White, and Thurgood Marshall, also framed the issue as one of access to the judicial proceeding, not one of prior restraint on the press. Blackmun, upon a lengthy historical examination, concluded that the criminally accused did not have a right to compel a private pretrial proceeding or trial. Only in certain circumstances, with appropriate procedural safeguards, might a court give effect to the accused's attempts to waive the right to a public trial.

—KIM MCLANE WARDLAW

GARCIA v. SAN ANTONIO METROPOLITAN TRANSIT AUTHORITY

469 U.S. 528 (1985)

In *National League of Cities* v. *Usery* (1976) a 5–4 majority of the Supreme Court sought to establish a new doctrinal foundation for the concept of states' rights. Overruling its eight-year-old precedent in *Maryland* v. *Wirtz* (1968), the Court held unconstitutional the application of the wage and hour provisions of the federal Fair Labor Standards Act to state and local government employees in areas of "traditional governmental functions" such as police and fire protection. After eight more years, *Garcia* followed *Wirtz* and overruled *Usery*—again by a 5–4 vote. Justice Harry A. Blackmun, whose change of vote produced this second about-face, wrote the opinion of the Court.

Lower court decisions following *Usery*, said Justice Blackmun, had failed to establish

In Gannett *the trial judge excluded the public, including the press, from a pretrial hearing in a highly publicized murder case.*

See also

Free Press/Fair Trial

Nebraska Press Association v. *Stuart*

Richmond Newspapers, Inc. v. *Virginia*

*The most maligned
aspect of the Garcia
opinion was its
announcement of
the Court's virtual
abdication from
judicial review of
acts of Congress.*

♦ **stare decisis**
*[Latin: to stand by what
has been decided] A
doctrine requiring that
courts, in deciding cases,
should adhere to the
principles of law
established in prior cases,
called precedents.*

See also

National League of Cities v.

Usery

any principle for determining which governmental functions were "traditional" and essential to state sovereignty, and thus immune from impairment by congressional regulations. Justice Blackmun did not mention his own contribution to the confusion, first in his *Usery* concurrence, which suggested that the reach of Congress's power depended on the importance of the national interests at stake, and later in his votes to uphold congressional power in cases only doubtfully distinguishable from *Usery*, such as *Federal Regulatory Commission* v. *Mississippi* (1982) and *Equal Employment Opportunity Commission* v. *Wyoming* (1983). The reasoning in those opinions—heatedly disputed by the four *Garcia* dissenters—had sapped *Usery*'s strength as a precedent by making the states pass through a doctrinal labyrinth before *Usery* could be applied.

The aspect of the *Garcia* opinion that drew the most fire, from within the Court and from the outside, was its announcement of the Court's virtual abdication from judicial review of acts of Congress challenged as invasions of state sovereignty. The principal remedy for such potential abuses of congressional power, said Justice Blackmun, is not judicial but political. The constitutional structure assures the states a significant role in the selection of the national government; the influence of the states was demonstrated in the federal government's financial aid to the states and in the numerous exemptions for state activities provided in congressional regulations. The Court's abdication was not complete; Justice Blackmun acknowledged that some "affirmative limits . . . on federal action affecting the States" may remain. Yet he explicitly left to another day the specification of what those limits might be.

Justice Lewis F. Powell wrote the main opinion for the four dissenters. He began with a lament for the demise of stare decisis—which he had not mourned when *Usery* overruled *Wirtz*. The *Usery* principle had been "reiterated consistently over the past

eight years," he said—not mentioning that those same opinions uniformly had sustained congressional regulations against challenges founded on *Usery*. Justice Powell argued that the majority had abandoned the federalism envisioned by the Framers, leaving the states' role to "the grace of elected federal officials." In any event, he contended, the "political safeguards of federalism" are not what they used to be. Congressional regulatory techniques have changed, increasingly displacing or commandeering the states' sovereign functions. Furthermore, although the people of the states are represented in the federal government, the state governments as institutions are apt to have little influence on national decision making, in comparison with nationwide interest groups.

Some of the dissenters left no doubt that they expect the *Usery* principle to return when members of the *Garcia* majority are replaced by new Justices more attuned to the symbolism of states' rights. But symbolism may be all that is left of that once vital principle, whatever the future may hold for the *Garcia* precedent. First, Congress can dragoon the state into its regulatory schemes as it did in *Hodel* v. *Virginia Surface Mining and Reclamation Association* (1981): regulating private conduct directly, but allowing a state to opt out of the federal regulation by adopting its own law under federal guidelines. Furthermore, if Congress wants to buy state sovereignty, it will find willing sellers. By placing conditions on federal grants-in-aid—which now amount to about one-fifth of state budgets—Congress can achieve through the spending power virtually anything it might achieve by direct regulation.

However, since *Garcia* the Court has made clear that the Tenth Amendment, protecting states' rights, still bars Congress from "commandeering" the states' police powers through federal fiat. In *New York* v. *United States* (1992) the Court held Congress could not direct the states to control nuclear waste by compelling the states to take title to, and assume liability for, nuclear waste that the states failed to regulate. This law, unlike the one in *Garcia*, applied to the states alone, not to private industry or municipalities.

Even if *Garcia* should be overruled and *Usery* reinstated, Congress can offer subsidies that are vital to local transit authorities or police departments, conditioned on promises to pay transit and police employees the federal minimum wage. The passion of the Justices on both sides may indicate that in these cases the symbolism is what counts.

—KENNETH L. KARST

Bibliography

Field, Martha A. (1985). *Garcia* v. *San Antonio Metropolitan Transit Authority:* The Demise of a Misguided Doctrine. *Harvard Law Review* 99:84–118.

Van Alstyne, William W. (1985). The Second Death of Federalism. *Michigan Law Review* 83:1709–1733.

GAULT, IN RE

387 U.S. 1 (1967)

In re Gault is the Supreme Court's most important landmark concerning juveniles, both because of its specific requirements for delinquency proceedings and because of its unequivocal declaration of the broad principle that young persons, as individuals, have constitutional rights of their own. Rejecting the informality that had long characterized state juvenile courts, the Supreme Court held that due process of law required four procedural safeguards in the adjudicatory (or guilt-determining) phase of delinquency proceedings: adequate written notice to the juvenile and his parents of the specific charges; notification of the right to counsel, with appointed counsel for those who lack the means to retain a lawyer; the right of confrontation and cross-examination of witnesses; and the notification of the right against self-incrimination. For the

first time the Supreme Court declared boldly, in a seminal opinion by Justice Abe Fortas, that "whatever may be their precise impact, neither the Fourteenth Amendment nor the Bill of Rights is for adults alone."

The facts of the case dramatically suggested the risks of procedural informality and "unbridled discretion," which the Court saw as a poor substitute for "principle and procedure." Fifteen-year-old Gerald Gault was found to be a delinquent and was committed for up to six years to the Arizona Industrial School for an offense that would have subjected an adult to a small fine and no more than two months' imprisonment. Neither Gerald nor his parents were ever served with a petition that disclosed the factual basis of the juvenile court proceedings. It was claimed that Gerald and a friend had made an obscene telephone call to a neighbor who never appeared in the proceedings. Although the judge subsequently reported that Gerald had made some sort of admission to him, no transcript was made of what was said at either of Gerald's two appearances before the judge, nor was Gerald offered counsel.

Although a few states had anticipated the Court's rulings in *Gault* by adopting new juvenile justice acts that provided greater safeguards, procedural informality had characterized most juvenile courts since their creation around 1900. This was typically justified on two interrelated grounds. First, the goal of juvenile proceedings was said to be treatment and rehabilitation, not punishment or deterrence. Second, investigation, diagnosis, and treatment required individualized determinations of what was best for each particular child. Legalistic formalities were seen as inconsistent and counterproductive in a benevolent and paternalistic institution committed to the rehabilitative ideal. State courts had refused to impose safeguards that "restrict the state when it seeks to deprive a person of his liberty," typically with conclusory statements that minors had no interest in liberty (because they would be subject in all events to

In re Gault *is the Supreme Court's most important landmark concerning juveniles.*

parental control) or that delinquency proceedings were civil, rather than criminal, because their purpose was not punitive.

Gault rejected these traditional justifications. Pointing to various empirical studies, the *Gault* majority challenged the rehabilitative effectiveness of the juvenile justice system by suggesting that juvenile crime had increased since the establishment of the juvenile courts; questioned the value of procedural informality as a means to shape desirable attitudes about justice in the young people caught up by the system; and disparaged the significance, in terms of loss of liberty, of the difference between detention in a "home" or "school" after a finding of delinquency and incarceration after conviction of a crime. The strength of much of the social science evidence cited by the Court has been subsequently challenged, but the Court's willingness to attach substantial weight to the interest of a young person in avoiding the serious practical consequences of an erroneous determination of delinquency is certainly justified.

The Court did not suggest in *Gault* or in its subsequent decisions that the Constitution requires the state to treat a juvenile accused of delinquency in all respects like an adult accused of a similar act. The Court has extended other procedural safeguards to juveniles in delinquency proceedings—in *In re Winship* (1970) it required proof beyond a reasonable doubt, for example, and in *Breed* v. *Jones* (1975) it held that the prohibition against double jeopardy applied—but it has refused, as in *McKeiver* v. *Pennsylvania* (1971), to require trial by jury in delinquency proceedings. Although the traditional goals of the juvenile courts do not justify the absence of certain safeguards, *Gault* and its progeny suggest that the Constitution does not require abolition of the separate juvenile court system with some distinctive procedural features. Nor does *Gault* require the states to impose identical sanctions on minors and adults after a determination that a criminal statute has been violated. Indeed, by emphasizing that the proce-

dural requirements extended only to the adjudicatory phase, and not to the dispositional phase, of delinquency proceedings, the Court in *Gault* argued that its decision did not threaten the emphasis juvenile courts have traditionally claimed to place on individualized treatment and rehabilitation.

—ROBERT H. MNOOKIN

Bibliography

Stapleton, W. Vaughan, and Teitelbaum, Lee E. (1972). *In Defense of Youth: A Study of the Role of Counsel in American Juvenile Courts.* New York: Russell Sage Foundation.

GERTZ v. ROBERT WELCH, INC.

418 U.S. 323 (1974)

In this major case on libel and the First Amendment, the Supreme Court in an opinion by Justice Lewis F. Powell held, 5–4, that the rule of *New York Times* v. *Sullivan* (1964) did not apply when the party seeking damages for libel is not a public official or a public figure. *New York Times* had applied the rule of "actual malice": the First Amendment bars a public official from recovering damages for a defamatory falsehood relating to his conduct in office unless he proves that the publisher or broadcaster made the statement knowing it to be false or "with reckless disregard of whether it was false or not." The Court had extended that rule in 1967 to public figures. In *Rosenbloom* v. *Metromedia, Inc.* (1971) a plurality ruled that if the defamation concerned a public issue the actual malice rule extended also to private individuals, who were not public figures. In *Gertz* the Court, abandoning that rule, held that a private plantiff had to prove actual malice only if seeking punitive damages; the First Amendment did not require him to produce such proof merely to recover actual damages for injury to reputation.

Powell reasoned that public officers and public figures had a far greater opportunity to counteract false statements than private persons. Moreover, an official or a candidate for public office knowingly exposes himself to close public scrutiny and criticism, just as public figures knowingly invite attention and comment. The communications media cannot, however, assume that private persons similarly expose themselves to defamation. Powell declared that they "are not only more vulnerable to injury than public officials and public figures; they are also more deserving of recovery." Their only effective redress is resort to a state's libel laws. So long as a state does not permit the press or a broadcaster to be held liable without fault and applies the actual malice rule to requests for punitive damages, the Court held that the First Amendment requires a "less demanding showing than that required by *New York Times*" and that the states may decide for themselves the appropriate standard of liability for media defendants who defame private persons.

Each of the dissenting Justices wrote a separate opinion. The dissents covered a wide spectrum from greater concern for the defamed party to alarm about the majority's supposedly constrictive interpretation of the First Amendment. Chief Justice Warren E. Burger worried that the party libeled in this case was a lawyer who ought not to be invidiously identified with his client. Justice William O. Douglas thought all libel laws to be unconstitutional. Justice William J. Brennan preferred the actual malice test to be applied to private individuals in matters of public concern. Justice Byron R. White, opposing the Court's restriction of the common law of libels, condemned the nationalization of so large a part of libel law.

—LEONARD W. LEVY

GIBBONS v. OGDEN

9 Wheaton 1 (1824)

Chief Justice John Marshall's great disquisition on the commerce clause in this case is the most influential in our history. *Gibbons* liberated the steamship business and much of American interstate commerce from the grip of state-created monopolies. More important, Marshall laid the doctrinal basis for the national regulation of the economy that occurred generations later, though at the time his opinion buttressed laissez-faire. He composed that opinion as if statecraft in the interpretation of a constitutional clause could decide whether the United States remained just a federal union or became a nation. The New York act, which the Court voided in *Gibbons,* had closed the ports of the state to steamships not owned or licensed by a monopoly chartered by the state. Other states retaliated in kind. The attorney general of the United States told the *Gibbons* Court that the country faced a commercial "civil war."

The decision produced immediate and dramatic results. Within two weeks, a newspaper jubilantly reported: "Yesterday the Steamboat *United States,* Capt. Bunker, from New Haven, entered New York in triumph, with streamers flying, and a large company of passengers exulting in the decision of the United States Supreme Court against the New York monopoly. She fired a salute which was loudly returned by huzzas from the wharves." Senator Martin Van Buren (Democrat, New York), who had recently advocated curbing the Court, declared that even those states whose laws had been nullified, including his own, "have submitted to their fate," and the Court now justly attracted "idolatry," its Chief respected as "the ablest Judge now sitting upon any judicial bench in the world." For a Court that had been under vitriolic congressional and state attack, *Gibbons* wedded a novel popularity to its nationalism.

One of the ablest judges who ever sat on an American court, James Kent of New York, whose opinion Marshall repudiated, grumbled in the pages of his *Commentaries on American Law* (1826) that Marshall's "language was too general and comprehensive for the case." Kent was right. The Court held

The dissents covered a wide spectrum from greater concern for the defamed party to alarm about the majority's supposedly constrictive interpretation of the First Amendment.

See also

New York Times v. *Sullivan*

Chief Justice John Marshall's great disquisition on the commerce clause in this case is the most influential in our history.

the state act unconstitutional for conflicting with an act of Congress, making Marshall's enduring treatise on the commerce clause unnecessary for the disposition of the case. The conflict between the two statutes, Marshall said, "decides the cause." Kent was also right in stating that "it never occurred to anyone," least of all to the Congress that had passed the Coastal Licensing Act of 1793, which Marshall used to decide the case, that the act could justify national supremacy over state regulations respecting "internal waters or commerce." The act of 1793 had been intended to discriminate against foreign vessels in the American coastal trade by offering preferential tonnage duties to vessels of American registry. Marshall's construction of the statute conformed to his usual tactic of finding narrow grounds for decision after making a grand exposition. He announced "propositions which may have been thought axioms." He "assume[d] nothing," he said, because of the magnitude of the question, the distinction of the judge (Kent) whose opinion he scrapped, and the able arguments, which he rejected, by Thomas Emmett and Thomas Oakely, covering over 125 pages in the report of the case.

Except for the arguments of counsel, the Court had little for guidance. It had never before decided a commerce clause case, and the clause itself is general: "Congress shall have power to regulate commerce with foreign nations and among the several states. . . ." The power to regulate what would later be called "interstate commerce" appears in the same clause touching foreign commerce, the regulation of which is necessarily exclusive, beyond state control. But the clause does not negate state regulatory authority over interstate commerce, and the framers of the Constitution had rejected proposals for a sole or exclusive power in Congress. Interstate commerce could be, as counsel for the monopoly contended, a subject of concurrent power. Marshall had previously acknowledged that although the Constitution vested in Congress

bankruptcy and tax powers, the states retained similar powers. *The Federalist* #32 recognized the principle of concurrent powers but offered no assistance on the commerce clause. Congress had scarcely used the commerce power except for the Embargo Acts, which had not come before the Supreme Court. Those acts had interpreted the power to "regulate" as a power to prohibit, but they concerned commerce with foreign nations and were an instrument of foreign policy.

Prior to *Gibbons* the prevailing view on the interstate commerce power was narrow and crossed party lines. Kent, a Federalist, differed little from the Jeffersonians. James Madison, for example, when vetoing a congressional appropriation for internal improvements, had declared in 1817 that "the power to regulate commerce among the several states cannot include a power to construct roads and canals, and to improve the navigation of water courses." In 1821, when James Monroe had vetoed the Cumberland Road Bill, whose objective was to extend national authority to turnpikes within the states, he had virtually reduced the commerce power to the enactment of duties and imports, adding that goods and vessels are the only subjects of commerce that Congress can regulate. "Commerce," in common usage at the time of *Gibbons,* meant trade in the buying and selling of commodities, not navigation or the transportation of passengers for hire. That was the business of Mr. Gibbons, who operated a steamship in defiance of the monopoly, between Elizabethtown, New Jersey, and New York City, in direct competition with Ogden, a licensee of the monopoly. Had Gibbons operated under sail, he would not have violated New York law; as it was, the state condemned his vessel to fines and forfeiture.

In *Gibbons,* then, the Court confronted a stunted concept of commerce, a strict construction of the commerce power, and an opinion bearing Kent's authority that New York had regulated only "internal" commerce. Kent had also held that the commerce power was a concurrent one and that the test for the constitutionality of a state act should be practical: Could the state and national laws coexist without conflicting in their operation? Marshall "assumed nothing" and in his step-by-step "axioms" repudiated any argument based on such premises.

He began with a definition of "commerce." It comprehended navigation as well as buying and selling, because "it is intercourse." This sweeping definition prompted a disgruntled states-rightist to remark, "I shall soon expect to learn that our fornication laws are unconstitutional." That same definition later constitutionally supported an undreamed of expansion of congressional power over the life of the nation's economy. Having defined commerce as every species of commercial intercourse, Marshall, still all-embracing, defined "commerce among the several states" to mean commerce intermingled with or concerning two or more states. Such commerce "cannot stop at the external boundary line of each State, but may be introduced into the interior"—and wherever it went, the power of the United States followed. Marshall did not dispute Kent's view that the "completely internal commerce" of a state (what we call intrastate commerce) is reserved for state governance. But that governance extended only to such commerce as was completely within one state, did not "affect" other states, "and with which it is not necessary to interfere, for the purpose of executing some of the general powers of the [United States] government." Marshall's breathtaking exposition of the national commerce power foreshadowed the stream of commerce doctrine and the Shreveport Doctrine of the next century. "If Congress has the power to regulate it," he added, "that power must be exercised whenever the subject exists. If it exists within the States . . . then the power of Congress may be exercised within a State."

Having so defined the reach of the commerce power, Marshall, parsing the clause, defined the power to "regulate" as the power "to prescribe the rule by which commerce is to be governed." It is a power that "may be exercised to its utmost extent, and acknowledges no limitations. . . ." In *Cohens* v. *Virginia* (1821) he had said that the United States form, for most purposes, one nation: "In war, we are one people. In making peace, we are one people. In all commercial regulations, we are one and the same people," and the government managing that people's interests was the government of the Union. In *Gibbons* he added that because the "sovereignty of Congress" is plenary as to its objects, "the power over commerce with foreign nations, and among the several states, is vested in Congress as absolutely as it would be in a single government. . . ." Were that true, the commerce power would be as exclusive as the treaty power or war powers and could not be shared concurrently with the states.

Marshall expressly denied that the states possessed a concurrent commerce power; yet he did not expressly declare that Congress possessed an exclusive commerce power, which would prevent the states from exercising a commerce power even in the absence of congressional legislation. That was Daniel Webster's argument in *Gibbons*, against the monopoly, and Marshall found "great force" in it. Notwithstanding the ambiguity in Marshall's opinion, he implicitly adopted Webster's argument by repeatedly rejecting the theory of concurrent commerce powers. He conceded, however, that the states can reach and regulate some of the same subjects of commerce as Congress, but only by the exercise of powers distinct from an interstate commerce power. Referring to the mass of state regulatory legislation that encompassed inspection laws, health laws, turnpike laws, ferry laws, "etc.," Marshall labeled them the state's "system of police," later called the police power. But his jurisprudence-by-label did not distinguish interstate from intrastate commerce powers. Having declared that Congress might regulate a state's "internal" commerce to effectuate a national policy, he

allowed the state police power to operate on subjects of interstate commerce, in subordination, of course, to the principle of national supremacy.

Following his treatise on the commerce clause, Marshall turned to the dispositive question whether the New York monopoly act conflicted with an act of Congress. The pertinent act of 1793 referred to American vessels employed in the "coasting trade." It made no exception for steamships or for vessels that merely transported passengers. The New York act was therefore "in direct collision" with the act of Congress by prohibiting Gibbons's steamship from carrying passengers in and out of the state's ports without a license from the monopoly.

Justice William Johnson, although an appointee of Thomas Jefferson, was even more nationalistic than Marshall. Webster later boasted that Marshall had taken to his argument as a baby to its mother's milk, but the remark better suited Johnson. Concurring separately, he declared that the commerce clause vested a power in Congress that "must be exclusive." He would have voided the state monopoly act even in the absence of the Federal Coastal Licensing Act: "I cannot overcome the conviction, that if the licensing act was repealed tomorrow, the rights of the appellant to a reversal of the decision complained of, would be as strong as it is under this license." Johnson distinguished the police power laws that operated on subjects of interstate commerce; their "different purposes," he claimed, made all the difference. In fact, the purpose underlying the monopoly act was the legitimate state purpose of encouraging new inventions.

In a case of first impression, neither Marshall nor Johnson could lay down doctrines that settled all conflicts between state and national powers relating to commerce. Not until 1851 did the Court, after much groping, seize upon the doctrine of selective exclusiveness, which seemed at the time like a litmus paper test. Yet *Gibbons* anticipated doctrines

concerning the breadth of congressional power that emerged in the next century and still govern. Marshall was as prescient as human ability allows. The Court today cannot construe the commerce clause except in certain state regulation cases without being influenced by Marshall's treatise on it. "At the beginning," Justice Robert Jackson declared in *Wickard* v. *Filburn* (1941), "Chief Justice Marshall described the federal commerce power with a breadth never exceeded."

—LEONARD W. LEVY

Bibliography

Baxter, Maurice G. (1972). *The Steamboat Monopoly:* Gibbons v. Ogden, *1824.* New York: Knopf.

Beveridge, Albert J. (1916–1919). *The Life of John Marshall.* 4 vols. Vol. 4:397–460. Boston: Houghton Mifflin.

Frankfurter, Felix (1937). *The Commerce Clause under Marshall, Taney and Waite.* Pages 1–45. Chapel Hill: University of North Carolina Press.

GIDEON v. WAINWRIGHT

372 U.S. 335 (1963)

From time to time in constitutional history an obscure individual becomes the symbol of a great movement in legal doctrine. Character and circumstance illuminate a new understanding of the Constitution. So it was in the case of Clarence Earl Gideon.

Gideon was a drifter and petty thief who had served four prison terms when, in 1961, he was charged with breaking and entering the Bay Harbor Poolroom in Panama City, Florida, and stealing a pint of wine and some coins from a cigarette machine. At the age of fifty he had the look of defeat: a gaunt wrinkled face, white hair, a trembling voice. But inside there was still passion—a concern for

See also

Cohens v. *Virginia*

Wickard v. *Filburn*

justice that approached obsession. Through it, in a manner of speaking, Gideon changed the Constitution.

When he went to trial in the Circuit Court of Bay County, Florida, on August 4, 1961, he asked the judge to appoint a lawyer for him because he was too poor to hire one himself. The judge said he was sorry but he could not do that, because the laws of Florida called for appointment of counsel only when a defendant was charged with a capital offense. Gideon said: "The United States Supreme Court says I am entitled to be represented by counsel." When the Florida courts rejected that claim, he went on to the Supreme Court. From prison he submitted a petition, handwritten in pencil, arguing that Florida had ignored a rule laid down by the Supreme Court: "that all citizens tried for a felony crime should have aid of counsel."

Gideon was wrong. The rule applied by the Supreme Court at that time was in fact exactly the opposite. The Constitution, it had held, did *not* guarantee free counsel to all felony defendants unable to retain their own. That was the outcome—the bitterly debated outcome—of a line of cases on the right to counsel.

The Supreme Court first dealt with the issue in 1932, in the *Scottsboro Case, Powell* v. *Alabama*. Due process of law required at least a "hearing," Justice George H. Sutherland said, and the presence of counsel was "fundamental" to a meaningful hearing.

But Sutherland said that the Court was not deciding whether poor defendants had a right to free counsel in all circumstances, beyond the aggravated ones of this case: a capital charge, tried in haste and under public pressure.

In *Johnson* v. *Zerbst* (1938) the Court read the Sixth Amendment to require the appointment of counsel for all indigent *federal* criminal defendants. But in *Betts* v. *Brady* (1942), when considering the right of poor *state* defendants to free counsel in noncapital cases, the Court came out the other way. Jus-

tice Owen J. Roberts said that "the states should not be straitjacketed" by a uniform constitutional rule. Only when particular circumstances showed that want of counsel denied fundamental fairness, he said, were such convictions invalid.

For twenty years the rule of *Betts* v. *Brady* applied. Counsel was said to be required only when a defendant suffered from "special circumstances" of disability: illiteracy, youth, mental illness, the complexity of the charges. But during that period criticism of the case mounted. No one could tell, it was said, when the Constitution required counsel. More and more often, too, the Supreme Court found "special circumstances" to require counsel.

That was the situation when Clarence Earl Gideon's petition reached the Court. The Justices seized on the occasion to think again about the Constitution and the right to counsel. Granting review, the Court ordered counsel to discuss: "Should this Court's holding in *Betts* v. *Brady* be reconsidered?" And

HE CHANGED THE CONSTITUTION

Petty thief Clarence Earl Gideon won the right to counsel for any citizen tried for a felony crime. (Corbis/Bettmann)

*To what extent does
a minor's own First
Amendment rights
constrain the state's
power to limit a
minor's access to
written or pictorial
materials?*

See also

Powell v. *Alabama*

then it appointed to represent Gideon, who had had no lawyer at his trial, one of the ablest lawyers in Washington, Abe Fortas—later to sit on the Supreme Court himself.

On March 18, 1963, the Court overruled *Betts* v. *Brady.* Justice Hugo L. Black, who had dissented in *Betts,* wrote the opinion of the Court: a rare vindication of past dissent. He quoted Justice Sutherland's words on every man's need for the guiding hand of counsel at every step of the proceeding against him. "The right of one charged with crime to counsel may not be deemed fundamental and essential to fair trials in some countries," Justice Black said, "but it is in ours."

The decision in *Gideon* v. *Wainwright* was an important victory for one side in a general philosophical debate on the Court about whether constitutional protections should apply with the same vigor to state as to federal action: a victory for Justice Black over Justice Felix Frankfurter's more deferential view of state power. But on this particular issue changing ideas of due process would have led Justice Frankfurter in 1963 to impose a universal rule; retired and ill, he told a friend that he would have voted to overrule *Betts.* The case thus showed how time may bring a new consensus on the meaning of the Constitution.

And, not least, the *Gideon* case showed that the courts still respond to individuals in a society where most institutions of government seem remote and unresponsive. The least influential of men, riding a wave of legal history, persuaded the Supreme Court to reexamine a premise of justice. The case in fact represented more than an abstract principle. It was a victory for Clarence Earl Gideon. After the Supreme Court decision he was tried again in Bay County, Florida, this time with a lawyer—and the jury acquitted him. Gideon stayed out of prison until he died, on January 18, 1972.

—ANTHONY LEWIS

Bibliography

Lewis, Anthony (1964). *Gideon's Trumpet.* New York: Random House.

GINSBERG v. NEW YORK

390 U.S. 629 (1968)

In *Ginsberg* the Supreme Court upheld the validity under the First Amendment and Fourteenth Amendment of a New York criminal statute that prohibited the sale to persons under seventeen years of age of sexually explicit printed materials that would not be obscene for adults. Drawing upon the criteria suggested in *Roth* v. *United States* (1957) and *Memoirs* v. *Massachusetts* (1966), the New York statute broadly defined sexually explicit descriptions or representations as "harmful to minors" when the material: "(i) predominantly appeals to the prurient, shameful or morbid interest of minors, and (ii) is patently offensive to prevailing standards in the adult community as a whole with respect to what is suitable material for minors, and (iii) is utterly without redeeming social importance for minors." Convicted for selling two "girlie" magazines to a sixteen-year-old, Ginsberg claimed that the statute was unconstitutional because the state was without the power to deny persons younger than seventeen access to materials that were not obscene for adults. Justice William J. Brennan, for the 6–3 majority, rejected this challenge by introducing the concept of "variable obscenity." According to the majority, the New York statute had "simply adjust[ed] the definition of obscenity to social realities by permitting the appeal of this type of material to be assessed in terms of the sexual interests . . . of such minors."

Although the decision rests on the legitimacy of protecting children from harm, the Court found it unnecessary to decide whether persons under seventeen were caused harm by exposure to materials proscribed by the statute. After suggesting that scientific studies neither proved nor disproved a causal connection, the majority held that it was "not irrational" for the New York legislature to find that "exposure to material condemned by the statute is harmful to minors."

To what extent do a minor's own First Amendment rights constrain the state's power to limit a minor's access to written or pictorial materials? Because of the nature of Ginsberg's challenge to the statute, the Court did not concern itself with the question whether a minor might have the constitutional right to buy "girlie" magazines. In *Erznoznik* v. *Jacksonville* (1975) the Court later indicated that while the First Amendment rights of minors are not coextensive with those of adults, "minors are entitled to a significant measure of First Amendment protection" and that under the *Ginsberg* variable obscenity standard "all nudity" in films "cannot be deemed as obscene even as to minors."

—ROBERT H. MNOOKIN

GINSBURG, RUTH BADER

(1933–   )

Coming two years after the bitterly divisive Senate confirmation hearings for Justice Clarence Thomas, the 1993 nomination of Judge Ruth Bader Ginsburg to replace retiring Justice Byron R. White was to many a profound relief. Her selection by President Clinton was also a reassurance that nominations to the Supreme Court, while not without political considerations, can be relatively free of public turmoil, political dissent, or accusations of political gamesmanship. And in contrast with the earlier nomination, there was in Ginsburg's case not a whisper of doubt about the nominee's qualifications. When the president echoed Janet Benshoof, president of the Center for Reproductive Law and Policy, in hailing Ruth Bader Ginsburg as "the Thurgood Marshall of gender equality law," he was not exaggerating. Erwin Griswold, former solicitor general and dean of the Harvard Law School, had said essentially the same thing in a 1985 speech commemorating

the fiftieth anniversary of the Supreme Court building.

Ruth Joan Bader was born on March 15, 1933, in Brooklyn, New York, the second daughter of Nathan and Celia Amster Bader. Her parents were Jewish Americans whose own parents had emigrated from central Europe and from Russia. Ruth grew up an only child after an older sister named Marilyn died in childhood of meningitis.

Nathan Bader worked as a furrier and as a haberdasher, and owned several clothing stores. Celia Bader had been an impressive student in her own time; she graduated from high school at the age of fifteen with top grades. She would surely have excelled in college, but instead she went to work in the garment industry in New York, giving part of her wages to help her older brother pay for college. She did the same for her daughter, as she was determined that Ruth should have the opportunities she was not able to enjoy herself. Celia Bader was a loving and stimulating influence on her daughter, impressing on her the importance of learning and excellence. Mother and daughter frequented a public library located above a Chinese restaurant in Brooklyn, and to this day Justice Ginsburg associates the aromas of Chinese cuisine with the pleasures of reading.

It is not difficult to imagine that Ruth Bader was all the more driven to extraordinary achievement as a consequence of her mother's illness and early death. Early in Ginsberg's high school years, Celia Bader was diagnosed with stomach cancer; she died the day before her daughter's graduation. During her years at James Madison High in Brooklyn—a school that has been described as a melting pot of overachievers—Ruth Bader excelled in her studies, twirled the baton, and won scholarships that would permit her to attend college without depleting the college savings her mother had methodically set aside from her own earnings.

Ruth Bader attended Cornell University from 1951 to 1954. She was elected to the

FIGHTING FOR WOMEN'S RIGHTS

Only the second female to be sworn in as a Supreme Court Justice, Ruth Bader Ginsburg has been hailed as "the Thurgood Marshall of gender equality law." (Reuters/Corbis-Bettmann)

honorary society of Phi Beta Kappa and graduated first among the women in her class. While at Cornell, she met her future husband, Martin D. Ginsburg. They decided they would both pursue careers in the law, but in an early instance of what was to become a series of "role reversals," it was the woman who convinced the man to attend law school, for Ruth Bader had already decided *she* was going. The couple married in June 1954 after Bader graduated with a B.A. degree.

Soon after their marriage, Martin Ginsburg served a two-year stint in the army in Fort Sill, Oklahoma, and Ruth Ginsberg worked in a Social Security office. It was during this time that she became pregnant with their first child, Jane. She did not attempt to conceal her pregnancy and was thus demoted—her first encounter with the gender discriminations that Ginsberg later came to question.

After two years in Oklahoma, the Ginsburgs entered Harvard Law School, Martin

one year ahead of Ruth. She was one of nine women in her class, and one of two selected for the *Harvard Law Review*. Ginsberg was already caring for a young child and excelling in the most demanding law school in the country when her husband was diagnosed with cancer. While he underwent surgery and radiation treatments, she covered his classes as well as her own, and typed his third-year paper; an elderly woman helped by babysitting Jane.

Martin Ginsburg graduated and was offered a position with a New York law firm, so Ruth Ginsberg transferred to the Columbia Law School where she again made law review. "We had heard that the smartest person on the East Coast was going to transfer, and that we were all going to drop down one rank," recalls Nina Appel, a Columbia classmate who later became dean of Loyola Law School in Chicago. Ginsburg finished tied for first place in the class of 1959.

Finding work was a different matter. Of all the firms she applied to, only two invited her to visit, and neither offered her a job. "In the Fifties, the traditional law firms were just beginning to turn around on hiring Jews," she has written. "But to be a woman, a Jew and a mother to boot—that combination was a bit too much." Finally she was offered a job as clerk to Judge Edmund L. Palmieri of Federal District Court in Manhattan. Twenty years later he recalled her as among the best clerks who ever worked for him.

In 1963 Ginsburg joined the law faculty of Rutgers University in New Jersey, the second woman to do so. She had not been granted tenure when she became pregnant with her second child, James. She hid her pregnancy for as long as possible by dressing in oversized clothing, fearing similar consequences as during her first pregnancy, when she'd been demoted at the Social Security Administration as a result. It was around the late 1960s that Ginsburg read Simone de Beauvoir's *The Second Sex*, and began to recognize a larger societal pattern to the obstacles and discrimination she had faced as a second-class citizen.

She began assisting the New Jersey affiliate of the American Civil Liberties Union in cases involving women who had been forced to quit their jobs when they became pregnant. While preparing to litigate these cases and putting together a course on sex-based discrimination, Ginsburg was surprised to discover how little literature existed on the subject. In the 1960s, although racial discrimination was increasingly viewed as an intolerable injustice requiring immediate correction, discrimination on the basis of sex was not regarded as a problem. Ginsburg has said that the few gender discrimination complaints that did trickle in to the ACLU were seen as "women's work." In time, she later recalled, "I began to wonder: 'How have people been putting up with such arbitrary distinctions? How have I been putting up with them?'"

Ginsburg came to understand that the most effective approach to battling gender discrimination would be a long-range, incremental strategy, like that used by Thurgood Marshall and partners in battling race discrimination in the 1940s and 1950s. Marshall began not with challenges to segregation in public elementary schools but in professional schools, where judges would more likely sympathize with the plaintiffs. As Ginsburg has explained it, "The courts needed to be educated. That requires patience: it may mean holding back a case until the way has been paved for it." Ginsburg believed that the efforts against gender discrimination would only succeed if the Court could be convinced of the need to apply a heightened standard of judicial scrutiny to gender-based legal distinctions; this "heightened sensitivity" did not come quickly.

A former colleague from the ACLU, Kathleen Peratis, testified at Ginsburg's Senate nomination hearings, "She insisted that we try to develop the law one step at a time. Present the Court with the next logical step . . . and then the next and then the next. Don't ask them to go too far too fast, or you'll lose what you might have won."

In 1971, while still teaching at Rutgers, Ginsburg founded the Women's Rights Project of the American Civil Liberties Union, where she supervised the selection of cases and the writing of briefs. From this position, she argued six gender discrimination cases before the Supreme Court. She chose the cases carefully, and of the six she won five. Ginsburg's strategy involved advocating for cases that could demonstrate to the Court that legislation ostensibly designed to protect women often harms them instead, and often men as well.

A dinner guest from around this time recalled a man at the table remarking once on Ginsburg's work for women's liberation. "She turned on him and said 'It is not *women's* liberation; it is women's *and men's* liberation.'" Ginsburg was normally calm and not particularly expressive, but this guest recalled, "I'd

Ginsburg came to understand that the most effective approach to battling gender discrimination would be a long-range, incremental strategy.

never seen her exercise such strength and ve-
hemence before."

The first case Ginsburg argued and won
before the Supreme Court, in 1973, involved
a female Air Force lieutenant, Sharron Frontiero, and her husband, Joseph. The couple
were challenging a statute that said a married
serviceman could claim his wife as a dependent and qualify for better housing even if his
wife did not depend on his income, whereas
for a woman in the armed forces to qualify for
the extra housing allowance, she would have
to prove that her husband received more than
half of his support from her paycheck. Why
the difference? Ginsburg's argument demonstrated that such differential treatment both
assumed and ensured that women were in an
inferior position. The Justices ruled 8 to 1 in
Sharron Frontiero's favor.

In arguing ACLU cases before the
Supreme Court, it was part of Ginsburg's
strategy to represent some male plaintiffs
who had been affected in some adverse way
by legal distinctions based on sex, and she
urged the Court to establish a legal rule for
evaluating gender discrimination in a way
that could be applied to either sex. In *Weinberger* v. *Wiesenfeld* (1975) she argued for
equal treatment for a father, Stephen
Wiesenfeld, whose wife, the principal wage
earner in the family, had died in childbirth.
He wanted to stay home and care for their
infant son, and applied for survivor's benefits, which had always been called "mother's
benefits," but he was ruled ineligible based
on a provision in the Social Security Act.
Ginsburg pointed out that the wife had paid
her Social Security taxes at the same rate as a
man, yet was not given equal protection for
her family. The discrepancy resulted from
society's assumption that husbands are always the wage earners and wives always the
dependents. The Court unanimously ruled
the Social Security Act provision unconstitutional, though without giving the case the
heightened scrutiny Ginsburg hoped to inspire.

It was in *Craig* v. *Boren* (1976) that the
Court at last accepted Ginsburg's argument,
expressed in an amicus curiae brief, that legal
distinctions based on gender deserved a
heightened standard of judicial review. In this
case, the Court struck down an Oklahoma
statute requiring that men be at least twenty-
one to buy 3.2 percent beer, while women
could buy the same at the age of eighteen. In
its ruling, the Court created a category
known as "intermediate scrutiny," meaning
that states could not arbitrarily enact laws
that discriminated on the basis of sex, but
must show the distinction to be substantially
related to an important state interest. The effect of the Court's ruling in *Craig* v. *Boren* was
to make it more difficult for states to enact
laws based on sexual stereotype.

Justice (later Chief Justice) William H.
Rehnquist was on the Court during Ginsburg's arguments, and dissented from some of
the gender-discrimination decisions she won.
In one oral argument, Justice Rehnquist
asked, apparently without irony, why women
were not satisfied with their place in the
world now that the image of Susan B. Anthony had been minted on a silver dollar.
Ginsburg maintained her composure and
held her silence, though, as she later recalled,
she was tempted to reply, "No, Your Honor,
tokens won't do."

In 1972 Ginsburg left Rutgers for the Columbia Law School, where she became the
first woman to receive tenure. In 1980 President Jimmy Carter appointed her to the U.S.
Court of Appeals, District of Columbia Circuit, where she would serve until President
Clinton called her name in 1993. As they
moved from New York to Washington, Martin Ginsburg left his law school chair at Columbia to take a law professorship at Georgetown.

On the Court of Appeals Justice Ginsburg
showed some of the traits she has exhibited
throughout her career. She dissented from a
decision that denied nuclear information
sought by a public-interest group under the

Freedom of Information Act in *Critical Mass Energy Project* v. *Nuclear Regulatory Commission* (1992). She deferred to the discretion of government agencies in a large number of cases reviewing agencies' rules and decisions, a steady diet of the D.C. Circuit Court of Appeals. She took a narrow view of citizens' standing to challenge agency decision-making.

After Justice Byron R. White announced his retirement in May 1993, Senator Daniel Patrick Moynihan (D-N.Y.) spoke to President Clinton during a flight aboard Air Force One from Washington to New York. Although Moynihan did not know Ginsburg personally, he had admired some of her writings and was aware of her excellent reputation. He was impressed by her pioneering work against gender discrimination and her judicial opinion that courts must respect the views of legislatures. After he spoke so convincingly, Moynihan was later appointed by the White House to shepherd Ginsburg's nomination in the Senate.

When Clinton nominated her to the Supreme Court, not all reaction was favorable. Ginsburg had attracted the attention of some feminists and abortion rights activists by her public criticism of the grounds on which *Roe* v. *Wade* was argued and won. In a lecture at the New York University Law School earlier in 1993, Ginsburg had asserted, as she had written before, that the right to abortion granted in *Roe* might have been more secure if it had been argued on grounds of women's right to equality, rather than on the right to privacy. "The *Roe* decision might have been less of a storm center," she said, if it had "homed in more precisely on the women's-equality dimension of the issue." Indeed, the equality argument had been included in the presentation to the Court in *Roe* v. *Wade*, but Blackmun's majority opinion was based on privacy issues.

The second point in Ginsburg's critique of *Roe*, regarding the scope of the decision, is the one that most disturbs abortion rights de-

fenders. Had the Court simply struck down the restrictive Texas law forbidding Jane Roe's abortion, she argued, that would have been a good initial step, and later cases could have been argued from that precedent. (Stopping here would show judicial restraint.) Instead, the Court issued a broad ruling that invalidated the abortion laws in most states, and it devised a trimester formula that prescribed to all fifty states how to govern abortion restrictions. In Ginsburg's view, the Court went too far, inviting a backlash that short-circuited a liberal trend that was just then getting under way in the early 1970s. Further, making the decision on these bases may have set a more vulnerable precedent than might otherwise have been the case. "Measured motions seem to me right, in the main, for constitutional as well as common-law adjudication," she said in her NYU address. "Doctrinal limbs too swiftly shaped, experience teaches, may prove unstable." In fact, although the Court has adhered to the holding in *Roe* that the states may not unduly burden a woman's ability to obtain an abortion, it did, in *Planned Parenthood of Southeastern Pennsylvania* v. *Casey*, ultimately abandon *Roe*'s trimester formula.

While some may have doubted her reliability as a defender of hard-won abortion rights, Ginsburg's comments during the confirmation hearings made her position on reproductive rights quite clear. She said that a woman's right to choose abortion is "something central to a woman's life, to her dignity. . . . And when government controls that decision for her, she's being treated as less than a full adult human being responsible for her own choices." Also unambiguous is a passage from an article on *Roe* that Ginsburg published in the *North Carolina Law Review* in 1985: "In the balance is a woman's autonomy of her full life's course . . . her ability to stand in relation to man, society, and the state as an independent sustaining equal citizen."

Ruth Bader Ginsburg was confirmed by a Senate vote of 97 to 3.

Justice Ginsburg reaffirmed her commitment to eradicating gender discrimination, writing the opinion of the Court in *United States* v. *Virginia* (1996), the historic decision that halted the century-old all-male admission policy at Virginia Military Institute (VMI). VMI, a bastion of gender discrimination operated by the state of Virginia, had maintained that admitting women would downgrade its stature and destroy the "adversative" system it used to instill self-discipline in its cadets. Justice Ginsburg sensibly dismissed these claims as "hardly different from other 'self-fulfilling prophecies' once routinely used to deny rights or opportunities." She noted, relying on language in *Mississippi University for Women* v. *Hogan*, that states must show "exceedingly persuasive justification" for gender-based discrimination.

Ginsburg went on to reject Virginia's argument that a jury-rigged program for women cadets at Mary Baldwin College would substitute for equal admission at VMI. As she pointed out, Mary Baldwin, a small private college, lacked VMI's prestige and alumni network, and offered far fewer academic choices. She aptly compared this proposal to earlier attempts by Southern states to avoid racial desegregation at state universities by offering inferior, hastily contrived alternatives for African Americans, as in *Sweatt* v. *Painter*.

Again, in *M.L.B.* v. *S.L.J.* (1996), Justice Ginsburg showed her abiding concern for women's rights. Writing for the Court, she held Mississippi was constitutionally obligated to furnish a free trial transcript to an indigent mother appealing a court order that found her an unfit parent. Earlier cases stemming from *Griffin* v. *Illinois* (1956) had held the Equal Protection Clause required the states to provide a trial transcript without charge to needy appellants in criminal cases. In *M.L.B.* Ginsburg extended this right to a civil appeal from an order depriving a mother of her child. She held these state "intrusions on family relationships" were more comparable to a criminal conviction in their impact than to routine civil litigation (where the Court had rejected claims of entitlement to a free transcript).

Justice Ginsburg wrote the majority opinion in *Chandler* v. *Miller* (1997), holding Georgia could not require candidates for public office to submit to drug testing. She ruled the state law "does not fit within the closely guarded category of constitutionally permissible suspicionless searches," and distinguished earlier decisions upholding drug testing of high school athletes and of railroad crews after serious accidents.

New Republic legal editor Jeffrey Rosen wrote in the *New York Times Magazine* (Oct. 5, 1997) that in Ginsburg's four years on the Court, she has shown the same qualities of judicial restraint that characterized her thirteen years on the court of appeals: "an affinity for resolving cases on narrow procedural grounds rather than appealing to broad principles of social justice; a preference for small steps over sweeping gestures, and an aversion to bold assertions of judicial power."

Ginsburg is widely described as not having a particular philosophy or ideology that would dictate her decisions, but a sensibility or manner of analysis that is careful, precise, and finely attuned to procedure. In the 1950s she studied under Professor Herbert Wechsler—coauthor of the great casebook on the jurisdiction of Federal court—who taught that the best way for attorneys to pursue the ideal of neutrality is by focusing on procedural questions. Peter Huber, a former Ginsburg clerk, says, "It is an extremely revealing fact about Ruth Ginsburg that she taught civil procedure for seventeen years." Because of what Huber calls her "almost Talmudic reverence and respect for the process of law," Ginsburg is "the most apolitical liberal you can be."

She tends not to reach farther than a case warrants, and her opinions are carefully worded. Her dissent in *Agostini* v. *Felton* provides a vivid example of her great concern with procedural correctness. *Agostini* involved separation of church and state: Was it constitutional for New York City public-school teachers to go into parochial schools to teach remedial programs? In her majority opinion, Justice Sandra Day O'Connor over-ruled a 1985 ruling (*Aguilar* v. *Felton*), and wrote that there was no need to fear that public-school teachers would "inculcate religion simply because they happen to be in a sectarian environment." The earlier decision, the Court held, had been undermined by later cases. Ginsburg was in the minority, along with Justices Breyer, Stevens, and Souter. In her dissent, rather than focusing on the constitutional meaning of the First Amendment, Ginsburg wrote that Justice O'Connor had misinterpreted Rule 60(b) of the Federal Rules of Civil Procedure, which permits courts to "relieve a party . . . from a final judgement [that] is no longer equitable. . . ." In her view, that rule was not intended to simply permit parties to relitigate cases because the legal precedents had shifted. It should, she wrote, be limited to situations where factual conditions have altered—and that was not the case here. Therefore the Court should not revisit the 1985 decision. She concluded that a proper reading of the rule "would lead us to defer reconsideration of *Aguilar* until we are presented with the issue in another case," in order to maintain the integrity of the procedural rule and avoid "invitations to reconsider old cases based on speculat[ion]."

Another instance of Justice Ginsburg's insistence on following proper procedure, even when it prevents the Court from reaching an important question, is her opinion denying review in a significant affirmative action case. In *Hopwood* v. *Texas* (1996) the United States Court of Appeals for the Fifth Circuit held the University of Texas Law School could not consider race in admitting students. This controversial ruling appeared to reject the Supreme Court's holding in *Regents of University of California* v. *Bakke* that race may be weighed as an element in admitting students, though it could not be the sole factor. Nonetheless, the Supreme Court turned down review of *Hopwood*. Though denials of review are usually ordered without a written opinion, Justice Ginsburg wrote here to explain that the denial was based on the case having become moot: the Law School had abandoned its policy and adopted a new one. Therefore, she stated, "We must await a final judgment on a program genuinely in controversy before addressing the important issues raised in this petition."

While one root of Ginsburg's judicial restraint is based on her respect for civil procedure, another is her particularism. She works by the specifics of a case rather than in obedience to an overarching judicial philosophy. As another former clerk, David Post, observes, "She narrows things down. She looks at a case and says, 'What's going on; why are they suing; who are the people; what's going on in the background?' She likes to look at larger questions through the lens of smaller stories of people's lives."

—PHILIP WEINBERG
AND MARK LAFLAUR

Bibliography

Cushman, Clare, ed. Ruth Bader Ginsburg. 1993– . *The Supreme Court Justices: Illustrated Biographies, 1789-1995.* 2nd ed. Washington, D.C.: Congressional Quarterly and The Supreme Court Historical Society.

Hill, Richard (1999). *Chandler* v. *Miller*: A New Standard for Evaluating State Statutes Requiring Disclosure of Information from Political Candidates. *George Mason Law Review* 7:453.

*This case
established the
eligibility of
conscientious
objectors to be
naturalized as
citizens of the
United States.*

GIROUARD v. UNITED STATES

328 U.S. 61 (1946)

An applicant for United States citizenship
declared that he could take the oath of allegiance ("support and defend the Constitution
and laws of the United States against all enemies . . .") only with the reservation that he
would not serve in the military in a combatant role.

The Court, speaking through Justice
William O. Douglas, held that despite *United
States* v. *Schwimmer* (1929), *United States* v.
MacIntosh (1931), and *United States* v. *Bland*
(1931), Girouard met the requirements for
naturalization. Justice Douglas argued that
Congress had not specifically insisted upon
willingness to perform combatant service.
Chief Justice Harlan F. Stone dissented,
joined by Justices Stanley F. Reed and Felix
Frankfurter.

This case established the eligibility of conscientious objectors to be naturalized as citizens of the United States.

—RICHARD E. MORGAN

GITLOW v. NEW YORK

268 U.S. 652 (1925)

Gitlow was convicted under a state statute
proscribing advocacy of the overthrow of
government by force. In a paper called *The
Revolutionary Age,* he had published "The
Left Wing Manifesto," denouncing moderate socialism and prescribing "Communist
revolution." There was no evidence of any effect resulting from the publication. Rejecting
the clear and present danger test that Oliver
Wendell Holmes and Louis D. Brandeis reasserted in their dissent, Justice Edward Sanford for the Court upheld the statute. Enunciating what subsequently came to be called
the remote bad tendency test, Sanford declared that the state might "suppress the
threatened danger in its incipiency." "It cannot reasonably be required to defer the adoption of measures for its own . . . safety until
the revolutionary utterances lead to actual
disturbances of the public peace or imminent
and immediate danger of its own destruction."

Unwilling to reverse its decision in *Schenck* v. *United States* (1919), the Court limited the clear and present danger test enunciated there to the situation in which a speaker is prosecuted under a statute prohibiting acts and making no reference to language. Under such a statute the legislature has made no judgment of its own as to the danger of any speech, and the unlawfulness of the speech must necessarily depend on whether "its natural tendency and probable effect was to bring about the substantive evil" that the legislature had proscribed. In short, Sanford sought to confine the danger test to its origin in the law of attempts and to strip it of its imminence aspect. He argued that where a legislature itself had determined that a certain category of speech constituted a danger of substantive evil, "every presumption [was] to be indulged in favor of the validity" of such an exercise of the police power.

The preferred freedoms doctrine that became central to the speech cases of the next two decades was largely directed toward undermining the *Gitlow* position that state statutes regulating speech ought to be subject to no more demanding constitutional standards than the reasonableness test applied to state economic regulation.

The *Gitlow* formula was rejected in the 1930s, but the Court returned to some of its reasoning in the 1950s, particularly to the notion that where revolutionary speech is involved, government need not wait until "the spark . . . has enkindled the flame or blazed into the conflagration." Such reasoning, bolstered by the *Gitlow* distinction between advocacy and abstract, academic teaching informed the *Dennis* v. *United States* (1951) and *Yates* v. *United States* (1951) decisions that upheld the Smith Act, a federal statute in part modeled on the New York criminal anarchy statute sustained in *Gitlow*.

The Court's language in *Gitlow* was equivocal, and it provided no rationale. Indeed, *Gitlow* is most often cited today for its dictum, "incorporating" First Amendment free speech guarantees into the due process clause of the Fourteenth Amendment, thus rendering the Amendment applicable to the states as well as to Congress.

Holmes's *Gitlow* dissent did not address the question so troublesome to believers in judicial

GITLOW v. NEW YORK

268 U.S. 652 (1925)

Gitlow was convicted under a state statute proscribing advocacy of the overthrow of government by force.

GOLDBERG v. KELLY
397 U.S. 254 (1970)

Residents of New York receiving welfare benefits brought suit challenging the state's procedures authorizing termination of a beneficiary's benefits without a prior hearing on his or her eligibility. The Supreme Court, 6–3, held that these procedures denied procedural due process.

For the majority, Justice William J. Brennan rejected the state's argument that because welfare benefits were a "privilege" and not a "right," their termination could not deprive a beneficiary of "property" within the meaning of the due process clause. Those benefits, said Brennan, were "a matter of statutory entitlement for persons qualified to receive them" and thus qualified as "property" interests whose termination must satisfy the requirements of due process.

These requirements included an evidentiary hearing prior to the termination of welfare benefits, including timely notice of the reasons for the proposed termination, the right to retain counsel, opportunity to confront any adverse witnesses, and opportunity to present the beneficiary's own evidence. The procedural safeguards thus required approximated those available in judicial proceedings; the Court underscored the point by insisting on an impartial decision maker who would "state the reasons for his determination and indicate the evidence he relied on."

Goldberg was the leading decision extending the guarantees of procedural due process in civil proceedings beyond the protection of traditional common law property interests to "entitlements" defined by statute, administrative regulation, or contract. It was aptly called the beginning of a "procedural due process revolution." By the mid-1970s, however, the counterrevolution had begun.

—KENNETH L. KARST

self-restraint: why should courts not defer to the legislature's judgment that a particular kind of speech is too dangerous to tolerate when, in applying the due process clause, they do defer to other legislative judgments? He did attack the majority's distinction between lawful abstract teaching and unlawful incitement in language that has become famous:

Every idea is an incitement. It offers itself for belief and if believed it is acted on unless some other belief outweighs it. . . . The only difference between the expression of an opinion and an incitement in the narrower sense is the speaker's enthusiasm for the result. . . . If in the long run the beliefs expressed in proletarian dictatorship are destined to be accepted by the dominant forces of the community, the only meaning of free speech is that they should be given their chance and have their way.

—MARTIN SHAPIRO

Bibliography

Chafee, Zechariah (1941). *Free Speech in the United States.* Cambridge, Mass.: Harvard University Press.

GOLDMAN v. WEINBERGER

475 U.S. 503 (1986)

Goldman, an orthodox Jew and ordained rabbi, was forbidden from wearing a yarmulke while on duty as an Air Force officer. The prohibition was pursuant to an Air Force regulation enjoining the wearing of headgear indoors "except by armed security police." Goldman sued, claiming that the prohibition violated his First Amendment right to the free exercise of religion. The Supreme Court disagreed, 5–4.

Writing for the majority, Justice William H. Rehnquist declined to require a govern-

ment showing of either a compelling state interest or a rational basis to justify the yarmulke prohibition. Rehnquist argued that the military must be accorded wide-ranging deference by the courts in order to carry out its mission; hence he refused to second-guess the Air Force's "professional judgment" about how to maintain a uniform dress code. Rehnquist used similar reasoning a year later to uphold the power of prison authorities to restrict the free-exercise rights of prisoners in *O'Lone* v. *Estate of Shabazz* (1987).

Justices William J. Brennan, Harry A. Blackmun, and Sandra Day O'Connor each filed separate dissents. All three believed that the Court should have attempted to weigh Goldman's free-exercise rights against the government interest at stake; they further agreed that the government interest should give way in this case because the military had made no attempt to show a reasonable basis for the regulation as applied to Goldman. They noted, in particular, that Goldman had been allowed to wear his yarmulke by the Air Force for almost four years before the practice was challenged.

—JOHN G. WEST, JR.

GRANGER CASES

(1877)

Chicago, Burlington & Quincy Railroad v. Iowa, 94 U.S. 155

Peik v. Chicago & Northwestern Railway Co., 94 U.S. 164

Chicago, Milwaukee & St. Paul Railroad Co. v. Ackley, 94 U.S. 179

Winona and St. Peter Railroad Co. v. Blake, 94 U.S. 180

Stone v. Wisconsin, 94 U.S. 181

The *Granger Cases*, decided on March 1, 1877, included *Munn* v. *Illinois,* in which state regulation of grain warehouse and elevator rates and practices was challenged, and

Goldman, an orthodox Jew and ordained rabbi, was forbidden from wearing a yarmulke while on duty as an Air Force officer.

See also

Dennis v. *United States*

Schenck v. *United States*

Yates v. *United States*

five railroad cases in which the companies attacked the validity of state legislatures' imposition of fixed maximum rates. In these decisions, the Supreme Court upheld the state regulations. Conservative, pro-business voices—and Justice Stephen J. Field, in vigorous dissent in *Munn*—regarded the decisions as a catastrophic surrender of due process values in law and a mortal blow to entrepreneurial liberty. They left legislatures, Field contended, with an unfettered power over private property rights of business firms. To the Court's majority, speaking through Chief Justice Morrison R. Waite, however, the issue of state regulation's legitimacy must turn on the difference in nature between business that was purely private and business that was affected with a public interest, hence peculiarly subject to regulation.

Laws for the regulation of railroads and grain warehouses, enacted in Illinois, Wisconsin, Iowa, and Minnesota during the period 1871–74, were at issue in the 1877 decisions. Until recent years, historians and students of constitutional law have tended to accept the view that the Grange and other farm organizations provided the political muscle in the midwestern reform movements that produced those laws. Indeed, it was customary to regard the legislation as radical, antibusiness, and anti-private property in intent and content. Recent research (particularly the work of historian George L. Miller) has shown, however, that there was no general antagonism between agrarian and business interests in the debates over the regulatory laws. Instead, reform was sought by coalitions, in a pattern of intrastate sectionalism; farmers lined up with commercial interests in some sections that favored regulation, and similar interests joined against regulation in other sections. The division of views depended much more upon calculations of local advantage and disadvantage from regulation than upon political ideology, "agrarian" or otherwise, or even upon political party alignments.

Contrary to another view long held by scholars, the Granger laws did not lack legislative precedent. The charters of early railway companies typically had carried maximum rate provisions and other features that bespoke the state's interest in the efficient provision of transport services. And in the 1850s several states (notably New York and Ohio) had prohibited local discrimination in railroad rate making and had levied special taxes on railroad companies to offset the effects of rail competition on state-owned canals. The Granger laws may be seen as an extension of a regulatory tradition well established in American railway law.

Still another common error of interpretation concerns the doctrinal basis of the "affectation" doctrine as employed in Waite's majority opinion in *Munn*. The concept of "business affected with a public interest," according to a long-standard view, was a surprising resort to a forgotten antiquity of English common law—a concept reintroduced in American law after a lapse of nearly two centuries. In fact, the concept of affectation was well known in American riparian and admiralty law; and equally familiar was the jurist from whose writings Waite drew the affectation concept for use in *Munn*, for Lord Chief Justice Matthew Hale's tracts on common law had been cited in scores of important American cases in riparian and eminent domain law.

The Court's majority in the *Granger Cases* rejected the contention of railroad counsel that if state legislatures were permitted to mandate fixed, maximum rates, the result would be to deprive business of fair profits, and thus to produce effective "confiscation" of private property. The majority also rejected the view that the equal protection and due process clauses of the Fourteenth Amendment warranted judicial review of the fairness of rates. Such regulatory power was subject to abuse, Waite conceded, but this was "no argument against its existence. For protection against abuses by legislatures the people must resort to the polls, not to the courts."

GRANGER CASES

Chicago, Burlington & Quincy Railroad *v.* Iowa, *94 U.S. 155*

Peik *v.* Chicago & Northwestern Railway Co., *94 U.S. 164*

Chicago, Milwaukee & St. Paul Railroad Co. *v.* Ackley, *94 U.S. 179*

Winona and St. Peter Railroad Co. *v.* Blake, *94 U.S. 180*

Stone *v.* Wisconsin, *94 U.S. 181*

Within fifteen years after the Granger Cases, *the Court had begun to strike down state regulations of interstate railroad operations.*

See also

Rational Basis

GRAVES v. NEW YORK
ex rel. O'KEEFE

306 U.S. 466 (1939)

G

By 1939 the Court had already begun to retrench its doctrines of reciprocal tax immunities enjoyed by "government" instrumentalities.

Thus, the *Granger Cases* decisions held back, at least for a time, the conservative efforts to make the Fourteenth Amendment a fortress for vested rights against the state police power. The decisions were also of enduring importance in constitutional development for their elaborate formulation of the "affectation with a public interest" doctrine. Relying upon the advice of his colleague Justice Joseph P. Bradley, who was learned in the English law of common carriers and in admiralty law, Waite explored in his opinion the legitimate reach of the police power in regulation of business. He concluded that modern railroad companies and warehouses played a role in commerce that was analgous to the role played by ferry operators and others who in the seventeenth century had exercised a "virtual monopoly" of vital commercial services, hence were held subject to regulations not ordinarily imposed on other businesses. Thus the Court indicated, by implication at least, that businesses not so affected with a special public interest could not be regulated.

Not long after publication of the decisions, Waite wrote privately: "The great difficulty in the future will be to establish the boundary between that which is private, and that in which the public has an interest. The Elevators furnished an extreme case, and there was no difficulty in determining on which side of the line they properly belonged." This proved an accurate forecast of the Court's future travails, until in *Nebbia* v. *New York* (1934) the Court finally abandoned the "affectation" doctrine, holding that *all* businesses were subject to state regulation under the police power.

Within fifteen years after the *Granger Cases,* moreover, the Court had begun to invoke both the commerce clause and the Fourteenth Amendment to strike down state regulations of interstate railroad operations and to review both procedural and substantive aspects of state regulation of business. The drive to establish a new constitutional foundation for vested rights, in sum, for many years relegated the *Granger Cases'* support of a broad legislative discretion to the status of a doctrinal relic.

—HARRY N. SCHEIBER

Bibliography

Fairman, Charles (1953). The So-Called *Granger Cases,* Lord Hale, and Justice Bradley. *Stanford Law Review* 5:587–679.

Magrath, C. Peter (1963). *Morrison R. Waite: The Triumph of Character.* New York: Macmillan.

Miller, George L. (1971). *Railroads and the Granger Laws.* Madison: University of Wisconsin Press.

Scheiber, Harry N. (1971). The Road to *Munn:* Eminent Domain and the Concept of Public Purpose in the State Courts. *Perspectives in American History* 5:327–402.

GRAVES v. NEW YORK ex rel. O'KEEFE

306 U.S. 466 (1939)

For practical purposes the decision in *Graves* by a 7–2 Supreme Court toppled an elaborate structure of intergovernmental tax immunities, which the Justices had erected from assumptions about the federal system. The right of self-preservation immunized the United States and the states from taxation by competing governments within the system. Obviously the United States cannot tax the Commonwealth of Massachusetts or the state capitol in Sacramento, California, any more than the states can tax a congressional investigation. From a sensible assumption first advanced in *McCulloch* v. *Maryland* (1819) protecting a national instrumentality from state taxation, the Court made progressively sillier decisions that hampered the taxing power of the state and national governments and allowed many commercial activities to escape taxation. *Collector* v. *Day* (1871) made the salaries of state judges exempt from federal income taxes. In time the Court held unconstitutional a federal tax on the income of a private corporation leasing state land, and a federal sales tax on a motorcycle sold by a private corporation to city police.

By 1939 the Court had already begun to retrench its doctrines of reciprocal tax immunities enjoyed by "government" instrumentalities. In *Graves*, Justice Harlan Fiske Stone faced the question whether a state tax on the salary of an employee of a federal instrumentality created by Congress violated the principles of national supremacy. Stone observed that the tax was imposed on an employee's salary, not on the instrumentality itself. Because the Constitution did not mandate tax immunity and such immunity should attach only to a government instrumentality, the Court not only sustained the tax but also overruled *Day* and several related cases. A state may tax the income of officers or employees of the national government, and vice versa. In *New York* v. *United States* (1946), the Court upheld a national tax on soft drinks bottled by the state. To the extent that government functions cannot be be taxed by another government the core doctrine from *McCulloch* endures.

—LEONARD W. LEVY

GRIFFIN v. ILLINOIS

351 U.S. 12 (1956)

Griffin was the first decision giving constitutional status to an indigent person's claim to invalidate an economic barrier to his or her access to the courts.

Illinois normally required persons appealing from their criminal convictions to provide trial transcripts to the appellate courts. The state supplied free transcripts to indigents appealing in capital cases, but not in other cases. The Supreme Court held, 5–4, that the state must furnish a free transcript to an appellant in a noncapital case.

The opinion of Justice Hugo L. Black, for four Justices, rested on both due process and equal protection grounds, asserting the state's constitutional obligation to provide "equal justice for poor and rich." Justice Felix Frankfurter, concurring, emphasized the irrationality of the capital/noncapital distinction. The dissenters found this distinction reasonable and argued that the state had no affirmative duty to alleviate the consequences of economic inequality.

Griffin, along with *Douglas* v. *California* (1963), raised expectations that the equal protection clause would be interpreted as a

Griffin *was the first decision giving constitutional status to an indigent person's claim to invalidate an economic barrier to his or her access to the courts.*

♦ **in personam**
[Latin: against the person] A manner of proceeding in a case so that the decision and remedy are directed against a particular person.

GRIGGS v. DUKE POWER CO.

401 U.S. 924 (1971)

Although subject to narrower interpretations, *Griggs* is viewed as establishing that employment selection criteria that disqualify blacks at higher rates than whites may violate Title VII of the Civil Rights Act of 1964 even if the selection criteria are not chosen for discriminatory purposes. *Griggs* opened the door to vast numbers of Title VII actions seeking to establish violations through statistical analysis of the relative effect of employment criteria on minorities. *Griggs*'s emphasis on effects also influenced non-Title VII cases. Until *Washington* v. *Davis* (1976) was decided, many courts and analysts relied in part on *Griggs* to interpret the equal protection clause to prohibit unequal effects. Even after *Davis*, *Griggs*'s effects test continued to influence litigation under Title VI of the Civil Rights Act of 1964, Title VIII of the Civil Rights Act of 1968, and other provisions.

—THEODORE EISENBERG

Many courts and analysts relied in part on Griggs *to interpret the equal protection clause to prohibit unequal effects.*

See also
Equal Protection of the Laws
Washington v. *Davis*

Griswold *stands
among the most
influential Supreme
Court decisions of
the latter part of the
twentieth century.*

broad guarantee against wealth discrimination, but these decisions are seen today as standing for a more modest proposition: that the right to state criminal appeals must not be foreclosed to the poor because of their poverty.

—KENNETH L. KARST

GRISWOLD v. CONNECTICUT

381 U.S. 479 (1965)

Seen in the perspective of the development of constitutional doctrine, *Griswold* stands among the most influential Supreme Court decisions of the latter part of the twentieth century. A full understanding of its effect on the constitutional future requires a look at *Griswold*'s antecedents. Even seen narrowly, *Griswold* was something of a culmination. The birth control movement had made two previous unsuccessful attempts to get the Court to invalidate Connecticut's law forbidding use of contraceptive devices. In *Tileston* v. *Ullman* (1943) a doctor was held to lack standing to assert his patients' constitutional claims, and in *Poe* v. *Ullman* (1961), when a doctor and his patients sued in their own rights, the Court again dismissed—this time on jurisdictional grounds that could charitably be called ingenuous. *Griswold* proved to be the charm; operators of a birth control clinic had been prosecuted for aiding married couples to violate the law, furnishing them advice and contraceptive devices. The Supreme Court held the law invalid, 7–2.

Griswold fanned into flames a doctrinal issue that had smoldered in the Supreme Court for nearly two centuries: the question of whether the Constitution protects natural rights or fundamental interests beyond those specifically mentioned in its text. In the modern era, that question of constitutional interpretation had focused on Justice Hugo L. Black's argument that the Fourteenth Amendment fully incorporated the specific guarantees of the Bill of Rights and made them applicable to the states. Black's dissent in *Adamson* v. *California* (1947) had scorned the competing view, limiting the content of the Fourteenth Amendment due process to the fundamentals of ordered liberty. This "natural-law-due-process formula," said Black, not only allowed judges to fail to protect rights specifically covered by the Constitution but also permitted them "to roam at large in the broad expanses of policy and morals," trespassing on the legislative domain. In *Adamson* Justice Frank Murphy had also dissented; accepting the incorporation doctrine, Murphy argued that other "fundamental" rights, beyond the specific guarantees of the Bill of Rights, were also protected by due process. *Griswold* offered a test of the Black and Murphy views.

Justice William O. Douglas, who had agreed with Black in *Adamson*, recognized that the Connecticut birth control law violated no specific guarantee of the Bill of Rights. A number of other guarantees, however, protected various aspects of privacy, and all of them had "penumbras, formed by emanations from those guarantees that [helped] give them life and substance." The *Griswold* case concerned "a relationship lying within the zone of privacy created by several fundamental constitutional guarantees." The Ninth Amendment recognized the existence of other rights outside those specifically mentioned in the Bill of Rights, and the right of marital privacy itself was "older than the Bill of Rights." Enforcement of Connecticut's law would involve intolerable state intrusion into the marital bedroom. The law was invalid in application to married couples, and the birth control clinic operators could not be punished for aiding its violation.

In form, this "penumbras" theory was tied to the specifics of the Bill of Rights; in fact, it embraced the Murphy contention. Justices John Marshall Harlan and Byron R. White, concurring, candidly rested on substantive due process grounds. Justice Black, dissenting, expressed distaste for the Connecticut law but could find nothing specific in the Constitution to prevent the state from forbidding the furnishing or the use of contraceptives. He chided the majority for using natural law to "keep the Constitution in tune with the times"—a function that lay beyond the Court's power or duty.

Griswold served as an important precedent eight years later when the Court held, in *Roe v. Wade* (1973), that the new constitutional right of privacy included a woman's right to have an abortion. The *Roe* opinion, abandoning the shadows of *Griswold*'s penumbras, located the right of privacy in the "liberty" protected by Fourteenth Amendment due process. *Griswold* thus provided a bridge from the Murphy view in *Adamson* to the Court's modern revival of substantive due process. Underscoring this transition, later decisions such as *Eisenstadt* v. *Baird* (1972) and *Carey* v. *Population Services International* (1977) have made plain that *Griswold* protected not only marital privacy but also the marital relationship—and, indeed, a freedom of intimate association extending to unmarried persons. If substantive due process is a vital part of today's constitutional protections of personal liberty, much of the credit goes to the *Griswold* decision and to Justice Douglas.

—KENNETH L. KARST

Bibliography

Kauper, Paul G. (1965). Penumbras, Peripheries, Emanations, Things Fundamental and Things Forgotten: The *Griswold Case*. *Michigan Law Review* 64:235–258.

GUEST, UNITED STATES v.

383 U.S. 745 (1966)

This case raised important questions about Congress's power to enforce the Fourteenth Amendment and about the scope of section 241 of Title 18 of the United States Code, a federal criminal civil rights statute deriving from section 6 of the Force Act of 1870. Section 241 outlaws conspiracies to interfere with rights or privileges secured by the Constitution or laws of the United States. A group of whites allegedly murdered Lemuel A. Penn, a black Army officer, while he was driving through Georgia on his way to Washington, D.C. Two of the whites were charged with murder and acquitted by a state court jury. They and others then were indicted under section 241 for conspiracy to deprive blacks of specified constitutional rights by shooting, beating, and otherwise harassing them and by making false criminal accusations causing the blacks to be arrested. The rights allegedly deprived included the right to use state facilities free of racial discrimination and the right to travel freely throughout the United States. The Supreme Court held that the alleged conduct constituted a crime under section 241, punishable by Congress under the Fourteenth Amendment.

Guest's principal significance stems from two separate opinions, joined by a total of six Justices, that addressed the question of whether the Fourteenth Amendment empowers Congress to outlaw private racially discriminatory behavior. In an opinion concurring in part and dissenting in part, Justice William J. Brennan, joined by Chief Justice Earl Warren and Justice William O. Douglas, stated that section 5 of the Fourteenth Amendment grants Congress authority to punish individuals, public or private, who interfere with the right to equal use of state facilities. Justice Tom C. Clark, in a concurring opinion joined by Justices Hugo L. Black and Abe Fortas, in effect agreed with the portion of Justice Brennan's opinion relating to Congress's power. Justice Clark's opinion stated that there could be no doubt about Congress's power to punish all public and private conspiracies that interfere with Fourteenth Amendment rights, "with or without state action."

Guest's generous attitude toward Congress's power has had less influence than might have been expected.

Guest also raised the question of whether, in light of the state action doctrine, the defendants, all private persons, were legally capable of depriving others of Fourteenth Amendment rights within the meaning of section 241. Justice Potter Stewart's opinion for the Court, which, as to this point, Justice Clark's opinion expressly endorsed, avoided the issue by construing the indictment's allegation that the conspiracy was accomplished in part by "causing the arrest of Negroes by means of false reports that such Negroes had committed criminal acts" to be an allegation of state involvement. Justice Brennan read Justice Stewart's opinion to mean that a conspiracy by private persons to interfere with Fourteenth Amendment rights was not a conspiracy to interfere with a right secured by the Constitution within the meaning of section 241. Justice Brennan rejected this interpretation, arguing that private persons could deprive blacks of rights "secured" by the Constitution "even though only governmental interferences with the exercise of that right are prohibited by the Constitution itself."

Other aspects of *Guest* generated less disagreement among the Justices. The case revived a question addressed in *Screws* v. *United States* (1945) when the Court interpreted section 242 (a remnant of the Civil Rights Act of 1866). Sections 241 and 242 define proscribed behavior as conduct violating constitutional rights. Since constitutional standards change, defendants argued that the sections were unconstitutionally vague. As in *Screws,* the Court construed the statute to require a specific intent to violate constitutional rights and, therefore, found section 241 not unconstitutionally vague. And the Court found the right to travel throughout the United States to be a basic constitutional right that, like freedom from involuntary servitude, is protected even as against private interference. Only Justice John Marshall Harlan dissented from the holding that the right to travel is protected against private interference.

Both the suggestion by six Justices (through the Brennan and Clark opinions) concerning Congress's power under section 5 of the Fourteenth Amendment and Justice Brennan's views about the scope of section 241 are difficult to reconcile with important nineteenth-century decisions. In *United States* v. *Cruikshank* (1876), one of the first

AMENDMENT XIV

Section 1. All persons born or naturalized in the United States, and subject to the jurisdiction thereof, are citizens of the United States and of the State wherein they reside. No State shall make or enforce any law which shall abridge the privileges or immunities of citizens of the United States; nor shall any State deprive any person of life, liberty, or property, without due process of law; nor deny to any person within its jurisdiction the equal protection of the laws.

Section 2. Representatives shall be apportioned among the several States according to their respective numbers, counting the whole number of persons in each State, excluding Indians not taxed. But when the right to vote at any election for the choice of electors for President and Vice President of the United States, Representatives in Congress, the Executive and Judicial officers of a State, or the members of the Legislature thereof, is denied to any of the male inhabitants of such State, being twenty-one years of age, and citizens of the United States, or in any way abridged, except for participation in rebellion, or other crime, the basis of representation therein shall be reduced in the proportion which the number of such male citizens shall bear to the whole number of male citizens twenty-one years of age in such State.

cases construing Reconstruction-era civil rights legislation, indictments charging violations of section 6 of the Force Act of 1870 were ordered dismissed in part on the ground that Fourteenth Amendment rights could not be violated by private citizens. In *United States* v. *Harris* (1883) the Court held unconstitutional a civil rights statute that punished private conspiracies to interfere with rights of equality. The provision struck down in *Harris*, which stemmed from section 2 of the Civil Rights Act of 1871, was so similar to section 241 that, until *Guest*, it seemed unlikely that section 241 could be applied to private conspiracies to interfere with rights of equality. And *Guest*'s expansive view of Congress's Fourteenth Amendment powers is difficult to reconcile with the Court's decision in the *Civil Rights Cases* (1883).

Guest thus represents a shift in attitude toward Congress's Fourteenth Amendment power to reach private discrimination. But *Guest* also is part of a larger shift in attitude toward the Civil War amendments. In *Katzenbach* v. *Morgan* (1966) and *South Carolina* v. *Katzenbach* (1966), cases decided during the same term as *Guest*, the Court for the first time found Congress to have broad powers to interpret and define the content of the Fourteenth and Fifteenth Amendments.

Guest's generous attitude toward Congress's power has had less influence than might have been expected. Prior to *Guest*, *Heart of Atlanta Motel, Inc.* v. *United States*, (1964) and *Katzenbach* v. *McClung* (1964) already had found Congress to have broad power under the commerce clause to reach discrimination in facilities affecting interstate commerce. In *Jones* v. *Alfred H. Mayer Co.*

(1968), the Court found Congress to have broad Thirteenth Amendment powers to reach private discrimination in all areas. *Jones* and the commerce clause cases rendered moot much of the question about Congress's Fourteenth Amendment powers. *Griffin* v. *Breckenridge* (1971), where the Court again faced the question of Congress's power to reach private discriminatory conspiracies, underscores *Guest*'s modest influence. *Griffin* involved a civil statute, section 1985(3), that is similar to section 241. By the time of *Griffin*, however, the Court could rely on Congress's Thirteenth Amendment powers to sustain legislation proscribing private racial conspiracies. *Guest*'s possible implications will be realized only in cases, if any, to which Congress's Thirteenth Amendment and commerce clause powers are inapplicable.

—THEODORE EISENBERG

Bibliography

Cox, Archibald (1966). Foreword: Constitutional Adjudication and the Promotion of Human Rights. *Harvard Law Review* 80:91–122.

Note (1974). Federal Power to Regulate Private Discrimination: The Revival of the Enforcement Clauses of the Reconstruction Era Amendments. *Columbia Law Review* 74:449–527.

Note (1967). Fourteenth Amendment Congressional Power to Legislate Against Private Discrimination: The *Guest Case*. *Cornell Law Quarterly* 52:586–599.

Tribe, Laurence H. (1978). *American Constitutional Law*. Pages 273–275. Mineola, N.Y.: Foundation Press.

See also

Cruikshank, United States v.

Heart of Atlanta Motel

v. *United States*

Jones v. *Alfred H. Mayer Co.*

Screws v. *United States*

South Carolina v. *Katzenbach*

H

HAGUE v. CONGRESS OF INDUSTRIAL ORGANIZATIONS

307 U.S. 496 (1939)

In separate opinions yielding no majority, over two dissents, and with only seven Justices participating, the Court enjoined enforcement of a local ordinance used to harass labor organizers. Justices Owen Roberts and Hugo L. Black and Chief Justice Charles Evans Hughes deemed the right to organize under and discuss the Wagner (National Labor Relations) Act a privilege or immunity of national citizenship. Justices Harlan Fiske Stone and Stanley F. Reed held it a right protected by the First Amendment. Justice Stone's separate opinion, which suggested that Section 1983's jurisdictional counterpart authorized federal courts to hear actions involving personal liberty but not to hear actions involving property rights, influenced subsequent civil rights cases. Some courts accepted the distinction and applied the dichotomy to section 1983 itself. *Lynch* v. *Household Finance Corp.* (1972) discredited the distinction.

—THEODORE EISENBERG

HAMMER v. DAGENHART

247 U.S. 251 (1918)

From 1903 to 1918, the Supreme Court consistently had approved national police power regulations enacted under the commerce clause. But in *Hammer* v. *Dagenhart,* the Court deviated from this tradition and invalidated the Keating-Owen Child Labor Act, which prohibited the interstate shipment of goods produced by child labor. The Court's restrictive doctrine nevertheless proved vulnerable and the decision itself eventually was overruled.

In *Champion* v. *Ames* (1903) the Justices had sustained a congressional prohibition against the interstate shipment of lottery tickets. The ruling actually was quite narrow, holding that such tickets were proper subjects of commerce and that Congress could prevent the "pollution" of interstate commerce. A more general, expansive doctrine seemed to emerge as the Court soon approved similar regulations of the interstate flow of adulterated foods and impure drugs, prostitutes, prize fight films, and liquor. The Court abruptly deviated from this course in the child labor case, perhaps signaling a reaction against some of the Progressive era's social reforms and the Court's prior tendency toward liberal nationalism.

Justice William R. Day, speaking for a 5–4 majority, maintained at the outset that in each of the other cases the Court had acknowledged that the "use of interstate transportation was necessary to the accomplishment of harmful results." But the child labor regulations, Day held, were different because the goods shipped were of themselves harmless in contrast with lottery tickets, impure foods, prize fight films, and liquor. It was an unsound distinction, but one perhaps anticipated by Justice John Marshall Harlan's remarks in the *Lottery Case* that the Court would not allow Congress arbitrarily to exclude every article from interstate commerce.

The Court enjoined enforcement of a local ordinance used to harass labor organizers.

H

HAMMER v. DAGENHART

247 U.S. 251 (1918)

The Hammer decision did not significantly diminish the Court's willingness or ability to sustain congressional police regulations under the commerce clause.

The ruling revealed that the Court seemed less concerned with the evils of child labor than Congress and was more interested in maintaining the purity of the federal system.

See also

Champion v. Ames

The Court refuted any suggestions that congressional authority extended to prevent unfair competition among the states, thus enabling it to ignore any discussion of the evils or deleterious effects of child labor. This argument was grounded in the majority's revival of rigid notions of dual federalism. Production, Day said, as he resurrected an older, dubious, and arbitrary distinction, was not commerce; the regulation of production was reserved by the Tenth Amendment to the states. "If it were otherwise," Day noted, "all manufacture intended for interstate shipment would be brought under federal control to the practical exclusion of the authority of the States, a result certainly not contemplated by the . . . Constitution." The regulation of child labor, he maintained, not only exceeded congressional authority but also invaded the proper sphere of local power. To allow such a measure, Day concluded, would end "all freedom of commerce," eliminate state control over local matters, and thereby destroy the federal system.

In dissent, Justice Oliver Wendell Holmes uttered his oft-quoted remark that "if there is any matter upon which civilized countries have agreed—far more unanimously than they have with regard to intoxicants and some other matters over which this country is now emotionally aroused—it is the evil of premature and excessive child labor." But Holmes offered more than his customary philosophical discourse on judicial restraint. Congress plainly had the power to regulate interstate shipments, and its motives of doing so were no less legitimate here than they had been in the regulations.

Whether "evil precedes or follows the transportation" was irrelevant, Holmes said; once states transported their goods across their boundaries, they were "no longer within their rights."

The *Hammer* decision did not significantly diminish the Court's willingness or ability to sustain congressional police regulations under the commerce clause. The ruling revealed that the Court seemed less concerned with the evils of child labor than Congress and was more interested in maintaining the purity of the federal system. In *Bailey* v. *Drexel Furniture* (1922), the Justices invalidated a congressional attempt to regulate child labor by using the taxing power, again despite ample precedents justifying national power. But three years later, Chief Justice William Howard Taft, who had written the child labor tax opinion, reverted to the Court's earlier police power decisions and broadly approved the National Motor Vehicle Act (1919), which made the transportation of stolen automobiles across state lines a federal crime. In *Brooks* v. *United States* (1925) Taft agreed that Congress could forbid the use of interstate commerce "as an agency to promote immorality, dishonesty or the spread of any evil or harm of other States from the State of origin." *Hammer* v. *Dagenhart* marred an otherwise consistent pattern in the precedents, but Taft quickly disposed of it by reiterating the distinction that the products of child labor were not harmful. Yet his 1925 opinion refuted such doctrine as he demonstrated that a perceived evil required national action and the question of harmfulness was secondary.

Throughout the 1920s the Supreme Court, following Taft's strong views, generally approved an ever expanding scope to the commerce clause. There was some retreat during the bitter constitutional struggle over the New Deal, but it proved temporary. After 1937 a number of decisions reaffirmed a broad nationalistic view of the commerce power. Finally, in 1941, the Court specifically overruled *Hammer*. Justice Harlan Fiske Stone, in *United States* v. *Darby*, rebuked the earlier decision as "novel," "unsupported," "a departure," and "exhausted" as a precedent.

The most poignant historical commentary on *Hammer* came from the supposed victor, Reuben Dagenhart, whose father had sued in order to sustain his "freedom" to allow his fourteen-year-old boy to work in a textile mill. Six years later, Reuben, a 105–pound man, recalled that his victory had earned him a soft drink, some automobile rides from his employer, and a salary of one dollar a day; he had also lost his education and his health.

—STANLEY I. KUTLER

Bibliography

Wood, Stephen (1968). *Constitutional Politics in the Progressive Era: Child Labor and the Law.* Chicago: University of Chicago Press.

HARPER v. VIRGINIA BOARD OF ELECTIONS

383 U.S. 663 (1966)

Harper epitomizes the Warren Court's expansion of the reach of the equal protection clause of the Fourteenth Amendment. Virginia levied an annual $1.50 poll tax on residents over twenty-one, and conditioned voter registration on payment of accrued poll taxes. The Supreme Court, 6–3, overruled *Breedlove* v. *Suttles* (1937), holding that the condition on registration denied the equal protection of the laws.

The *Harper* opinion, by Justice William O. Douglas, played an important part in crystallizing equal protection doctrine by justifying heightened levels of judicial scrutiny. The Court did not quite hold that wealth or indigency was a suspect classification, saying only that "lines drawn on the basis of wealth of property, like those of race, are traditionally disfavored." It did say, following *Reynolds* v. *Sims* (1964), that voting was a fundamental interest, requiring strict scrutiny of its restriction. The poll tax by itself might be constitutionally unobjectionable; wealth as a condition on voting, however, not only failed the test of strict scrutiny; it was a "capricious or irrelevant factor."

For Justice Hugo L. Black, dissenting, *Harper* represented a relapse into judicial subjectivism through a variation on the "natural-law-due-process" formula he had decried in *Adamson* v. *California* (1947). The Virginia scheme was not arbitrary; it might increase revenues or ensure an interested electorate. The Court should not substitute its judgment for the Virginia legislature's. Justice John Marshall Harlan also dissented, joined by Justice Potter Stewart. Harlan, who shared Black's views, added that it was arguable that "people with some property have a deeper stake in community affairs, and are consequently more responsible, more educated, more knowledgeable, more worthy of confidence, than those without means." That this belief was not his own did not matter; it was arguable, and that was all the rational basis standard demanded.

Commentators saw in *Harper* and other contemporary decisions a major shift away from the tradition of minimal judicial scrutiny of laws challenged under the equal protection clause. Invasions of interests of great importance, or discrimination against disadvantaged groups, appeared to call for judicial scrutiny more demanding than that required by the relaxed rational basis standard. Soon the Court found a formula for two levels of review: rational basis for most "social and economic" legislation, and strict scrutiny for laws invading fundamental interests or employing suspect classifications.

The Court has not pursued *Harper*'s suggestion that wealth discrimination is suspect. Voting rights, however, are firmly established as interests whose invasion demands strict scrutiny. Implicitly, as in cases involving aliens or illegitimacy, and explicitly, as in cases on sex discrimination, the Court has transformed its two levels of judicial scrutiny into a sliding-scale approach that is interest balancing by another name: the more important the interest invaded, or the more "suspect" the classification, the more the state must justify its legislation. In broad outline

The Harper *opinion played an important part in crystallizing equal protection doctrine by justifying heightened levels of judicial scrutiny.*

See also

Adamson v. *California*

Equal Protection of the Laws

Reynolds v. *Sims*

Warren Court

H

The restrictions went beyond the law sustained in Maher v. Roe *(1977) by refusing funding even for medically necessary abortions.*

this development was portended in *Harper,* which exemplified not only Warren Court egalitarianism but also Justice Douglas's doctrinal leadership.

—KENNETH L. KARST

Bibliography

Karst, Kenneth L. (1969). Invidious Discrimination: Justice Douglas and the Return of the "Natural-Law-Due-Process Formula." *UCLA Law Review* 16:716–750.

HARRIS v. MCRAE

448 U.S. 297 (1980)

A 5–4 Supreme Court here sustained a series of restrictions on congressional appropriations for the Medicaid program. The restrictions went beyond the law sustained in *Maher* v. *Roe* (1977) by refusing funding even for medically necessary abortions.

Justice Potter Stewart's opinion for the Court relied heavily on *Maher* in rejecting claims based on the substantive due process right of privacy and on the equal protection clause. A woman's right to be free from governmental interference with her decision to have an abortion did not imply a right to have government subsidize that decision. Equal protection demanded only a rational basis for the law's discrimination between therapeutic abortions and other medical necessities, and such a basis was found in the protection of potential life. Justice Stewart also rejected a claim that the law amounted to an establishment of religion. Opposition to abortion might be a tenet of some religions, but the establishment clause did not forbid governmental action merely because it coincided with religious views.

The *Maher* dissenters were joined in *McRae* by Justice John Paul Stevens, who had joined the *Maher* majority. The cases were different, he argued; here an indigent woman was denied a medically necessary abortion for lack of funds, at the same time that the government was funding other medically necessary services. *Roe* v. *Wade* (1973), allowing a state to forbid abortions in the later stages of pregnancy, had excepted abortions necessary to preserve pregnant women's lives or health. The government could not create exclusions from an aid program, Justice Stevens argued, solely to promote a governmental interest (preservation of potential life) that was "constitutionally subordinate to the individual interest that the entire program was designed to protect."

—KENNETH L. KARST

HARRIS v. NEW YORK

401 U.S. 222 (1971)

This case is significant as a limitation on *Miranda* v. *Arizona* (1966). Harris sold narcotics to undercover police officers. The police failed to inform him, after his arrest, that he had a right to counsel during a custodial police interrogation and they ignored his request for an attorney. Harris eventually admitted that he had acted as an intermediary, buying heroin for the undercover agent, but he denied selling it to the agent. During the trial Harris contradicted the statement that he had made during interrogation; the judge overruled defense objections that the custodial statement was inadmissible under the *Miranda* rules because it was made involuntarily and in violation of his rights. The judge instructed the jury that although the statement was unavailable as evidence of guilt, they might consider it in assessing Harris's credibility as a witness.

The Supreme Court, 5–4, upheld Harris's conviction. *Miranda* dissenters John Marshall Harlan, Byron R. White, and Potter J. Stewart along with Justice Harry A. Blackmun joined in Chief Justice Warren E. Burger's opinion holding that testimony secured without the necessary warnings could nevertheless be used to impeach contradictory testimony at trial. Burger flatly asserted that Harris made "no claim that the unwarned statements were coerced or involuntary"—a statement clearly controverted by the record. Burger also dismissed, as obiter dictum, the assertion in *Miranda* that all such statements were inadmissible for any purpose. The majority relied heavily on *Walder* v. *United States* (1954), in which evidence secured in an unreasonable search was admitted to impeach testimony although the exclusionary rule would have prohibited its use as evidence of guilt.

Justice William J. Brennan, dissenting, said that *Miranda* prohibited the use of any statements obtained in violation of its guarantees and denied the contention that that was obiter dictum. Brennan also distinguished *Walder:* the statement there had no connection to the crime with which the defendant had been charged; in *Harris* the defendant's statements related directly to the crime. Moreover, the evidence there could have been used to assess credibility; here the jury could have misused it as evidence of guilt because the statement provided information about the crime charged.

—DAVID GORDON

Bibliography

Levy, Leonard W. (1974). *Against the Law: The Nixon Court and Criminal Justice.* New York: Harper & Row.

HAWAII HOUSING AUTHORITY v. MIDKIFF

467 U.S. 229 (1984)

The system of feudal land tenure developed under the Hawaiian monarchy had modern

♦ **exclusionary rule**
A rule excluding evidence obtained in violation of a defendant's rights from admission at the defendant's trial as proof of guilt.

DISTORTED LAND MARKET

Seventy-two landowners owned 47 percent of the land in Hawaii; the federal and state governments owned 49 percent, leaving only 4 percent of the state's land for other owners. (Corbis/Galen Rowell)

See also

Miranda v. *Arizona*

The system of feudal land tenure developed under the Hawaiian monarchy had modern consequences.

The Supreme Court held that school officials could not interfere with students' speech unless that speech threatened disorder.

consequences. Seventy-two landowners owned 47 percent of the land in the state, and the federal and state governments owned 49 percent; only 4 percent of the land was left for other owners. The Hawaii legislature, finding that this system distorted the land market, in 1967 adopted a land reform act. The law authorized use of the state's eminent domain power to condemn residential plots and to transfer ownership to existing tenants. Landowners challenged the law as authorizing takings of property for private benefit rather than public use. The Supreme Court unanimously rejected this argument, upholding the law's validity. The legislature's purpose to relieve perceived evils of land concentration was legitimately public, and the courts' inquiry need extend no further. Apart from issues of just compensation, the taking of property has virtually ceased to present a judicial question.

—KENNETH L. KARST

HAZELWOOD SCHOOL DISTRICT v. KUHLMEIER

484 U.S. 260 (1988)

In *Tinker* v. *Des Moines Independent School District* (1969) the Supreme Court held that school officials could not interfere with students' speech unless that speech threatened substantial disorder, a material disruption of the educational program, or invasion of the rights of others. The *Kuhlmeier* decision continues the erosion of *Tinker* that had begun in *Bethel School District* v. *Fraser* (1986).

A journalism class in a Missouri public high school wrote and edited the school newspaper. The school's principal, after reviewing proofs, ordered the deletion of two of the paper's projected six pages to avoid publi-

cation of two articles: one detailing the experiences of three pregnant students and another on students' feelings about their parents' divorces. The first story, the principal said, was inappropriate for the school's younger students; the second contained derogatory comments by a named student about her father. With no notice to the student writers or editors, the paper was printed with the offending pages deleted. Three of the students brought suit against school officials, seeking a declaratory judgment that the censorship violated their First Amendment rights. They lost in the federal district court, but prevailed in the court of appeals on the theory of the *Tinker* decision. The Supreme Court reversed, 5–3.

Justice Byron R. White, for the Court, first concluded that the paper was not a public forum because its pages had not been opened up to students generally or to any other segment of the general public. He distinguished *Tinker* in two main ways. First, the school could legitimately seek to inculcate the community's values, and thus could act to avoid the inference that it endorsed the conduct that led to student pregnancy. Second, the principal's control over the school paper was a series of decisions about the educational content of the journalism curriculum, and courts must pay deference to educators in such matters. Thus, the proper standard of review was not strict scrutiny but one of "reasonableness"—a standard satisfied by the principal's decision.

For the three dissenters, Justice William J. Brennan argued that the majority's "reasonableness" test effectively abandoned the much more demanding standards of *Tinker*. Surely some members of the *Kuhlmeier* majority would be satisfied to paint *Tinker* into a corner where its value as a precedent would be severely limited. Whether the Court will complete this process of doctrinal retrenchment remains to be seen.

—KENNETH L. KARST

HEART OF ATLANTA MOTEL v. UNITED STATES

379 U.S. 241 (1964)

KATZENBACH v. MCCLUNG

379 U.S. 294 (1964)

In these cases the Supreme Court unanimously upheld the portion of the Civil Rights Act of 1964 forbidding racial discrimination by hotels, restaurants, theaters, and other public accommodations.

Congressional debates had discussed the appropriate source of congressional power to prohibit private racial discrimination. The commerce clause was proposed as a safe foundation for the bill; since 1937 the Supreme Court had upheld every congressional regulation of commerce that came before it. Because Congress obviously was seeking to promote racial equality, some thought the commerce clause approach "artificial" and thus "demeaning." They argued for reliance on the power of Congress to enforce the Fourteenth Amendment. That amendment's state action limitation, however, seemed to obstruct reaching private discrimination. As enacted, the 1964 act's public accommodations provisions were limited to establishments whose operations "affect commerce" or whose racial discrimination is "supported by state action."

The Supreme Court moved swiftly, accelerating decision in these two cases. The majority relied on the commerce power, validating the act in application not only to a large whites-only motel that mainly served out-of-state guests but also to a restaurant with no similar connection to interstate travel. The latter case, *McClung*, illustrates how far the commerce power has been stretched in recent years to allow Congress to legislate on matters of national concern. The restaurant mainly served a local clientele; it served blacks, but only at a take-out counter. Almost half the food used by the restaurant had come from other states, but even the Court recognized that this fact was trivial. More persuasive was

---

CIVIL RIGHTS ACT OF 1964—TITLE II

Injunctive Relief against Discrimination in Places of Public Accommodation

Section 201 (a) All persons shall be entitled to the full and equal enjoyment of the goods, services, facilities, privileges, advantages, and accommodations of any place of public accommodation, as defined in this section, without discrimination or segregation on the ground of race, color, religion, or national origin.

(b) Each of the following establishments which serves the public is a place of public accommodation within the meaning of this title if its operations affect commerce, or if discrimination or segregation by it is supported by state action:

(1) any inn, motel, or other establishment which provides lodging to transient guests, other than an establishment located within a building which contains not more than five rooms for rent or hire and which is actually occupied by the proprietor of such establishment as his residence;

(2) any restaurant, cafeteria, lunch room, lunch counter, soda fountain, or other activity principally engaged in selling food for consumption on the premises . . .

(3) any motion picture house, theater, concert hall, sports arena, stadium, or other place of exhibition or entertainment . . .

♦ **state action**
Official action by a state or under color of state law, an essential element of a claim of right raised under the "due process" or "equal protection" clause of the Fourteenth Amendment.

See also

Bethel School District v. *Fraser*

Freedom of Speech

Tinker v. *Des Moines Independent School District*

The Court unanimously upheld the portion of the Civil Rights Act of 1964 forbidding racial discrimination by hotels, restaurants, theaters, and other public accommodations.

If an act breaches the laws of two states, it constitutes distinct offenses for double-jeopardy purposes.

the fact, fully documented in congressional hearings, that discrimination in public accommodations severely hindered interstate travel by blacks. Justices William O. Douglas and Arthur J. Goldberg, concurring, argued that both the commerce clause and the Fourteenth Amendment empowered Congress to impose these regulations.

In retrospect the pre-enactment debate over which power Congress should assert seems unimportant, in either institutional or doctrinal terms. Congress need not, after all, specify which of its powers it is using. And the Supreme Court has not needed to explore the full reach of Congress's Fourteenth Amendment power, because in *Jones* v. *Alfred H. Mayer Co.* (1968) it held that the Thirteenth Amendment empowered Congress to prohibit private racial discrimination.

—KENNETH L. KARST

HEATH v. ALABAMA

474 U.S. 82 (1985)

By the same act, Heath committed crimes in two states. Men whom he hired kidnapped his wife in one state and killed her in another. He pleaded guilty in one state to avoid capital punishment and he received a life sentence. However, the other state tried him for essentially the same offense, convicted him, and sentenced him to death. Heath claimed that the second trial exposed him to double jeopardy in violation of the clause of the Fifth Amendment, applicable to the states via the incorporation doctrine.

In many cases, the Court had held that a state and the federal government may prosecute the same act if it was a crime under the laws of each. Never had the Court previously decided whether two states could prosecute the same act.

Justice Sandra Day O'Connor, for a 7–2 Court, declared that although the Fifth Amendment's double-jeopardy clause pro-

tects against successive prosecutions for the same act, if that act breached the laws of two states, it constituted distinct offenses for double-jeopardy purposes. The "dual sovereignty" rule in such cases meant that each affronted sovereign had criminal jurisdiction. The states are as sovereign toward each other as each is toward the United States. In a sense, the case created no new law because the double-jeopardy clause had never previously barred different jurisdictions from trying the same person for the same act. Nevertheless, Justices William J. Brennan and Thurgood Marshall sharply dissented.

—LEONARD W. LEVY

HELVERING v. DAVIS

301 U.S. 619 (1937)

Plaintiff, a stockholder of an affected corporation, challenged Titles II and VIII of the 1935 Social Security Act. Title II creates the old age benefits program, popularly known as "social security," and Title VIII contains the funding mechanism for that program. Under Title VIII, an employer must take a payroll deduction from each employee's wages and pay it, together with an equal amount directly from the employer, to the treasury.

Plaintiff's primary argument was that Congress lacked constitutional power to levy a tax for the purpose of providing old-age benefits. Justice Benjamin N. Cardozo, writing an opinion in which six other Justices joined, resoundingly rejected the argument that Congress had transgressed the Tenth Amendment reservation to the states of powers not delegated to the federal government. Only Justices James C. McReynolds and Pierce Butler dissented. The majority classified the old age benefits program as a legitimate exercise of Congress's power "to lay and collect taxes . . . to . . . provide . . . for the general welfare of the United States." The Court adopted a fluid definition of the general welfare. "Nor is the concept of the general welfare static. Needs that were narrow or parochial a century ago may be interwoven in our day with the well-being of a nation." The Court then examined the effects on older workers of the "purge of nationwide calamity that began in 1929" and concluded that the problem was national in scope, acute in severity, and intractable without concerted federal effort. State governments were deficient in economic resources and reluctant to finance social programs that would place them at comparative economic disadvantage with competitor states: industry would flee the new taxes and indigents would flock to any state that provided the new social benefits. (Justice Cardozo's analysis proved prescient. In the 1960s and 1970s a number of socially progressive northeastern and western states experienced these twin problems when they far exceeded national benefit norms in the federal-state cooperative programs of Aid to Families with Dependent Children and Medicaid.) Having determined that the purpose of Title II was well within the scope of the "general welfare" clause, the Court sustained the Title VIII funding provisions.

In its broad, though imprecise, reading of the term "general welfare," *Helvering* v. *Davis*, even more than its companion case, *Steward Machine Co.* v. *Davis* (1937), rejects the view that Congress, in exercising its power to tax for the general welfare, is required by the Tenth Amendment to eschew regulation of matters historically controlled by the states. In so doing, it repudiates that vein of case law, exemplified by *United States* v. *Butler* (1936), that treats the Tenth Amendment as a limitation on the federal taxing and spending power. Though *Butler* is factually distinguishable, the analysis used by Justice Cardozo in *Steward Machine Co.* and *Helvering* v. *Davis* would surely have sustained the agricultural price support provisions struck down in *Butler* a year earlier.

—GRACE GANZ BLUMBERG

HERBERT v. LANDO

441 U.S. 153 (1979)

In *Herbert* v. *Lando* a majority of the Supreme Court soundly rejected the argument that the constitutional protections afforded journalists should be expanded to bar inquiry into the editorial processes of the press in libel actions. Anthony Herbert, a Vietnam veteran, received widespread media attention when he accused his superior officers of covering up atrocities and other war crimes. Herbert sued for libel when CBS broadcast a report and *The Atlantic Monthly* published an article, both by Barry Lando, about Herbert and his accusations. Herbert conceded that he was a public figure required by *New York Times* v. *Sullivan* (1964) to prove that the media defendants acted with "actual malice." During pretrial discovery, Lando refused to answer questions on the ground that the First Amendment precluded inquiry into the state of mind of those who edit, produce, or publish, and into the editorial process.

The Court recognized that the First Amendment affords substantial protection to media defendants in libel actions, citing specifically the *Sullivan* requirement that

The plaintiff's primary argument was that Congress lacked constitutional power to levy a tax for the purpose of providing old age benefits.

♦ **plaintiff**
The party who brings an action. At the appellate level, the moving party is called the appellant or the petitioner.

See also

Butler, United States v.

H

**HODGSON v.
MINNESOTA**

110 S.Ct. 2841 (1990)

**OHIO v. AKRON
CENTER FOR
REPRODUCTIVE
HEALTH**

110 S.Ct. 2841 (1990)

*Herbert conceded
that he was a public
figure to prove that
the media
defendants acted
with "actual
malice."*

See also

New York Times v. *Sullivan*

public figures and officials must prove knowing or reckless untruth. The Court noted, however, that the Framers did not abolish civil or criminal liability for defamation when adopting the First Amendment. It reasoned that upholding a constitutional privilege that barred inquiry into facts relating directly to the central issue of the defendant's state of mind would effectively deprive plaintiffs of the very evidence necessary to prove their case. That result would substantially eliminate recovery by plaintiffs who were public figures or public officials.

Justice Lewis F. Powell separately elaborated upon the majority's admonition that in supervising discovery in libel actions, trial judges should exercise appropriate controls to prevent abuse, noting the courts' duty to consider First Amendment interests along with plaintiffs' private interest. Justice William J. Brennan, dissenting in part, asserted that the First Amendment provided a qualified editorial privilege that would yield once the plaintiff demonstrated a *prima facie* defamatory falsehood. Separately dissenting, Justice Potter J. Stewart argued that inquiry into the editorial process is irrelevant, and Justice Thurgood Marshall rejected the majority's balance of the competing First Amendment and private interests.

—KIM MCLANE WARDLAW

HODGSON v. MINNESOTA

110 S.Ct. 2841 (1990)

OHIO v. AKRON CENTER FOR REPRODUCTIVE HEALTH

110 S.Ct. 2841 (1990)

Minnesota and Ohio adopted laws requiring that parents be notified before abortions were performed on minors. By shifting 5–4 votes, the Supreme Court struck down one version of Minnesota's law and upheld another. The Court upheld the Ohio law, 6–3. Four Justices thought all the laws were valid, and three thought they were all invalid; the swing votes were Justices Sandra Day O'Connor and John Paul Stevens.

Minnesota required notification to both of a minor's biological parents before she could have an abortion. A majority concluded that this law "[did] not reasonably further any legitimate state interest." This formulation avoided the question whether a restriction on the right to have an abortion must pass the test of strict scrutiny, as *Roe* v. *Wade* (1973) had held. Whatever the rhetoric, the effective standard of review was a demanding one. Justice Stevens, for the majority, acknowledged the state's interest in supporting parents' authority and counseling, but said that any such interest could be served by a one-parent notification rule. He also conceded that the state might wish to protect parents' interests in shaping their children's values, but said this interest could not "overcome the liberty interests of a minor acting with the consent of a single parent or court." Justice O'Connor, too, found this version of the Minnesota law "unreasonable," especially considering that only half the minors in the state lived with both biological parents.

The Minnesota legislature, anticipating that the Court might hold the statute invalid, had adopted a fall-back procedure: If a minor could convince a judge that she was mature enough to give her informed consent to an abortion or that an abortion without two-parent notification was in her best interests, the judge might dispense with that notification. This "judicial bypass" was enough to secure the approval of Justice O'Connor, and so was upheld, 5–4.

The Ohio law required notification of only one parent. Here Justices O'Connor and Stevens joined the four Justices who had considered both Minnesota laws valid. Justice

Anthony M. Kennedy wrote the principal opinion, most of which was joined by a majority of the Court. The dissenters in this case, who also dissented as to the Court's disposition of Minnesota's fallback law, emphasized the severe costs of any parental notification requirement to a minor who dared not tell her parents she was pregnant and who was likely to find a judicial proceeding intimidating. As Justice Thurgood Marshall said, those costs are not merely psychological; the fear of confronting parents may cause a young woman to delay an abortion, with attendant increases in risks to her health.

Justice Antonin Scalia, who voted to uphold all three laws, took note of the way in which different majorities were pieced together in these cases and concluded that the reason lay in the lack of a principled way to distinguish the results when the Court persists in "this enterprise of devising an Abortion Code." But the Court in *Planned Parenthood of Southeastern Pennsylvania* v. *Casey* (1992), just two years later, showed its intention that *Roe* not be overruled.

—KENNETH L. KARST

HOLMES, OLIVER WENDELL, JR.

(1841–1935)

When he was appointed to the Supreme Court in 1902, at the age of sixty-one, he was best known to the general public as the son of a famous poet and man of letters; when he retired, thirty years later, he had been called "the greatest of our age in the domain of jurisprudence, and one of the greatest of the ages." Oliver Wendell Holmes's thirty years on the Supreme Court unquestionably made his reputation, and yet those years, given the aspirations of Holmes's earlier career, were years in which his mood as a judge can best be described as resignation. He was not able to achieve anything like what he thought he

could achieve as a judge; regularly he confessed his inability to do anything other than ratify "what the crowd wants." He wryly suggested that on his tombstone should be inscribed "here lies the supple tool of power," and he allegedly told John W. Davis that "if my country wants to go to hell, I am here to help it." For these expressions of resignation he was called "distinguished," "mature," and "wise," the "completely adult jurist." The constitutional jurisprudence of Holmes could be called a jurisprudence of detachment, indifference, or even despair; yet it was a jurisprudence in which contemporary commentators reveled.

Holmes's career hardly began with his appointment to the Court. He had previously written *The Common Law,* a comprehensive theoretical organization of private law subjects, taught briefly at Harvard Law School, and served for twenty years as a justice on the Massachusetts Supreme Judicial Court. Although he had not considered many constitu-

The fear of confronting parents may cause a young woman to delay an abortion, with attendant increases in risks to her health.

THE COMPLETELY ADULT JURIST

Despite Oliver Wendell Holmes's distinguished reputation, he often confessed his inability to do anything other than ratify "what the crowd wants." (Corbis)

See also

Abortion and the
    Constitution
Roe v. *Wade*
Strict Scrutiny

*Holmes was called
the "Great
Dissenter," and
some of his
dissenting opinions
were memorable for
the pithiness of their
language.*

tional cases as a state court judge, he had a distinctive philosophy of judging. There was little difficulty in the transition from the Massachusetts court to the Supreme Court; Holmes simply integrated a new set of cases with his preexistent philosophy. That philosophy's chief postulate was that judicial decisions were inescapably policy choices, and that a judge was better off if he did not make his choices appear too openly based on the "sovereign prerogative" of his power.

Arriving at that postulate had been an unexpected process for Holmes. He was convinced, at the time he wrote *The Common Law* (1881), that private law could be arranged in a "philosophically continuous series." His lectures on torts, criminal law, property, and contracts stressed the ability of those subjects to be ordered by general principles and the desirability of having judges ground their decisions in broad predictive rules rather than deferring to the more idiosyncratic and less predictable verdicts of juries. Holmes had accepted a judgeship in part because he believed that he could implement this conception of private law. Academic life was "half-life," he later said, and judging gave him an opportunity to "have a share in the practical struggle of life."

In practice, however, Holmes found that the law resisted being arranged in regular, predictable patterns. Too many factors operated to create dissonance: the need for court majorities to congeal on the scope and language of a decision; the insignificance of many cases, which were best decided by routine adherence to precedent; the very difficult and treacherous policy choices truly significant cases posed, fostering caution and compromise among judges. The result, for Holmes, was that legal doctrine developed not as a general progression toward a philosophically continuous series but rather as an uneven clustering of decisions around opposing "poles" that represented alternative policy judgments. "Two widely divergent cases"

suggested "a general distinction," which initially was "a clear one." But "as new cases cluster[ed] around the opposite poles, and beg[a]n to approach each other," the distinction became "more difficult to trace." Eventually an "arbitrary . . . mathematical line" was drawn, based on considerations of policy.

Thus judging was ultimately an exercise in making policy choices, but since the choices were often arbitrary and judges had "a general duty not to change but to work out the principles already sanctioned by the practice of the past," bold declarations of general principles were going to be few and far between. Indeed in many cases whose resolution he thought to turn on "questions of degree," or "nice considerations," or line drawing, Holmes attempted, as a state court judge, to avoid decision. He delegated "questions of degree" to juries where possible; he relied on precedents even where he felt that they had ceased to have a functional justification; he adhered to the findings of trial judges; he resorted to "technicalities" to "determine the precise place of division." And on those relatively few occasions when he was asked to consider the impact of a legislature's involvement, Holmes tended to defer to legislative solutions, especially in close cases. "Most differences," he said in one case, were "only one[s] of degree," and "difference of degree is one of the distinctions by which the right of the legislature to exercise the state police power is determined." Deference to the legislature was another means of avoiding judicial policy choices.

Holmes thus brought a curious, if consistent, theory of judging with him to the Supreme Court. Although his original aim as a legal scholar had been the derivation of general guiding principles in all areas of law, as a judge he had concluded that principles were not derived in a logical and continuous but in a random and arbitrary fashion, and that in hard cases, where principles competed, policy considerations dictated the outcome. Judges should be sensitive to the fact that cases did involve policy choices, but they should exercise great caution in making them. Hard cases, turning on "questions of degree" or "nice considerations" should be delegated to other lawmaking bodies, such as the jury and the legislature, that were closer to the "instinctive preferences and inarticulate convictions" of the community. What started out as a theory of bold, activist judicial declarations of principle had ended as a theory of deference to lawmakers who were more "at liberty to decide with sole reference . . . to convictions of policy and right." The creative jurist of *The Common Law* had become the apostle of judicial self-restraint.

In his first month on the Supreme Court Holmes wrote to his longtime correspondent Sir Frederick Pollock that he was "absorbed" with the "variety and novelty of the questions." And indeed Holmes's docket was strikingly different from that he had encountered as a Massachusetts state judge: more federal issues, a greater diversity of issues, and far more cases involving the constitutionality of legislative acts. But the new sets of cases did not require Holmes to modify his theory of judging; they merely emphasized his inclination to defer hard policy choices to others. As a Massachusetts state judge Holmes had found only one act of the Massachusetts legislature constitutionally invalid; as a Supreme Court justice he was to continue that pattern. His first opinion, *Otis v. Parker* (1902), sustained a California statute prohibiting sales of stock shares on margin on the ground that although the statute undoubtedly restricted freedom of exchange, that "general proposition" did not "take us far." The question was one of degree: How far could the legislature restrict that freedom? Since the statute's ostensible purpose, to protect persons from being taken advantage of in stock transactions, was arguably rational, Holmes's role was to defer to the legislative judgments.

Otis v. Parker set a pattern for Holmes's decisions in cases testing the constitutionality of economic regulations. Rarely did he find that questions posed by statutes were not ones of "degree"; rarely did he fail to uphold the legislative judgment. He believed that the New York legislature could regulate the hours of bakers (*Lochner v. New York*, 1905) even though he thought that hours and wages laws merely "shift[ed] the burden to a different point of incidence." He supported prohibition and antitrust legislation notwithstanding his beliefs that "legislation to make people better" was futile and that the Sherman Act was "damned nonsense." His position, in short, was that "when a State legislature has declared that in its opinion policy requires a certain measure, its actions should not be disturbed by the courts . . . unless they clearly see that there is no fair reason for the law."

Deference for Holmes did not mean absolute passivity. He thought Congress and the states had gone too far in convicting dissidents in a number of war-related speech cases, including *Abrams v. United States* (1919) (the case in which he proposed the clear and present danger test), *Gitlow v. New York* (1924), and *United States v. Schwimmer* (1928). He invalidated a Pennsylvania statute that regulated mining operations without adequate compensation in *Pennsylvania Coal Company v. Mahon* (1922). He did not think that Congress could constitutionally allow the postmaster general to deny "suspicious" persons access to the mails, and said so in two cases, *Milwaukee Socialist Democratic Publishing Co. v. Burleson* (1920) and *Leach v. Carlile Postmaster* (1921). And he struck down a Texas statute denying blacks eligibility to vote in primary elections in *Nixon v. Herndon* (1922), declaring that "states may do a good deal of classifying that it is difficult to believe rational, but there are limits."

Holmes was called, especially in the 1920s, the "Great Dissenter," and some of his dissenting opinions were memorable for the pithiness of their language. In *Lochner* v. *New York* (1905), Holmes protested against the artificiality of the freedom of contract argument used by the majority by saying that "the Fourteenth Amendment does not enact Mr. Herbert Spencer's *Social Statics.*" In *Abrams* he said that "the best test of truth is the power of the thought to get itself accepted in the competition of the market," and that "every year . . . we have to wager our salvation upon some prophecy based on imperfect knowledge." And in *Olmstead* v. *United States* (1928), he decried the use of wiretapping by federal agents: "I think it a less evil that some criminals should escape than that the government should play an ignoble part."

Each of these dissents was subsequently adopted as a majority position by a later Court. Freedom of contract was repudiated as a constitutional doctrine in *West Coast Hotel* v. *Parrish* (1937); Holmes's theory of free speech was ratified by the Court in such decisions as *Herndon* v. *Lowry* (1937) and *Yates* v. *United States* (1957); and *Katz* v. *United States* (1967) and *Berger* v. *New York* (1967) overruled the majority decision in *Olmstead.* Despite the eventual triumph of Holmes's position in these cases and despite the rhetorical force of his dissents, "Great Dissenter" is a misnomer by any standard other than a literary one. Holmes did not write an exceptionally large number of dissents, given his long service on the Court, and his positions were not often vindicated.

Holmes's dissents also gave him the reputation among commentators as being a "liberal" justice. But for every Holmes decision protecting civil liberties one could find a decision restricting them. The same Justice who declared in *Abrams* v. *United States* (1919) that "we should be eternally vigilant against attempts to check the expression of opinions" held for the Court in *Buck* v. *Bell* (1927) that a state could sterilize mental defectives without their knowing consent. "It is better for all the world, if instead of waiting to execute de-

generate offspring for crime, or to let them starve for their imbecility, society can prevent those who are manifestly unfit from continuing their kind," Holmes argued. "Three generations of imbeciles are enough."

Holmes supported the constitutionality of laws prohibiting child labor, defended the right of dissidents to speak, and resisted government efforts to wiretap bootleggers. At the same time he upheld the compulsory teaching of English in public schools, supported the rights of landowners in child trespasser cases, and helped develop a line of decisions giving virtually no constitutional protection to aliens. For a time critics ignored these latter cases and followed the *New York Times* in calling Holmes "the chief liberal of the supreme bench for twenty-nine years," but recent commentary has asserted that Holmes was "largely indifferent" to civil liberties.

Holmes's constitutional thought, then, resists ideological characterization and is notable principally for its limited interpretation of the power of judicial review. How thus does one explain Holmes's continued stature? In an age where judicial activism, especially on behalf of minority rights, is a commonplace phenomenon, Holmes's interpretation of his office appears outmoded in its circumscription. In an age where the idea of rights against the state has gained in prominence, Holmes's decisions appear to tolerate altogether too much power in legislative majorities. Only in the speech cases does Holmes seem to recognize that the contribution of dissident minorities can prevent a society's attitudes from becoming provincial and stultifying. Elsewhere Holmes's jurisprudence stands for the proposition that the state, as agent of the majority, can do what it likes until some other majority seizes power. That hardly seems a posture inclined to elicit much contemporary applause.

Yet Holmes's reputation remains, on all the modern polls, among the highest of those Justices who have served on the Supreme

Court. It is not likely to change for three reasons. First, in an era that was anxious to perpetuate the illusion that judicial decision making was somehow different from other kinds of official decision making, since judges merely "found" or "declared" law, Holmes demonstrated that judging was inescapably an exercise in policy making. This insight was a breath of fresh air in a stale jurisprudential climate. Against the ponderous intonations of other judges that they were "making no laws, deciding no policy, [and] never entering into the domain of public action," Holmes offered the theory that they were doing all those things. American jurisprudence was never the same again.

Second, Holmes, as a sitting judge, followed through the implications of his insight. If judging was inevitably an exercise in policy choices, if all legal questions eventually became "questions of degree," then there was much to be said for judges' avoiding the arbitrary choice. Other institutions existed whose mandate for representing current community sentiment seemed clearer than the judiciary's; judging could be seen as an art of avoiding decision in cases whose resolution appeared to be the arbitrary drawing of a line. In a jurisprudential climate that was adjusting to the shock of realizing that judges were making law, Holmes's theory of avoidance seemed to make a great deal of sense. Federal judges were not popularly elected officials; if they made the process of lawmaking synonymous with their arbitrary intuitions, the notion of popularly elected government seemed threatened. The wisdom in Holmes's approach to judging seemed so apparent that it took the Warren Court to displace it.

These first two contributions of Holmes, however, can be seen as having a historical dimension. To be sure, seeing judges as policy makers was a significant insight, but it is now a commonplace; judicial deference was undoubtedly an influential theory, but it has now been substantially qualified. The enduring quality of Holmes appears to rest on his having a first-class mind and in his unique manner of expression: his style. No judge has been so quotable as Holmes; no judge has come closer to making opinion writing a form of literature. Paradoxically, Holmes's style, which is notable for its capacity to engage the reader's emotions in a manner that transcends time and place, can be seen as a style produced out of indifference. The approach of Holmes to his work as a judge was that of a person more interested in completing his assigned tasks than in anything else. Holmes would be assigned opinions at a Saturday conference and seek to complete them by the following Tuesday; his opinions are notable for their brevity and their assertiveness. The celebrated epigrams in Holmes's opinions were rarely essential to the case; they were efforts to increase the emotional content of opinions whose legal analysis was often cryptic.

Holmes's style of writing was of a piece with his general attitude toward judging. Since judging was essentially an effort in accommodating competing policies, the outcome of a given case was relatively insignificant. Just where the line was drawn or where a given case located itself in a "cluster" of related cases was insignificant. One might as well, as a judge, announce one's decision as starkly and vividly as one could. A sense of the delicacy and ultimate insignificance of the process of deciding a case, then, fostered a vivid, emotion-laden, and declarative style.

Thus the legacy of Holmes's constitutional opinions is an unusual one. As contributions to the ordinary mine run of legal doctrine, they are largely insignificant. Their positions are often outmoded, their analyses attenuated, their guidelines for future cases inadequate. One feels, somehow, that Holmes has seen the clash of competing principles at stake in a constitutional law case, but has not probed very far. Once he discovered what was at issue, he either avoided decision or argued for one resolution in a blunt, assertive, and arbitrary manner. One cannot take a Holmes precedent and spin out the resolution of

See also

Abrams v. *United States*

Buck v. *Bell*

Gitlow v. *New York*

Katz v. *United States*

Lochner v. *New York*

West Coast Hotel Co. v. *Parrish*

H

**HOUSTON, EAST &
WEST TEXAS RAILWAY
CO. v. UNITED STATES
(SHREVEPORT
RATE CASE)**

234 U.S. 342 (1914)

*The Interstate
Commerce
Commission ordered
the Texas Railroad
Commission to raise
intrastate rates to
equal interstate
rates.*

See also

Minnesota Rate Cases

companion cases; one cannot go to Holmes to find the substantive bottomings of an area of law. Holmes's opinions are like a charismatic musical performance: one may be inspired in the viewing but one cannot do much with one's impressions later.

As literary expressions, however, Holmes's opinions probably surpass those of any other Justice. While it begs questions and assumes difficulties away to say that "a policeman may have a constitutional right to talk politics, but he has no constitutional right to be a policeman," the vivid contrast catches one's imagination. While "three generations of imbeciles are enough" was a misstatement of the facts in *Buck* v. *Bell* and represents an attitude toward mentally retarded persons one might find callous, it engages us, for better or worse. In phrases like these Holmes will continue to speak to subsequent generations; his constitutional opinions, and consequently his constitutional thought, will thus endure. It is ironic that Holmes bequeathed us those vivid phrases because he felt that a more painstaking, balanced approach to judging was futile. He thought of judging, as he thought of life, as "a job," and he got on with it.

—G. EDWARD WHITE

Bibliography

Burton, David (1980). *Oliver Wendell Holmes, Jr.* Boston: Twayne Publishers.

Frankfurter, Felix (1938). *Mr. Justice Holmes and the Supreme Court.* Cambridge, Mass.: Harvard University Press.

Howe, Mark DeWolfe (1957). *Justice Oliver Wendell Holmes: The Shaping Years, 1841–1870.* Cambridge, Mass.: Harvard University Press.

——— (1963). *Justice Oliver Wendell Holmes: The Proving Years, 1870–1882.* Cambridge, Mass.: Harvard University Press.

Konefsky, Samuel J. (1956). *The Legacy of Holmes and Brandeis: A Study in the Influence of Ideas.* New York: Macmillan.

Lerner, Max (1943). *The Mind and Faith of Justice Holmes.* Boston: Little, Brown.

Rogat, Yosel (1963). Mr. Justice Holmes: A Dissenting Opinion. *Stanford Law Review* 15:3–44, 254–308.

White, G. Edward (1971). The Rise and Fall of Justice Holmes. *University of Chicago Law Review* 39:51–77.

——— (1982). The Integrity of Holmes' Jurisprudence. *Hofstra Law Review* 10: 633–671.

HOUSTON, EAST & WEST TEXAS RAILWAY CO. v. UNITED STATES (SHREVEPORT RATE CASE)

234 U.S. 342 (1914)

To relieve a competitive inequality in rail rates, the Interstate Commerce Commission (ICC) ordered the Texas Railroad Commission to raise intrastate rates to equal interstate rates. Shreveport, Louisiana, to east Texas rates, set by the ICC, were higher than west Texas to east Texas rates, fixed by the states, thereby placing interstate commerce at a competitive disadvantage. With only Justices Horace Lurton and Mahlon Pitney dissenting, Justice Charles Evans Hughes relied on the Interstate Commerce Act and the commerce clause in upholding the ICC order. Hughes distinguished the *Minnesota Rate Cases* (1913) as neither involving an attempt at federal regulation nor adversely affecting or burdening interstate commerce. Emphasizing Congress's "complete and paramount" power over interstate commerce, he announced the Shreveport doctrine: "Wherever the interstate and intrastate transactions of carriers are so related that the government of the one involves the control of the other, it is Congress and not the state, that is entitled to prescribe the final and dominant rule."

—DAVID GORDON

HUDGENS v. NATIONAL LABOR RELATIONS BOARD

424 U.S. 507 (1976)

In terminating its experiment with extending *Marsh* v. *Alabama* (1946) to privately owned shopping centers, the Supreme Court, 7–2, announced in *Hudgens* that the refusal of owners to permit union picketing did not constitute state action and thus did not violate the First Amendment, even though the private property was "open to the public." That vast shopping plazas, which are central features of American culture, are not required by the First Amendment to grant freedom of speech is a highly significant feature of contemporary constitutional law.

—MARTIN SHAPIRO

HUGHES, CHARLES EVANS

(1862–1948)

The only child of a Baptist minister and a strong-willed, doting mother who hoped their son would become a man of the cloth, Charles Evans Hughes compiled a record of public service unparalleled for its diversity and achievement by any other member of the Supreme Court with the exception of William Howard Taft. In addition to pursuing a lucrative career at the bar, Hughes taught law at Cornell, served as a two-term governor of New York, was secretary of state under two presidents during the 1920s, and served as associate Justice and Chief Justice of the United States. By the narrowest of margins, he lost the electoral votes of California in 1916 and thus the presidency to the incumbent, Woodrow Wilson. Hughes was a man of imposing countenance and intellectual abilities, who left an indelible mark upon the nation's politics, diplomacy, and law.

First appointed to the Court as associate justice by President William Howard Taft, Hughes brought to the bench the social and intellectual outlook of many American progressives, those morally earnest men and women from the urban middle class who wished to purge the nation's politics of corruption, infuse the business world with greater efficiency and concern for the public welfare, and minister to the needs of the poor in the great cities. In an earlier era, such people had found an outlet for their moral energies in religion. By the turn of the twentieth century, they practiced a social gospel and undertook a "search for order" through secular careers in law, medicine, public administration, journalism, engineering, and social welfare.

"We are under a Constitution," Governor Hughes remarked shortly before his appointment to the bench, "but the Constitution is what the judges say it is, and the judiciary is the safeguard of our liberty and of our property under the Constitution." This statement

That vast shopping plazas are not required by the First Amendment to grant freedom of speech is a highly significant feature of contemporary constitutional law.

UNPARALLELED PUBLIC SERVICE

Hughes left an indelible mark upon the nation's politics, diplomacy, and law. (Corbis/Oscar White)

See also

Freedom of Speech

347

reflected the ambivalence of many progressives about the nation's fundamental charter of government and its judicial expositers on the Supreme Court. On the one hand, Hughes and other progressives clearly recognized that constitutional decision making was a subjective process, strongly influenced by the temper of the times and by the social biases and objectives of individual jurists. The Constitution, they believed, was flexible enough to accommodate the growing demands for reform that sprang from the manifold desires of businessmen, consumers, farmers, and industrial workers who wished to use government to promote economic security in an increasingly complex, interdependent capitalist economy. Like other progressives, Hughes saw government, both state and federal, as a positive instrument of human welfare that could discipline unruly economic forces, promote moral uplift, and guarantee domestic social peace by protecting the citizen from the worst vicissitudes of the marketplace.

At the same time, Hughes and other middle-class reformers had a morbid fear of socialism and resisted endowing government with excessive power over persons and property. They wanted social change under the rule of law, in conformity with American traditions of individualism, and directed by a disinterested elite of lawyers, administrators, and other experts of enlightened social progress.

By the time Hughes took his seat on the nation's highest court, the Justices had grappled inconclusively for almost five decades with the question of the reach of the constitutional power of the states and the national government to regulate economic activity. One group of Justices, influenced by the Jacksonian legacy of entrepreneurial individualism, equality, and states' rights, had combined an expansive reading of the Fourteenth Amendment's due process clause and a narrow interpretation of the commerce clause and the taxing and spending power in order to restrict both state and federal regulation of private economic decision making. Another group of Justices, heirs to the radical Republican tradition of moral reform and positive government, had been more receptive to governmental efforts at economic regulation and redistribution.

Hughes placed his considerable intellectual resources on the side of the economic nationalists and those who refused to read the due process clause as a mechanical limitation upon state regulation of economic affairs. In *Miller* v. *Wilson* (1915), for example, he wrote for a unanimous bench to sustain California's eight-hour law for women in selected occupations against a challenge that the law violated freedom of contract. The liberty protected by the due process clause, he noted, included freedom from arbitrary restraint, but not immunity from regulations designed to protect public health, morals, and welfare.

More significant, he joined the dissenters in *Coppage* v. *Kansas* (1915), where six members of the Court, speaking through Justice Mahlon Pitney, invalidated a Kansas law prohibiting yellow dog contracts on the ground that the regulation deprived employers of their contractual liberty. Hughes endorsed the dissent by Justice William R. Day that argued that the law attempted only to protect the right of individual workers to join labor unions if they so pleased and represented a legitimate exercise of the state police power, "not to require one man to employ another against his will, but to put limitations upon the sacrifice of rights which one may exact from another as a condition of employment."

Hughes's views on the federal commerce power were equally generous during this period. He wrote the two leading opinions of the era supporting the authority of Congress and the Interstate Commerce Commission (ICC) to regulate both interstate railroad rates and purely intrastate rates that undermined the efficiency of the nation's transportation network. In the *Minnesota Rate Cases* (1913) he upheld the particular exercise of rate making by the state, although he and the majority affirmed that the power of Congress "could not be denied or thwarted by the commingling of interstate and intrastate operations" of the railroad. A year later, in the landmark *Shreveport Case, Houston, East & West Texas Railway Company* v. *United States*, (1914), he spoke for all but two Justices in sustaining an order of the ICC that effectively required an increase in intrastate rates in order to bring them into line with those fixed by the commission for interstate carriers over the same territory. The power of Congress to regulate interstate commerce, he wrote, was "complete and paramount"; Congress could "prevent the common instrumentality of interstate and intrastate commercial intercourse from being used in their intrastate operations to the injury of interstate commerce."

Most progressives displayed little sympathy for the plight of either American blacks or the foreign immigrants who entered the country in large numbers during the decades before World War I. Hughes was a striking exception to the usual pattern of collaboration with the forces of racial and ethnic intolerance. He began to speak out in these years against various forms of oppression and bigotry and to lay the foundation for many of his subsequent opinions on civil rights during the 1930s.

In *McCabe* v. *Atchison, Topeka & Santa Fe Railroad* (1914), Hughes led a five-Justice majority in striking down a state law that authorized intrastate railroads to provide dining and sleeping cars only for members of the white race. The state and the carriers argued that the statute was reasonable in light of the limited economic demand by black passengers for such services, a point of view that also appealed to Justice Oliver Wendell Holmes. Hughes, however, flatly condemned the law as a violation of the Fourteenth Amendment's equal protection clause. With support from all but one of the Justices, he also overturned, in *Truax* v. *Raich* (1915), an Arizona law that

had limited the employment of aliens in the state's principal industries to 20 percent of all workers in firms with five or more employees. Discrimination against such inhabitants "because of their race or nationality," he declared, "clearly falls under the condemnation of the fundamental law."

His most impressive effort in this regard came in the famous debt peonage case, *Bailey* v. *Alabama* (1911), where he both invalidated the state's draconian statute and gained a notable rhetorical victory over Justice Holmes. Under the Alabama law, as under similar ones in force throughout the South, a person's failure to perform a labor contract without just cause and without paying back money advanced was prima facie evidence of intent to defraud, punishable by fine or imprisonment. The accused, furthermore, could not rebut the presumption with testimony "as to his uncommunicated motives, purposes, or intention." Hughes condemned this "convenient instrument for . . . coercion" as a violation of both the Thirteenth Amendment and the Anti-Peonage Act of 1867.

With a few exceptions, the progressives also displayed more concern for the suppression of crime than for the rights of the accused. The due process clause had seldom been invoked successfully against questionable methods of law enforcement and criminal procedure on the state level. In this field, too, Hughes attempted to break new ground that anticipated the jurisprudence of a later era. One case in point is *Frank* v. *Mangum* (1915), arising out of the notorious Leo Frank trial in Georgia. A young Jewish defendant had been convicted of murder and sentenced to death with a mob shouting outside the courtroom, "Hang the Jew, or we'll hang you." Frank and his lawyers had not been present during the reading of the verdict, because the trial judge could not guarantee their safety in the event of an acquittal.

Despite this evidence of intimidation, the Georgia Supreme Court upheld the conviction and sentence; a federal district judge

*Hughes's views on
the federal
commerce power
were equally
generous during this
period.*

refused Frank's petition for habeas corpus, which raised a host of due process challenges; and a majority of the Supreme Court affirmed that decision. Hughes joined a powerful dissent written by Holmes, which chastised the majority for its reasoning and called upon the Justices to "declare lynch law as little valid when practiced by a regularly drawn jury as when administered by one elected by a mob intent on death."

Hughes's initial appointment to the Court, following in the wake of his progressive achievements as governor of New York, had been received with almost unanimous acclaim. However, his nomination as Chief Justice by President Herbert Hoover in 1930 sparked furious debate. Twenty-six senators, led by the redoubtable George Norris of Nebraska, voted against his confirmation. Many of them believed, as Norris did, that the former Justice's profitable law practice during the 1920s had turned him into a pliant tool of the "powerful combinations in the political and financial world" and therefore rendered him incapable of fairly deciding the "contests between organized wealth and the ordinary citizen." Events proved Norris to be half right.

Beginning in 1930, Hughes was called upon to pilot the Court through the years of social and economic crisis spawned by the financial collapse of 1929 and the Great Depression. These were the most turbulent years in the Court's history since the decade before the Civil War and the economic crisis of the 1890s—two earlier occasions when the Justices had attempted to hold back the tide of popular revolt against the status quo.

Under Hughes's leadership, the Court majority became aggressively liberal with respect to the protection of civil liberties and civil rights, often building upon the doctrinal structure erected by the Chief Justice himself during the Progressive Era. In *Stromberg* v. *California* (1931), *Near* v. *Minnesota* (1931), and *DeJonge* v. *Oregon* (1937) Hughes's distinguished opinions significantly enlarged the scope of First Amendment rights protected against state abridgment via the due process clause. He personally drove the first judicial nail into the coffin of the separate but equal doctrine with his opinion in *Missouri ex rel. Gaines* v. *Canada* (1938), holding that a state university's refusal to admit a qualified black resident to its law school constituted a denial of equal protection. He endorsed Justice George H. Sutherland's opinion in the initial Scottsboro case, *Powell* v. *Alabama* (1932), and wrote the second one, *Norris* v. *Alabama* (1935), himself. Both opinions tightened the Supreme Court's supervision over state criminal trials involving the poor and members of racial minorities.

Hughes contributed to Justice Harlan F. Stone's famous fourth footnote in *United States* v. *Carolene Products Company* (1938), where the latter suggested that the Court had a special role to play in defending preferred freedoms, including freedom of the press, and voting rights, from legislative abridgment and also to protect discrete and insular minorities from the tyranny of the majority. Under Hughes, finally, the Court broadened the reach of habeas corpus to attack constitutionally defective state criminal convictions, and greatly expanded the *in forma pauperis* docket, which permitted indigent defendants to seek Supreme Court review of their convictions. By any yardstick, Hughes as Chief Justice compiled a civil liberties record of impressive range and impact.

The Hughes who regularly cast his vote on the libertarian side in cases touching civil liberties and civil rights during the 1930s also voted in 1935 and 1936 against many of the social and economic reforms sponsored by the Franklin D. Roosevelt administration and state governments in their efforts to cope with the economic crisis of the decade. It is this side of his performance as Chief Justice that has fueled the most controversy—and puzzlement, too, considering Hughes's toleration for many of the early anti-Depression nostrums of both the New Deal and the individual states. It was Hughes, after all, who wrote for the five-Justice majority in *Home Building & Loan Association* v. *Blaisdell* (1934), upholding a far-reaching mortgage moratorium law that many observers found to be in flat violation of the Constitution's contract clause. He also wrote for the narrow majority in the *Gold Clause Cases*, where the Justices sustained the New Deal's monetary experiments over the protests of Justice James C. McReynolds who declared, "This is Nero at his worst. The Constitution is gone."

The Chief Justice sided as well with Justice Owen J. Roberts's views in *Nebbia* v. *New York* (1934), which expanded the sphere of business activities subject to state regulation, and he spoke out forcefully against the crabbed interpretation of the federal commerce power in *Railroad Retirement Board* v. *Alton Railroad Company* (1935), where five Justices voted to strike down a mandatory pension plan for railway workers. In 1935 and 1936, however, Hughes began to vote more consistently with Roberts and the Court's four conservatives—Justices McReynolds, Pierce Butler, Willis Van Devanter, and Sutherland—against the New Deal and various state reform programs.

Six months later, in the aftermath of Roosevelt's crushing reelection victory and his threats to reorganize the federal judiciary, the Court reversed gears once again when a bare majority of the Justices—including Hughes and Roberts—sustained a minimum wage law in *West Coast Hotel Co.* v. *Parrish* (1937) and the New Deal's major labor law in the *Wagner Act Cases* (1937). Hughes wrote both landmark opinions, the first laying to rest "liberty of contract" and the second affording Congress ample latitude to regulate labor-management conflicts under the commerce clause.

Various explanations have been advanced since the 1930s to explain both Hughes's alignment with the conservatives and his eventual return to the progressive fold in 1937. Hughes justified his behavior during the first period by casting blame upon the New Deal's lawyers, who, he complained, wrote vague, unconstitutional statutes. This thesis has some credibility with respect to the controversial National Industrial Recovery Act, which the Court invalidated in *Schechter Poultry Corporation* v. *United States* (1935), but none at all when one reflects upon the care with which very good lawyers wrote both the Agricultural Adjustment Act and the Guffey Bituminous Coal Act. Others have suggested that Hughes voted with Roberts and the four conservatives on several occasions in 1935 and 1936 in order to avoid narrow 5–4 decisions that might damage the Court's reputation for constitutional sagacity. But this hypothesis does not explain why he found 5–4 decisions in favor of the New Deal any less injurious to the Court in 1937.

A more plausible explanation may be that Hughes regarded many New Deal regulatory programs and some on the state level as dangerously radical, both to the inherited constitutional system and to the social order, because of their redistributive implications. Other old progressives also fought the New Deal for similar reasons after 1935. Those who resisted the leftward drift of the administration in 1935 hoped that the electorate would repudiate Roosevelt's course of action in the 1936 referendum, but Roosevelt's landslide victory left them with few alternatives but capitulation to the popular will. In bowing to the election returns, Hughes became the leader of the Court's progressive wing once again, salvaged the basic power of judicial review, and at the same time administered a fatal blow to the president's misconceived reorganization bill. It was a stunning triumph for the Chief Justice.

Hughes accomplished this feat without serious damage to his intellectual integrity. The Justice who wrote *Miller* v. *Wilson* in 1915 did not find it too difficult to sustain minimum wage legislation two decades later. And the ideas expressed in *NLRB* v. *Jones & Laughlin* (1937) had already been given initial shape in the *Minnesota Rates Cases* and the *Shreveport Case*. For a Justice as brilliant and as crafty as Hughes, leading the constitutional revolution in 1937 was as easy as resisting it a year before, but the latter course assured his place in history.

—MICHAEL E. PARRISH

Bibliography

Freund, Paul A. (1967). Charles Evans Hughes. *Harvard Law Review* 81:34–48.

Hendel, Samuel (1951). *Charles Evans Hughes and the Supreme Court.* New York: Russell Russell.

Pusey, Merlo J. (1951). *Charles Evans Hughes.* 2 vols. New York: Harper & Row.

HUGHES COURT

(1930–1941)

The years in which Chief Justice Charles Evans Hughes presided over the Supreme Court of the United States, 1930–41, are notable for the skillful accomplishment of a revolution in constitutional interpretation. The use of the due process clauses of the Fifth Amendment and Fourteenth Amendment to protect freedom of contract and economic Darwinism against government regulation yielded to legislative supremacy and judicial self-restraint. The prevailing limits on the regulatory powers of Congress under the commerce clause were swept away. The Hamiltonian view that Congress has power to spend money for any purpose associated with the general welfare was solidified by judicial approval. The Court acquiesced in the delegation of vast lawmaking power to administrative agencies. The groundwork was laid for expanding the constitutionally guaranteed freedom of speech and freedom of the press.

Change was all about the Hughes Court. Of the eight Justices who flanked Hughes when he took his seat as Chief Justice, seven left the Court before he retired. The Court moved across the street from the cozy, old Senate Chamber in the Capitol to the gleaming white marble palace and ornate conference room used today. More profound changes were occurring in the social, economic, and political conditions that give rise to constitutional litigation, that shape the briefs and arguments of counsel, and that the Court's decisions must address.

The preceding era had been marked by the rise to dominance of large-scale business and financial enterprise. Vast aggregations of men and women and material wealth were needed to develop America's resources, to harness the power unleashed by science and technology, and to capture the efficiencies of mass production for mass markets. Unlocking America's agricultural and industrial wealth made for higher standards of living and an extremely mobile society. With the gains had come corruption, hardships, injustices, and pressure for political action; but in the general prosperity of the 1920s the costs were too often ignored.

Yet the farmers were left behind and too much of the wealth was committed to speculation in corporate securities. The bursting of the latter bubble in November 1929 heralded an economic depression of unprecedented length and depth. Ninety percent of the market value of stock in industrial corporations was wiped out in three years. Twenty-five percent of the land in Mississippi was auctioned off in mortgage foreclosure sales. Factory payrolls were cut in half. One out of every four persons seeking employment was without work. The Depression destroyed people's faith in the industrial magnates and financiers, even in the ethic of individual self-reliance. The stability of American institutions seemed uncertain.

The election of Franklin D. Roosevelt as president of the United States brought a new, more active political philosophy to government. Government, Roosevelt asserted, should seek to prevent the abuse of superior economic power, to temper the conflicts, and to work out the accommodations and adjustments that a simpler age had supposed could safely be left to individual ability and the free play of economic forces. Government should also meet the basic need for jobs and, in the case of those who could not work, for food, clothing, and shelter. For the most part these responsibilities must be met by the federal government, which alone was capable of dealing with an economy national in scope and complexity.

Roosevelt's "New Deal" not only provided money and jobs for the worst victims of the Depression, it enacted the legislation and established the government agencies upon which national economic policies would rest for at least half a century: the Agricultural Adjustment Acts, the Wagner National Labor Relations Act, the Fair Labor Standards Act, the Social Security Act, and the Securities and Exchange Act.

Judicial review permits those who lose battles in the executive and legislative branches to carry the war to the courts. Earlier in the century many courts, including the Supreme Court, had clung to the vision of small government, economic laissez-faire, and unbounded opportunity for self-reliant individuals. Judges had thus struck down as violations of the due process clauses of the Fifth and Fourteenth Amendments many measures now generally accepted as basic to a modern industrial and urban society: maximum hours and minimum wage laws, laws forbidding industrial homework, and laws protecting the organization of labor unions. The critical question for the Supreme Court in the Hughes era would be whether the Court would persevere or change the course of American constitutional law.

The response of Justices Willis Van Devanter, James C. McReynolds, George Sutherland, and Pierce Butler was predictable: they would vote to preserve the old regime of limited federal government and economic laissez-faire. Three Justices—Louis D. Brandeis, Harlan F. Stone, and Benjamin N. Cardozo—could be expected to eschew the use of judicial power to protect economic liberty, and might not condemn broader congressional interpretation of the commerce clause. The balance rested in the hands of Chief Justice Hughes and Justice Owen J. Roberts.

At first the Court challenged the New Deal. The National Recovery Administration sought to halt the downward spiral in wages and prices by stimulating the negotiation of industry-by-industry and market-by-market codes of "fair competition" fixing minimum prices and wages and outlawing "destructive" competitive practices. In *Schechter Poultry Corporation* v. *United States* (1935) the Court held the underlying legislation unconstitutional. The major New Deal measure for dealing with the plight of the farmers was held unconstitutional in *United States* v. *Butler* (1936) as "a statutory plan to regulate and control agricultural production, a matter beyond the powers delegated to the federal government." *Carter* v. *Carter Coal Company* (1936) held that, because production was a purely local activity, Congress lacked power to legislate concerning the wages and hours of bituminous coal miners. In *Morehead* v. *New York ex rel. Tipaldo* (1936) the four conservative Justices, joined by Justice Roberts, reaffirmed the 1923 decision in *Adkins* v. *Children's Memorial Hospital* invalidating a law fixing minimum wages for women. These opinions seemed to presage invalidation of such other fundamental New Deal measures as the National Labor Relations Act, a proposed federal wage and hour law, and even the Social Security Act.

President Roosevelt responded with strong criticism. The *Schechter* ruling, he said, was evidence that the Court was still living "in the horse and buggy age." On February 5, 1937, the president sent a special message to Congress urging enactment of a bill to create one new judgeship for every federal judge over the age of seventy who railed to retire.

Much more than legal logic lay behind the Hughes Court's recognition of virtually unlimited congressional power under the commerce clause.

The message spoke of the heavy burden under which the courts—particularly the Supreme Court—were laboring, of the "delicate subject" of "aged or infirm judges," and of the need for "a constant infusion of new blood in the courts." No one doubted Roosevelt's true purpose. Six of the nine Supreme Court Justices were more than seventy years old. Six new Justices would ensure a majority ready to uphold the constitutionality of New Deal legislation. A month later the president addressed the nation more candidly, acknowledging that he hoped "to bring to the decision of social and economic problems younger men who have had personal experience and contact with modern facts and circumstances under which average men have to live and work."

Despite overwhelming popular support for New Deal legislation and despite the president's landslide reelection only a few months earlier, the court-packing plan was defeated. The president's disingenuous explanation was vulnerable to factual criticism. Justice Brandeis, widely known as a progressive dissenter from his colleagues' conservative philosophy, joined Chief Justice Hughes in a letter to the Senate Judiciary Committee demonstrating that the Court was fully abreast of its docket and would be less efficient if converted into a body of fifteen Justices. Much of the political opposition came from conservative strongholds, but the current ran deeper. The American people had a well-nigh religious attachment to constitutionalism and the Supreme Court. They intuitively realized that packing the Court in order to reverse the course of its decisions would destroy its independence and erode the essence of constitutionalism. Yet no explanation is complete without recalling the contemporary quip: "A switch in time saves nine." The final defeat of the court-packing plan came after a critical turning in the Court's own interpretation of constitutional limitations.

The shift first became manifest in *West Coast Hotel Co.* v. *Parrish* (1937), a 5–4 decision upholding the constitutionality of a state statute authorizing a board to set minimum wages for women. The Chief Justice's opinion overruled the *Adkins* case and markedly loosened the standards of substantive due process that had previously constricted regulation of contractual relations. To the old state police power doctrine confining the permissible objectives of government to health, safety, and morals, the Chief Justice added broadly the "welfare of the people" and "the interests of the community." Where the old opinions declared as an abstract truth that "The employer and the employee have equality of right and any legislation that disturbs the equality is an arbitrary interference with liberty of contract," the new majority more realistically asserted that a legislature may consider the "relatively weak bargaining power of women" and may "adopt measures to reduce the evils of the "sweating system." There were also hints of greater judicial deference to legislative judgments: "regulation which is reasonable in relation to its subject and is adopted in the interests of the community is due process."

The *West Coast Hotel* case inaugurated a line of decisions sustaining every challenged economic regulation enacted by a state legislature or by the Congress. General minimum wage and maximum hour laws, price regulations, and labor relations acts—all were upheld. Even prior to Hughes's retirement, the trend was intensified by the normal replacement of all but one of the Justices who had sat with Hughes on his first day as Chief Justice. The philosophy of judicial self-restraint gradually became dominant on the Court, in the laws, and throughout the legal profession.

The troublesome problems of constitutional interpretation often call for striking a balance between the opposing ideals of democratic self-government and judicial particularization of majestic but general and undefined constitutional limitations. The philosophy of legislative supremacy and judicial self-restraint that came to dominate constitutional interpretation in the time of the Hughes Court was often asserted and widely accepted as broadly applicable to all constitutional adjudication except the enforcement of clear and specific commands. The Hughes Court thus set the stage for the central constitutional debate of the next major era in constitutional history. As claims to judicial protection of civil liberties and civil rights became the focus of attention, judicial activism would be revived by substituting strict scrutiny for judicial deference in many areas of preferred freedoms and fundamental rights. Many of the new judicial activists would be liberals or progressives of the same stripe that had pressed for democratic self-government in the days when their political power confronted conservative dominance of the courts. But the opinions of the Hughes Court still mark the end of effective constitutional challenges to legislative regulation of economic activity.

The Hughes Court broke new ground in interpretation of the commerce clause only a few months after the minimum wage decision. In *National Labor Relations Board* v. *Jones & Laughlin Steel Corporation* (1937) the Labor Board, under authority delegated by the Wagner Act, had ordered Jones & Laughlin to reinstate four employees discharged from production and maintenance jobs in a basic steel mill because of their union activity. Both Jones & Laughlin's antiunion activities and the order for reinstatement were beyond the reach of federal power as delimited by the old line between production and interstate movement. The lower court had so decided. Led by Chief Justice Hughes, a bare majority of the Supreme Court Justices reversed that decision. Rejecting the old conceptualism that had asked whether the regulated activity had a "legal or logical connection to interstate commerce," the Court appraised the relation by "a practical judgment drawn from experience." Congress could reasonably conclude that an employer's antiunion activities and refusal to bargain collectively might result in strikes, and that a strike at a basic steel mill drawing its raw materials from, and shipping its products to, many states might in fact affect the movement of interstate commerce.

The *Jones & Laughlin* opinion appeared to retain some judicially enforceable constitutional check upon the congressional power under the commerce clause: "Undoubtedly the scope of this power must be considered in the light of our dual system of government and may not be extended so far as to embrace effects upon interstate commerce so indirect and remote that to embrace them, in view of our complex society, would effectually obliterate the distinction between what is national and what is local and create a completely centralized government." But the check proved illusory. The quoted admonition, while operable as a political principle guiding congressional judgment, yields no rule of law capable of judicial administration. Once the distinctions between interstate movement and production and between "direct" and "indirect" effects upon interstate commerce are rejected, the number of links in the chain of cause and effect becomes irrelevant. Federal power would reach to the local machine shop that repaired the chain saws that cut the trees that yielded the pulp wood that yielded the pulp that made the paper bought by the publisher to print the newspaper that circulated in interstate commerce. The size of the particular establishment or transaction also became irrelevant, for the cumulative effect of many small local activities might have a major impact upon interstate commerce. The new judicial deference, moreover, called for leaving such questions to Congress.

A second doctrinal development accelerated the trend. The Fair Labor Standards Act of 1938 required employers to pay workers engaged in the production of goods for shipment in interstate commerce no less than a specified minimum wage. The act also forbade shipping in interstate commerce any goods produced by workers who had not received the minimum wage. Congress claimed the power to exclude from the pipeline of interstate commerce things that would, in its judgment, do harm in the receiving state. Goods produced at substandard wages and shipped in interstate commerce might depress wages paid in the receiving states, and also in other producing states. The theory had been applied as early as 1903 to uphold a congressional law forbidding the interstate shipment of lottery tickets, but in 1918, under the doctrine barring federal regulation of production, the Court had struck down an act of Congress barring the interstate shipment of goods made with child labor. Having rejected that doctrine in the *Labor Board Cases*, the Hughes Court readily upheld the constitutionality of the Fair Labor Standards Act upon the theory of the lottery cases. The direct prohibition against paying less than the specified minimum wage was also upheld as a necessary and proper means of preventing goods made under substandard conditions from moving in interstate commerce and doing harm in other states. Years later similar reasoning supported broader decisions upholding the power of Congress to regulate or prohibit the local possession or use of firearms and other articles that have moved in interstate commerce.

Much more than legal logic lay behind the Hughes Court's recognition of virtually unlimited congressional power under the commerce clause. The markets of major firms had become nationwide. A complex and interconnected national economy made widely separated localities interdependent. A century earlier layoffs at the iron foundry in Saugus, Massachusetts, would have had scant visible effect in other states. During the Great Depression no one could miss the fact that layoffs at the steel mills in Pittsburgh, Pennsylvania, reduced the demand for clothing and so caused more layoffs at the textile mills in Charlotte, North Carolina, and Fall River, Massachusetts. Even as the Hughes Court deliberated the *Labor Board Cases*, a strike at a General Motors automobile assembly plant in Michigan was injuring automobile sales agencies in cities and towns throughout the United States.

The states were incapable of dealing with many of the evils accompanying industrialization. Many states were smaller and less powerful than the giant public utilities and industrial corporations. Massachusetts might forbid the employment of child labor, or fix a minimum wage if the due process clause permitted, but the cost of such measures was the flight of Massachusetts industries to North Carolina or South Carolina. New York might seek to ensure the welfare of its dairy farmers by setting minimum prices that handlers should pay for milk, only to watch the handlers turn to Vermont farmers who could sell at lower prices. The commerce clause barred the states from erecting protective barriers against out-of-state competition.

A shift in intellectual mode was also important. The rise of legal realism stimulated by publication of Oliver Wendell Holmes's *The Common Law* in 1881 had made it increasingly difficult for courts to find guidance in such abstractions as the equality of right between employer and employee or in such rhetorical questions as "What possible legal or logical connection is there between an employee's membership in a labor organization and the carrying on of interstate commerce?" The harsh facts of the Depression made both impossible.

The proper division of regulatory activity between the nation and the states is and may always be a much debated question of constitutional dimension. Today the question is nonetheless almost exclusively political. The Hughes Court yielded the final word to Congress.

The enormous expansion of the federal establishment that began in the 1930s and continued for half a century finds a second constitutional source in the power that Article I, Section 8, grants to Congress: "to lay and collect taxes . . . and provide for the common defense and general welfare of the United States." Here, too, the key judicial precedents of the modern era are decisions of the Hughes Court.

The scope of the taxing and spending power had been disputed from the beginning. Jeffersonian localists argued that the words "general welfare" encompassed only the purposes expressly and somewhat more specifically stated later in Article I. Spending for internal improvements gradually became accepted practice in the political branches, but the Supreme Court had had no occasion to adjudicate the issue of constitutional power because no litigant could show that he or she had suffered the kind of particular injury that would sustain a cause of action.

The Roosevelt administration not only spent federal funds on an unprecedented scale in order to relieve unemployment; it also broke new ground in using subsidies to shape the conduct of both state governments and private persons. The Agricultural Adjustment Act of 1933 levied a tax upon processors in order to pay subsidies to farmers who would agree to reduce the acreage sown to crops. The aim was to stabilize the prices of agricultural commodities. Linking the subsidy payments to the processing tax gave the processors standing to challenge the tax on the ground that the payments exceeded the limits of the federal spending power. In *United States* v. *Butler* (1936) the Hughes Court held the act unconstitutional because conditioning the farmer's allotments upon the reduction of his planted acreage made the whole "a statutory plan to regulate and control agricultural production, a matter beyond the power delegated to the federal government."

The decision was a prime target of President Roosevelt's criticism. It aroused fears that the Hughes Court would also invalidate the Social Security Act, a key New Deal measure establishing systems of unemployment and old-age and survivors insurance. The title of the act dealing with unemployment levied a federal payroll tax upon all employers of eight or more individuals but gave a credit of up to 90 percent of the federal tax for employer contributions to a state employment fund meeting federal standards specified in the act. Very few states had previously established unemployment insurance, but the act's combination of pressure and inducement proved effective. The combination was attacked as a coercive, unconstitutional invasion of the realm reserved exclusively to the states by the Tenth Amendment, which, if generalized, would enable federal authorities to induce, if not indeed compel, state enactments for any purpose within the realm of state power, and generally to control state administration of state laws. In *Steward Machine Company* v. *Davis* (1937) the five-Justice majority answered that offering a choice or even a temptation is not coercion. Spending to relieve the needs of the army of unemployed in a nationwide depression serves the general welfare, the majority continued; the spending power knows no other limitation.

In later decades congressional spending programs would grow in size, spreading from agriculture and social insurance to such areas as housing, highway construction, education, medical care, and local law enforcement. Many federal grants-in-aid to both state and private institutions are conditioned upon observance of federal standards. The balance to be struck between federal standards and state autonomy is sharply debated, but in this area, as under the commerce clause, the question is now almost exclusively left to political discretion as a result of the decisions of the Hughes Court.

Questions concerning the delegation of power gave rise to the fourth major area of constitutional law shaped by the Hughes Court. Congress makes the laws, it is said; the executive carries out the laws; and the judiciary interprets the laws and resolves controversies between executive and legislative officials. Never quite true, this old and simple division of functions proved largely incompatible with the new role established for federal government by the Roosevelt administration. Much law, however denominated, would have to be made by executive departments or new administrative agencies authorized by Congress, such as the Securities and Exchange Commission and the Civil Aeronautics Board. Under the traditional division the new arrangements were subject to attack as unconstitutional attempts to delegate to other agencies part of the legislative power that Congress alone can exercise.

The flow of decisions in the Hughes Court upon this question paralleled the course taken under the due process, commerce, and spending clauses. At first the majority seemed disposed to resist the new political order as in *Panama Refining Company* v. *Ryan* (1935) and *Schechter Poultry Corporation* v. *United States* (1935). Later decisions, however, reversed the initial trend. *United States* v. *Rock Royal Cooperative, Inc.,* (1939) is illustrative. The Agricultural Marketing Agreement Act gave the secretary of agriculture broad authority to regulate the marketing of eight agricultural commodities, including milk, with a view to reestablishing the purchasing power of farmers at the level in a base period, usually 1909–14. In the case of milk, however, if the secretary found the prices so determined to be unreasonable, he was authorized to fix producer prices at a level that would reflect pertinent economic conditions in local milk markets, provide an adequate supply of wholesome milk, and be in the public interest. The purported standards were numerous and broad enough to impose no significant limit upon the secretary's decisions. Nevertheless, the Court upheld the delegation. It was enough that Congress had limited the secretary's power to specified commodities, had specifically contemplated price regulation, and had provided standards by which the secretary's judgment was to be guided after hearing interested parties. The decision set the pattern for all subsequent legislative draftsmen and judicial determinations.

The contributions of the Hughes Court to the law of the First Amendment were less definitive than in the areas of the commerce clause, economic due process, the spending power, and delegation; but they were not less important. The Hughes Court infused the First Amendment with a new and broader vitality that still drives the expansion of the constitutional protection available to both individual speakers and institutional press.

Apart from the World War I prosecution of pacifists and socialists for speeches and pamphlets alleged to interfere with the production of munitions or conscription for the armed forces, federal law posed few threats to freedom of expression. State laws were more restrictive. The illiberal decisions of the 1920s sustaining the prosecution of leftists under state criminal syndicalism laws assumed that the First Amendment's guarantees against congressional abridgment of freedom of expression are, by virtue of the Fourteenth Amendment, equally applicable to the states. These obiter dicta encouraged constitutional attack upon state statutes, municipal ordinances, and judge-made doctrines restricting political and religious expression. In this area Chief Justice Hughes and Justice Roberts quickly allied themselves with the three Justices of established liberal reputation.

Two early opinions highlight the protection that the First and Fourteenth Amendments afford the press against previous restraints. *Near* v. *Minnesota* (1931) was decided upon appeal from a state court's injunction forbidding further publication of *The Saturday Press,* a weekly newspaper, upon the ground that it was "largely devoted to malicious, scandalous and defamatory articles." The newspaper had charged Minneapolis officials with serious offenses in tolerating gambling, bootlegging, and racketeering; the articles were scurrilous and anti-Semitic in tone and content. The decree was authorized by a Minnesota statute. Minnesota had experienced a rash of similar scandal sheets, some of whose publishers were believed to use their journals for blackmail. In an opinion by Chief Justice Hughes, the Supreme Court held that the injunction against publication was an infringement upon the liberty of the press guaranteed by the Fourteenth Amendment regardless of whether the charges were true or false. For any wrong the publisher had committed or might commit, public and private redress might be available; but this prior restraint was inconsistent with the constitutional liberty.

The law's strong set against previous restraints was underscored a few years later by *Grosjean* v. *American Press Company* (1936), where a review of history led the Hughes Court to conclude that the First and Fourteenth Amendments bar not only censorship but also taxes that single out the press and are thus calculated to limit the circulation of information.

The chief danger to freedom or expression by the poor, the unorthodox, and the unpopular lies in state statutes and municipal ordinances that give local authorities wide discretion in preserving the peace and public order. Such laws not only invite suppression of unorthodox ideas by discriminatory enforcement but they also encourage self-censorship in hope of avoiding official interference. The Hughes Court laid the foundations for current constitutional doctrines narrowing the opportunities for abuse.

Lovell v. *City of Griffin* (1938) introduced the doctrine that a law requiring a license for the use of the streets or parks for the distribution of leaflets, speeches, parades, or other forms of expression must, explicitly or by prior judicial interpretation, confine the licensing authority to considerations of traffic management, crowd control, or other physical inconvenience or menace to the public. From there it was only a short step to holding in *Cantwell* v. *Connecticut* (1941) that a man may not be punished for words or a street demonstration, however offensive to the audience, under a broad, general rubric that invites reprisal for the expression of unorthodox views instead of requiring a narrow judgment concerning the risk of immediate violence. *Thornhill* v. *Alabama* (1941), once important for the ruling that peaceful picketing in a labor dispute is a form of expression protected by the First Amendment, also introduced the then novel and still controversial doctrine that an individual convicted under a law drawn so broadly as to cover both expression subject to regulation and constitutionally protected expression may challenge the constitutionality of the statute "on its face" even though his own conduct would not be constitutionally protected against punishment under narrower legislation.

Supreme Court Justices and other constitutionalists still debate the theoretical question how far the First and Fourteenth Amendments secure individuals a right to some public forum for the purposes of expression. The Hughes Court's decision in *Hague* v. *Congress of Industrial Organizations* (1939) recognized such a right to the use of streets, parks, and like public places traditionally open for purposes of assembly, communication, and discussion of public questions: "Such use of the streets and public places has, from ancient times, been a part of the privileges, immunities, rights and liberties of citizens. The privilege . . . to use the streets and parks for communication of views on national questions may be regulated in the interest of all; . . . but must not in the guise of regulation be abridged or denied." On this ground *Schneider* v. *State* (1939) invalidated four city ordinances banning the use of the streets to hand out leaflets. Against this background later Justices would wrestle with the constitutional problems raised by restrictions upon house-to-house canvassing and the use of other government properties for the purpose of expression.

The Hughes Court presided over a revolution in constitutional interpretation. Many conservatives were convinced that in joining the liberal Justices, the Chief Justice and Justice Roberts unconscionably distorted the law

H

HUMPHREY'S EXECUTOR v. UNITED STATES

295 U.S. 602 (1935)

Humphrey was a blatantly probusiness, antiadministration official who thwarted the objectives of the FTC.

to suit the winds of politics. Yet while the revolution is plain, the groundbreaking decisions did appreciably less violence than some reforming decisions of the later Warren Court and Burger Court to the ideal of a coherent, growing, yet continuing body of law binding the judges as well as the litigants. Doubtless the presence of two competing lines of authority in the Court's earlier decisions often made it easier for the Hughes Court to perform this part of the judicial function. Liberty of contract had never been absolute. The Court had previously sustained, in special contexts, the power of Congress to regulate local activities affecting interstate commerce. Acceptance of the Hughes Court's changes was also the easier because the Hughes Court was diminishing judicial interference with legislative innovations whereas the Warren and Burger Courts pressed far-reaching reforms without legislative support and sometimes against the will expressed by the people's elected representatives. That the old structure and powers of government should be shaped to industrialization, urbanization, and a national economy seemed more inevitable than that public schools should be integrated by busing, that prayer and Bible-reading should be banned from the public schools, or that abortion should be made a matter of personal choice. Yet even when the differences are acknowledged, much of the success of the Hughes Court in managing its revolution in constitutional interpretation seems attributable to the Chief Justice's belief in the value of a coherent, though changing, body of law, to his character, and to his talents combining the perception and sagacity drawn from an earlier, active political life with his extraordinary legal craftsmanship, earlier fine-honed as an Associate Justice.

—ARCHIBALD COX

Bibliography

Alsop, Joseph, and Catledge, Turner (1938). *The 168 Days.* Garden City, N.Y.: Doubleday.

Jackson, Robert H. (1941). *The Struggle for Judicial Supremacy.* New York: Knopf.

Murphy, Paul (1972). *The Constitution in Crisis Times 1918–1969* New York: Harper & Row.

Pusey, Merlo J. (1951). *Charles Evans Hughes.* New York: Macmillan.

Stern, Robert L. (1946). The Commerce Clause and the National Economy, 1933–1946. *Harvard Law Review* 59: 645–693.

Swindler, William F. (1970). *Court and Constitution in the Twentieth Century,* Part I. Indianapolis: Bobbs-Merrill.

HUMPHREY'S EXECUTOR v. UNITED STATES

295 U.S. 602 (1935)

This decision probably more than any other contributed to President Franklin D. Roosevelt's animus against the Supreme Court. As Attorney General Robert H. Jackson wrote, the opinion of the unanimous Court by Justice George Sutherland gave the impression "that the President had flouted the Constitution, rather than that the Court had simply changed its mind within the past ten years." In *Myers* v. *United States* (1926) a 6–3 Court had sustained the removal power of the president in a case involving a postmaster. Sutherland had joined the opinion of the Court, including its obiter dictum that the removal power extended even to members of independent regulatory commissions. Roosevelt, relying on *Myers,* removed from the Federal Trade Commission (FTC) William Humphrey, who had been reappointed for a six-year term in 1931. The Federal Trade Commission Act provided for removal for cause, including inefficiency or malfeasance.

Humphrey was a blatantly probusiness, antiadministration official who thwarted the objectives of the FTC. After he died, his executor sued for Humphrey's back pay, raising the question of whether a member of an administrative tribunal created by Congress to implement legislative policies can be removed as if he were a member of the executive department. Ruling against the removal power, Sutherland distinguished *Myers,* overruled the dictum, and failed to mention that Roosevelt had acted in good faith when he relied on *Myers.* Liberal Justices joined Sutherland for the reason given privately by Justice Louis D. Brandeis: if a Huey Long were president and the administration's argument prevailed, the commissions would become compliant agents of the executive.

Despite the Court's unanimity, its strict reliance on a simplistic separation of powers theory ignored the fact that the administrative agencies, however mixed their powers, were executive agencies and Congress acknowledged that fact. Moreover, had Roosevelt chosen to remove Humphrey for cause, the Court would not likely have challenged his judgment. The Court followed *Humphrey* in *Wiener* v. *United States* (1958), ruling that President Dwight D. Eisenhower could not remove a member of a quasi-judicial agency without cause.

—LEONARD W. LEVY

HURTADO v. CALIFORNIA

110 U.S. 516 (1884)

Due process of law reached a watershed in *Hurtado.* For centuries due process had stood for a cluster of specific procedures associated especially with trial by jury. Sir Edward Coke, for example, explicitly associated due process with indictment by grand jury. The Bill of Rights enumerated many of the rights that the concept of due process spaciously accommodated. The Fourteenth Amendment's due process clause was copied verbatim from the Fifth Amendment, where the same clause sat cheek-by-jowl with a number of specific guarantees that due process had embodied as a common law concept. The framers of the Fifth Amendment had added the due process clause as an additional assurance, a rhetorical flourish, and a genuflection toward the traditions of Magna Carta. In *Hurtado,* the Supreme Court began to whittle away at the conventional meanings of procedural due process and did not pause until *Moore* v. *Dempsey* (1923).

California tried and convicted Hurtado on an information for murder, filed by his prosecutor. He claimed that because the state had denied him indictment by grand jury, it had violated the due process clause of the Fourteenth Amendment. The Court, sustaining the conviction, 7–1, rejected Hurtado's claim on the ground that "any legal proceeding" that protects "liberty and justice" is due process. Justice Stanley Matthews, for the Court, reasoned that the Constitution, having been framed for an undefined and expanding future, must recognize new procedures. To hold otherwise, he said, would render the Constitution "incapable of progress and improvement. It would be to stamp upon our jurisprudence the unchangeableness attributed to the Medes and the Persians. . . ." Matthews also argued that no part of the Constitution was superfluous; the fact that the Fifth Amendment included both a guarantee of grand jury proceedings in federal prosecutions and the guarantee of due process showed that the latter did not mean the former.

Justice John Marshall Harlan, dissenting, had history on his side when he found grand jury proceedings to be an indispensable requisite of due process, but whether history should have disposed of the question is a different issue. Harlan did not think that prosecuting individuals for their lives by information inaugurated a new era of progress in the constitutional law of criminal procedure. The Court's inexorable logic, he asserted, as if asserting the unthinkable, would lead to the

In Hurtado, *the Supreme Court began to whittle away at the conventional meanings of procedural due process and did not pause until* Moore v. Dempsey.

♦ **indictment**
A formal statement by a grand jury charging a person with a criminal offense.

See also

Myers v. *United States*

conclusion that due process did not even guarantee the traditional trial by jury. Later cases justified his fears.

—LEONARD W. LEVY

HUSTLER MAGAZINE AND LARRY FLYNT v. JERRY FALWELL

485 U.S. 46 (1988)

On first glance, this appears to be a case in which the First Amendment ran amok because the Supreme Court extended its constitutional protection to a malevolent libel that in no way expressed an opinion or an idea. *Hustler* magazine, which caters to prurient interests, published a parody of an advertise-

ment in which Jerry Falwell, a nationally syndicated television preacher and head of a political organization called the Moral Majority, was purportedly interviewed. By innuendo, the parody suggested that his first experience with sexual intercourse was with his mother in an outhouse when he was drunk. At the bottom of the page in small print was a disclaimer, "ad parody—not to be taken seriously."

Falwell sued for damages, claiming libel and the intentional infliction of emotional distress. A jury found for him on the issue of emotional distress but against him on the libel claim because the parody could not reasonably be understood to describe actual facts. *Hustler* appealed the verdict on the emotional distress issue, arguing that the "actual malice" standard of *New York Times* v. *Sullivan* (1964) must be met before one could recover for emotional distress. The Fourth Circuit sustained the verdict on the ground that the *Sullivan* standard had been met because *Hustler* acted recklessly. Unanimously, the Supreme Court sustained *Hustler* in an opinion by Chief Justice William H. Rehnquist.

His opinion makes little sense unless one understands that the dispositive fact was the trial jury's refusal to find that *Hustler* had libeled Falwell. One might think that if the parody was not believable, it was false, and if it was false and recklessly published with malice, the *Sullivan* standard had been met; but the Court took as decisive the jury's finding that *Hustler* had not published a libel because no one would reasonably believe the parody described a fact. Accordingly, the question before the Court was not whether Falwell's reputation had been maliciously and recklessly libeled. Rather, the question was whether his emotional distress overcame a First Amendment protection for offensive speech calculated to inflict psychological injury, "even when that speech could not reasonably have been interpreted as stating actual facts about the public figure involved."

See also

Moore v. *Dempsey*

In response to this question, Rehnquist discoursed on the importance of the First Amendment to the free flow of "ideas and opinions" and the need for "robust debate" concerning public figures involved in important public issues. One might read this section of the opinion as a parody of the Court's great free-speech opinions, for nothing in *Hustler*'s alleged interview with Falwell related to any public issues or reflected the expression of ideas or opinions.

More persuasive was Rehnquist's argument that to hold that public figures or public officials might recover damages for the infliction of emotional distress might mean that "political cartoonists and satirists would be subjected to damages awards without any showing that their work falsely defamed its subject." Nevertheless, Thomas Nast's depictions of the Tweed Ring or Herblock's of Richard Nixon seem wholly different from *Hustler*'s of Falwell; *Hustler* carried no ring of truth and addressed no issues other than, broadly speaking, Falwell's moral character. The outrageousness of the allegation against him places it apart from traditional political cartooning and satire, but the Court was unable to make distinctions. It relied on the *Sullivan* standard by concluding that a public figure victimized by a publication inflicting emotional injury could not recover damages without showing false facts published with actual malice.

Justice Byron R. White in an inch of space, separately concurring, noted that as he saw the case, the *Sullivan* precedent was irrelevant because the jury found that the *Hustler* parody contained no assertion of fact. That being so, one may conclude that the Court correctly decided that the First Amendment barred Falwell from recovering damages on the sole ground that he had suffered emotional distress.

—LEONARD W. LEVY

On first glance, this appears to be a case in which the First Amendment ran amok.

See also

New York Times v. Sullivan

I

ILLINOIS v. PERKINS

110 S.Ct. 2394 (1990)

An eight-member majority of the Supreme Court held that the right against self-incrimination is not abridged when prisoners incriminate themselves in statements voluntarily made to a cellmate who is an undercover officer. Justice Anthony M. Kennedy for the Court reasoned that the officer posing as a prisoner did not have to give *Miranda* warnings before asking questions that sought incriminating responses because Perkins, although in custody, was not in a coercive situation when he boasted to his cellmate about a murder. He spoke freely to a fellow inmate. He was tricked, but the *Miranda* rules prohibit coercion, not deception. Any statement freely made without compelling influences is admissible in evidence. The Court also held that because the prisoner had not yet been charged for the crime that was the subject of the interrogation, the right to counsel had not yet come into play. Therefore, the prisoner suffered no violation of his Sixth Amendment right. Justice William J. Brennan, who concurred separately, agreed completely on the Fifth Amendment issue, but believed that the police deception raised a question of due process of law.

Justice Thurgood Marshall, the lone dissenter, contended that because the prisoner was in custody, the interrogation should not have occurred without *Miranda* warnings. He believed that the Court had carved out of *Miranda* an undercover-agent exception.

—LEONARD W. LEVY

IMMIGRATION AND NATURALIZATION SERVICE v. CHADHA

462 U.S. 919 (1983)

Immigration and Naturalization Service v. *Chadha* cast serious doubt on the use of the legislative veto, a device by which Congress seeks to retain control over the use of delegated powers. *Chadha* involved a provision in the immigration and nationality act that permitted either house of Congress, by resolution, to overturn orders of the attorney general suspending deportation of aliens.

The Supreme Court held, 7–2, that congressional review of such cases was legislative in character, and was therefore subject to the provisions of Article I requiring the concurrence of both houses and an opportunity for the president to exercise his veto power before the resolution can have the force of law. The majority opinion, by Chief Justice Warren E. Burger, declared that the one-house legislative veto violated the constitutional principles of separation of powers and bicameralism.

Justice Byron R. White, dissenting, ascribed to the decision much greater scope than did the majority. White asserted that the *Chadha* decision effectively invalidated every legislative veto provision in federal law. A majority in future cases, however, may choose not to apply the *Chadha* rationale to two-house legislative vetoes or to legislative vetoes of agency actions that are clearly legislative rather than executive or quasi-judicial. It

> Immigration and Naturalization Service *v.* Chadha *casts serious doubt on the use of the legislative veto.*

See also

Miranda Rules

Miranda v. *Arizona*

would be curious indeed if administrative agencies promulgating regulations with the force of law were freed from congressional oversight by a Court intent on preserving the separation of powers and bicameralism.

—DENNIS J. MAHONEY

IMPACT OF SUPREME COURT DECISIONS

The Supreme Court's decisions have regularly embroiled it in controversy. Its rulings have considerable impact. In its early years, the Court, over strenuous objection from the states, shaped our federal system and helped establish the national government's supremacy. The Court also had substantial effects on the economy, aiding in the creation of an American economic common market and providing opportunities for the private sector to develop. The Court's major effects on federalism and the economy subsided after the 1930s. However, its effect on civil rights, visible earlier with respect to slavery and its emasculation of Reconstruction civil rights statutes, again became apparent as questions such as school desegregation came to the fore in the 1950s.

The Supreme Court's impact includes ways in which federal and state agencies and lower federal and state courts carry out the Court's decisions, but it also includes the ways in which the agencies and courts delay, circumvent, misunderstand, and erode them. It includes the response to decisions by different "populations"—those who explain or elaborate its rulings, those supposed to apply or implement them, those for whom the rulings are intended, and the general population. Because the Court, "the least dangerous branch," lacks the capacity to enforce its rulings directly, assistance from those at whom a ruling is directed or from others (legislatures, executive agencies, courts) is required. The Court is now recognized to be a political actor, but one must abandon the tacit assumption held by earlier scholars that Supreme Court decisions are self-executing and recognize that the law is what the judges say it is only after all others have had their say.

Impact and compliance are not identical but are related. Compliance, the process by which individuals accept a decision prior to its impact or effect, cannot occur unless a person knows of the ruling and is required to take or abstain from a certain action. Compliance means an individual's intentionally conforming behavior to the ruling's dictates, that is, doing what the decision commands because of the ruling. Because noncompliance, or refusal to obey, occurs relatively seldom despite the attention it receives, it is important to pay heed to implementation of decisions, the process by which they are put into effect. Short-run resistance may blend into longer-run obedience, as resulted in the aftermath of the reapportionment decisions.

Impact includes all effects, direct and indirect, resulting from a ruling of the Court, regardless of whether those affected knew about the decision; it includes the results of rulings permitting but not requiring the adoption of certain policies. When effects of a ruling indirectly induce behavior congruent with the ruling, that behavior is better viewed as impact than as compliance. Impact encompasses actions neither directly defiant nor clearly obedient, such as attempts at evasion coupled with technical obedience and efforts to anticipate the Court's decisions ("anticipatory compliance"). Impact also includes both short-term and long-run consequences of a decision, for example, massive resistance to school desegregation rulings and the rulings' arguable contribution to "white flight" to the suburbs. There will also be situations in which no response occurs, that is, where there is an absence of obvious impact.

The Supreme Court's effect on the president has generally been one of support and reinforcement. The Court has been least willing to overturn his acts in time of war, when presidential resistance to Court decisions would be most likely. Although limiting somewhat the president's authority to remove certain government employees, the Court, since the New Deal, has sustained delegations of power to the president and the executive branch and has generally been deferential to the regulatory commissions since World War II. Confrontations between Court and president have been relatively infrequent; when the Court invalidates policies the president had espoused, for example, wiretapping, it is not attacking the presidency as an institution. Presidents may have been reluctant to assist in enforcing the Court's decisions, but direct defiance is rare indeed. Both President Harry S Truman and President Richard M. Nixon complied with orders when their actions (seizure of the steel mills and withholding of tapes) were ruled improper. In those situations, as with impoundment of appropriated funds, the Court insisted that the president follow the law as interpreted by the courts rather than determine for himself whether he should be subject to it; in the case of the steel seizure, the Court insisted that he follow a course of action legislated by Congress.

The Court has had considerable impact on Congress's internal processes—its authority to exclude members, legislative investigations, and the contempt power. Congressional reaction to the Court's decisions has been manifested in a number of ways. After the Court has engaged in statutory interpretation or, less frequently, has invalidated statutes for vagueness, Congress has often rewritten or reenacted the laws to reestablish its "legislative intent," in effect establishing a continuing dialogue between Court and Congress. Congress has also shown negative reaction to the Court's ruling through proposals to eliminate appellate jurisdiction in particular classes of cases, for example, internal security, abortions, and school prayer, but these attempts have been less frequent and far less successful than those to rewrite statutes. Efforts to overturn the Court's rulings have

also resulted in introduction of numerous proposals to amend the Constitution, but most such proposals die. Only a few—the Eleventh Amendment, Civil War Amendments, Sixteenth Amendment, and Twenty-Sixth Amendment—have been both submitted and ratified.

The impact of the Supreme Court's decisions extends well beyond the other branches of the national government. Controversial Supreme Court rulings have affected public opinion and have produced divided editorial reaction on a wide range of decisions. Changes in the public's feelings of trust or confidence in the Court have paralleled changes in feeling about the presidency and Congress but generally have been somewhat more positive. Such ratings have changed rapidly, but shifts in the Court's doctrine on controversial topics (such as criminal procedure) in the direction of public opinion usually are not immediately reflected in changed public opinion ratings.

The public generally supports the Court's work. Those giving the Court general (or "diffuse") support, however, outnumber those giving the Court specific support (for particular rulings) by a large ratio. The proportion of the public that feels the Court may legitimately produce structural political change is quite small. Acquiescence in the Court's rulings, which helps produce compliance, has been more common than active approval of the decisions.

The public also has little information about the Court. Even many controversial decisions fail to penetrate the general public's consciousness. The greater the knowledge, however, the greater the *dis*approval, but those reporting negative views on specific cases outnumber those whose general view of the Court is negative. Those with negative views also tend to hold them more intensely, but seldom would most members of the public do more than write letters of protest; demonstrations and other overt protest are atypical. Negative views about the Court are

The Supreme Court's decisions have regularly embroiled it in controversy.

usually accounted for by reactions to the few specific decisions that catch the attention of large proportions of the public. Those salient decisions change with considerable rapidity, shifting in the 1960s from civil rights and school prayer to criminal procedure.

The Supreme Court's impact on the states and local communities is varied. Effectuating many decisions involves little controversy, and implementation may be prompt and complete, particularly if actions of only a few public officials are necessary. Other rulings, such as those on school desegregation, school prayer, and criminal procedure, produce a disproportionate amount both of resistance or attempts to evade and of critical rhetoric—rhetoric at times not matched by reality. Despite claims that the warnings required by *Miranda* v. *Arizona* (1966) would have a negative impact on police work, suspects and defendants often talk to police after being "read their rights." However, even these criticized rulings have definite impacts, for example, more professional police work as a result of criminal procedure rulings. Although opponents of the rule that improperly seized evidence should be excluded (the exclusionary rule of *Mapp* v. *Ohio,* 1961) have claimed that the rule does not deter illegal seizures and is too costly because guilty defendants are set free, some studies have suggested that the rule might be having some of its intended effect. At least in some cities, few cases were dropped after motions to suppress evidence and a higher proportion of searches conducted after the rule was promulgated were constitutional.

If people are to comply with Supreme Court rulings or if the rulings are to have an impact, they must be communicated to those expected to implement or adhere to them. One cannot, however, assume that effective communication takes place. A ruling may have to be transmitted through several levels, at each of which distortion can be introduced, before reaching its ultimate audience. Lawyers may be accustomed to easy access to the Court's published opinions, but many others, such as police or school officials, often do not receive the opinions or have such direct access to them and must therefore rely on other means of communication through which to learn of them.

The mass media, with the exception of a few newspapers, provide only sketchy information about the Court's decisions. Specialized media, for example, trade publications, provide only erratic coverage even of decisions relevant to the groups for which they are published. Most newspapers and radio and television stations must rely on the wire services for information about Supreme Court rulings. Disproportionate nationwide emphasis is given to decisions the wire services emphasize, with little or no coverage given to other rulings. The media also have different patterns of coverage ("profiles"). Newspapers, for example, give more attention to postdecision events, while the wire services and television pay more attention to cases before they are decided. All the media, however, generally convey much information about immediate reaction to, or impact of, decisions instead of emphasizing the content of, or rationale for, the Court's rulings.

The lower courts do not constitute a bureaucratic structure through which decisions are fully communicated downward. Lawyers thus become particularly important in transmitting the Court's rulings, as they are in transmitting any law. Lower court judges who do not routinely follow the Court's decisions may find out about them only if lawyers arguing cases cite the decisions, which they do not always do accurately. Lawyers, either individually or through their bar associations, do little to inform the general public about developments in the law. Some state attorneys general and local prosecutors undertake to inform state and local officials of recent rulings affecting their work. The failure of these officials to do so in most locations has led some local agencies that can afford to do so to hire their own lawyers, for example, police department "police legal advisers," to monitor the Court's rulings, provide appropriate information to the agency, and arrange for implementation.

Training programs—effective because they combine printed materials with oral presentation—can be particularly important in the transmission of rulings. They are especially necessary because the educational system has generally done little to educate students, later to be members of the general public, about the Court's functioning or its rulings. Training programs are, however, not available to all those expected to be cognizant of or familiar with the Court's rulings. Many members of some important occupational groups such as the police do not receive adequate legal training about the Court's decisions. Even if initially well trained, they are less likely to receive adequate follow-up through in-service training.

The impact of the Court's decisions is, of course, affected by far more than deficiencies and distortions in the lengthy, often convoluted process by which the decisions are communicated. Numerous other factors affect both the communication process, thus indirectly affecting impact, and impact itself. One is the legitimacy attributed to the Court and its work. If a particular audience, for example, the police during the Warren Court's "criminal procedure revolution," feels that the Court is not acting fairly or lacks appropriate information on which to base its decisions, that audience will heed the Court's word less carefully even when the opinions are fully communicated. Characteristics of the Court's rulings, such as their relative unanimity and relative clarity or ambiguity, are also important, as both unanimity and clarity are thought to produce greater compliance. In new and sensitive areas of policy such as civil rights and criminal procedure, the lower courts can exercise power over the Supreme Court by their resistance. Rulings by lower court judges applying and extending (or narrowing) the Court's decisions are particularly important in such situations

and in those where gaps in doctrinal development—a result of case-by-case development of the law—leave unanswered questions. In many, perhaps most, areas of the law, however, lower court judges enforce Supreme Court rulings because those rulings are a matter of relative personal indifference for the judges, because they have been socialized to follow those rulings, and because they wish to avoid being reversed.

Whether someone follows up a decision, who that "someone" is, and how that someone acts, also affect a decision's impact. Elites' support for a decision may be able to calm negative public reaction. The likelihood that desegregation would be accepted in either the short or long run was decreased because southern elites were not favorably disposed toward either the result of *Brown* v. *Board of Education* (1954) or the Court's opinion. Because most rulings of the Court are not self-enforcing, follow-up by government agencies is often crucial for effective implementation. Officials not committed to the values in the Court's rulings are less likely to be assiduous in their follow-up; thus the attitudes of individual decision makers, particularly those in key policy-making or enforcement positions, are of considerable importance.

The situation into which a Supreme Court ruling is "injected"—whether in a crisis or in normal times—also affects the ruling's impact. A local community's belief system and its past history both are part of that situation. So are community pressures on the individuals expected to carry out the Court's dictates. Often a wide variety of enforcement mechanisms must be used before compliance is achieved. Incentive systems in organizations can lead individuals either to follow the Court's rulings or to continue existing practices. Because organizations have considerable interest in maintaining such practices, externally imposed penalties may be insufficient to produce required change.

To overcome problems of communicating Supreme Court rulings so that they reach the appropriate audience might seem insuperable. The Court's rulings are, however, often complied with and do have widespread impact. Were it otherwise, we should not hear so much about the problems occurring in particularly sensitive areas of the law such as civil rights and civil liberties. The difficulties in implementing the Court's decisions to achieve their greatest impact should remind us that, as an active policy maker, the Supreme Court faces many of the same problems faced by other policy-making institutions.

—STEPHEN L. WASBY

Bibliography

Becker, Theodore L., and Feeley, Malcolm, eds. (1973). *The Impact of Supreme Court Decisions: Empirical Studies.* 2d ed. New York: Oxford University Press.

Johnson, Charles A., and Canon, Bradley C. (1984). *Judicial Policies: Implementation and Impact.* Washington, D.C.: Congressional Quarterly Press.

Krislov, Samuel, ed. (1972). *Compliance and the Law: A Multidisciplinary Approach.* Beverly Hills, Calif.: Sage Publications.

Wasby, Stephen L. (1970). *The Impact of the United States Supreme Court: Some Perspectives.* Homewood, Ill.: Dorsey Press.

INCITEMENT TO UNLAWFUL CONDUCT

Incitement to unlawful conduct raises a central and difficult issue about the proper boundaries of freedom of expression and of the First Amendment. Many of the Supreme Court's most important freedom of speech decisions have involved some form of incitement. Though the term incitement sometimes refers to emotionally charged appeals to immediate action, the word is most often used to cover any urging that others commit illegal acts.

See also

Brown v. *Board of Education*

Civil Rights

Mapp v. *Ohio*

Miranda v. *Arizona*

The basic problem about incitement is fairly simple, involving a tension between a criminal law perspective and a free speech perspective. Any society seeks to minimize the number of crimes that are committed. Some people commit crimes because others urge them to do so. Although the person who actually commits a crime may usually seem more to blame than someone who encourages him, on other occasions the inciter, because of greater authority, intelligence, or firmness of purpose, may actually be more responsible for what happens than the person who is the instrument of his designs. In any event, because the person who successfully urges another to commit a crime bears some responsibility and because effective restrictions on incitement are likely to reduce the amount of crime to some degree, sound reasons exist for punishing those who incite.

Anglo-American criminal law, like the law of other traditions, has reflected this view. In 1628 Edward Coke wrote that "all those that incite . . . any other" to commit a felony are guilty of a crime; and, at least by 1801, unsuccessful incitement was recognized as an offense in England. Modern American criminal law generally treats the successful inciter on a par with the person who performs the criminal act; the unsuccessful inciter is guilty of criminal solicitation, treated as a lesser crime than the one he has tried to incite.

From the free speech perspective, the problem of incitement takes on a different appearance. A basic premise of a liberal society is that people should be allowed to express their views, especially their political views. Some important political views support illegal actions against actual or possible governments. Indeed, one aspect of the political tradition of the United States is that revolutionary overthrow of existing political authority is sometimes justified. Other views deem certain illegal acts justified even when the government is acceptable. Were all encouragements of illegal activity suppressed, an important slice of political and social opinions would be silenced. Further, in the practical administration of such suppression some opinions that did not quite amount to encouragement would be proceeded against and persons would be inhibited from saying things that could possibly be construed as encouragements to commit crimes. Thus, wide restrictions on incitement have been thought to imperil free expression, particularly when statutes penalizing incitement have been specifically directed to "subversive" political ideologies.

The tension between criminal law enforcement and freedom of expression is addressed by both legislatures and courts. Legislatures must initially decide what is a reasonable, and constitutionally permissible, accommodation of the conflicting values. When convictions are challenged, courts must decide whether the statutes that legislatures have adopted and their applications to particular situations pass constitutional muster.

Most states have statutes that make solicitation of a crime illegal. These laws are drawn to protect speech interests to a significant extent. To be convicted of solicitation, one must actually encourage the commission of a specific crime. Therefore, many kinds of statements, such as disinterested advice that committing a crime like draft evasion would be morally justified, approval of present lawbreaking in general, or urging people to prepare themselves for unspecified future revolutionary acts, are beyond the reach of ordinary solicitation statutes.

One convenient way to conceptualize the First Amendment problems about incitement is to ask whether any communications that do amount to ordinary criminal solicitation are constitutionally protected and whether other communications that encourage criminal acts but fall short of criminal solicitation lack constitutional protection.

All major Supreme Court cases on the subject have involved political expression of one kind or another and have arisen under statutes directed at specific kinds of speech.

Some of the cases have involved criminal conspiracy charges, but because the conspiracy has been to incite or advocate, the constitutionality of punishing communications has been the crucial issue. In *Schenck* v. *United States* (1919) the Court sustained a conviction under the 1917 Espionage Act, which made criminal attempts to obstruct enlistment. The leaflet that Schenck had helped to publish had urged young men to assert their rights to oppose the draft. Writing the majority opinion that found no constitutional bar to the conviction, Justice Oliver Wendell Holmes penned the famous clear and present danger test: "The question in every case is whether the words used are used in such circumstances and are of such a nature as to create a clear and present danger that they will bring about the substantive evils that Congress has a right to prevent." Much was unclear about this test as originally formulated and as subsequently developed, but the results in *Schenck* and companion cases show that the Court then did not conceive the standard as providing great protection for speech. During the 1920s, while the majority of Justices ceased using the test, eloquent dissents by Holmes and Louis D. Brandeis forged it into a principle that was protective of speech, requiring a danger that was both substantial and close in time in order to justify suppressing communication. Even these later opinions, however, did not indicate with clarity whether the test applied to ordinary criminal solicitation or whether an intent to create a clear and present danger would be sufficient for criminal punishment.

During the 1920s the majority of the Supreme Court was willing to affirm convictions for expression, so long as the expression fell within a statutory prohibition and the statutory prohibition was reasonable. Thus, in *Gitlow* v. *New York* (1925) the Court upheld a conviction under a criminal anarchy statute that forbade teaching the propriety of illegally overthrowing organized government. The Court concluded that the legislature could

Many of the Supreme Court's most important freedom of speech decisions have involved some form of incitement.

reasonably anticipate that speech of this type carried the danger of a "revolutionary spark" kindling a fire. The standard applied in *Gitlow* and similar cases would permit suppression of virtually any type of speech that a legislature might consider to create a danger of illegal activity, a category far broader than ordinary criminal solicitation.

In the 1930s the Supreme Court began to render decisions more protective of speech, and in *Herndon* v. *Lowry* (1937) the Court reversed a conviction for attempting to incite insurrection, when the evidence failed to show that the defendant, a Communist party organizer, had actually urged revolutionary violence. The majority in *Herndon* referred to the clear and present danger test with approval. In a series of subsequent decisions, that test was employed as an all-purpose standard for First Amendment cases.

In 1951 the Supreme Court reviewed the convictions of eleven leading communists in *Dennis* v. *United States*. The defendants had violated the Smith Act by conspiring to advocate the forcible overthrow of the United States government. As in *Gitlow*, the expressions involved (typical communist rhetoric) fell short of inciting to any specific crime. The plurality opinion, representing the views of four Justices, accepted clear and present danger as the appropriate standard, but interpreted the test so that the gravity of the evil was discounted by its improbability. In practice, this formulation meant that if the evil were very great, such as overthrow of the government, communication creating a danger of that evil might be suppressed even though the evil would not occur in the near future and had only a small likelihood that it would ever occur. The dissenters and civil libertarian observers protested that this interpretation undermined the main point of "clear and present" danger. *Dennis* is now viewed by many as a regrettable product of unwarranted fears of successful communist subversion. In subsequent cases, the Court emphasized that the Smith Act reached only advocacy of illegal action, not advocacy of doctrine. In the years since *Dennis* only one conviction under the act has passed this stringent test.

The modern constitutional standard for incitement cases arose out of the conviction of a Ku Klux Klan leader for violating a broad criminal syndicalism statute, not unlike the statute involved in *Gitlow*. Unsurprisingly, the Court said in *Brandenburg* v. *Ohio* (1969) that the broad statute was unconstitutional. But it went on to fashion a highly restrictive version of clear and present danger: that a state may not "forbid or proscribe advocacy of the use of force or of law violation except where such advocacy is directed to inciting or producing imminent lawless action and is likely to incite or produce such action." This test requires lawless action that is likely, imminent, and intended by the speaker. Only rarely could such a test possibly be met by speech that does not amount to criminal solicitation, and under this test both solicitation of crimes in the distant future and solicitation unlikely to be acted upon are constitutionally protected. In *Brandenburg*, however, the Court had directly in mind public advocacy; it is unlikely that this stringent test also applies to private solicitations of crime that are made for personal gain. The present law provides significant constitutional protection for political incitements, but how far beyond political speech this protection may extend remains uncertain.

—KENT GREENAWALT

Bibliography

American Law Institute (1985). *Model Penal Code*, Section 5.02 and Commentary. St. Paul, Minn.: West Publishing Co.

Greenawalt, Kent (1980). Speech and Crime. *American Bar Foundation Research Journal* 1980:647–785.

Linde, Hans A. (1970). "Clear and Present Danger" Reexamined: Dissonance in the *Brandenburg* Concerto. *Stanford Law Review* 22:1163–1186.

INGRAHAM v. WRIGHT

430 U.S. 651 (1977)

Two Florida junior high school students, disciplined by severe paddling, sued school officials for damages and injunctive relief, claiming that the paddling constituted cruel and unusual punishment. They also claimed that they had been deprived of their right to a prior hearing in violation of their procedural due process rights. The lower federal courts denied relief, and the Supreme Court affirmed, 5–4.

For the majority, Justice Lewis F. Powell, a former school board president, concluded that the guarantee against cruel and unusual punishment was limited to cases of punishment for criminal offenses and thus had no application to paddling as a means of school discipline. The openness of public schools provided a safeguard against abusive punishments of the kind that might be visited on prisoners. Common law restraints on the privilege of school officials to administer corporal punishment were sufficient to prevent excesses. As for due process, Powell conceded that the paddling had implicated a "liberty" interest, but he concluded that due process required no hearing, in view of the availability of common law remedies or damages.

For the dissenters, Justice Byron R. White argued that it was anomalous to conclude that some punishments are "cruel and unusual" when inflicted on convicts but raise no such problem when they are inflicted on children for breaches of school discipline. The relevant inquiry, White argued, was not the label of criminal punishment but the purpose to punish. While some spanking might be permissible in public schools, the majority was wrong in saying "that corporal punishment in the public schools, no matter how barbaric, inhumane, or severe, is never limited by the Eighth Amendment." Here the record showed not just spanking but severe beatings. Furthermore, the risk of erroneous punishment—a crucial aspect of the due

Two junior high school students claimed that paddling constituted cruel and unusual punishment.

SCHOOL DISCIPLINE

The Ingraham *decision reflected nostalgia for a day when children were seen and not heard. (UPI/Corbis-Bettmann)*

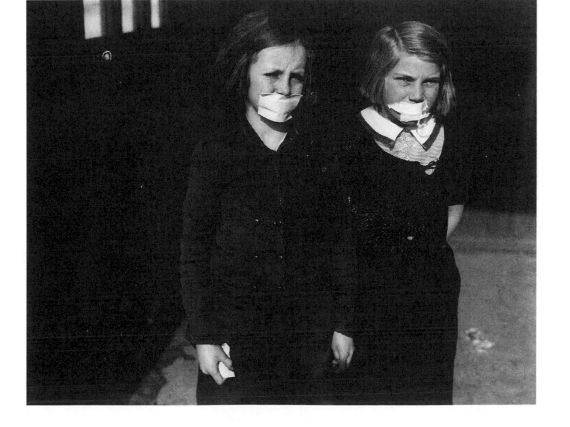

INGRAHAM v. WRIGHT

430 U.S. 651 (1977)

See also

Mathews v. Eldridge

process calculus established in *Mathews* v. *Eldridge* (1976)—demanded at least some informal discussion between student and disciplinarian before paddling was administered. The common law damages remedy offered no redress for punishments mistakenly administered in good faith and obviously could not undo the infliction of pain.

Ingraham seems an unstable precedent. Constitutional law, following social practice, has increasingly insisted that children be treated as persons, as members of the community deserving of respect. The due process right to a hearing rests partly on the premise that the dignity of being heard, before the state takes away one's liberty or property, is one of the differences between being a participating citizen and being an object of administration. The *Ingraham* majority, unmoved by such concerns, reflected nostalgia for a day when children were seen and not heard.

—KENNETH L. KARST

J

JACKSON v. METROPOLITAN EDISON CO.

419 U.S. 345 (1974)

In the Warren Court years, the state action doctrine was progressively weakened as a limitation on the Fourteenth Amendment; more and more "private" conduct fell under the amendment's reach. The *Jackson* decision illustrates how the Burger Court called a halt to this trend, limiting the substantive scope of the amendment by giving new life to the state action limitation.

Metropolitan Edison turned off Jackson's supply of electricity, asserting that she had not paid her bill. She sued for damages and injunctive relief under federal civil rights laws, claiming procedural due process rights to notice, hearing, and an opportunity to pay any amounts due the company. The lower courts denied relief, holding that the company's conduct did not amount to state action. The Supreme Court affirmed, 6–3, in an opinion by Justice William H. Rehnquist, systematically rejecting a series of arguments supporting the contention that state action was present in the case.

The fact of state regulation was held insufficient to constitute state action. As in *Moose Lodge No. 107* v. *Irvis* (1972), there was no showing of a "close nexus" between the company's no-hearing policy and the state. The approval by the state's public utilities commission of the company's tariff, stating the right to terminate service for nonpayment, was held insufficient to demonstrate explicit state approval of the no-hearing policy. Where *Moose Lodge* had relied on the absence of a monopoly under a state liquor license, *Jackson* characterized *Moose Lodge* as a near-monopoly case and said there was no showing of a connection between the utility's monopoly status and its no-hearing policy. Finally, the Court rejected the notion that Metropolitan Edison was performing a "public function" by supplying electricity, saying there had been no delegation to the company of a power "traditionally associated with sovereignty." The latter comment looked forward to the Court's decision in *Flagg Bros., Inc.* v. *Brooks* (1978).

Justice William J. Brennan dissented without reaching the merits. Justices William O. Douglas and Thurgood Marshall dissented on the merits, pointing out how the majority was departing from the teaching of the Warren Court—something that Justice Rehnquist likely did not need to have explained. *Jackson* did more than reverse currents in the various individual streams of state action doctrine (public functions, monopolies, state encouragement). By taking up each of these arguments separately and rejecting them one by one, the Court also implicitly abandoned the approach of *Burton* v. *Wilmington Parking Authority* (1961), which had called for determining state action questions by looking at the totality of circumstances in a particular case.

—KENNETH L. KARST

JACOBELLIS v. OHIO

378 U.S. 184 (1964)

The Supreme Court reversed Jacobellis's conviction for possessing and exhibiting an

When Metropolitan Edison turned off Jackson's supply of electricity, asserting that she had not paid her bill, she sued for damages and injunctive relief under federal civil rights laws.

♦ **bill of attainder**
A legislative finding of guilt and imposition of punishment without a court trial.

See also
Burton v. *Wilmington Parking Authority*

*Stewart declined to
define the material
hard-core
pornography
included, stating
only, "I know it
when I see it."*

obscene motion picture, finding the movie not obscene under *Roth* v. *United States* (1957). Justice William J. Brennan's plurality opinion announced two significant constitutional developments and presaged a third. First, in any case raising the issue of whether a work was obscene, the Court would determine independently whether the material was constitutionally protected. Second, in judging the material's appeal to prurient interests against "contemporary community standards," courts were to apply a national standard, not the standards of the particular local community from which the case arose. Finally, purporting to apply standards based on *Roth* and foreshadowing his opinion in *Memoirs* v. *Massachusetts* (1965), Brennan noted that a work could not be proscribed unless it was " 'utterly' without social importance."

Jacobellis is best known, however, for Justice Potter J. Stewart's concurring opinion. Contending that only hard-core pornography constitutionally could be proscribed, Stewart declined to define the material that

term included, stating only, "I know it when I see it."

—KIM MCLANE WARDLAW

JACOBSON v. MASSACHUSETTS

197 U.S. 11 (1905)

A Massachusetts statute required vaccination of a town's inhabitants when health authorities so ordered. For the Supreme Court, Justice John Marshall Harlan concluded the regulation was within the police power of the commonwealth and violated no federal constitutional right.

The First Amendment was not then interpreted to apply to the states. Jacobson relied on the liberty guaranteed by the Fourteenth Amendment's due process clause, although his objection to vaccination was religious. Harlan concluded that substantive due process implied no absolute right to control one's body. Justices David Brewer and Rufus Peckham dissented.

—RICHARD E. MORGAN

*This exceptionally
influential decision
reflected laissez-
faire principles
against government
regulation of the
economy.*

JACOBS, IN RE

98 N.Y. 98 (1885)

This exceptionally influential decision, cited hundreds of times by state and federal courts, reflected laissez-faire principles against government regulation of the economy. New York in 1884 enacted a statute to improve the public health by penalizing the manufacture of cigars on the same floor of tenement houses where people lived. Jacobs, a tenement occupant prosecuted under the statute, somehow retained William M. Evarts, "the Prince of the American Bar," whose powerful defense of free enterprise convinced the New York Court of Appeals to decide unanimously against the constitutionality of the regulation. Judge Robert Earl, drawing heavily on Evarts's argument, larded his

opinion with polemics against state infringement on liberty and property conducted under the pretext of the police power. The constitutional basis of the opinion is not clear because Earl stopped short of invoking the doctrine of freedom of contract, but the rhetoric of substantive due process as a limitation on legislative power to regulate the economy stands out. "Under the mere guise of police regulations," Earl said, "personal rights and private property cannot be arbitrarily invaded," and judicial review determines whether the legislative power exceeded the limits. The court found that the state plainly had not passed a health law but had trampled personal liberty.

—LEONARD W. LEVY

JAPANESE AMERICAN CASES

Hirabayashi v. United States
320 U.S. 81 (1943)

Korematsu v. United States
323 U.S. 214 (1944)

Ex Parte Endo
323 U.S. 283 (1944)

For more than a month after the Japanese attack on Pearl Harbor in December 1941, no one of high authority in the armed services or elsewhere in the national government suggested seriously that persons of Japanese ancestry should be moved away from the West Coast. The Army's historian wrote that in February and March of 1942 the military estimates were that "there was no real threat of a Japanese invasion" of the area. Yet by March 1942 a program was fully underway to remove about 120,000 persons from their West Coast homes and jobs and place them in internment camps in the interior of the country. About 70,000 of these people were citizens of the United States; two out of every five people sent to the camps were under the age of fifteen or over fifty. All were imprisoned for an indefinite time without any individualized determination of grounds for suspicion of disloyalty, let alone charges of unlawful conduct, to be held in custody until their loyalty might be determined. The basis for their imprisonment was a single common trait—their Japanese ancestry.

The military services came to discover the "military necessity" of relocating the Japanese Americans in response to pressure from the West Coast congressional delegations and from other political leaders in the region—including, to his later regret, Earl Warren, then attorney general of California. These politicians were responding, in turn, to a clamor from certain newspapers and labor unions, along with (as U.S. Attorney General Francis Biddle later listed them) "the Ameri-can Legion, the California Joint Immigration Committee, the Native Sons and Daughters of the Golden West, the Western Growers Protective Association, the California Farm Bureau Federation [and] the Chamber of Commerce of Los Angeles." The groups' campaign was aided by newspaper accounts of American military defeats and Japanese atrocities in the early days of the war, and by false reports of sabotage at Pearl Harbor. Anti-Asian racism, long a feature of California, now had a focus. In Hawaii, which *had* been attacked, no evacuation was proposed; persons of Japanese ancestry constituted almost one third of that territory's population. On the West Coast, Japanese Americans barely exceeded one percent of the population; thus, no political force resisted the mixture of fear, racism, and greed. "The Japanese race is an enemy race," said General John De-Witt in his official report to the War Department. Once the Army urged wholesale evacuation, the opposition of Biddle and the Justice Department was unavailing. President Franklin D. Roosevelt sided with the Army, and the evacuation began.

The program, first established by Executive Order 9066 and then partly ratified by Congress, called for three measures in "military areas"—that is, the entire West Coast. First, persons of Japanese descent were placed under curfew at home from 8:00 P.M. to 6:00 A.M. Second, they would be excluded from "military areas" upon military order. Third, they would be "relocated" in internment camps until their "loyalty" could be determined. The loyalty-determining process was leisurely; as late as the spring of 1945 some 70,000 persons remained in the camps.

The three parts of the program, all of which raised serious constitutional problems, were considered separately by the Supreme Court in three cases: *Hirabayashi* v. *United States* (1943), *Korematsu* v. *United States* (1944), and *Ex Parte Endo* (1944).

The *Hirabayashi* case offered the Court a chance to rule on the validity of both the

J

JAPANESE AMERICAN
CASES

Hirabayashi *v.*
United States
320 U.S. 81 (1943)

Korematsu *v.*
United States
323 U.S. 214 (1944)

Ex Parte Endo
323 U.S. 283 (1944)

The Japanese American Cases *have made two positive contributions to the development of egalitarian constitutional doctrine.*

J

**JAPANESE AMERICAN
CASES**

Hirabayashi v.
United States
320 U.S. 81 (1943)

Korematsu v.
United States
323 U.S. 214 (1944)

Ex Parte Endo
323 U.S. 283 (1944)

**JAPANESE
INTERNMENT**

*Children of Japanese ancestry
await transportation to one of
several relocation camps for
Japanese Americans during
World War II. (Corbis)*

curfew and the exclusion orders. A young
American citizen was charged with violating
the curfew and refusing to report to a control
station to be evacuated from Seattle, where
he lived. He was convicted on both counts,
and sentenced to three months of imprisonment. In June 1943 the Supreme Court
unanimously upheld the curfew violation
conviction, and said that it need not consider
the validity of the exclusion order, because
the two sentences were to run concurrently.

Not until December 1944 did the Court
reach the other parts of the evacuation program. In *Korematsu,* the Court divided 6–3 in

upholding an order excluding an American citizen from his home town, San Leandro, California. On the same day, the Court in *Endo* avoided deciding on the constitutional validity of internment. Instead, it concluded that the act of Congress ratifying the evacuation program had not authorized prolonged detention of a citizen whose loyalty was conceded. The Court assumed that some brief detention was implicitly authorized as an incident of an exclusion program aimed at preventing espionage and sabotage. Any further detention would have to rest on an assumption the Court was unwilling to make: that citizens were being detained because of their ancestry, in response to community hostility. Justice Owen Roberts, concurring in the result, found congressional authority for internment in the appropriation of funds to operate the camps. Reaching the constitutional issues the majority had avoided, he concluded that Endo's detention violated "the guarantees of the Bill of Rights . . . and especially the guarantee of due process of law."

The *Japanese American Cases* have made two positive contributions to the development of egalitarian constitutional doctrine. The *Hirabayashi* and *Korematsu* opinions were links in a chain of precedent leading to the Supreme Court's recognition that the Fifth Amendment's due process clause contains a guarantee of equal protection as a substantive limit on the conduct of the national government. And *Korematsu* first announced the principle that legal restrictions on the civil rights of a racial group are "suspect." Even so, these decisions deserve Eugene Rostow's epithet: "a disaster." The Supreme Court's evasion of issues, its refusal to examine the factual assumptions underlying the "military necessity" of evacuation—in short, its failures to perform as a court—are easier to forgive than to excuse. There is little comfort in the fact that the Court's *Hirabayashi* and *Korematsu* opinions were authored by Justices celebrated as civil libertarians.

Chief Justice Harlan Fiske Stone wrote for a unanimous Court in *Hirabayashi*, approaching the validity of the curfew not so much as a question about the liberties of a citizen but as a question about congressional power. The war powers, of course, are far-reaching; they include, as Justices often repeat, "the power to wage war successfully." Thus, for Stone, the only issue before the Court was whether there was "a rational basis" for concluding that the curfew was necessary to protect the country against espionage and sabotage in aid of a threatened invasion. As to that necessity, the Chief Justice said: "We cannot close our eyes to the fact, demonstrated by experience, that in time of war residents having ethnic affiliations with an invading enemy may be a greater source of danger than those of a different ancestry." There was no effort to examine into the likelihood of invasion, or to specify what experience demonstrated the "fact" assumed. The one hard fact was that no sabotage or espionage had been committed by persons of Japanese ancestry at the time of the Hawaii attack or afterward. (California's Attorney General Warren had been equal to that challenge, however: ". . . that is the most ominous sign in our whole situation. It convinces me more than perhaps any other factor that the sabotage we are to get, the fifth column activities that we are to get, are timed just like Pearl Harbor was timed. . . .")

Another question remained: Why impose wholesale restrictions on persons of Japanese ancestry, when Germans and Italians were being investigated individually? Here the Court took refuge in a presumption: "We cannot say that the war-making branches of the Government did not have ground for believing that in a critical hour [disloyal] persons could not readily be isolated and separately dealt with. . . ." This is the classical language of "rational basis" review; government officials have made a factual determination, and a court "cannot say" they are mistaken. That standard of review serves well enough to test the reasonableness of a congressional conclusion that some type of activity substantially affects interstate commerce. It is utterly inappropriate to test the justification for selectively imposing restrictions on a racial minority.

Justice Hugo L. Black began his opinion for the majority in *Korematsu* by recognizing this difference. Racial distinctions, he said, were "immediately suspect," and must be subjected to "the most rigid scrutiny." Following that pronouncement, however, all judicial scrutiny of the racial discrimination at hand was abandoned. The opinion simply quoted the "We cannot say" passage from the *Hirabayashi* opinion; stated, uncritically, the conclusions of the military authorities; observed that "war is an aggregation of hardships"; and—unkindest cut—concluded that "citizenship has its responsibilities as well as its privileges."

Justice Roberts, dissenting, argued that Korematsu had been subjected to conflicting orders to leave the military area and to stay put, a plain due process violation. It was left to Justice Frank Murphy—in his finest hour—to expose the absence of imperial clothing. He demonstrated how the "military" judgment of the necessity for evacuation had departed from subjects in which Army officers were expert and had embarked on breathtaking sociological generalization: the Japanese American community were "a large, unassimilated, tightly knit racial group, bound to an enemy nation by strong ties of race, culture, custom and religion" (quoting General DeWitt).

Decades later, Peter Irons discovered in government archives irrefutable evidence that government officers had deliberately misled the Supreme Court on questions directly related to the claim of military necessity for the evacuations. In response to this evidence, in the mid-1980s federal district courts set aside the convictions of Gordon Hirabayashi, Fred Korematsu, and Minoru Yasui (whose conviction had been affirmed along with Hirabayashi's).

Justice Robert H. Jackson, dissenting in *Korematsu*, said, in effect: There is nothing courts can do to provide justice in this case, or in any case in which the military and the president are determined to take action in wartime; yet we should not lend our approval to this action, lest we create a precedent for similar extraconstitutional action in the future. Of all the oft-noted ironies of the Japanese American cases, this topsy-turvy prediction may be the most ironic of all. *Korematsu* as a judicial precedent has turned out to provide a strong doctrinal foundation for the Supreme Court's vigorous defense of racial equality in the years since mid-century. The disaster of the *Japanese American Cases* was not doctrinal. It was instead the betrayal of justice there and then for Gordon Hirabayashi, Fred Korematsu, Minoru Yasui, and some 120,000 other individuals—and thus for us all.

—KENNETH L. KARST

Bibliography

Grodzins, Morton (1949). *Americans Betrayed: Politics and the Japanese Evacuation.* Chicago: University of Chicago Press.

Irons, Peter (1983). *Justice at War.* New York: Oxford University Press.

Rostow, Eugene V. (1949). The Japanese American Cases—A Disaster. *Yale Law Journal* 54:489–533.

JAY, JOHN

(1745-1829)

John Jay was a major figure during the Revolutionary era. Born into one of colonial New York's leading families, he was aristocratic in appearance, well educated, and a hard worker with a precise and orderly mind. He graduated from King's College in 1764, was admitted to the bar four years later, and soon had a prosperous practice. He early took an interest in the constitutional debate between England

and the American colonies; although uneasy about the radical implication of some of the resistance to imperial policies in the 1770s, he nevertheless was a firm patriot. He served as a member of the New York Committee of Correspondence and in the Provincial Congress, as well as in the first and second Continental Congresses in Philadelphia. In 1776 he returned to New York to help draft a state constitution (1777) and to become New York's first chief justice. His major interests, however, lay in the field of diplomacy: he became the United States Minister to Spain in 1779 and later joined Benjamin Franklin and John Adams in Paris to negotiate the treaty of 1783 that recognized American independence and formally ended the fighting with Great Britain.

Returning to the United States in 1784 Jay assumed the position of secretary of foreign affairs under the Articles of Confederation. Unhappy over the weakness of the central government during the 1780s, he sympathized with the movement to create a new constitution that would strengthen the power of the federal government over the states. Jay was not a member of the Constitutional Convention of 1787, but he strongly advocated adoption of the Constitution in the closely contested ratification struggle in New York the following year. Joining forces with Alexander Hamilton and James Madison, Jay contributed several pieces (#2–#5 and, after a bout with illness, #64) to *The Federalist*. In these essays Jay warned that failure to adopt the new government would probably lead to the dissolution of the Union and the creation of separate confederacies. He also stressed that only through the creation of a strong and energetic central government could the discord and jealousies of the various states be brought under control and the territorial integrity of the United States be protected from foreign encroachment.

Shortly after becoming president, George Washington appointed Jay the first Chief Justice of the United States, a position he held from 1789 to 1795. Two main themes ran through Jay's decisions. The first stressed the supremacy of the newly created national government. *Chisholm* v. *Georgia* (1793) involved the constitutional question of whether a state could be sued in a federal court by a citizen of a different state without its permission, thus limiting its sovereignty. The question had been raised during the debate over ratification, and the supporters of the Constitution had given assurances that such suits would not be allowed. Nevertheless, under Jay's leadership the Court handed down an affirmative decision, couched in extremely nationalistic terms. Jay stressed the role of the people of the United States in the creation of the Union, and deemphasized the powers and sovereignty of the states. A very controversial decision, *Chisholm* was vitiated when reaction to it culminated in the adoption of the Eleventh Amendment.

While riding circuit in 1793 Jay delivered a dissenting opinion in *Ware* v. *Hylton* arguing that a Virginia statute sequestering prerevolutionary debts of British creditors was invalid because it had been nullified by the Treaty of Paris (1783), which specifically indicated that such debts would be honored.

J

JAY, JOHN

(1745–1829)

John Jay was a major figure during the Revolutionary era.

FIRST CHIEF JUSTICE

John Jay's decisions stressed the supremacy of the newly created national government. (Corbis/Bettmann)

*The use of prearrest
silence to impeach a
defendant's
credibility does not
violate any
constitutional
rights.*

See also

Chisholm v. Georgia

Ware v. Hylton

The case was appealed in 1796, and the Supreme Court, from which Jay had already resigned, adopted the former Chief Justice's reasoning and reversed the lower court's decision. In another important case, *Glass v. The Sloop Betsy* (1794), the Supreme Court overturned a Maryland District Court ruling that allowed French consuls in America to function as prize courts and dispose of prizes captured by French privateers. Writing for the Court, Jay concluded that United States sovereignty required that these cases be handled by American courts.

Jay's other major concern as Chief Justice was to protect the independence of the Supreme Court by insisting on a strict separation of powers. He rejected various attempts to incorporate the Court into the activities of the legislative and executive branches. For example, when Congress passed an act that required the circuit courts to review the applications of military invalids for pensions, Jay, while riding circuit in New York, declared that "neither the Legislative nor Executive branch can constitutionally assign to the Judicial any duties but such as are properly judicial and to be performed in a judicial manner." This position was upheld a short time later by the United States Circuit Court of Pennsylvania, in what has become known as *Hayburn's Case* (1792), when the constitutionality of the law was actually challenged. Jay also rejected occasional requests from the president and Secretary of the Treasury Alexander Hamilton for advisory opinions on controversial matters, arguing that the Supreme Court should render opinions only in actual lawsuits brought by contending parties.

Jay was never happy serving on the Court. He thought the circuit riding duties too arduous. He also believed the Court lacked "the energy, weight and dignity which are essential to its affording due support to the national government." Hoping to return to a more active political life, he was defeated in a bid to become governor of New York in 1792. In 1794, while still holding the position of Chief

Justice, he went on a special diplomatic mission to try to resolve existing controversies with Great Britain. The result was the controversial but successful Jay's Treaty. Resigning his post on the Court, Jay became governor of New York in 1795 for two terms. Following the Jeffersonian successes in 1800 he declined reappointment as Chief Justice of the United States Supreme Court and retired from public life.

—RICHARD E. ELLIS

Bibliography

Monaghan, Frank (1935). *John Jay*. Indianapolis: Bobbs-Merrill.

Morris, Richard B. (1967). *John Jay, the Nation and the Court*. Boston: Boston University Press.

JENKINS v. ANDERSON

447 U.S. 231 (1980)

The Fifth Amendment allows a criminal defendant to remain silent during his trial and prevents the prosecution from commenting on his silence, in order to prevent the jury from drawing adverse inferences. In *Jenkins* the defendant surrendered to the police two weeks after killing a man and claimed that he had acted in self-defense. When he told that self-defense story at his trial, the prosecutor countered that he would have surrendered immediately had he killed in self-defense. After conviction the defendant, seeking habeas corpus relief, argued that the use of his prearrest silence violated his right against self-incrimination and fundamental fairness. The Supreme Court, like the federal courts below, denied relief. Justice Lewis F. Powell, for a 7–2 Court, ruled that the use of prearrest silence to impeach a defendant's credibility, if he testifies in his own defense, does not violate any constitutional rights. Powell's murky reasoning provoked Justices Thurgood Marshall and William J. Brennan, dissenting, to declare that a duty to incriminate oneself now replaced the right to remain silent. Powell had supported no such duty, but he rejected a "right to commit perjury," which no one claimed. His opinion weakened the right to remain silent.

—LEONARD W. LEVY

JIMMY SWAGGART MINISTRIES v. BOARD OF EQUALIZATION OF CALIFORNIA

110 S.Ct. 688 (1990)

In conjunction with its evangelistic activities in the state of California, Jimmy Swaggart Ministries sold religious books, tapes, records, and other merchandise. The group agreed to pay state sales tax on the nonreligious merchandise sold, but maintained that merchandise with specific religious content—such as Bibles, sermons, and Bible study manuals—was exempt from taxation on the basis of the First Amendment. The Supreme Court unanimously disagreed, holding that application of a sales tax to the religious merchandise did not violate either the free exercise clause or the excessive entanglement provision read into the establishment clause by the *Lemon* test.

The Court distinguished the case from prior precedents that had invalidated the application of general licensing fees to those who sold and distributed religious materials door-to-door. In both *Murdock* v. *Pennyslvania* (1943) and *Follett* v. *McCormick* (1944), the Court had objected to such licensing fees because they acted as a prior retraint on the free exercise of religion. In the same cases, however, the Court made clear that the First Amendment did not exempt religious groups from generally applicable taxes on income and property. The Court reaffirmed that principle

here, noting that the tax under attack was a general levy on revenues raised from the sale of certain products. The Court acknowledged that in some cases a generally applicable tax of this sort might "effectively choke off an adherent's religious practices," but reserved for the future a determination on whether such a tax would violate the free exercise clause.

—JOHN G. WEST, JR.

JOHNSON v. LOUISIANA

406 U.S. 356 (1972)

APODACA v. OREGON

406 U.S. 404 (1972)

In *Duncan* v. *Louisiana* (1968) the Supreme Court declared that every criminal charge must be "confirmed by the unanimous suffrage of twelve jurors," and in *Williams* v. *Florida* (1970) the Court found little reason

See also

Establishment Clause

J

For centuries the standard of proof of guilt beyond reasonable doubt was inextricably entwined with the reasonable principle of a unanimous verdict.

♦ **error**
A form of writ issued by a higher court directing a lower court to submit a case for appellate review. The writ of error is no longer used in the federal courts, having been superseded by appeal.

See also

Duncan v. *Louisiana*

Williams v. *Florida*

to believe that a jury of six people functions differently from a jury of twelve "particularly if the requirement of unanimity is retained." Justice Byron R. White, the Court's spokesman in these cases, also wrote its opinion in *Johnson* and for a plurality of four Justices in *Apodaca;* he found nothing constitutionally defective in verdicts by a "heavy" majority vote and no constitutional mandate for verdicts by unanimous vote. The Court upheld the laws of two states that permitted verdicts of 9–3 and 10–2 respectively. These 1972 cases, according to the dissenters, diminished the burden of proof beyond reasonable doubt and made convictions possible by a preponderance of jurors.

For centuries the standard of proof of guilt beyond reasonable doubt was inextricably entwined with the principle of a unanimous verdict, creating a hedge against jury bias. The requirement of jury unanimity had meant that a single juror might veto all others, thwarting an overwhelming majority. Accordingly, Johnson contended that due process of law, by embodying the standard of proof beyond a reasonable doubt, required unanimous verdicts and that three jurors who possessed such doubt in his case showed that his guilt was not proved beyond such doubt. White answered that no basis existed for believing that the majority jurors would refuse to listen to the doubts of the minority. Yet Johnson's jurors, who were "out" for less than twenty minutes, might have taken a poll before deliberating, and if nine had voted for a guilty verdict on the first ballot, they might have returned the verdict without the need of considering the minority's doubts. The dissenters saw the jury as an entity incapable of rendering a verdict by the undisputed standard of proof beyond a reasonable doubt if any juror remained unconvinced. The Court majority saw the jury as twelve individuals, nine of whom could decide the verdict if they were satisfied beyond a reasonable doubt, regardless of minority views.

If the prosecution's burden of proving guilt beyond a reasonable doubt does not change when a 9–3 verdict is permissible, verdicts returned by a nine-juror majority ought to be the same as those returned by unanimous juries of twelve. In fact, the 9–3 system yields a substantially higher conviction ratio and substantially fewer hung juries by which defendants avoid conviction, thus substantially lowering the prosecution's burden of proof.

Johnson also contended that Louisiana's complicated three-tier system of juries—unanimous verdicts of twelve in some cases, unanimous verdicts of five in others, and 9–3 verdicts in still others—denied him the equal protection of the laws. In fact, the standard of proof varied with the crime, but White rejected the equal protection argument, claiming instead that Louisiana's three-tier scheme was "not invidious" because it was rational: it saved time and money. The Court hardly considered whether it diluted justice.

In *Apodaca*, the 10–2 verdict came under attack from an argument that the Fourteenth Amendment extended to the states the same standard as prevailed in federal courts, where unanimity prevails. Four Justices, led by White, would have ruled that the Sixth Amendment does not require unanimous verdicts even in federal trials; four, led by Justice William O. Douglas, believed that because the amendment embodies the requirement of unanimous jury verdicts, no state can permit a majority verdict. Lewis F. Powell's opinion was decisive. He concurred with the Douglas wing to save the unanimous verdict in federal criminal trials and with the White wing to allow nonunanimous verdicts for states wanting them. In *Apodaca*, White contradictorily conceded that the reasonable doubt standard "has been rejected in *Johnson* v. *Louisiana*." Douglas proved, contrary to White, that the use of the nonunanimous jury altered the way the jury functioned, stacking it against the defendant. He interpreted the majority opinions as reflecting "a 'law and order' judicial mood."

—LEONARD W. LEVY

Bibliography

Levy, Leonard W. (1974). *Against the Law: The Nixon Court and Criminal Justice.* Pages 276–298. New York: Harper & Row.

JOHNSON v. TRANSPORTATION AGENCY

480 U.S. 616 (1987)

Paul Johnson sought promotion to the position of road dispatcher with the Transportation Agency of Santa Clara County, California; he was deemed the best-qualified applicant for the job by a board of interviewers and by the Road Operations Division Director, who normally would have made the promotion decision. But the agency's affirmative-action officer intervened, recommending to the agency director that a woman seeking the position be appointed instead. The agency director agreed, and the woman was selected over Johnson. Johnson subsequently filed a suit alleging sex discrimination, and a federal district court found gender to be "the determining factor" in the promotion. The Supreme Court nevertheless sustained the agency's action, 6–3.

Writing for the majority, Justice William J. Brennan invoked the language of *United Steelworkers* v. *Weber* (1979) and argued that the agency's affirmative-action program was justified because it sought to correct a "manifest imbalance" that existed in job categories that had been "traditionally segregated" on the basis of gender. According to Brennan, the determination of whether a "manifest imbalance" exists usually rests on the disparity between the percentage of a protected group employed in specific job categories and the percentage of the protected group in the local labor force who are qualified to work in those categories. Precisely how high the disparity has to be before a "manifest imbalance" arises, Brennan did not say; but he did indicate that the requisite disparity was something less than that required in cases like *Wygant* v. *Jackson Board of Education* (1986), where employees had to establish a prima facie case of discrimination against their employer.

Concurring, Justice John Paul Stevens sought to push open the door to affirmative action still further. He implied that private employers should be able to discriminate in favor of "disadvantaged" racial and gender groups for a wide variety of reasons, including improving education, "averting racial tension over the allocation of jobs in a community," and "improving . . . services to black constituencies."

Justice Sandra Day O'Connor concurred in the Court's judgment, but on narrower grounds than the majority. She maintained that affirmative-action programs can be invoked only to remedy past discrimination. But her standard of proof for past discrimination was nearly the same as the majority's standard for "manifest imbalance": a statistical disparity between the percentage of an organization's employees who are members of a protected group and the percentage of the relevant labor pool that is made up of members of the group. Unlike Brennan, however, O'Connor did claim that the disparity must be enough to establish a prima facie case that past discrimination in fact occurred. In the present case this was a distinction without a difference, because O'Connor found that her standard had been met.

Writing for the dissenters, Justice Antonin Scalia attacked the Court for converting "a statute designed to establish a color-blind and gender-blind workplace . . . into a powerful engine of racism and sexism. . . ." Scalia noted that although Brennan cited *Weber* as controlling, he had in fact dramatically

Justice Antonin Scalia attacked the Court for converting "a statute designed to establish a color-blind and gender-blind workplace . . . into a powerful engine of racism and sexism. . . ."

extended *Weber* by redefining the meaning of the phrase "traditionally segregated job categories." In *Weber,* the phrase had "described skilled jobs from which employers and unions had systematically and intentionally excluded black workers. . . ." But in the present case, few women were employed in categories such as road maintenance workers because women themselves did not want the jobs. "There are, of course, those who believe that the social attitudes which cause women themselves to avoid certain jobs and to favor others are as nefarious as conscious, exclusionary discrimination. Whether or not that is so . . . the two phenomena are certainly distinct. And it is the alteration of social attitudes, rather than the elimination of discrimination, which today's decision approves as justification for state-enforced discrimination. This is an enormous expansion. . . ."

—JOHN G. WEST, JR.

Bibliography

Urofsky, Melvin I. (1991). *A Conflict of Rights: The Supreme Court and Affirmative Action.* New York: Scribners.

U.S. Commission on Civil Rights (1987). *Toward an Understanding of Johnson.* Clearinghouse Publication 94. Washington, D.C.: U.S. Government Printing Office.

JONES v. ALFRED H. MAYER CO.

392 U.S. 409 (1968)

This opinion contains important interpretations of a civil rights statute and of Congress's power to prohibit private discrimination. Jones alleged that the defendants had refused to sell him a home because he was black. He brought an action under section 1982 of Title 42, United States Code, a remnant of the Civil Rights Act of 1866, which states in part that all citizens shall have the same right as white citizens to purchase property.

This opinion contains important interpretations of a civil rights statute and of Congress's power to prohibit private discrimination.

See also

Affirmative Action

United Steelworkers v. Weber

Wygant v. Jackson Board of Education

Because Jones relied on a federal law to challenge private discrimination, and because the Supreme Court found that section 1982 encompassed Jones's claim, the case raised the question whether the Constitution grants Congress authority to outlaw private discrimination. The degree to which Congress may do so under the Fourteenth Amendment has been a recurring unsettled question. In *Jones,* Justice Potter Stewart's opinion for the Court avoided that complex matter by sustaining section 1982's applicability to private behavior under Congress's Thirteenth Amendment power to eliminate slavery. But even this holding generated tension with the Court's nineteenth-century pronouncements on Congress's power to reach private discrimination.

In the *Civil Rights Cases* (1883) the Court seemed to concede that the Thirteenth Amendment vests in Congress power to abolish all badges or incidents of slavery. In that case, however, the Court viewed those badges or incidents narrowly and limited Congress's role in defining them. In striking down the Civil Rights Act of 1875, a provision barring discrimination in public accommodations, the Court commented, "It would be running the slavery argument into the ground" to make it apply to every act of private discrimination in the field of public accommodations. In *Jones,* however, the Court acknowledged Congress's broad discretion not merely to eliminate the badges or incidents of slavery but also to define the practices constituting them.

Jones thus granted Congress virtually unlimited power to outlaw private racial discrimination. In later cases, *Jones* provided support for Congress's power to outlaw private racial discrimination in contractual relationships. Section 1981, another remnant of the Civil Rights Act of 1866, confers on all persons the same right "enjoyed by white citizens" to make and enforce contracts, to be parties or witnesses in lawsuits, and to be protected by law in person and property.

Runyon v. *McCrary* (1976) held section 1981 to prohibit the exclusion of blacks from private schools, and *Johnson* v. *Railway Express Agency, Inc.* (1974) held it to prohibit discrimination in employment.

As Justice John Marshall Harlan's dissent noted, *Jones*'s interpretation of section 1982 established it, more than a hundred years after its enactment, as a fair housing law discovered within months of passage of the Civil Rights Act of 1868, which itself contained a detailed fair housing provision. In finding that section 1982 reaches private discrimination not authorized by state law, *Jones* offers a questionable interpretation of the 1866 act's structure and manipulates legislative history. Whether a candid opinion could support *Jones*'s interpretation of section 1982 remains a subject of debate.

—THEODORE EISENBERG

Bibliography

Casper, Gerhard (1968). *Jones v. Mayer:* Clio, Bemused and Confused Muse. *Supreme Court Review* 1968:89–132.

Fairman, Charles (1971). *Reconstruction and Reunion 1864–88: Part One.* Volume 6 of *The Oliver Wendell Holmes Devise History of the Supreme Court of the United States.* New York: Macmillan.

JUDGE PETERS, UNITED STATES v.

5 Cranch 115 (1809)

This case bears historical significance as an episode in defiance, expressed in nullification and bordering on rebellion, by a state against the United States courts. The state was Pennsylvania, which suggests that doctrines of state sovereignty have never been merely sectional. The case was the occasion of Chief Justice John Marshalls's first nationalist opinion, but more important is the fact that Pennsylvania successfully thwarted the federal courts, exposing their helplessness in enforcing their writs, until a president of the Virginia dynasty unhesitatingly backed the judiciary, still Federalist-dominated, against the political machine of his own party in Pennsylvania.

The case originated during the Revolution as the result of a dispute between the state and Gideon Olmstead over the proceeds from the sale of a captured enemy ship. A state court denied Olmstead's claim, but a prize court established by Congress ruled in his favor; the state court refused to obey the federal order and the state treasurer retained the money. Litigation went on for years. In 1803 Judge Richard Peters of the United States District court in Philadelphia decided in favor of Olmstead in his suit against the treasurer's estate, which held the money for the state. The state legislature, invoking the Eleventh Amendment, resolved that Peters had "illegally usurped" jurisdiction and instructed the governor to protect the rights of the state. In 1808 Olmstead, then in his eighties, obtained from the Supreme Court an order against Peters to show cause why a writ of mandamus should not be issued compelling him to enforce his decision of 1803. The judge stated that the state legislature had commanded the governor "to call out an armed force" to prevent the execution of a federal process. Peters asked for a resolution of the issue by the supreme tribunal of the nation, saying that he had withheld process to avoid a conflict between the state and federal governments.

In 1809, at a time when New England was disobeying the Embargo Acts, Marshall, speaking for the Court, declared:

> *If the legislatures of the several states may, at will, annul the judgments of the courts of the United States, and destroy the rights acquired under those judgements, the constitution itself becomes a solemn mockery, and the nation is deprived of the means of enforcing its laws by the instrumentality of*

♦ **mandamus**
[Latin: we command] A form of writ directed to a government official or a lower court directing the performance of an act appropriate to that official's or court's duties.

See also

Civil Rights

Racial Discrimination

Runyon v. McCrary

J

*The supremacy of
the Supreme Court
had by no means
been established yet.*

*its own tribunals. So fatal a result must be
deprecated by all; and the people of Pennsylvania, not less than the citizens of every
other state, must feel a deep interest in resisting principles so destructive of the
Union, and in averting consequences so fatal to themselves.*

(That passage was quoted by the Court in the
1950s and 1960s in cases involving southern
defiance of federal orders commanding desegregation.) The Court awarded a "peremptory mandamus" against Peters, but neither he
nor Marshall could force the state to comply.

The state governor called out the militia,
and the state legislature, supporting him,
announced that "*as guardians of the State
rights,* we cannot permit an infringement of
those rights by an unconstitutional exercise
of power in the United States Courts."
Those actions were not the only reply to
Marshall's declaration that the Eleventh
Amendment did not apply inasmuch as
the suit had not been commenced against
the state. Pennsylvania also denied that the
Supreme Court had appellate powers over
the state courts or that it was the final arbiter in a dispute between the United States
and any state. When a federal marshal attempted to execute Peters's judgment, 1,400
men of the state militia opposed him; he
summoned a federal *posse comitatus* of 2,000
men, but to avoid bloodshed fixed the day
for service in three weeks. At this juncture,
while the papers in the country were still
carrying news about Federalist New England's defiance of the Embargo Acts, the
Democratic governor of Pennsylvania turned
to the Democratic national administration
for support. "The issue is in fact come to
this," said *The Aurora*, the administration
newspaper in Philadelphia, "whether the
Constitution of the United States is to remain in force or to become a dead letter. . . .
The decree of the Court must be obeyed."
President James Madison, mindful of the
repercussions of the case, chastised the state

governor. "The Executive," he replied, "is
not only unauthorized to prevent the execution of a decree sanctioned by the Supreme
Court of the United States, but is expressly
enjoined, by statute, to carry into effect any
such decree, where opposition may be made
to it."

The incipient rebellion immediately collapsed. The state withdrew its militia and appropriated the money to pay Olmstead. In
the aftermath of the affair, the United States
arrested and tried the commanding general of
the state militia and eight of his officers for
having obstructed the federal marshal. A federal jury convicted them in a trial before Justice Bushrod Washington, who sentenced the
defendants to fines and imprisonment, but
the president pardoned them. Eleven state
legislatures adopted resolutions condemning
Pennsylvania's resistance to the federal
courts. Every southern state rejected Pennsylvania's doctrines of states' rights. That
northern state had also proposed the establishment of "an impartial tribunal" to settle
disputes between "the general and state governments." The legislature of Virginia replied
that "a tribunal is already provided by the
Constitution of the United States, *to wit:* the
Supreme Court, more eminently qualified . . .
to decide the disputes aforesaid . . . than any
other tribunal which could be erected." In a
few years, however, Virginia would be playing Pennsylvania's tune. The supremacy of
the Supreme Court had by no means been established yet.

—LEONARD W. LEVY

Bibliography

Higginbotham, Sanford W. (1952). *The Keystone in the Democratic Arch: Pennsylvania
Politics 1800–1816.* Pages 177–204. Har-
risburg: Pennsylvania Historical and Museum Commission.

Treacy, Kenneth W. (1957). The Olmstead
Case, 1778–1809. *Western Political Quarterly* 10:675–691.

See also

Martin v. Hunter's Lessee

Warren, Charles (1923). *The Supreme Court in American History*, 3 vols. Vol. 1: 375–387. Boston: Little, Brown.

JUDICIAL STRATEGY

That judges shape much public policy is a fact of political life. The significant questions are how, how often, how effectively, and how wisely they influence policy. Each of these inquiries poses normative as well as empirical problems. Here we shall be concerned only with legitimate strategies that a Justice of the United States Supreme Court can employ to maximize his or her influence. We shall focus mainly on marshaling the Court.

A Justice, like any strategist, must coordinate limited resources to achieve goals. He or she must make choices—about goals and priorities among goals and also about means to achieve those goals. Intelligent choices among means depend in part on accurate assessments of the resources the Justice controls and of the limitations that others may impose on use of those resources.

The Justices can order litigants, including government officials, to act or not act in specified ways. Less tangibly, judges also have the prestige of their office, supported by a general cultural ethos of respect for the rule of law. In particular, a Justice has a powerful weapon, an opinion—a document that will be widely distributed by the Government Printing Office and several private firms. That opinion will justify—well or poorly—a particular decision and, explicitly or implicitly, the public policy it supports.

A Justice's power is limited by the nature of judicial institutions. Judges lack self-starters. Someone has to bring a case to them. Furthermore, while they can hold acts of other public officials constitutional or unconstitutional and so allow or forbid particular policies, it is much more difficult for judges to compel government to act. The Supreme Court can rule that blacks are entitled to vote, but it cannot force Congress to pass a civil rights law to make that right effective. Moreover, the Court can hear only a limited number of cases. It depends on thousands of state and federal judges to carry out its jurisprudence. And no Justice plays an *official* role in selecting, retaining, or promoting judges.

Second, a Supreme Court Justice needs the agreement of at least four colleagues. And each Justice can write a separate opinion, dissenting or concurring, in any case.

Third, and more broadly, the Court is dependent on Congress and the president for appropriations and enforcement of decisions. Each of these branches has other important checks: the House can impeach and the Senate can then remove a Justice. Congress can increase the size of the Court, remove at least part of its appellate jurisdiction, propose constitutional amendments to erase the effects of decisions or strike at judicial power itself, and use its access to mass media to challenge the Court's prestige. The president can even more effectively attack the Court's prestige, and he can persuade Congress to use any of its weapons against the Justices. He can also choose new judges who, he hopes, will change the course of constitutional interpretation.

Fourth, state officials can influence public opinion to pressure Congress and the president. State officers can also drag their heels in carrying out judicial decisions and select judges who are hostile to the Court's jurisprudence.

Fifth, leaders of interest groups can pressure elected officials at all levels of government. And when judicial decisions threaten or support their values, these people seldom hesitate to apply whatever political leverage is in their self-interest.

Commentators—journalists and social scientists as well as law professors—constitute a sixth check. If judges make law, Edward S. Corwin said, so do commentators. Justices who want their jurisprudence to endure must look not only to immediate reactions but also

That judges shape much public policy is a fact of political life.

to the future. What commentators write may influence later generations of voters, lawyers, and public officials.

A Justice confronts these limitations simultaneously, and each of these groups will include a range of opinion. Any ruling will elate some and infuriate others, and the political power of various factions is likely to vary widely. In short, problems of synchronizing activities are always present and are typically complex.

The first audience a Justice must convince is composed of other Justices. The most obvious way of having one's views accepted by one's colleagues is to have colleagues who agree with one's views. Thus ability to influence the recruiting process is a difficult but fruitful means of maximizing influence. Justices who cannot choose their colleagues must consider how to persuade them.

Although treating others with courtesy may never change a vote or modify an opinion, it does make it more likely that others will listen. When others listen, intellectual capacity becomes critical. The Justice who knows "the law," speaks succinctly, writes clearly, and analyzes wisely gains distinct advantages.

Practical experience can be a valuable adjunct. Logic is concerned with relations among propositions, not with their desirability or social utility. According to William O. Douglas, several Justices were converted to Chief Justice Earl Warren's position in *Brown v. Board of Education* (1954) because of his vast political experience. Strength of character is also crucial. Although neither learned nor gifted as a writer, Warren led the Court and the country through a constitutional revolution. It was his "passion for justice," his massive integrity, Douglas also recalled, that made Warren such a forceful leader. "Is it right?" was his typical question, not "Do earlier decisions allow it?"

In another sense, intellect alone is unlikely to suffice. Justices are all apt to be intelligent, strong-willed people with divergent views

about earlier rulings as well as public policy. They are also apt to differ about the Court's proper roles in the political system—in sum, about fundamentals of jurisprudence. At that level of dispute, it is improbable that one Justice, no matter how astute and eloquent, will convert another.

Facing disagreements that cannot be intellectually reconciled, a Justice may opt for several courses. Basically, he can negotiate with his colleagues or go it alone. Most often, it will be prudent to negotiate. Like policy making, negotiation, even bargaining, is a fact of judicial life. Writing the opinion of the Court requires "an orchestral, not a solo performance." All Justices can utilize their votes and freedom to write separate opinions. The value of each depends upon the circumstances. If the Court divides 4–4, the ninth Justice, in effect, decides the case. On the other hand, when the Court votes 8–0, the ninth Justice's ability to negotiate will depend almost totally on his capacity to write a separate opinion that, the others fear, would undermine their position.

To be effective, negotiations must be restrained and sensitive. Justices are likely to sit together for many years. Driving a hard bargain today may damage future relations. The mores of the Court forbid trading of votes. The Justices take their oaths of office seriously; and, while reality pushes them toward accommodation, they are not hagglers in a market, peddling their views.

The most common channels of negotiating are circulation of draft opinions, comments on those drafts, and private conversations. A Justice can nudge others, especially the judge assigned the task of producing the opinion of the Court, by suggesting additions, deletions, and rephrasings. In turn, to retain a majority, the opinion writer must be willing to accede to many suggestions, even painful ones, as he tries to persuade the Court to accept the core of his reasoning. Oliver Wendell Holmes once complained that "the boys generally cut one of the genitals" out of his drafts, and he made no claim to have restored their manhood.

Drafts and discussions of opinions can and do change votes, even outcomes. Sometimes those changes are not in the intended direction. After reading Felix Frankfurter's dissent in *Baker* v. *Carr* (1961), Tom C. Clark changed his vote, remarking that if those were the reasons for dissenting he would join the majority.

Although the art of negotiation is essential, a Justice should not wish to appear so malleable as to encourage efforts to dilute his jurisprudence. He would much prefer a reputation of being reasonable but tough-minded. He thus might sometimes find it wise to stand alone rather than even attempt compromise. It is usually prudent for a Justice, when with the majority, to inject as many of his views as possible into the Court's opinion, and when with the minority to squeeze as many hostile ideas as possible out of the Court's opinion. There are, however, times when both conscience and prudence counsel standing alone, appealing to officials in other governmental processes or to future judges to vindicate his jurisprudence.

Although Justices have very limited authority to make the other branches of government act, they are not powerless. Judges can often find more in a statute than legislators believe they put there. Obiter dicta in an opinion can also prod other officials to follow the "proper" path. The Court might even pursue a dangerous course that might push a reluctant president to carry out its decisions lest he seem either indifferent to the rule of law or unprotective of federal power against state challenges.

Lobbying with either branch is also possible. Indeed, judicial lobbying has a venerable history running back to John Jay. Advice delivered through third parties may have been even more common. Over time, however, expectations of judicial conduct have risen so that even a hint of such activity triggers an outcry. Thus a judge must heavily discount the benefits of direct or indirect contacts by the probability of their being discovered.

The most obvious weapon that a Justice has against unwelcome political action is the ability to persuade his colleagues to declare that action unconstitutional or, if it comes in the shape of a federal statute or executive order, to disarm it by interpretation. These are the Court's ultimate weapons, and their overuse or use at the wrong time might provoke massive retaliation.

A Justice must therefore consider more indirect means. Delay is the tactic that procedural rules most readily permit. The Justices can deny a writ of certiorari, dismiss an appeal, remand the case for clarification, order reargument, or use a dozen other tactics to delay deciding volatile disputes until the political climate changes.

Under other circumstances, it might be more prudent for a Justice to move the Court step by step. Gradual erosion of old rules and accretion of new ones may win more adherents than sudden statements of novel doctrines. The Court's treatment of segregation provides an excellent illustration. If *Missouri ex rel. Gaines* v. *Canada* (1938) had struck down separate but equal, the Court could never have made the decision stick. Indeed, years later, when it excommunicated Jim Crow, enforcement created a generation of litigation that still continues.

Strategy is concerned with efficient utilization of scarce resources to achieve important objectives. Its domain is that of patience and prudence, not of wisdom in choosing among goals nor of courage in fighting for the right. The messages that a study of judicial strategy yields are: a web of checks restrains a judge's power; and if he or she wishes to maximize his or her ability to do good, a judge must learn to cope with those restrictions, to work within and around them, and to conserve available resources for the times when he or she must, as a matter of conscience, directly challenge what he or she sees as a threat to the basic values of constitutional democracy.

—WALTER F. MURPHY

Bibliography

Bickel, Alexander M. (1957). *The Unpublished Opinions of Mr. Justice Brandeis.* Cambridge, Mass.: Harvard University Press.

——— (1961). The Passive Virtues. *Harvard Law Review* 75:40–79.

Douglas, William O. (1980). *The Court Years, 1939–1975.* New York: Random House.

Kluger, Richard (1976). *Simple Justice.* New York: Knopf.

Murphy, Bruce (1982). *The Brandeis/Frankfurter Connection.* New York: Oxford University Press.

Murphy, Walter F. (1964). *Elements of Judicial Strategy.* Chicago: University of Chicago Press.

O'Brien, David M. (1986). *Storm Center: The Supreme Court in American Politics.* New York: Norton.

JUDICIAL SUPREMACY

Stripped of the partisan rhetoric that usually surrounds important decisions of the Supreme Court, debate about judicial supremacy raises a fundamental question: Who is the final, authoritative interpreter of the Constitution? The response of judicial supremacy is that courts perform that function and other officials are bound not only to respect judges' decisions in particular cases but also, in formulating future public policy, to follow the general principles judges have laid down.

Judicial review does not necessarily entail or logically imply judicial supremacy. One can, as Thomas Jefferson did, concede the legitimacy of courts' refusing on constitutional grounds to enforce statutes and executive orders and still deny either that officials of a coordinate branch must obey a decision or follow its rationale in the future. This view, called "departmentalism," sees the three branches of the national government as equal in constitutional interpretation. Each department has authority to interpret the Constitution for itself, but its interpretations do not bind the other two.

There are other possible answers to the basic question: Congress, the president, the states, or the people. A claim for the states presupposes the Constitution to be a compact among sovereign entities who reserved to themselves authority to construe their obligations. Such was Jefferson's assertion in the Kentucky Resolutions (1798), and it echoed down decades of dreary debates on nullification and secession. The Civil War settled the matter, though some southern states briefly tried to resurrect nullification to oppose *Brown* v. *Board of Education* (1954).

A claim for the president as the ultimate, authoritative interpreter smacks too much of royalty for the idea to have been seriously maintained. On the other hand, presidents have frequently and effectively defended their independent authority to interpret the Constitution for the executive department.

A case for the people as the final, authoritative interpreter permeates the debate. American government rests on popular consent. The people can elect officials to amend the Constitution or create a new constitution and so shape basic political arrangements as well as concrete public policies. Jefferson advocated constitutional conventions as a means of popular judging between conflicting departmental interpretations.

Although even James Madison rejected Jefferson's solution, indirect appeals to the people as the ultimate interpreters are reflected in claims to the supremacy of a popularly elected legislature. On the other hand, in *The Federalist* #78, Alexander Hamilton rested his argument for judicial review on the authority of the people who have declared their will in the Constitution. Judicial review,

See also

Baker v. *Carr*

Brown v. *Board of Education*

he argued, does not imply that judges are superior to legislators but that "the power of the people is superior to both."

Although John Marshall partially incorporated this line of reasoning in *Marbury* v. *Madison* (1803), neither he nor Hamilton ever explicitly asserted that the Supreme Court's interpretation of the Constitution was binding on other branches of the federal government. One might, however, infer that conclusion from Marshall's opinions in *Marbury* and in *McCulloch* v. *Maryland* (1819), where he expressly claimed supremacy as far as state governments were concerned.

We know little of the Framers' attitudes toward judicial supremacy. In *The Federalist* #51, Madison took a clear departmentalist stand, as he did in the First Congress. In 1788 Madison wrote a friend that the new Constitution made no provision for settling differences among departments' interpretations: "[A]nd as ye Courts are generally the last in making the decision, it results to them by refusing or not refusing to execute a law, to stamp it with its final character. This makes the Judiciary Dept paramount in fact to the Legislature, which was never intended and can never be proper."

In the Senate in 1802, however, Gouverneur Morris argued that the judges derived their power to decide on the constitutionality of laws "from authority higher than this Constitution. They derive it from the constitution of man, from the nature of things, from the necessary progress of human affairs. The decision of the Supreme Court is and, of necessity, must be final."

What turns a brief for judicial review into one for judicial supremacy is, of course, the claim of finality. Partially, that claim rests on the notion that interpretation of law is a uniquely judicial function (and, by its own terms, the Constitution is "the supreme law"); partially, on the ambiguity of the Constitution about the interpretive authority of other branches; and partially on the need for a supreme arbiter to assure the supremacy and uniform interpretations of the Constitution. The claim also rests on the belief that judges, because they are protected from popular pressures, are more apt to act fairly and coherently than elected officials. "It is only from the Supreme Court," Charles Evans Hughes once asserted, "that we can obtain a sane, well-ordered interpretation of the Constitution." The Court itself has seldom explicitly claimed judicial supremacy and has never articulated a full argument for it vis-à-vis Congress or the president. Indeed, through such doctrines as the presumption of constitutionality and political questions, the Court often defers to interpretations by other departments.

The first modern, categorical claim by the Court to supremacy came in *Cooper* v. *Aaron*

THE BUCK STOPS HERE

The Supreme Court is generally accepted as the final, authoritative interpreter of the Constitution. (Corbis/Kelly–Mooney Photography)

J

JUDICIAL SUPREMACY

Although the constitutional text does not require judicial supremacy, Congress and the president have usually gone along with the Court's constitutional interpretations.

(1958), where the Justices said that "the federal judiciary is supreme in the exposition of the law of the Constitution," and thus that *Brown* v. *Board of Education* was "the supreme law of the land." But *Cooper* involved state officials as did *Baker* v. *Carr* (1962), where the Court first referred to itself as the "ultimate interpreter of the Constitution." Still, it was not until *Powell* v. *McCormack* (1969) that the Court so designated itself in a dispute involving Congress, an assertion the Justices repeated about the president in *United States* v. *Nixon* (1974) and about both in *Immigration and Naturalization Service* v. *Chadha* (1983). *Powell*, however, addressed only the authority of the House to exclude a duly elected member and it did not require that he be readmitted or be given back pay. *Nixon* upheld a subpoena to a president whose political situation was already desperate. What would have happened to the Court's claim as "ultimate interpreter" had it faced a politically secure chief executive in *Nixon* or tried to force Congress to take action in *Powell* might well have produced examples of departmentalism, as did Jefferson's refusal to obey Marshall's subpoena in *United States* v. *Burr* (1807). And early congressional reactions to *Chadha*'s declaring the legislative veto unconstitutional have been mixed. Formally as well as informally, Congress has continued the practice, though in a more guarded fashion and on a smaller scale.

Although the constitutional text does not require judicial supremacy, Congress and the president have usually gone along with the Court's constitutional interpretations. Yet the exceptions have been sufficiently frequent and important that it is difficult to demonstrate a firm tradition requiring coordinate federal branches to accept the Court's doctrines. In matters strictly judicial—whether or not courts will enforce particular statutes—judges have been supreme, though subject to checks regarding jurisdiction and appointment of new personnel. The other branches, however, have frequently denied that they have an obligation, when setting policy, to follow the Court's constitutional interpretations.

There is a stronger argument for a duty of enforcing a judicial decision in a particular case. Certainly where the government has brought the case to the courts, an obligation to obey is obvious, as even Jefferson admitted. Where, however, the government is the defendant, the matter is much more complicated, especially when a court commands an official to perform a positive action. Jefferson and Andrew Jackson said they had no duty to obey such orders; Abraham Lincoln acted as if he did not; and Franklin D. Roosevelt was prepared to ignore the *Gold Clause Cases* (1934) had they been decided against the government.

Typically, Congress and the president acquiesce in judicial interpretations of the Constitution because they agree with the results of judicial decisions, or fear public opinion, or recognize the difficulty of securing a congressional response. Often, too, the Justices reinforce Congress's tendency toward inertia by not pressing a claim to supremacy. Always hovering in the background of any department's assertion of supremacy is the possibility of an appeal to "the people" through the amending process. Yet even such an appeal, when directed against the Court's jurisprudence, implies an admission of the tactical if not theoretical superiority of the Court as constitutional interpreter.

—WALTER F. MURPHY

Bibliography

Corwin, Edwin S. (1914). *Marbury* v. *Madison* and the Doctrine of Judicial Review. *Michigan Law Review* 12:538–572.

Fisher, Louis (1985). Constitutional Interpretation by Members of Congress. *North Carolina Law Review* 63:701–741.

Mikva, Abner J. (1983). How Well Does Congress Support and Defend the Constitution? *North Carolina Law Review* 61:587–611.

Murphy, Walter F.; Fleming, James E.; and Harris, William F., II (1986). *American Constitutional Interpretation*. Chaps. 6–7. Mineola, N.Y.: Foundation Press.

JUDICIAL SYSTEM, FEDERAL

The charter of the federal judicial system is Article III of the Constitution, authorizing the creation of federal tribunals vested with the judicial power of the United States, that is, the authority to adjudicate a specifically enumerated set of cases and controversies. Article III also specifies the method of appointment of federal judges and lays down rules designed to guard their independence.

The Framers, mindful of the problems that the absence of a national judiciary had caused under the Articles of Confederation, easily agreed that there must be a national Supreme Court with power to assure the uniformity and supremacy of federal law. But the Framers were divided over the question of whether further provision should be made for national courts. Some favored the creation of a complete system of federal courts. Some thought that this would unnecessarily narrow the preexisting general jurisdiction of the state courts; they argued that national interests could be sufficiently protected by providing for Supreme Court review of state court decisions involving questions of federal law. This division was settled by a compromise: Article III itself mandates that there shall be "one Supreme Court"; but beyond this the federal judicial power is simply vested in "such inferior Courts as the Congress may from time to time ordain and establish."

Article III specifies that the Supreme Court (and whatever inferior federal courts Congress may establish) are to be courts of a strictly limited jurisdiction: they may adjudicate only nine enumerated categories of cases. Some of these were included because they touch on issues of national interest: most important, cases "arising under" the Constitution and laws of the United States (the federal question jurisdiction); cases of admiralty and maritime jurisdiction; and cases to which the United States is a party. Federal courts were also empowered to decide certain controversies implicating the nation's foreign affairs (for example, disputes affecting ambassadors and other alien parties; cases arising under treaties). The remaining categories authorize the federal courts to engage in interstate umpiring in cases where it was feared that parochial interests would prevail in the state courts. Examples are controversies between states, between a state and a citizen of another state, and between citizens of different states.

Article III's specification that the judicial power consists of adjudicating "cases" or "controversies" itself embodies a fundamental political decision: the national courts were to exercise only a judicial power. Thus the Constitutional Convention of 1787 repeatedly and explicitly rejected a variety of proposals to allow federal courts or judges to participate as advisers or revisers in the legislative process or to render advisory opinions; their authority was to be limited to "cases of a judiciary nature." On the other hand, the historical evidence establishes the Framers' understanding that the grant of the judicial power was to include the authority, where necessary to the lawful decision of a case properly within a court's jurisdiction, to disregard federal or state statutes found to be unconstitutional. This power of judicial review, occasionally challenged as a usurpation because it is not explicitly mentioned in Article III, has been settled since *Marbury* v. *Madison* (1803).

Besides defining the outer bounds of the federal judicial power, Article III protects federal judges from political pressures by guaranteeing tenure during good behavior without reduction in compensation.

Article III is not self-executing; it needs legislation to bring it to life, most particularly because Congress must determine whether there should be "inferior" federal courts and what should be the scope of their jurisdiction. It is to this task that the First Congress turned in its twentieth enactment: the seminal Judiciary Act of 1789. Obeying the Constitution's command, the act constituted a Supreme Court, consisting of a Chief Justice and five associates. Next, the act, establishing a tradition persisting without interruption to this day, took up the constitutional option to create a system of federal courts of original jurisdiction. The structure created was curious, but survived for a century. The country was divided into districts (at least one for each state), with a district court manned by a district judge. In addition, the country was divided into circuits (originally three), each with another trial court—a circuit court—manned not by its own judges but by two Supreme Court Justices (sitting "on circuit") and a district judge.

Only a fraction of the constitutional potential for original federal court jurisdiction was exploited by the first Judiciary Act, attesting to the clear contemporaneous understanding of the Constitution that it is for Congress to determine which (if any) of the cases and controversies encompassed by the federal judicial power should be adjudicated in the first instance in a lower federal (rather than a state) court. (The modest original jurisdiction of the Supreme Court, limited to controversies where a state is a party and certain cases involving foreign diplomats, is thought to flow "directly" from the Constitution and thus represents a special case.) The district courts were given the jurisdiction most clearly felt to be a national one: authority to adjudicate admiralty cases. In a controversial decision, the First Congress set a precedent by opening the circuit courts to some cases involving controversies between citizens of different states and involving aliens. The federal trial courts were also granted jurisdiction over most civil suits brought by the United States and over the

then negligible federal criminal caseload. Notably, the act did not give the federal trial courts jurisdiction over cases "arising under" federal law, leaving these to be adjudicated in the state courts.

The appellate structure of the new court system was rudimentary. Federal criminal cases were left without direct review (and remained so for a century). The circuit courts were given a limited appellate jurisdiction over the district courts, and the Supreme Court was authorized to review civil cases decided by the circuit courts involving more than $2,000.

Finally, in its famous section 25, the act—consistent with the Framers' intention to assure the supremacy of federal law—gave the Supreme Court power to review final state court judgments rejecting claims of right or immunity under federal law. (State court judgments upholding claims of right under federal law were not made reviewable until 1914.) Supreme Court review of state judgments involving questions of federal law has been a feature of our judicial federalism ever since 1789, and has served as a profoundly significant instrument for consolidating and protecting national power.

The institutional structure created by the first Judiciary Act proved to be remarkably stable; major structural change did not come until 1891. The Supreme Court has had a continuous existence since 1789, with changes only in the number of Justices. So also have the district courts (though their number has of course undergone major change). Even the circuit courts—architecturally the weakest feature of the system—survived for more than a century.

As to the jurisdiction of the federal courts, changes were incremental in the pre-Civil War period, with the state courts acting as the primary enforcers of the still rudimentary corpus of national law. But the Civil War brought a sea change: Congress was no longer prepared to depend on the state judiciaries to enforce rights guaranteed by the new Fourteenth Amendment and by the Reconstruction legislation. By the Habeas Corpus Act of 1867 and the various Civil Rights Acts, Congress extended the lower federal courts' jurisdiction to include claims against state officials for invasion of federal constitutional and statutory rights. These extensions were in turn overtaken by the Judiciary Act of 1875, giving the federal courts a general jurisdiction to adjudicate civil cases arising under federal law, subject only to a minimum amount-in-controversy. These expansions, supplemented by subsequent numerous specific extensions of federal trial jurisdiction over various sorts of actions involving national law, signaled the transformation of the federal courts from narrow forums designed to resolve maritime and certain interstate disputes into catholic tribunals playing a principal role in enforcing the growing body of national rights, privileges, and immunities.

The growth of the federal judicial business in the post–Civil War era placed an ever-growing pressure on the federal judicial system. The Supreme Court was especially burdened by the duties of circuit riding and by an increasing caseload. By 1890 the Court had a backload of 1,800 cases; in the same year, 54,194 cases were pending in the lower federal courts. Congress responded to the crisis in the Circuit Courts of Appeals Act (Evarts Act) of 1891, which fixed the outline of the contemporary federal judicial system. The act established a system of intermediate appellate courts called Circuit Courts of Appeals (not to be confused with the old circuit courts, which were finally abolished in 1911), one for each of (the then) nine circuits and staffed with its own judges. Although a narrow category of district court decisions continued (and continue) to be reviewed directly by the Supreme Court, the Evarts Act created the standard modern practice: appeals went normally from the district courts to the new courts of appeals; the judgments of the latter were in turn reviewable by the Supreme Court.

The second major and seminal innovation of the Evarts Act related to appellate review in the Supreme Court: the act introduced the principle of review at the Court's own discretion (by writ of certiorari) of judgments in the lower courts. This principle was in turn greatly expanded in the so-called Judges' Bill of 1925, which sharply reduced the availability of Supreme Court review as of right of decisions of state and federal courts and substituted for it discretionary review on certiorari—the method of review that, to this day, dominates the Court's docket.

Changes in the structure of the federal judicial system have been few and minor since 1925, although both the statutory jurisdiction and the business of the courts have undergone major transformations. In essence the system remains a three-tier system, with the district courts serving as the trial courts, the courts of appeals as the appellate tribunals of first instance, and the Supreme Court as the court of final review (having also the power to review state court decisions involving issues of federal law). The picture is completed by the existence of special federal tribunals empowered to decide particular categories of cases, and by numerous federal administrative tribunals; the decisions of all of these are typically subject to review in the regular federal courts.

The most important component of the contemporary statutory jurisdiction of the United States District Courts encompasses diversity cases involving more than $75,000, criminal prosecutions and civil actions brought by the United States, a large range of actions against the United States and its agencies and officials, federal habeas corpus, and—most significant—all civil cases in which a plaintiff sues on a claim arising under the Constitution and laws of the United States. The latter, all-encompassing rubric includes not only cases brought pursuant to the hundreds of federal statutes specifying a right to sue but also the numerous cases where that right is a judge-created ("implied") right to enforce a federal statutory or—(of profound significance)—constitutional provision not itself explicitly containing a right of action. In addition, the statutes allow certain diversity and federal question cases brought in the state courts to be removed for trial to a federal district court. Finally, the district courts exercise a significant jurisdiction to review the work of many federal administrative agencies and to review and supervise the work of the system of bankruptcy courts. The jurisdiction of the district courts is occasionally specified as exclusive of the state courts (for example, admiralty, copyright, and patent); most of their civil jurisdiction is, however, concurrent with that of the state courts.

The country was, in the mid-1980s, divided into ninety-seven districts (including the District of Columbia and Puerto Rico). Each state had at least one district; districts had never encompassed more than one state. The district courts were staffed by 576 active district judges—almost three times the 1950 figure (182 new district judgeships were created between 1978 and 1984 alone). The growth in number of judges has, nevertheless, failed to keep pace with the explosive increase in the caseload that has occurred since the 1960s. In 1940 about 70,000 criminal and civil (nonbankruptcy) cases were filed in the federal courts; in 1960, about 80,000; by 1980, the figure was almost 200,000, and in 1984 it exceeded 275,000. (The compound annual rate of increase in the federal district court case load was under 1 percent between 1934 and 1960; it has been 5 percent since 1960.) The increase is due primarily and naturally to the vast growth in the total corpus of federal (constitutional, statutory, common, and administrative) law applied in turn to a growing country with an expansive and mobile economy. It was also fed, however, over twenty-five years by congressional and court-initiated changes in substantive and remedial rules that made the federal courts into powerful litigation-attracting engines for the cre-

ation and expansion of rights and the redistribution of entitlements and powers in our society. Thus open-ended constitutional and statutory formulas have been used to fuel aggressive judicial review of the validity of federal and state legislative and administrative action and to create an expansive system of remedies against federal and state government (including affirmative claims on the resources of these governments). Justiciability requirements (such as standing) that previously narrowed the scope of jurisdiction over public law actions have been significantly eroded. And federal court litigation has become increasingly attractive to plaintiffs as a result of provisions for attorneys' fees, the elimination (or inflation-caused erosion) of amount-in-controversy requirements, and the increasing use of class actions.

These developments are reflected in the changing content of the federal district courts' workload. There were 6,000 suits against the United States in 1960, and almost 30,000 in 1983. There were only 300 civil rights cases in 1960, almost 20,000 in 1983; 2,100 prisoner postconviction cases in 1960, more than 30,000 in 1983; 500 social security law cases in 1960, more than 20,000 in 1983. In general, about 35 to 40 percent of the mid-1980s district court civil caseload involved the United States or its officials as a plaintiff or defendant; 60 to 65 percent of the civil caseload was "private" (including, however, litigation against state and local governments and officials). Diversity cases contributed about 20 percent of the caseload since the 1970s. The number of criminal prosecutions has, historically, fluctuated widely in response to special federal programs (peaking during prohibition); since the mid-1970s the criminal caseload has been quite stable and in the mid-1980s contributed about 15 to 20 percent of the total.

In response to the explosive caseload Congress has acted to allow the district courts to rely substantially on the work of so-called federal magistrates—officials appointed by district judges with wide powers (subject to review by the district judge) to issue warrants, conduct preliminary hearings, try minor criminal offenses, supervise civil discovery, rule on preliminary motions and prisoner petitions, and (with the consent of the parties) even to hear and enter judgment generally in civil cases. The conferring of additional powers on magistrates has evoked controversy as well as some (so far unsuccessful) constitutional attacks.

The United States Courts of Appeals (as they are now called) have jurisdiction to review all final (and some interlocutory) decisions of the district courts. Pursuant to special statutory provisions they also review some cases coming directly from federal administrative agencies (this being an especially significant component of the business of the Court of Appeals for the District of Columbia Circuit). About 15 percent of their cases are criminal cases, and another 15 percent are federal and state prisoner postconviction and civil rights cases; only 14 percent of their docket consists of diversity cases.

The caseload of the courts of appeals increased dramatically over twenty-five years and was, in the mid-1980s, commonly described as constituting a crisis. In the forty years before 1960 that caseload hovered between 1,500 and the peak of 3,700 reached in 1960. In 1970 the figure was almost 11,500, and in 1980 it was over 21,000. From 1980 to 1983 the caseload jumped again to 29,580. From 1960 to 1983 there was an increase of almost 800 percent in the number of appeals from the district courts; the compound annual rate of increase for all cases from 1960 to 1983 was 9.4 percent (compared to 0.5 percent in the preceding twenty-five years).

To manage this workload there existed (in the mid-1980s) twelve courts of appeals assigned to geographical circuits (eleven in the states and one for the District of Columbia) and an additional one (described below) for certain special categories of subject matter. The number of judges in each circuit ranged from six (First) to twenty-eight (Ninth). There were 156 authorized circuit judgeships; in 1960 there were sixty-eight (and in 1978 only ninety-seven). Cases are typically heard by panels of three judges; a few cases of special importance are in turn reheard by the court sitting en banc. The increase in number of judges by no means kept pace with the expansion of the caseload since 1960. As a result, there were substantial changes in the procedures of these courts: opportunities for oral argument (and even for briefing) were sharply curtailed and an increasing proportion of cases disposed of summarily, without opinion. Central staff attorneys (as well as a growing army of conventional law clerks) assisted the judges.

From the beginning of our national history Congress has perceived a need to create special tribunals for the adjudication of cases falling outside the traditional areas of federal court jurisdiction. Military tribunals have, from the outset, administered a special body of law through special procedures. The administration of justice in the territories in transition toward statehood was perceived as requiring special temporary federal tribunals that would become state courts upon statehood; the District of Columbia and the territories and dependencies of the United States also require a full panoply of special federal courts to administer local law. Beginning in 1855, with the establishment of a rudimentary Court of Claims, Congress has created a series of special tribunals to adjudicate money claims against the United States. And, particularly with the advent in this century of the modern administrative state, Congress has created numerous administrative agencies and tribunals whose business includes adjudication.

Unlike the ordinary federal courts, the institutional hallmark of most of these tribunals has been specialization. Further, the transitory nature of some of these tribunals, the perceived need to allow some of them to function inexpensively with expeditious or informal procedures, and (in the case of the administrative agencies) the equally strongly perceived need to endow them with a range of policy-making functions in addition to adjudicative functions, has typically led Congress to create them not as tribunals constituted under Article III (with lifetime judges performing an exclusively judicial function) but as special legislative courts or administrative tribunals. Their judges typically serve temporary terms and are removable for misfeasance without impeachment. The constitutional authority for such tribunals has been much discussed and litigated; Congress's authority to constitute them has virtually always been upheld.

The most important specialized tribunals in the current federal judicial system are the local courts of the District of Columbia, Puerto Rico, and the territories and dependencies; the system of military courts; the system of bankruptcy courts; the Tax Court and the Claims Court, adjudicating certain tax refund claims and certain damage actions against the federal government; the Court of International Trade, adjudicating certain customs disputes; and a large and variegated array of administrative tribunals and agencies. The work of all of these tribunals is typically subject to review, through various forms of proceedings, in the regular federal courts.

In addition, in 1982 Congress created a thirteenth court of appeals, the United States Court of Appeals for the Federal Circuit. This is a regular Article III court, whose jurisdiction is not territorial but is defined in terms of subject matter, including appeals from the Claims Court and the Court of International Trade and many patent and trademark cases.

Continuously since 1789 the Supreme Court has been the single institution with nationwide authority to supervise the infe-rior federal courts and to give voice to a uniform national law. The Court's size has varied from five to ten Justices; since 1869 it has consisted of a Chief Justice and eight associate Justices. The Supreme Court acts *en banc*, not in panels, though individual Justices have the conventional authority to issue stays and take emergency action. The Court acts by majority, but in this century the practice has been to grant a certiorari petition (setting the case for plenary review) if four Justices are in favor.

The caseload explosion in the lower federal courts imposed major burdens on the Court. The Court disposed of over 4,000 cases in its 1983 term (compared to about 3,300 in 1970, 1,900 in 1960, and 1,200 in 1950). The task was possible because only a small number of cases (usually about 150) were decided on the merits by full opinion after plenary briefing and oral argument. Another 100 to 150 cases were decided on the merits by memorandum order. The remaining dispositions consisted of summary denials of petitions for certiorari (or other writs); there were almost 3,900 of these in 1983–84. In 1960 there were just under 2,000 new cases docketed in the Court; in 1970, about 3,400; in 1983, about 4,200. The increase in cases docketed means more and more resources devoted to "screening" cases for decision and less to the hearing and disposition of cases on the merits. Thus the time devoted to oral argument has shrunk steadily in this century and now almost never exceeds one hour per case. The length of briefs is limited; and an ever-growing battery of law clerks assists in legal research and in the drafting of opinions.

The content of the Court's work reflects the scope and content of the national law. In the 1983 term the Court's decisions by full opinion included three cases within the original jurisdiction; ninety-six civil cases coming from the lower federal courts (of which forty-six involved the federal government, twenty-eight involved state and local governments, and twenty-two were private cases); sixteen federal habeas corpus cases; and thirty-two cases from the state courts (eighteen civil and fourteen criminal). Diversity cases are rarely reviewed. The Court is, increasingly, a constitutional court; about half of its cases tend to involve a constitutional question as the (or a) principal issue. The United States (as party or amicus curiae) participates in over half of the cases that the Court decides on the merits.

Although the federal judicial system has grown substantially in its 200 years, the federal courts continue to constitute only a small—though disproportionately powerful—component of the American judicial system. (Fewer than 3 percent of the country's judges are federal Article III judges; the biggest states have judicial systems larger than the federal system.)

The relations between state and federal courts are multifarious and exceedingly complex. Except where Congress has specified that federal court jurisdiction is exclusive, state courts of general jurisdiction exercise a normal competence to adjudicate cases involving issues of federal law (particularly in that many such issues arise by way of defense in civil and criminal cases arising under state law). Their decisions of these cases are subject to Supreme Court review, usually on certiorari; but that Court's jurisdiction in such a case is limited to the federal question in the case and may not be exercised at all if the judgment rests on a valid and dispositive state-law ground. State court judgments on issues of federal law (unless reversed by the Supreme Court) have normal res judicata effect.

The federal district courts, in turn, adjudicate many questions of state law, not only in diversity cases but also in cases arising under federal law where state law governs one or more issues. No provision for review by the state courts of the correctness of federal court decisions on issues of state law has ever existed, but in a narrow class of cases federal courts will abstain from exercising an otherwise proper federal jurisdiction in order to allow a state law issue to be determined in the state courts. Under the decision in *Erie Railroad* v. *Tompkins* (1938), on issues of state law (including issues of state common law) state court precedents are accepted as authoritative by the federal courts.

Special problems are presented by the politically sensitive role of the federal courts in controlling the legality of the actions of state and local governments and their officials. Although the Eleventh Amendment bars the federal courts from asserting jurisdiction over actions against a state as such, a wide range of remedies against state and local governments and their officials exists in the federal courts. Federal courts routinely review the constitutional validity of state criminal convictions through the writ of habeas corpus. Since the adoption of the Civil Rights Act of 1871, they have exercised jurisdiction to grant injunctions and damages against state and local officials (and, more recently, against local governmental entities as such) for conduct under color of state law—including conduct by officials asserting official power even where the conduct is prohibited by state law—that infringes on the ever-growing corpus of federal constitutional and statutory rules governing state action. Federal courts may enjoin state officials from enforcing unconstitutional state statutes and administrative schemes; moreover, the courts' injunctive remedial powers are frequently exercised to assume broad managerial supervision over state agencies and bureaucracies (for example, schools, mental hospitals, prisons). And the ever-burgeoning array of federal conditions and restrictions that accompany federal economic and social programs available to the states are, as a matter of routine, enforceable in the federal courts.

The political sensitivities aroused by the federal courts' jurisdiction to control the validity of state and local government action has led to some statutory and judge-made restrictions on the exercise of this jurisdiction. For over half a century federal court actions to enjoin the enforcement of state statutes on constitutional grounds had to be litigated before three-judge courts and were subject to direct review by appeal to the Supreme Court. (The institution of the three-judge district court was virtually abolished in 1976.) During the New Deal, statutory restrictions were placed on the jurisdiction of the federal courts to interfere with state tax statutes and public utility rate orders. Statutory and judge-made rules restrict the power of the federal courts to enjoin or interfere with pending state court proceedings; and state prisoners who fail to exhaust state court remedies or fail to comply with state procedural rules do not have access to federal habeas corpus.

The federal judicial system appears to operate on one-hundred-year cycles. The structure created in 1789 became increasingly unwieldy after the Civil War and was—after some twenty years of pressure for reform—finally transformed by the Evarts Act of 1891. That act created a stable system that has, in turn, come under increasing pressure from the caseload explosion that began in the 1960s. Relief could come in the form of diminutions in the district courts' original jurisdiction (such as a long-discussed abolition of or reduction in the diversity jurisdiction); but the need for architectural revision has also become increasingly clear in the 1970s and 1980s.

Structural problems center on the appellate tiers. Further substantial increases in the number of circuit judges is an uncertain remedy. Some circuits are already unwieldy and are finding it increasingly difficult to maintain stability and uniformity in the intracircuit law. Increasing the number of circuits would increase intercircuit instability and disuniformity and place further pressure on the finite appellate capacity of our "one Supreme Court"—the latter constituting the obvious structural bottleneck in the system.

More generally, a judicial system administering an enormous and dynamic corpus of national law and adjudicating a rising caseload (approaching 300,000 cases a year) cannot operate forever on an appellate capacity that is limited to some 150–200 judicial opinions with nationwide authority. There is rising concern, too, about the quality of federal justice as the growing caseload leads to an increasing bureaucratization of the federal judicial process, with the judges reduced to an oversight capacity in managing a growing array of magistrates, central staff, and law clerks.

Since the 1970s, two methods of increasing the system's capacity to provide authoritative and uniform judicial pronouncements on issues of national law have been discussed. One consists of greater subject-matter specialization at the appellate level, with special courts of appeals having nationwide authority to deal with specified subjects of federal litigation (for instance, tax cases, administrative appeals); such courts would remove pressure from the regional courts of appeals and the Supreme Court. The alternative (or additional) possibility is to create an additional appellate "tier": a national court of appeals with power to render decisions of nationwide authority, receiving its business by assignment from the Supreme Court or by transfer from the regional courts of appeals. In addition, if the number of certiorari petitions continues to mount, the Supreme Court will eventually have to make some adjustments in its screening procedures (perhaps dealing with these petitions in panels).

Behind these structural problems lie more fundamental questions about the enormous power that the federal courts have come to exercise over the political, economic, and social policies of the nation. Throughout our history intense controversy has surrounded the question whether (and to what extent) a small corps of appointed life-tenured officials should exercise wide-ranging powers to supervise and invalidate the actions of the political branches of federal, state, and local governments. From time to time these debates have threatened to affect the independence of the federal judicial system. Thus, in the 1930s, facing wholesale invalidations of the New Deal program by a "conservative" Supreme Court, President Franklin D. Roosevelt proposed to "pack" the Court with additional judges; his plan was widely perceived to be contrary to the spirit of the Constitution and was defeated in Congress. (Shortly thereafter a Court with a new membership and a new judicial philosophy in effect accomplished Roosevelt's purposes.)

In the second half of the twentieth century retaliatory proposals have mostly consisted of attempts to strip a "liberal" Supreme Court of appellate jurisdiction in certain categories of constitutional litigation (for example, reapportionment or abortion), leaving the state courts to be the final arbiters of federal law in these areas. Intense controversy surrounds the question of whether Congress has constitutional power to divest the Supreme Court of appellate jurisdiction over specific categories of constitutional litigation. (The one explicit Supreme Court pronouncement on the question, the celebrated *Ex Parte McCardle* [1869], in sweeping language upheld this power pursuant to the explicit provision of Article III providing that the Court's appellate jurisdiction is subject to "such Exceptions" and "such Regulations" as "the Congress shall make.") Even if Congress has jurisdiction-stripping power, however, its exercise—much like the exercise of the power to "pack" the Court—would be widely perceived as anticonstitutional in spirit. In fact, no such legislation has come near to achieving acceptance, attesting to the vast reservoir of ideological and political strength that the ideal of an independent federal judiciary continues to possess.

The more important and authentic debate that continues to rage as the federal court system enters its third century relates to the proper role of an independent federal judiciary in a nation that is democratic but also committed to the ideal of fidelity to law. The federal courts have come to exercise a power over the political, economic, and social life of this nation that no other independent judicial system in the history of mankind has possessed. Whether that power is wholly benign—or whether it should and can be reduced—is one of the great questions to which the twenty-first century will have to attend.

—PAUL M. BATOR

Bibliography

American Law Institute (1969). *Study of the Division of Jurisdiction Between State and Federal Courts*. Washington D.C.: American Law Institute.

Bator, Paul M.; Mishkin, Paul J.; Shapiro, David L.; and Wechsler, Herbert (1973). *The Federal Courts and the Federal System*, 2nd ed., with 1981 Supplement. Mineola, N.Y.: Foundation Press.

Carrington, Paul D.; Meador, Daniel J.; and Rosenberg, Maurice (1976). *Justice on Appeal*. St. Paul, Minn.: West Publishing Co.

Director of the Administrative Office of the United States Courts [annually] *Annual Reports*. Washington, D.C.: United States Government Printing Office.

Frankfurter, Felix, and Landis, James M. (1928). *The Business of the Supreme Court: A Study in the Federal Judicial System*. New York: Macmillan.

Friendly, Henry J. (1973). *Federal Jurisdiction: A General View*. New York: Columbia University Press.

Posner, Richard A. (1985). *The Federal Courts: Crisis and Reform*. Cambridge, Mass.: Harvard University Press.

Wright, Charles Alan (1983). *The Law of Federal Courts*. St. Paul, Minn.: West Publishing Co.

See also

Certiorari, Writ of

Marbury v. *Madison*

K

KASTIGAR v. UNITED STATES

406 U.S. 441 (1972)

Until this case the rule was that the Fifth Amendment requires a grant of transactional immunity to displace a claim of the right against self-incrimination. Title II of the Organized Crime Control Act of 1970 fixed a single comprehensive standard applicable to grants of immunity in all federal judicial, grand jury, administrative, and legislative proceedings. The new law provided that when a witness is required to testify over his claim of the Fifth Amendment right, "no testimony or other information compelled under the order (or any information directly or indirectly derived from such testimony or other information) may be used against the witness in any criminal cases," except in a prosecution for perjury or failure to comply. The statute thus provided for use immunity, permitting a pros-

ecution based on evidence not derived from the testimony forced by a grant of immunity.

Kastigar was cited for contempt after he persisted in his refusal to testify concerning unnecessary dental services affecting the draft status of persons seeking to evade the draft. His refusal to testify raised the question of whether the grant of use immunity was sufficient to displace the Fifth Amendment right.

A seven-member Supreme Court, voting 5–2, sustained the constitutionality of use immunity. Justice Lewis F. Powell declared: "We hold that such immunity from use and derivative use is coextensive with the scope of the privilege against self-incrimination, and therefore is sufficient to compel testimony over a claim of the privilege. . . . Transactional immunity, which accords full immunity from prosecution for the offense to which the compelled testimony relates, affords the witness considerably broader protection than does the Fifth Amendment privilege. The privilege has never been construed to mean

> *Kastigar's refusal to testify raised the question of whether the grant of use immunity was sufficient to displace the Fifth Amendment right.*

♦ **immunity**
An exemption from a legally imposed duty or liability; along with privileges, immunities are protected by Article IV and by the Fourteenth Amendment.

THE RIGHT AGAINST SELF-INCRIMINATION

"No person," the Fifth Amendment unequivocally states, "shall be . . . compelled in any criminal case to be a witness against himself. . . ." It does not add, "unless such person cannot be prosecuted or punished as a result of his testimony," and it does not refer to self-incrimination. Yet, if the government wants evidence concerning a crime, it can compel a witness to testify by granting immunity from prosecution. In law, such immunity means that the witness cannot incriminate himself and therefore has suffered no violation of his right against self-incrimination. The common sense of the matter is that to "incriminate" means to implicate criminally; in law, however, it means exposure to prosecution or penalties. The law indulges the fiction that when one receives a grant of immunity, removing him from criminal jeopardy, the right not to be a witness against oneself is not violated. If the witness cannot be prosecuted, the penalties do not exist for him, so that his testimony can be compelled without forcing him to incriminate himself or "be a witness against himself."

See also

Counselman v. Hitchcock

Katz ended an era of constitutional protection for Fourth Amendment rights and began another.

that one who invokes it cannot subsequently be prosecuted." Powell dismissed *Counselman* v. *Hitchcock* (1892) and its progeny, which established the transactional immunity standard, as obiter dicta and therefore not binding. Powell reasoned that a witness who had use immunity against his compelled testimony is in substantially the same position as if he had invoked the Fifth Amendment in the absence of a grant of immunity.

But one who relies on his constitutional right to silence gives the state no possible way to use his testimony, however indirectly, against him, and he has not remotely, from the standpoint of the law, criminally implicated himself. Use immunity permits compulsion without removing the implication of criminality. On the other hand, the values of the Fifth Amendment are not infringed if the state prosecutes on evidence not related to the compelled testimony, and the state has the burden of proving that the prosecution relies on evidence from sources independent of the compelled testimony. The trouble is, as Justice Thurgood Marshall pointed out in dissent, that only the prosecuting authorities know, if even they can know, the chains of information by which evidence was gathered. In any case, use immunity compels a person to be a witness against himself criminally.

—LEONARD W. LEVY

Bibliography

Levy, Leonard W. (1974). *Against the Law: The Nixon Court and Criminal Justice.* Pages 173–187. New York: Harper & Row.

KATZ v. UNITED STATES

389 U.S. 347 (1967)

Katz ended one era of constitutional protection for Fourth Amendment rights and began another. In *Olmstead* v. *United States* (1928) the Supreme Court had virtually exempted from the Fourth Amendment's ban on unreasonable searches and seizures any search that did not involve a physical intrusion on property and a seizure of tangible things. Although eroded by subsequent decisions, and superseded by a federal statute where wiretapping was required, *Olmstead*'s physical intrusion requirement inhibited constitutional control of aural and visual surveillance for forty years, until *Katz* was decided.

Federal agents, believing that Katz was using a pay telephone to transmit gambling information, attached a listening and recording device to the outside of the phone booth without trying to meet Fourth Amendment requirements. With the information obtained from the device, the police were able to convict Katz, but the Supreme Court overturned the conviction. The Court ruled that Katz was entitled to Fourth Amendment protection for his conversations and that a physical intrusion into an area occupied by Katz was not necessary to bring the amendment into play. "The Fourth Amendment protects people, not places," wrote Justice Potter Stewart for a virtually unanimous Court (only Justice Hugo L. Black dissented). Justice John Marshall Harlan, concurring, developed a test for determining what interests are protected, which has come to be the accepted standard: "first that a person have exhibited an actual (subjective) expectation of privacy and second, that the expectation be one 'that society is prepared to recognize as reasonable.' "

The Court also set out some of the requirements for lawful electronic eavesdropping, supplementing those in *Berger* v. *New York* (1967), many of which were incorporated in Title III of the Omnibus Crime Control and Safe Streets Act of 1968.

—HERMAN SCHWARTZ

KENNEDY, ANTHONY M.

(1936–   )

Anthony M. Kennedy has largely fulfilled the objectives of President Ronald Reagan in

See also

Olmstead v. *United States*

choosing him to fill the vacancy on the Supreme Court created by the retirement of Justice Lewis F. Powell.

First, President Reagan expected that Kennedy's noncontroversial background would ensure him swift confirmation by the Senate. After graduating from Harvard Law School in 1961, Kennedy had worked as a lawyer and lobbyist in California until President Gerald R. Ford appointed him to the Ninth Circuit Court of Appeals in 1975. While on the bench, Kennedy, who also taught constitutional law at McGeorge School of Law, evolved as a relatively colorless, nonideological conservative, but gained notoriety for writing the lower court opinion striking down the legislative veto—a result subsequently affirmed by the Supreme Court in *Immigration and Naturalization Service* v. *Chadha* (1983). In February 1988 the Senate unanimously confirmed Kennedy.

President Reagan also hoped that Kennedy would join Chief Justice William H. Rehnquist and Justices Byron R. White, Sandra Day O'Connor, and Antonin Scalia to form a conservative majority that would curtail the initiatives of both the Warren Court and the Burger Court. Kennedy has in fact cast the crucial fifth vote with these Justices in several 5–4 decisions expanding state control in the fields of abortion, capital punishment, criminal procedure, and civil rights.

However, Kennedy has demonstrated strong support for free speech and the right of privacy, writing the important opinion in *Romer* v. *Evans* (1996) striking down a state constitutional amendment that restricted the civil rights of homosexuals. In general, Kennedy has emerged as a classically conservative Justice: he has thus far avoided articulating any overarching philosophy of constitutional interpretation and has been reluctant to challenge precedent.

Kennedy's votes support a view of federalism under which the states check federal power and are responsible for matters on which the Constitution provides no clear prohibitions. For example, Kennedy wrote a concurring

opinion in *United States* v. *Lopez* (1995), overturning a federal law that made it a crime to possess a gun within 1,000 feet of a school as exceeding the power of Congress. Although he expressed reluctance to hold Congress had gone beyond its power to legislate under the commerce clause, he noted that "here neither the actors nor their conduct have a commercial character," so that Congress had "intrude[d] upon an area of traditional state concern." Similarly, Kennedy maintained in dissent in *Missouri* v. *Jenkins* (1990) that by upholding a federal court order commanding a school district to impose a tax, the majority impermissibly expanded federal court power at the expense of "fundamental precepts for the democratic control of public institutions."

Similarly, Kennedy's opinions show a concern for property rights and a hesitancy to uphold legislation restricting those rights. Concurring separately in *Eastern Enterprises* v. *Apfel* (1998), he concluded that a federal law requiring former coal mine operators to retroactively fund health care for employees and their dependents deprived the employers of their property without due process of law.

Kennedy wrote the Court's opinion in *City of Boerne* v. *Flores* (1997) invalidating the Religious Freedom Restoration Act, a federal law aimed at requiring courts to strictly scrutinize laws substantially burdening the free exercise of religion. His opinion, holding Congress lacked power to interpret the Constitution, emphasized that this power remains with the judiciary.

Kennedy's opinions reflect his belief in a living constitution that recognizes, even against claims of individual liberties, the need for government to adapt to changes in technology and its responsibilities. For example, in *Skinner* v. *Railway Labor Executives Association* (1989) and *Treasury Employees Union* v. *Von Raab* (1989) Kennedy explained that the Fourth Amendment did not preclude drug testing of railway workers after railroad accidents and of customs workers when there was no individualized suspicion and no evidence of drug abuse in the customs service. Simi-

KENNEDY, ANTHONY M.

(1936–)

Kennedy's steadfast refusal to offer a sophisticated alternative to the grander constitutional visions of his fellow conservatives may foretell a modest role for him.

K

KENNEDY, ANTHONY M.

(1936–)

larly, Kennedy rejected First Amendment challenges to a municipal regulation in *Ward* v. *Rock Against Racism* (1989) that required performers at an outdoor theater to use the city's sound system and technician, even though the requirement restricted certain speakers and messages.

Kennedy's hesitancy to reverse or to expand precedent reflects his preference for deciding cases on the narrowest available grounds and to affect settled doctrine as little as possible. Accordingly, in *Saffle* v. *Parks* (1990) Kennedy read precedents narrowly in order to deny federal habeas corpus relief because the respondent had raised a new legal claim that could not be applied retroactively on collateral review. Kennedy also hewed closely to precedent in *Barnard* v. *Thorstenn* (1989) in holding that residency requirements for admission to the Virgin Islands bar violated the privileges and immunities clause of Article IV.

In *Webster* v. *Reproductive Health Services* (1989) Kennedy refused to join Justice Scalia's concurrence urging overruling of *Roe* v. *Wade* (1973), but joined Chief Justice Rehnquist's plurality opinion that rejected the trimester analysis by the *Roe* Court for measuring the importance of the state's interest. Shortly thereafter, Kennedy joined Justices O'Connor and David H. Souter in *Planned Parenthood of Southeastern Pennsylvania* v. *Casey* (1992) in reaffirming the holding of *Roe*, though again rejecting *Roe*'s trimester framework. Similarly, in *Richmond (City of)* v. *J. A. Croson Co.* (1989) Kennedy refused to join Justice Scalia's concurrence challenging a city's set-aside of public funds for minority contractors, as well as the congressional program on which it was modeled, which had been upheld in *Fullilove* v. *Klutznick* (1980). Kennedy's concurrence emphasized that *Fullilove* posed a difficult but separate issue concerning the scope of congressional power under section 5 of the Fourteenth Amendment.

Kennedy showed great concern for privacy rights in his opinion for the Court in *Romer* v. *Evans*. Colorado had amended its constitution to bar the state or its municipalities from allowing homosexuals to raise a claim of discrimination. Although adhering to the Court's ruling in *Bowers* v. *Hardwick* (1986) that the Constitution's fundamental right of privacy did not encompass homosexual acts, Kennedy nonetheless held under the amendment "[h]omosexuals are forbidden the safeguards that others enjoy or may seek," so that the provision had the impermissible intent of "singling out a certain class of citizens for disfavored legal status."

In *Patterson* v. *McLean Credit Union* (1989) Kennedy narrowly reaffirmed *Runyon* v. *McCrary* (1976). Although the *Runyon* Court had applied 42 U.S.C. section 1981 to restrict racial discrimination in private school admissions, Kennedy refused to apply the statute's prohibitions of discrimination in the "formation" or "making" of contracts to racial harassment in the conditions of employment.

Dissenting in *James* v. *Illinois* (1990), Kennedy reluctantly accepted precedents imposing the exclusionary rule on the states, but suggested the rule should not have been applied to prevent the prosecution from using illegally obtained evidence to impeach the defendant and other defense witnesses in a criminal trial. Similarly, in *Jones* v. *Thomas* (1989), Kennedy acknowledged, but refused to extend, the traditional double jeopardy prohibition (against multiple sentences for the same offense) to preclude the petitioner's continued confinement under a longer sentence after he had completed a commuted sentence imposed for the same offense. He also explained in *Washington* v. *Harper* (1990) that the involuntary administration of antipsychotic drugs to a violent prisoner comported with both substantive due process and procedural due process.

However, in his dissent in *County of Allegheny* v. *ACLU* (1989), Kennedy urged abandoning the Court's traditional test in establishment clause cases. He argued that the

Court's test separated church and state more than the Framers intended. Three years later, though, in *Lee* v. *Weisman* (1992), Kennedy wrote for the Court that even under the traditional test a school board had violated the establishment clause when it invited a cleric to give an invocation at a public high school graduation. He noted that this had a subtly coercive effect on the students present.

The major exception to Kennedy's narrow construction of individual rights is his concurrence in *Texas* v. *Johnson* (1989), in which the Court held 5–4 that the First Amendment protected flag burning as political speech. Kennedy explained that "the flag protects even those who would hold it in contempt."

Kennedy's steadfast refusal to offer a sophisticated alternative to the grander constitutional visions of his fellow conservatives may foretell a modest role for him. Ironically, such a role would reflect Kennedy's vision of the Court's modest role in a system governed by traditional notions of federalism.

—MICHAEL J. GERHARDT

Bibliography

Chemerinsky, Erwin (1989). Foreword: The Vanishing Constitution. *Harvard Law Review* 103:43–104.

Maltz, Earl M. (1990). The Prospects for a Revival of Conservative Activism in Constitutional Jurisprudence. *Georgia Law Review* 24:629–668.

KEYISHIAN v. BOARD OF REGENTS

385 U.S. 589 (1967)

Adler v. *Board of Education* (1952) was one of the cases in which the Supreme Court upheld a wide range of regulations barring "subversives" from government employment. *Keyishian* overruled *Adler* and was the culmination of a series of later decisions restricting loyalty-security programs, typically by invoking the vagueness and overbreadth doctrines. *Keyishian* struck down some parts of a complex New York law limiting employment in public teaching; the law's use of the term "seditious" was unconstitutionally vague. Other parts of the law were invalid because they prohibited *mere* knowing membership in the Communist party without the specific intent required by *Elfbrandt* v. *Russell* (1966). *Keyishian* confirmed the Court's previous decisions rejecting the doctrine that public employment is a privilege to which government may attach whatever conditions it pleases.

—MARTIN SHAPIRO

KILBOURN v. THOMPSON

103 U.S. 168 (1881)

Until this case Congress believed that its power of conducting investigations was unlimited and that its judicial authority to punish contumacious witnesses for contempt was unquestionable. After this case both the investigatory and contempt powers of Congress were distinctly limited and subject to judicial review. Not until *McGrain* v. *Daugherty* (1927) did the Court firmly establish the constitutional basis for oversight and investigatory powers. The decision in *Kilbourn* was so negative in character that the legitimate area of legislative investigations seemed murky.

Kilbourn developed out of the House's investigation, by a select committee, into the activities of a bankrupt banking firm that owed money to the United States. The committee subpoenaed Kilbourn's records, which he refused to produce, and interrogated him, but he refused to answer on the ground that the questions concerned private matters. The House cited him for contempt and jailed him. He in turn sued for false arrest, and on a writ of habeas corpus he obtained a review of his case before the Supreme Court.

KILBOURN v. THOMPSON

103 U.S. 168 (1881)

Keyishian *overruled* Adler v. Board of Education, *which barred "subversives" from government employment.*

Kilbourn *developed out of the House's investigation into the activities of a bankrupt banking firm that owed money to the United States.*

See also

McGrain v. *Daugherty*

Unanimously, in an opinion by Justice Samuel F. Miller, the Court held that neither house of Congress can punish a witness for contumacy unless his testimony is required on a matter concerning which "the House has jurisdiction to inquire," and, Miller added, neither house has "the general power of making inquiry into the private affairs of the citizen." The subject of this inquiry, Miller said, was judicial in nature, not legislative, and a case was pending in a lower federal court. The investigation was fruitless also because "it could result in no valid legislation" on the subject of the inquiry. Thus, the courts hold final power to decide what constitutes a contempt of Congress, and Congress cannot compel a witness to testify in an investigation that cannot assist remedial legislation.

—LEONARD W. LEVY

KIRBY v. ILLINOIS

406 U.S. 682 (1972)

Kirby leaves untouched the possible due process objections to an unfair pretrial confrontation.

In an effort to eviscerate *United States* v. *Wade* (1967) without overruling it, a plurality of the Supreme Court held that the right to counsel does not apply to pretrial identification procedures that occur before indictment or other indicia of formal criminal charges. The case involved the most suggestive confrontation imaginable: a one-to-one presentation of the person upon whom police had found a robbery victim's credit cards. Yet the Court held that because this confrontation occurred before Kirby had been formally charged, it was not a "critical stage" of the proceedings requiring counsel to preserve a future right to a fair trial.

The distinction between pre- and postindictment identification procedures is dubious for two reasons. First, the vast majority of lineups occur while cases are under investigation, and thus before indictment. Second, all the dangers of irreparable mistaken identification and the inability of counsel to reconstruct the pretrial confrontation—which had been the foundation of *Wade*—apply whether the identification occurs before or after formal charging. The plurality's startling misreading of precedent was highlighted when Justice Byron R. White, who dissented in *Wade*, dissented in *Kirby* also, saying that *Wade* compelled the opposite result.

Kirby leaves untouched the possible due process objections to an unfair pretrial confrontation. Proof of unfairness would require suppression of testimony about the pretrial procedure as well as the in-court identification by a witness whose perceptions were possibly tainted. A due process objection may be made whether the pretrial confrontation has occurred before or after formal charging. Of course, it is much more difficult for the accused to show that a confrontation was fundamentally unfair than to prove that it was done without counsel.

—BARBARA ALLEN BABCOCK

KNIGHT COMPANY, E. C., UNITED STATES v.

156 U.S. 1 (1895)

The issue in the Supreme Court's first interpretation of the Sherman Antitrust Act hung on the lawfulness of the Sugar Trust's acquisition of its competitors, and the decision nearly eviscerated the act. An 8–1 Court used the doctrine of dual federalism in dismissing a government suit to dissolve the trust.

When the American Sugar Refining Company (the Sugar Trust) acquired four Philadelphia refineries in 1892 it controlled 98 percent of domestic sugar manufacturing. Attorney General Richard Olney, who inherited the case from his predecessor, believed that the Sherman Act was founded on a false economic theory; he believed that free competition had been "thoroughly discredited" and that the act should have regulated trusts as a natural development, not prohibited them. There is, however, little evidence of deliberate carelessness in Olney's preparation of the case. Although the majority opinion commented upon a lack of evidence to demonstrate a restraint of trade, the government never believed that such a showing was necessary. Prior decisions had clearly held sales to be a part of commerce; the majority would admit as much here, and a lower court conceded that the trust had sought control of both refining and sales. Clever defense strategy successfully shifted the Court's attention from restraint of interstate commerce to a consideration whether the commerce power extended to manufacturing.

Chief Justice Melville W. Fuller's opinion for the Court endorsed the defendants' argument. By repeating that manufacturing was separable from commerce, the Court made a formally plausible distinction based solely on precedent. Although the Sugar Trust had monopolized manufacturing, the Court found no Sherman Act violation because the acquisition of the Philadelphia refineries involved intrastate commerce. Although manufacturing "involves in a certain sense the control of its disposition . . . this is a secondary and not the primary sense." The trust did not lead to control of interstate commerce and so "affects it only incidentally and indirectly." This direct/indirect effects test of the reach of federal regulation had been mentioned in earlier cases and was here employed to reach unrealistic ends: "Contracts, combinations, or conspiracies to control domestic enterprise in manufacture, agriculture, mining, production in all its forms, or to raise or lower prices or wages, might unquestionably tend to restrain external as well as domestic trade, but the restraint would be an indirect result, however inevitable and whatever its extent, and such result would not necessarily determine the object of the contract, combination or conspiracy."

Justice John Marshall Harlan, dissenting, posed the basic question: "What, in a legal sense, is a restraint of trade?" The trust was in business to sell as well as manufacture sugar, and most of its sales obviously constituted interstate commerce. Relying on *Gibbons* v. *Ogden* (1824), Harlan posited a broad view of the commerce power. Any obstruction of commerce among the states was an impairment of that commerce and must be treated as such. The majority's construction of the Sherman Act left the public "at the mercy of combinations." The Sugar Trust's inevitable purpose of preventing free competition doomed it as a restraint of trade. "The general government is not placed by the Constitution in such a condition of helplessness that it must fold its arms and remain inactive while capital combines . . . to destroy competition." Harlan correctly believed that the issue should not have been the contracts of acquisition but rather the trust's control over commerce in sugar.

By excluding manufacturing monopolies from the scope of the antitrust act, the decision in *Knight* cleared the way for the greatest merger and consolidation movement in American history. Chief among the industries taking advantage of the opportunities given them by the Supreme Court were manufacturing and the railroads. Such massive combines as United States Steel Corporation, American Can Company, International Harvester, and Standard Oil of New Jersey can trace their origins to this period. From 1879 to 1897 fewer than a dozen important combinations had been formed, with a total capital of around one billion dollars. Before the century ended, nearly two hundred more combinations formed, with a total capital exceeding three billion dollars. Of some 318 corporations in business in 1904, nearly 75 percent had been formed after 1897.

The Court's opinion also seriously injured the concept of national supremacy; Fuller's

KNIGHT COMPANY, E. C., UNITED STATES v.

156 U.S. 1 (1895)

The decision in Knight *cleared the way for the greatest merger and consolidation movement in American history.*

See also

Gibbons v. *Ogden*

Northern Securities Co. v. *United States.*

K

KNIGHT COMPANY, E. C., UNITED STATES v.

156 U.S. 1 (1895)

distinction between production and commerce lasted until 1937. In the meantime, the Court had created what Edward S. Corwin called a "twilight zone" in which national regulation of corporations was uncertain and haphazard. Although the Court would apply the Sherman Act to railroads within two years, not until the reinterpretation in *Northern Securities Co.* v. *United States* (1904) would the Sherman Act become an effective tool against big business.

—DAVID GORDON

Bibliography

Eichner, Alfred S. (1969). *Emergence of Oligopoly: Sugar Refining as a Case Study.* Westport, Conn.: Greenwood Press.

LABOR AND EMPLOYMENT LAW

The Supreme Court is the ultimate judicial recourse for the resolution of disputes in labor and employment law. Many aspects of labor and employment law, however, are resolved through various federal and state administrative agencies, in state courts, or through alternative dispute resolution processes such as arbitration. For example, a discharged white-collar manager, not represented by a union, will usually sue the employer directly in state court, invoking the state law against wrongful discharge, or, in some instances, seek arbitration without any labor union involvement. Workers represented by labor unions, on the other hand, generally have disputes resolved through labor contract grievance arbitration mechanisms, or through the administrative procedures of the National Labor Relations Board, pursuant to the federal National Labor Relations Act. Thus, only a fraction of labor and employment law matters ever successfully reach the Supreme Court for resolution. Most of the labor and employment law matters that do reach the Supreme Court emanate from one of several likely sources: disputes alleging employment discrimination in violation of the Constitution or various federal statutory law, such as the landmark Title VII of the Civil Rights Acts of 1964 and 1991 (which prohibit discrimination on the bases of race, religion, color, sex, sexual harassment, pregnancy, national origin), the Age Discrimination in Employment Act of 1967, the Employee Retirement Income Security Act of 1974 (ERISA), or the Americans with Disabilities Act of 1990, and, historically, the National Labor Relations Act.

For most of the twentieth century, however, labor law, rather than employment discrimination law, framed most of the labor and employment law cases proceeding to the Supreme Court. For example, in the labor relations context, where employees are represented by labor unions negotiating with management regarding the hours, wages, and terms and conditions of employment on behalf of the union's constituents and encapsulating their joint agreements through collectively bargained labor contracts, cases may reach the Supreme Court only after long and intricate litigation before the federal National Labor Relations Board and after subsequently exhausting often extensive and protracted appeals of NLRB decisions through the various federal circuit courts of appeals.

Prior to 1937, relatively few, and until then only isolated, labor and employment law cases ever reached the Supreme Court; and, in almost all of its pertinent decisions before 1937, employees lost. For example, in *Adair* v. *United States* (1908) and in *Coppage* v. *Kansas* (1915), the Supreme Court upheld the notorious antiunion device of the "yellow dog" contract. Many employers insisted that prospective employees first sign contracts as a precondition to beginning work, with the contracts designed to prohibit employees from joining unions as a contractually enforceable precondition of employment; thus, if the employee later reneged and presumed to join a union, the employer would successfully terminate the employee for the employee's breach of the employee's earlier contractual "promise" to the employer, via the "yellow dog" contract, to refrain from unionization. In

*In almost all of the
pertinent labor and
employment law
cases before 1937,
employees lost.*

the *Coppage* decision, the Court struck down the statutory effort by the Kansas state legislature to outlaw "yellow dog" contracts in Kansas. Likewise, a decade earlier, in the infamous decision of *Lochner* v. *New York* (1905), the Court invoked abstract principles of freedom of contract to prohibit the state of New York from limiting the maximum number of hours that bakers could lawfully work each week. New York had sought unsuccessfully to protect the health of the bakers from exhaustion and ruthless exploitation by unscrupulous employers. Thus, prior to the New Deal of President Franklin D. Roosevelt during the depths of the Great Depression, the pro-employer laissez-faire principle of freedom of contract reigned virtually supreme and free from any effective interference from workers or from protective legislation on behalf of workers, and whether the unsuccessful workers in the earlier cases were represented by labor unions.

In 1935, however, Congress enacted the National Labor Relations Act, sometimes popularly called the Wagner Act in honor of New York senator Robert Wagner, the law's chief sponsor in the United States Senate. In 1937 the Supreme Court pronounced the NLRA constitutional, in *NLRB* v. *Jones & Laughlin Steel Corp.* (1937). Most private sector employees represented by, or seeking to be represented by, labor unions have since operated under the statutory and administrative agency framework of the NLRA Wagner Act, which is administered by the National Labor Relations Board. The NLRA is a thorough regulatory mechanism that sets both the parameters for unionization and the operative rules governing collective bargaining throughout most of the private sector. In addition, the NLRA defines most of the major terms, such as who is an "employee," what it means to bargain collectively in good faith, and, perhaps most important, it sets forth series of unfair labor practices that can ultimately result in significant liability on the part of the offending employers (section 8a of

the Act) and unions (section 8b). Disputes that arise regarding the NLRA are resolved, in most instances, under the auspices of the National Labor Relations Board; the NLRB is the federal administrative agency, created by Congress, that is responsible for the implementation, effectuation, enforcement, and adjudication of disputes arising under the NLRA Wagner Act. Dissatisfied losing parties before the NLRB can, in some instances, appeal to the federal courts of appeals, and, failing to prevail in the federal appellate court, can endeavor to seek a final decision from the United States Supreme Court. In many of the private labor relations law decisions of the Supreme Court, the essential dispute implicates fundamental principles of the employer's right to control its property and to manage the business enterprise as the employer sees fit, in obvious tension with the Wagner Act's conferral of certain rights upon labor to intrude into the employer's previously unfettered ownership prerogatives. Most of the intricate details of these labor-management relationships are decided through the administrative apparatus of the National Labor Relations Board and the federal courts of appeals for the various circuits. Thus, when such decisions are issued by the Supreme Court, they necessarily involve matters of complex administrative law and process, as well as pronouncements on particular core issues of labor relations law. For example, in *Lechmere, Inc.* v. *NLRB* (1992), the Supreme Court reversed a National Labor Relations Board decision that had deviated from well-established NLRB and Supreme Court precedential law; the Court also reaffirmed the particular labor law principle that labor union organizers who are not themselves active current employees have extremely limited access, if any, to the employer's private property during the union's campaign to organize the workers. And, as one can imagine, over the course of more than sixty years, the Supreme Court has issued scores of labor law decisions, ranging from elaborating the scope of the duty of fair representation that unions owe to the workers whom they represent (as decided in *Vaca* v. *Sipes*, 1967, the union must discharge its duties in a way that is not "arbitrary, discriminatory, or in bad faith"), to the Court's preference that the parties use internal grievance arbitration mechanisms within labor contracts to resolve labor disputes, rather than seek external litigation in the courts (the *Steelworkers Trilogy*, 1960), to the circumstances under which the Court will order strikers to return to work while concurrently ordering arbitration of the particular dispute (*Boys Markets, Inc.* v. *Retail Clerks Union*, 1970). In labor law, the significant constitutional law principle of preemption operates to broadly preclude most state courts from applying state law, rather than federal law, to resolve disputes that implicate issues arising under the federal National Labor Relations Act. [*San Diego Building Trades Council* v. *Garmon* (1959).]

In 1999, however, only approximately 10 percent of the private sector workforce of more than one hundred thirty million persons in the United States is represented by labor unions. Thus, the vast majority of the private sector workforce—that is, those not employed by the federal, state, county, or municipal governments—generally have no recourse to invoke the protections of the NLRA, unless they seek to unionize under the Act for purposes of collective bargaining. Thus, absent some particular federal statute, such as the NLRA or one of the employment discrimination laws coming into play, the plethora of employment law disputes that arise are decided largely by state courts according to state law, such as breach of contract claims or various other workplace injuries, as in workers' disability compensation insurance claims.

Since the enactment of the landmark Civil Rights Act of 1964, however, and especially its Title VII provisions, which prohibit unlawful employment discrimination on the basis of several categories, such as race, religion, color, sex, sexual orientation, and national origin, and analogous federal laws prohibiting discrimination in employment on the basis of age (the Age Discrimination in Employment Act of 1967) or disability (the Americans with Disabilities Act of 1990) or interference with pensions or related benefits (the Employee Retirement Income Security Act of 1974), many workers not represented by labor unions have succeeded in reaching the Supreme Court for resolution of their particular employment law dispute. Some of the Court's employment law decisions beyond the unionized employment context have ranged from the (un)lawfulness of affirmative action in employment (*Adarand* v. *Pena; Richmond (City of)* v. *J. A. Croson; Paradise* v. *United States; United Steelworkers of America* v. *Weber; Wygant* v. *Jackson Board of Education*) to the Court's unequivocal and repeated condemnation of unlawful, unwelcome sexual harassment in employment, as in *Meritor Savings Bank* v. *Vinson.*

Finally, and perhaps most directly, the Supreme Court resolves constitutional issues in the context of labor and employment law disputes involving public sector workers— the multimillions of employees of the federal, state, county, and municipal governments. In such public sector government employment, a significantly higher percentage of employees are represented by labor unions, which operate pursuant to federal and state civil service laws for the most part, than is the percentage of employees—about 10 percent— represented by labor unions in the much larger private (nongovernmental) workforce. Whether or not the particular government worker is represented by a labor union, public sector employees, unlike private sector workers, are protected much more directly by the Constitution and by the Bill of Rights, such as First Amendment rights to free speech and press, Fourth Amendment right against unreasonable search and seizure, and Fifth Amendment and Fourteenth Amendment rights to due process of law and to equal protection of the laws.

Originally, however, just as in the private sector prior to the enactment of the NLRA Wagner Act in 1935, government workers received very little protection from the federal or state courts. Government employment was often acquired, and retained, through Tammany Hall–like systems of raw and overt political patronage, with little, if any, civil service, legal, statutory, or administrative protections until the twentieth century. And, just as in the private sector, nonfederal government workers—those employed at the state, county, and municipal levels—generally continue to bring their disputes into various state and municipal administrative systems and to state courts to decide under state law, including state constitutional law. Thus, even in the public, government employment sector, only a small fraction of public sector labor and employment law cases reach the Supreme Court. Those that do generally implicate constitutional law considerations, ranging from First Amendment rights of freedom of speech and of press, as in *Perry Education Association* v. *Perry Local Education Association,* to the circumstances under which public sector, government workers may be constitutionally subjected to employer testing for drug or alcohol use in the public, governmental workplace. For example, the Court set forth the conditions under which the government, as the employer, may subject government employees to searches for drug use without violating the Fourth Amendment constitutional provision against unreasonable search and seizure, in *National Treasury Employees Union* v. *von Raab,* 489 U.S. 656 (1989) and in the companion case of *Skinner* v. *Railway Labor Executive Association.* Many of the Supreme Court's decisions in public sector labor and employment law involve determining the constitutional boundaries and contours of the employee's rights to, for example, First Amendment speech and to procedural due process. Thus, for example, in

Connick v. *Myers* (1983) the Court found that an assistant district attorney in New Orleans did not have a First Amendment right to criticize internally within the office, by means of distributing internal memos and surveys, the district attorney's various employment policies with which the assistant disagreed. In other public sector employment contexts, the Court has found that the government employer can discharge workers even when the "facts" upon which the government employer has relied, in good faith, are ultimately proved nonexistent or to be markedly different from those the employer originally thought, in good faith, to be extant at the time the employer disciplined or discharged the employee from government employment. Thus, in *Waters* v. *Churchill* (1994) the Court ruled that the public employer did not violate the First Amendment if it fired an employee for what the employer reasonably believed was speech on a matter of private concern, even if the employer's original belief subsequently turned out to have been mistaken. The range of constitutional issues in the public sector, governmental workplace will continue to be as varied and as extensive as the Constitution and the Bill of Rights themselves.

Over the course of the next several decades, the Supreme Court is likely to decide more cases arising under statutory laws that protect against unlawful employment discrimination and that provide related statutory protections for various employment benefits, such as pensions and health care. With the continuing decline in the percentage of private sector workers represented by labor unions, the previously historically significant number of labor law cases under the National Labor Relations Act is likely to diminish over time, as a steadily declining percentage of the Court's labor and employment law decisions. Public sector government cases will continue to be an important part of the Court's labor and employment law jurisprudence, due to the always evolving jurisprudential dynamics under the Constitution, the Bill of Rights, and the Fourteenth Amendment.

—DAVID L. GREGORY

Bibliography

Atleson, James B. (1983). *Values and Assumptions in American Labor Law.* Amherst: University of Massachusetts Press.

Forbath, William E. (1991). *Law and the Shaping of the American Labor Movement.* Cambridge, Mass.: Harvard University Press.

Gould, William B. (1993). *Agenda for Reform: The Future of Employment Relationships and the Law.* Cambridge, Mass.: MIT Press.

Reich, Robert. (1991). *The Work of Nations.* New York: Vintage Books.

LALLI v. LALLI

439 U.S. 259 (1978)

In *Lalli* a fragmented Supreme Court brought further confusion to the body of equal protection doctrine governing classifications based on illegitimacy. A 5–4 majority upheld a New York law that allowed an illegitimate child to inherit from his or her father only if a court, during the father's lifetime and no later than two years after the child's birth, had declared the father's paternity. Justice Lewis F. Powell, who had written the majority opinion in *Trimble* v. *Gordon* (1977), wrote for a plurality of three Justices. Powell distinguished *Trimble* as a case in which even a judicial order declaring paternity would not have allowed inheritance; only the marriage of the child's parents would suffice. In *Lalli* the state could properly insist on the "evidentiary" requirement of a judicial order to establish paternity. The other six Justices all thought *Lalli* and *Trimble* indistinguishable: the four *Lalli* dissenters, plus two who joined the majority in upholding the law. The latter two Justices voted in accordance with their *Trimble* dissents.

The precedential force of *Trimble* may be uncertain, but at least seven Justices (the *Lalli* plurality and dissenters) all agreed that the standard of review for testing classifications based on illegitimacy was more rigorous than the rational basis test. Such classifications, said the plurality, would be invalid unless they were "substantially related to permissible state interests."

The state's interest in *Lalli* was the achievement of finality in the settlement of decedents' estates. The court order requirement provided sure proof of paternity. The artificiality of the requirement, however, was illustrated dramatically by the facts of *Lalli* itself, as Justice Byron R. White, for the dissenters, made clear. The decedent had often acknowledged his children openly; he had even executed a notarized document referring to one of them as "my son" and consenting to his marriage. Paternity had been proved clearly; what was missing was the formality of a court order. Such a judicial proceeding, of course, is least likely in the case in which the father and his illegitimate child are closest, and the father's acknowledgment of paternity has been most clearly established by nonjudicial means. The New York estate planners who wrote the law contrived its inertia to lean against the children of informal unions. *Lalli* is thus reminiscent of an earlier legal order designed to assure a man that his wealth and status would attach to a woman only when he chose to formalize their union and would pass only to the children of such a union.

—KENNETH L. KARST

LARSON v. DOMESTIC AND FOREIGN COMMERCE CORPORATION

337 U.S. 682 (1949)

This is a leading decision concerning the sovereign immunity of the United States.

In Lalli *a fragmented Supreme Court brought further confusion to the body of equal protection doctrine governing classifications based on illegitimacy.*

LARSON v. DOMESTIC AND FOREIGN COMMERCE CORPORATION

337 U.S. 682 (1949)

Plaintiff sued the head of the War Assets Administration (WAA), alleging that the administrator had sold certain surplus coal to plaintiff, had refused to deliver the coal, and had entered into a contract to sell the coal to others. Because plaintiff sought injunctive relief against WAA officials, ordering them not to sell the coal or to deliver it to anyone other than plaintiff, and because the suit concerned property of the United States, the Supreme Court found the suit to be one against the United States and, therefore, to be barred by sovereign immunity. The Court distinguished *Larson* from suits against officers for acts beyond their statutory powers and from suits seeking to enjoin allegedly unconstitutional behavior, both of which the Court stated would not constitute suits against the

LARKIN v. GRENDEL'S DEN, INCORPORATED

459 U.S. 116 (1982)

Dissenting alone, Justice William H. Rehnquist observed that "silly cases" like this one, as well as great or hard cases, make bad law. Chief Justice Warren E. Burger for the Court aimed its "heavy First Amendment artillery," in Rehnquist's phrase, at a statute that banned the sale of alcoholic beverages within 500 feet of a school or church, should either object to the presence of a neighboring tavern. Originally, Massachusetts had absolutely banned such taverns but found that the objective of the state police power, promoting neighborhood peace, could be fulfilled by the less drastic method of allowing schools and churches to take the initiative of registering objections. In this case a church objected to a tavern located ten feet away. Burger held that vesting the church with the state's veto power breached the prohibition against an establishment of religion, on the grounds that the church's involvement vitiated the secular purposes of the statute, advanced the cause of religion, and excessively entangled state and church. Rehnquist argued that a sensible statute had not breached the wall of separation of church and state.

—LEONARD W. LEVY

SEPARATION OF CHURCH AND STATE?

Churches like the one behind this pub cannot take the initiative of registering objections to nearby bars. (Corbis/Michael Busselle)

sovereign, even if the plaintiff alleges the officer acted unconstitutionally or beyond his statutory powers, "if the relief requested cannot be granted merely by ordering the cessation of the conduct complained of but will require affirmative action by the sovereign or the disposition of unquestionably sovereign property." In cases involving suits against state officials, part of this passage apparently was contradicted by *Edelman* v. *Jordan* (1974) and *Milliken* v. *Bradley* (1977). In each of these cases the Court found that litigation to require a state to pay the costs of future compliance with the Constitution did not constitute a suit against the sovereign. The precise holding in *Larson* became an important and debated issue in *Pennhurst State School and Hospital* v. *Halderman* (1984), where the Court relied in part on *Larson* to hold that actions in federal court against state officials, alleging violations of state law, are prohibited by the Eleventh Amendment.

—THEODORE EISENBERG

LAW OF THE LAND

The phrase "law of the land" has two connotations of constitutional dimension. In general usage it refers to a higher law than that of common law declaration or legislative enactment. As a result of the supremacy clause, the Constitution is such a higher law; it is the "supreme law of the land." In the exercise of judicial review, the Supreme Court claims the office of ultimate interpreter of the Constitution. It has thus become commonplace to think of decisions of the Court as the law of the land.

A second connotation has a specialized meaning that reaches far back into English history and leaves its indelible mark on American constitutional law. In 1215 the barons of England forced King John to sign Magna Carta, pledging his observance of obligations owed to them in return for their fealty to him. Among the provisions was one

that declared (in translation from the Latin): "No freeman shall be taken or imprisoned or dispossessed or outlawed or banished, or in any way destroyed, nor will we go upon him, nor send upon him, except by the judgment of his peers, or by the law of the land." Magna Carta was necessarily a feudal document, but this provision was so worded that it retained meaning long after feudalism gave way to the modern constitutional state.

The term "law of the land" consequently continued in English usage, representing that body of fundamental law to which appeal was made against any oppression by the sovereign, whether procedural or substantive. By 1354 there had appeared an alternate formulation, "due process of law." In his *Second Institute of the Laws of England* (1642), Sir Edward Coke asserted that "law of the land" and "due process of law" possessed interchangeable meanings; nevertheless, the older version was not thereby supplanted. The Petition of Right (1628) played no favorites with the two terms, demanding "that freemen be imprisoned or detained only by the law of the land, or by due process of law and not by the king's special command, without any charge."

In the politically creative period after Independence, American statesmen preferred "law of the land" to "due process," apparently because of its historic association with Magna Carta. All eight of the early state constitutions incorporating the guarantee in full or partial form employed the term "law of the land"; and the same was true of the Northwest Ordinance (1787). The first appearance of "due process of law" in American organic law occurred in the Fifth Amendment to the United States Constitution (1791). But that switch of usage did not displace "law of the land." Throughout the nineteenth century state constitutions and state courts spoke in one voice or the other, or even both. As of 1903 a listing by Thomas M. Cooley of state constitutions incorporating the legacy from Magna Carta showed "law of the land" outrunning "due process of law." The trend subsequently

Larson is a leading decision concerning the sovereign immunity of the United States.

See also
Edelman v. *Jordan*
Milliken v. *Bradley*
Pennhurst State School and Hospital v. *Halderman*

In the exercise of judicial review, the Supreme Court claims the office of ultimate interpreter of the Constitution.

has been to the latter phrase; yet a 1980 count found eleven states still expressing the guarantee as "law of the land."

The Glorious Revolution of 1688, embodying the political theory that parliamentary enactment was the practical equivalent of the "law of the land," presented a dilemma in interpretation when the versions of the guarantee were introduced into American thought and incorporated into most American constitutions. Legislative supremacy was unacceptable in the New World; the American view was that when sovereignty changed hands the English concept of limitations upon the crown now applied to the legislative as well as the executive branch. It followed that to construe the guarantee as forbidding deprivation of life, liberty, or property except by legislative enactment would be to render its protection meaningless. The puzzlement of American judges is understandable; only in the latter part of the nineteenth century had the concept been fully disentangled from the related concepts of regularized legislative process and separation of powers.

The guarantee inherited from Magna Carta is unusual among constitutional limitations. On its face it is not absolute but conditional. The government may not act against persons except by the law of the land or by due process. The thrust is arguably procedural, suggesting original intent may have been to guarantee the protection of a trial. But it can carry substantive meanings as well; those meanings emerged early and had fully developed in England by the late seventeenth century.

Although the wording and position of the state constitutional guarantees varied—some using "law of the land," others "due process of law"; some appending the guarantee to a list of procedural rights, others making it a separate provision—the variation made little difference in judicial response at the procedural level. Not so, however, with respect to substantive content. Where, as in the constitutions of the Carolinas, Illinois, Maryland, and Tennessee, the wording was close to a literal translation of Magna Carta, the guarantee was extended to vested rights, independently of the criminal provisions of the procedural connotation. On the other hand, Connecticut and Rhode Island courts sustained prohibition laws in the 1850s, holding that the phrase "due process of law" in their state constitutions was so enmeshed with entitlements of the criminally accused as to preclude inclusion of substantive right. A third series of cases, from Massachusetts, New Hampshire, New York, and Pennsylvania, read substantive content into the guarantee despite close interrelation with procedural protections. *Wynehamer* v. *New York* (1856) requires special consideration. In that case the state's highest court invalidated a prohibition law, insofar as it destroyed property rights in existing liquor stocks, resting its decision on separate constitutional guarantees of both "due process" and "law of the land." Contrary to the opinion of some scholars, *Wynehamer* was not overruled by *Metropolitan Board* v. *Barrie* (1866); the former case applied to a law with retroactive application, the latter to one that was purely prospective.

The Fifth Amendment associates "due process" with other constitutional guarantees clearly procedural in character, and separates the guarantee of due process from the right against self-incrimination only by a comma. Yet in major decisions, *Dred Scott* v. *Sandford* (1857), *Hepburn* v. *Griswold* (1870), and *Adair* v. *United States* (1908), the Supreme Court found substantive content in the clause.

In the Fourteenth Amendment, due process is not linked to criminal procedure protections, but resembles those state constitutional provisions that had been held in state courts to have substantive content. However, the Supreme Court has disregarded the distinction between the two due process clauses in the federal Constitution. The Court has been abetted by numerous commentators on the constitution who, intent on denying the

See also

Dred Scott v. *Sandford*

Due Process of Law

Judicial Supremacy

Lochner v. *New York*

Slaughterhouse Cases

Wynehamer v. *People of New York*

substantive element in due process, have ignored or misinterpreted the history of state constitutional guarantees of "due process" and "law of the land." The freedom from procedural connotation of Fourteenth Amendment due process made easier the path of substantive content from dissent in the *Slaughterhouse Cases* (1873), to reception in *Chicago, Milwaukee & St. Paul Railway Company* v. *Minnesota* (1890), to full embrace in *Lochner* v. *New York* (1905). The Court's acceptance of the incorporation doctrine, with consequent reading into the Fourteenth Amendment of the various procedural protections enumerated in the Bill of Rights, largely equates the content of the two due process clauses. This development has written the final chapter in the reinterpretation of "law of the land."

—FRANK R. STRONG

Bibliography

Howard, A. E. Dick (1968). *The Road from Runnymede: Magna Carta and Constitutionalism in America.* Charlottesville: University Press of Virginia.

Rembar, Charles (1980). *The Law of the Land: The Evolution of Our Legal System.* New York: Simon & Schuster.

LEISY v. HARDIN

135 U.S. 100 (1890)

Chief Justice Melville W. Fuller, speaking for a six-member majority, ruled that because Congress possesses an exclusive power under the commerce clause to regulate interstate transportation, no state may enact a liquor prohibition statute that bars the sale in that state of liquors imported from other states and sold in their original packages. That Congress had not exercised its commerce power was equivalent to a declaration that commerce shall be free. Any doctrine to the contrary, deriving from the *License Cases* (1847), said

Fuller, was "overthrown." Congress might, however, specifically authorize a state to ban interstate liquors; the Court sustained such an act of Congress in *In re Rahrer* (1891).

—LEONARD W. LEVY

LEMON v. KURTZMAN

403 U.S. 602 (1971) (I)

411 U.S. 192 1973) (II)

This case resulted in the "*Lemon* test" used by the Court to weigh whether a law violates the Establishment Clause of the First Amendment. It involved one of the school aid statutes produced by state legislatures in the wake of *Board of Education* v. *Allen* (1968). *Lemon I* stands for three cases joined for decision by the Court. *Lemon* challenged the constitutionality of a Pennsylvania statute that authorized the Superintendent of Public Instruction to reimburse nonpublic schools for teachers' salaries, textbooks, and instructional materials in secular subjects. *Erley* v. *DiCenso* and *Robinson* v. *DiCenso* (1971) challenged a Rhode Island statute that made available direct payments to teachers in nonpublic schools in amounts of up to 15 percent of their regular salaries.

Both statutes were unconstitutional, Chief Justice Warren Burger concluded, and he set forth a threefold test that continues to be invoked in establishment of religion cases: any program aiding a church-related institution must have an adequate secular purpose; it must have a primary effect that neither advances nor inhibits religion; and government must not be excessively entangled with religious institutions in the administration of the program. The Pennsylvania and Rhode Island schemes provided government aid to religious institutions. Burger argued that in order to see that these dollars were not used for religious instruction, the states would have to monitor compliance in ways involving excessive entanglement.

This case involved one of the school aid statutes produced by state legislatures in the wake of Board of Education v. Allen *(1968).*

♦ **equity**
A system of jurisprudence parallel to and corrective of the common law, based on principles of fairness rather than on the letter of the law. In most American jurisdictions, law and equity have been merged.

See also
Board of Education v. *Allen*
Establishment Clause
Establishment of Religion

*For three decades
the decision
influenced the Court
as it scrutinized
carefully and often
struck down
economic
regulations as
violations of
substantive due
process.*

See also

Griswold v. *Connecticut*

Roe v. *Wade*

Lemon v. *Kurtzman* returned to the Court (*Lemon II*) two years later on the question of whether the Pennsylvania schools could retain the monies that had been paid out in the period between the implementation of the law and the decision of the Supreme Court invalidating it in *Lemon I*. In a plurality opinion for himself and Justices Harry Blackmun, Lewis F. Powell, and William H. Rehnquist, Chief Justice Burger held that they could. An unconstitutional statute, he suggested, is not absolutely void but is a practical reality upon which people are entitled to rely until authoritatively informed otherwise. Justice Byron R. White concurred. Justice William O. Douglas, joined by Justices William J. Brennan and Potter Stewart, dissented. Douglas argued that there was "clear warning to those who proposed such subsidies" that they were treading on unconstitutional ground. "No consideration of equity," Douglas suggested, should allow them "to profit from their unconstitutional venture."

The *Lemon* test continues to be used by the courts, although Justice Sandra Day O'Connor has argued that it be modified by a test to determine whether the government has endorsed religion, a view the Court has moved toward espousing in recent years. In *Lee* v. *Weisman* (1992) the Court, while using the *Lemon* test, emphasized the "subtle coercive" effect of having a member of the clergy give an invocation at a public high school graduate.

—RICHARD E. MORGAN

LOCHNER v. NEW YORK

198 U.S. 45 (1905)

Lochner v. *New York*, a landmark decision of 1905, has been discredited by the evolution of constitutional law. Justice Rufus W. Peckham, writing for a 5–4 majority of the Supreme Court, invalidated a New York state statute forbidding employment in bakeries for more than sixty hours a week or ten hours a day. The rationale for the Court's opinion was that the statute interfered with the freedom of contract and thus the Fourteenth Amendment's right to liberty afforded both the employer and the employee. The Court stated that under the statute, viewed as a labor law, the state had no reasonable ground for interfering with liberty by determining the hours of labor. Seen as a health law, the statute affected only the bakers and not the public. Accordingly, the Court concluded that the law was neither necessary nor appropriate to accomplish its health objective. Moreover, the Court was of the view that if the law were upheld for the bakers, laws designed to protect other workers would also have to be upheld. In either case, said the Court, the statute was an illegal interference with the right to contract.

Justice Oliver Wendell Holmes, in an important and historic dissent, concluded that the legislature had the power to enact a law that interfered with full freedom to contract and that the personal biases of judges could not justify declaring a statute unconstitutional. Said Justice Holmes: "The constitution is not intended to embody a particular economic theory," an obvious reference to the laissez-faire view then widely accepted. Holmes's view was that a law interfered with the Fourteenth Amendment's guarantee of liberty only if "a rational and fair man necessarily would admit that the statute proposed would infringe fundamental principles of our people and our law." The dissent's view was that the statute, viewed either as a health or a labor law, did not violate these principles.

Justice John Marshall Harlan also dissented, arguing with Justice Holmes that the wisdom of the statute or of a particular economic theory is judicially irrelevant. Citing studies that showed the hazards of bakery work, Harlan noted that legislatures in many states had enacted legislation dealing with the number of hours in a work day. Said Justice Harlan: "[I]t is enough for the determination of this case, and it is enough for this Court, to know that the question is one about which there is room for debate and for at least honest difference of opinion." If there are "weighty substantial" reasons for enacting a law it ought "to be the end of [the] case, for the State is not amenable to the judiciary, in respect of its legislative enactments, unless such enactments are plainly, palpably, beyond all question, inconsistent with the Constitution of the United States."

The Court implicitly overruled the *Lochner* result in *Bunting* v. *Oregon* (1917), but for three decades the decision influenced the Court as it scrutinized carefully and often struck down economic regulations as violations of substantive due process. It was not until the mid-1930s, in the wake of the court-packing furor and especially the Court's approval of the constitutionality of the National Labor Relations Act in *National Labor Relations Board* v. *Jones & Laughlin Steel Corporation* (1937), that judicial intervention in economic legislation declined. Although *Lochner*

is now discredited, its focus upon substantive due process and fundamental rights has emerged in cases dealing with both contraception and abortion, namely *Griswold* v. *Connecticut* (1965) and *Roe* v. *Wade* (1973).

—WILLIAM B. GOULD

LOEWE v. LAWLOR

208 U.S. 274 (1908)

This case fits a pattern of antilabor decisions that supported injunctions against trade unions and struck down maximum hours acts, minimum wage acts, and acts prohibiting yellow dog contracts. In *Loewe*, the Court, while crippling secondary boycotts, held that unions were subject to the antitrust laws and therefore were civilly liable for triple damages to compensate for injuries inflicted by their restraints on interstate commerce.

Loewe originated in an attempt by the United Hatters Union, AFL, to organize a manufacturer of hats in Danbury, Connecticut. Most hat firms in the country were unionized. The few nonunion firms sweated

Loewe presents the phenomenon of a labor union being held within the terms of an antitrust act and contrasting opinions of the court.

YELLOW DOG CONTRACTS

The yellow dog contract was a device used by employers prior to the New Deal era to prevent collective bargaining by employees. By signing a yellow dog contract a worker agreed not to join or remain a member of a labor organization and to quit his job if he joined one. At a time in our history when the courts shaped the law so that its major beneficiary was industrial capitalism, yellow dog contracts were enforceable, even though workers had little choice in accepting their terms. Workers either signed such contracts or forfeited the opportunity of working. In effect, a

yellow dog contract blackmailed an employee into promising not to join a union; his supposed free choice to accept a job or look elsewhere for work turned out to be a choice between being blackmailed or blacklisted. In one perspective, yellow dog contracts robbed workers of their freedom of contract. The courts thought otherwise, however.

In the 1890s fifteen states enacted laws that promoted collective bargaining by outlawing yellow dog contracts, and in 1898 section 10 of the Erdman Act, passed by Congress, also outlawed their use by interstate railroads.

In *Adair* v. *United States* (1908) the Supreme Court held the Erdman Act unconstitutional. Substantive due process of law provided one ground of decision. The Court reasoned that section 10 abridged freedom of contract, a liberty the Court found in the Fifth Amendment's due process clause, because Congress had violated the right of workers to make contracts for the sale of their labor. In *Coppage* v. *Kansas* (1915) the Court applied this reasoning to state statutes that had banned yellow dog contracts.

L

LOEWE v. LAWLOR

208 U.S. 274 (1908)

♦ **injunction**
A form of writ prohibiting or requiring the performance of a specific act by a particular person. An injunction is a form of remedy available under a court's equity power.

See also

Labor and Employment Law

Knight Company, E.C., United States v.

their workers and were able to undersell unionized competitors, threatening their survival as well as the jobs of their unionized labor. Loewe's firm refused to negotiate a union contract and defeated a strike. The union retaliated with a secondary boycott, a refusal by the national membership of the AFL to buy Loewe's hats or patronize retailers who sold them. Loewe sued the union under the Sherman Antitrust Act after the boycott resulted in a substantial loss of orders. The union demurred to the charges, admitting that it had engaged in the boycott but alleging that it had not violated the antitrust law, because that law did not cover the activities of trade unions and because the boycott in this case was not a conspiracy in restraint of commerce among the states. Invoking the doctrine of the *Sugar Trust Case* (*United States* v. *E. C. Knight Co.*, 1895) that manufacturing is a purely local activity, the union claimed that neither it nor the manufacturer engaged in interstate commerce. Although Loewe's hats, once manufactured, were shipped to purchasing retailers in twenty-one states, the union argued that it did not interfere with the actual transportation across state lines and that any restraint on interstate commerce resulting from the boycott was, according to the *Sugar Trust Case,* remote and indirect.

Overruling a lower federal court decision in favor of the union, the Supreme Court, in a unanimous opinion by Chief Justice Melville W. Fuller, for the first time held that the Sherman Act applied to union activities; that a secondary boycott conducted across state lines is a conspiracy in restraint of interstate commerce; and that even if the restraint were remote and indirect, the Sherman Act applied because it covered "every" combination in the form of a trust "or otherwise" in restraint of interstate commerce. In 1911, however, the Court embraced the rule of reason, enabling it subsequently to find that corporations, not unions, might engage in reasonable restraints; that is, the act did not prohibit all restraints except by unions. In *Loewe,* however, the

Court construed the act broadly, even to the point of using the stream of commerce doctrine to show the scope of the commerce power. There is no evidence, however, that Congress, when adopting the Sherman Act, intended to cover union activities.

The case presents the phenomenon of a labor union being held within the terms of an antitrust act and contrasting opinions of the Court. In the *Sugar Trust Case* the Court held a 98 percent monopoly not to violate the act because manufacturing is local and any effect upon or relationship with interstate commerce is necessarily indirect; here, though, a small hatmakers' union came within the act because its boycott was interstate, despite its having done nothing to control the price or transportation of the product of a manufacturer. Moreover, the decision in this case came one week after the decision in *Adair* v. *United States* (1908), where the Court declared that there is "no connection between interstate commerce and membership in a labor organization," as it struck down an act of Congress prohibiting the use of yellow dog contracts by railroads against railroad workers engaged in interstate commerce. If *Adair* correctly invalidated the attempt by Congress to protect railroad workers under the commerce power, then a week later the Court should have decided that Congress under the same commerce power cannot, via the Sherman Act, reach an admittedly indirect relationship between a hatters' union and interstate commerce. Both the legislative history of the antitrust law and the *Sugar Trust* and *Adair* precedents opposed the decision in the *Danbury Hatters' Case.* Following the Court's decision, a triple-damages suit against the union in the lower federal court resulted in a fine of $252,000. The Danbury hatters went unorganized, hatmakers everywhere suffered, and unionization everywhere was thwarted to an inestimable extent by the threat of Sherman Act suits. *Loewe* is one of the major cases on the subject of labor and the Constitution.

—LEONARD W. LEVY

Bibliography

Lieberman, Elias (1960). *Unions Before the Bar.* Pages 56–70. New York: Harper & Row.

LOPEZ v. UNITED STATES

373 U.S. 427 (1963)

The Supreme Court held that a government agent may surreptitiously record a conversation with a criminal suspect and use the recording to corroborate his testimony. Lopez, a tavern keeper, offered a bribe to a federal tax agent who thereupon recorded the conversation. The Court refused to exclude the recording. Because the agent was on the premises with Lopez's consent, there was no trespass and therefore no violation of the Fourth Amendment. Because the agent could

testify to the conversation, he could use the recording to corroborate his testimony.

—HERMAN SCHWARTZ

LOVING v. VIRGINIA

388 U.S. 1 (1967)

For more than a decade following its decision in *Brown* v. *Board of Education* (1954) the Supreme Court avoided direct confrontation with the constitutionality of miscegenation laws. In *Loving,* the Court faced the issue squarely and held invalid a Virginia law forbidding any interracial marriage including a white partner. The decision is a major precedent in the area of racial discrimination as well as the foundation of the modern "freedom to marry."

A black woman and a white man, Virginia residents, went to the District of Columbia to

In Lopez *the Supreme Court held that a government agent may surreptitiously record a conversation with a criminal suspect and use the recording to corroborate his testimony.*

INTERRACIAL MARRIAGE

Mr. and Mrs. Loving married in violation of the Racial Integrity Act, which the Supreme Court found to be unconstitutional. (Corbis/Bettmann)

In Loving, *Earl Warren said that a "heavy burden of justification" must be carried by a state seeking to sustain any racial classification.*

Chief Justice Roger B. Taney provided the first judicial exposition of the clause of the Constitution guaranteeing republican forms of government.

be married, and returned to live in Virginia. They were convicted of violating the Racial Integrity Act and given one-year prison sentences, suspended on condition that they leave Virginia. The Virginia appellate courts modified the sentences but upheld the constitutionality of the law. The Supreme Court unanimously reversed; Chief Justice Earl Warren wrote for the Court.

Citing the suspect classification language of *Korematsu* v. *United States* (1944), Warren said that a "heavy burden of justification" must be carried by a state seeking to sustain any racial classification. The fact that the law punished both the white and black partners to a marriage did not relieve the state of that burden. The law's announced goal of "racial integrity" was promoted only selectively. A white was prohibited from marrying any nonwhite except the descendants of Pocahantas; a black and an Asian, for example, could lawfully marry. The law's obvious goal was the maintenance of white supremacy; it had no legitimate purpose independent of racial discrimination and thus violated the equal protection clause. *Pace* v. *Alabama* (1883) was assumed to be overruled.

The Court's opinion also rested on an alternative ground: the statute violated substantive due process, by interfering with "the freedom to marry." Quoting from the sterilization case, *Skinner* v. *Oklahoma* (1942), Chief Justice Warren called marriage "one of the "basic civil rights of man,' fundamental to our very existence and survival."

Justice Potter Stewart, concurring, merely repeated his earlier statement in *McLaughlin* v. *Florida* (1964) that a state could never make an act's criminality depend on the race of the actor.

—KENNETH L. KARST

LUTHER v. BORDEN

7 Howard (48 U.S.) 1 (1849)

In *Luther* v. *Borden*, a case arising from the aftermath of the Dorr Rebellion (1842), Chief Justice Roger B. Taney enunciated the doctrine of political questions and provided the first judicial exposition of the clause of the Constitution guaranteeing republican forms of government (Article IV, section 4).

Though Rhode Island was in the forefront of the Industrial Revolution, its constitutional system, derived from the royal charter of 1663 (which was retained with slight modifications as the state's organic act after the Revolution), was an archaic and peculiar blend of democratic and regressive features. Malapportionment and disfranchisement grew intolerably severe as the industrial cities and mill villages filled with propertyless native and immigrant workers. (Perhaps as many as 90 percent of the adult males of Providence were voteless in 1840.) Reform efforts through the 1820s and 1830s were unsuccessful. In 1841–42, suffragist reformers adopted more radical tactics derived from the theory of the Declaration of Independence, asserting that the people had a right to reform or replace their government, outside the forms of law if need be. They therefore drafted a new state constitution (the "People's Constitution") and submitted it to ratification by a vote open to all adult white male citizens of the state. The regular government, meanwhile, also submitted a revised constitution (the "Freeholders' Constitution") to ratification, but only by those entitled to vote under the Charter. The People's Constitution was ratified, the Freeholders' rejected. Reform leaders then organized elections for a new state government, in which Thomas Wilson Dorr was elected governor. The two governments organized, each claiming exclusive legitimacy. The Freeholders' government declared martial law and, with the tacit support of President John Tyler, used state militia to suppress the Dorrites in an almost bloodless confrontation. It then submitted another revised constitution, ratified in late 1842, that alleviated the problems arising under the Charter.

Dorrites dissatisfied with this outcome created a test case from an incident of militia harassment and requested the Supreme Court to determine that the Freeholders' government and the subsequent 1842 constitution were illegitimate, on the grounds that the Freeholders' government was not republican and that the people of the state had a right to replace it, without legal sanction if necessary. Taney, for a unanimous Court (Justice Levi Woodbury dissenting in part on a martial law point), declined to issue any such ruling. After noting the insuperable practical difficulties of declaring the previous seven years of Rhode Island's government illegitimate, Taney stated that "the courts uniformly held that the inquiry proposed to be made belonged to the political power and not to the judicial." He went on to explain that Dorrite contentions "turned upon political rights and political questions, upon which the court has been urged to express an opinion. We decline doing so." Taney thus amplified a distinction, earlier suggested by Chief Justice John Marshall, between judicial questions, which a court can resolve, and political ones, which can be resolved only by the political branches of government (executive and legislative).

Taney further held that the guarantee clause committed the question of the legitimacy of a state government to Congress for resolution, and that Congress's decision was binding on the courts, a point later reiterated by Chief Justice Salmon P. Chase in cases involving the legitimacy of congressional Reconstruction policies. Taney concluded his opinion with an empty concession to the political theory of the Dorrites: "No one, we believe, has ever doubted the proposition that, according to the institutions of this country, the sovereignty in every State resides in the people of the State, and that they may alter and change their form of government at their pleasure. But whether they have changed it or not," Taney repeated, "is a question to be settled by the political power," not the courts.

Though the political question doctrine thereby created has never been explained by a definitive rationale, it has proved useful in enabling the courts to avoid involvement in controversies that are not justiciable, that is, not suitable for resolution by judges.

—WILLIAM W. WIECEK

LUTHER v. BORDEN

7 Howard (48 U.S.) 1 (1849)

The U.S. Forest Service planed to build a paved road and allow timber harvesting in an area held sacred by certain American Indians.

LYNG v. NORTHWEST INDIAN CEMETERY

485 U.S. 439 (1988)

The U.S. Forest Service planned to build a paved road and allow timber harvesting in an area held sacred by certain American Indians. The Indians used the area, now part of a national forest, to perform religious rituals. The Supreme Court held 5–3 that the Forest Service action would not violate the free exercise clause of the First Amendment.

Writing for the majority, Justice Sandra Day O'Connor maintained that the free exercise clause was not implicated here because the Indians would not be coerced by the government's action into violating their religious beliefs. Hence, the government did not have to supply a compelling state interest to justify its action. The fact that the government activity would interfere with the Indians' religion was irrelevant because "the Free Exercise Clause is written in terms of what the govenment cannot do to the individual, not in terms of what the individual can extract from the government." Moreover, even if the Forest Service actions should " 'virtually destroy the Indians' ability to practice their religion,' . . . the Constitution simply does not provide a principle that could justify upholding" their claims.

Writing for the dissenters, Justice William J. Brennan rejected the majority's narrow reading of the free exercise clause and argued that because the beliefs and activities implicated by the government action were "central" to the religion of the American Indians, the government must supply a compelling state interest to justify its action.

—JOHN G. WEST, JR.

The Supreme Court significantly lowered the wall of separation of church and state by sanctioning an official display of a sacred Christian symbol.

See also

Separation of Church and State

LYNCH v. DONNELLY

465 U.S. 668 (1984)

The Supreme Court significantly lowered the wall of separation of church and state by sanctioning an official display of a sacred Christian symbol. Pawtucket, Rhode Island, included a crèche, or nativity scene, in its annual Christmas exhibit in the center of the city's shopping district. The case raised the question of whether Pawtucket's crèche violated the Constitution's prohibition of establishment of religion.

Chief Justice Warren Burger for a 5–4 Court ruled that despite the religious nature of the crèche, Pawtucket had a secular purpose in displaying it, as evinced by the fact that it was part of a Christmas exhibit that proclaimed "Season's Greetings" and included Santa Claus, his reindeer, a Christmas tree, and figures of carolers, a clown, an elephant, and a teddy bear. That the First Amendment, Burger argued, did not mandate complete separation is shown by our national motto, paid chaplains, presidential proclamations invoking God, the pledge of allegiance, and religious art in publicly supported museums.

Justice William Brennan, dissenting, construed Burger's majority opinion narrowly, observing that the question was still open on the constitutionality of a public display on public property of a crèche alone or of the display of some other sacred symbol, such as a crucifixion scene. Brennan repudiated the supposed secular character of the crèche; he argued that "[f]or Christians the essential message of the nativity is that God became incarnate in the person of Christ." The majority's insensitivity toward the feelings of non-Christians disturbed Brennan.

A spokesman for the National Council of Churches complained that the Court had put Christ "on the same level as Santa Claus and Rudolph the Red-Nosed Reindeer." Clearly, the Court had a topsy-turvy understanding of what constitutes an establishment of religion, because in *Larkin* v. *Grendel's Den* (1982) it saw a forbidden establishment in a state police power measure aimed at keeping boisterous patrons of a tavern from disturbing a church, yet here saw no establishment in a state-sponsored crèche.

A few years later in *Allegheny County* v. *ACLU* (1989) the Court, distinguishing *Lynch*, ruled a crèche in a government building without any secular accompaniment did violate the establishment clause. The same decision followed *Lynch* in allowing a menorah, along with a Christmas tree, as part of generalized winter holiday display.

—LEONARD W. LEVY

M

MAHER v. ROE

432 U.S. 464 (1977)

The Supreme Court here sustained, 6–3, a Connecticut law limiting state medicaid assistance for abortions in the first trimester of pregnancy to "medically necessary" abortions (including "psychiatric necessity"), but providing such aid for childbirth. Justice Lewis F. Powell, for the Court, rejected both the claim that the law violated the right of privacy recognized in *Roe* v. *Wade* (1973) and the claim that the state's wealth discrimination violated the equal protection clause.

There was to be "no retreat from *Roe,*" but Connecticut had placed "no obstacles . . . in the pregnant woman's path to an abortion." An indigent woman suffered no disadvantage from the state's funding of childbirth; she might still have an abortion if she could find the wherewithal; Connecticut had not created her indigency. Nor did the scheme deny equal protection. There was no suspect classification requiring strict scrutiny of the law; neither had the state invaded any fundamental interest by discriminating against the exercise of a constitutional right. The law satisfied the rational basis standard, for it was rationally related to promoting the state's interest in protecting potential life—an interest recognized in *Roe* itself.

Two companion decisions, *Poelker* v. *Doe* and *Beal* v. *Doe,* upheld a city's refusal to provide hospital services for an indigent woman's nontherapeutic abortion, and read the Social Security Act not to require a state to aid nontherapeutic abortions in order to receive federal medicaid grants.

Justices William J. Brennan, Thurgood Marshall, and Harry Blackmun all filed opinions dissenting in the three cases. They emphasized the "coercive" effect on poor women of the state's financial preference for childbirth, and the particularly harsh effect of adding unwanted children to poor households.

Even before *Roe,* wealthy women could have abortions by traveling to other states or abroad. *Roe* brought abortion within the means of middle-class women. The *Maher* majority Justices declined to extend the effective right to have an abortion beyond the boundaries of their own socioeconomic environment.

—KENNETH L. KARST

MALLOY v. HOGAN

378 U.S. 1 (1964)

This is one of a series of cases in which the Warren Court nationalized the rights of the criminally accused by incorporating provisions of the Fourth through the Eighth Amendments into the Fourteenth Amendment. In *Malloy* it was the right against self-incrimination. Malloy, a convicted felon on probation, was ordered to testify in a judicial inquiry into gambling activities. He refused to answer any questions concerning the crime for which he had been convicted, and he was held in contempt. Connecticut's highest court, relying on *Twining* v. *New Jersey* (1908) and *Adamson* v. *California* (1947), ruled that Malloy's invocation of the Fifth Amendment right had no constitutional basis in the state and that the Fourteenth Amendment did not extend the right to a state proceeding.

The Court declined to extend the effective right to have an abortion beyond the boundaries of the woman's socioeconomic environment.

See also

Abortion and the
  Constitution

Roe v. *Wade*

Malloy stands for the doctrine that the Fourteenth Amendment protects against state abridgement the same right that the Fifth protects against federal abridgment.

The Supreme Court reversed on the ground that the "same standards must determine whether an accused's silence in either a federal or a state proceeding is justified." Had the inquiry been a federal one, said Justice William J. Brennan for a 5–4 majority, Malloy would have been entitled to refuse to answer because his disclosures might have furnished a link in a chain of evidence to connect him to a new crime for which he might be prosecuted. The Court held that "the Fifth Amendment exception from compulsory self-incrimination is also protected by the Fourteenth against abridgment by the States." *Twining* and *Adamson,* which had held to the contrary, were overruled, although the specific holding in *Adamson* relating to comments on the accused's failure to testify was not overruled until *Griffin* v. *California* (1965). Thus, *Malloy* stands for the doctrine that the Fourteenth Amendment protects against state abridgment the same right that the Fifth protects against federal abridgment. Justices Byron R. White and Potter Stewart did not expressly dissent from this doctrine; they contended, rather, that Malloy's reliance on his right to silence was groundless on the basis of the facts. Justices John Marshall Harlan and Tom C. Clark opposed the incorporation of the Fifth Amendment right into the Fourteenth.

—LEONARD W. LEVY

MAPP v. OHIO

367 U.S. 643 (1961)

Mapp v. *Ohio* brought to a close an abrasive constitutional debate within the Supreme Court on the question whether the exclusionary rule, constitutionally required in federal trials since 1914, was also required in state criminal cases. *Mapp* imposed the rule on the states.

Wolf v. *Colorado* (1949) had applied to the states the Fourth Amendment's prohibition against unreasonable searches, but it had not required state courts to exclude from trial evidence so obtained. *Mapp's* extension of *Wolf* was based on two considerations. First, in *Wolf* the Court had been persuaded by the rejection of the exclusionary rule by most state courts; by 1961, however, a narrow majority of the states had independently adopted the rule. Second, the *Wolf* majority was convinced that other remedies, such as suits in tort against offending officers, could serve equally in deterring unlawful searches; time, however, had shown that such remedies were useless. "Nothing can destroy a government more quickly than its failure to observe its own laws," wrote Justice Tom C. Clark for the Court, "or worse, its disregard of the charter of its own existence."

In *Mapp* v. *Ohio* the Court asserted emphatically that the exclusionary rule was "an essential part" of the Fourth Amendment and hence a fit subject for imposition on the states despite "passing references" in earlier cases to its being a nonconstitutional rule of evidence. Yet, in some hazy phrasing, the opinion also suggested that the Fifth Amendment's right against self-incrimination was the exclusionary rule's constitutional backbone. Equally confusing was the Court's characterization of the rule as "the most important constitutional privilege" (that is, personal right) guaranteed by the Fourth Amendment while at the same time pointing to the rule's deterrent effect as justification for its imposition. More recently, the Court has settled on deterrence as the crucial consideration, and thus has refused to apply the rule in situations, such as grand jury proceedings in *Calandra* v. *United States* (1974), where in the Court's view the deterrent effect is minimal.

Three dissenters, in an opinion by Justice John Marshall Harlan, expressed "considerable doubt" that the federal exclusionary rule of *Weeks* v. *United States* (1914) was constitutionally based and argued that, in any event, considerations of federalism should allow the states to devise their own remedies for unlawful searches.

The court asserted emphatically that the exclusionary rule was "an essential part" of the Fourth Amendment.

(Unlike the well-entrenched federal exclusionary rule, which has gone well-nigh unchallenged on the Court from the beginning, controversy concerning the rule for the states has continued unabated, both on and off the Court, since *Mapp* was decided.)

Several later decisions have limited *Mapp*, holding, for example, the exclusionary rule inapplicable to grand jury proceedings and to cases where the police acted in good faith under a warrant they believed valid.

—JACOB W. LANDYNSKI

MARBURY v. MADISON

1 Cranch 137 (1803)

Marbury has transcended its origins in the party battles between Federalists and Republicans, achieving mythic status as the foremost precedent for judicial review. For the first time the Court held unconstitutional an act of Congress, establishing, if only for posterity, the doctrine that the Supreme Court has the final word among the coordinate branches of the national government in determining what is law under the Constitution. By 1803 no one doubted that an unconstitutional act of government was null and void, but who was to judge? What *Marbury* settled, doctrinally if not in reality, was the Court's ultimate authority over Congress and the president. Actually, the historic reputation of the case is all out of proportion to the merits of Chief Justice John Marshall's unanimous opinion for the Court. On the issue of judicial review, which made the case live, he said nothing new, and his claim for the power of the Court occasioned little contemporary comment. The significance of the case in its time derived from its political context and from the fact that the Court appeared successfully to interfere with the executive branch. Marshall's most remarkable accomplishment, in retrospect, was his massing of the Court behind a poorly reasoned opinion

that section 13 of the Judiciary Act of 1789 was unconstitutional. Though the Court's legal craftsmanship was not evident, its judicial politics—egregious partisanship and calculated expediency—was exceptionally adroit, leaving no target for Republican retaliation beyond frustrated rhetoric.

Republican hostility to the United States courts, which were Federalist to the last man as well as Federalist in doctrine and interests, had mounted increasingly and passed the threshold of tolerance when the Justices on circuit enforced the Sedition Act. Then the lame-duck Federalist administration passed the Judiciary Act of 1801 and, a week before Thomas Jefferson's inauguration, passed the companion act for the appointment of forty-two justices of the peace for the District of Columbia, prompting the new president to believe that "the Federalists have retired into the Judiciary as a stronghold . . . and from that battery all the works of republicanism are to be beaten down and erased." The new Circuit Court for the District of Columbia sought in vain to obtain the conviction of the editor of the administration's organ in the capital for the common law crime of seditious libel. The temperate response of the new administration was remarkable. Instead of increasing the size of the courts, especially the Supreme Court, and packing them with Republican appointees, the administration simply repealed the Judiciary Act of 1801. On taking office Jefferson also ordered that the commissions for the forty-two justices of the peace for the district be withheld, though he reappointed twenty-five, all political enemies originally appointed by President John Adams.

Marbury v. *Madison* arose from the refusal of the administration to deliver the commissions of four of these appointees, including one William Marbury. The Senate had confirmed the appointments and Adams had signed their commissions, which Marshall, the outgoing secretary of state, had affixed with the great seal of the United States. But in the rush of the "midnight appointments" on the evening of March 3, the last day of the

MARBURY v.
MADISON

1 Cranch 137 (1803)

See also

Exclusionary Rule

Weeks v. *United States*

Wolf v. *Colorado*

outgoing administration, Marshall had neglected to deliver the commissions. Marbury and three others sought from the Supreme Court, in a case of original jurisdiction, a writ of mandamus compelling James Madison, the new secretary of state, to issue their commissions. In December 1801 the Court issued an order commanding Madison to show cause why the writ should not be issued.

A congressman reflected the Republican viewpoint when saying that the show-cause order was "a bold stroke against the Executive," and John Breckinridge, the majority leader of the Senate, thought the order "the most daring attack which the annals of Federalism have yet exhibited." When the debate began on the repeal bill, Federalists defended the show-cause order, the independence of the judiciary, and the duty of the Supreme Court to hold void any unconstitutional acts of Congress. A Republican paper declared that the "mandamus business" had first appeared to be only a contest between the judiciary and the executive but now seemed a political act by the Court to deter repeal of the 1801 legislation. In retaliation the Republicans passed the repealer and altered the terms of the Court so that it would lose its June 1802 session and not again meet until February 1803, fourteen months after the show-cause order. The Republicans hoped, as proved to be the case, that the Justices would comply with the repealer and return to circuit duty, thereby averting a showdown and a constitutional crisis, which the administration preferred to avoid.

By the time the Court met in February 1803 to hear arguments in *Marbury,* which had become a political sensation, talk of impeachment was in the air. A few days before the Court's term, Federalists in Congress moved that the Senate should produce for Marbury's benefit records of his confirmation, provoking Senator James Jackson to declare that the Senate would not interfere in the case and become "a party to an accusation which may end in an impeachment, of which

the Senate were the constitutional Judges." By no coincidence, a week before the Court met, Jefferson instructed the House to impeach a U.S. District Court judge in New Hampshire, and already Federalists knew of the plan to impeach Justice Samuel Chase. Jefferson's desire to replace John Marshall with Spencer Roane was also public knowledge. Right before Marshall delivered the Court's opinion in *Marbury,* the Washington correspondent of a Republican paper wrote: "The attempt of the Supreme Court . . . by a mandamus, to control the Executive functions, is a new experiment. It seems to be no less than a commencement of war. . . . The Court must be defeated and retreat from the attack; or march on, till they incur an impeachment and removal from office."

Marshall and his Court appeared to confront unattractive alternatives. To have issued the writ, which was the expected judgment, would have been like the papal bull against the moon; Madison would have defied it, exposing the Court's impotence, and the Republicans might have a pretext for retaliation based on the Court's breach of the principle of separation of powers. To have withheld the writ would have violated the Federalist principle that the Republican administration was accountable under the law. Alexander Hamilton's newspaper reported the Court's opinion in a story headed "Constitution Violated by President," informing its readers that the new president by his first act had trampled on the charter of the peoples' liberties by unprincipled, even criminal, conduct against personal rights. Yet the Court did not issue the writ; the victorious party was Madison. But Marshall exhibited him and the president to the nation as if they were arbitrary Stuart tyrants, and then, affecting judicial humility, Marshall in obedience to the Constitution found that the Court could not obey an act of Congress that sought to aggrandize judicial powers in cases of original jurisdiction, contrary to Article III of the Constitution.

The Court was treading warily. The statute in question was not a Republican measure, not, for example, the repealer of the Judiciary Act of 1801. Indeed, shortly after *Marbury*, the Court sustained the repealer in *Stuart* v. *Laird* (1803) against arguments that it was unconstitutional. In that case the Court ruled that the practice of the Justices in sitting as circuit judges derived from the Judiciary Act of 1789, and therefore derived "from a contemporary interpretation of the most forcible nature," as well as from customary acquiescence. Ironically, another provision of the same statute, section 13, was at issue in *Marbury*, not that the bench and bar realized it until Marshall delivered his opinion. The offending section, passed by a Federalist Congress after being drafted by Oliver Ellsworth, one of the Constitution's Framers and Marshall's predecessor, had been the subject of previous litigation before the Court without anyone having thought it was unconstitutional. Section 13 simply authorized the Court to issue writs of mandamus "in cases warranted by the principles and usages of law," and that clause appeared in the context of a reference to the Court's appellate jurisdiction.

Marshall's entire argument hinged on the point that section 13 unconstitutionally extended the Court's original jurisdiction beyond the two categories of cases, specified in Article III, in which the Court was to have such jurisdiction. But for those two categories of cases, involving foreign diplomats or a state as a litigant, the Court has appellate jurisdiction. In quoting Article III, Marshall omitted the clause that directly follows as part of the same sentence: the Court has appellate jurisdiction "with such exceptions, and under such regulations as the Congress shall make." That might mean that Congress can detract from the Court's appellate jurisdiction or add to its original jurisdiction. The specification of two categories of cases in which the Court has original jurisdiction was surely intended as an irreducible minimum,

but Marshall read it, by the narrowest construction, to mean a negation of congressional powers.

In any event, section 13 did not add to the Court's original jurisdiction. In effect it authorized the Court to issue writs of mandamus in the two categories of cases of original jurisdiction and in all appellate cases. The authority to issue such writs did not extend or add to the Court's jurisdiction; the writ of mandamus is merely a remedial device by which courts implement their existing jurisdiction. Marshall misinterpreted the statute and Article III, as well as the nature of the writ, in order to find that the statute conflicted with Article III. Had the Court employed the reasoning of *Stuart* v. *Laird* or the rule that the Court should hold a statute void only in a clear case, giving every presumption of validity in doubtful cases, Marshall could not have reached his conclusion that section 13 was unconstitutional. That conclusion allowed him to decide that the Court was powerless to issue the writ because Marbury had sued for it in a case of original jurisdiction.

Marshall could have said, simply, this is a case of original jurisdiction but it does not fall within either of the two categories of original jurisdiction specified in Article III; therefore we cannot decide: writ denied, case dismissed. Section 13 need never have entered the opinion, although, alternatively, Marshall could have declared: section 13 authorizes this Court to issue such writs only in cases warranted by the principles and usages of law; we have no jurisdiction here because we are not hearing the case in our appellate capacity and it is not one of the two categories in which we possess original jurisdiction: writ denied, case dismissed. Even if Marshall had to find that the statute augmented the Court's original jurisdiction, the ambiguity of the clause in Article III, which he neglected to quote, justified sustaining the statute.

Holding section 13 unconstitutional enabled Marshall to refuse an extension of the Court's powers and award the judgment to

**MARBURY v.
MADISON**

1 Cranch 137 (1803)

For the first time the Court held an act of Congress unconstitutional.

Madison, thus denying the administration a pretext for vengeance. Marshall also used the case to answer Republican arguments that the Court did not and should not have the power to declare an act of Congress unconstitutional, though he carefully chose an inoffensive section of a Federalist statute that pertained merely to writs of mandamus. That he gave his doctrine of judicial review the support of only abstract logic, without reference to history or precedents, was characteristic, as was the fact that his doctrine swept way beyond the statute that provoked it.

If Marshall had merely wanted a safe platform from which to espouse and exercise judicial review, he would have begun his opinion with the problems that section 13 posed for the Court; but he reached the question of constitutionality and of judicial review at the tail end of his opinion. Although he concluded that the Court had to discharge the show-cause order, because it lacked jurisdiction, he first and most irregularly passed judgment on the merits of the case. Everything said on the merits was obiter dicta and should not have been said at all, given the judgment. Most of the opinion dealt with Marbury's unquestionable right to his commission and the correctness of the remedy he had sought by way of a writ of mandamus. In his elaborate discourse on those matters, Marshall assailed the president and his cabinet officer for their lawlessness. Before telling Marbury that he had initiated his case in the wrong court, Marshall engaged in what Edward S. Corwin called "a deliberate partisan *coup.*" Then Marshall followed with a "judicial *coup d'etat,*" in the words of Albert J. Beveridge, on the constitutional issue that neither party had argued.

The partisan *coup* by which Marshall denounced the executive branch, not the grand declaration of the doctrine of judicial review for which the case is remembered, was the focus of contemporary excitement. Only the passages on judicial review survive. Cases on the removal power of the president, especially concerning inferior appointees, cast doubt on the validity of the dicta by which Marshall lectured the executive branch on its responsibilities under the law. Moreover, by statute and by judicial practice the Supreme Court exercises the authority to issue writs of mandamus in all appellate cases and in the two categories of cases of original jurisdiction. Over the passage of time *Marbury* came to stand for the monumental principle, so distinctive and dominant a feature of our constitutional system, that the Court may bind the coordinate branches of the national government to its rulings on what is the supreme law of the land. That principle stands out from *Marbury* like the grin on the Cheshire cat; all else, which preoccupied national attention in 1803, disappeared in our constitutional law. So too might have disappeared national judicial review if the impeachment of Chase had succeeded.

Marshall himself was prepared to submit to review of Supreme Court opinions by Congress. He was so shaken by the impeachment of Chase and by the thought that he himself might be the next victim in the event of Chase's conviction, that he wrote to Chase on January 23, 1804: "I think the modern doctrine of impeachment should yield to an appellate jurisdiction in the legislature. A reversal of those legal opinions deemed unsound by the legislature would certainly better comport with the mildness of our character than a removal of the judge who has rendered them unknowing of his fault." The acquittal of Chase meant that the Court could remain independent, that Marshall had no need to announce publicly his desperate plan for congressional review of the Court, and that *Marbury* remained as a precedent. Considering that the Court did not again hold unconstitutional an act of Congress until 1857, when it decided *Dred Scott* v. *Sandford,* sixty-eight years would have passed since 1789 without such a holding, and but for *Marbury,* after so long a period of congressional omnipotence, national judicial review might never have been established.

—LEONARD W. LEVY

Bibliography

Beveridge, Albert J. (1916–1919). *The Life of John Marshall.* 4 vols. Vol. 3:50–178. Boston: Houghton Mifflin.

Corwin, Edward S. (1914). *The Doctrine of Judicial Review.* Pages 1–78. Princeton, N.J.: Princeton University Press.

Haines, Charles Grove (1944). *The Role of the Supreme Court in American Government and Politics, 1789–1835.* Pages 223–258. Berkeley: University of California Press.

Van Alstyne, William W. (1969). A Critical Guide to *Marbury v. Madison. Duke Law Journal* 1969:1–47.

Warren, Charles (1923). *The Supreme Court in United States History.* 3 vols. Vol. 1:200–268. Boston: Little, Brown.

MARSH v. ALABAMA

326 U.S. 501 (1946)

When a person sought to distribute religious literature on the streets of a company town, the Supreme Court, 5–3, upheld her First Amendment claim against the owner's private property claims. Stressing the traditional role of free speech in town shopping districts open to the general public, Justice Hugo L. Black for the Court noted that, aside from private ownership, this town functioned exactly as did other towns that were constitutionally forbidden to ban leafleting. *Marsh* served as the basis for the later attempt, aborted in *Hudgens* v. *NLRB* (1976), to extend First Amendment rights to users of privately owned shopping centers.

—MARTIN SHAPIRO

MARSHALL, JOHN

(1755–1835)

John Marshall, the third Chief Justice of the Supreme Court (1801–35), is still popularly known as the "Great Chief Justice" and the "Expounder of the Constitution." He was raised in the simple circumstances of backwoods Virginia, but his mother was pious and well educated and his father was a leader of his county and a friend of George Washington. Even though Marshall had little formal education, his extraordinary powers of mind, coupled with equity and good humor, made him a natural leader as a young soldier of the Revolution, as a member of the Richmond bar (then outstanding in the country), and as a general of the Virginia militia. He became nationally prominent as a diplomat, having outwitted the wily Charles Talleyrand while negotiating with France's Directory (1797–98), and as a legislator, having supported Washington's federalism first in the Virginia Assembly (1782–91, 1795–97) and then in the House of Representatives (1799–1800). In June 1800 President John Adams named Marshall to replace the Hamiltonian John Pickering as secretary of state, and in January 1801, after the strife-ridden Federalists' epochal defeat, appointed him Chief Justice when John Jay, the first Chief Justice, declined to preside again over "a system so defective."

From its inception Marshall had defended the Constitution. His experience in Washington's ragtag army had made him a national patriot while rousing his disgust with the palsied Confederation. At the crucial Virginia ratifying convention (June 1788) he replied in three important speeches to the fears of Patrick Henry and other anti-federalists. The proposed Constitution, he argued, was not undemocratic, but a plan for a "well-regulated democracy." It set forth in particular the great powers of taxing and warring needed by any sound government. The state governments would retain all powers not given up expressly or implicitly; they were independently derived from the people. A mix of dependence upon the people and independence and virtue in the judges would prevent federal overreaching. If a law were not "warranted by any of the powers enumerated," Marshall remarked prophetically, the judges would declare it "void" as

MARSHALL, JOHN

(1755–1835)

Can religious literature be distributed on the streets of a company town?

See also

Hudgens v. *NLRB*

infringing "the Constitution they are to guard." Two other nonjudicial interpretations of the Constitution are notable. In 1799 Marshall wrote a report of the Virginia Federalists defending the constitutionality of the ill-famed Sedition Act of 1798 (a law he nevertheless had opposed as divisive in the explosive political atmosphere surrounding the French Revolution). If the necessary and proper clause authorizes punishment of actual resistance to law, he argued, it also authorizes punishment of "calumnious" speech, which is criminal under the common law and prepares resistance. A speech to Congress in 1800, once famous in collections of American rhetoric, defended the president's power required by Jay's Treaty to extradite a British subject charged with murder on a British ship. Because the criminal and the location were foreign, Marshall argued, the question was not a case in law or equity for United States courts; although a treaty is a law, it is a "political law," the execution of which lies with the president, not the courts. The judiciary has no political power whatever; the president is "the sole organ of the nation in its external relations."

As Chief Justice, Marshall raised the office and the Supreme Court to stature and power previously lacking. After having two Chief Justices in eleven years, the Court had Marshall for thirty-four, the longest tenure of any Chief Justice before or since. Individual opinions seriatim largely ceased, and dissents were discouraged. The Court came to speak with one voice. Usually the voice was Marshall's. He delivered the opinion of the Court in every case in which he participated during the decisive first five years, three-quarters of the opinions during the next seven years, and almost all the great constitutional opinions throughout his tenure. Marshall's captivating and equable temper helped unite a diverse group of justices, many appointed by Republican presidents bent on reversing the Court's declarations of federal power and restrictions of state power. In the face of triumphant Jeffersonian Republicans, suspicious of an unelected judiciary stocked with Federalists, Marshall was wary and astute. His Court never erred as the Jay Court did in *Chisholm* v. *Georgia* (1793), which had provoked the Eleventh Amendment as a corrective. Nor did he cast antidemocratic contentions in the teeth of the Jeffersonians or their Jacksonian successors, thus to provoke (as had Justice Samuel Chase) impeachment proceedings. Marshall's judicial opinions encouraged grave respect for law, treated the Constitution as sacred and its Founding Fathers as sainted men, and fashioned a protective and compelling shield of purpose, principle, and reasoning.

His crucial judicial accomplishment was *Marbury* v. *Madison* (1803), which laid down the essentials of the American rule of law. Judges are to oversee executive and legislature alike, keeping the political departments faithful to applicable statutes, to the written Constitution, and to "general principles" of law protecting individual rights and delimiting the functions of each department. A se-

"EXPOUNDER OF THE CONSTITUTION"

As Chief Justice, Marshall raised the office and the Supreme Court to a stature previously lacking. (Corbis/Bettmann-UPI)

ries of important decisions secured individual rights, especially the right to acquire property by contract, against state and general governments. *United States* v. *Burr* (1807) expounded a narrow constitutional definition of treason and made prosecution difficult. *Sturges* v. *Crowninshield* (1819) set strict standards for voiding debts by bankruptcy. *Fletcher* v. *Peck* (1810) and *Dartmouth College* v. *Woodward* (1819) enforced as judicially protected contracts a state's sale of land and a state's grant of a corporate charter. Finally, several of Marshall's most famous opinions elaborated great powers for the national government and protected them from state encroachment. *McCulloch* v. *Maryland* (1819) sustained Congress's authority to charter a bank and in general to employ broad discretion as to necessary and proper means for carrying out national functions. *Gibbons* v. *Ogden* (1824), the *Steamboat Case,* interpreted congressional power under the commerce clause to protect a national market, a right of exchange free from state-supported monopoly. *Cohens* v. *Virginia* (1821) eloquently defended Supreme Court review of state court decisions involving federal questions.

The presupposition of Marshall's constitutionalism was that the Constitution is fundamental law, not merely a fundamental plan, written to impose limits, not just to raise powers, and designed to be permanent, not to evolve or to be fundamentally revised. Interpretation is to follow the words and purposes of the various provisions; amendment is for subordinate changes that will allow "immortality" to the Framers' primary work. Marshall called a written constitution America's "greatest improvement on political institutions." It renders permanent the institutions raised by popular consent, which is the only basis of rightful government. Besides, the American nation was fortunate in its founding: it benefited from a remarkable plan, from a fortunate ratification in the face of jealousy and suspicion in states and people, and from the extraordinary firmness of the first presi-

dent. Washington had settled the new federal institutions and conciliated public opinion, despite the "infinite difficulty" of ratification and a crescendo of attacks upon his administration as monarchic, aristocratic, and anglophile. So Marshall argued in the penetrating (if somewhat wooden) *Life of George Washington,* a biography he condensed into a schoolbook to impress on his countrymen the character and political principles of "the greatest man in the world."

Marshall understood the Constitution to establish a government, not a league such as that created by the Articles of Confederation. The new government possessed sovereign powers of two sorts, legal (the judicial power) and political (legislative and executive). The special function of judges is to apply the law to individuals. It is a power extensive although not, Marshall consistently said, political or policy-oriented. Judicial jurisdiction extends as far as does the law: common law, statute law, Constitution, treaties, and the law of nations (which Marshall influenced by several luminous opinions). In applying the law to individuals, courts are to care for individual rights, the very object of government in general. By "nature" or by "definition," courts are "those tribunals which are established for the security of property and to decide on human rights." Such rights are contained either in explicit constitutional provisions and amendments, or in "unwritten or common law," which the Constitution presupposes as the substratum of our law (and which Marshall thought was spelled out in traditional law books, such as Sir William Blackstone's *Commentaries on the Laws of England*). In short, courts are to construe all law in the light of the rights of person and property that are the object of law—as well as in the light of the constitutional authority of the other branches.

Marshall was fond of contrasting the Americans' "rational liberty," which afforded "solid safety and real security," with revolutionary France's "visionary" civic liberty, which had led to a despotism "borrowing the garb and usurping the name of freedom." While trying Aaron Burr, Marshall repeatedly noted the "tenderness" of American law for the rights of the accused. His *Life of Washington* mixes praise of freedom of speech and of conscience with attacks on religious persecution. Yet Marshall also said that morals and free institutions need to be "cherished" by public opinion; he would not suppose that a free marketplace of ideas insures progress in public enlightenment. He did suppose that a rather free economic marketplace would lead to progress in national wealth. Marshall defended property rights in the sense of rights of contract or vested rights, rights that vest under contract and originate in a right to the fruits of one's labor and enterprise. By protecting industrious acquisitions the judiciary fosters the dynamic economy of free enterprise. Rational liberty is prudent liberty, which breeds power as well as wealth: the "legitimate greatness" of a "widespreading, rising empire," extending from "the Ste. Croix to the Gulph of Mexico, from the Atlantic to the Pacific." By directly securing the rights of property, courts indirectly secure the "vast republic."

While courts are "the mere instruments of the law, and can will nothing," or at most possess a legal discretion governed by unwritten principles of individual rights, the executive and legislature enjoy broad political discretion for the safety and interrelation of all. President and Congress are indeed subordinate to the Constitution of enumerated powers and explicit restrictions. Marshall did not follow Alexander Hamilton, and would not have followed some later Supreme Courts, in inferring a plenary legislative power. His arguments, however, take aim at enemies on the other flank, at Jeffersonian strict constructionists who allowed only powers explicit in the Constitution or necessarily deduced from explicit powers. A constitution of government is not a "legal code," Marshall replied, and its enumerated powers are vested fully and encompass the full panoply of appropriate means. In *McCulloch,* Marshall set forth the core of the American doctrine of sovereignty: the need for great governmental powers to confront inevitable crises. Maryland had placed a prohibitive tax on a branch of the national bank, and its counsel denied federal authority to charter a bank (a power not explicit in the Constitution). Ours is a constitution, Marshall replied, "intended to endure for ages to come, and, consequently, to be adapted to the various *crises* of human affairs." Armies must be marched and taxes raised throughout the land. "Is that construction of the Constitution to be preferred which would render these operations difficult, hazardous, and expensive?" In a similar spirit Marshall defended an executive vigorous in war and foreign affairs and able to overawe faction and rebellion at home. He struck down, as violating Congress's power to regulate commerce among the states, state acts imposing import taxes or reserving monopolistic privileges. The arguments are typical. Great powers are granted for great objects. A narrow interpretation would defeat the object: the words must be otherwise construed. Thus a nation is raised. Individual enterprise, a national flow of trade, and the bonds of mutual interest breach barriers of state, section, and custom. The machinery of government is geared for great efforts of direction and coercion. The national sovereign, limited in its tasks, supreme in all means needed for their accomplishment, rises over the once independent state sovereignties. Marshall acknowledged the states' independent powers as well as the complexities of federalism: America was "for many purposes an entire nation, and for others several distinct and independent sovereignties." He tried above all to protect the federal government's superior powers from what the Framers had most feared, the encroachments of the states, more strongly entrenched in the people's affections.

Like virtually all of the Framers, Marshall was devoted to popular government. Yet Shays' Rebellion of western Massachusetts farmers (1786–87) had made him wonder whether "man is incapable of governing himself." He thought the new Constitution a republican remedy for the flaws of republican government, and for some time he thought constitutional restraints might suffice to rein the people to sound government. Marshall's republicanism encompassed both representative government and balanced government. The people are to grant their sovereignty to institutions for exercise by their representatives. A more substantial, virtuous, and enlightened Senate and president would balance the more popular House of Representatives, the dangerous house in a popular republic. Marshall came to be troubled by a decline in the quality of American leaders, from the great statesmen of the Revolution and founding, notably Washington, to the "superficial showy acquirements" of "party politicians." He came to be deeply disheartened by the tumultuous growth of democratic control, inspired by Thomas Jefferson and consummated by Andrew Jackson. A "torrent of public opinion," inflamed by the French Revolution, aroused the old debtor and states' rights party during Washington's administration. It led to democratic societies, set up to watch the government, and then to a legislature that conveyed popular demands without much filtering. Marshall had anticipated that Jefferson would ally himself with the House of Representatives, and become leader of the party dominating the whole legislature, thus increasing his own power while weakening the office of president and the fundamentals of balanced government. During Jackson's terms (1828–36), with the presidency transformed from a check on the majority to the tribune of the majority, Marshall favored reduction of its power, a tenure limited to one

term, and even selection of the president by lot from among the senators. He called his early republicanism "wild and enthusiastic democracy," and came to doubt that the constitutional Union could endure in the face of resurgent sectionalism and populism.

The eventual dissolution of political balances made crucial Marshall's decisive accomplishment as he and Jefferson began their terms of office: the confirmation of the judiciary as interpreter and enforcer of the fundamental law. Although Marshall's opinion in *Marbury* denied that courts can exercise political power, it gave courts power to circumscribe the forbidden sphere, to determine the powers of legislatures and executives. Marshall's argument for this unprecedented judicial authority recalled "certain principles . . . long and well established." In deciding cases judges must declare what the law is. The Constitution is the supreme law. Judges must apply the Constitution in preference to statute when the two conflict—else the Constitution is not permanent but "alterable when the legislature shall please to alter it." The argument established the Supreme Court as enforcer of the constitutional government central to America's constitutional democracy. Marshall pointed to the horrors of "legislative omnipotence," only inconspicuously bestowing on courts a ruling potency as the voice of the Constitution. Marshall's opinion, the object of intense scrutiny ever since, was faithful to the Constitutional Convention's supposition that there will be some judicial review of statutes and to its suspicion of democratic legislatures. It did not confront certain difficulties, notably those of a Supreme Court (like the Taney Court in *Dred Scott* v. *Sandford*, 1857) whose decisions violate the principles of the Constitution. Marshall's judicial reasonings were his attempt to keep judges, and his country, from violating the Constitution that preserves those principles.

—ROBERT K. FAULKNER

Bibliography

Beveridge, Albert J. (1916–1919). *The Life of John Marshall.* 4 vols. Boston: Houghton Mifflin.

Corwin, Edward S. (1919). *John Marshall and the Constitution.* New Haven, Conn.: Yale University Press.

Faulkner, Robert K. (1968). *The Jurisprudence of John Marshall.* Princeton, N.J.: Princeton University Press.

Holmes, Oliver Wendell (1952). John Marshall. Pages 266–271 in *Collected Legal Papers.* New York: Peter Smith.

White, G. Edward (1976). *The American Judicial Tradition.* Pages 7–34. New York: Oxford University Press.

Ziegler, Benjamin Munn (1939). *The International Law of John Marshall.* Chapel Hill: University of North Carolina Press.

MARSHALL COURT

(1801–1835)

In 1801 the Supreme Court existed on the fringe of American awareness. Its prestige was slight, and it was more ignored than respected. On January 20, 1801, the day President John Adams nominated John Marshall for the chief justiceship, the commissioners of the District of Columbia informed Congress that the Court had no place to hold its February term. The Senate consented to the use of one of its committee rooms, and Marshall took his seat on February 4 in a small basement chamber. At the close of 1809, Benjamin Latrobe, the architect, reported that the basement had been redesigned to enlarge the courtroom and provide an office for the clerk and a library room for the Justices. In 1811, however, Latrobe reported that the Court "had been obliged to hold their sittings in a tavern," because Congress had appropriated no money for "fitting up and furnishing the Court-room. . . ." After the British burned the Capitol in 1814 Congress again

neglected to provide for the Court. It held its 1815 term in a private home, and for several years after met in temporary Capitol quarters that were "little better than a dungeon." The Court moved into permanent quarters in 1819. In 1824 a New York correspondent described the Court's Capitol chamber: "In the first place, it is like going down cellar to reach it. The room is on the basement story in an obscure part of the north wing. . . . A stranger might traverse the dark avenues of the Capitol for a week, without finding the remote corner in which Justice is administered to the American Republic." He added that the courtroom was hardly large enough for a police court.

The Supreme Court, however, no longer lacked dignity or respect. It had become a force that commanded recognition. In 1819 a widely read weekly described it as so awesome that some regarded it with reverence. That year Thomas Jefferson complained that the Court had made the Constitution a "thing of wax," which it shaped as it pleased, and in 1824 he declared that the danger he most feared was the Court's "consolidation of our government." Throughout the 1820s Congress debated bills to curb the Court, which, said a senator, the people blindly adored—a "self-destroying idolatry." Alexis De Tocqueville, writing in 1831, said: "The peace, the prosperity, and the very existence of the Union are vested in the hands of the seven Federal judges. Without them, the Constitution would be a dead letter. . . ." Hardly a political question arose, he wrote, that did not become a judicial question.

Chief Justice Marshall was not solely responsible for the radical change in the Court's status and influence, but he made the difference. He bequeathed to the people of the United States what it was not in the political power of the Framers of the Constitution to give. Had the Framers been free agents, they would have proposed a national government that was unquestionably dominant over the states and possessed a formidable array of powers breathtaking in flexibility and scope. Marshall in more than a figurative sense was the supreme Framer, emancipated from a local constituency, boldly using his judicial position as an exalted platform from which to educate the nation to the true meaning, his meaning, of the Constitution. He wrote as if words of grandeur and power and union could make dreams come true. By the force of his convictions he tried to will a nation into being.

He reshaped the still malleable Constitution, giving clarification to its ambiguities and content to its omissions that would allow it to endure for "ages to come" and would make the government of the Union supreme in the federal system. Marshall is the only judge in our history whose distinction as a great nationalist statesman derives wholly from his judicial career. Justice Oliver Wendell Holmes once remarked, "If American law were to be represented by a single figure, sceptic and worshipper alike would agree without dispute that the figure could be one alone, and that one, John Marshall." That the Court had remained so weak after a decade of men of such high caliber as John Jay, Oliver Ellsworth, James Wilson, James Iredell, William Paterson, and Samuel Chase demonstrates not their weakness but Marshall's achievement in making the Court an equal branch of the national government.

Until 1807 he cast but one of six votes, and after 1807, when Congress added another Justice, but one of seven. One Justice, one vote has always been the rule of the Court, and the powers of anyone who is Chief Justice depend more on the person than the office. From 1812, Bushrod Washington and Marshall were the only surviving Federalists, surrounded by five Justices appointed by Presidents Thomas Jefferson and James Madison; yet Marshall dominated the Court in a way that no one has ever since. During Marshall's thirty-five-year tenure, the Court delivered 1,106 opinions in all fields of law, and he wrote 519; he dissented only eight times. He wrote forty of the Court's sixty-four opinions in the field of constitutional law, dissenting only once in a constitutional case. Of the twenty-four constitutional opinions for the Court that he did not write, only two were important: *Martin* v. *Hunter's Lessee* (1816), a case in which he did not sit, and *Ogden* v. *Saunders* (1827), the case in which he dissented. He virtually monopolized the constitutional cases for himself and won the support of his associates, even though they were members of the opposing political party.

Marshall's long tenure coincided with the formative period of our constitutional law. He was in the right place at the right time, filling, as Holmes said, "a strategic place in the campaign of history." But it took the right man to make the most of the opportunity. Marshall had the character, intellect, and passion for his job that his predecessors lacked. He had a profound sense of mission comparable to a religious "calling." Convinced that he knew what the Constitution should mean and what it was meant to achieve, he determined to give its purposes enduring expression and make them prevail. The Court was, for him, a judicial pulpit and political platform from which to address the nation, to compete, if possible, with the executive and legislative in shaping public opinion.

Marshall met few of the abstract criteria for a "great" judge. A great judge should possess intellectual rectitude and brilliance. Marshall was a fierce and crafty partisan who manipulated facts and law. A great judge should have a self-conscious awareness of his biases and a determination to be as detached as human fallibility will allow. In Marshall the judicial temperament flickered weakly; unable to muzzle his deepest convictions, he sought to impose them on the nation, sure that he was right. He intoxicated himself with the belief that truth, history, and the Constitution dictated his opinions, which merely declared the law rather than made the law. A great judge should have confidence in majority rule, tempered by his commitment to personal freedom and fairness. Marshall did not think men capable of self-government and inclined to favor financial and industrial capitalism over most other interests. A great judge should have a superior technical proficiency, modified by a sense of justice and ethical behavior beyond suspicion. Marshall's judicial ethics were not unquestionable. He should have disqualified himself in *Marbury* v. *Madison* (1803) because of his negligent complicity. He overlooked colossal corruption in *Fletcher* v. *Peck* (1810) to decide a land title case by a doctrine that promoted his personal interests. He wrote the opinion in *McCulloch* v. *Maryland* (1819) before hearing the case. Marshall's "juridical learning," as Justice Joseph Story, his reverent admirer and closest colleague, conceded, "was not equal to that of the great masters in the profession. . . ." He was, said Story, first, last, and always, "a Federalist of the good old school," and in the maintenance of its principles "he was ready at all times to stand forth a determined advocate and supporter." He was, in short, a Federalist activist who used the Constitution to legitimate predetermined results. A great judge should have a vision of national and moral greatness, combined with respect for the federal system. Marshall had that—and an instinct for statecraft and superb literary skills. These qualities, as well as his activism, his partisanship, and his sense of mission, contributed to his inordinate influence.

So too did his qualities of leadership and his personal traits. He was generous, gentle, warm, charming, considerate, congenial, and open. At a time when members of the Court lived together in a common boardinghouse during their short terms in Washington, his charismatic personality enabled him to preside over a judicial family, inspire loyalty, and convert his brethren to his views. He had a cast-iron will, an astounding capacity for hard work (witness the number of opinions he wrote for the Court), and formidable powers of persuasion. He thought audaciously in terms of broad and basic principles that he expressed axiomatically as absolutes. His arguments were masterful intellectual performances, assuming that his premises were valid. Inexorably and with developing momentum he moved from an unquestioned premise to a foregone conclusion. Jefferson once said that he never admitted anything when conversing with Marshall. "So sure as you admit any position to be good, no matter how remote from the conclusion he seeks to establish, you are gone." Marshall's sophistry, according to Jefferson, was so great, "you must never give him an affirmative answer or you will be forced to grant his conclusion. Why, if he were to ask me if it were daylight or not, I'd reply, 'Sir, I don't know. I can't tell.' " Marshall could also be imperious. He sometimes gave as the opinion of the Court a position that had not mustered a majority. According to one anecdote, Marshall is supposed to have said to Story, the greatest legal scholar in our history, "That, Story, is the law. You find the precedents."

The lengthy tenure of the members of the Marshall Court also accounts for its achievements. On the pre-Marshall Court, the Justices served briefly; five quit in a decade. The Marshall Court lasted—Brockholst Livingston seventeen years, Thomas Todd nineteen, Gabriel Duvall twenty-four, William Johnson thirty, Bushrod Washington thirty-one, and Marshall outlasted them all. Story served twenty-four years with Marshall and ten more after his death; Smith Thompson served fifteen years with Marshall and eight years after. This continuity in personnel contributed to a consistent point of view in constitutional doctrine—a view that was, substantially, Marshall's. From 1812, when the average age of the Court's members was only forty-three, through 1823—twelve successive terms—the Court had the same membership, the longest period in its history without a change, and during that period the Marshall Court decided its most important cases except for *Marbury*.

Marshall also sought to strengthen the Court by inaugurating the practice of one

Justice's giving the opinion of the Court. Previously the Justices had delivered their opinions seriatim, each writing an opinion in each case in the style of the English courts. That practice forced each Justice to take the trouble of understanding each case, of forming his opinion on it, and showing publicly the reasons that led to his judgment. Such were Jefferson's arguments for seriatim opinions; and Marshall understood that one official opinion augmented the Court's strength by giving the appearance of unity and harmony. Marshall realized that even if each Justice reached similar conclusions, the lines of argument and explanation of doctrine might vary with the style and thought of every individual, creating uncertainty and impairing confidence in the Court as an institution. He doubtless also understood that by massing his Court behind one authoritative opinion and by assigning so many opinions to himself, his own influence as well as the Court's would be enhanced. Jefferson's first appointee, Justice Johnson, sought to buck the practice for a while. He had been surprised, he later informed Jefferson, to discover the Chief Justice "delivering all the opinions in cases in which he sat, even in some instances when contrary to his own judgment and vote." When Johnson remonstrated in vain, Marshall lectured him on the "indecency" of judges' "cutting at each other," and Johnson soon learned to acquiesce "or become such a cypher in our consultations as to effect no good at all." Story, too, learned to swallow his convictions to enhance the "authority of the Court." His "usual practice," said Story, was "to submit in silence" to opinions with which he disagreed. Even Marshall himself observed in an 1827 case, by which time he was losing control of his Court, that his usual policy when differing from the majority was "to acquiesce silently in its opinion."

Like other trailblazing activist judges, Marshall squeezed a case for all it was worth, intensifying its influence. For Marshall a constitutional case was a medium for explaining his philosophy of the supreme and fundamental law, an occasion for sharing his vision of national greatness, a link between capitalism and constitutionalism, and an opportunity for a basic treatise. Justice Johnson protested in 1818, "We are constituted to decide causes, and not to discuss themes, or digest systems." He preferred, he said, to decide no more in any case "than what the case itself necessarily requires." Ordinary Justices decide only the immediate question on narrow grounds; but Marshall, confronted by some trivial question—whether a justice of the peace had a right to his commission or whether peddlers of lottery tickets could be fined—would knife to the roots of the controversy, discover that it involved some great constitutional principle, and explain it in the broadest possible way, making the case seem as if the life of the Union or the supremacy of the Constitution were at stake. His audacity in generalizing was impressive; his strategy was to take the highest ground and make unnerving use of obiter dicta; and then, as a matter of tactics, almost unnoticeably decide on narrow grounds. *Marbury* is remembered for Marshall's exposition of judicial review, not for his judicial humility in declining jurisdiction and refusing to issue the writ of mandamus. *Cohens* v. *Virginia* (1821) is remembered for Marshall's soaring explication of the supremacy of the judicial power of the United States, not for the decision in favor of Virginia's power to fine unlicensed lottery ticket peddlers. *Gibbons* v. *Ogden* (1824) is remembered for its sweeping discourse on the commerce clause of the Constitution, not for the decision that the state act conflicted with an obscure act of Congress.

Marshall's first major opinion, in *Marbury*, displayed his political cunning, suppleness in interpretation, doctrinal boldness, instinct for judicial survival, and ability to maneuver a case beyond the questions on its face. Having issued the show cause order to Madison, the Court seemingly was in an impossible position once Jefferson's supporters called that

Time has hardly withered the influence and achievements of the Marshall Court.

order a judicial interference with the executive branch. To decide for Marbury would provoke a crisis that the Court could not survive: Madison would ignore the Court, which had no way to enforce its decision, and the Court's enemies would have a pretext for impeachment. To decide against Marbury would appear to endorse the illegal acts of the executive branch and concede that the Court was helpless. Either course of action promised judicial humiliation and loss of independence. Marshall therefore found a way to make a tactical retreat while winning a great strategic victory for judicial power. After upbraiding the executive branch for violating Marbury's rights, Marshall concluded that the Court had no jurisdiction in the case, because a provision of an act of Congress conflicted with Article III. He held that provision unconstitutional by, first, giving it a sweeping construction its text did not bear and, second, by comparing it to his very narrow construction of Article III. Thus he reached and decided the great question, not argued by counsel, whether the Court had the power to declare unconstitutional an act of Congress. By so doing he answered from the bench his critics in Congress who, now that they were in power, had renounced judicial review during the debate on the repeal of the Judiciary Act of 1801. Characteristically Marshall relied on no precedents, not even on the authority of *The Federalist* #78. Significantly, he chose a safe act of Congress to void—section 13 of the Judiciary Act of 1789, which concerned not the province of the Congress or the president but of the Supreme Court, its authority to issue writs of mandamus in cases of original jurisdiction. But Marshall's exposition of judicial review was, characteristically, broader than the holding on section 13. Jefferson, having been given no stick with which to beat Marshall, privately fumed: "Nothing in the Constitution has given them a right to decide for the Executive, more than to the Executive to decide for them," he wrote in a letter. "The

opinion which gives to the judges the right to decide what laws are constitutional, and what not, not only for themselves in their own sphere of action, but also for the Legislature and Executive also, in their spheres, would make the judiciary a despotic branch."

The Court did not dare to declare unconstitutional any other act of Congress, which remained hostile to it throughout Marshall's tenure. *Stuart* v. *Laird* (1803), decided shortly after *Marbury*, upheld the repeal of the Judiciary Act of 1801. A contrary decision would have been institutionally suicidal for the Court. Marshall's opinion in *Marbury* was daring enough; in effect he courageously announced the Court's independence of the other branches of the government. But he was risking retaliation. Shortly before the arguments in *Marbury*, Jefferson instructed his political allies in the House to start impeachment proceedings against John Pickering, a federal district judge; the exquisite timing was a warning to the Supreme Court. Even earlier, Jeffersonian leaders in both houses of Congress openly spoke of impeaching the Justices. The threats were not idle. Two months after *Marbury* was decided, Justice Chase on circuit attacked the administration in a charge to a grand jury, and the House prepared to impeach him. Senator William Giles of Virginia, the majority leader, told Senator John Quincy Adams that not only Chase "but all the other Judges of the Supreme Court," except William Johnson, "must be impeached and removed." Giles thought that holding an act of Congress unconstitutional was ground for impeachment. "Impeachment was not a criminal prosecution," according to Giles, who was Jefferson's spokesman in the Senate. "And a removal by impeachment was nothing more than a declaration by Congress to this effect: you hold dangerous opinions, and if you are suffered to carry them into effect, you will work the destruction of the Union. We want your offices for the purposes of giving them to men who will fill them better."

Intimidated by Chase's impending impeachment, Marshall, believing himself to be next in line, wrote to Chase that "impeachment should yield to an appellate jurisdiction in the legislature. A reversal of those legal opinions deemed unsound by the legislature would certainly better comport with the mildness of our character than a removal of the Judge who has rendered them unknowing of his fault." Less than a year after his *Marbury* opinion the fear of impeachment led an anguished Marshall to repudiate his reasoning and favor Congress as the final interpreter of the Constitution. Fortunately, the greatest crisis in the Court's history eased when the Senate on March 1, 1805, failed to convict Chase on any of the eight articles of impeachment. Marshall and his Court were safe from an effort, never again repeated, to politicize the Court by making it subservient to Congress through impeachment.

The Court demonstrated its independence even when impeachment hung over it. In *Little* v. *Barreme* (1804) Marshall for the Court held that President Adams had not been authorized by Congress to order an American naval commander to seize a ship sailing from a French port. Justice Johnson on circuit vividly showed his independence of the president who had appointed him. To enforce the Embargo Acts, Jefferson had authorized port officers to refuse clearance of ships with "suspicious" cargoes. In 1808 Johnson, on circuit in Charleston, ordered the clearance of a ship and denounced the president for having exceeded the power delegated by the Embargo Acts. Jefferson could not dismiss as partisan politics Johnson's rebuke that he had acted as if he were above the law. Justice Brockholst Livingston, another Jefferson appointee, also had occasion in 1808 to show his independence of the president. Jefferson supported a federal prosecution for treason against individuals who had opposed the embargo with violence. Livingston, who presided at the trial, expressed "astonishment" that the government would resort to a theory of "constructive treason" in place of the Constitution's definition of treason as levying war against the United States, and he warned against a "precedent so dangerous." The jury speedily acquitted. After the tongue-lashing from his own appointees, Jefferson won an unexpected victory in the federal courts in the case of the brig *William* (1808). Federal district judge John Davis in Massachusetts sustained the constitutionality of the Embargo Acts on commerce clause grounds. Davis, a lifelong Federalist, showed how simplistic was Jefferson's raving about judicial politics.

The evidence for the Court's nonpartisanship seems plentiful. For example, Justice Story, Madison's appointee, spoke for an independent Court in *Gelston* v. *Hoyt* (1818), a suit for damages against government officials whose defense was that they had acted under President Madison's orders. Story, finding no congressional authority for these orders, "refused an extension of prerogative" power and added, "It is certainly against the general theory of our institutions to create discretionary powers by implication. . . ."

On the other hand, the Court supported the theory of implied powers in *McCulloch* v. *Maryland* (1819), which was the occasion of Marshall's most eloquent nationalist opinion. *McCulloch* had its antecedent in *United States* v. *Fisher* (1804), when the Court initially used broad construction to sustain an act of Congress that gave to the government first claim against certain insolvent debtors. Enunciating the doctrine of implied powers drawn from the necessary and proper clause, Marshall declared that Congress could employ any useful means to carry out its enumerated power to pay national debts. That the prior claim of the government interfered with state claims was an inevitable result, Marshall observed, of the supremacy of national laws. Although a precursor of *McCulloch*, *Fisher* attracted no opposition because it did not thwart any major state interests.

When the Court did confront such interests for the first time, in *United States* v. *Judge*

Peters (1809), Marshall's stirring nationalist passage, aimed at states that annulled judgments of the federal courts, triggered Pennsylvania's glorification of state sovereignty and denunciation of the "unconstitutional exercise of powers in the United States Courts." The state called out its militia to prevent execution of federal judgments and recommended a constitutional amendment to establish an "impartial tribunal" to resolve conflicts between "the general and state governments." State resistance collapsed only after President Madison backed the Supreme Court. Significantly, eleven state legislatures, including Virginia's, censured Pennsylvania's doctrines and endorsed the Supreme Court as the constitutionally established tribunal to decide state disputes with the federal courts.

The *Judge Peters* episode revealed that without executive support the Court could not enforce its mandate against a hostile state, which would deny that the Court was the final arbiter under the Constitution if the state's interests were thwarted. The episode also revealed that if other states had no immediate stake in the outcome of a case, they would neither advance doctrines of state sovereignty nor repudiate the Court's supreme appellate powers. When Virginia's high court ruled that the appellate jurisdiction of the Supreme Court did not extend to court judgments and that section 25 of the Judiciary Act of 1789 was unconstitutional, the Marshall Court, dominated by Republicans, countered by sustaining the crucial statute in *Martin* v. *Hunter's Lessee* (1816). Pennsylvania and other states did not unite behind Virginia when it proposed the constitutional amendment initiated earlier by Pennsylvania, because *Martin* involved land titles of no interest to other states. The fact that the states were not consistently doctrinaire and became aggressive only when Court decisions adversely affected them enabled the Court to prevail in the long run. A state with a grievance typically stood alone. But for the incapacity or unwillingess of the Court's state enemies to act together in their proposals to cripple it, the great nationalist decisions of the Marshall Court would have been as impotent as the one in *Worcester* v. *Georgia* (1832). *Worcester* majestically upheld the supreme law against the state's despoliation of the Cherokees, but President Andrew Jackson supported Georgia, which flouted the Court. Even Georgia, however, condemned the South Carolina Ordinance of Nullification, and several state legislatures resolved that the Supreme Court was the constitutional tribunal to settle controversies between the United States and the states.

The Court made many unpopular decisions that held state acts unconstitutional. *Fletcher* v. *Peck,* which involved the infamous Yazoo land frauds, was the first case in which the Justices voided a state act for conflict with the Constitution itself. *Martin* v. *Hunter's Lessee,* which involved the title to the choice Fairfax estates in Virginia, was only the first of a line of decisions that unloosed shrill attacks on the Court's jurisdiction to decide cases on a writ of error to state courts. In *McCulloch* the Court supported the "monster monopoly," the Bank of the United States chartered by Congress, and held unconstitutional a state tax on its Baltimore branch. In *Cohens* the Court again championed its supreme appellate powers under section 25 of the Judiciary Act of 1789 and circumvented the Eleventh Amendment. In *Sturges* v. *Crowninshield* (1819) the Court nullified a state bankruptcy statute that aided victims of an economic panic. In *Green* v. *Biddle* (1821) the Court used the contract clause when voiding Kentucky acts that supported valuable land claims. In *Osborn* v. *Bank of the United States* (1824) it voided an Ohio act that defied *McCulloch* and raised the question whether the Constitution had provided for a tribunal capable of protecting those who executed the laws of the Union from hostile state action.

When national supremacy had not yet been established and claims of state sovereignty bottomed state statutes and state judicial decisions that the Court overthrew, state assaults on the Court were inevitable, imperiling it and the Union it defended. Virginia, the most prestigious state, led the assault, which Jefferson encouraged and Spencer Roane directed. Kentucky's legislature at one point considered military force to prevent execution of the *Green* decision. State attacks were vitriolic and intense, but they were also sporadic and not united. Ten state legislatures adopted resolutions against the Marshall Court, seven of them denouncing section 25 of the 1789 Act, which was the jurisdictional foundation for the Court's power of judicial review over the states. In 1821, 1822, 1824, and 1831 bills were introduced in Congress to repeal section 25. The assault on the Court was sharpest in the Senate, whose members were chosen by the state legislatures. Some bills to curb the Court proposed a constitutional amendment to limit the tenure of the Justices. One bill would have required seriatim opinions. Others proposed that no case involving a state or a constitutional question could be decided except unanimously; others accepted a 5–2 vote. One bill proposed that the Senate should have appellate powers over the Court's decisions.

Throughout the 1820s the attempts to curb the Court created a continuing constitutional crisis that climaxed in 1831, when Marshall despondently predicted the repeal of section 25 and the dissolution of the Union. In 1831, however, the House, after a great debate, defeated a repeal bill by a vote of 138–51; southerners cast forty-five of the votes against the Court. What saved the Court was the inability of its opponents to mass behind a single course of action; many who opposed section 25 favored a less drastic measure. The Court had stalwart defenders, of course, including Senators Daniel Webster and James Buchanan. Most important, it had won popular approbation. Although the Court had enemies in local centers of power, Americans thrilled to Marshall's paeans to the Constitution and the Union, and he

taught them to identify the Court with the Constitution and the Union.

A perceptible shift in the decisions toward greater tolerance for state action also helped dampen the fires under the Court in Marshall's later years. The coalition that Marshall had forged began to dissolve with the appointments of Justices Smith Thompson, John McLean, and Henry Baldwin. *Brown* v. *Maryland* (1827), *Martin* v. *Mott* (1827), *American Insurance Company* v. *Canter* (1828), *Weston* v. *Charleston* (1829), *Craig* v. *Missouri* (1830), and the *Cherokee Indian Cases* (1832) continued the lines of doctrine laid down by the earlier Marshall Court. But the impact of new appointments was felt in the decisions of *Ogden* v. *Saunders* (1827), *Willson* v. *Blackbird Creek Marsh Company* (1829) and *Providence Bank* v. *Billings* (1830). In Marshall's last decade on the Court, six decisions supported nationalist claims against seventeen for state claims. During the same decade there were ten decisions against claims based on vested rights and only one sustaining such a claim. The shift in constitutional direction may also be inferred from the inability of the Marshall Court, because of dissension and illness, to resolve *Charles River Bridge* v. *Warren Bridge*, *Mayor of New York* v. *Miln*, and *Briscoe* v. *Bank of Kentucky*, all finally decided in 1837 under Marshall's successor against the late Chief Justice's wishes. Before his last decade the only important influence on the Court resulting from the fact that Republicans had a voting majority was the repudiation of a federal common law of crimes.

What was the legacy of the Marshall Court? It established the Court as a strong institution, an equal and coordinate branch of the national government, independent of the political branches. It established itself as the authoritative interpreter of the supreme law of the land. It declared its rightful authority to hold even acts of Congress and the president unconstitutional. It maintained continuing judicial review over the states to support the supremacy of national law. In so doing,

MARSHALL COURT

(1801–1835)

the Court sustained the constitutionality of the act of Congress chartering the Bank of the United States, laying down the definitive exposition of the doctrine of implied powers. The Court also expounded the commerce clause in *Gibbons* v. *Ogden* (1824), with a breadth and vigor that provided the basis for national regulation of the economy generations later. Finally, the Court made the contract clause of the Constitution into a bulwark protecting both vested rights and risk capital. *Fletcher* supported the sanctity of public land grants to private parties, encouraging capital investment and speculation in land values. *New Jersey* v. *Wilson* (1812) laid down the doctrine that a state grant of tax immunity constituted a contract within the protection of the Constitution, preventing subsequent state taxation for the life of the grant. *Dartmouth College* v. *Woodward* (1819) protected private colleges and spurred the development of state universities; it also provided the constitutional props for the expansion of the private corporation by holding that a charter of incorporation is entitled to protection of the contract clause. The Marshall Court often relied on nationalist doctrines to prevent state measures that sought to regulate or thwart corporate development. Just as national supremacy, judicial review, and the Court's appellate jurisdiction were often interlocked, so too the interests of capitalism, nationalism, and judicial review were allied. Time has hardly withered the influence and achievements of the Marshall Court.

—LEONARD W. LEVY

Bibliography

Baker, Leonard (1974). *John Marshall.* New York: Macmillan.

Beveridge, Albert J. (1919). *The Life of John Marshall.* Vols. 3 and 4. Boston: Houghton Mifflin.

Corwin, Edward S. (1919). *John Marshall and the Constitution: A Chronicle of the Supreme Court.* New Haven: Yale University Press.

Haines, Charles G. (1944). *The Role of the Supreme Court in American Government and Politics, 1789–1835.* Berkeley: University of California Press.

Haskins, George Lee, and Johnson, Herbert Q. (1981). *Foundations of Power: John Marshall, 1801–1815.* Volume 2 of the *Oliver Wendell Holmes Devise History of the Supreme Court of the United States.* New York: Macmillan.

Konefsky, Samuel J. (1964). *John Marshall and Alexander Hamilton.* New York: Macmillan.

Morgan, Donald G. (1954). *Justice William Johnson: The First Great Dissenter.* Columbia: University of South Carolina Press.

Warren, Charles (1923). *The Supreme Court in United States History.* 3 vols. Boston: Little, Brown.

MARSHALL, THURGOOD

(1908–1993)

Thurgood Marshall earned a unique place in American history on the basis of a long, varied, and influential career as a private attorney, government lawyer, and appellate jurist. Two achievements in particular stand out. First, as counsel for the National Association for the Advancement of Colored People (NAACP), he shaped the litigation that destroyed the constitutional legitimacy of state-enforced racial segregation. Second, as an Associate Justice of the Supreme Court—the nation's first black Justice—he boldly articulated a liberal jurisprudence on a Court dominated by conservatives. No person in the history of the Supreme Court better illustrated the limits and possibilities of the jurist as dissenter.

Marshall was born July 2, 1908, in Baltimore, Maryland, attended that city's racially segregated public schools, and was graduated from Lincoln University. Excluded from the University of Maryland Law School by that state's racial policies, he received his law degree from Howard Law School. He excelled at Howard and came to the attention of the school's dean, Charles H. Houston, a pioneer in the use of litigation as a vehicle of social reform. Although Marshall embarked on a conventional commercial practice upon graduation, he also participated, under Houston's guidance, in important, albeit unremunerative, civil rights cases. Appropriately enough, his first consisted of a successful suit against the same state university system that had earlier excluded him. In *Murray* v. *Maryland* (1937) Marshall convinced the Court of Appeals of Maryland that the Constitution required the state to do more for black residents seeking legal education than merely offer them scholarships to attend out-of-state law schools.

In 1939 Marshall succeeded Houston as special counsel of the NAACP. Over the next two decades he traveled ceaselessly, addressing problems of racial inequality in a wide array of settings: from obscure local courts in which he sought to extract from hostile juries and judges a measure of justice for black defendants, to Korea where he investigated the treatment of black soldiers by United States military authorities, to black churches and lodges where he encouraged people in aggrieved communities to seek to vindicate their rights. He also argued thirty-two cases before the Supreme Court, prevailing in twenty-nine of them. His brilliant advocacy helped to convince the Supreme Court to invalidate practices that excluded blacks from primary elections (*Smith* v. *Allwright* [1944]), to prohibit segregation in interstate transportation (*Morgan* v. *Virginia* [1946]), to overturn convictions obtained from juries from which blacks had been illicitly barred (*Patton* v. *Mississippi* [1947]), and to prohibit state courts from enforcing racially restrictive real estate covenants (*Shelley* v. *Kraemer*

[1948]). Marshall's greatest triumph arose from the skillfully orchestrated litigation that culminated in *Brown* v. *Board of Education of Topeka* (1954), which invalidated state-enforced racial segregation in public schooling. By the close of the 1950s Marshall had attained widespread recognition as a leading public figure and was known affectionately in much of black America as "Mr. Civil Rights."

The next stage in Marshall's career was marked by a series of high-level appointments. In 1961 President John F. Kennedy appointed him to the United States Court of Appeals for the Second Circuit over the strong objections of segregationist senators who delayed his confirmation for nearly a year. In 1965 President Lyndon B. Johnson appointed Marshall solicitor general of the United States. The first black American to hold this post, Marshall argued several important cases before the Court, including *Miranda* v. *Arizona* (1966), in which he successfully urged the Court to impose greater limitations on the power of police to interrogate criminal suspects; *Harper* v. *Virginia State Board of Elections* (1966), in which he successfully argued that state poll taxes violated the federal Constitution; and *United States* v. *Guest* (1966), in which he successfully defended the federal prosecution of white supremacists in Georgia who committed a racially motivated murder during the era of the civil rights movement.

In 1967 President Johnson set the stage for Marshall to cross the color line in another area of governmental service when he named him to a seat on the Supreme Court. Marshall's elevation vividly symbolized the ascendancy of values and interests he had long sought to advance. At the outset of Marshall's career on the Court, it was presided over by Chief Justice Earl Warren and animated by a decidedly reformist ethos. Ironically, however, the liberal wing whose ranks Marshall fortified began to disintegrate soon after he took his seat. By the mid-1970s the

appointments of Chief Justice Warren E. Burger and associate Justices Lewis F. Powell and William H. Rehnquist had brought to the fore a conservative ethos that long confined Justice Marshall to the periphery of judicial power.

During his years on the Court, Justice Marshall seldom held sway in the middle as a "swing" vote. Rather, he made his mark as a judicial maverick—always independent, consistently bold, frequently dissenting. Keenly attentive to allegations of invidious discrimination, Justice Marshall was strongly favorable to the claims of members of historically oppressed groups. However, he repeatedly found himself at odds with the Court. *Memphis* v. *Greene* (1981) involved a city's decision to close a street, mainly used by blacks, which traversed a predominantly white neighborhood. The Court upheld the legality of the city's action. Justice Marshall perceived a violation of the Thirteenth Amendment, concluding that the city's ac-

tion constituted a racially prejudiced "badge or incident of slavery." *Personnel Administrator of Massachusetts* v. *Feeney* (1979) called into question a state law that provided an absolute preference for veterans of the Armed Forces in civil service positions, a system of selection that tended overwhelmingly to disadvantage women in relation to men. The Court upheld the statute. Justice Marshall condemned it as a violation of the equal protection clause of the Fourteenth Amendment. *Mobile* v. *Bolden* (1980) concerned an at-large voting scheme under which, for almost seventy years, no black had ever been elected to a seat on the ruling city commission in Mobile, Alabama, even though blacks constituted nearly a third of the city's population. The Court held that this electoral arrangement could be invalidated only if it were used as a vehicle of purposeful discrimination. Justice Marshall concluded that the system's racially disparate impact violated the Fifteenth Amendment. *Rostker* v. *Goldberg* (1981) brought into question the constitutionality of a federal statute that requires men but not women to register for the military draft. Differing with the majority of his colleagues, Justice Marshall declared that the Court erred in placing its "imprimatur on one of the most potent remaining public expressions of 'ancient canards about the proper role of women.'"

Critical of the Court for showing too little solicitude for those who have been historically victimized on the basis of race and gender, Justice Marshall also rebuked the Court for displaying undue aggressiveness in defending the asserted rights of those who challenge affirmative action policies that provide preferences to women and racial minorities. Sharply distinguishing between benign and invidious discrimination, he voted to uphold every affirmative action plan the Court reviewed. Here, too, he was forced into dissent, objecting bitterly to decisions that increasingly limited the permissible scope of affirmative action measures. In *Re-*

"MR. CIVIL RIGHTS"

Marshall shaped the litigation that destroyed the constitutional legitimacy of state-enforced racial segregation. (Corbis)

gents of University of California v. Bakke (1978), the first affirmative action case that the Court resolved, Justice Marshall declared that "it must be remembered that during most of the past 200 years, the Constitution as interpreted by the [Supreme] Court did not prohibit the most ingenious and pervasive forms of discrimination against the Negro. Now, when a State acts to remedy the effects of that legacy of discrimination, I cannot believe that this same Constitution stands as a barrier."

A decade later, Justice Marshall continued to rail against an interpretation of the Fourteenth Amendment that he considered perverse. In *Richmond* v. *J. A. Croson Co.* (1989), for instance, he dissented against a ruling that invalidated Richmond, Virginia's, policy of reserving for enterprises owned by racial minorities a designated percentage of business generated by the city. Observing that "it is a welcome symbol of racial progress when the former capital of the Confederacy acts forthrightly to confront the effects of racial discrimination in its midst," he angrily chided his colleagues for taking "a deliberate and giant step backward." The Court's decision, he predicted, "will inevitably discourage or prevent governmental entities, particularly States and localities, from acting to rectify the scourge of past discrimination. This is the harsh reality of the majority's decision, but it is not the Constitution's command."

Other areas in which Justice Marshall's strongly held views were frequently at odds with the Court's conclusions involve capital punishment, abortion, and the legal status of the poor—areas in which Marshall's jurisprudential commitments frequently overlapped. Insisting that death penalties under all circumstances violate the Eighth Amendment's prohibition against cruel and unusual punishment, Justice Marshall filed dissents against all executions that the Court sanctioned. In *Ake* v. *Oklahoma* (1985), his advocacy on behalf of those charged with capital crimes suc-

ceeded in wringing from his colleagues a rare broadening of rights to which criminal defendants are entitled. Writing for the Court, Justice Marshall held that, at least in cases possibly involving the death penalty, due process requires states to afford indigent defendants the means to obtain needed psychiatric experts.

With respect to abortion, Justice Marshall was among the most stalwart defenders of *Roe* v. *Wade* (1973), dissenting in every case in which the Court upheld legislative inroads on what he viewed as a woman's broad right to decide whether or not to terminate a pregnancy. An example of his allegiance to *Roe* v. *Wade* (1973) is his dissenting opinion in *Maher* v. *Roe* (1977), where he maintained that a state violated the Constitution by denying poor women funding for abortions while making funds available to them for expenses of childbirth. "Since efforts to overturn [*Roe* v. *Wade*] have been unsuccessful," he charged, "the opponents of abortion have attempted every imaginable means to circumvent the commands of the Constitution and impose their moral choices upon the rest of society." Articulating his anger with characteristic sharpness, Justice Marshall asserted that this case involved "the most vicious attacks yet devised" in that they fell on poor women— "those among us least able to help or defend themselves."

Throughout Justice Marshall's career on the Court he vigorously attempted to improve the legal status of the poor. He argued, for instance, that the federal courts should subject to heightened scrutiny state laws that explicitly discriminate on the basis of poverty. For the most part, however, his efforts were stymied. One particularly memorable expression of Justice Marshall's empathy for the indigent is his dissent in *United States* v. *Kras* (1973), a case in which the Court held that federal law did not violate the Constitution by requiring a $50 fee of persons seeking the protections of bankruptcy. Objecting to the Court's assumption

MARSHALL, THURGOOD

(1908–1993)

Most of Marshall's major contributions to the constitutional development have come through dissents.

that the petitioner could readily accumulate this amount, Justice Marshall wrote that he could not agree with the majority

> *that it is so easy for the desperately poor to save $1.92 each week over the course of six months. . . . The 1970 Census found that over 800,000 families in the Nation had annual incomes of less than $1,000 or $19.23 a week. . . . I see no reason to require that families in such straits sacrifice over 5% of their annual income as a prerequisite to getting a discharge in bankruptcy. . . . It may be easy for some people to think that weekly savings of less than $2 are no burden. But no one who has had close contact with poor people can fail to understand how close to the margin of survival many of them are. . . . It is perfectly proper for judges to disagree about what the Constitution requires. But it is disgraceful for an interpretation of the Constitution to be premised upon unfounded assumptions about how people live.*

On occasion Justice Marshall's dissents succeeded in changing the mind of the Court. An example is the Court's response to claims of racially invidious discrimination in peremptory challenges. In *Swain* v. *Alabama* (1965) the Court had ruled that prosecutors could properly use race as a basis for peremptorily excluding potential jurors so long as they did so as a matter of strategy relating to a particular trial and not for the purpose of barring blacks routinely from participation in the administration of justice. By repeatedly dissenting from orders in which the Court refused to reconsider *Swain* and by showing in detail this decision's dismal practical consequences, Marshall finally convinced the Court to reverse itself—though even when it did, in *Batson* v. *Kentucky* (1986), Marshall still maintained that his colleagues had neglected to go far enough in ridding the criminal justice system of invidious practices.

For much of Justice Marshall's career on the bench, he seemed to deliberately avoid any extrajudicial controversies. Beginning in the 1980s, however, he appeared to have altered his habits. He publicly criticized Ronald Reagan, declaring that his civil rights record as president of the United States was among the worst in the twentieth century. He also chided President George Bush for selecting David H. Souter to occupy the seat on the Court vacated by Justice Marshall's longtime ally Justice William J. Brennan. In an unprecedented action, Justice Marshall declared on a televised broadcast that, in his view, the president's choice was inappropriate.

Although Justice Marshall received considerable criticism for his comments on Presidents Reagan and Bush, extrajudicial remarks that generated an even greater amount of controversy stemmed from a speech that he gave in 1987 in the midst of the bicentennial celebration of the United States Constitution. Boldy challenging the iconography of American constitutionalism, he asserted that he did not find "the wisdom, foresight, and sense of justice exhibited by the framers [to be] particularly profound. To the contrary," he declared, "the government they devised was defective from the start," omitting, for example, blacks and women as protected members of the polity. Eschewing "flag waving fervor," Justice Marshall noted his intention to commemorate the bicentennial by recalling "the suffering, struggle, and sacrifice that has triumphed over much of what was wrong with the original document" and by also acknowledging the Constitution's unfulfilled promise.

Some detractors fault Justice Marshall on the grounds that his penchant for dissent robbed him of influence that he might otherwise have wielded. Judging influence, however, is a dangerous endeavor. Justices John Marshall Harlan, Oliver Wendell Holmes Jr., and Louis D. Brandeis are as well respected on the basis of their dissenting opinions as they are respected for any other aspect of their illustrious careers. History may well bequeath the same fate to Justice Thurgood Marshall. Justice Marshall resigned from the Court in 1991, and he died on January 24, 1993.

—RANDALL KENNEDY

MARTIN v. HUNTER'S LESSEE

1 Wheaton 304 (1816)

Appomattox ultimately settled the issue that bottomed this case: Were the states or was the nation supreme? As a matter of law, the opinion of the Supreme Court supplied the definitive answer, but law cannot settle a conflict between competing governments unless they agree to abide by the decision of a tribunal they recognize as having jurisdiction to decide. Whether such a tribunal existed was the very issue in this case; more precisely the question was whether the Supreme Court's appellate jurisdiction extended to the state courts. In 1810 Virginia had supported the Court against state sovereignty advocates. Pennsylvania's legislature had resolved that "no provision is made in the Constitution for determining disputes between the general and state governments by an impartial tribunal." To that Virginia replied that the Constitution provides such a tribunal, "the Supreme Court, more eminently qualified . . . to decide the disputes aforesaid in an enlightened and impartial manner, than any other tribunal which could be erected." The events connected with the *Martin* case persuaded Virginia to reverse its position. The highest court of the state, the Virginia Court of Appeals, defied the Supreme Court, subverted the judicial power of the United States as defined by Article III of the Constitution, circumvented the supremacy clause (Article VI), and held unconstitutional a major act of Congress—all for the purpose of repudiating judicial review, or the Supreme Court's appellate jurisdiction over state courts and power to declare state acts void.

The *Martin* case arose out of a complicated and protracted legal struggle over land titles. Lord Fairfax died in 1781, bequeathing valuable tracts of his property in Virginia's Northern Neck to his nephew, Denny Martin, a British subject residing in England. During the Revolution Virginia had confiscated Loyalist estates and by an act of 1779, which prohibited alien enemies from holding land, declared the escheat, or reversion to the state, of estates then owned by British subjects. That act of 1779 did not apply to the estates of Lord Fairfax, who had been a Virginia citizen. The Treaty of Peace with Great Britain in 1783, calling for the restitution of all confiscated estates and prohibiting further confiscations, strengthened Martin's claim under the will of his uncle. In 1785, however, Virginia had extended its escheat law of 1779 to the Northern Neck, and four years later had granted some of those lands to one David Hunter. Jay's Treaty of 1794, which protected the American property of British subjects, also buttressed Martin's claims. By then a Virginia district court, which included Judge St. George Tucker, decided in Martin's favor; Hunter appealed to the state's high court. John Marshall, who had represented Martin, and James Marshall, his brother, joined a syndicate that arranged to purchase the Northern Neck lands. In 1796 the state legislature offered a compromise, which the Marshall syndicate accepted: the Fairfax devisees relinquished claim to the undeveloped lands of the Northern Neck in return for the state's recognition of their claim to Fairfax's manor lands. The Marshall syndicate accepted the compromise, thereby seeming to secure Hunter's claim, yet thereafter completed their purchase. In 1806 Martin's heir conveyed the lands to the syndicate, and in 1808 he appealed to the Court of Appeals, which decided in favor of Hunter two years later.

The Martin-Marshall interests, relying on the Treaty of 1783 and Jay's Treaty, took the

The issue at the bottom of this 1816 case was: Are the states or the nation supreme?

case to the Supreme Court on a writ of error under section 25 of the Judiciary Act of 1789. That section provided in part that the nation's highest tribunal on writ of error might reexamine and reverse or affirm the final judgment of a state court if the state court sustained a state statute against a claim that the statute was repugnant to the Constitution, treaties, or laws of the United States, or if the state court decided against any title or right claimed under the treaties or federal authority. Chief Justice Marshall took no part in the case, and two other Justices were absent. Justice Joseph Story, for a three-member majority and against the dissenting vote of Justice William Johnson, reversed the judgment of the Virginia Court of Appeals, holding that federal treaties confirmed Martin's title. In the course of his opinion Story sapped the Virginia statutes escheating the lands of alien enemies and ignored the "compromise" of 1796. The mandate of the Supreme Court to the state Court of Appeals concluded: "You therefore are hereby commanded that such proceedings be had in said cause, as according to right and justice, and the laws of the United States, and agreeable to said judgment and instructions of said Supreme Court . . ." (*Fairfax's Devisee* v. *Hunter's Lessee,* 1813).

The state court that received this mandate consisted of eminent and proud men who regarded the Supreme Court as a rival; the man who dominated the state court was Spencer Roane, whose opinion Story had reversed. Roane, the son-in-law of Patrick Henry, was not just a judge; he was a state political boss, an implacable enemy of John Marshall, and the man whom Thomas Jefferson would have appointed Chief Justice, given the chance. To Roane and his brethren, Story's opinion was more than an insulting encroachment on their judicial prerogatives. It raised the specter of national consolidation, provoking the need to rally around the states' rights principles of the Virginia and Kentucky Resolutions. Roane consulted with Jefferson and

James Monroe, and he called before his court the leading members of the state bar, who spoke for six days. Munford, the Virginia court reporter, observed: "The question whether this mandate should be obeyed excited all that attention from the Bench and Bar which its great importance truly merited." The reporter added that the court had its opinions ready for delivery shortly after the arguments. That was in April 1814, when the Republican political organization of Virginia dared not say anything that would encourage or countenance the states' rights doctrines of Federalist New England, which opposed the War of 1812 and thwarted national policies. Not until December 1815, when the crisis had passed and secessionism in the North had dissipated, did the Virginia Court of Appeals release its opinions.

Each of four state judges wrote opinions, agreeing that the Constitution had established a federal system in which sovereignty was divided between the national and state governments, neither of which could control the other or any of its organs. To allow the United States or any of its departments to operate directly on the states or any of their departments would subvert the independence of the states, allow the creature to judge its creators, and destroy the idea of a national government of limited powers. Although conflicts between the states and the United States were inevitable, the Constitution "has provided no umpire" and did not authorize Congress to bestow on the Supreme Court a power to pass final judgment on the extent of the powers of the United States or of its own appellate jurisdiction. Nothing in the Constitution denied the power of a state court to pass finally upon the validity of state legislation. The states could hold the United States to the terms of the compact only if the state courts had the power to determine finally the constitutionality of acts of Congress. Section 25 of the Judiciary Act was unconstitutional because it vested appellate powers in the Supreme Court in a case where the highest court of a state has authoritatively construed state acts. In sum, the position of the Court of Appeals was that the Supreme Court cannot reverse a state court on a matter of state or even federal law, but a state court can hold unconstitutional an act of the United States. Thus, Roane, with Jefferson's approval, located in the state courts the ultimate authority to judge the extent of the powers of the national government; in 1798 Jefferson had centered that ultimate authority in the state legislatures. At the conclusion of their opinions, the Virginia judges entered their judgment:

> *The court is unanimously of opinion, that the appellate power of the Supreme Court of the United States does not extend to this court, under a sound construction of the constitution of the United States; that so much of the 25th section of the act of Congress to establish the judicial courts of the United States, as extends the appellate jurisdiction of the Supreme Court to this court, is not in pursuance of the constitution of the United States; that the writ of error, in this cause, was improvidently allowed, under the authority of that act; that the proceedings thereon in the Supreme Court were* Coram non judice *[before a court without jurisdiction], in relation to this court, and that obedience to its mandate be declined by the court.*

When the case returned a second time to the Supreme Court on writ of error, Marshall again absented himself and Story again wrote the opinion. The *Martin* Court, consisting of five Republicans and one Federalist, was unanimous, though Johnson concurred separately. Story's forty-page opinion on behalf of federal judicial review is a masterpiece, far superior to Marshall's performance in *Marbury v. Madison* (1803) on behalf of national judicial review. In its cadenced prose, magisterial tone, nationalist doctrine, incisive logic, and driving repetitiveness, Story's opinion fore-shadowed Marshall's later and magnificent efforts in *McCulloch* v. *Maryland* (1819), *Cohens* v. *Virginia* (1821), and *Gibbons* v. *Ogden* (1824), suggesting that they owe as much to Story as he to Marshall's undoubted influence on him. Because the Constitution, as Roane pointed out, had neither expressly empowered Congress to extend the Court's appellate jurisdiction to the state courts nor expressly vested the Court itself with such jurisdiction, Story had to justify broad construction. The Constitution, he observed, was ordained not by the sovereign states but by the people of the United States, who could subordinate state powers to those of the nation. Not all national powers were expressly given. The Constitution "unavoidably deals in general language," Story explained, because it was intended "to endure through a long lapse of ages, the events of which were locked up in the inscrutable purpose of Providence." The Framers of the Constitution, unable to foresee "what new changes and modifications of power might be indispensable" to achieve its purposes, expressed its powers in "general terms, leaving to the legislature, from time to time, to adopt its own means to effectuate legitimate objects. . . ." From such sweeping premises on the flexibility and expansiveness of national powers, Story could sustain section 25. He found authority for its enactment in Articles III and VI.

Article III, which defined the judicial power of the United States, contemplates that the Supreme Court shall be primarily an appellate court, whose appellate jurisdiction "shall" extend to specified cases and controversies. "Shall" is mandatory or imperative: the Court *must* exercise its appellate jurisdiction in *all* cases, in law and equity, "arising under the Constitution, the Laws of the United States, and Treaties made. . . ." It is, therefore, the case, not the court from which it comes, that gives the Supreme Court its appellate jurisdiction, and because cases involving the Constitution, federal laws, and treaties may arise in state courts, the Supreme

Court must exercise appellate jurisdiction in those cases. Contrary to Roane, that appellate jurisdiction did not exist only when the case came from a lower federal court. The Constitution required the establishment of a Supreme Court but merely authorized Congress to exercise a discretionary power in establishing lower federal courts. If Congress chose not to establish them, the Court's mandatory appellate jurisdiction could be exercised over only the state courts. The establishment of the lower federal courts meant that the appellate jurisdiction of the Supreme Court extended concurrently to both state and federal courts.

Article VI, the supremacy clause, made the Constitution itself, laws in pursuance to it, and federal treaties the supreme law of the land, binding on state courts. The decision of a state court on a matter involving the supreme law cannot be final, because the judicial power of the United States extends specifically to all such cases. To enforce the supremacy clause, the Supreme Court must have appellate jurisdiction over state court decisions involving the supreme law. That a case involving the supreme law might arise in the state courts is obvious. Story gave the example of a contract case in which a party relied on the provision in Article I, section 10, barring state impairments of the obligations of a contract, and also the example of a criminal prosecution in which the defendant relied on the provision against ex post facto laws. The Constitution, he pointed out, was in fact designed to operate on the states "in their corporate capacities." It is "crowded" with provisions that "restrain or annul the sovereignty of the States," making the Court's exercise of appellate power over state acts unconstitutional no more in derogation of state sovereignty than those provisions or the principle of national supremacy. Not only would the federal system survive the exercise of federal judicial review; it could not function without such review. The law must be uniform "upon all subjects within the purview of the Constitution. Judges . . . in different States, might differently interpret a statute, or a treaty of the United States, or even the Constitution itself: If there were no revising authority to control these jarring and discordant judgments, and harmonize them into uniformity, the laws, the treaties and the Constitution of the United States would be different in different states," and might never have the same interpretation and efficacy in any two states.

Story's opinion is the linchpin of the federal system and of judicial nationalism. It remains the greatest argument for federal judicial review, though it by no means concluded the controversy. Virginia's hostility was so intense that a case was contrived in 1821 to allow the Supreme Court to restate the principles of *Martin*. As a matter of fact, though, federal judicial review and the constitutionality of section 25 remained bitterly contested topics to the eve of the Civil War.

—LEONARD W. LEVY

Bibliography

Beveridge, Albert J. (1916–1919). *The Life of John Marshall*. 4 vols. Vol. 4:145–167. Boston: Houghton Mifflin.

Crosskey, William Winslow (1953). *Politics and the Constitution*. 2 vols. Pages 785–817. Chicago: University of Chicago Press.

Haines, Charles Grove (1944). *The Role of the Supreme Court in American Government and Politics, 1789–1835*. Pages 340–351. Berkeley: University of California Press.

MARYLAND v. CRAIG

110 S.Ct. 3157 (1990)

This is another Sixth Amendment case in which the Supreme Court declined to follow the express words of the text. Although the

See also

Gibbons v. *Ogden*
Marbury v. *Madison*
McCulloch v. *Maryland*

Court engaged in what is usually described as judicial activism, it acted in a good cause and had precedent for its exception to the confrontation clause of the amendment. In every case in which hearsay evidence of any sort is admitted, the right of the accused to confront the witnesses against him or her becomes empty. In this case the Court held, 5–4, that the victim of child abuse may testify on closed circuit television to avoid the trauma of face-to-face confrontation with the accused.

Justice Sandra Day O'Connor, for the Court, reasoned that the state had a legitimate interest in protecting the child witness from psychological trauma. Face-to-face confrontation, assured by the text of the Sixth Amendment, turned out not to be an indispensable element of the confrontation guarantee.

Justice Antonin Scalia, an unlikely spokesman for the liberal Justices who joined him, rested his dissent on the clear language of the text. He accused the majority of a line of reasoning that "eliminates the right." But his view on the admission of hearsay ("not expressly excluded by the Confrontation Clause") would also justify admission of television testimony in the presence of defense counsel—because the amendment does not expressly exclude such a procedure. Scalia further questioned whether the evidence of a frightened child was reliable. But the state, not the Court, should decide whether

the child required protection. Scalia's final proposition, that the Court is not at liberty to ignore the confrontation clause, was at war with his several illustrations to the contrary.

—LEONARD W. LEVY

MASSES PUBLISHING COMPANY v. PATTEN

244 Fed. 535 (1917)

Judge Learned Hand's *Masses* opinion was one of the first federal opinions dealing with free speech. It remains influential even though Hand was reversed by the court of appeals and many years later himself abandoned his initial position. A postmaster had refused to accept the revolutionary monthly *The Masses* for mailing, citing the Espionage Act. Hand, sitting in a federal district court, interpreted the act not to apply to the magazine. He noted that any broad criticism of a government or its policies might hinder the war effort. Nevertheless, to suppress such criticism "would contradict the normal assumption of democratic government." Hand advanced a criminal incitement test. He conceded that words can be "the triggers of action" and, if they counseled violation of law, were not constitutionally protected. If, however, the words did not criminally incite and if the words stopped short "of urging upon

♦ **precedent**
A past decision, resolving issues of law, that is relied on in the decision of later cases.

A postmaster refused to accept the revolutionary monthly The Masses *for mailing, citing the Espionage Act.*

AMENDMENT VI

In all criminal prosecutions, the accused shall enjoy the right to a speedy and public trial, by an impartial jury of the State and district wherein the crime shall have been committed, which district shall have been previously ascertained by law, and to be informed of the nature and cause of the accusation; to be confronted with the witnesses against him; to have compulsory process for obtaining witnesses in his favor, and to have Assistance of Counsel for his defence.

See also
Clear and Present Danger
Freedom of Speech

The Supreme Court established its basic test for determining whether a particular procedure satisified the demands of due process.

others that it is their duty or their interest to resist the law . . . one should not be held to have attempted to cause its violation."

Hand's concentration on the advocacy content of the speech itself is thought by some to be more speech-protective than the clear and present danger rule's emphasis on the surrounding circumstances.

—MARTIN SHAPIRO

MATHEWS v. ELDRIDGE

424 U.S. 319 (1976)

Goldberg v. *Kelly* (1970) established a procedural due process right to an evidentiary hearing prior to the termination of state welfare benefits. Eldridge, whose Social Security disability benefits had been terminated without a prior hearing, could be pardoned for thinking that *Goldberg* controlled his case. In the event, a 6–2 Supreme Court explained how that view was mistaken, and established its basic test for determining whether a particular procedure satisfied the demands of due process.

The government conceded that the disability benefit was the sort of statutory "entitlement" that constituted a "property" interest protected by the due process guarantee. The government nonetheless argued that a *prior* hearing was not required; rather, due process was satisfied by a post-termination hearing at which the beneficiary might review the evidence, submit evidence of his own, and make arguments for reconsideration. Under the existing procedures, a beneficiary who prevailed in such a post-termination hearing was entitled to full retroactive relief. A majority of the Court agreed with the government's argument.

In a passage often quoted in later opinions, the Court set out the factors relevant to determining "the specific dictates of due process," once a "liberty" or "property" interest is impaired: "First, the private interest that will be affected by the official action; second, the risk of an erroneous deprivation of such interest through the procedures used, and the probable value, if any, of additional or substitute procedural safeguards; and finally, the Government's interest, including the function involved and the fiscal and administrative burdens that the additional or substitute procedural requirement would entail." Here, eligibility for disability benefits was not based on need, the standard for welfare eligibility in *Goldberg*. The Court assumed that a delayed payment would harm the typical disability beneficiary less than the typical welfare recipient. The medical question of disability, in contrast with the "need" question in a welfare case, was more focused and less susceptible to erroneous decision. The costs of pretermination hearings would be great. In short, the Court balanced its factors on the government's side.

The *Eldridge* due process calculus implies a strong presumption of constitutionality of whatever procedures a legislative body or government agency may choose to provide persons deprived of liberty or property. This presumption grows naturally out of the Court's limited choice of factors to be balanced, emphasizing material costs and benefits and ignoring the role of procedural fairness in maintaining each individual's sense of being a respected, participating citizen.

KENNETH L. KARST

MCCARDLE, EX PARTE

7 Wallace (74 U.S.) 506 (1869)

In *Ex Parte McCardle,* Chief Justice Salmon P. Chase, for the Supreme Court, validated congressional withdrawal of the Court's jurisdiction over appeals in habeas corpus proceedings under an 1867 statute but reasserted the Court's appellate authority in all other habeas cases.

See also

Goldberg v. *Kelly*

A federal circuit court remanded William McCardle, a Mississippi editor hostile to Republican Reconstruction policies, to military custody. When he appealed to the Supreme Court, Democrats predicted that the Justices would use his case as a vehicle to hold unconstitutional the trial of civilians by military commissions in southern states undergoing Reconstruction. Democrats inferred from the earlier decision of *Ex Parte Milligan* (1866) that a majority of the Court believed that military commissions could not constitutionally try civilians accused of crimes where courts were functioning in peacetime. Alarmed congressional Republicans, seeing this essential machinery of Reconstruction threatened, enacted a narrow statute in 1868 that revoked Supreme Court appellate authority in habeas cases under the Habeas Corpus Act of 1867.

In the *McCardle* opinion, Chief Justice Chase acknowledged the validity of this repeal under the "exceptions clause" of Article III, section 2, but pointedly reminded the bar that the 1868 repealer "does not affect the jurisdiction which was previously exercised." In *Ex Parte Yerger* (1869), the Court promptly affirmed this obiter dictum, accepting a habeas appeal under section 14 of the Judiciary Act of 1789 and rebuking Congress for the 1868 repealer. *McCardle* is therefore historically significant as evidence not of judicial submission to political threats during Reconstruction but rather of the Court's uninterrupted determination to preserve its role in questions of civil liberties.

McCardle remains important in the modern debate on congressional power to curtail the Supreme Court's appellate jurisdiction over cases raising controversial issues such as school busing, school prayer, and abortion. Some constitutional scholars have argued that Congress cannot erode the substance of the judicial power of the United States vested in the Supreme Court by Article III, section 1, through jurisdictional nibbling at the Court's appellate authority, but the extent to which Congress can affect substantive rights by jurisdictional excisions remains controverted.

—WILLIAM M. WIECEK

MCCLESKEY v. KEMP

481 U.S. 279 (1987)

McCleskey, a black Georgian, on being sentenced to death for the murder of a white person, sought a writ of habeas corpus on the claim that Georgia's capital-sentencing procedures violated the equal protection clause of the Fourteenth Amendment and the cruel and unusual punishment clause of the Eighth Amendment. He based his claim on "the Baldus study," a statistical examination of Georgia's more than 2,000 murder cases during the 1970s. The study showed a significant correlation between race and prosecutors' decisions to seek the death penalty and jurors' recommendations of the death penalty. For example, death was the sentence in 22 percent of the cases involving black defendants and white victims, in 8 percent of the cases involving white defendants and white victims, and in 3 percent of the cases involving white defendants and black victims. The Supreme Court held 5–4, that McCleskey did not show that Georgia had acted unconstitutionally in sentencing him to capital punishment.

The infirmity of McCleskey's argument, according to Justice Lewis F. Powell, for the Court, consisted in his failure to prove that he personally had been the target of racial discrimination or that the race of his victim had anything to do with his sentence. Anyone invoking the equal protection clause in a capital-sentencing case has the burden of showing that deliberate discrimination had a discriminatory effect "in *his* case." McCleskey's reliance on the Baldus study proved nothing with respect to him; moreover, every jury is unique, so that statistics concerning

McClesky based his claim on "the Baldus study," a statistical examination of Georgia's more than 2,000 murder cases during the 1970s.

many juries do not establish anything regarding a particular one.

McCleskey also argued that the state violated the equal protection clause by enacting the death penalty statute and retaining it despite its supposedly discriminatory application. Powell dismissed this argument because it had no support from proof that the legislature passed and kept a capital punishment act because of its racially discriminatory effect. The Court had previously held in *Gregg* v. *Georgia* (1976) that Georgia's capital-sentencing system could operate fairly.

The Court found McCleskey's Eighth Amendment argument no more persuasive. In *Gregg* it had ruled that the jury's discretion was controlled by clear and objective standards. The statute even required the trial court to review every sentence to determine whether it was imposed under the influence of prejudice, whether the evidence supported it, and whether the sentence was disproportionate to sentences in similar cases. Moreover, the judge had to consider the question whether race had any role in the trials. Absent proof that the Georgia system operated arbitrarily, McCleskey could not prove a violation of the Eighth Amendment by showing that other defendants had not received the death penalty.

McCleskey also argued that Georgia's system was arbitrarily applied "because racial considerations may influence capital sentencing decisions." Statistics, Powell replied, show only a "likelihood," which was insufficient to establish an "unacceptable risk" of racial prejudice.

Justice William J. Brennan, for the dissenters, argued the Eighth Amendment issue. He believed that a death sentence should be voided if there was a risk that it might have been imposed arbitrarily. Brennan believed that McCleskey should not have to prove discrimination in his own case; it was enough that the risk of prejudice, which Brennan believed was established by the statistical study, "might have infected the sentencing decision." McCleskey's claim warranted the Court's support because his was the first case challenging the system, not on how it might operate but "on empirical documentation of how it does operate." Black Georgians who killed whites were sentenced to death at nearly twenty-two times the rate of blacks who killed blacks and at more than seven times the rate of whites who kill blacks. This proved the point about disproportionate sentencing for the dissenters.

Justice Harry A. Blackmun, who also spoke for them, used similar evidence to maintain that Georgia's capital-sentencing procedures conflicted with the equal protection clause. Racial factors impermissibly affected the system from indictment to sentencing: "The Baldus study demonstrates that black persons are a distinct group that are singled out for a different treatment in the Georgia capital sentencing system." The burden of proof, Blackmun contended, should be on the state to demonstrate that racially neutral procedures yielded the racially skewed results shown by the study.

The Court's opinion is not easy to explain, unless one accepts the belief of dissenters that the Court did not wish to open a can of worms. McCleskey's claims taken to their logical conclusion undermined principles that buttressed the entire criminal justice system. His equal protection and "cruel and unusual punishment" arguments, if accepted, could have applied to punishments in noncapital cases and to procedures before sentencing and might have resulted in abolition of the death penalty as well.

—LEONARD W. LEVY

MCCULLOCH v. MARYLAND

4 Wheat. 316 (1819)

Speaking for a unanimous Supreme Court, Chief Justice John Marshall delivered an

See also

Capital Punishment

Equal Protection

Racial Discrimination

opinion upon which posterity has heaped lavish encomiums. James Bradley Thayer thought "there is nothing so fine as the opinion in *McCulloch* v. *Maryland.*" Albert Beveridge placed it "among the very first of the greatest judicial utterances of all time," while William Draper Lewis described it as "perhaps the most celebrated judicial utterance in the annals of the English speaking world." Such estimates spring from the fact that Marshall's vision of nationalism in time became a reality, to some extent because of his vision. Beveridge was not quite wrong in saying that the *McCulloch* opinion "so decisively influenced the growth of the Nation that, by many, it is considered as only second in importance to the Constitution itself." On the other hand, Marshall the judicial statesman engaged in a judicial coup, as his panegyrical biographer understood. To appreciate Marshall's achievement in *McCulloch* and the intense opposition that his opinion engendered in its time, one must also bear in mind that however orthodox his assumptions and doctrines are in the twentieth century, they were in their time unorthodox. With good reason Beveridge spoke of Marshall's "sublime audacity," the "extreme radicalism" of his constitutional theories, and the fact that he "rewrote the fundamental law of the Nation," a proposition to which Beveridge added that it would be more accurate to state that he made of the written instrument "a living thing, capable of growth, capable of keeping pace with the advancement of the American people and ministering to their changing necessities."

The hysterical denunciations of the *McCulloch* opinion by the aged and crabbed Thomas Jefferson, by the frenetically embittered Spencer Roane, and by that caustic apostle of localism, John Taylor, may justly be discounted, but not the judgment of the cool and prudent "Father of the Constitution," James Madison. On receiving Roane's "Hampden" essays assaulting *McCulloch*, Madison ignored the threat of state nullification and the repudiation of judicial review, but he agreed with Roane that the Court's opinion tended, in Madison's words, "to convert a limited into an unlimited Government." Madison deplored Marshall's "latitude in expounding the Constitution which seems to break down the landmarks intended by a specification of the Powers of Congress, and to substitute for a definite connection between means and ends, a Legislative discretion as to the former to which no practical limit can be assigned." Few if any of the friends of the Constitution, declared Madison, anticipated "a rule of construction . . . as broad & as pliant as what has occurred," and he added that the Constitution would probably not have been ratified if the powers that Marshall claimed for the national government had been known in 1788–89. Madison's opinion suggests how far Marshall and the Court had departed from the intentions of the Framers and makes understandable the onslaught that *McCulloch* provoked. Although much of that onslaught was a genuine

"FATHER OF THE CONSTITUTION"

James Madison felt that the Court's opinion in McCulloch *tended "to convert a limited into an unlimited Government." (Corbis/Bettmann)*

Albert Beveridge said the McCulloch *opinion "so decisively influenced the growth of the Nation that, by many, it is conisdered as only second in importance to the Constitution itself."*

concern for the prostration of states' rights before a consolidating nationalism, Taylor hit the nail on the head for the older generation of Jeffersonians when he wrote that *McCulloch* reared "a monied interest."

The case, after all, was decided in the midst of a depression popularly thought to have been caused by the Bank of the United States, a private corporation chartered by Congress; and *McCulloch* was a decision in favor of the hated bank and against the power of a state to tax its branch operations. The constitutionality of the power of Congress to charter a bank had been ably debated in Congress and in Washington's cabinet in 1791, when Alexander Hamilton proposed the bank bill. Constitutional debate mirrored party politics, and the Federalists had the votes. The Court never passed judgment on the constitutionality of the original Bank of the United States Act, though it had a belated opportunity. In 1809 a case came before the Court that was remarkably similar to *McCulloch:* state officials, acting under a state statute taxing the branches of the bank, forcibly carried away from its vaults money to pay the state tax. In *Bank of the United States* v. *Deveaux* (1809), Marshall for the Court, deftly avoiding the questions that he confronted in *McCulloch,* found that the parties lacked the diversity of citizenship that would authorize jurisdiction. With the bank's twenty-year charter nearing expiration, a decision in favor of the bank's constitutionality might look like pro-federalist politics by the Court, embroiling it in a dispute with President Madison, who was on record as opposing the bank's constitutionality, and with Congress, which supported Madison's policies.

The United States fought the War of 1812 without the bank to help manage its finances, and the results were disastrous. The war generated a new wave of nationalism and a change of opinion in Madison's party. In 1816 President Madison signed into law a bill chartering a second Bank of the United States, passed by Congress with the support

of young nationalists like Henry Clay and John C. Calhoun and opposed by a Federalist remnant led by young Daniel Webster. The political world was turned upside down. The bank's tight credit policies contributed to a depression, provoking many states to retaliate against "the monster monopoly." Two states prohibited the bank from operating within their jurisdictions; six others taxed the operations of the bank's branches within their jurisdictions. The constitutionality of Maryland's tax was the issue in *McCulloch,* as well as the constitutionality of the act of Congress incorporating the bank.

Six of the greatest lawyers of the nation, including Webster, William Pinkney, and Luther Martin, argued the case over a period of nine days, and only three days later Marshall delivered his thirty-six-page opinion for a unanimous Court. He had written much of it in advance, thus prejudging the case, but in a sense his career was a preparation for the case. As Roane conceded, Marshall was "a man of profound legal attainments" writing "upon a subject which has employed his thoughts, his tongue, and his pen, as a politican, and an historian for more than thirty years." And he had behind him all five Jeffersonian-Republican members of the Court.

Arguing that Congress had no authority to incorporate a bank, counsel for Maryland claimed that the Constitution had originated with the states, which alone were truly sovereign, and that the national government's powers must be exercised in subordination to the states. Marshall grandiloquently turned these propositions around. When Beveridge said that Marshall the solider wrote *McCulloch* and that his opinion echoed "the blast of the bugle of Valley Forge" (where Marshall served), he had a point. Figuratively, Old Glory and the bald eagle rise up from the opinion—to anyone stirred by a nationalist sentiment. The Constitution, declared Marshall, had been submitted to conventions of the people, from whom it derives its authority. The government formed by the Constitution proceeded "directly from the people" and in the words of the preamble was "ordained and established" in their name, and it binds the states. Marshall drove home that theme repeatedly. "The government of the Union . . . is, emphatically, and truly, a government of the people. In form and in substance it emanates from them. Its powers are granted by them, and are to be exercised directly on them, and for their benefit." A bit later Marshall declared that the government of the Union though limited in its powers "is supreme within its sphere of action. . . . It is the government of all; its powers are delegated by all; it represents all, and acts for all." And it necessarily restricts its subordinate members, because the Constitution and federal laws constitute the supreme law of the land. Reading this later, Abraham Lincoln transmuted it into "a government of the people, by the people, for the people."

Marshall's opinion is a state paper, like the Declaration of Independence, the Constitution itself, or the Gettysburg Address, the sort of document that puts itself beyond analysis or criticism. But there were constitutional issues to be resolved, and Marshall had not yet touched them. Madison agreed with Roane that "the occasion did not call for the general and abstract doctrine interwoven with the decision of the particular case," but *McCulloch* has survived and moved generations of Americans precisely because Marshall saw that the "general and abstract" were embedded in the issues, and he made it seem that the life of the nation was at stake on their resolution in the grandest way.

Disposing affirmatively of the question of whether Congress could charter a bank was a foregone conclusion, flowing naturally from unquestioned premises. Though the power of establishing corporations is not among the enumerated powers, seeing the Constitution "whole," as Marshall saw it, led him to the doctrine of implied powers. The Constitution ought not have the "prolixity of a legal code"; rather, it marked only "great outlines,"

with the result that implied powers could be "deduced." Levying and collecting taxes, borrowing money, regulating commerce, supporting armies, and conducting war are among the major enumerated powers; in addition, the Constitution vests in Congress the power to pass all laws "necessary and proper" to carry into execution the powers enumerated. These powers implied the means necessary to execute them. A banking corporation was a means of effectuating designated ends. The word "necessary" did not mean indispensably necessary; it did not refer to a means without which the power granted would be nugatory, its object unattainable. "Necessary" means "useful," "needful," "conducive to," thus allowing Congress a latitude of choice in attaining its legitimate ends. The Constitution's Framers knew the difference between "necessary" and "absolutely necessary," a phrase they used in Article I, section 10, clause 2. They inserted the necessary and proper clause in a Constitution "intended to endure for ages to come, and, consequently, to be adapted to the various crises of human affairs." They intended Congress to have "ample means" for carrying its express powers into effect. The "narrow construction" advocated by Maryland would abridge, even "annihilate," Congress's discretion in selecting its means. Thus, the test for determining the constitutionality of an act of Congress was: "Let the end be legitimate, let it be within the scope of the Constitution, and all means which are appropriate, which are plainly adapted to that end, which are not prohibited, but consist with the letter and spirit of the Constitution, are constitutional." That formula yielded the conclusion that the act incorporating the bank was valid.

Such was the broad construction that "deduced" implied powers, shocking even Madison. The Court, he thought, had relinquished control over Congress. He might have added, as John Taylor did, that Marshall neglected to explain how and why a private bank chartered by Congress was necessary, even in a

loose sense, to execute the enumerated powers. In *Construction Construed* (1820) Taylor gave five chapters to *McCulloch*, exhibiting the consequences of Marshall's reasoning. Congress might legislate on local agriculture and manufactures, because they were necessary to war. Roads were still more necessary than banks for collecting taxes. And:

> *Taverns are very necessary or convenient for the offices of the army. . . . But horses are undoubtedly more necessary for the conveyance of the mail and for war, than roads, which may be as convenient to assailants as defenders; and therefore the principle of implied power of legislation will certainly invest Congress with a legislative power over horses. In short, this mode of construction completely establishes the position, that Congress may pass any internal law whatsoever in relation to things, because there is nothing with which war, commerce and taxation may not be closely or remotely connected.*

All of which supported Taylor's contention that Marshall's doctrine of implied powers would destroy the states and lead to a government of unlimited powers, because "as ends may be made to beget means, so means may be made to beget ends, until the co-habitation shall rear a progeny of unconstitutional bastards, which were not begotten by the people."

Marshall's reasoning with respect to the second question in the case incited less hostility, though not by much. Assuming Congress could charter the bank, could a state tax its branch? Marshall treated the bank as a branch or "instrument" of the United States itself, and relying on the supremacy clause (Article VI), he concluded that if the states could tax one instrument to any degree, they could tax every other instrument as well—the mails, the mint, even the judicial process. The result would cripple the government, "prostrating it at the foot of the States." Again, he was deducing from general principles in or-

der to defeat the argument that nothing in the Constitution prohibits state taxes on congressionally chartered instruments. Congress's power to create, Marshall reasoned, implied a power to preserve. A state power to tax was a power to destroy, incompatible with the national power to create and preserve. Where such repugnancy exists, the national power, which is supreme, must control. "The question is, in truth, a question of supremacy," with the result that the Court necessarily found the state act unconstitutional.

That was Marshall's *McCulloch* opinion. Roane and Taylor publicly excoriated it, and Jefferson spurred them on, telling Roane, who rejected even federal judicial review, "I go further than you do." The Virginia legislature repudiated implied powers and recommended an amendment to the Constitution "creating a tribunal for the decision of all questions, in which the powers and authorities of the general government and those of the States, where they are in conflict, shall be decided." Marshall was so upset by the public criticism that he was driven for the first and only time to reply in a series of newspaper articles. Still, Ohio allied itself with Virginia and literally defied, even nullified, the decision in *McCulloch*. Pennsylvania, Indiana, Illinois, and Tennessee also conducted a guerrilla war against the Court, and Congress seriously debated measures to curb its powers. Fortunately the common enemies of the Court shared no common policies. *McCulloch* prevailed in the long run, providing, together with *Gibbons* v. *Ogden* (1824), the constitutional wherewithal to meet unpredictable crises even to our time. *McCulloch* had unforeseen life-giving powers. Marshall, Beveridge's "supreme conservative," laid the constitutional foundations for the New Deal and the Welfare State.

—LEONARD W. LEVY

Bibliography

Beveridge, Albert J. (1916–1919). *The Life of John Marshall.* 4 vols. Vol. 4:283–339. Boston: Houghton Mifflin.

See also

Gibbons v. *Ogden*

Marshall, John

Haines, Charles Grove (1944). *The Role of the Supreme Court in American Government and Politics, 1789–1835.* Pages 351–368. Berkeley: University of California Press.

Warren, Charles (1923). *The Supreme Court in United States History.* 3 vols. Vol. 1:499–540. Boston: Little, Brown.

MCGRAIN v. DAUGHERTY

273 U.S. 135 (1927)

In *Kilbourn* v. *Thompson* (1881) the Supreme Court had held that because Article I of the Constitution assigned Congress no power beyond the lawmaking power, Congress might constitutionally investigate "the private affairs of individuals" only for the purpose of gathering information to write new legislation. *McGrain* restated this requirement of legislative purpose, but rejected, 8–0, a challenge to the contempt conviction of the brother of Harry M. Daugherty who had failed to appear before a Senate committee investigating the failure of former attorney general Daugherty to prosecute the malefactors in the Teapot Dome scandal.

In reality the investigation was not aimed at developing new legislation but at exposing malfeasance in the executive branch, a task that might have been deemed constitutionally appropriate for Congress if it were not for the simplistic *Kilbourn* theory. The gap between theory and reality was bridged by the creation of a presumption that congressional investigations had a legislative purpose, a presumption that was not to be overcome simply by showing that an investigation also had a purpose of public exposure.

The *McGrain* technique of requiring a legislative purpose for a congressional investigation, and then invoking a presumption of legislative purpose even when exposure was clearly a principal motive, had important consequences in post–World War II cases

HELD IN CONTEMPT

McGrain *upheld the contempt conviction of Harry M. Daugherty's brother, as well as Congress's power to investigate individuals only for the purpose of gathering information to write new legislation. (Corbis/Bettmann)*

where anticommunist investigating committees were seeking to punish leftist speakers by public exposure precisely because the First Amendment prohibited Congress from passing legislation punishing such speech. The Court invoked the presumption of legislative purpose both to blind itself to the actual "exposure for exposure's sake" being conducted and to establish a congressional interest in lawmaking that outweighed whatever incidental infringement on speech the Court was willing to see.

—MARTIN SHAPIRO

McGrain had important consequences in post–World War II cases where anticommunist investigating committees sought to punish leftist speakers by public exposure.

MCNABB-MALLORY RULE

Partly in response to the problem posed by the voluntariness test, the Supreme Court made an unexpected departure from that test in *McNabb* v. *United States* (1943) and *Mallory* v. *United States* (1957). Under the "McNabb-Mallory Rule," a confession obtained

See also

Kilbourn v. Thompson

*The Court decided
that due process of
law does not
guarantee trial by
jury to juvenile
offenders.*

by law enforcement officers during a period of unnecessary delay in bringing an arrested person before a magistrate for arraignment was inadmissible in federal prosecutions. The rule was based not on constitutional grounds but on the Court's supervisory authority over the administration of criminal justice in the federal courts. The rule created more problems than it attempted to solve, and in 1968, Congress abolished it.

In *McNabb*, five brothers were arrested for murder and held in barren detention cells for forty-eight hours. Isolated from friends and family, and without the assistance of counsel, they were repeatedly interrogated until confessions were obtained. Only after they confessed were they taken before a magistrate for arraignment. The confessions were admitted into evidence at trial and the McNabbs were convicted.

The Court, with only Justice Stanley F. Reed dissenting, reversed the convictions on the ground that they were unlawfully obtained during a period of prolonged custodial delay. Federal laws in effect at the time of the Court's decision required officers to take an arrested person "immediately" before a magistrate for arraignment. At arraignment, the magistrate advises the defendant of the charges against him, of his constitutional rights, and sets a preliminary hearing date at which the government must show legal cause for the detention.

Justice Felix Frankfurter devoted much of his opinion for the Court to an analysis of the policies behind the immediate arraignment laws. He concluded that they were intended to protect the rights of arrested persons and to deter the police from secret third-degree interrogation of persons not yet arraigned.

Finding that the officers who arrested the McNabbs had acted in willful disobedience of the laws requiring immediate arraignment, the Court suppressed the confessions. Suppression, Frankfurter explained, would promote the policies behind the laws and ensure the fair and effective administration of the federal criminal justice system by disallowing convictions based on unfair police procedures.

Two years after *McNabb*, Congress adopted Rule 5(a) of the Federal Rules of Criminal Procedure. The rule required that an arrested person be taken, "without unnecessary delay," before the nearest available commissioner or any other nearby officer em-

MCKEIVER v. PENNSYLVANIA

403 U.S. 528 (1971)

Although *In re Gault* (1967) extended some basic procedural rights to juvenile offenders, young people continued to be tried in most states before judges who exercised great discretion, supposedly to protect juveniles. McKeiver, a juvenile defendant, faced possible incarceration for five years and requested trial by jury, which the state denied. By a 6–3 vote, the Supreme Court decided that due process of law does not guarantee trial by jury to juvenile offenders. Justice Harry Blackmun for a plurality of four wrote an opinion based on the unrealistic premise that the juvenile system is fundamentally sound and enlightened, but he did not explain how it assured fundamental fairness. Justice John Marshall Harlan found Blackmun's opinion romantic but concurred nevertheless because he still opposed *Duncan* v. *Louisiana* (1968), which extended trial by jury to the states. Justice William J. Brennan concurred because he thought, mistakenly, that publicity served as a check on juvenile court judges. Justices William O. Douglas, Hugo L. Black, and Thurgood Marshall dissented. *McKeiver* short-circuited expectations that the Court would require essentially all the rights of the criminally accused for juveniles who commit adult crimes and face the prospect of serious punishment.

—LEONARD W. LEVY

powered to commit persons charged with offenses against the laws of the United States. The rule, by failing to include remedies for its violation, left intact the *McNabb* mandate that confessions obtained during a period of unlawful detention be suppressed. Any questions regarding the continuing viability of the *McNabb* rule were put to rest by the Court's opinion in *Mallory*.

Mallory was arrested with two other suspects on rape charges. Although the police had sufficient evidence to consider Mallory the prime suspect, he was not arraigned until ten hours after his arrest, during which time he was continually interrogated and finally signed a written confession. At trial, the signed confession was introduced into evidence; Mallory was convicted and received the death sentence.

Frankfurter delivered the opinion of a unanimous Court, which held the confession inadmissible because Mallory had not been arraigned without unnecessary delay as required by Rule 5(a). The Court's interpretation of Rule 5(a) was based on the principles announced earlier in the *McNabb* decision. Delays in arraignment must be prevented in order to prevent abusive and unlawful law enforcement practices aimed at obtaining confessions of guilt from suspects in custody who have not been informed by a judicial officer of the charges against them or of their constitutional rights.

After *Mallory* the law prevailing in the federal courts, commonly referred to as the "McNabb-Mallory Rule," was that any confession made by a suspect under arrest, in violation of Rule 5(a), was inadmissible in evidence. The problem with the McNabb-Mallory Rule was that it operated arbitrarily to exclude from evidence otherwise free and voluntary confessions merely because of delay in arraignment. In other words, the United States Supreme Court had failed to consider the obvious: a delayed arraignment does not imply the involuntariness of a confession.

Criticized as illogical and unrealistic, the McNabb-Mallory Rule was abolished in 1968 when Congress enacted Title II of the Omnibus Crime Control and Safe Streets Act. The act provides in part that confessions shall not be inadmissible solely because of delay in arraignment, if they are voluntary and made within six hours of arrest or during a delay in arraignment that is reasonable, considering the transportation problems in getting a defendant before a magistrate. Thus, the voluntary nature of the confession is the test of its admissibility, and delay in arraignment is only one factor for the judge to consider.

—WENDY E. LEVY

Bibliography

Stephens, Otis H., Jr. (1973). *The Supreme Court and Confessions of Guilt.* Pages 63–89. Knoxville: University of Tennessee Press.

MEMOIRS v. MASSACHUSETTS

383 U.S. 413 (1966)

Nine years after *Roth* v. *United States*, still unable to agree upon a constitutional definition of obscenity, the Supreme Court reversed a state court determination that John Cleland's *Memoirs of a Woman of Pleasure*, commonly known as *Fanny Hill*, was obscene. The three-Justice plurality opinion, written by Justice William J. Brennan, held that the constitutional test for obscenity was: "(a) the dominant theme of the material taken as a whole appeals to a prurient interest in sex; (b) the material is patently offensive because it affronts contemporary community standards relating to the description or representation of sexual matters; and (c) the material is utterly without redeeming social value."

McNabb deemed a confession obtained by law officers during a period of unnecessary delay in bringing an arrested person before a magistrate for arraignment inadmissible in federal prosecutions.

The Court reversed a state court decision that John Cleland's Fanny Hill was obscene.

See also

Jacobellis v. *Ohio*

Obscenity

Roth v. *United States*

*The Supreme Court
issues thousands of
memorandum orders
each year, some
effectively deciding
cases.*

Despite an obiter dictum in *Jacobellis* v. *Ohio* (1964), it was believed—and the Massachusetts courts had held—that *Roth* did not require unqualified worthlessness before a book might be deemed obscene. Justice Brennan twisted the *Roth* reasoning (that obscenity was unprotected because it was utterly worthless) into a constitutional test that was virtually impossible to meet under criminal standards of proof. Thus a finding of obscenity would become rare, even where the requisite prurient interest appeal and offensiveness could be demonstrated.

The Massachusetts courts had tried the book in the abstract; a host of literary experts testified to its social value. The circumstances of the book's production, sale, and publicity were not admitted. Justice Brennan noted that evidence that distributors commercially exploited *Fanny Hill* solely for its prurient appeal could have justified a finding, based on the purveyor's own evaluation, that *Fanny Hill* was utterly without redeeming social importance.

Justices Hugo L. Black, William O. Douglas, and Potter J. Stewart concurred in the result, Black and Douglas adhering to their view that obscenity is protected expression. Stewart reiterated his view that the First Amendment protected all but "hard-core pornography."

Justice Tom C. Clark, dissenting, rejected the importation of the "utterly without redeeming social value" standard into the obscenity test, which he believed would give the "smut artist free rein." Reacting against the continuous flow of pornographic materials to the Supreme Court, he reasserted that the Court should apply a "sufficient evidence" standard of review of lower courts' obscenity decisions.

Justice John Marshall Harlan, dissenting, argued that although the federal government could constitutionally proscribe only hard-core pornography, the states could prohibit material under any criteria rationally related to accepted notions of obscenity.

Justice Byron R. White, also dissenting, argued that *Roth* counseled examination of the predominant theme of the material, not resort to minor themes of passages of literary worth to redeem obscene works from condemnation.

The *Memoirs* notion that the government must prove a work to utterly lack social value—never adopted by a majority—was expressly rejected by the Court in *Miller* v. *California* (1973).

—KIM MCLANE WARDLAW

MEMORANDUM ORDER

Most orders of any court are not accompanied by opinions, but are simply stated in memorandum form. The Supreme Court issues thousands of such memorandum orders each year, granting or denying such requests as applications for review, applications for permission to appear *in forma pauperis*, applications for permission to file briefs amici curiae, or petitions for rehearing.

Some memorandum orders effectively decide cases; the denial of a petition for certiorari is one example, and another is the dismissal of an appeal "for want of a substantial federal question." Occasionally the Court summarily affirms the decision of a lower court, issuing no opinion but only a memorandum order. The denial of certiorari generally has little force as a precedent; however, both lower courts and commentators do draw conclusions concerning the Court's view when they see a consistent pattern of refusal to review lower court decisions reaching the same conclusion. The summary affirmance of a decision in a memorandum order does establish a precedent, but the precedent is limited to the points necessarily decided by the lower court, and does not extend to the reasoning in that court's opinion. The practice of deciding major issues through memorandum orders is often criticized on the ground that decisions will not be understood as principled if they are not explained.

—KENNETH L. KARST

Bibliography

Brown, Ernest J. (1958). The Supreme Court, 1957 Term—Foreword: Process of Law. *Harvard Law Review* 72:77–95.

MERE EVIDENCE RULE

A search warrant must identify the place to be searched and the items to be seized. Such items may include fruits or instrumentalities of crime (such as stolen money or burglars' tools) or contraband (such as illegal drugs). In *Gouled* v. *United States* (1921) the Supreme Court held that search warrants could not issue to seize mere evidence of crime.

In *Warden* v. *Hayden* (1967), however, the Court held that warrants could issue for mere evidence so long as there was a "nexus" between the evidence and the criminal behavior. *Zurcher* v. *Stanford Daily* (1978) illustrates the effect of the rule's abandonment. The Stanford University student newspaper published photographs of a campus disturbance between the police and demonstrators. Because the police observed only two of their assailants, a warrant was obtained for a search of the newspaper's offices. The warrant affidavit did not allege any involvement in the unlawful acts by newspaper staff members. During the search, police examined the paper's photographic labs, files, desks, and waste paper baskets. Since no new evidence was discovered, no items were taken.

One commentator has summarized the "mere evidence rule" after *Zurcher* as follows: *Zurcher* represents a case in which none of the items searched for by the police was a fruit or instrumentality of a crime, or contraband. Under the pre-*Hayden* rule, the warrant used in *Zurcher* could not have been is-

sued. Yet the present broad rule is so well established that the Supreme Court's majority opinion did not even discuss the issue.

—CHARLES H. WHITEBREAD

Bibliography

Whitebread, Charles H. (1980). *Criminal Procedure.* Mineola, N.Y.: Foundation Press.

MERITOR SAVINGS BANK v. MECHELLE VINSON

477 U.S. 57 (1986)

This Supreme Court decision attempted for the first time to define what standard a court should use to determine sexual harassment under Title VII of the Civil Rights Act of 1964. The two main issues were whether a plaintiff's claim of sexual harassment could succeed if based on psychological aspects without tangible loss of an economic character, and whether employers are absolutely liable in cases of sexual harassment by supervisors. Mechelle Vinson was an employee at Meritor Savings Bank under the supervision of the vice president and branch manager, Sidney Taylor, and Vinson had earned various promotions on the basis of merit. Vinson testified that Taylor invited her to dinner, repeatedly proposed sexual relations, leading to forty or fifty occasions of intercourse, fondled her in front of employees, followed her into the women's restroom, exposed himself to her, and raped her on several occasions. At first Vinson resisted but ceased to do so out of fear of losing her job. She testified she never reported the incidents or used the bank's complaint procedure out of fear and because she would have to make the claim directly to her supervisor, Taylor. He stopped sexually harassing her when Vinson began dating someone steadily. She was fired for taking an excessive leave of absence.

The bank argued that the prohibitions of Title VII of the Civil Rights Act were limited to discrimination causing economic or tangible loss, not psychological harm.

See also

Warden v. *Hayden*

Zurcher v. *Stanford Daily*

Subsequently, she filed a sexual harassment claim for violations of Title VII. Both the bank and Taylor denied Vinson's accusations and insisted that the claim arose from a business-related dispute. The bank asserted that if Vinson's claims were true, the supervisor's activities were unknown to the bank's executive managers and engaged in without its consent. The federal district court held that for a sexual harassment claim to prevail the plaintiff had to demonstrate a tangible economic loss. The court also held that the bank was not liable for the misconduct of its supervisors. On both counts the circuit court reversed in favor of Vinson. The bank appealed to the Supreme Court, which in a unanimous decision decided for Vinson on the first point, but held that employers were not automatically liable for sexual harassment by supervisors. Similarly, however, absence of notice to an employer did not insulate the business from liability for the acts of supervisors. In such cases the issue was one of fact, which required meeting a burden of proof. The case placed sexual harassment resulting from a hostile work environment on an equal footing with sexual harassment resulting in the loss of job or promotion. The case put employers on notice that they must review supervisors' conduct because mere absence of notice of improper conduct is no longer a defense.

—TONY FREYER

METRO BROADCASTING, INC. v. F.C.C.

110 S. Ct. 2997 (1990)

In this decision the Supreme Court, 5–4, upheld two aspects of an affirmative action program approved by Congress in the area of broadcasting. In 1986 members of racial and ethnic minorities, who constitute about one-fifth of the nation's population, owned just over two percent of the radio and television broadcasting stations licensed by the Federal Communications Commission (FCC). Two FCC policies aim to bring a greater racial and ethnic diversity to broadcast ownership. First, the FCC considers minority ownership as one factor among many in making comparative judgments among applicants for new licenses. Second, the FCC seeks to increase minority ownership through a "distress sale" policy. Normally, a licensee cannot transfer its license during the time when the FCC is considering whether the license should be revoked. As an exception to this policy, such a broadcaster may sell its license before the revocation hearing to a minority-controlled broadcaster that meets the FCC's qualifications, provided that the price does not exceed seventy-five percent of the station's value. Congress, in appropriating money for the FCC, ordered that these programs be continued.

In *Metro Broadcasting* both of these policies were challenged as denials of the guarantee of equal protection that the Court has recognized in the Fifth Amendment's due process clause. Writing for the majority, Justice William J. Brennan strongly emphasized Congress's adoption of the two minority ownership policies. The proper standard of review for congressional affirmative action was not strict scrutiny but the intermediate standard that the Court has previously used, for example, in cases of sex discrimination. This standard requires that Congress have an "important" purpose for its legislation and that the racial classification be "substantially related" to achieving that purpose.

For the majority of the Court, the FCC's policies easily satisfied this test. The interest in diversifying broadcast programming accorded with the long-recognized policy of the Federal Communications Act to ensure the presentation of a wide variety of views. The Supreme Court had recognized this

See also

Civil Rights

Sex Discrimination

need in the context of the scarcity of electronic frequencies in *Red Lion Broadcasting Co. v. F.C.C.* (1969), sustaining the FCC's "fairness doctrine." The FCC had quite reasonably determined that racial and ethnic diversity in broadcast ownership would promote diversity in programming, and Congress had repeatedly endorsed this view by rejecting proposals that would arguably reduce opportunities for minority ownership, such as a proposal to deregulate broadcasting. The Court, said Justice Brennan, must give great weight to the joint administrative-congressional determination of a connection between minority ownership and programming diversity. The minority ownership policies did not rest on impermissible stereotyping, but on the need to diversify programming. The FCC had considered other means of achieving this diversification and had reasonably concluded that these means were relatively ineffective. The burden imposed by these two policies on nonminority applicants for broadcast licenses was not impermissibly great.

Justice Sandra Day O'Connor wrote for the four dissenters. Arguing that any race-conscious program must pass the test of strict scrutiny, she rejected the claim that broadcasting diversity was a compelling state interest or even an important one. Furthermore, the policies were not narrowly tailored; they assumed a connection between minority ownership and program content, and they ignored other race-neutral means of assuring programming to serve a diversity of audiences, such as direct regulation of programming.

The importance of *Metro Broadcasting* as a precedent was short-lived. Just five years later in *Adarand* v. *Pena* (1995) the Court ruled that federal affirmative action programs were subject to strict scrutiny and that *Metro,* to the extent it was inconsistent with that holding, was overruled.

—KENNETH L. KARST

Bibliography

Eule, Julian N. (1990). Promoting Speaker Diversity: Austin and *Metro Broadcasting.* *Supreme Court Review* 1990: 105–132.

METROPOLITAN LIFE INSURANCE CO. v. WARD

470 U.S. (1985)

This decision departed from a long series of Supreme Court decisions upholding the constitutionality of state taxes against attack under the equal protection clause. Alabama taxed the gross premiums of insurance companies by imposing a 1 percent tax on companies organized in Alabama, and a tax of 3 percent or 4 percent on companies organized in other states. In an opinion by Justice Lewis F. Powell, the Supreme Court held, 5–4, that this discrimination failed even the rational basis test, because its only articulated purpose—to create a tax advantage for domestic economic interests over out-of-state interests—was illegitimate. Congress, in its 1945 act permitting the states to discriminate in favor of local insurance companies, had insulated such laws from attack under the commerce clause, but had not purported to speak to any issue of equal protection.

In an unusual division of the Court, Justice Sandra Day O'Connor dissented, joined by Justices William J. Brennan, Thurgood Marshall, and William H. Rehnquist. Justice O'Connor pointed to previous decisions recognizing the legitimacy of state efforts to promote domestic industry, and made the unanswerable point that Alabama's tax scheme was rationally related to such a purpose. Furthermore, she said, Congress in 1945 understood that it was authorizing laws of this very kind. She also accused the majority of reviving active judicial scrutiny of state

In an unusual division of the Court, Sandra Day O'Connor dissented, joined by Justices Brennan, Marshall, and Rehnquist.

economic regulation. Although the latter prediction seems unlikely to come true, the fear that it expresses is not dispelled by the majority's opinion.

—KENNETH L. KARST

Bibliography

Cohen, William (1985). Federalism in Equality Clothing: A Comment on *Metropolitan Life Insurance Company v. Ward*. *Stanford Law Review* 38:1–27.

MEYER v. NEBRASKA

262 U.S. 390 (1923)

Meyer represented an early use of substantive due process doctrine to defend personal liberties, as distinguished from economic ones. Nebraska, along with other states, had prohibited the teaching of modern foreign languages to grade school children. Meyer, who taught German in a Lutheran school, was convicted under this law. The Supreme Court, 7–2, held the law unconstitutional. Justice James C. McReynolds wrote for the Court in *Meyer* and in four companion cases from Iowa, Ohio, and Nebraska. Justice Oliver Wendell Holmes, joined by Justice George Sutherland, dissented in all but the Ohio cases.

McReynolds began with a broad reading of the "liberty" protected by the Fourteenth Amendment: "It denotes not merely freedom from bodily restraint, but also the right of the individual to contract, to engage in any of the common occupations of life, to acquire useful knowledge, to marry, establish a home and bring up children, to worship God according to the dictates of his own conscience, and, generally, to enjoy those privileges long recognized at common law as essential to the orderly pursuit of happiness by free men." State regulation of this liberty must be reasonably related to a proper state objective; the legisla-

ture's view of reasonableness was "subject to supervision by the courts." The legislative purpose to promote assimilation and "civic development" was readily appreciated, given the hostility toward our adversaries in World War I. However, "no adequate reason" justified interfering with Meyer's liberty to teach or the liberty of parents to employ him during a "time of peace and domestic tranquillity."

Holmes concurred in the Ohio cases, because Ohio had singled out the German language for suppression. But he could not say it was unreasonable for a state to forbid teaching foreign languages to young children as a means of assuring that all citizens might "speak a common tongue." Because "men might reasonably differ" on the question, the laws were not unconstitutional.

Meyer was thus a child of *Lochner* v. *New York* (1905), taking *Lochner*'s broad view of the judicial role in protecting liberty. Yet, although substantive due process has lost its former vitality in the field of economic regulation, *Meyer*'s precedent remains vigorous in the defense of personal liberty. *Meyer* was reaffirmed in *Griswold* v. *Connecticut* (1965), *Loving* v. *Virginia* (1967), and *Zablocki* v. *Redhail* (1978), three modern decisions protecting the freedom of intimate association.

—KENNETH L. KARST

MIAMI HERALD PUBLISHING COMPANY v. TORNILLO

418 U.S. 241 (1974)

It may be argued that freedom of speech is meaningless unless it includes access to the mass media so that the speech will be heard. Here the Supreme Court unanimously struck

---

Nebraska, along with other states, had prohibited the teaching of modern foreign languages to grade school children.

See also

Griswold v. *Connecticut*

Lochner v. *New York*

Loving v. *Virginia*

Zablocki v. *Redhail*

down a Florida statute requiring a newspaper to provide a political candidate free space to reply to its attacks on his personal character. Noting that the statute infringed upon "editorial control and judgment," the Court held that "any [governmental] compulsion to publish that which 'reason' tells . . . [the editors] . . . should not be published is unconstitutional."

Tornillo was a major blow to proponents of a right of access. When compared to *Red Lion Broadcasting Co.* v. *F.C.C.* (1969), it raises the question of whether the First Amendment provides greater protection for the press than for the electronic media. In light of the large number of one-newspaper towns, the scarcity rationale for allowing government to compel access to broadcast channels would seem to apply even more strongly to the print media. Ultimately the distinction may be between the public ownership of the channels and the private ownership of the print media. If so, the Court has not explained or defended this linking of speech rights to property rights.

—MARTIN SHAPIRO

MICHAEL M. v. SUPERIOR COURT

450 U.S. 464 (1981)

A boy of seventeen was convicted of rape under a California statute making it a crime for a male to have intercourse with a female under eighteen; the girl's age was sixteen. A fragmented Supreme Court voted 5–4 to uphold the conviction against the contention that the statute's sex discrimination—the same act was criminal for a male but not for a female—denied the equal protection of the laws.

There was no opinion for the Court. The majority Justices, however, agreed in accepting the California Supreme Court's justification for the law: prevention of illegitimate teenage pregnancies. The risk of pregnancy itself, said Justice William H. Rehnquist, served to deter young females from sexual encounters; criminal sanctions on young males only would roughly "equalize" deterrents.

The dissenters argued that California had not demonstrated its law to be a deterrent;

Should a California law be struck down as denying equal protection because it convicts underage boys who have intercourse with underage females but does not punish the females?

EDITORIAL CONTROL

The Miami Herald *denied a political candidate free space to respond to its attacks on his personal character. (Corbis/Tony Arruza)*

thirty-seven states had adopted gender-neutral statutory rape laws, no doubt on the theory that such laws would provide even more deterrent, by doubling the number of persons subject to arrest. When both parties to an act are equally guilty, argued Justice John Paul Stevens, to make the male guilty of a felony while allowing the female to go free is supported by little more than "traditional attitudes toward male-female relations."

—KENNETH L. KARST

MICHIGAN DEPARTMENT OF STATE POLICE v. SITZ

110 S.Ct. 2481 (1990)

Recent Fourth Amendment cases reflect a pattern of rejection by the Supreme Court of claims based on the right against unreasonable search and seizure. This case fits that pattern, yet the decision of the Court seems right.

Because of the slaughter on public highways caused by drunk drivers, the Michigan State Police instituted a program of sobriety checkpoints. All drivers passing through a checkpoint, usually after midnight, were stopped and examined briefly for signs of intoxication. Suspected drunk drivers were directed out of the flow of traffic for further investigation; all others were permitted to continue. The average stop took twenty-five seconds.

A 6–3 Supreme Court held that although the stop was a seizure in the sense of the Fourth Amendment, it was a reasonable one because the intrusion was slight and served a substantial public interest. The dissenters, led by Justice John Paul Stevens, believed that the intrusion violated the Fourth Amendment. Much of Stevens's opinion challenged the wisdom of the legislative policy authorizing the sobriety-checkpoint program. His

*A 6-3 Supreme
Court held that
when Michigan
state police stopped
drivers at sobriety
checkpoints it was a
seizure, but a
reasonable one.*

See also

Equal Protection of the Laws

Sex Discrimination

challenge to its constitutionality was founded on the absurd proposition that "unannounced investigatory seizures are, particularly when they take place at night, the hallmarks of regimes far different from ours," and he referred to Nazi Germany. Moreover, Stevens weakened his argument based on the Fourth Amendment by offering the opinion that a permanent, nondiscretionary checkpoint program would not violate the amendment. He supposed that a state could condition the use of its roads on the uniform administration of a breathalizer test to all drivers, thereby keeping drunks off the roads.

The intrusiveness of the means upheld by the Court's majority, led by Chief Justice William H. Rehnquist, was considerably less than that of the means favored by Stevens. In addition, the majority did not debate the wisdom of the policy before it. Its deference to the legislature seemed submissive, however, and its constitutional analysis stopped when it took notice of the twenty-five-second intrusion.

—LEONARD W. LEVY

MILKOVICH v. LORAIN JOURNAL CO.

110 S.Ct. 2695 (1990)

This is a major free press case that has been widely misunderstood, especially by the news media. The *Los Angeles Times,* for example, called it a "huge setback" for freedom of the press. Under the heading, "Supreme Court Strips Away 'Opinion' as Libel Defense," the *Times* announced that the Court had unanimously demolished "a widely used media defense against libel suits, ruling that a writer or speaker may be sued for statements that express opinion." The *Times* censured the Court for having acted "with astonishing recklessness . . . when it overturned nearly two decades of precedent and ruled that the

First Amendment does not automatically protect expressions of opinion from being found libelous." A dramatic increase in libel litigation was foreseen as a result of the Court's chilling just the sort of "serious speech the First Amendment was intended to protect." Every critic, editorialist, cartoonist, and commentator faced trial, the *Times* predicted.

In fact, the Court did not diminish the First Amendment's protection of opinion and overruled no precedents, let alone two decades of them. It did hold, however, that opinion requires no new constitutional protection because the conventional safeguards of freedom of expression adequately protect opinion in libel cases. It held, too, that if an expression of opinion implied an assertion of objective fact on a matter of public concern, no liability for defamation would exist unless the party bringing suit proved that the publication was false and published with malice in the case of a public official or a public figure, or false and published with "some level of fault" in the case of a private individual involved in a matter of public concern.

In this case, the publication accused a private individual of perjuring himself in a judicial proceeding on a matter of public concern, but the accusation was couched in terms of opinion, for example, "anyone who attended the [wrestling] meet . . . knows in his heart that [Coach] Milkovich . . . lied at the hearing." Chief Justice William H. Rehnquist, for the Court, observed that the writer should not escape liability merely because he used words such as "I think," because he might do as much damage to an individual's reputation as he would by saying flatly that he had lied.

The publishing company sought a special rule distinguishing "fact" from "opinion" and exempting opinion from the law of libel. This is what the Court refused to do because some opinions connoted facts for which their authors ought to be responsible. The Court made clear, however, that "a statement of opinion relating to a matter of public concern which does not contain a provably false factual connotation will receive full constitutional protection."

Justices William J. Brennan and Thurgood Marshall dissented, but only on the question as to whether the publisher in this case should be held accountable for libel. Significantly, Brennan, who was the Court's foremost exponent of freedom of the press in libel cases, declared that Rehnquist addressed the issue of First Amendment protection of opinion "cogently and almost entirely correctly. I agree with the Court that . . . only defamatory statements that are capable of being proved false are subject to liability under state libel law." Thus, the Court did not diminish constitutional protections of opinion and held, properly, that existing First Amendment doctrines adequately served to insulate from libel prosecutions the expression of sheer opinion in matters of public interest.

—LEONARD W. LEVY

MILLER, SAMUEL F.

(1816–1890)

Samuel Freeman Miller was a towering figure on the Supreme Court from his appointment by Abraham Lincoln in 1862 until his death in 1890. He sat with four Chief Justices, participated in more than 5,000 decisions of the Court, and was its spokesman in ninety-five cases involving construction of the Constitution. No previous member of the Court had written as many constitutional opinions. Miller's contemporaries regarded him as one of the half-dozen great Justices in American history, a remarkable achievement for a self-educated lawyer who had never held public office, either in his native Kentucky or in adopted Iowa, prior to his appointment to the Court. Justice Horace Gray

Milkovich is a major free press case that's been widely misunderstood.

See also

Freedom of the Press

claimed that if his legal training had been less "unsystematic and deficient," Miller would have been "second only to [John] Marshall."

Miller looked and acted the part of a great magistrate. He was tall and massive; he had a warm, unaffected disposition and was said to be "as ready to talk to a hod-carrier as to a cardinal." His instinct for what he often called "the main points, the controlling questions," his impatience with antique learning and philosophical abstraction, and his unrivaled reputation for industry, integrity, and independence all enhanced his stature. Candor and intellectual self-reliance pervaded his opinions, and he often stated quite bluntly his assumption that law and practical good sense were of one piece: "This is the honest and fair view of the subject, and we think it conflicts with no rule of law" (*Pettigrew* v. *United States,* 1878); "if this is not due process of law it ought to be" (*Davidson* v. *New Orleans,* 1878); "this is just and sound policy" (*Iron Silver Mining Co.* v. *Campbell,* 1890).

Statecraft rather than formal jurisprudence was Miller's forte, and he emerged as the Court's balance wheel soon after coming to the bench. His career ultimately spanned three tumultuous decades in which the Justices constantly quarreled, often rancorously, about the scope of federal and state powers and the Court's role in protecting private rights against the alleged usurpations of both. Scores of cases involved highly charged political issues. Yet Miller always remained detached. He never permitted differences of opinion to affect personal relations with his brethren; he met counsels of heat and passion with chilly distaste. Miller's capacity for detachment was, in part, a matter of personality. But it was also a function of his modest view of the Court's role in the American system of government. He resisted doctrinal formulations that curtailed the discretion of other lawmakers, spoke self-consciously about "my conservative habit of deciding no more than is necessary in any case," and often succeeded in accommodating warring factions of more

doctrinaire colleagues by narrowing the issue before the Court. As early as 1870, Chief Justice Salmon P. Chase said he was "beyond question, the dominant personality upon the bench."

The first principles of Miller's constitutional understanding were derived from Henry Clay and the Whig party. Although he abandoned the Whigs for the Republican party in 1854, Miller never ceased to regard Clay as the quintessential American statesman or to reaffirm the Kentucky sage's belief in a broad construction of national powers, the primacy of the legislative department in shaping public policy, and the duty of government at all levels to encourage material growth. Miller's adherence to the first two principles was especially apparent in his work on the Chase Court. In *Ex Parte Milligan* (1866), he joined the minority of four, concurring, who suggested that Congress might constitutionally have established martial rule in Indiana. And in *Tyler* v. *Defrees* (1870), a confiscation case, Miller flatly rejected the doctrine "long inculcated, that the Federal Government, however strong in a conflict with a foreign foe, lies manacled by the Constitution and helpless at the feet of a domestic enemy." Early in 1868, when the movement to impeach President Andrew Johnson gathered momentum and the Court initially established jurisdiction in *Ex Parte McCardle,* Miller conceded privately that "in the threatened collision between the Legislative branch of the government and the Executive and judicial branches I see consequences from which the cause of free government may never recover in my day." He added, however, that "the worst feature I now see is the passion which governs the hour in all parties and persons who have a controlling influence." In contrast, Miller not only counseled caution and delay while Congress proceeded to divest the Court of jurisdiction over *McCardle* but also dissented in *Texas* v. *White* (1869). He regarded the status of states still undergoing military reconstruction as a political question that only Congress could decide. *Hepburn* v. *Griswold* (1870), the first of the *Legal Tender Cases*, evoked his most celebrated defense of congressional authority. There Miller sharply criticized the majority's reliance on the "spirit" of the Constitution, which, he insisted, "substitutes . . . an undefined code of ethics for the Constitution, and a court of justice for the National Legislature. . . . Where there is a choice of means, the selection is for Congress, not the Court."

Miller was not always such a positivist in rejecting considerations arising from the spirit of the Constitution. In the *Slaughterhouse Cases* (1873), which came up during fierce public debate over the Enforcement and Klu Klux Klan Acts, Miller intervened decisively to preserve "the main features" of the federal system. Although the powers of Congress were not directly at issue, his opinion for the Court undercut every Fourteenth Amendment theory that had been advanced in other cases to justify federal jurisdiction over perpetrators of racially motivated private violence. The Fourteenth Amendment's privileges and immunities clause, Miller explained for a majority of five, protected only the handful of rights that necessarily grew out of "the relationship between the citizen and the national government." The really fundamental privileges and immunities of citizenship, including the rights to protection by the government, to own property, and to contract, still remained what they had been since 1789—rights of state citizenship. To bring all civil rights under the umbrella of national citizenship, Miller concluded, would be "so great a departure from the structure and spirit of our institutions" and would so "fetter and degrade the State governments by subjecting them to the control of Congress" that it should not be permitted "in the absence of language which expresses such purpose too clearly to admit of doubt."

Over the succeeding seventeen years, Miller's voting record in civil rights cases remained consistent with the views he expounded in 1873. He joined the majority in *United States* v. *Cruikshank* (1876) and the *Civil Rights Cases* (1883), both of which severely reduced the range of "appropriate legislation" Congress was authorized to enact; he voted to invalidate the Ku Klux Klan Act altogether in *United States* v. *Harris* (1883). In *Ex Parte Yarbrough* (1884), an important Enforcement Act case, Miller consolidated his formal approach to protecting civil rights in a federal system. Speaking for a unanimous Court, he sustained federal jurisdiction over persons who violently interfered with the exercise of voting rights in a federal election. Congress's authority to reach private action in *Yarbrough*, he explained, flowed not from the Fifteenth Amendment but from both its power to regulate the time, place, and manner of federal elections and its duty "to provide, in an election held under its authority, for security of life and limbs to the voter." By emphasizing the national ramifications of private action in *Yarbrough*, Miller managed to distinguish *Cruikshank* in much the same way that he had distinguished between rights of national citizenship and rights of state citizenship in the *Slaughterhouse Cases*. Both formulations were designed to set principled limits to the exercise of Congress's affirmative powers to protect civil rights.

The impulse to preserve "the main features" of the federal system also shaped Miller's work in cases involving governmental interventions in economic life. He was certainly not immune to the laissez-faire ethos of the late nineteenth century, and his opinion for the Court in *Loan Association* v. *Topeka* (1875) has long been regarded as one of the most significant expressions of natural law constitutionalism in American history and as an important building block in the growth of substantive due process. There he held that a contract for $100,000 in municipal bonds, issued to lure a manufacturing firm to Topeka, was unenforceable. The people's tax dollars, he proclaimed, could not "be used for purposes of private interest instead

MILLER, SAMUEL F.

(1816–1890)

of public use." Yet Miller resisted the urge, spearheaded by Justice Stephen J. Field, to link the "public use" principle with the Fourteenth Amendment and the concept of "general jurisprudence" in order to limit the exercise of all the states' inherent powers—police, taxation, and eminent domain.

The sweeping doctrines advanced by Field and other doctrinaire advocates of laissez-faire conflicted with three working principles of Miller's constitutional understanding, each of which militated against dramatic enlargement of federal judicial power at the expense of the states. The first was his Whiggish predisposition to allow state governments ample room to channel economic activity and develop resources for the general good. A broad construction of the Fourteenth Amendment, he asserted in the *Slaughterhouse Cases*, "would constitute this Court a perpetual censor upon all legislation of the States" and generate state inaction, even in the face of clear public interests, for fear of endless litigation. Miller also believed that it was not the function of federal courts to sit in judgment on state courts expounding state law. He repeatedly invoked this second working principle in the long line of cases that began with *Gelpcke* v. *Dubuque* (1864). There the Court insisted that municipal bonds issued to subsidize railroad construction were unquestionably for a "public use" despite recent state court decisions to the contrary. The *Gelpcke* majority defended federal judicial intervention on the ground that municipal bonds were a species of commercial paper and therefore the question of bondholder rights "belong[ed] to the domain of general jurisprudence." Miller dissented. In his view, extension of the principle of *Swift* v. *Tyson* (1842) to the construction of state statute law was an unconscionable act of federal usurpation, and he accurately predicted that it would spawn a generation of conflict between federal courts and recalcitrant state and local officials.

The apparent inconsistency between Miller's opinion in *Loan Association* v. *Topeka* and his stance in the *Slaughterhouse Cases* and in the *Gelpcke* line of municipal-bond cases is readily explained. All of them did raise similar conceptual issues; each hinged, in part, on the application of the "public use" principle to governmental aid of private enterprise in the form of either monopoly grants or cash subsidies. But for Miller, if not for his colleagues, the controlling factor in *Loan Association* v. *Topeka* was that it had been tried under the diversity jurisdiction of a federal court, and pertinent state law had not yet been framed on the subject. As a result, Miller later explained in *Davidson* v. *New Orleans* (1878), the Court had been free to invoke "principles of general constitutional law" that the Kansas court was equally free to adopt or reject in subsequent cases involving similar circumstances. The concepts of substantive due process and "general jurisprudence," on the other hand, failed to maintain the ample autonomy for state governments that Miller regarded as an indispensable component of the American polity.

Miller ultimately failed to stave off the luxuriation of substantive due process, just as he had failed to curb the majority's impulse to invoke *Swift* in the municipal-bond cases. "It is in vain to contend with judges who have been at the bar the advocates for forty years of rail road companies, and all the forms of associated capital," he told his brother-in-law late in 1875. "I am losing interest in these matters. I will do my duty but will fight no more." Yet Miller's views did make a difference, particularly in the conference room. What remained influential was Miller's third working principle of constitutional interpretation. He recommended resistance to Field's syllogistic reasoning and quest for immutable principles; he suggested, instead, that once the Court had determined to protect private rights against state interference, it was best to decide cases on the narrowest possible grounds, to employ open-ended doctrinal formulas amenable to subsequent alteration, and to elaborate the meaning of due process through what he called a "gradual process of inclusion and exclusion." Thus Miller described local aid of manufactures as "robbery" in *Loan Association* v. *Topeka*, but he added that "it may not be easy to draw the line in all cases so as to decide what is a public use in this sense and what is not." He also endorsed the notoriously vague doctrine of "business affected with a public interest" in *Munn* v. *Illinois* (1877). And in *Chicago, Milwaukee & St. Paul Ry.* v. *Minnesota* (1890), when the Court finally invalidated a state law on due process grounds, Miller concurred "with some hesitation" but filed an opinion cautioning his colleagues against the adoption of a rigid formula, such as "fair value," to determine whether rate-making authorities had acted "arbitrarily and without regard to justice and right."

Miller's immediate successors disregarded the advice, but during the 1930s interest revived in his conception of the judicial function, particularly among Felix Frankfurter's circle at the Harvard Law School. Frankfurter, who called Miller "the most powerful member of his Court," insisted in 1938 that judging was not at all like architecture. Rather than framing doctrinal structures with clean lines and the appearance of permanence, Frankfurter explained, "the Justices are cartographers who give temporary location but do not ultimately define the ever-shifting boundaries between state and national power, between freedom and authority." Miller could not have described his own views with greater clarity or force.

—CHARLES W. MCCURDY

Bibliography

Fairman, Charles (1938). *Mr. Justice Miller and the Supreme Court, 1862–1890.* Cambridge, Mass.: Harvard University Press.

Frankfurter, Felix ([1938] 1961). *Mr. Justice Holmes and the Supreme Court.* Cambridge, Mass.: Harvard University Press.

Gillette, William (1969). Samuel Miller. Pages 1011–1024 in Leon Friedman and Fred Israel, eds., *The Justices of the Supreme Court, 1789–1965.* New York: Chelsea House.

MILLER v. CALIFORNIA

413 U.S. 15 (1973)

PARIS ADULT THEATRE I v. SLATON

413 U.S. 49 (1973)

For the first time since *Roth* v. *United States* (1957), a Supreme Court majority agreed on a definition of obscenity. The Court had adopted the practice of summarily reversing obscenity convictions when at least five Justices, even if not agreeing on the appropriate test, found the material protected. The states were without real guidelines; and the requirements of *Jacobellis* v. *Ohio* (1964) that each Justice review the material at issue had transformed the Court into an ultimate board of censorship review.

To escape from this "intractable" problem, the *Miller* Court reexamined obscenity standards. Chief Justice Warren E. Burger's majority opinion, reaffirming *Roth*, articulated specific safeguards to ensure that state obscenity regulations did not encroach upon protected speech. The Court announced that a work could constitutionally be held to be obscene when an affirmative answer was appropriate for each of three questions:

> *(a) whether "the average person applying contemporary community standards" would find that the work, taken as a whole, appeals to the prurient interest . . . ;*
> *(b) whether the work depicts or describes, in a patently offensive way, sexual conduct specifically defined by the applicable state law; and*
> *(c) whether the work, taken as a whole, lacks serious literary, artistic, political or scientific value.*

*In this case a
majority of Justices
agreed on a
definition of
obscenity.*

*Millet contracted
with his miners to
pay wages by the
boxload rather than
by weight, in
violation of Illinois
state statute.*

Three aspects of the *Miller* formula are noteworthy. First, the work need not be measured against a single national standard, but may be judged by state community standards. Second, state obscenity regulations must be confined to works that depict or describe sexual conduct. Moreover, the states must specifically define the nature of that sexual conduct to provide due notice to potential offenders. Third, the Court rejected the "utterly without redeeming social value" standard of *Memoirs* v. *Massachusetts* (1966). To merit First Amendment protection, the work, viewed as a whole, must have serious social value. A token political or social comment will not redeem an otherwise obscene work; nor will a brief erotic passage condemn a serious work.

In a companion case, *Paris Adult Theater I,* the Court held that regulations concerning the public exhibition of obscenity, even in "adult" theaters excluding minors, were permissible if the *Miller* standards were met. The prohibition on privacy grounds against prosecuting possession of obscene material in one's home, recognized in *Stanley* v. *Georgia* (1969), does not limit the state's power to regulate commerce in obscenity, even among consenting adults.

Justice William J. Brennan, joined by Justices Potter J. Stewart and Thurgood Marshall, dissented in both cases. Abandoning the views he expressed in *Roth* and *Memoirs,* Brennan concluded that the impossibility of definition rendered the outright suppression of obscenity irreconcilable with the First Amendment and the Fourteenth Amendment. The Court's inability to distinguish protected speech from unprotected speech created intolerable fair notice problems and chilled protected speech. Furthermore, "institutional stress" had resulted from the necessary case-by-case Supreme Court review. Instead of attempting to define obscenity, Brennan would balance the state regulatory interest against the law's potential danger to free expression. He recognized the protection

of juveniles or unconsenting adults as a state interest justifying the suppression of obscenity. Justice William O. Douglas, separately dissenting, also denounced the vague guidelines that sent persons to jail for violating standards they could not understand, construe, or apply.

The Court's attempt to articulate specific obscenity standards was successful to the extent it reduced the number of cases on the Supreme Court docket. Nevertheless, as Justice Brennan noted, and the history of obscenity decisions confirms, any obscenity definition is inherently vague. The Court thus remains the ultimate board of censorship review.

—KIM MCLANE WARDLAW

Bibliography

Lockhard, William B. (1975). Escape from the Chill of Uncertainty: Explicit Sex and the First Amendment. *Georgia Law Review* 9:533–587.

MILLETT v. PEOPLE OF ILLINOIS

117 Illinois 294 (1886)

This was the first case in which a court held a regulatory statute unconstitutional on the ground that it violated the doctrine of freedom of contract. Illinois required coal mine owners to install scales for the weighing of coal in order to determine the wages of miners. Millett, an owner, contracted with his miners, in violation of the statute, to pay by the boxload rather than by weight. The state supreme court, overturning his conviction, unanimously declared that the statute deprived him of due process substantively construed. Miners, the court said, could contract as they pleased in regard to the value of their labor, and owners had the same freedom of contract. The court summarily dismissed the contention that the regulation was a valid exercise of the police power on the ground that the legislature had not protected the miners' safety or the property of others. A few months later the Pennsylvania high court, in *Godcharles* v. *Wigeman* (1886), held unconstitutional a state act that prohibited owners of mines or factories from paying workers in kind rather than in money wages. Such cases were forerunners of *Lochner* v. *New York* (1905) and its progeny.

—LEONARD W. LEVY

MILLIGAN, EX PARTE

4 Wallace 2 (1866)

In 1861 Chief Justice Roger B. Taney contrived a possibility of executive-judicial, civil-military clashes (*Ex Parte Merryman*); in 1863 the Supreme Court averted similar confrontations (*Ex Parte Vallandigham; Prize Cases*). But in 1866–67, the Chase Court, in the Test Oath and *Ex Parte Milligan* decisions, overcame its restraint.

In 1864 an Army court sentenced Lambden (spelling various) Milligan, a militantly antiwar, Negrophobe Indianan, to death for overtly disloyal activities. President Andrew Johnson commuted the sentence to life imprisonment. Milligan's lawyer, employing the 1863 Habeas Corpus Act, in 1865 appealed to the federal circuit court in Indiana for release. The judges, including Justice David Davis, divided on whether a civil court had jurisdiction over a military tribunal and on the legitimacy of military trials of civilians. This division let the petition go to the Supreme Court. There, in 1866, Attorney General Henry Stanbery denied that any civil court had jurisdiction; special counsel Benjamin F. Butler insisted on the nation's right to use military justice in critical areas.

Milligan's lawyers included James A. Garfield, Jeremiah Black, and David Dudley Field. Milligan, they argued, if indictable, was triable in civil courts for treason. Alternatively, they insisted that the Army court had failed to obey the 1863 Habeas Corpus Act's requirement to report on civilian prisoners. Further, they asserted that the Constitution's barriers against the use of military power in a state not in rebellion were fixed and unmodifiable, though Congress, they admitted, had authority to use military justice in the South.

All the Justices concurred about the military court's dereliction in not reporting Milligan's arrest. For the Court's bare majority, Justice Davis held that neither president nor Congress could establish military courts to try civilians in noninvaded areas, and, implicitly, that the final decision as to what areas were critical was the Court's. Martial law must never exist where civil courts operated, he stressed, although both had coexisted since the war started. Salmon P. Chase, speaking also for Justices Samuel Miller, Noah Swayne, and James Wayne, disagreed. Congress could extend military authority in Indiana under the war powers without lessening Bill of Rights protections, Chase asserted. The option was Congress's, not the Court's.

The majority view in *Milligan* was at once seized upon by supporters of President Johnson, the white South, and the Democratic party, though even Justice Davis stressed that he referred not at all to the South. Until military reconstruction clarified matters, the duties of the Army, acting under President Johnson's orders and the Freedmen's Bureau statute, were complicated greatly by misuses of the *Milligan* decision in the southern state courts, complications increased by the Test Oath decisions. Taken together, the *Milligan* and the Test Oath decisions greatly limited the capacity of both the nation and the states to provide more decent, color-blind justice in either civil or military courts (including those of the Freedmen's Bureau), and to exclude

MILLIGAN, EX PARTE

4 Wallace 2 (1866)

Martial law must never exist where civil courts operated, said Justice Davis for a bare Court majority, although both court systems had coexisted since the Civil War had started.

See also

Lochner v. *New York*

481

from leadership in politics and the professions persons who had sparked secession and war.

In subsequent decades, legal writers Thomas Cooley and Zechariah Chafee reconstructed *Milligan* into a basic defense of individual liberty and of civilian primacy over the military. Both men were flaying dragons perceived by Victorian Social Darwinists and by critics of World War I witch-hunts. Milligan was never a merely theoretical threat. Neither the civil police and courts of Indiana nor the federal government, except for the Army, evidenced capacity to deal with him. In light of existing alternatives, the Army's decision to try Milligan (not its failure to report its decision and verdict) is defensible.

Republican criticism of the *Milligan* decision never threatened the Court. Instead, from 1863 through 1875, the Congress increased the Court's habeas corpus jurisdiction as well as that in admiralty, bankruptcy, and claims. The *Milligan* decision, paradoxically, became a major step in the Court's successful effort to regain the prestige that it had squandered in *Dred Scott* v. *Sandford* (1857), and that Taney had risked dissipating altogether in *Merryman*.

—HAROLD M. HYMAN

Bibliography

Gambione, Joseph G. (1970). *Ex Parte Milligan:* The Restoration of Judicial Prestige? *Civil War History* 16:246–259.

Kutler, Stanley I. (1968). *Judicial Power and Reconstruction Politics.* Chaps. 6–8. Chicago: University of Chicago Press.

MILLIKEN v. BRADLEY

418 U.S. 717 (1974)

433 U.S. 267 (1977)

The desegregation of public schools in many large cities poses a problem: the cities are running out of white pupils, as white families move to the suburbs. In the early 1970s, some federal district judges began to insist on desegregation plans embracing not only city districts but also surrounding suburban districts. In the first such case to reach the Supreme Court, the Justices divided 4–4, thus affirming without opinion the decision of the court of appeals, which had reversed the district court's order for metropolitan relief. The case had come from Richmond, Virginia; Justice Lewis F. Powell, the former president of the Richmond school board, had disqualified himself.

Milliken, the Detroit school desegregation case, came to the Court the next year. Justice Powell participated, and a 5–4 Court held that interdistrict remedies were inappropriate absent some showing of a constitutional violation by the suburban district as well as the city district. Chief Justice Warren E. Burger wrote for the majority, joined by the other three appointees of President Richard M. Nixon and by Justice Potter Stewart. Justices Thurgood Marshall, Byron R. White, and William O. Douglas all wrote dissenting opinions, and Justice William J. Brennan also dissented.

This decision was the first major setback for school desegregation plaintiffs, but it did not entirely foreclose metropolitan relief. Justice Stewart, who joined the majority opinion, concurred separately as well, saying he would be prepared to accept metropolitan relief not only where a suburban district had committed a constitutional violation, but also where state officials had engaged in racially discriminatory conduct such as racial gerrymandering of district lines or discriminatory application of housing or zoning laws.

When the Detroit case returned to the Court three years later, it added a weapon to the arsenal of desegregation remedies. As part of a desegregation decree, the district court ordered the establishment of remedial education programs; the Supreme Court unanimously affirmed, with the Chief Justice again

In the early 1970s some federal district judges began to insist on desegregation plans embracing not only city districts but also surrounding suburban districts.

See also

Dred Scott v. *Sandford*

writing for the Court. The remedy must not exceed the constitutional violation, he wrote, but here, unlike the situation in *Milliken I,* the remedy was "tailored to cure the condition that offend[ed] the Constitution."

—KENNETH L. KARST

MINNESOTA RATE CASES

230 U.S. 352 (1913)

In these cases a unanimous Supreme Court reaffirmed state power to regulate intrastate commerce even if it should indirectly affect interstate commerce. Justice Charles Evans Hughes stressed the supremacy of federal authority but, reaching back to *Cooley* v. *Board of Wardens of Philadelphia* (1852), held that states could regulate interstate commerce when Congress had not yet chosen to act.

The cases before the Court represented extensive litigation throughout the country. The Railroad Warehouse Commission of Minnesota and the state legislature had issued orders fixing maximum rail rates within the state. Although the rates they set were purely intrastate, both sides agreed that interstate rates would be affected. The cases arose as stockholders' suits to prevent the application of the prescribed rates to interstate operators. On the principal question whether the orders fixed rates that interfered with interstate commerce, Hughes agreed that if the rates imposed a direct burden on commerce, they must fall. He then began a lengthy exposition of the nature of commercial regulation in the federal system, concluding that "it is competent for a state to govern its internal

A unanimous Court reaffirmed state power to regulate intrastate commerce even if it should indirectly affect interstate commerce.

INTRASTATE COMMERCE

The Railroad Warehouse Commission of Minnesota and the state legislature had issued orders fixing maximum rail rates within the state. (Corbis/Bettmann)

commerce . . . although interstate commerce may incidentally or indirectly be involved." Unless and until Congress acted, state action might well be legal even if touching interstate commerce. Only Congress could judge the necessity for action and, having decided to, it could intervene "at its discretion for the complete and effective government" of even local conduct affecting interstate commerce. The Minnesota actions were, therefore, within the state's power but would be superseded if Congress acted. The Court thus broadly upheld state rate making authority; it also implicitly affirmed federal power over intrastate railroad activity affecting interstate commerce, a significant step it would take explicitly the following year in *Houston, East & West Texas Railway Company* v. *United States* (1914).

—DAVID GORDON

MIRANDA v. ARIZONA

384 U.S. 436 (1966)

Miranda is the best known as well as the most controversial and maligned self-incrimination decision in the history of the Supreme Court. Some of the harshest criticism came from the dissenters in that case. Justice Byron R. White, for example, declared that the rule of the case, which required elaborate warnings and offer of counsel before the right against self-incrimination could be effectively waived, would return killers, rapists, and other criminals to the streets and have a corrosive effect on the prevention of crime. The facts of *Miranda,* one of four cases decided together, explain the alarm of the four dissenters and of the many critics of the Warren Court. The majority of five, led by Chief Justice Earl Warren, reversed the kidnap-and-rape conviction of Ernesto Miranda, who had been picked out of a lineup by his victim, had been interro-

gated without mistreatment for a couple of hours, and had signed a confession that purported to have been voluntarily made with full knowledge of his rights, although no one had advised him that he did not need to answer incriminating questions or that he could have counsel present. The Court reversed because his confession had been procured in violation of his rights, yet had been admitted in evidence. Warren conceded that the Court could not know what had happened in the interrogation room and "might not find the . . . statements to have been involuntary in traditional terms." Justice John Marshall Harlan, dissenting, professed to be "astonished" at the decision. Yet the Court did little more than require that the states follow what was already substantially FBI procedure with respect to the rights of a suspect during a custodial interrogation.

The doctrinal significance of the case is that the Fifth Amendment's self-incrimination clause became the basis for evaluating the admissibility of confessions. The Court thus abandoned the traditional due process analysis that it had used in state cases since *Brown* v. *Mississippi* (1936) to determine whether a confession was voluntary under all the circumstances. Moreover, the Court shifted to the Fifth Amendment from the Sixth Amendment analysis of *Escobedo* v. *Illinois* (1964), when discussing the right to counsel as a means of protecting against involuntary confessions. *Miranda* stands for the proposition that the Fifth Amendment vests a right in the individual to remain silent unless he chooses to speak in the "unfettered exercise of his own will." The opinion of the Court lays down a code of procedures that must be respected by law enforcement officers to secure that right to silence whenever they take a person into custody or deprive him of his freedom in any significant way.

In each of the four *Miranda* cases, the suspect was not effectively notified of his constitutional rights and was questioned incommunicado in a "police-dominated" atmosphere;

This case is the best known and the most controversial and maligned self-incrimination decision in the history of the Supreme Court.

See also

Cooley v. *Board of Wardens*

Houston, East & West Texas Railway Company v. *United States*

**THE RIGHT TO
REMAIN SILENT**

*The Court overturned Ernesto
Miranda's kidnap-and-rape
conviction because no one had
advised him that he did not
need to answer incriminating
questions or that he could have
counsel present. (UPI/Corbis-
Bettmann)*

each suspect confessed, and his confession was introduced in evidence against him at his trial. The Court majority demonstrated a deep distrust for police procedures employed in station-house interrogation, aimed at producing confessions. The *Miranda* cases showed, according to Warren, a secret "interrogation environment," created to subject the suspect to the will of his examiners. Intimidation, even if only psychological, could undermine the will and dignity of the suspect, compelling him to incriminate himself. Therefore, the inherently compulsive character of in-custody interrogation had to be offset by procedural safeguards to insure obedience to the right of silence. Until legislatures produced other procedures at least as effective, the Court would require that at the outset of interrogation a person be clearly informed that he has the right to remain silent, that any statement he makes may be used as evidence against him, that he has the right to

the presence of an attorney, and that if he cannot afford an attorney, one will be appointed to represent him.

These rules respecting mandatory warnings, Warren declared, are "an absolute prerequisite to interrogation." The presence of a lawyer, he reasoned, would reduce coercion, effectually preserve the right of silence for one unwilling to incriminate himself, and produce an accurate statement if the suspect chooses to speak. Should he indicate at any time before or during interrogation that he wishes to remain silent or have an attorney present, the interrogation must cease. Government assumes a heavy burden, Warren added, to demonstrate in court that a defendant knowingly and intelligently waived his right to silence or to a lawyer. "The warnings required and the waiver necessary in accordance with our opinion today are prerequisites," he emphasized, "to the admissibility of any statement made by a defendant."

Warren insisted that the new rules would not deter effective law enforcement. The experience of the FBI attested to that, and its practices, which accorded with the Court's rules, could be "readily emulated by state and local law enforcement agencies." The Constitution, Warren admitted, "does not require any specific code of procedures" for safeguarding the Fifth Amendment right; the Court would accept any equivalent set of safeguards.

Justice Tom C. Clark, dissenting, observed that the FBI had not been warning suspects that counsel may be present during custodial interrogation, though FBI practice immediately altered to conform to Warren's opinion. Clark, like Harlan, whose dissent was joined by Justices Potter Stewart and Byron White, would have preferred "the more pliable dictates" of the conventional due process analysis that took all the circumstances of a case into account. Harlan also believed that the right against self-incrimination should not be extended to the police station and should not be the basis for determining whether a confession is involuntary. White wrote a separate dissent, which Harlan and Stewart joined, flaying the majority for an opinion that had no historical, precedential, or textual basis. White also heatedly condemned the majority for weakening law enforcement and for prescribing rules that were rigid, but still left many questions unanswered.

—LEONARD W. LEVY

Bibliography

Kamisar, Yale (1980). *Police Interrogations and Confessions.* Pages 41–76. Ann Arbor: University of Michigan Press.
Whitebread, Charles H. (1980). *Criminal Procedure.* Pages 292–310. Mineola, N.Y.: Foundation Press.

MIRANDA RULES

Miranda v. *Arizona* (1966) held that a statement obtained from a criminal defendant through custodial interrogation is inadmissible against that defendant unless the police obtained a waiver of the right against self-incrimination after warning the suspect of both the right to remain silent and the right to counsel. Recently, the Supreme Court has issued decisions favorable to the government concerning several *Miranda* issues: the definition of custodial interrogation, in *Arizona* v. *Mauro* (1989); the adequacy of warnings provided to persons in custody, in *Duckworth* v. *Eagan* (1989); and the standard that governs the validity of waiver, in *Colorado* v. *Spring* (1987) and *Colorado* v. *Connelly* (1986). Although in *Arizona* v. *Robertson* (1988) the Court reaffirmed the proscription of questioning until counsel appears, once the suspect requests counsel, the police need not advise the suspect of a lawyer's efforts to consult with him or her, as the Court held in *Moran* v. *Burbine* (1986).

The most significant of these developments is the holding in *Connelly* and *Spring*

MIRANDA RIGHTS

1. You have the right to remain silent.
2. Anything you say can and will be used against you in a court of law.
3. If you are under the age of 18, anything you say can be used against you in a juvenile court prosecution for a juvenile offense and can also be used against you in an adult court criminal prosecution if the juvenile court decides that you are to be tried as an adult.
4. You have the right to talk to an attorney before answering any questions.
5. You have the right to have your attorney present during questioning.
6. If you cannot afford an attorney, one will be appointed for you without cost, before or during questioning, if you desire.
7. Do you understand these rights?

See also

Brown v. Mississippi

Right to Counsel

that a *Miranda* waiver is valid so long as the police did not obtain the waiver through conduct that would render a confession "involuntary" as a matter of procedural due process. The *Miranda* opinion stated that "a heavy burden rests on the Government to demonstrate that the defendant knowingly and intelligently waived his privilege against self-incrimination and his right to . . . counsel." Connelly, a lunatic, confessed at the behest of "the voice of God." Spring waived *Miranda* rights after government agents led him to believe that the questioning would concern an illegal firearms transaction, but the interrogation eventually included questions about a homicide. Spring's waiver was not knowing, and Connelly's was not intelligent. The Court nonetheless approved admission of both confessions, stating in *Connelly* that "there is obviously no reason to require more in the way of a 'voluntariness' inquiry in the *Miranda* waiver context than in the Fourteenth Amendment confession context."

The Justices would not likely approve waiver of the right to counsel *at trial* by a person in Connelly's condition or by a person like Spring, who misunderstood the seriousness of the charge. Yet in *Patterson* v. *Illinois* (1988), the Court held that in the interrogation context the claimed waiver of the Sixth Amendment right to counsel, a right initiated by a formal charge with the prospect of a trial, is tested under the *Connelly* standard. Ironically, the standard governing the waiver of rights is strictest in the courtroom, where coercion and deception are least likely, and most lenient in the stationhouse or the police cruiser, where these dangers are greatest.

Not many police departments are likely to depart from the verbal formulation of the warnings given by the *Miranda* opinion, and in few cases does a lawyer attempt to advise an arrested person who did not invoke the *Miranda* right to counsel. Commonly, however, the government claims that the accused waived his or her *Miranda* rights. The ability of police interrogators to induce suspects to waive their rights explains the consistent empirical finding that the *Miranda* doctrine has had a negligible effect on police effectiveness. Because *Miranda* was inspired by dissatisfaction with the vacuous and unpredictable due process approach, stating the test for waiver in the same terms as the voluntariness test comes close to full circle from the law that preceded *Miranda*.

But the Court's retrenchment of the *Miranda* doctrine is not the whole story. In one sense, the most important development in confessions law is *Miranda*'s continued survival, emphasized by cases such as *Roberson*, in which the Court approved the exclusion of valuable evidence obtained without police brutality. At least since *Harris* v. *New York* (1971), a majority of the Justices have believed that *Miranda* was wrongly decided. A majority continues to describe the *Miranda* rules as prophylactic safeguards rather than constitutional entitlements, a distinction that is not compatible with *Miranda*'s presumption that statements obtained without a valid waiver are compelled within the meaning of the Fifth Amendment. Despite the erosion of their Fifth Amendment foundation, the Court refuses to abandon the *Miranda* rules.

The failure of recent efforts to have *Miranda* overruled confirms that stare decisis, even without more, will sustain the decision. During the presidency of Ronald Reagan, the Justice Department's Office of Legal Policy issued a lengthy report calling for *Miranda*'s demise. The report effectively pointed out the inconsistency of *Harris* and its progeny with *Miranda* itself; but on several points, including the key issue of law enforcement effectiveness, the report made an embarrassingly weak case for obliterating a landmark. Not only did the Court as a whole reject the department's effort; the report was not approved by a single Justice in any concurring or dissenting opinion.

So *Miranda* lives, a symbol of commitment to civil liberty that conveniently does

At the borders of the Miranda *rules, a skeptical Supreme Court majority has taken frequent opportunities to limit the rules' scope.*

little to obstruct the suppression of crime. But at the borders of the *Miranda* rules, a skeptical Supreme Court majority has taken frequent opportunities to limit their scope. The most likely future development along these lines is approval of the suggestion advanced by two Justices, concurring in *Duckworth* v. *Eagan*, to the effect that claims by state prisoners that their convictions violated *Miranda* should not be cognizable in federal habeas corpus proceedings.

—DONALD A. DRIPPS

Bibliography

Kamisar, Yale; Lafave, Wayne; and Israel, Jerold (1989). *Modern Criminal Procedure.* 6th ed. St. Paul, Minn.: West Publishing Co.

United States Department of Justice, Office of Legal Policy (1986). *Report to the Attorney General on the Law of Pre-trial Interrogation.* Washington, D.C.: U.S. Government Printing Office.

MISSISSIPPI UNIVERSITY FOR WOMEN v. HOGAN

458 U.S. 718 (1982)

The Court held that an all-female school of nursing could not exclude a male registered nurse.

Joe Hogan, a male registered nurse, was rejected by a state university's all-female school of nursing. A 5–4 Supreme Court held that Hogan's exclusion violated his right to equal protection of the laws. For the majority, Justice Sandra Day O'Connor rejected the argument that, by excluding males, the university was compensating for discrimination against women. Rather, the all-female policy "tends to perpetuate the stereotyped view of nursing as an exclusively woman's job." The university thus failed the test set by *Craig* v. *Boren* (1976) for sex discrimination cases. The dissenters, making a case for diversity of types of higher education, empha-

sized that Hogan could attend a coeducational state nursing school elsewhere in Mississippi.

—KENNETH L. KARST

MISSOURI v. HOLLAND

252 U.S. 416 (1920)

Missouri v. *Holland* confirmed the status of treaties as supreme law. Although becoming "perhaps the most famous and most discussed case in the constitutional law of foreign relations" it arose from a narrower Progressive Era desire to prevent indiscriminate killing of migratory birds, which key states had proved unable or unwilling to end by themselves. Congress first legislated hunting restrictions in March 1913, but lower federal courts invalidated them on Tenth Amendment grounds as exceeding the federal government's commerce power, intruding on state police powers, and usurping the states' well-established position in American law as trustees for their citizens of wild animals. The federal government feared the outcome of a final test of the 1913 act sufficiently to delay Supreme Court action. Instead, responding to suggestions from Elihu Root and others, the Wilson administration concluded the Migratory Bird Treaty of 1916 with Great Britain (acting on behalf of Canada). This committed both nations to restrict hunting of the birds, and in the United States President Woodrow Wilson signed implementing legislation in July 1918.

Several lower courts, including one that had ruled against the 1913 legislation, quickly upheld the 1918 act. In one of these cases the state of Missouri had sought to enjoin federal game warden Ray P. Holland from enforcing the new law. Appealing to the Supreme Court, Missouri argued that because, in the absence of a treaty, the legisla-

See also

Craig v. Boren
Equal Protection of the Laws
Sex Discrimination

tion would be clearly invalid on Tenth Amendment grounds, it must fall even with a treaty base, for otherwise constitutional limitations would become a nullity. The Supreme Court upheld the 1918 legislation in a 7–2 vote (but with no written dissent filed).

Echoing the government's defense of the challenged act, the core of Justice Oliver Wendell Holmes's opinion for the Court was a standard federal supremacy argument. Whether or not the 1913 legislation had been invalid, the 1918 act implemented a treaty; because the Constitution explicitly delegated the treaty power to the federal government and gave status as supreme law to treaties made "under the authority of the United States," Tenth Amendment objections had no force.

Less restrained, even cryptic, was Holmes's language, which provided a basis for years of controversy. After questioning whether the requirement that treaties be made under the authority of the United States meant more than observance of the Constitution's prescribed forms for treaty making, Holmes defended an organic, expansive conception of the Constitution. Its words had "called into life a being the development of which could not have been foreseen completely by the most gifted of its begetters." The Migratory Bird Case needed consideration "in light of our whole experience." The question finally became whether the treaty was "forbidden by some invisible radiation from the general terms of the 10th Amendment." Holmes thereby camouflaged his admissions that treaties must involve matters of national interest and must not contravene specific constitutional prohibitions.

In the 1920s and early 1930s, when the Court often adhered to the doctrine of dual federalism, *Missouri* v. *Holland* arguably offered constitutional grounds for otherwise suspect federal legislation if appropriate treaties were concluded. (Proponents of child labor regulation toyed with the approach.) Fears about its potential in this respect lingered into the 1950s, when the case was a frequent target for backers of the Bricker Amendment. Yet after 1937 the Supreme Court routinely accepted broader interpretations of taxing and spending powers, the commerce clause, and the Fourteenth Amendment, so in practice the case's importance diminished.

—CHARLES A. LOFGREN

Bibliography

Henkin, Louis (1972). *Foreign Affairs and the Constitution.* Mineola, N.Y.: Foundation Press.

Lofgren, Charles A. (1975). *Missouri* v. *Holland* in Historical Perspective. *Supreme Court Review* 1975:77–122.

MISSOURI V. JENKINS

110 S.Ct. 1651 (1990)

Jenkins produced a unanimous result but with two sharply differing opinions on an important question concerning the power of federal courts to remedy school desegregation. A federal district court, after ordering the desegregation of the Kansas City school district, ordered the state of Missouri and the district to share the costs of the remedy, which included substantial capital improvements to make the integrated schools more attractive and thus to reduce "white flight." The district had exhausted its capacity to tax as defined by state law, and so the court ordered the district's property-tax levy increased through the next several fiscal years. The court of appeals affirmed the tax increase order, but the Supreme Court unanimously reversed. The majority, in an opinion by Justice Byron R. White, held that the district court had abused its discretion in imposing the tax itself when an alternative to such an intrusive order was available. That alternative, said Justice White, would be for the district court to order the school district to

Missouri is "perhaps the most famous and most discussed case in the constitutional law of foreign relations."

♦ **diversity jurisdiction**
The legitimate authority of federal courts to hear cases in which the parties have "diversity of citizenship," that is, when they are citizens of different states or of a state and a foreign country.

INTEGRATED

The Supreme Court had differing opinions on an important question concerning the power of federal courts to remedy school segregation. (Corbis/Bettmann)

Desegregating schools was an important objective, but the limits on judicial power must be strictly observed.

See also

Desegregation

levy property taxes at a rate adequate to fund the desegregation remedy.

Justice Anthony M. Kennedy, joined by three other Justices, concurred in the result but disagreed strongly with the majority's conclusion that the district court had power to order the district to levy such a tax. That order, he said, would exceed the judicial power of the United States established in Article III of the Constitution. Taxation would be a legislative function, and the hiring and supervision of a staff to administer the funds so levied would be a political function. Justice Kennedy distinguished *Griffin* v. *County*

School Board of Prince Edward County (1964), in which the Court had upheld the power of a district court to order a school district to levy taxes to reopen schools that had been closed in evasion of a desegregation order. *Griffin*, he said, involved an order to exercise an existing power to tax; in *Jenkins*, the school district would have to exceed its powers under state law. He suggested that the district court might have accomplished the desegregation of Kansas City's schools—although not with the particular remedies chosen—by means that did not require funding beyond the district's current means. Desegregating schools was an important objective, he said, but the limits on judicial power must be strictly observed.

—KENNETH L. KARST

MISTRETTA v. UNITED STATES

488 U.S. 361 (1989)

In *Mistretta* the Supreme Court, 8–1, upheld the Sentencing Reform Act of 1984 against the constitutional challenges that it was an unconstitutional delegation of power and that it violated the principle of separation of powers by intruding the federal judiciary into functions that are legislative.

Congress has the power to fix the sentence for a federal crime. Historically Congress has, in practical effect, delegated a considerable part of this power to the judicial branch through the mechanism of setting a range of possible sentences for the same offense—for example, one to five years of imprisonment. This scheme gives the judge authority to select the sentence appropriate in a particular case—typically including the possibility of probation—in light of the circumstances of the offense, the defendant's history and sense of responsibility, and the like. The possibility of a presidential pardon remained. In recent years, too, Congress allowed the judge to sentence the defendant to an indeterminate term, leaving the actual release date to the U.S. Parole Commission, an agency located in the executive branch. The system not only divided power among the three branches of the federal government, but also produced wide-ranging variation in the severity of sentences.

These disparities persisted despite the best efforts of sentencing institutes, judicial councils, and the Parole Commission. Concern for sentencing inequities, combined with a desire to express a tough attitude toward crime, led Congress to adopt the 1984 act. This act authorized the creation of the United States Sentencing Commission, "an independent commission in the judicial branch" composed of seven members appointed by the president with the advice and consent of the Senate. Three of the members must be federal judges chosen by the president from a list of six submitted by the Judicial Conference of the United States. The commission was authorized to prepare guidelines for essentially determinate sentencing, specifying sentences for various types of crimes and categories of defendants. A judge must adhere to the guidelines except when a case presents aggravating or mitigating circumstances of a kind not specified in the guidelines. The commission is to review and revise the guidelines periodically.

John Mistretta, sentenced on the basis of the guidelines by a federal district court for the sale of cocaine, appealed to the United States Court of Appeals and petitioned the Supreme Court for certiorari before judgment in the court of appeals. The Supreme Court granted the petition and affirmed the sentence. Justice Harry A. Blackmun, writing for the Court, quickly rejected *Mistretta*'s delegation of power challenge. Congress can constitutionally delegate its legislative power to an agency if it specifies clear standards for the agency to follow in carrying out its rulemaking power. Congress gave the Sentencing Commission a clear set of specific goals, including lists of the factors to be considered in establishing grades of offense and categories of defendants. These lists leave considerable discretion to the commission, but the statute's standards are sufficiently clear to allow a reviewing court to determine whether the commission had followed the will of Congress.

Justice Blackmun wrote at greater length in rejecting the broader separation of powers challenge that the Sentencing Commission was a judicial body exercising legislative powers. The commission's work undoubtedly involved political judgment, but the practical

Congress can constitutionally delegate its legislative power to an agency if it specifies clear standards for the agency to follow.

♦ **certification**
A procedure by which a lower court requests from a higher court (or a federal court requests from a state court) guidance on questions of law relative to a case pending in the lower court.

consequences of locating the commission within the judicial branch did not threaten to undermine either the integrity of the judiciary or the power of Congress. On the question of locating the commission within the judicial branch, Justice Blackmun emphasized that the commission is not a court and does not exercise judicial power; that Congress can override the commission's determinations at any time; and that the questions assigned to the commission had long been exercised by the judiciary in the aggregate, deciding case by case.

Justice Blackmun found "somewhat troublesome" the participation in the commission of judges appointed under Article III of the Constitution. Nonetheless, he concluded that the constitution does not prohibit Article III judges from taking on extrajudicial functions in their individual capacities, that Congress and the president had historically acquiesced in federal judges' assumption of such duties, and that the Court's own precedents supported the constitutionality of the practice. Some kinds of extrajudicial service might have adverse effects on the public's sense of the judiciary's independence, but the commission's work was "essentially neutral" in the political sense and designed primarily to govern tasks done entirely within the judicial branch. Although the president could remove the commission members for neglect of duty or malfeasance, this power did not extend to the dismissal of federal judges as judges. Justice Blackmun made clear that there were limits to such extrajudicial services by judges of the constitutional courts, but he could find no constitutionally significant practical effect on the work of the judicial branch from these judges' service on this commission. The emphasis on "practical" and "functional" considerations is the central theme throughout Justice Blackmun's opinion.

Justice Antonin Scalia dissented, arguing that Congress could not constitutionally delegate its legislative power to an agency whose sole power was to make laws, even laws going under the name of "guidelines." This opinion represents the strongest effort in the modern era to revive the delegation doctrine as a serious limit on congressional authority to enlist other agencies in lawmaking. Justice Scalia lamented the Court's tendency to tolerate blurring of the lines separating the powers of the three branches of the federal government. Scolding the majority in a manner now familiar, he offered a restatement of today's operative rule: "The functions of the Branches should not be commingled too much—how much is too much to be determined, case-by-case, by this Court." If we disregard the tone, this restatement seems exactly on the mark. Even so, it is not clear how the national government can be run on a formalistic model of separation of powers that already seemed too confining in 1794 when John Jay, while he was Chief Justice of the United States, went to London to negotiate the agreement we now call Jay's Treaty.

—KENNETH L. KARST

MOORE v. CITY OF EAST CLEVELAND

431 U.S. 494 (1977)

Although it produced no opinion of the court, *Moore* is a major modern Supreme Court precedent confirming the Constitution's protection of the family. A 5–4 Court held invalid a city ordinance limiting occupancy of certain residences to single families and defining "family" in a way that excluded a family composed of Inez Moore, her son, and two grandsons who were not brothers but cousins. Justice Lewis F. Powell, for a plurality of four Justices, concluded that "such an intrusive regulation of the family" required careful scrutiny of the regulation's justification. The city's asserted justifications—avoiding overcrowding, traffic and parking problems, and burdens on its schools—were served only marginally by the ordinance. The plurality thus concluded that the ordinance denied Mrs. Moore liberty without due process of law.

Justice John Paul Stevens, concurring, characterized the ordinance as a taking of property without due process or compensation. Chief Justice Warren E. Burger, dissenting, would have required Moore to exhaust her state administrative remedies before suing in federal court. Three other Justices dissented on the merits, rejecting both due process and equal protection attacks on the ordinance and more generally opposing heightened judicial scrutiny of legislation merely on the basis of its effect on a family like the Moores.

The plurality opinion has become a standard citation for the reemergence of substantive due process, and more specifically for a constitutional right of an extended—but traditional—family to choose its own living arrangements. In a wider perspective the decision can be seen as part of the growth of a freedom of intimate association. The decision was not, however, a blow against covert racial discrimination. East Cleveland was a predominantly black city, with a black commission and city manager. The ordinance, like ordinances in many white communities, was designed to maintain middle-class nuclear family arrangements. In this perspective, the plurality opinion is seen to collide with *Village of Belle Terre* v. *Boraas* (1974), which had upheld an ordinance excluding "unrelated" groups from single-family residences. Justice Powell's distinction of *Belle Terre* amounted to this: families are different. But he offered no definition of "family" apart from a generalized bow to "a larger conception of the family," including an extended family of blood relatives, for which he found support in "the accumulated wisdom of civilization." Of such stuff is substantive due process made.

—KENNETH L. KARST

Bibliography

Burt, Robert A. (1979). The Constitution of the Family. *Supreme Court Review* 1979: 329, 388–391.

MOORE v. DEMPSEY

261 U.S. 86 (1923)

Moore was a landmark for two of the twentieth century's most important constitutional developments: the emergence of the due process clause of the Fourteenth Amendment as a limitation on state criminal procedure, and the assumption by the federal judiciary of a major responsibility for supervising the fairness of state criminal processes, through habeas corpus proceedings.

For all its importance, the case began as a squalid episode of racist ferocity. Returning from World War I, a black Army veteran sought to organize black tenant farmers of Phillips County, Arkansas, into a farmers' union. In October 1919—a year disfigured by racial violence in both North and South—these farmers held a meeting in a rural church to plan efforts to obtain fair accountings from their white landlords. At this remove in time it requires effort to understand that such a meeting, in such a place, for such a purpose, was seen as revolutionary. A sheriff's deputy fired at the church; blacks who were armed fired back, killing the deputy and wounding his companion. Hundreds of new deputies were sworn; they and hundreds of troops arrested most of the county's black farmers, killing resisters. Responsible estimates of the black dead ranged from twenty-five to 200.

About 120 blacks were indicted for various crimes, including the murder of the deputy. The trial juries, like the grand jury that had issued the indictments, were all white. Twelve men were convicted of murder and sentenced to death; dozens of others were sentenced to long prison terms. The twelve sentenced to death filed appeals in two groups of six each. One group, after multiple appeals, was released in 1923 by order of the Arkansas Supreme Court, for excessive delay in their retrial. The convictions of the remaining six, however, were affirmed by the state supreme

For all its importance, the case began as a squalid episode of racist ferocity.

court, and the U.S. Supreme Court denied certiorari. They unsuccessfully sought habeas corpus in the state courts, and again the Supreme Court declined to review the case.

· By now the NAACP had mounted a national fund-raising drive to support the six petitioners. Their execution, set for September 1921, was postponed by the filing of a habeas corpus petition in the federal district court. That court dismissed the writ. On direct appeal, the Supreme Court reversed, 7–2, with an opinion by Justice Oliver Wendell Holmes. (The opinion refers, apparently erroneously, only to the five petitioners who were tried together; the petition of the sixth was consolidated for hearing and decision.)

On remand to the district court, counsel for the six petitioners struck a deal; the habeas corpus petition would be dismissed and the sentence commuted to twelve years' imprisonment, making the men eligible for immediate parole. In 1925 the governor of Arkansas granted an "indefinite furlough," releasing them along with the others convicted following the Phillips County "insurrection."

The federal habeas corpus petition in *Moore* alleged that counsel appointed to represent the five defendants tried together did not consult with his clients before the trial; requested neither delay nor change of venue nor separate trials; challenged not a single juryman; and called no defense witnesses. The trial took forty-five minutes, and the jury "deliberated" less than five minutes. A lynch mob had been dissuaded from carrying out its purpose by a local committee, appointed by the governor to combat the "insurrection," who assured the mob that justice would be done swiftly. Two black witnesses swore they had been whipped and tortured into testifying as the prosecution wished. Holmes summarized the petition: "no juryman could have voted for an acquittal and continued to live in Phillips county, and if any prisoner, by any chance, had been acquitted by a jury, he could not have escaped the mob."

The Supreme Court held that these facts, if proved, justified two conclusions: the state

had violated procedural due process, and the federal district court should grant the writ of habeas corpus. Today both conclusions seem obvious. In 1923, however, the Supreme Court had not yet begun to impose significant federal constitutional limitations on the fairness of state criminal proceedings. *Moore* lighted the path that would lead, in less than half a century, to an expansion of the liberty protected by the due process clause, applying virtually the entire Bill of Rights to the states.

Moore's other conclusion, concerning the reach of federal habeas corpus, also broke new ground. In *Frank* v. *Mangum* (1915), a case involving strikingly similar facts, the Court had rejected a claim to federal habeas corpus relief on the ground that the state courts had provided a full "corrective process" for litigating the accused's federal constitutional claims. Only in the absence of such a corrective process, the Court had held, could a federal habeas corpus court intervene. *Moore* did not explicitly overrule *Frank*, but it did look in a different direction. Justice Holmes, in his characteristically laconic way, said only that if "the whole proceeding is a mask," with all participants in the state trial swept to their conclusion by a mob, and if the state courts fail to correct the wrong, "perfection in the [state's] machinery for correction" could not prevent the federal court from securing the accused's constitutional rights. The right claimed in *Moore*, of course, goes to the essence of due process of law; when the basic fairness of a state criminal trial is challenged, the fact that the state courts have already had a chance to look into the matter seems a weak justification for barring federal habeas corpus.

From *Moore* through *Fay* v. *Noia* (1963), the Supreme Court steadily widened access to federal habeas corpus for persons challenging constitutionality of state convictions. *Stone* v. *Powell* (1976) and *Wainwright* v. *Sykes* (1977) marked the Burger Court's reversal of the direction of doctrinal change. Indeed, *Stone* revived the doctrine of *Frank* v. *Mangum* in cases involving claims based on

See also

Fay v. *Noia*

Frank v. *Mangum*

the Fourth Amendment's guarantee against unreasonable searches and seizures. Yet, despite these limitations, *Moore*'s legacy, even in the field of federal habeas corpus, remains vital to a system of national constitutional standards of fairness for persons accused of crime.

—KENNETH L. KARST

Bibliography

Bator, Paul M. (1963). Finality in Criminal Law and Federal Habeas Corpus for State Prisoners. *Harvard Law Review* 76:441, 483–493.

Waterman, J. S., and Overton, E. E. (1933). The Aftermath of *Moore* v. *Dempsey*. *St. Louis Law Review* (now *Washington University Law Review*) 18:117–126.

MOREHEAD v. NEW YORK ex rel. TIPALDO

298 U.S. 587 (1936)

In June 1936 the Supreme Court ended its term with an opinion so startling that even the Republican party repudiated it at the party's national convention. The Republican plank read: "We support the adoption of State laws to abolish sweatshops and child labor and to protect women and children with respect to maximum hours, minimum wages and working conditions. We believe that this can be done within the Constitution as it now stands." "This" was precisely what the Court had ruled could not be done. It had defended states' rights as it struck down national legislation, and in *Nebbia* v. *New York* (1934) it had declared, "So far as the requirement of due process of law is concerned, a state is free to adopt whatever economic policy may reasonably be deemed to promote public welfare. . . ." Just two weeks before the *Tipaldo* decision, the Court had announced, in *Carter* v. *Carter Coal Company* (1936), as it

had in *Schechter Poultry Corporation* v. *United States* (1935), that the regulation of labor was a local matter reserved by the Tenth Amendment to the states, and specifically the Court had referred to the fixing of wages as a state function. Thus the resolution of *Tipaldo* came as a surprise. The Court used the freedom of contract doctrine, derived from substantive due process, to hold that the states lack power to enact minimum wage laws. The precedent that controlled the case, the Court ruled, was *Adkins* v. *Children's Hospital* (1923).

Although *Adkins* had seemed to block minimum wage legislation, the Court grounded that decision on the statute's failure to stipulate that prescribed wages should not exceed the value of labor services. New York had carefully framed a minimum wage law for women and children that embodied the Court's *Adkins* standard: the state labor commission was empowered to fix wages "fairly and reasonably commensurate with the value of the service or class of service rendered." By a 5–4 vote the Court held the state act unconstitutional. Justice Pierce Butler, speaking for the majority, declared, "Forcing the payment of wages at a reasonable value does not make applicable the principle and ruling of the Adkins Case." The right to make contracts for wages in return for work "is part of the liberty protected by the due process clause," Butler said, and the state was powerless to interfere with such contracts. Women were entitled to no special consideration. Any measure that deprived employers and women employees the freedom to agree on wages, "leaving employers and men employees free to do so, is necessarily arbitrary."

Chief Justice Charles Evans Hughes dissented on ground that the statute was a reasonable exercise of the police power, and he distinguished this case from *Adkins* because the *Tipaldo* statute laid down an appropriate standard for fixing wages. Justices Harlan Fiske Stone, Louis D. Brandeis, and Benjamin N. Cardozo concurred in Hughes's opinion but in a separate dissent by Stone they went much further. Stone accused the

"We support the adoption of State laws to abolish sweatshops and child labor and to protect women and children with respect to maximum hours, minimum wages and working conditions."

This was the first transportation segregation case brought to the Supreme Court by the NAACP.

majority of having decided on the basis of their "personal economic predilections." He repudiated the freedom of contract doctrine, adding: "There is grim irony in speaking of the freedom of contract of those who, because of their economic necessities, give their services for less than is needful to keep body and soul together." Following the reasoning of Justice Oliver Wendell Holmes, dissenting in *Adkins,* Stone declared that it made no difference what wage standard the statute fixed, because employers were not compelled to hire anyone and could fire employees who did not earn their wages. Stone would have followed the principle of *Nebbia,* which the majority ignored, and he would have overruled *Adkins.* A year later, after President Franklin D. Roosevelt proposed packing the Court, it overruled *Adkins* and *Tipaldo* in *West Coast Hotel Co.* v. *Parrish* (1937).

—LEONARD W. LEVY

Bibliography

Leonard, Charles A. (1971). *A Search for a Judicial Philosophy: Mr. Justice Roberts and the Constitutional Revolution of 1937.* Pages 88–93. Port Washington, N.Y.: Kennikat Press.

MORGAN v. VIRGINIA

328 U.S. 373 (1946)

This was the first transportation segregation case brought to the Supreme Court by the NAACP; counsel for the appellant were Thurgood Marshall and William H. Hastie. A Virginia law required racial segregation of passengers on buses. A black woman, riding from Virginia to Maryland, refused to move to a rear seat; she was convicted of a misdemeanor and fined $10. Eighteen states forbade such segregation of passengers, and ten states required it. In 1878 the Supreme Court had invalidated a state law forbidding racial segregation on an interstate carrier as an undue burden on interstate commerce in *Hall* v. *Decuir.* The NAACP lawyers rested on the *Hall* precedent, and did not argue that the Virginia law violated the Fourteenth Amendment.

In an opinion by Justice Stanley F. Reed, the Supreme Court held, 7–1, that the law unduly burdened interstate commerce. Although the usual analysis of a state regulation of commerce involves a balance of burdens on commerce against competing state interests such as health or safety, the Court avoided any discussion of a state interest in segregation, saying only that a uniform national rule of passenger seating was required for interstate carriers, if any rule was to be adopted. Justice Harold Burton dissented.

—KENNETH L. KARST

MUELLER v. ALLEN

463 U.S. 388 (1983)

In this major case on the separation of church and state, the Supreme Court altered constitutional law on the issue of state aid to parents of parochial school children. The precedents had established that a state may not aid parochial schools by direct grants or indirectly by financial aids to the parents of the children; whether those aids took the form of tax credits or reimbursements of tuition expenses did not matter. In this case the state act allowed taxpayers to deduct expenses for tuition, books, and transportation of their children to school, no matter what school, public or private, secular or sectarian.

Justice William H. Rehnquist for a 5–4 Court ruled that the plan satisfied all three parts of the purpose, effect, and no-entanglement test of *Lemon* v. *Kurtzman* (1971). That all taxpaying parents benefited from the act made the difference between this case and the precedents, even though parents of public school children could not take advantage of the major tax deduction. Rehnquist declared that the state had not aided religion generally or any particular denomination and had not excessively entangled the state with religion even though government officials had to disallow tax deductions for instructional materials and books that were used to teach religion. According to the dissenters, however, the statute had not restricted the parochial schools to books approved for public school use, with the result that the state necessarily became enmeshed in religious matters when administering the tax deductions. The dissenters also rejected the majority point that the availability of the tax deduction to all parents distinguished this case from the precedents. The parents of public school children simply were unable to claim the large deduction for tuition. Consequently the program had the effect of advancing the religious mission of the private sectarian schools.

LEONARD W. LEVY

MUGLER v. KANSAS

123 U.S. 623 (1887)

In *Mugler* the Supreme Court took a significant step toward the acceptance of substantive due process, announcing it would henceforth examine the reasonableness involved in an exercise of state police power. A Kansas statute prohibited the manufacture or sale of intoxicating liquor; the state arrested Mugler for making and selling malt liquor and also closed a brewery for being a public nuisance.

Justice John Marshall Harlan addressed the issue: did the Kansas statute violate the Fourteenth Amendment guarantee of due process of law? He declared that such a prohibition "does not necessarily infringe" any of those rights. Although an individual might have an abstract right to make liquor for his own purposes, as Mugler contended, that right could be conditioned on its effect on others' rights. The question became who would determine the effects of personal use on the community? Harlan found that power lodged squarely in the legislature, which, to protect the public health and morals, might exercise its police power. But, bowing to Joseph Choate's argument, he admitted that such power was limited. Harlan asserted that the courts would not be bound "by mere forms [or] . . . pretenses." They had a "solemn duty—to look at the substance of things"; absent a "real or substantial relation" of the act to its objects, the legislation must fall as a "palpable invasion of rights secured by the fundamental law." The Kansas statute easily passed this test, however, and Harlan denied any interference or impairment of property rights. Harlan likewise dismissed the contention that the closing of a brewery amounted to a taking of property without just compensation, thereby depriving its owners of due process. Justice Stephen J. Field dissented in part, urging the Court to adopt substantive due process.

Mugler's more important legacy lies in its analysis of the plaintiff's claim that the state had taken his property by denying him all its reasonable use. The Court rejected that contention, holding the state law had declared the brewery a public nuisance, and since the Constitution did not require the state to compensate the owner of a nuisance, Kansas did not have to pay here either. A century later, in *Lucas* v. *South Carolina Coastal Council* (1992), the Court, relying in part on *Mugler*, held a land-use regulation depriving a

MUGLER v. KANSAS

123 U.S. 623 (1887)

The Supreme Court altered constitutional law on the issue of state aid to parents of parochial school children.

A Kansas statute prohibited the manufacture or sale of intoxicating liquor.

See also

Lemon v. *Kurtzman*

Separation of Church and State

The Justices unanimously sustained an Oregon statute limiting women to ten hours' labor in "any mechanical establishment, or factory, or laundry."

beachfront owner of all reasonable value of his property to be a compensable taking in violation of the Constitution unless—as in *Mugler*—the owner had created a nuisance, or had otherwise offended common-law principles of ownership.

—DAVID GORDON

MULLER v. OREGON

208 U.S. 412 (1908)

Despite the Supreme Court's previous rejection of a maximum hour law for bakers in *Lochner* v. *New York* (1905), here the Justices unanimously sustained an Oregon statute limiting women to ten hours' labor in "any mechanical establishment, or factory, or laundry." The sole issue was the law's constitutionality as it affected female labor in a laundry. Lawyers for Muller contended that

MUSKRAT v. UNITED STATES

219 U.S. 346 (1911)

In one of a series of test cases, the Court here refused to hear the suits involved because the parties failed to meet the constitutional requirement of cases or controversies (Article III, section 2). Congress had authorized certain Indians to sue the United States in the Court of Claims and directed the attorney general to defend. The object was to determine the validity of certain congressional acts regarding Indian lands. The Court dismissed the suits, denying that Congress had the authority to create a case and designate parties to it.

Muskrat became the fountainhead of a long line of decisions requiring plaintiffs to allege a case or controversy under Article III, as discussed under Cases and Controversies and Standing.

—DAVID GORDON

the law violated freedom of contract, that it was class legislation, and that it had no reasonable connection with the public health, safety, or welfare. The state countered with Louis D. Brandeis's famous brief elaborately detailing similar state and foreign laws, as well as foreign and domestic experts' reports on the harmful physical, economic, and social effects of long working hours for women.

Justice David Brewer, speaking for the Court, based his opinion on the proposition that physical and social differences between the sexes justified a different rule respecting labor contracts, thereby allowing him to distinguish *Lochner*. Although the Constitution imposed unchanging limitations on legislative action, Brewer acknowledged that the Fourteenth Amendment's liberty of contract doctrine was not absolute. He invoked *Holden* v. *Hardy* (1898), sustaining an eight-hour day for Utah miners, and portions of *Lochner* that similarly approved some exceptional regulations. Brewer declared that although the legislation and opinions cited in the Brandeis brief were not "authorities," the Court would "take judicial cognizance of all matters of general knowledge."

The accepted wisdom that women were unequal and inferior to men animated Brewer's opinion. Women's physical structure and their maternal functions, he said, put them at a disadvantage. Long hours of labor, furthermore, threatened women's potential for producing "vigorous" children; as such their physical well-being was a proper object of interest "in order to preserve the strength and vigor of the race." Beyond Brewer's concerns for the "future well-being of the race," he contended that the long historical record of women's dependence upon men demonstrated a persistent reality that women lacked "the self-reliance which enables one to assert full rights." Legislation such as the Oregon maximum hour law, Brewer concluded, was necessary to protect women from the "greed" and "passion" of men and therefore validly

See also

Adkins v. *Children's Hospital*

Lochner v. *New York*

and properly could "compensate for some of the burdens" imposed upon women.

Taken out of context, Brewer's remarks obviously reflected paternalistic and sexist notions. Yet they also reflected prevailing sentiments, which he invoked to justify an exception to his normally restrictive views of legislative power. The same arguments were advanced by those who sought an opening wedge for ameliorating some of the excesses of modern industrialism.

Although the *Muller* decision did not overrule *Lochner*, it reinforced a growing line of precedents to counter *Lochner*. *Muller* eventually led to *Bunting* v. *Oregon* (1917), approving maximum hour laws for both sexes, a decision that Chief Justice William Howard Taft believed in 1923 had tacitly overruled *Lochner*—mistakenly, as it turned out, for the Court invoked *Lochner* to strike down a minimum wage law in *Adkins* v. *Children's Hospital* (1923).

—STANLEY I. KUTLER

Bibliography

Mason, Alpheus T. (1946). *Brandeis: A Free Man's Life.* New York: Viking Press.

MYERS v. UNITED STATES

272 U.S. 52 (1926)

An 1876 statute authorized presidential appointment and removal of postmasters with the advice and consent of the Senate. President Woodrow Wilson appointed Myers with Senate consent but later removed him without consulting that body. Myers filed suit in the Court of Claims and appealed that court's adverse decision to the Supreme Court.

Chief Justice, and former president, William Howard Taft, in a broad construc-

POWER OF REMOVAL

President Woodrow Wilson (left) appointed Myers with Senate consent but later removed him without consulting that body. (Corbis/Hulton-Deutsch Collection)

tion of Article II, found the statute unconstitutional. For a 6–3 majority he insisted upon the necessity for the nation's chief executive officer to be able to remove subordinates freely: "To hold otherwise would make it impossible for the President . . . to take care that the laws be faithfully executed."

Justices Oliver Wendell Holmes, James C. McReynolds, and Louis D. Brandeis dissented. Brandeis declared that implying an unrestricted power of removal from the power of appointment "involved an unnecessary and indefensible limitation upon the constitutional power of Congress." History and present state practice demonstrated "a decided tendency to limit" the executive's removal power, and he also cited the doctrines of checks and balances and the separation of powers.

The Court limited the doctrinal reach of *Myers* in *Humphrey's Executor* v. *United States* (1935).

—DAVID GORDON

See also

Advice and Consent

Humphrey's Executor v. *United States*

NAACP v. ALABAMA

357 U.S. 449 (1958)

In this decision the Supreme Court first recognized a freedom of association guaranteed by the First Amendment. Alabama, charging that the NAACP had failed to qualify as an out-of-state corporation, had sought an injunction preventing the association from doing business in the state. In that proceeding, the state obtained an order that the NAACP produce a large number of its records. The association substantially complied, but refused to produce its membership lists. The trial court ruled the NAACP in contempt and fined it $100,000. The state supreme court denied review, and the U.S. Supreme Court unanimously reversed.

Justice John Marshall Harlan wrote for the Court. First, the NAACP had standing to assert its members' claims; to rule otherwise would be to require an individual member to forfeit his or her political privacy in the act of claiming it. On the constitutional merits, Harlan wrote: "Effective advocacy . . . is undeniably enhanced by group association"; thus "state action which may have the effect of curtailing the freedom to associate is subject to the closest scrutiny." The privacy of association may be a necessary protection for the freedom to associate "where a group espouses dissident beliefs." Here, disclosure of NAACP membership in Alabama during a time of vigorous civil rights activity had been shown to result in members' being fired from their jobs, physically threatened, and otherwise harassed. Only a compelling state interest could justify this invasion of political privacy. That compelling interest was not shown here. The names of the NAACP's rank-and-file members had no substantial bearing on the state's interest in assuring compliance with its corporation law.

This same technique—solemnly accepting the state's account of its purposes, ignoring possible improper motives, and concluding that those state interests were not "compelling"—was employed in other cases involving efforts by southern states to force disclosures of NAACP membership such as *Bates* v. *Little Rock* (1960) and *Shelton* v. *Tucker* (1960).

—KENNETH L. KARST

NATIONAL LEAGUE OF CITIES v. USERY

426 U.S. 833 (1976)

This case proved that obituaries for dual federalism were premature. It arose after Congress amended the Fair Labor Standards Act (FLSA), in 1974, to extend wages-and-hours coverage to nearly all public employees. Several states, cities, and intergovernmental organizations sought to enjoin enforcement of the new provisions. Admitting that the employees in question would come within the federal commerce power if they worked in the private sector, the plaintiffs argued that congressional regulation of employment conditions for state and municipal workers violated "the established constitutional doctrine of intergovernmental immunity." A three-judge district court disagreed, ruling that under *Maryland* v. *Wirtz* (1968), which had upheld the application of wages-and-hours regulations to public schools and hospitals, an employee's public

> *In* NAACP v.
> Alabama *the Court*
> *first recognized a*
> *freedom of*
> *association*
> *guaranteed by the*
> *First Amendment.*

See also

Compelling State Interest

♦ **dual federalism**
A doctrine of constitutional interpretation according to which the reserved powers of the states operate as limitations on the power of the national government.

status was irrelevant to the scope of congressional authority. On appeal, the Supreme Court reversed the lower court, 5–4, holding that the FLSA amendments could not constitutionally be applied to public employees performing "traditional governmental functions."

Writing for the Court, Justice William H. Rehnquist initially confronted the sweep of the commerce clause recognized in *Gibbons* v. *Ogden* (1824). The grant of congressional power was plenary, he conceded, but did not override "affirmative limitations" on Congress. The Tenth Amendment provided the most explicit source for such a limitation, for in *Fry* v. *United States* (1975) the Court had offered the dictum that the amendment "expressly declared the constitutional policy that Congress may not exercise power in a fashion that impairs the States' integrity or their ability to function effectively in a federal system." Yet Rehnquist emphasized a less explicit limitation—the overall federal structure. Within it, states perform essential governmental functions, and state decisions about these functions, which include fire protection and law enforcement, must be free from federal interference. Wages-and-hours legislation constituted a forbidden infringement, because it "operate[s] directly to displace the States' freedom to structure integral operations in areas of traditional governmental functions. . . ." Indeed, he expressly held the Court had wrongly decided *Wirtz*.

But the meaning of *National League of Cities* as precedent is not clear. Justice Harry A. Blackmun qualified his crucial fifth vote with a concurrence that interpreted the Court as "adopt[ing] a balancing approach." For him, the decision did not preclude regulation of states in areas, such as environmental protection, where the federal interest was demonstrably greater. And the Court itself expressly left open the power of Congress to regulate even traditional state functions by employing the taxing and spending power or by enforcing the Fourteenth Amendment.

In dissent, Justice William J. Brennan charged that the decision contained "an ominous portent of destruction of our constitutional structure" and delivered a "catastrophic body blow" to the commerce power. In his view, Rehnquist had misread earlier case law and had abandoned the plain meanings of the commerce and supremacy clauses. Moreover, Rehnquist's "essential function test" was "conceptually unworkable," for it failed to

NATIONAL TREASURY EMPLOYEES UNION v. VON RAAB

489 U.S. 656

In this companion case to *Skinner* v. *Railway Labor Executives Association*, the Supreme Court upheld 5–4 the constitutionality of federal regulations requiring urine testing of all Customs employees involved in drug interdiction, carrying weapons, or handling classified materials. Justices Antonin Scalia and John Paul Stevens, who had supported the majority in *Skinner*, joined the *Skinner* dissenters in this case.

Scalia believed that considerations of public safety and the relation between drugs and accidents had justified the departure from individualized suspicion in *Skinner*. These considerations did not prevail in this case. No evidence existed to show that Customs employees used drugs, let alone that such use jeopardized the public. Accordingly, the public safety could not be furthered by the urinalysis required

of these employees. The search itself, Scalia believed, was "particularly destructive of privacy and offensive to personal dignity." The Court majority, however, remained convinced that the government had a compelling interest in ensuring the physical fitness of the employees required to submit to urine testing.

—LEONARD W. LEVY

clarify the distinction between essential and other state activities.

The Court's opinion did lack a reasoned test for determining the essential functions of states "*qua* states." It also ran counter to forty years of judicial acceptance of broad congressional power under the commerce clause. Accordingly, *National League of Cities* led to further litigation over state immunity from federal regulation and injected the Supreme Court into issues long dormant. In *Garcia* v. *San Antonio Metropolitan Transit Authority* (1985) a different 5–4 majority flatly overruled *National League of Cities,* but the dissenters promised that disinterment of the 1976 decision awaited only one more vote.

—CHARLES A. LOFGREN

Bibliography

Barber, Sotirios A. (1976). *National League of Cities* v. *Usery:* New Meaning for the Tenth Amendment? *Supreme Court Review* 1976:161–182.

Lofgren, Charles A. (1980). The Origins of the Tenth Amendment: History, Sovereignty, and the Problem of Constitutional Intention. Pages 331–357 in Ronald K. L. Collins, ed., *Constitutional Government in America.* Durham, N.C.: Carolina Academic Press.

Nagel, Robert F. (1981). Federalism as a Fundamental Value: *National League of Cities* in Perspective. *Supreme Court Review* 1981:81–109.

NEAL v. DELAWARE

103 U.S. 370 (1881)

Justice John Marshall Harlan, for a majority of 7–2, laid down an important principle in jury discrimination cases: the fact that no black person had ever been summoned as a juror in the courts of a state presents "a *prima facie* case of denial, by the officers charged with the selection of grand and petit jurors, of that equality of protection" secured by the

Fourteenth Amendment. *Neal* differed from *Virginia* v. *Rives* (1880), here reaffirmed, because the prisoner in *Rives* had merely alleged the exclusion of blacks, which the state denied, while here the state conceded the exclusion. The state chief justice explained that "the great body of black men residing in this State are utterly unqualified by want of intelligence, experience or moral integrity, to sit on juries." Harlan called that a "violent presumption." *Neal* did nothing to prevent the elimination of blacks from juries in the South, because in the absence of a state confession of constitutional error, blacks had the burden of proving deliberate and systematic exclusion of their race.

—LEONARD W. LEVY

NEAR v. MINNESOTA

283 U.S. 697 (1931)

Although *Gitlow* v. *New York* (1925) had accepted for the sake of argument that the First Amendment's freedom of speech guarantees were applicable to the states through the due process clause of the Fourteenth Amendment, *Near* was the first decision firmly adopting the incorporation doctrine and striking down a state law in its totality on free speech grounds. Together with *Stromberg* v. *California* (1931), decided in the same year and also with a 5–4 majority opinion by Chief Justice Charles Evans Hughes, *Near* announced a new level of Supreme Court concern for freedom of speech.

A Minnesota statute authorizing injunctions against a "malicious, scandalous and defamatory newspaper, magazine or other periodical" had been applied against a paper that had accused public officials of neglect of duty, illicit relations with gangsters, and graft. Arguing that hostility to prior restraint and censorship are the very core of the First Amendment, the Court struck down the statute. Yet *Near,* the classic precedent against prior restraints, is also the doctrinal starting

No black person had ever been summoned as a juror in the courts of a state.

♦ **subpoena**
[Latin: under penalty]
An order to appear and testify at a proceeding (subpoena ad testificandum) *or to produce physical evidence at a proceeding* (subpoena duces tecum).

Near *was the first decision firmly adopting the incorporation doctrine and striking down a state law in its totality on free speech grounds.*

See also
Racial Discrimination

point for most defenses of prior restraint. The Court commented in obiter dictum that "the protection even as to previous restraint is not absolutely unlimited," and listed as exceptions wartime obstruction of recruitment and publication of military secrets, obscenity, incitements to riot or forcible overthrow of the government, and words that "may have all the effect of force."

In emphasizing the special First Amendment solicitude for criticisms of public officials, whether true or false, *Near* was an important way station between *Gitlow*'s implicit acceptance of the constitutional survival in the United States of the English common law concept of seditious libel and the rejection of that concept in *New York Times* v. *Sullivan* (1964).

—MARTIN SHAPIRO

NEBBIA v. NEW YORK

291 U.S. 502 (1934)

Both the desperate economic conditions in the American dairy industry and the legal responses to the dairy crisis, during the depression years 1929–33, exemplified the dilemmas that the Great Depression posed for American law. Vast, unmarketable surpluses of fluid milk and other dairy products, widespread mortgage foreclosures in dairy centers of rural America, and wild swings in dairy prices and consumption, all spelled extreme distress for the industry and its marketing institutions.

Among the states that responded with new legislation was New York, whose dairy industry constituted about half the value of its farm income and served the great urban concentration of population in the city of New York and its metropolitan area. In framing a program to deal with the crisis, New York's lawmakers knew they were forced to walk through a constitutional minefield. Despite provisions of the 1933 federal Agricultural Adjustment Act intended to give the states some latitude in control of dairy commerce involving interstate milksheds, federal district courts around the country had struck down state laws seeking to control interstate movements of fluid milk or the terms on which it could be marketed. In addition, even laws seeking to regulate only in-state production and distribution were challenged as invalid under the "affected with a public interest" rule; indeed, in numerous previous decisions the Supreme Court had in obiter dicta listed dairies among the

INCORPORATION DOCTRINE

According to the incorporation doctrine the Fourteenth Amendment incorporates or absorbs the Bill of Rights, making its guarantees applicable to the states. Whether the Bill of Rights applied to the states, restricting their powers as it did those of the national government, was a question that arose in connection with the framing and ratification of the Fourteenth Amendment. Before 1868 nothing in the Constitution of the United States prevented a state from imprisoning religious heretics or political dissenters, or from abolishing trial by jury, or from torturing suspects to extort confessions of guilt. The Bill of Rights limited only the United States, not the states. James Madison, who framed the amendments that became the Bill of Rights, had included one providing that "no State shall violate the equal rights of conscience, of the freedom of the press, or the trial by jury in criminal cases." The Senate defeated that proposal. History, therefore, was on the side of the Supreme Court when it unanimously decided in *Barron* v. *Baltimore* (1833) that "the fifth amendment must be understood as restraining the power of the general government, not as applicable to the States," and said that the other amendments composing the Bill of Rights were equally inapplicable to the States.

enterprises that clearly were "ordinary" or "purely private" businesses, not affected with a public interest and therefore not subject to price regulation. In *New State Ice Co.* v. *Liebmann* (1932), for example, the Court had denied the legislature of Oklahoma authority to regulate ice manufacturing and selling on the ground that it was "a business as essentially private in its nature as the business of the grocer, the dairyman, the butcher, the baker, the shoemaker, or the tailor."

Mindful of this background, the New York legislature conducted a lengthy investigation of the fluid milk industry and its travails. In addition to making a record, thereby, as to the condition of the farmers and distribution system, the price collapse and its consequences, and the extensive effects of the crisis on the state's economy, when the legislature drafted a new Milk Control Law in March 1933, it explicitly denominated it as emergency legislation and provided for its termination one year following. By this maneuver, the legislators hoped to slip the knot of "affected with a public interest" and give the Milk Control Law safe harbor in the emergency powers and police power area in the event that courts proved unimpressed with the statute's assertion that the milk industry was "a business affecting the public health and interest."

Like similar legislation enacted in New Jersey, Illinois, and other dairy states, the New York law included power to fix prices in the virtually plenary grant of authority to the milk control agency that was established. The board was also empowered to license producers, establish maximum retail prices and the spread between prices paid producers and charged consumers, and regulate interstate fluid milk entrants to the New York market.

The price-fixing provision came before the bench in an appeal from the conviction of a storekeeper for selling milk at retail below the price established by the new milk control agency. When the New York Court of Appeals affirmed the conviction, the case was carried to the Supreme Court. Counsel contended that price control violated the "affected with a public interest" standard, subjecting Nebbia to improper regulation in violation of his Fourteenth Amendment right to due process.

By a 5–4 vote, the Court upheld the New York law. Justice Owen J. Roberts's opinion did not rest on the narrow grounds that the milk control program was of an emergency nature; instead, it addressed in broadest possible terms the nature of the police power and the constitutional limitations upon which states might exercise it. The long history of the "affected with a public interest" doctrine came to an end with *Nebbia,* the majority opinion going back to Chief Justice Morrison R. Waite's language in *Munn* v. *Illinois* (1877). Waite had used the phrase "affected with a public interest" as the equivalent of "subject to the exercise of the police power," the Court now declared: "It is clear that there is no closed class or category of businesses affected with a public interest, and the function of courts in the application of the Fifth and Fourteenth Amendments is to determine in each case whether circumstances vindicate the challenged regulation as a reasonable exertion of governmental authority or condemn it as arbitrary or discriminatory." By repudiating the doctrine of affection with a public interest, which was based on substantive due process of law, the Court weakened the due process clause as a bastion of property rights. The due process clause, Roberts observed, made no mention of sales, prices, business, contracts, or other incidents of property. Nothing, he added, was sacred about the prices one might charge. The state, Roberts declared, "may regulate a business in any of its aspects, including the prices to be charged for the products or commodities it sells." The crux of this opinion, which prefigured a transformation in constitutional law, was this statement: "So far as the requirement of due process is concerned . . . a state is free to adopt whatever economic policy may reasonably be deemed to promote public welfare,

NEBBIA v. NEW YORK

291 U.S. 502 (1934)

A storekeeper was convicted for selling milk at retail below the price established by the new milk control agency.

♦ **appeal**
Review of a court decision by a higher court to determine whether errors of law were made. Appeal is a particular type of review, but the word is sometimes used more generally, to refer to any review of a lower court decision.

and to enforce that policy by legislation adapted to its purpose. The courts are without authority either to declare such policy, or, when it is declared by the legislature, to override it."

Handed down not long after *Home Building & Loan Association* v. *Blaisdell* (1934), a decision that did extensive damage to once sacrosanct contract clause doctrine, the *Nebbia* decision was anathema to property-minded conservatives who saw the juridical scaffolding for vested rights as collapsing in the early New Deal years, even before the Court fight and the wholesale reversal of doctrine that came after 1935. Indeed, *Nebbia* may be read as present-day constitutional law.

—HARRY N. SCHNEIBER

Bibliography

Goldsmith, Irving B., and Winks, Gordon W. (1938). Price Fixing: From *Nebbia* to *Guffey*. Pages 531–553 in Douglas B. Maggs, ed., *Selected Essays on Constitutional Law*. Chicago: Association of American Law Schools.

NEBRASKA PRESS ASSOCIATION v. STUART

427 U.S. 539 (1976)

In *Nebraska Press Association* v. *Stuart* the Court addressed for the first time the constitutionality of a prior restraint on pretrial publicity about a criminal case. Noting the historic conflict between the First and Sixth Amendments, the Court refused to give either priority, recognizing that the accused's right to an unbiased jury must be balanced with the interests in a free press. At issue was a narrowly tailored gag order in a sensational murder case restraining the press from publishing or broadcasting accounts of the accused's confessions or admissions or "strongly implicative" facts until the jury was impaneled.

Applying the standard of *Dennis* v. *United States* (1951) and inquiring whether "the gravity of the 'evil,' discounted by its improbability justified such invasion of free speech as is necessary to avoid the danger," the Court struck down the gag order. To determine whether the record supported the extraordinary measure of a prior restraint on publication, the Court considered the nature and extent of pretrial news coverage, the likelihood that other measures would mitigate the effects of unrestrained pretrial publicity, and the effectiveness of a restraining order to prevent the threatened danger, and, further, analyzed the order's terms and the problems of managing and enforcing it. The gag order was critically flawed because it prohibited publication of information gained from other clearly protected sources.

Justice William J. Brennan, joined by Justices Potter J. Stewart and Thurgood Marshall, concurring, argued that a prior restraint on the press is an unconstitutionally impermissible method for enforcing the Sixth Amendment. Refusing to view the First and Sixth Amendments as in irreconcilable conflict, he noted that there were numerous less restrictive means by which a fair trial could be ensured. Justice Byron R. White doubted whether prior restraints were ever justifiable, but did not believe it wise so to announce in the first case raising that question. Justice Lewis F. Powell emphasized the heavy burden resting on a party seeking to justify a prior restraint.

—KIM MCLANE WARDLAW

NEW JERSEY v. T.L.O.

469 U.S. 325 (1985)

In *New Jersey* v. *T.L.O.* a unanimous Supreme Court held that the Fourth Amendment's prohibition against unreasonable searches

---

At issue was a gag order in a sensational murder case restraining the press from publishing or broadcasting accounts of the accused's confessions.

See also

Dennis v. *United States*

Free Press/Fair Trial

Prior Restraint and
Censorship

and seizures applies to searches of students conducted by public school officials. A majority of the Court (6–3) also held that school officials need not obtain a search warrant before searching a student under their authority and that their searches can be justified by a lower standard than probable cause to believe that the subject of the search has violated or is violating the law. Instead, the legality of the search depends on the reasonableness of the search under all the circumstances.

According to Justice Byron R. White's majority opinion, determining reasonableness requires a twofold inquiry: first, whether the search was justified at its inception, and, second, whether the search as actually conducted was reasonably related in its scope to the circumstances that initially justified it. Ordinarily, the search is justified at its inception if there are reasonable grounds for suspecting that the search will produce evidence that the student has violated or is violating either the law or the school rules. The search is permissible in scope if the measures adopted are reasonably related to the objectives of the search and are not excessively intrusive in light of the age and sex of the student and the nature of the infraction.

—PATRICK DUTTON

Bibliography

Dutton, Patrick (1985). School Searches: Recent Applications of the United States and California Constitutions. *Journal of Juvenile Law* 9:106–128.

NEW JERSEY v. WILSON

7 Cranch 164 (1812)

This case was the vehicle by which the Supreme Court made a breathtaking expansion of the contract clause. In the colonial period New Jersey had granted certain lands to an Indian tribe in exchange for a waiver by the Indians of their claim to any other lands. The grant provided that the new lands would be exempt from taxation in perpetuity. In 1801, over forty years later, the Indians left the state after selling their lands with state permission. The legislation repealed the tax exemption statute and assessed the new owners, who challenged the constitutionality of the repeal act.

A unanimous Supreme Court, overruling the state court, held that the grant of a tax immunity was a contract protected by the contract clause. By some species of metaphysics the Court reasoned that the tax immunity attached to the land, not to the Indians, and therefore the new holders of the land were tax exempt. Chief Justice John Marshall's opinion, voiding the state tax, gave a retroactive operation to the contract clause; the grant of tax immunity predated the clause by many years. More important, Marshall ignored the implications of his doctrine that such a grant was a contract. According to this decision, a state, by an act of its legislature, may contract away its sovereign power of taxation and prevent a successive legislature from asserting that power. The doctrine of vested rights, here converted into a doctrine of tax immunity, handicapped the revenue capabilities of the states, raising grave questions about the policy of the opinion. As a matter of political or constitutional theory, the Court's assumption that an attribute of sovereignty can be surrendered by a legislative grant to private parties or to their property was, at the least, dubious. Although Marshall restricted the states, he allowed them to cede tax powers by contract rather than thwart the exercise of those powers on rights vested by contract.

The growth of corporations revealed the significance of the new doctrine of tax immunity. States and municipalities, eager to promote the establishment of banks, factories, turnpikes, railroads, and utilities, often granted corporations tax immunity or other tax advantages as an inducement to engage in

A unanimous Supreme Court held that the grant of a tax immunity was a contract protected by the contract clause.

See also

Search and Seizure

such enterprises, and the corporations often secured their special privileges by corrupt methods. This case permitted the granting of tax preferences and constitutionally sanctioned political corruption and the reckless development of economic resources. But permission is not compulsion; the legislatures, not the judiciary, granted the contracts. The Court simply extended the contract clause beyond the intentions of its framers to protect vested rights and promote business needs.

—LEONARD W. LEVY

NEW YORK v. QUARLES

467 U.S. 649 (1984)

Justice William Rehnquist, for a 5–4 Supreme Court, announced a public safety exception to the *Miranda* rules. In a situation where concern for the public safety must supersede adherence to *Miranda* v. *Arizona* (1966), the prosecution may use in evidence incriminating statements made during a custodial interrogation before the suspect receives notice of his constitutional rights.

Here, the Court reinstated a conviction based on the evidence of a gun and information concerning its whereabouts. Dissenters disagreed on whether the case showed a threat to the public safety, but produced no principled argument against the exception to *Miranda*.

—LEONARD W. LEVY

NEW YORK TIMES CO. v. SULLIVAN

376 U.S. 254 (1964)

Martin Luther King Jr. was arrested in Alabama in 1960 on a perjury charge. In New York a group of entertainers and civil rights activists formed a committee to help finance King's defense. They placed a full-page advertisement in the *New York Times* appealing for contributions. The ad charged that King's arrest was part of a campaign to destroy King's leadership of the movement to integrate public facilities and encourage blacks in the South to vote. It asserted that "Southern violators" in Montgomery had expelled King's student followers from college, ringed the campus with armed police,

The Court reinstated a conviction based on the evidence of a gun and information concerning its whereabouts.

See also

Miranda Rules

Miranda v. *Arizona*

NEW YORK v. FERBER

458 U.S. 747 (1982)

This decision demonstrated the Burger Court's willingness to add to the list of categories of speech excluded from the First Amendment's protection. New York, like the federal government and most of the states, prohibits the distribution of material depicting sexual performances by children under age 16, whether or not the material constitutes obscenity. After a New York City bookseller sold two such films to an undercover police officer, he was convicted under this law.

The Supreme Court unanimously affirmed his conviction.

Justice Byron R. White, for the Court, denied that state power in this regulatory area was confined to the suppression of obscene material. The state's interest in protecting children against abuse was compelling; to prevent the production of such materials, it was necessary to forbid their distribution. Child pornography—the visual depiction of sexual conduct by children below a specified age—was "a category of material outside the protection of the First Amendment."

The Court also rejected the argument that the law was overbroad, thus abandoning a distinction announced in *Broadrick* v. *Oklahoma* (1973) to govern overbreadth challenges. Henceforth the overbreadth doctrine would apply only in cases of "substantial overbreadth," whether or not the state sought to regulate the content of speech.

—KENNETH L. KARST

**RECKLESS
DISREGARD?**

Libel suits were being used to discourage the press from supporting the civil rights movement, led by Martin Luther King Jr. (Corbis/Flip Schulke)

padlocked the dining hall to starve them into submission, bombed King's home, assaulted his person, and arrested him seven times for speeding, loitering, and other dubious offenses.

L. B. Sullivan, a city commissioner of Montgomery, filed a libel action in state court against the *Times* and four black Alabama ministers whose names had appeared as endorsers of the ad. He claimed that because his duties included supervision of the Montgomery police, the allegations against the police defamed him personally.

Under the common law as it existed in Alabama and most other states, the *Times* had little chance of winning. Whether the statements referred to Sullivan was a fact issue; if the jury found that readers would identify him, it was immaterial that the ad did not name him. Because the statements reflected

adversely on Sullivan's professional reputation they were "libelous per se"; that meant he need not prove that he actually had been harmed. The defense of truth was not available because the ad contained factual errors (for example, police had not "ringed the campus," though they had been deployed nearby; King had been arrested four times, not seven). A few states recognized a privilege for good faith errors in criticism of public officials, but Alabama was among the majority that did not.

The jury awarded Sullivan $500,000. In the Alabama Supreme Court, the *Times* argued such a judgment was inconsistent with freedom of the press, but that court merely repeated what the United States Supreme Court had often said: "The First Amendment of the United States Constitution does not protect libelous publications."

Under the common law as it existed in Alabama and most other states, the Times *had little chance of winning.*

See also

Civil Rights

Public Figures

When the case reached the Supreme Court in 1964, it was one of eleven libel claims, totaling $5,600,000, pending against the *Times* in Alabama. It was obvious that libel suits were being used to discourage the press from supporting the civil rights movement in the South. The *Times* urged the Court to equate these uses of libel law with the discredited doctrine of seditious libel and to hold that criticism of public officials could never be actionable.

Only three Justices were willing to go that far. The majority adopted a more limited rule, holding that public officials could recover for defamatory falsehoods about their official conduct or fitness for office only if they could prove that the defendant had published with "actual malice." This was defined as "knowledge that [the statement] was false or with reckless disregard of whether it was false or not." The Court further held that this element had to be established by "clear and convincing proof," and that, unlike most factual issues, it was subject to independent review by appellate courts. The Court then reviewed Sullivan's evidence and determined that it did not meet the new standard.

The decision was an important breakthrough, not only for the press and the civil rights movement but also in First Amendment theory. Until then, vast areas of expression, including libel and commercial speech, had been categorically excluded from First Amendment protection. Also, the decision finally repudiated the darkest blot on freedom of expression in the history of the United States, the Sedition Act of 1798.

Over the next few years, the Court went out of its way to make the new rule effective. It defined "reckless disregard" narrowly (*St. Amant v. Thompson,* 1967). It extended the *Sullivan* rule to lesser public officials (*Rosenblatt* v. *Baer,* 1966), to candidates for public office (*Monitor Patriot Co.* v. *Roy,* 1971), to public figures (*As-*

AMENDMENT I

"Congress shall make no law respecting an establishment of religion, or prohibiting the free exercise thereof; or abridging the freedom of speech, or of the press; or the right of the people peaceably to assemble, and to petition the Government for a redress of grievances."

Within the legal culture, the First Amendment is typically understood to protect from government abridgment a broad realm of what might be called "symbolic activity," including speech, religion, press, association, and assembly. Because these symbolic activities are intertwined with many other activities that the government is clearly empowered to regulate—for instance, education and economic relations—the courts have experienced considerable difficulty in distinguishing impermissible infringement on First Amendment freedoms from legitimate exercises of government authority. Much of Supreme Court doctrine in the First Amendment area is an attempt to develop and refine precisely this sort of distinction.

One dominant principle that has informed the Supreme Court's doctrinal development of this distinction is the principle of content neutrality. The principle of content neutrality suggests that government must be neutral as to the conceptual content of speech, religion, press, and symbolic activity in general. Hence, according to First Amendment doctrine, it is only in extreme circumstances and for the most important reasons that the Court will allow government to regulate symbolic activity because of its conceptual content. The converse of this judicial principle is that the Court will recognize a relatively broad governmental power to regulate symbolic activity because of its effects or its form. Putting these two principles side by side, the result is that content-based regulation is often found unconstitutional, whereas content-neutral regulation is often found to be constitutional. These two broad imperatives with their sharply divergent implications for case outcomes place great conceptual pressure on distinguishing the content-based from the content-neutral, or more specifically on distinguishing the conceptual or substantive content of symbolic activity from its form and effects.

sociated Press v. Walker, 1967), and to criminal libel (Garrison v. Louisiana, 1964). After 1971 the Court retreated somewhat, declining to extend the Sullivan rule to private plaintiffs and permitting a de facto narrowing of the public figure category.

From its birth the rule has been criticized, by public officials and celebrities who believe it makes recovery too difficult, and by the news media, which argue that the rule still exposes them to long and expensive litigation, even though ultimately they usually win. The Court, however, has shown no inclination to revise the rule. In *Bose Corp.* v. *Consumers Union* (1984) the Court was invited to dilute it by abandoning independent appellate review of findings of "actual malice." The Court refused, holding such review essential "to preserve the precious liberties established and ordained by the Constitution."

—DAVID A. ANDERSON

Bibliography

Kalven, Harry, Jr. (1964). The New York Times Case: A Note on "The Central Meaning of the First Amendment." *Supreme Court Review* 1964:191–221.

Pierce, Samuel R., Jr. (1965). The Anatomy of an Historic Decision: *New York Times Co.* v. *Sullivan. North Carolina Law Review* 43:315–363.

NEW YORK TIMES CO. v. UNITED STATES

403 U.S. 713 (1971)

New York Times Co. v. *United States,* more commonly known as the Pentagon Papers case, is one of the landmarks of contemporary prior restraint doctrine. Only *Near* v. *Minnesota* (1931) rivals it as a case of central importance in establishing the First Amendment's particular and extreme aversion to any form of official restriction applied prior to the act of speaking or the act of publication.

THE PENTAGON PAPERS

Daniel Ellsberg leaked classified Defense Department studies to the *New York Times. (Corbis/Bettmann)*

The dramatic facts of the case served to keep it before the public eye even as it was being litigated and decided. On June 12, 1971, the *New York Times* commenced publication of selected portions of a 1968 forty-seven-volume classified Defense Department study entitled "History of United States Decision Making Process on Vietnam Policy" and a 1965 classified Defense Department study entitled "The Command and Control Study of the Tonkin Gulf Incident Done by the Defense Department's Weapons Systems Evaluation Group in 1965." Collectively these documents came to be known as the Pentagon Papers. Within a few days other major newspapers, including the *Washington Post,* the *Los Angeles Times,* the *Detroit Free Press,* the *Philadelphia Inquirer,* and the *Miami Herald* also commenced publication of the Pentagon Papers. The papers had been provided to the *New York Times* by Daniel Ellsberg, a former Defense Department official and former government consultant. Ellsberg had no official authority to take the Pentagon Papers; his

N

**NEW YORK TIMES CO.
v. UNITED STATES**

403 U.S. 713 (1971)

*This case is one of
the landmarks of
contemporary prior
restraint doctrine.*

turning over the papers to the *New York Times* was similarly unauthorized.

When the newspapers commenced publication, the United States was still engaged in fighting the Vietnam War. Claiming that the publication of the Pentagon Papers jeopardized national security, the government sought an injunction against any further publication of the papers, including publication of scheduled installments yet to appear. In the United States District Court for the Southern District of New York, Judge Murray Gurfein issued a temporary restraining order against the *New York Times*, but then denied the government's request for a preliminary injunction against publication, finding that, in light of the extremely high hurdle necessary to justify a prior restraint against a newspaper, "the publication of these historical documents would [not] seriously breach the national security." The United States immediately appealed, and the Court of Appeals for the Second Circuit, on June 23, 1971, remanded the case for further consideration in light of documents filed by the United States indicating that publication might pose "grave and immediate danger to the security of the United States." The Second Circuit continued to enforce the stay it had previously issued, in effect keeping the *Times* under the restraint of the temporary restraining order. On the same day, however, the United States Court of Appeals for the District of Columbia Circuit, in a case involving the *Washington Post*'s publication of the Pentagon Papers, affirmed a decision of the district court refusing to enjoin further publication. On June 24, the *New York Times* filed a petition for a writ of certiorari and motion for expedited consideration in the Supreme Court, and on the same day the United States asked that Court for a stay of the District of Columbia circuit's ruling in the *Washington Post* case. The two cases were consolidated and accelerated, with briefs filed on June 26, oral argument the same day, and a decision of the Supreme Court on June 30,

only seventeen days after the first publication of the papers in the *New York Times*.

In a brief per curiam opinion, the Supreme Court affirmed the District of Columbia Circuit, reversed the Second Circuit, and vacated the restraints. Noting the "heavy presumption" against prior restraints, and the consequent "heavy burden of . . . justification" necessary to support a prior restraint, the Court found that the United States had not met that especially heavy burden.

The Court's per curiam opinion was accompanied by a number of important separate opinions by individual Justices. Justices Hugo L. Black and William O. Douglas made it clear that in their view prior restraints were never permissible. Justice William J. Brennan would not go this far, but found it noteworthy that "never before has the United States sought to enjoin a newspaper from publishing information in its possession." For him "only governmental allegation and proof that publication must inevitably, directly, and immediately cause the occurrence of an evil kindred to imperiling the safety of a transport already at sea [citing *Near* v. *Minnesota*] can support even the issuance of an interim restraining order." In agreeing that the restraint was improper, Justice Thurgood Marshall emphasized the absence of statutory authorization for governmental action to enjoin a newspaper. And Justice John Marshall Harlan, joined by Chief Justice Warren E. Burger and Justice Harry A. Blackmun, dissented. The dissenters were disturbed by the alacrity of the proceedings, and in addition thought that the executive's "constitutional primacy in the field of foreign affairs" justified a restraint at least long enough to allow the executive to present its complete case for the necessity of restriction. The most doctrinally illuminating opinions, however, were those of Justices Potter J. Stewart and Byron R. White. For them only the specific nature of the restriction rendered it constitutionally impermissible. Had the case involved criminal or civil sanctions imposed after publication—subsequent punishment rather than prior restraint—they indicated that the First Amendment would not have stood in the way.

As highlighted by the opinions of Justices Stewart and White, therefore, the Pentagon Papers case presents the problem of prior restraint in purest form. The judges had the disputed materials in front of them, and thus there was no question of a restraint on materials not before a court, or not yet published. And the evaluation of the likely effect of the materials was made by the judiciary, rather than by a censorship board, other administrative agency, or police officer. Under these circumstances, why might a prior restraint be unconstitutional when a subsequent punishment for publishing the same materials would be upheld? What justifies a constitutional standard higher for injunctions than for criminal sanctions? It cannot be that prior restraints in fact "prevent" more things from being published, for the deterrent effect of a criminal sanction is likely to inhibit publication at least as much as an injunction. Someone who is willing knowingly to violate the criminal law, in order to publish out of conscience, may also be willing to violate an injunction. Is the special aversion against prior restraint, visible in the Pentagon Papers case, based on principle, or is it little more than an anachronism inherited from John Milton and William Blackstone, and transferred from a milieu in which prior restraint was synonymous with unreviewable determinations of an administrative censorship board?

The result in the Pentagon Papers case was not inconsistent with prior cases. The case did, however, present more clearly the puzzling nature of the virtually absolute prohibition against prior restraints under circumstances in which subsequent punishment of the very same material would have been permissible. Yet the case is also significant for reasons that transcend the doctrine of prior restraint. When confronted with a constitutional objection to a governmental policy, a court typically must evaluate the justification for the policy, and assess the likelihood of some consequences that the policy is designed to prevent. When that consequence and the governmental attempt to forestall it relates to war, national security, or national defense, judicial deference to governmental assertions of likely consequences has traditionally been greatest, even if the putative restriction implicates activities otherwise protected by the Constitution. When national security has been invoked, constitutional protection has often been more illusory than real. At every level in the Pentagon Papers case the courts conducted their own independent assessments of the likely dangers to national security and to troops overseas. The Supreme Court's decision was at least partly a function of the Justices' unwillingness to accept governmental incantation of the phrase "national security" as dispositive. Certainly executive determinations concerning the effect of publications on national security still receive greater deference than do other executive predictions about the effect of publications. But the Pentagon Papers case stands for the proposition that even when national security is claimed the courts will scrutinize for themselves the necessity of restriction. The decision, therefore, speaks not only to prior restraint but also, and more pervasively, to the courts' willingness to protect constitutional rights even against wartime governmental restrictions imposed in the name of national security.

—FREDERICK SCHAUER

Bibliography

Henkin, Louis (1971). The Right to Know and the Duty to Withhold: The Case of the Pentagon Papers. *University of Pennsylvania Law Review* 120:271–280.

Junger, Peter (1971). Down Memory Lane: The Case of the Pentagon Papers. *Case Western Reserve Law Review* 23:3–75.

Kalven, Harry, Jr. (1971). Foreword: Even When a Nation Is at War. *Harvard Law Review* 85:3–36.

See also

Memoris v. Massachusetts

Near v. Minnesota

A federal grand jury had indicted seven defendants, including Nixon's former attorney general and closest White House aides.

NIXON, UNITED STATES v.

418 U.S. 683 (1974)

This litigation unfolded contemporaneously with congressional investigation of the Watergate affair and with proceedings in the House of Representatives for the impeachment of President Richard M. Nixon. A federal grand jury had indicted seven defendants, including Nixon's former attorney general and closest White House aides, charging several offenses, including conspiracy to obstruct justice by "covering up" the circumstances of a burglary of Democratic party offices in Washington. The grand jury named Nixon as an unindicted coconspirator. A special prosecutor had been appointed to handle this prosecution. To obtain evidence, the special prosecutor asked Judge John Sirica to issue a subpoena ordering Nixon to produce electronic tapes and papers relating to sixty-four White House conversations among persons named as conspirators, including Nixon himself.

Judge Sirica issued the subpoena in mid-April 1974; on May 1 Nixon's counsel moved to quash the subpoena and to expunge the grand jury's naming of the president as a coconspirator. Sirica denied both motions and ordered Nixon to produce the subpoenaed items. When Nixon appealed, the special prosecutor asked the Supreme Court to hear the case, bypassing the court of appeals. The Court granted that motion and advanced argument to July 8. On July 24 the Court upheld the subpoena, 8–0, including the votes of three Nixon appointees. Justice William H. Rehnquist, formerly a Justice Department official under the indicted ex-attorney general, had disqualified himself. A week following the decision, before Nixon had complied with it, the House Judiciary Committee recommended his impeachment. When Nixon turned over the tapes on August 5, they included a conversation that even his strongest supporters called a "smoking gun." On August 9 the president resigned.

A year earlier a White House press officer had said Nixon would obey a "definitive" decision of the Supreme Court about the tapes. At oral argument in the Supreme Court, however, Nixon's counsel, pressed to say that the president had "submitted himself" to the Court's decision, evaded any forthright promise of compliance. Even after the Court's decision, the press reported, Nixon and his aides debated for some hours whether he should comply with the subpoena. Some have reported that the Court's unanimity was an important factor influencing that decision.

The Court itself seems to have been impressed with the need for unanimity; its bland opinion, formally attributed to Chief Justice Warren E. Burger, bore the external marks of a document hurriedly negotiated— as investigative reporters have said it was. The Court brushed aside objections to its jurisdiction, such as the final judgment rule. Nixon also argued that the courts had no jurisdiction over an "intra-branch" dispute between the president and his subordinate, the special prosecutor. Responding, the Court emphasized the "uniqueness" of the conflict, but apart from that comment its argument bordered on incoherence. After gratuitously remarking that the executive branch had exclusive discretionary control over federal criminal prosecutions, the Court reversed field, discovering a guarantee of independence for the special prosecutor in the regulation that appointed him and promised not to remove him absent a consensus among certain congressional leaders. Both the Court's propositions were dubious. Yet the Court marched on to some heroic constitutional issues concerning relations between the executive and judicial branches.

Both sides had appealed to the abstraction of separation of powers. Nixon argued first that the judiciary lacked power "to compel the President in the exercise of his discretion," and second that the president enjoyed

COCONSPIRATOR

*President Richard M. Nixon
was accused of covering up a
burglary of Democratic party
offices at the Watergate complex
in Washington.
(Corbis/Bettmann)*

♦ **petit jury**
*The ordinary trial jury: a
body of lay persons who
hear evidence and decide
questions of fact in a civil
or criminal case.*

an executive privilege to keep confidential his conversations with his advisers. The first argument blurred two separate issues: the president's immunity from judicial process and the political question issue of his discretion to control disclosure of his conversations. This latter claim of absolute executive privilege overlapped his second main argument. That argument began with an absolute privilege claim, but if that claim failed the president sought to persuade the Court to recognize a wide scope for a qualified privilege.

The special prosecutor, opposing both presidential immunity and the claim of absolute privilege, assumed the existence of a qualified privilege. That privilege was lost, he argued, when there was substantial reason to believe that the participants in a presidential conversation had been planning a crime.

The Court's opinion, like Nixon's argument, blurred the boundaries of separate issues in the case. The decision to uphold the subpoena, however, implicitly rejected the claim of presidential immunity, and the Court expressly rejected the claim of absolute privilege. A qualified privilege did exist, the Court said—by way of assumption, not demonstration—but the privilege was defeated when the specific confidential information sought was shown to be relevant, admissible evidence for a pending federal prosecution. The Court thus disposed of the case without mentioning Nixon's own possible complicity in crime; it dismissed the question whether the president could constitutionally be named as a coconspirator.

Today some form of a qualified executive privilege is assumed to exist, but the scope of the privilege remains largely undefined. *Nixon*'s most important contribution to our constitutional law, however, lay elsewhere: in its reaffirmation that even the highest officer of government is not beyond the reach of the law and the courts. Nixon's brief had included this remark, designed to reassure: "it must be stressed we do not suggest the President has the attributes of a king. *Inter alia,* a king rules by inheritance and for life." The *Nixon* decision reminded us that there are also other differences.

—KENNETH L. KARST

Bibliography

Symposium (1974). *United States* v. *Nixon. UCLA Law Review* 22:1–140.

Woodward, Bob, and Armstrong, Scott (1979). *The Brethren: Inside the Supreme Court.* Pages 285–347. New York: Simon & Schuster.

NIXON v. FITZGERALD

457 U.S. 731 (1982)

HARLOW v. FITZGERALD

457 U.S. 800 (1982)

In these cases the Supreme Court significantly expanded the scope of executive immunity in actions for damages brought by persons injured by official action. Fitzgerald sued former president Richard M. Nixon and two of his aides, alleging that he had been dismissed from an Air Force job in retaliation for revealing to a congressional committee a two billion dollar cost overrun for a transport aircraft.

In *Nixon* the Court held, 5–4, that the president is absolutely immune from civil damages—not merely for the performance of particular functions but for all acts within the "outer perimeter" of his official duties. Justice Lewis F. Powell, for the majority, rested his decision not on the text of the Constitution but on "the constitutional tradition of the separation of powers." Unlike other executive officers, who have only a qualified immunity from damages actions, the president occupies a unique place in the government. He must be able to act without fear of intrusive inquiries into his motives. The dissenters

agreed that some of the president's functions should be clothed in absolute immunity, but argued that a qualified immunity from suit was sufficient in most cases to protect presidential independence.

In *Harlow* the Court, 8–1, rejected the aides' claim of absolute immunity, but broadened the scope of qualified executive immunity. Under previous decisions, this immunity was lost when the official negligently violated "clearly established" rights or acted with malicious intention to deprive constitutional rights or to cause harm. The Court here eliminated the "malicious intention" test for losing the immunity. A great many actions for damages against executive officials are based on claims of right that are not "clearly established." *Harlow* forbids damages in such a case even though the official acts with malice.

—KENNETH L. KARST

NORRIS v. ALABAMA

294 U.S. 587 (1935)

Clarence Norris, one of the Scottsboro boys on retrial, moved to quash the indictment and trial venire (pool of potential jurors) on the ground that qualified black citizens were systematically excluded from jury service solely on the basis of race. On denial of his motion by the trial judge, Norris was retried and again found guilty. The state supreme court affirmed the judgment of the trial court that no jury discrimination existed. The Supreme Court, voting 8–0, reversed the judgment after reviewing the evidence for itself for the first time in such a case. The evidence showed that for a generation or more no black person had been called for jury service in the county and that a substantial number of black persons qualified under state law. In an opinion by Chief Justice Charles Evans Hughes, the Court ruled that the evidence of black exclusion made a *prima facie* case of denial of the equal protection guaranteed by the Fourteenth Amendment. *Norris* began a line of

The Court held that the president is absolutely immune from civil damages.

See also

Racial Discrimination

cases that led to the virtual extinction of racial discrimination in the composition of juries.

—LEONARD W. LEVY

NORTHERN SECURITIES CO. v. UNITED STATES

193 U.S. 197 (1904)

A bare majority of the Supreme Court, in a broad construction of congressional power under the commerce clause, upheld the constitutionality of the Sherman Antitrust Act as applied to holding companies. The Court thus extended the scope of the Sherman Act to companies not directly engaged in such commerce that nevertheless controlled interstate commerce.

The formation in 1901 of the Northern Securities Company, a holding company comprising both the Hill-Morgan and the Harriman interests, united parallel competing lines. In March 1902 the government filed an equity suit to dissolve the company. The question was clear: Was a holding company, whose subsidiaries' operations were its only connection with interstate commerce, exempt from the Sherman Act? The Court split 5–4 but without a majority opinion.

Justice John Marshall Harlan, for the plurality, followed *United States* v. *Trans-Missouri Freight Association* (1897) and other cases, arguing that the Sherman Act established competition as a test for interstate commerce. Harlan declared that a combination need not be directly in commerce to restrain it: intent to restrain or potential for restraint was all that was needed, and here potential restraint could be found in the reduction of competition resulting from the holding company's formation. Harlan refused to interpret the statute using the rule of reason. He also broadly construed the commerce clause, curtly dismissing defense allegations that the injunction violated state sovereignty

and the Tenth Amendment. Justice David J. Brewer concurred only in Harlan's result. Abandoning his earlier opinions, Brewer now embraced the rule of reason but concluded that even under that rule the Northern Securities Company clearly constituted an unlawful restraint of trade.

Justices Edward D. White and Oliver Wendell Holmes each wrote dissents. The former followed the definition of interstate commerce in *United States* v. *E. C. Knight Company* (1895), stressing that stock ownership did not place the defendants within the scope of the Sherman Act. Holmes's first written dissent on the Supreme Court emphasized a common law reading of the statute. He believed that the holding company device was neither a combination nor a contract in restraint of trade. Holmes asserted that this case so nearly resembled *Knight* as to require no deviation from that opinion.

Counted by Theodore Roosevelt "one of the greatest achievements of my administration because it emphasized the fact that the most powerful men in this country were held to accountability before the law," this decision's importance lay both in Harlan's insistence on the supremacy of federal law and in the reinvigoration of a law that business had hoped the Court rendered ineffectual in *Knight*.

—DAVID GORDON

Bibliography

Appel, R. W., Jr. (1975). The Case of the Monopolistic Railroadman. In John A. Garraty, ed., *Quarrels That Have Shaped the Constitution*. New York: Harper & Row.

NORTHWESTERN FERTILIZER CO. v. HYDE PARK

97 U.S. 659 (1878)

In 1867 the Illinois legislature chartered the company for a term of fifty years to

The formation in 1901 of the Northern Securities Company united parallel competing lines.

See also

E. C. Knight Co., United States v.

See also

Boston Beer Co. v.
   Massachusetts

manufacture fertilizer, from dead animals, outside the city limits of Chicago. The nearby village of Hyde Park regarded the company's factory as an unendurable nuisance, injurious to the public health. Immediately before the legislature chartered the company it empowered the village to abate public nuisances excepting the company. The village passed an ordinance prohibiting the existence of any company engaged in any offensive or unwholesome business within a distance of one mile. The ordinance put the fertilizer company out of business. It invoked its chartered rights against the ordinance, which it claimed violated the contract clause.

On the basis of past decisions the Court should have accepted the company's argument, holding that the village had no authority to abate its factory. By a vote of 7–1, however, the Supreme Court ruled that the village had validly exercised its police power to protect the public health. Justice Noah Swayne for the Court declared that the company's charter must be construed narrowly and held that it provided no exemption from liability or nuisances. Swayne quoted from the decision earlier that term in *Boston Beer Co.* v. *Massachusetts* in which the Court announced the doctrine of inalienable police power. Both cases had the result of weakening the contract clause's traditional protection of chartered rights.

—LEONARD W. LEVY

O

O'BRIEN,
UNITED STATES v.

391 U.S. 367 (1968)

The *O'Brien* opinion is today widely cited in briefs and judicial opinions defending governmental action against claims of violation of the freedom of speech. In 1965 Congress amended the Selective Service Act to make it a crime to destroy or mutilate a draft registration card. The amendment's legislative history made clear that it was aimed at antiwar protest, but the Supreme Court nonetheless upheld, 8–1, the conviction of a protester for draft card burning, rejecting his First Amendment claims.

Writing for the Court, Chief Justice Earl Warren assumed that symbolic speech of this kind was entitled to First Amendment protection. However, he announced a doctrinal formula now dear to the hearts of government attorneys, a formula that seemed to apply generally to all First Amendment cases: "[W]e think it clear that a government regulation is sufficiently justified if it is within the constitutional power of the Government; if it furthers an important or substantial governmental interest; if the governmental interest is unrelated to the suppression of free

♦ **brief**
A document filed on behalf of a litigant, at a trial or on appeal, stating the facts of the case and arguing the legal basis for a decision in the litigant's favor.

**NO FIRST
AMENDMENT
PROTECTION**

Antiwar protestors burn their draft cards in violation of the O'Brien *decision. (Corbis/Bettmann)*

expression; and if the incidental restriction on alleged First Amendment freedoms is no greater than is essential to the furtherance of that interest."

This very case seemed appropriate for application of the formula to overturn the protesters' conviction, but it was not to be. Here, Warren said, the power of the federal government to "conscript manpower" was clear; further, he placed great importance on the government's interests in keeping draft cards intact. As for the purpose to suppress expression, the Chief Justice took away what he had just given to First Amendment challengers: the Court should not inquire, he said, into possible improper congressional motivations for an otherwise valid law. Finally, he said, the government's interests could not be served by any less restrictive means.

It is hard to avoid the conclusion that the Justices, embattled on political fronts ranging from segregation to school prayers, thought it prudent not to add to the Court's difficulties a confrontation with Congress and the president over the Vietnam War. Justice William O. Douglas, however, dissented alone on the ground that the Court should consider the constitutionality of military conscription in the absence of a declaration of war by Congress.

—KENNETH L. KARST

Bibliography

Ely, John Hart (1975). Flag Desecration: A Case Study in the Roles of Categorization and Balancing in First Amendment Analysis. *Harvard Law Review* 88: 1482–1508.

Nimmer, Melville B. (1973). The Meaning of Symbolic Speech under the First Amendment. *UCLA Law Review* 21:29–62.

OBSCENITY

Obscenity laws embarrass Alexis De Tocqueville's claim that there is "hardly a political question in the United States which does not sooner or later turn into a judicial one." It is not merely that the obscenity question became a serious judicial issue rather much later than sooner. It is that the richness of the questions involved have been lost in their translation to the judicial forum.

Obscenity laws implicate great questions of political theory including the characteristics of human nature, the relationship between law and morals, and the appropriate role of the state in a democratic society. But these questions were barely addressed when the Court first seriously considered a constitutional challenge to obscenity laws in the 1957 cases of *Roth* v. *United States* and *Alberts* v. *California*.

The briefs presented the Court with profoundly different visions of First Amendment law. Roth argued that no speech including obscenity could be prohibited without meeting the clear and present danger test, that a danger of lustful thoughts was not the type of evil with which a legislature could be legitimately concerned, and that no danger of antisocial conduct had been shown. On the other hand, the government urged the Court to adopt a balancing test that prominently featured a consideration of the value of the speech involved. The government tendered an illustrative hierarchy of nineteen speech categories with political, religious, economic, and scientific speech at the top; entertainment, music, and humor in the middle; and libel, obscenity, profanity, and commercial pornography at the bottom. The government's position was that the strength of public interest needed to justify speech regulation diminished as one moved down the hierarchy and increased as one moved up.

In response to these opposing contentions, the Court took a middle course. Relying on cases like *Beauharnais* v. *Illinois* (1952), the Court seemed to embrace what Harry Kalven Jr. later called the two-level theory of the First Amendment. Under this theory, some speech is beneath the protection of the

See also

Freedom of Speech

Symbolic Speech

First Amendment; only that speech within the amendment's protection is measured by the clear and present danger test. Thus some speech is at the bottom of a two-level hierarchy, and the *Roth* Court sought to explain why obscenity deserved basement-level non-protection.

History, tradition, and consensus were the staple of the Court's argument. Justice William J. Brennan explained that all "ideas having even the slightest redeeming social importance" deserve full First Amendment protection. But, he said, "implicit in the history of the First Amendment is the rejection of obscenity as utterly without redeeming social importance." Then he pointed to the consensus of fifty nations, forty-eight states, and twenty obscenity laws passed by the Congress from 1842 to 1956. Finally, relying on an obiter dictum from *Chaplinsky* v. *New Hampshire* (1942), the Court explained that obscene utterances "are of such slight social value as a step to truth that any benefit that may be derived from them is clearly outweighed by the social interest in order and morality."

From the perspective of liberal, conservative, or feminist values, the Court's reliance on the *Chaplinsky* quotation amounts to a cryptic resolution of fundamental political questions. Liberals would advance several objections. Some would suggest that the Court underestimates the contribution to truth made by sexually oriented material. David Richards, for example, has suggested that

> pornography can be seen as the unique medium of a vision of sexuality . . . a view of sensual delight in the erotic celebration of the body, a concept of easy freedom without consequences, a fantasy of timelessly repetitive indulgence. In opposition to the Victorian view that narrowly defines proper sexual function in a rigid way that is analogous to ideas of excremental regularity and moderation, pornography builds a model of plastic variety and joyful excess in sexuality. In opposition to the sorrowing

> Catholic dismissal of sexuality as an unfortunate and spiritually superficial concomitant of propagation, pornography affords the alternative idea of the independent status of sexuality as a profound and shattering ecstasy [1974, p. 81].

Even some liberals might find these characterizations overwrought as applied to Samuel Roth's publications, such as *Wild Passion* and *Wanton by Night*. Nonetheless, many of them would argue that even if such publications have no merit in the marketplace of ideas, individuals should be able to decide for themselves what they want to read. Many would argue along with John Stuart Mill that "[t]he only purpose for which power can be rightfully exercised over any member of a civilized community, against his will, is to prevent harm to others." Such a principle is thought to advance the moral nature of humanity, for what distinguishes human beings from animals is the capacity to make autonomous moral judgments. From this perspective, the *Roth* opinion misunderstands the necessity for individual moral judgments and diminishes liberty in the name of order without a proper showing of harm.

Conservatives typically agree that humans are distinguished from animals by their capacity to make rational moral judgments. They believe, however, that liberals overestimate human rational capacity and underestimate the importance of the state in promoting a virtuous citizenry. Moreover, they insist that liberals do not sufficiently appreciate the morally corrosive effects of obscenity. From their perspective, obscenity emphasizes the base animality of our nature, reduces the spirituality of humanity to mere bodily functions, and debases civilization by transforming the private into the public. As Irving Kristol put it, "When sex is a public spectacle, a human relationship has been debased into a mere animal connection."

Feminists typically make no objection to erotic material and make no sharp separation

*Obscenity laws
implicate great
questions of political
theory.*

between reason and passion. Their principal objection is to the kind of sexually oriented material that encourages male sexual excitement in the domination of women. From their perspective, a multibillion dollar industry promotes antifemale propaganda encouraging males to get, as Susan Brownmiller put it, a "sense of power from viewing females as anonymous, panting playthings, adult toys, dehumanized objects to be used, abused, broken and discarded." From the feminist perspective, the *Roth* opinion's reference to the interests in order and morality obscures the interest in equality for women. From the conservative perspective, the opinion is underdeveloped. From the liberal perspective, it is wrongheaded.

Liberals gained some post-*Roth* hope from the Court's treatment of the obscenity question in *Stanley* v. *Georgia* (1969). In *Stanley* the Court held that the possession of obscenity in the home could not be made a criminal offense without violating the First Amendment. More interesting than the holding, which has since been confined to its facts, was the Court's rationale. The Court insisted that "our whole constitutional heritage rebels at the thought of giving government the power to control men's minds." It denied the state any power "to control the moral content of a person's thoughts." It suggested that the only interests justifying obscenity laws were that obscene material might fall into the hands of children or that it might "intrude upon the sensibilities or privacy of the general public."

Many commentators thought that *Stanley* would be extended to protect obscene material where precautions had been taken to avoid exposure to children or nonconsenting adults. Indeed such precautions were taken by many theaters, but the Supreme Court (the composition of which had changed significantly since *Stanley*) reaffirmed *Roth* and expanded on its rationale in *Paris Adult Theatre I* v. *Slaton* (1973).

The Court professed to "hold that there are legislative interests at stake in stemming the tide of commercialized obscenity, even assuming it is feasible to enforce effective safeguards against exposure to the juvenile and the passerby. These include the interest of the public in the quality of life and the total community environment, the tone of commerce in the great city centers, and, possibly, the public safety itself." The Court did not suggest that the link between obscenity and sex crimes was anything other than arguable. It did insist that the "States have the power to make a morally neutral judgment that public exhibition of obscene material, or commerce in such material, has a tendency to injure the community as a whole . . . or to jeopardize, in Chief Justice Earl Warren's words, the State's "right . . . to maintain a decent society."

Several puzzles remain after the Court's explanation is dissected. First, "arguable" connections to crime do not ordinarily suffice to justify restrictions of First Amendment liberties. A merely arguable connection to crime supports restriction only if the speech involved is for some other reason outside First Amendment protection. Second, as the Court was later to recognize in *Young* v. *American Mini Theatres, Inc.* (1976), the reference to quality of life, the tone of commerce in the central cities, and the environment have force with respect to all sexually oriented bookstores and theaters whether or not they display obscene films or sell obscene books. The Court in *Miller* v. *California* (1973) limited the definition of obscenity to that material which the "average person, applying contemporary community standards" would find that "taken as a whole appeals to the prurient interest" and "depicts and describes, in a patently offensive way, sexual conduct specifically defined by the applicable state law"; and which, "taken as a whole, lacks serious literary, artistic, political, or scientific value." No one has suggested that these restrictions on the definition bear any relationship to the tone of commerce in the cities.

Moreover, if the intrusive character of public display were the issue, mail order sales of obscene material should pass muster under the First Amendment; yet there is no indication that the Court is prepared to protect such traffic. As interpreted in the *Paris Adult Theatre* opinion, *Stanley* v. *Georgia* appears to protect only those obscene books and films created and enjoyed in the home; the right to use in the home amounts to no more than that. There is no right to receive obscene material—even in plain brown wrappers.

Perhaps least convincing is the Court's attempt to harmonize its *Paris Adult Theatre* holding with liberal thought. It claims to have no quarrel with the court's insistence in *Stanley* that the state is without power "to control the moral content of a person's thoughts." Because obscene material by the Court's definition lacks any serious literary, artistic, political, or scientific value, control of it is said to be "distinct from a control of reason and the intellect." But this is doubletalk. The power to decide what has serious artistic value is the power to make moral decisions. To decide that material addressing "reason" or the "intellect" is all that is important to human beings is ultimately to make a moral decision about human beings. Implicit in the latter idea, of course, is the belief that the enjoyment of erotic material for its own sake is unworthy of protection. But the view is much more general. The Court supposes that human beings have a rational side and an emotional side, that the emotional side needs to be subordinated and controlled, and that such suppression or control is vital to the moral life. That is why the Court believes that the contribution of obscenity to truth is outweighed by the state's interest in morality. The Court's insistence on the right to maintain a decent society is in fact an insistence on the state's interest in the control of the "moral content of a person's thoughts."

Finally, it is simply dazzling for the Court to suggest that the states are engaged in a "morally neutral" judgment when they decide that obscene material jeopardizes the right to maintain a decent society. When states decide that "a sensitive key relationship of human existence, central to family life, community welfare, and the development of human personality can be debased and distorted by commercial exploitation of sex," they operate as moral guardians, not as moral neutrals. Nonetheless, the Court's bows to liberal theory in *Paris Adult Theatre* are revealing, and so are the guarded compromises of the obscenity test adopted in *Miller* v. *California*. The bows and compromises reflect, as do the opinions of the four dissenting Justices in *Paris Adult Theatre,* that America is profoundly divided on the relationship of law to morality and on the meaning of free speech. Since *Paris Adult Theatre* and *Miller,* and despite those decisions, the quantity of erotic material has continued to grow. At the same time, feminist opposition to pornography has ripened into a powerful political movement. The Supreme Court's decisions have neither stemmed the tide of commercial pornography nor resolved the divisions of American society on the issue. These political questions will continue to be judicial questions.

—STEVEN SHIFFRIN

Bibliography

Clor, Harry M. (1969). *Obscenity and Public Morality.* Chicago: University of Chicago Press.

Kalven, Harry, Jr. (1960). The Metaphysics of the Law of Obscenity. *Supreme Court Review* 1960:1–45.

Lederer, Laura, ed. (1980). *Take Back the Night: Women on Pornography.* New York: Bantam Books.

Richards, David A. J. (1974). Free Speech and Obscenity Law: Toward a Moral Theory of the First Amendment. *University of Pennsylvania Law Review* 123:45–99.

See also

Beauharnais v. *Illinois*

Chaplinsky v. *New Hampshire*

Miller v. *California*

Roth v. *United States*

Stanley v. *Georgia*

Young v. *American Mini Theaters, Inc.*

*O'Connor has
refused to accept the
prevailing view that
the Constitution is
merely a procedural
instrument.*

O'CONNOR,
SANDRA DAY

(1930–)

Sandra Day O'Connor was born in Arizona in 1930. After leaving high school at the age of sixteen, she completed both her undergraduate and law degrees at Stanford University in five years. She spent the next decade as a county attorney and in private practice in Arizona and elsewhere, and she became an Arizona assistant attorney general in 1965. She served in the Arizona state senate from 1969 until 1974, when she moved into the state judiciary—first as a trial judge and later on the state's intermediate court of appeals. President Ronald Reagan nominated her as the first female Justice of the Supreme Court of the United States in 1981.

O'Connor took the oath of office on September 25, 1981, as the first Supreme Court appointee of the most conservative president since Calvin Coolidge. Not surprisingly, she immediately became part of the conservative wing of the Court, voting with Justice William H. Rehnquist more than 90 percent of the time by 1984. She has continued to be a reliable conservative vote in criminal procedure and federalism cases. After 1984, however, she began striking out on her own in several areas. She became considerably less predictable in cases involving substantive due process, discrimination, and complex jurisdictional or procedural questions.

O'Connor soon became a pivotal center vote on the Court. Although this change resulted in part from the appointment of three more conservative Justices, it was also the result of the changes in O'Connor's own views: by 1987 she was voting with Rehnquist only 78 percent of the time. Moreover, O'Connor often writes separate concurrences and dissents, approaching cases from independent points of view; and her originally solo viewpoints have commanded majorities in several doctrinal areas. Four topics illustrate both her influence and her central position on the Court: the establishment clause of the First Amendment, affirmative action, capital punishment, and abortion.

At the time O'Connor joined the Court, establishment clause challenges were virtually always governed by the test of *Lemon* v. *Kurtzman* (1971): a statute violates the establishment clause if it has a primary purpose or a primary effect of advancing or inhibiting religion, or if it causes excessive government entanglement with religion. Beginning with *Lynch* v. *Donnelly* (1984), O'Connor proposed a "refinement" of the *Lemon* test emphasizing the questions "whether the government's purpose is to endorse religion and whether the statute actually conveys a message of endorsement." Unlike the standard view of the *Lemon* test, which centers on the practical effect of governmental action, O'Connor's test focuses on the communicative or symbolic aspects of that action. Thus, O'Connor would find a constitutional violation when "[e]ndorsement sends a message to non-adherents that they are outsiders, not full members of the political community, and an accompanying message to adherents that they are insiders, favored members of the political community."

Between 1984 and 1989 O'Connor's application of this principle made her the swing vote in many establishment-clause cases. She provided the fifth vote to uphold a public Christmas display including a crèche in *Lynch* v. *Donnelly* and to uphold federal funding of religious family-planning organizations in *Bowen* v. *Kendrick* (1988). She also provided the fifth vote to invalidate a state-mandated moment of silence for meditation or prayer at the beginning of the public school day in *Wallace* v. *Jaffree* (1985) and to invalidate a public Christmas display of a crèche alone in *County of Allegheny* v. *ACLU* (1989). In *County of Allegheny*, moreover, she appeared to have converted a majority of the Court to her test, at least where the display of religious symbols is at issue. And in *Agostini*

v. *Felton* (1997) she led the court in overruling two prior decisions so as to allow public school teachers to enter sectarian schools to furnish remedial instruction.

O'Connor also fashioned what has become the majority test for constitutional challenges to affirmative action programs. For over a decade, the Court was unable to produce a majority opinion in any constitutional case involving affirmative action. Badly fragmented, the Court could not agree on either the level of scrutiny to be applied to such challenges or the factual prerequisites that might make an affirmative action program valid. Beginning with *Wygant* v. *Jackson Board of Education* (1986), O'Connor wrote several separate opinions answering both questions with great specificity: affirmative action programs should be tested by strict scrutiny, and such scrutiny typically requires that there be a remedial need for the program, shown by some evidence—not necessarily contemporaneous—of prior government discrimination (remedying past societal discrimination is an insufficient governmental interest). In 1989, in *Richmond (City of)* v. *J. A. Croson Co.*

(1989), O'Connor obtained majority support for her position.

O'Connor's influential role in affirmative action continues. She held for the Court in *Johnson* v. *Transportation Agency of Santa Clara County* (1987) that a male applicant for promotion lacked a claim under Title VII of the Civil Rights Act when a female applicant got the position, even though she had scored slightly lower in the agency's evaluation procedure. As she pointed out, the vast statistical disparity—the county had never chosen a female road dispatcher—justified selecting the female applicant. However in *Adarand Constructors* v. *Pena* (1995) she wrote the Court's important opinion extending her ruling in *Croson* to mandate strict scrutiny review for federal as well as state affirmative action programs.

Similarly, in *Shaw* v. *Reno* (1993), O'Connor wrote for the Court that voting districts drawn with race as the main factor likewise are to be judged under the strict scrutiny test.

O'Connor has also had a significant influence in cases dealing with the death penalty for juveniles. Although she has not generally

FIRST FEMALE JUSTICE

Sandra Day O'Connor immediately became part of the conservative wing of the Court. (Corbis/Bettmann)

been the swing vote in ordinary capital cases, her vote has been crucial in deciding whether the state may execute persons who committed crimes when they were under the age of majority. In *Thompson v. Oklahoma* (1988), she voted with the four liberal Justices to overturn a death sentence imposed on a girl who had committed murder at the age of fifteen. O'Connor did not join Justice John Paul Stevens's plurality opinion, however, because it categorically denied the constitutionality of executing anyone who was under sixteen when the crime was committed. Instead, O'Connor concluded that the legislature, in failing to set any minimum age limit, did not give proper consideration to a question on which no national consensus existed and, thus, that the penalty was cruel and unusual punishment.

This distinctive approach allowed her to vote the very next year in *Stanford* v. *Kentucky* (1989) to uphold death sentences imposed on two juveniles who had committed crimes at the ages of sixteen and seventeen. Again she was the fifth vote, this time combining with the conservative wing of the Court, and again she wrote a separate concurrence basing her decision on a "sufficiently clear . . . national consensus." In a case decided the same day as *Stanford, Penry* v. *Lynaugh* (1989), O'Connor provided the pivotal vote (and wrote the majority opinion) for two separate majorities: one concluding that the Eighth Amendment generally permits the execution of mentally retarded adults and the other reversing the death sentence of the particular mentally retarded defendant on the ground that the jury instructions deprived the jury of any meaningful opportunity to take the defendant's handicap into account as a mitigating factor.

Finally, O'Connor proved to be the crucial vote on abortion. From 1981 to 1989 O'Connor consistently voted to uphold all antiabortion laws; and in *Akron* v. *Akron Center for Reproductive Health* (1983), she even wrote that the trimester framework of *Roe* v. *Wade* (1973) was "on a collision course with itself." In *Webster* v. *Reproductive Health Services*

(1989), however, O'Connor declined to join with the four other Justices wishing to modify *Roe.* Instead, she wrote a separate concurrence upholding the challenged statute under *Roe* itself and explicitly refusing to reach the question of *Roe's* continued validity. Indeed, her earlier opinions had suggested that the Court abandon the trimester approach to abortion and instead ask whether a challenged statute "unduly burdens" a woman's right to an abortion. In *Webster,* Rehnquist's plurality opinion adopted this approach almost verbatim, but O'Connor nevertheless declined to join his opinion.

Then in *Planned Parenthood of Southeastern Pennsylvaniaa* v. *Casey* (1992) O'Connor, together with Justices Anthony M. Kennedy and David H. Souter, wrote to emphasize that the Court would adhere to *Roe's* basic holding, though it discarded *Roe's* trimester approach and upheld some restrictions placed on the ability to obtain an abortion. In addition, O'Connor's opinion in *Casey* enunciated that the test for legislation restricting abortions would be whether it placed an "undue burden" on the right to obtain an abortion—a test that some see as a partial retreat from *Roe.*

O'Connor made her presence felt in another critical pair of decisions. In *Employment Division, Department of Human Resources of Oregon* v. *Smith* (1990), the Court held those challenging laws of general applicability as interfering with the free exercise of religion must show those laws lack a rational basis. O'Connor wrote a concurring opinion, agreeing with the three dissenters that in such cases the government should have to show the law to be narrowly tailored to meet a compelling state interest. However, she concurred with the majority because she believed a law criminalizing peyote, even when used in religious ceremonies, met that strict test. Later, in *Boerne (City of)* v. *Flores* (1997), when the Court held Congress was without power to legislate that strict scrutiny be the test for laws alleged to substantially burden the free exercise of religion, O'Connor, accompanied by Justice Stephen G, Breyer, contended *Smith* was wrongly decided and should be reexamined.

Two additional trends are evident in O'Connor's opinions. First, she frequently writes separately in order to "clarify" the majority's opinion. Her clarifying concurrences are often attempts to point out the limits of the Court's decision or to minimize the distance between the majority and dissent. In *Wygant,* for example, her concurrence stressed that there was little difference in application between a "compelling" governmental interest and an "important" one and that both majority and dissenting opinions agreed that remedying past discrimination constitutes such an interest. In other cases she has made a great effort to specify what issues the Court has not decided.

The second common thread during O'Connor's tenure on the Court to date is her tendency to demand fact-specific decision making in a wide variety of contexts. For example, in *Lanier* v. *South Carolina* (1985), she wrote a separate concurrence to a per curiam opinion on the voluntariness of a confession, stressing that on remand the court should look at the particular circumstances of the confession. In two cases involving the appropriate state statute of limitations to be borrowed in section 1983 actions, she dissented from nearly unanimous Court decisions imposing a single standard, preferring instead to examine the circumstances of each section 1983 suit (*Wilson* v. *Garcia* [1985] and *Goodman* v. *Lukens Steel Co.* [1987]). In a series of habeas corpus cases, she wrote majority opinions fashioning a test whereby defendants who could produce evidence of "actual innocence" might avoid the newly strengthened strictures of the "cause and prejudice" test (*Smith* v. *Murray* [1986] and *Murray* v. *Carrier* [1986]). In *Coy* v. *Iowa* (1988) she concurred in a decision invalidating on confrontation clause grounds a state statute permitting courts to place a screen between the accused and the accuser in child sexual abuse cases, but refused to join the majortity's conclusion that such screens *always* violate the right to confrontation. In *Allen* v. *Wright* (1984) she demanded greater specificity by parents seeking standing to challenge Internal Revenue Service regulations that they alleged were inadequate to prevent discriminatory private schools from obtaining and keeping charitable exemption status. Finally, her position on affirmative action, noted above, makes clear the need for some factual predicate for the adoption of any affirmative-action plan.

When O'Connor joined the Court in 1981, it was expected that her votes would reflect three influences: her conservatism would align her with the right wing of the Court, her state legislative background would give her a strong states' rights tilt, and her gender would make her more receptive to claims of sex discrimination. The last two of these expectations has proved both accurate and significant. Although as already indicated, she has voted conservatively on some issues, in other cases she has followed an independent path. Her deference to state legislatures has been reasonably consistent.

She furnished the deciding vote holding Congress had exceeded its authority in *United States* v. *Lopez* (1995) and *Printz* v. *United States* (1997), and wrote the Court's opinion in *New York* v. *United States* (1992) holding states' rights limited the ability of Congress to compel states to regulate nuclear waste on pain of being required to assume financial liability for that waste if they failed to do so.

O'Connor has, however, been a consistent supporter of gender equality. During her tenure on the Court, she has joined the majority—and sometimes provided a crucial vote—in making partnership decisions subject to Title VII (*Hishon* v. *King Spalding* [1984]), declaring sexual harassment as actionable under the same statute (*Meritor Savings Bank* v. *Vinson* [1986]), rejecting a preemption challenge to a state law requiring employers to give pregnancy leave to employ-

O

O'CONNOR, SANDRA DAY

(1930–)

ees who want one (*California Federal Savings & Loan* v. *Guerra* [1987]), upholding discrimination claims based on sexual stereotyping (*Price Waterhouse* v. *Hopkins* [1989]), invalidating an all-female state nursing school (*Mississippi University for Women* v. *Hogan* [1982]), and, as noted, upholding an affirmative action program for women (*Johnson* v. *Transportation Agency* [1987]).

Thus, after eighteen years on the Court, O'Connor has proved herself an independent and sometimes unpredictable thinker. It is clear, however, that the first female Supreme Court Justice has already left her mark on the Court and will continue to do so.

—SUZANNA SHERRY

Bibliography

Cordray, Richard M., and Vradelis, James I. (1985). The Emerging Jurisprudence of Justice O'Connor. *University of Chicago Law Review* 52:389–459.

O'Connor, Sandra Day (1981). Trends in the Relationship Between the Federal and State Courts from the Perspective of a State Court Judge. *William and Mary Law Review* 22:801–815.

Shea, Barbara C. S. (1986). Sandra Day O'Connor—Woman, Lawyer, Justice: Her First Four Terms on the Supreme Court. *University of Missouri, Kansas City Law Review* 55:1–32.

Sherry, Suzanna (1986). Civic Virtue and the Feminine Voice in Constitutional Adjudication. *Virginia Law Review* 72:543–616.

O'CONNOR v. DONALDSON

422 U.S. 563 (1975)

Donaldson was initially billed as the case that would decide whether a mental patient held in custody had a constitutional "right to treatment." Ultimately the Court did not decide that issue, but it did make some important pronouncements on the relation between mental illness and the Constitution.

Kenneth Donaldson was committed to a state hospital at the request of his father; the committing judge found that he suffered from "paranoid schizophrenia." Although the commitment order specified "care, maintenance, and treatment," for almost fifteen years Donaldson received nothing but "milieu therapy"—the hospital superintendent's imaginative name for involuntary confinement. Donaldson finally sued the superintendent and others for damages under section 1983, Title 42, United States Code, claiming they had intentionally denied his constitutional rights. The federal district judge instructed the jury that Donaldson's rights had been denied if the defendants had confined him against his will, knowing that he was neither dangerous nor receiving treatment. The jury awarded damages, and the court of appeals affirmed, specifically endorsing the district court's theory of a mental patient's constitutional right to treatment.

The Supreme Court unanimously held that Donaldson had stated a valid claim, but remanded the case for reconsideration of the hospital superintendent's assertion of executive immunity. Justice Potter Stewart, for the Court, said that a finding of mental illness alone could not justify a state's confining a person indefinitely "in simple custodial confinement." The Court did not reach the larger question of a "right to treatment"; it disclaimed any need to decide whether persons dangerous to themselves or others had a right to be treated during their involuntary confinement by the state, or whether a nondangerous person could be confined for purposes of treatment. But when the state lacked any of the usual grounds for confinement of the mentally ill—the safety of the person confined or others, or treatment for illness—involuntary confinement was a denial of liberty without due process of law. Confinement was not justified, for example, in order to provide the mentally ill with superior living standards, or to shield the public from unpleasantness. To support the latter point, the Court cited First Amendment decisions including *Cohen* v. *California* (1971). Chief Justice Warren E. Burger concurred in the Court's opinion, but wrote separately to express his opposition to any constitutional "right to treatment."

—KENNETH L. KARST

OGDEN v. SAUNDERS

12 Wheaton 213 (1827)

Ogden established the doctrine that a state bankruptcy act operating on contracts made after the passage of the act does not violate the obligation of a contract. The majority reasoned that the obligation of a contract, deriving from positive law, is the creature of state laws applicable to contracts. A contract made after the enactment of a bankruptcy statute is, therefore, subject to its provisions; in effect the statute enters into and becomes part of all contracts subsequently made, limiting their obligation but not impairing it.

For a minority of three, Chief Justice John Marshall dissented, losing control of his Court in a constitutional case for the first and only time during his long tenure. He would have voided all state bankruptcy acts that affected the obligation of contracts even prospectively. Grounding his position in the immutable higher law principles of morality and natural justice, he maintained that the right of contract is an inalienable right not subject to positive law. The parties to a contract, not society or government, create its obligation. Marshall believed that the majority's interpretation of the contract clause would render its constitutional prohibition on the states "inanimate, inoperative, and unmeaning." Had his opinion prevailed, contractual rights of property vested by contract would have been placed beyond government regulation, making the contract clause the instrument of protecting property that the Court

later fashioned out of the due process clause substantively construed. Until then, despite Marshall's fears, the contract clause remained the principal bastion for the doctrine of vested rights. This case, however, ended the Court's doctrinal expansion of that clause. *Ogden* prevented constitutional law from confronting the nation with a choice between unregulated capitalism and socialism.

—LEONARD W. LEVY

OLMSTEAD v. UNITED STATES

277 U.S. 438 (1928)

Federal agents installed wiretaps in the basement of a building where Roy Olmstead, a suspected bootlegger, had his office and in streets near his home. None of Olmstead's property was trespassed upon. A sharply divided Supreme Court admitted the wiretap evidence in an opinion that virtually exempted electronic eavesdropping from constitutional controls for forty years. The dissents by Justices Oliver Wendell Holmes and

AMENDMENT V

No person shall be held to answer for a capital, or otherwise infamous crime, unless on a presentment or indictment of a Grand Jury, except in cases arising in the land or naval forces, or in the Militia, when in actual service in time of War or public danger; nor shall any person be subject for the same offence to be twice put in jeopardy of life or limb; nor shall be compelled in any criminal case to be a witness against himself, nor be deprived of life, liberty, or property, without due process of law; nor shall private property be taken for public use, without just compensation.

Ogden established the doctrine that a state bankruptcy act operating on contracts made after the passage of the act does not violate the obligation of a contract.

*Olmstead argued
that because the
prosecution's
evidence came
entirely from the
wiretaps, it could
not be used against
him.*

Louis D. Brandeis are classic statements of the government's obligation to obey the law.

Olmstead argued that because the prosecution's evidence came entirely from the wiretaps, it could not be used against him; wiretapping, he claimed, was a search and seizure under the Fourth Amendment, and because the amendment's warrant and other requirements had not been met, the wiretap evidence was illegally obtained. He also claimed that use of the wiretap evidence violated his right against self-incrimination under the Fifth Amendment; further, that because the agents had violated a state statute prohibiting wiretapping, the evidence was inadmissible, apart from the Fourth and Fifth Amendments.

Chief Justice William Howard Taft, writing for a five-Justice majority, rejected all Olmstead's contentions. The self-incrimination claim was dismissed first: the defendants had not been compelled to talk over the telephone but had done so voluntarily. This aspect of *Olmstead* has survived to be applied in cases such as *Hoffa* v. *United States* (1966). As to the Fourth Amendment claims: first, the Court ruled that the amendment was violated only if officials trespassed onto the property of the person overheard, and no such trespass had taken place—the agents had tapped Olmstead's telephones without going onto his property. Second, the Court limited Fourth Amendment protection to "material things," not intangibles like conversations. Third, the Court seemed to deny any protection for the voice if projected outside the house. As to the claim that the agents' violation of the state statute required excluding the evidence, the Chief Justice found no authority for such exclusion.

Justice Holmes wrote a short dissent, condemning the agents' conduct as "dirty business." Justice Brandeis wrote the main dissent in which he disagreed with the majority's reading of the precedents, its very narrow view of the Fourth Amendment, and its willingness to countenance criminal activity by the government. For him, the Fourth Amendment was designed to protect individual privacy, and he warned that the "progress of science in furnishing the Government with means of espionage" called for a flexible reading of the amendment to "protect the right of personal security." He stressed that because a tap reaches all who use the telephone, including all those who either call the target or are called, "writs of assistance or general warrants are but puny instruments of tyranny and oppression when compared with wiretapping." Responding to the argument that law enforcement justified both a narrow reading of the amendment and indifference to the agents' violation of state law, he wrote: "Experience should teach us to be most on our guard to protect liberty when the Government's purposes are beneficent. . . . The greatest dangers to liberty lurk in insidious encroachment by men of zeal, well-meaning but without understanding. . . . Our Government is the potent, the omnipresent teacher. For good or for ill, it teaches the whole people by its example."

Although the decision was harshly criticized, it endured. In *Goldman* v. *United States* (1942), *Olmstead* was read to allow police to place a microphone against the outside of a wall, because no trespass onto the property was involved. Wiretapping itself remained outside constitutional controls, though section 605 of the Communications Act of 1934 was construed by the Supreme Court in *Nardone* v. *United States* (1937) to bar unauthorized interception and divulgence of telephone messages.

In 1954, however, *Olmstead* began to be undermined. In *Irvine* v. *California* (1954), the Court indicated that intangible conversations were protected by the Fourth Amendment. The Court found a trespass when the physical penetration was only a few inches into a party wall as in *Silverman* v. *United States* (1961) or by a thumbtack as in *Clinton* v. *Virginia* (1964). Finally, in *Katz* v. *United States* (1967), the Supreme Court overruled

Olmstead, holding that a trespass was unnecessary for a violation of the Fourth Amendment and that the amendment protects intangibles, including conversations.

—HERMAN SCHWARTZ

Bibliography

Murphy, Walter F. (1966). *Wiretapping on Trial: A Case Study in the Judicial Process.* New York: Random House.

OPINION OF THE COURT

An appellate court would give little guidance to inferior courts, the legal community, or the general public concerning the law if it merely rendered a decision and did not explain the ratio decidendi, or the grounds for its decision. It is the court's reading of the law and the application of legal principles to the facts that gives a reported case value as precedent and permits the judicial system to follow the doctrine of stare decisis. By ancient custom, Anglo-American judges, at least at the appellate level, publish opinions along with their decisions.

The general practice of English courts at the time of the American Revolution, and the general practice today in most of the British Commonwealth, is for the members of multijudge courts to deliver their opinions seriatim, that is, severally and in sequence. This practice was followed by the United States Supreme Court during its early years. However, when John Marshall became Chief Justice in 1801 he instituted the practice of delivering a single "opinion of the court." The effect of this change was to put the weight of the whole Court behind a particular line of reasoning (usually Marshall's), and so to make that line of reasoning more authoritative. At the time, Marshall's innovation was criticized by many, including President Thomas Jefferson, either because it permit-

ted lazy Justices to evade the responsibility of thinking through the cases on their own or because it fortified the Federalist majority in its conflicts with Republican legislators and state governments.

The opinion of the court is not necessarily unanimous. A majority of the Justices customarily endorses a single opinion, however, and that majority opinion is issued as the opinion of the court, with the Chief Justice—or the senior Justice, if the Chief Justice is not in the majority—assigning responsibility for writing the opinion. A Justice who disagrees with the decision of the case may file a dissenting opinion; a Justice who agrees with the result, but disagrees with the rationale, or desires to supplement the majority opinion, may file a concurring opinion. When there is no majority opinion, the opinion signed by the largest number of Justices in support of the decisions is called the plurality opinion, and no opinion of the court is issued. In some important cases in the past, and increasingly during the Burger Court years, the number of separate opinions presented an appearance resembling a return to seriatim opinions.

—DENNIS J. MAHONEY

ORAL ARGUMENT

Lawyers argue points of law orally before courts at all levels. The Supreme Court regulates oral argument by court rule. Some cases are decided summarily, without full briefing and argument, on the papers filed by the parties seeking and opposing Supreme Court review. About 150 cases per term are decided with briefs and oral argument. The arguments begin in October, early in the term, and (absent extraordinary circumstances) end in the following April, so that all opinions can be finished by the end of the term.

In the Court's early years oral argument was a leisurely affair; argument in *McCulloch v. Maryland* (1819) lasted nine days. Today,

A majority of the Justices customarily endorses a single opinion and that majority opinion is issued as the opinion of the Court.

♦ **seriatim**
[Latin: serially] One at a time, in sequence; used to describe the opinions of judges on multimember tribunals where custom does not permit a single "opinion of the court."

The Supreme Court regulates oral argument by court rule.

See also

McCulloch v. Maryland

given the increase in the Court's business and increasing doubt that illumination is proportional to talk, argument is normally limited to one-half hour for each side. More time may be allocated to a case that is unusually complicated or important. Permission to argue is only rarely granted to an amicus curiae, except for the solicitor general, who is often allowed to argue orally for the United States as amicus curiae.

The Justices have already read the briefs when they hear counsel. Accordingly, oral argument is no longer a place for oratory. Justices interrupt with their questions and even conduct debates with each other through rhetorical questions to counsel. Time limits on argument are strictly enforced; the red light flashes on the lectern, and counsel stops.

Normally within a few days after oral argument the Justices meet in conference to discuss groups of cases and vote tentatively on their disposition. The Justices regularly say that oral argument, fresh in their minds, influences their thinking in "close" cases. Whether a case is close, however, is a characterization very likely formed before a Justice hears what counsel have to say.

—KENNETH L. KARST

Bibliography

Stern, Robert L., and Gressman, Eugene (1978). *Supreme Court Practice.* 5th ed. Chap. 14. Washington, D.C.: Bureau of National Affairs.

OREGON v. MITCHELL

400 U.S. 112 (1970)

Mitchell reviewed the question of Congress's power to interpret and alter the scope of the Fourteenth Amendment.

This decision suggested some short-lived constitutional limits on Congress's power to regulate voting. The 1970 amendments to the Voting Rights Act of 1965 lowered from twenty-one to eighteen the minimum voting age for federal, state, and local elections, suspended literacy tests throughout the nation, prohibited states from imposing residence requirements in presidential elections, and provided for uniform national rules for absentee registration and voting in presidential elections. The Supreme Court unanimously upheld the suspension of literacy tests and over Justice John Marshall Harlan's dissent, found the residency and absentee voting provisions valid. Four Justices found the age limit reduction constitutional for all elections and four Justices found it unconstitutional for all elections. Because Justice Hugo T. Black found the age limit reduction constitutional only for federal elections, the case's formal holding, though reflecting only Justice Black's view, was to sustain the age reduction only in federal elections. The many separate opinions in *Mitchell* also reviewed the question, first addressed in *Katzenbach* v. *Morgan* (1966), of Congress's power to interpret and alter the scope of the Fourteenth Amendment. In 1971, in reponse to *Mitchell*, the Twenty-Sixth Amendment lowered the voting age to eighteen in all elections.

More important, *Oregon* v. *Mitchell* halted the Court's expansion of section 5 of the Fourteenth Amendment as a lever for Congressional enactments declaring activities to be unlawful. The Court emphasized here that section 5 only authorizes Congress to "enforce" the Fourteenth Amendment—to adopt remedial laws to correct historical abuses and discrimination, but not to interpret the Amendment any way Congress sees fit. Therefore for Congress to bar literacy tests for voting was permissible because of their long history as a device to bar blacks from voting. But Congress lacked power to reduce the voting age in state elections. (It could do so for federal elections under powers given it in Article I.)

A few years later, in *Boerne (City of)* v. *Flores* (1997), invalidating a law designed to alter the level of judicial scrutiny in religious freedom cases, the Court built on *Mitchell* to underscore that Congress lacked power under section 5 to interpret the Fourteenth Amendment unless it was remedying past abuses.

—THEODORE EISENBERG

ORIGINAL JURISDICTION

The original jurisdiction of a court (as distinguished from appellate jurisdiction) is its power to hear and decide a case from the beginning. In the federal court system, the district courts originally hear the overwhelming majority of cases. Most discussion and litigation concerning the jurisdiction of federal courts centers on the district courts' original jurisdiction. Yet the term "original jurisdiction" is heard most frequently in discussion and litigation concerning the jurisdiction of the Supreme Court.

The Constitution itself establishes the Supreme Court's original jurisdiction. After setting out the types of cases subject to the judicial power of the United States, Article III distributes the Supreme Court's jurisdiction over them: "In all cases affecting ambassadors, other public ministers and consuls, and those in which a state shall be a party, the Supreme Court shall have original jurisdiction. In all other cases mentioned, the Supreme Court shall have appellate jurisdiction. . . ."

From the beginning, Congress has given the district courts concurrent jurisdiction over some of the cases within the Supreme Court's original jurisdiction, offering plaintiffs the option of commencing suit in either court. The Supreme Court has given this practice its stamp of constitutional approval. Furthermore, because the Court is hard-pressed by a crowded docket, it has sought ways of shunting cases to other courts. Thus, even when a case does fall within the Court's original jurisdiction, the court has conferred on itself the discretion to deny the plaintiff leave to file an original action. Typically the Court decides only three or four original jurisdiction cases each year, conserving its institutional energies for its main task: guiding the development of federal law by exercising its appellate jurisdiction.

Congress, however, cannot constitutionally diminish the Court's original jurisdiction. Nor can Congress expand that jurisdiction; the dubious reading of Article III in *Marbury* v. *Madison* (1803) remains firmly entrenched. However, the Supreme Court does entertain some actions that have an "original" look to them, even though Article III does not list them as original jurisdiction cases: habeas corpus is an example; so are the common law writs of mandamus and prohibition. The Court hears such cases only when they can be characterized as "appellate," calling for Supreme Court supervision of actions by lower courts.

Of the two types of original jurisdiction cases specified in Article III, the state-as-party case has produced all but a tiny handful of the cases originally decided by the Supreme Court. Officers of foreign governments enjoy a broad diplomatic immunity from suit in our courts, and, for motives no doubt similarly diplomatic, they have not brought suits in the Supreme Court. (The "ambassadors" and others mentioned in Article III, of course, are those of foreign governments, not our own.)

The state-as-party cases present obvious problems of sovereign immunity. The Eleventh Amendment applies to original actions in the Supreme Court; indeed, the amendment was adopted in response to just such a case, *Chisholm* v. *Georgia* (1793). Thus a state can no more be sued by the citizen of another state in the Supreme Court than in a district court. However, when one state sues another, or when the United States or a foreign government sues a state, there is no bar to the Court's jurisdiction.

The spectacle of nine Justices of the Supreme Court jointly presiding over a trial has a certain Hollywood allure, but the Court

In the federal court system, the district courts originally hear the overwhelming majority of cases.

♦ **original jurisdiction**
The legitimate authority of a court to hear and decide cases in the first instance. Original jurisdiction is distinguished from appellate jurisdiction.

consistently avoids such proceedings. The Seventh Amendment commands trial by jury in any common law action, and at first the Supreme Court did hold a few jury trials. The last one, however, took place in the 1790s. Since that time the Court has always managed to identify some feature of an original case that makes it a suit in equity; thus jury trial is inappropriate, and findings of fact can be turned over to a special master, whose report is reviewed by the Court only as to questions of law.

The source of the substantive law applied in original actions between states is federal common law, an amalgam of the Anglo-American common law, policies derived from congressional statutes, and international law principles. Thus far no state has defied the Supreme Court sufficiently to test the Court's means of enforcing its decrees, but some states have dragged out their compliance for enough years to test the patience of the most saintly Justice.

—KENNETH L. KARST

Bibliography

Note (1959). The Original Jurisdiction of the United States Supreme Court. *Stanford Law Review* 11:665–719.

ORIGINAL PACKAGE DOCTRINE

In *Brown* v. *Maryland* (1827) the Supreme Court had before it a challenge to a state statute requiring all importers of goods from foreign countries to take out a $50 license. Instead of simply holding that such a license tax imposed only on importers from foreign countries violated the constitutional clause prohibiting states from laying "any imposts or duties on imports or exports," Chief Justice John Marshall used the occasion to decide just when goods imported from abroad ceased being imports exempted from taxation

by the states. He concluded that no tax could be imposed on the goods or their importer so long as the goods had not been sold and were held in the original packages in which they were imported. He also said the principles laid down "apply equally to importations from a sister state."

The original package doctrine had a long career as applied to goods imported from abroad. In *Low* v. *Austin* (1872) the Court held that a state could not collect its uniform property tax on cases of wine which the importer held in their original package on tax day. Much later, in *Hooven & Allison Co.* v. *Evatt* (1945), the Court applied the doctrine to immunize bales of hemp from state property taxation, so long as the importer held them in their original package—the bales. Along the way, not surprisingly, the Court struggled in many cases with such problems as what constitutes the original package, and when it is broken.

Finally, in *Michelin Tire Corp.* v. *Wages* (1976) the Court upheld the imposition of a nondiscriminatory property tax upon tires imported from abroad and held in their original packages. It discussed at length the decision in *Low* v. *Austin,* overruled it, and appeared to be saying that only taxes discriminating against foreign commerce will be held invalid. Hence, it appears that the rules governing taxation of imports will now be similar to those applied to taxing such goods from other states, with the original package doctrine playing no part in the decisions.

Marshall's suggestion in *Brown* v. *Maryland* that the original package doctrine applied to state *taxation* of goods imported from other states was early rejected. In *Woodruff* v. *Parham* (1869) the Court upheld a state sales tax applied to an auctioneer who brought goods from other states and sold them in the taxing state in the original and unbroken packages. The import-export clause was determined to apply only to traffic with foreign nations, not to interstate traffic.

Chief Justice John Marshall used the occasion to decide just when goods imported from abroad ceased being imports exempted from taxation by the states.

See also

Chisholm v. *Georgia*

Marbury v. *Madison*

The Court indicated its feeling that it would be grossly unfair if a resident of a state could escape from state taxes on all merchandise that he was able to import from another state and keep in its original package.

In 1890, however, the Court held that the original package doctrine applied to invalidate state *regulations* of goods imported from other states until the goods were sold or the package broken. The decision, *Leisy* v. *Hardin* (1890), invalidated a state prohibition law as applied to sales within the state by the importer of kegs and cases of beer. Federal statutes were then enacted permitting states to exclude alcohol even in original packages. But the original package doctrine persisted with reference to other state regulations for nearly half a century. The Court found reasons in many cases to avoid applying the doctrine but did not effectively repudiate it until 1935. In *Baldwin* v. *G. A. F. Seelig* (1935) the Court, after reviewing the cases applying the original package doctrine said:

> In brief, the test of the original package is not an ultimate principle. . . . It makes a convenient boundary and one sufficiently precise save in exceptional conditions. What is ultimate is the principle that one state in its dealing with another may not place itself in a position of economic isolation. Formulas and catchwords are subordinate to this overmastering requirement.

Today the original package doctrine is of interest only to historians.

—EDWARD L. BARRETT, JR.

Bibliography

Nowak, John E.; Rotunda, Ronald D.; and Young, Nelson J. (1979). *Handbook on Constitutional Law.* Pages 285–290. St. Paul, Minn.: West Publishing Co.

Powell, Thomas R. (1945). State Taxation of Imports: When Does an Import Cease to Be an Import? *Harvard Law Review* 58:858–876.

Ribble, F. D. G. *State and National Power over Commerce.* Pages 196–199. New York: Columbia University Press.

OVERBREADTH

Judges frequently encounter the claim that a law, as drafted or interpreted, should be invalidated as overbroad because its regulatory scope addresses not only behavior that constitutionally may be punished but also constitutionally protected behavior. The normal judicial response is confined to ruling on the law's constitutionality as applied to the litigant's behavior, leaving the validity of its application to other people and situations to subsequent adjudication. Since *Thornhill* v. *Alabama* (1940), however, the Supreme Court has made an exception, most frequently in First Amendment cases but applicable to other precious freedoms, when it is convinced that the very existence of an overbroad law may cause knowledgeable people to refrain from freely exercising constitutional liberties because they fear punishment and are unwilling to litigate their rights. In such cases, the aggregate inhibition of guaranteed freedom in the regulated community is thought to justify both holding the overbroad law invalid on its face and allowing one to whom a narrower law could be applied constitutionally to assert the overbreadth claim. Unlike the alternative of narrowing the unconstitutional portions of an overbroad statute case by case, facial invalidation prevents delay in curing the improper deterrence. Moreover, courts most effectively can address the inhibition of those who neither act nor sue by allowing those who do to raise the overbreadth challenge.

Like a vagueness challenge, an overbreadth challenge implicates judicial governance in two controversial ways. First, if successful, the challenge completely prohibits the law's enforcement, even its constitutional applications, until it is narrowed through

Judges frequently encounter the claim that a law, as drafted or interpreted, should be invalidated as overbroad.

See also

Leisy v. *Hardin*

reenactment or authoritative interpretation. Second, the challenge requires a court to gauge the law's applications to unidentified people in circumstances that must be imagined, often ignoring the facts of the situation before them—a practice of hypothesizing that is at odds with the courts' usual application of law to the facts of concrete cases or controversies.

Overbreadth differs from vagueness in that the constitutional defect is a law's excessive reach, not its lack of clarity; yet the defects are related. A law that punished "all speech that is not constitutionally protected" would, by definition, not be overbroad, but it would be unduly vague because people would have to speculate about what it outlawed. A law that prohibited "all speaking" would be unconstitutionally overbroad, but it also might be vague. Although clear enough if taken literally, it might be understood that the legislature did not intend the full reach of its broadly drafted law, and the public would have to speculate about what the contours of the intended lesser reach might be. A law that banned "all harmful speech" would be both overbroad and vague on its face. The key connection, however, is the improper inhibiting effect of the broad or vague law.

As with vagueness, the federal courts approach overbreadth challenges to state and federal laws differently. A federal court must interpret a federal law before judging its constitutionality. In doing so, the court may reduce the law's scope, if it can do so consistently with Congress's intent, a course that may minimize constitutional problems of overbreadth. Only state courts may authoritatively determine the reach of state laws, however. Consequently, when the Supreme Court reviews an overbreadth challenge to a state law on appeal from a state court—which review usually occurs because the challenger raised the claim in defense of state court proceedings against him—the Court must accept the state court's determination of the law's scope and apply its own constitutional

judgment to the law as so construed. By contrast, if parties threatened with enforcement of a state statute sue in federal court to have the law declared unconstitutionally overbroad before they are prosecuted or sued in state court, the federal court faces the additional complication of determining the overbreadth question without the guidance of any state court interpretation of the law in this case. If past interpretations of the law's terms make its breadth clear, there is no more difficulty than in Supreme Court review of a state court case. But if there is some question whether a state court might have narrowed the state law, especially in light of constitutional doubts about it, the federal court faces the possibility of making its own incorrect interpretation and basing an overbreadth judgment on that unstable premise.

With other constitutional claims involving uncertain state laws, a federal court normally will abstain from deciding the constitutional question until clarification is sought in state court. However, because the prolongation of chilling effects on constitutionally protected conduct is the basis of the vagueness of overbreadth doctrines, the Supreme Court indicated in *Dombrowski* v. *Pfister* (1965) and *Baggett* v. *Bullitt* (1964) that abstention is generally inappropriate if the problem would take multiple instances of adjudication to cure. *Babbitt* v. *United Farm Workers* (1979) followed the implicit corollary, requiring abstention where a single state proceeding might have obviated the need to reach difficult constitutional issues. But *Brockett* v. *Spokane Arcades, Inc.,* (1985) shunned abstention in a case where state court clarification was feasible in an expeditious single proceeding, but where the litigants objecting to overbreadth were not people to whom the law could be validly applied but people who desired to engage in constitutionally protected speech. In that circumstance, at least where the unconstitutional portion of the statute was readily identifiable and severable from the remainder, the Court chose to strike that portion rather than abstain to see if the state court would remove it by interpretation.

Brockett also expressed a preference for partial over facial invalidation whenever challengers assert that application of a statute to them would be unconstitutional. The Court's ultimate objective is to invalidate only a statute's overbroad features, not the parts that legitimately penalize undesirable behavior. It permits those who are properly subject to regulation to mount facial overbreadth attacks only to provide an opportunity for courts to eliminate the illegitimate deterrent impact on others. Partial invalidation would do such people no good, and those who are illegitimately deterred from speaking may never sue. In order to throw out the tainted bathwater, the baby temporarily must go too, until the statute is reenacted or reinterpreted with its flaws omitted. Where, as in *Brockett,* one asserts his own right to pursue protected activity, however, no special incentive to litigate is needed. The Court can limit a statute's improper reach through partial invalidation and still benefit the challenger. *Brockett*'s assumption that the tainted part of the statute does not spoil the whole also undercuts Henry Monaghan's important argument that allowing the unprotected to argue overbreadth does not depart from normal standing rules because they always assert their own right not to be judged under an invalid statute. The part applied to them is valid, and they are granted standing to attack the whole only to protect others from the invalid part. Finally, the claim that a law is invalid in all applications because based on an illegitimate premise has elements of both partial and facial invalidation. As the invalid premise affects the challenger as well as everyone else, there is no need to provide a special incentive to litigate, but because the whole law is defective, total invalidation is appropriate.

The seriousness of striking the whole of a partially invalid law at the urging of one to whom it validly applies, together with doubts about standing and the reliability of constitu-

tional adjudication in the context of imagined applications, renders overbreadth an exceptional and controversial doctrine. The determination of what circumstances are sufficiently compelling to warrant the doctrine's use has varied from time to time and among judges. The Warren Court focused mainly on the scope of the laws' coverage, the chilling effect on protected expression, and the ability of the legislature to draw legitimate regulatory boundaries more narrowly. The Court seemed convinced that overbroad laws inhibited freedom substantially, and thus made that inhibition the basis of invalidation, especially when the laws were aimed at dissidents and the risk of deliberate deterrence was high, as in *Aptheker* v. *Secretary of State* (1964), *United States* v. *Robel* (1967), and *Dombrowski* v. *Pfister* (1965). The Burger Court continued to employ the overbreadth doctrine when deterrence of valued expression seemed likely, as in *Lewis* v. *New Orleans* (1974), which struck down a law penalizing abusive language directed at police, and in *Schad* v. *Mt. Ephraim* (1981), which struck down an extremely broad law banning live entertainment.

Justice Byron R. White led that Court, however, in curtailing overbreadth adjudication. As all laws occasionally may be applied unconstitutionally, there is always a quantitative dimension of overbreadth. White's majority opinion in *Broadrick* v. *Oklahoma* (1973) held that the overbroad portion of a law must be "real and substantial" before it will be invalidated. That standard highlights the magnitude of deterrent impact, which depends as much on the motivations of those regulated as on the reach of the law. *Broadrick* also emphasized the need to compare and offset the ranges of a statute's valid and invalid applications, rather than simply assess the dimensions of the invalid range. This substituted a judgment balancing a statute's legitimate regulation against its illegitimate deterrence of protected conduct for a judgment focused predominantly on the improper inhibition.

Broadrick initially limited the "substantial overbreadth" approach to laws seemingly addressed to conduct, leaving laws explicitly regulating expression, especially those directed at particular viewpoints, to the more generous approach. In *New York* v. *Ferber* (1982) and *Brockett,* however, substantial overbreadth was extended to pure speech cases as well. That these cases involved laws regulating obscenity might suggest that some Justices find the overbreadth doctrine an improper means to counter deterrence of marginally valued expression. More likely, however, the Court generally is abandoning its focus on the subject of a law's facial coverage in favor of a comparative judgment of the qualitative and quantitative dimensions of a law's legitimate and illegitimate scope, whatever speech or conduct be regulated.

Still, the reality of deterrence and the value of the liberty deterred probably remain major factors in overbreadth judgments, even if more must be considered. For example, the Court's pronouncement in *Bates* v. *State Bar of Arizona* (1977) that overbreadth analysis generally is inappropriate for profit-motivated advertising rested explicitly on a judgment that advertising is not easily inhibited and implicitly on the historic perception of commercial speech as less worthy of protection.

Overbreadth controversies nearly always reflect different sensitivities to the worth of lost expression and of lost regulation of unprotected behavior, or different perceptions of the legitimacy and reliability of judicial nullification of laws that are only partially unconstitutional, or different assessments of how much inhibition is really likely, how easy it would be to redraft a law to avoid overbreadth, and how important broad regulation is to the effective control of harmful behavior. Despite controversy and variations in zeal for application of the overbreadth doctrine, however, its utility in checking repression that too sweepingly inhibits guaranteed liberty should assure its preservation in some form.

—JOHNATHAN D. VARAT

See also

New York v. *Ferber*

Thornhill v. *Alabama*

Bibliography

Alexander, Lawrence A. (1985). Is There an Overbreadth Doctrine? *San Diego Law Review* 22:541–554.

Monaghan, Henry P. (1981). Overbreadth. *Supreme Court Review* 1981:1–39.

Note (1970). The First Amendment Overbreadth Doctrine. *Harvard Law Review* 83:844–927.

OVERRULING

The authority of the Supreme Court to reconsider and overrule its previous decisions is a necessary and accepted part of the Court's power to decide cases. By one estimate, the Supreme Court overruled itself on constitutional issues 159 times through 1976 and in each case departed from the doctrine of *stare decisis.*

The basic tenet of *stare decisis,* as set forth by William Blackstone, is that precedents must generally be followed unless they are "flatly absurd" or "unjust." The doctrine promotes certainty in the law, judicial efficiency (by obviating the constant reexamination of previously settled questions), and uniformity in the treatment of litigants. The roots of the doctrine, which is fundamental in Anglo-American jurisprudence, have been traced to Roman civil law and the Code of Justinian.

Justices and commentators have disagreed about the proper application of *stare decisis* to constitutional decision making. Justice (later Chief Justice) Edward D. White, in his dissenting opinion in *Pollock* v. *Farmers Loan & Trust Co.* (1895), observed:

The fundamental conception of a judicial body is that of one hedged about by precedents which are binding on the court without regard to the personality of its members. Break down this belief in judicial continuity, and let it be felt that on great constitutional questions this court is to depart from the settled conclusions of its pre-

cedessors, and to determine them all according to the mere opinion of those who temporarily fill its bench, and our Constitution will, in my judgment, be bereft of value and become a most dangerous instrument to the rights and liberties of people.

Under this view, *stare decisis* should be applied with full force to constitutional issues.

The more commonly accepted view is that *stare decisis* has a more limited application in constitutional interpretation than it does in the interpretation of statutes or in ordinary common law decision making. Although Congress, by a simple majority, can override the Supreme Court's erroneous interpretation of a congressional statute, errors in the interpretation of the Constitution are not easily corrected. The amending process is by design difficult. In many instances only the Court can correct an erroneous constitutional decision.

Moreover, the Court will on occasion make decisions that later appear to be erroneous. As Chief Justice John Marshall remarked in *McCulloch* v. *Maryland* (1819), the Constitution requires deductions from its "great outlines" when a court decides specific cases. Because the modern Supreme Court generally accepts for review only cases in which principles of broad national importance are in competition, its decisions necessarily involve difficult questions of judgment. In view of the difficulties inherent in amending the Constitution, any errors made by the Court in the interpretation of constitutional principles must be subject to correction by the Court in later decisions.

The classic statement of this view was expressed by Justice Louis D. Brandeis in his dissenting opinion in *Burnet* v. *Coronado Oil & Gas Co.* (1932): "[I]n cases involving the Federal Constitution, where correction through legislative action is practically impossible, this Court has often overruled its earlier decisions. The Court bows to the lessons of experience and the force of better reasoning, recognizing that the process of trial and error, so fruitful in the physical sciences, is appropriate also in the judicial function." The Court has relied on Brandeis's reasoning in later decisions, such as *Edelman* v. *Jordan* (1974), overruling previous constitutional precedents.

An additional reason for applying *stare decisis* less rigidly to constitutional decisions is that the judge's primary obligation is to the Constitution itself. In the words of Justice Felix Frankfurter, concurring in *Graves* v. *New York* (1939), "the ultimate touchstone of constitutionality is the Constitution itself and not what we have said about it."

Some critics of *stare decisis* suggest that it has no place whatsoever in constitutional cases. For example, Chief Justice Roger B. Taney reasoned in the *Passenger Cases* (1849) that a constitutional question "is always open to discussion" because the judicial authority of the Court should "depend altogether on the force of the reasoning by which it is supported." The more generally accepted view, however, was stated by the Court in *Arizona* v. *Rumsey* (1984): "Although adherence to precedent is not rigidly required in constitutional cases, any departure from the doctrine of *stare decisis* requires special justification." Consistent with this view, the Supreme Court generally seeks to provide objective justification for the overruling of past precedents, apart from the fact that the Court's personnel may have changed.

One of the most commonly expressed reasons for overruling a previous decision is that it cannot be reconciled with other rulings. This rationale is in a sense consistent with *stare decisis* in that the justification for the overruling decision rests on competing but previously established judicial principles. In *Gideon* v. *Wainwright* (1963), for example, which overruled *Betts* v. *Brady* (1942), the Court asserted not only that the rationale of *Betts* was erroneous but also that *Betts* had abruptly departed from well-established prior decisions. *Betts* had held that the due process

By one estimate, the Supreme Court overruled itself on constitutional issues 159 times through 1976.

clause of the Fourteenth Amendment does not impose on the states, as the Sixth Amendment imposes on the federal government, the obligation to provide counsel in state criminal proceedings. *Gideon* expressly rejected this holding, thereby ruling that indigent defendants have the right to appointed counsel in such cases. Similarly, in *West Coast Hotel Co.* v. *Parrish* (1937) the Court concluded that it had no choice but to overrule its earlier decision in *Adkins* v. *Children's Hospital* (1923), which had held a minimum wage statute for women unconstitutional under the due process clause. The Court reasoned that *Adkins* was irreconcilable with other decisions permitting the regulation of maximum hours and other working conditions for women.

The Court frequently argues, too, that the lessons of experience require the overruling of a previous decision. In *Erie Railroad Co.* v. *Tompkins* (1938), for example, the Court reasoned that in nearly one hundred years the doctrine of *Swift* v. *Tyson* (1842) "had revealed its defects, political and social." And in *Mapp* v. *Ohio* (1961) the Court held the exclusionary rule applicable to the states, saying that the experience of various states had made clear that remedies other than the exclusionary rule could not effectively deter unreasonable searches and seizures. The Court therefore overruled *Wolf* v. *Colorado* (1949), which only two decades earlier had ruled that states were free to devise their own remedies for enforcing search and seizure requirements applicable to the states through the due process clause of the Fourteenth Amendment.

The Court also justifies overruling decisions on the basis of changed or unforeseen circumstances. In *Brown* v. *Board of Education* (1954), for example, the Court referred to the change in status of the public schools in rejecting the application of the separate but equal doctrine of *Plessy* v. *Ferguson* (1896). And in *Propeller Genesee Chief* v. *Fitzhugh* (1851), one of the earliest overruling decisions, the Court stressed that when it had erroneously held in

The Thomas Jefferson (1825) that the admiralty and maritime jurisdiction of the federal government was limited "to the ebb and flow of the tide," commerce on the rivers of the West and on the Great Lakes had been in its infancy and "the great national importance of the question . . . could not be foreseen."

Other considerations may also suggest a decision's susceptibility to being overruled. Thus a decision on an issue not fully briefed and argued may be entitled to less precedential weight than one in which the issue received full and deliberate consideration. Or, the fact that an issue was decided by a closely divided Court may suggest a higher probability of error and make later reconsideration more likely. By contrast, as the Court recognized in *Akron* v. *Akron Center for Reproductive Health* (1983), a carefully considered decision, repeatedly and consistently followed (in that case, *Roe* v. *Wade* [1973]), may be entitled to more respect than other constitutional holdings under principles of *stare decisis*.

A decade after *Akron* in *Plannd Parenhood of Southeastern Pennsylvania* v. *Casey* (1992), Justices Sandra Day O'Connor, Anthony M. Kennedy, and David H. Souter clarified the Court's adherence to *Roe* v. *Wade*. They held for the Court that "principles of institutional integrity" as well as *stare decisis* required that result. They contrasted the Court's two earlier dramatic overrulings of earlier precedents in *West Coast Hotel* and *Brown* v. *Board of Education* as resting on "an understanding of facts" so different from "the claimed justifications for the earlier constitutional resolutions" in *Adkins* and *Plessy* that those cases were no longer supportable. (One might well ask whether they ever were, or whether the dissenters in the overruled decisions were simply correct all along.) The *Casey* authors further pointed out that "[t]he legitimacy of the Court would fade with the frequency of its vacillation," and that a generation of Americans had organized their relationships and made personal choices on the assumption that *Roe* was the law and would remain so.

As the Court develops constitutional doctrine, it may limit or distinguish a previous decision, gradually eroding its authority without expressly overruling it. Such a doctrinal evolution may both portend an overruling decision and establish the groundwork for it.

The Court's willingness to reconsider its prior constitutional decisions and in some instances to overrule itself is implicit in the general understanding of the Constitution as a document of broad outlines intended to endure the ages. Yet it has been suggested that the Court risks a loss of confidence as a disinterested interpreter of the Constitution whenever it overrules itself. Because of its antimajoritarian character, the Court must be sensitive to the need for restraint in exercising its power of judicial review. If it overrules itself too frequently and without adequate justification, its reputation may suffer. The Constitution's general language, however, leaves wide room for honest differences as to its interpretation and application. An objective and detached overruling opinion, which faithfully seeks to apply constitutional principles on the basis of the constitutional text and history, is on occasion to be expected and need not jeopardize public confidence in the Court.

—JAMES R. ASPERGER

OVERRULING

Bibliography

Bernhardt, Charlotte C. (1948). Supreme Court Reversals on Constitutional Issues. *Cornell Law Quarterly* 34:55–70.

Blaustein, Albert P., and Field, Andrew H. (1958). "Overruling" Opinions in the Supreme Court. *Michigan Law Review* 57: 151–194.

Israel, Jerold H. (1963). *Gideon* v. *Wainwright:* The "Art" of Overruling. *Supreme Court Review* 1963:211–272.

Noland, Jon D. (1969). *Stare Decisis* and the Overruling of Constitutional Decisions in the Warren Years. *Valparaiso University Law Review* 4:101–135.

Reed, Stanley (1938). *Stare Decisis* and Constitutional Law. *Pennsylvania Bar Association Quarterly* 1938:131–150.

PALKO v.
CONNECTICUT

302 U.S. 319 (1937)

Palko, decided in the sesquicentennial year of the Constitution, highlights the difference between the constitutional law of criminal justice then and now. The *Palko* Court, which was unanimous, included five of the greatest judges in our history—Charles Evans Hughes, Louis D. Brandeis, Harlan Fiske Stone, Hugo L. Black, and the Court's spokesman, Benjamin N. Cardozo. In one respect Cardozo's opinion is a historical relic, like *Hurtado* v. *California* (1884), *Maxwell* v. *Dow* (1900), and *Twining* v. *New Jersey* (1908), which he cited as governing precedents. In another respect, *Palko* rationalized the Court's incorporation doctrine of the Fourteenth Amendment by which it selected fundamental rights to be safeguarded against state violation.

Palko was sentenced to life imprisonment after a jury found him guilty of murder in the second degree. The state sought and won a new trial on the ground that its case had been prejudiced by errors of the trial court. Palko objected that a new trial on the same indictment exposed him to double jeopardy, but he was overruled. At the second trial the jury's verdict of murder in the first degree resulted in a sentence of death. Had the case been tried in a federal court, the double jeopardy claim would have been good. The question raised by Palko's case was whether a double standard prevailed—one for state courts and the other for federal—or whether the Fifth Amendment's guarantee against double jeop-ardy applied to the state through the due process clause of the Fourteenth Amendment.

Cardozo declared that Palko's contention was even broader: "Whatever would be a violation of the original Bill of Rights (Amendments 1 to 8) if done by the federal government is now equally unlawful by force of the Fourteenth Amendment if done by a state." The Court answered, "There is no such general rule," thus rejecting the theory of total incorporation. Nevertheless, said Cardozo, by a "process of absorption"—now referred to as selective incorporation—the Court had extended the due process clause of the Fourteenth Amendment to include First Amendment freedoms and the right to counsel in certain cases, yet it had rejected the rights of

Palko *highlights the difference between the constitutional law of criminal justice then and now.*

**COURT
SPOKESMAN**

Benjamin N. Cardozo alleged that the right against double jeopardy was not a fundamental right. (Corbis/Bettmann)

See also

Benton v. *Maryland*

Double Jeopardy

Hurtado v. *California*

the criminally accused, excepting representation by counsel for ignorant indigents in capital prosecutions. The rationalizing principle that gave coherence to the absorption process, Cardozo alleged, depended on a distinction among the various rights. Some were "fundamental" or "of the very essence of a scheme of ordered liberty," like freedom of speech or religion. By contrast, trial by jury, indictment by grand jury, and the right against self-incrimination were not: justice might be done without them. The right against double jeopardy, the Court ruled summarily, did not rank as fundamental and therefore received no protection against the states from the due process clause of the Fourteenth Amendment. *Benton* v. *Maryland* (1969) overruled *Palko,* showing that even "fundamental" value judgments change with time. All that remains of *Palko* is the abstract principle of selective incorporation.

—LEONARD W. LEVY

Bibliography

Abraham, Henry J. (1977). *Freedom and the Court.* 3rd ed. Pages 64–70. New York: Oxford University Press.

PANAMA REFINING CO. v. RYAN

293 U.S. 388 (1935)

In 1933 the price of wholesale gasoline had fallen to two and a half cents a gallon, that of crude oil to ten cents a barrel. The states, unable to cut production and push up prices, clamored for national controls. Congress responded with section 9(c) of the National Industrial Recovery Act, authorizing the president to prohibit the shipment in interstate commerce of petroleum produced in excess of quotas set by the states. By a vote of 8–1 the Supreme Court, in an opinion by Chief Justice Charles Evans Hughes, for the first time in history held an act of Congress unconstitutional because it improperly delegated legislative powers to the president without specifying adequate standards to guide his discretion. Moreover, the act did not require him to explain his orders. Vesting the president with "an uncontrolled legislative power," Hughes said, exceeded the limits of delegation; he did not explain how much delegation is valid and by what standards.

TOO MUCH OIL

In Panama, *the states demanded national controls over petroleum production. (Corbis/Morton Beebe, S. F.)*

Justice Benjamin N. Cardozo disagreed. He found adequate standards in section 1 of the statute: the elimination of unfair competitive practices and conservation of natural resources. These objectives guided the president's discretion, Cardozo explained. The principle of separation of powers, which the majority used to underpin its opinion, should not be applied with doctrinaire rigor. Moreover, the statute, Cardozo observed, "was framed in the shadow of a national disaster" that raised unforeseen contingencies that only the president could face from day to day. The standards for his discretion had to be broad, and he need never give reasons for executive orders. Cardozo's opinion notwithstanding, the Court in effect removed the oil industry from effective controls, to its detriment and that of the national economy. This case marked the New Deal's debut before the Court.

—LEONARD W. LEVY

PARADISE, UNITED STATES v.

480 U.S. 149 (1987)

For several decades, the Alabama Department of Public Safety excluded blacks from employment as state troopers. Only after a federal district court imposed a hiring quota in the early 1970s did the department finally change its ways. Even then, however, the department failed to promote the black officers it hired. Thereafter, the district court again intervened, this time requiring the department to institute promotion procedures without an adverse impact on black officers. When the department failed to institute such procedures within a timely period, the court imposed a promotion quota until the department developed acceptable promotion procedures of its own. Under the court's scheme, one black officer had to be promoted for every white officer promoted. The United

States challenged the court's order, claiming that it violated the equal protection clause of the Fourteenth Amendment. The Supreme Court disagreed and upheld the order 5–4.

Writing for a plurality, Justice William J. Brennan noted that members of the Court disagreed about what level of scrutiny to apply to discrimination remedy cases, but argued that this did not matter because the race-conscious remedy under review survived even the Court's highest standard of strict scrutiny because it was "narrowly tailored" to serve a compelling state interest.

Rejecting the strict scrutiny approach in discrimination-remedy cases, Justice John Paul Stevens concurred in the judgment, but stressed that the federal judiciary has "broad and flexible authority" to fashion even race-conscious remedies once a violation of the Fourteenth Amendment has occurred.

Justice Sandra Day O'Connor vigorously disagreed. Writing for three of the dissenters, O'Connor not only insisted that all remedies be subjected to strict scrutiny but she also took the plurality to task for adopting "a standardless view" of strict scrutiny's requirement that a remedy be narrowly tailored to accomplish its purpose. Maintaining that "there is simply no justification for the use of racial preferences if the purpose of the order could be achieved without their use," O'Connor argued there was no evidence that the district court considered any alternatives to the racial quota, even though several alternatives in fact existed, including an invocation of the court's contempt power.

—JOHN G. WEST, JR.

PARHAM v. J. R.

442 U.S. 584 (1979)

The notion of "voluntary" civil commitment of mental patients takes on a special meaning when the patients are children: under a typical state's law they can be committed by the joint decision of their parents and mental

P

PARHAM v. J. R.

442 U.S. 584 (1979)

The Alabama Department of Public Safety excluded blacks from employment as state troopers.

*The notion of
"voluntary" civil
commitment of
mental patients
takes on a special
meaning when the
patients are
children.*

hospital authorities. This case, a class action on behalf of all children detained in Georgia mental hospitals, was brought in order to establish a child's procedural due process right to an adversary hearing before being so committed. Although the lower federal court agreed with the plaintiff's theory, the Supreme Court reversed in an opinion by Chief Justice Warren E. Burger.

The Court was unanimous in rejecting the broadest due process claim in behalf of the children. There were constitutionally protected "liberty" interests at stake in a commitment, both the freedom from bodily restraint and the freedom from being falsely labeled as mentally ill. However, applying the interest-balancing calculus suggested in *Mathews* v. *Eldridge* (1976), the Court concluded that a child's due process rights did not extend to an adversary precommitment hearing. The majority concluded that due process required no more than informal "medical" inquiries, once near the time of commitment and periodically thereafter, by a "neutral fact-finder" who would determine whether the standards for commitment were satisfied. There need be no adversary proceeding, but this neutral decision maker should interview the child.

The Court's opinion emphasized the importance of maintaining parents' traditional role in decision making for their children. Although some parents might abuse their authority, the law had historically "recognized that natural bonds of affection lead parents to act in the best interests of their children." On the surface, *J. R.* is a "family autonomy" decision. Yet, as Robert Burt has shown, the Court's solicitude for parental authority was expressed in the context of parental decisions validated by state officials. Other decisions suggest that the Court's primary deference runs not to parents but to "state-employed behavioral professionals."

Justice William J. Brennan, for three partially dissenting Justices, agreed that pre-confinement hearings were not constitutionally required in all cases where parents sought

to have their children committed, but he argued that due process did require at least one postadmission hearing. The informal inquiries approved by the Court did not meet this standard.

—KENNETH L. KARST

Bibliography

Burt, Robert A. (1979). The Constitution of the Family. *Supreme Court Review* 1979: 329–395.

PATTERSON v. MCLEAN CREDIT UNION

109 S.Ct. 2363 (1989)

This decision's constitutional significance lies in what the Supreme Court did not do. The Civil Rights Act of 1866 guarantees "all persons . . . the same right . . . to make and enforce contracts . . . as is enjoyed by white persons." In *Runyon* v. *McCrary* (1976) the Court had held that this provision not only required a state to give blacks and whites the same legal rights in contracting but also forbade private racial discrimination in the making of contracts. Later decisions had applied the same section to employment contracts. *Patterson* raised the issue of whether this section gave a black employee a right to damages against her employer for acts of racial harassment. In 1988, after oral argument on this issue and without any prompting from the parties, a 5–4 majority of the Court set the case down for reargument and asked the parties to consider whether *Runyon* v. *McCrary* should be overruled.

Four Justices bitterly dissented from this order, and outside the Court a clamor of protest rose. The majority that supported the order consisted of the two *Runyon* dissenters and the three Justices appointed by President Ronald Reagan, and the order appeared to be the opening salvo in an assault on some of the major gains of the civil rights movement. If *Runyon* were overruled, why should the Court not overrule *Jones* v. *Alfred H. Mayer Co.* (1968)? *Jones* was the landmark decision that (1) interpreted a parallel provision of the 1866 Act to forbid private racial discrimination in the disposition of property, and (2) upheld the law, as so interpreted, on the basis of Congress's power to enforce the Thirteenth Amendment. The latter possibility seems, in retrospect, to have been unlikely, but the depth of concern is understandable. Sixty-six United States senators and 118 representatives filed a brief urging the Court not to overrule *Runyon,* and so did the attorneys general of forty-seven states.

In the event, the Court unanimously reaffirmed the *Runyon* precedent. The majority opinion (the same majority that had agreed on the reargument order) simply applied the doctrine of *stare decisis.* The Court went on to read the 1866 act extremely narrowly, rejecting the conclusion of most lower federal courts that the law allowed damages for a private employer's racial harassment of an employee.

Patterson's narrow interpretation of the 1866 act quickly became vulnerable to criticism, as the opinion of the four dissenters attested, and Congress overturned it in 1991, amending the 1866 act so that it now applies to condition sof employment. But the Court's reaffirmation of *Runyon* stands as the doctrinal consolidation of a broad political consensus on civil rights that had seemed threatened in the 1980s.

—KENNETH L. KARST

Bibliography

Karst, Kenneth L. (1989). Private Discrimination and Public Responsibility: *Patterson* in Context. *Supreme Court Review* 1989:1–51.

PAUL v. DAVIS
424 U.S. 693 (1976)

Even before *Goldberg* v. *Kelly* (1970) the Supreme Court assumed that the guarantee of procedural due process attached to state impairments of "liberty" or "property" interests—concepts that bore their own constitutional meanings as well as their traditional common law meanings. *Goldberg* and its successors added to those meanings a new category of protected "entitlements" established by statute or other state action. *Bishop* v. *Wood* (1976) and *Paul* v. *Davis* turned this development upside

PAUL v. VIRGINIA
8 Wallace 168 (1869)

In 1866 Virginia prohibited out-of-state insurance companies from doing business without a substantial deposit; domestic companies were not so required. Convicted of violating the 1866 act, Paul filed a writ of error and Benjamin R. Curtis argued his case. Justice Stephen J. Field, for a unanimous Supreme Court, rejected Paul's Article IV privileges and immunities argument, declaring that citizenship could apply only to natural persons. Field further asserted that insurance contracts were not articles of commerce and that the issuance of a policy was not a transaction in interstate commerce. *Paul* was often cited as a limitation on congressional power on the incorrect assumption that congressional and state regulatory power were mutually exclusive. *Paul* remained law until virtually overturned in *United States* v. *South-Eastern Underwriters Association* (1944), involving congressional power, after which Congress authorized state regulation.

—DAVID GORDON

In 1866 Virginia prohibited out-of-state insurance companies from doing business without a substantial deposit.

*Police officers
circulated a flyer
containing the
names and
photographs of
persons desccribed
as "active
shoplifters."*

down, using the idea of "entitlements" under state law to *confine* the reach of due process.

In *Paul*, police officers circulated a flyer containing the names and photographs of persons described as "active shoplifters." Davis, one of those listed, had been arrested and charged with shoplifting, but the case had not been prosecuted and the charge had been dismissed. He sued a police officer in a federal district court, claiming damages for a violation of his federal constitutional rights. The Supreme Court held, 5–3, that the alleged harm to Davis's reputation did not, of itself, amount to impairment of a "liberty" interest protected by the due process guarantee. For the majority, Justice William H. Rehnquist manhandled precedents that had established reputation as a "core" constitutionally protected interest, asserting that the Court had previously offered protection to reputation only when it was harmed along with some other interest established by state law, such as a right to employment. Justice William J. Brennan, for the dissenters, showed how disingenuous was this characterization of the precedents.

Probably the majority's main concern was to keep the federal civil rights laws from becoming a generalized law of torts committed by state officers, with the federal courts as the primary forum. Yet the majority opinion cannot be taken at face value. Unquestionably the notion of "liberty" interests protected by due process still includes a great many interests not defined by state law, such as First Amendment liberties.

—KENNETH L. KARST

PAYTON v. NEW YORK

445 U.S. 573 (1980)

The Fourth Amendment, which the Fourteenth makes applicable to the states, says that the "right of people to be secure in their . . . houses . . . shall not be violated." *Payton* was the first case in which the Supreme Court confronted the issue whether police may enter a private home, without an arrest warrant or consent, to make a felony arrest. New York, sustained by its courts, authorized warrantless arrests, by forcible entry if necessary, in any premises, if the police had probable cause to believe a person had committed a felony. In Payton's case the police seized evi-

*This case helped
delineate the
boundaries between
the traditional First
Amendment
freedoms and the
expanding area of
prisoners' rights.*

PELL v. PROCUNIER

417 U.S. 817 (1974)

In a case that helped delineate the boundaries between the traditional First Amendment freedoms and the expanding area of prisoners' rights, several prisoners and professional journalists challenged the constitutionality of a California prison regulation that forbade press interviews with particular inmates. The argument for the prisoners' rights was that this regulation abridged their freedom of speech; the journalists claimed the rule inhibited their newsgathering capabilities, thus violating the freedom of press. The Justices voted 6–3 against the inmates and 5–4 against the journalists. Because the prisoners had alternative means of communication (friends or family, for example) the California regulation did not violate their rights. The majority based its rejection of the journalists' position on the purpose of the regulation—to prevent particular individuals from gaining excessive influence through special attention—and the reporters' otherwise free access to prisoners. Furthermore, the regulation did not prohibit the press from publishing what it chose.

—DAVID GORDON

dence in plain view at the time of arrest and used it to convict him.

A 6–3 Supreme Court, in an opinion by Justice John Paul Stevens, reversed and held the state statute unconstitutional. Absent exigent circumstances, "a man's house is his castle" and unlike a public place may not be invaded without a warrant. Stevens found slight guidance in history for his position on the special privacy of the home in the case of a felony arrest, but he insisted that the Fourth Amendment required a magistrate's warrant. Justice Byron R. White for the dissenters declared that the decision distorted history and severely hampered law enforcement; the amendment required only that a warrantless felony arrest be made on probable cause in daytime.

—LEONARD W. LEVY

PENN CENTRAL TRANSPORTATION CO. v. NEW YORK CITY

438 U.S. 104 (1978)

Some governmental regulations of the use of property are severe enough to be called takings of property, for which just compensation must be made under the explicit terms of the Fifth Amendment (governing federal government action) or interpretations of the Fourteenth Amendment's due process clause (governing state action). This decision illustrates how difficult it is to persuade the Supreme Court that a regulation constitutes a "taking."

A New York City ordinance required city approval before a designated landmark's exterior could be altered. The owner of Grand Central Terminal sought to build a tall office building on top of the terminal, and was refused permission on aesthetic grounds. The Supreme Court held, 6–3, that this regulation did not constitute a "taking."

Justice William J. Brennan, for the majority, conceded that the taking/regulation distinction had defied clear formulation, pro-

P

PENN CENTRAL TRANSPORTATION CO. v. NEW YORK CITY

438 U.S. 104 (1978)

COURT NOT CONVINCED

A city ordinance restricting an addition to New York's Grand Central Terminal did not constitute a "taking." (Corbis/G. E. Kidder Smith)

ducing a series of "ad hoc factual inquiries." This regulation, however, was analogous to zoning under a comprehensive plan; over 400 landmarks had been designated. Further, the owner's loss was reduced by transferring its air-space development rights to other property in the city.

For the dissenters, Justice William H. Rehnquist argued that the law's severely destructive impact on property values was not justified by either of the usual "exceptions": the banning of "noxious uses," or the imposition of widely shared burdens to secure "an average reciprocity of advantage" (as in the case of zoning). Penn Central had suffered a huge loss of value, not offset by benefits under the landmark law.

Penn Central itself became a landmark, not only because it eloquently sustained historic preservation laws for the future, but also because Justice Brennan's opinion so clearly delineated the law with regard to land-use controls challenged as takings.

—KENNETH L. KARST

A New York City ordinance required city approval before a designated landmark's exterior could be altered.

PENNHURST STATE SCHOOL & HOSPITAL v. HALDERMAN

451 U.S. 1 (1981)

457 U.S. 1131 (1984)

Pennhurst worked major changes in the interpretation of the Eleventh Amendment and in the pendent jurisdiction of federal courts over claims based on state law. These changes remove one important weapon from the arsenal of civil rights plaintiffs.

Terri Lee Halderman, a resident of Pennhurst, a state institution for the mentally retarded, commenced a class action in federal district court against Pennhurst and a number of state and local officials. She alleged that squalor, abuse of residents, and other conditions at Pennhurst violated the federal Developmentally Disabled Assistance and Bill of Rights Act of 1975, the due process clause of the Fourteenth Amendment, and Pennsylvania's statute governing mental retardation. After a long trial, the district court agreed with her on all counts, and held that mentally retarded people in the state's care had a due process right to live in "the least restrictive setting" that would serve their needs. The court's injunction ordered the defendants to close Pennhurst and place its residents in "suitable living arrangements." The court of appeals affirmed, but rested decision only on the federal statute. The Supreme Court reversed, instructing the lower courts to consider whether the district court's order was justified on the basis of the Constitution or state law. On remand, the court of appeals avoided the constitutional issue, holding that state law required reaffirmation of the "least restrictive setting" ruling. When the case returned to the Supreme Court, the Court held, 5–4, that the Eleventh Amendment barred the district court's injunction. (The case was then settled, with the state agreeing to close Pennhurst and to move its residents to their home communities, or to other institutions if they were aged or ill.)

Justice Lewis F. Powell's opinion of the Court announced that the doctrine of sovereign immunity is a constitutional principle, based on the Eleventh Amendment, which gives a state immunity from suit in a federal court by an individual plaintiff. In Powell's novel reading, *Ex Parte Young* (1908) stands for a narrow exception to this immunity, allowing a suit in federal court for an injunction against a state officer only when the plaintiff's claim is based on a violation of the federal Constitution. (Perhaps violations of federal statutes will fit within this category, because of the operation of the supremacy clause.) Suits in federal court against state officers—even suits for injunctive relief—are thus barred by the Eleventh Amendment when they are based on claimed violations of state law.

Prior to *Pennhurst* an action in federal court founded on federal question jurisdiction could include a claim for relief on state law grounds, when both the federal and state claims arose out of the same facts. However, Powell said, this doctrine of pendent jurisdiction rests only on concerns for efficiency and convenience, concerns that must give way to the force of the Eleventh Amendment.

For the dissenters, Justice John Paul Stevens decried the Court's overruling of some two dozen precedents, and defended the long-established understanding of *Ex Parte Young*: that when a state officer's conduct is illegal (under either federal or state law), the officer is "stripped" of the cloak of the sovereign's immunity. Here it was perverse to clothe Pennsylvania's officers with the state's Eleventh Amendment immunity when they were acting in violation of their sovereign's commands as embodied in state law. Justice William J. Brennan, dissenting separately, argued that the amendment does not bar a suit by a citizen against the citizen's own state.

The *Pennhurst* majority opinion is vulnerable to criticism for its historical analysis of the Eleventh Amendment, for its casual dismissal of the importance of the federal courts' pendent jurisdiction, and for its choice to confer immunity on wrongdoing officials in the name of the sovereignty of the very state that had made the officials' conduct illegal. These criticisms seem minor, however, in the light of another one that is far more grave. The majority, in denying private citizens a vital judicial remedy against official lawlessness, weakened the rule of law.

—KENNETH L. KARST

Bibliography

Shapiro, David L. (1984). Wrong Turns: The Eleventh Amendment and the *Pennhurst* Case. *Harvard Law Review* 98:61–85.

PENRY v. LYNAUGH

492 U.S. 302 (1989)

In this case on the prohibition against cruel and unusual punishment imposed by the Eighth Amendment and the Fourteenth Amendment, the Court ruled that to inflict capital punishment on a mentally retarded prisoner was not necessarily unconstitutional. The Court, speaking through Justice Sandra Day O'Connor, also held that the ban on cruel and unusual punishments would be violated in a capital case if the sentencing jury were not instructed to consider all circumstances mitigating against the imposition of the death penalty. In this case, the jury had not properly considered whether Penry's mental retardation and history of childhood abuse diminished his moral culpability and made capital punishment a disproportionate sentence. Because the Eighth Amendment mandates an individualized assessment of the appropriateness of the death penalty, no mit-

igating factor may be withheld from the jury. Punishment must be directly related to the personal culpability of the criminal. Accordingly, the Court vacated the death sentence and remanded the case for resentencing under proper jury instruction.

Nonetheless, Justice O'Connor, for the Court, rejected Penry's second claim, ruling that the Eighth Amendment does not categorically prohibit the execution of a criminal who is mentally retarded. One who is profoundly or severely retarded and wholly lacking in the capacity to understand the wrongfulness of his or her actions cannot, in the face of the amendment, be executed. But the degree of mental retardation must be considered. In Penry's case, that of an adult with the reasoning capacity of a child not more than seven years of age, there was some proof that his diminished abilities disabled him from controlling his impulses and learning from his mistakes; yet a jury could properly conclude that his disabilities did not substantially reduce his level of blameworthiness for a capital offense. The Court refused to accept mental age as a line-drawing principle in such cases.

Four dissenters argued that the execution of mentally retarded prisoners invariably violates the "cruel and unusual punishment" clause because such people lack the culpability that is prerequisite to the proportionate imposition of the death penalty.

The *Penry* decision also made law on the subject of habeas corpus relief in federal courts, extending the nonretroactivity principle of *Teague* v. *Lane* (1989) to capital cases.

—LEONARD W. LEVY

PENUMBRA THEORY

Writing for the Supreme Court in *Griswold* v. *Connecticut* (1965), Justice William O. Douglas commented that "specific guarantees in

The Court ruled that to inflict capital punishment on a mentally retarded prisoner was not necessarily unconstitutional.

See also

Capital Punishment

*The "penumbra"
theory is best
understood as a
last-ditch effort by
Justice William O.
Douglas to avoid a
confrontation with
Justice Hugo L.
Black over a
doctrinal issue.*

See also

Adamson v. *California*

Griswold v. *Connecticut*

Right of Privacy

Search and Seizure

the Bill of Rights have penumbras, formed by emanations from those guarantees that help give them life and substance." The occasion for this shadowy suggestion was the Court's decision holding unconstitutional the application to a birth control clinic of a state law forbidding the use of contraceptive devices, even by the married couples whom the clinic had aided. Although nothing in the Constitution specifically forbade such a law, Justice Douglas rested decision on a right of privacy founded in this "penumbra" theory. A number of constitutional guarantees created "zones of privacy." One such zone included the "right of association contained in the First Amendment." Other protections of privacy were afforded by the Third Amendment's limitations on the quartering of troops, the Fourth Amendment's protections against unreasonable searches and seizures, and the Fifth Amendment's right against self-incrimination. "The present case, then, concerns a relationship lying within the zone of privacy created by several fundamental constitutional guarantees."

This "penumbra" theory, which has had no generative power of its own, is best understood as a last-ditch effort by Justice Douglas to avoid a confrontation with Justice Hugo L. Black over a doctrinal issue dear to Black's heart. In his famous dissent in *Adamson* v. *California* (1947), Black had derided "the natural-law-due-process formula" that allowed judges, with no warrant in the constitutional text, "to trespass, all too freely, on the legislative domain of the States as well as the Federal Government." Douglas had joined Black's *Adamson* dissent, and perhaps hoped that his *Griswold* opinion, by maintaining a formal tie to the specifics of the Bill of Rights, might persuade Black to come along. Black, of course, would have none of it: "I get nowhere in this case by talk about a constitutional 'right of privacy' as an emanation from one or more constitutional provisions. I like my privacy as well as the next one, but I am

nevertheless compelled to admit that government has a right to invade it unless prohibited by some specific constitutional provision."

The Court subsequently relocated its new right of privacy in the liberty protected by the due process clause of the Fourteenth Amendment, and no further "penumbras" have been seen in the land. Nonetheless, the *Griswold* decision has been an unusually influential precedent, not only for the Supreme Court's abortion decisions but also for the development of a generalized freedom of intimate association. Not every penumbra darkens the road ahead.

—KENNETH L. KARST

Bibliography

Kauper, Paul G. (1965). Penumbras, Peripheries, Emanations, Things Fundamental and Things Forgotten: The *Griswold* Case. *Michigan Law Review* 64:235–282.

PEOPLE v. CROSWELL

*3 Johnson's Cases (N.Y.)
336 (1804)*

The state of New York, run by Jeffersonians, indicted Harry Croswell, a Federalist editor, for the crime of seditious libel, because he wrote that President Thomas Jefferson had paid a scurrilous journalist to defame George Washington. Croswell was convicted at a trial presided over by the Jeffersonian chief justice of the state, Morgan Lewis, who embraced the position of the prosecution in *Zenger's Case* (1735). Lewis ruled that truth was not a defense against a charge of seditious libel and that the jury's sole task was to decide whether the defendant had published the statements charged, leaving the court to decide their criminality as a matter of law.

Alexander Hamilton, representing Croswell on his appeal to the state's highest court, advocated the protections of the Sedition Act of 1798: truth as a defense and determination by the jury of the criminality of the publication. Freedom of the press, declared Hamilton, was "the right to publish, with impunity, truth, with good motives for justifiable ends, though reflecting on government, the magistracy, or individuals." Spenser Ambrose, the Jeffersonian prosecutor, defended the remote bad tendency test. By the time the court decided the case, Ambrose had become a member of it. Had he been eligible to vote, the court would have supported the suppressive views of Lewis and Ambrose. As it was, the court split 2–2. Judge Brockholst Livingston joined Lewis, while Judge Smith Thompson joined the opinion of James Kent, a Federalist who adopted Hamilton's argument.

In 1805 the state legislature enacted a bill allowing the jury to decide the criminality of a publication and permitted truth as a defense if published "with good motives for justifiable ends." On the whole that was the standard that prevailed in the United States until *New York Times* v. *Sullivan* (1964).

—LEONARD W. LEVY

PERRY EDUCATION ASSOCIATION v. PERRY LOCAL EDUCATORS' ASSOCIATION

460 U.S. 37 (1983)

Perry provided the leading modern opinion setting guidelines governing First Amendment claims of access to the public forum. A school district's collective bargaining agreement with a union (PEA) provided that PEA, but no other union, would have access to the interschool mails and to teacher mailboxes. A rival union (PLEA) sued in federal district court, challenging the constitutionality of its exclusion from the school mails. The district court denied relief, but the court of appeals held that the exclusion violated the equal protection clause and the First Amendment. The Supreme Court reversed, 5–4, rejecting both claims.

Justice Byron R. White wrote for the Court, setting out a three-category analysis that set the pattern for later "public forum" cases such as *Cornelius* v. *NAACP Legal Defense and Educational Fund, Inc.* (1985). First, the streets and parks are "traditional" public forums, in which government cannot constitutionally forbid all communicative activity. Any exclusion of a speaker from such a traditional public forum based on the content of the speaker's message must be necessary to serve a compelling state interest. Content-neutral regulations of the "time, place, and manner" of expression in such places may be enforced when they are narrowly tailored to serve significant state interests and they leave open "ample alternative channels" of communication.

Second, the state may open up other kinds of public property for use by the public for expressive activity. The state may close such a "designated" public forum, but so long as it remains open it must be made available to all speakers, under the same constitutional guidelines that govern traditional public forums.

Third, communicative uses of public property that is neither a traditional nor a designated public forum may be restricted to those forms of communication that serve the governmental operation to which the property is devoted. The only constitutional limits on such restrictions on speech are that they be reasonable, and that they not be imposed in order to suppress a particular point of view. The *Perry* case, said Justice White, fit this third category: the school mail system was neither a traditional public forum nor designated for public communicative use; rather it could be limited to school-related

P

PERRY EDUCATION ASSOCIATION v. PERRY LOCAL EDUCATORS' ASSOCIATION

460 U.S. 37 (1983)

In 1805 the state legislature enacted a bill allowing the jury to decide the criminality of a publication.

Justice Byron R. White wrote for the Court, setting out a three-category analysis that set the pattern for later "public forum" cases.

See also

Freedom of the Press
New York Times v. *Sullivan*

communications, including those from PEA, the teachers' elected bargaining agent. Such a limitation did not exclude PLEA because of its point of view.

Justice William J. Brennan, for the four dissenters, argued that the exclusion of PLEA was "viewpoint discrimination," and thus that the case did not turn on the characterization of the school mails as a public forum.

The *Perry* formula capped a process of doctrinal development focused on what Harry Kalven Jr. named "the concept of the public forum." In its origin, the concept expanded the First Amendment's protections of speech. *Perry* marks the success of a campaign, highlighted by Justice William H. Rehnquist's opinion in *United States Postal Service* v. *Greenburgh Civic Association* (1981), to convert the public forum concept into a preliminary hurdle for would-be speakers to clear before they can establish their claims to the freedom of speech on government prop-

erty or in government-managed systems of communication.

—KENNETH L. KARST

PERSONNEL ADMINISTRATOR OF MASSACHUSETTS v. FEENEY

442 U.S. 256 (1979)

In selecting applicants for state civil service positions, Massachusetts preferred all qualifying veterans of the armed forces over any qualifying nonveterans. Because fewer than two percent of Massachusetts veterans were women, the preference severely restricted women's public employment opportunities. A nonveteran woman applicant challenged the preference as a denial of the equal protec-

See also

Compelling State Interest

Equal Protection of the Laws

Freedom of Speech

tion of the laws; the Supreme Court, 7–2, upheld the preference's constitutionality.

The Court, speaking through Justice Potter Stewart, followed *Washington* v. *Davis* (1976) and held that sex discrimination, like racial discrimination, is to be found only in purposeful official conduct. A discriminatory impact, of itself, is thus insufficient to establish the sex discrimination that demands the judicial scrutiny set out in *Craig* v. *Boren* (1976). Here the veterans preference disadvantaged nonveteran men as well as women; there was no basis for assuming that the preference was "a pretext for preferring men over women." Rather it was aimed at rewarding the sacrifices of military service and easing the transition from military to civilian life.

Justice Thurgood Marshall dissented, joined by Justice William J. Brennan: legislators act for a variety of reasons; the question is whether an improper purpose was one motivating factor in the governmental action. Here the discriminatory impact of the law was not merely foreseeable but inevitable. The result was to relegate female civil servants to jobs traditionally filled by women. Other less discriminatory means were available for rewarding veterans (bonuses, for example); the state's choice of this preference strongly suggested intentional gender discrimination. A similar "foreseeability" argument was persuasive to a majority of the Court four weeks later, in the context of school segregation.

—KENNETH L. KARST

PIERCE v. SOCIETY OF SISTERS

268 U.S. 510 (1925)

Pierce provided a doctrinal link between the substantive due process of the era of *Lochner* v. *New York* (1905) and that of our own time. The Supreme Court unanimously invalidated an Oregon law requiring children to attend public schools. A church school and a military school, threatened with closure, sued to enjoin the law's enforcement. Although the law threatened injury to the schools, their challenge to it was based not on their own constitutional rights but on the rights of their pupils and the children's parents. By allowing the schools to make this challenge, the Court made a major exception to the usual rule denying a litigant's standing to assert the constitutional rights of others. Here there was a close relationship between the schools and their patrons, and failure to allow the schools to assert the patrons' rights might cause injury to the schools that no one would contest in court. Parents, fearing prosecution and unwilling to bear the expense of suit, might simply send their children to public schools.

In an opinion by Justice James C. McReynolds, the Court held that the law unconstitutionally invaded the parents' liberty, guaranteed by the Fourteenth Amendment's due process clause, to direct their children's education and upbringing. The decision rested squarely on the notion that important personal liberties could be seriously restricted by the state only upon a showing of great public need. Although *Pierce* thus traced its lineage to earlier decisions protecting economic liberty, it provided support for a later generation of decisions protecting marriage and family relationships against state intrusion.

Pierce is also cited regularly as a religious liberty precedent, defending the right of parents to choose religious education for their children.

—KENNETH L. KARST

PINK, UNITED STATES v.

315 U.S. 203 (1942)

In *Pink,* the Supreme Court reaffirmed a doctrine articulated five years earlier in *United States* v. *Belmont* (1937): that the president has exclusive constitutional authority to

By allowing the schools to make this challenge, the Court made a major exception to the usual rule denying a litigant's standing to assert the constitutional rights of others.

See also

Lochner v. *New York*

Religious Liberty

Standing

P

PIQUA BRANCH OF THE STATE BANK OF OHIO v. KNOOP

16 Howard 369 (1854)

The president has exclusive constitutional authority to recognize foreign governments and to take all steps necessary to effect such recognition.

recognize foreign governments and to take all steps necessary to effect such recognition. In *Belmont,* the Court recognized the federal government's standing to sue to enforce an executive agreement known as the "Litvinov Agreement." As part of the process of recognition of the Soviet Union by the United States in 1933, this agreement assigned to the United States nationalized Russian assets located within the United States.

In *Pink,* the Court was again confronted with the controversial Litvinov Agreement. In this case, while recognizing the federal government's rights under the Litvinov Assignment as required by *Belmont,* the New York courts rejected the government's claims of ownership of the assets in question, contending that to enforce the assignment would violate New York public policy against the confiscation of private property. The Supreme Court reversed, 5–2, emphasizing that an executive agreement, like a treaty, is part of the "supreme law of the land" that no state may frustrate without interfering unconstitutionally with the federal government's exclusive competence in respect of foreign affairs. In so doing, the Court reasserted the supremacy of an executive agreement over all inconsistent state law or policy.

—BURNS H. WESTON

Bibliography

Cardozo, Michael H. (1962). The Authority in Internal Law of International Treaties: The *Pink* Case. *Syracuse Law Review* 13: 544–553.

Forkosch, Morris D. (1975). The Constitution and International Relations. *California Western International Law Journal* 5: 219, 246–249.

Henkin, Louis (1972). *Foreign Affairs and the Constitution.* Mineola, N.Y.: Foundation Press.

Leary, M. A. (1979). International Executive Agreements: A Guide to the Legal Issues and Research Sources. *Law Library Journal* 72:1–11.

PIQUA BRANCH OF THE STATE BANK OF OHIO v. KNOOP

16 Howard 369 (1854)

In *New Jersey* v. *Wilson* (1812) the Supreme Court had held that a state grant of a tax immunity was a contract within the protection of the contract clause. In this case Ohio chartered a bank with the proviso that six percent of its net profits would be taxed in lieu of other taxation. The states competed with each other to entice private business to settle within their borders on the supposition that the more banks, railroads, and factories a state had, the greater would be its prosperity. Special privileges to corporations were common, and they often wrote their own charters. Ohio, gripped by an anticorporate movement, reneged by passing an act to tax banks at the same rate as other properties. The bank refused to pay the new tax on the ground that its charter was a contract the obligation of which had been impaired by the tax. By a vote of 6–3 the Supreme Court invalidated the tax. To the contention that the power to tax was an inalienable attribute of sovereignty, which could not be contracted away, the Court replied that the making of a public contract is an exercise of sovereignty. To the argument that one legislature, by granting a charter of tax immunity, could not bind its successors, the Court replied that the contract clause made the charter binding. In effect the Court cautioned the states to govern wisely, because the Court would not shield them from their imprudence if it took the form of contracts. Corporations throughout the country profited enormously.

—LEONARD W. LEVY

See also

New Jersey v. *Wilson*

PLANNED PARENTHOOD OF CENTRAL MISSOURI v. DANFORTH

428 U.S. 52 (1976)

Following *Roe* v. *Wade* (1973), Missouri adopted a comprehensive law regulating abortion. Planned Parenthood, which operated an abortion clinic, and two eminent physicians sued in federal district court challenging the constitutionality of most of the law's provisions. On appeal, the Supreme Court unanimously upheld three of the state's requirements and by divided vote invalidated four others. Justice Harry A. Blackmun wrote for the Court.

The Court sustained the law's definition of "viability" of a fetus: "when the life of the unborn child may be continued indefinitely outside the womb by natural or artificial life-supportive systems." The state's failure to set a specific time period survived a challenge for vagueness; the Court assumed that the physician retained the power to determine viability. The Court also upheld a requirement of written certification by a woman of her "informed" consent to an abortion, and certain record-keeping requirements.

The Court invalidated, 6–3, a requirement of consent to an abortion by the husband of the pregnant woman, and invalidated, 5–4, a parental consent requirement for unmarried women under age eighteen. Recognizing the husband's strong interest in the abortion decision, the Court concluded that when spouses disagreed, only one of them could prevail; that one must be the woman. As for parental consent, the opinion offered no broad charter of children's rights but concluded that a "mature" minor's right to have an abortion must prevail over a parent's contrary decision (*H. L.* v. *Matheson*, 1981). The state had little hope of restoring a family structure already "fractured" by such a conflict.

The question of the doctor's role in determining viability and preserving fetal life returned to the Court.

AFTER ROE v. WADE

Planned Parenthood is an outspoken opponent of the Court's attempts to regulate abortion. (Corbis/Henry Diltz)

See also

The Court invalidated, 6–3, a prohibition on saline amniocentesis as an abortion technique. The procedure was used in more than two-thirds of all abortions following the first trimester of pregnancy; its prohibition would undermine *Roe*. Finally, the state had required a physician performing an abortion to use professional skill and care to preserve the life and health of a fetus. The requirement was held invalid, 6–3, because it was not limited to the time following the stage of fetal viability.

The question of the doctor's role in determining viability and preserving fetal life returned to the Court in *Colautti* v. *Franklin* (1979). There the Court invalidated, 6–3, on vagueness grounds, a Pennsylvania law requiring a doctor to exercise care to protect a fetus when there was "sufficient reason to believe that the fetus may be viable." As in *Roe* and *Danforth*, the Court paid considerable deference to physicians, leaving undefined their control over their patients' constitutional rights.

—KENNETH L. KARST

Bibliography

Cohen, Leslie Ann (1980). Fetal Viability and Individual Autonomy: Resolving Medical and Legal Standards for Abortion. *UCLA Law Review* 27:1340–1364.

PLANNED PARENTHOOD OF SOUTHEASTERN PENNSYLVANIA v. CASEY

112 Supreme Court 2791 (1992)

This case is best known for what it did not do—overrule *Roe* v. *Wade* (1973). By 1992 five associate justices had been appointed to the Supreme Court by Presidents Ronald Reagan and George Bush, both of whom pledged to

select judges committed to overturning *Roe*, which had legalized abortion. Reagan had named William Rehnquist, one of the original dissenters in *Roe*, as chief justice in 1986. *Webster* v. *Reproductive Health Services* (1989) and *Rust* v. *Sullivan* (1991) had upheld laws limiting access to abortion and seemed indicators of doctrinal shifts. The Pennsylvania Abortion Control Act at issue in *Casey* did not ban abortion, but the Court upheld all of the restrictions on abortion imposed by Pennsylvania except for mandatory husband notification. These included a twenty-four-hour waiting period, informed consent of one parent for pregnant teenagers, reporting requirements, and a state-scripted warning against the medical procedure. As a result of *Casey*, restrictions on abortion would no longer be judged by a strict scrutiny standard requiring a "compelling state interest," as did restrictions on other constitutional rights. Instead, an "undue burden" standard was substituted, allowing states to place restrictions on abortion unless they posed "substantial obstacles" to a woman's right of privacy recognized in *Roe*. For Justices Sandra Day O'Connor, Anthony Kennedy, and David Souter, all appointed by Presidents Reagan and Bush, "the reservations any of us may have in reaffirming the central holding of *Roe* are out-weighed by the expectation of individual liberty." Hence, *Casey* was a defeat for both sides on the abortion issue. It represented a victory for centrist judicial politics.

—JUDITH A. BAER

Bibliography

Craig, Barbara Hinkson, and O'Brien, David M. (1993). *Abortion and American Politics.* Chatham, N.J.: Chatham House.

PLESSY v. FERGUSON

163 U.S. 537 (1896)

Until *Brown* v. *Board of Education* (1954), *Plessy* was the constitutional linchpin for the entire structure of Jim Crow in America. Borrowed from Lemuel Shaw in *Roberts* v. *Boston* (1851), the *Plessy* Court established the separate but equal doctrine: black persons were not denied the equal protection of the laws safeguarded by the Fourteenth Amendment when they were provided with facilities substantially equal to those available to white persons.

Florida enacted the first Jim Crow transportation law in 1887, and by the end of the century the other states of the old Confederacy had followed suit. Louisiana's act, which was challenged in *Plessy*, required railroad companies carrying passengers in the state to have "equal but separate accommodations" for white and colored persons by designating coaches racially or partitioning them. Black citizens, who denounced the innovation of Jim Crow in Louisiana as "unconstitutional, un-american, unjust, dangerous and against sound public policy," complained that prejudiced whites would have a "license" to maltreat and humiliate inoffensive blacks. *Plessy* was a test case. Homer A. Plessy, an octoroon (one-eighth black), boarded the East Louisiana Railroad in New Orleans bound for Covington in the same state and sat in the white car; he was arrested when he refused to move to the black car. Convicted by the state he appealed on constitutional grounds, invoking the Thirteenth and Fourteenth Amendments. The Court had already decided in *Louisville, New Orleans & Texas Pacific Ry.* v. *Mississippi*, (1890) that Jim Crow cars in intrastate commerce did not violate the commerce clause.

FORESHADOWING

In 1944 demonstrators call for the "death" of Jim Crow laws, which would not be declared unconstitutional for ten more years, until Brown *v.* Board of Education. *(Corbis)*

Until Brown v.
Board of Education,
Plessy *was the
constitutional
linchpin for the
entire structure of
Jim Crow in
America.*

Justice John Marshall Harlan was the only dissenter from the opinion by Justice Henry B. Brown. That the state act did not infringe the Thirteenth Amendment, declared Brown, "is too clear for argument." The act implied "merely a legal distinction" between the two races and therefore had "no tendency to destroy the legal equality of the two races, or reestablish a state of involuntary servitude." Harlan, believing that state action could have no regard to the race of citizens when their civil rights were involved, would have ruled that compulsory racial segregation violated the Thirteenth Amendment by imposing a badge of servitude.

The chief issue was whether the state act abridged the Fourteenth Amendment's equal protection clause. One reads Brown's opinion with an enormous sense of the feebleness of words as conveyors of thought, because he conceded that the object of the amendment "was undoubtedly to enforce the absolute equality of the two races before the law," yet he continued the same sentence by adding, "but in the nature of things it could not have been intended to abolish distinctions based on color. . . ." As a matter of historical fact the intention of the amendment was, generally, to abolish legal distinctions based on color. The Court pretended to rest on history without looking at the historical record; it did not claim the necessity of adapting the Constitution to changed conditions, making untenable the defense often heard in more recent years, that the decision fit the times. *Plessy* makes sense only if one understands that the Court believed that segregation was not discriminatory, indeed that it would violate the equal protection clause if it were discriminatory. Brown conceded that a statute implying a legal inferiority in civil society, lessening "the security of the right of the colored race," would be discriminatory, but he insisted that state-imposed segregation did not "necessarily imply the inferiority of either race to the other. . . ." There was abundant evidence to the contrary, none of it understandable to a Court that found fallacious the contention that "the enforced separation of the two races stamps the colored race with a badge of inferiority. If this be so, it is not by reason of anything found in the act, but solely because the colored race chooses to put that construction on it." That segregation stamped blacks with a badge of inferiority was not fallacious. The fallacy was that only they imputed inferiority to segregation. Jim Crow laws were central to white supremacist thought. That blacks were inherently inferior was a conviction being stridently trumpeted by white supremacists from the press, the pulpit, and the platform, as well as from the legislative halls, of the South. The label "For Colored Only" was a public expression of disparagement amounting to officially sanctioned civil inequality. By the Court's own reasoning, state acts compelling racial segregation were unconstitutional if inferiority was implied or discrimination intended.

The separate but equal doctrine was fatally vulnerable for still other reasons given, ironically, by the Court in *Plessy*. It sustained the act as a valid exercise of the police power yet stated that every exercise of that power "must be reasonable, and extend only to such laws as are enacted in good faith for the promotion of the public good, and not for the annoyance or oppression of a particular class." Jim Crow laws were not only annoying and oppressive to blacks; they were not reasonable or for the public good. The Court asserted that the question of reasonableness must be determined with reference "to the established usages, customs and traditions" of the people of the state. The proper standard of reasonableness ought to have been the equal protection clause of the Constitution, not new customs of the white supremacists of an ex-slave state. Even if the custom of segregation had been old, and it was not, the Court was making strange doctrine when implying that discrimination becomes vested with constitutionality if carried on long enough to become customary. Classifying people by race for the purpose of transportation was unreasonable because the classification was irrelevant to any legitimate purpose.

The only conceivable justification for the reasonableness of the racial classification was that it promoted the public good, which Brown alleged. The effects of segregation were inimical to the public good, because, as Harlan pointed out, it "permits the seeds of race hate to be planted under the sanction of law." It created and perpetuated interracial tensions. Oddly the Court made the public-good argument in the belief that the commingling of the races would threaten the public peace by triggering disorders. In line with that assumption Brown declared that legislation is powerless to eradicate prejudice based on hostile "racial instincts" and that equal rights cannot be gained by "enforced commingling." These contentions seem cynical when announced in an opinion sanctioning inequality by sustaining a statute compelling racial segregation. The argument that prejudice cannot be legislated away overlooked the extent to which prejudice had been legislated into existence and continued by Jim Crow statutes.

Harlan's imperishable dissent repeated the important Thirteenth Amendment argument that he had made in the *Civil Rights Cases* (1883) on badges of servitude. That amendment, he declared, "decreed universal civil freedom in the country." Harlan reminded the Court that in *Strauder* v. *West Virginia* (1880), it had construed the Fourteenth Amendment to mean that "the law in the States shall be the same for the black as for the white" and that the amendment contained "a necessary implication of a positive immunity, or right . . . the right to exemption from unfriendly legislation against them distinctively as colored—exemption from legal discriminations, implying inferiority in civil society, lessening the security of their enjoyment of rights which others enjoy. . . ." To Harlan, segregation was discriminatory per se. The state act was unreasonable because

segregation was not germane to a legitimate legislative end. He meant that the Fourteenth Amendment rendered the state powerless to make legal distinctions based on color in respect to public transportation. A railroad, he reminded the Court, was a public highway exercising public functions available on the same basis to all citizens. "Our Constitution," said Harlan, "is color-blind, and neither knows nor tolerates classes among citizens." He thought the majority's decision would prove in time to be as pernicious as *Dred Scott* v. *Sandford* (1857). As for the separate but equal doctrine, he remarked that the "thin disguise" of equality would mislead no one "nor atone for the wrong this day done."

Plessy cleared the constitutional way for legislation that forced the separation of the races in all places of public accommodation. Most of that legislation came after *Plessy*. In the *Civil Rights Cases,* the Court had prevented Congress from abolishing segregation, and in *Plessy* the Court supported the states in compelling it. Not history and not the Fourteenth Amendment dictated the decision; it reflected its time, and its time was racist. As Justice Brown pointed out, even Congress in governing the District of Columbia had required separate schools for the two races. The Court did not invent Jim Crow but adapted the Constitution to it.

—LEONARD W. LEVY

Bibliography

Kluger, Richard (1973). *Simple Justice: The History of* Brown *v.* Board of Education *and Black America's Struggle for Equality.* Pages 71–83. New York: Knopf.

Oberst, Paul (1973). The Strange Career of *Plessy* v. *Ferguson. Arizona Law Review* 15:389–418.

Olson, Otto, ed. (1967). *The Thin Disguise: Turning Point in Negro History:* Plessy v. Ferguson. New York: Humanities Press.

Woodward, C. Vann (1971). The National Decision Against Equality. Pages 212–233 in Woodward, *American Counterpoint:*

P

In some cases the majority of Justices of the Supreme Court do not agree on the reasoning behind a decision.

Slavery and Racism in the North–South Dialogue. Boston: Little, Brown.

PLURALITY OPINION

In some cases the majority of Justices of the Supreme Court, although agreeing on the decision, do not agree on the reasoning behind the decision. In such cases, there is no opinion of the court; instead there are two or more opinions purporting to explain the decision. If one opinion is signed by more Justices than any other, it is called the "plurality opinion." A plurality opinion may be cited as precedent in later cases, but, unlike a majority opinion, it is not an authoritative statement of the Court's position on the legal or constitutional issues involved.

—DENNIS J. MAHONEY

PLYLER v. DOE

457 U.S. 202 (1982)

Experimenting with ignorance, the Texas legislature authorized local school boards to exclude the children of undocumented aliens from the public schools, and cut off state funds to subsidize those children's schooling. The Supreme Court, 5–4, held that this scheme denied the alien children the equal protection of the laws. The opinion of the Court, by Justice William J. Brennan, contains the potential for important future influence on equal protection doctrine.

The Court was unanimous on one point: the Fourteenth Amendment's guarantee of equal protection for all persons extends not only to aliens lawfully admitted for residence but also to undocumented aliens. The question that divided the Court was what that guarantee demanded—an issue that the Court's recent opinions had typically discussed in language about the appropriate standard of review. In *San Antonio Independent School District* v. *Rodriguez* (1973) the

Court had rejected the claim that education was a fundamental interest, and had subjected a state system for financing schools to a deferential rational basis standard. A significant obiter dictum, however, had suggested that a total denial of education to a certain group of children would have to pass the test of strict scrutiny. Furthermore, although alienage was, for some purposes, a suspect classification, the Court had not extended that characterization to laws discriminating against aliens who were not lawfully admitted to the country.

Justice Brennan's analysis blurred the already indistinct lines dividing levels of judicial scrutiny in equal protection cases. He suggested that some form of "intermediate scrutiny" was appropriate, and even hinted at a preference for strict scrutiny. Eventually, though, he came to rest on rhetorical ground that could hold together a five-Justice majority. Because the Texas law imposed a severe penalty on children for their parents' misconduct, it was irrational unless the state could show that it furthered "some substantial goal of the State," and no such showing had been made. In a concurring opinion, Justice Lewis F. Powell remarked that heightened scrutiny was proper, on analogy to the Court's decisions about classifications based on illegitimacy. Justice Thurgood Marshall, also concurring, repeated his argument for recognition of a "sliding scale" of standards of review, and accurately noted that this very decision illustrated that the Court was already employing such a system. No one should be surprised when the Court holds invalid a supremely stupid law that imposes great hardship on a group of innocent people.

Chief Justice Warren E. Burger, writing for the four dissenters, agreed that the Texas policy was "senseless." He argued nonetheless that the Court, by undertaking a "policymaking role," was "trespass[ing]" on the assigned function of the political branches. In allocating scarce state resources, Texas could rationally choose to prefer citizens and lawfully admitted aliens over aliens who had entered

The Texas legislature authorized local school boards to exclude the children of undocumented aliens from the public schools.

the country without permission; for the dissenters, that was enough to validate the law.

The *Plyler* opinion was narrow, leaving open the question whether a similar burden of substantial justification would be imposed on a discrimination against undocumented aliens who were adults, or even against innocent children when the discrimination was something less than a total denial of education. Justice Brennan did suggest that judicial scrutiny might properly be heightened in cases of discrimination against aliens—even undocumented aliens—who had established "a permanent attachment to the nation." Although it is unlikely that this view could command a majority of the Court today, the remark may bear fruit in the future.

—KENNETH L. KARST

POLICE DEPARTMENT OF CHICAGO v. MOSLEY

408 U.S. 92 (1972)

Mosley is the leading modern decision linking equal protection doctrine with the First Amendment. Chicago adopted an ordinance prohibiting picketing within 150 feet of a school during school hours, but excepting peaceful labor picketing. Earl Mosley had been picketing on the public sidewalk adjoining a high school, carrying a sign protesting "black discrimination," and after the ordinance was adopted he sought declaratory and injunctive relief, arguing that the ordinance was unconstitutional. The Supreme Court unanimously agreed with him.

Justice Thurgood Marshall, for the Court, concluded that the exemption of labor picketing violated the equal protection clause of the Fourteenth Amendment. This conclusion followed the lead of Justice Hugo L. Black, concurring in *Cox* v. *Louisiana* (1965). Yet Justice Marshall's opinion speaks chiefly to First Amendment values and primarily cites First Amendment decisions. "[A]bove all else, the First Amendment means that government has no power to restrict expression because of its message, its ideas, its subject matter, or its content." As Chief Justice Warren E. Burger noted in a brief concurrence, so broad a statement is not literally true; the Court has upheld regulations of speech content in areas ranging from defamation to obscenity. Yet *Mosley* properly stakes out a presumption in favor of "equality of status in the field of ideas"—a phrase borrowed from Alexander Meiklejohn.

The *Mosley* opinion makes two main points. First, regulations of message content are presumptively unconstitutional, requiring justification by reference to state interests of compelling importance. Second, "time, place, and manner" regulations that selectively exclude speakers from a public forum must survive careful judicial scrutiny to ensure that the exclusion is the minimum necessary to further a significant government interest. Together, these statements declare a principle of major importance: the principle of equal liberty of expression.

—KENNETH L. KARST

Bibliography

Karst, Kenneth L. (1976). Equality as a Central Principle of the First Amendment. *University of Chicago Law Review* 43:20–68.

POLLOCK v. FARMERS' LOAN & TRUST CO.

157 U.S. 429 and 158 U.S. 601 (1895)

Charles Evans Hughes called these decisions a "self-inflicted wound" comparable to the decision in *Dred Scott* v. *Sandford* (1857). Here the Supreme Court held unconstitutional an 1894 act of Congress that fixed a flat tax of 2 percent on all annual incomes over $4,000. Pollock filed a stockholder's suit against the trust company to prevent it from

Mosley is the leading modern decision linking equal protection doctrine with the First Amendment.

See also

Equal Protection of the Laws

P

complying with the statute that, he claimed, imposed a direct tax without apportioning it among the states on the basis of population. The trust company, the party of record on the side of the tax, avoided the appearance of collusion by hiring the president of the American Bar Association, James Coolidge Carter; Richard Olney, attorney general of the United States, was on the same side as amicus curiae. Theirs was the easy task because history and all the precedents proved that the clause of Article 1, section 9, referring to direct taxes, meant only taxes on people or on land. The Court had so declared in *Hylton* v. *United States* (1796) and in several other cases, especially *Springer* v. *United States* (1881), a direct precedent; the Court there had unanimously sustained an earlier income tax as imposing an indirect tax and therefore

not subject to the requirement of apportionment.

Counsel for Pollock, led by Joseph H. Choate, buttressed a weak case with an impassioned argument intended to provoke judicial fear and reflecting the panic felt by many conservatives. Choate warned that the Court had to choose between "the beginning of socialism and communism" and the preservation of private property, civilization, and the Constitution. He appealed to the Court to substitute its discretion for that of Congress.

Justice Howell E. Jackson not having participated, an eight-member Court decided the case. All agreed that the federal tax on municipal bonds was unconstitutional, because government instrumentalities were exempt from taxation. On the question of the validity of the

AMENDMENT XVI

"The Congress shall have power to lay and collect taxes on incomes, from whatever source derived, without apportionment among the several States, and without regard to any census or enumeration."

The Sixteenth Amendment was designed to circumvent *Pollock* v. *Farmers' Loan & Trust Co.* (1895), in which the Supreme Court had held that a federal tax on income from property was a direct tax on that property and therefore invalid for want of apportionment among the states on the basis of population (Article I, sections 2 and 9). Following *Pollock*, powerful political forces continued to press for an income tax to replace the regressive consumption

taxes then employed to finance the federal government. Indeed, an amendment might have been unnecessary, given the Supreme Court's philosophical shift in *Flint* v. *Stone Tracy Co.* (1911), upholding a corporate income tax as an excise on doing business in corporate form, not a tax on property.

Although there was sentiment for challenging *Pollock* by reenacting a personal income tax, President William Howard Taft urged a constitutional amendment. The Sixteenth Amendment was speedily passed and ratified in 1913.

Since the enactment of a new income tax statute in 1913, only a single Supreme Court decision has held an income tax provision unconstitutional.

Eisner v. *Macomber* (1920) ruled that a stock dividend of common stock on common stock was not "income" because the element of "realization" was lacking. *Macomber* has been greatly undermined by subsequent cases, such as *Helvering* v. *Bruun* (1940), which treated the return of a lessor's property to him at the termination of a lease as a realization of income. Indeed, the current Court would probably dispense entirely with any constitutional requirement of a realization (or alternatively view a stock dividend as a realization). In *Helvering* v. *Griffiths* (1943) three dissenters would have overruled *Macomber* but the majority held that the constitutional issue had not been presented by the statute.

tax on income from personal property, the Court divided evenly. But on the question of the validity of the tax on income from real estate, the Court voted 6–2 that it was a direct tax unconstitutionally assessed. Nothing favorable can be said about Chief Justice Melville W. Fuller's opinion for the majority. He took for granted the very proposition he should have proved, asserting that a tax on the income from land was indistinguishable from a tax on the land itself. Clearly, however, the income that may derive from rents, timber, oil, minerals, or agriculture is distinguishable from a tax on acreage or on the assessed value of the land itself. Fuller distinguished away the precedents: *Hylton* had decided only that a tax on carriages was not a direct tax, and *Springer* had decided only the narrow point that a tax on a lawyer's fees was not a direct one. Neither case, Fuller declared, dealt with a tax on the income from land, and he made much of the point that such a tax is unique because of the undisputed fact that a tax on the land itself is undoubtedly a direct tax. Justices Edward D. White and John Marshall Harlan, dissenting, concluded that history and *stare decisis* demanded a different ruling, and they warned that when the Court virtually annulled its previous decisions on the basis of the policy preferences of a majority that happened to dominate the bench, the Constitution was in jeopardy.

The tie vote of the Court on all other issues meant that the decision of the circuit court prevailed, leaving in force the taxes on corporate income, wages and salaries, and returns from investments. Accordingly, Choate moved for a rehearing, which was granted, and Justice Jackson attended. The trust company, which was supposed to defend the income tax act, did not retain Carter or replace him, thus leaving Olney to defend it. He took half the time permitted by the Court for his presentation.

The arguments the second time focused on the validity of the tax on the income from personal property, mainly interest and dividends. Fuller, speaking for a bare majority, again read the Court's opinion. Six weeks earlier he had based his position on the uniqueness of a tax on the income from land; now he took the opposite view, reasoning that if a tax on the income from land is a direct tax, so is a tax on the income from personal property. Having found the statute void in significant respects, he reasoned next that the invalidity of some sections contaminated the rest: since the sections were inseparable, all were void because some were.

When Fuller finished his opinion, Harlan began to read his dissent; it sizzled in its language and delivery. He ended a systematic refutation by pounding his desk, shaking his finger in the face of the Chief Justice, and shouting, "On my conscience I regard this decision as a disaster!!" (*The Nation* magazine described Harlan as an "agitator" who expounded "the Marx gospel from the bench.") He accused the majority of an unprecedented use of judicial power on behalf of private wealth by striking down a statute whose policy they disliked and by doing it against all law and history. He also pointed out, as did the other dissenters, Justices White, Jackson, and Henry B. Brown, that the parts of the statute that were not unconstitutional per se, and might be reenacted if Congress chose, taxed the income of people who earned their money from wages and salaries but who derived no income from land or invested personal property. The decision, said Brown, is "nothing less than a surrender of the taxing power to the moneyed class" making for "a sordid despotism of wealth." It "takes invested wealth," said White, and "reads it into the Constitution as a favored and protected class of property. . . ." It was, said Jackson, "the most disastrous blow ever struck at the constitutional power of congress" and made the tax burden fall "most heavily and oppressively upon those having the least ability" to pay.

Here the Supreme Court held unconstitutional an 1894 act of Congress that fixed a flat tax of 2 percent on all annual incomes over $4,000.

See also

Dred Scott v. Sandford

Public opinion was opposed to the Court, though it had vigorous supporters especially among the Republican newspapers in the East. The *New York Sun* exclaimed in delight, "Five to Four, the Court Stands Like a Rock." The *New York Herald Tribune* hailed the Court for halting a "communist revolution." The Democratic party, however, recommended an amendment to the Constitution vesting Congress with the power denied by the Court. The Sixteenth Amendment was not ratified, though, until 1913, by which time the nation's maldistribution of wealth had intensified. For eighteen years, as Edward S. Corwin wrote, "the veto of the Court held the sun and moon at pause," while the great fortunes went untaxed. The government during that time raised almost all of its revenues from excise taxes and tariffs, whose burden fell mainly on consumers. In 1913 the average annual income in the United States was $375 per capita.

—LEONARD W. LEVY

Bibliography

Corwin, Edward S. (1932). *Court over Constitution.* Pages 177–209. Princeton, N.J.: Princeton University Press.

King, Willard L. (1950). *Melville Weston Fuller.* Pages 193–221. New York: Macmillan.

Paul, Arnold M. (1960). *Conservative Crisis and the Rule of Law: Attitudes of Bar and Bench, 1887–1895.* Pages 159–220. Ithaca, N.Y.: Cornell University Press.

Shiras, George, III, and Shiras, Winfield (1953). *Justice George Shiras Jr. of Pittsburgh.* Pages 160–183. Pittsburgh: University of Pittsburgh Press.

POLYGAMY

Because polygamy was one of the early tenets of the Mormon Church, the movement to eradicate plural marriage became bound up with religious persecution. The Supreme Court has consistently held that the First Amendment's protections of religious liberty do not protect the practice of plural marriage. Thus *Reynolds* v. *United States* (1879) upheld a criminal conviction for polygamy in the Territory of Utah, and *Davis* v. *Beason* (1880) upheld a conviction for voting in the Territory of Idaho in violation of an oath required of all registrants forswearing belief in polygamy. The corporate charter of the Mormon Church in the Territory of Utah was revoked, and its property forfeited to the government, in *Church of Jesus Christ of Latter-Day Saints* v. *United States* (1890). The church's First Amendment claim was waved away with the statement that belief in polygamy was not a religious tenet but a "pretense" that was "contrary to the spirit of Christianity."

It would be comforting if this judicial record were confined to the nineteenth century, but it was not. In *Cleveland* v. *United States* (1946) the Court upheld a conviction of Mormons under the Mann Act for transporting women across state lines for the purpose of "debauchery" that took the form of living with them in polygamous marriage. The Court's opinion, citing the nineteenth-century cases and even quoting the "spirit of Christianity" language with approval, was written by none other than Justice William O. Douglas.

More recently, the Court has recognized a constitutional right to marry, and in a number of contexts has afforded protection for a freedom of intimate association. With or without the ingredient of religious freedom, substantive due process doctrine seems amply to justify an extension of these rights to plural marriage among competent consenting adults. Yet the force of conventional morality in constitutional adjudication should not be underestimated; the Supreme Court is not just the architect of principle but an institution of government. Polygamy is not on the verge of becoming a constitutional right.

—KENNETH L. KARST

The movement to eradicate plural marriage became bound up with religious persecution.

See also

Reynolds v. *United States*

Bibliography

Larson, Gustave O. (1971). *The "American-ization" of Utah for Statehood.* San Marino, Calif.: Huntington Library.

PORNOGRAPHY

The Supreme Court's obscenity decisions define the forms of pornography that are protected from censorship by the First Amendment. As a practical matter, this protection is quite broad. Most pornography is also a unique kind of speech: about women, for men. In an era when sexual equality is a social ideal, the constitutional protection of pornography is a vexing political issue. Should pornographic imagery of male dominance and female subordination be repudiated through censorship, or will censorship inevitably destroy our commitment to free speech?

In *Roth* v. *United States* (1957) the Court found obscene speech to be unworthy of First Amendment protection because it forms "no essential part of any exposition of ideas." Yet precisely because of pornography's ideational content, some of it was deemed harmful and made criminal. The Court could avoid examining the specific nature of this harm, once it had located obscenity conveniently outside the constitutional pale. But it could not avoid defining obscenity, and thereby identifying the justification for its censorship.

The essential characteristic of "obscene" pornography is its appeal to one's "prurient interest," which is a genteel reference to its capacity to stimulate physical arousal and carnal desire. But such pornography must also be "offensive," and so, to be censored, sex-stimulant speech must be both arousing and disgusting. The meaning of offensiveness depends upon the subjective judgment of the observer, and is best captured by Justice Potter Stewart's famous aphorism in *Jacobellis* v. *Ohio* (1964): "I know it when I see it."

Given the limitations of the criminal process, obscenity laws did not make offensive

PRURIENT INTERESTS

Obscenity laws have not made offensive pornography unavailable in the marketplace, as evidenced by these adult theaters in New York City. (Corbis/Bettmann)

Most pornography is a unique kind of speech: about women, for men.

pornography unavailable in the marketplace. As Harry Kalven Jr. pointed out, few judges took the evils of obscenity very seriously, although constitutional rhetoric made the law appear to be "solemnly concerned with the sexual fantasies of the adult population." The Court's chief goal was the protection of admired works of art and literature, not the elimination of pornographic magazines at the corner drug store. Sporadic obscenity prosecutions may occur in jurisdictions where the "contemporary community standard" of offensiveness allows convictions under *Miller* v. *California* (1973). But the constitutional validity of a legal taboo on "hard-core" pornography became largely irrelevant to its suppliers and consumers, even as that material became sexually explicit and more violent in its imagery during the 1970s.

That same decade saw a legal revolution in equality between the sexes, embodied in judicial decisions based on the guarantees of equal protection and due process. Women won legal rights to control and define their own sexuality, through litigation establishing rights to contraception and abortion, and through legislative reforms easing restrictions on prosecutions for sexual assault. Pornography also became a women's issue, as feminists such as Catharine MacKinnon attacked it as "a form of forced sex, a practice of sexual politics, an institution of gender inequality." Women marched and demonstrated against films and magazines portraying them as beaten, chained, or mutilated objects of sexual pleasure for men. In 1984 their protests took a legal form when MacKinnon and Andrea Dworkin drafted an ordinance adopted by the Indianapolis City Council, outlawing some types of pornography as acts of sex discrimination.

By using the concept of equal protection as a basis to attack pornographic speech, the council set up a dramatic assault upon First Amendment doctrine, making embarrassed enemies out of old constitutional friends. As a strategic matter, however, the council needed a compelling state interest to justify

censorship of speech that did not fall into the obscenity category. The ordinance defined offensive pornography more broadly than *Miller*'s standards allow, because it went beyond a ban on displays of specific human body parts or sexual acts. Instead, it prohibited the "graphic sexually explicit subordination of women" through their portrayals as, for example, "sexual objects who enjoy pain or humiliation," or "sexual objects for domination, conquest, violation, exploitation, possession or use."

As a philosophical matter, sex discrimination is a good constitutional metaphor for the harms attributed to pornography, namely, the loss of equal citizenship status for women through the "bigotry and contempt" promoted by the imagery of subordination. But as a matter of doctrine, the causal link between the social presence of pornography and the harms of discrimination is fatally remote. Free speech gospel dictates that "offensive speech" may be censored only upon proof of imminent, tangible harm to individuals, such as violent insurrection (*Brandenburg* v. *Ohio*, 1969), a physical assault (*Cohen* v. *California*, 1971), or reckless tortious injury to reputation (*New York Times* v. *Sullivan*, 1964). The closest historical analogue to the creation of a cause of action for classwide harm from speech is the criminal group libel statute upheld by a 5–4 Supreme Court in *Beauharnais* v. *Illinois* (1952). But this remedy has been implicitly discredited by *New York Times* and *Brandenburg*, given its chilling effect upon uninhibited criticism of political policies and officials.

It came as no surprise when early court decisions struck down Indianapolis-type ordinances as void for vagueness, as an unlawful prior restraint on speech, and as an unjustified restriction of protected speech as defined by the earlier obscenity decisions. The courts could accept neither the equal protection rationale nor the breadth of the ordinances' scope, as both would permit too great an encroachment upon the freedoms of expression and consumption of art, literature, and political messages. Ironically, it is the potentially endemic quality of the imagery of women's subordination that defeats any attempt to place a broad taboo upon it.

Eva Feder Kittay has posed the question, "How is it that within our society, men can derive a sexual charge out of seeing a woman brutalized?" Her answer to that loaded question is that our conceptions of sexuality are permeated with conceptions of domination, because we have eroticized the relations of power: men eroticize sexual conquering, and women eroticize being possessed. Pornography becomes more than a harmless outlet for erotic fantasies when it makes violence appear to be intrinsically erotic, rather than something that is eroticized. The social harm of such pornography is that it brutalizes our moral imagination, "the source of that imaginative possibility by which we can identify with others and hence form maxims having a universal validity."

The constitutional source for an analysis of brutalizing pornography lies in the richly generative symbols of First Amendment law itself. That law already contains the tolerance for insistence "on observance of the civic culture's norms of social equality," in the words of Kenneth L. Karst. Any acceptable future taboo would be likely to take the form of a ban on public display of a narrowly defined class of pictorial imagery, simply because that would be a traditional, readily enforceable compromise between free speech and equality. Any taboo would be mostly symbolic, but it would matter. Only by limiting the taboo can we avoid descending into the Orwellian hell where censorship is billed as freedom.

—CATHERINE HANCOCK

Bibliography

Bryden, David (1985). Between Two Constitutions: Feminism and Pornography. *Constitutional Commentary* 2:147–189.

Kalven, Harry, Jr. (1960). The Metaphysics of Obscenity. *Supreme Court Review* 1960:1–45.

Kittay, Eva Feder (1983). Pornography and the Erotics of Domination. Pages 145–174 in Carol C. Gould, ed., *Beyond Domination: New Perspectives on Women and Philosophy*. Totowa, N.J.: Rowman & Allanheld.

MacKinnon, Catharine A. (1984). Not a Moral Issue. *Yale Law & Policy Review* 2:321–345.

Note (1984). Anti-Pornography Laws and First Amendment Values. *Harvard Law Review* 98:460–481.

POSADAS DE PUERTO RICO ASSOCIATES v. TOURISM COMPANY OF PUERTO RICO

478 U.S. 328 (1986)

In *Posadas* the Supreme Court upheld, 5–4, a Puerto Rico statute that authorized casino gambling but forbade advertising of casino gambling when the advertising was aimed at Puerto Rican residents. The majority, in an opinion by Justice William H. Rehnquist, followed the doctrinal formula in *Central Hudson Gas and Electric Corp. v. Public Service Commission* (1980) for testing the constitutionality of regulations of commercial speech. The advertising concerned a lawful activity and was not misleading or fraudulent. Thus, the Court proceeded to the interest-balancing part of the formula. The governmental interest was the reduction of demand for casino gambling; Puerto Rico's concerns for its residents' health, safety, and welfare was obvious, considering that a majority of the states prohibit such gambling altogether. The restrictions on advertising, said the Court, directly advanced that interest. Furthermore, the Commonwealth of Puerto Rico was not required to resort to advertising of its own as a least restrictive means for discouraging casino gambling. In support of the latter point Justice Rehnquist cited lower court decisions ap-

*There is little doubt
that Congress or a
state legislature
could constutionally
ban the sale or use
of cigarettes.*

See also

Central Hudson Gas and
   Electric Corp. v. Public
   Service Commission

P

proving restrictions on advertising of cigarettes and alcohol. Puerto Rico could have banned casino gambling altogether; this greater power included the lesser power to regulate advertising.

Justice William J. Brennan, writing for three Justices, dissented, arguing the the Commonwealth had not met its burden of substantial justification for regulating commercial speech. In particular, the Commonwealth had not shown that less restrictive means would suffice. Justice John Paul Stevens focused his dissent on the law's discrimination based on the advertising's intended audience.

There is little doubt that Congress or a state legislature could constitutionally ban the sale or use of cigarettes. Although some commentators suggested that *Posadas* implies that even if such a prohibition law were not adopted, a ban on cigarette advertising would be constitutional, the court's decision a few years later in *44 Liquormart* v. *Rhode Island* (1996) enormously deflated *Posadas*. The court there invalidated a law that banned the display or advertising of liquor prices, rejecting the theme of *Posadas* that because the government may ban a product or activity it may therefore curb commercial speech advertising it. Four of the justices were ready to overrule *Posadas* outright. The others, annulling the Rhode Island law, scarcely defended the *Posadas* ruling. It now has little precedential value.

—KENNETH L. KARST

POWELL, LEWIS F.

(1907–   )

Lewis Franklin Powell Jr. has always eluded conventional portraiture. In broad brush, Powell appears the archetypal conservative: a successful corporate lawyer, a director of eleven major companies, a pillar of Richmond, Virginia's civic and social life. The roll call of legal honors—president of the American Bar Association, the American College of Trial Lawyers, and the American Bar Foundation—does little to dispel the impression.

The portrait, however, needs serious refinement. During Virginia's "massive resistance," when the Byrd organization chose to close public schools rather than accept racial integration, Powell, as chairman of the Richmond Public School Board, fought successfully to keep Richmond's open. As vice-president of the National Legal Aid and Defender Society, he helped persuade the organized bar to support publicly financed legal services for the poor. Jean Camper Cahn, a black leader with whom he worked in that endeavor, found Powell "so curiously shy, so deeply sensitive to the hurt or embarrassment of another, so self-effacing that it is difficult to reconcile the public and private man—the honors and the acclaim with the gentle, courteous, sensitive spirit that one senses in every conversation, no matter how casual. . . ."

The portrait of the private practitioner parallels that of the Supreme Court Justice. The broad picture is again one of orthodox adherence to the canons of restraint. Powell labored diligently to limit the powers of the federal courts. He sought to narrow the standing of litigants invoking federal jurisdiction to instances of actual injury in *Warth* v. *Seldin* (1975). He dissented when the Court in *Cannon* v. *University of Chicago* (1979) inferred from federal statutes a private cause of action. He greatly restricted the power of federal judges to review claims of unlawful search and seizure raised by state defendants in *Stone* v. *Powell* (1976). And he urged the sharp curtailment of federal equitable remedies such as student busing for racial balance, in cases like *Keyes* v. *Denver School District #1* (1973).

While working to limit federal judicial power, Powell championed the power of others to operate free of constitutional strictures. Thus prosecutors should enjoy discretion in initiating prosecution, police and grand juries in pursuing evidence, trial judges in questioning jurors, welfare workers in terminating assistance, and military officers in conducting training. The "hands-off" view applied especially to public education. Powell, a former member of the Virginia Board of Education, wrote the Court opinion preserving the rights of states to devise their own systems of public school finance in *San Antonio School District* v. *Rodriguez* (1973). And the former chairman of the Richmond School Board spoke for the broad discretion of school authorities to administer student suspensions and corporal punishment, dissenting in *Goss* v. *Lopez* (1975) and writing for the Court in *Ingraham* v. *Wright* (1977).

Even so, a corner of the jurist's nature has been reserved for personal circumstances of particular poignancy. An early opinion afforded a black construction worker in Mississippi, father of nine, the opportunity to confront his accusers and establish his innocence in *Chambers* v. *Mississippi* (1973). Another Powell opinion, in *Moore* v. *East Cleveland* (1977), voided a municipal housing ordinance that prevented an elderly woman from living with her adult sons and grandchildren. Another, *Solem* v. *Helm* (1983), held unconstitutional a life sentence without parole imposed by state courts on the perpetrator of seven nonviolent felonies. Even in the sacrosanct area of education, the Justice concurred in *Plyler* v. *Doe* (1982) rather than leave children of illegal aliens "on the streets uneducated."

The cases of compassion are remarkable in one respect. Vindication of the individual claims meant overriding the most cherished of Powell's conservative tenets: the protection of state criminal judgments from meddlesome review on petition for federal writs of habeas corpus, and the recognition of only those rights tied closely to the constitutional text. Powell, plainly nervous about damaging these principles, narrowed the rulings almost to their actual facts. The cases thus testify

both to a strength and a weakness in the jurist, the strength being that of an open mind and heart, the weakness being that of cautious case-by-case adjudication that leaves law bereft of general guidance and sure content.

The dichotomy between the cases of compassion and the towering doctrinal efforts of the school finance case (*Rodriguez*) and the search and seizure case (*Stone*) illustrates the different dimensions of the man himself. Powell, for example, privately deplored the arrogance of the national communications media and the maleficence of the criminal element. But he was, by nature, reserved, considerate, as eager to listen as to talk. Thus, even on subjects of strong feeling, the tempered judgment often triumphed. This quality marked his opinions dealing with the press. In a concurrence more libertarian than the Court opinion he joined in *Branzburg* v. *Hayes* (1972), Powell urged that "a proper

THE ARCHETYPAL CONSERVATIVE?

Known for his compassion, Powell's vindication of the individual sometimes meant overriding the most cherished of his conservative tenets. (Corbis)

While working to limit federal judicial power, Powell championed the power of others to operate free of constitutional strictures.

balance" be struck on a "case-by-case basis" between the claims of newsmen to protect the confidentiality of sources and the need of grand juries for information relevant to criminal conduct. In *Gertz* v. *Robert Welsh Inc.* (1974), perhaps his most important opinion on the First Amendment, Powell balanced a plaintiff's interest in his good reputation against press freedoms, permitting private citizens to recover in libel on a standard less than "knowing or reckless falsehood" but greater than liability without fault. Balancing of individual and societal claims characterized Powell's opinions involving the rights of radical campus organizations, the unconventional use of national symbols, and even many criminal cases, where fact-specific rulings on the admissibility of suspect lineups, for example, began to replace the per se exclusionary rules of the Warren Court.

Balancing does not permit confident forecasting of appellate outcomes. Case-by-case weighing of facts and circumstances can constitute a dangerous delegation of the Supreme Court's own authority on constitutional matters to trial judges, police and prosecutors, and potential litigants, all of whom capitalize on the uncertainty of law to work their own wills. But balancing suited Powell's preference for a devolution of authority and, in cases like *Gertz*, achieved a thoughtful accommodation of competing interests.

In his most famous opinion, *Regents of University of California* v. *Bakke* (1978), Powell, the balancer, struck a middle course on the flammable question of benign preferences based on race. The immediate question in *Bakke* was whether the medical school of the University of California at Davis could set aside sixteen of one hundred places in its entering class for preferred minorities. Eight Justices took polar positions. Four argued that Title VI of the Civil Rights Act of 1964 prohibited any preference based on race. Four others contended that both the act and the constitution permitted the Davis program. Powell, the ninth and deciding Justice, alone sought to accommodate both the American

belief in the primacy of the individual and the need to heal a history of oppression based on race.

It has become common to note that the Supreme Court under Warren E. Burger did not, as some feared, dismantle the activist legacy of the Warren Court. Many of the influential Justices, Powell, Potter Stewart, and Byron R. White among them, were more pragmatic than ideological. Thus the Court trimmed here, expanded there, and approached complex questions cautiously. Powell's opinions exhibit, as much as those of any Justice, this Court's composite frame of mind. Like him, the Court he served has eluded conventional description.

—J. HARVIE WILKINSON III

Bibliography

Gunther, Gerald (1972). In Search of Judicial Quality in a Changing Court: The Case of Justice Powell. *Stanford Law Review* 24:1001–1035.

Howard, A. E. Dick (1972). Mr. Justice Powell and the Emerging Nixon Majority. *Michigan Law Review* 70:445–468.

Symposium (1977). [Justice Lewis F. Powell] *University of Richmond Law Review* 11:259–445.

Symposium (1982). [Justice Lewis F. Powell] *Virginia Law Review* 68:161–458.

POWELL v. ALABAMA

287 U.S. 45 (1932)

Powell was the famous "Scottsboro boys" case in which "young, ignorant, illiterate blacks were convicted and sentenced to death without the effective appointment of counsel to aid them. The trials were in a hostile community, far from the defendants' homes; the accusation was rape of two white women, a crime "regarded with especial horror in the community."

In an early major use of the due process clause to regulate the administration of criminal justice by the states, the Supreme Court held that the trials were fundamentally unfair. The facts of the case made this portentous holding an easy one: the defendants were tried in one day, the defense was entirely pro forma, and the death sentence was immediately imposed on all seven defendants without regard to individual culpability or circumstance. *Powell* was not a Sixth Amendment right to counsel case; three decades would pass before that guarantee was imported into due process in *Gideon* v. *Wainwright* (1963). But the language of the Court in expounding the importance of counsel to a fair trial was repeatedly quoted as the Sixth Amendment right developed: "[The layman] lacks both the skill and knowledge adequately to prepare his defense, even though he has a perfect one. He requires the guiding hand of counsel at every step in the proceedings against him. Without it, though he be not guilty, he faces the danger of conviction because he does not know how to establish his innocence."

Although *Powell* is usually cited as a case in which defendants had no counsel at all, there was actually a lawyer at their side, but he came late into the case and was unfamiliar with Alabama law. In discussing the failure of due process, the Court referred to the lack of investigation and consultation by this last-minute volunteer. Thus, *Powell* has implications for the developing doctrine of ineffective assistance of counsel.

—BARBARA ALLEN BABCOCK

PRECEDENT

In *Marbury* v. *Madison* (1803) Chief Justice John Marshall rested the legitimacy of judicial review of the constitutionality of legislation on the necessity for courts to "state what the law is" in particular cases. The implicit assumption is that the Constitution is law, and that the content of constitutional law is determinate—that it can be known and applied by judges. From the time of the nation's founding, lawyers and judges trained in the processes of the common law have assumed that the law of the Constitution is to be found not only in the text of the document and the expectations of the Framers but also in judicial precedent: the opinions of judges on "what the law is," written in the course of deciding earlier cases.

Inevitably, issues that burned brightly for the Framers of the Constitution and of its various amendments have receded from politics into history. The broad language of much of the Constitution's text leaves open a wide range of choices concerning interpretation. As the body of judicial precedent has grown, it has taken on a life of its own; the very term "constitutional law," for most lawyers today, primarily calls to mind the interpretations of the Constitution contained in the Supreme Court's opinions. For a lawyer writing a brief, or a judge writing an opinion, the natural style of argumentation is the common law style, with appeals to one or another "authority" among the competing analogies offered by a large and still growing body of precedent.

The same considerations that support reliance on precedent in common law decisions apply in constitutional adjudications: the need for stability in the law and for even-handed treatment of litigants. Yet adherence to precedent has also been called the control of the living by the dead. Earlier interpretations of the Constitution, when they seem to have little relevance to the conditions of society and government here and now, do give way. As Chief Justice Earl Warren wrote in *Brown* v. *Board of Education* (1954), "In approaching [the problem of school segregation, we cannot turn the clock back to 1868 when the [Fourteenth] Amendment was adopted, or even to 1896 when *Plessy* [v. *Ferguson*] was written. We must consider public education in the light of its full development and its present place in American life. . . ." Justice Oliver Wendell Holmes put the matter more pungently: "It is revolting to have no better reason for a rule of law than that so it was laid down in the time of Henry IV."

Although Powell *is usually cited as a case in which defendants had no counsel at all, there was actually a lawyer at their side, but he came late into the case and was unfamiliar with Alabama law.*

See also

Gideon v. *Wainwright*

Right to Counsel

Although the Supreme Court decides only those issues that come to it in the ordinary course of litigation, the Court has a large measure of control over its own doctrinal agenda. The selection of about 150 cases for review each year (out of more than 4,000 cases brought to the Court) is influenced most of all by the Justices' views of the importance of the issues presented. And when the Court does break new doctrinal ground, it invites further litigation to explore the area thus opened. For example, scores of lawsuits were filed all over the country once the Court had established the precedent, in *Baker* v. *Carr* (1962), that the problem of legislative reapportionment was one that the courts could properly address. The Justices see themselves, and are seen by the Court's commentators, as being in the business of developing constitutional doctrine through the system of precedent. The decision of particular litigants' cases today appears to be important mainly as an instrument to those lawmaking ends. The theory of *Marbury* v. *Madison*, in other words, has been turned upside down.

Lower court judges pay meticulous attention to Supreme Court opinions as their main source of guidance for decisions in constitutional cases. Supreme Court Justices themselves, however, give precedent a force that is weaker in constitutional cases than in other areas of the law. In a famous expression of this view, Justice Louis D. Brandeis, dissenting in *Burnet* v. *Coronado Oil & Gas Co.* (1932), said, "In cases involving the Federal Constitution, where correction through legislative action is practically impossible, this court has often overruled its earlier decisions. The court bows to the lessons of experience and the force of better reasoning, recognizing that the process of trial and error, so fruitful in the physical sciences, is appropriate also in the judicial function."

Although this sentiment is widely shared, Justices often are prepared to defer to their reading of precedent even when they disagree with the conclusions that produced the earlier decisions. Justice John Marshall Harlan, for example, regularly accepted the authoritative force of Warren Court opinions from which he had dissented vigorously. The Court as an institution occasionally takes the same course, making clear that it is following the specific dictates of an earlier decision because of the interest in stability of the law, even though that decision may be out of line with more recent doctrinal developments.

The Supreme Court is regularly criticized, both from within the Court and from the outside, for failing to follow precedent. But a thoroughgoing consistency of decision cannot be expected, given the combination of three characteristics of the Court's decisional process. First, the Court is a collegiate body, with the nine Justices exercising individual judgment on each case. Second, the body of precedent is now enormous, with the result that in most cases decided by the Court there are arguable precedents for several alternative doctrinal approaches, and even for reaching opposing results. Indeed, the system for selecting cases for review guarantees that the court will regularly face hard cases—cases that are difficult because they can plausibly be decided in more than one way. Finally, deference to precedent itself may mean that issues will be decided differently, depending on the order in which they come before the Court. The Court's decision in *In re Griffiths* (1973), that a state cannot constitutionally limit the practice of law to United States citizens, is still a good precedent; yet, if the case had come up in 1983, almost certainly it would have been decided differently.

On the other hand, though the Court is certainly prepared to overrule earlier decisions it finds to have utterly lost their precedential value, as with *Plessy* v. *Ferguson*, in *Planned Parenthood of Southeastern Pennsylvania* v. *Casey* (1992) it stated that "principles of institutional integrity," along with *stare decisis*, supported adhering to precedent unless its "claimed justifications" had disappeared. The Court noted that its "legitimacy . . . would fade with the frequency of its vacillation."

The result of this process is an increasingly fragmented Supreme Court, with more plurality opinions and more statements by individual Justices of their own separate views in concurring opinions and dissents—thus presenting an even greater range of materials on which Justices can draw in deciding the next case. In these circumstances, it is not surprising that some plurality opinions, such as that in *Moore* v. *City of East Cleveland* (1977), are regularly cited as if they had a precedent value equal to that of opinions of the Court.

The range of decisional choice offered to a Supreme Court Justice by this process is so wide as to call into the question the idea of principled decision on which the legitimacy of judicial review is commonly assumed to rest. Yet the hard cases that fill the Supreme Court's docket—the very cases that make constitutional law and thus fill the casebooks that law students study—do not typify the functioning of constitutional law. A great many controversies of constitutional dimension never get to court, because the law seems clear, on the basis of precedent; similarly, many cases that do get to court are easily decided in the lower courts. Although we celebrate the memory of our creative Justices—Justices who are remembered for setting precedent, not following it—the body of constitutional law remains remarkably stable. In a stable society it could not be otherwise. As Holmes himself said in another context, "historic continuity with the past is not a duty, it is only a necessity."

—KENNETH L. KARST

Bibliography

Easterbrook, Frank H. (1982). Ways of Criticizing the Court. *Harvard Law Review* 95:802–832.

Levi, Edward H. (1949). *An Introduction to Legal Reasoning.* Chicago: University of Chicago Press.

Llewellyn, Karl N. (1960). *The Common Law Tradition.* Boston: Little, Brown.

Monaghan, Henry P. (1979). Taking Supreme Court Opinions Seriously. *Maryland Law Review* 39:1–26.

PRICE, UNITED STATES v.

383 U.S. 787 (1966)

Eighteen defendants implicated in the murder of three civil rights workers in Mississippi challenged the indictments against them under the federal Civil Rights Act of 1866 and that of 1870. One act applied only to persons conspiring to violate any federally protected right, the other only to persons acting "under color of law" who willfully violated such rights. Previous decisions of the Supreme Court had limited the two statutes. "Under color of law" covered only officers and in effect meant state action, thus excluding private persons from prosecution. The language of the conspiracy statute notwithstanding, the Court had previously applied it to protect only the narrow class of rights that Congress could, apart from the Fourteenth Amendment, protect against private individuals' interference, thus excluding the bulk of civil rights. Justice Abe Fortas for a unanimous Court ruled that when private persons act in concert with state officials they all act under color of law, because they willfully participate in the prohibited activity (deprivation of life without due process of law) with the state or its agents. Fortas also ruled that the 1870 act meant what it said: it safeguarded *all* federally protected rights secured by the supreme law of the land. By remanding the cases for trial, the Court made possible the first conviction in a federal prosecution for a civil rights murder in the South since Reconstruction.

—LEONARD W. LEVY

PRINCE v. MASSACHUSETTS

321 U.S. 158 (1944)

Massachusetts law provided that no boy under twelve or girl under eighteen could engage in street sale of any merchandise. Prince was

By remanding the cases for trial, the Court made possible the first conviction in a federal prosecution for a civil rights murder in the South since Reconstruction.

♦ **remand**
The action of a higher court in returning a case to a lower court for decision or for further proceedings.

See also
Civil Rights

the guardian of a nine-year-old girl. Both were Jehovah's Witnesses and sold Witness literature. The question was whether the statute impermissibly infringed on the free exercise of religion.

Writing for the Court, Justice Wiley B. Rutledge balanced the broad powers of the state to protect the health and welfare of minors against the First Amendment claims and held that the state's power prevailed. Justices Frank Murphy and Robert H. Jackson dissented.

Prince follows the "secular regulation" approach to religious liberty introduced by *United States* v. *Reynolds* (1879).

—RICHARD E. MARGAN

PRIOR RESTRAINT AND CENSORSHIP

History has rooted in our constitutional tradition of freedom of expression the strongest aversion to official censorship. We have learned from the English rejection of press licensing and from our own experiences that the psychology of censors tends to drive them to excess, that censors have a stake in finding things to suppress, and that—in systems of wholesale review before publication—doubt tends to produce suppression. American law tolerated motion picture censorship for a time, but only because movies were not thought to be "the press" in First Amendment terms. Censorship of the movies is now virtually dead, smothered by stringent procedural requirements imposed by unsympathetic courts, by the voluntary rating system, and, most of all, by public distaste for the absurdities of censorship in operation.

American law has tolerated requirements of prior official approval of expression in several important areas, however. No one may broadcast without a license, and the government issues licenses without charge to those it believes will serve the "public interest." Li-

censing is also grudgingly tolerated—because of the desirability of giving notice and of avoiding conflicts or other disruptions of the normal functions of public places—in the regulation of parades, demonstrations, leafleting, and other expressive activities in public places. But the courts have taken pains to eliminate administrative discretion that would allow officials to censor public forum expression because they do not approve its message.

Notwithstanding these areas where censorship has been permitted, the clearest principle of First Amendment law is that the least tolerable form of official regulation of expression is a requirement of prior official approval for publication. It is easy to see the suffocating tendency of prior restraints where all expression—whether or not ultimately deemed protected by the First Amendment for publication—must be submitted for clearance before it may be disseminated. The harder question of First Amendment theory has been whether advance prohibitions on expression in specific cases should be discredited by our historical aversion to censorship. The question has arisen most frequently in the context of judicial injunctions against publication. Even though injunctions do not involve many of the worst vices of wholesale licensing and censorship, the Supreme Court has tarred them with the brush of "prior restraint."

The seminal case was *Near* v. *Minnesota* (1931), handed down by a closely divided Court but never questioned since. A state statute provided for injunctions against any "malicious, scandalous, and defamatory newspaper," and a state judge had enjoined a scandal sheet from publishing anything scandalous in the future. The Minnesota scheme did not require advance approval of all publications, but came into play only after a publication had been found scandalous, and then only to prevent further similar publications. Nevertheless, the majority of the Justices concluded that to enjoin future editions under such vague standards in effect put the newspaper under judicial censorship. Chief Justice Charles Evans Hughes's historic opinion made clear, however, that the First Amendment's bar against prior restraint was not absolute. Various exceptional instances would justify prior restraints, including this pregnant one: "No one would question but that a government might prevent actual obstruction to its recruiting service or the publication of the sailing dates of transports or the number and location of troops."

It was forty years before the scope of the troop ship exception was tested. The Pentagon Papers decision of 1971, *New York Times Co.* v. *United States*, reaffirmed that judicial injunctions are considered prior restraints and are tolerated only in the most compelling circumstances. This principle barred an injunction against publication of a classified history of the government's decisions in the Vietnam war, although—unlike *Near*—the government had sought to enjoin only readily identifiable material, not unidentified similar publications in the future. Ten different opinions discussed the problem of injunctions in national security cases, and the only proposition commanding a majority was the unexplained conclusion that the government had not justified injunctive relief.

The central theme sounded in the opinions of the six majority Justices was reluctance to act in such difficult circumstances without guidance from Congress. Accepting the premise that there was no statutory authority for an injunction, several considerations support the Court's refusal to forge new rules concerning the disclosure of national secrets. First, the Court's tools are inadequate for the task; ad hoc evaluations of executive claims of risk are not easily balanced against the First Amendment's language and judicial interpretation. Second, dissemination of secret information often arises in the context of heated disagreements about the proper direction of national policy. One's assessment of the disclosure's impact on security will depend on one's reaction to the policy. Third, it would be particularly unsatisfactory to build a judge-made system of rules in an area where much litigation must be done *in camera*. Thus, general rules about specific categories of defense-related information cannot be fashioned by courts. The best hope in a nuclear age for accommodating the needs of secrecy and the public's right to know lies in the legislative process where, removed from pressures of adjudicting particular cases, general rules can be fashioned. The courts' proper role in this area is to review legislation, not try to devise rules of secrecy case by case.

Chilling this victory for freedom of the press were admonitions, loosely endorsed by four Justices, that the espionage statutes might support criminal sanctions against the *New York Times* and its reporters. No journalists were indicted, but the prosecutions of Daniel Ellsberg and Anthony Russo rested on a view of several statutes that would reach the press by punishing news-gathering activities necessarily incident to publication. Since the dismissal of these cases for reasons irrelevant to these issues, the extent of possible criminal liability for publishing national security secrets remains unclear.

The Pentagon Papers case underlines how little the United States has relied on law to control press coverage of national defense and foreign policy matters. For most of our history the press has rarely tested the limits of its rights to publish. Secrets were kept because people in and out of government with access to military and diplomatic secrets shared basic assumptions about national aims. The Vietnam War changed all that. The Pentagon Papers dispute marked the passing of an era in which journalists could be counted on to work within understood limits of discretion in handling secret information.

The third major decision striking down a judicial order not to publish involved neither national security nor scandal but the right of a criminal defendant to a fair trial. A state

P

PRIOR RESTRAINT AND CENSORSHIP

Some decisions have firmly established that the First Amendment tolerates virtually no prior restraints.

court enjoined publication of an accused's confession and some other incriminating material on the ground that if prospective jurors learned about it they might be incapable of impartiality. In *Nebraska Press Association* v. *Stuart* (1976) the Supreme Court decided that the potential prejudice was speculative, and it rejected enjoining publication on speculation. The majority opinion examined the evidence to determine the nature and extent of pretrial publicity, the effectiveness of other measures in mitigating prejudice, and the effectiveness of a prior restraint in reducing the dangers. This opinion determined that the impact of pretrial publicity was necessarily speculative, that alternative measures short of prior restraint had not been considered by the lower courts, and that prior restraint would not significantly reduce the dangers presented.

On one issue of considerable importance, the Court seemed to be in full agreement. The opinions endorsed controls on parties, lawyers, witnesses, and law enforcement personnel as sources of information for journalists. These gag orders have been controversial among many journalists and publishers who think the First Amendment should guarantee the right to gather news. Although freeing the press from direct control by limiting prior restraint, the Court approved an indirect method of reaching the same result, guaranteeing that the press print no prejudicial publicity, by approving direct controls on sources of prejudicial information. The Court has subsequently held that pretrial motions may be closed to the public and the press with the consent of the prosecutor and the accused but over the objection of the press, in *Gannett Co. v. DePasquale* (1979). This case involved access to judicial proceedings, not prior restraints on the press, and was decided largely on Sixth Amendment grounds. The Court reached the opposite result with respect to trials in *Richmond Newspapers* v. *Virginia* (1980), but acknowl-

edged that the right of access to trials is not absolute.

These decisions and others have firmly established that the First Amendment tolerates virtually no prior restraints. This doctrine is one of the central principles of our law of freedom of the press. On the surface, the doctrine concerns only the form of controls on expression. It bars controls prior to publication, even if imposition of criminal or civil liability following publication would be constitutional. But, as with most limitations of form, the prior restraint doctrine has important substantive consequences. Perhaps the most important of these consequences is that the doctrine is presumably an absolute bar to any wholesale system of administrative licensing or censorship of the press, which is the most repellent form of government suppression of expression. Second, the prior restraint doctrine removes most of the opportunities for official control of those types of expression for which general rules of control are difficult to formulate. The message of the prior restraint doctrine is that if you cannot control expression pursuant to general legislative standards, you cannot control it at all—or nearly at all, as the Pentagon Papers decision suggests, by suggesting an exception allowing an injunction in a truly compelling case of national security. A third effect of the doctrine is that by transferring questions of control over expression from the judiciary to the legislatures, it provides an enormously beneficial protection for the politically powerful mass media, if not for other elements of society with strong First Amendment interests but weaker influence in the legislative process.

Although the Supreme Court has exceeded its historical warrant in subjecting judicial injunctions to the full burden of our law's traditional aversion to prior restraints, there are sound reasons for viewing all prior controls—not only wholesale licensing and censorship—as dangerous to free expression.

Generally it is administratively easier to prevent expression in advance than to punish it after the fact. The inertia of public officials in responding to a *fait accompli,* the chance to look at whether expression has actually caused harm rather than speculate about the matter, public support for the speaker, and the interposition of juries and other procedural safeguards of the usual criminal or civil process all tend to reinforce tolerance when expression can only be dealt with by subsequent punishment. Moreover, all prior restraint systems, including injunctions, tend to divert attention from the central question of whether expression is protected to the subsidiary problem of promoting the effectiveness of the prior restraint system. Once a prior restraint is issued, the authority and prestige of the restraining agent are at stake. If it is disobeyed, the legality of the expression takes a back seat to the enforcement of obedience to the prior restraint process. Moreover, the time it takes a prior restraint process to decide produces a systematic delay of expression. On the other hand, where law must wait to move against expression after it has been published, time is on the side of freedom. All in all, even such prior restraints as judicial injunctions—which are more discriminating than wholesale censorship—tend toward irresponsible administration and an exaggerated assessment of the dangers of free expression.

—BENNO C. SCHMIDT, JR.

Bibliography

Blasi, Vincent (1981). Toward a Theory of Prior Restraint: The Central Linkage. *Minnesota Law Review* 66:11.

Emerson, Thomas (1955). The Doctrine of Prior Restraint. *Law and Contemporary Problems* 20:648.

Schmidt, Benno C., Jr. (1977). *Nebraska Press Association:* An Expansion of Freedom and Contraction of Theory. *Stanford Law Review* 29:431.

PRIZE CASES

2 Black (67 U.S.) 635 (1863)

In the *Prize Cases,* a 5–4 majority of the Supreme Court sustained the validity of President Abraham Lincoln's blockade proclamations of April 1861, refusing to declare unconstitutional his unilateral actions in meeting the Confederacy's military initiatives.

Lincoln proclaimed a blockade of southern ports on April 19 and 27, 1861. Congress authorized him to declare a state of insurrection by the Act of July 13, 1861, thereby, at least in the view of the dissenters, giving formal legislative recognition to the existence of civil war. By the Act of August 6, 1861, Congress retroactively ratified all Lincoln's military actions. The *Prize Cases* involved seizures of vessels bound for Confederate ports prior to July 13, 1861.

For the majority, Justice Robert C. Grier held that a state of civil war existed de facto after the firing on Fort Sumter (April 12, 1861) and that the Supreme Court would take judicial notice of its existence. Though neither Congress nor president can declare war against a state of the Union, Grier conceded, when states waged war against the United States government, the president was "bound to meet it in the shape it presented itself, without waiting for Congress to baptize it with a name." Whether the insurgents were to be accorded belligerent status, and hence be subject to blockade, was a political question to be decided by the president, whose decision was conclusive on the courts. Grier reproved the dissenters by reminding them that the court should not "cripple the arm of the government and paralyze its power by subtle definitions and ingenious sophisms."

Justice Samuel Nelson for the dissenters (Chief Justice Roger B. Taney, and Justices John Catron and Nathan Clifford) argued that only Congress can declare a war and that

*The Supreme Court
sustained the
validity of President
Abraham Lincoln's
blockade
proclamations of
April 1861.*

*The actual malice
rules apply to both
public officials and
public figures.*

consequently the president can neither declare nor recognize it. A civil war's "existence in a material sense . . . has no relevancy or weight when the question is what constitutes war in a legal sense." Lincoln's acts before July 13, 1861, constituted merely his "personal war against those in rebellion." Therefore seizures under the blockade proclamations were illegal.

The *Prize Cases* permitted the federal government the convenient ambiguity of treating the Confederacy as an organized insurgency and as a conventional belligerent. The opinions also had an implicit relevance to other disputed exercises of presidential authority. Defenders of a broad executive power could argue that the majority opinion's reasoning supported the constitutionality of Lincoln's call for volunteers, of his suspension of the writ of habeas corpus, and perhaps also of the Emancipation Proclamation.

—WILLIAM M. WIECEK

PRUNEYARD
SHOPPING CENTER
v. ROBINS

447 U.S. 74 (1980)

Hudgens v. *N.L.R.B.* (1976) had held that the First Amendment did not compel private owners of shopping centers to permit their property to be used for expressive activity. In *PruneYard,* California's supreme court held that the state constitution required a shopping center owner to permit the collection of signatures on a petition. The Supreme Court unanimously affirmed. Justice William H. Rehnquist, for the Court, concluded that the state law did not work an uncompensated taking of property. Nor did it violate the owner's First Amendment rights by compelling it to convey a message. Justice Lewis F. Powell, concurring, argued that under

PROCEDURAL DUE PROCESS OF LAW

The Fifth Amendment forbids the United States to "deprive" any person of "life, liberty, or property without due process of law." The Fourteenth Amendment imposes an identical prohibition on the states.

Due process is the ancient core of constitutionalism. It is a traditional legal expression of concern for the fate of persons in the presence of organized social power. The question of according due process arises when governments assert themselves adversely to the interests of individuals.

In modern usage "due process" connotes a certain normative ideal for decisions about the exercise of power. Very broadly, it has come to mean decisions that are not arbitrary, but are aligned with publicly accepted aims

and values; are not dictatorial, but allow affected persons a suitable part in their making; and are not oppressive, but treat those affected with the respect owed political associates and fellow human beings. It is from the liberal individualist tradition that these abstract due process standards—of reason, voice, and dignity—have drawn their more concrete content. That content includes the definition of proper aims for state activity, the canons of legitimating participation and consent, and the conceptions of human personality that set the threshold of respectful treatment.

The courts recognize two sorts of due process concerns: substantive and procedural. Substantive due process informs the idea that government lacks

power to deprive its citizens of life, liberty, or property with regard to a particular subject. Procedural due process focuses on whether government has furnished its citizens with an opportunity to contest a charge that one has violated a statute—in other words, a "day in court." This is the essence of due process for one accused of a crime. However, procedural due process also applies to civil cases, as well as decisions by executive or administrative agencies that deprive one of liberty or property. In those situation one is entitled to an opportunity to refute a claim that he or she has violated the law or is not entitled to a license, government employment, a government benefit (such as Social Security) or the like.

other circumstances an owner might have such a First Amendment right.

—KENNETH L. KARST

PUBLIC FIGURE

The concept of a public figure features prominently in modern First Amendment law involving libel suits. *New York Times* v. *Sullivan* (1964) prevented public officials (officeholders and candidates for office) from recovering damages for defamation without proof of actual malice, that is, proof that the statement was made with the knowledge that it was false or with reckless disregard whether it was or not. In *Curtis Publishing Company* v. *Butts* (1967) the Supreme Court extended the actual malice rule to public figures, described by the Court as private persons in positions of considerable influence or able to attract attention because they had thrust themselves into public controversies. A public figure commands public interest and therefore has sufficient access to the mass media to be able, like an officeholder, to publicize his response to falsehoods about him. He invites comment and his remarks make news. The Justices unanimously agreed that for the sake of a robust freedom of the press, the actual malice rule applies to public figures, but they disagreed in specific cases on the question whether a particular person, such as the former wife of the scion of a famous family, is a public figure, the question before the court in *Time Incorporated* v. *Firestone* (1976). The Court has tended to deny the press's claim that the party suing for damages is a public figure.

—LEONARD W. LEVY

See also

New York Times v. *Sullivan*

R

RACIAL BALANCE

The idea of racial balance is a product of the desegregation of public schools in the years since *Brown* v. *Board of Education* (1954–55). The term refers to the racial distribution of students in particular schools in relation to the racial distribution of school children in an entire district. If a district's children are 70 percent white and 30 percent black, then a hypothetically perfect balance would produce these same percentages in each school. By extension, the notion of racial balance may be used in discussing other institutions: a housing project, a factory's work force, a state university's medical school.

In the school cases, the Supreme Court has held that racial balance is an appropriate "starting point" for a lower court to use in fashioning a remedy for de jure segregation. However, even where segregation has been deliberately caused by school board actions, there is no constitutional requirement of racial balance throughout the district's schools. Although one-race schools are presumptively to be eliminated, the school board will be allowed to prove that the racial distribution in those schools results from something other than the board's deliberate policy. School busing over very long distances, for example, would not be required under this approach; distance alone would be a racially neutral explanation for the board's failure to remedy racial imbalance.

In the absence of previous legislation commanding or authorizing school segregation, or school board actions with segregative intent, the fact of racial imbalance in a district's schools, standing alone, does not amount to a constitutional violation. However, intentional acts of segregation by the board in the remote past, coupled with current racial imbalance, will place on the board an almost impossible burden of proving that it has dismantled its "dual" (segregated) system.

The term racial balance is sometimes used in a different sense. Some discussions of school segregation use the term to describe a school that includes a "critical mass" of students from each race. Social scientists disagree over the educational value to minority students of having a significant number of white students in the classroom. The suggestion that minority students learn better in the company of whites has roots in the Supreme Court's pre-*Brown* decisions on graduate education. And where segregation is imposed by official action, *Brown* itself takes the view that the resulting stigma impairs minority students' ability to learn. But the abstract proposition that minority students cannot learn effectively outside the presence of whites is more than a little patronizing. And the notion of racial balance in this sense is immensely complicated in a multiethnic community: is a school integrated if it contains significant numbers of both white and minority students, or should the category of minority students be broken down into its black, Hispanic, and other components? Merely to ask this question is to understand why the Supreme Court has avoided speaking of racial balance in this latter sense and has used the idea in its mechanical racial-percentages sense only as a "starting point."

—KENNETH L. KARST

Bibliography

Fiss, Owen M. (1975). The Jurisprudence of Busing. *Law and Contemporary Problems* 1975:194–216.

If a district's children are 70 percent white and 30 percent black, then a hypothetically perfect balance would produce these same percentages in each school.

See also
Brown v. *Board of Education*
Segregation

RACIAL DISCRIMINATION

In the 1980s and 1990s most observers would have said that the Supreme Court's view of racial discrimination was in equipoise. Some of the Justices seemed sympathetic to the aggressive purposeful use of racial criteria to end the legacy of racial subordination; others were skeptical of "benign discrimination" and looked instead to a constitutional principle of color-blindness as the cornerstone of a society free of discrimination. The last decade has made plain the ascendancy of the latter view. It is now evident that a majority of the Justices are prepared to view with suspicion and hold to the highest standard of constitutional scrutiny governmental efforts to use racial classifications even to assist members of racial minorities. At the same time, governmental actions that disadvantage racial minorities will be sustained absent clear and unambiguous evidence of impermissible racial animus.

Affirmative action advocates are particularly concerned about the Court's recent willingness to view benign racial classifications with the same suspicion with which it has traditionally treated classifications intended to oppress. Where this leaves racially conscious programs is unclear, except that as before the stronger the showing that a racial preference is related to a bona fide remedial goal, the greater the likelihood the Court will sustain it.

Thus in *Wygant* v. *Jackson Board of Education* (1986) the Justices overturned a plan under which a school board extended to minority teachers what a plurality of the Court called "preferential protection against layoffs." The plan was part of the collective-bargaining agreement between the board and the union representing school teachers and was defended before the Court as an effort to alleviate "social discrimination" by providing a diverse set of role models in public school-rooms. A three-Justice plurality declared that the proper test was strict scrutiny and held the plan invalid because more specific findings of prior discrimination were necessary before the layoff protection could be said to serve a compelling state interest.

In contrast, in *Paradise* v. *United States* (1987) the Justices voted 5–4 to sustain a federal district court's imposition of a "one-for-one" hiring plan, pursuant to which the Alabama Department of Public Safety was obliged to remedy its past failure to hire black troopers by hiring one black trooper for each white trooper hired. The solicitor general argued that even when a racially conscious remedial program was ordered by a court, strict scrutiny was the proper test, and the program could survive only on a showing of a compelling state interest. Four Justices, in an opinion by Justice William J. Brennan, refused to decide this question, ruling that the program could meet any level of scrutiny because it was "justified by a compelling interest in remedying the discrimination that permeated entry-level practices and the promotional process alike." The plurality further noted that the district court had imposed the one-for-one plan only after the department had repeatedly failed to comply with earlier decrees.

Probably the most controversial benign discrimination decision—and the one with the most far-reaching implications—was *Richmond (City of)* v. *J. A. Croson Co.* (1989), in which the Justices struck down a program under which the City of Richmond required its prime contractors to subcontract thirty percent of the dollar amount of each contract to minority-owned firms. In *Croson*, a majority of the Justices ruled explicitly that strict scrutiny was the proper level of review for benign discrimination cases. Although there was no majority opinion on the point, six Justices repudiated as insufficiently narrow the city council's defense that the program was needed to eliminate the effects of societal discrimination.

Although it is true that the Justices have always taken the position that even benign classifications are subject to the highest level of constitutional scrutiny, they had not previously applied the rule with quite the strictness used in *Croson*. Indeed, *Fullilove v. Klutznick* (1980), which sustained a federally mandated set-aside program for certain construction projects, is in one sense indistinguishable: in *Fullilove* and in *Croson*, the relevant body (in the first case the Congress, in the other the city council) had before it no record of past discrimination. However, in *Adarand Constructors v. Pena* (1995) the Court unequivocally held federal affirmative action programs are to be judged by the same strict scrutiny as state and local efforts. *Adarand* rejected the argument that Congress's authority under section 5 of the Fourteenth Amendment to enforce the equal protection clause warranted giving it greater deference than the states in devising affirmative action plans. However, the Court has stopped short of limiting affirmative action only to cases, like *Paradise*, that redress discrimination by the particular entity involved. It seems clear that affirmative action narrowly tailored to achieve diversity among a state university's students, as in *Bakke*, or in a city's police force, will be sustained.

The Court has also ruled that the drawing of voting districts primarily based on racial lines is subject to strict scrutiny, as in *Shaw v. Reno* (1993).

At the same time, the Court has arguably shown increasing sensitivity to certain claims of racial discrimination in the criminal justice system. Thus in *Hunter v. Underwood* (1985), a unanimous Court struck down a neutrally applied disenfranchisement of persons convicted of misdemeanors involving "moral turpitude" on the ground that it was originally enacted decades earlier for the purpose of discriminating against black citizens. The following term, in *Batson v. Kentucky* (1986), the Justices eased the burden of a defendant seeking to prove that the prosecution had used its peremptory challenges to exclude jurors on the basis of race. On the same day, the Justices decided in *Turner v. Murray* that a defendant in a capital case has the right to examine prospective jurors about racial bias.

But the trend has gone only so far. In the following term, the Justices made plain their resistance to inferring impermissible discriminatory motivation from circumstantial evidence, especially statistical evidence. In *McCleskey v. Kemp* (1987), a black convicted of murder argued that Georgia's decision to sentence him to death violated the Eighth and Fourteenth Amendments because statistics demonstrated that black defendants, especially black defendants whose victims were white, were far more likely than white defendants to receive capital punishment. The statistics (generally referred to as the Baldus study, after the principal author of the underlying work) were stark indeed; they indicated, among other disparities, that capital juries in Georgia handed down death sentences to black defendants whose victims were white twenty-two times more frequently than they did to black defendants whose victims were black.

The *McCleskey* majority, however, was unimpressed, responding tersely, "We refuse to assume that what is unexplained is invidious." This answer in a sense eluded McCleskey's point, which was that the disparity was great enough to place the burden of explanation on the state. The Court replied that other explanations were plausible, adding that juror discretion should not be condemned or disturbed simply because of an "inherent lack of predictability." As long as forbidden racial animus was not the only possible explanation, the Court would not assume that animus was at work.

As the dissenters pointed out, the result in *McCleskey* seemed to stand as a departure from the Burger Court decision in *Arlington Heights v. Metropolitan Housing Development Corp.* (1977). In *Arlington Heights* the Justices suggested that racial animus might be inferred from "a clear pattern" of official behav-

The Civil War brought slavery to an end and reversed the basic commitment of the Constitution toward blacks.

ior, "unexplainable on grounds other than race." The *McCleskey* majority was correct that other explanations for the Baldus data are conceivable, and some critics have offered them. But in *McCleskey* the Justices declined even to speculate.

Nevertheless, in important respects, *McCleskey* differed from other racial-discrimination cases. First, as several observers have noted, the Baldus study most strongly supports an argument that the murderers of black people are systematically treated with greater leniency than the murderers of white people. If one believes that the death penalty deters the crime of murder, then the implication is that the state is doing less to protect the lives of black people than to protect the lives of white people. Warren McCleskey, convicted of killing a police officer while committing another felony, was not a particularly attractive candidate to raise this issue. The better case (unfortunately for the Supreme Court's paradoxical ruling in *Linda R.S.* v. *Richard D.* [1973], which denied standing to raise a claim that the law is inadequately enforced) would be one brought by law-abiding black citizens seeking to protect their lives and property.

A second distinction between *McCleskey* and other cases is that, had it gone the other way, *McCleskey* might have opened up a Pandora's box of claims that blacks in the criminal process—from arrests to sentencing—are treated more harshly than whites, claims that are supported by considerable empirical literature. Even if the literature is accurate (again, there are critics), it is difficult to imagine what practical relief might be fashioned in such cases. For those who are convicted, mandatory resentencing is one possibility, although the continued judicial monitoring of sentencing disparities could produce a procedural nightmare. The fear that this slippery slope lay ahead might well have been a part of the majority's calculus.

The Justices have also worked important changes in the interpretation of one of the keystones of the "Second Reconstruction," Title VII of the Civil Rights Act of 1964. In *Ward's Cove* v. *Antonio* (1989) the Justices reexamined the burden of proof of a plaintiff relying on the Court's decision in *Griggs* v. *Duke Power Co.* (1971). *Griggs* had read Title VII to prohibit an employment practice with racially identifiable disparate impacts unless the employer was able to show a business necessity for the test. In *Ward's Cove* the Court ruled 5–4 that the plaintiff must carry the burden of demonstrating the causal link to the composition of the market of people qualified to do the job in question. Critics of *Ward's Cove* argued that the decision had shifted the burden from the employer to the employees and would make employment-discrimination cases more difficult to prove; defenders responded that Title VII plaintiffs should be required to prove all elements of their claims. Congress later amended Title VII to overrule *Ward's Cove* with regard to the burden of proof.

Depending on one's point of view, then, the recent work of the Supreme Court in the area of racial-discrimination law has represented either a tragic abandonment of the judiciary's traditional role as protector of the racially oppressed or a return to the shining principles of color-blindness as the fundamental rule for government action. But not all significant changes in the area of racial discrimination require judicial action. In fact, one of the most important developments of recent years involved an attempted legislative correction of a judicial wrong. The World War II decisions sustaining the internment of Japanese Americans are widely regarded as among the most horrific judicial decisions of the twentieth century (although it must be said that the programs could never have been approved had the president and Congress not imposed them in the first place). In the mid-1980s federal courts vacated the convictions of Gordon Hirabayashi, Minoru Yasui, and Fred Korematsu for evading registration for internment. A damages claim by former de-

tainees was rejected by the Federal Circuit in 1988 on statute of limitations grounds, but in August of that year, the Congress adopted legislation apologizing for the internment program and granting to each surviving internee compensation of roughly $20,000—not perhaps the same as justice, but at least an acknowledgment that justice was due.

In short, the Court continues to view with great skepticism any discrimination based on race, tending in recent decades to equate benign measures to remedy past discrimination with traditional, obnoxious discrimination against disfavored minorities.

—STEPHEN L. CARTER

Bibliography

Areen, Judith, et al. (1989). Constitutional Scholars' Statement on Affirmative Action After *City of Richmond* v. *J. A. Croson Co. Yale Law Journal* 98:1711–1716.

Fried, Charles (1989). Affirmative Action After *City of Richmond* v. *J. A. Croson Co.:* A Response to the Scholars' Statement. *Yale Law Journal* 99:155–161.

Kennedy, Randall L. (1988). *McCleskey* v. *Kemp:* Race, Capital Punishment, and the Supreme Court. *Harvard Law Review* 101:1388–1443.

RACIAL QUOTAS

Programs of affirmative action, aimed at increasing opportunities for women and members of racial and ethnic minorities in employment and higher education, have sometimes taken the form of numerical quotas. In *Regents of University of California* v. *Bakke* (1978) sixteen places in a state university medical school's entering class were reserved for minority applicants; in *Fullilove* v. *Klutznick* (1980) 10 percent of funds in a federal public works program were reserved for minority-owned businesses. Such quotas have been challenged as denials of the equal protection of the laws, with mixed doctrinal results.

Opponents of racial quotas maintain that it is offensive to penalize or reward people on the basis of race—in short, that the Constitution is, or ought to be, color blind. Opponents discern in quotas a subtle but pervasive racism, in the patronizing assumption that persons of particular colors or ethnic backgrounds cannot be expected to meet the standards that apply to others. This assumption, the opponents argue, is, in its own way, a badge of servitude, stigmatizing the quotas' supposed beneficiaries. Some opponents see quotas as part of a general trend toward dehumanization, robbing individuals of both personal identity and human dignity, lumping them together in a collectivity based on other people's assumptions about racially defined traits.

Unfortunately for today's America, race has never been a neutral fact in this country.

REVERSE DISCRIMINATION?

Allan Bakke challenged a University of California racial quota when he was denied admission despite test scores that were higher than those of minorities who had been accepted. (Corbis/Bettmann)

R

RACIAL QUOTAS

Those who defend affirmative action generally admit to some uneasiness about the potential abuse of racial distinctions. They argue, however, that there is no real neutrality in a system that first imposes on a racial group harsh disadvantages, readily transmitted through the generations, and then tells today's inheritors of disadvantages that from now on the rules prohibit playing favorites. If either compensation for past racial discrimination or the integration of American institutions is a legitimate social objective, the proponents argue, a government in pursuit of those objectives can hardly avoid taking race into account.

The recent attack on racial quotas draws fuel from an emotional reservoir filled two generations ago by universities that limited admission of racial and religious minorities—most notably Jews—to specified small quotas. This ugly form of discrimination was part of a systematic stigmatization and subordination of minority groups by the dominant majority. The recent quotas are designed to remedy the effects of past discrimination, and—when they serve the objective of compensation or integration—are not stigmatizing. They do, however, use race or ethnic status as a means of classifying persons, and thus come under fire for emphasizing group membership rather than "individual merit."

The right to equal protection is, indeed, an individual right. Yet the term "individual merit" misleads in two ways. The word "individual" misleads by obscuring the fact that every claim to equality is a claim made on behalf of the group of persons identified by some set of characteristics: race, for example, or high college grades and test scores. To argue against a racial preference is not to support individual merit as against a group claim, but to argue that some other group, defined by other attributes, is entitled to preference.

"Merit" misleads by conveying the idea of something wholly intrinsic to an individual, apart from some definition of community needs or purposes. When we reward achievement, we are not merely rewarding effort, but are also giving out prizes for native talents and environmental advantages. Mainly, we reward achievement because society wants the goods produced by the combination of talents, environment, and effort. But it is also reasonable to look to past harms and potential contributions to society in defining the characteristics that deserve reward. We admit college achievers to law schools not to reward winners but to serve society with good lawyers. If it be legitimate to seek to end a system of racial caste by integrating American society, nothing in the idea of individual merit stands in the way of treating race as one aspect of "merit."

Race-conscious remedies for past governmental discrimination were approved in decisions as early as *Swann* v. *Charlotte-Mecklenburg Board of Education* (1971). Affirmative action quotas pose another question: Can government itself employ race-conscious remedies for the effects of past societal discrimination? In *Fullilove*, six Justices agreed on an affirmative answer to that question, at least when Congress prescribes the remedy. *Bakke* was complicated by a statutory claim; its result—and its practical effect in professional school admissions—was a distinction between racial or ethnic quotas, which are unlawful, and the use of racial or ethnic status as "one factor" in admission, which is lawful.

The distinction was a political success; it drew the fangs from a controversy that had turned venomous. But the distinction between a quota and a racial factor is more symbol than substance. If race is a factor, it will decide some cases. How many cases? The weight assigned to race surely will be determined by reference to the approximate number of minority admittees necessary to achieve the admitting university's goals of educational "diversity." The difference between saying "sixteen out of a hundred" and "around sixteen percent" is an exercise in constitutional cosmetics—but it seems to have saved affirmative action during a critical season.

After *Bakke* and *Fullilove*, the Court swung to the view that racial quotas must be viewed with great skepticism. In *Richmond (City of)* v. *J. A. Croson Co.* (1989) it overturned a municipal quota requirement for minority businesses engaged in city contracting, holding the program was not narrowly tailored to meet a compelling government interest. A program that favored minority businesses without imposing a quota might well have passed muster. A few years later, in *Adarand Constructors* v. *Pena* (1995), the Court examined a federal program similarly benefiting minority highway subcontractors, though whether this was an actual quota was not as clear as in *Croson*. The Court nonetheless ruled the program to be subject to strict scrutiny. It rejected the view that Congress had more flexibility than states and localities in creating affirmative action programs.

—KENNETH L. KARST

Bibliography

Karst, Kenneth L., and Horowitz, Harold W. (1974). Affirmative Action and Equal Protection. *Virginia Law Review* 60: 955–974.

Van Alstyne, William W. (1979). Rites of Passage: Race, the Supreme Court, and the Constitution. *University of Chicago Law Review* 46:775–810.

RAILWAY EXPRESS AGENCY v. NEW YORK

336 U.S. 106 (1949)

Railway Express is a leading modern example of the Supreme Court's deference to legislative judgments in the field of economic regulation. The Court unanimously upheld a New York City "traffic safety" ordinance forbidding advertisements on vehicles but exempting delivery vehicles advertising their owners' businesses. No one mentioned the First Amendment. Justice William O. Douglas, for the Court, first waved away a due process attack on the ordinance. Turning to the companion equal protection attack, Douglas said that the city "may well have concluded" that advertising vehicles presented a greater traffic hazard than did trucks carrying their owners' messages. "We cannot say that that judgment is not an allowable one." The opinion typifies the Court's use of the most deferential rational basis review of economic regulation.

Justice Robert H. Jackson expressed some doubt as to the Court's reasoning but concurred, referring to the law's historic distinctions between "doing in self-interest and doing for hire." Along the way he uttered the decision's most memorable words: "there is no more effective practical guarantee against arbitrary and unreasonable government than to require that the principles of law which officials would impose on a minority must be imposed generally."

Since the Court's decisions, commencing with *Virginia State Board of Pharmacy* v. *Virginia Citizens Consumer Council* (1976), affording constitutional protection to commercial speech, a law such as the one upheld in *Railway Express* would be subjected to greater scrutiny. It would be sustained only if shown to be substantially related to an important governmental interest, and might well not meet that test.

—KENNETH L. KARST

RATIONAL BASIS

The "rational basis" standard of review emerged in the late 1930s, as the Supreme Court retreated from its earlier activism in the defense of economic liberties. We owe the phrase to Justice Harlan Fiske Stone, who used it in two 1938 opinions to signal a new judicial deference to legislative judgments. In *United States* v. *Carolene Products*

The opinion typifies the Court's use of the most deferential rational basis review of economic regulation.

R

RATIONAL BASIS

We owe the phrase "national basis" to Justice Harlan Fiske Stone, who used it in two 1938 opinions to signal a new judicial deference to legislative judgments.

Co. (1938), Stone said that an economic regulation, challenged as a violation of substantive due process or of equal protection, would be upheld unless demonstrated facts should "preclude the assumption that it rests upon some rational basis within the knowledge and experience of the legislators." In *South Carolina State Highway Department* v. *Barnwell Brothers, Inc.* (1938), Stone proposed "rational basis" as the standard for reviewing state regulations of commerce. (Later, Stone would accept the necessity for more exacting judicial scrutiny of such laws.) To complete the process, the Court adopted the same deferential posture toward congressional judgments that local activities substantially affected interstate commerce and thus might be regulated by Congress under the commerce power. In all its uses, "rational basis" represents a strong presumption of the constitutionality of legislation.

Yet even so minimal a standard of judicial review does, in theory, call for some judicial scrutiny of the rationality of the relationship between legislative means and ends. And that scrutiny of means makes sense only if we assume that the ends themselves are constitutionally required to serve general, public aims; otherwise, every law would be self-justifying, as precisely apt for achieving the advantages and disadvantages it achieves. Although the Court has sometimes suggested in economic regulation cases that even a search for legislative rationality lies beyond the scope of the judicial function, some such judicial scrutiny is required if our courts are to give effect to generalized constitutional guarantees of liberty and equality. Today's assumption, therefore, is that a law depriving a person of liberty or of equal treatment is invalid unless, at a minimum, it is a rational means for achieving a legitimate legislative purpose.

Even so relaxed a standard of review appears to call for a judicial inquiry always beset by uncertainties and often dominated by fictitious assumptions. Hans Linde has demonstrated the unreality attendant on judicial efforts to identify the "purposes" served by a law adopted by legislators with diverse objectives, or objectives only tenuously connected to the public good. Lacking sure guidance as to those "purposes"—which may have changed in the years since the law was adopted—a court must rely on counsel's assertions and its own assumptions. But in its inception the rational basis standard was not so much a mode of inquiry as a formula for validating legislation. Thus, in *McGowan* v. *Maryland* (1961) the Supreme Court said, "A statutory discrimination will not be set aside if any state of facts reasonably may be conceived to justify it." Part of the reason why the rational basis standard survives in federal constitutional law is that it is normally taken seriously only in its permissive feature (*United States Railroad Retirement Board* v. *Fritz,* 1980). A number of state courts, interpreting state constitutional law, do take the rational basis standard to require a serious judicial examination of the reasonableness of legislation. And the Supreme Court itself, in its late-1960s forays into the reaches of equal protection doctrine lying beyond racial equality, sometimes labeled legislative classifications as "irrational" even as it insisted that state-imposed inequalities be justified against more exacting standards of review. Since that time, the explicit recognition of different levels of judicial scrutiny of legislation has allowed the Court to reserve the rhetoric of rational basis for occasions thought appropriate for judicial modesty, in particular its review of "economic and social regulation." Some substantive interests call for heightened judicial scrutiny of legislative incursions into them; absent such considerations, the starting point for constitutional analysis remains the rational basis standard.

—KENNETH L. KARST

Bibliography

Linde, Hans A. (1976). Due Process of Lawmaking. *Nebraska Law Review* 55: 197–255.

See also

Carolene Products Co., United States v.

Standard of Review

REASONABLE DOUBT

Proof beyond a reasonable doubt is the highest level of proof demanded in American courts. It is the usual standard for criminal cases, and in criminal litigation it has constitutional grounding in decisions of the United States Supreme Court. Although the reasonable doubt standard is not often used in noncriminal settings, there are exceptional situations, usually where liberty is placed in jeopardy, when a jurisdiction will borrow the criminal standard of proof for a civil case.

Any standard of proof chosen by an American court recognizes that in all litigation there is the chance of a mistake. If opposing litigants agree on the various matters that constitute their case, usually the case is settled. There is little for a judge or a jury to do. Once a dispute arises, however, adversaries offer conflicting evidence and conflicting interpretations of evidence to decision makers. Rarely, if ever, is there a dispute in which every witness and every aspect of physical and scientific evidence presented by opposing parties point with perfect certainty to one specific conclusion. Witnesses may suffer from ordinary human frailties—they have memory problems; they sometimes confuse facts; they see events differently from each other; they have biases and prejudices that call into question their judgment; and they may be frightened and have trouble communicating on the witness stand. Physical evidence might be damaged or destroyed and thus of minimal or no use at trial. Or, it might be difficult to connect physical evidence with the parties before the court. Even scientific tests often provide little more than probabilities concerning the relationship of evidence to the issues in a case.

Were judges and juries required to decide cases on the basis of absolute certainty about what occurred, it is doubtful that they ever would find the standard satisfied. Whoever was required to prove the case would always lose. Recognizing that absolute certainty is not reasonably possible, American courts have chosen to demand less. How much less determines the extent to which they are willing to accept the risk of error in the course of litigation.

In criminal cases the typical requirement is that the government must prove the essential elements of any offense it chooses to charge beyond a reasonable doubt. This means that, although the decision maker need not be certain that a defendant is guilty before convicting, any reasonable doubt requires that it find the defendant not guilty. Such a standard allocates most of the risk of error in criminal cases to the state. It cannot assure that no innocent person will ever be convicted, but the standard is demanding enough to make it most unlikely that someone who is actually innocent will be found guilty. It is more likely that truly guilty persons may go free, but that is the price American criminal justice pays to avoid mistakes that harm the innocent.

It is uncertain when this standard of proof was first used in criminal cases. In early England, whether or not a person would be convicted depended on his ability to produce compurgators or to avoid misfortune in an ordeal. Subsequently, success turned on whether or not a suspect could succeed in trial by combat. As trial by jury replaced other forms of proof, the jurors originally decided cases on the basis of their own knowledge, and even if they relied on informants, the jurors themselves were responsible for the accuracy of the facts. Not until the notion of an independent fact finder, typically a jury, developed was a standard of proof very meaningful. With the development of the independent and neutral fact finder, the "beyond a reasonable doubt" concept took on importance.

Although there is no mention of the proof beyond a reasonable doubt concept in the United States Constitution, trial by jury is in all but petty cases guaranteed by the Sixth Amendment, and with the Supreme Court's decision in *Duncan* v. *Louisiana* (1968), this right is now binding on the states. By the time the Sixth Amendment was adopted, proof be-

Proof beyond a reasonable doubt is the highest level of proof demanded in American courts.

See also

Duncan v. *Louisiana*

Reese *was the first
voting rights case
under the Fifteenth
Amendment and,
among the early
decisions, the most
consequential.*

See also

Voting Rights

yond a reasonable doubt was closely associated with the right to an impartial jury guaranteed by the Constitution in criminal cases.

Thus, it is not surprising that the Supreme Court has found the proof beyond a reasonable doubt standard to be constitutionally required in criminal cases with respect to all essential elements of offenses charged, whether the criminal case is litigated in state or federal court (*In re Winship*, 1970). The Court associated the high proof standard with the strong presumption of innocence in criminal cases and observed that before a defendant may be stigmatized by criminal conviction and punished for criminal wrongdoing, due process requires the state to prove guilt beyond a reasonable doubt.

There is little agreement on exactly what a reasonable doubt is. No single definition of reasonable doubt has ever gained acceptance in American courts. There does seem to be some consensus that a decision maker should understand that a reasonable doubt is one based in reason as applied to the proof offered in a case. This elaboration of the standard is consistent with the oath that judges administer to jurors who are called upon to decide a case. Beyond this, it is difficult to define the term. Any language that is used is likely to be challenged as being either too demanding or not demanding enough.

Judges and juries have come to know that the proof beyond a reasonable doubt standard represents American regard for liberty and the dignity of the individual who stands against the state and who seeks to preserve his freedom and independence. A reasonable doubt will protect him.

—STEPHEN A. SALTZBURG

Bibliography

Kalven, Harry, Jr., and Zeisel, Hans (1966). *The American Jury.* Boston: Little, Brown.

Tribe, Laurence H. (1971). Trial by Mathematics: Precision and Ritual in the Legal Process. *Harvard Law Review* 84: 1329–1393.

REESE v. UNITED STATES

92 U.S. 214 (1876)

Reese was the first voting rights case under the Fifteenth Amendment and, among the early decisions, the most consequential. The Supreme Court crippled the attempt of the federal government to protect the right to vote and made constitutionally possible the circumvention of the Fifteenth Amendment by formally nonracial state qualifications on the right to vote. Congress had made election officials subject to federal prosecution for refusing to qualify eligible voters or not allowing them to vote. Part of the statute specified denial on account of race, part did not. One

---

RED LION BROADCASTING CO. v. FEDERAL COMMUNICATIONS COMMISSION

395 U.S. 367 (1969)

The Federal Communications Commission promulgated fairness rules requiring balanced broadcasting on public issues. The Court answered First Amendment challenges by arguing that different media required different constitutional standards, and that the scarcity of frequencies both necessitated government allocation and justified requirements that allocatees insure balanced programming. Comparing *Red Lion* to *Miami Herald Publishing Co.* v. *Tornillo* (1974) indicates that electronic media enjoy less editorial freedom than do the print media. As technological developments undercut the scarcity rationale, the Court shifted toward an intrusiveness-into-the-home rationale for greater regulation of broadcasters.

—MARTIN SHAPIRO

section, for example, provided for the punishment of any person who prevented any citizen from voting or qualifying to vote. A black citizen offered to pay his poll tax to vote in a municipal election, but the election officials refused to receive his tax or to let him vote. The United States prosecuted the officials.

The Court, by an 8–1 vote, in an opinion by Chief Justice Morrison R. Waite, held the act of Congress unconstitutional because it swept too broadly: two sections did not "confine their operation to unlawful discriminations on account of race, etc." The Fifteenth Amendment provided that the right to vote should not be denied because of race, but Congress had overreached its powers by seeking to punish the denial on any ground. The Court voided the whole act because its sections were inseparable, yet refused to construe the broadly stated sections in terms of those sections that did refer to race. By its pinched interpretation of the amendment, the Court made it constitutionally possible for the states to deny the right to vote on any ground except race, thus allowing the use of poll taxes, literacy tests, good character tests, understanding clauses, and other devices to achieve black disfranchisement.

—LEONARD W. LEVY

REGENTS OF UNIVERSITY OF CALIFORNIA v. BAKKE

438 U.S. 265 (1978)

Perhaps the Supreme Court's majority in *De-Funis* v. *Odegaard* (1974) thought a delay in deciding on the constitutionality of racial preferences in state university admissions would give time for development of a political consensus on the issue. The result was just the opposite; by the time *Bakke* was decided, the question of racial quotas and preferences had become bitterly divisive. Bakke, a nonminority applicant, had been denied admission to the university's medical school at Davis. His state court suit had challenged the school's program setting aside for minority applicants sixteen places in an entering class of 100. Bakke's test scores and grades exceeded those of most minority admittees. The California Supreme Court held that the racial preference denied Bakke the equal protection of the laws guaranteed by the Fourteenth Amendment.

A fragmented United States Supreme Court agreed, 5–4, that Bakke was entitled to admission, but concluded, in a different 5–4 alignment, that race could be taken into account in a state university's admissions. Four Justices thought the Davis quota violated Title VI of the Civil Rights Act of 1964, which forbids the exclusion of anyone on account of race from any program aided by federal funds. This position was rejected, 5–4. Four other Justices argued that the Davis quota was constitutionally valid as a reasonable, nonstigmatizing remedy for past societal discrimination against racial and ethnic minorities. This view was rejected by Justice Lewis F. Powell, who concluded that the Davis quota was a denial of equal protection. His vote, along with the votes of the four Justices who found a Title VI violation, placed Bakke in Davis's 1978 entering class.

Justice Powell's opinion on the constitutional question began by rejecting the notion of a "benign" racial classification. He concluded that the burden of remedying past societal discrimination could not constitutionally be placed on individuals who had no part in that discrimination—absent the sort of constitutional violation that had been found in school desegregation cases such as *Swann* v. *Charlotte-Mecklenburg Board of Education* (1971), where color-conscious remedies had been approved. While rejecting quotas, Justice Powell approved the use of race as one factor in a state university's admissions policy for the purpose of promoting diversity in its student body.

Race is relevant to "diversity," of course, mainly because past societal discrimination

Race is relevant to "diversity," of course, mainly because past societal discrimination has made race relevant to a student's attitudes and experiences.

See also

Affirmative Action

Equal Protection of the Laws

Racial Quotas

Swann v. *Charlotte-Mecklenburg Board of Education*

has made race relevant to a student's attitudes and experiences. And if one's membership in a racial group may be a factor in the admissions process, it may be the decisive factor in a particular case. The Powell opinion thus anticipates a preference for minority applicants; how much of a preference will depend, as he says, on "some attention to numbers"—that is, the number of minority students already admitted. The difference between such a system and a racial quota is mostly symbolic.

The press hailed Justice Powell's opinion as a judgment of Solomon. As a contribution to principled argument about equal protection doctrine, it failed. As a political solution, however, it was a triumph. The borders of preference became blurred, so that no future applicant could blame her rejection on the preference. At the same time, a university following a "diversity" approach to admissions was made safe from constitutional attack. Affirmative action was thus saved, even as Bakke was ushered into medical school and racial quotas ringingly denounced. Solomon, it will be recalled, succeeded in saving the baby.

However, in subsequent cases the Court has repeatedly had to deal with the validity of affirmative action programs, and the issue of such programs at state universities has continued to smolder. California itself enacted a law by referendum in 1996 abolishing racial preferences at state universities (as well as other state and municipal agencies). But in the absence of such statutes, and despite a pair of lower court decisions holding racial preferences at state universities to be invalid, *Bakke* remains the law.

—KENNETH L. KARST

Bibliography

Blasi, Vincent (1979). Bakke as Precedent: Does Mr. Justice Powell Have a Theory? *California Law Review* 67:21–68.

Karst, Kenneth L., and Horowitz, Harold W. (1979). The Bakke Opinions and Equal Protection Doctrine. *Harvard Civil Rights-Civil Liberties Law Review* 14:7–29.

Wilkinson, J. Harvie, III (1979). *From Brown to Bakke*. New York: Oxford University Press.

REHNQUIST, WILLIAM H.

(1924–   )

William H. Rehnquist grew up in Milwaukee and was educated at Stanford, Harvard, and Stanford Law School. He served as a law clerk to Supreme Court Justice Robert H. Jackson and then entered into private practice in Phoenix. In 1969, through his association with Deputy Attorney General Richard Kleindienst and work as a Republican party official in Phoenix, he went to Washington as Assistant Attorney General for the Office of Legal Counsel. On January 7, 1972, he, along with Lewis F. Powell, was sworn in as an Associate Justice of the Supreme Court. On September 26, 1986, he was sworn in as Chief Justice of the United States, only the third sitting Justice to be so elevated. Despite widespread disagreement with Rehnquist's views among legal academics, there is little dispute that he is among the ablest Justices who have ever served on the Court.

Justice Rehnquist's vision of the nation's constitutional structure, emphasizing the words and history of that document, is expressed in three doctrines: strict construction (of both the Constitution and of statutes), judicial restraint, and federalism. He summarized this vision in a 1976 speech at the University of Texas:

> It is almost impossible . . . to conclude that the [Founding Fathers] intended the Constitution itself to suggest answers to the manifold problems that they knew would confront succeeding generations. The Constitution that they drafted was intended to endure indefinitely, but the reason for this well-founded hope was the general language by which national authority was

granted to Congress and the Presidency. These two branches were to furnish the motive power within the federal system, which was in turn to coexist with the state governments; the elements of government having a popular constituency were looked to for the solution of the numerous and varied problems that the future would bring.

In other words, as he stated, dissenting, in *Trimble* v. *Gordon* (1977), neither the original Constitution nor the Civil War amendments made "this Court (or the federal courts generally) into a council of revision, and they did not confer on this Court any authority to nullify state laws which were merely felt to be inimical to the Court's notion of the public interest."

During his early years on the Court, despite the presence of three other Republican appointees, Justice Rehnquist was often in lone dissent, espousing a view of states' rights and limited federal judicial power that many regarded as anachronistic. For example, in *Weber* v. *Aetna Casualty and Surety Company* (1972), *Sugarman* v. *Dougall* (1973), and *Frontiero* v. *Richardson* (1973), he resisted the view of the other eight members of the Court that the equal protection clause of the Fourteenth Amendment applied to, and required heightened scrutiny of, state-sponsored discrimination against illegitimate children, resident aliens, and women, respectively. Indeed, he insisted that the equal protection clause had only marginal application beyond cases of racial discrimination. In the area of criminal procedure Rehnquist urged that the Court overrule *Mapp* v. *Ohio* (1961), which applied the exclusionary rule to the states. Rehnquist also seemed hostile to *Miranda* v. *Arizona* (1966), though he never directly argued that it should be reversed. Still, even in his early years on the Court, Justice Rehnquist was less likely to be in dissent than the liberal Justices William O. Douglas, William J. Brennan, and Thurgood Marshall; and the

ideas expressed in some of Rehnquist's early dissents, such as in *Cleveland Board of Education* v. *LaFleur* (1974) and *Fry* v. *United States* (1975) were influential in majority opinions in the years to come.

The 1975 term saw Justice Rehnquist come into his own as the leader of the (evershifting) conservative wing of the Court. In that term he wrote for the Court in *Paul* v. *Davis* (1976), holding that reputation, standing alone, was not a constitutionally protected "liberty" interest subject to vindication under the guarantee of procedural due process of law; in *National League of Cities* v. *Usery* (1976), holding that the Tenth Amendment limited Congress's power under the commerce clause to regulate the states; and in *Rizzo* v. *Goode* (1976), holding that "principles of federalism" forbade federal courts from ordering a restructuring of a city police force in response to constitutional violations. In *National League of Cities*, Rehnquist used an

AMONG THE ABLEST

Rehnquist's vision of the nation's constitutional structure is expressed in three doctrines: strict construction, judicial restraint, and federalism. (Corbis)

expansive reading of the Tenth Amendment to strike down a federal statute that regulated the wages and hours of state government employees, although such regulation was otherwise concededly within Congress's commerce power. The opinion showed that when faced with a choice between judicial restraint/strict constructionism and states' rights, Justice Rehnquist was prepared to defend the latter aggressively. However, the potential significance of the first decision limiting Congress's use of the commerce power since 1936 was eroded by subsequent Court majorities, first refusing to follow, and then overruling, *National League of Cities* in *Garcia* v. *San Antonio Metropolitan Transit Authority* (1985). Despite Justice Rehnquist's prediction in dissent that this issue would return to haunt the Court, it seems unlikely that the Court will really disable Congress from establishing national control of virtually any area in which Congress chooses to assert itself, provided Congress has chosen a rational relationship with commerce or some other power given to Congress by the Constitution. However, in recent years Rehnquist has led the Court in holding that Congress has exceeded those powers, as in *United States* v. *Lopez* (1995), where the Court invalidated a federal law making it a crime to possess a gun within 1,000 feet of a school. The Court, in an opinion by Rehnquist, found this law not to be substantially related to interstate commerce, as a law regulating the sale of guns, for example, would be. He also was part of the majority in *New York* v. *United States* (1992) and *Printz* v. *United States* (1997) where the Court held the state's reserved powers under the Tenth Amendment limited the ability of Congress to direct states to act according to federal directives—a partial vindication of his views in *National League of Cities*.

When dissenting, Rehnquist makes his most telling points in opposing the majority's efforts to enact "desirable" social policy with little support from the constitutional or statutory provisions that they purport to be interpreting. An example is *United Steel Workers of America* v. *Weber* (1979). In that case, Kaiser Aluminum Company and the United Steelworkers had devised a "voluntary" affirmative action plan under which half of available positions in an on-the-job training plan would be reserved for blacks. Weber, excluded solely because he was white, filed suit based on Title VII of the Civil Rights Act of 1964. The statute provides that "it shall be unlawful for an employer . . . to fail or refuse to hire . . . any individual . . . because of such individual's race." The statute goes on to say that its provisions are not to be interpreted "to require any employer . . . to grant preferential treatment to any individual or group." Moreover, as a unanimous Court had recognized only three years before in *McDonald* v. *Santa Fe Trail Transportation Co.* (1976), the "uncontradicted legislative history" showed that Title VII "prohibited racial discrimination against the white petitioners . . . upon the same standards as would be applicable were they Negroes." Nevertheless, in *Weber*, a 5–2 majority, reversing the lower courts, found that discrimination against whites was not within the "spirit" of Title VII and consequently not prohibited. In a bitter dissent, Justice Rehnquist accused the majority of Orwellian "newspeak" and concluded that "close examination of what the Court proffers as the spirit of the Act reveals it as the spirit of the present majority, not the 88th Congress." Similarly in *Roe* v. *Wade* (1973), where the majority based a woman's right to an abortion on a constitutional right of privacy that arose not from the terms but from the "penumbras" of the Bill of Rights, Rehnquist wrote, "To reach its result, the Court necessarily has had to find within the scope of the Fourteenth Amendment a right that was apparently completely unknown to the drafters of the Amendment." Whatever the wisdom of the policies announced in these cases, it is difficult to disagree that Rehnquist's reading of the textual material in question was the more accurate one.

It is ironic that Rehnquist, often condemned as a right-wing ideologue was, in *Weber* and *Roe,* as in many other cases, advocating a view of the Court's role that had previously been vigorously advanced by the progressive members of the Court. In *Morehead* v. *New York ex rel. Tipaldo* (1936), for example, the dissenting opinion of Justice Harlan F. Stone, joined by Justices Louis Brandeis and Benjamin Cardozo, declared: "It is not for the Court to resolve doubts whether the remedy by regulation is as efficacious as many believe, or better than some other, or is better even than blind operation of uncontrolled economic forces. The legislature must be free to choose unless government is rendered impotent. The Fourteenth Amendment has no more imbedded in the Constitution our preference for some particular set of economic beliefs, than it has adopted in the name of liberty the system of theology which we happen to approve." The distinction made by the Court is that the rights enunciated in *Roe* and similar cases are "fundamental," unlike the property rights at stake in the economic regulation decisions of the 1930s, so that legislation circumscribing those fundamental rights is subjected to stricter scrutiny than legislation governing property.

Similarly, in a series of opinions, Rehnquist has succeeded in limiting the role of the federal courts in reviewing actions alleged to violate the Constitution, using the requirement that there be "state action" in order to show a Constitutional violation. In *Moose Lodge* v. *Irvis* (1972) he wrote for the Court that racial discrimination by a club with a state liquor license was not unconstitutional, since licensing by the state did not render the club an arm of the state, and in *Jackson* v. *Metropolitan Edison Co.* (1974) he held that a heavily regulated private electric utility was not likewise engaged in "state action" and therefore not subject to a claim that it deprived a subscriber of procedural due process when it terminated service to her. Finally, in *Flagg Bros.* v. *Brooks* (1978), he led the Court

in ruling that a warehouse operator that sold a customer's goods after she failed to pay for their storage, as authorized by a state statute, was not engaged in state action, so that its acts could not be challenged as violative of due process.

In criminal procedure, Rehnquist's views are driven by the same narrow view of the role of courts in a tripartite federal system, and he frankly admits that his goal when he came on the Court was to "call a halt to a number of sweeping rulings of the Warren Court in this area." In this objective he generally was joined by the other appointees of Richard M. Nixon and by Justice Byron White. Consequently, the 1970s and 1980s saw a series of decisions aimed at making it easier for the police to investigate crimes and harder for defendants to upset their convictions because of police investigatory errors. For example, in *Rakas* v. *Illinois* (1978) the Court, per Rehnquist, made it more difficult for a defendant to establish standing to litigate search and seizure violations; in *United States* v. *Robinson* (1973) the scope of police searches incident to arrest was expanded; and in *United States* v. *Leon* (1984) the Court, per Justice White, established a good faith exception to the exclusionary rule in search warrant cases. However, neither Rehnquist nor any of his fellow conservatives sought to undercut the fundamental rights to counsel, appeal, and trial by jury that had been applied to the states by the Warren Court. In a 1985 interview, despite the feeling of most Court watchers that the Burger Court had not dismantled the major criminal procedure protections of the Warren Court, including the Miranda rules and the exclusionary rule, Justice Rehnquist pronounced himself satisfied that the law was "more evenhanded now than when I came on the Court."

If Rehnquist has not been successful in exempting states from congressional control, he has frequently prevailed in his efforts to exempt state courts from federal court interference. To do this, he has taken the 1971 deci-

*Justice Rehnquist is
not always cavalier
in distinguishing or
narrowing
unpleasant
precedents.*

sion in *Younger* v. *Harris,* which counseled restraint by federal courts in enjoining ongoing state criminal proceedings, and extended it greatly. In *Rizzo* and in *Real Estate Association* v. *McNary* (1981) he held that "principles of federalism" limited a federal court's ability to enjoin not just the judicial branch but the executive branch of state governments as well and that this comity limitation was not confined to criminal proceedings. Nor, as he held in *Doran* v. *Salem Inn, Inc.* (1975), was it necessary that a state criminal proceeding predate a federal action for the federal action to be barred by principles of comity.

Similarly, in the area of federal habeas corpus for state prisoners, Rehnquist and his conservative colleagues have advanced the dual goals of limiting federal court interference with state court adjudications and enhancing the finality of criminal convictions. The most significant holding in this line of cases is the decision in *Wainwright* v. *Sykes* (1977). In this case, Rehnquist, writing for a six-Justice majority, held that a defendant's failure to raise an issue at the appropriate stage of a state criminal proceeding barred the federal courts from considering that issue later under habeas corpus, absent a showing by the defendant of good cause for the failure and prejudice to his case. *Sykes* thus largely overruled *Fay* v. *Noia* (1963), which had allowed new issues to be raised on federal habeas corpus unless they had been deliberately bypassed by the defendant in state proceedings. *Sykes* represented a significant diminution of the power of federal courts to interfere with state convictions. The trend continued in 1989 in the significant case of *Teague* v. *Lane,* authored by Justice Sandra Day O'Connor, where the Court held that "new" rules of criminal procedure generally should not apply retroactively on habeas corpus to defendants whose state convictions had become final before the new law was established. In *Butler* v. *McKellar* (1990) Justice Rehnquist defined "new" broadly so as to make it very difficult for state prisoners to obtain federal habeas relief.

Consistent with his stance on federalism and judicial restraint, Rehnquist is the Court's leading advocate of a restrictive interpretation of the establishment clause of the First Amendment. He set forth his view in detail in a dissenting opinion in *Wallace* v. *Jaffree* (1985), where the majority struck down Alabama's statutorily required moment of silence for "meditation or voluntary prayer" in public schools. Rehnquist rejected the "wall of separation between church and state" principle of *Everson* v. *Board of Education* (1947), arguing that history did not support this rigid interpretation of the First Amendment. According to Rehnquist, James Madison viewed the purpose of the establishment clause as simply "to prohibit the establishment of a national religion, and perhaps to prevent discrimination among sects. He did not see it as requiring neutrality on the part of the government between religion and irreligion." Consequently, Rehnquist would have found no defect in a state statute that openly endorsed prayer, much less a "moment of silence."

In a similar vein, in *First National Bank* v. *Bellotti* (1978), Rehnquist, in a sole dissent, refused to recognize a First Amendment commercial speech right for corporations, and in *Virginia State Board of Pharmacy* v. *Virginia Consumer Council* (1976) he refused to recognize a First Amendment right of consumers to receive commercial information. In short, in the First Amendment area, as in all others, he would generally give the legislative branch, whether state or federal, greater freedom to plot its own course than his colleagues would.

When, in June of 1986, Warren Burger announced his resignation as Chief Justice and President Ronald Reagan nominated Rehnquist as his replacement, there was a firestorm of protest among liberals. Senator Edward Kennedy denounced Justice Rehnquist as having an "appalling record on race" and liberal columnists branded him a right-wing extremist. A concerted effort was undertaken to find something in his past that might provide a basis for defeating the nomination. Assorted allegations were raised concerning contacts with black voters when he was a Republican party official in Phoenix, the handling of a family trust, a memo he had written to Justice Jackson as a law clerk urging that the separate-but-equal doctrine not be overruled in *Brown* v. *Board of Education of Topeka* (1954, 1955), and a racially restrictive covenant in the deed to his Phoenix house. The Senate perceived that these allegations were either unproved or, if true, were "ancient history" and irrelevant to his fitness for the post of Chief Justice. Significantly, no serious charge of misconduct was shown as to Rehnquist's fourteen and a half years as an Associate Justice on the Supreme Court. In the end, after much sound and fury, he was confirmed by a vote of 65–13.

If the 1975 term saw Rehnquist "arrive" as a major force on the Court, it was the 1987 term, his second year in the post, that saw him mature as Chief Justice. In a speech given in 1976 he had discussed the role of Chief Justice, citing Charles Evans Hughes as his model: "Hughes believed that unanimity of decision contributed to public confidence in the Court. . . . Except in cases involving matters of high principle he willingly acquiesced in silence rather than expose his dissenting views. . . . Hughes was also willing to modify his own opinions to hold or increase his majority and if that meant he had to put in disconnected thoughts or sentences, in they went."

Following his own advice, in the 1987 term he achieved a high level of agreement with his fellow Justices (ranging from 57.6 percent with Justice Thurgood Marshall to 83.1 percent with Justice Anthony Kennedy). His administrative abilities in the 1987 term won the praise of Justice Harry Blackmun, who deemed him a "splendid administrator in conference." For the first time in years, the Court concluded its work prior to July 1. During that term, Rehnquist showed that he

could be flexible, joining with the more liberal Justices to subject the dismissal of a homosexual CIA agent to judicial review and to support the First Amendment claims of *Hustler* magazine to direct off-color ridicule at a public figure. Most significantly, in *Morrison* v. *Olson* (1988) Rehnquist wrote for a 7–1 majority upholding the office of independent counsel against a challenge by the Reagan administration. In a decision termed an "exercise in folly" by the lone dissenter, Justice Antonin Scalia, Rehnquist held that the appointments clause was not violated by Congress's vesting the power to appoint a special prosecutor in a "Special Division" of three United States Court of Appeals judges. Nor did the act violate separation of powers principles by impermissibly interfering with the functions of the executive branch. While the act can be shown to have theoretical flaws, Rehnquist could not be faulted if he perceived that a truly independent prosecutor was a necessary check on the many abuses of executive power, including criminal violations, that were occurring during the latter years of the Reagan administration and in upholding a check on those abuses in an opinion that gained the concurrence of a substantial majority of his colleagues. Rehnquist's performance during the 1988 term led the *New York Times*, which had vigorously opposed his elevation to Chief Justice, to praise him with faint damnation. "While he is certainly no liberal, or even a moderate, his positions are not always responsive to the tides of fashionable opinion among his fellow political conservatives."

Indeed, while Rehnquist's judicial philosophy is undoubtedly born of a staunch political conservatism, the principles of federalism and strict construction will frequently prevail even when they lead to a "liberal" result. For example, in *PruneYard Shopping Center* v. *Robins* (1980) he wrote the opinion upholding state constitutional provisions that allowed political demonstrators to solicit signatures for a petition in a shopping center.

R

REHNQUIST, WILLIAM H.

(1924–)

He recognized "the authority of the state to exercise its police power or its sovereign right to adopt in its own Constitution individual liberties more expansive than those conferred by the Federal Constitution." Similarly, in *Hughes* v. *Oklahoma* (1979) he dissented when the Court invalidated a state's attempt to preserve its wildlife. And, in *Pennell* v. *City of San Jose* (1988), he upheld the city's rent control ordinance in the face of a due process challenge by landlords. In numerous criminal cases, such as *United States* v. *Maze* (1974) and *Ball* v. *United States* (1985), he has voted to reverse criminal convictions on the ground that the government had failed to prove that the defendant's conduct had violated the terms of the (strictly construed) statute.

But if the 1987 term showed that Rehnquist could be flexible as Chief Justice, that term and the 1988 term also had him, in most cases, leading the Court in a conservative direction. In a series of close cases decided in the 1987 term, ranging across the landscape of the Bill of Rights, the Court denied an equal protection challenge to user fees for bus transportation to school, denied a claim by Indians that a Forest Service logging road through a national forest would interfere with their free exercise of religion, denied food stamps to striking workers, allowed censorship of a school newspaper, upheld federal tort immunity for defense contractors, and allowed illegally discovered evidence to be used against a criminal defendant under the "independent source" exception to the exclusionary rule.

The 1988 term demonstrated that Rehnquist was still prepared to be flexible. For example, in *City of Canton* v. *Harris* he joined an opinion by Justice White that held that a city could be liable for damages under Section 1983, Title 42, U. S. Code for poor training of police officers and that a new trial was not barred; Justices O'Connor, Kennedy, and Scalia, on the other hand, wanted to dismiss the plaintiff's case because the plaintiff could not have met the "deliberate indifference"

standard of proof. Such flexibility was rarely called for during the 1988 term, however, and the conservatives stayed together most of the time. The leading case of the term was *Webster* v. *Reproductive Health Services* (1988). Here Chief Justice Rehnquist and four others upheld a Missouri statute that forbade public funding and the use of public hospitals for abortions. The decision was consistent with Rehnquist's views of state's rights and strict construction of the federal Bill of Rights. Rehnquist observed that "our cases have recognized that the due process clauses generally confer no affirmative right to government aid, even where such aid may be necessary to some life, liberty or property interests of which the government itself may not deprive the individual." Because a state is under no constitutional obligation to provide public hospitals at all, it is free to condition their use however it wishes. This notion, that beneficiaries of public largess must accept the "bitter [restrictions] with the sweet" has been a hallmark of Rehnquist's jurisprudence since he first expressed it in *Arnett* v. *Kennedy* in 1974. However, Rehnquist was unable to convince a majority of the Court that it was time to abandon the "rigid" framework of *Roe* v. *Wade* that gave a woman an absolute right to an abortion during the first trimester of pregnancy. Indeed, in *Planned Parenthood of Southeastern Pennsylvania* v. *Casey* (1992), over Rehnquist's dissent, the Court announced it would adhere to the "essential holding" of *Roe*, though it lowered the standard of judicial review and sustained some state restrictions on the right to obtain an abortion.

It seems unlikely that the country in the foreseeable future will be confronted with a constitutional problem of the magnitude of the legal discrimination against blacks (and the closely related problem of police abuse of the rights of criminal suspects) that faced the Warren Court. Consequently, it is also unlikely that the judicial activism displayed by the Warren Court to deal with these problems will seem as morally necessary or politically desirable in the future. Thus, while Justice Rehnquist's vision of a vigorous Tenth Amendment checking Congress's power vis-à-vis the states seems unlikely to totally prevail in the long term, his view of a more limited role for the federal Constitution, and hence for the federal courts, probably will be the wave of the future. Having reached its highest point in the 1960s, the "Rights Revolution"—already dying during the Burger Court years—terminated with the appointment of William Rehnquist as Chief Justice of the United States; it probably will not recur after he steps down.

—CRAIG M. BRADLEY

Bibliography

Bradley, Craig M. (1987). Criminal Procedure in the Rehnquist Court: Has the Rehnquisition Begun? *Indiana Law Journal* 62:273–294.

Davis, Sue (1989). *Justice Rehnquist and the Constitution.* Princeton, N.J.: Princeton University Press.

Powell, H. Jefferson (1982). The Compleat Jeffersonian: Justice Rehnquist and Federalism. *Yale Law Journal* 91:1317–1370.

Rehnquist, William H. (1976). Chief Justices I Never Knew. *Hastings Constitutional Law Quarterly* 3:637.

——— (1976). The Notion of a Living Constitution. *Texas Law Review* 54:693–706.

——— (1987). *The Supreme Court: How It Was, How It Is.* New York: Morrow.

Shapiro, David L. (1976). Mr. Justice Rehnquist: A Preliminary View. *Harvard Law Review* 90:293–357.

REHNQUIST COURT

(1986–   )

The Rehnquist Court began its reign in September of 1986 when President Ronald Reagan appointed William H. Rehnquist Chief Justice to replace retiring Chief Justice Warren E. Burger. Before his appointment as Chief Justice, however, Rehnquist had served as an Associate Justice on the Burger Court for almost fifteen years. Like Burger, he was originally appointed by President Richard M. Nixon to redeem a specific campaign promise to promote law and order through Court appointments that would stem the tide of Warren Court decisions protecting the rights of the criminally accused and to pursue his more general philosophical commitment to appoint "strict constructionists . . . to interpret the law, not to make law."

The Burger Court itself made a fairly quick start in redeeming Mr. Nixon's law-and-order pledge, although the Rehnquist Court has continued and in some ways even accelerated this redemption. It seems highly likely that the elevation of Rehnquist, in conjunction with two subsequent appointments by President Reagan and two by President George Bush, will complete the more general transformation of the Court contemplated by President Nixon's commitment to strict construction. However, two later justices appointed by President Bill Clinton are more moderate and will likely temper that process.

This broader transformation has been steady but slow. It has been steady because Republican presidents holding the conservative values associated with "strict construction" controlled the White House continuously from Nixon's election to Clinton's, except for the four-year interlude of President Jimmy Carter, who did not have the opportunity to appoint a single Justice. It has been slow partly because some of the appointees did not turn out as conservative as expected and partly because some of the conservatives replaced other conservatives rather than liberals. Of President Nixon's four appointments, only one, Chief Justice Burger, remained consistently faithful to the conservative cause, whereas Justice Lewis F. Powell proved to be a moderate and Justice Harry A. Blackmun became increasingly liberal. Justice

John Paul Stevens, appointed by President Gerald Ford, has also proved to be a moderate; one of President Reagan's first two appointments replaced a moderate, Justice Sandra Day O'Connor replacing Justice Potter J. Stewart, and the other, Justice Antonin Scalia, replaced conservative Chief Justice Burger.

Since then, President Reagan's final appointment, Justice Anthony M. Kennedy, again replaced the moderate Justice Powell. Of President Bush's two appointments, Justice David H. Souter, a moderate, replaced the liberal Justice William J. Brennan, while Justice Clarence Thomas, a conservative, replaced the liberal Justice Thurgood Marshall. These were followed by President Clinton's naming Justice Ruth Bader Ginsburg to replace Justice Byron R. White and Justice Stephen G. Breyer to replace Justice Blackmun—in both cases, moderate-to-liberal justices replacing a moderate and a liberal respectively.

"Strict construction" is sometimes equated with a strategy of interpreting the Constitution according to the "plain meaning" of the text or the intention of its Framers. In fact, however, this interpretive strategy had not proved so far to be of great importance, except with regard to the methodology used by the Court to decide whether rights not expressly mentioned in the text are impliedly protected, where a variation of it has gained prominence. The form of strict construction, or conservatism, that has gradually come to dominate the Court, however, has been based more on institutional and political than on historical or textual commitments.

Institutionally, most of the Republican appointees have been inclined to resolve any doubts about how the Constitution should be interpreted by upholding actions of other agencies of government. This inclination probably rests mainly on three interconnected institutional commitments: a vision of democracy that pictures majoritarian-responsive institutions as its centerpiece and the life-tenured Court as antidemocratic; a vision of the management of society as a complex matter best delegated to various experts and professionals, like school boards and other administrative agencies; and a vision of federalism that views with suspicion the intrusion of federal power including the judicial power, into areas of decision making traditionally left to state and local government.

Politically, most of the Republican appointees have been guided or at least disciplined by the values associated with the constituency of the Republican party in late twentieth-century America. The Burger Court sat and the Rehnquist Court is sitting in an era when the historically dispossessed are actively seeking possession: blacks and other racial minorities; the poor and the homeless; women; gays; and other groups, like the handicapped, who have in different ways been marginalized in our society.

The Republican party has sought in a variety of ways to accommodate the interests of these groups, but it has been the party of mainstream America, not the party of the dispossessed. While Republicans and Democrats have vied for the "law and order" vote, the Republican party has been the more consistently and vocally anticriminal. The party has sought a moderate, compromising posture on the matters touching the protection of minority groups, women, and the handicapped. It has generally aligned itself at least rhetorically with traditional and to some extent religiously inspired moral views on controversial social questions such as abortion and homosexuality. While it has often conformed to the realities of interest-group politics, it has tended to resist governmental redistributive programs that would tax or otherwise interfere with property interests, preferring to rely instead on a relatively unregulated market to provide full employment and thus help the poor.

The behavior of the Rehnquist Court has been quite consistent with these political commitments, although at the same time, it is worthy of emphasis that a consistent and cohesive "Rehnquist Court" does not yet exist in one important sense. Even the conservative Justices sometimes disagree over outcomes and often, in important ways, over the rationale for decisions. As a result, the Court is often at least doctrinally splintered.

The Supreme Court, like the Republican party, has often sought what might be characterized as compromises; but on the whole, it is the Court of mainstream America, not the dispossessed. In a high percentage of important constitutional cases, its institutional and political commitments have pointed in the same direction. When these commitments have conflicted, it has to this point usually refrained from imposing its values, instead deferring to the governmental agencies whose decisions are challenged. There are some important exceptions, most notably in its resistance to affirmative action programs, but these have been few and on the whole restrained. For example, although it has sometimes protected property rights against governmental regulation, its rulings to this point do not remotely promise a return to pre-New Deal ideology. Occasionally, chiefly in freedom of speech cases, it has acted in ways that might be interpreted as neither institutionally nor politically conservative, as in upholding against regulation the speech rights of flag burners, but such cases are also rare. The Rehnquist Court has been, largely but not completely, a passively rather than an actively conservative court.

In one view the Court's overall performance shows only that the system is working as it is supposed to work: the presidential appointment power is the main effective check on these nine Justices who are accountable to no electorate, and twenty years of Republican presidents has had an effect on the Supreme Court.

The Rehnquist Court has continued the Burger Court's contraction of the rights of the criminally accused and convicted, in general subordinating these rights to law-and-order concerns, except in a subclass of cases in which the prosecution behaved outrageously in a way that might have tainted the guilt determination. Both courts have restricted the application of the Fourth Amendment's prohibition of unreasonable searches and seizures and the Fifth Amendment's prohibition of compulsory self-incrimination, limited the scope of the exclusionary rule, interpreted the Eighth Amendment so as to allow the states great discretion in reinstituting and administering capital punishment, and virtually eliminated the possibility of habeas corpus and other postconviction challenges to final judgments of criminal conviction.

United States v. *Salerno* (1987), in which the Court upheld against Eighth Amendment attack the pretrial detention of dangerous defendants, exemplifies the Court's law-and-order commitment. *Maryland* v. *Buie* (1990) is an example of the priority the Court gives to law enforcement goals over Fourth Amendment rights claims. In this case, the Court sanctioned the use of evidence turned up after an arrest in a "protective sweep" of a house, on less than probable cause, that someone dangerous might have been in the areas searched. The Court seems prepared in many contexts to abandon not only the probable cause requirement but any concept of individualized suspicion as a condition to search, as in *Michigan Department of State Police* v. *Sitz,* (1990) where it upheld highway-checkpoint sobriety testing. *Teague* v. *Lane* (1989) made it much more difficult for constitutional claims by prisoners to be heard in the federal courts, holding that federal habeas corpus is unavailable for the assertion of a right not clearly established by precedent unless the right would apply retroactively. For all practical purposes, this ruling requires a prisoner to show that fundamentally unfair governmental practices might have led to the conviction of someone innocent.

The seeds of the Rehnquist Court's more general conservative agenda, also sown during the Burger Court era, include both broad propositions of law that serve to eliminate whole categories of potential constitutional rights and smaller but continuous doctrinal innovations that cumulatively have made ever more difficult the establishment of a violation of rights. The most important developments of the former have been the following: (1) the Court's unwillingness to interpret the Constitution to protect "implied" rights not explicitly mentioned in the text; (2) its limitation of the concept of constitutional rights to negative private rights against governmental interference, rejecting claims of rights to affirmative governmental assistance or subsidy; and (3) its understanding that the government's fundamental constitutional obligation is to refrain from targeting racial, gender, or religious groups for relatively disadvantageous treatment. It rejects any obligation of government to make accommodations in order to protect or benefit any such groups, and to some extent restricts government from making such accommodations for racial (although not for religious) groups. In addition, the Court has circumscribed the power of Congress to legislate in areas it sees as reserved to the states under the Constitution.

Illustrative of the Rehnquist Court's narrow approach to defining the rights protected by the Constitution are *Michael H.* v. *Gerald D.* (1989) and *Burnham* v. *Superior Court of California* (1990). The former case raised the question as to how the term "liberty" in the due process clause of the Fourteenth Amendment should be interpreted; and the latter raised the question as to how the term "due process of law" should be interpreted.

In *Michael H.*, state law conclusively presumed that a child born to a married woman living with her husband was a child of the marriage. A genetic father argued that this law infringed on his "liberty" interest in establishing his paternity. In many prior cases, the Court had held that "liberty," in the due process clause, included implied fundamental rights not expressly mentioned in the Constitution when they were "implicit in the con-

cept of ordered liberty" or "deeply rooted in this Nation's history and tradition." These formulations do not answer the questions of how and at what level of abstractness traditional values should be identified. The *Michael H.* plurality, following the Burger Court's lead in *Bowers* v. *Hardwick* (1986), chose to conceptualize this question very narrowly, asking not even whether our traditions recognize the rights of natural fathers, but rather whether they recognize those of adulterous natural fathers; on this basis the Court rejected the claim.

This historically concrete way of identifying constitutional rights does not necessarily eliminate implied constitutional rights, first, because the Court might (or might not) let stand previously announced implied rights, and second, because it is always possible that some small number of states might in the future restrict rights that have been traditionally and widely respected by all the other states. But it does very substantially limit the potential category of implied rights. Moreover, it does so in an odd way, given the traditional assumption that the main point of constitutional rights is to protect minorities: after *Bowers* and *Michael H.,* the stronger, more widespread, and more historically entrenched a rights-restrictive majoritarian imposition, the less likely the Court will find a constitutional violation. However, in *Romer* v. *Evans* (1996) the Court overturned a state constitutional amendment forbidding state and municipal agencies from allowing homosexuals to assert any "claim of discrimination." Although *Bowers* v. *Hardwick* had held homosexual conduct not to be within the fundamental right of privacy, the Court in *Romer* v. *Evans* held the state had unconstitutionally legislated "for the purpose of disadvantaging the group burdened by the law," thus denying homosexuals the equal protection of the laws.

The *Bowers* approach was applied by four Justices in *Burnham,* with the concurrence of enough others to constitute a majority, to reject a claim that subjecting an individual to a state's jurisdiction on the basis of his fleeting presence within the state amounted to a denial of liberty "without due process of law." The opinion of the four by Justice Scalia found that fleeting physical presence, which would have been thought a sufficient predicate for jurisdiction when the Fourteenth Amendment was adopted, had been assumed to be sufficient since then in many state decisions. This "continuing tradition" was sufficient to validate the practice of founding jurisdiction on a fleeting presence, whether or not it might otherwise be thought unfair.

Cruzan v. *Director of Missouri Dept. of Health* (1990) suggests that the Court is not prepared to scuttle the implied-rights doctrine completely, but is also not disposed to use it aggressively. The Court found a sufficiently concrete tradition recognizing the right of individuals to refuse medical treatment to imply that this choice was a protected liberty that included the right to die under at least some circumstances. Nonetheless, it held that the state's interest in insisting that the choice be shown by clear and convincing evidence was sufficiently strong in the case at hand to justify disallowing a patient's parents from making the decision, even though the patient herself could not make it because she was in a vegetative state.

Although *Cruzan* made clear that one has a constitutionally protected right to refuse unwanted medical treatment, the Court in *Washington* v. *Glucksberg* (1997) refused to extend that right to encompass physician-assisted suicide, and sustained a state law making that a crime.

The best known and most practically important of the pre-Rehnquist Court's decisions protecting implied constitutional rights is *Roe* v. *Wade* (1973), where the Court ruled that the Constitution impliedly protects a woman's right to have an abortion. The Rehnquist Court's general unreceptiveness to implied-rights claims does not bode well for the future of this right, and some of the sitting Justices have already announced their willingness to overrule *Roe*. Whether the right to abort will survive may depend on the vote of Justice Souter, but even if the right survives, smaller but incrementally important shifts in doctrine by the Rehnquist Court have already weakened it significantly.

These shifts had their genesis in Burger Court decisions protecting the implied "privacy" right of individuals to decide their own family living arrangements, but only if the challenged regulation "substantially interfered" with the right. This substantial-interference concept has so far been important mainly in privacy right cases, although it is theoretically transplantable to other areas of constitutional law. Its patent importance at this point is in the abortion rights controversy where, in *Planned Parenthood of Southeastern Pennsylvania* v. *Casey* (1992), the Court made clear its adherence to *Roe* v. *Wade*, though it did show its willingness to uphold greater state control over abortions than prior decisions allowed. *Casey* announced that the proper test for such restrictions is whether they place an "undue burden" on the right to obtain an abortion, and went on to sustain a state twenty-four-hour waiting period and a provision requiring physicians to supply information about the consequences of an abortion. (Medical emergencies were exempt from both of these provisions.) On the other hand the Court overturned a requirement of spousal consent for an abortion as resting on an archaic and discredited view of marriage.

The ancestry of the Court's refusal to recognize positive constitutional rights to governmental assistance are decisions of the Burger Court that effectively terminated enlargement of the "fundamental interest" branch of equal protection jurisprudence bequeathed to it by the Warren Court, along with decisions that rejected the claim that liberties protected against governmental interference are also entitled to affirmative governmental protection.

The Warren Court has held that individuals had an equality-based right to the subsi-

R

The behavior of the Rehnquist Court has been quite consistent with political commitments, yet a cohesive "Rehnquist Court" does not yet exist.

dized provision of "fundamental" services or rights they were too poor to afford, such as counsel and other important defense services in criminal cases. Warren Court decisions had suggested that which rights were "fundamental" for these purposes would depend on the degree to which they were of practical importance to people. The Burger Court did not overturn the particular rulings of the Warren Court, but early in its tenure, did effectively undercut the equal-protection basis of the doctrine and consequently its future growth, ruling that henceforth rights would be regarded as fundamental only if they were constitutional rights, irrespective of their practical importance. These opinions, however, left open the possibility that such "real" constitutional rights might sometimes include subsidy rights.

Burger Court decisions eventually repudiated this suggestion in holding that the right to abort, although a constitutional right, did not include the right to governmental Medicaid payments for abortions for those too poor to afford them. According to these decisions, constitutional rights are negative entitlements available to individuals only to stop governmental interference with the use of private resources.

The Rehnquist Court has perpetuated this jurisprudence of negative rights, holding in the abortion context, for example, that the closing of state hospitals to abortions did not violate the right to abort because the state's action left women who wanted abortions exactly where they would have been had the state never operated public hospitals—that is, dependent on their private resources.

DeShaney v. *Winnebago County Department of Social Services* (1989) suggests, moreover, that the Rehnquist Court's commitment to the jurisprudence of negative rights is pervasive and extends beyond the abortion issue. In this case, the Court held that governmental social-service officials did not violate the rights of a boy by failing to remove him from a father who they knew was continuously

beating him and whose beatings eventually resulted in severe brain damage to the boy. The Court found no violation of the boy's right not to be deprived of liberty without due process. It ruled that due process protects individuals only against the government's interfering with their liberty and imposes no "affirmative obligation" on government to take action to protect that liberty. Just as the "culprit" in abortion-subsidy cases is not the government, but rather the pregnant woman's poverty, so (in this view) the boy's father, not the state, was the source of his problem.

The Rehnquist Court's pursuit of a "neutrality" concept of the government's basic constitutional obligation arguably has fairly deep roots in constitutional history, but is grounded most immediately in the Burger Court's *Washington* v. *Davis* (1976) decision, which held that unless the plaintiff is challenging a law that expressly classifies people on the basis of race, he or she can successfully challenge a governmental action as racially discriminatory only by proving that it was undertaken for a discriminatory purpose. The vision of racial justice that *Washington* has retrospectively been understood to endorse in subsequent Burger and Rehnquist Court decisions interpreting it is one of neutrality in a double sense: first because the Constitution requires governmental racial neutrality, *any* use by government of race as a classifying trait in law is suspect and likely to be struck down. And second, because the Constitution requires nothing more of government than racial neutrality, its actions are immune from attack so long as it does not act for a racially bad purpose.

This vision has substantially constrained attempts on behalf of minority groups to use law and legal institutions to better their lots in two distinct fashions, one by way of constitutional legitimation and the other by way of constitutional restriction. First, a governmental action that produces effects that disadvantage minority groups to a greater extent than other groups is constitutionally legitimate unless a plaintiff can meet the difficult burden of proving that this relative racial disadvantage was a purpose of the action. Second, voluntary attempts by government specifically and expressly to benefit racial minority groups—commonly called benign or reverse discrimination or affirmative action—are seriously vulnerable to constitutional invalidation. Indeed, the Court held in *Richmond (City of)* v. *J. A. Croson Co.* (1989) and *Adarand Constructors* v. *Pena* (1995) that both state and federal affirmative action programs must be shown to be narrowly tailored to serve a compelling government interest.

The Rehnquist Court has vigorously confirmed and extended both the legitimation and restriction branches of the neutrality principle bequeathed to it. In *McCleskey* v. *Kemp* (1987), for example, it rejected, on the ground of a failure of proof of discriminatory purpose, a claim by a black criminal defendant sentenced to death that the state's death penalty was administered in a racially discriminatory fashion. McCleskey's discrimination claim was based on a statistical study that, controlling for extraneous variables, found that a black defendant charged with killing a white in Georgia was four times more likely to be sentenced to death than someone charged with killing a black. The Court conceded, arguendo, the statistical reliability of the evidence, but found that even this statistical pattern would not prove that McCleskey himself was sentenced to death because of racial considerations. The case evidently shows the depth of the Rehnquist Court's commitment to its neutrality principle. Even conceding the correctness of the Court's criticism of the proof as to this individual defendant, the statistical evidence showed systematic racial discrimination and therefore proved that *some* (even if nonidentifiable) individual black murderers of whites were being sentenced to death for racial reasons. Even proof of a pattern of purposeful racial discrimination that might well have infected McCleskey's sentence was not sufficient to establish constitutional illegitimacy without evidence linking this nonneutrality to McCleskey himself.

The depth of the Rehnquist Court's commitment to its neutrality principle is also illustrated by its interpretation of the Civil Rights Act of 1964, which prohibits among other things racial discrimination by employers. Burger Court decisions had held that proof that an employment practice disadvantaged minority group members to a greater extent than others, although insufficient to establish a presumptive constitutional violation by government, *was* sufficient to establish a presumptive violation of the statute by either governmental or private employers. On such a showing, the burden shifted to the employer to establish the business necessity of the challenged practice, failing which the practice would be found illegal.

In *Wards Cove Packing Co., Inc.* v. *Antonio* (1989) the Rehnquist Court changed this evidentiary framework in a way that requires the plaintiff to prove almost as much as he or she would need to establish intentional discrimination. After *Wards Cove*, the employer, in response to a showing that the challenged practice disproportionately disadvantages minority group members, need only come forward with some evidence of a business justification, after which the plaintiff must prove that the practice does not serve "in a significant way, the legitimate employment goals of the employer." A plaintiff who can meet this difficult burden will have come very close to proving that the discrimination was intentional because he or she would have shown that the putatively innocent purpose for the racial injury was a bogus explanation. In the wake of *Ward's Cove* Congress amended the applicable statute, Title VII of the Civil Rights Act of 1964, to restore the burden of proof to the employer as it was before that decision.

The restrictive branch of the neutrality principle arises in cases involving benign or reverse discrimination, a practice whose constitutionality was left extremely uncertain by a series of Burger Court decisions. The Rehnquist Court's decisions in *Croson* and *Adarand* communicate at a minimum that a majority of the Justices (1) see governmental actions that allocate benefits to minority races on the express basis of race as equally or almost as constitutionally troublesome as actions that expressly disadvantage them on the basis of race; (2) believe that few goals are adequate to justify such actions; and (3) will insist that these goals be pursued through race-neutral means whenever possible.

The "degree of troublesomeness" issue is important because it directly affects the "level of scrutiny" or burden of justification that reverse discrimination cases trigger. Under basic principles of constitutional law that have largely been settled for some time, most laws are constitutional so long as they rationally promote legitimate goals of government. One major historical exception to this rule is laws that expressly classify people for burdens or benefits on the basis of race, which are unconstitutional unless the government establishes that they are necessary to serve goals of compelling importance, a justification burden that is very difficult to satisfy.

The special rule for race cases, however, developed in a line of cases involving governments' acting out of racial hostility or prejudice to the detriment of minority groups. Some have argued and some Justices have agreed that reverse discrimination, which does not share this characteristic, is not so constitutionally troublesome and therefore should be judged under a less demanding justification standard. Since *Croson* and *Adarand* a majority of Justices agree on the burden of justification applicable in reverse-discrimination cases. They found such cases sufficiently troublesome to invoke the demanding justification standard historically applied in hostile-discrimination cases, effectively adopting a broad rule requiring governmental neutrality with regard to race.

The remaining important question was under what conditions, if any, this demanding justification standard might be met. A variety of claims have been historically made in an attempt to justify governmental programs that expressly allocate benefits like admission to state medical or law schools or governmental contracts to minority racial groups. Some, for example, see such programs as justified by the goal of preventing the perpetuation of racial underclasses or castes, promoting racial integration in the professions or work force, or creating role models for minority youth. A majority of the Court indicates that such goals will be treated skeptically.

The neutrality principle that has played such an important role in the development of race law has been equally important in sex discrimination cases, where the same basic rule applies: laws that expressly discriminate on gender grounds are suspect (although subject to a less demanding justification than racial classifications), and in the absence of express gender classification, a plaintiff must prove that a challenged action was taken for a gender-discriminatory purpose. In *United States* v. *Virginia* (1995) the Court, with but one dissent, annulled the refusal of that state to admit women to its prestigious Virginia Military Institute. The Court ruled that the state had failed to show the required "exceedingly persuasive" justification for it's discrimination based on gender.

The Court has continued, as in *Virginia*, to adhere to its neutrality principle. In fact, its assimilation of the free exercise of religion clause to the neutrality principle indicates that its commitment to that principle is quite robust.

This assimilation occurred in *Employment Division, Department of Human Resources of Oregon* v. *Smith* (1990), which presented the question as to whether Oregon's penalization of the religious use of peyote violated Smith's right to the free exercise of his religion. Before *Smith*, a law that had the effect of burdening a person's ability to follow a religion was unconstitutional unless shown necessary to the accomplishment of a goal of compelling importance. *Smith* holds that with certain very limited exceptions a "*neutral* law of general applicability" cannot be challenged as an interference with the free exercise of religion. The upshot is that, in the future, adjudication under the free exercise clause will parallel racial and gender equal protection adjudication. Laws that expressly require or prohibit religious practices are not religion neutral and will therefore trigger a heavy burden of justification. But laws that are of general applicability, like those prohibiting drug use, are religion neutral and are not subject to successful constitutional attack unless they were adopted or enforced for the purpose of discriminating against a religion, notwithstanding that their effect burdens certain religious practices. Thus, for example, a law prohibiting the serving of alcohol to minors could be enforced against the Catholic use of wine in communion, although the major religions probably have enough political influence to secure accommodating legislation, and the brunt of *Smith* will likely be borne, as in *Smith* itself, by minority religions.

An attempt by Congress to overrule *Smith* and restore strict scrutiny in free exercise cases was itself rebuffed by the Court in *Boerne (City of)* v. *Flores* (1997). The Court held Congress was without power to legislate a different level of constitutional scrutiny in the absence of some showing of a history of discrimination.

To say that a principle of "neutrality" pervades the Rehnquist Court's jurisprudence of race, gender, and religion is not of course the same as saying that the Court is employing the only tenable, or the right, or even an internally consistent concept of neutrality, for neutrality is no more self-defining than "equality." With regard to race, for example, critics might argue that for the government to act in a truly neutral way its actions should not disproportionately disadvantage members of some racial groups relative to others, irrespective of its purpose, at least when the subject of the disadvantageous treatment is important. They might also say that even if purpose rather than effect is a proper measure of neutrality, the evidence system through which the Court determines purpose is nonneutral, for it rests implicitly on the assumption that government does not usually engage in racial discrimination, rather than the opposite assumption. Finally, these critics might say that the neutrality of current governmental actions cannot be fairly judged without regard to its past actions and, consequently, that what might appear to be a nonneutral conferral of governmental advantages to racial groups previously purposefully disadvantaged by government is better characterized as the pursuit of racial neutrality over time. The Rehnquist Court's neutrality concept might be seen as an attempt to compromise competing political interests, but the underlying questions of principle and policy certainly cannot be resolved by reference to the unadorned concept of neutrality.

No question in contemporary constitutional law better illustrates this proposition than what constitutes an unconstitutional establishment of religion. The Rehnquist Court has addressed this question several times, but has not yet supplied a clear answer. All of the Justices who disagree with its answer appear to believe they are being religiously neutral, yet their answers differ significantly. Three answers have figured prominently: (1) the government may not take actions that in fact benefit religion (a major part of the pre-Rehnquist Court test and one favored by some current Justices); (2) it may not take actions that amount to active proselytizing for a religion (the test favored by four Justices); and (3) it may not take actions that create the appearance that it is endorsing religion (the test favored by two "swing" Justices and therefore likely in the short run to prove determinative of the outcome of many cases).

These competing visions of neutrality were all at work in *County of Allegheny* v. *American Civil Liberties Union* (1989), where the Court was called on to decide whether either of two Christmas displays by the city of Pittsburgh violated the establishment clause. One was a crèche in the county courthouse, and the other a side-by-side display of a Christmas tree and a menorah in front of a public building. A majority of the Court, apparently pursuing what appeared to five Justices a neutral principle that would simultaneously assure that government does not help or hurt religion too much, applied the "no appearance of endorsement" test, and held the crèche unconstitutional and the other display constitutional. The Court found that the factual context of the first display created the appearance of an endorsement of religion, whereas that of the second created the appearance of a celebration of a winter holiday season. Those Justices who applied the "no benefit in fact" test would have held both displays unconstitutional for their nonneutral favoring of the Christian and Jewish religions. Those who applied the "no proselytizing" test criticized the other opinions for their nonneutral hostility toward religion and would have upheld both because neither coerced anyone to support or participate in a religion.

The establishment clause cases illustrate not only the elusiveness of the "neutrality" concept but also, when read together with the free exercise cases, an asymmetry in Rehnquist Court jurisprudence between racial and religious neutrality apparently reflective of the Court's "mainstream America" predisposition.

With regard to its legitimation function, the neutrality concept operates similarly in race and religion cases: regulations are legitimate even if they produce nonneutral effects, so long as they are facially and purposively neutral. With regard to its restrictive function, however, Rehnquist Court neutrality presumptively prohibits regulations that specially benefit minority races, but permits those that specially benefit religious groups, so long as they do not appear to endorse a religion (or, perhaps, so long as they do not actually proselytize).

The Court has also returned to its earlier view, largely abandoned after the mid-1930s, that the Constitution imposes definite limits on the power of Congress to legislate. We have seen one instance of this in *Boerne (City of)* v. *Flores*. In addition, in *United States* v. *Lopez* (1995), it ruled Congress was without authority to make carrying a gun within 1,000 feet of a school a federal crime. The Court held this activity was not substantially related to commerce so as to be a valid exercise of the commerce power. It noted that criminal law was a traditional area for state legislation, which Congress could only enter where interstate commerce or some other federal interest was involved. Again, in *New York* v. *United States* (1992), the Court ruled that Congress had invaded the states' rights, reserved under the Tenth Amendment, when it enacted a law requiring states to regulate nuclear waste on pain of becoming financially responsible for the waste if they failed to do so. And in *Printz* v. *United States* (1997) it similarly found Congress could not direct state law enforcement officials to conduct background checks of prospective handgun purchasers.

The Rehnquist Court has also pursued its conservative agenda through numerous smaller but cumulatively important doctrinal avenues. One example is the privacy rights doctrine that interferences must be "substantial" before they will be regarded as constitutionally troublesome. Many other examples might be given, but one will suffice: the Court's use in free-speech cases of the threshold public forum concept effectively to

foreclose speech rights on most kinds of public property and its related apparent willingness to accept without serious scrutiny governmentally proffered justifications for regulating speech activities in the few public places where individuals do have the right to engage in expressive activities.

In free speech cases, the Rehnquist Court has been reasonable if sporadically protective of traditional constitutional rights. It has struck down many regulations restricting speech, not only in well-publicized cases, such as those involving flag desecration, see *Texas* v. *Johnson* (1989), but in more mundane settings, such as newsrack placements and handbilling. One area in which it has been less protective, however, concerns the right to engage in expressive activities in public places, a right that has historically been particularly important to the dispossessed who lack the resources to project their views through other media.

The Court's tolerance toward restrictions of speech in public places derives from the Burger Court's legacy, but again, it seems fairly clear that the Rehnquist Court enthusiastically subscribes to the intuitions that informed that legacy. The questions as to whether and to what extent the free speech clause entitles individuals to engage in expressive activity on public property has been implicit in constitutional law for a long time, but for a variety of reasons went largely unaddressed in early cases. The Court was not forced to confront it directly until the mid-1960s, when civil rights demonstrators began to use unconventional sites such as libraries and jails as demonstration locations. The early decisions often rested on unclear reasoning, although for at least a time, the dominant trend was to protect the demonstrators' rights unless the government could prove that the demonstration actually interfered with the normal use of the property.

The Burger Court eventually decided on a tripartite classification of public places and hence speech rights. Streets and parks were labeled "public forums," and speech regulation in these places was "sharply circumscribed." In particular, even so-called content-neutral or "time, place, and manner" restrictions were unconstitutional unless, among other things, they were "narrowly tailored to serve a significant government interest." A second type of public forum consisted of places the government had voluntarily opened for speech purposes, and regulations here were subject to the same constitutional limits. All other kinds of public property were not public forums, and speech activity in such places could be prohibited unless, in substance, the government was simply trying to suppress views it opposed.

Because relatively few places were true public forums and therefore available for speech activities as a matter of right, one important question that remained concerned the circumstances in which the Court would find that property had been voluntarily opened for speech. Additionally, because content-neutral regulation of true public forums is far more common than content-based regulation, the practical effect of these rules on access even to streets and parks depended largely on the circumstances in which the Court would find that "time, place, and manner" regulations were adequately "narrowly tailored."

The current answers to these questions come largely from Rehnquist Court decisions and are not very speech protective. With regard to voluntarily opened forums, the main case is *Hazelwood School District* v. *Kuhlmeier* (1988), where the Court upheld the authority of public school officials to censor from a student newspaper articles about student pregnancy and the effect of divorce on students. Although the Court might have decided the case as it did on alternative grounds, its decision suggests that the category of voluntarily opened forums is a very small if not an empty one. It held that the newspaper was not such

R

a forum because school officials had retained curricularly based editorial rights; therefore, even though the paper had always been open to the student body at large to submit opinions and articles, it had not been opened for general student speech purposes. The same theory would seem available for a wide variety of public property. Managers of public auditoriums, for example, might make their facilities broadly available, but retain the right to exclude certain subject matters (although perhaps not viewpoints). After *Hazelwood,* the Court, in this same vein, held in *United States* v. *Kokinda* (1990) that handbilling and fund solicitation on the sidewalk leading from a parking lot to a post office could be banned because the sidewalk was neither a true nor opened public forum, having been built for post office business purposes. And a narrowly divided Court later ruled, in *International Society for Krishna Consciousness* v. *Lee* (1992), that a publicly owned airport was not a public forum, and could restrict solicitation, though not the handing out of leaflets.

The most important case on the related question of when a content-neutral regulation is sufficiently "narrowly tailored" to survive constitutional attack is *Ward* v. *Rock Against Racism* (1989), where the Court appeared to hold that this requirement is met so long as the government can accomplish its goal better with the regulation at issue than without it. The Court did say that a regulation may not burden speech more than is necessary to accomplish the government's legitimate goal, but it simultaneously rejected the view that the government must use the means that would accomplish its goal with the least restriction of speech; it is unclear how these two propositions can coexist. For example, a ban on all picketing on a certain sidewalk would be more effective in accomplishing the goal of pedestrian free movement than no ban would. Thus, it would seem to be constitutional under *Ward,* unless

it burdens speech more than is necessary; if it does so, it would seem that this is because pedestrian free movement could have been assured by means that are less restrictive of speech. How *Ward* will ultimately be interpreted is uncertain, but if one takes seriously the idea that any contribution toward a goal validates a content-neutral regulation—and related decisions of the Rehnquist Court suggest that it does take this idea seriously—the Court will have given speech rights so little weight in the balance that virtually all non-content-based restrictions on access, even to true public forums, will survive constitutional attack.

A final important free-speech decision by the Rehnquist Court, *R.A.V.* v. *City of St. Paul* (1992), struck down an ordinance prohibiting cross-burning or other symbols or objects "arous[ing] anger, alarm or resentment" based on race, religion, or gender. The law was clearly overbroad in its attempt to outlaw fighting words, and the four concurring justices so ruled. However, the majority found the ordinance unconstitutional because it improperly discriminated among categories of fighting words, proscribing only those based on race, religion, or gender, and not those that might be based on political views, for example.

The Rehnquist Court has narrowed the ability of litigants to assert constitutional claims by limiting the standing required in order for one to invoke the federal courts' jurisdiction. It has found in a series of cases that plaintiffs did not have sufficient standing to show that a "case" or "controversy" existed to furnish court jurisdiction under Article III of the Constitution.

In addition, the Court has broadened the concept of an unconstitutional "taking" in order to protect property rights, holding in several cases that laws regulating land use deprived the property owner of various attributes of ownership in violation of the Constitution. Most recently, in *Eastern En-*

terprises v. *Apfel* (1998), the Court invalidated a federal law requiring companies that had operated coal mines to be responsible for health benefits for their former employees. In short, while narrowing the scope of fundamental rights such as privacy, the Rehnquist Court has augmented the rights of property owners to be free of government regulation.

In the criminal procedure area the Rehnquist Court has continued in the direction set by its predecessor in cabining the Warren Court's expansive decisions. The Court has upheld death sentences in numerous cases, sustained forfeitures of vehicles, funds and other property used in connection with criminal activity, and upheld searches and drug testing.

—LARRY G. SIMON

Bibliography

Abrams, J. Marc, and Goodman, S. Mark (1988). End of an Era? The Decline of Student Press Rights in the Wake of *Hazelwood School District* v. *Kuhlmeier. Duke Law Journal* 1988:706–732.

Constitutional Scholars' Statement on Affirmative Action After *City of Richmond* v. *J. A. Croson Co.* 1988 *Yale Law Journal* 98:1711–1716.

Estrich, Susan R., and Sullivan, Kathleen M. (1989). Abortion Politics: Writing for an Audience of One. *University of Pennsylvania Law Review* 138:119–155.

Fried, Charles (1989). Affirmative Action After *City of Richmond* v. *J. A. Croson Co.*: A Response to the Scholars' Statement. *Yale Law Journal* 99:155–161.

Karst, Kenneth L. (1989). Private Discrimination and Public Responsibility: *Patterson* in Context. *Supreme Court Review* 1989: 1–51.

Soifer, Aviam (1989). Moral Ambition, Formalism, and the "Free World" of *DeShaney. George Washington Law Review* 57: 1513–1532.

Tushnet, Mark (1988). The Emerging Principle of Accommodation of Religion (Dubitante). *Georgetown Law Journal* 76: 1691–1714.

R

REHNQUIST COURT

(1986–)

The Reitman *decision implies an affirmative state obligation to protect against private racial discrimination in housing.*

REITMAN v. MULKEY

387 U.S. 369 (1967)

By an overwhelming majority, California's voters adopted an initiative measure ("Proposition 14") adding to the state constitution a provision repealing existing open housing laws and forbidding the enactment of new ones. Following the lead of the state supreme court, the Supreme Court held, 5–4, that the circumstances of Proposition 14's adoption demonstrated state encouragement of private racial discrimination in the sale and rental of housing. Justice Byron R. White, for the majority, said this encouragement amounted to state action in violation of the Fourteenth Amendment. Justice John Marshall Harlan, for the dissenters, argued that Proposition 14 merely withdrew the state from regulation of private conduct; the state court determinations of "encouragement" were not fact findings, but mistaken readings of the Supreme Court's own precedents.

Taken seriously, the *Reitman* decision implies an affirmative state obligation to protect against private racial discrimination in housing. The Supreme Court, far from reading the decision in this manner, has consistently rejected litigants' efforts even to invoke the "encouragement" doctrine there announced. *Reitman* thus lies in isolation, awaiting resurrection. But the trumpet call announcing the end of the world of state action doctrine, seemingly so close in the final years of the Warren Court, now seems far away.

—KENNETH L. KARST

R

The Supreme Court invalidated a provision making the Uniform Code of Military Justice applicable to civilians accompanying the armed forces abroad.

Werhan, Keith (1987). The O'Briening of Free Speech Methodology. *Arizona State Law Review* 19:635–679.

REID v. COVERT
KINSELLA v. KRUEGER

354 U.S. 1 (1957)

In a 6–2 decision, the Supreme Court invalidated a provision making the Uniform Code of Military Justice applicable to civilians accompanying the armed forces abroad, and reversed the court-martial convictions of two women who had murdered their servicemen husbands on military bases overseas.

Justice Hugo L. Black, for a plurality, held that neither the power to make rules for governing the armed forces nor any international agreement could free the government from the procedural requirements of Article III, Section 2, and the Fifth and Sixth Amendments.

—DENNIS J. MAHONEY

RELIGION IN
PUBLIC SCHOOLS

Despite several Supreme Court decisions on religion in public schools, conflict in this area has proliferated in recent years. One example is the discord that persists over the teaching of evolution. In *Epperson* v. *Arkansas* (1968) the Court struck down a statute prohibiting the teaching of evolution. In *Edwards* v. *Aguillard* (1987) the Court invalidated a Louisiana statute requiring that "creation science" be given equal exposure in public schools where evolution is taught. (Among other things, creation science teaches that plants and animals were created substantially as they now exist.) The majority reasoned that the statute was intended to promote the biblical version of creation or to hamper the teaching of evolution for religious reasons. However, the Court did not hold that teaching creationism is unconstitutional.

In several cases, religious parents have tried to turn the Court's expansive interpretation of the establishment clause to their advantage by alleging that public schools were unconstitutionally establishing a religion of secular humanism. Although the Supreme Court has not tackled this issue, the lower federal courts have uniformly rejected these claims. These results seem appropriate. The Supreme Court has stated that nontheistic faiths, including secular humanism, can qualify as First Amendment religions. However, if secular humanism is defined narrowly enough to be a specific religion, the public schools are not establishing it, for they promote no particular dogma or rituals. In contrast, if secular humanism is defined broadly enough to include the education given in public schools, it ceases to be a religion for First Amendment purposes. A contrary conclusion would impel the untenable result that virtually any secular enthusiasm, such as music, art, or sports, would be considered a religion and thus barred from the public schools.

This conclusion does not end all controversy, however; parents often charge that teaching in public schools is inimical to their religious beliefs and therefore violates their right to free exercise of religion. The Supreme Court has not yet dealt with this issue, and its pronouncements elsewhere offer little guidance. The Court has often stated that a substantial burden of free exercise can be justified only by a compelling state interest pursued by the least restrictive means. Public schools have denied that their teaching burdens free exercise at all because their teaching is secular, not religious; children need not accept what is taught, and children are not compelled to attend public schools, but are free to attend private schools. Dissatisfied parents reply that free exercise is burdened if children are taught that their religion is wrong, although the children do not have to profess acceptance of the schools' teaching, and although others consider the issues in question secular. These parents stress that young impressionable children may not understand that they are free to reject the school's teaching or may be too intimidated to express their disagreement. They also argue that the option of attending private schools is too expensive to remove the burden on free exercise.

Even if the curriculum does burden free exercise, public schools claim a compelling state interest in giving all children this education. Most observers concede that states have an interest in teaching basic skills such as reading and writing. However, it is debatable how important the state's interest is in other areas, including moral values and sex education. If a public school does burden free exercise without compelling justification, some accommodation of the religious students may be necessary as a remedy. Many school systems excuse students from certain programs to which they have religious objections, and some schools provide students with alternative instruction. The latter approach can be expensive and administratively burdensome; the former may prevent the child from obtaining essential skills. Suggestions that children be given vouchers to attend private schools, meanwhile, have been attacked as both violative of the establishment clause and destructive of the objectives of public education.

The legal need for accommodation may no longer be as pressing as it once was, however. The Supreme Court has indicated in *Employment Division, Department of Human Resources of Oregon* v. *Smith* (1990) that it has abandoned the "compelling state interest" standard. If the Court adheres to this position, public schools would not be constitutionally required to show a compelling reason for subjecting children to teaching that is hostile to their religion.

In addition to controversies over school curriculum, disputes have also multiplied over the use of public school facilities by student religious groups. In *Widmar* v. *Vincent* (1981), the Supreme Court insisted that public university facilities generally available to student groups and speakers also be open to student religious groups. In 1984 Congress tried to extend this principle to secondary schools by adopting the Equal Access Act, which forbids public secondary schools from discriminating on the basis of the content of speech when affording student groups access to school facilities outside school hours. However, the school may not sponsor, and school employees may not participate in, student religious groups.

Some critics believed that the act was unconstitutional because of the possibility that school employees would become involved and that students would perceive the provision of facilities to student religious groups as endorsing religion. The Court disagreed in *Board of Education of Westside Community Schools* v. *Mergens* (1990), holding that the act did not violate the establishment clause.

Although the Court has repeatedly struck down daily school prayers, many schools have included prayers or benedictions in special school events. The Supreme Court has upheld the opening of legislative sessions with prayers in *Marsh* v. *Chambers* (1983), but the differences in the public school context have persuaded some lower courts that the practice cannot be permitted there.

The Supreme Court has said that public schools may study the Bible as literature and history, but not for devotional purposes. This has required lower courts to decide case by case whether particular programs meet this standard or improperly include religious indoctrination. In *Wallace* v. *Jaffree* (1985) the Court annulled state law mandating a moment of silence "for meditation or voluntary prayer" in public schools. It found the legislative history and actual practice under this law were a mask for reintroducing daily school prayers, though the opinion leaves room for a genuine moment-of-silence requirement.

Public school teachers occasionally endorse or criticize religious beliefs in the classroom. Courts generally have tried to distinguish between teachers' statements of their own be-

Colonial schools established on the American shores naturally reflected a religious orientation.

liefs, which are permissible and protected by the rights of free speech and free exercise, and propagandizing, which infringes on both the students' right of free exercise and the establishment clause. Lower courts have also upheld regulations against teachers' regularly wearing distinctively religious garb. And the Court has held a member of the clergy's invocation at a public school graduation was in violation of the First Amendment.

—GEORGE W. DENT

Bibliography

Dent, George W. (1988). Religious Children, Secular Schools. *Southern California Law Review* 61:863–941.

Strossen, Nadine (1986). "Secular Humanism" and "Scientific Creationism": Proposed Standards for Reviving Curricular Decisions Affecting Students' Religious Freedom. *Ohio State Law Journal* 47: 333–407.

RELIGIOUS LIBERTY

Although the First Amendment's mandate that "Congress shall make no law respecting an establishment of religion, or prohibiting the free exercise thereof" is expressed in unconditional language, religious liberty, insofar as it extends beyond belief, is not an absolute right. The First Amendment, the Supreme Court said in *Cantwell* v. *Connecticut* (1940), "embraces two concepts—freedom to believe and freedom to act. The first is absolute but, in the nature of things, the second cannot be. Conduct remains subject to regulation of society."

Although the Court has repeated this dualism many times, it does not explain what the free exercise clause means. There is no need for a constitutional guarantee protecting freedom to believe, for, as the common law had it, "the devil himself knows not the thoughts of man." Even if freedom to believe encompasses freedom to express what one

believes, the clause adds nothing, since freedom of speech and freedom of the press are specifically guaranteed in the amendment. Indeed, before *Cantwell* was decided, the Court applied the free speech rather than free exercise guarantee to challenges against state laws allegedly impinging upon religious liberty. Moreover, the word "exercise" connotes action or conduct, thus indicating that the framers had in mind something beyond the mere expression of a belief even if uttered in missionary activities.

In America the roots of religious liberty can be traced to Roger Williams, whose pamphlet "The Bloudy Tenent of Persecution for cause of Conscience, discussed in a Conference between Truth and Peace" asserted that it was God's command that "a permission of the most Paganish, Jewish, Turkish, or Antichristian consciences and worships, be granted to all men in all Nations and Countries." Another source was Thomas Jefferson's Virginia Statute of Religious Liberty, adopted in 1786, which declared that no person should be compelled to frequent or support any religious worship nor suffer on account of religious opinions and beliefs.

By the time the First Amendment became part of the Constitution in 1791, practically every state in the Union, to a greater or lesser degree, had enacted constitutional or statutory provisions securing the free exercise of religion. Indeed, it was the absence of a Bill of Rights whose proponents invariably called for a guarantee of religious freedom, that was the most frequently asserted objection to the Constitution presented to the states for approval. The necessary approval was obtained only because the Constitution's advocates promised that such a bill would be added by amendment after the Constitution was adopted.

Although the First Amendment was framed as a limitation of congressional powers, Supreme Court decisions have made it clear that executive and judicial action were likewise restricted by the amendment. Thus

See also

Compelling State Interest

Employment Division,
Department of Human
Resources of Oregon v.
Smith

Establishment of Religion

in *Anderson* v. *Laird* (1971) the Supreme Court refused to review a decision that the secretary of defense violated the First Amendment in requiring cadets in governmental military academies to attend chapel. As to the judiciary, unquestionably a federal court could not constitutionally disqualify a person from testifying as a witness because he was an atheist.

Since the Court's decision in *Cantwell* the states are subject to the restrictions of the free exercise clause no less than the federal government. Because our federal system leaves to the states what is generally called the police power, there were few occasions, prior to *Cantwell,* when the Supreme Court was called upon to define the meaning of the clause. The few that did arise involved actions in the territories, which were subject to federal laws and thus to the First Amendment. Most significant of these was *Reynolds* v. *United States* (1879), wherein the Supreme Court upheld the constitutionality of an act of Congress criminalizing polygamy in any American territory. In rejecting the defense that polygamy was mandated by doctrines of the Holy Church of Latter-Day Saints (Mormons) and thus was protected by the free exercise clause, the Court stated what was later echoed in *Cantwell,* that although laws "cannot interfere with mere religious belief, they may with practice." It could hardly be contended, the Court continued, that the free exercise clause barred prosecution of persons who engaged in human sacrifice as a necessary part of their religious worship.

Since Reynolds was charged with practicing polygamy, the Court's decision did not pass upon the question whether teaching it as a God-mandated duty was "mere religious belief" and therefore beyond governmental interference. In *Davis* v. *Beason* (1890) the Court decided that such teaching was "practice," and therefore constitutionally subject to governmental restrictions.

Teaching or preaching, even if deemed action, is however not beyond all First Amendment protection, which encompasses freedom of speech as well as religion. In *Gitlow* v. *New York* (1925) the Supreme Court declared for the first time that the free speech guarantee of the First Amendment was incorporated into the Fourteenth Amendment by virtue of the due process clause in the latter and thus was applicable to the states. Accordingly, the Jehovah's Witnesses cases that first came to the Court in the 1930s were initially decided under the speech rather than the religion clause (*Lovell* v. *Griffin,* 1938; *Schneider* v. *Irvington,* 1939). It was, therefore, natural for the Court to decide the cases under the clear and present danger test that had first been announced in *Schenck* v. *United States* (1919), a case involving prosecution for speaking against United States involvement in World War I.

In another sense, this too was quite natural since, like Schenck, the Witnesses were pacifists, at least in respect to wars in this world. (In *Sicurella* v. *United States* the Court in 1955 ruled that a member of the sect was not disqualified from conscientious objector exemption because the sect's doctrines encompassed participation by believers in serving as soldiers in the Army of Christ Jesus at Armageddon.) Nevertheless, unlike Schenck and other opponents to American entry in World War I, the Witnesses (like the Friends) did not vocally oppose American entry into the war but limited themselves to claiming conscientious objection status.

The Court did not apply the clear and present danger test in a case involving a member of the Jehovah's Witnesses whose child was expelled from public school for refusing to participate in the patriotic program of flag salute. In that case, *Minersville School District* v. *Gobitis* (1940), the Court, in an opinion by Justice Felix Frankfurter, rejected the assertion as a defense of religious freedom. The antipolygamy law, he stated, was upheld in *Reynolds* not because it concerned action rather than belief, but because it was a valid general law, regulating the secular practice of marriage.

The majority of the Court, however, soon concluded that *Gobitis* had been incorrectly decided, and three years later the Court overruled it in *West Virginia State Board of Education* v. *Barnette* (1943). There the Court treated the Witnesses' refusal to salute the flag as a form of speech and therefore subject to the clear and present danger test. In later decisions, the Court returned to *Cantwell* and treated religious freedom cases under the free exercise rather than free speech clause, although it continued to apply the clear and present danger test.

Unsatisfied with that test, Justice Frankfurter prevailed upon his colleagues to accept a differently worded rule, that of balancing competing interests, also taken from Court decisions relating to other freedoms secured in the Bill of Rights. When a person complains that his constitutional rights have been infringed by some law or action of the state, it is the responsibility of the courts to weigh the importance of the particular right in issue as against the state's interest upon which its law or action is based. For example, the right of an objector not to violate his religious conscience by engaging in war must be weighed against the nation's interest in defending itself against foreign enemies, and, in such weighing, the latter interest may be adjudged the weightier.

The majority of the Court accepted this rule, but in recent years it has added an element that has almost turned it around. Justice Frankfurter believed that a citizen who challenged the constitutionality of state action had the burden of convincing the court that his interest was more important than the state's and should therefore be adjudged paramount. Establishing an individual's right superior to the state's interest was a particularly heavy burden to carry, but it was made even heavier by Justice Frankfurter's insistence that any doubt as to relative weights must be resolved in favor of the state, which would prevail unless its action were patently unreasonable. Recently, however, the Court has taken a more libertarian approach, requiring the state to persuade the courts that the values it seeks to protect are weightier. In the language of the decisions, the state must establish that there is a compelling state interest that justifies infringement of the citizen's right to the free exercise of his religion. If it fails to do so, its law or action will be adjudged unconstitutional.

In accord with this rule, the Court, in the 1972 case of *Wisconsin* v. *Yoder*, expressly rejected the belief-action test, holding that Amish parents could not be prosecuted for refusing to send their children to school after they had reached the age of fourteen. "Only those interests of the highest order," the Court said, "and those not otherwise served can overbalance the legitimate claim to the free exercise of religion."

Religious liberty is protected not only by the free exercise clause but also by the clause against establishments of religion. In *Everson* v. *Board of Education* (1947) and later cases, the Court has stated that under the establishment clause, government cannot force a person to go to church or profess a belief in any religion. In later decisions, the Court has applied a three-pronged purpose-effect-entanglement test as a standard of constitutionality under the establishment clause. The Court has held, in *Committee for Public Education and Religious Liberty* v. *Nyquist* (1973), for example, that a challenged statute must have a primary effect that neither advances nor inhibits religion, and must avoid government entanglement with religion.

The Supreme Court's decisions in the arena of conflict between governmental concerns and individuals' claims to religious liberty can be considered in relation to the four categories suggested by the Preamble to the Constitution: national defense, domestic tranquillity, the establishment of justice, and general welfare. In resolving the issues before it in these decisions the Court has spoken in terms of clear and present danger, balancing of competing interests, or determination of compelling governmental interests, depending upon the date of the decision rendered.

Probably no interest of the government is deemed more important than defense against a foreign enemy. Individual liberties secured by the Constitution must yield when the nation's safety is in peril. As the Court ruled in the *Selective Draft Law Cases* (1918), the prohibition by the Thirteenth Amendment of involuntary servitude was not intended to override the nation's power to conscript an army of—if necessary—unwilling soldiers, without which even the most just and defensive war cannot be waged.

By the same token, exemption of Quakers and others whose religious conscience forbids them to engage in military service cannot be deemed a constitutional right but only a privilege accorded by Congress and thus subject to revocation at any time Congress deems that to be necessary for national defense. However, even in such a case, Congress must exercise its power within the limitations prescribed by the First Amendment's mandate of neutrality among religions and by the equal protection component of the Fifth Amendment's due process clause. Hence, in exercising its discretion, Congress could not constitutionally prefer some long-standing pacifist religions over others more recently established.

Exemption of specific classes—the newly betrothed, the newly married, the fainthearted, and others—goes back as far as Mosaic times (Deuteronomy 20:1–8). Since all biblical wars were theocratic, there was no such thing as religious exemption. In England, Oliver Cromwell believed that those whose religious doctrine forbade participation in armed conflict should constitute an exempt class. So too did the legislatures in some of the American colonies, the Continental Congress, and a number of the members of the Congress established under the Constitution. Madison's original draft of what became the Second Amendment included a provision exempting religious objectors from compulsory militia duty; but that provision was deleted before Congress proposed the amendment to the states. The first national measure exempting conscientious objectors was adopted by Congress during the Civil War; like its colonial and state precedents, it was limited to members of well-recognized religious denominations whose articles of faith forbade the bearing of arms.

The Selective Service Act of 1917 exempted members of recognized denominations or sects, such as the Friends, Mennonites, and Seventh-Day Adventists, whose doctrine and discipline declared military service sinful. The 1940 act liberalized the requirements for exemption to encompass anyone who by "reason of religious training and belief" possessed conscientious scruples against "participation in war in any form." In 1948, however, the 1940 act was further amended, first, to exclude those whose objection to war was based on "essentially political, sociological or philosophical views or a mere personal code," and second, to define religion as a belief in a "Supreme Being."

In view of the Court's holding in *Torcaso* v. *Watkins* (1961) that the Constitution did not sanction preferential treatment of theistic religions over other faiths, limitation of exemption to persons who believe in a "Supreme Being" raised establishment clause issues. In *United States* v. *Seeger* (1965) the Court avoided these issues by interpreting the statute to encompass a person who possessed a sincere belief occupying a place in the life of its possessor parallel to that filled by the orthodox belief in God of one who clearly qualified for the exemption. Applying this definition to the three cases before it, the Court held that Selective Service boards had erroneously denied exemption: to one who expressed a "belief in and devotion to goodness and virtues for their own sakes, and a religious faith in a purely ethical creed"; to another who rejected a relationship "vertically towards Godness directly," but was committed to relationship "horizontally towards Godness through Mankind and the

Teaching or preaching, even if deemed action, is not beyond all First Amendment protection.

World"; and to a third who defined religion as "the supreme expression of human nature," encompassing "man thinking his highest, feeling his deepest, and living his best."

Because exemption of conscientious exemption is of legislative rather than constitutional origin, Congress may condition exemption on possession of belief forbidding participation in all wars, excluding those whose objection is selective and forbids participation only in what they personally deem unjust wars, such as that in Vietnam. The Court sustained such an act of Congress in *Gillette* v. *United States* (1971). However, independent of any statutory exemption, the Court held in *Thomas* that, at least in peacetime, disqualification of a person from unemployment insurance benefits for conscientious refusal to accept an offered job in a plant that manufactured arms violated the free exercise clause.

Closely related to military service as an aspect of national defense is national unity, cultural as well as political. The relevant constitutional issues reached the Supreme Court in 1923 in three cases involving Lutheran and Reformed schools, and, two years later, in two cases involving a Roman Catholic parochial and a nonsectarian private school. The former cases, reflecting post–World War I hostility to German-speaking Americans, were decided by the Court in *Meyer* v. *Nebraska* (1923) and two companion cases. These involved the conviction of teachers of German who violated statutes forbidding the teaching of a foreign language to pupils before they had completed eight grades of elementary schooling. The Court, in reversing the convictions, relied not only on the constitutional right of German teachers to pursue a gainful occupation not inherently evil or dangerous to the welfare of the community, but also the right of parents to have their children taught "Martin Luther's language" so that they might better understand "Martin Luther's dogma." The cases were decided long before the Court held that the free exercise clause was incorporated in the Fourteenth Amendment's due process

clause and therefore were technically based upon the teachers' due process right to earn a livelihood and the parents' due process right to govern the upbringing of their children.

In *Pierce* v. *Society of Sisters* and its companion case, *Pierce* v. *Hill Military Academy* (1925), the Court invalidated a compulsory education act that required all children, with limited exceptions, to attend only public schools. A single opinion, governing both cases, relied upon *Meyer* v. *Nebraska* and based the decision invalidating the law on the due process clause as it related to the school owners' contractual rights and the parents' right to control their children's education, rather than to the free exercise rights of teachers, parents, or pupils. Nevertheless, since the Court's ruling in *Cantwell* that the free exercise clause was applicable to the states, *Pierce* has often been cited by lawyers, scholars, and courts as a free exercise case, and particularly one establishing the constitutional rights of churches to operate parochial schools. Had *Pierce* been decided after *Cantwell* it is probable that free exercise would have been invoked as an additional ground in respect to the Society of Sisters' claim; the opinion as written did note that the child was not the mere creature of the state and that those who nurtured him and directed his destiny had the right, coupled with the high duty, to recognize and prepare him for additional obligations.

Reference has already been made to the Supreme Court's decision in *West Virginia State Board of Education* v. *Barnette* upholding the First Amendment right of Jehovah's Witnesses public school pupils to refrain from participating in flag salute exercises, although there the Court predicated its decision on the free speech rather than the free exercise mandate of the Amendment.

Jehovah's Witnesses' creed and conduct affected not only national defense through pacifism and alleged failure to pay respect to the flag but also governmental concern with domestic tranquillity. What aggravated hostility to the sect beyond its supposed lack of patriotism were its militant proselytizing methods, encompassing verbal attacks on organized religion in general and Roman Catholicism in particular. In their 1931 convention the Witnesses declared their mission to be "to inform the rulers and the people of and concerning Satan's cruel and oppressive organization, and particularly with reference to Christiandom, which is the most visible part of that visible organization." God's purpose was to destroy Satan's organization and bring quickly "to the obedient peoples of the earth peace and prosperity, liberty and health, happiness and life."

This is hardly new or surprising. Practically every new religion, from Judaism through Christianity and Islam to the present, has been predicated upon attacks against existing faiths; indeed, this is implied in the very term "Protestant." Clearly, those who wrote the First Amendment intended it to encompass attacks upon existing religions. (In *Burstyn* v. *Wilson*, 1952, the Court invalidated a statute banning "sacrilegious" films.) Attacks on existing religions are almost invariably met with counterattacks, physical as well as verbal, by defenders of the accepted faiths.

The assaults upon the Jehovah's Witnesses were particularly widespread and intense for a number of reasons. Their conduct enraged many who felt that their refusal to salute the flag was unpatriotic, if not treasonous. Their attacks upon the Christian religion infuriated many others. The evidence in *Taylor* v. *Mississippi* (1943), for example, included a pamphlet suggesting that the Roman Catholic Church was responsible for flag saluting. The book *Religion,* by the Witnesses' first leader, Charles T. Russell, described their operations: "God's faithful servants go from house to house to bring the message of the kingdom to those who reside there, omitting none, not even the houses of the Roman Catholic hierarchy, and there they give witness to the kingdom because they are commanded by the Most High to do so. . . . They do not loot nor break into the houses, but they set up their phonographs before the doors and windows and send the message of the kingdom right into the ears of those who might wish to hear; and while those desiring to hear are hearing, some of the 'sourpusses' are compelled to hear."

The predictably resulting resort to violence and to law for the suppression of the Witnesses' activities gave rise to a host of Supreme Court decisions defining for the first time both the breadth and the limitations of the free exercise clause (and also, to some extent, the free speech clause). Most of the Jehovah's Witnesses cases were argued before the Supreme Court by Hayden Covington; his perseverance, as well as that of his client, was manifested by the fact that before *Minersville School District* v. *Gobitis* was decided, the Court had rejected his appeals in flag salute cases four times. The Court had accepted jurisdiction in *Gobitis,* as well as its successor *Barnette,* because, notwithstanding these previous rejections, the lower courts had decided both cases in the Witnesses' favor.

The Witnesses were not the only persons whose aggressive missionary endeavors and verbal attacks upon other faiths led to governmental actions that were challenged as a violation of the free exercise clause and were defended as necessary to secure domestic tranquillity. In *Kunz* v. *New York* (1951), the Court held that a Baptist preacher could not be denied renewal of a permit for evangelical street meetings because his preachings, scurrilously attacking Roman Catholicism and Judaism, had led to disorder in the streets. The Court said that appropriate public remedies existed to protect the peace and order of the communities if the sermons should result in violence, but it held that these remedies did not include prior restraint under an ordinance that provided no standards for the licensing official.

Jehovah's Witnesses were the major claimants to religious liberty in the two decades between 1935 and 1955. During that period they brought to the Supreme Court a large number of cases challenging the application to them of a variety of laws forbidding disturbing the peace, peddling, the use of soundtrucks, as well as traffic regulations, child labor laws, and revenue laws.

In *Cantwell* v. *Connecticut* (1940) the Court held that the First Amendment guaranteed the right to teach and preach religion in the public streets and parks and to solicit contributions or purchases of religious materials. Although a prior municipal permit might be required, its grant or denial might not be based upon the substance of what is taught, preached, or distributed but only upon the need to regulate, in the interests of traffic control, the time, place, and manner of public meetings. In *Cox* v. *New Hampshire* (1940) the Court ruled that religious liberty encompassed the right to engage in religious processions, although a fee might be imposed to cover the expenses of administration and maintenance of public order. The Constitution, however, does not immunize from prosecution persons who in their missionary efforts use expressions that are lewd, obscene, libelous, insulting, or that contain "fighting" words which by their very utterance, the Court declared in *Chaplinsky* v. *New Hampshire* (1942), inflict injury or tend to incite an immediate breach of the peace. The Constitution also secures the right to distribute religious handbills in streets and at publicly owned railroad or bus terminals, according to the decision in *Jamison* v. *Texas* (1943), and, according to *Martin* v. *City of Struthers* (1943), to ring doorbells in order to offer house occupants religious literature although, of course, not to force oneself into the house for that purpose.

Related to the domestic tranquillity aspects of Jehovah's Witnesses claims to use public streets and parks are the claims of other feared or unpopular minority religious groups (often referred to as "sects" or, more recently, "cults") to free exercise in publicly owned areas. In *Heffron* v. *International Society for Krishna Consciousness (ISKCON)* (1981) the Court held that a state rule limiting to specific booths the sale or distribution of merchandise, including printed material, on public fair grounds did not violate the free exercise clause when applied to members of ISKCON whose ritual required its members to go into all public places to distribute or sell its religious literature and to solicit donations.

Discriminatory treatment, however, is not constitutionally permissible. Thus, in *Cruz* v. *Beto* (1972) the Supreme Court upheld the claim of a Buddhist prisoner in Texas that his constitutional rights were violated by denying him use of the prison chapel, punishing him for sharing his Buddhist religious materials with other prisoners, and denying him other privileges, such as receiving points for attendance at religious services, which enhanced a prisoner's eligibility for early parole consideration. While a prisoner obviously cannot enjoy the free exercise of religion to the same extent as nonprisoners, the Court said, he is protected by the free exercise clause subject only to the necessities of prison security and discipline, and he may not be discriminated against simply because his religious belief is unorthodox. This does not mean that every sect within a prison, no matter how few in number, must have identical facilities or personnel; but reasonable opportunities must be afforded to all persons to exercise their religion without penalty.

One of the most difficult problems facing a court arises when it is called upon to decide between free exercise and the state's interest in preventing fraud. The leading case on the subject is *United States* v. *Ballard* (1944), which involved a prosecution for mail fraud. The indictment charged that the defendants, organizers of the "I Am" cult, had mulcted money from elderly and ill people by falsely representing that they had supernatural powers to heal and that they themselves had communicated personally with Heaven and with Jesus Christ.

The Court held that the free exercise clause would be violated if the state were allowed to seek to prove to a jury that the defendants' representations were false. Neither a jury nor any other organ of government had power to decide whether asserted religious experiences actually occurred. Courts, however, could constitutionally determine whether the defendant himself believed that what he recounted was true, and if a jury determined that he did not, they could convict him of obtaining money under false pretenses. The difficulty with this test, as Justice Robert H. Jackson noted in his dissenting opinion, is that prosecutions in cases such as *Ballard* could easily degenerate into religious persecution; juries would find it difficult to accept as believed that which, by reason of their own religious upbringing, they deemed unbelievable.

In providing for "affirmation" as an alternative to "oath" in Article II, section 1, and Article VI, section 3, the framers of the Constitution, recognizing that religious convictions might forbid some persons (specifically Quakers) to take oaths, manifested their intention that no person in the judicial system—judge, lawyer, court official, or juryman—should be disqualified from governmental service on the ground of religion. In *Torcaso* v. *Watkins* (1961) the Court reached the same conclusion under the First Amendment as to state officials (for example, notaries public), and in *In re Jenison* (1963), the Court refused to uphold a conviction for contempt of court of a woman who would not serve on a jury because of the biblical command "Judge not that ye not be judged."

Resort to secular courts for resolution of intrachurch disputes (generally involving ownership and control of church assets) raises free exercise as well as establishment problems. As early as 1872 the Court held in *Watson* v. *Jones* that judicial intervention in such controversies was narrowly limited: a court could do no more than determine and enforce the decision of that body within the church that was the highest judicatory body according to appropriate church law. If a religious group (such as Baptist and Jewish) were congregational in structure, that body would be the majority of the congregation; if it were hierarchical (such as Roman Catholic or Russian Orthodox), the authority would generally be the diocesan bishop.

That principle was applied by the Supreme Court consistently until *Jones* v. *Wolf* (1979). There the court held that "neutral principles of law developed for use in all property disputes" could constitutionally be applied in church schism litigation. This means that unless the corporate charter or deeds of title provide that the faction loyal to the hierarchical church will retain ownership of the property, such a controversy must be adjudicated in accordance with the laws applicable to corporations generally, so that if recorded title is in the name of the local church, the majority of that body is entitled to control its use and disposition. The Court rejected the assertion in the dissenting opinion that a rule of compulsory deference to the highest ecclesiastical tribunal is necessary in order to protect the free exercise of those who formed the association and submitted themselves to its authority.

Where a conflict exists between the health of the community and the religious conscience of an individual or group, there is little doubt that the free exercise clause does not mandate risk to the community. Thus, as the Court held in *Jacobson* v. *Massachusetts* (1905), compulsory vaccination against communicable diseases is enforceable notwithstanding religious objections to the procedure. So, too, fluoridation of municipal water supplies to prevent tooth cavities cannot be enjoined because of objection by some that drinking fluoridated water is sinful.

Where the life, health, or safety of individuals, rather than communities at large, is involved the constitutional principles are also fairly clear. When the individuals are children, a court may authorize blood transfusions to save their lives notwithstanding objection by parents (such as Jehovah's Witnesses) who believe that the procedure violates the biblical command against the drinking of blood. The underlying principle was stated by the Court in *Prince* v. *Massachusetts* (1944) upholding the conviction of a Jehovah's Witness for violating the state's child labor law in allowing her nine-year-old niece to accompany and help her while she sold the sect's religious literature on the city's streets. "Parents," the Court said, "may be free to become martyrs themselves. But it does not follow that they are free, in identical circumstances, to make martyrs of their children before they have reached the age of full and legal discretion when they can make that choice for themselves." It follows from this that unless mental incompetence is proved, a court may not authorize a blood transfusion upon an unconsenting adult.

The Court also balances competing interests in determining the constitutionality of enforcing compulsory Sunday laws against those whom religious conscience forbids labor or trade on the seventh rather than the first day of the week. In *McGowan* v. *Maryland* and *Two Guys from Harrison-Allentown* v. *McGinley* (1961) the Court upheld the general validity of such laws against an establishment clause attack. Although their origin may have been religious, the Court said, the laws' present purpose was secular: to assure a weekly day for rest, relaxation, and family companionship.

Two other cases, *Gallagher* v. *Crown Kosher Super Market* (1961) and *Braunfeld* v. *Brown* (1961), decided at the same time, involved Orthodox Jews who observed Saturday as their day of rest and refrained from business on that day. In these cases the Court rejected the argument that requiring a Sabbatarian either to abstain from engaging in his trade or business two days weekly or to sacrifice his religious conscience, while requiring his Sunday-observing competitors to abstain only one day, imposed upon the Sabbatarian a competitive disadvantage, thereby penalizing him for his religious beliefs in violation of the free exercise clause. Exempting Sabbatarians, the Court held, might be administratively difficult, might benefit non-Sabbatarians motivated only by a desire for a competitive advantage over merchants closing on Sundays, and might frustrate the legitimate legislative goal of assuring a uniform day of rest. Although state legislatures could constitutionally elect to grant an exemption to Sab-

batarians, the free exercise clause does not require them to do so.

In *Sherbert* v. *Verner* (1963), however, the Court reached a conclusion difficult to reconcile with that in *Gallagher* and *Braunfeld*. Denial of unemployment insurance benefits to a Seventh-Day Adventist who refused to accept tendered employment that required working on Saturday, the Court held, imposed an impermissible burden on the free exercise of religion. The First Amendment, it said, forbids forcing an applicant to choose between following religious precepts and forfeiting government benefits on the one hand, or, on the other, abandoning the precepts by accepting Sabbath work. Governmental imposition of such a choice, the Court said, puts the same kind of burden upon the free exercise of religion as would a fine imposed for Saturday worship.

The Court upheld statutory tax exemptions for church-owned real estate used exclusively for religious purposes in *Walz* v. *Tax Commission* (1970), rejecting an establishment clause attack. In *Murdock* v. *Pennsylvania* (1943) and *Follett* v. *Town of McCormack* (1944), however, the Court ruled that under the free exercise clause a revenue-raising tax on the privilege of canvassing or soliciting orders for articles could not be applied to Jehovah's Witnesses who sold their religious literature from door to door; in the same cases, the Court stated that an income tax statute could constitutionally be applied to clergymen's salaries for performing their clerical duties.

In *United States* v. *Lee* (1982) the Court upheld the exaction of social security and unemployment insurance contributions from Amish employers. The employers argued that their free exercise rights had been violated, citing 1 Timothy 5:8: "But if any provide not . . . for those of his own house, he hath denied the faith, and is worse than an infidel." Compulsory contribution, the Court said, was nonetheless justified; it was essential to accomplish the overriding governmental interest in the effective operation of the social security system.

Although *Sherbert* v. *Verner* and other cases had used strict scrutiny in free exercise cases, requiring the government to show the law allegedly restricting religious freedom to be narrowly tailored to serve a compelling state interest, in *Employment Division, Department of Human Resources of Oregon* v. *Smith* (1990) the Court ruled that laws of general application, not specifically aimed at religious practices, need only have a rational basis. The Court therefore sustained a state law criminalizing the use of the drug peyote even when used in a religious ceremony. An attempt by Congress to restore the strict scrutiny test for laws that substantially burden the free exercise of religion was itself overturned by the Court in *Boerne (City of)* v. *Flores* (1997) as an unconstitutional limit on the judiciary's authority to interpret the Constitution.

To sum up, the Supreme Court's decisions in the arena of religious liberty manifest a number of approaches toward defining its meaning, specifically clear and present danger, the balancing of competing interests, and the rejection of a compelling state interest justifying intrusion on free exercise. On the whole, though, the Court has been loyal to the original intent of the generation that wrote the First Amendment to accord the greatest degree of liberty feasible in our society.

—LEO PFEFFER

Bibliography

Gianella, Donald (1968). Religious Liberty: Non-Establishment and Doctrinal Development: Part I, The Religious Liberty Guarantee. *Harvard Law Review* 80: 1381–1431.

Howe, Mark DeWolfe (1965). *The Garden and the Wilderness: Religion and Government in American Constitutional History.* Chicago: University of Chicago Press.

Kauper, Paul G. (1964). *Religion and the Constitution.* Baton Rouge: Louisiana State University Press.

Manwaring, David R. (1962). *Render unto Caesar: The Flag Salute Controversy.* Chicago: University of Chicago Press.

Pfeffer, Leo ([1953] 1967). *Church, State and Freedom.* Boston: Beacon Press.

Stokes, Anson P. (1950). *Church and State in the United States.* New York: Harper & Brothers.

———, and Pfeffer, Leo (1965). *Church and State in the United States.* New York: Harper & Row.

Tribe, Lawrence H. (1978). *American Constitutional Law.* Mineola, N.Y.: Foundation Press.

RELIGIOUS SYMBOLS IN PUBLIC PLACES

In 1984 the Supreme Court, in *Lynch* v. *Donnelly*, rejected a constitutional challenge to the display of a publicly financed nativity scene—a crèche—in a private park in Pawtucket, Rhode Island. Chief Justice Warren E. Burger's decision for a 5–4 majority evoked deep resentment in many quarters, particularly among non-Christians who opposed the use of public funds to depict an event—the birth of Jesus to the Virgin Mary—that is a central tenet of Christianity. Moreover, the decision appeared to be a sharp departure from the Court's establishment clause precedents, particularly *Lemon* v. *Kurtzman* (1971), in which the Court set forth the three "tests" that the establishment clause imposes on government actions involving religion: "The statute must have a secular legislative purpose . . . its principal or primary effect must be one that neither advances nor inhibits religion . . . [and] the statute must not foster 'an excessive government entanglement with religion.' "

Conceding that the crèche was a religious symbol, the majority opinion nevertheless perceived the Pawtucket display as essentially a secular recognition of the historical origins of the Christmas season and therefore a permissible accommodation to religion. The Chief Justice's opinion observed that the display contained a Santa Claus, sleigh, candy-striped poles, and some reindeer.

Critics chided the Court for creating a "two-reindeer" rule and, more seriously, for demonstrating extreme insensitivity to non-Christians.

As lower courts and local governments addressed the questions that *Lynch* v. *Donnelly* left unanswered, they were guided in large part by Justice Sandra Day O'Connor's concurring opinion in which she reformulated the three-part Lemon test by emphasizing that the "purpose" and "effect" prongs of the test are designed to prevent government practices that endorse or disapprove of religion. "Endorsement," she wrote, "sends a message to adherents that they are outsiders, not full members of the political community." Based on this interpretation of *Lemon*, Justice O'Connor concluded that the purpose of the crèche was not to endorse Christianity but to celebrate a public holiday of secular significance, notwithstanding its religious aspect. As for the effect of the crèche, its "overall holiday setting . . . negates any message of endorsement" of the religious aspect of the display. Justice O'Connor's "endorsement" test provided a more focused approach than the open-ended emphasis on "accommodation" in Chief Justice Burger's opinion and has been widely followed in subsequent cases even by Justices who disagreed with her conclusion that the Pawtucket crèche was constitutional.

After five years of extensive litigation and public controversy, the Supreme Court revisited the religious-display issue in 1989 when, in *County of Allegheny* v. *American Civil Liberties Union*, it ruled that (1) a privately financed crèche, without holiday trappings and embell-

**TOO CLOSE FOR
COMFORT?**

*Does a menorah in the Ellipse
across from the White House
constitute government endorsement of religion?
(Corbis/Mark Thiessen)*

ished with a banner proclaiming "Gloria in Excelsis Deo," was unconstitutional as displayed in the main staircase of a county courthouse; and (2) an eighteen-foot menorah situated outside a county office building was constitutional as part of a display that featured the menorah alongside a forty-five-foot Christmas tree and a "Salute to Liberty" sign reminding viewers that "We are the keepers of the flame of liberty and our legacy of freedom." In light of the retirement of Justice William J. Brennan in July of 1990, the division on the Court in the *Allegheny* case was significant. Four Justices (William H. Rehnquist, Byron R. White, Antonin Scalia, and Anthony M. Kennedy) would have upheld both displays because there was no governmental effort to coerce or proselytize, and three Justices (Brennan, Thurgood Marshall, and John Paul Stevens) found both displays unconstitutional. Thus, the votes of Justices Harry A. Blackmun and O'Connor produced majorities upholding one display (the menorah) and invalidating the other (the crèche).

The Pawtucket crèche posed a risk of government endorsement because it was publicly financed. The Allegheny County displays, although privately financed, posed a similar danger because they were located in or near government buildings. By eschewing a clear test that would bar all government-financed displays with religious messages, or privately financed displays adjacent to government buildings, certain Justices on the Court were compelled in both cases to emphasize the design of the display as the key element of constitutionality. It was predictable, therefore, that governments would almost certainly invite litigation if they paid for holiday displays containing religious symbols or placed them in front of or in government buildings. Such displays require a fact-specific evaluation to determine whether the religious message has been sufficiently mixed with the secular holiday observance to avoid the overall impression of governmental endorsement of religion. A subject as intensely personal as religion is likely to evoke strong reactions if religious displays are constructed with public funds or if they are placed in locations that give them some type of official status.

These disputes, and the attendant divisiveness, can be minimized, however, if private groups, rather than the government, pay for holiday displays that contain religious symbols and if such displays are placed in traditional forums, like parks and plazas, that are normally used for speeches, displays, or other expressions of opinion. Indeed, the free-speech provisions of the First Amendment probably protect the right of a private group to display a crèche or menorah in a public forum, even without holiday trappings, as the symbolic expression of the celebration of the holiday season.

Since the Supreme Court's decision in *Allegheny County*, there is evidence that local communities have indeed adopted policies that avoid the divisiveness that the establishment clause was intended to prevent. They have relied increasingly on private groups to sponsor religious holiday displays and have selected locations that are not adjacent to public buildings such as city halls and courthouses. This development has the salutary effect of compelling governments, private parties, and courts to consider the nature of the forum rather than the numbers of reindeer, the prominence of Santa Claus, or the relative sizes of a menorah and a Christmas tree.

If governments desire to participate more actively in celebrating the Christmas season, the traditional Christmas tree provides a constitutionally acceptable alternative. Christmas trees have acquired a sufficiently secular meaning as a symbol of the holiday season so that their display does not endorse Christianity regardless of who bears the cost or wherever the tree may be located. If communities display understanding and restraint, the Constitution need not prevent the Christmas holiday season from serving as an occasion for uniting Americans rather than dividing them along religious lines.

—NORMAN REDLICH

Religious displays are likely to evoke strong reactions if they are constructed with public funds or if they are placed in locations that give them some type of official status.

R

The act here hamstrung use of the Internet for communication between adults.

Bibliography

Dorsen, Norman, and Sims, Charles (1985). The Nativity Scene Case; An Error of Judgment. *University of Illinois Law Review* 1985:837–868.

Redlich, Norman (1984). "Nativity Ruling Insults Jews." *New York Times*, March 26, 1984.

Van Alstyne, William (1984). Trends in the Supreme Court: Mr. Jefferson's Crumbling Wall—A Comment on *Lynch* v. *Donnelly*. *Duke University Law Journal* 1984:770–787.

RENO v. AMERICAN CIVIL LIBERTIES UNION

521 U.S. 844 (1997)

This important decision overturned the Communications Decency Act, a 1996 statute enacted by Congress to limit so-called indecent speech on the Internet. The Court held the Act's challenged provisions to be unconstitutionally vague and overbroad. These sections of the Act prohibited knowingly transmitting an indecent message to a person under eighteen years of age or knowingly sending or displaying a patently offensive message in a manner that makes it available to one under eighteen.

The Court in *Miller* v. *California* laid down a three-part test to define obscenity. In order to be prohibited as obscene, speech must appeal to a prurient interest, be patently offensive, as explicitly defined by statute, and lack serious literary, artistic, political, or scientific value. Unless it falls within these narrow confines, erotic, indecent, or even pornographic speech is protected by the First Amendment. However, the Court has also held that in the area of broadcasting, indecent speech that would otherwise be protected may be regulated, as the Court ruled in *Federal Communications Commission* v. *Pacifica Foundation* (1978). Thus a prime issue in deciding the validity of the Communications Decency Act was whether the Internet should be subject to the stricter controls applicable to broadcasting or is, on the other hand, more comparable to speech in writing, the telephone and other media, where the *Miller* test applies.

The Court gave two related reasons in *Pacifica* for allowing more stringent government regulation of broadcasting. First, broadcasting is subject to greater governmental control because of the limited number of broadcast frequencies available. Second, and more to the point, is the invasive nature of broadcasting, with its ability to enter the home and workplace and reach a virtually captive audience, including children. However, in the wake of *Pacifica* the Court ruled that telephone and cable television were not subject to this greater degree of governmental control, because they lack the captive-audience nature of broadcasting.

In the Internet suit Justice John Paul Stevens, writing for the Court, similarly held neither the scarcity of available frequencies nor the invasive quality of broadcasting applied to cyberspace. Internet communications, the Court noted, "do not 'invade' an individual's home or appear on one's computer screen unbidden. Users seldom encounter content 'by accident.'" Nor is there any scarcity of channels of expression on the Internet, the Court ruled, where 40 million Americans use it daily, with Web sites, e-mail, and other arenas for dialogue available to hosts of speakers. Therefore the government may only ban speech on the Internet that meets the narrow definition of obscenity in *Miller*. The definition in the Act, however, related only to offensiveness, and made no mention of appeal to a prurient interest or lack of serious value—two of the three prongs of the *Miller* test.

In response, the government contended that the Court had ruled in *Ginsberg* v. *New York* that indecent speech addressed to minors may be constitutionally regulated, as long as the restriction does not curtail the First Amendment rights of adults. The Act's provisions, it therefore argued, only restricted sending indecent material, or making it available, to persons under eighteen. But unlike the law upheld in *Ginsberg*, which simply barred the sale of books depicting nudity to minors, the Act here hamstrung use of the Internet for communication between adults. As the Court pointed out, "[G]iven the size of the potential audience for most messages, in the absence of a viable age verification process, the sender must be charged with knowing that one or more minors will likely view it." There is, it noted, currently no effective way of screening Internet messages from children. As the Court famously pointed out in *Butler* v. *Michigan* (1957), in overturning a law that barred adults from purchasing books and magazines unsuitable for children, "this is to burn the house to roast the pig."

Finally, the Court was concerned over the vagueness of the Act's definitions of "indecent" and "patently offensive" material. It pointed out that without a more specific prohibition, speech regarding birth control practices, homosexuality, or prison rape might be criminal. The sole defining language for "patently offensive" material in the Act merely speaks of an "image or other communication that . . . depicts or describes, in terms patently offensive as measured by contemporary community standards, sexual or excretory activities or organs. . . ." This lack of specificity is particularly dangerous to First Amendment values since the Internet reaches virtually every community. Thus a communicator is subject to the lowest common denominator of whatever state or county his or her message might reach. This falls far short, as the Court observed, of the constitutional requirement that restrictions on the content

SCREEN YOUR MESSAGES

Attorney General Janet Reno challenged the Communications Decency Act as it pertained to the transmission of messages via the Internet. (Corbis/Matthew Mendelsohn)

of speech be narrowly tailored to serve a compelling governmental interest.

Justice Sandra Day O'Connor, joined by Chief Justice William H. Rehnquist, concurred in part and dissented in part. She agreed that the ban on sending or displaying a patently offensive message was unconstitutional. However, she viewed the restrictions on transmitting indecent material as valid if construed to apply only where the sender knows the intended recipient of the message to be a minor. Since the Court has authority to interpret a federal statute narrowly in order to preserve its constitutionality, she contended it should do so here. So construed, the Act would bar a conversation between an adult and one or more minors that the adult knew to contain indecent material. How a sender could be assured that the sole recipients of the message were adults, and how criminalizing the message if a minor listens would not chill protected speech, were issues Justice O'Connor's opinion did not directly address.

The *Reno* decision leaves open the possibility of state attempts to control Internet speech, which several states' legislatures are considering. Any state legislation would of course be subject to the First Amendment concerns that invalidated the congressional provisions here. Another potential issue relates to attempts by other countries to restrict speech on the Internet—an especially vexing concern since many nations limit speech far more severely than the Constitution allows here.

—PHILIP WEINBERG

REPRODUCTIVE AUTONOMY

Commencing in 1942 in *Skinner* v. *Oklahoma*, and most intrepidly in 1973 in *Roe* v. *Wade*, the Supreme Court has secured against unwarranted governmental intrusion a decision fundamental to the course of an individual's life—the decision whether to beget or bear a child. Government action in this area bears significantly on the ability of women, particularly, to plan and control their lives. Official policy on reproductive choice may effectively facilitate or retard women's opportunities to participate in full partnership with men in the nation's social, political, and economic life. Supreme Court decisions concerning birth control, however, have not yet adverted to evolving sex equality-equal protection doctrine. Instead, high court opinions rest dominantly on substantive due process analysis; they invoke basic liberty-autonomy values difficult to tie directly to the Constitution's text, history, or structure.

Skinner marked the first occasion on which the Court referred to an individual's procreative choice as "a basic liberty." The Court invalidated a state statute providing for compulsory sterilization of habitual offenders. The statute applied after a third conviction for a felony "involving moral turpitude," defined to include grand larceny but exclude embezzlement. The decision ultimately rested on an equal protection ground: "Sterilization of those who have thrice committed grand larceny, with immunity for those who are embezzlers, is a clear, pointed, unmistakable discrimination." Justice William O. Douglas's opinion for the Court, however, is infused with substantive due process tones: "We are dealing here with legislation which involves one of the basic civil rights of man. Marriage and procreation are fundamental to the very existence and survival of the race." Gerald Gunther has noted that, in a period marked by a judicial hands-off approach to economic and social legislation, *Skinner* stood virtually alone in applying a stringent review standard favoring a "basic liberty" unconnected to a particular constitutional guarantee.

Over two decades later, in *Griswold* v. *Connecticut* (1965), the Court grappled with a state law banning the use of contraceptives. The Court condemned the statute's application to married persons. Justice Douglas's opinion for the Court located protected "zones of privacy" in the penumbras of several specific Bill of Rights guarantees. The law in question impermissibly intruded on the marriage relationship, a privacy zone "older than the Bill of Rights" and "intimate to the degree of being sacred."

In *Eisenstadt* v. *Baird* (1972) the Court confronted a Massachusetts law prohibiting the distribution of contraceptives, except by a registered pharmacist on a doctor's prescription to a married person. The Court avoided explicitly extending the right announced in *Griswold* beyond use to distribution. Writing for the majority, Justice William J. Brennan rested the decision on an equal protection ground: "Whatever the rights of the individual to access to contraceptives may be," the Court said, "the right must be the same for the unmarried and the married alike." *Eisenstadt* thus carried constitutional doctrine a considerable distance from "the sacred precincts of marital bedrooms" featured in *Griswold*.

The Court's reasoning in *Eisenstadt* did not imply that laws prohibiting fornication, because they treat married and unmarried persons dissimilarly, were in immediate jeopardy. Rather, Justice Brennan declined to attribute to Massachusetts the base purpose of "prescrib[ing] pregnancy and the birth of an unwanted child as punishment for fornication."

In 1977, in *Carey* v. *Population Services International*, the Court invalidated a New York law prohibiting the sale of contraceptives to minors under age sixteen and forbidding commercial distribution of even nonprescription contraceptives by anyone other than a licensed pharmacist. Justice Brennan reinterpreted the pathmarking precedent. *Griswold*, he noted, addressed a "particularly 'repulsive'" intrusion, but "subsequent decisions have made clear that the constitutional protection of individual autonomy in matters of childbearing is not dependent on [the marital privacy] element." Accordingly, "*Griswold* may no longer be read as holding only that a State may not prohibit a married couple's use of contraceptives. Read in light of [*Eisenstadt* and *Roe* v. *Wade*], the teaching of *Griswold* is

that the Constitution protects individual decisions in matters of childbearing from unjustified intrusion by the State."

Roe v. *Wade* declared that a woman, guided by the medical judgment of her physician, has a fundamental right to abort her pregnancy, a right subject to state interference only upon demonstration of a compelling state interest. The right so recognized, Justice Harry L. Blackmun wrote for the Court, falls within the sphere of personal privacy recognized or suggested in prior decisions relating to marriage, procreation, contraception, family relationships, child-rearing and education. The "privacy" or individual autonomy right advanced in *Roe* v. *Wade* is not explicit in our fundamental instrument of government, Justice Blackmun acknowledged; however, the Court viewed it as "founded in the Fourteenth Amendment's [and presumably the Fifth Amendment's] concept of personal liberty and restrictions upon state action." Justice Blackmun mentioned, too, the district court's view, derived from Justice Arthur J. Goldberg's concurring opinion in *Griswold*, that the liberty at stake could be located in the Ninth Amendment's reservation of rights to the people.

The Texas criminal abortion law at issue in *Roe* v. *Wade* was severely restrictive; it excepted from criminality "only a *lifesaving* procedure on behalf of the mother, without regard to pregnancy stage and without recognition of the other interests involved." In the several years immediately preceding the *Roe* v. *Wade* decision, the Court noted, the trend in the states had been "toward liberalization of abortion statutes." Nonetheless, the Court's rulings in *Roe* v. *Wade* and in a companion case decided the same day, *Doe* v. *Bolton* (1973), called into question the validity of the criminal abortion statutes of every state, even those with the least restrictive provisions.

The sweeping impact of the 1973 rulings on state laws resulted from the precision with which Justice Blackmun defined the state interests that the Court would recognize as

Official policy on reproductive choice may effectively facilitate or retard women's opportunities to participate in full partnership with men in the nation's social, political, and economic life.

compelling. In the first two trimesters of a pregnancy, the state's interest was confined to protecting the woman's health: during the first trimester, "the abortion decision and its effectuation must be left to the medical judgment of the pregnant woman's attending physician"; in the next three-month stage, the state may, if it chooses, require other measures protective of the woman's health. During "the stage subsequent to viability" (roughly, the third trimester), the state may protect the "potentiality of human life"; at that stage, the state "may, if it chooses, regulate, and even proscribe, abortion except where it is necessary, in appropriate medical judgment, for the preservation of the life or health of the mother."

Sylvia Law has commented that no Supreme Court decision has meant more to women. Wendy Williams has noted that a society intent on holding women in their traditional role would attempt to deny them reproductive autonomy. Justice Blackmun's opinion indicates sensitivity to the severe burdens, mental and physical, immediately carried by a woman unable to terminate an unwanted pregnancy, and the distressful life she and others in her household may suffer when she lacks the physical or psychological ability or financial resources necessary for child-rearing. But *Roe* v. *Wade* bypassed the equal protection argument presented for the female plaintiffs. Instead, the Court anchored stringent review to the personal autonomy concept found in *Griswold.* Moreover, *Roe* v. *Wade* did not declare an individual right; in the Court's words, the decision stated a joint right of "the woman and her responsible physician . . . in consultation."

The 1973 abortion rulings have been called aberrational, extraordinarily activist interventions by a Court reputedly deferential to states' rights and legislative judgments. John Hart Ely criticized *Roe* v. *Wade* as a decision the Court had no business making because freedom to have an abortion "lacks connection with any value the Constitution marks as special."

Archibald Cox described his own view of *Roe* v. *Wade* as "less rigid" then Ely's. He said in a 1975 lecture: "The Court's persistent resort to notions of substantive due process for almost a century attests the strength of our natural law inheritance in constitutional adjudication." Cox considered it "unwise as well as hopeless to resist" that strong tradition. *Roe* v. *Wade* nevertheless foundered, in his judgment, because the Court did not (and, he believed, could not) articulate an acceptable "precept of sufficient abstractness." The critical parts of the opinion, he commented, "read like a set of hospital rules and regulations."

Paul Freund expressed a similar concern in 1982. He thought *Roe* v. *Wade* epitomized a tendency of the modern Supreme Court (under Chief Justice Warren E. Burger as well as Chief Justice Earl Warren) "to specify by a kind of legislative code the one alternative pattern which will satisfy the Constitution, foreclosing further experimentation by Congress or the states." In his view, "a law which absolutely made criminal all kinds and forms of abortion could not stand up; it is not a reasonable accommodation of interests." But the Court "adopted what could be called the medical point of view—making distinctions that turn on trimesters." The Court might have drawn other lines, Freund suggested; it might have adopted an ethical rather than a medical approach, for example, by immunizing abortions, in a manner resembling the American Law Institute proposal, "where the pregnancy was the result of rape or incest, where the fetus was severely abnormal, or where the mother's health, physical or mental, would be seriously impaired by bringing the fetus to term." (The Georgia statutes struck down in *Doe* v. *Bolton,* companion case to *Roe* v. *Wade,* were patterned on the American Law Institute's model.) If the Court had proceeded that way, Freund commented, perhaps "some of the bitter debate on the issue might . . . have been averted; at any rate the animus against the Court might have been diverted to the legislative halls."

Animus there has been, in the form of antiabortion constitutional amendments introduced in Congress in 1973 and each session thereafter; proposals for "human life" legislation, in which Congress, upon the vote of a simple majority, would declare that the Fourteenth Amendment protects the life of "persons" from the moment of conception; and bills to strip the Supreme Court of jurisdiction to decide abortion cases. State legislatures reacted as well, adopting measures aimed at minimizing the impact of the 1973 ruling, including notice and consent requirements, prescriptions for the protection of fetal life, and bans on public expenditures or access to public facilities for abortion.

Some speculated that the 7–2 judgments in the 1973 cases (Justices Byron R. White and William H. Rehnquist dissented) were motivated in part by population concerns and the specter of unwanted children born to women living in grinding poverty. But in 1977 the Court voted 6–3 against pleas to extend the 1973 rulings to require public assistance for an indigent woman's elective (not medically necessary) abortion. First, in *Beal* v. *Doe,* the Court held that the federally established Medicaid program did not require Pennsylvania, as a condition of participation, to fund elective abortions. Second, in *Maher* v. *Roe* the Court ruled that the equal protection clause did not command Connecticut, which furnished Medicaid funds for childbirth, to pay as well for elective abortions. Finally, *Poelker* v. *Doe* held that the city of St. Louis did not violate the equal protection clause by providing publicly financed hospital services for childbirth but not for elective abortions.

The impoverished Connecticut women who sought Medicaid assistance in *Maher* maintained that, so long as their state subsidized childbirth, it could not withhold subsidy for abortion, a far less expensive and, at least in the first trimester, less risky procedure. Stringent equal protection review was required, they urged, because the state had intruded on the "fundamental right" declared in *Roe* v. *Wade.* Justice Lewis F. Powell, writing for the Court, responded that the right recognized in *Roe* did not require government neu-

trality as to the abortion decision; it was not a right to make a choice unchecked by substantive government control. Rather, it was a right restraining government from obstructing a woman's access to private sources to effectuate her decision. Because the right *Roe* v. *Wade* secured, as explained in *Maher,* was not impinged upon (and because disadvantageous treatment of needy persons does not alone identify suspect classification requiring close scrutiny), Connecticut's funding refusal could be sustained if it related "rationally" to a "constitutionally permissible" purpose. The policies to encourage childbirth in preference to abortion and to protect potential life supported the *Maher* regulation. There was, in the Court's view, no issue here, as there had been in *Roe* v. *Wade,* of an attempt "to impose [the state's] will by force of law."

Although criticized as irrational in the reproductive choice context, the distinction Justice Powell drew between government carrot and government stick had been made previously in other settings. But in *Maher,* unlike other cases in which the carrot/stick distinction had figured, the state could not justify its funding bar as an attempt to conserve public funds. In comparison to the medical costs of childbirth and the subsequent costs of child-rearing borne by public welfare programs, the costs of elective abortions are insubstantial.

The *Maher* logic was carried further in *Harris* v. *McRae* (1980). The federal law at issue, known as the Hyde Amendment, excluded even therapeutic (medically needed) abortions from the Medicaid program. In holding, 5–4, that the Hyde Amendment survived constitutional review, the Court reiterated the distinction drawn in *Maher.* Justice John Paul Stevens, who had joined the majority in *Maher,* switched sides in *McRae* because he discerned a critical difference between elective and therapeutic abortions in the context of the Medicaid program. Congress had established two neutral criteria for Medicaid benefits—financial need and medical need. The pregnant women who challenged the Hyde Amendment met both criteria. By creating an exception to the medical need criterion for the sole purpose of deterring exercise of the right declared "fundamental" in *Roe* v. *Wade,* Justice Stevens reasoned, the sovereign had violated its "duty to govern impartially."

Following the bold step in the 1973 abortion rulings, the public funding rulings appear incongruous. The direct, practical effect of the funding rulings will not endure, however, if the legislative trend again turns in the direction discernible at the time of the *Roe* v. *Wade* decision. National and state legislators may come to question the wisdom of a childbirth-encouragement policy trained on Medicaid-eligible women, and to comprehend more completely the centrality of reproductive autonomy to a woman's control of her life's course.

May the state require spousal consent to the abortion decision of a woman and her physician when the state itself may not override that decision? In *Planned Parenthood* v. *Danforth* (1976) the Court held unconstitutional Missouri's requirement of spousal consent to a first-trimester abortion. Justice Blackmun, for the six-member majority, declared that the state may not delegate authority to any person, even a spouse, to veto abortions which the state may not proscribe or regulate. A husband, of course, has a vital interest in his wife's pregnancy, Justice Blackmun acknowledged. But the woman's stake is more compelling; therefore the final decision must rest with her.

Although government may not remove the abortion decision from the woman and her physician unless its action demonstrably serves a compelling interest in the woman's health or in potential life, a state may act to ensure the quality of the decision. In *Danforth* the Court unanimously upheld Missouri's requirement that, prior to a first-trimester abortion, a woman certify that she has given her informed, uncoerced consent. The abortion decision is stressful, the Court observed; it should be made with "full knowledge of its nature and consequences." A state's authority in this regard, however, is

limited. Regulations must be genuinely necessary to secure enlightened consent; they must be designed to inform rather than persuade; and they must not interfere with the physician's counseling discretion.

In *Akron* v. *Akron Center for Reproductive Health* (1983) the Court, 6–3, speaking through Justice Powell, struck down a series of regulations that exceeded these limits. One regulation required the physician to tell any woman contemplating an abortion that the unborn child is a human life from conception; to tell her the details of the anatomical characteristics of the fetus; and to enumerate the physical and psychological risks of abortion. The Court held this regulation invalid because it was designed to persuade women to forgo abortions, and because it encroached upon the physician's discretion to decide how best to advise the patient. The Court also invalidated as unnecessary to secure informed, uncoerced consent, a twenty-four-hour waiting period between consent and abortion, and a requirement that the physician personally convey information to the woman.

The Court has not yet had occasion to pass upon a regulation designed to render the birth-control-through-contraception decision an informed one. In *Bolger* v. *Young's Drug Product Corporation* (1983), however, a majority held that government may not block dissemination of information relevant to that decision. At issue was a federal statute (the Comstock Act) prohibiting the mailing of contraceptive advertisements. All eight participating Justices held the statute unconstitutional as applied to the promotional and informational literature in question because the legislation impermissibly regulated commercial speech. (Earlier, in *Carey,* the Court had invalidated an analogous state regulation on the same ground.) Five Justices joined in a further ruling that the federal statute violated the right to reproductive autonomy because it denied adults truthful information relevant to informed contraception decisions.

The trimester scheme established in *Roe* v. *Wade* guided the Court's ruling on state regulation of abortion procedures until the *Casey* decision in 1992, discussed below. Under that scheme, the state may not interfere with a physician's medical judgment concerning the place and manner of first-trimester abortions because abortions performed at that stage are less risky than childbirth. Thus in *Doe* v. *Bolton* (1973), the companion case to *Roe* v. *Wade,* the Court invalidated a Georgia requirement that even first-trimester abortions be performed in a full-service hospital. In *Connecticut* v. *Menillo* (1975), however, the Court, per curiam, explicitly relied upon one of the underpinnings of *Roe* v. *Wade,* the need for a physician's medical judgment, to uphold a state's conviction of a nonphysician for performing an abortion.

The ban on state regulation of a physician's performance of first-trimester abortions is not absolute; it does not exclude regulation serving an important state health interest without significantly affecting the abortion decision. A unanimous bench in *Danforth* so indicated in upholding a Missouri regulation requiring maintenance of records of all abortions, for disclosure only to public health officials, for seven years.

Roe v. *Wade* declared that after the first trimester, because an abortion entails greater risks, the state's interest in women's health could justify "place and manner" regulations even if the abortion decision itself might be affected. However, the Court has attentively scrutinized procedural regulations applicable after the first trimester to determine whether, in fact, they are reasonably related to the protection of the patient's health in light of current medical knowledge. Several regulations have failed to survive the court's scrutiny. In *Doe* v. *Bolton*, for example, the Court struck down Georgia's requirement that a hospital committee and two doctors, in addition to the woman's physician, concur in the abortion decision. And in *Danforth*, the Court struck down a Missouri ban on use, after the first trimester, of saline amniocentesis, then the most widely used second-trimester abortion procedure. Justice Blackmun, for the majority, observed that although safer procedures existed, they were not generally available. Consequently, the regulation in practice would either require the use of more dangerous techniques or compel women to forgo abortions.

The Court had three 1983 encounters with regulations alleged to connect sufficiently with a women's health: *Akron, Planned Parenthood Association* v. *Ashcroft,* and *Simopoulos* v. *Virginia.* In *Akron* and *Ashcroft,* the Court invalidated regulations requiring that abortions, after the first trimester, be performed in licensed acute-care hospitals. Justice Powell, for the majority, said that although current medical knowledge justified this requirement during much of the relevant period, it was unnecessary during the first four weeks of the second trimester; medical advances had rendered abortions safe at that stage even when performed in less elaborate facilities. The hospital requirement significantly burdened a woman's access to an abortion by raising costs substantially; therefore it must be tied more precisely to the period in which it was necessary. In *Simopoulos,* on the other hand, the Court upheld the limitation of second-trimester abortions to licensed facilities (including nonacute care facilities licensed to perform abortions during the first four to six weeks of the second trimester).

These three decisions indicated the Court's readiness to test specific second-trimester regulations that increase the cost of abortions against advances in medical technology. However, the majority in *Akron,* although aware that medical advances had rendered early second-trimester abortions safer than childbirth, explicitly refused to extend beyond the first trimester an across-the-board proscription of burdensome "place and manner" regulations.

Only in the last stage of pregnancy, after viability, does the state's interest in potential life become sufficiently compelling to allow the state to forbid all abortions except those necessary to preserve the woman's health, according to *Roe.* The point at which viability occurs is a medical judgment, the Court said in *Roe* v. *Wade, Danforth,* and *Colautti* v. *Franklin* (1979); the state may not establish a fixed measure of that point after which nontherapeutic abortions are illegal.

When post-viability abortions occur, may the state impose manner requirements in the interest of preserving a viable fetus? The answer appears to be yes, if the regulations are not overbroad. In *Danforth* the Court invalidated a regulation requiring the physician to exercise due care to preserve the fetus; the regulation was not limited to post-viability abortions. In *Ashcroft,* however, a 5–4 majority sustained a law requiring a second physician to attend a post-viability abortion and attempt to preserve the life of the fetus. Even the dissenters agreed that such a regulation could stand if trimmed; they objected to Missouri's regulation because it required a second physician even at abortions using techniques that eliminated any possibility of fetal survival.

Dissenting in *Akron,* Justice Sandra Day O'Connor, joined by Justices White and Rehnquist, strongly criticized the Court's trimester approach to the regulation of abortion procedures. *Roe* v. *Wade's* medical model, she maintained, had been revealed as unworkable in subsequent cases. Advances in medical technology would continue to move forward the point during pregnancy when regulation could be justified as protective of a woman's health, and to move backward the point of viability, when the state could forbid abortions unless they were necessary to preserve the patient's life or health. The *Roe* v. *Wade* framework thus impelled legislatures to adjust their laws to changing medical practices, and called upon courts to examine legislative judgments, not as jurists applying "neutral principles" but as "science review boards."

More fundamentally, Justice O'Connor disapproved the interest balancing exhibited by the Court in the 1973 decisions. Throughout pregnancy, she said, the state has "compelling interests in the protection of potential human life and in maternal health." (In *Beal* the Court had said that the state does have an interest in potential life throughout a pregnancy, but that the interest becomes *compelling* only in the postviability stage.) Justice O'Connor's analysis, it appears, would permit from the beginning of pregnancy the regulation *Roe* v. *Wade* permits only in the final trimester: state proscription of abortion except to preserve a woman's health.

Vagueness doctrine has occasionally figured in the Court's review of state regulation of abortion procedures. In *Colautti,* the Court invalidated as too vague to supply adequate notice a statute attaching a criminal sanction to a physician's failure to exercise due care to preserve a fetus when there is "sufficient reason to believe that the fetus may be viable." And in *Akron,* a vagueness handle was employed to strike down a provision mandating the sanitary and "humane" disposal of aborted fetuses.

Minors have constitutional rights, but state authority over children's rights is greater than over adults'; the state may protect minors because of their immaturity and "peculiar vulnerability," and in recognition of "the importance of the parental role in child rearing." Justice Powell so observed in his plurality opinion in *Bellotti* v. *Baird* (1979), and no Justice has disagreed with these general statements. In concrete cases concerning the reproductive autonomy of minors, however, the Court has been splintered.

In *Danforth,* the Court invalidated, 5–4, a law requiring a parent's consent for most abortions performed on unmarried women under the age of eighteen. The majority did not foreclose a parental consent requirement for minors unable to make the abortion decision in an informed, mature manner.

The Court "continue[d] the inquiry" in *Bellotti.* Massachusetts required unmarried minors to obtain the consent of both parents or, failing that, the authorization of a state judge "for good cause shown." The Court voted 8–1 to invalidate the law, but split 4–4 on the rationale. Justice Stevens, writing for four Justices, thought the case governed by *Danforth.* Justice Powell, writing for four other Justices, attempted to provide guidance for state legislators. The abortion decision is unique among decisions facing a minor, he observed; it cannot be postponed until attainment of majority, and if the fetus is carried to term, the new mother will immediately face adult responsibilities. A blanket requirement of parental consent, using age as a proxy for maturity, was too sweeping. Yet the state's interest in ensuring the quality of a minor's abortion decision and in encouraging family participation in that decision would justify a law requiring either parental consent or the determination of an independent decision maker that abortion is in the minor's best interest, or that she is mature enough to decide for herself.

Justice Powell's *Bellotti* framework, although by 1983 only a two-member view, became, in *Akron* and *Ashcroft,* the de facto standard governing consent statutes. In *Ashcroft,* the Court upheld, 5–4, a statute conditioning a minor's abortion on either parental consent or a juvenile court order. Justice Powell and Chief Justice Burger voted to uphold the provision because, as indicated in *Bellotti,* the juvenile court must authorize an abortion upon finding that the abortion is in the minor's best interest or that the minor is mature enough to make her own decision. Three other Justices viewed the consent requirement as imposing "no undue burden on any right that a minor [arguably] may have to undergo an abortion." Four Justices dissented because the statute permitted an absolute veto, by parent or judge, "over the decision of the physician and his patient."

In *Akron,* however, the Court struck down, 6–3, an ordinance requiring all minors under age fifteen to have either parental or judicial consent. Because *Akron* failed to provide explicitly for a judicial determination of the minor's maturity, Justice Powell and the Chief Justice joined the four *Ashcroft* dissenters in condemning the consent provision. Most recently in *Hodgson* v. *Minnesota* (1990) a divided Court upheld a law requiring both parents to be notified before a minor's abortion, but only because the statute contained a judicial bypass for mature minors or those for whom an abortion was in their best interests.

With respect to contraception, no clear statement has emerged from the Court on the extent of state and parental authority over minors. In *Carey* the Court, 7–2, struck down a ban on the distribution of contraceptives to persons under age sixteen. The state sought to justify the measure as a means of deterring sexual activity by minors. There was no majority decision, but six Justices recognized that banning birth control would not in fact deter sexual activity.

May the state require parental consent to the minor's use of contraceptives? At least five Justices, it appears from the *Carey* decision, would state unequivocally that minors have no right to engage in sexual activity in face of disapproval of the state and of their parents. But it is hardly apparent that any minor-protective interest supports stopping the young from effectuating a decision to use nonhazardous contraceptives when, despite the views or commands of the state and their parents, they do engage in sexual activity.

Arguably, such a provision would serve to preserve parental authority over a decision many people consider a moral one. *Danforth* indicated that this end is insufficient to justify requiring parental consent for an abortion. Yet, as Justice Powell's *Bellotti* opinion illustrates, at least some Justices consider the abortion decision unique. Perhaps the issue will remain undecided. For practical reasons, lawmakers may be deterred from conditioning a minor's access to contraceptives on parental consent or notification. Many minors whose parents would wish them to use birth control if they engaged in sexual activity would nevertheless fail to seek parental consent for fear of disclosing their sexual activities. As five Justices indicated in *Carey,* deliberate state policy exposing minors to the risk of unwanted pregnancies is of questionable rationality.

In *Akron,* which came to the Court a decade after *Roe* v. *Wade,* Justice Powell acknowledged the continuing argument that the Court "erred in interpreting the Constitution." Nevertheless, *Akron* commenced with a reaffirmation of the 1973 precedent.

R

REPRODUCTIVE AUTONOMY

As *Akron* itself illustrates, the Court typically has applied *Roe* v. *Wade* to restrict state efforts to impede privately financed access to contraceptives and abortions.

Two important decisions left *Roe's* essential holding intact but upheld state restrictions on the right to obtain an abortion. *Webster* v. *Reproductive Health Services* (1989) sustained a Missouri law that barred abortions in public hospitals and required physicians to determine whether fetuses of twenty or more weeks were viable. *Planned Parenthood of Southeastern Pennsylvania* v. *Casey* (1992) upheld a twenty-four-hour waiting period and a requirement that physicians furnish information about adoption and the risks of abortion, except in medical emergencies. However, *Casey* overturned a provision requiring spousal consent. That decision is also noteworthy for rephrasing the standard of judicial review in the abortion area to whether a law places an "undue burden" on the right to an abortion, as well as expressly abandoning *Roe's* trimester framework.

It appears safe to predict continued "adher[ence] to *stare decisis* in applying the principles of *Roe* v. *Wade."* But other issues remain beyond the zone of secure prediction. Current opinions do not indicate whether the Court eventually will relate its reproductive autonomy decisions to evolving law on the equal status of men and women. Nor can one forecast reliably how science and population will influence the next decades' legislative and judicial decisions in this area.

The development of a safe, efficient, inexpensive morning-after pill, for example, may alter the reproductive autonomy debate by further blurring distinctions between contraceptives and abortifacients, and by sharply reducing occasions for resort to clinical procedures. A development of this order may diminish in incidence and detail both legislative activity and constitutional review of the kind sparked in the decade following *Roe* v. *Wade.* Moreover, it is at least possible that a different question will confront the Court by the turn of the century: If population size becomes a larger governmental concern, legislators may change course, and measures designed to limit childbirth may become the focus of constitutional controversy.

—RUTH BADER GINSBURG

Bibliography

Brest, Paul (1981). The Fundamental Rights Controversy: The Essential Contradictions of Normative Constitutional Scholarship. *Yale Law Journal* 90:1063–1112.

Byrn, Robert (1973). An American Tragedy: The Supreme Court on Abortion. *Fordham Law Review* 41:807–862.

Cox, Archibald (1976). *The Role of the Supreme Court in American Government.* New York: Oxford University Press.

Dembitz, Nanette (1980). The Supreme Court and a Minor's Abortion Decision. *Columbia Law Review* 80:1251–1263.

Destro, Robert (1975). Abortion and the Constitution: The Need for a Life Protective Amendment. *California Law Review* 63:1250–1351.

Ely, John Hart (1973). The Wages of Crying Wolf: A Comment on *Roe* v. *Wade. Yale Law Journal* 82:920–949.

Estreicher, Samuel (1982). Congressional Power and Constitutional Rights: Reflections on Proposed "Human Life" Legislation. *Virginia Law Review* 68:333–458.

Freund, Paul (1983). Storms over the Supreme Court. *American Bar Association Journal* 69:1474–1480.

Heymann, Philip, and Barzelay, Douglas (1973). The Forest and the Trees: *Roe* v. *Wade* and Its Critics. *Boston University Law Review* 53:765–784.

Law, Sylvia (1984). Rethinking Sex and the Constitution. *University of Pennsylvania Law Review* 132:955–1040.

Perry, Michael (1976). Abortion, the Public Morals, and the Police Power: The Ethical Function of Substantive Due Process. *UCLA Law Review* 23:689–736.

——— (1978). The Abortion Funding Cases: A Comment on the Supreme

Court's Role in American Government. *Georgetown Law Journal* 66:1191–1245.

Regan, Donald (1979). Rewriting *Roe* v. *Wade*. *Michigan Law Review* 77:1569–1646.

Tribe, Laurence H. (1978). *American Constitutional Law* Pages 921–934. Mineola, N.Y.: Foundation Press.

REYNOLDS v. SIMS

377 U.S. 533 (1964)

Once the Supreme Court declared in *Baker* v. *Carr* (1962) that legislative districting presented a justiciable controversy, lawsuits were filed in more than thirty states challenging existing legislative apportionments. Six of these cases were decided by the Court on the same day, and the Court held all six states' apportionments unconstitutional. The main opinion was written in *Reynolds* v. *Sims,* the Alabama case; all six opinions of the Court were by Chief Justice Earl Warren, who believed until his death that *Reynolds* was the most important decision rendered by the Court during his tenure. The vote in four of the cases was 8–1, and in the other two, 6–3. Justice John Marshall Harlan dissented in all six cases, joined in two of them by Justices Potter Stewart and Tom C. Clark.

Baker v. *Carr* had been a response to decades of stalemate in the political process. Population shifts from rural areas to cities in the twentieth century had not been accompanied by changes in the electoral maps of most states. As a result, vast disparities in district populations permitted control of both houses of the typical state legislature to be dictated by rural voters. In Alabama, for example, Mobile County, with a population over 300,000, had three seats in the lower house, while Bullock County's two representatives served a population under 14,000. If judicial review normally defers to majoritarian democracy, here the premise for that deference was lacking; legislators favored by these apportionment inequalities were not apt to remedy them.

Baker had rested decision not on the guarantee clause but on the equal protection clause of the Fourteenth Amendment. In the early 1960s, the Court had heightened the standard of review in equal protection cases only when racial discrimination was present; for other cases, the relaxed rational basis standard prevailed. Some Justices in the *Baker* majority had based their concurrence on the total arbitrariness of the Tennessee apportionment scheme there challenged. Justice William O. Douglas, concurring, had even said, "Universal equality is not the test; there is room for weighting." The *Baker* dissenters and academic critics had argued that the apportionment problem was unsuitable for judicial determination because courts would be unable to devise principled standards to test the reasonableness of the "weighting" Justice Douglas had anticipated; the problem belonged, they had said, in the category of political questions. The *Baker* majority had replied blandly: "Judicial standards under the Equal Protection Clause are well developed and familiar," and courts could determine that malapportionment represented "*no* policy, but simply arbitrary and capricious action." The suggestion was plain: departures from district population equality would be valid if they rested on legitimate policies.

Reynolds belied this suggestion. In a sweeping opinion that Archibald Cox called a *coup de main,* the Court discarded almost all possible justifications for departing from a strict principle of equal district populations and established for state legislative districts the one person, one vote formula it had recently used in other electoral contexts. The Court thus solved *Baker*'s problem of judicially manageable standards by resort to a mechanical test that left no "room for weighting"—and, not incidentally, no room for legislative evasion. The companion cases to *Reynolds* demonstrated the strength of the majority's conviction. *Maryland Committee for Fair Representation* v. *Tawes* (1964) rejected the "federal analogy" and imposed the population equality principle on both houses of a bicameral legislature, and *Lucas* v. *Forty-fourth General*

Academic criticism of the Warren Court has prominently featured Reynolds *as a horrible example.*

See also

Baker v. *Carr*

Assembly of State of Colorado (1964) insisted on the principle in the face of a popular referendum approving an apportionment that departed from it. In *Reynolds* itself the Court made clear that the states must keep their legislative apportionments abreast of population shifts as reported in the nation's decennial census.

In short, numbers were in, and a political theory of interest representation was out: "Citizens, not history or economic interests, cast votes." Justice Stewart, dissenting in two of the cases, took another view: "Representative government is a process of accommodating group interests through democratic institutional arrangements." Fairness in apportionment thus requires effective representation of the various interests in a state, a concern that the principle of district population equality either ignored or defeated. But Justice Stewart's premise—that equal protection required only an apportionment scheme that was rationally based and did not systematically frustrate majority rule—was rejected by the Court. Because voting "is a fundamental matter in a free society," the Chief Justice said, the dilution of the strength of a citizen's vote "must be carefully and meticulously scrutinized." *Reynolds* was the crucial decision in the line of equal protection cases developing the doctrine that voting is a fundamental interest, whose impairment calls for strict scrutiny.

The Court's disposition of the six reapportionment cases, and its memorandum orders in other cases in succeeding months, left little doubt that the Justices had learned a lesson from their experience in *Brown* v. *Board of Education* (1954–55). Here there would be no all deliberate speed formula to extend the time for compliance with the decision. Lower courts were expected to move quickly—and did move quickly—to implement the doctrine announced in *Reynolds*. Even so, politicians had some time to mount a counterattack. Thirty-two state legislatures requested the calling of a constitutional convention to overturn *Reynolds*. Senator Everett Dirksen

gained substantial support when he introduced a proposed constitutional amendment to the same end. Bills were offered in both houses of Congress to withdraw the federal courts' jurisdiction over reapportionment cases. But all these efforts came to nothing. The jurisdictional bills failed; the Dirksen proposal did not pass either house; the constitutional convention proposal, which had been carried forward with little publicity, withered in the remaining state legislatures when it was exposed to political sunlight.

The reason for the politicians' protest was obvious to all: many of them anticipated losing their own seats, and many others foresaw reduced influence for certain interests that rural representatives had favored. The public, however, overwhelmingly approved the principle of "one person, one vote" when the issue was tested in opinion polls; the politicians' counterattack failed because the people sided with the Court.

Academic criticism of the Warren Court has prominently featured *Reynolds* as a horrible example. The Court, the critics say, failed to write an opinion that reasoned from generally accepted premise to logically compelled conclusion. That is a telling criticism if, as Henry Hart was fond of saying, "reason is the life of the law." But reason is not the *life* of the law, or of anything else. It is a mental instrument to be used by judges and other humans along with their capacities for other ways of knowing: recognizing textures, patterns, analogies, relations that are not demonstrated by "if . . . then" syllogisms but grasped intuitively and at once. Perhaps the public was more ready to accept "one person, one vote" than were the Warren Court's critics because people who are not lawyers understand that the Supreme Court's most important product is justice. Surely they understood that the *Reynolds* formula, for all its inflexibility, more truly reflected our national sense of political justice than did the "cancer of malapportionment"—the term is Professor Cox's—that preceded it.

It is, by definition, hard to justify innovation by reference to the conventional wisdom. The beginnings of judicial doctrine, like other beginnings, may be more easily felt than syllogized. Ultimately, if constitutional intuitions are to be translated into constitutional law, coherent explanation must come to replace the vague sense of doing the right thing; consolidation is an essential part of the Supreme Court's task. Yet to deny the legitimacy of a decision whose underlying value premises are clear, on the ground that the decision does not follow deductively from what has gone before, is to deny the legitimacy of judicial creativity—and it is our creative judges whom we honor most.

Reynolds v. *Sims* did not remake the political world; it mostly transferred power from rural areas to the conservative suburbs of large cities. But the decision touched a deep vein of American political egalitarianism and gave impetus to a doctrinal development as important as any in our time: recognition of the values of equal citizenship as the substantive core of the Fourteenth Amendment.

—KENNETH L. KARST

Bibliography

Casper, Gerhard (1973). Apportionment and the Right to Vote: Standards of Judicial Scrutiny. *Supreme Court Review* 1973:1–32.

Dixon, Robert G., Jr. (1968). *Democratic Representation: Reapportionment in Law and Politics.* New York: Oxford University Press.

McKay, Robert B. (1965). *Reapportionment: The Law and Politics of Equal Representation.* New York: Twentieth Century Fund.

REYNOLDS v. UNITED STATES

98 U.S. 145 (1879)

This case established the principle that under the guarantee of religious liberty, government

*Government may
not punish religious
beliefs but may
punish religiously
motivated practices
that injure the
public interest.*

may not punish religious beliefs but may punish religiously motivated practices that injure the public interest. Reynolds violated a congressional prohibition on bigamy in the territories and appealed his conviction in Utah on First Amendment grounds, alleging that as a Mormon he had a religious duty to practice polygamy. Chief Justice Morrison R. Waite for a unanimous Supreme Court ruled that although government might not reach opinions, it could constitutionally punish criminal activity. The question, Waite declared, was whether religious belief could be accepted as justification of an overt act made criminal by the law of the land. Every government, he answered, had the power to decide whether polygamy or monogamy should be the basis of social life. Those who made polygamy part of their religion could no more be exempt from the law than those who believe that human sacrifice was a necessary part of religious worship. Unless the law were superior to religious belief, Waite reasoned, every citizen might become a law unto himself and government would exist in name only. He did not explain why polygamy and human sacrifice were analogous, nor did he, in his simplified exposition, confront the problem whether an uncontrollable freedom of belief had much substance if the state could punish the dictates of conscience: belief without practice is an empty right. Moreover, Waite did not consider whether belief should be as absolutely free as he suggested; if polygamy was a crime, its advocacy had limits.

—LEONARD W. LEVY

RHODE ISLAND
v. INNES

446 U.S. 291 (1980)

Innes explained the meaning of "interrogation" under *Miranda* v. *Arizona* (1966). *Miranda* declared, "If the individual states that he wants an attorney, the interrogation must cease until an attorney is present." Everyone agreed that the suspect in *Innes* had received his *Miranda* warnings and invoked his right to counsel, and that he was in custody. The question was whether he had been interrogated.

Police arrested a man suspected of a shotgun murder. Repeatedly they advised him of his *Miranda* rights, and a captain instructed officers about to transport him to the stationhouse not to question him in any way. During a brief automobile ride, one officer said to another, within the suspect's hearing, that they ought to try to find the shotgun because a child might discover it and kill herself. The suspect promptly volunteered to take the police to the shotgun. Again the police gave the *Miranda* warnings. The suspect replied that he understood his rights but wanted the gun removed from the reach of children. His statements and the gun were introduced in evidence at his trial, over his objection. The state supreme court reversed his conviction, finding a violation of *Miranda*.

A 6–3 Supreme Court decided that the police had not interrogated the suspect. Justice Potter Stewart for the majority construed *Miranda* broadly to mean that interrogation includes questioning or a "functional equivalent"—any words or actions by the police reasonably likely to elicit any response from their suspect. Here there was no interrogation, only a spontaneous admission. The dissenters believed that an officer deliberately referred to the missing gun as a danger to innocent children in the hope of eliciting from the suspect an incriminating statement; whether that happened cannot be known. If the Court majority had believed that the officer making the remark had understood the suspect's psychological makeup and that an appeal to his conscience might have worked, that majority would have decided that the suspect had been interrogated. Contrary to the view of Justice John Paul Stevens, dissenting, *Miranda* was not narrowed.

—LEONARD W. LEVY

See also

Polygamy

Religious Liberty

RICHMOND (CITY OF) v. J. A. CROSON CO.

488 U.S. 469 (1989)

In *Fullilove* v. *Klutznick* (1980) the Supreme Court upheld an act of Congress requiring that 10 percent of certain federal subsidies to local governments be set aside for contractors that were minority-owned business enterprises (MBE). In *Croson* the Court invalidated a similar affirmative action ordinance adopted by a city. The ordinance, adopted for a five-year term, required a prime contractor to allocate 30 percent of the dollar amount of the contract to MBE subcontractors. A waiver was authorized in the event that MBE were not available. The Court held, 6–3, that this scheme denied nonminority businesses the equal protection of the laws.

Justice Sandra Day O'Connor wrote an opinion that was in part the opinion of the court and in part a plurality opinion. A majority concurred in the opinion's basic building blocks: that the appropriate standard of review for a state and local affirmative action program was strict scrutiny; that the city had not offered sufficient evidence of "identified discrimination" that could justify a race-conscious remedy; and that the city's program, even if it were remedial, was not sufficiently narrowly tailored to such discrimination. In addition, she spoke for a plurality in concluding that Congress's remedial powers, unlike those of the states, could extend to remedying past societal discrimination. Justice Anthony M. Kennedy, concurring, dissociated himself from the latter position, and Justice Antonin Scalia, also concurring, argued that the city had power to use race-conscious remedies only for its own discrimination. Justice John Paul Stevens concurred only in the view that Richmond's plan was not justified by sufficient evidence of past discrimination and was not narrowly tailored.

Justice O'Connor concluded that Richmond could constitutionally provide a race-conscious remedy not only for its own past discrimination but also for past discrimination by private contractors or trade associations in the Richmond area. She also concluded that such discrimination might be proved by statistics showing a serious disparity between the percentage of qualified MBE in the area and the percentage of contracts awarded to MBE. Here, however, the city had shown only that the MBE contracts were extremely low in comparison with the percentage of minorities in Richmond's general population. To achieve a "narrowly tailored" program, she said, Richmond would have to show that race-neutral alternatives were unworkable, and to peg its MBE set-aside percentage at a figure that bore a clearly stated relation to the percentage of qualified MBE.

Justice Thurgood Marshall wrote a sharply worded opinion for the three dissenters. He argued that strict scrutiny was inappropriate and that Richmond's ordinance served the important purposes of remedying the effects of a pattern of past discrimination and keeping the city from reinforcing that pattern. He found the Richmond council's conclusions about past discrimination, both by the city and by private contractors, to be soundly based. Justice Harry A. Blackmun also dissented.

Although many civil rights advocates regarded *Croson* as a serious setback for affirmative action, it may turn out, like *Regents of University of California* v. *Bakke* (1978), to be a blessing in disguise for their cause. Certainly, *Croson*'s standards for affirmative action in state and local government contracting will, in some communities, prevent any effective affirmative action. One of the legacies of racial discrimination is the paucity of minority businesses in many of the fields in which governments offer contracts. However, Justice O'Connor's explicit approval of statistical proof of past discrimination offers considerable opportunity, particularly for states and for large cities, to satisfy the Court's requirements. More important, six Justices not

R

RICHMOND (CITY OF)
v. J. A. CROSON CO.

488 U.S. 469 (1989)

Although many civil rights advocates regarded Croson *as a serious setback for affirmative action, it may turn out to be a blessing in disguise for their cause.*

only reaffirmed the *Fullilove* precedent, which had seemed vulnerable, but also issued to Congress a sweeping invitation to engage in broadscale affirmative action of its own aimed at remedying the effects of past societal discrimination.

—KENNETH L. KARST

Bibliography

Constitutional Scholars' Statement on Affirmative Action After *City of Richmond* v. *J. A. Croson Co.* (1989). *Yale Law Journal* 98:1711–1716.

Fried, Charles (1989). Affirmative Action After *City of Richmond* v. *J. A. Croson Co.*, A Response to the Scholars' Statement. *Yale Law Journal* 99:155–161.

Scholars' Reply to Professor Fried (1989). *Yale Law Journal* 99:163–168.

RICHMOND NEWSPAPERS, INC. v. VIRGINIA

448 U.S. 555 (1980)

Richmond Newspapers recognized a constitutional right of access to criminal trials. It marked the first time a majority embraced any such First Amendment claim. Yet division and bitterness obviously remained from the splintered decision a year earlier in *Gannett* v. *DePasquale*, which had held that the Sixth Amendment did not preclude closing a pretrial suppression hearing to the press and public.

In *Richmond Newspapers*, a 7–1 majority distinguished *Gannett* and held that the press and public share a right of access to actual criminal trials, though the press may enjoy some preference. In the plurality opinion, Chief Justice Warren E. Burger found a right to attend criminal trials within "unarticulated rights" implicit in the First Amendment rights of speech, press, and assembly, as well as within other constitutional language and

the uninterrupted Anglo-American tradition of open trials. This right to an open trial prevailed over efforts by Virginia courts to close a murder trial, premised on the defendant's request to do so. The trial judge had made no particularized finding that a fair trial could not be guaranteed by means less drastic than total closure.

Justice William H. Rehnquist was alone in dissent, but only Justices Byron R. White and John Paul Stevens concurred in Burger's opinion. Justice Lewis F. Powell took no part in the decision. Four Justices concurred separately in the judgment. They differed about whether *Gannett* actually was distinguishable, what weight to give history, and what particular constitutional basis mandated the result.

Richmond Newspapers decided only the unconstitutionality of a total ban on public access to actual criminal trials when there is no demonstration that alternative means could not guarantee a fair trial. Yet the decision is significant for its recognition of a First Amendment right to gather newsworthy information; moreover, some Justices identified a broad right to receive information about government, including the activities of the judicial branch.

—AVIAM SOIFER

RIGHT OF PRIVACY

Following extensive litigation and commentary, the right of privacy now is firmly established in constitutional law since *Griswold* v. *Connecticut* (1965). The abortion decision in *Roe* v. *Wade* (1973) raised the level of controversy about the right of privacy without clarifying the scope or nature of the rights understood under this concept. Sharp criticism of the vagueness of the concept of privacy and persistent doubts about its supporting constitutional text and traditions have not hampered the vitality of the right of privacy. In some areas, such as the right to die, pri-

Richmond Newspapers *recognized a constitutional right of access to criminal trials.*

See also

Free Press/Fair Trial
Gannett v. *DePasquale*
Plurality Opinion

vacy and related concepts have made notable advances in constitutional law.

The Supreme Court has identified the Fourteenth Amendment's guarantee of "liberty" as the source of privacy rights. This is a notable shift for two reasons. First, it signals the willingness on the part of recent Justices to accept substantive due process as a legitimate concept in constitutional law, so long as it does not touch on economic or labor matters. To Justices of the generation of William O. Douglas and Hugo L. Black, adjudication under such a general rubric was perilous. It encouraged judicial excess. Douglas went to great, perhaps absurd, lengths in *Griswold* to find textual sources for a right to privacy in the First, Third, Fourth, Fifth, and Eighth Amendments. Arthur Goldberg sought to find privacy in the Ninth Amendment. This is now widely understood as a fool's errand.

Second, the preference for due process liberty as the source of the right to privacy reflects its permanence in the constitutional galaxy. Whatever its source, Justice Harry A. Blackmun wrote in *Roe* v. *Wade,* "[T]his right of privacy . . . is broad enough to encompass a woman's decision whether or not to terminate her pregnancy." Justices in some decisions have sometimes altogether avoided the term privacy, with conservatives often speaking of "liberty interests" and liberals of personal or "intimate" decisions. In *Cruzan* v. *Missouri Department of Health* (1990), the "right to die" case, Chief Justice William H. Rehnquist made this avoidance explicit: "Although many state courts have held that a right to refuse treatment is encompassed by a generalized constitutional right of privacy, we have never so held." The issue, he added, "is more properly analyzed in terms of a 14th Amendment liberty interest."

Outside of the law of search and seizure, privacy has proven extremely hard to define. Scholars have been unable to agree on the elements of ordinary usage, constitutional history, or moral philosophy from which to construct a normative concept. The concept itself

has been of little but rhetorical help in deciding particular cases in which, typically, regulation is seen to invade an individual's preference for seclusion or immunity. All this has made the precedents of *Griswold* and *Roe* hard to confine by ordinary arguments. The steps from privacy in marital sexuality to privacy in abortion and from heterosexuality to homosexuality have not been easy to resist when arguments are made in terms of a right to privacy possessed by all persons. However, in *Bowers* v. *Hardwick* (1986) a narrow majority of the Court made clear its unwillingness to extend the right to homosexual conduct. The Court there stated that the right to privacy in this context was limited to the areas of marriage, family, and procreation. In *Washington* v. *Glucksberg* (1997) the Court similarly refused to extend *Cruzan* to encompass physician-assisted suicide.

However disappointing to those awaiting clarification, the turn from privacy to liberty may nonetheless make good legal and political sense. Privacy as a term has no plain reference or meaning for most of us. "The right to be let alone," as Earl Warren and Louis Brandeis called it, covered many situations and many abuses. In criminal procedure, the protection of "persons, papers, and effects" refers to those things (including one's own body) over which we normally exercise complete control. But the transportation from one context to another—search and seizure, for example, to sexuality—leaves much of the force of argument, as well as precedent and tradition, behind. We are left then with an argument for immunity unaided by the concept under which immunity is claimed. Obviously, private life—*la vie privée*—must shelter information, decisions, and behaviors of many different kinds. The question is, which ones are to be protected against regulation or governmental intrusion?

Liberty is not much more helpful in this regard than is privacy. Yet liberty offers a plainer inquiry with less confusion and less of a temptation to believe that we will find our

Not until 1977 did the Supreme Court begin to map out the territory occupied by the constitutional right of privacy.

rights by simply defining a concept. Moreover, liberty, unlike privacy, is a concept with a long constitutional history.

The inquiry that now seems to govern adjudication is whether or not fundamental liberties extend to certain aspects of private life, including sexuality, reproduction, and perhaps dying. Often, regulations have reached these matters in connection with medical treatment. Thus, the right to die is the right to refuse medical treatment where it might prolong life. The right to abortion is the right to choose whether or not to terminate a pregnancy before the fetus is viable outside the womb. We may generalize from these instances to a concept of privacy in intimate associations or intimate decisions, but the Supreme Court's response to this generalization remains equivocal: sexuality between consenting adults of the opposite sexes seems at this point effectively protected. Although *Griswold* relied on the context of marriage for its extension of protection to information about the use of birth control, *Eisenstadt* v. *Baird* (1972) seemed to make clear that this context was unnecessary. We should note, however, that the effective protection for disapproved behavior lies in a conjunction of privacy decisions from the Supreme Court and, of equal or greater importance, regulatory reforms from the various state legislatures that permit a greater range of behaviors than heretofore. Sodomy statutes remain on the books in many states, and it is not yet clear that unmarried heterosexual sodomy would be held to be protected by the Supreme Court.

In *Bowers* v. *Hardwick* (1986) the Court upheld a Georgia statute that made sodomy a felony in a case in which charges had been filed and then withdrawn against two consenting adult males. The 5–4 decision sharply divided the Court. "The issue presented," wrote Justice Byron R. White, for the majority, "is whether the Federal constitution confers a fundamental right upon homosexuals to engage in sodomy. . . ." Justices Blackmun, William J. Brennan, Thurgood Marshall, and John Paul Stevens dissented. "This case is no more about a fundamental right to engage in homosexual sodomy," Justice Blackmun wrote, "than *Stanley* v. *Georgia* (1969) was about a fundamental right to watch obscene movies, or *Katz* v. *United States* (1967) was about a fundamental right to place interstate bets from a telephone booth." For the dissenters, Brandeis's dissent in *Olmstead* v. *United States* (1928) provided the applicable concept, "the right to be let alone," as Warren and Brandeis had described it (without any reference to sexuality) in their famous *Harvard Law Review* article on the "Right to Privacy." Thus, Blackmun insisted on a certain understanding of the concept of privacy: "I believe we must analyze respondent's claim in the light of the values that underlie the constitutional right to privacy. If that right means anything, it means that, before Georgia can prosecute its citizens for making choices about the most intimate aspects of their lives, it must do more than assert that the choice they have made is an "abominable crime not fit to be named among Christians."

The incommensurability of these points of view may be understood from at least three angles. First, and most obvious to students of the concepts of privacy and liberty, there is a difference over the level of abstraction at which the argument will be joined. The majority refused to accept the claim that adult homosexuals might shelter their consensual sexual practices under the same general liberty as adult heterosexuals. To the majority, the assertion is of an immunity to engage in a homosexual act consistently condemned in our tradition. The dissenters argue that this act must be understood in relation to other sexual intimacies protected by the Fourteenth Amendment. It is, after all, an expression of sexuality between consenting adults in the bedroom of a private apartment. (A houseguest had admitted the policeman into the apartment and directed him to Hardwick's bedroom.) Neither position is refutable as illogical or inconsistent. The choice of a level of abstraction will often decide a dispute over rights; yet there seems to be no conclusive argument that one level of abstraction is the appropriate one for a given case. What makes one level preferable to another is the sense of coherence and completeness at that level of whatever issues are understood as pertinent. This is inevitably a circular process of reasoning. Intimacy and sexuality seem the relevant terms to the dissenters, but not to the majority, which focuses on homosexuality. A simpler way to understand this difference is to note that, as always, each side in legal argument denies the applicability of the other side's precedents. In this case, the majority will not accept the force and bearing of *Griswold*, *Eisenstadt*, and *Roe* v. *Wade*. For the dissenters, however, these are the relevant precedents, pointing the way to a different result.

Finally, there is an important line of argument, going back to the younger Justice John Marshall Harlan in *Poe* v. *Ullman* (1961), that tradition should inform our understanding of the concept of liberty. Constitutional traditions, like others, are notoriously inexact. Moreover, there are good traditions and bad ones. Yet it is undeniable that legal and institutional traditions give us a context in which to understand the terms and arrangements provided for in the Constitution. Due process is one example, judicial review is another, and privacy may be a third.

Harlan, in *Poe* and *Griswold*, relied on a specific tradition, namely, marriage. The various measures of restriction and permission attached to it by law suggested to him that the concept of privacy had constitutional standing in protecting the uses of sexuality— including contraception—by husband and wife. He never went beyond this point, however, retiring from the Court in 1971, one year before the *Eisenstadt* decision and two years before *Roe* v. *Wade*.

Eisenstadt's majority opinions had relied on an equal protection argument that left the factual question of the marital status of the recipient of a contraceptive unresolved. Justice Brennan's language, however, was unambiguous: "If the right of privacy means anything, it is the right of the *individual*, married or single, to be free from unwarranted governmental intrusion into matters so fundamentally affecting a person as the decision whether to bear or beget a child." This language may be said either to disregard tradition or to generalize it, raising it to a more abstract level. Only in *Moore* v. *City of East Cleveland* (1977) has the Court openly pursued Harlan's approach. In this case, the Court invalidated a zoning ordinance disallowing residence in the same house of a grandmother and two grandchildren who were cousins rather than siblings. Justice Lewis F. Powell cited Harlan's reasoning in *Poe* in a plurality opinion insisting on "the sanctity of the family." "Ours is by means a tradition limited to respect for the bonds uniting the members of the nuclear family," he wrote. *Bowers* v. *Hardwick* made clear, as noted earlier, that the right to privacy encompassed marriage, the family, and procreation.

In *Planned Parenthood of Southeastern Pennsylvania* v. *Casey* (1992) the Court enunciated a new and less restrictive standard of review in abortion cases. Regulation that does not "unduly" burden abortion will survive judicial scrutiny. Many would foresee the likelihood of an extension of privacy protections to homosexuals as inescapable, however conservative the Court. If so, cultural acceptance may ultimately prove more crucial in constitutional debate than the conclusions of scholarship or formal argument.

Similarly, the right to die as an aspect of privacy, liberty, or both, seems at this point to have secured its toehold in constitutional law. Like sexual privacy at the time of *Griswold*, this right remains uncertain in scope and definition, and the concept at work—once we move beyond a narrow statement of the right to refuse treatment—is both elastic and ambiguous. But these are not fatal intellectual flaws in constitutional law. Privacy, like many legal concepts, is not so much a philosophical conception as a practical one, more readily

R

identified by its messy precedents than by its tidy definition.

—TOM GERETY

Bibliography

Baker, Richard Allan (1989). The Senate of the United States: "Supreme Executive Council of the Nation," 1787–1800. *Prologue* 21:299–313.

Bickford, Charlene Bangs, and Bowling, Kenneth R. (1989). *Birth of the Nation: The First Federal Congress 1789–1791*. Madison, Wis.: Madison House.

Bowling, Kenneth R. (1968). Politics in the First Congress 1789–1791. Ph.D. diss., University of Wisconsin.

Silbey, Joel H. (1987). "Our Successors Will Have an Easier Task": The First Congress Under the Constitution, 1789–1791. *This Constitution* 17:4–10.

Smock, Raymond W. (1989). The House of Representatives: First Branch of the New Government. *Prologue* 21:287–297.

RIGHT TO COUNSEL

The constitutional right to counsel in American law encompasses two broad categories of rights: first, rights of persons to retain and employ counsel in official proceedings and, second, rights of persons who because of financial incapacity or other reasons are unable to procure the assistance of lawyers, to have counsel appointed in their behalf.

The modern rights to counsel are the product of a historical evolution extending over a half-millennium. English criminal procedure in the early modern era diverged sharply from today's institutions of adversary criminal justice. In the Tudor and Stuart regimes, legal proceedings in which the crown's interests were strongly implicated were heavily tilted in favor of the state and against the accused. Thus it was only in the least serious cases, those involving misde-meanors, that the privilege of the accused to present his defense by counsel was recognized. Not until the end of the seventeenth century was a similar right granted defendants in treason trials (along with the right to have counsel appointed by the court when requested). Over 140 years were to elapse before Parliament recognized the right of the accused to retain and employ counsel in felony trials. The earlier recognition of the right to counsel in treason cases reflects the fact that members of Parliament were themselves frequent targets of treason prosecutions launched by the crown. Throughout the eighteenth century the incongruity of a system that recognized counsel rights in misdemeanor and treason cases but withheld them in felony cases at a time when as many as 150 felonies were punishable by death was widely perceived and sometimes protested.

In the American colonies there was great variation in practices and statutory provisions relating to rights of counsel in criminal cases. By 1776, however, the right of attorneys retained by the accused to perform defense functions in courts appears to have been widely conceded, and in several of the colonies practices were considerably in advance of those then prevailing in England. In Pennsylvania, for example, the appointment of counsel for impoverished defendants in capital cases was mandated by statute; and in Connecticut even more liberal practices of appointment were established in the quarter-century before the American revolution.

Rights to counsel entered American constitutional law through provisions included in the early state constitutions and with the ratification of the Sixth Amendment to the federal Constitution in 1791. Seven of the original states and Vermont adopted constitutional provisions relating to the rights to counsel, and the right so protected was that to retain and employ lawyers in criminal trials. By the beginning of the nineteenth century only two states, Connecticut and New

Jersey, appear clearly to have recognized a right in the accused to request appointment of counsel in all serious cases; and in neither was the privilege created by a constitutional provision.

Included in the Sixth Amendment, upon which most of the modern law of counsel rights depends, is the following clause: "In all criminal prosecutions, the accused shall enjoy the right . . . to have the Assistance of Counsel for his defense." There is no direct evidence of the framers' intentions in drafting the language or of the understanding of those who ratified the amendment. Yet the general assumption until well into the present century was that the right constitutionally protected was one to employ counsel, not to have counsel assigned.

One of the most remarkable features of Sixth Amendment history is the paucity of judicial authority on the counsel clause for nearly a century and a half after the amendment's ratification. There was no comprehensive exegesis in the Supreme Court, and only a scattering of holdings in the lower federal courts. The relative absence of authoritative interpretation may be explained in part by the long delay in establishing a system of federal criminal appeals and the strict limitations applied to the habeas corpus remedy in the federal courts. The landmark decision in *Johnson* v. *Zerbst* was not handed down until 1938, six years after the Court had begun its delineation of the rights to counsel protected by the due process clause of the Fourteenth Amendment in state criminal prosecutions. *Johnson* was comprehensive and far-reaching. The Court, through Justice Hugo L. Black, without pausing to canvass the historical understanding of the counsel clause, held that a federal trial court lacked power "to deprive an accused of his life and liberty unless he has or waives the assistance of counsel." Second, the assistance of counsel "is an essential jurisdictional prerequisite" to a federal court's power to try and sentence a criminal defendant.

Hence the habeas corpus remedy may be invoked by a prisoner to set aside his conviction if the Sixth Amendment right to counsel was withheld at his trial. Third, although the right to have counsel assigned may be waived, allegations of waiver will be closely scrutinized. Waiver of constitutional rights involves "an intentional relinquishment of a known right or privilege." The trial judge has a "protecting duty" to see that the accused understands his rights to legal assistance, and if the judge determines that the defendant has waived his rights, the record of the trial should clearly reveal the judge's determination and the basis for it.

In holding that the counsel clause not only creates a right to make use of a retained lawyer in federal criminal proceedings but also mandates the assignment of counsel for an accused otherwise unable to procure legal assistance, *Johnson* v. *Zerbst* upset the long-prevailing understanding to the contrary. Yet the decision did not immediately produce a major alteration in the actual practices of federal criminal justice. Many federal district courts before 1938, with the active encouragement of the Department of Justice, had been assigning counsel to indigent defendants in felony cases. The lawyers so appointed typically received no compensation for their services and were hampered in having no resources for pretrial investigations of their cases or for many other incidents of trial. *Johnson* v. *Zerbst* did little to improve this situation. It was not until a quarter-century later that Congress enacted the Criminal Justice Act of 1964 and for the first time provided, however inadequately, a system of compensated legal assistance in the federal courts.

In the celebrated case of *Powell* v. *Alabama*, decided in 1932, the Supreme Court made its first significant contribution to the constitutional law of counsel rights in Fourteenth Amendment cases. *Powell*, in addition, was one of the great seminal decisions in the Court's history and strongly influenced the development of the entire modern constitutional law of criminal procedure. The decision arose out of one of the most famous of twentieth-century criminal prosecutions, that of the Scottsboro defendants. Seven illiterate young blacks were arrested on the charge of raping two white women. After indictment the accused were divided into groups and tried in three separate trials. No lawyer having come forward to represent the defendants, the trial judge appointed "all the members of the bar" to assist in the arraignment, an act later described by the Supreme Court as merely "an expansive gesture." At the trial no lawyer was designated to assume personal responsibility for protecting the defendants' interests. Each trial was completed in a single day, and in each the jury convicted the accused and sentenced them to death. The convictions were affirmed in the Alabama Supreme Court, the chief justice vigorously dissenting.

At the time of the *Powell* decision, the Supreme Court had rarely employed the federal judicial power to upset state criminal prosecutions. The determination of the Court that the procedures in the Alabama trial had violated the accused's rights to due process of law protected by the Fourteenth Amendment was, therefore, an event of portentous significance. The Court held that both the right of the defendants to retain counsel and the right to have counsel assigned in their behalf had been nullified. The speed with which the Scottsboro defendants had been rushed to trial and conviction deprived them of an opportunity to secure legal assistance, and the arrival of lawyers eager to provide representation for the defendants shortly thereafter indicated that the haste was seriously prejudicial. Beyond this, the Court found that the failure to make an effective appointment of counsel in behalf of the accused, given the circumstances of the case, constituted a denial of due process.

The constitutional theory of Justice George Sutherland's opinion for the court is important, for it dominated thought about the rights of counsel for the next three decades. Whatever else the protean phrase "due process of law" contemplates, argued the Court, it encompasses the requirement of notice and hearing in criminal cases. A fair hearing, in turn, encompasses the right to counsel. In one of the Court's best-known obiter dicta, Justice Sutherland wrote: "The right to be heard would be, in many cases, of little avail if it did not comprehend the right to be heard by counsel. [Even the intelligent and educated layman] requires the guiding hand of counsel at every step of the proceedings against him. Without it, though he be not guilty, he faces the danger of conviction because he does not know how to establish his innocence."

Although the *Powell* decision was placed on a broad constitutional base, one susceptible of future doctrinal development, the actual holding of the case was narrowly drawn. Thus the right of the accused to receive an assignment of counsel in *Powell* was made to rest on such considerations as that the charge was a capital offense, that the defendants were young, inexperienced, illiterate, and the like. The question that immediately became pressing was how far the *Powell* precedent would be extended when one or more of the circumstances in that case were absent. It was widely assumed that the Fourteenth Amendment might require the state to appoint counsel for an indigent defendant in any capital case, even though a considerable interval elapsed before the proposition was authoritatively stated in *Bute* v. *Illinois* (1948). The more important question, however, was whether a "flat requirement" of counsel similar to the Sixth Amendment rule imposed on the federal courts in *Johnson* v. *Zerbst* would also be found applicable to state prosecutions by reason of the Fourteenth Amendment. A definitive negative answer came in *Betts* v. *Brady* (1942).

In *Betts* the defendant was convicted of robbery, a noncapital felony. At his trial in the state court, the accused, an unemployed farm hand said by the Supreme Court to be "of ordinary intelligence," requested the appointment of counsel to assist in his defense. The request was denied by the trial judge, and the accused participated in the defense by examining his own witnesses and cross-examining those of the prosecution. When, after conviction, defendant was denied habeas corpus relief in the state courts, he took his case to the Supreme Court alleging that the denial of counsel at his trial violated due process of law. Justice Owen Roberts for the Court denied that due process required the assignment of counsel for indigent defendants in every state felony case. There was, in the view of the Court's majority, nothing in historical or contemporary practice to validate the claim. Rather, the question in each case was whether in the totality of circumstances presented, appointment of counsel was required to insure the accused a fair hearing. In the present case, the Court said, there was no such necessity. The issue upon which the defense rested, that of alibi, was simple and straightforward. There were no special circumstances of mental incapacity or inexperience that placed defendant at a serious disadvantage in maintaining his defense.

Criticism of the *Betts* decision began with Justice Black's vigorous dissent in that case and was promptly amplified in the press and the writings of legal commentators. Two principal reasons for the reluctance of the Court's majority to impose the obligation of assigning counsel in all state felony prosecutions can be identified. First, the prevailing opinion in *Betts* reflected the Court's deference to state autonomy, a deference widely believed at the time to be mandated by the nature of American federalism. The administration of criminal justice was an area in which state powers of self-determination were thought to be particularly broad. Sec-

ond, there was the related concern that the states were poorly prepared suddenly to assume the obligation of providing legal aid for unrepresented defendants in all state felony cases. The problem was not only that lawyers and resources would have to be supplied in pending and future cases, but also that hundreds of state prisoners had been convicted in trials in which no assistance of counsel was received. The concern was freely articulated by Justice Felix Frankfurter when in *Foster* v. *Illinois* (1947) he wrote: "Such an abrupt innovation . . . would furnish opportunities hitherto uncontemplated for opening wide the prison doors of the land."

Nevertheless, with the passage of time opinion increasingly supported the overturning of *Betts* and recognition of a "flat requirement" of counsel in state as well as federal prosecutions. The *Betts* rule, far from strengthening federalism, exacerbated the relations of state and federal courts. Because under *Betts* the requirement of appointing counsel depended on the unique circumstances of the particular case, the resulting decision often provided little guidance to state judges dealing with cases in which the facts were significantly different. Many state judges came to favor the broader rule of *Johnson* v. *Zerbst* because of its greater certainty. It became apparent to many state officials that ultimately *Betts* v. *Brady* would be overruled, and in anticipation of the event they created systems of legal aid on their own initiative, supplying counsel for unrepresented defendants in all serious state cases. Meanwhile it had become increasingly difficult for the states to protect convictions in the Supreme Court when defendants argued that "special circumstances" had required appointment of counsel at the trial. In the thirteen years before *Betts* was overruled in *Gideon* v. *Wainwright* (1963), no state conviction was upheld by the Court against a claim of special circumstances. It is significant also that when the *Gideon* case was pending before the

Court, the attorneys general of twenty-two states filed amicus curiae briefs asking that *Betts* be overruled and the broader rule of appointment recognized.

Although the opinion of Justice Black for the court is unprepossessing, *Gideon* v. *Wainwright* marked a new era in the constitutional law of counsel rights. Portions of the opinion appear to pay deference to the older theories of fair hearing, and others seem to suggest that counsel must be assigned to unrepresented defendants on grounds of equality. Ultimately, however, *Gideon's* constitutional basis is the Sixth Amendment: the Sixth Amendment is "subsumed" in the provisions of the Fourteenth Amendment, and hence the same obligations relating to assignment of counsel for the indigent accused in federal courts are also owed in state prosecutions. Since the *Gideon* case there has been a flowering of constitutional doctrine relating to counsel rights in many important areas of the criminal process.

Although the prevailing opinion in the *Gideon* case did not specifically limit its holding to felony trials, most observers believed that the right to counsel for indigent defendants would not apply in all misdemeanor cases. Following *Gideon*, state and lower federal courts devised various formulas for dealing with counsel rights in small-crime prosecutions. The state of Florida, borrowing from cases involving the constitutional right to jury trial, provided that counsel rights should not attach in prosecutions for "petty offenses," that is, crimes punishable by not more than six months' imprisonment. (Cf. *Baldwin* v. *New York*, 1970.) In *Argersinger* v. *Hamlin* (1972), nine years after *Gideon*, the Supreme Court rejected Florida's use of the petty-offense concept. In effect, the Court ruled that any deprivation of liberty, even for a few days, is a sanction of significant gravity. Accordingly, no unrepresented defendant may be jailed for any term unless he has waived counsel at the trial. The *Argersinger*

holding dramatically expanded the legal aid obligations of state systems of criminal justice. Adequate practical implementation of counsel rights in small-crimes courts is yet to be fully attained in many jurisdictions.

The right recognized in *Argersinger* was defined further in *Scott* v. *Illinois* (1979). In the latter case an unrepresented defendant was sentenced for an offense that under state law was punishable by both fines and imprisonment. The sentence actually imposed, however, was a monetary fine. The Court, through Justice William H. Rehnquist, ruled that because the unrepresented accused was not actually sentenced to jail, his constitutional rights had not been denied. Ironically, Scott's rights were given less protection than he would have received if the Court had adopted the petty-offense formula in *Argersinger;* that formula would have looked to the penalties authorized by a statute, not solely to those actually imposed.

Because of the comparative modernity of criminal appeals in Anglo-American legal history, the Supreme Court's consideration of constitutional rights of representation in appellate proceedings was not preceded by extensive common law experience. The first substantial discussion of constitutional rights to counsel on appeal occurred in *Douglas* v. *California* (1963) decided on the same day as the *Gideon* case. A California rule of court authorized the state intermediate appellate court to scrutinize the record in a pauper's appeal "to determine whether it would be of advantage to the defendant or helpful to the appellate court to have counsel appointed." Pursuant to this authority the court denied counsel to defendant, adjudicated his appeal, and affirmed his criminal conviction. In the Supreme Court the defendant successfully asserted that the California procedures violated his Fourteenth Amendment rights.

In reaching its result the Court relied primarily on an obligation in the state to accord equal treatment to rich and poor appellants and revived an earlier dictum of Justice Black in *Griffin* v. *Illinois* (1956): "There can be no equal justice where the kind of trial a man gets depends on the amount of money he has." Here the obligation of equal treatment was not met. Had defendant been able to retain his own lawyer, his appeal, regardless of its merits, would have been presented by counsel. Because of his poverty and the decision of the appellate court not to assign a lawyer to him, he was unrepresented on appeal. Whatever the implications of the Court's theory, the obligation of the state to provide "equal treatment" to the poor does not necessarily mean that the treatment must be identical to that meted out to appellants able to hire their own lawyers. Thus, the opinion asserts, "absolute equality is not required." In illustrating this possibility, the Court strongly implied that the constitutional obligation to assign counsel involved in *Douglas* may apply only to the first appeal. If an indigent represented by an assigned counsel is unsuccessful in the intermediate appellate court and decides to seek further review in the state's highest court, he may submit to the latter the brief prepared by counsel in the intermediate court, but the highest court may not be under obligation to assign a lawyer to conduct the second appeal. A decade later the Court made explicit what had been suggested in the *Douglas* case. In *Ross* v. *Moffitt* (1974) the Court sustained the validity of North Carolina procedures that provided the indigent with counsel in the first appeal but denied his requests for representation when he sought a discretionary review in the state supreme court and later, when seeking a writ of certiorari in the United States Supreme Court.

The limitations recognized by the Court, however, do not appear to have seriously inhibited the availability of appellate remedies to indigent defendants. Arguably, this may be true in part because the Court was essentially correct in concluding that the decencies of fair hearing and reasonable equality of treatment can be accorded such appellants without offering counsel in all stages of the appellate procedure. Also, many jurisdictions have gone beyond the constitutional minima and supply counsel throughout the review process. Perhaps of equal importance is a series of cases that have overcome many of the difficulties that earlier confronted impoverished criminal litigants in the appellate courts. As early as 1956 the Court in *Griffin* v. *Illinois* held that a convicted defendant may not be denied access to an appellate remedy because of his poverty. Under state law the appellant could perfect his appeal only by use of a stenographic transcript of the trial proceedings, the latter being unavailable to him because he had no funds to purchase it. Under these circumstances, the Court ruled, the state must furnish the prisoner with a transcript. In the years following, the *Griffin* principle was broadly applied.

Recognition of counsel rights and the removal of obstacles to review for indigent prisoners have greatly widened opportunities for appellate regulation of the trial process. They have, at the same time, created substantial problems for the administration of justice in the appellate courts. Economic constraints may operate on appellants "paying their own way" so as to deter the filing of frivolous appeals. No such constraints influence the indigent prisoner. The resulting problems go beyond the swelling of the dockets of appellate courts and also include certain difficulties for lawyers assigned by the courts to represent indigent appellants. Many such attorneys believe, often rightly, that the appeals of their clients cannot be supported on any substantial legal grounds. Yet efforts by the lawyers to withdraw from representation may, on occasion, prejudice the interests of their clients and, in some instances, may be motivated by the lawyers' design to escape onerous and unprofitable obligations. Efforts to balance such considerations have not as yet resulted in a satisfactory resolution. The rule

The modern rights to counsel are the product of a historical evolution extending over a half-millennium.

announced by the Supreme Court requires the appointed lawyer seeking to be relieved of the case to allege that it is "wholly frivolous." The motion must be accompanied by a brief referring to anything in the record that might arguably support the appeal. How matters may be both "arguable" and "wholly frivolous" is not explained, and the effect of the rule must be to induce the lawyer to remain in the case regardless of his professional judgment of frivolity. The Massachusetts Supreme Judicial Court, in *Commonwealth* v. *Moffett* (1981) recognizing this effect, simply refused to permit counsel to withdraw solely on grounds of absence of merit in the appeal.

Other questions relating to counsel rights have arisen in the postconviction criminal process. As early as *Mempa* v. *Ray* (1967) a unanimous Court held that an indigent defendant, who had been placed on probation after conviction and given a deferred sentence, was entitled to be represented by counsel when his probation was revoked and he was sentenced to imprisonment. In *Gagnon* v. *Scarpelli* (1973), however, the Court ruled that although due process requires a hearing whenever a probation or parole is revoked, counsel need not be appointed unless special circumstances dictate the need for legal representation. This dubious resurrection of the *Betts* v. *Brady* doctrine, long since rejected at the criminal trial, was justified in part by the need to preserve "flexibility" in procedures leading to revocation. The American Bar Association in its *Standards of Criminal Justice* repudiated the *Gagnon* rule and called for appointment of counsel in such cases.

One of the most striking characteristics of the Warren Court was its allegiance to the adversarial system of criminal justice. This dedication inevitably resulted in the expansion of constitutional rights to counsel. Thus, the adversary system was strengthened in areas where it already existed, such as the criminal trial, and also extended to other areas where it had had little or no operation, such

as pretrial police interrogations. Clearly the Court's attitudes toward a rejuvenated adversarial process reflected some of its deepest convictions about the proper containment of state power in the administration of criminal justice. Introducing lawyers into the interrogation rooms of police stations, for example, was intended to achieve values going beyond those ordinarily associated with counsel rights. In addition to advising his client, the lawyer could serve as a witness to police interrogatory activity and a deterrent to police abuse. His presence might often be indispensable to the preservation of the suspect's right against self-incrimination and other constitutional rights.

Concern with proper representation of defendants' interests in the pretrial phases of the criminal process was expressed by the Supreme Court in its earliest cases involving rights to counsel. Even in *Powell* v. *Alabama* (1932) the Court had referred to the pretrial preparation of the defense as "the most critical" period in the criminal proceedings. Before the decision of *Gideon* v. *Wainwright* (1963) the Court had begun mandating the appointment of counsel for unrepresented accused persons at various "critical stages of the proceedings." Thus in *Hamilton* v. *Alabama* (1961) the murder conviction of the indigent accused was reversed because of the absence of defense counsel at the pretrial arraignment.

The more difficult problems, however, were those of the accused's rights after arrest but before formal commencement of the judicial proceedings by bringing the accused into court for preliminary hearing or arraignment. The issues were squarely drawn in the companion cases of *Crooker* v. *California* and *Cicenia* v. *La Gay* (1958). In the former, petitioner, who was under sentence of death, complained that the confession introduced against him at his trial had been obtained in a period of incommunicado questioning during which time he was denied the opportunity to confer with his own attorney. A narrowly divided Court affirmed the conviction, Justice Tom C. Clark emphasizing the "devastating effect" of the presence of counsel in the interrogation room on criminal law enforcement.

Crooker and *Cicenia* were overruled in *Escobedo* v. *Illinois* (1964), which represented the high-water mark of judicial protection of Sixth Amendment counsel rights in the pretrial interrogatory process. In a 5–4 decision the Court ruled that at the point in questioning when suspicions of the police have "focused" on the party being interrogated, even if this occurs before defendant is indicted for a criminal offense, the right of the party to consult with an attorney cannot constitutionally be denied. Two years later the Court decided the famous case of *Miranda* v. *Arizona* (1966), holding that whenever a suspect has been taken into custody he may not be interrogated until he has been given the "fourfold" warning: the arrested party must be advised that he has a right to remain silent, that he is entitled to consult with a lawyer, that the lawyer may be present at the interrogation, and that if he is unable to hire an attorney, counsel will be supplied.

Although the prevailing opinion in *Miranda* reaffirmed the holding of the *Escobedo* case, the impact of the latter was considerably modified. Thus, use of the "focus" concept, while not expressly rejected, was for practical purposes abandoned. Again, although the *Miranda* opinion reaffirmed the existence of Sixth Amendment counsel rights in pretrial interrogation, the emphasis of the opinion is significantly different. The dominant view regarded the right to counsel in the interrogation situation as an incident to and a necessary means for protection of the Fifth Amendment's right against self-incrimination. The emphasis on that right is so dominant that the rights to representation recognized in *Miranda* have sometimes been referred to as Fifth Amendment rights to counsel.

The *Miranda* case did not bring lawyers into interrogation rooms so frequently as was hoped or feared at the time the decision was handed down. One principal weakness of the prevailing opinion was its failure to insist that a suspect's decision to waive the presence of counsel must itself be made only with the advice of a lawyer. In consequence, rights to counsel are frequently waived by persons in police custody. One study published shortly after the *Miranda* ruling revealed as few as 7 percent of the suspects requesting stationhouse counsel. The tendency toward widespread waiver of *Miranda* rights appears to have continued in the intervening years.

Even before *Escobedo,* the Court had contributed another important strand to counsel doctrine in *Massiah* v. *United States* (1964). After the defendant in that case had been indicted for a narcotics offense, government agents induced an accomplice of Massiah to draw him into conversation in an electronically "bugged" automobile. Incriminating admissions made by the defendant were overheard by the agents and introduced against him at the trial. In reversing Massiah's conviction, the Court ruled that the electronic eavesdropping violated defendant's rights to counsel, which rights had "attached" when the indictment against him was returned. Contemporary reaction to the *Massiah* decision was generally critical. Many commentators believed that if a wrong had been done to Massiah it consisted not of a denial of counsel rights, but rather an invasion of his Fourth Amendment right to privacy, or perhaps of the introduction of an "involuntary" confession against him. Again, to conceive of the rights to counsel attaching only at the return of the indictment leaves open to police officials an opportunity of frustrating the rule by simply delaying the indictment or information.

After the decision of *Escobedo* it was widely assumed that the *Massiah* precedent had been drained of vitality. Yet in the widely noted case of *Brewer* v. *Williams* (1977) *Massiah* was invested with renewed significance. Although *Brewer* might readily have been decided by an application of the *Miranda* rule, the Court chose instead to reverse the conviction on the grounds of denial of counsel, reliance being placed on the *Massiah* precedent. Later decisions, building on *Massiah*, appear to assert a right in the defendant not to be approached by the government for evidence of his own guilt in the absence of counsel, once judicial proceedings are initiated by return of an indictment or other in-court proceedings (*United States* v. *Henry,* 1980). In New York the state courts have transcended the *Massiah* precedent by interpreting state law to mean that whenever a lawyer enters a case in behalf of the defendant, even when this occurs before indictment, the accused in custody may not waive his right to counsel in the absence of his lawyer (*People* v. *Hobson,* 1976). Although the New York rule alleviates the restrictions imposed by the Supreme Court on the *Massiah* doctrine, it is of limited value to indigent defendants, who ordinarily do not acquire counsel before the commencement of judicial proceedings.

A final area of pretrial counsel rights involves lineups. Misidentification of the accused by prosecution witnesses constitutes perhaps the most prolific source of erroneous convictions; police lineups and other identification procedures often spawn such errors. In *United States* v. *Wade* (1967) the Court responded to these problems by designating the pretrial identification confrontation between witnesses and the accused as a "critical stage" of the proceedings and hence one requiring the presence of the accused's attorney. An identification made at a lineup in which the suspect's right to counsel was not honored may not be introduced at the criminal trial. An in-court identification is not summarily barred, but before it can be employed as evidence, the prosecution must establish by "clear and convincing evidence" that it was based on observations other than those made at the flawed lineup. After this promising beginning the Court backed away, and the view appears established that unless the identification evidence was obtained by methods so defective as to deny due process of law, an identification obtained in the absence of counsel may be introduced in court if the lineup occurred before return of an indictment. Limiting rights of counsel to the postindictment period is especially devastating in these areas because identification efforts are typically undertaken before formal charges are made. In *United States* v. *Ash* (1973) the Court has also refused to supervise other identification procedures, such as those involving the use of photographic files. The problems of convicting the innocent through misidentification persist, and the Court has relegated their solutions largely to administrative and legislative action.

Basic to the rights of counsel is the quality of the legal representation supplied the criminal accused. Yet growth of the law in this area is inhibited by the fear that close judicial scrutiny of the competency of such representation will provide numerous and unwarranted opportunities for disappointed criminal litigants to attack their convictions. Such administrative concerns resulted in the once widely recognized rule that convictions were not to be reversed on incompetency grounds unless the performance of defense counsel constituted a "mockery of justice." The formula employed in the Supreme Court today is considerably more demanding: counsel's advice must not fall "outside the range of competence demanded of attorneys in criminal cases" (*Tollet* v. *Henderson,* 1953). The application of the "ordinary competence" test, however, results in the reversal of comparatively few criminal convictions. Thus in *United States* v. *Decoster* (1979) the District of Columbia Court of Appeals refused to upset a conviction in which a court-appointed lawyer failed to interview his client's co-defendants or any other witnesses before trial. Failures to achieve the objective of adequate defense in criminal cases are often not the product of the professional incompetence of lawyers. In many cases the court-appointed lawyer is on the staff of an inadequately funded legal aid agency that must impose wholly unrealistic case loads on its attorneys. Similar problems also often affect the privately retained lawyer who because of the economics of criminal law practice may be under pressure to accept more cases than he can adequately handle. The courts alone cannot be expected to solve problems of this sort, but it is doubtful that instances of inadequate defense will be significantly abated until the courts articulate and apply specific minimum standards of counsel performance.

The right of an indigent litigant to demand appointment of counsel from the state in noncriminal proceedings has received comparatively little judicial consideration or development. In the famous case of *In re Gault* (1967) the Court recognized a right to counsel in a state juvenile court delinquency proceeding. Some courts have held that, where necessary to a fair hearing, a similar right is possessed by an indigent petitioner in an habeas corpus action. Since juvenile court and habeas corpus proceedings, although "civil" in form, are analogous or intimately related to the criminal process, the precedents in neither category represent a significant expansion of counsel rights into noncriminal areas.

In *Lassiter* v. *Department of Social Services* (1981) the question was whether counsel must be appointed to represent an indigent mother in a proceeding brought by the state to terminate her parental rights. In such a proceeding the defendant faces a sanction often considered more severe than a sentence of imprisonment, and, given the nature of the issues, the defendant's need for professional assistance is at least as great as that of the accused in many criminal cases. Although recognizing these considerations, the Court's majority limited the right to counsel to the situation in which all the circumstances in a particular case make legal representation necessary for a fair hearing, and it concluded that such considerations were not shown to be present in the *Lassiter* case. This latter-day revival of the *Betts* v. *Brady* precedent is regrettable in view of the needs for counsel in these proceedings and the comparatively small social costs involved in making counsel available routinely in all such cases. Like *Betts*, however, the *Lassiter* holding may represent a step toward a more satisfactory ultimate result.

In the development of the modern constitutional law of criminal procedure, questions of the rights of counsel have held a central position. This centrality is not surprising; counsel rights are integral to an adversarial system of justice, and the expansion and refurbishing of that system have been a dominant objective of constitutional procedural law from the decision of *Powell* v. *Alabama* in 1932 to the present. In the intervening years, issues of counsel rights have continued to emerge in a variety of contexts. It may be anticipated that this course of constitutional events will continue so long as the Supreme Court places significant reliance on the adversarial system as the principal mechanism to control and order the applications of state power in the criminal process.

—FRANCIS A. ALLEN

Bibliography

Allen, Francis A. (1975). The Judicial Quest for Penal Justice: The Warren Court and the Criminal Cases. *Illinois Law Forum* 1975:518–542.

Attorney General's Committee (1963). *Poverty and the Administration of Federal Criminal Justice.* Washington, D.C.: Government Printing Office.

Beaney, William A. (1955). *The Right to Counsel in American Courts.* Ann Arbor: University of Michigan Press.

Holtzoff, A. (1944). Right to Counsel under the Sixth Amendment. *New York University Law Review* 20:1–22.

Kamisar, Yale (1962). *Betts* v. *Brady* Twenty Years Later. *Michigan Law Review* 61: 219–282.

———— (1978). *Brewer* v. *Williams, Massiah and Miranda:* What Is Interrogation? When Does It Matter? *Georgetown Law Journal* 67:1–101.

Levine, F., and Tapp, J. (1973). The Psychology of Criminal Identification: The Gap from Wade to Korley. *University of Pennsylvania Law Review* 121:1079–1131.

RIGHT TO DIE

The "right to die" is an ambiguous, and therefore expansive, phrase. It can encompass the right to refuse life-sustaining medical treatment, the right to commit suicide, the right to have a doctor assist a person in suicide, and the right of third parties to kill legally incompetent patients by administering lethal doses of drugs or by removing food, water, respirators and/or other medical care.

The constitutional arguments for the right to die are premised on either the right of privacy or on the right to liberty guaranteed by the due process clause of the Fourteenth Amendment. Several lower federal courts, as well as state supreme courts, have held that the right of privacy includes at least a limited right to die. In *Cruzan* v. *Director, Missouri Department of Health* (1990), however, the Supreme Court suggested that right-to-die cases fit more appropriately within the due process framework.

Cruzan involved the tragic plight of Nancy Cruzan, who sustained severe head injuries in a car accident in 1983. After three weeks in a coma, she improved sufficiently that she could chew and swallow food. A feeding tube was nevertheless inserted into her stomach in order to make long-term care easier. Subsequent efforts to rehabilitate her failed.

In 1987 Nancy's parents sought to stop the food and hydration provided through the tube, arguing that their daughter was in a "persistent vegetative state," manifesting no awareness of herself or her environment. They further said that previous to her accident Nancy had indicated that she would not want to be kept alive in such a condition. The trial court granted the Cruzans' request, but the Missouri state supreme court reversed, ruling that not enough evidence had been presented to demonstrate that Ms. Cruzan would in fact choose to forgo food and liquids if she were competent to make the choice. The U.S. Supreme Court narrowly upheld the constitutionality of this determination by a vote of 5–4.

Writing for the majority, Chief Justice William H. Rehnquist said that according to previous decisions of the Court, "a competent person has a constitutionally protected liberty interest in refusing unwanted medical treatment" based on the due process clause. This liberty interest is not inviolable, however. It must be weighed against various state interests, including the state's commitment to the preservation of human life. According to Rehnquist, this commitment justifies prohibitions against both homicide and assistance to commit suicide. It also justifies state measures to prevent suicide. In Rehnquist's words, "We do not think a State is required to remain neutral in the face of an informed and voluntary decision by a physically able adult to starve to death."

Nancy Cruzan, of course, was not physically able; and for the purpose of this case, Rehnquist assumed that while competent able persons may not have the constitutional right to starve themselves to death, competent persons requiring artificially administered food and fluids do. The question was how this right could be applied to an incompetent individual like Nancy Cruzan. Concerned about the possible abuse of the power to remove life-sustaining treatment from others, Missouri had stipulated that food and hydration can be removed from an incompetent patient only when there is clear and convincing evidence that this is what the patient would have wanted under the circumstances.

In the case of Nancy Cruzan, the Missouri supreme court held that insufficient evidence had been presented to make this determination. Rehnquist and the majority concluded that in this particular case this was a permissible way to safeguard the state's interest in protecting human life.

However, the Court also hinted that a different result might be required in a situation where a person had duly appointed a third party to make decisions in the case of the person's incompetency. In other words, had Nancy Cruzan made clear prior to her accident that she wanted her parents to make medical decisions for her if she ever became incompetent, the Court might have compelled the state to carry out the parents' wishes. Justice Sandra Day O'Connor emphasized this point in her concurring opinion.

Dissenting, Justice William J. Brennan claimed that more than enough evidence existed to show that Nancy Cruzan did not want to be kept alive in her present condition. Even if there had not been sufficient evidence to determine Cruzan's wishes, however, the state still had no right to maintain her life according to Brennan. Instead, it was obligated by the due process clause to leave the decision over whether or not to remove medical treatment to "the person whom the patient himself would most likely have chosen as proxy or . . . to the patient's family."

Justice John Paul Stevens, in a separate dissent, adopted a different approach. He articulated an objective "best interests" test whereby the courts would determine if it is in the best interests of the patient to continue to receive life support. Reviewing Nancy Cruzan's tragic condition, Stevens concluded that her "best interests" unquestionably dictated that food and fluids be shut off. Some might find chilling Stevens's expansive definition of "best interests," however, for it apparently included a patient's interest in not being a burden to others. At the end of his opinion, Stevens spoke of Nancy's "interest in minimizing the burden that her own illness imposes on others . . . [and] in having their memories of her filled predominantly with thoughts about her past vitality rather than her current condition."

Several aspects of the right to die raise difficult questions. In *Washington* v. *Glucksberg* (1997) the Court made clear that the right did not extend to physician-assisted suicide, for example, because suicide wishes are often fleeting and irrational, and if society makes suicide too easy, efforts to prevent suicide may be undermined. Advocates for persons with disability claim this is already happening, pointing to a case in California where a court sanctioned the request of a disabled woman to starve herself to death in a hospital—despite clear evidence that the woman was severely depressed because of recent personal tragedies. Although the Court in *Glucksberg* viewed physician-assisted suicide as best left to the legislative process, only Oregon has legalized it.

The power of third parties to deny life-sustaining measures to incompetent patients is equally problematic. Underlying much of the discussion over incompetent patients is the assumption that these persons are not fully human. This came out with force in the dissents in *Cruzan,* where Justices Brennan and Stevens both claimed that Nancy existed in a state "devoid of thought, emotion and sensation." This contention was fundamental to their arguments, because it allowed them to claim that the state could have no legitimate interest in preserving Nancy's life, because no human life in fact existed for the state to protect.

There are serious problems, however, with premising the right to die on judgments about someone else's humanity. Such judgments are not nearly so clear or so objective as many presume. Nancy Cruzan, for example, was supposed to be oblivious to her environment. Yet the trial court heard testimony from nurses who testified that Nancy tracked with her eyes, smiled after being told stories, and cried after family visits. Even in cases

The "right to die" is an ambiguous, and therefore expansive, phrase.

where a patient cannot respond at all, one may question whether this alone is a sufficient indicator of a person's loss of cognitive faculties. Research on coma victims who have recovered shows that the mere fact that they could not respond outwardly while comatose did not mean they had lost their humanity. They could hear what others said about them in their hospital room. They experienced emotions. They dreamt. But if persons in a persistent vegetative state retain their humanity in some fundamental sense, the assumption that the state has *no* interest in protecting their lives becomes much less persuasive.

The application of the right to die to incompetent patients other than those in persistent vegetative states is even more problematic. The right to die has been used to justify withholding food, fluids, and basic medical treatment from a wide array of incompetent individuals, from conscious stroke victims to infants with Down's Syndrome or treatable physical disabilities such as spina bifida. Disability groups complain that in these cases the right to die is nothing more that the right to discriminate against the physically and mentally hadicapped. They argue that not only is such discrimination not constitutionally protected, it is constitutionally proscribed by guarantees of due process and equal protection.

Like abortion, the right to die implicates some of the most fundamental beliefs humans hold about the nature of human life. Right-to-die cases often require judges to be physicians and philosophers as well as jurists, and few would pretend that a judge's role in such cases is either enviable or easy.

—JOHN G. WEST, JR.

Bibliography

Arkes, Hadley (1987). "Autonomy" and the "Quality of Life": The Dismantling of Moral Terms. *Issues in Law and Medicine* 2:421–433.

Barry, Robert (1988). *Protecting the Medically Dependent: Social Challenge and Ethical Imperative.* Stafford, Va.: Castello Institute.

Bopp, Jr., James (1987). Is Assisted Suicide Constitutionally Protected? *Issues in Law and Medicine* 3:113–140.

Longmore, Paul K. (1987). Elizabeth Bouvia, Assisted Suicide and Social Prejudice. *Issues in Law and Medicine* 3:141–168.

RIPENESS

People who anticipate harm occasionally attack a law's constitutionality before it is applied to them, or even before the law takes effect. A federal court may decline to decide such a case for lack of ripeness if it is unclear that adjudication is needed to protect the challengers, or if information sufficient to permit intelligent resolution is not yet available. A matter of timing and degree, ripeness is grounded both in Article III's case or controversy requirement and the federal courts' reluctance to issue constitutional decisions needlessly or prematurely. Delaying decision may cause interim hardship and allow unconstitutional harm to occur, but further developments may narrow the issues, or produce important information, or even establish that no decision is needed.

The Supreme Court's ripeness decisions display varying sensitivity to these sometimes conflicting factors. Normally, a court is more likely to defer resolution of fact-dependent issues, like those based on a particular application of a law, than it is to defer adjudication of strictly legal issues. A single case may present some issues ripe for adjudication, but others not ripe. Ripeness decisions mainly respond, however, to the degree of contingency or uncertainty of the law's expected effect on the challenger.

Where leeway exists, the court may be influenced by determining whose interests a quicker decision would serve. Thus, when federal civil servants fearing dismissal for violation of the Hatch Act asked that the political activities they were contemplating be declared constitutionally protected in *United*

See also

Washington v. *Glucksberg*

Public Workers v. *Mitchell* (1947), the Court found the case unripe absent enforcement of the act against some particular employee behavior. Similarly, a challenge to immigration policy was held unripe in *International Longshoremen's Union* v. *Boyd* (1954) despite a strong indication that, without a ruling, resident aliens risked jeopardizing their right to return to the United States. With little doubt that the laws would be applied, the challengers nonetheless were forced to act at their peril. By contrast, when a delay in decision has threatened to frustrate government policy, the Court has resolved anticipatory challenges to laws whose future application appeared inevitable, including legislation restructuring some of the nation's railroads in the *Regional Rail Reorganization Act Cases* (1974) and the Federal Election Campaign Acts in *Buckley* v. *Valeo* (1976).

Sensitivity to the government's interest in quick resolution even led the Court to uphold a federal statute limiting aggregate operator liability for nuclear power plant explosions in *Duke Power Co.* v. *Carolina Environmental Study Group, Inc.* (1978), despite evidence that explosions are unlikely and serious doubt that this statute would ever be applied. Because injury to the asserted right of unlimited recovery for nuclear disaster was unlikely to occur soon, if at all, the constitutional issues did not seem ripe; yet the Court concluded that the case was ripe, because the normal operation of nearby nuclear plants (whose development the statute had facilitated) threatened imminent pollution—even though the suit had not questioned the pollution's legality.

More recently, in *Ohio Forestry Association* v. *Sierra Club* (1998), the Court showed its reluctance to hear a suit if considered not yet ripe, reminding us that ripeness concerns are alive and well.

As the *Duke Power* case illustrates, the inherent policy choice in ripeness decisions—between finding constitutional adjudication premature and finding prevention of harm or validation of government policy timely—embodies important perceptions of judicial role in a regime characterized by the separation of powers.

—JONATHAN D. VARAT

Bibliography

Wright, Charles A.; Miller, Arthur R.; and Cooper, Edward H. (1984). *Federal Practice and Procedure.* Vol. 13A:112–214. St. Paul, Minn.: West Publishing Co.

ROBERTS v. CITY OF BOSTON

5 Cush. (Mass.) 198 (1850)

In *Brown* v. *Board of Education* (1954) the Court observed that the separate but equal doctrine "apparently originated in *Roberts* v. *City of Boston*." Chief Justice Lemuel Shaw's opinion in that case had an extraordinary influence. The courts of at least ten states relied on it as a precedent for upholding segregated education. In *Hall* v. *DeCuir* (1878) the Supreme Court cited it as an authority for the rule that "equality does not mean identity." In *Plessy* v. *Ferguson* (1896) the Court relied on it as the leading precedent for the validity of state legislation requiring racial segregation in places where whites and blacks "are liable to be brought in to contact," and in *Gong Lum* v. *Rice* (1927) the Court explained *Roberts* as having sustained "the separation of colored and white schools under a state constitutional injunction of equal protection, the same as the Fourteenth Amendment. . . ."

Roberts arose as a test case to determine the validity of Boston's requirement that black children attend segregated schools. Charles Sumner, attacking that requirement, denied that a racially separate school could be equal, because it imposed a stigma of caste and fostered prejudice.

Shaw, for a unanimous Supreme Judicial Court, agreed that the case presented the question of whether the separate schools for

Shaw agreed that the case presented the question of whether the separate schools for blacks violated their constitutional right to equality.

See also

Brown v. *Board of Education*

Equal Protection

Plessy v. *Ferguson*

Segregation

Separate but Equal Doctrine

Until 1984, only males between eighteen and thirty-five could be full members of the Jaycees.

blacks violated their constitutional right to equality. But he reasoned that all rights must depend on laws adapted to the "respective relations and conditions" of individuals. He believed that the school committee had exercised "a discriminating and honest judgment" in deciding that the good of both races was best promoted by the separate education of their children. The law, Shaw said in reply to Sumner, did not create prejudice, probably could not change it, and might only foster it by "compelling" both races to attend "the same schools." Thus, by a singular absence of considered judgment, the court found no constitutional violation of equal protection in compulsory racial segregation as long as blacks had an equal right to attend public schools.

—LEONARD W. LEVY

ROBERTS ET AL. v. UNITED STATES JAYCEES

468 U.S. 609 (1984)

In this case, the Supreme Court ruled that the states may forbid sex discrimination not only in public accommodations but also in private associations whose membership is restricted. The Civil Rights Act of 1964 exempted private clubs from its coverage, but by the 1980s California and Minnesota had extended their bans on sex discrimination to cover these groups. Minnesota's law led to a confrontation between the local and national organizations of the Junior Chamber of Commerce (the Jaycees), which encouraged members to participate in community activities, including running for office. Membership is open to any eligible person who pays the dues, and the Jaycees have welcomed all races, religions, and nationalities since it was founded in 1920. Until 1984, however, only males between the ages of eighteen and thirty-five could be full members. Women began demanding Jaycee membership in the 1970s, arguing that exclusion denied them

equal professional and civic opportunities. Some local chapters began admitting women, and when the national organization threatened to revoke the charters of the Minneapolis and Saint Paul chapters, the case ended up in the Supreme Court. The justices ruled unanimously that, in light of the Jaycees' traditionally inclusive membership, they "have demonstrated no serious burden on their male members' freedom of association." *Roberts* did not ban all sex discrimination in private associations; it held only that the Constitution did not bar the states from prohibiting sex discrimination in a group like the Jaycees. Nevertheless, one month after the decision, the national organization voted to admit women.

—JUDITH A. BAER

Bibliography

Baer, Judith A., *Women in American Law* (New York, 1985–1991).

ROBINSON, UNITED STATES v.

414 U.S. 218 (1973)

The Supreme Court here resolved the question of whether the Fourth Amendment permits a full search of the person incident to arrest for a minor offense. This question is particularly acute in cases of traffic offenses, where police commonly make arrests in order to search drivers and their automobiles.

In *Robinson* the police stopped an automobile and arrested its driver for operating the vehicle without a license. A search of his clothing uncovered heroin. Because searches incident to arrest are allowed for the purpose of discovering concealed weapons and evidence, Robinson's counsel argued that such searches are unjustified in connection with routine traffic arrests: they will seldom yield evidence related to the traffic offense itself, and the chances of the driver's being armed are usually minimal.

The Supreme Court ruled, however, that a search incident to a custodial arrest requires no justification beyond the arrest; it is not an exception to the warrant requirement, but rather is itself a reasonable search. It was "speculative" to believe that those arrested for driving without a license "are less likely to be armed than those arrested for other crimes." Any lawful arrest justifies "a full search of the person."

—JACOB W. LANDYNSKI

ROE v. WADE

410 U.S. 113 (1973)

DOE v. BOLTON

410 U.S. 179 (1973)

In these cases the Supreme Court confronted the emotionally charged issue of abortion. The decisions invalidated two states' abortion laws—and, by inference, similar laws in a majority of states. As a result, the Court was plunged into prolonged and intense controversy, ranging from questions about the bearing of morality on constitutional law to questions about the proper role of the judiciary in the American system of government. The Court held unconstitutional a Texas law forbidding abortion except to save the pregnant woman's life and also invalidated several features of a Georgia law regulating abortion procedures and limiting abortion to Georgia residents.

The two women whose fictitious names grace the cases' titles were pregnant when they filed their actions in 1970, but not at the time of the Supreme Court's decision. The Court nonetheless held that their cases were not moot; rigid application of the mootness doctrine would prevent appellate review of an important issue that was capable of repetition. Nine doctors were also held to have standing to challenge the Georgia law; the intervention of a doctor under prosecution in Texas was held improper under the equitable abstention principle of *Younger* v. *Harris* (1971); and a Texas married couple was de-

nied standing because the woman had not been pregnant. The Court thus proceeded to the constitutional merits.

The *Roe* opinion, by Justice Harry A. Blackmun, reviewed the history of abortion laws and the recent positions on abortion taken by medical groups and the American Bar Association, but the Court grounded its decision on neither history nor current professional opinion. Instead, the Court relied on a constitutional right of privacy previously recognized in *Griswold* v. *Connecticut* (1965) and now relocated in the "liberty" protected by the due process clause of the Fourteenth Amendment. This right included "a woman's decision whether or not to terminate her pregnancy," which decision was a fundamental interest that could be restricted only on a showing of a compelling state interest.

The Court identified two state interests that would qualify as "compelling" at different stages in pregnancy: protection of maternal health and protection of potential life. Before discussing these interests, however, the Court dealt with a preliminary question: whether a fetus was a person within the meaning of the Fourteenth Amendment. In an abortion, of course, it is not the state that denies life to a fetus; presumably the point of the Court's question was that if a fetus were a "person," the amendment should not be read to bar a state from protecting it against being aborted. The Court concluded, however, that a fetus was not a "person" in the amendment's contemplation. In reaching this conclusion, Justice Blackmun said: "We need not resolve the difficult question of when life begins." Absent a consensus among doctors, philosophers, or theologians on the issue, "the judiciary, at this point in the development of man's knowledge, is not in a position to speculate as to the answer." In any event, the law had never recognized the unborn "as persons in the whole sense." That conclusion alone, however, could not dispose of the question of the state's power. A state can constitutionally protect beings (or even things) that are not persons—including fetuses, which surely can

See also

Search and Seizure

663

be protected by law against certain kinds of experimentation or disposal, even though the law may be motivated by a feeling that fetuses share our common humanity.

The Court did recognize the state's interests in protecting maternal health and potential life; each would become "compelling" at successive stages of pregnancy. During the first trimester of pregnancy, neither interest is compelling; the abortion decision and its implementation must be left to the woman and her doctor. During the second trimester, the interest in maternal health becomes sufficiently compelling to justify some state regulations of the abortion procedure. When the fetus becomes "viable"—capable of life outside the womb, around the beginning of the third trimester of pregnancy—the state's interest in potential life becomes sufficiently

compelling to justify prohibiting abortion except to preserve the "life or health" of the mother.

This scheme of constitutional rights has the look of a statute and evidently was influenced by New York's liberal law and the American Bar Association's model abortion law. Investigative reporters tell us that the three-part scheme resulted from negotiation among the Justices, and it is hard to see it as anything but a compromise between banning abortion altogether and turning over the entire abortion decision to the pregnant woman.

Justice Byron R. White, dissenting, complained that the Court had permitted abortion to satisfy "the convenience, whim or caprice of the putative mother." Chief Justice Warren E. Burger, concurring, responded that the Court had rejected "any claim that the Constitution requires abortion on demand" in favor of a scheme relying on doctors' "medical judgments relating to life and health." The Court's opinion deals ambiguously with the doctor's decisional role. At one point it states that the abortion decision "must be left to the medical judgment of the pregnant woman's attending physician." Yet the Court's decision rests on the constitutional right to privacy, which includes "a woman's decision whether or not to terminate her pregnancy." Very likely Justice Blackmun, a former general counsel of the Mayo Clinic, was influenced by the medical authorities he cited. Indeed, the Blackmun and Burger opinions both convey an inclination to convert abortion issues into medical questions. Linking the state's power to forbid abortions with "viability" is one example—although it is unclear how the Court will respond when medical technology permits the preservation of very young fetuses outside the womb. Similarly, a supposed lack of medical consensus made the Court reluctant to decide when life begins.

The issues in *Roe*, however, were not medical issues. First, there is no medically correct decision concerning an abortion when the pregnant woman's health is not endangered.

Second, there is no lack of medical consensus about what happens in the normal process of reproduction from insemination to birth. In some sense "life" begins at conception; to say otherwise is not to make a medical judgment but to decide a question of law or morality. The problem before the Court in *Roe* was to determine whether (or when) a state could constitutionally protect a fetus. The state's interest in potential life surely begins at the time of conception, and arguably before. Yet if *Griswold* and *Eisenstadt* v. *Baird* (1972) remained good law, the state could not constitutionally protect that interest by forbidding contraception. Most people do not equate the use of "morning after" pills or intrauterine devices with murder, although these forms of "contraception" are really ways of effecting abortion after conception. In 1973 no state was enforcing its abortion laws against such practices. Yet the argument that "life" begins at conception, for purposes of defining legal or moral rights, embraced the claims of both the newest embryo and the eight-month fetus. There was evident artificiality in the Court's selection of "viability" as the time when the state's concerns for potential life became "compelling," but there would have been artificiality in any resolution of the issue of state power other than an all-or-nothing decision.

In *Roe*'s companion case, *Doe* v. *Bolton*, the Court held invalid four provisions of Georgia law, requiring that abortions be (1) performed in hospitals accredited by the Joint Commission on Accreditation of Hospitals; (2) approved by hospital staff committees; (3) approved in each case by two physicians other than the pregnant woman's doctor; and (4) limited to Georgia residents. The latter requirement was an obvious violation of Article IV's privileges and immunities clause, and the other three were held to impose unreasonable restrictions on the constitutional right recognized in *Roe*.

The *Roe* opinion has found few defenders; even the decision's supporters are inclined to offer substitute justifications. *Roe*'s critics divide roughly into two groups: those who regard abortion as murder, and those who think the Supreme Court exceeded its proper institutional bounds, failing to ground its decision in the Constitution and merely substituting its own policy judgment for that of the people's elected representatives.

The latter criticism touched off an impressive succession of essays on judicial review. It was the former group of critics, however, who dominated the politics of abortion. The "right to life" movement was, for a time, one of the nation's most effective "single issue" groups, achieving enough respect from legislators to permit the adoption of laws withdrawing governmental financial aid to poor women who seek abortions. Various constitutional amendments to overturn *Roe* were proposed in Congress, but none was submitted to the states for ratification. In the early 1980s Congress considered, but did not adopt, a bill declaring that "human life begins from the moment of conception." Congress also heard proposals to withdraw federal court jurisdiction over abortion cases. Yet the *Roe* decision has weathered all these political storms. Indeed, in 1992, in *Planned Parenthood of Southeastern Pennsylvania* v. *Casey*, the Court reaffirmed the "essential holding" of *Roe* in the clearest of terms.

Roe's stability as a precedent is founded on the same social and political base that initially supported the decision. It was no accident that *Roe* was decided in the 1970s, when the movement against sex discrimination was winning its most important constitutional and political victories. The abortion question was not merely an issue between pregnant women and their unwanted fetuses; it was also a feminist issue, going to women's position in society in relation to men. Even today American society imposes a greater stigma on unmarried women who become pregnant than on the men who father their children, and society still expects women to take the major responsibility for contraception and

The Court's decision rests on the constitutional right to privacy, which includes "a woman's decision whether or not to terminate her pregnancy."

child care. The implications of an unwanted pregnancy or parenthood for a woman's opportunities in education, employment, and personal association—indeed, for the woman's definition of self—are enormous. Justice White's dissenting remark, that abortion regulation is an issue about which "reasonable men may easily and heatedly differ," perhaps said more than he intended to say.

—KENNETH L. KARST

Bibliography

Ely, John Hart (1973). The Wages of Crying Wolf: A Comment on *Roe* v. *Wade*. *Yale Law Journal* 82:920–949.

Henkin, Louis (1974). Privacy and Autonomy. *Columbia Law Review* 74:1410–1433.

Symposium on the Law and Politics of Abortion (1979). *Michigan Law Review* 77: 1569–1646.

Tribe, Laurence H. (1978). *American Constitutional Law.* Pages 923–934. Mineola, N.Y.: Foundation Press.

Woodward, Bob, and Armstrong, Scott (1979). *The Brethren: Inside the Supreme Court.* Pages 165–189, 229–240. New York: Simon & Schuster.

ROMER v. EVANS

517 U.S. 620 (1996)

This decision overturned an amendment to the Colorado Constitution, adopted by referendum, that purported to bar homosexuals from claiming discrimination by any state or local government agency or private business. Specifically, the amendment barred the state and its municipalities and other political subdivisions, as well as school districts, from enacting or enforcing any statute, regulation, ordinance, or policy through which homosexuals might claim protected status or discrimination. The plaintiffs challenged it as a denial of equal protection under the Fourteenth Amendment.

Vital to the courts' treatment of an equal protection claim is the degree of scrutiny the court employs. Ordinarily a law will be upheld as against an equal protection challenge as long as it has a rational basis. However, classifications involving a fundamental right like free speech or privacy, or "suspect classifications" based on race, gender, or the like, receive more intensive scrutiny from the courts. Sexual orientation, however, has not been considered a suspect classification, nor has homosexual conduct been encompassed in the fundamental right of privacy, which includes marriage, procreation, and family decision making. The Court so held in *Bowers* v. *Hardwick*. This placed the difficult burden on the plaintiffs in *Romer* v. *Evans* to prove the Colorado amendment lacked a rational basis. Yet the Court, in an opinion by Justice Anthony M. Kennedy, held just that, and set the amendment aside.

Justice Kennedy noted that the rational-basis test still requires that classification not be "drawn for the purpose of disadvantaging the group burdened by the law." And, the Court found, that was the sole intent of the amendment. It was aimed at overturning several state and local laws that barred discrimination in employment, housing, and access to places of business based on one's sexual orientation. In addition, it purported to annul a governor's executive order barring discrimination against state employees based on their sexual orientation, as well as similar rules at state colleges.

Colorado argued the amendment did no more than put homosexuals "in the same position as all other persons." But, as the Court found, it went much further, and forbade the state and its municipalities from ever enacting or reinstating such laws and policies. Therefore it did not simply return the pendulum to its midpoint, but swung it to the opposite extreme. In addition, the amendment likely even prevented one from claiming under ordinary common-law principles that he or she had been arbitrarily denied a license or permit because of the applicant's homosexuality. This

Colorado argued that the amendment did no more than put homosexuals "in the same position as all other persons." But, as the Court found, it went much further.

See also

Abortion and the
   Constitution
Griswold v. *Connecticut*
Right of Privacy
Younger v. *Harris*

means "the amendment imposes a special disability upon those persons alone." Homosexuals are "forbidden the safeguards that others enjoy or may seek" without hindrance.

In the Court's view it was hard to avoid the inference that the amendment was "born of animosity toward" homosexuals. This in itself strongly suggested that the amendment lacked any rational link to a legitimate governmental goal, but was instead simply intended to stigmatize and injure a class of persons.

The state's last-ditch defense was that the amendment protected other people's freedom of association, such as landlords and employers not wishing to deal with homosexuals. But it found the breadth of the amendment "so far removed from these particular justifications that we find it impossible to credit them." In any event, the state's argument surely proves too much, for it could as well be used to justify an amendment to a state's constitution to bar laws against discrimination based on race, gender, or national origin.

Justice Antonin Scalia, joined by two other Justices, dissented. He argued the amendment "prohibits *special treatment* of homosexuals, and nothing more" (emphasis in original). And since *Bowers* v. *Hardwick* upheld state laws criminalizing homosexual conduct, Colorado was free to deny protected status to that group. This glosses over the fact that the amendment was aimed not just at homosexual conduct but at homosexual orientation. In Justice Scalia's view, though, if the state may criminalize the conduct, it may rationally deny "special favor and protection to those with a self-avowed tendency or desire to engage in the conduct." Therefore, in his opinion, Coloradans are in fact "*entitled* to be hostile toward homosexual conduct" (emphasis in original).

The decision makes clear that though the Court is unwilling so far to find laws criminalizing homosexual acts unconstitutional, it will not tolerate an attempt to deny to homosexuals basic rights enjoyed by every citizen, such as the right to be free of arbitrary conduct by government agencies or officials. However, the Court left open whether a law doing no more than denying homosexuals protected status would be valid. One recent lower federal court decision in fact has upheld a local law of that nature, though the thrust of *Romer* v. *Evans* suggests that a law of that nature is equally grounded in hostility to homosexuals as a group and therefore without a rational basis as well.

—PHILIP WEINBERG

ROSENBERG v. UNITED STATES

346 U.S. 273 (1953)

Over the vehement protests of three of its members (Hugo Black, Felix Frankfurter, and William O. Douglas), the Vinson Court vacated a stay of execution issued by Douglas that had halted the scheduled electrocution of Julius and Ethel Rosenberg. The Rosenbergs had been convicted and sentenced to death in 1951 for allegedly violating the 1917 Espionage Act by passing secret information about the atomic bomb to the Soviet Union. Douglas had refused to join Black, Frankfurter, and Harold Burton in earlier efforts to review the case by means of certiorari and habeas corpus, but on June 17, 1953, after the Court had recessed for the term, he stayed the Rosenbergs' execution on the ground that their lawyers had raised a new argument deserving judicial scrutiny—the couple should have been tried under the Atomic Energy Act of 1946 rather than the earlier statute.

Responding to intense pressure from the Eisenhower administration, Chief Justice Fred Vinson recalled the Justices to Washington for special session. On June 19 a 6–3 majority overturned the stay and rejected Douglas's interpretation of the Atomic Energy Act. The Rosenbergs were executed that same evening. Frankfurter, who, with Black,

Justice Frankfurter called this case "the most disturbing single experience I have had during my term of service on the Court."

Ross *altered the constitutional law of automobile searches.*

See also

Search and Seizure

had urged a full review of the case since the earliest appeals, later wrote that this last act of the Vinson Court was "the most disturbing single experience I have had during my term of service on the Court."

—MICHAEL E. PARRISH

Bibliography

Radosh, Ronald, and Milton, Joyce (1983). *The Rosenberg File: A Search for the Truth.* New York: Holt, Rinehart & Winston.

ROSS, UNITED STATES v.

456 U.S. 798 (1982)

Ross altered the constitutional law of automobile searches. A United States Court of Appeals, following Supreme Court prece-

dents, had held that although police had probable cause to stop an automobile and make a warrantless search of its interior, including its closed areas, they should have had a search warrant before opening closed containers that they had searched for evidence. And in *Robbins* v. *California* (1981) the Court had declared that unless a closed container, by its shape or transparency, revealed contraband, it might not be opened without a warrant. The rationale of requiring a warrant for such a search turned on the reasonable expectation of privacy protected by the Fourth Amendment. *Ross,* however, substantially expanded the automobile exception to the warrant requirement.

Justice John Paul Stevens for a 6–3 Court declared that the question for decision was whether the police, making a warrantless search with probable cause, had a right to open containers found in a vehicle. A lawful search of any premises extended to the whole area where the object of the search might be found. Thus a warrant to search a vehicle authorizes the search of all closed areas within it, including containers. "The scope of a warrantless search based on probable cause," Stevens said, "is no narrower—and no broader—than the scope of a search authorized by a warrant supported by probable cause." Accordingly, the scope of the search depended on the evidence sought for, not on the objects containing that evidence. Having so reasoned, the Court necessarily overruled the *Robbins* holding.

Justices Thurgood Marshall, William J. Brennan, and Byron R. White, dissenting, lamented that "the majority today not only repeals all realistic limits on warrantless automobile searches, it repeals the Fourth Amendment warrant requirement itself"—patently an exaggeration. *Ross* did make a shambles of the reasoning in earlier cases on searching closed containers in automobiles, but the Court finally delivered an unambiguous opinion for the guidance of law enforcement officers. Whether or not the Court based the new rule on expediency for the purpose of assisting prosecutorial forces, it will likely have serious implications for the privacy of Americans using their vehicles.

—LEONARD W. LEVY

ROSTKER v. GOLDBERG

453 U.S. 57 (1981)

Men subject to registration for possible military conscription challenged the exclusion of women from the registration requirement as a denial of equal protection. The Supreme Court, 6–3, rejected this claim. Justice William H. Rehnquist, for the majority, paid great deference to Congress's authority over military affairs; with the most minimal judi-

cial second-guessing of the congressional judgment, he concluded that men and women were "not similarly situated," because any draft would be designed to produce combat troops, and women were ineligible for combat. Sex discrimination, in other words, was its own justification.

As the dissenters demonstrated, the exclusion of women from draft registration had resulted from no military judgment at all; the president and the Joint Chiefs of Staff had urged that women be registered. Rather, Congress had heard the voice of public opinion. It is not impossible that the Court itself heard that voice. Thus do sex-role stereotypes perpetuate themselves.

—KENNETH L. KARST

ROTH v. UNITED STATES

354 U.S. 476 (1957)

ALBERTS v. CALIFORNIA

354 U.S. 476 (1957)

Until *Roth* and *Alberts*, argued and decided on the same days, the Supreme Court had assumed that the First Amendment did not protect obscenity. Squarely confronted with the issue by appeals from convictions under the federal obscenity statute (in *Roth*) and a California law outlawing the sale and advertising of obscene books (in *Alberts*), the Court held that obscenity was not constitutionally protected speech.

Justice William J. Brennan, for the majority, relied on historical evidence that the Framers of the First Amendment had not intended to protect all speech, but only speech with some redeeming social value. Thus, the First Amendment protected even hateful ideas that contributed toward the unfettered exchange of information that might result in

R

ROTH v.
UNITED STATES

354 U.S. 476 (1957)

ALBERTS v.
CALIFORNIA

354 U.S. 476 (1957)

The exclusion of women from draft registration had resulted from no military judgment at all.

♦ **judgment**
The official decision by a court of a case or controversy, including the remedy ordered, excluding the reasons for the ruling.

See also

Equal Protection

Sex Discrimination

desired political and social change. Obscenity, however, was utterly without redeeming social importance, and was not constitutionally protected.

Neither statute before the Court defined obscenity; nor did the Court examine the materials to determine whether they were obscene. The Court nevertheless rejected the appellants' due process objections on the grounds that the statutes had given sufficient warning as to the proscribed conduct and the trial courts had applied the proper standard for judging obscenity.

The Court rejected the widely used test based on *Queen* v. *Hicklin* (1868), which judged a work's obscenity by the effect of an isolated excerpt upon particularly susceptible persons. The proper standard was "whether to the average person, applying contemporary community standards, the dominant theme taken as a whole appeals to prurient interest," that is, has a tendency to excite lustful thoughts. Because the obscenity of the materials involved in *Roth* was not at issue, the Court escaped the task of applying its definition. Ironically, the definition of obscenity was to preoccupy the Court for the next sixteen years. The Court, having designated a category of speech that could be criminally proscribed, now confronted the critical task of delineating that category.

Chief Justice Earl Warren and Justice John Marshall Harlan, separately concurring, sought to limit the scope of the majority opinion. Warren, concurring in the result, agreed that the defendants' conduct in commercially exploiting material for its appeal to prurient interest was constitutionally punishable. Harlan, concurring in *Alberts* and dissenting in *Roth*, believed the Court was required to examine each work individually to determine its obscene character, and argued that the Constitution restricted the federal government in this field more severely than it restricted the states. Justices William O. Douglas and Hugo L. Black, dissenting in

both cases, enunciated the positions they were to take in the wave of obscenity cases soon to overwhelm the Court: obscenity, like every other form of speech, is absolutely protected by the First Amendment.

—KIM MCLANE WARDLAW

RULE OF FOUR

Even before Congress expanded the Supreme Court's discretionary certiorari jurisdiction in 1925, the Court had adopted the practice of granting certiorari whenever four of the nine Justices agreed that a case should be heard. This "rule of four" was first made public in testimony concerning the bill that became the 1925 act. Some commentators have seen the adoption of that act as a congressional ratification of the practice; in any case, the rule is well established. In *Rogers* v. *Missouri Pacific R.R.* (1957) a majority agreed that the rule required the Court to hear a petition granted on the vote of four Justices, even though the other five might still think the case unworthy of review, unless new considerations had come to light in the meanwhile. As *New York* v. *Uplinger* (1984) makes clear, however, the vote of four Justices to *hear* a case does not require the Court to *decide* it if the other five Judges think a decision inappropriate.

The Court follows a similar practice in appeal cases coming from the state courts. The Court has even dismissed such an appeal "for want of a substantial federal question" over the expressed dissent of three Justices. When three members of the Court argue that a question is a substantial one, it probably is. The dismissal of an appeal under these circumstances reinforces the view that appeal, despite its theoretically obligatory nature as defined by Congress, has taken on much of the discretionary quality of the Court's certiorari policy.

—KENNETH L. KARST

Bibliography

Leiman, Joan Meisel (1957). The Rule of Four. *Columbia Law Review* 57:975–992.

RULE OF REASON

The rule of reason was a statutory construction of the Sherman Antitrust Act by the Supreme Court. Nothing better illustrated judicial policymaking than the rule of reason, which held that the Sherman Act excepted from its scope "good trusts" or "reasonable restraints of trade." The statute expressly declared illegal "every" contract, combination, and conspiracy in restraint of trade, and as a result the Court in several early cases rejected the argument that "every" did not mean what it said. The Court also denied that the statute should be construed in the light of the common law, which had recognized the legality of certain ancillary restraints of trade on the ground that they were reasonable. For example, in *United States* v. *Trans-Missouri Freight Association* (1897) the Court rejected the proposition that "Congress, notwithstanding the language of the [Sherman] act, could not have intended to embrace all contracts, but only such contracts as were in unreasonable restraint of trade." Said Justice Rufus Peckham for the Court: "[W]e are, therefore, asked to hold that the act of Congress excepts contracts which are not in unreasonable restraint of trade." To read that rule of reason into the statute, Peckham answered, would be an exercise of judicial legislation.

That remained the Court's view until 1911, when it ignored its precedents, the text of the statute, and the views of the Senate and the president. In 1909 the Senate had rejected a bill that proposed to amend the Sherman Act by incorporating the rule of reason. "To amend the antitrust act, as suggested by this bill," declared a subcommittee of the Senate Judiciary Committee, "would be to entirely emasculate it, and for all practical purposes render it nugatory as a remedial statute." In 1910 President William Howard Taft in a

The Court found no cruel and unusual punishment in Rummel's mandatory life sentence after his third felony conviction.

RUMMEL v. ESTELLE
445 U.S. 263 (1980)

Oliver Wendell Holmes once said that the Supreme Court sits to expound law, not do justice. This case is proof. On the premise that the length of a sentence is "purely a matter of legislative judgment," Justice William H. Rehnquist for a 5–4 Court found no cruel and unusual punishment in Rummel's mandatory life sentence after his third felony conviction for obtaining $120.75 by false pretenses. Rummel argued that his sentence was disproportionate to his crime. Rehnquist replied that the possibility of a parole in twelve years and the right of a state legislature to fix penalties against recidivists overcame Rummel's argument. Rehnquist declared that the state legislature was acting within its competence in prescribing punishment and that the state has a legitimate interest in requiring extended incarceration of habitual criminals. The Court would not substitute its judgment for the legislature's and overturn a sentence that was neither inherently barbarous nor grossly disproportionate to the offense.

Justice Lewis F. Powell for the dissenters believed that Rummel's life sentence "would be viewed as grossly unjust by virtually every layman and lawyer." The cruel and unusual punishment clause of the Eighth Amendment, extended by the Fourteenth Amendment to the states, Powell argued, prohibited grossly disproportionate punishments as well as barbarous ones. Rummel's three felonies netted him about $230 in frauds. He never used violence, threatened anyone, or endangered the peace of society. Texas treated his crimes as no different from those of a three-time murderer. The Court's decision weakened the use of the cruel and unusual punishment clause in noncapital cases.

—LEONARD W. LEVY

The school operators argued unsuccessfully that the application of the 1866 act to their admissions practices violated rights of association, parental rights, and the right of privacy.

See also

Civil Rights

Jones v. Alfred H. Mayer Co.

Racial Discrimination

Right of Privacy

message to Congress had argued that no need existed to amend the scope of the Sherman Act. Yet in 1911, in two major antitrust cases, *United States* v. *Standard Oil Company of New Jersey* and *United States* v. *American Tobacco Co.,* Chief Justice Edward D. White, who had dissented from earlier opinions repudiating the rule of reason, explicitly adopted it for an 8–1 Court. The sole dissenter, Justice John Marshall Harlan, echoing the *Trans-Missouri Freight* case, assaulted "judicial legislation"— the usurpation by the Court of a congressional function. The Sherman Act, Harlan insisted, included "every" restraint of trade, even a reasonable one. But Congress, in its 1914 antitrust legislation of the Clayton Act and the Federal Trade Commission Act, by failing to attack the rule of reason acquiesced in it.

As a result of its rule of reason, the Supreme Court prevented effective use of the Sherman Act to prevent industrial consolidations of a monopolistic character. Thus, in *United States* v. *United Shoe Machinery Company* (1918), the Court held that the antitrust act did not apply to the company even though its dominating position in the industry approached that of an absolute monopoly which had restrained trade by its use of exclusive patent rights. In *United States* v. *United States Steel Corporation* (1920) the Court held that the nation's largest industrial enterprise had reasonably restrained trade despite its "attempt to monopolize" in violation of the act. Similarly, in *United States* v. *International Harvester Company* (1927) the rule of reason defeated the government's case once again even though the company controlled a big proportion of the market and used exclusive dealer contracts to eliminate competition. Although the Court ruled that trade union activities came within the scope of the antitrust act, no union ever benefited from a Court finding that its restraint of trade was reasonable. The rule of reason, in short, proved to be of considerable importance in the history of judicial review, of the economy,

and of government efforts to regulate monopolistic practices.

—LEONARD W. LEVY

Bibliography

Neale, A. D. (1970). *The Antitrust Laws of the United States of America.* Cambridge: At the University Press.

RUNYON v. MCCRARY

427 U.S. 160 (1976)

The Civil Rights Act of 1866 gives all persons "the same right . . . to make and enforce contracts . . . as is enjoyed by white persons." In the *Runyon* case the Supreme Court, following its 1968 decision in *Jones* v. *Alfred H. Mayer Co.,* relied on the Thirteenth Amendment as a source of congressional power and upheld the application of this provision to two private schools' exclusion of qualified black applicants.

Justice Potter Stewart, writing for the Court, made clear that several issues concerning the act's coverage were being left open. The Court was not deciding whether the act forbade a private social organization to impose a racial limitation on its membership; nor was it deciding whether a private school might limit its students to boys or girls, or to members of some religious faith. *Runyon* itself involved "private, commercially operated, non-sectarian schools."

Although Congress is empowered to enforce the Thirteenth Amendment, the provisions of the Bill of Rights limit congressional power here as elsewhere. The school operators argued unsuccessfully that the application of the 1866 act to their admissions practices violated rights of association, parental rights, and the right of privacy.

In responding to the associational freedom claim, Justice Stewart came close to saying that the freedom to practice racial discrimination in the choice of one's associates is not entitled to constitutional protection—a view that surely would not survive in the context of marriage or other intimate association. Concurring specially, Justice Lewis F. Powell remarked on the strength of the associational freedoms that would be involved if the 1866 Act were applied to a racially discriminatory selection of a home tutor or babysitter.

The Court dismissed the parental rights claim with the comment that parents and school operators retained the right to use the schools to inculcate the values of their choice. The privacy claim was similarly rejected; parents had a right to send their children to private schools, but the schools remained subject to reasonable government regulation.

Justices Byron R. White and William H. Rehnquist dissented, arguing that *Jones* was wrongly decided and that the 1866 act had not been intended to forbid a private, racially motivated refusal to contract. Justice John Paul Stevens, in a special concurrence, agreed with the dissenters' view of the 1866 act's purposes. However, he concluded, "for the Court now to overrule *Jones* would be a significant step backwards" in the process of eliminating racial discrimination; thus he joined the Court's opinion. It was ever so; today's history almost always prevails in a contest with yesterday's.

—KENNETH L. KARST

RUST v. SULLIVAN

111 Supreme Court 1759 (1991)

Congress enacted a law in 1970 that supported family-planning services by making available federal funds under Title X but forbade the use of federal funds for abortions. Over a fifteen-year period the Department of Health and Human Services (HHS) so regulated use of the funds under the law, but in 1986 HHS tightened regulations, attempting to limit the ability of clinics to provide information about abortions. Two years later, with

the strong support of President George Bush, HHS imposed a gag rule upon clinics and their physicians, prohibiting references to abortion in family-planning programs. The first issue in *Rust* was whether the 1970 law could be construed to allow the gag rule even though Congress had not granted federal authorities such power. The second was whether the regulations including the rule violated freedom of expression guaranteed by the First Amendment and the due process of law protected by the Fifth Amendment. On both issues the Court decided in favor of the government. Conceding that the intent of Congress was ambiguous, the Court nonetheless held that it should defer to the judgment of those charged with applying the law. Regarding the second issue, the Court found that discussion of abortions could occur outside the federal program and thus there was no violation of either the First or Fifth Amendment. *Rust* affected 4,500 facilities serving nearly 4 million women and raised the question of whether the government could impose free-speech restrictions on other institutions receiving Title X funds. It marked a further limit of a woman's right to an abortion since the Court's landmark decision of *Roe* v. *Wade* (1973). The impact of the decision declined, however, when the administration of President Bill Clinton lifted the gag rule in 1993.

—TONY FREYER

Bibliography

Garrow, David, *Liberty and Sexuality: The Right to Privacy and the Making of* Roe *v.* Wade (New York, 1994).

RUTAN v. REPUBLICAN PARTY OF ILLINOIS

110 S.Ct. 2729 (1990)

The governor of Illinois prohibited state entities under his control from hiring any

The decision in Rust v. Sullivan *affected 4,500 facilities serving nearly 4 million women.*

RUTLEDGE, JOHN

(1739–1800)

employees without his express consent. Because more than 5,000 state positions become vacant in Illinois each year, this policy allowed the governor to make several thousand additional appointments. Evidence suggested that the governor's hiring policy operated as a patronage system, with the governor restricting appointments to people who belonged to his political party. Persons alleging that they had been denied jobs, promotions, transfers, or recall after layoffs because of their party affiliation filed suit, claiming that these employment practices violated their rights of speech and association guaranteed by the First Amendment. The challenge was based on previous cases such as *Elrod* v. *Burns* (1976), where the Court had held that the First Amendment barred political affiliation from being used as a reason for dismissal from most governmental jobs. In *Rutan,* the Court ruled 5–4 to extend the doctrine of *Elrod* v. *Burns* to promotions, transfers, recall from layoffs, and hiring decisions.

Writing for the majority, Justice William J. Brennan applied the compelling state interest test used by the Court in many other types of cases, arguing that patronage clearly violates the First Amendment unless it is "narrowly tailored to further vital government interests." In Brennan's view, a general patronage system manifestly fails this test because it is not necessary to maintain either strong political parties or employee loyalty; these goals can be achieved by other means, such as having a handful of senior positions filled by political appointees.

Justice Antonin Scalia, writing for the dissenters, argued that the compelling-interest standard was inappropriate for this case because the government was acting in the role of employer. Numerous decisions have upheld the idea that the government has more leeway in regulating the conduct of its employees than it does in regulating the behavior of ordinary citizens. According to Scalia,

as long as the benefits of an employment practice can "reasonably be deemed to outweigh its " 'coercive' effects," the practice should pass constitutional muster. In this case, Scalia believed that the perceived benefits clearly outweighed the coercive effects, because patronage has long been regarded as a cornerstone of our party system, "promoting political stability and facilitating the social and political integration of previously powerless groups." Scalia disputed the majority's contention that "parties have already survived" the demise of patronage. Saying the Court's assessment had "a positively whistling-in-the-graveyard character to it," Scalia noted recent evidence of party decline, including the substantial decrease in party competition for congressional seats. Reasonable men and women can differ about the appropriateness of patronage in various contexts, said Scalia, but this is precisely why the Court should respect the federal system and not impose its own will in the matter.

—JOHN G. WEST, JR.

RUTLEDGE, JOHN

(1739–1800)

John Rutledge, a wealthy lawyer, represented South Carolina in the Stamp Act Congress (1765) and chaired that state's delegations to the First and Second Continental Congresses. He was a member of the committee that drafted the South Carolina Constitution (1776) and was elected the state's first president (1776–78) and second governor (1779). He led his state's delegation to the Constitutional Convention of 1787, where he used his oratorical skill to advance a moderate states' rights position and to defend the interests of the southern slaveholding aristocracy. He opposed creation of a separate federal judiciary, but favored a provision making the federal Constitution and laws binding on state courts. After signing the Constitution, he

See also

Compelling State Interest

SIGNER OF THE CONSTITUTION

John Rutledge was one of the original Associate Justices of the Supreme Court, appointed by George Washington in 1789.

John Rutledge led his state's delegation to the Constitutional Convention of 1787.

served as a member of the South Carolina ratifying convention.

In 1789 President George Washington appointed Rutledge one of the original Associate Justices of the Supreme Court, but he resigned in 1791—having done only circuit duty—to become Chief Justice of South Carolina. In 1795 Washington appointed him Chief Justice of the United States, and he presided over the August 1795 term of the Court; but an intemperate speech against Jay's Treaty alienated the Federalists, and the Senate refused to confirm his nomination.

—DENNIS J. MAHONEY

S

SALERNO,
UNITED STATES v.

481 U.S. 739 (1987)

In many nations of the world, governments imprison people believed to be dangerous because of their opinions. This does not happen in a free society. However, since the Bail Reform Act, passed by Congress in 1984, persons arrested for a specific category of serious offenses, those violating the Racketeer Influences and Corrupt Organizations Act (RICO), may be imprisioned while awaiting trial. This is preventive detention, which is based on the supposition that the prisoner will likely commit other crimes if let out on bail. When the Court sustained the constitutionality of the 1984 statute, Justice Thurgood Marshall, dissenting, joined only by Justice William J. Brennan, made the following remarkable statement:

> *This case brings before the Court for the first time a statute in which Congress declares that a person innocent of any crime may be jailed indefinitely, pending the trial of allegations which are legally presumed to be untrue, if the Government shows to the satisfaction of a judge that the accused is likely to commit crimes, unrelated to the pending charges, at any time in the future. Such statutes, consistent with the usages of tyranny and the excesses of what bitter experience teaches us to call the police state, have long been thought incompatible with the fundamental human rights protected by our Constitution. Today a majority of this Court holds otherwise. Its decision disregards basic principles of justice established centuries ago and enshrined beyond the reach of governmental interference in the Bill of Rights.*

Justice John Paul Stevens, dissenting separately, agreed with Marshall that the statute violated both the presumption of innocence and the Eighth Amendment's excessive-bail clause.

Chief Justice William H. Rehnquist, for the majority, first rejected the contention that the statute conflicted with the Fifth Amendment's due process clause. No conflict existed, he held, because Congress's purpose in authorizing pretrial detention was not penal, but merely regulatory. So construed, the statute did not authorize impermissible punishment without trial; it merely employed pretrial detention to protect the community against danger. Not only was substantive due process not violated; the statute conformed with procedural due process as well, because it provided for a full adversary hearing before a judge. The government had the burden of proving that to offer bail to the prisoner endangered society and that the prisoner had the right to counsel and all other trial rights.

Rehnquist also rejected the argument based on the Eighth Amendment's excessive-bail clause. It did not guarantee a right to bail, only that, when available, bail should not be excessive. In murder cases, bail can be denied. Moreover, in *Schall* v. *Martin* (1984), the Court had permitted pretrial detention of juveniles following a showing before a judge that the person might commit crimes if bailed. Finally, the bail clause bound courts, not Congress. Given the Court's extraordinary deference to Congress on an important Bill of Rights issue, *Salerno* may deserve a

Rehnquist first rejected the contention that the statute conflicted with the Fifth Amendment's due process.

*Under Texas law,
the financing of
local school districts
relies heavily on
local property taxes.*

good part of Justice Marshall's denunciation and show the risks of judicial faineance. However, the risk comes from Congress, not an acquiescent Court, and Congress is controllable by the people.

—LEONARD W. LEVY

SAN ANTONIO INDEPENDENT SCHOOL DISTRICT v. RODRIGUEZ

411 U.S. 1 (1973)

Rodriguez was the Burger Court's definitive statement on the subject of equal protection guarantees against wealth discrimination—and the statement was that the Court wanted the subject to go away.

Under Texas law, the financing of local school districts relies heavily on local property taxes. Thus a district rich in taxable property can levy taxes at low rates and still spend almost twice as much per pupil as a poor district can spend, even when the poor district taxes its property at high rates. A federal district court, relying on Warren Court precedents, concluded that wealth was a suspect classification, that education was a fundamental interest, and thus that strict judicial scrutiny of the state-imposed inequalities was required. The trial court also concluded that, even if the permissive rational basis standard of review were appropriate, the Texas school finance system lacked any reasonable basis. The Supreme Court reversed, 5–4, in an opinion by Justice Lewis F. Powell that was plainly designed as a comprehensive pronouncement about equal protection doctrine.

The opinion was definitive, as a coffin is definitive. Despite what the Court had said in *Brown* v. *Board of Education* (1954) about education as the key to effective citizenship, here it said that education was not a fundamental interest in the sense that triggered strict scrutiny—at least not when some minimal level of education was being provided. Indeed, said the majority, the courts lacked power to create new substantive rights by defining interests as "fundamental," unless those interests were already guaranteed elsewhere in the Constitution. Here was for-

WEALTH DISCRIMINATION

Wealth discrimination—the state's allocation of resources on the basis of ability to pay—has received the attention of the courts only recently. Sensitivity to the plight of the poor was an outgrowth of the civil rights movement of the 1960s. Thus, the first constitutional issue raised by equal protection claims of the poor was whether poverty-based discrimination is analogous to racial discrimination for purposes of the applicable standard of review.

Advocates of this analogy stress the poor's lack of political power and the public's antipathy to the poor and to programs, such as welfare, enacted to ameliorate poverty. They argue that the Supreme Court should give less deference to legislative judgments when reviewing poverty discrimination claims than it does when reviewing economic regulations challenged by those able to pursue nonjudicial means of redress. However, at no time during the more than quarter of a century since the Court's first decision in this area, *Griffin* v. *Illinois* (1956), has a majority of the Court ever embraced the analogy to

race for purposes of equal protection review.

The *Griffin* decision held unconstitutional a state's refusal to provide an indigent convicted criminal defendant with a free transcript necessary to obtain meaningful appellate review. In so holding, *Griffin* enunciated a potentially expansive principle of "equal justice": "[A] state can no more discriminate on account of poverty than on account of religion, race, or color. . . . There can be no equal justice when the kind of trial [or appeal] a man gets depends on the amount of money he has."

mal recognition of the Burger Court's zero-population-growth policy for fundamental interests.

Nor was wealth a suspect classification. Decisions such as *Griffin* v. *Illinois* (1956) and *Douglas* v. *California* (1963) had involved indigents "completely unable to pay" for the benefits at stake, who "sustained an absolute deprivation" of the benefits. Here, the deprivation was only relative; pupils in poor districts were receiving some education. Furthermore, although the trial court had found a significant correlation between district wealth and family wealth, the Supreme Court held the proof of that correlation insufficient; poor children, after all, might live in the shadows of a rich district's factories. In any case, Justice Powell concluded, the evidence was mixed on the question of whether school spending affected the quality of education.

Because there was no occasion for strict scrutiny, the Court employed the rational basis standard of review. Contrary to the district court's conclusion, the Texas financing scheme was rationally designed to maintain local control over school spending and educational policy. Justice Byron R. White, dissenting, attacked this asserted rationality. If "local control" flowed from control over the spending of money, then Texas, by relying heavily on the property tax and by drawing its district lines, had parceled out that choice in an irrationally selective way, to rich districts and not to poor ones.

Justice Thurgood Marshall's dissent was the most powerful equal protection opinion of the Burger Court era. He elaborated on his *Dandridge* v. *Williams* (1970) dissent, rejecting a two-tier system of standards of review in favor of a "sliding-scale" approach tying the level of judicial scrutiny to the importance of the interests at stake and the degree to which the state's classification bore on the powerless. Here, on both counts, judicial scrutiny should be heightened well above the level of requiring only minimal rationality. In any case, the Court had not, in the *Griffin/Douglas* line of cases, insisted on a showing of absolute deprivation as a condition of strict scrutiny of wealth discrimination; the problem in those cases was the *adequacy* of an appeal, as affected by a discrimination between rich and poor. The Texas scheme could not survive any heightened judicial scrutiny—as the majority itself had virtually conceded.

Justice Powell, a former school board president, surely feared judicial intrusion into the decisions of local school officials. Beyond that narrow concern, the majority undoubtedly worried about judicial intrusion into the allocation of state resources. These are legitimate concerns. The question was, and remains, what kinds of economic inequality, *imposed by the state itself,* can be tolerated in the face of a constitutional guarantee of the equal protection of the laws.

—KENNETH L. KARST

Bibliography

Michelman, Frank I. (1969). The Supreme Court, 1968 Term—Foreword: On Protecting the Poor Through the Fourteenth Amendment. *Harvard Law Review* 83: 7–59.

SCALIA, ANTONIN

(1936–   )

Associate Justice Antonin "Nino" Scalia became the 103rd Justice of the United States Supreme Court on September 27, 1986. Justice Scalia came to the Court after a distinguished career in law, teaching, government, and as a federal appellate judge. He is the first Italian-American to be appointed to the Court and was second of three conservative Supreme Court Justices appointed by President Ronald Reagan. Scalia has established himself as an outspoken proponent of a jurisprudence that is profoundly at odds with the jurisprudence of later twentieth-century liberalism (i.e., the liberalism of the Warren

See also

Court) and differs in significant detail from current judicial conservatism of the role it assigns the judiciary. Before analyzing this jurisprudence, it is important to place it in the context of Scalia's life and professional career, both of which had revealed him as an articulate exponent of political conservative opinions.

Scalia was born in Trenton, New Jersey, on March 11, 1936, the only child of Italian immigrant parents. The family moved later to Queens, New York, where Scalia's father, S. Eugene Scalia, was a college professor, and his mother, Catherine Louise Panaro Scalia, was an elementary school teacher. S. Eugene Scalia was a scholar of romance language and literature who wrote several monographs on Italian literary history and criticism and translated Italian works into English.

Antonin Scalia was a brilliant student. He graduated first in his class at a Manhattan Jesuit military academy, Xavier High School, and then repeated that accomplishment at Georgetown University, from which he graduated in 1957. He attended Harvard Law School, where he again excelled scholastically and was elected Note Editor of the *Harvard Law Review*. After graduation he entered practice with Jones, Day, Cockley & Reavis in Cleveland. He practiced corporate law with the firm until 1967, when he declined a partnership offer. Instead, he accepted a position on the faculty of the University of Virginia Law School.

At Virginia, Scalia began, both through his teaching and research, to develop a specialty in administrative law. He published several articles critical of procedural aspects of federal agencies before leaving Virginia to work in Washington, D.C. Scalia's conservative political orientation, which friends and colleagues identify as having been held by him consistently since college, led him to leave teaching to accept several positions in the administration of President Richard M. Nixon. He first served as general counsel in the executive office of telecommunications policy and then

was appointed chairman of the Administrative Conference of the United States. The conference is responsible for studying common legal and management issues affecting federal executive branch agencies and for recommending improvements in administrative procedures. Scalia next became embroiled in the political battles of Watergate when he moved to the Department of Justice in the summer of 1974 as assistant attorney general in charge of the Office of Legal Counsel, the office that provides legal advice to the president. Among Scalia's first duties was drafting a defense of the president's claim that the tapes and records that Congress sought were his property, not the government's, and that they were protected from congressional subpoena by executive privilege. After Nixon's resignation, following the Supreme Court's rejection of his argument, Scalia remained at the Justice Department until January 1977 when President Gerald R. Ford left office. He subsequently spent six months at the American Enterprise Institute, a conservative research organization, and then accepted a position as a professor at the University of Chicago School of Law.

Scalia taught at Chicago until his appointment to the federal appellate court bench in 1982. (He served one year as a visiting professor at Stanford Law School.) During his time at Chicago, Scalia established himself as a leading voice among conservative academics. He continued to write and teach in the area of administrative law, and he edited the American Enterprise Institute's journal *Regulation*, which was largely devoted to attacking regulatory excesses and advocating deregulation. Scalia also attacked judicial inattention to the provisions of the Administrative Procedure Act—most notably, the U.S. Court of Appeals for the District of Columbia's review of the work of the Nuclear Regulatory Commission in the *Vermont Yankee Nuclear Power Corp.* case (1978). From 1981 to 1982 Scalia served as chair of the administrative law section of the American Bar

Association, and he used his office to call for lawyers to become involved in reforming administrative procedure to make it fit the new environment of deregulation.

Scalia's writings addressed other items on the conservative political agenda as well. He attacked affirmative action in a 1979 article in the *Washington University Law Quarterly* both on principle and because he believed that it could not effectively overcome discrimination. He ridiculed white Anglo-Saxon judges such as Justice Lewis F. Powell and Judge John Minor Wisdom for justifying affirmative action as "restorative justice" when the members of white ethnic groups—such as Scalia's own Italian family—most often bore the cost of compensating blacks for the WASPs' prior treatment of blacks. Scalia further denounced the Freedom of Information Act for imposing prohibitive costs on the government and promoting openness at the cost of law enforcement, privacy, and national security, and at an American Enterprise Institute conference in 1978, he blasted the Supreme Court's 1973 ruling in *Roe* v. *Wade* for being an illegitimate exercise in judicial lawmaking.

Hence, by the early 1980s, when President Reagan was showing propensity to fill federal court positions with conservative legal academics, Nino Scalia was a prime candidate. He was first offered a position on the United States Court of Appeals for the Seventh Circuit in Chicago, but he turned it down, preferring instead the Court of Appeals for the District of Columbia. A vacancy on that court occurred in 1982, and he resigned his professorship at the University of Chicago to move his wife, Maureen, and their nine children to Washington, D.C.

Judge Scalia's tenure on the federal appellate bench was marked by the political conservatism of his opinions and by his ability to maintain strong personal working relationships on a court that had been politically and socially divided for many years. Among Scalia's notable opinions on the D.C. Circuit were those that supported the executive branch over both the legislative branch and independent federal agencies. For example, Scalia wrote an opinion striking down the Gramm-Rudman-Hollings Act, on separation of powers grounds. According to Scalia, the act impermissibly delegated executive branch functions to an official who was subject to removal by Congress. Scalia further gained attention by narrowing press protection from libel suits in two opinions: one against the *Washington Post* and one in which his dissent would have allowed a suit against two political columnists. He also narrowly read Title VII contending in a dissent that sexual harassment on the job did not violate the provisions of the act.

Judge Scalia's conservative politics and his performance as a judge made him the choice of the Reagan administration in 1986 for the Supreme Court seat of Associate Justice William H. Rehnquist when the president elevated Rehnquist to the position of Chief Justice. The American Bar Association en-

SCALIA, ANTONIN

(1936–)

JURISPRUDENTIAL VISION

Antonin Scalia is noted for the intellectual tenacity of his position as a Justice. (Corbis/Bettmann)

Judge Scalia's conservative politics and his performance as a judge made him the choice of the Reagan administration in 1986.

dorsed Scalia without qualification, and only a few feminist and civil rights groups opposed him at his confirmation hearings. He was subjected to far less criticism and hostile questioning than Rehnquist, and he avoided the political battle his fellow circuit judge Robert Bork experienced two years later when he was nominated to the court. The Senate approved Justice Scalia's nomination unanimously on September 16, 1986.

As a Supreme Court Justice, Scalia has received attention for the intellectual tenacity of his positions and for his jurisprudential methodology. Not unexpectedly, he voted most often with the Court's conservatives: Chief Justice Rehnquist, Justice Anthony M. Kennedy, Justice Sandra Day O'Connor, Justice Byron R. White, and more recently Clarence Thomas. Over the years he has been on the Court, Scalia and the Chief Justice have agreed in about 85 percent of the Court's cases, which is similar to his rate of agreement with Justice Kennedy and only slightly higher than the rate with Justice O'-Connor. He agreed with Justice White at a slightly lower rate (75 percent), whereas his agreement rates with Justices William J. Brennan, Thurgood Marshall, Harry A. Blackmun, and John Paul Stevens were closer to 50 percent. That he has voted in support of conservative policies is not surprising. For example, Justice Scalia's dissents in *Webster* v. *Reproductive Health Services* (1989) and *Planned Parenthood of Southeastern Pennsylvania* v. *Casey* (1992) argued that *Roe* v. *Wade* should be overturned. He joined the majority in striking down affirmative action plans in *Richmond (City of)* v. *J. A. Croson Co.* (1989) and *Adarand Constructors* v. *Pena* (1995), and he has rejected challenges to the constitutionality of capital punishment.

What has been noted by commentators, however, is the jurisprudential vision that Justice Scalia has forcefully constructed through his opinions. The cornerstone of his jurisprudence is the limited role of the judge and the judiciary in the American constitutional system. In Scalia's understanding of American democracy, the Constitution granted the legislature and (by delegation) the executive the power to define rights and to determine the wisdom of specific policies designed or executed within their respective constitutional spheres. This may sound similar to the familiar criticism judicial conservatives have made to "judicial legislation" engaged in by liberal justices since the Warren Court. However, Scalia has taken the position further by advancing the argument for judicial restraint across all areas of judging, building on the critiques of judicial activism offered by liberals such as Justices Louis D. Brandeis and Felix Frankfurter and later elaborated by professors such as Harvard's Henry Hart and Herbert Wechsler. This position must be contrasted to the post-New Deal liberals as well as to many twentieth-century conservatives. Both have had at the core of their jurisprudence an active role for the judiciary as the balancers of society's interests. The liberals have envisioned the judge as the protector of individuals against majoritarian legislatures and thus have used concepts such as due process and equal protection to create rights and strike down both federal and state legislation. Conservatives, typified by Chief Justice William Howard Taft, have believed that judges should ensure that the majority's legislative actions (which generally have taken the form of increased regulation of social and economic activities) are gradual and that property interests are protected.

Justice Scalia's differences with such conservatives can be illustrated through both his writings and his opinions. Perhaps the most striking comparison that can be made is between his article "The Rule of Law as a Law of Rules" and the writings of Chief Justice Taft. Taft celebrated the creation of "the rule of reasonableness" in determining violations of the provisions of the Sherman Antitrust Act precisely because it left the federal judiciary as the arbiter of which monopolies were unlawful. Also, for Taft the glory of the common law process was that judges made law incrementally and directed change through their opinions by the elaboration of rules and the application of facts to those rules. Scalia's article directly challenges both these points. He argues that judges should attempt to formulate general rules rather than gradually developing standards through common law case-by-case determinations. He maintains that cases decided by such standards are determined by the weight individual judges place on particular facts, thus allowing the individual to decide outcomes by his or her individual preferences. An example of what Justice Scalia means, as well as how his approach differs from both liberals and conservatives on the Supreme Court, can be found in a recent punitive damages case decided by the Court, *Pacific Mutual Life Insurance Co. v. Haslip* (1991). In this opinion, the majority (Justices Blackmun, Rehnquist, White, Marshall, and Stevens) considered the constitutionality of an award of punitive damages by an Alabama jury. The Court held in an opinion by Blackmun that punitive damages were not per se unconstitutional but that due process considerations required that both the process for instructing the jury as well as the amount awarded must be "reasonable" in order to be constitutional. The majority then discussed the factors that should be considered in testing the reasonableness of the award. Justice O'Connor in dissent argued that the Alabama punitive-damages scheme did not meet due process standards as it was impermissibly vague. Justice Scalia concurred in the result reached by the majority, but rejected both its reasoning and that of Justice O'Connor. He rejected the inquiry into the reasonableness or fairness of the procedures because "this jury-like verdict provides no guidance as to whether any *other* procedures are sufficiently 'reasonable,' and thus perpetuates the uncertainty that . . . this case was intended to resolve." Justice Scalia instead derived a per se rule that these damages were constitutional by broadly canvassing this history of their use and concluding that, since

they had been "a part of our living tradition that dates back prior to 1868, I would end the suspense and categorically affirm their validity." He stated that "it is not for the Members of this Court to decide from time to time whether a process approved by the legal traditions of our people is 'due' process, nor do I believe such a rootless analysis to be dictated by our precedents."

As this example reveals, Justice Scalia's attempt to implement judicial restraint requires an interpretive methodology that can derive categorical rules that are founded on something other than the judges' individual sense of what is right. He does not totally embrace originalism as do other conservatives such as Robert Bork, although he acknowledges that the intent of the Framers is where analysis must begin. Instead, Justice Scalia has adopted a literalistic approach in which the plain and ordinary meaning of the language of texts— whether they be the U.S. Constitution, statutes, or regulations—must govern the judge's decision. For example, in *Morrison v. Olson* (1989), Justice Scalia issued the only dissent in the case that upheld the federal law governing the appointment of special prosecutors. His strongly worded attack on the majority's opinion centered on the wording of Article I. All executive power was vested in the president by the wording of Article I, and this law removed some of this power and thus was unconstitutional. He rejected any idea that the Court could balance the interests of the two branches to decide the reasonableness of this statutory scheme. Similarly, in *Cruzan v. Missouri Department of Health* (1990), Scalia concurred in the majority's decision to refuse to create a constitutional right to die. He differed from the majority in that he would have forthrightly declared that no such right existed because to do so would be "to create out of nothing (for it exists neither in text nor tradition)."

This methodology requires several subsidiary rules. Because the ordinary meaning of the words are to govern, the intent of the drafters of legislation have no place in judicial analysis. Thus, Justice Scalia refused to resort to an inquiry into the legislative history of statutes. If the plain meaning of a law creates a hardship that was unintended or if enforcement of a law as written is unworkable, it is for the legislative branch to redraft the act rather than for judges to amend it through their interpretations. Scalia outlined this position in his first term on the Court in a concurrence in *Immigration & Naturalization Service* v. *Cardoza Fonseca* (1987). He stated that the Court's result was correct, but that it could reach the result through the plain meaning of the statute. Not only was the majority's inquiry into the legislative history unnecessary, it was also irrelevant. He thus rejected a technique not only used consistently by the Warren Court but also accepted by conservative Justices. Second, when the ordinary meaning of a text is not determinative, the judge should look to "objective" standards, such as the history and tradition of a particular practice. These would require consultation of historical sources and monographs, as well as judicial precedents. An example of this approach was *Pacific Mutual*, where Justice Scalia relied on American common law history of punitive damages to determine what due process meant in this context. Similarly, in *Stanford* v. *Kentucky* (1989) Justice Scalia determined that executing a juvenile was not "cruel and unusual" under the Eighth Amendment because, in part, a canvass of state laws showed that a majority allowed execution of sixteen-year-olds. Thus, he reasoned, the practice could not be considered unusual.

An important Scalia opinion, in *R.A.V.* v. *City of St. Paul* (1992), overturned an ordinance barring cross-burning or other symbols that arouse "anger, harm or resentment" based on race, religion, or gender because it was discriminatory. His concern was not the plain overbreadth of the ordinance, which the four justices who concurred found unconstitutional, but rather the fact that it did not prohibit other "fighting words" not based on race, religion, or gender.

In addition, Justice Scalia has authored several majority opinions limiting the standing of plaintiffs to bring suit in the federal courts and has relied heavily on the "case or controversy" requirement of the Constitution to deny plaintiffs access to the courts, a position that effectively bars even Congress from legislating to provide standing in such cases. In these decisions, as in others discussed earlier, he has emphasized separation of powers and the narrow role the judiciary, in his view, ought to play.

In *Employment Division, Department of Human Resources of Oregon* v. *Smith* (1990) Justice Scalia held for the Court that challenges to laws asserting a denial of the free exercise of religion are to be rebuffed as long as the government had a rational basis for the enactment. At issue was an Oregon law that criminalized the use of peyote even in religious ceremonies. This opinion once more illustrated the Scalia view that the courts ought not overturn actions of the legislative or executive branches except in the most egregious cases. He did allow that laws directly intended to inhibit religious practice should undergo strict scrutiny.

Two points should be made in concluding a review of Justice Scalia's strikingly innovative jurisprudential methodology. As several of the examples reveal, his approach is often made in concurrences or individual dissents. At the Supreme Court he has not played the role of a consensus builder, and in fact, his sharp attacks on other Justices in dissent (most notably against Justice O'Connor in *Webster*) have received critical comment. Although there is some evidence that the Court has moved toward him on some issues, such as ignoring legislative history, he has yet to emerge as the intellectual leader of the Court, as opposed to a single highly intelligent voice. Second, his jurisprudence has been developed at a time when political conservatives have enjoyed considerable success in both legislative and executive branches on the state and federal levels. Although there is certainly some evidence that he has followed his methodology even when it has surprisingly resulted in liberal outcomes (he voted to strike down the flag desecration statute in *Johnson* v. *Texas* [1989] and has reached pro-defendant positions in several criminal procedure cases, it remains to be seen what might happen if the future were to bring a strongly liberal executive and legislature intent on expanding federal social and economic reform.

—RAYMAN L. SOLOMON

Bibliography

Comment (1987). The Appellate Jurisprudence of Justice Antonin Scalia. *University of Chicago Law Review* 54:705–739.

Eskridge, William N., Jr. (1990). The New Textualism. *University of California at Los Angeles Law Review* 37:621–691.

Kannar, George (1990). The Constitutional Catechism of Antonin Scalia. *The Yale Law Journal* 99:849–865.

Scalia, Antonin (1989). Originalism; The Lesser Evil. *University of Cincinnati Law Review* 57:849–865.

——— (1989). The Rule of Law as a Law of Rules. *University of Chicago Law Review* 56:1175–1188.

SCHECHTER POULTRY CORP. v. UNITED STATES

295 U.S. 495 (1935)

After the decision in this case, striking down the National Industrial Recovery Act, a conservative gave thanks that the Constitution still stood, while a liberal wondered whether it stood still. The Supreme Court's "horse and buggy" interpretation, as President Franklin D. Roosevelt called it, imperiled the power of the United States to control any part of the economy that the Court regarded as subject to the exclusive control of the states. Chief Justice Charles Evans Hughes, for the Court, first held the statute void because it improperly delegated legislative powers. Private business groups might frame codes governing their industries as long as NRA officials approved and the president promulgated them. Hughes said the president's discretion was "unfettered," and even Justice Benjamin N. Cardozo, who had dissented in *Panama Refining Co.* v. *Ryan* (1935), separately concurred and spoke of "delegation running riot." Improper delegation [of power] could have been rectified by new legislation, but the Court also held the act unauthorized by the commerce clause, leaving the impression that labor matters and trade practices were beyond the scope of congressional power unless in interstate commerce or directly affecting it.

The government argued that although Schechter sold only in the local market, its business was in the stream of commerce. Ninety-six percent of the poultry sold in New York City came from out of state. Hughes rejected that argument by ruling that the flow of interstate commerce had ceased, because the poultry had come to a permanent rest in the city: it was sold locally and did not again leave the state. The government also invoked the Shreveport Doctrine, arguing that even if the commerce here were local, it had so close and substantial a relationship to interstate commerce that its federal regulation was necessary to protect interstate commerce. Schechter's preferential trade practices, low wages, and long hours, in violation of the poultry code, enabled it to undersell competitors, diverting the interstate flow of poultry to its own market, injuring interstate competitors, and triggering a cycle of wage and price cutting that threatened to extend beyond the confines of the local market. This entire line of reasoning, Hughes said, proved too much. It laid the basis for national regulation of the entire economy, overriding state authority. It also ignored the fundamental distinction between direct and indirect ef-

The government argued that although Schechter sold only in the local market, its business was in the stream of commerce.

See also

Delegation of Power

Panama Refining Co. v. *Ryan*

*In 1917 Congress
passed an
Espionage Act
making it a crime to
cause or attempt
to cause
insubordination in
the armed forces
and obstruct
recruitment or
enlistment.*

♦ **presentment**
*A formal report of a
grand jury charging a
person with a criminal
offense. Different from
an indictment, a
presentment is prepared
on the grand jury's own
initiative while an
indictment is initiated by
the public prosecutor.*

fects upon interstate commerce. What that distinction was Hughes did not explain, but he asserted that Schechter's violations of the code only indirectly affected interstate commerce and therefore stood beyond national reach. Even Cardozo, joined by Justice Harlan Fiske Stone, declared that "to find immediacy or directness here is to find it almost everywhere."

Schechter temporarily ended national regulation of industry and allowed Roosevelt to blame the Court, even though the NRA's code programs were cumbersome, unpopular, and scheduled for political extinction. The Court's views of the commerce clause made no substitute constitutionally feasible.

—LEONARD W. LEVY

SCHENCK v. UNITED STATES

249 U.S. 47 (1919)

The freedom of speech provisions of the First Amendment played a singularly retiring role in American constitutional law until the time of World War I or, more precisely, until the Russian Revolution and the Red Scare that it generated in the United States. The Sedition Act of 1798 obviously posed serious First Amendment questions but was not tested in the Supreme Court and was soon repealed. A scattering of free speech claims and oblique pronouncements by the federal courts occurred after 1900, but speech issues, even when they did arise, typically appeared in state courts in the contexts of obscenity prosecutions and labor disputes. The Court did not declare the First Amendment applicable to the states through the due process clause of the Fourteenth Amendment until *Gitlow* v. *New York* (1925). Furthermore, in its most direct pronouncement on the freedom of speech provision of the First Amendment, *Patterson* v. *Colorado* (1907), the Court, speaking through Justice Oliver Wendell

Holmes, had suggested that the provision barred only prior restraints, a position that Holmes abandoned in *Schenck.*

In 1917 Congress passed an Espionage Act making it a crime to cause or attempt to cause insubordination in the armed forces, obstruct recruitment or enlistment, and otherwise urge, incite, or advocate obstruction or resistance to the war effort. Although there had been much bitter debate about U. S. entry into World War I, the speakers whose prosecutions raised First Amendment issues that ultimately reached the Supreme Court were not German sympathizers. They were left-wing sympathizers with the Russian Revolution who were provoked by the dispatch of Allied expeditionary forces to Russia. If the American war machine was to be turned on the Revolution, it must be stopped.

Prosecutions of such revolutionary sympathizers triggered three important federal court decisions that initiated the jurisprudence of the First Amendment: *Masses Publishing Company* v. *Patten* (1917), *Schenck* v. *United States,* and *Abrams* v. *United States* (1919). *Schenck* was the first major Supreme Court pronouncement on freedom of speech.

Schenck was general secretary of the Socialist Party, which distributed to prospective draftees a leaflet denouncing conscription and urging recipients to assert their opposition to it. He was convicted of conspiracy to violate the Espionage Act by attempting to obstruct recruiting. Following his own earlier writing on attempts, Holmes, writing for a unanimous Court, said: "It seems to be admitted that if an actual obstruction of the recruiting service were proved, liability for words that produced that effect might be enforced. The statute of 1917 . . . punishes conspiracies to obstruct as well as actual obstruction. If the act (speaking, or circulating a paper), its tendency and the intent with which it is done are the same, we perceive no ground for saying that success alone warrants making the act a crime." In response to Schenck's First Amendment claims, Holmes said:

We admit that in many places and in ordinary times the defendants in saying all that was said in the circular would have been within their constitutional rights. But the character of every act depends upon the circumstances in which it is done. The most stringent protection of free speech would not protect a man in falsely shouting fire in a theatre and causing a panic. . . . The question in every case is whether the words used are used in such circumstances and are of such a nature as to create a clear and present danger that they will bring about the substantive evils that Congress has a right to prevent. It is a question of proximity and degree.

That the clear and present danger test was first announced in a context in which speech was treated as an attempt to commit an illegal act rather than in a situation in which the statute declared certain speech itself criminal was important for several reasons. First, the attempts context necessarily drew the judicial focus to the nexus between speech and criminal action and thus to the circumstances in which the speech was uttered rather than to the content of the speech itself. Questions of intent and circumstances, crucial to the law of attempts, thus became crucial to the danger test. Second, if the link between speech and illegal act was necessarily a question of degree, then much discretion was necessarily left to the judge. The clear and present danger test has often been criticized for leaving speakers at the mercy of judicial discretion. Having invoked the danger test, the Court affirmed Schenck's conviction. Third, supporters of judicial self-restraint subsequently sought to narrow the scope of the danger test by insisting that it was to be employed only in situations where the government sought to prosecute speech under a statute proscribing only action. In this view, the test was inapplicable when the legislature itself had proscribed speech, having made its own independent, prior judgment that a certain class

of speech created a danger warranting suppression.

Although Holmes wrote in *Schenck* for a unanimous court, he and Justice Louis D. Brandeis were the danger test's sole supporters in the other leading cases of the 1920s: *Abrams, Gitlow,* and *Whitney* v. *California* (1927). A comparison of these cases indicates that Holmes's "tough guy" pose was deeply implicated in his clear and present danger decisions. In the later cases, Holmes seemed to be saying that a self-confident democracy ought not to descend to the prosecution of fringe-group rantings about socialist revolution. In *Schenck,* however, where the speech was concretely pointed at obstructing war time recruitment, Holmes said: "When a nation is at war, many things that might be said in time of peace are such a hindrance to its effort that their utterance will not be endured so long as men fight and that no Court could regard them as protected by any constitutional right."

—MARTIN SHAPIRO

Bibliography

Chafee, Zechariah (1941). *Free Speech in the United States.* Cambridge, Mass.: Harvard University Press.

SCHOOL BUSING

Before *Brown* v. *Board of Education* (1954–55) was decided, many a southern child rode the bus to school, passing on the way a bus headed in the other direction, loaded with children of another race. The busing of children was "one tool" used to maintain a system of school segregation. As late as 1970, before the Supreme Court had approved a single busing order, about 40 percent of the nation's children rode buses to school. The school bus had permitted the replacement of rural one-room schoolhouses with consolidated schools; in the city, riding the bus had been thought safer than walking. School busing did not become the object of

In a rural southern county, the simplest form of desegregation might drastically reduce school busing.

majoritarian anger until the 1970s, when the Supreme Court described it as "one tool" for dismantling a segregated system and affirmed its use not only in the South but also in the cities of the North and West.

In a rural southern county, the simplest form of desegregation might drastically reduce school busing; racial living patterns would permit integration of the schools through the discontinuation of racial assignments and assignment of children to the schools nearest their homes. In the cities, however, residential segregation had been so thorough that the abandonment of racial assignments and the substitution of a neighborhood school policy would not end the separation of school children by race. The question was asked: Would the Supreme Court insist on more than the end of racial assignments—on the actual mixing of black and white children in the schools—by way of dismantling segregation produced by deliberate official policy? In *Swann* v. *Charlotte-Mecklenburg Board of Education* (1971), the Court answered that question affirmatively. Then, in *Keyes* v. *School District No. 1* (1973) and *Columbus Board of Education* v. *Penick* (1979), the Court extended *Swann*'s commands to the North and West, in ways that blurred the *de facto/de jure* distinction. Once a constitutional violation is found, even in remote acts of deliberate segregation by a school board, then as a practical matter the district court's remedial goal becomes "the greatest possible degree of actual desegregation"—and that, in a large city, means the busing of massive numbers of children for the purpose of achieving the maximum practicable racial balance.

Apart from the busing ordered by courts, some busing for integration purposes has resulted from voluntary programs, mostly involving the busing of minority children to schools formerly populated by non-Hispanic whites. Political resistance has been directed not to those programs but to busing ordered by a court over the opposition of the school board and of large numbers of parents and children.

The most outspoken protest has come from white parents. The responses of school board majorities have varied, from political warfare in Boston and Los Angeles to the "let's-make-it-work" attitude in Columbus.

President Richard M. Nixon, whose first electoral campaign adopted a "Southern strategy" and whose campaign for reelection included an attack on school busing, proposed congressional legislation to restrict busing. In 1974 Congress purported to forbid a federal court to order a student's transportation to a school "other than the school closest or next closest to his place of residence." This statute's constitutionality would have been dubious but for a proviso that canceled its effect: the law was not to diminish the authority of federal courts to enforce the Constitution.

The school busing issue has forced a reevaluation of the goals of desegregation. In *Brown* the chief harm of school segregation imposed by law was said to be the stigma of inferiority, which impaired black children's motivation to learn. The fact of separation of the races in urban schools may or may not have the same stigmatic effect—even though deliberately segregative governmental actions have contributed to residential segregation in cities throughout the nation. Stigma aside, it is far from clear that racial isolation alone impairs minority children's learning. In communities with substantial Hispanic or Asian-American populations, concerns about the maintenance of cultural identity are apt to be expressed in opposition to taking children out of neighborhood schools and away from bilingual education programs. The call for "community control" of schools is heard less frequently in black communities today than it was around 1970, but some prominent black civil rights leaders have placed increasing emphasis on improvement of the schools and decreasing emphasis on the busing of children.

Part of the reason for this shift in emphasis surely is a sense of despair over the prospects of busing as an effective means of achieving integration. Social scientists disagree on the amount of "white flight" that has resulted from court-ordered busing. Some demographic changes are merely extensions of a long-established pattern of middle-class migration to the suburbs. The Supreme Court in *Milliken* v. *Bradley* (1974) made clear that metropolitan relief, combining city and suburban districts for purposes of school integration, was allowable only in rare circumstances. "White flight" can also take the form of withdrawal of children from public schools; recent estimates suggest that about one-fifth of the students in the nation's private schools have fled from desegregation orders. In this perspective, the neighborhood school is seen not only as a focus for community but also, less appetizingly, as a means for controlling children's associations and passing social advantage from one generation to the next. Either strategy of "white flight" costs money. It is no accident that the hottest opposition to court-ordered school busing has come from working-class neighborhoods, where people feel that they have been singled out to bear a burden in order to validate an ideal they have come to doubt.

School busing for integration purposes has come under strong political attack. Neither Congress nor a state can constitutionally prohibit busing designed to remedy *de jure* segregation. However, state measures limiting busing designed to remedy *de facto* segregation may or may not be upheld, depending on the legislation's purposes and effects.

Sadly, it is realistic to assume the continuation of urban residential segregation, which has diminished only slightly since 1940, despite nearly half a century of civil rights litigation and legislation. (Even the migration of increasing numbers of middle-class black families to the suburbs has not significantly diminished residential segregation.) Given that assumption, the nation must choose between accepting racially separate schools and using school busing to achieve integration. The first choice will seem to many citizens a betrayal of the promise of *Brown*. The second choice faces opposition strong enough to threaten not only the nation's historic commitment to public education but also its commitment to obedience to law. The resolution of this dilemma is a challenge not only to courts but also to school board members and citizens, demanding imagination, patience, and good will in quantities far beyond their recent supply.

—KENNETH L. KARST

Bibliography

Bell, Derrick A., Jr. (1976). Serving Two Masters: Integration Ideals and Client Interests in School Desegregation Litigation. *Yale Law Journal* 85:470–516.

Dimond, Paul R. (1985). *Beyond Busing: Inside the Challenge to Urban Segregation.* Ann Arbor: University of Michigan Press.

Fiss, Owen M. (1975). The Jurisprudence of Busing. *Law and Contemporary Problems* 39:194–216.

TITLE 18 § 242.
DEPRIVATION OF RIGHTS UNDER COLOR OF LAW

Whoever, under any color of law, statute, ordinance, regulation, or custom, willfully subjects any inhabitant of any State, Territory, or District to the deprivation of any rights, privileges, or immunities secured or protected by the Constitution or laws of the United States, or to different punishments, pains, or penalties, on account of such inhabitant being an alien, or by reason of his color, or race, than are prescribed for the punishment of citizens, shall be fined not more than $1,000 or imprisoned not more than one year, or both; and if bodily injury results shall be fined under this title or imprisoned not more than ten years, or both; and if death results shall be subject to imprisonment for any term of years or for life.

*Screws raised the
question of whether
federal criminal
civil rights
statutes are
unconstitutionally
vague.*

Wilkinson, J. Harvie, III (1979). *From Brown to Bakke.* New York: Oxford University Press.

SCREWS v. UNITED STATES

325 U.S. 91 (1945)

Southern law enforcement officers were prosecuted under section 242 of Title 18, United States Code, a federal civil rights statute, for beating to death a black arrestee. Because section 242 proscribes only action "under color of law," and because congressional power to enforce the Fourteenth Amendment was assumed to be limited to reaching state action, the question arose whether behavior not authorized by state law could be either state action or action under color of law. The Court's affirmative answer, which relied in part on *United States* v. *Classic* (1941), both established section 242 as a weapon against police misconduct and nourished the post-1960 expansion of noncriminal civil rights litigation. *Monroe* v. *Pape* (1961), relying on *Screws* and *Classic,* similarly interpreted the "under color of" law requirement for noncriminal civil rights actions brought under Section 1983, Title 42, United States Code. Exclusive reliance on state law to remedy police misconduct, a position advocated in dissent in *Screws* by Justices Owen Roberts, Felix Frankfurter, and Robert H. Jackson, would never again be the rule.

Screws also raised the question of whether federal criminal civil rights statutes are unconstitutionally vague. Section 242 outlaws willful deprivations of rights secured by the Constitution. Because constitutional standards change constantly, there was doubt that section 242 provided potential defendants with adequate warning of proscribed behavior. In *Screws,* the Court sought to avoid this difficulty by holding that the word "willfully" in section 242 connotes "a purpose to deprive a person of a specific constitutional right."

The Court's remand of the case to reinstruct the jury on the meaning of "willful" prompted Justice Frank Murphy to dissent, pointing out that the officers had contrived to beat their victim for fifteen minutes after he lost consciousness and arguing that the right to "life" protected by the Fourteenth Amendment surely included a right not to be murdered by state officials. The specific intent requirement has generated confusion in subsequent interpretations of the criminal civil rights statutes.

—THEODORE EISENBERG

SEARCH AND SEIZURE

Since 1985 the Supreme Court has refined and expanded upon previously articulated exceptions to the search warrant requirement, the probable cause requirement, and the exclusionary rule. Few decisions have addressed novel issues or fashioned new approaches to the Fourth Amendment.

Earlier cases, beginning with *Camara* v. *Municipal Court,* (1967) and *Terry* v. *Ohio* (1968), established that a warrant and probable cause may not be needed when a search is undertaken primarily for noncriminal purposes or is limited in scope. Rather, the essential criterion of the Fourth Amendment is "reasonableness," which requires balancing the intrusiveness of a particular category of search against the special law enforcement needs served by the search. In recent years, the Court has increasingly applied a balancing test to permit the government to conduct warrantless searches and searches with less than probable cause, in pursuit of special law enforcement interests aimed at particular groups, including government employees, schoolchildren, probationers, prisoners, and automobile owners.

Two recent decisions upholding government employee drug testing programs illustrate both the advantages and the difficulties of a balancing approach to the Fourth Amendment. Balancing is attractive because it permits the Court to give a full account of competing interests and to adjust constitutional limitations accordingly. In *Skinner* v. *Railway Labor Executives Association* (1989), which upheld mandatory blood and urine testing of all railroad workers involved in train accidents or certain safety violations, the Court engaged in a two-stage analysis. First, the pervasively regulated nature of the railroad industry and railroad employees' awareness of the testing regime lessened the employees' reasonable expectation of privacy concerning their bodily fluids. Second, the government's interest in deterrence and detection of drug use by railroad workers, in order to ensure safety on the railroads, was sufficiently compelling to outweigh any residue of legitimate privacy expectations with respect to testing of bodily fluids.

The limitations of balancing analysis become apparent in a companion case, *National Treasury Employees* v. *Von Raab* (1989). At issue in *Von Raab* was a more sweeping program that required drug testing of all Customs Service employees hired or promoted into positions in which they would carry guns or come into contact with drugs. Yet *Skinner*—which, like all balancing opinions, was inherently fact-specific and conclusory— shed little light on how *Von Raab* should be resolved. Ultimately, a bare majority upheld the Customs Service program, concluding that the government's special need for honest "frontline offices" in the midst of a national illicit drug crisis outweighed any individual Customs Service employee's expectation of privacy. For Justice Antonin Scalia, in dissent, the balance came out differently in *Von Raab* because there was no record of a history of substance abuse in the Customs Service, as there had been in the railroad industry of *Skinner*. Yet others might strike the opposite balance, upholding the program in *Von Raab* but not that in *Skinner*, on the ground that the Customs Service program contained a significant internal limitation not present in the railroad program: that the government

could not use drug test results in criminal prosecutions.

The Customs Service program is almost unique in actually prohibiting introduction of acquired evidence in criminal trials, but in several other recent search cases the Court has invoked government interests other than criminal prosecution. Noncriminal motivation was critical in the school search case *New Jersey* v. *T.L.O.* (1984). In the Court's view, the special interest of school authorities in maintaining order permits them to search a student when there are "reasonable" grounds for believing the search will yield evidence of a violation of a law or a school rule and the search is not especially intrusive. *T.L.O.* expressly withheld judgment as to whether the police, as opposed to school officials, could likewise conduct school searches without a warrant and on less than probable cause. Yet, in *New York* v. *Burger* (1987), the Court permitted evidence seized from automobile junkyards in warrantless administrative searches conducted by police officers to be used for penal, as well as administrative, purposes because the two purposes were sufficiently related.

The government's interest in effective supervision of particular groups was also determinative in *Griffin* v. *Wisconsin* (1987), which held that probation officers may search probationers' homes if there are "reasonable grounds" to suspect a probation violation, and in *O'Connor* v. *Ortega* (1987), which held that government supervisors may search employee offices for "work-related purposes" (in this case, to investigate alleged misconduct). The Court has declined to establish an explicit middle-tier cause standard somewhere between probable cause and the *Terry* "reasonable suspicion" standard. Nevertheless, the "reasonable scope" test of *T.L.O.* may implicitly create such an intermediate standard governing focused searches for primarily noncriminal purposes.

In several other recent cases, the Court has refused to impose Fourth Amendment limita-

*Some decisions
reflect the Court's
belief that certain
police intrusions are
more serious than
others.*

tions on particular categories of investigative activity on the basis that the activities at issue were not "searches" at all under the Fourth Amendment. In *California* v. *Ciraolo* (1985) and *Florida* v. *Riley* (1989), the Court concluded that there are no Fourth Amendment restrictions on aerial surveillance from publicly navigable airspace (by plane and by helicopter, respectively). In *California* v. *Greenwood* (1988) the Court agreed with the great majority of lower courts in holding that police need neither particularized suspicion nor a warrant to seize trash placed for roadside pickup. In each of these cases the Court applied the two-pronged test set forth in *Katz* v. *United States* (1967) for determining when government action invades privacy protected by the Fourth Amendment: first, whether the individual has an actual expectation of privacy and, second, whether any such expectation of privacy is reasonable or legitimate. The majority in each case concluded that any expectation of privacy was not one "the society" at large was prepared to accept as reasonable. The Court made clear that state law is not controlling either as to the creation of privacy expectations or as to their reasonableness, although FAA regulations apparently are highly relevant to both prongs of the test. Despite the invocation of *Katz*, each decision is more persuasive by analogy to the pre-*Katz* test for determining what constitutes a search under the Fourth Amendment: whether there has been a trespass upon traditionally recognized property interests.

The Supreme Court has continued to cast an unfavorable eye on the exclusionary rule, which precludes admission at trial of evidence obtained through an illegal search or seizure. Previously, in *Nix* v. *Williams* (1984), the Court had ruled that illegally seized evidence is admissible if it would have been "inevitably discovered" through an "independent source." In *Murray* v. *United States* (1988) a four-Justice majority (Justices William J. Brennan and Anthony Kennedy not participating) applied the logic of the inevitable discovery and "independent source" exceptions to permit admission of evidence first viewed in an illegal search as long as the evidence was subsequently seized pursuant to an independently valid search warrant. The moral hazard of these two exceptions to the exclusionary rule is especially apparent in *Murray,* which may be read to provide an incentive to make an illegal search to determine whether obtaining a search warrant later would be worthwhile. Yet the Court is intent upon reminding us that there is also hazard—to society at large and to the integrity of criminal trials—in suppressing probative evidence, especially where probable cause existed apart from any illegal search.

The Court has also expanded the exclusionary rule's good faith exception, first developed in *United States* v. *Leon* (1984), to include warrantless administrative searches authorized by statutes later held to be unconstitutional; *Illinois* v. *Krull* (1987) held that the exception applies whenever the police officer acts "in good-faith reliance on an apparently valid statute." *Krull* thus signals a departure from *Leon*, which had given much weight to institutional considerations justifying reliance on search warrants issued by neutral, independent judicial officers. As Justice Sandra Day O'Connor indicated in dissent for herself and three others, legislative schemes authorizing warrantless searches do not invite such reliance, because legislators are not expected to operate as independent, politically detached interpreters of the Constitution.

Some recent cases have articulated the new Fourth Amendment standards. In *Winston* v. *Lee* (1984) the Court recognized that the Fourth Amendment may prohibit as unreasonable certain forms of search and seizure (in this case extracting a bullet from the body) even when there is probable cause. Similarly, *Tennessee* v. *Garner* (1984) held that the shooting death of a fleeing felon is an unreasonable form of seizure, even though there was probable cause to believe that the burglary involved violence or that the felon otherwise presented a threat to someone's physical safety.

It was unclear after *Garner* whether successful termination of freedom of movement is a sine qua non for a "seizure" under the Fourth Amendment. The majority in *Michigan* v. *Chesternut* (1988) rejected both the state's argument that no seizure occurs "until an individual stops in response" to a show of authority and the defendant's contention that a seizure occurs as soon as the police "pursue" an individual; rather, the Court appeared to reaffirm the test of *Florida* v. *Royer* (1983) and *Immigration and Naturalization Service* v. *Delgado* (1984): there is a seizure when the police's actions would cause a reasonable person to believe she is not free to leave. During the term after *Chesternut,* however, in *Brower* v. *County of Inyo* (1989), a bare majority of the Court concluded that a seizure under the Fourth Amendment does not occur until there is an actual "termination of freedom through intentionally applied means."

In other cases the Court has refused to develop new Fourth Amendment principles. *United States* v. *Sokolow* (1989) declined to hold a stop unconstitutional merely because it was based on a drug-courier profile; as long as there is *Terry*'s "reasonable suspicion" in the particular case, the police may stop the suspect. In *United States* v. *Verdugo-Urquidez* (1990), the Court refused to apply Fourth Amendment limitations to U.S. law enforcement agents operating against aliens in foreign jurisdictions.

—KATE STITH

Bibliography

Goldstein, Abraham S. (1987). The Search Warrant, the Magistrate, and Judicial Review. *New York University Law Review* 62:1173–1217.

Grano, Joseph (1984). Probable Cause and Common Sense: A Reply to the Critics of *Illinois* v. *Gates. University of Michigan Journal of Law Reform* 17:465–521.

Kamisar, Yale (1987). Comparative Reprehensibility and the Fourth Amendment Exclusionary Rule. *University of Michigan Law Review* 86:1–50.

SEARCH INCIDENT TO ARREST

Weeks v. *United States* (1914) recognized, as an exception to the Fourth Amendment's requirement of a search warrant, the authority of police to search a person incident to his arrest in order to discover concealed weapons or evidence. This principle has remained essentially unchallenged, although its application to a person arrested for a minor offense, such as a traffic violation, involving small likelihood of danger to the officer, was severely criticized by some Justices in *United States* v. *Robinson* (1973). Extension of the allowable search from the person of the arrestee to include the area "in his control," in *Agnello* v. *United States* (1925), planted the seed of conflict between those Justices who would allow a complete search of the premises and those who would limit the search to the area from which the arrestee could conceivably reach for weapons to wield or evidence to destroy.

Marron v. *United States* (1927) allowed the search to cover "all parts of the premises," but in *Go Bart* v. *United States* (1931) and *United States* v. *Lefkowitz* (1932) the Court condemned wholesale "rummaging of the place." Again, *Harris* v. *United States* (1947) upheld the search of an entire apartment, but *Trupiano* v. *United States* (1948) forebade even the seizure of contraband in plain view of the arresting officers. The pendulum again swung in *United States* v. *Rabinowitz* (1950), which authorized search of the whole place. By now the field was "a quagmire," as Justice Tom C. Clark exclaimed, dissenting in *Chapman* v. *United States* (1961). One group of Justices took the position, essentially, that once officers are legitimately on premises to make an arrest, the accompanying search, no matter how extensive, is only a minor additional invasion of privacy and therefore reasonable. They conceded that the arrest must not serve as a pretext for the search, and that the search must be limited to objects for which the arrest was made, but these limitations are easily evaded. Justice Felix Frankfurter provided in-

S

tellectual leadership for the opposing view, arguing that when a search incident to arrest is allowed to extend beyond the need that gave rise to it, the exception swallows up the rule that a warrant must be obtained save in exigent circumstances. Moreover, because a warrant often will strictly limit the area to be searched, to authorize search of the entire premises has the novel effect of allowing searches incident to arrest a broader scope than searches under warrant.

So the matter stood until *Chimel* v. *California* (1969). There the Court restored the balance between theory and practice by overruling *Harris* and *Rabinowitz* and limiting the scope of incident searches to the person of the arrestee and his immediate environs. Still, the *Chimel* limitation may not always apply. Where the police have strong reason to believe that confederates of the arrestee are hidden on the premises, they are presumably entitled, under the "hot pursuit" doctrine of *Warden* v. *Hayden* (1967), to make a "sweep" of the place in order to minimize the danger. The reverse would also seem to follow: once the arrestee has been subdued (assuming there is no reason to suspect the presence of confederates), the police no longer have authority to search even a limited area.

An important legal difference between search of the person's clothing and search of property within the area of his reach should be noted. Property under the arrestee's control, which might have been searched without a warrant immediately following the arrest, may not be searched later; to be lawful under *United States* v. *Chadwick* (1977) the search must be substantially contemporaneous with the arrest. However, in a radical departure from the spirit, if not the letter, of the *Chimel* rule, the Court held in *United States* v. *Edwards* (1974) that authority to search the arrestee's clothing is not lost by the passage of time and may be exercised hours later, following his incarceration. The rationale for this difference appears to be that the arrestee's expectation of privacy in property not associ-

ated with his person remains undiminished. Absent a warrant, the property search must therefore be carried out promptly, as an exigency measure, or not at all.

Under *Illinois* v. *Lafayette* (1983), an arrestee's possessions may be inventoried in the police station prior to his incarceration so as to safeguard them against theft and protect the officers against spurious claims. Because it is considered a reasonable administrative procedure, "the inventory search constitutes a well-defined exception to the warrant requirement."

—JACOB W. LANDYNSKI

Bibliography

LaFave, Wayne R. (1978). *Search and Seizure: A Treatise on the Fourth Amendment.* Vol. 2:406–466. St. Paul, Minn.: West Publishing Co.

Landynski, Jacob W. (1966). *Search and Seizure and the Supreme Court.* Pages 87, 98–117. Baltimore: Johns Hopkins University Press.

——— (1971). The Supreme Court's Search for Fourth Amendment Standards. *Connecticut Bar Journal* 45:2–30.

SEGREGATION

From the beginning, racial discrimination in America has been a national phenomenon. Jim Crow was a southern name for the segregation of the races as part of a system of caste. But segregation antedated Jim Crow, and it began in the North and the West. The leading judicial decision upholding school segregation before the Civil War bears a name Northerners prefer to forget: *Roberts* v. *Boston* (1850). Blacks were either excluded entirely from public accommodations such as hotels, railroads, and theaters, or given separate accommodations. They were segregated in prisons and in churches. Several northern and western states even sought to bar the immigration of blacks; such a legal provision was

---

There is an important difference between search of a person's clothing and search of property.

See also

Chimel v. *California*

Search and Seizure

Weeks v. *United States*

adopted by Oregon voters by an eight-to-one margin.

Nor has this country's segregation been limited to blacks. As late as 1947, a federal court of appeals held that the segregation of Chicano children in a school district in California was invalid. The decision's ground was itself depressing: the state's statute authorized only the segregation of children whose ancestry was Indian, Chinese, Japanese, and Mongolian.

Still, it was the post-abolition South that carried the segregation of the races to its fullest development, and blacks were the chief victims of the practice. Before slavery was abolished, of course, the dominance of whites was assured without any call for segregation. After abolition, the southern states adopted severe legal restrictions on blacks, which served to maintain white supremacy. When the Civil Rights Act of 1866 and the

Fourteenth Amendment not only ended these legal restrictions but also positively declared the citizenship of the freed slaves, segregation was the southern response. By 1870 Tennessee had forbidden interracial marriages and later came the "Jim Crow car" laws segregating railroad passenger seating.

Segregation was not, however, merely a creature of state legislation. It also resulted from private action: a hotel would refuse to take black guests; homeowners in a neighborhood would agree not to sell to black buyers. In such cases law played a role that was less obvious on the surface of events but was vital nonetheless. A black who sought the aid of the state courts in overcoming private discrimination would simply be turned away; state laws would deny any remedy.

Late in the nineteenth century, the Supreme Court gave its support to this system of interlocking discriminations. In the

DENIAL OF CITIZENSHIP

Separate drinking fountains exemplify the tragic and ludicrous extremes that characterized early twentieth-century segregation in the South. (Corbis/Bettmann)

Civil Rights Cases (1883), the Court held invalid a congressional statute forbidding racial discrimination by railroads, hotels, theaters, and restaurants. And in *Plessy* v. *Ferguson* (1896) the Court upheld a Jim Crow car law against an equal protection attack. By the early twentieth century, the South was racially segregated to extremes that were at once tragic and ludicrous: separate telephone booths for blacks in Oklahoma; separate storage for textbooks used by black children in North Carolina and Florida schools; separate elevators for blacks in Atlanta; separate Bibles for swearing black witnesses in Georgia courts. The point of all this was nothing less than the denial to blacks of membership in a white-dominated society—the denial of citizenship itself, in defiance of the Fourteenth Amendment.

Some of the harms caused by racial segregation are harms to material interests: a black is denied accommodation at a hotel, or admission to a state university medical school (and thus to the medical profession), or the chance to live in a particular neighborhood or be a factory foreman. These material harms are serious, but the worst harms of segregation are psychic harms. The primary reason for segregating railroad passengers, of course, is to symbolize a caste system. The stigma of inferiority is a denial of a person's humanity, and the result is anguish and humiliation. The more the races are separated, the more natural it is for members of the dominant white race to see each black person not as an individual but simply as a black. Ralph Ellison, in his novel *Invisible Man* (1952), makes the point: "I am invisible, understand, simply because people refuse to see me. . . . When they approach me they see only my surroundings, themselves, or figments of their imagination—indeed, everything and anything except me. . . . You ache with the need to convince yourself that you do exist in the real world." To be a citizen, on the other hand, is to be respected as a person and recognized as a participating member in the society.

This country's segregation has not been limited to blacks.

Jim Crow was a complex living system, and its dismantling would be no simple task. The field of segregation in housing exemplifies the difficulties. The NAACP's first major victory against segregation came in *Buchanan* v. *Warley* (1917), when the Supreme Court struck down a local zoning ordinance aimed at maintaining segregated residential neighborhoods. But the decision by no means ended housing segregation, which continued as a result of private conduct. When the private discrimination was sufficiently connected with state action, as in the case of racially restrictive covenants enforced by state courts, the Fourteenth Amendment was an effective weapon against residential segregation. But in the absence of such state support, a landowner might simply refuse to rent or sell to blacks, and the would-be buyers would be without remedy. Two events in 1968 altered this portion of the doctrinal landscape. In *Jones* v. *Alfred H. Mayer Co.* the Supreme Court concluded that the Civil Rights Act of 1866 forbade private discrimination in the sale of property. In the same year, Congress adopted a comprehensive fair housing law as part of the Civil Rights Act of 1968. The new law forbade various forms of racial discrimination by lenders and brokers as well as private landlords and sellers. The combination of constitutional litigation and legislation aimed at ending housing segregation had achieved a radical restructuring of the law.

The restructuring of racial patterns in the neighborhoods where people live, however, has proved to be quite another matter. Middle-class blacks have largely left the core cities to live in suburbs, but the degree of racial segregation in residences has changed only slightly since 1940. The term "white flight," coined in the context of school desegregation, seems even more clearly applicable to residential patterns. It is hard to find stable interracial neighborhoods in any large city in the country, at any income level.

In contrast, racial segregation in transportation and other public accommodations has come to an end. And laws forbidding interracial marriage collapsed under the double weight of equal protection and due process in *Loving* v. *Virginia* (1967). Employment discrimination, too, is in retreat—including the segregation of job categories by race—as a result of enforcement of the fair employment portions of the 1964 Act.

The segregation that remains in American society, then, is chiefly residential segregation—with its concomitant, a substantial extent of separation of the races in the public schools. There is irony here: the decision in the school segregation case, *Brown* v. *Board of Education* (1954), was the critical event in the demise of Jim Crow, but our big city schools are the one set of public institutions in which the races remain largely separated. Yet *Brown*'s impact on American life was important. The decision began more than a doctrinal movement; its implicit affirmation of the equal citizenship of all our people accelerated forces that have markedly changed not only race relations but also a wide range of other relationships formerly characterized by dominance and dependency.

It is easy now to see the social and economic changes in the country that permitted the success of the movement to end officially sponsored segregation. World War II was the great watershed. By the time the war began, there was a critical mass of educated blacks, enough to provide a national movement not only with its great chiefs but with local leadership as well—and with a trained cadre of lawyers. The war produced waves of migration of blacks out of the rural South and into the cities of the North and West, where they very soon found a political voice. In part, too, the war had been billed as a war against Nazi racism—whatever we might be doing on the home front. The expected postwar depression failed to appear, and the 1950s and 1960s were a time of economic expansion, conducive to a sympathetic reception for egalitarian claims. All this is familiar learning. Yet in the early 1950s there was no sense of inevitability surrounding the assault on segregation. If the sudden collapse of Jim Crow now seems inevitable, that in itself is a measure of the distance we have come. And if the end of segregation did not end a system of racial caste, that is a measure of the distance we have yet to travel.

—KENNETH L. KARST

Bibliography

Bell, Derrick (1980). *Brown* v. *Board of Education* and the Interest-Convergence Dilemma. *Harvard Law Review* 93: 518–533.

Levy, Leonard W., and Jones, Douglas (1972). Jim Crow Education: Origins of the "Separate but Equal" Doctrine. In Levy, Leonard W., *Judgments: Essays on American Constitutional History*. Chicago: Quadrangle Books.

Litwack, Leon F. (1961). *North of Slavery*. Chicago: University of Chicago Press.

Myrdal, Gunnar (1944). *An American Dilemma*. New York: Harper & Brothers.

Woodward, C. Vann (1966). *The Strange Career of Jim Crow*. 2nd rev. ed. New York: Oxford University Press.

SELECTIVE EXCLUSIVENESS

Selective exclusiveness, or the *Cooley* doctrine, derives from the opinion of Justice Benjamin R. Curtis for the Supreme Court in *Cooley* v. *Board of Port Wardens* (1852). Before that case, conflict and confusion characterized the Court's decisions in commerce clause cases. Some Justices believed that Congress's power to regulate interstate and foreign commerce was an exclusive power and others that the states shared concurrent power over commerce. Some believed that a distinction existed between the national power over commerce and the state police power.

Cooley provided a compromise doctrine that transformed judicial thinking. The Court recognized that commerce embraces a

Cooley provided a compromise doctrine that transformed judicial thinking.

See also

Brown v. *Board of Education*

Buchanan v. *Warley*

Civil Rights Cases

Jones v. *Alfred H. Mayer Co.*

Loving v. *Virginia*

Plessy v. *Ferguson*

Racial Discrimination

Roberts v. *Boston*

vast field of diverse subjects, some demanding a single uniform rule that only Congress might make, and others best served by state regulations based on local needs and differences. Thus the doctrine treated congressional power as exclusive on a selective basis—in only those cases requiring uniform legislation; and the states shared a concurrent power in other cases. In cases of conflict, of course, congressional action would prevail.

The *Cooley* formulation necessarily failed to provide a means by which the Court could discern which subjects were national and which local. Accordingly the Justices were able to manipulate the doctrine to sustain or invalidate state legislation as they wished. In time, judicial analysis focused on the purposes of the legislation and the degree to which it adversely affected the flow of commerce, rather than on the nature of the subject regulated. No formulation could diminish the free play of judicial discretion.

—LEONARD W. LEVY

Bibliography

Frankfurter, Felix (1937). *The Commerce Clause under Marshall, Taney, and Waite.* Chapel Hill: University of North Carolina Press.

In railroad cars, it was easy to achieve a rough equality of physical facilities.

See also

Cooley v. *Board of Wardens*

SEPARATE BUT EQUAL DOCTRINE

The first type of racial segregation law to spread over the South was the "Jim Crow car" law, requiring blacks and whites to be seated separately in railroad passenger cars. When the Supreme Court held such a law valid in *Plessy* v. *Ferguson* (1896), the majority concluded that, so long as the facilities for each race were equal, the enforced separation of the races did not itself impose any inequality on black persons. In support of this separate but equal doctrine, the Court drew on a pre-Civil War decision in Massachusetts, upholding racial segregation in the public schools.

Although the doctrine originated in the context of state regulation of private conduct, it was soon extended to validate segregation in state-operated facilities. The races were separated by the law's command in courtrooms; in the public schools; in state offices; in public parks, beaches, swimming pools, and golf courses; in prisons and jails. Some state institutions, such as universities, simply excluded blacks altogether; in most southern states there were separate state colleges for blacks. Throughout this system of segregation, the formal assumption was that facilities for blacks and whites might be separate, but they were equal.

Given the undoubted fact that segregation was imposed for the purpose of maintaining blacks in a condition of inferiority, the very term separate but equal is internally inconsistent. But the *Plessy* opinion had rejected the claim that racial separation itself imposed on blacks an inequality in the form of inferiority. Yet *Plessy* set the terms of judicial inquiry in a way that ultimately undermined the separate but equal principle. The question of *justifications* for inequality was largely neglected; the Court focused on the question whether inequality *existed*.

In railroad cars, it was easy to achieve a rough equality of physical facilities. Similarly, a public swimming pool might be reserved for whites three days a week, reserved for blacks three days, and closed the other day. In education, however, inequalities of enormous proportion persisted up to the decision in *Brown* v. *Board of Education* (1954) and beyond. Black colleges lacked professional schools; black high schools emphasized vocational training and minimized preparation for college. In physical plants, teachers' salaries, levels of teacher training, counseling services, curricula—in every measurable aspect—the separate education offered blacks was anything but the equal of the education offered whites.

One strategy devised by the NAACP for ending school segregation was thus the filing of lawsuits aimed at forcing school boards to equalize spending for black education—at crushing expense. At the same time, a direct assault was made on segregation in higher education, and especially graduate education, where it was easiest to prove the inequality of facilities. These decisions, following *Plessy*'s lead, focused on the bare question of inequality. Inevitably, these cases came to touch the question whether segregation itself implied unequal education. The *Brown* opinion pursued that inquiry, found educational inequality in the fact of enforced separation, and—without discussing any purported justifications for segregation—held school segregation unconstitutional.

Separate but equal thus ended its doctrinal sway in the field of education. Within a few years the Supreme Court, in a series of per curiam opinions consisting entirely of citations to *Brown*, had invalidated all state-sponsored segregation. The separate but equal doctrine was laid to rest.

—KENNETH L. KARST

Bibliography

Levy, Leonard W., and Jones, Douglas (1972). Jim Crow Education: Origins of the "Separate but Equal" Doctrine. In Levy, Leonard W., *Judgments: Essays on American Constitutional History.* Chicago: Quadrangle Books.

Oberst, Paul (1973). The Strange Career of *Plessy* v. *Ferguson. Arizona Law Review* 15:389–418.

Woodward, C. Vann (1966). *The Strange Career of Jim Crow.* 2nd rev. ed. New York: Oxford University Press.

SEPARATION OF CHURCH AND STATE

In the law concerning religion and the Constitution, the period from the end of World War II until the mid-1980s can be best characterized as the separationist period. Since 1985, however, two major developments have altered the face of the constitutional landscape. The first concerns interpretation of the establishment clause of the First Amendment, upon which much separationist history and law is based. Although some establishment clause principles have been reaffirmed, others have been strongly questioned and several are in flux. Second, the role of the free exercise clause of the First Amendment has been decisively limited by the Court's decision in *Employment Division, Department of Human Resources* v. *Smith* (1990) discussed below.

Establishment clause problems generally fall into three categories—government aid to religious institutions, the role of religion in public schools, and government support of religious symbols in public places or activities. In all three categories, a crucial and overarching question is whether the clause demands maximum separation of government and religious institutions (separationism) or, alternatively, whether government support of religion is acceptable so long as sectarian discrimination is avoided (accommodationism).

These competing themes remained submerged when an important principle related to the provision of aid to religious institutions was reinforced in the Supreme Court decision in *Witters* v. *Washington Department of Services for the Blind* (1986). In *Witters* the Court built upon *Mueller* v. *Allen* (1983) in ruling that the establishment clause did not require a state to deny aid to a blind applicant who would use the grant to pay tuition in a program of preparation for the Christian ministry. Though the Justices differed among themselves on the rationale, all seemed to agree that the individual, not the state, was responsible for selecting the program in which the funds would be spent. Such a private choice creates no risk of forbidden church-state interaction and, when viewed in the aggregate with other individual choices of

See also

Brown v. *Board of Education*

Plessy v. *Ferguson*

Segregation

One of the nation's most politically divisive issues has been the proper place of religion in public schools.

how to spend such grants, creates quantitatively little religious consequences.

This distinction between grants to individuals, which may be "spent" in religious institutions, and grants to the institutions themselves, which the state may not make, may be in danger of collapsing. Only a narrow and shaky majority on the Court reaffirmed the legal principles governing financial aid to religious institutions in the 1985 cases of *Grand Rapids School District* v. *Ball* and *Aguilar* v. *Felton*. Each case produced another in the line of dissents complaining of the "catch-22" of school aid law: categorical grants of benefits to parochial schools are impermissible aid to religion unless the benefits are monitored to eliminate the possibility of their use to promote religion, but the acts required to monitor restrictions on benefits produce forbidden interaction between church and state.

By 1988 these dissents had ripened into what may well signal a major change in the law governing aid programs. In *Bowen* v. *Kendrick* (1988) a 5–4 majority upheld portions of the Adolescent Family Life Act, which provides federal funds to religious as well as secular institutions for counseling teenagers on matters of sexuality and pregnancy. Despite the obvious dangers of religious indoctrination built into any program that enlists religiously affiliated institutions in counseling on such theologically charged matters, the Court shifted the basic focus of establishment clause analysis by asking whether such indoctrination had occurred in fact. Under its prior cases, the risk of such indoctrination would have been enough to doom the program. Although it is possible that litigants can prove in an individual case that government money is subsidizing religious counsel, the process of judicial decision making in aid to religion cases will be profoundly altered if the *Bowen* approach is extended to aid to schools and other kinds of church-supported programs. Such proof may be difficult to obtain, and the consequences

of such proof will be to condemn isolated instances of abuse rather than to invalidate entire programs of state assistance.

Then in 1997, in *Agostini* v. *Felton*, the Court overruled *Ball* and *Aguilar* and upheld the very programs those cases had rejected.

The establishment clause principle that has changed least and seems strongest is that which prohibits the introduction of religious worship or sectarian theology into the public schools. Such an effort was handed a ringing defeat in *Edwards* v. *Aguillard* (1987), which invalidated a Louisiana statute requiring public schools to teach "creation science" whenever they teach biological theories of evolution. Despite the state's defense of the requirement as a protection of the academic freedom of those interested in pursuing creationism, the Court found this scheme to be a deliberate attempt to introduce sectarian religious teachings (in particular, the teaching of the Book of Genesis that God created the universe and all its life forms in six days) into the public schools. As such, the law ran afoul of the principle enunciated in the various school prayer cases that the public school must remain free of efforts at religious indoctrination. While teaching about religion may be permissible, teaching designed to inculcate or reinforce religious beliefs is not.

A third context for establishment clause litigation—government involvement with the display or production of religious symbols—has been the most volatile over the past several years. *Lynch* v. *Donnelly* (1984) upheld the validity of a city's sponsorship of a Christmastime display that included a Nativity scene at its center. The uncertain scope of *Lynch* as authority for government support of displays with some religious significance led to a flurry of litigation in the lower courts involving both Christmas displays and other symbols with religious origins. One lower court, for example, found an establishment clause violation in the adornment of San Bernardino, California, police cars with a shield bearing a Latin cross and Spanish words translating to "With This We Conquer."

In 1989 the Supreme Court tried again to draw lines concerning government sponsorship of such symbols and displays. In *County of Allegheny* v. *ACLU* (1989), a case arising from the celebration of winter holidays in Pittsburgh, Pennsylvania, the Court reached mixed results: a Nativity scene displayed on the grand staircase of the Allegheny County Courthouse was held to constitute a violation of the establishment clause, while an eighteen-foot Hanukkah menorah displayed near a larger Christmas tree outside the city-county building was held not to violate the Constitution. This pair of results is explicable only by reference to the three main groupings on the Court that the *County of Allegheny* case produced. One group of four Justices—Anthony M. Kennedy, William H. Rehnquist, Antonin Scalia, and Byron R. White—would have upheld both displays on the ground that they were temporary and noncoercive, and therefore did not threaten to establish Christianity or Judaism or any combination of the two. Another group of three Justices—William J. Brennan, Thurgood Marshall, and John Paul Stevens—would have invalidated both displays on the grounds that they included objects "which retain a specifically (religious) meaning" and therefore may not be supported by the government. The deciding votes in the cases were cast by Justices Harry A. Blackmun and Sandra Day O'Connor, who adopted the view that government may display, but may not endorse, symbols that have religious meaning for some. Viewing both displays in their seasonal context, these two Justices found that the county had endorsed Christianity with its crèche display but was simply recognizing the secular aspects of the season's holidays with its Christmas tree and menorah combination.

These cases are troubling, and the problems they represent are difficult to solve. Atheists feel offended by any government ac-

knowledgment of the existence of God; many religious people are deeply disturbed by the state's embrace or exploitation of religious symbols; and a line of cases that permits government to display menorahs and crèches next to Christmas trees, but not crèches standing alone, does not inspire confidence in the Court's judgment about law or religion. Solutions at the extreme—eliminating practices such as imprinting "In God We Trust" on coins and currency, on the one hand, or tolerating blatant endorsement by government of sectarian religious symbols, on the other—appear inconsistent with America's national traditions and values. A principled middle ground is hard to articulate and defend, however, as the *Allegheny County* case reveals.

The symbols cases may reflect a movement away from separationism and toward accommodationism. Though the latter takes many forms, the narrowest and most defensible version involves exemptions for religious activity from legislative burdens otherwise imposed on comparable activity. In *Corporation of Presiding Bishop* v. *Amos* (1987), for example, the Supreme Court upheld as an accommodation the exemption for religious institutions from the federal statutory ban on religious discrimination in employment.

Yet not all legislative efforts at accommodation survive establishment clause attack. In *Texas Monthly, Inc.* v. *Bullock* (1989) a closely divided Court held it impermissible for a state to exempt only religious publications from the state's sales tax. Such an exemption involves the state in distinguishing religious from nonreligious activity and preferring the former. Accommodationism permits such a preference; separationism does not.

The provision protecting the "free exercise of religion" shifted dramatically with the 1990 decision in *Employment Division, Department of Human Resources of Oregon* v. *Smith*. Justice Scalia there held for the Court that laws of general application should be sustained when challenged as interfering with free exercise unless they lack a rational basis. Thus a state law that barred the use of the drug peyote was upheld as against a claim that it violated the free exercise clause as applied to its use in a religious ceremony. Only laws aimed directly at interference with the exercise of religion need meet strict scrutiny. The Court furnished an example of this uncommon sort of enactment when it later set aside a law that prohibited ritual animal sacrifice, clearly aimed at particular religious practices. An attempt by Congress to alter the *Smith* holding was itself declared unconstitutional in *Boerne (City of)* v. *Flores* (1997), on the ground that Congress lacked power to interpret the Constitution, a role reserved to the judiciary.

Even before *Smith*, some claims that appeared meritorious under the Court's announced standards fared equally poorly. In *Goldman* v. *Weinberger* (1986) the Court held that the Air Force need not accommodate the religious concern of an Orthodox Jewish captain to wear a skullcap while on duty. Deferring to what seemed decidedly trivial objectives on the part of the military to preserve uniformity of appearance, the Court's majority treated the free exercise claim as deserving little respect. *O'Lone* v. *Estate of Shabazz* (1987) extended this approach by granting wide authority to prison officials to refuse to accommodate the religious concerns of prison inmates through any prison regulations that are "reasonably related to legitimate penological interests." And, in what may be the most disturbing of this trio of cases about government enclaves, *Lyng* v. *Northwest Indian Cemetery* (1988), a 5–4 majority concluded that the free exercise clause was not even implicated, much less violated, when the United States government proposed to build in a national forest a road that would disturb, by sight and sound, places of religious significance to several Native American tribes. Despite the use of open lands by the tribes for spiritual purposes over many centuries, the *Lyng* result effectively forecloses any and all free exercise litigation by Indian tribes against government land-use decisions that may despoil Indian holy places. Earlier, in *Bowen* v. *Roy* (1986), the Court had also rejected a free exercise claim by a Native American concerning the use of Social Security numbers on government files pertaining to his family.

Fundamentalist Christians have fared little better in free exercise cases than have the Native American tribes. State courts have been unreceptive to attempts by parents to educate their children at home without state approval. And in a celebrated 1987 case that reached the United States Court of Appeals for the Sixth Circuit, *Mozert* v. *Hawkins County School Board,* a group of fundamentalist parents unsuccessfully sought to have their children exempted from a reading program in the public schools that they found objectionable to their religious beliefs. In the battle over education generally, and the public schools in particular, the separationists continue to prevail.

Characterized most generally, the trend in the Supreme Court has been toward easing some of the restrictions imposed on government by the establishment clause while increasing the hurdles for free exercise claims. In such a world of deference to legislative judgment, accommodation is far more likely to emerge from the legislative branch than from the judicial branch. Accommodationism, so practiced, presents a substantial risk of favoritism for majority religions—that is, of replicating the evils that the religion clauses of the First Amendment were intended to combat.

—IRA C. LUPU

Bibliography

Levy, Leonard W. (1986). *The Establishment Clause: Religion and the First Amendment.* New York: Macmillan.

Lupu, I. C. (1989). Where Rights Begin: The Problem of Burdens on the Free Exercise of Religion. *Harvard Law Review* 102:933–989.

McConnell, Michael W. (1985). Accommodation of Religion. *Supreme Court Review* 1985:1–59.

SEX DISCRIMINATION

During the 1980s and 1990s intense disagreement arose over the appropriate strategy for eliminating sex discrimination. Some courts and commentators argued for gender-neutral rules that defined categories in purely functional terms. Others, who pointed out that gender-neutral rules promised equality only for women who can meet a "male standard," think that legal distinctions between the sexes are not only appropriate but necessary, at least in cases involving perceived biological differences. Still others refuse to think in terms of sameness and difference. They analyze each issue by asking whether the disputed rule furthers the domination of men and the subordination of women.

Those who favor gender-neutral rules argue that the equality and liberty of women is best furthered by treating women, like men, as autonomous individuals capable of exercising free choice. Their opponents believe that legal rules ought to acknowledge the degree to which many women are actually constrained in ways men are not—by direct and indirect pressures to engage in intercourse, to become pregnant, and to assume parenting and nurturing responsibilities. The disagreement is most painfully joined over laws, such as those granting unique benefits to pregnant women or mothers, that seem intended to help women but resemble earlier, unconstitutional "protective" legislation in assuming difference and dependency between men and women.

Although no case directly raised the constitutional question, several Title VII cases gave the Court an opportunity to respond to the debate among advocates of women's rights. The question was posed most starkly by *California Federal Savings & Loan* v. *Guerra* (1987), a challenge to a California statuatory requirement that employers provide unpaid pregnancy disability leave. As amended by the Pregnancy Disability Act, Title VII of the Civil Rights Act of 1964 specifies that discrimination on the basis of pregnancy is sex discrimination. Opponents of the California law argued that it was pre-empted by federal law because it required benefits for pregnant women that were not required for temporarily disabled men. The Court, in an opinion by Justice Thurgood Marshall, found no conflict with the Title VII. Earlier protective legislation that had been held invalid under equal protection clause and Title VII was distinguished on the ground that it "reflected archaic or stereotypical notions about pregnancy and the abilities of pregnant workers." Justice Marshall found that Title VII and the state law shared a common goal of equal employment opportunity for women: "By taking pregnancy into account, California's . . . statue allows women, as well as men, to have families without losing their jobs."

Because the Court has not modified its holding in *Geduldig* v. *Aiello* (1974) that discrimination on the basis of pregnancy is not unconstitutional because it is not gender-based, *Guerra* raised no equal protection questions. But the decision indicates that the Court is willing to permit governmental distinctions between men and women when those distinctions appear to benefit women without perpetuating pernicious sex-role stereotypes. The decision leaves ambiguous exactly how the Court will determine whether such stereotyping exists. Justice Marshall described the statute as "narrowly drawn to cover only the period of *actual physical disability*." Yet "disability" seems an odd description for a common human condition like reproduction.

In 1961, the Court's decision in Hoyt v. Florida *recognized women's place at the "center of home and family life."*

The term suggests that mandatory pregnancy leave is necessary only because of real biological differences between men and women, and not as a remedy for the problem of inequality caused by the allocation of child-rearing responsibilities to women. Some commentators fear that in the long run mandatory pregnancy leave, like earlier forms of protective legislation, will decrease the actual employment opportunities of women by increasing the cost of hiring them.

A related question is whether the law ought to recognize a practice as discriminatory when it is said to harm women though it presents no threat to men who seem, at least superficially, to be similarly situated. Just as it has been difficult for the court to see pregnancy discrimination as sex discrimination, some lower courts refused to characterize sexual harassment claims as sex discrimination claims, especially when both men and women worked in an environment that only women perceived as hostile. In another Title VII case, *Meritor Savings Bank* v. *Vinson* (1986), the Supreme Court emphatically affirmed that claims of a hostile work environment are actionable under the statute as sex discrimination. Again, the Court was willing to look beyond formal equality of treatment to determine whether practices have different social meanings for, and thus different impacts on, men and women.

Many of the earliest constitutional sex discrimination cases decided by the Court involved challenges by men to "benign" gender distinctions that could be eliminated by simply extending the challenged benefit to men as well as women. In this respect, sex discrimination law differed from cases involving race; few racial classifications benefited blacks at the expense of whites. However, in challenges brought by men to affirmative action programs, the claim is the same as in race cases: the preference ought to be eliminated, not simply be available without reference to gender or race. This similarity may explain why the Court's approach to gender-based affirmative action has tended to merge with its approach to race-based affirmative action, even though racial classifications are theoretically subject to a stricter level of scrutiny. In *Johnson* v. *Transportation Agency* (1987) the Court found no violation of Title VII in a public employer's voluntary affirmative action plan that permitted the sex of an employee to be considered as one factor in promotion decisions for jobs in which women historically had been underrepresented. The Court approved the plan as a "moderate, flexible, case-by-case approach to effecting a gradual improvement in the representation of minorities and women in the Agency's work force." Title VII imposes identical restrictions on gender-based and race-based affirmative action plans, but the Court also cited *Wygant* v. *Jackson Board of Education* (1986), a racial affirmative action case decided under the equal protection clause, as if it would provide the standards for evaluating a constitutional challenge to the *Johnson* plan. Thus, the Court, although reserving the question, suggested that the constitutional approach, like the Title VII approach, may be identical for both kinds of affirmative action.

Two years later, in *Richmond* v. *J. A. Croson Co.* (1989), a constitutional case in which strict scrutiny, was applied to overturn a municipal set-aside plan for racial minorities, the Court signaled a new reluctance to approve government affirmative action plans that could not be justified by evidence of identified past discrimination. Whether the constitutional approach in *Richmond* will be applied to gender-based governmental affirmative action plans depends on whether gender classifications will be distinguished as calling for less searching scrutiny. Since intermediate review has been the standard in other gender-preference cases, governmental affirmative action designed to benefit women may, if the suggestion in *Johnson* is not followed, be found to raise no constitutional problems, even where identical plans benefiting racial minorities are unconstitutional.

Some efforts by local governments to further sex equality have been challenged as unconstitutional under the First Amendment. Those that further women's claims for equal access to all-male institutions have proved most resistant to constitutional attack. In *Board of Directors of Rotary International* v. *Rotary Club* (1987) and *New York State Club Association* v. *New York City* (1988), the Supreme Court upheld state and local requirements that women not be excluded from membership in certain private organizations, despite the claim that the local laws infringed upon male members' First Amendment right to freedom of assembly and association. The effort to impose local restrictions on pornography as a step toward the elimination of the subordinate status of women has proved more vulnerable to constitutional challenge. In *Hudnut* v. *American Booksellers Association* (1986), a divided Supreme Court summarily affirmed a lower federal court's conclusion that a municipally created civil rights action for women injured by pornography impermissibly burdened protected speech.

A major sex discrimination decision, *United States* v. *Virginia* (1996), held unconstitutional the refusal to admit female applicants to Virginia Military Institute, a state-operated school. Analogizing this to earlier racial discrimination cases such as *Sweatt* v. *Painter* (1950), the Court ruled the state's offer of an inferior program at a private women's college to be a blatantly inadequate substitute. The Court's opinion, by Justice Ruth Bader Ginsburg, also noted that the state must furnish "exceedingly persuasive justification" for discrimination based on gender. Although this language in fact came from an earlier decision, it was construed by some as heightening the standard of review somewhat from middle-tier scrutiny. Chief

Justice Rehnquist, concurring, specifically noted that the majority had in fact, in his view, "adhere[d] to" the traditional middle-tier standard.

—CHRISTINA BROOKS WHITMAN

Bibliography

Becker, Mary (1987). Prince Charming: Abstract Equality. *Supreme Court Review* 1987:201–247.

Finley, Lucinda M. (1986). Transcending Equality Theory: A Way Out of the Maternity and the Workplace Debate. *Columbia Law Review* 86:1118–1182.

MacKinnon, Catharine A. (1987). *Feminism Unmodified: Discourses on Life and Law.* Cambridge, Mass.: Harvard University Press.

——— (1989). *Toward a Feminist Theory of the State.* Cambridge, Mass.: Harvard University Press.

Olsen, Frances (1986). Statutory Rape: A Feminist Critique of Rights Analysis. *Texas Law Review* 63:387–432.

Rhode, Deborah (1989). *Justice and Gender.* Cambridge, Mass.: Harvard University Press.

West, Robin (1988). Jurisprudence and Gender. *University of Chicago Law Review* 55:1–72.

Williams, Joan C. (1989). Deconstructing Gender. *Michigan Law Review* 1989: 797–845.

SEXUAL ORIENTATION

Today government officially and systematically stigmatizes persons of homosexual orientation in two principal ways. The first is embodied in the sodomy laws that remain in about half of the states, and the second is embodied in laws and regulations restricting government employment to persons who are heterosexual. Most prominent among the employment restrictions are the federal government's regulations barring gay men and lesbians from serving in the armed forces.

In *Bowers* v. *Hardwick* (1986) the Supreme Court, 5–4, upheld the application to homosexual sex of a Georgia law making sodomy a crime punishable by imprisonment up to twenty years. The majority rejected a claim that the law violated the right of privacy that had been recognized within the doctrine of substantive due process. Justice Lewis F. Powell, who provided the crucial fifth vote for the majority, originally voted with the dissenters, but after the Court's conference switched his vote to uphold the law. In a concurring opinion, however, he noted that the case would be different for him if the state actually enforced the law by putting someone in prison.

Justice Powell's effort at accommodation leaves wholly untouched the most serious harm caused to gay and lesbian Americans by the sodomy laws. Although such a law played a role in the harassment of Michael Hardwick, the sodomy laws are rarely enforced by prosecution. Their mission today is to symbolize society's disapproval of persons who are gay or lesbian, legitimizing the identification of homosexuals as outsiders and thus encouraging not only police harassment but privately inflicted harm, from insults to trashing to violence. Stigma, in other words, is not just a by-product of the sodomy laws; it is their main function.

The *Hardwick* majority not only failed to deal with this problem of stigmatic harm but evaded the whole question of inequality. The Court noted that the Georgia law, despite its general language, was never applied to heterosexual sodomy; accordingly, the Court would not pronounce on the constitutionality of any such application. Having thus raised a serious issue of discrimination, the majority ignored the question of whether the discrimination violated the guarantee of equal protection of the laws.

A decade after *Hardwick* the Court somewhat blunted its impact by overturning a Colorado constitutional amendment that forbade the state or any municipality from allowing any "minority status" or "claim of discrimination" by homosexuals. In *Romer* v. *Evans* (1996) it found this enactment lacked a rational basis since it singled out homosexuals "for the purpose of disadvantaging" them. As the Court pointed out, this law actually "withdraws from homosexuals, but no others, specific legal protection from the injuries caused by discrimination."

An equal protection issue similar to the one in *Hardwick* has been presented to a number of lower courts in the years since that decision, most frequently in contexts involving exclusion of persons identified as lesbians and gay men from government employment, notably service in the armed forces. Some judges have been sympathetic to these equal protection claims, but to date the prevailing view has rejected them, and thus far the Supreme Court has declined to review these decisions. The military exclusion policy, which seems likely to confront the Court with the equality issues in antigay discrimination, illustrates those issues as they may arise in other contexts as well.

The judges who conclude that heightened judicial scrutiny is appropriate for discriminations based on the status of homosexual orientation make a number of persuasive arguments. Gay men and lesbians have historically suffered from pervasive discrimination, both governmental and private. Despite some recent improvement in the lot of persons of homosexual orientation, this historic pattern continues today, seriously impairing the ability of lesbians and gay men to end discrimination through the political process. Sexual orientation bears little relation to the capacity to perform military tasks or any other tasks. Although a person's behavior and self-identification are subject to his or her control, the sexual orientation of persons who are exclusively homosexual is immutable. The usual indicia of suspect classifications, in other words, are present in these cases.

Furthermore, discriminations against lesbians and gay men reinforce traditional stereotypes of gender; indeed, this reinforcement appears to be the main point of the military services' policy of exclusion. Putting the preservation of military secrets to one side, the main arguments of the Department of Defense are that ending the policy of exclusion would harm discipline, morale, and mutual trust; would invade the privacy of service members; and would prejudice recruiting and "the public acceptability of military service." These arguments rest on the assumption that the existence of discrimination justifies government's imposition of further discrimination—an argument soundly rejected by the Supreme Court in the context of racial discrimination, as *Palmore* v. *Sidoti* (1984) made clear. If the services' arguments supporting the exclusion policy seem familiar, the reason is that during World War II the leaders of the armed forces offered the same arguments—all of them—as reasons why racial integration of the services would impede the military mission.

The proposition that gay orientation increases security risk has no factual support. The concern expressed by the military services rests on the idea that homosexual orientation implies susceptibility to blackmail. In considerable measure, any such risk to security would be created by the policy of exclusion itself, which punishes disclosure of homosexuality with discharge. In any case, the risk disappears in the case of service members known to be homosexual—who are the only ones excluded by these policy directives. The circularity of reasoning here is so obvious that even the Department of Defense has stopped barring civilians who are openly homosexual from receiving security clearances.

During World War II the military induction system examined eighteen million men and women and routinely (but perfunctorily) inquired into their sexual orientation. Eventually, sixteen million of the examinees served in the armed forces. The number of gay and lesbian service members during the war is estimated between 650,000 and 1,600,000; the induction examiners excluded between 4,000 and 5,000 persons on grounds of homosexual orientation, and the services discharged another 10,000 on these grounds. Today, too, scores, and perhaps hundreds, of thousands of gay and lesbian service members are performing their jobs without incident. Despite several well-publicized group investigations of lesbians (called "witch-hunts" by proponents and victims alike), the services generally deal with the exclusion policy in a reactive way, taking action in individual cases when they are directly confronted with the issue.

It was the military exclusion that introduced the American public, during World War II, to the idea that one's personal identity could focus on sexual orientation. Today, the service regulations require dismissal of a member who acknowledges being "a homosexual," provided that the relevant decision makers believe that statement. In such a case no conduct need be proved; the status of "homosexual" requires discharge even if the member is celibate. The regulations also require dismissal for a "homosexual act" (a category that includes not only sodomy but also touching and kissing), but make an exception for the case in which such an act is found to be out of line with the service member's general sexual behavior in the past and his or her desires or intentions for the future. If the decision makers conclude that the act is unlikely to recur, and the member declares his or her heterosexuality, then the member can be retained if his or her retention is for the good of the service. Thus, it is the member's public identity as "a homosexual" that requires discharge. The perceived harm in this situation is not that the member is unquali-

Today government officially and systematically stigmatizes persons of homosexual orientation in two principal ways.

fied to perform his or her assigned tasks—the records in these cases are replete with praise from commanders and other work associates—but that the image of the services will be tarnished. The focus of concern is the gender line, the maintenance of what a Marine general once called "the manliness of war."

The crucial question for the services in determining whether to exclude a member on this ground is the member's sexual identity. Although the regulations require a yes-or-no answer to the question of whether the member is "a homosexual," the question of identity is far more complex than can be comprehended in so simple a categorization. Humans are distributed over a considerable range of modes of sexual behavior and over an even greater range of thoughts and feelings about their sexual orientations. The result is that the exclusion regulations are a powerful inducement for servicemembers to resolve private ambivalence by suppressing the parts of themselves that are homosexual, or, even if they privately consider themselves to be gay, to adopt public identities that are unambiguously heterosexual. Whatever degree of self-betrayal one might find in either of these responses, undeniably both kinds of behavior serve the regulations' main purpose of maintaining the armed forces' public image.

The centrality of questions about public identity—for individual service members and for the services themselves—naturally suggests a role for the First Amendment in challenges to the military's exclusion policy. One of the values protected by the freedom of intimate association is the power to shape one's own public identity by reference to one's intimate associations. The experience of the "gay liberation" movement shows that an individual's public avowal of homosexual orientation is not merely a self-defining statement; it is also a political act. Several recently litigated cases have involved discharges of service members with sterling records in direct response to their "coming

out," that is, publicly expressing their homosexual identity. Although some judges have found merit in First Amendment attacks on these discharges, most lower courts have rejected these claims. Ultimately, First Amendment doctrine in this context will surely follow the Supreme Court's disposition of parallel equal protection claims. Just as *Bowers* v. *Hardwick* is this generation's version of *Plessy* v. *Ferguson* (1896), a generous protection of the freedom to express one's gay or lesbian identity probably must await another generation's version of *Brown* v. *Board of Education* (1954).

—KENNETH L. KARST

Bibliography

Benecke, Michelle M, and Dodge, Kirstin S. (1990). Recent Developments—Military Women in Nontraditional Job Fields: Casualties of the Armed Forces' War on Homosexuals. *Harvard Women's Law Journal* 13:215–250.

Bérubé, Allan (1990). *Coming Out Under Fire: The History of Gay Men and Women in World War Two.* New York: Free Press/Macmillan.

Developments in the Law—Sexual Orientation and the Law (1989). *Harvard Law Review* 102:1508–1671.

Halley, Janet E. (1989). The Politics of the Closet: Towards Equal Protection for Gay, Lesbian, and Bisexual Identity. *UCLA Law Review* 36:915–976.

Harris, Seth (1989–1990). Permitting Prejudice to Govern: Equal Protection, Military Deference, and the Exclusion of Lesbians and Gay Men from the Military. *New York University Review of Law and Social Change* 17:171–223.

Law, Sylvia A. (1988). Homosexuality and the Social Meaning of Gender. *Wisconsin Law Review* 1988:187–235.

Mohr, Richard D. (1988). *Gays/Justice: A Study of Ethics, Society, and Law.* New York: Columbia University Press.

See also

Bowers v. *Hardwick*

Equal Protection of the Laws

Romer v. *Evans*

Strict Scrutiny

Sunstein, Cass R. (1988). Sexual Orientation and the Constitution: A Note on the Relationship Between Due Process and Equal Protection. *University of Chicago Law Review* 55:1161–1179.

SHAPIRO v. THOMPSON

394 U.S. 618 (1969)

Two states and the District of Columbia denied welfare benefits to new residents during a one-year waiting period. The Supreme Court, 6–3, held that the state schemes denied the equal protection of the laws and that the District's law violated the Fifth Amendment's equal protection component, as recognized in *Bolling* v. *Sharpe* (1954).

Justice William J. Brennan wrote for the Court. The right to travel from one state to settle in another was a fundamental interest, whose impairment was justified only on a showing of a compelling state interest. These statutes served to deter the entry of indigents and to discourage interstate travel for the purpose of obtaining increased welfare benefits, but those objectives were constitutionally illegitimate efforts to restrict the right to travel. Equal protection considerations forbade a state to apportion its benefits and services on the basis of past tax contributions. The saving of welfare costs similarly could not "justify an otherwise invidious classification." Various arguments addressed to administrative convenience were also insufficiently compelling.

The Court also hinted that wealth discrimination against the indigent might constitute a suspect classification, or, alternatively, that minimum subsistence might be a fundamental interest. Both these suggestions were sidetracked in later decisions such as *San Antonio Independent School District* v. *Rodriguez* (1973).

Chief Justice Earl Warren dissented, joined by Justice Hugo L. Black. Warren ar-

gued that Congress had approved the one-year waiting periods in the Social Security Act. The majority rejected this statutory interpretation but added that in any event "Congress may not authorize the States to violate the Equal Protection Clause."

Justice John Marshall Harlan, in a long dissent, mounted a frontal attack on the Warren Court's expansion of the judicial role in equal protection cases through its heightening of the standards of review in cases involving fundamental interests and suspect classifications. Here, as in other decisions of the same period, the Harlan dissent illuminates the Court's doctrinal path more effectively than does the majority opinion. It has always been possible for a Justice to combine clarity of vision with the wrong conclusion.

—KENNETH L. KARST

SHELLEY v. KRAEMER

334 U.S. 1 (1948)

HURD v. HODGE

334 U.S. 24 (1948)

In 1926, in *Corrigan* v. *Buckley*, the Supreme Court rejected a constitutional attack on judicial enforcement of racially restrictive covenants—contractual agreements between neighboring residential landowners limiting the occupancy of their houses to white persons. From that time forward, the NAACP sought to persuade the Court to reconsider and find the covenants' enforcement to constitute state action in violation of the Fourteenth Amendment. Finally, in *Shelley,* the Court granted review in two such cases, one from Missouri and one from Michigan. In both, white neighbors obtained injunctions forbidding black buyers to occupy houses subject to racial covenants. The decision was widely anticipated to be important, both doctrinally and practically. Eighteen amicus curiae briefs supported the NAACP's position,

States denied welfare benefits to first-year residents.

See also

Compelling State Interest

Equal Protection of the Laws

San Antonio Independent

School District v.

Rodriguez

S

SHELLEY v. KRAEMER

334 U.S. 1 (1948)

HURD v. HODGE

334 U.S. 24 (1948)

FIGHTING RACIAL COVENANTS

In Shelley, *counsel for the NAACP included Charles Houston, shown, and future Justice Thurgood Marshall. (Corbis/Bettmann)*

Shelley's result seems inescapable. Yet hardly anyone has a kind word for the Shelley *opinion.*

See also

Equal Protection of the Laws

NAACP v. *Alabama*

Racial Discrimination

Segregation

and on the other side three white "protective associations" filed briefs, as did the National Association of Real Estate Boards. Counsel for the NAACP included Charles Houston and Thurgood Marshall.

The time was ripe for an overruling of *Corrigan*'s casual acceptance of racially restrictive covenants as a "private" means of imposing residential segregation. The armed forces had integrated at the end of the World War II; in 1947 the President's Committee on Civil Rights had published a report calling attention to the importance of judicial enforcement to the effectiveness of the covenants; and President Harry S Truman, a strong civil rights advocate, had placed the weight of the executive branch on the NAACP's side by authorizing the solicitor general to file an amicus curiae brief. The Supreme Court held, 6–0, that state courts could not constitutionally enjoin the sale to black buyers of property covered by restrictive covenants.

Shelley's result seems inescapable. Yet hardly anyone has a kind word for the *Shelley* opinion, written by Chief Justice Fred Vinson. *Corrigan* was not overruled but was characterized as a case involving only the validity of restrictive covenants and not their enforcement in courts. Standing alone, said Vinson, the racial covenants violated no rights; their enforcement by state court injunctions, however, constituted state action in violation of the Fourteenth Amendment. Taken for all it is worth, this reasoning would spell the end of the state action limitation—a loss many could cheerfully bear. But it is plain the Court had no such heroics in mind. The Justices were not ready to find state action in any private conduct the state might fail to prohibit. Yet the opinion never quite explained why, given the *Shelley* result, those larger doctrinal consequences do not follow. The opinion's elusive quality led Philip Kurland to call it "constitutional law's *Finnegans Wake*."

Two decades later, in *Evans* v. *Abney* (1970), the Court picked up the first shoe. *Shelley* was limited severely, and the power of a private owner to call on the courts to enforce his or her control over property was largely freed from constitutional limitations.

A companion case to *Shelley, Hurd* v. *Hodge* (1948), involved a racial covenant covering land in the District of Columbia. Without reaching the question of whether the Fifth Amendment guaranteed equal protection, the Court held the judicial enforcement of the covenant to violate "the public policy of the United States."

—KENNETH L. KARST

Bibliography

Henkin, Louis (1962). *Shelley* v. *Kraemer:* Notes for a Revised Opinion. *University of Pennsylvania Law Review* 110:473–505.

Horowitz, Harold W. (1957). The Misleading Search for "State Action." *Southern California Law Review* 30:208–221.

SHERBERT v. VERNER

374 U.S. 398 (1963)

Sherbert, a Seventh-Day Adventist, lost her job after the mill at which she had been working went on a six-day work week and she refused Saturday work. She filed for unemployment compensation, was referred to a job, but declined it because it would have required Saturday work. By declining proffered employment she was no longer "available for work" under South Carolina's rules and hence no longer eligible for unemployment benefits.

Justice William J. Brennan, speaking for the Supreme Court, concluded that the disqualification imposed a burden on Mrs. Sherbert's free exercise of religion. The First Amendment, he declared, protected not only belief but observance. Even an incidental burdening of religion could be justified only if the state could show a compelling state interest in not granting an exemption.

This decision was a significant departure from the secular regulation approach to free exercise claims which had been affirmed by the Court as recently as *Braunfeld* v. *Brown* (1961). Brennan made little attempt to distinguish *Sherbert* from *Braunfeld.* Justice William O. Douglas, concurring, rejected the secular regulation approach.

Justice Potter Stewart concurred in the result, disassociating himself from Brennan's reasoning. Stewart saw tension developing between the Court's interpretation of the free exercise and establishment clauses. To grant free exercise exemptions from otherwise valid secular regulations preferred religious over nonreligious people. In establishment clause cases, however, any governmental action that had the effect of advancing religion was forbidden. Stewart would have relieved the tension by relaxing the establishment clause rule.

Justice John Marshall Harlan, joined by Justice Byron R. White, dissented. For Harlan, the notion of a constitutional compulsion

to "carve out an exception" based on religious conviction was a singularly dangerous one.

—RICHARD E. MORGAN

SHIELD LAWS

In *Branzburg* v. *Hayes* (1972) and later decisions relating to an asserted reporter's privilege, the Supreme Court rejected the claim that the First Amendment should privilege reporters from having to respond to proper inquiries incident to legal proceedings. However, before and after *Branzburg,* more than half the states have passed legislation, called shield laws, that give reporters such a privilege. These laws vary considerably, as has their reception in the state courts. Some laws privilege reporters as to all information gathered in the course of their journalistic activities. Others privilege reporters only as to information gathered from confidential informants. Some laws make an exception to the privilege if a reporter has witnessed the commission of a crime.

A number of state courts have found state constitutional grounds for cutting back on shield laws. Thus one California decision held that a shield law could not immunize a reporter from having to answer a judge's questions about who had violated a judicial gag order against informing the press about evidence in a notorious criminal trial. And New Jersey's supreme court held that the state's law could not shield a reporter from inquiries by a defendant in a criminal case concerning information relevant to his defense.

—BENNO C. SCHMIDT, JR.

SIERRA CLUB v. MORTON

405 U.S. 727 (1972)

Acting as a public defender of the environment, the Sierra Club sued the secretary of

S

SIERRA CLUB v. MORTON

405 U.S. 727 (1972)

Shield laws grant reporters the privilege to not respond to legal proceeding inquiries.

See also

Branzburg v. *Hayes*

the interior to enjoin approval of a ski resort development at Mineral King Valley in Sequoia National Forest. The Supreme Court, 4–3, denied the Club's right to judicial review of claimed statutory violations, for failure to allege harm to its members in their personal use of Mineral King. Significantly, however, the Court declared aesthetic and environmental interests, though widely shared, to be as deserving of judicial protection as economic interests. Thus, persons whose individual enjoyment of the environment is impaired by government action have standing to contest the action's legality.

—JONATHAN D. VARAT

SILVER PLATTER DOCTRINE

Weeks v. *United States* (1914), which formulated the exclusionary rule for federal prosecutions, made an exception for evidence seized by state officers in searches that did not meet Fourth Amendment standards. The evidence was usable in a federal trial when it was handed by the state to federal officers on "a silver platter" (Justice Felix Frankfurter's phrase in *Lustig* v. *United States*, 1949). Participation by federal officers in the state search, no matter how minor, rendered the evidence inadmissible in federal cases under *Byars* v. *United States* (1927), as did even a search conducted by state officers alone if its purpose was the gathering of evidence for the federal government under *Gambino* v. *United States* (1927).

A combination of several factors led to the overruling of the silver platter doctrine in *Elkins* v. *United States* (1960). First, in *Wolf* v. *Colorado* (1949), the Supreme Court had applied "the core" of the Fourth Amendment's standard (which did not, however, include the exclusionary rule) to the states. It therefore became incongruous to admit in federal court evidence which state officials had seized in violation of the Constitution. In ad-

dition, about half the states had adopted an exclusionary rule for unlawfully seized evidence; to allow federal authorities to use evidence which would have been excluded in the state courts served to frustrate the exclusionary policies of those states and to undermine the principle of federalism on which the silver platter doctrine was itself premised. The expansion of federal criminal law also undermined the vitality of the doctrine: a growing catalogue of crimes punishable by both federal and state governments evidently alerted the Court to the attendant possibilities of abuse by cooperative law enforcement.

Thus far the *Elkins* principle applies only to evidence in criminal cases. In *Janis* v. *United States* (1976), the Court held that evidence unlawfully seized by state officers can be used by the federal government (and vice versa) in civil proceedings (for instance, in a tax assessment case). The Court reasoned that the main purpose of the exclusionary rule is to deter unlawful searches, and that application of the rule should be tailored to this end. When the officer is prevented from using the seized evidence to further a criminal prosecution, the principle of deterrence is amply served; exclusion of the evidence in a civil case would provide no significant reinforcement for Fourth Amendment values.

—JACOB W. LANDYNSKI

Bibliography

Landynski, Jacob W. (1966). *Search and Seizure and the Supreme Court.* Pages 70–73, 149–158. Baltimore: Johns Hopkins University Press.

SILVERTHORNE LUMBER CO. v. UNITED STATES

251 U.S. 385 (1920)

Silverthorne was the first case to test the scope of the exclusionary rule, formulated in

*Evidence was usable
in a federal trial
when it was handed
by the state to
federal officers on
"a silver platter."*

See also

Exclusionary Rule

Weeks v. *United States*

Wolf v. *Colorado*

Weeks v. *United States* (1914), requiring exclusion from a federal trial of evidence obtained in an unconstitutional search.

Federal officers searched the Silverthorne Company's office; "without a shadow of authority," in Justice Oliver Wendell Holmes's words, they "made a clean sweep of all the books, papers, and documents found there." Compounding the "outrage," the records were copied and photographed, and an indictment was framed on the basis of the information uncovered. The district court ordered the return of the originals but allowed the copies to be retained by the government, which then subpoenaed the originals. The Supreme Court reversed.

Holmes asserted that to allow the government to use the derivatively acquired evidence would mean that "only two steps are required [to render the evidence admissible] instead of one. In our opinion such is not the law. It reduces the 4th Amendment to form of words." Holmes added: "The essence of a provision forbidding the acquisition of evidence in a certain way is that not merely evidence so acquired shall not be used, but that it shall not be used at all." On this principle, an admission made by a suspect while he is under illegal arrest, as in *Wong Sun* v. *United States* (1963), like a lead furnished by an illegally placed wiretap, as in *Nardone* v. *United States* (1939), may not be introduced into evidence because it is directly derived from an unlawful act. In *Nardone*, Justice Felix Frankfurter dubbed the doctrine of the *Silverthorne* case as the fruit of the poisonous tree.

—JACOB W. LANDYNSKI

SKINNER v. OKLAHOMA

315 U.S. 535 (1942)

In *Skinner* the Supreme Court laid a doctrinal foundation for two of the most important constitutional developments of the twentieth century: the expansion of the reach of the equal protection clause and the reemergence of substantive due process as a guarantee of personal freedoms. The case arose out of an Oklahoma law authorizing sterilization of a person convicted three times of "felonies involving moral turpitude." Skinner, convicted first of chicken stealing and then twice of armed robbery, was ordered sterilized by the state courts. The Supreme Court unanimously reversed, holding the sterilization law unconstitutional. Surely the decision seemed easy; no doubt the only serious question was the appropriate ground for decision.

The opinion of the Court, by Justice William O. Douglas, rested on equal protection grounds. The sterilization law contained an exception for violations of "prohibitory [liquor] laws, revenue acts, embezzlement, or political offenses." Although the state might constitutionally impose different penalties on embezzlement and other forms of stealing, it could not use so artificial a distinction as the basis for depriving someone of the right of procreation, "one of the basic civil rights of man." Because sterilization permanently deprived a person of a "basic liberty," said Justice Douglas, the judiciary must subject it to "strict scrutiny." Here the state had offered no justification for the belief that inheritability of criminal traits followed the line between embezzlement and chicken stealing.

Surely the Court also recognized that the sterilization law's exceptions were white collar crimes. Justice Douglas said, "In evil or reckless hands" sterilization could "cause races or types which [were] inimical to the dominant group to wither and disappear." (The year was 1942; the Nazi theory of a "master race" was a major ideological target in World War II.) Sterilization of some but not all who commit "intrinsically the same quality of offense" was "invidious" discrimination in the same way that racial discrimination was.

Chief Justice Harlan Fiske Stone, concurring, found the Court's equal protection rationale unpersuasive, but found a denial of procedural due process in the sterilization

Federal officers searched the Silverhorne Company's office "without a shadow of authority."

See also

Exclusionary Rule

Weeks v. *United States*

Skinner, convicted first of chicken stealing and then twice of armed robbery, was ordered sterilized by the state courts.

law's failure to give a three-time felon like Skinner an opportunity to show that his criminal tendencies were not inheritable. Given the prevailing scientific opinion that criminal traits were not generally inheritable, an individual should have a chance to contest the law's assumption. (This style of reasoning was in vogue briefly during the 1970s under the name of irrebuttable presumptions.) Justice Robert H. Jackson agreed with both the Douglas and the Stone approaches.

Close to the surface of both the Douglas and the Stone opinions was a strong skepticism that any criminal traits were inheritable. Such an objection would seem fatal to Oklahoma's law on substantive due process grounds. But the Court had very recently abandoned substantive due process as a limit on economic regulation, and in doing so had used language suggesting the complete demise of substantive due process. Both Douglas and Stone seemed to be avoiding the obvious ground that the law arbitrarily deprived Skinner of liberty. But *Skinner* can be seen today as not only a forerunner of a later Court's strict scrutiny analysis of equal protection cases involving fundamental interests and suspect classifications but also a major early precedent for the development of a constitutional right of privacy as a branch of substantive due process.

—KENNETH L. KARST

Bibliography

Karst, Kenneth L. (1969). Invidious Discrimination: Justice Douglas and the Return of the "Natural-Law-Due-Process Formula." *UCLA Law Review* 16:716–750.

SLAUGHTERHOUSE CASES

16 Wallace 36 (1873)

Most histories of the Constitution begin consideration of the judicial interpretation of the Thirteenth and Fourteenth Amendments with the *Slaughterhouse* decision of 1873. The decision is, to be sure, of vast significance. Justices Joseph P. Bradley and Stephen J. Field, dissenting, expressed embryonic doctrines of freedom of contract and substantive due process that were to dominate American jurisprudence for two generations.

In 1869 Louisiana, ostensibly as a public health measure, incorporated the Crescent City Stock Landing and Slaughterhouse Company and granted it a monopoly of licensed butchering in New Orleans. Butchers not parties to the lucrative arrangement, after failing to crack the monopoly in the state courts, employed as counsel, in an appeal to the federal courts, former Supreme Court Justice John A. Campbell, who more recently had been a Confederate assistant secretary of war. Campbell argued before the Supreme Court that the excluded butchers had been deprived of their livelihoods by the state's deliberate discrimination, although Louisiana had disguised the corrupt monopoly as a health measure. Therefore the disputed statute violated the Thirteenth Amendment's ban on involuntary servitude, the 1866 Civil Rights Act's enforcements of that ban, and the Fourteenth Amendment's guarantees of equal protection of the laws, and due process.

Among prominent counsel for the state, Senator Matthew Hale Carpenter responded to Campbell's innovative brief. Carpenter easily assembled case law that sustained state restrictions on private economic relationships. He insisted that the state police power amply undergirded the Louisiana statute. No federal constitutional question existed, Carpenter asserted. Both the Thirteenth and the Fourteenth Amendments were irrelevant to the litigants' rights and remedies. And, he prophesied, the federal system would be virtually revolutionized if the Court accepted Campbell's notions and legitimized a federal interest in individuals' claims to be exempt from state regulation.

Speaking through Justice Samuel F. Miller, a majority of the Court was unready to accept Campbell's view that federal guarantees to individuals extended to trades (although, in the *Test Oath Cases*, 1867, the Court had extended other federal guarantees to lawyers, ministers, and teachers). Instead, having accepted Carpenter's arguments, Miller reviewed the tradition of judicial support for state determination of ways to meet police power responsibilities. Miller denied that exclusion from butchering deprived the appellants of federally protected rights to freedom, privileges and immunities, equal protection, or due process; the "one pervading purpose" of the postwar amendments, he said, was to liberate black slaves, not to enlarge whites' rights. The monopoly created by the state law could not be perceived as imposing servitude; the Thirteenth Amendment was irrelevant as a protection for livelihoods.

Turning to the Fourteenth Amendment, Miller separated federal from state privileges and immunities. He assigned to the states the definition of ordinary marketplace relationships essential to the vast majority of people. More important, he assigned to state privileges and immunities all basic civil liberties and rights, excluding them from federal protection. Miller's sweeping interpretation relegated everyone, including Negroes, who had assumed that the Fourteenth Amendment had assigned the federal government the role of "guardian democracy" over state-defined civil rights, to the state governments for effective protection. The national government could protect only the few privileges and immunities of national citizenship: the right to travel, access to Washington, D.C., freedom of assembly and petition, and habeas corpus. Miller and the majority ignored contemporary evidence that many of the framers of both amendments and of the 1866 Civil Rights Act did perceive federally protectable privileges and immunities in broad terms; did assign to federal courts the duty to protect those rights; did envision national civil rights

as the essential bridge connecting individuals and states to the nation in a more perfect union. And the majority overlooked earlier contrary case law that spoke directly to the point of the amendments as requirements for federal protection against both state and private discriminations: *In re Turner* (1867) and *Blyew* v. *U.S.* (1872).

Ignoring also prewar uses of due process in *Dred Scott* v. *Sandford* (1857) and in law of the land clauses in state constitutions, and shrugging off the equal protection argument Campbell had advanced for the appellants, Miller reiterated his position that the postwar amendments protected only blacks against state action. The federal protection the Court allowed was minimal and virtually irrelevant to the needs of freedmen, and, for all Americans, left the protection of rights fundamentally unchanged from the prewar condition.

Dissenting, Justices Joseph P. Bradley and Stephen J. Field dredged up Justice Samuel Chase's 1798 opinion in *Calder* v. *Bull* and that of Justice Bushrod Washington in his much-quoted 1823 circuit opinion in *Corfield* v. *Coryell*, plus the augmented emphases on judicial discretion in a long line of decisions. Bradley emphasized the Fourteenth Amendment's due process clause. Advancing beyond the views of Chief Justice Roger B. Taney in *Dred Scott*, he justified judicial intervention to defend substantive due process rights and insisted that a right to choose a calling is a property, a fundamental right that no state might demean casually. That right was the base for all liberty. The federal courts must repel any state attack on that right, even though the attack might be disguised as a health measure under police powers.

Field argued that the butchering monopoly created servitudes forbidden by the Thirteenth Amendment, but he concentrated on the Fourteenth's privileges and immunities clause. It embraced all the fundamental rights belonging to free men. The national Constitution and laws affirmed those rights. Arbitrary state inhibitions on access to a

The Slaughterhouse *decision is, to be sure, of vast significance.*

See also

Calder v. *Bull*

Dred Scott v. *Sandford*

trade or professions demeaned national rights. Field conceded that states were free to exercise their police powers, even to regulate occupations. But state regulations must apply equally to all citizens who met the standards of the state regulations.

Later, jurists less respectful than Field of state-based federalism were to cut his *Slaughterhouse* dissent free of its privileges and immunities moorings. Combining his views with Bradley's emphases on the broad effect of the Fourteenth Amendment, later jurists and legal commentators were to transform them into doctrines of freedom of contract and substantive due process. Those doctrines, which were to reign until the twentieth century was well advanced, constrained needful state actions in numerous areas of life and labor.

—HAROLD M. HYMAN

Bibliography

Beth, Loren P. (1963). The Slaughter-House Cases—Revisited, *Louisiana Law Review* 23:487–505.

Fairman, Charles (1971). Reconstruction and Reunion, 1864–1868. Chap. 21 in Vol. 6, part 1, of the *Oliver Wendell Holmes Devise History of the Supreme Court of the United States*. New York: Macmillan.

Hamilton, Walton H. (1938). The Path of Due Process of Law. Pages 167–179 in Conyers Read, ed., *The Constitution Reconsidered.* New York: Columbia University Press.

Hyman, Harold M., and Wiecek, William M. (1982). *Equal Justice under Law: Constitutional Development 1835–1875.* Pages 472–483. New York: Harper & Row.

SMITH v. ALLWRIGHT

321 U.S. 649 (1944)

In 1935 the Supreme Court had held in *Grovey* v. *Townsend* that the Texas Democratic party convention's rule excluding black voters from primary elections was not state action and thus violated no constitutional rights. *Allwright* involved the same question, raised in the same manner; Smith alleged that he was excluded from the Texas Democratic primary because of his race and sought damages from election officials under federal civil rights laws. The case had become a plausible candidate for Supreme Court review because in *United States* v. *Classic* (1941) the Court had reconsidered the nature of a primary election by way of upholding Congress's power to forbid fraud in primary elections of nominees for federal offices. In *Classic*, the Court had concluded that Louisiana primary elections were, by law, an integral part of the machinery for electing officers.

Applying the *Classic* reasoning in *Allwright*, the Court overruled *Grovey* v. *Townsend* and held that the state's provision of machinery for primary elections was sufficiently connected with the party's conduct of those elections to satisfy the state action limitation of the Fifteenth Amendment. Because that amendment forbade a state to deny or abridge the right to vote on account of race, Smith was entitled to damages if he could prove his allegations. Justice Stanley F. Reed wrote for the Court.

Justice Owen Roberts, who had written for a unanimous Court in *Grovey*, dissented, complaining that the overruling of a decision after only nine years tended "to bring adjudications of this tribunal into the same class as a restricted railroad ticket, good on this day and train only." The obvious question was: Why had Roberts joined in the *Classic* decision? Contemporary accounts suggest that at least some of the other Justices thought Roberts had been "duped" into concurring in *Classic*, and that Roberts knew they thought so. In the years between *Grovey* and *Allwright*, President Franklin D. Roosevelt had made seven appointments to the Court. Justice Roberts's lone companion

Smith alleged that he was excluded from the Texas Democratic primary because of his race.

See also

Classic, United States v.

ENTITLED TO DAMAGES

As a result of the Court's decision in Smith, *blacks could no longer be excluded from voting in primary elections. Here, a black man registers to vote as others wait their turn. (Corbis/Bettmann)*

from the earlier days was Chief Justice Harlan Fiske Stone, who had written the *Classic* opinion.

—KENNETH L. KARST

SMYTH v. AMES

169 U.S. 466 (1898)

A unanimous Supreme Court, in this arrogation of power, proclaimed its acceptance of substantive due process in rate regulation. The Court refused to "shrink from the duty" of exercising its judgment in a highly technical area of economic regulation best left to experts. For the next forty years, the Court would review the rate schedules of regulatory commissions seeking to accommodate shifting and illusory judicial standards of fairness.

In 1893 a Nebraska statute prescribed maximum rail rates for intrastate transportation. William Jennings Bryan defended the state legislature's power to fix reasonable rates for intrastate commerce; James Coolidge Carter urged that the Court limit the power when unreasonable rates effectively divested a railroad of its property. The question presented by the three cases consolidated here was whether those rates amounted to a taking of property without just compensation, thereby depriving the railroads of their property without due process of law. Justice David J. Brewer, sitting as a circuit judge in one of the cases, invented a "fair return on fair value"

Regulatory commissions of all sorts would spend four decades attempting to second-guess the courts' efforts to determine what constituted a "fair return" on "fair value."

test. He struck down the rates because they failed to provide a fair return on a fair valuation of the railroad property and thereby they effectively destroyed property.

Accepting Brewer's opinion, Justice John Marshall Harlan, for the Court, asserted that *Reagan* v. *Farmers' Loan & Trust Company* (1894) demonstrated the appropriateness of a judicial determination of the question. Courts, he said, must be free to inquire into the sufficiency of the rates set by the state legislature, even though the Nebraska constitution only granted the legislature the power to prescribe " 'reasonable' maximum rates." Admitting that the question could be "more easily determined by a commission" of experts, Harlan pursued the "considerations" that, "given such weight as may be just and right in each case," would allow a determination of reasonable rate. He declared that the "basis of all calculations . . . must be the fair value of the property being used." Then he listed a number of various aids to determine fair value: original construction costs, replacement or reproduction costs, stock values, the cost of permanent improvements, earning power under the prescribed rate structure, operating expenses, and other unspecified matters. The company, he concluded, was justified in asking a "fair return upon the value of that which it employs for the public convenience." The Nebraska statute had failed to provide that fair return and so deprived the railroad of its property without just compensation, thereby depriving it of due process of law under the Fourteenth Amendment.

In *Smyth* the Court readily substituted its judgment on a question of policy for other branches of government. Regulatory commissions of all sorts would spend four decades attempting to second-guess the courts' efforts to determine what constituted a "fair return" on "fair value." Over those decades, the Court manipulated the fair value standards to the benefit of corporations. The Court relied primarily on two of Harlan's factors in assessing fair value. Until about 1918, high original costs governed the Court's determination of fair value. When the war ended and both costs and prices rose, the Court turned to replacement costs as a means of deciding fair value, again keeping rates high. The Court consistently avoided using earnings—perhaps the best economic measure—as a guide. Justices Louis D. Brandeis and Oliver Wendell Holmes denounced the fair return rule throughout the 1920s and 1930s; their views gained adherents by the early 1940s. In *Federal Power Commission* v. *Natural Gas Company* (1942) the Court asserted that property value was not an essential factor in calculating a fair return, and the Supreme Court finally disavowed a judicial control of the question in *Federal Power Commission* v. *Hope Natural Gas Company* (1944).

—DAVID GORDON

Bibliography

Hale, Robert Lee (1952). *Freedom through Law: Public Control of Private Governing Power.* Pages 461–500. New York: Columbia University Press.

SNEPP v. UNITED STATES

444 U.S. 507 (1980)

A former Central Intelligence Agency (CIA) employee, Frank W. Snepp III, published a book containing unclassified information about CIA activities in South Vietnam. Snepp did not submit the book to the CIA for prepublication review, in breach of his express employment agreement not to publish any information without the agency's prior approval or to disclose any *classified* information. In a decision remarkable for its procedural setting and for its failure to meet head-on the First Amendment issues implicated by the prior restraint, the Supreme Court, per curiam, sanctioned the imposition of a constructive trust on all proceeds from the book's sales.

The Court recognized, as the government conceded, that Snepp had a First Amendment right to publish unclassified information. The Court found, however, that by virtue of his employment as a CIA agent, Snepp had entered a fiduciary relationship with the agency. Snepp breached the special trust reposed in him by failing to submit *all* material, whether classified or not, for prepublication review. That breach posed irreparable harm to the CIA's relationships with foreign governments and its ability to perform its statutory duties. The constructive trust remedy was thereby warranted.

Justice John Paul Stevens, joined by Justices William J. Brennan and Thurgood Marshall, dissented, arguing that the remedy was unsupported by statute, the contract, or case law. He urged that the contract be treated as an ordinary employment covenant. On this theory, its enforcement would be governed by a rule of reason that would require a balancing of interests, including Snepp's First Amendment rights, and might justify an equity court's refusal to enforce the prepublication review covenant. Further, the alleged harm suffered by the government did not warrant the Court's "draconian" remedy, especially because the government had never shown that other remedies were inadequate. Stevens noted that the Court seemed unaware that it had fashioned a drastic new remedy to enforce a species of prior restraint on a citizen's right to criticize the government.

—KIM MCLANE WARDLAW

SOUTER, DAVID H.

(1939–   )

David Hackett Souter, who became Associate Justice of the Supreme Court of the United States in 1990, was born on September 17, 1939, in Melrose, Massachusetts. He was graduated from Harvard College in 1961 and was awarded a Rhodes Scholarship. From 1961 to 1963 he studied at Oxford University. He then returned to Harvard for his legal education and graduated from Harvard Law School in 1966.

Following law school, Justice Souter practiced law at a private firm in Concord, New Hampshire, for two years. This is the only time that Justice Souter spent in the private sector. In 1968 he accepted a position as assistant attorney general for the State of New Hampshire. During the next ten years he rose to the top of the state attorney general's office, becoming deputy attorney general in 1971 and attorney general in 1976.

In 1978 Justice Souter was appointed to the Superior Court of New Hampshire. Five years later, he was elevated to the New Hampshire Supreme Court, where he served until 1990. In early 1990 he was appointed by president George Bush to the United States Court of Appeals for the First Circuit. He served on that court for only five months, participating in only one week of oral arguments and writing no opinions.

On July 20, 1990, Justice William J. Brennan Jr. resigned from the Supreme Court of the United States after thirty-four years of service. Five days later, President Bush nominated Justice Souter to be Associate Justice of the Supreme Court. Justice Souter's nomination was perceived by both supporters and opponents to be historically significant. This was true for several reasons, few of them related to Justice Souter himself.

First, during Justice Brennan's long and distinguished tenure, Brennan became the leading symbol of the "liberal" approach identified with the Supreme Court under Chief Justice Earl Warren—an approach concerned with promoting equality and protecting individual rights against the government. Supporters of that approach viewed with alarm the prospect that Justice Brennan

S

SOUTER, DAVID H.

(1939–)

Justice Souter's nomination was perceived by both supporters and opponents to be historically significant for several reasons, though few of them related to Souter himself.

would be replaced by the appointee of a Republican president who had made a campaign issue of Supreme Court decisions supported by the liberal wing of the Court.

Second, Justice Souter was the ninth consecutive Justice to have been appointed by a Republican president; no Democratic president had made an appointment to the Supreme Court for twenty-three years, since President Lyndon B. Johnson appointed Justice Thurgood Marshall in 1967. While there had been comparable periods in history—Democratic presidents Franklin D. Roosevelt and Harry S Truman, for example, appointed thirteen consecutive Justices—those were periods in which one party thoroughly dominated national politics. By contrast, Justice Souter was appointed at a time when Democrats held a majority in the Senate, as they had for all but six of the previous thirty-two years. This long-standing division of power in Washington, combined with the perception among Democratic senators that President Bush and President Ronald Reagan consciously sought to make judicial appointments that would change the political orientation of the federal courts, made partisan controversy over Justice Brennan's replacement almost inevitable no matter who the replacement was.

Third, both supporters and opponents perceived Justice Souter to be a crucial appointment in determining the direction of the Court. Senate Judiciary Committee Chair Joseph Biden, for example, asserted that no nomination had been so significant to the future of the Court since the 1930s. In particular, both supporters and opponents of the nomination expected that Justice Souter would cast the decisive vote on whether the Constitution permits the states to outlaw abortion. After the Supreme Court's 1989 decision in *Webster* v. *Reproductive Health Services*, which upheld significant state restrictions on abortion, supporters of the right to an abortion believed that four Justices were

prepared to overrule *Roe* v. *Wade* (1973), the decision that first established that right. Partly in response to *Webster*, abortion was an important issue in several closely watched political campaigns in 1989. Justice Souter had made few significant public statements about *Roe* v. *Wade* or the constitutional right to an abortion, and his views on abortion were the subject of intense investigation, and speculation, in the period between his nomination and his eventual confirmation by the Senate in October 1990.

Finally, Souter's nomination to the Court occurred in the shadow of the rejection of President Ronald Reagan's nomination of Judge Robert Bork to the Supreme Court, in 1987. The nationally televised hearings on the Bork nomination were the longest confirmation hearings on any Supreme Court nomination in history, and during the confirmation battle Bork's fate became a major national political issue. Bork had made extensive public statements on many issues of constitutional law and philosophy and was a nationally known, highly controversial figure in legal circles. Justice Souter, by contrast, had made virtually no public statements on broad issues of constitutional law and was unknown outside of New Hampshire. Those inclined to be suspicious of Justice Souter suggested that President Bush had deliberately sought out an unknown candidate who would pursue the president's agenda but who did not have the record that made Bork vulnerable. Others, including supporters of Bork, argued that the Souter nomination confirmed their fears that the treatment of Bork made it impossible for anyone except an undistinguished anonymity to be confirmed to the Supreme Court.

Souter's record was revealing in certain respects. Even among his opponents, few criticized the overall quality of the more than 100 opinions he wrote while a justice of the New Hampshire Supreme Court. Few questioned his general intellectual ability. His opinions as a state supreme court justice showed a tendency to favor the interests of the government over those of criminal suspects. Apart from that, however, his New Hampshire opinions revealed few clear patterns. Accordingly, reporters and investigators for concerned interest groups made extraordinary efforts to uncover information that might shed light on Souter's views, particularly on the abortion issue. Ultimately little such material was uncovered.

Souter's confirmation hearings were the third longest in history (after those of Bork and Justice Louis D. Brandeis). Justice Souter himself testified for almost twenty hours, the second longest time for any Supreme Court nominee (after Bork). The hearings were notable in several respects.

Perhaps most significant, senators asked, and Souter answered, numerous substantive questions about the nominee's views on specific issues of constitutional law. Justice Souter made specific statements about his views on racial discrimination; affirmative action to aid racial minorities; sex discrimination; legislative reapportionment and the principle of one person, one vote; congressional power to enforce the Fourteenth Amendment's guarantees of due process and equal protection against the states; the enforcement of the Bill of Rights against the states through the Fourteenth Amendment's due process clause; the free speech clause, free exercise clause, and establishment clause of the First Amendment; and the decision in *Miranda* v. *Arizona* (1966), which required police officers to warn suspects in custody before interrogating them. Souter commented specifically on several Supreme Court decisions—endorsing, for example, the landmark expansions of free speech rights in *New York Times* v. *Sullivan* (1964) and *Brandenburg* v. *Ohio* (1969), but criticizing the standard for judging establishment clause issues specified in the *Lemon* test and the approach that Justice Antonin Scalia took to the role of tradi-

tion in determining the rights protected by the due process clause. Justice Souter also engaged in broad-ranging discussions with members of the Senate Judiciary Committee on the significance of the intentions of the Framers of the Constitution and on a Supreme Court Justice's obligation to follow precedent.

Souter's extensive substantive answers were significant principally because, before the Senate hearings, there had been considerable controversy over whether it was proper for senators to ask Supreme Court nominees their views on specific issues, and whether it was obligatory, or even appropriate, for the nominee to answer. Some recent nominees (notably Justice Scalia) had refused to answer substantive questions about constitutional issues, and many thought that Bork's uninhibited willingness to answer contributed to his downfall. Souter's extensive answers buttressed the position of those who maintained that nominees should be expected to give their views on constitutional issues in detail to the Senate committee.

Souter's hearings were also significant for what he did not disclose. Despite repeated questioning, he declined to state his views on whether the Constitution protected the right to an abortion and on whether *Roe* v. *Wade* should be overruled. Ultimately, many senators who believed that this issue was of the first importance, and that a Supreme Court nominee was obligated to disclose his views on it, voted to confirm Justice Souter despite his reticence.

Another conspicuous aspect of Souter's confirmation process was the role of groups of private citizens interested in specific issues. Those groups had played a significant role in mobilizing public opinion against the Bork nomination, and many—especially groups concerned about the possible overruling of *Roe* v. *Wade*—testified against Justice Souter and attempted, unsuccessfully, to rally public opinion against him. In this respect as well,

S

SOUTER, DAVID H.

(1939–)

the Souter nomination confirmed the trend toward the increased politicization of the Supreme Court nomination process.

Finally, Souter's confirmation hearings were significant because of the extraordinary degree of preparation that preceded them and the increasing tendency of confirmation hearings to take on the aspect of choreographed productions. The Bush administration assigned several officials to help Souter prepare for the Senate hearings, and Souter spent most of the period between his nomination and the hearings studying intensely and practicing his responses to anticipated questions from the senators. His preparation was manifestly successful: most observers considered his testimony at the hearings to be a virtuoso performance in which he demonstrated careful thought on a wide range of constitutional issues to which he had not been greatly exposed while on the New Hampshire Supreme Court. Justice Souter was confirmed by an overwhelming vote in the Senate despite the salience of the abortion issue and his refusal to indicate his views on that issue. This emphasis on careful preparation to defuse political difficulties is another respect in which it seems likely that Justice Souter's confirmation process established a lasting pattern.

The cases decided through April 1991 of Justice Souter's first term on the Supreme Court revealed little about his orientation, and what they did reveal was not surprising. The most important cases during that period dealt with criminal procedure, and in each of them Justice Souter voted in favor of the government. Perhaps the most significant single vote was in *Arizona* v. *Fulminante* (1991), where a 5–4 majority of the Court (in an opinion by Chief Justice William H. Rehnquist) ruled that the admission of a coerced confession in a criminal trial can be harmless error. Observers speculated, plausibly, that Justice Brennan would have reached the opposite conclusion and that Justice Souter's appointment determined the result on this issue. In *McClesky* v. *Zant* (1991), Justice Souter joined a six-Justice majority (in an opinion by Justice Kennedy) in adopting a rule that sharply limited the ability of prisoners to bring successive federal habeas corpus petitions. The ruling was issued in a capital case, and its most marked effect will be to cut off the avenues of federal judicial review available to defendants who have been sentenced to death. Finally, in *California* v. *Hodari D.* (1991), Justice Souter, with six of his colleagues, joined an opinion (written by Justice Scalia) that adopted a narrow construction of the term "seizure" in the Fourth Amendment: The Court ruled that a suspect who ran away when a police officer ordered him to stop was seized not at the time the order was given but only when he was finally restrained. In all of these cases, Justice Souter's votes confirmed the strong tendency he had shown in his opinions on the New Hampshire Supreme Court to favor the government in criminal cases.

Justice Souter has continued to be a significant centrist on the Court, often dissenting from its more conservative decisions, especially with regard to congressional power and states' rights. Similarly, in *Planned Parenthood of Southeastern Pennsylvania* v. *Casey* (1992) he joined the opinion of Justices Sandra Day O'Connor and Anthony M. Kennedy sustaining the "essential holding" of *Roe* v. *Wade*, but abandoning *Roe*'s trimester framework and rephrasing the standard of judicial scrutiny in abortion cases to whether a restriction is an undue burden on the right to seek an abortion. In other cases Justice Souter has written thoughtful concurrences, often adopting a narrower view than the majority to support the same conclusion. In short, Justice Souter has confounded those of his original critics who saw him as a predictable judicial conservative, and has become an influential moderate voice on a divided Court.

—DAVID A. STRAUSS

Bibliography

Nomination of David H. Souter to Be an Associate Justice of the United States Supreme Court, Senate Executive Report No. 101–32, 101st Cong., 2d Sess. (October 1, 1990).

SOUTH CAROLINA v. KATZENBACH

383 U.S. 301 (1966)

The decision upheld the constitutionality of portions of the Voting Rights Act of 1965. Southern states attacked, as an intrusion upon state sovereignty and on other grounds, portions of the act suspending tests or devices used to measure voter qualifications, barring new voter qualifications pending approval by federal authorities, providing for the appointment of federal voting examiners to register voters, and determining which states and political subdivisions were subject to the act's coverage. In sustaining the legislation under the Fifteenth Amendment, the Supreme Court, in an opinion by Chief Justice Earl Warren, rejected the argument that Congress could do no more than forbid violations of the Fifteenth Amendment and must leave the fashioning of remedies for violations to the courts. Congressional findings that case-by-case litigation was inadequate to vindicate voting rights justified the decision "to shift the advantage of time and inerta from the perpetrators of the evil to its victims."

—THEODORE EISENBERG

SOUTH DAKOTA v. NEVILLE

459 U.S. 553 (1983)

In this case the Supreme Court answered a question left unresolved by earlier decisions: Can a state use as evidence the fact that a person arrested for drunk driving refused to take a blood-alcohol test? *Griffin* v. *California* (1965) had held that adverse comment on a defendant's refusal to testify impermissibly burdened the right against self-incrimination, and *Schmerber* v. *California* (1966) had held that a state could compel the taking of a blood-alcohol test without violating that right, which protected against testimonial compulsion only, not compulsion of physical evidence drawn from the body. In *Neville* the Court ruled that a state that authorized a driver to refuse a blood-alcohol test could introduce that refusal as evidence against him. The Court relied not on the earlier distinction between testimonial and nontestimonial compulsion but on the fact that the element of compulsion was altogether absent here because the state did not require the test.

—LEONARD W. LEVY

SOUTHERN PACIFIC CO. v. ARIZONA

325 U.S. 761 (1945)

Arizona prohibited operation of a railroad train more than fourteen passenger cars or seventy freight cars long. The Supreme Court, 7–2, held the law an unconstitutional burden on interstate commerce. Chief Justice Harlan Fiske Stone, for the Court, emphasized the magnitude of that burden; the law forced the railroad to operate thirty percent more trains in the state, and to break up and remake trains; its total yearly cost to both railroads operating in the state was a million dollars. Stone also noted that requiring more trains would produce more accidents; the state's safety argument was weak. This interest-balancing analysis was far more demanding than the "rational basis" standard of review Stone had employed in *South Carolina State Highway Department* v. *Barnwell Bros., Inc.* (1938), upholding limits on truck widths and weights. *Southern Pacific* set the standard for future challenges to state regulations of commerce in the transportation field.

—KENNETH L. KARST

Can a state use as evidence the fact that a person arrested for drunk driving refused to take a blood-alcohol test?

Southern Pacific set the standard for future challenges to state regulations of commerce in the transportation field.

See also

Rational Basis

Standard of Review

STANDARD OF REVIEW

Some constitutional limitations on government are readily susceptible to "interpretation," in the sense of definition and categorization. Once a court categorizes a law as a bill of attainder, for example, it holds the law invalid. Other limitations, however, are expressed in terms that make this sort of interpretation awkward: the freedom of speech, the equal protection of the laws, due process of law. The judicial task in enforcing these open-ended limitations implies an inquiry into the justifications asserted by government for restricting liberty or denying equal treatment. The term "standards of review," in common use since the late 1960s, denotes various degrees of judicial deference to legislative judgments concerning these justifications.

The idea that there might be more than one standard of review was explicitly suggested in Justice Harlan Fiske Stone's opinion for the Supreme Court in *United States* v. *Carolene Products Co.* (1938). Confirming a retreat from the judicial activism that had invalidated a significant number of economic regulations over the preceding four decades, Stone concluded that such a law would be valid if the legislature's purpose were legitimate and if the law could rationally be seen as related to that purpose. Stone added, however, that this permissive rational basis standard might not be appropriate for reviewing laws challenged under certain specific prohibitions of the Bill of Rights, or laws restricting the political process, or laws directed at discrete and insular minorities. Such cases, Stone suggested, might call for a diminished presumption of constitutionality, a "more exacting judicial scrutiny."

The Warren Court embraced this double standard in several doctrinal areas, most notably in equal protection cases. The permissive rational basis standard continued to govern review of economic regulations, but strict scrutiny was given to laws discriminating against the exercise of fundamental interests such as voting or marriage and to laws employing suspect classifications such as race. The strict scrutiny standard amounts to an inversion of the presumption of constitutionality: the state must justify its imposition of a racial inequality, for example, by showing that the law is necessary to achieve a compelling state interest. Today active judicial review of both the importance of legislative purposes and the necessity of legislative means is employed not only in some types of equal protection cases but also in fields such as the freedom of speech and religious liberty. It has even attended the rebirth of substantive due process.

Inevitably, however, cracks appeared in this two-tier system of standards of review. The Court used the language of "rational basis" to strike down some laws, and in cases involving sex discrimination it explicitly adopted an intermediate standard for reviewing both legislative ends and means: discrimination based on sex is invalid unless it serves an "important" governmental purpose and is "substantially related" to that purpose. A similar intermediate standard is now part of the required analysis of governmental regulations of commercial speech. In practical effect, the Court has created a "sliding scale" of review, varying the intensity of judicial scrutiny of legislation in proportion to the importance of the interests invaded and the likelihood of legislative prejudice against the persons disadvantaged. The process, in other words, is interest-balancing, pure and simple. Justice William H. Rehnquist, writing for the Court in *Rostker* v. *Goldberg* (1981), remarked accurately that the Court's various levels of scrutiny "may all too readily become facile abstractions used to justify a result"—a proposition well illustrated by the *Rostker* opinion itself.

—KENNETH L. KARST

Bibliography

Gunther, Gerald (1972). The Supreme Court, 1971 Term—Foreword: In Search

In practical effect, the Court has created a "sliding scale" of review, varying the intensity of judicial scrunity of legislation.

of Evolving Doctrine on a Changing Court: A Model for a Newer Equal Protection. *Harvard Law Review* 86:1–48.

STANDARD OIL COMPANY v. UNITED STATES

221 U.S. 1 (1911)

UNITED STATES v. AMERICAN TOBACCO COMPANY

211 U.S. 106 (1911)

John D. Rockefeller, owner of the nation's first, largest, and richest trust and controller of the nation's oil business, scorned his competitors and condemned the law. His disregard for the Sherman Antitrust Act helped earn him, in 1909, a dissolution order which the trust appealed to the Supreme Court. Rockefeller thereby provided Chief Justice Edward D. White with the occasion to celebrate the conversion of a majority of the Court to his viewpoint, enabling him to write the rule of reason into antitrust law. After nearly fifteen years of effort, White had managed to enlarge judicial discretion in antitrust cases, even though the oil trust did not urge the doctrine upon the Court; indeed, it was unnecessary to the case's disposition.

Chief Justice White, leading an 8–1 Court, ruled that only an "unreasonable" contract or combination in restraint of trade would violate the law. White had effectively amended the law to insert his test: section 1 of the Sherman Act would henceforth be interpreted as if it said, "Every unreasonable contract, combination . . . or conspiracy in restraint of trade . . . is hereby declared to be illegal."

Standard Oil, however, lost the case. The record, said White, showed clearly and convincingly that this trust was unreasonable. Systematic attempts to exclude or crush rivals

and the trust's astounding success demonstrated the violation beyond any doubt.

Justice John Marshall Harlan concurred in the result but dissented from the Court's announcement of the rule of reason. Harlan observed that Congress had refused to amend the act to incorporate the rule of reason, and he lashed out at the majority's "judicial legislation," predicting that the new policy would produce chaos. His call echoed in Congress where Democratic pressure grew to write the rule of reason out of the Sherman Act. That pressure would eventually find partial release in supplementary antitrust legislation, passage of the Clayton Act in 1914. The rule of reason prevailed, however, although the Court applied a double standard. When massive business combinations such as United States Steel Corporation, United Shoe Machinery Company, and International Harvester came before the Court, they were

DISREGARD FOR THE LAW

In this undated cartoon, John D. Rockefeller is depicted as "The King of the World," a reference to his ownership of the Standard Oil monopoly. (Corbis/Bettmann)

Systematic attempts to exclude or crush rivals and the trust's astounding success demonstrated the violation beyond any doubt.

found to have acted reasonably, restraints of trade notwithstanding. In antitrust action against labor unions, however, the Court ignored that rule.

In the companion *American Tobacco* case, Chief Justice White attempted to mitigate a too vigorous federal antitrust policy by ordering reorganization, not dissolution, of the Tobacco Trust. He thereby heartened business interests by showing solicitousness for property rights and a stable economy.

—DAVID GORDON

Bibliography

Bringhurst, Bruce (1979). *Antitrust and the Oil Monopoly: The Standard Oil Cases, 1890–1914*. Westport, Conn.: Greenwood Press.

STANDING

In the United States, unelected, life-tenured federal judges may decide legal issues only when they are asked to do so by appropriate litigants. Such litigants are said to have standing to raise certain legal claims, including constitutional claims, in the federal courts.

A litigant's standing depends on two sets of criteria, one constitutionally required and one not, each ostensibly having three parts. The constitutional criteria derive from Article III's job description for federal judges, which permits them to declare law only when such a declaration is necessary to decide cases and controversies. These criteria center on the notion of an injured person's asking a court for a remedy against the responsible party, and each criterion corresponds to one of the three participants—to the plaintiff, the defendant, and the court, respectively. The plaintiff must assert that he suffered a cognizable personal injury; that the defendant's conduct caused the injury; and that the court's judgment is substantially likely to relieve it. The three nonconstitutional criteria for standing are "prudential" rules, self-imposed by the courts for their own governance,

rules that Congress can eliminate if it chooses. These criteria, too, serve to diminish the frequency of substantive pronouncements by federal judges, but they focus on the legal basis of the suit, not on the plaintiff's actual injury. The first nonconstitutional criterion concerns representation: to secure judicial relief, injured litigants normally must assert that the injurious conduct violated their own legal rights, not the rights of third parties. The second assumes that government violations of everyone's undifferentiated legal rights are best left to political, not judicial, response: no one has standing if his or her legal position asserts "only the generalized interest of all citizens in constitutional governance." The third "prudential" criterion for standing seeks assurance that the law invoked plausibly protects the legal interest allegedly invaded: whatever interest is asserted must be "arguably within the zone of interests to be protected or regulated by the statute or constitutional guarantee in question."

Standing issues rarely surface in traditional suits, but federal courts applying these guidelines frequently deny standing to "public interest" plaintiffs anxious to challenge the legality of government behavior. The aim is not only to prevent federal judges from proclaiming law unless such declarations are needed to resolve concrete disputes, but also to promote proper conditions for intelligent adjudication (including adversary presentation of the facts and legal arguments) and to foster adequate representation of affected interests. When litigants ask federal courts to restrict the constitutional authority of politically accountable public officials, moreover, apprehension about unwise or excessive judicial intervention heightens, and the standing limitations may be applied with particular force.

Collectively, the Supreme Court's standing criteria often overlap; they are applied flexibly—sometimes inconsistently—to give the Supreme Court considerable discretion to exercise or withhold its power to declare law. The way that discretion is exercised reflects any particular Court's ideology of judicial activism and restraint and the substantive, constitutional rights it is either eager or reluctant to enforce.

The refinements of standing doctrine illustrate this flexibility and discretion. The core requirement of cognizable personal injury, for example, demands that the plaintiff have suffered injury to an interest deemed deserving of judicial protection. Over time, the Court has expanded the category of judicially acknowledged injuries beyond economic harm to include reputational, environmental, aesthetic, associational, informational, organizational, and voter harms, among others. Because of its vision of constrained judicial power in a representative democracy, however, the Court steadfastly forbids taxpayers' suits and citizens' suits asserting purely ideological harm, particularly the harms of frustration, distress, or apprehension born of unlawful government conduct. Resting on lack of cognizable injury, the ban on citizen standing thus appears constitutionally compelled, although it effectively duplicates the nonconstitutional barrier to asserting generalized grievances, which appears to rest on the absence of a cognizable legal interest. Less diffuse, but in *Allen* v. *Wright* (1984) nonetheless held an insufficiently personal injury, is the feeling of stigma arising from discrimination directed, not personally, but against other members of the plaintiff's race. If the type of injury is judicially approved and the plaintiff personally suffered it, however, the fact that many others have suffered it will not negate standing. For example, in *United States* v. *SCRAP* (1973) a student activist group was deemed to have standing based on widespread environmental injury.

Flexibility also characterizes the Court's degree of insistence on the remaining constitutional criteria. The closeness of the causal link between defendant's conduct and plaintiff's injury has varied from *United States* v. *SCRAP*, which accepted a loose connection between the Interstate Commerce Commission's approval of freight rate increases for scrap materials and increased trash problems in national parks, to *Allen* v. *Wright* (1984),

which found too attenuated a seemingly closer link between the Internal Revenue Service's allegedly inadequate enforcement of the law requiring denial of tax exemptions to racially discriminatory private schools and "white flight" in public school districts undergoing desegregation. Similarly, insistence that judicial relief be substantially likely to redress plaintiff's injury has varied from *Linda R. S.* v. *Richard D.* (1973), where mothers of illegitimate children seeking to force prosecution of the fathers for nonsupport were denied standing because a court order supposedly would result only in jailing the fathers, not in increased support, to *Duke Power Co.* v. *Carolina Environmental Study Group* (1978), where neighbors of nuclear power plants, seeking relief from present injury caused by normal plant operation, were granted standing to contest (unsuccessfully) the constitutional validity of a federal statute limiting recovery of damages for potential nuclear disasters, despite considerable uncertainty that a legal victory for the plaintiffs would stop the plants' normal operations.

In the 1990s the Court used the Constitution's case or controversy requirement to deny standing in a series of decisions, several of which Justice Antonin Scalia authored. These emphasized both the limited role that, in the majority's view, the federal courts should play in reviewing executive actions and the need for "redressability": the courts' ability to actually redress some injury, as opposed to merely declaring the law.

Of the nonconstitutional criteria, only the usual prohibition against representing third-party rights needs elaboration, primarily because of its different forms and its significant exceptions. When a personally injured plaintiff seeks to argue that the injurious conduct violated the legal rights of others, the prohibition, beyond serving the usual objectives of standing, serves also to protect nonlitigants who may not wish to assert their own rights or would do so differently (and perhaps more effectively) if they became litigants. Major exceptions to that prohibition respond to this

Like other justiciability doctrines, standing rules often thwart attempts to induce federal courts to make or reform constitutional or other law.

See also

Cases and Controversies

NAACP v. *Alabama*

policy by allowing representation, even of constitutional rights, when the Court concludes that the absent third parties would benefit rather than suffer from a substantive decision. One important example of this exception is the case in which third parties would have difficulty asserting their own rights, as in *NAACP v. Alabama* (1958), where the civil rights group was permitted to assert its members' right to remain anonymous. Another example is the case in which the disputed conduct affects special plaintiff-third party relationships in ways suggesting that the plaintiff and third-party interests coincide. Under this exception doctors can represent patient rights to abortion, private schools can represent parent rights to choose private education, and sellers can represent the rights of young consumers to buy beer or contraceptives.

The Court generally denies standing when persons constitutionally subject to regulation urge that the regulation would be unconstitutional in application to others. This rule preserves legislative policy in cases where the law is applied constitutionally. Again, however, there is an exception, invoked most often in First Amendment challenges of vagueness and overbreadth, when the law's very existence would significantly inhibit others from exercising important constitutional rights and thus deter them from mounting their own challenge. However, in recent decisions the Court has limited standing in free speech overbreadth cases to situations involving "substantial overbreadth"—applications of the statute that are truly likely to occur.

A final example is the case in which uninjured representatives seek to champion the legal rights of injured persons they represent outside of litigation. Thus, associations, not injured themselves, may sue on behalf of their members' injuries, provided that the members would have standing, the associations seek to protect interests germane to their purposes, and the claims and requested relief do not require individual member participation. And a state, which normally lacks standing as *parens patriae* to represent the claims of individual citizens, or even of all its citizens in opposition to the federal government, may represent its citizens when the injury alleged substantially affects the state's general population, especially if suit by individual citizens seems unlikely.

Like other justiciability doctrines, standing rules often thwart attempts to induce federal courts to make or reform constitutional or other law. How often the rules have that result will depend not only on the articulated criteria of standing but also on the Supreme Court's receptivity to the substance of the underlying claims and its judgment of the desirability and likelihood of political solutions.

—JONATHAN D. VARAT

Bibliography

Nichol, Gene R., Jr. (1984). Rethinking Standing. *California Law Review* 72: 68–102.

Scott, Kenneth E. (1973). Standing in the Supreme Court: A Functional Analysis. *Harvard Law Review* 86:645–692.

Vining, Joseph (1978). *Legal Identity: The Coming of Age of Public Law.* New Haven, Conn.: Yale University Press.

STANFORD v. KENTUCKY

492 U.S. 361 (1989)

By a 5–4 vote, the Court held that the infliction of capital punishment on juveniles who committed their crimes at sixteen or seventeen years of age did not violate the cruel and unusual punishment clause of the Eighth Amendment, applied to the states by the Fourteenth Amendment.

Justice Antonin Scalia, for the majority, acknowledged that whether a punishment conflicts with evolving standards of decency depends on public opinion. But in examining the laws of the country, Scalia found that a majority of the states permit the execution of

Public opinion polls and the views of professional associations seemed to invite constitutional law to rest on "uncertain foundations."

See also

Capital Punishment

juvenile offenders. He refused to consider indicia of society's opinion other than by examination of jury verdicts and statutory law. Public opinion polls and the views of professional associations seemed to invite constitutional law to rest on "uncertain foundations." The Court also ruled that the imposition of death on juvenile offenders did not conflict with the legitimate goals of penology.

The four dissenters, led by Justice William J. Brennan, argued that the Eighth Amendment prohibits the punishment of death for a person who committed a crime when under eighteen years of age. The dissenters relied on a far wider range of indicia of public opinion than did the majority to reach their conclusion that evolving standards of decency required a different holding. They argued too that the death penalty is disproportionate when applied to young offenders and significantly fails to serve the goals of capital punishment.

—LEONARD W. LEVY

STANLEY v. GEORGIA

394 U.S. 557 (1969)

Authorized by a search warrant, federal and state agents entered and searched Stanley's home for evidence of bookmaking activities. Instead they found film, which was used to convict him for possession of obscene material. The Supreme Court reversed, holding that mere possession of obscenity in one's home cannot constitutionally be made a crime.

Prior obscenity decisions had recognized a legitimate state interest in regulating public dissemination of obscene materials. In *Stanley*, however, the Court recognized two fundamental constitutional rights that outweighed the state interest in regulating obscenity in a citizen's home: the First Amendment right to receive information and ideas, regardless of their social worth, and the constitutional right to be free from unwanted government intrusion into one's privacy.

As justification for interfering with these important individual rights, the state asserted the right to protect individuals from obscenity's effects. The Court rejected that argument, viewing such "protection" as an attempt to "control . . . a person's thoughts," a goal "wholly inconsistent with the philosophy of the First Amendment."

Justices Potter J. Stewart, William J. Brennan, and Byron R. White concurred in the result, on the ground that the search and seizure were outside the lawful scope of the officers' warrant, and thus violated Stanley's Fourth Amendment rights.

—KIM MCLANE WARDLAW

STATE ACTION

The phrase "state action," a term of art in our constitutional law, symbolizes the rule—or supposed rule—that constitutional guarantees of human rights are effective only against *governmental* action impairing those rights. (The word "state," in the phrase, denotes any unit or element of government, and not simply one of the American states, though the "state action" concept has been at its most active, and most problematic, with respect to these.) The problems have been many and complex; the "state action" doctrine has not reached anything near a satisfactory condition of rationality.

A best first step toward exploring the problems hidden in the "state action" phrase may be a look at its development in constitutional history. The development has revolved around the first section of the Fourteenth Amendment, wherein the problem is in effect put forward by the words here italicized:

> *All persons born or naturalized in the United States, and subject to the jurisdiction thereof, are citizens of the United States and of the State wherein they reside.* No State *shall make or enforce any law which shall abridge the privileges or immu-*

In Stanley *the Court recognized two fundamental constitutional rights that outweighed the state interest in regulating obscenity in a citizen's home.*

nities of citizens of the United States; nor shall any State deprive any person of life, liberty, or property, without due process of law; nor deny to any person within its jurisdiction the equal protection of the laws.

An early "state action" case under this section, *Ex Parte Virginia* (1880), raised an audacious claim as to the limiting effect of the words emphasized above. A Virginia judge had been charged under a federal statute forbidding racial exclusion from juries. He was not directed by a state statute to perform this racial exclusion. The judge argued that the action was not that of the state of Virginia, but rather the act of an official, proceeding wrongfully on his own. On this theory, a "state" had not denied equal protection. The Fourteenth Amendment, the judge contended, did not therefore forbid the conduct charged, or authorize Congress to make it criminal. The Supreme Court, however, declined to take such high ground.

"The constitutional provision," it said, ". . . must mean that no agency of the state, or of the officers or agents by whom its powers are exerted, shall deny . . . equal protection of the laws." But probably the only fully principled and maximally clear rule as to "state action" would have been that the "state," as a state, does not "act" except by its official enactments—and so does not "act" when one of its officers merely abuses his power. "Fully principled and maximally clear"—but, like so many such "rules," aridly formalistic, making practical nonsense of any constitutional rule it limits. There were gropings, around the year of this case, toward a "state action" requirement with bite, but the modern history of the concept starts with the *Civil Rights Cases* of 1883, wherein many modern problems were foreshadowed. In the Civil Rights Act of 1875, Congress had enacted "[t]hat all persons . . . shall be entitled to the full and equal enjoyment of the accommodations, advantages, facilities, and privileges of inns, public conveyances on land or water, theatres,

and other places of public amusement . . . [regardless of race]."

Persons were indicted for excluding blacks from hotels, theaters, and railroads. The Court considered that the only possible source of congressional power to make such a law was section 5 of the Fourteenth Amendment: "The Congress shall have power to enforce, by appropriate legislation, the provisions of this article." This section the Court saw as authorizing only those laws which *directly* enforced the guarantees of the amendment's section 1 (quoted above), which in turn referred only to a *state*. The amendment therefore did not warrant, the Court held, any congressional dealing with racially discriminatory actions of individuals or corporations.

Few judicial opinions seem to rest on such solid ground; at the end of Justice Joseph Bradley's performance, the reader is likely to feel, "Q.E.D." But this feeling of apparent demonstration is attained, as often it is, by the passing over in silence of disturbing facts and thoughts. Many of these were brought out in the powerful dissent of Justice John Marshall Harlan.

One of the cases involved racial discrimination by a railroad. The American railroads, while they were building, were generally given the power of eminent domain. Eminent domain is a sovereign power, enjoyed par excellence by the state, and given by the state to "private" persons for public purposes looked on as important to the state; the Fifth Amendment's language illustrates the firmness of the background assumption that "private property" shall be taken, even with just compensation, only for public use. The American railroads were, moreover, very heavily assisted by public subsidy from governmental units at all levels. Both these steps—the clothing of railroad corporations with eminent-domain power, and their subsidization out of public funds—were justified, both rhetorically and as a matter of law, on the grounds that the railroads were *public instrumentalities*, fulfilling the classic state function of furnishing a transportation system. Regulation of railroads was undertaken under the same theory.

Railroads and hotel keepers, moreover, followed the so-called common callings, traditionally entailing an obligation to take and carry, or to accommodate, all well-behaved persons able to pay. The *withdrawal* of protection of such a right to equal treatment might be looked on as "state action," and Congress might well decide, as a practical matter, either that the right had been wholly withdrawn as to blacks (which was in many places the fact of the matter) or that the state action supporting these rights of access was insufficient and required supplementation; only the most purposefully narrow construction could deny to such supplementation the name of "enforcement."

Indeed, this line of thought, whether as to the *Civil Rights Cases* or as to all other "equal protection" cases, is fraught with trouble for the whole "state action" doctrine, in nature as in name. "Action" is an exceedingly inapt word for the "denial" of "protection." Protection against lynching was, for example, usually "denied" by "inaction." Inaction by the state is indeed the classic form of "denial of protection." The *Civil Rights Cases* majority did not read far enough, even for the relentless literalist; it read as far as "nor shall any State . . ." but then hastily closed the book before reading what follows: ". . . *deny* to any person . . . the equal *protection* of the laws." Contrary to the majority's reading, the state's affirmative obligation of protection should have extended to the protection of the traditional rights of resort to public transport and common inns; it was notorious that the very people (blacks) whose "equal protection" was central to the Fourteenth Amendment were commonly the only victims of nominally "private" denial of these rights.

Justice Harlan pointed out that in its first sentence, conferring citizenship on the newly emancipated slaves, the first section of the Fourteenth Amendment did not use any language in any way suggesting a "state action" requirement, so that there was not even the verbal support for the "state action" requirement that the Court had found in the other phrases of that section. The question then became, in Harlan's view, what the legal consequences of "citizenship" were; for purposes of the particular case at hand, he said:

> *But what was secured to colored citizens of the United States—as between them and their respective States—by the national grant to them of State citizenship? With what rights, privileges, or immunities did this grant invest them? There is one, if there be no other—exemption from race discrimination in respect of any civil right belonging to citizens of the white race in the same State . . . . Citizenship in this country necessarily imports at least equality of civil rights among citizens of every race in the same State. It is fundamental in American citizenship that, in respect of such rights, there shall be no discrimination by the State, or its officers, or by individuals or corporations exercising public functions or authority, against any citizen because of his race or previous condition of servitude. . . .*

There is a third, most interesting aspect to Harlan's dissent. The majority had summarily rejected the argument that under the Thirteenth Amendment—forbidding slavery and involuntary servitude and giving Congress enforcement power—racial exclusion from public places was one of the "badges and incidents" of slavery. Harlan argued that forced segregation in public accommodations was a badge of servitude, and he pointed out that no "state action" requirement could be found in the words of the Thirteenth Amendment. This argument was plowed under and was heard from no more for many decades, but it is of great interest because it was revived and made the basis of decision in a leading case in the 1960s, *Jones* v. *Alfred H. Mayer Co.* (1968).

The *Civil Rights Cases*, in the majority opinion, brushed past contentions that were in no way frivolous. Very many discriminatory actions of public scope are taken by persons or corporations enjoying special favor from government and heavily regulated by government; one cannot easily see their actions as isolated from public power. "Denial of equal protection," the central constitutional wrong in racial cases, seems to refer at least as naturally to inaction as it does to action. If any positive rights at all inhere in citizenship—and if there are no such rights, the citizenship clause is a mere matter of nomenclature—these rights are set up by the Fourteenth Amendment without limitation as to the source of their impairment. Nevertheless, the holdings and doctrine of the *Civil Rights Cases* fell on a thirstily receptive society. The "state action" doctrine became one of the principal reliances of a racist nation, North as well as South.

In a society where so much of access to goods and values is managed by nominally "private" persons and corporations—railroads, restaurants, streetcars, cinemas, even food and clothing—a protection that runs only against the government, strictly defined, can work out to very little effective protection. If the official justice system is hampered by inconvenient constitutional safeguards, the sheriff can play cards while the lynch mob forms, and there is "no state action." A nightclub may refuse to serve a black celebrity, and there is "no state action." The "state action" doctrine protected from constitutional scrutiny an enormous network of racial exclusion and humiliation, characterizing both North and South.

Paradoxically, the "state action" requirement may for a long time have been more important to the maintenance of northern racism than to that of the cruder racism of the South. The South developed segregation by law, in all phases of public life, and this regime was broadly validated by the notorious 1896 decision in *Plessy* v. *Ferguson*. For complex political reasons—and perhaps because of a faintly lingering adherence to scraps of Civil War idealism—segregation by

official law was not widely imposed in the North. But the practices of real-estate agents, mortgage lenders, restaurant keepers, and a myriad of other "private" people and corporations added up to a pervasive custom of racial segregation in many phases of life, a custom less perfectly kept than the official legal dictates of the southern regime, but effectively barring most blacks from much of the common life of the communities they lived in.

A striking case in point was *Dorsey* v. *Stuyvesant Town Corporation* (1949–50). The Metropolitan Life Insurance Company, having much money to invest, struck a complicated deal with the State and the City of New York. The contemplated end result was the conversion of a large section of New York City—from 14th to 23rd Streets, and from Avenue A to the East River—into a vast complex of apartments, to be owned and run by a Metropolitan subsidiary. By formal statute and ordinance, the state and city acquiesced in this scheme, agreeing to use (and later using) the sovereign "eminent domain" power to acquire title to all the needed land, which was, as prearranged, later transferred to Metropolitan. Again by formal arrangement, a quarter-century tax exemption was granted on "improvements"—that is to say, on the immensely valuable apartment buildings. The public easement on certain streets was extinguished, and control over them turned over to Stuyvesant Town Corporation, a Metropolitan subsidiary; various water, sewage, and fire protection arrangements were altered to suit the needs of the project. And all this was done, visibly and pridefully, as a joint effort of public and "private" enterprise; politicians as well as insurance men took bows. Then, when the whole thing was built, with "title" safely vested in "private" hands, Stuyvesant Town Corporation announced that no blacks need apply for apartments. The suit of a black applicant reached the highest court of New York, and that court held, 4–3, that there was not enough "state action" in all this to make applicable the

Fourteenth Amendment prohibition of racial discrimination. The Supreme Court of the United States denied certiorari.

The *Stuyvesant Town* case illustrates very well what could be done with the "state action" formula. With the fullest cooperation from government at all levels, as much of any city as might be desired (strictly public buildings alone excepted) could be turned into a "whites only" preserve. With the necessary cooperation, the process could be extended to a whole county, or a whole state. If they were prudent, the political partners in such deals would not put anything in writing about the racial exclusion contemplated.

But the essentiality of the "state action" formula to the success of northern racism must not obscure its considerable strategic importance even in the South. Segregation by law had in the main been validated, and this was the South's main reliance, but there were gaps, and the "state action" formula filled them in.

First, there was the role of nominally "private" violence against blacks, as the ultimate weapon of the racist regime—with lynching at the top of the arsenal's inventory. At this point the disregard of the Fourteenth Amendment's words "nor shall any State *deny* . . . equal *protection* of the laws" is most surprising. But for a long time a whole lot of seemingly serious people saw no "denial of protection" in the de facto denial of protection to blacks against a great deal of "private" violence.

Second, outright racial residential zoning by law—just one form of segregation—had been struck down by the Supreme Court, in the 1917 case of *Buchanan* v. *Warley.* The opinion in that case does not adequately distinguish *Plessy* v. *Ferguson,* but it was the law, and nominally "private" methods of racial zoning had often to be resorted to in the South—just as they were, pervasively, in the North. Real-estate agents and mortgage banks played their accustomed part; until astonishingly recent times, the actually pub-lished codes of "ethics" of "realtors" forbade (under some transparent euphemism) actions tending toward spoiling the racial homogeneity of any neighborhood. But more was needed, and that more was found—South and North—in the "racially restrictive covenant." These "covenants" were neither necessarily nor commonly mere casual contractual arrangements between parties dickering at random. Very commonly, when an "addition" was "subdivided," all the first deeds restricted ownership or occupancy, or both, to whites only—or to white Gentiles only, or to white Gentiles of northern European extraction. These covenants, recorded at the courthouse in a registry furnished by the state for this purpose, were ordained by many states' laws to "run with the land"—that is, they had to be put in all subsequent deeds forever, and usually were binding whether so inserted or not, since any buyer, examining title, could find them in the title-chain. These "covenants"—often functionally equivalent to racial zoning by law, enforced by court orders, and kept on file at the courthouse—were for a long time looked on as "merely private" action, in no way traceable to the state, and so not amenable to constitutional command.

A third and even more important use of the "state action" doctrine (or a doctrine closely akin) was peculiar to the South, and was the rotting-out base of southern politics for generations. The Fifteenth Amendment forbade racial exclusions from voting—but, like the Fourteenth, it directed its prohibition at governments: "The right of citizens of the United States to vote shall not be denied or abridged by the United States or by any State on account of race, color, or previous condition of servitude."

The general response in the South to this politically inconvenient constitutional mandate was the all-white Democratic primary election. This primary was colloquially known as "the election"; its nominees virtually always won in the November balloting, when all the whites who had voted in the Democratic primary were expected to vote for its nominee, and enough did so to wipe out any scattered Republican votes, including the votes of those blacks who could surmount the other barriers to their voting—literacy tests, difficult registration procedures, and even more violent discouragements. This plain fraud on the Constitution did not rest wholly on the concept that the action of the Democratic party was not "state action," but the even bolder idea behind it—the idea, namely, that the practical substitution of a "party" election for the regular election could altogether escape the Fifteenth Amendment mandate, even when the state commanded the all-whiteness of the Party—was related in more than spirit to the "state action" doctrine as illustrated in the Stuyvesant Town case. Its basis was the thought that racial voting requirements were not "official" if a nominally "private" organization was put in as a buffer between the wrong done and state power. And the all-white primary in the end had to rely (vainly, as at last it turned out) on the "state action" requirement.

The "state action" doctrine is not a mere interesting footnote in constitutional law. It has served as an absolutely essential and broadly employed component in the means by which black equality, theoretically guaranteed by the post–Civil War amendments, was made to mean next to nothing. It could do this because of the fact that, in our society, vast powers over all of life are given to formally private organizations—the Democratic party, the realtors' association, the mortgage bank, the telephone company, and so on—and because, further and indispensably, the courts were (as is illustrated by a line of decisions from the *Civil Rights Cases* to the Stuyvesant Town case) willing in case after case to gloss over the fact that large organized enterprises can rarely if ever be successfully conducted without very considerable help from the government. Intermixed in these racial cases was, moreover, the disregard of

the Fourteenth Amendment's textual condemnation of governmental *inaction*, where that inaction amounted to *denial of equal protection*, as inaction obviously may. And constitutional guarantees that were implicit rather than explicit as limits on government were mostly ignored. A doctrine that went to the length of seeming to make of lynching a thing untouched by the Constitution and (as in *United States* v. *Cruikshank*, 1875) untouchable by Congress was and could be again a powerful tool indeed for bringing national human rights, nationally enjoyed, to nothing, on the plane of life as lived.

The "state action" requirement thus served the major strategic goal of a nation to which racism, in practice, was utterly essential. But even outside the field of race, its incidence, though spotty, was wide-ranging. As late as 1951, in *Collins* v. *Hardyman*, the Supreme Court, obviously under the influence of the doctrine though not directly relying on it, forcibly construed a federal statute, in plain contradiction to the law's clear terms, as not to reach the "private" and violent breaking up of a political meeting of citizens.

But a strong countercurrent developed in the 1940s. Without entire consistency, the Supreme Court uttered a striking series of decisions that promised to clip the claws of the "state action" requirement. The Court declared the all-white Democratic primary unlawful in *Smith* v. *Allwright* (1944) and extended this ruling in *Terry* v. *Adams* (1953) to a local primary serving the same function under another name and form. *Marsh* v. *Alabama* (1946) held that the First Amendment, as incorporated into the Fourteenth, forbade the barring of Jehovah's Witnesses from distributing leaflets in a company-owned town. And *Shelley* v. *Kraemer* (1948) held that judicial enforcement of restrictive covenants was unlawful.

In the "white primary" cases the Court was doing no more than refusing to persevere in self-induced blindness to an obvious fraud on the Fifteenth Amendment. But *Marsh* v. *Al-*

abama suggested that the formality of "ownership" could not immunize from constitutional scrutiny the performance of a governmental function—an idea big with possibility. And the *Shelley* case even more profoundly stirred the foundations. Of course it was difficult to say that judicial enforcement of a racial-restrictive covenant, recorded at the courthouse, with the attendant implication that such covenants are not (as some others are) "against public policy," did not amount to "state action of some kind"—the requirement as worded in the fountainhead *Civil Rights Cases* of 1883. The difficulty in assimilation of *Shelley* arose from the fact that "state action of some kind" underpins and in one way or another enforces every nominally "private" action; the states had facilitated and lent their aid, indeed, to the very acts of discrimination considered in the 1883 cases. *Shelley*, therefore, forced a more searching analysis of the theory of "state action"; academic commentators became exceedingly eager and thorough, and in later decisions the Court became more willing to find "state action" and to move toward a fundamental doctrinal revision.

This process was accelerated by the civil rights movement that gained strength in the late 1950s, and grew to major force in the 1960s. In 1954 the famous case of *Brown* v. *Board of Education* had outlawed racial segregation in the public schools; a number of other decisions had extended this rule to all forms of segregation imposed by law or by uncontestable official action. Though enforcement of these decisions was to be difficult, the first of two principal jural supports of American racism—legal prohibition of participation by blacks in the common society—had crumbled. Naturally attention turned—whether with the aim of continuing racism or of completing its demolition—to the second of the pillars of American racism, the "state action" requirement.

Segregation and state action were now clearly seen to have a close functional similarity. Before the decisions following *Brown*, the blacks in a typical southern town could not eat in the good restaurants because state law commanded their exclusion. After these decisions, the proprietors of the restaurants, by and large, went on excluding blacks. (In this they were simply following a practice widely followed in the North already.) There was a difference in legal theory, but no difference to the black people. The city-owned bus system could not make black people sit in the back— but most bus companies were "private" in form; seating in the back was "privately" commanded.

The resistance to this widespread public segregation under "private" form was led (actively in part and symbolically throughout) by Dr. Martin Luther King Jr. Thousands of black people—most, but not all, young—defied the system by "sitting in"—insisting upon service at "private" establishments open to the general public. They were in great numbers convicted of "crimes" selected with careful attention to the appearance of neutrality, such as "trespass after warning" or breach of the peace, and their cases reached the Supreme Court in some number.

The net result up to about 1965 was a considerable practical loosening up of the "state action" requirement, but no satisfactory theoretical reworking of that doctrine. A very few examples must be selected from the abundant case law.

The 1961 case of *Burton* v. *Wilmington Parking Authority* is an interesting example. The parking authority, a state agency, leased space in its parking building to a restaurateur, who forthwith refused to serve blacks. One might have thought it all but frivolous to contend that "state action of some kind" was absent here. The state had gone with open eyes into a transaction that empowered the restaurateur to insult and inconvenience citizens, in a public building owned by itself, and its police stood ready to make his rule stick. The state had done this—in effect certainly, if not in intent—for rent money. It had had the easy recourse of inserting in the lease a provision against racial discrimination; one has to wonder how the omission of that provision, obviously available under "the laws," can be anything but a "denial" of "equal protection of the laws," on the part of government. Yet the Court majority, though striking down the discrimination in the very case, roamed back and forth amongst the minutiae of facts—gas, service for the boiler room, responsibility for structural repairs—and carefully confined its ruling to a lease of public property "in the manner and for the purpose shown to have been the case here. . . ." Still, the Wilmington case might have contributed toward some generality of constitutional theory.

As the "sit-in" issue heated up, however, the Court became even more evasive of the central issues. As cases reached the Court in great numbers, no "sit-in" conviction was ever affirmed. But neither the whole Court nor any majority ever reached and decided the central issue—whether *Shelley* v. *Kraemer* fairly implied that the knowing state use of state power to enforce discrimination, in publicly open facilities, constituted such action of the state as "denied equal protection of the laws." Instead the cases were decided on collateral grounds peculiar to each of them.

The culminating case was *Bell* v. *Maryland* (1964). Trespass convictions of Maryland civil-rights "sitters-in" were reversed, on the grounds (available by chance) that a newly enacted Maryland antidiscrimination statute might be held, in the state courts, to "abate" prosecution for prior attempts to get the service now guaranteed; nothing was actually decided on the more fundamental issues. Six Justices reached the "state action" issue, but of those six, three would have found it and three would not.

At this dramatic moment, with indefinite postponement of a major doctrinal decision seemingly impossible, Congress stepped in and solved the immediate problem, by passing the Civil Rights Act of 1964, Title 2 of which made unlawful nearly all the discriminatory exclusions that had generated the sit-in prosecutions, making future prosecutions of sit-ins impossible. Then, in 1964, in *Hamm* v. *City of Rock Hill,* the Court held that the act compelled dismissal of all such prosecutions begun before its passage. Thus vanished the immediate problem of the sit-ins, and of many other claims to nondiscrimination previously based purely on the Constitution. It is noteworthy that Congress chose to base this Title 2, dealing with public accommodations, mainly on the commerce clause rather than on the Fourteenth Amendment. This legislative decision reflected uncertainty as to whether the Court could be persuaded to overrule the 1883 *Civil Rights Cases,* which had severely limited congressional power to enforce the Fourteenth Amendment. In *Heart of Atlanta Motel* v. *United States* (1964) and *Katzenbach* v. *McClung* (1964) the Court construed the 1964 provisions broadly, and upheld them under the commerce clause theory that Congress had emphasized. The public accommodations crisis was over, and with it the really agonizing social crisis as to "state action."

Nevertheless, important problems continued to present themselves after 1964. It seemed for a time that, though no longer under the intense pressure of the public accommodations issue, the Court might be moving along the road toward relaxation of the state action requirement—a road along which travel had begun at least as early as the cases of *Smith* v. *Allwright* (1944—knocking out the all-white Democratic primary), *Marsh* v. *Alabama* (1946—the "company-town" case), and *Shelley* v. *Kraemer* (1948—the case of the racial-restriction covenants). (Indeed, no case actually denying relief on the "no-state-action" ground was decided by the Supreme Court from 1906 to 1970, except the 1935 case upholding the white primary, overruled nine years later.)

In 1966 the Court held, in *Evans* v. *Newton,* that a huge public park in the center of Macon, Georgia, could no longer be operated as a park "for whites only," pursuant to the directions in the 1911 will of the man who had given it to the city, even though the city, for the purpose of seeing this all-white status maintained, had resigned as trustee, and had acquiesced in the appointment of a set of "private" trustees. In *Amalgamated Food Employees* v. *Logan Valley Plaza* (1968) the Court applied *Marsh* v. *Alabama* to hold a large shopping center subject to the First Amendment, and *Reitman* v. *Mulkey* (1967) struck down under the Fourteenth Amendment a California constitutional amendment that would have forbidden state or local "fair" (i.e., antiracist) housing ordinances until such time as the state constitution might be amended again—a process substantially more difficult than the enactment of ordinary legislation. This opinion, by Justice Byron R. White, encouraged much hope, because it explicitly undertook to judge this state constitutional amendment "in terms of its "immediate objective,' its "ultimate effect,' and its "historical context and the conditions existing prior to its enactment." This attitude, if adhered to, would in every case bring the "state action" question down to the earth of reality. The Court would recognize the impact of formal state "neutrality" on the actual patterns of American racism, and would ask in each case whether such seeming "neutrality" operated as a denial of equal protection to the group principally marked for protection. This hope was further encouraged in 1969 in *Hunter* v. *Erickson* wherein the Court struck down an Akron, Ohio, requirement that fair-housing ordinances run an especially difficult gauntlet before they became effective; it was especially striking that Justices John Marshall Harlan and Potter Stewart, who had dissented in *Reitman,* found the Akron provision too much, because on its face it discriminated against antiracist laws.

But the current of doctrine changed after President Richard M. Nixon made the most of his chance to put his stamp on the Court. The change was signaled by the 1970 decision in *Evans* v. *Abney,* a follow-up to the first Macon park case, *Evans* v. *Newton,* above. After the Newton decision, the heirs of the donor of the park applied for a reverter to them. The Court held this time that the state court's decision in their favor, in effect imposing a penalty on the citizens of Macon for their being unable under the Fourteenth Amendment to keep the park all white, did not constitute "such state action" as to implicate the equal protection clause.

In 1971, in *Palmer* v. *Thompson,* the Court upheld the City of Jackson in its closing the city swimming pools and leasing one of them to the "private" YMCA, rather than having blacks swim in them. Here the Court found no state encouragement of discrimination, although the pools had been closed in response to a desegregation order. This was a total turnabout, in just four years, from the *Reitman* v. *Mulky* resolution to tie the operation of state-action law to the facts of life, and Justice White, the author of the *Reitman* opinion, dissented, with three other pre-Nixon Justices.

In 1974 the Court decided *Jackson* v. *Metropolitan Edison Company.* A heavily regulated "private" electric company, enjoying a monopoly and a state-issued certificate of public convenience, terminated service to a customer without offering her any chance to be heard. This practice was allowed by a "tariff" on file with and at the least acquiesced in by the Public Utilities Commission. Justice William H. Rehnquist's opinion for the Court found insufficient "state action" in any of this to implicate the due process clause. This opinion and judgment, if adhered to in all their implications, would put us at least as far back as the 1883 *Civil Rights Cases.* Then, in 1976, *Hudgens* v. *National Labor Relation Board* explicitly overruled the Logan Valley Shopping Center case and made authoritative for the time being a very narrow view of *Marsh* v. *Alabama.*

Meanwhile, however, a new doctrinal thread had become visible. In the 1883 *Civil*

Rights Cases the first Justice Harlan had argued that the Thirteenth Amendment, which contains no language to support a state-action requirement, proscribes all "badges and incidents" of slavery—which, historically, would mean a great many if not all racially discriminatory and degrading actions. This argument was a long time in coming into its own, but in 1968, in *Jones* v. *Alfred H. Mayer Co.,* the Court made it the ground of a decision upholding an old act of Congress which the Court interpreted to command nondiscrimination in the sale of housing. And in 1976, *Griffin* v. *Breckenridge,* overruling *Collins* v. *Hardyman,* based decision solidly on the Thirteenth Amendment, holding that the amendment authorizes Congress to secure its beneficiaries against "racially discriminatory private action aimed at depriving them of . . . basic rights. . . ." Under the very formula of the 1883 *Civil Rights Cases* themselves—Congress may "enforce" only that which is substantively there—this should imply a large substantive content in the Thirteenth Amendment, far beyond literal "slavery." In *Runyon* v. *McCrary* (1976) the Court extended much the same rationale to the condemnation of racial exclusion from a "private, commercially operated, nonsectarian" school.

"State action" doctrine has remained intractable to being made rational. What is wanted is attention to these points:

1. In almost any impingement by one person or more on another person or more, there is some contribution by the state: empowerment, support, or threatened support. Thus the presence or absence of "state action" is not a "test" at all; this has led to the spinning out of enormous series of subtests, hard to express and even harder to comprehend, none of which has much if any warrant in law.

2. Concomitantly, "state action" may not legitimately be confined—as the Supreme Court's recent opinions have confined it—to one or more neatly defined categories such as "command," "encouragement," or "public function." One may identify ten ways in which so infinitely complicated and subtle a being as the "state" may act—and the "state" may then act in an eleventh and then in a twelfth way—*all* "state action."

3. There is no warrant whatever in law for the assumption that "state action," to be significant, must be at a *high level* of involvement, or that a *very close* "nexus" must be found between "state action" and the wrong complained of.

4. Many constitutional guarantees do not explicitly require "state action" as a component. The modern "state action" requirement purported to draw its life from the words of the Fourteenth Amendment. Many rights and relationships set up by the Constitution and enforceable by Congress do not refer to the state at all, for example, the prohibition of slavery (and, as now held, its badges and incidents), the right to vote for congressmen and senators, the right to travel. It is only custom-thought, which usually means half-thought, that would think it obvious that an impediment to interstate commerce would be unconstitutional only if it were state created.

5. A citizen of the United States should be regarded as having *relational* rights—rights of membership in the organized community—which nobody, state or private person, may interfere with. This principle has some life in the cases; in *Bewer* v. *Hoxie School District* (8th Cir. 1956), for example, an injunction was upheld that restrained private persons from interfering with state officials' attempts to comply with the national Constitution. But the principle deserves a greater generality. Anybody who tries forcibly to keep another person from getting his mail is interfering with a legitimate relation between citizen and government, even though the wrongdoer's own actions may not be "state action" at all.

6. There is broad scope in the natural meaning of the Fourteenth Amendment's words: "deny to any person within its jurisdiction the equal protection of the laws." These

words, even as a matter of "narrow verbal criticism," do not require "action."

7. Above all, while much of the defense of the "state action" requirement is conducted in the name of the private, personal lives of people whose conduct, it is said, ought not to be constitutionalized, it is very, very rare that any real "state action" case involves these values at all. The conduct of public transportation and restaurants, the operation of carnivals and parks, dealings with city swimming pools, the way the light company collects its bills, the character of a whole section of town—these are the usual stuff of "state action" problems in real life. If anybody ever files a lawsuit praying a mandatory injunction that he be included on somebody else's dinner list, that will be time enough to begin devising a well-founded "rule of reason" fencing constitutional prohibition out of the genuinely private life. This "genuinely private" life may be hard to define, but surely no harder to define than the "state action requirement" has turned out to be, and continues to be. And at least one would be trying to define the right thing.

CHARLES L. BLACK, JR.

Bibliography

Black, Charles L., Jr. (1962). The Constitution and Public Power. *Yale Review* 52:54–66.

Black, Charles L., Jr. (1967). "State Action," Equal Protection, and California's Proposition 14. *Harvard Law Review* 81:69–109.

Hale, Robert L. (1952). *Freedom through Law.* Chap. 11. New York: Columbia University Press.

Horowitz, Harold W. (1957). The Misleading Search for "State Action" under the Fourteenth Amendment. *Southern California Law Review* 30:208–221.

Van Alstyne, William W. (1965). Mr. Justice Black, Constitutional Review, and the Talisman of State Action. *Duke Law Journal* 1965:219–247.

STATE ACTION DOCTRINE

(Update)

America's federal constitutional system generally protects individual rights only against violation by the national and state governments, their agencies, and officials. State action doctrine limits the scope of constitutional rights guarantees. If a state police officer arrests a criminal suspect without an arrest warrant, for example, state action is clearly present and the Constitution's Fourth Amendment and Fourteenth Amendment search and seizure prohibitions apply. By contrast, if a private individual or organization infringes on another private person's constitutional liberties, the courts may well not find state action, and the federal Constitution will not provide a remedy. The more controversial extensions of the state action doctrine involve cases where constitutional injuries are caused in part by ostensibly private actors. At its furthest reaches, then, the doctrine depends on workable and principled standards for attributing the constitutionally harmful conduct of a private person to the public sector.

In Lugar v. *Edmonson Oil Co.* (1982) Edmonson had obtained an invalid attachment order from a state court clerk to sequester Lugar's property. Lugar contended that Edmonson had acted jointly with the state to deprive him of property in an unconstitutional manner. Justice Byron R. White's opinion in *Lugar* explained that in order for any constitutional rights claimant to attribute a private defendant's wrongful conduct to the federal or state government, the claimant must satisfy two independent inquiries. First, the private defendant must be sufficiently identified with the government to be fairly labeled a state actor. This might be called the "identity" inquiry. Second, the defendant's wrongful conduct must have been the direct and affirmative cause of a constitutional injury; the government will not be held liable for an error of omission or a failure to prevent constitutional injury. This might be called the "causality" inquiry. Because the state court official had assisted Edmonson in using the state's constitutionally defective procedures to sequester Lugar's property, the Court held that the identity and causality requirements were met.

Two critical decisions in the 1970s, *Jackson* v. *Metropolitan Edison Company* (1974) and *Flagg Brothers, Inc.* v. *Brooks* (1978), set extremely narrow terms for the current identity and causality standards. Even if a government delegates general law enforcement powers to a private individual (as in state self-help repossession statutes) or heavily regulates a private industry (as in state utility rate regulation), the private party will be identified with the government only if these powers and operations had been exercised traditionally and exclusively by the government. Even if the government knew, or should have known, of the private party's wrongdoing, causality now requires evidence that the government affirmatively compelled or specifically approved the practice that harmed a constitutional liberty.

Today the Supreme Court guards these narrow boundaries of the state action doctrine with a rigorous and sterile formalism. In two unusual cases emerging from the arena of amateur sports, the Court recently shielded private organizations from constitutional liability by discounting their functional relationships with the government. After the United States Olympic Committee refused to license use of the name Gay Olympic Games for a homosexual international athletic event, a Fifth Amendment challenge for discrimination in *San Francisco Arts & Athletics* v. *United States Olympic Committee* (1987) failed on the basis that the committee was not a governmental actor to whom constitutional prohibitions apply. Because the committee coordinated activities that were not traditional government functions, even Con-

gress's unprecedented grant to the committee of exclusive regulatory authority over American athletic organizations and of unlimited trademark rights in the name Olympic did not satisfy the identity tests. Furthermore, because the committee's trademark enforcement decisions went unsupervised by any federal official, causality could not be attributed to the national government.

In *National Collegiate Athletic Association* v. *Tarkanian* (1988) the Court insulated the NCAA from liability for violation of a state university basketball coach's civil rights, ruling that the university's voluntary compliance with NCAA disciplinary recommendations did not transform the NCAA's private conduct into state action. Although the NCAA's findings made at NCAA hearings of NCAA rules violations had influenced the university's decision to suspend Tarkanian in accord with its NCAA membership agreement, the Court reasoned that NCAA had neither imposed the sanction directly nor compelled the university to act within the meaning of the causality standards.

Theoretically, the state action doctrine may serve two important purposes. Jurists defend the doctrine as a safeguard of federalism: by preventing the federal judiciary from enforcing constitutional rights guarantees against private violators, the doctrine preserves the traditional realm of state police power to regulate private civil rights. Additionally, the doctrine may promote liberal legal values: to the extent that it limits the Constitution's interference with private exercise of federal and state statutory or common law rights, the doctrine fosters a realm of individual freedom of action.

To serve federalism and liberalism meaningfully, however, state action requires a dichotomy between public and private action that is both definite and defensible. The current standards for identity and causality could be challenged on both accounts. Given the highly bureaucratic state of modern America, characterized by government penetration into most private economic and social dealings, the integrated public and private venture is a commonplace. Yet, identity and causality demand the conceptual division of integrated operations into discrete practices that are traditionally governmental, governmentally compelled, and injury-causative. Practical rules for this division will be difficult for courts to formulate and apply; reliance on criteria such as tradition and government compulsion will result in line-drawing of the most arbitrary and unprincipled sort.

Moreover, the doctrine undermines its own raison d'être; with its narrow focus, it will not rip the veil away from nominally private actors who wield governmentally delegated powers to destroy individual rights. Although the Constitution permits government to "privatize" the functions that it otherwise would perform, the state action doctrine ought not to immunize the government from liability for private violations of its constitutional obligations.

However appropriate for federal constitutional purposes, the state action doctrine is often an anomaly in state constitutional law interpretation. The texts of many state bill of rights provisions do not explicitly target state action for their prohibitions; indeed, a number of state constitutions directly regulate specific transactions among private individuals and corporations. Because the states do not recognize county and municipal governments as coordinate sovereigns, state action need not reinforce federalism interests. State high courts might reject the conceptual limitations of the federal state action doctrine to provide stronger protection of civil liberties under their state constitutions against private infringements.

DAVID M. SKOVER

Bibliography

Alexander, Larry A., and Horton, Paul (1988). *Whom Does the Constitution Control?* Westport, Conn.: Greenwood Press.

Chemerinsky, Erwin (1985). Rethinking State Action. *Northwestern University Law Review* 80:503–557.

Skover, David M. (1992). State Action Doctrine. In Collins, Skover, Cogan, and Schuman, *State Constitutional Law and Individual Rights: Cases Commentary.* Durham, N.C.: Carolina Academic Press.

Symposium (1982). The Public/Private Distinction. *University of Pennsylvania Law Review* 130: 1289–1608.

Van Alstyne, William, and Karst, Kenneth L. (1961). State Action. *Stanford Law Review* 14:3–58.

STATE OF TENNESSEE v. SCOPES

289 SW 363 (1925)

In 1925 Dayton, Tennessee, authorities arrested a local high school teacher, John T. Scopes, for violating the state's Butler Act, which prohibited public school instructors from teaching "any theory that denies the story of the Divine Creation of man as taught in the Bible, and to teach instead that man has descended from a lower order of animals." Scopes admitted to teaching about evolution from George Hunter's *Civic Biology,* a book approved by Tennessee's textbook commission. The Scopes trial, soon known throughout the nation as "the monkey trial," came in the middle of a decade punctuated by the Red Scare, increased urban-rural tensions, and the resurgence of the Ku Klux Klan. The Dayton courtroom soon became an arena of cultural and political conflict between fundamentalist Christians and civil libertarians.

The former, led by William Jennings Bryan, a three-time presidential candidate and ardent prohibitionist who joined the prosecution staff, argued that the Butler Act was a traditional exercise of state police power with respect to public education, little different from mandating other curricula and fixing the qual-

S

"THE MONKEY TRIAL"

Clarence Darrow, left, defended Tennessee teacher John Scopes against charges that he violated the state's Butler Act, which prohibited teaching of evolution. Ardent prohibitionist William Jennings Bryan, right, testified for the prosecution. (Corbis/Bettmann)

The Scopes trial, soon known throughout the nation as "the monkey trial," became an arena of cultural and political conflict between fundamentalist Christians and civil libertarians.

See also

Civil Liberties

Freedom of Speech

Separation of Church and
    State

ifications of teachers. They also saw the statute as a defense of traditional folk values against the moral relativism of modern science and other contemporary religious beliefs. Scopes's defenders, including the American Civil Liberties Union (ACLU) and the celebrated criminal lawyer Clarence Darrow, saw in the Butler Act a palpable threat to several constitutional guarantees, including separation of church and state and freedom of speech.

The trial judge, John T. Raulston, rejected all constitutional attacks against the statute; he also declined to permit testimony by scientific and religious experts, many of whom hoped to argue the compatibility between evolution and traditional religious values, including the belief in a supreme being. The only issue for the jury, Raulston noted, was the narrow one of whether or not John Scopes had taught his class that man had descended from a lower form of animals. Because Scopes has already admitted doing so, the jury's verdict was never in doubt. Darrow and the defense gained a public relations tri-

umph by putting Bryan on the stand to testify as an expert about the Bible. The Great Commoner, who collapsed and died several days after the trial ended, affirmed his faith in biblical literalism, including the story of Jonah and the whale. The jury, however, found Scopes guilty and Raulston fined him the statutory minimum of $100.

Darrow and the ACLU encountered only frustration when they attempted to appeal the conviction. The state supreme court, with one judge dissenting, upheld the constitutionality of the Butler Act. However, they reversed Scopes's conviction on a technicality, holding that the Tennessee constitution prohibited trial judges from imposing fines in excess of $50 without a jury recommendation. The state supreme court also urged Tennessee officials to cease further prosecution of John Scopes—advice that the attorney general followed. The Butler Act remained on the Tennessee statute books but was not enforced against other educational heretics.

—MICHAEL E. PARRISH

Bibliography

Ginger, Ray (1958). *Six Days or Forever? Tennessee v. John Thomas Scopes.* New York: Oxford University Press.

STATE VERSUS STATE LITIGATION

The Supreme Court is the only court in which one state may sue another. The Constitution, in Article III, § 2, specifies that the Supreme Court has original jurisdiction in all cases "in which a State shall be party." Original jurisdiction in this context means that the Supreme Court is the court in which the suit is originally brought – as opposed to the appellate jurisdiction that is the usual route to the Supreme Court.

As early as the Judiciary Act of 1789 Congress provided that the Supreme Court "shall have exclusive jurisdiction of all controversies of a civil nature where a state is a party, except between a state and its citizens [or] citizens of other states, or aliens. . . ." Current federal law, 28 U.S.C. § 1251, more succinctly states that "[t]he Supreme Court shall have original and exclusive jurisdiction of all controversies between two or more States." Suits by citizens (individuals or corporations) against states in the federal courts are now greatly circumscribed by the Eleventh Amendment.

The accepted rationale for the Supreme Court's exclusive jurisdiction in state-versus-state suits is that the courts of either state would likely be biased, or at least render the appearance of being biased. Scholars have explained these suits as an alternative to resolving these differences through combat, the remedy that history shows independent countries have repeatedly invoked.

Ever since an 1838 case, *Rhode Island* v. *Massachusetts*, it has been clear that Congress has the power to make the Supreme Court the exclusive, or sole, forum for state-versus-state litigation. Although the states enjoy sovereign immunity from suits by individuals in certain situations, that immunity does not bar a suit by another state under these provisions.

The first category of these actions to be brought had to do with boundary disputes. That was the issue in the 1838 litigation between Rhode Island and Massachusetts, and continues to be very much alive. For example, the Court in 1998 resolved a dispute between New York and New Jersey over the ownership of Ellis Island in New York harbor. Where two states have agreed for decades on a boundary, the Court will be quite reluctant to alter it, as it held in *California* v. *Nevada* (1980). On the other hand, where boundaries are genuinely in dispute, and neither state has acquiesced, the Court will look to historical events, including decrees of the British crown issued during the Colonial period, as in *New Hampshire* v. *Maine* (1976). In the Ellis Island litigation the Court relied on an 1834 interstate compact setting the border, under which New York owned the island, though it was in New Jersey waters. However, acreage later added to the island during its use as an immigration station did not, the Court ruled, add to New York's ownership, which continued to be limited to the island as it existed at the time of the compact. Title often shifts with alterations in the channels of rivers forming state borders, as along the Mississippi and Missouri rivers. As one would expect, the Court's rulings regarding boundaries are binding on landowners within those states.

Another major area of state-versus-state litigation concerns the apportionment of water rights. Here the Court has been called upon to interpret interstate compacts dividing water rights, as well as apportioning those rights where no compact exists. Where a compact fails to provide a mechanism for deciding disputes, as in *Texas* v. *New Mexico* (1983), the Court is obliged to do so. One suit of vital significance to the development of the Western states ruled Arizona was entitled to a major share of the Colorado River's water,

**BOUNDARY
DISPUTES**

*The Supreme Court in 1998
resolved a dispute between
New York and New Jersey over
the ownership of Ellis Island in
New York harbor. (Corbis/Gail
Mooney)*

*The Supreme Court
is the only court in
which one state may
sue another.*

rejecting an attempt by California to divert much of it. [*Arizona* v. *California* (1963).]

Other suits between states have involved environmental issues, such as the pollution of an interstate river or lake, as in *New Jersey* v. *New York* (1931), as well as the division of unclaimed funds that escheat to the state where the owners had contacts with two or more states. [*Pennsylvania* v. *New York* (1972).]

The dividing of Virginia and West Virginia during the Civil War led to a suit over whether West Virginia assumed a proportion of Virginia's debt. The Court took half a century to finally rule in 1915 that West Virginia was liable. [*Virginia* v. *West Virginia* (1915).]

Another fertile area of interstate litigation has to do with state attempts to tax citizens of other states. The Court has declined jurisdiction in some cases involving taxation of nonresidents on the theory that the taxpayer, not the state, has standing to question the validity of the tax. The Court so held in *New York* v. *New Jersey* (1976). In another suit the Court had to rule on the domicile of a decedent where two states sought to tax his estate. [*California* v. *Texas* (1982).]

In one unique suit, Alabama challenged the laws of five states that barred the sale of goods made by convict labor. The Court here too declined jurisdiction, ruling the firms involved had better standing than Alabama. [*Alabama* v. *Arizona* (1934).] However, the Court later held Wyoming had standing to question an Oklahoma law requiring utilities in that state to use a percentage of locally mined coal. It ruled the statute directly injured Wyoming by depriving that state of tax revenue from the sale of its coal. [*Wyoming* v. *Oklahoma* (1992).]

In determining whether to exercise jurisdiction, the Court will examine the seriousness of the nature of the plaintiff state's interest, as well as whether there are alternative forums to resolve the issue. Although the Supreme Court has final power to interpret, and determine the validity of, compacts between states, it will defer to the rulings of the states' courts on issues of state law. In deciding whether to accept jurisdiction over a state-versus-state suit, as Justice Oliver Wendell Holmes stated in the oft-cited *Missouri* v. *Illinois* (1906), "the case should be of serious magnitude" and "the principle to be applied should be one which the court is prepared deliberately to maintain."

A related area of Supreme Court original jurisdiction concerns suits between states and the United States. These, also within the

Court's original jurisdiction, have dealt with the states' title to undersea lands, important in connection with drilling for offshore oil. In one major suit the Court sustained the jurisdiction of the United States over underwater lands, and its entitlement to the royalties from oil leases on those lands, dismissing state claims based on royal patents issued in the Colonial era. [*United States* v. *Maine* (1975).]

In fact these original jurisdiction suits amount to a small proportion of the Supreme Court's caseload—typically three or four a year. But their importance often transcends their small number.

—PHILIP WEINBERG

Bibliography

McCusick, Vincent L. (1993). Discretionary Gatekeeping: The Supreme Court's Management of its Original Jurisdiction Docket since 1961, 45 Me. L. Rev. 185.

Wright, Miller & Cooper (1996). Federal Practice and Procedure (West Pub. Co.), §§ 4044, 4045.

STERILIZATION

Late in the nineteenth century, when simple and safe medical procedures for sterilization became available, the eugenics movement began to promote compulsory sterilization laws. A few laws were enacted specifying sterilization as punishment for sex crimes, but they were rarely enforced. In 1907 Indiana adopted a law authorizing sterilization of persons deemed "feebleminded," or, as one leading proponent put it, "socially defective." Other states soon followed. The Supreme Court lent both practical and moral support in its 1927 decision in *Buck* v. *Bell*, upholding the constitutionality of Virginia's law. By 1935 more than thirty states had adopted forced sterilization laws, and 20,000 "eugenic" sterilizations had been performed. The victims of such laws tended to be poor; indeed, in the view of eugenics proponents, poverty and other forms of dependence were the marks of the "socially inadequate classes" that needed eradication.

Times have changed, and constitutional law has changed. Concurring in *Griswold* v. *Connecticut* (1965), Justice Arthur Goldberg said, "Surely the Government, absent a showing of a compelling subordinating state interest, could not decree that all husbands and wives must be sterilized after two children have been born to them." After *Skinner* v. *Oklahoma* (1942) the point seems incontestable. Yet some state courts, following *Buck,* still uphold laws authorizing the involuntary sterilization of institutionalized mental patients. Although only fifteen years separated the *Buck* and *Skinner* decisions, their doctrinal foundations were worlds apart. *Skinner,* calling procreation "one of the basic civil rights of man," insisted on strict scrutiny by the Court of the justifications supporting a compulsory sterilization law. *Buck,* on the other hand, had employed a deferential form of rational basis review, analogizing forced sterilization to forced vaccination.

Skinner's crucial recognition was that sterilization was more than an invasion of the body; it was an irrevocable deprivation of the right to define one's life and one's identity as a biological parent. Vaccination implies no such consequences for one's self-identification and social role. The constitutional issues presented by sterilization thus bear a strong analogy to the issues raised by laws restricting other forms of birth control and abortion. The Supreme Court has characterized all these forms of state interference with reproductive autonomy as invasions of fundamental interests, and has subjected them to close scrutiny in the name of both equal protection, as in *Skinner,* and that form of substantive due process that goes by the alias of a right of privacy, as in *Griswold* and *Roe* v. *Wade* (1973).

The issue of *Buck* seems certain to return to the Supreme Court one day, to be decided on the basis of a much heightened standard of

In 1907 Indiana adopted a law authorizing sterilization of persons deemed "feebleminded," or "socially defective."

review. Similarly, a state law requiring consent of a spouse before a person could be sterilized would surely be held invalid, on analogy to *Planned Parenthood of Missouri* v. *Danforth* (1976). If a law calling for involuntary sterilization must pass the test of strict scrutiny, and if a competent adult has a corresponding right to choose to be sterilized, then the critical ingredient is choice. An "informed consent" requirement thus seems defensible against constitutional attack, provided that the required "informing" procedure does not unreasonably burden the decision to be sterilized. (An informed consent requirement for abortion was upheld by the Supreme Court in *Danforth*.)

As Justice William O. Douglas noted in his *Skinner* opinion, sterilization in "evil or reckless hands" can be an instrument of genocide. Even the most devoted partisan of reproductive choice cannot be entirely comfortable knowing that the percentage of sterilized nonwhite women in the United States is almost triple that for white women, or that among public assistance recipients blacks are twice as likely to "choose" sterilization as are whites. Under current interpretations the Constitution has nothing to say about the bare fact of this disparity; yet it reflects a condition of constitutional dimension that deserves to be addressed, at least in the domain of procedural due process. And if nonwhite women are led by government officers to believe that sterilization is voluntary in theory but somehow compulsory in fact, that form of "engineering of consent" appears reachable in actions for damages under Section 1983, Title 42, United States Code, based on the deprivation of substantive due process.

—KENNETH L. KARST

Bibliography

Kelly, Mary E. (1979). Sterilization Abuse: A Proposed Regulatory Scheme. *DePaul Law Review* 28:731–768.

Kevles, Daniel J. (1985). *In the Name of Eugenics: Genetics and the Uses of Human Heredity.* New York: Knopf.

Pilpel, Harriet F. (1969). Voluntary Sterilization: A Human Right. *Columbia Human Rights Law Review* 7:105–119.

STEVENS, JOHN PAUL

(1920–)

In 1975 President Gerald R. Ford sought a "moderate conservative" of unimpeachable professional qualifications to fill the Supreme Court seat vacated by William O. Douglas. John Paul Stevens of Chicago, an intellectually gifted antitrust lawyer, former law clerk to Justice Wiley B. Rutledge, occasional law professor, and federal court of appeals judge for the preceding five years, seemed to fit the bill. Justice Stevens in fact has more often been described as a "moderate liberal" of sometimes unpredictable or even idiosyncratic bent or as a "moderate pragmatist." A prolific writer of separate opinions frequently offering a different perspective, he generally is not a coalition builder. Even the common term "moderate" reflects his agreement in result with sometimes one and sometimes another more readily identifiable group of Justices on the Court or his balanced accommodation of community rights to govern and individual freedoms rather than his judicial substance or style.

Such labels usually mislead more than instruct, and in Justice Stevens's case conservative, moderate, and liberal strands of constitutional thought blend in a singular combination. He shares the judicial conservatism of Douglas's (and thus his) predecessor Justice Louis D. Brandeis, who frequently urged the Court to reach constitutional questions only when necessary and to resolve constitutional disputes as narrowly as possible. He shares the moderate rationalist's antipathy to excessive generalization that Nathaniel Nathanson, Brandeis's law clerk and Stevens's admired constitutional law teacher, abhorred. He also shares the liberal substantive vision of Justice Rutledge, whom Stevens once admiringly described as a Justice who "exhibited great respect for experience and practical considerations," whose "concern with the importance of procedural safeguards was frequently expressed in separate opinions," and most important, who believed that "the securing and maintaining of individual freedom is the main end of society." Each of these elements of his intellectual lineage appear centrally in Justice Stevens's own constitutional writings.

His particular mixture of judicial restraint and vigorous judicial enforcement of individual liberty, although akin to those of Brandeis and Rutledge, sets Stevens apart from his contemporaries on both the Burger Court and the Rehnquist Court. His is not the judicial restraint of extreme deference to government authority, but the judicial restraint of limiting the occasions and the breadth of Supreme Court rulings, particularly when he concludes that a ruling is unnecessary to protect liberty. His adjudicative approach is to balance all the relevant factors in a particular context with thorough reasoning whose ultimate aim is resolving the particular dispute, not declaring broad propositions of law. Yet, because Stevens sees protection of liberty as a peculiarly judicial obligation, there is no conflict for him between judicial restraint and liberty-protecting judicial intervention, however narrow the basis of that intervention might be. Thus, his frequent criticism of "unnecessary judicial lawmaking" by his colleagues, although it extends to reliance on any intermediate doctrinal standard of review that is a judicial gloss on constitutional text, is most bitterly voiced when judge-made doctrines stand in the way of vindicating individual freedom. In *Rose* v. *Lundy* (1982), for example, his dissent objected to several judicially imposed procedural obstacles to federal habeas corpus review of claims of fundamental constitutional error in the conviction of state criminal defendants. In contrast, Stevens, always sensitive to matters of degree, expressed his inclination to address constitu-

HARD TO DEFINE

Justice Stevens blends conservative, moderate, and liberal strands of constitutional thought into a single combination. (Corbis)

tional claims more readily the more fundamental they are and to husband scarce judicial resources for the occasions when judicial action is most acutely needed. Accordingly, he urged the Court to confine "habeas corpus relief to cases that truly involve fundamental fairness."

The same preference for employing judicial power to secure and maintain individual freedom, rather than to vindicate government authority, appears in other positions he has taken on the proper scope of the Court's institutional role. He has waged a lengthy, but largely unsuccessful, battle to convince the court to curtail its use of discretionary certiorari jurisdiction to review cases in which the claim of individual liberty prevailed in lower courts. In *New Jersey* v. *T.L.O.* (1984) he inveighed against the Court's "voracious appetite for judicial activism in its Fourth

Amendment jurisprudence, at least when it comes to restricting the constitutional rights of the citizen." To Stevens, the Court should not be concerned with legitimating prosecution practices or other governmental controls that lower courts have erroneously restricted through overly generous interpretations of federal law. In general, he sees dispersal of judicial power as a positive good, especially when state courts restrain state officials from interfering with individuals, even when those courts have applied the federal Constitution more stringently than the Supreme Court might. He has argued with respect to *stare decisis* that the Court should adhere more readily to prior rulings that recognized a liberty claim than to those that rejected one. Similarly, he appears more likely to find a "case or controversy" calling for decision on the merits in an individual challenge to government action than in review of a claim that the government's prerogatives have been unreasonably limited. This distinction can be seen in a comparison of his dissents on the issue of standing in *Allen* v. *Wright* (1984) and *Duke Power Co.* v. *Carolina Environmental Study Group* (1978). Similarly, he has argued for reduction in the Court's reliance on the doctrine of "harmless error," which allows convictions to be affirmed where arguably nonprejudicial error has occurred; in his view, saving convictions should have a low priority.

His substantive conception of the source and content of constitutional liberty is as distinctive as his view of the systemic judicial role in protecting it. Unlike protections for property rights, which Stevens agrees originate in positive law, he believes liberty stems from natural law. His dissents in *Hewitt* v. *Helms* (1983) and *Meachum* v. *Fano* (1976) illustrate his belief that even justifiably confined inmates retain claims to liberty, including the right to be treated with dignity and impartiality. The source of that liberty "is not state law, nor even the Constitution itself." Rather, drawing on the Declaration of Inde-

pendence, he found it "self-evident that all men were endowed by their Creator with liberty as one of the cardinal inalienable rights." Not surprisingly, given this view, he has embraced judicial recognition of a wide spectrum of textually unenumerated fundamental liberties that cannot be infringed without strong justification, including those implicated by criminal and civil commitment proceedings, termination of parental rights, loss of citizenship, restrictions on abortion and consensual sex, and laws limiting prisoners' rights to refuse antipsychotic drugs and terminal patients' rights to refuse unwanted, life-prolonging medical intervention. As to the last, his dissent in *Cruzan* v. *Missouri Department of Health* (1990) opined that "choices about death touch the core of liberty" and are "essential incidents of the unalienable rights to life and liberty endowed us by our Creator" and that the "Constitution presupposes respect for the personhood of every individual, and nowhere is strict adherence to that principle more essential than in the Judicial Branch." Stevens has been particularly distressed by the Court's rejection of a wide liberty to retain counsel in government-benefit disputes and the right to government-provided counsel in proceedings to terminate parental status, because he thinks these rulings substantially undervalue the fundamental liberty of legal representation. Of his general approach, he has written that judges are to use the common-law method of adjudication to ascertain the content of liberty: "The task of giving concrete meaning to the term 'liberty,' like the task of defining other concepts such as 'commerce among the States,' 'due process of law,' and 'unreasonable searches and seizures,' was a part of the work assigned to future generations of judges."

Contained in his conception of liberty are government obligations of impartiality, rational decision making, and procedural fairness. These obligations are tempered, however, by two factors. First, Justice Stevens is willing to search broadly for acceptable regulatory justifications, especially the justification that a particular regulation enhances rather than diminishes liberty. Second, he is a candid interest balancer, willing to distinguish among degrees of liberty and degrees of regulatory interference, as well as among degrees of strength of governmental interests to be served. The result is to give government at least some leeway. Moreover, he would hold judges to at least the same level of obligation, a fact that sometimes enlarges the regulatory freedom of political actors. Thus, although Justice Stevens starts from the presumption that government must justify its interference with liberty, rather than a presumption of judicial deference to regulation, he can be quite generous in accepting certain forms of regulation.

For Stevens, government treatment of individuals as equals with dignity and respect is a portion of their liberty, not just a derivation of the equal protection clause of the Fourteenth Amendment. His particular brand of equality analysis would eschew judicial searching for biased subjective motivations of decision makers in favor of an inquiry into whether a law's objectively identifiable purposes are legitimate and sufficiently served. His aversion to motive inquiry is founded largely on two concerns: judges lack capacity to assess motivation accurately and reliance on motive might mean that identical laws would be valid in one jurisdiction and invalid in another, depending on their sponsors' motives. Lack of nationwide uniformity of federal constitutional restraints on regulatory power is anathema to Stevens because it tends to undermine the judicial obligation of evenhandedness.

Justice Stevens opposes the Court's long-standing articulation of different tiers of equal-protection review depending on the nature of the group disadvantaged. He also opposes sharply differentiating between discriminatory intent and disproportionate impact as the dividing line between permissible and impermissible laws. Sacrificing guid-

ance to others for sensitive analysis—an easy accommodation for one who sees the judicial role as dispute resolution, not pronouncement of law—he would consider such factors relevant, but not determinative. Instead of categories, he insisted in *Craig* v. *Boren* (1976) that there is "only one Equal Protection Clause" and that its requirement is "to govern impartially." To be impartial, classifications may not be based on insulting assumptions or allow "punishment of only one of two equally guilty wrongdoers," as he wrote in dissent in *Michael M.* v. *Superior Court* (1981). His version of impartiality requires that people be treated as equals in dignity and moral respect, not that they necessarily receive equal treatment; so that unlike the "insulting" law held invalid in *Craig,* which forbade young men, but not young women, from buying beer, and the statutory rape law that he would have invalidated in *Michael M.,* which punished only males, he voted in *Rostker* v. *Goldberg* (1981) to uphold Congress's male-only draft law—a law that did not assume greater moral culpability of males than females.

When assessing impartiality, Justice Stevens would also consider whether persons other than the complainants are disadvantaged and whether members of the complaining group could rationally support the disadvantaging classification. Thus, he refused to invalidate a veterans' preference for jobs in *Personnel Administrator of Massachusetts* v. *Feeney* (1979), despite its disproportionately disadvantageous effect on women, because the law also disadvantaged nonveteran men in large numbers. And in *Cleburne* v. *Cleburne Living Center, Inc.* (1985) he left open the possibility that some restrictive regulations based on mental retardation might be permissible because a mentally retarded person, like an impartial lawmaker, could accept some regulation to protect himself or herself, or others.

Attention to the full composition of the disadvantaged group and to their views is related to political limits on discrimination and

*At times the power
of Stevens's attack
has swept away
entrenched dogma
and cleared the way
for new thinking.*

treatment with moral respect. In particular, adjusting judicial aggressiveness to the level of political protection that a constitutional challenger might otherwise have available pervades Justice Steven's jurisprudence. Most obviously, this view of the judicial function underlies his preference for reserving judicial power for vindicating the constitutional claims of individuals, not government. Less obviously, it is also reflected in his fervor for addressing the substance of unpopular claims, especially those raised by prisoners, to whose conditions politicians are seldom responsive. Conversely, Justice Stevens is unlikely to overturn arrangements that disadvantage those with considerable political clout. His majority opinion in *Lyng* v. *Castillo* (1986) upholding a food-stamp policy that disfavored close relatives in contrast to more distant relatives noted that families are hardly politically powerless. Outside the equal-protection arena, similar considerations explain his support of the current Court position that judicial enforcement of Tenth Amendment limits on Congress's power to regulate the states is generally inappropriate given the states' ability to apply political pressure in Congress. On similar ground, he agreed in *Goldwater* v. *Carter* (1979) that, given congressional power to protect its perogatives, whether the president may terminate a treaty with a foreign power without Senate consent is a nonjusticable "political question." Likewise in *United States* v. *Munoz-Flores* (1990) he argued unsuccessfully that the Court should not address a claimed violation of the constitutional provision requiring revenue bills to originate in the House of Representatives. It is the "weakest imaginable justification for judicial invaliadation of a statue" to contend "that the judiciary must intervene in order to protect a power of the most majoritarian body in the Federal Government, even though that body has absolute veto over any effort to unsurp that power." In yet another sphere he was the sole dissenter from the ruling in *Davis* v. *Michigan Department of Treasury* (1989) that a state

may not extend a tax on employee retirement benefits to retired federal employees if the state and local retirees are exempt. So long as the state taxed retirement benefits of private sector employees—"the vast majority of the voters in the State"—he thought the tax on federal retirees was allowable.

The obligation of impartiality also embraces another theme that extends beyond the realm of equal protection: judges should not adopt constitutional standards that themselves risk arbitrary or uneven treatment. Evenhandedness does not mean equal concern for governmental power and individual liberty, but equal liberty for all. This is a judicial obligation that sometimes has led Justice Stevens to limit, and sometimes to approve, governmental regulation. For example, unlike his colleagues, who tend either to favor or disfavor *both* establishment of religion and "free exercise of religion" arguments, he is simultaneously receptive to claims of strict separation of church and state, but unreceptive to claims that the free-exercise clause requires exemption from generally applicable laws for religiously motivated conduct. His singular stance appears grounded in an emphasis on evenhandedness. To Justice Stevens, preference for one religion over another or seeming endorsement of a limited set of religions that would offend others, violates the government's obligation of religious neutrality imposed by the establishment clause. In contrast, neutral laws that apply generally do not impugn governmental evenhandedness, and religion-based claims to a selective exemption would reintroduce this problem. Accordingly, he concurred in decisions refusing to exempt the Amish from paying social-security taxes, an Orthodox Jew from an Air Force regulation barring headgear indoors, and members of the Native American Church from a ban on drug use, including peyote, which they smoked as part of a religious ceremony.

A similar emphasis on evenhandedness surfaces in his public forum and other free-speech opinions, with alternately restrictive and permissive results. As with equal-protection standards of review, Justice Stevens doubts the value of public forum doctrine to resolve First Amendment issues of access to public property for free speech. But he is simultaneously intolerant of viewpoint discrimination and tolerant of broad but neutral exclusions of expression from public property. His majority opinion in *Los Angeles* v. *Taxpayers for Vincent* (1984) upheld an ordinance broadly banning posting of signs on public property after noting its viewpoint neutrality and its evenhanded enforcement. He rejected a claim for exemption of political signs because such an exemption "might create a risk of engaging in constitutionally forbidden content discrimination." Similarly, although he has adamantly opposed prohibitions on speech when the government's justification rests solely on the offensiveness of the message, he accepts restrictions designed to maintain government neutrality in the marketplace of ideas, even though the restrictions significantly lessen speech. This distinction is explained in *FCC* v. *League of Women Voters* (1984), where he dissented from the Court's invalidation of Congress's ban on all editorializing by publicly funded broadcasters. Finally, he is particularly critical of the Court's judge-made standards for defining obscenity unprotected by the First Amendment. As he wrote in his separate opinion in *Marks* v. *United States* (1977), those standards "are so intolerably vague that evenhanded enforcement of the law is a virtual impossibility," and "grossly disparate treatment of similar offenders is a characteristic of the criminal enforcement of obscenity law."

Justice Stevens's evenhandedness standard does not completely reject qualitative assessments of the comparative value of different kinds of speech. In particular, if speech is of limited social value, and its form, rather than its viewpoint, is found offensive—a distinction he, but not others, can perceive as viable—he would acknowledge government's

right to regulate its nuisance effects, although probably not to ban it altogether. In accepting zoning laws restricting the location of businesses offering "almost but not quite obscene" materials, and in permitting the Federal Communications Commission to declare that a profane radio broadcast during the day might be disciplined, Justice Stevens took explicit account of the low value of the speech, as well as of the limited nature of the governmental restriction. He concluded that the justification for both restrictions was offensiveness of the form of communication, not the message. In the profanity case, *Federal Communications Commission* v. *Pacifica Foundation* (1978), he reasoned that it is "a characteristic of speech such as this that both its capacity to offend and its 'social value' . . . vary with the circumstances."

The moderating tendency of accepting regulation of limited intrusiveness into liberty of lesser dimension so long as discernible, nonrepressive governmental purposes are present has often led Justice Stevens to emphasize the validity of civil nuisance-type regulations where he might find criminalization unacceptable. Indeed, there is evidence that he would uphold innovative moderate forms of regulation as a means of accommodating the tension between individual freedom and the right of communities to protect against the harm that exercising such freedom may do to others. There is much of John Stuart Mill in Justice Stevens's severely limited view of government power to restrain individual liberty that does no tangible harm to others, but his more generous view of government's power to protect against the nuisance effects of unrestrained freedom. This view is evident not only in his obscenity opinions and opinions regarding civil damages for recovery for libel such as *Philadelphia Newspapers, Inc.* v. *Hepps* (1986), but also in opinions addressing whether regulation of private property constitutes a deprivation of property without due process or a "taking of property" requiring payment of just compensation. In *Moore* v. *East Cleveland* (1977), for example, he separately concurred in the Court's judgment invalidating the city's single-family zoning ordinance, which defined a family to exclude a grandmother and two grandsons who were cousins to each other. In that opinion he located the ordinance's constitutional defect in its interference with the grandmother's "right to use her own property as she sees fit" with respect to the "relationship of the occupants." He distinguished zoning ordinances forbidding unrelated individuals from living together as legitimately based on controlling transient living arrangements that arguably might impair a sense of permanence in the community. Stevens generously approaches zoning ordinances based on arguable external effects, but is unsympathetic to those that fail to accord the reciprocal advantages to all in the community that zoning regulations normally create. These views are reflected in his majority opinion allowing an uncompensated prohibition on coal mining that would cause subsidence of others' property in *Keystone Bituminous Coal Association* v. *DeBendictis* (1987), from which Chief Justice William H. Rehnquist dissented. The same views surely explain his joining of Rehnquist's dissent in *Penn Central Transportation Co.* v. *New York City* (1978), which upheld a historic landmarks-preservation law as applied to prevent development in the airspace above Grand Central Terminal. Moreover, Stevens's tendency to allow moderate regulation of the use of property that affects others and his openness to a wide scope of legitimate, potentially innovative forms of regulation, underlies his dissenting view in *First English Evangelical Lutheran Church* v. *Los Angeles* (1987). He believed that the government should not be obligated to pay for the loss of property use during the temporary period that a land-use regulation is challenged as a compensable "taking." He was concerned that if government was required not only to lift its regulation, but also to pay for the loss during the period of the constitutional challenge, offi-

cials would be deterred from acting, and "the public interest in having important governmental decisions made in an orderly informed way" would be sacrificed.

A final distinctive theme of Justice Stevens—one he admired in Justice Rutledge—is that, even if government decision makers have broad latitude in choosing what goals to pursue and considerable discretion in choosing the means to achieve them, judges should carefully review the decision-making process to assure that the responsible officials sufficiently considered the rights of those whose constitutional interests are sacrificed. Moreover, his version of this "due process of lawmaking," which sometimes provides procedural safeguards in lieu of substantive limitations, tailors the intensity of the required process to the magnitude of the liberty and equality interests implicated by the decision or policy. His capital punishment opinions illustrate this concern, as well as his reluctance to narrow government goals and his deep attachment to impartiality. He would not prohibit imposition of the death penalty altogether, but he supports a variety of significant limitations on the process of its administration to limit arbitrariness. He insists on narrowing the category of those eligible for capital punishment, policing against its racially disproportionate infliction, and limiting, through defined and acceptable criteria, discretion of the prosecution to seek death sentences and discretion of the jury to impose them. He would not permit any death sentence not approved by a jury—in his view, the only acceptable voice for so irrevocable an expression of the community's sense of moral outrage. Furthermore, although he finds individualized guided jury discretion essential in all cases, he would preserve the jury's absolute discretion to spare life, as his powerful dissents in *Spaziano* v. *Florida* (1984) and *Walton* v. *Arizona* (1990) demonstrate.

Justice Stevens has expressed this preference for a calibrated review of process in a variety of circumstances. He readily protects the foundational rights of free and equal political participation against governmental action that would distort a fair political regime, just as he would broadly uphold governmental efforts to protect the purity of the political process. Not only do his influential and forceful opinions favoring constitutional limits on partisan gerrymandering and political patronage in cases like *Karcher* v. *Daggett* (1983), *Davis* v. *Bandemer* (1986), and *Branti* v. *Finkel* (1980) reflect this; so do his concurring opinion favorable to government-imposed anticorruption limits on corporate expenditures to support candidates in *Austin* v. *Michigan Chamber of Commerce* (1990), his dissent from the Court's refusal to extend the federal mail-fraud statute to cover deprivation of rights to honest government in *McNally* v. *United States* (1987), and his unwillingness in dissent in *Brown* v. *Socialist Workers '74 Campaign Committee* (1982) to require a First Amendment exemption for the Socialist Workers Party from a law mandating that political parties disclose their contributors. Not consistent judicial deference, but an overriding concern for a properly functioning political system, underlies his alternately restrictive or generous view of political efforts at domination or reform.

As many of these opinions suggest, he would require fair process for application as well as formulation of law, process whose demands increase the more fundamental the interest at issue. His dissent in *Bethel School District* v. *Fraser* (1986) acknowledged that school officials could consider the content of vulgar speech in setting rules of student conduct, but especially since speech was involved, he would not have allowed a student who made sexually suggestive remarks at a school assembly to be suspended without sufficient warning that his speech would provoke punishment. He would also distinguish between the process fit for legislation and that suited for adjudication. Dissenting in *City of Eastlake* v. *Forest City Enterprises* (1976), he would have found "manifestly unreasonable" a requirement that zoning changes be approved by fifty-five percent of the vote in a city-wide

referendum. He insisted that "[t]he essence of fair procedure is that the interested parties be given a reasonable opportunity to have their dispute decided on the merits by reference to articulable rules." Although he had "no doubt about the validity of the initiative or the referendum as an appropriate method of deciding questions of community policy," he thought it "equally clear that the popular vote is not an acceptable method of adjudicating the rights of individual litigants."

A distinctive element of Stevens's expectation of a rational decision-making process is found in his oft-noted inventive opinion in *Hampton* v. *Mow Sun Wong* (1976), which insisted that if questionable policies are to be implemented, at least the appropriate authority must adopt them. His plurality opinion invalidated a rule barring employment of aliens in the federal civil service, not because it violated equal protection, but because it was adopted by the Civil Service Commission to serve governmental interests that only the president or Congress could assert. More generally, he adheres closely to a constitutional vision in which all government officials, including judges, carry out the responsibilities particularly assigned to them. Several opinions aim to prevent Congress from abdicating its policy-making responsibilities. One is his separate concurrence in *Bowsher* v. *Synar* (1986), arguing that although "Congress may delegate legislative power to independent agencies or to the Executive," if it elects to exercise lawmaking power itself, it cannot "authorize a lesser representative of the Legislative Branch to act on its behalf," but must follow the normal process of enactment by both Houses of Congress and presentment to the president. In that case, Congress had inappropriately given power under the Gramm-Rudman-Hollings Act to the comptroller general, one of its own agents, to make important economic policy that binds the nation. Similarly, in his plurality opinion in *Industrial Union Department* v. *American Petroleum Institute* (1980), Stevens interpreted the Occupational Health and Safety Act to prohibit the secretary of labor from adopting

♦ **concurrent powers**
Governmental powers that may be exercised either by the national or by the state government.

standards for controlling potentially hazardous substances unless reasonably necessary to prevent significant harm in the workplace, rather than to achieve absolute safety. Construing Congress's intent more broadly would assume a delegation of "unprecedented power over American industry" that might constitute an unconstitutional transfer of legislative power—a conclusion that Justice Rehnquist's concurrence embraced.

Finally, Justice Stevens's vision of the minimal elements of an acceptably rational decision-making process builds on his presumption that government must justify its actions and entails a realistic appraisal of whether an identifiable and legitimate public purpose supports the challenged act, even if that purpose is not identified by the decision maker itself. Although broadly defining the legitimate goals that government may pursue—particularly including latitudinous conceptions of environmental or aesthetic improvements in the quality of community life and programs providing veterans benefits—he will not strain his imagination to prop up conduct that realistically could not have been aimed at legitimate objectives. Thus, he is not loath to ferret out protectionist state purposes that are invalid under the dormant commerce clause or the absence of secular purposes for religion-connected decisions that are invalid under the establishment clause. Moreover, he condemns harmful classifications adopted out of "habit, rather than analysis," as he shows in several of his opinions involving sex discrimination and distinctions based on legitimacy of birth. Although he will not impose on legislative bodies a duty to articulate their "actual purposes" for legislation, he will not accept, as a majority of the Court does, any "plausible" or "conceivable" purpose. Rather, as he wrote in his separate concurrence in *United States Railroad Retirement Board* v. *Fritz* (1980), he demands "a correlation between the classification and either the actual purpose of the statute or a legitimate purpose that we may reasonably presume to have motivated an impartial legislature." As his lone dissenting opinion in *Delaware Tribal Business Committee* v. *Weeks* (1977) demonstrates, it is not enough for him that a disadvantaging classification is not invidious; it cannot be neglectful, purposeless, or unthinking.

Several of these themes coalesce in his otherwise seemingly inconsistent pattern of positions in the Court's affirmative action cases. He dissented in *Fullilove* v. *Klutznick* (1980) from the Court's sustaining of Congress's setting aside ten percent of public works employment funds for minority business enterprises, largely because Congress gave only "perfunctory consideration" to a racial classification of "profound constitutional importance." He detected a decision illegitimately based on pure racial politics, generally urged that "the procedural character of the decisionmaking process" should affect any constitutional assessment, and specifically insisted that "because classifications based on race are potentially so harmful to the entire body politic, it is especially important that the reasons for any such classification be clearly identified and unquestionably legitimate." He did not assume that all race classifications were impermissible, however, and in *Wygant* v. *Jackson Board of Education* (1986) he dissented from the invalidation of a race-based preference for minority teachers contained in a lay-off provision of a collective bargaining agreement. Here he thought the interests of the disadvantaged white teachers were adequately represented and considered in the collective-bargaining process. He also urged that the validity of racial classifications must not be evaluated solely in relation to the justification of compensating for past discrimination, but also by considering their relevance to any valid public purposes, including achievement of the benefits of future diversity—a position subsequently adopted by the Court in *Metro Broadcasting, Inc.* v. *Federal Communications Commission* (1990). In fact, he suggested in his concurring opinion in *Richmond (City of)* v. *J. A. Croson Company* (1989), where he voted to nullify the city's *Fullilove*-style set-aside program, that "identifying past wrongdoers" and fashioning remedies for past discrimination is better suited to judicial than to legislative bodies.

And in *Adarand Constructors* v. *Pena* (1995), where the Court held federal as well as state affirmative action programs to require strict judicial scrutiny, he dissented, finding "no moral or constitutional equivalence between a policy that is designed to perpetuate a caste system and one that seeks to eradicate racial subordination."

A series of Stevens opinions in the 1990s demonstrates his judicial independence and insistence that the courts furnish a remedy for unconstitutional actions. In *Clinton* v. *New York* (1998) he wrote the Court's opinion invalidating the line-item veto adopted by Congress as unconstitutional. Similarly, in *U.S. Term Limits* v. *Thornton* (1998) he held for the Court that the Constitution's specific provisions governing elections to Congress barred a state from imposing term limits for its Congressional delegation. In *Reno* v. *American Civil Liberties Union* (1997) he again wrote for the Court that the Communications Decency Act, restricting "indecent" speech on the Internet, was overbroad and ran afoul of the First Amendment. And in *44 Liquormart* v. *Rhode Island* (1996) he invalidated a law that barred the advertising of liquor prices as an invalid attempt to keep people in ignorance "for what the government perceives to be their own good."

Finally, Stevens held in *Clinton* v. *Jones* (1997) that the president was not immune from suit involving his actions outside his official capacity.

Matching purposes to appropriate decision makers and requiring deliberation adequate to the liberty affected, yet remaining open to a multiplicity of valid governmental objectives, are essential characteristics of this rational, liberty-devoted and open-minded judge.

—JONATHAN D. VARAT

Bibliography

Burris, Scott (1987). Death and a Rational Justice: A Conversation on the Capital Jurisprudence of Justice John Paul Stevens. *Yale Law Journal* 96:521–546.

Carlson, Jonathan C., and Smith, Alan D. (1976). The One Hundred and First Justice: An Analysis of the Opinions of Justice John Paul Stevens, Sitting as a Judge on the Seventh Circuit Court of Appeals. *Vanderbilt Law Review* 29:125–209.

——— (1978). The Emerging Constitutional Jurisprudence of Justice Stevens. *University of Chicago Law Review* 46: 155–213.

——— (1987). Justice Stevens' Equal Protection Jurisprudence. *Harvard Law Review* 100:1146–1165.

O'Brien, David M. (1989). Filling Justice William O. Douglas's Seat: President Gerald R. Ford's Appointment of Justice John Paul Stevens. *Supreme Court Historical Society Yearbook* 1989:20–39.

Sickels, Robert Judd (1988). *John Paul Stevens and the Constitution: The Search for Balance.* University Park and London: The Pennsylvania State University Press.

Stevens, John Paul (1983). The Life Span of a Judge-Made Rule. *New York University Law Review* 58:1–21.

——— (1986). The Third Branch of Liberty. *San Diego Law Review* 22:437–452.

STEWARD MACHINE COMPANY v. DAVIS

301 U.S. 548 (1937)

Plaintiff, an employer, challenged the 1935 Social Security Act unemployment compensation provisions, which imposed a payroll tax on employers and directed that the tax receipts be paid to the general revenue. To offset part of this tax, the act granted employers a credit for taxes paid to a state unemployment fund conforming to federal benefit and solvency requirements. One such requirement was that state funds be held for safekeeping by the secretary of the treasury and invested in federal government

Steward is noteworthy for its sympathetic appraisal of joint federal-state welfare ventures.

securities. Plaintiff invoked *United States* v. *Butler* (1936), which had invalidated Agricultural Adjustment Act price support provisions that enabled the secretary of agriculture to contract with farmers to reduce agricultural production in exchange for payments funded by a federal tax levied on agricultural commodity processing. *Butler* had generally addressed the scope of Congress's power "to lay and collect taxes . . . to . . . provide . . . for the general welfare of the United States." While ostensibly rejecting the narrowest reading of the clause, originally proposed by James Madison, that the taxation power could be exercised only to carry out specifically enumerated powers, and purporting to adopt a broader, though undefined, interpretation of the taxing and spending power, *Butler* nevertheless had treated the Tenth Amendment as a limitation on the federal taxation power. In *Steward Machine Co.*, plaintiff argued that the unemployment taxation scheme, like the agricultural price support provisions, exceeded congressional powers because it infringed the Tenth Amendment's reservation to the states of power not delegated by the Constitution to the United States.

The unemployment compensation scheme was sustained, 5–4. Justice Benjamin N. Cardozo, writing for the majority, distinguished *United States* v. *Butler* on two grounds: the unemployment tax proceeds were to be used for the "general welfare" because they were not earmarked for any special group; and the unemployment compensation plan did not infringe state prerogatives because state participation in this cooperative federal-state program was entirely voluntary. The Court described unemployment as a "problem . . . national in area and dimensions." Many states wished to develop unemployment compensation programs but feared economic competition from those states without such plans. Hence a federal tax was necessary to enable states to accomplish their general welfare goals.

In its permissive, though vague, interpretation of the term "general welfare," *Steward Machine Co.* and its companion case, *Helvering* v. *Davis* (1937), seem to repudiate the *United States* v. *Butler* view that Congress, in exercising its power to tax for the general welfare, is required by the Tenth Amendment to eschew regulation of matters historically controlled by the states. *Steward Machine Co.* is also noteworthy for its sympathetic appraisal of joint federal-state welfare ventures. Justice Cardozo amply demonstrated that the competitive pressures of a national economy make it increasingly difficult for the states to perform traditional welfare functions without the national uniformity made possible by federal assistance and regulation.

—GRACE GANZ BLUMBERG

STONE, HARLAN F.

(1872-1946)

After finishing Amherst College and Columbia Law School (where in 1906 he became dean), Harlan F. Stone divided his time between teaching and practice in New York City. In 1923 President Calvin Coolidge, a former college mate from Amherst, appointed him attorney general of the United States. Less than a year later he became Associate Justice of the United States Supreme Court. In 1941 President Franklin D. Roosevelt, ignoring party labels, appointed him Chief Justice.

Experience gained as a teacher at the Columbia Law School had contributed directly to his preparation for the supreme bench. At the university, where he had time and opportunity for study and reflection, he developed ideas about the nature of law and the function of courts. Before donning judicial robes, Stone had argued only one case, *Ownbey* v. *Morgan* (1921), before the Supreme Court, adumbrating what was to become the major theme of his constitutional jurisprudence—judicial self-restraint. The correction of out-

See also

Butler, United States v.

Helvering v. *Davis*

moded processes, he argued, ought to be left to legislatures rather than assumed by courts.

It seems ironical that Stone, a solid, peace-loving man, should have been in the crossfire of controversy throughout his judicial career. On the Taft Court, and also during a good part of Chief Justice Charles Evans Hughes's regime, he differed from colleagues on the right who interposed their economic and social predilections under the guise of interpreting the Constitution. During his own chief justiceship Stone was sometimes at odds with colleagues on the left who were equally intent on using their judicial offices to further particular preferences.

Stone's moderate approach is revealed in his consideration of intergovernmental immunities from taxation—a vexing problem throughout the chief justiceships of Taft and Hughes. Rejecting the facile reciprocal immunities doctrine established in *McCulloch* v. *Maryland* and *Collector* v. *Day*, respectively, he held that the federal system does not establish a total want of power in one government to tax the instrumentalities of the other. For him, the extent and locus of the tax burden were the important considerations. No formula, no facile "black and white" distinctions sufficed to determine the line between governmental functions that were immune from taxation and those that were not. Stone elaborated these views in *Helvering* v. *Gerhardt* (1938) and *Graves* v. *New York ex rel. O'Keefe* (1939). Similarly, in cases concerning state regulations of economic affairs and state taxation of commerce, Stone rejected question-begging formulas such as "business affected with a public interest" or "direct and indirect effects."

Though habitually a Republican, Stone believed that increased use of governmental power was a necessary concomitant of twentieth-century conditions. "Law," he said, "functions best only when it is fitted into the life of a people." He made this point specific in his law lectures. This conviction sometimes aligned him with Oliver Wendell

IRONIC

Stone, a solid, peaceloving man, was in the crossfire of controversy throughout his judicial career.

Holmes and Louis D. Brandeis. Uniting the triumvirate was their view that a Justice's personal predilections must not thwart the realization of legislative objectives not clearly violative of the Constitution.

Stone's constitutional jurisprudence crystallized during 1936, the heyday of the Court's resistance to President Roosevelt's program of government control and regulation. In the leading case of *United States* v. *Butler* (1936) the Court voted 6–3 to invalidate the Agricultural Adjustment Act (AAA). Justice Owen J. Roberts and dissenting Justice Stone were about equally skeptical of the wisdom of the AAA. Their differences concerned the scope of national power and the Court's role in the American system of government. Stone thought that the majority had come to believe that any legislation it considered "undesirable" was necessarily unconstitutional. The Court had come to think of itself, as Stone said, as "the only agency of government that must be assumed to have capacity to govern."

The majority was haunted by the possibility that Congress might become "a parliament of the whole people, subject to no restrictions save such as are self-imposed." But, Stone countered, "consider the status of our own power." The president and Congress are restrained by the "ballot box and the processes of democratic government," and "subject to judicial restraint. The only check on our own exercise of power is our own sense of self-restraint."

Butler was neither the first nor the last time a dissenter expressly accused the court of "torturing" the Constitution under the guise of interpreting it. But no other Justice had previously used such strong language in condemning the practice.

In *Adkins* v. *Children's Hospital* (1923) the Court had declared unconstitutional the minimum wage for women. Justice George H. Sutherland was the spokesman. Holmes dissented as did Chief Justice Taft. *Adkins* was still in good standing in *Morehead* v. *New York ex rel. Tipaldo* (1936) when Stone repeated his indictment: "It is not for the Court to resolve doubts whether the remedy by regulation is as efficacious as many believe, or better than some other, or is better even than blind operation of uncontrolled economic forces. The legislature must be free to choose unless government is rendered impotent. The Fourteenth Amendment has no more imbedded in the Constitution our preference for some particular set of economic beliefs, than it has adopted in the name of liberty the system of theology which we happen to approve."

In his war on the recalcitrant four (Pierce Butler, James C. McReynolds, Sutherland, and Willis Van Devanter) Stone was sometimes allied with Holmes and Brandeis. Chief among points of agreement was their recognition of the need for a living law. As Holmes put it: "A slumber when prolonged means death." The essence of their creed was judicial self-restraint, recognized as a desirable rather than a realizable role.

The bond uniting them strengthened as the majority's doctrinaire approach became increasingly reactionary. Differences were exposed when Holmes, Brandeis, and Stone sometimes filed separate opinions in support of the same decision. In dissent Holmes, a gifted essayist addicted to generalization, often avoided the tough issues and "failed to meet the majority on its own ground." "This is a pretty good opinion," Stone remarked on one occasion, "but the old man leaves out all the troublesome facts and ignores all the tough points that worried the lower courts." "I wish," he once observed in grudging admiration, "I could make my cases sound as easy as Holmes makes his."

Stone's divergence from Brandeis was likewise most vividly portrayed in dissent. When the Court struck down legislation Brandeis favored in terms of policy, the erstwhile "People's Attorney" did not hesitate to use the Court as a forum to persuade others of its wisdom. "I told him [Brandeis] long ago," Holmes commented in 1930, "that he really was an advocate rather than a judge. He is affected by his interest in a cause, and if he feels it, he is not detached." Stone took specific exception to Brandeis's judicial activism. In reply to a note in which Brandeis invited Stone to join his dissent in *Liggett Co.* v. *Lee* (1931), Stone said: "Your opinion is a very interesting and powerful document. But it goes further than I am inclined to go, because I do not think it necessary to go that far in order to deal with this case. . . . I think you are too much an advocate of this particular legislation. I have little enthusiasm for it, although I think it constitutional. In any case, I think our dissents are more effective if we take the attitude that we are concerned with power and not with the merit of its exercises. . . ."

Without minimizing the great contributions of Holmes and Brandeis, it seems fair to conclude that in a logical as well as a chronological sense Stone was the one who, in both the old and the new Court, carried their tradition to fulfillment. Perforce it fell to him, as his former law clerk Herbert Wechsler said, "to carry through to victory and consolidate the gain."

Chief Justice Taft paid high tribute to Stone's pioneering, even as he warned of the danger in the former law teacher's method. Said Taft: "He is a learned lawyer in many ways, but his judgement I do not altogether consider safe and the ease with which he expresses himself, and his interest in the whole branch of the law in which he is called upon to give an opinion on a single principle makes the rest of the Court impatient and doubtful. . . . Without impeaching at all his good faith in matters of that sort, we find we have to watch closely the language he uses."

Viewing Stone's dissent in *United States* v. *Butler* as a "lodestar for due regard between legislative and judicial power," some commentators interpreted the 1937 judicial about-face as signifying well-nigh complete withdrawal of the Court from the governing process.

After 1937, when the Court's Maginot Line crumbled, Justice Stone feared that the guarantees of civil liberties might be wanting in effective safeguards. At first glance it does seem paradoxical that the leader of the campaign for judicial self-restraint in cases involving governmental economic regulation should have articulated the preferred freedoms doctrine. In an otherwise obscure case, Stone suggested in the body of the opinion that he would not go so far as to say that no economic legislation would ever violate constitutional restraints, but he did indicate that in this area the Court's role would be strictly confined. Attached to this opinion is a famous footnote suggesting special judicial responsibility in the orbit of individual liberties.

Two years later, in *Minersville School District* v. *Gobitis* (1940), the Court voted 8–1 to uphold Pennsylvania's compulsory flag salute as applied to Jehovah's Witnesses schoolchildren against their parents' religious beliefs. Justice Felix Frankfurter, who spoke for the majority, wrote privately to Stone: "We are not the primary resolver of the clash. What weighs strongly on me in this case is my anxiety that while we lean in the direction of the libertarian aspect, we do not exercise our judicial power unduly, and as though we ourselves were legislators by holding too tight a rein on organs of popular government."

When Frankfurter learned that Stone was the lone dissenter, he was deeply disturbed. He pleaded: "That you should entertain doubts has naturally stirred me to an anxious re-examination of my own view. . . . I can assure you that nothing has weighed as much on my conscience since I came on this Court as has this case. . . . I'm aware of the important distinction which you so skillfully adumbrated in your footnote 4 in the *Carolene Products Co.* Case. I agree with that distinction: I regard it as basic. I have taken over that distinction in its central aspect."

Adolf Hitler had already unleashed his diabolical forces in Europe, and a widening conflict seemed inevitable. Frankfurter continued: "For time and circumstances are surely not irrelevant in resolving the conflict that we have to resolve in this particular case. . . . But certainly it is relevant to make the adjustment that we have to make within the framework of present circumstances and those that are clearly ahead of us."

Reflecting his New England heritage of religious liberty, Stone was not convinced. He replied: "I am truly sorry not to go along with you. The case is peculiarly one of the relative weight of imponderables and I cannot overcome the feeling that the Constitution tips the scales in favor of religion."

Stone won this battle in a second case involving the compulsory flag salute, *West Virginia State School Board of Education* v. *Barnette* (1943). By 1943 three other justices, Hugo L. Black, William O. Douglas, and Frank Murphy, who had joined Frankfurter in upholding the compulsory flag salute in *Gobitis,* changed their minds. Two new appointees, Robert H. Jackson and Wiley B. Rutledge, agreed with Stone's dissent in the

The bench Stone headed was the most frequently divided, the most quarrelsome in history.

earlier case, thus transforming a vote of 8–1 to uphold the compulsory salute to a vote of 6–3 striking it down. Speaking through Justice Jackson, the Court declared: "If there is any fixed star in our constitutional constellation, it is that no official, high or petty, can prescribe what shall be orthodox in politics, nationalism, religion, or other matters of opinion, or force citizens to confess by word or act their faith therein. If there are any circumstances which permit an exception, they do not occur to us."

Stone had initially expressed the "preferred freedoms" doctrine tentatively, merely raising the question whether in the case of legislation touching rights protected by the First Amendment there may be "narrower scope for the operation of the presumption of constitutionality" and whether such legislation might not be "subjected to more exacting judicial scrutiny." He first used the expression "preferred freedoms" in *Jones* v. *Opelika* (1942).

After Stone's death in 1946, the passing of Justices Murphy and Rutledge in 1949, and the intensification of the Cold War, the "preferred freedoms" doctrine fell into a constitutional limbo. Justice Frankfurter, still smarting from the second flag salute case, attacked the doctrine fiercely in *Kovacs* v. *Cooper* (1949) where, referring to "preferred freedoms," he wrote: "This is a phrase which has crept into some recent decisions of the Court. I deem it a mischievous phrase if it carries the thought, which it may subtly imply, that any law touching communication is infected with invalidity. . . . I say that the phrase is mischievous because it radiates a constitutional doctrine without avowing it."

Dennis v. *United States* (1951), a case involving the last stage of the 1949 trial of eleven leaders of the Communist party of the United States for violation of the Smith Act of 1940, dealt the doctrine a serious blow. Yet even after *Dennis* some substance of the doctrine remained. In dissent Justice Black expressed the hope "that in calmer times, when present pressure, passions, and fear subside, this or some later Court will restore the First Amendment liberties to the high preferred place where they belong in a free society."

Stone's guiding rule was judicial self-restraint, not self-abnegation. Before 1937 he criticized right-wing colleagues who equated what they considered economically undesirable legislation with unconstitutionality. After Roosevelt had reconstructed the Court, he was at loggerheads with judges on the left, equally intent, he thought, on reading their preferences into the constitution.

Repeated conflicts with Black and Douglas, who, he felt, were prone to resolve all doubt in labor's favor, alienated him. Stone's creativity was confined by the boundaries of the known. Any marked departure from existing principles left him "a little hurt, a little bewildered and sometimes even a little angry." When in 1945 he found himself pitted against judicial activists on the left, he dolefully reminisced: "My more conservative brethren in the old days enacted their own economic prejudices into law. What they did placed in jeopardy a great and useful institution of government. The pendulum has now swung to the other extreme, and history is repeating itself. The Court is now in as much danger of becoming a legislative Constitution making body, enacting into law its own predilections, as it was then. The only difference is that now the interpretation of statutes, whether 'over-conservative' or 'over-liberal' can be corrected by Congress."

Stone's conception of judicial conduct was almost monastic. He strove against almost insuperable odds to keep the Court within what he considered appropriate bounds. A judge should limit himself precisely to the issue at hand. Contradictory precedents should usually be specifically overruled. The Court ought "to correct its own errors, even if I help in making them." Stone's judicial technique recognized complexity. "The sober second thought of the community," he urged, "is the firm base on which all law must ultimately rest."

Stone advocated restraint, not because he believed a judge's preference should not enter law, but precisely because it inevitably did. The sharp barbs of his thought were intended for the flesh of judges, both right and left, who, without weighing social values, prematurely enforced private convictions as law. He strove not to eliminate subjectivity but to tame it.

As Chief Justice he was less impressive. In 1929, when it was rumored that President Herbert C. Hoover might elevate Stone as Taft's successor, the Chief Justice had opposed it, saying that the Associate Justice was "not a great leader and would have a great deal of trouble in massing the Court." Years later, Taft's assessment proved true. The bench Stone headed was the most frequently divided, the most quarrelsome in history. If success be measured by the Chief's ability to maintain harmony, he was a failure. Solid convictions handicapped him. Nor would he resort to the high-pressure tactics of Chief Justices Taft and Hughes. Believing profoundly in freedom of expression for others, no less than himself, he was slow to cut off debate.

Stone had an abiding faith in free government and in judicial review as an essential adjunct to its operation. He believed that radical change was neither necessary not generally desirable. Drastic change could be avoided "if fear of legislative action, which Courts distrust or think unwise, is not overemphasized in interpreting the document." A free society needed continuity, "not of rules but of aims and ideals which will enable government in all the various crises of human affairs, to continue to function and to perform its appointed task within the bounds of reasonableness."

—ALPHEUS THOMAS MASON

Bibliography

Douglas, William O. (1946). Chief Justice Stone. *Columbia Law Review* 46:693–695.

Dowling, Noel T. (1941). The Methods of Mr. Justice Stone in Constitutional Cases. *Columbia Law Review* 41:1160–1181.

Dowling, Noel T.; Cheatham, E. E.; and Hale, R. L. (1936). Mr. Justice Stone and the Constitution. *Columbia Law Review* 36:351–381.

Frank, John P. (1957). Harlan Fiske Stone: An Estimate. *Stanford Law Review* 9:621–632.

Hand, Learned (1946). Chief Justice Stone's Conception of the Judicial Function. *Columbia Law Review* 46:696–699.

Konefsky, S. J. (1946). *Chief Justice Stone and the Supreme Court.* New York: Macmillan.

Mason, Alpheus Thomas (1956). *Harlan Fiske Stone: Pillar of the Law.* New York: Viking.

Wechsler, Herbert (1946). Stone and the Constitution. *Columbia Law Review* 46:764–800.

STONE COURT

(1941–1946)

When Associate Justice Harlan Fiske Stone moved over to the central seat of the Chief Justice in October 1941, he presided over a bench seven of whose nine members had been appointed to the Court by President Franklin D. Roosevelt. All seven, who were sympathetic to the mass of new regulatory laws and welfare measures sponsored by the president, could be expected to develop approvingly the constitutional revolution of 1937. Surely they would sustain vast congressional expansion of federal power under the commerce clause and drastically curtail the scope of judicial review. Stone himself had been appointed Associate Justice by President Calvin Coolidge, but he had long advocated newly dominant constitutional principles in dissenting opinions. Owen J. Roberts, now the senior Associate Justice, was a Republican appointed by President Herbert C. Hoover, but it was the shift of his vote, along with Chief Justice Charles Evans Hughes's, that had tipped the scales for change. Outside observers expected "a new unity in Supreme Court doctrine, based upon a clearer philosophy of government than has yet been expressed in the swift succession of decisions rendered by a Court standing in the shadow of political changes."

But there was no unity. The new Chief Justice soon came to view his brethren as "a

See also

Adkins v. *Children's Hospital*

Butler, United States v.

Dennis v. *United States*

Flag Salute Cases

Graves v. *New York*

McCulloch v. *Maryland*

Morehead v. *New York ex rel.*

Tipaldo

S

STONE COURT

(1941–1946)

team of wild horses." Dissenting opinions and concurring opinions proliferated in numbers previously inconceivable. The controversies ranged from major jurisprudential differences to unworthy personal squabbles over such matters as the phrasing of the Court's letter to Justice Roberts upon his retirement.

The sources of disunity were both philosophical and temperamental. All but one or two of the Justices were highly individualistic, each was accustomed to speak his mind. All, with the possible exception of Justice Roberts, accepted the new regulatory and welfare state; but there were sharp differences over the proper pace and extent of change. The Chief Justice and Justices Roberts, Stanley F. Reed, James F. Byrnes, and to a lesser degree Justices Felix Frankfurter and Robert H. Jackson, were more conservative in disposition than Justices Hugo L. Black, William O. Douglas, Frank Murphy, and Justice Byrnes's successor, Wiley B. Rutledge. The temperamental differences were sometimes matched by differences in legal philosophy. The Chief Justice, Justice Frankfurter, and to a lesser degree Justice Jackson, were craftsmen of the law deeply influenced by a strong sense of the importance of the judge's loyalty to a growing, changing, but still coherent set of legal principles. For them, such institutional concerns were often more important than immediate, practical consequences. Justices Black, Douglas, and Murphy gave far more emphasis to the redistribution of social and economic power and to progressive reform. In conflicts between the individual and his government outside the economic area, the conservatives' instinct for order would often clash with the progressive liberals' enthusiasm for civil liberties and civil rights. The marked dissension indicates the difficulty any president of the United States faces in stamping one pattern upon the work of the Court.

Viewed in the sweep of constitutional history, the Stone years, 1941–46, were the first part of a period of transition also encompassing the Vinson Court, 1946–53. By 1940 the main lines of constitutional interpretation under the commerce clause and general welfare clause had been adapted to centralized economic regulation and the welfare state. After 1953, when Earl Warren became Chief Justice of the United States, the driving force would be a new spirit of libertarianism, egalitarianism, and emancipation. It remained for the Stone Court to complete the reinterpretation of the commerce clause and to pursue the philosophy of judicial deference to legislative determinations, whether state or federal. But harbingers of the new age of reform by constitutional adjudication also began to appear. The first explicit challenges to an across-the-board philosophy of judicial self-restraint were raised in the Stone Court. From the seeds thus scattered would grow the doctrinal principles supporting the subsequent vast expansion of constitutionally protected civil liberties and civil rights.

In interpreting the commerce clause, the Stone Court, whenever faced with a clear assertion of congressional intent to exercise such wide authority, did not shrink from pressing to its logical extreme the doctrine that Congress may regulate any local activities that in fact affect interstate commerce. For example, in *Wickard* v. *Filburn* (1942) the Court sustained the imposition of a federal penalty upon the owner of a small family farm for sowing 11.9 acres of wheat in excess of his 11.1 acre federal allotment, upon the ground that Congress could rationally conclude that small individual additions to the total supply, even for home consumption, would cumulatively affect the price of wheat in interstate markets. The reluctance of the more conservative Justices to sanction unlimited expansion of federal regulation into once local affairs took hold when federal legislation was couched in terms sufficiently ambiguous to permit limitation. Decisions putting marginal limits upon the coverage of the federal wage and hour law are the best examples. Only a bare majority of four of the seven Justices participating could be mustered in *United States* v. *Southeastern Underwriters Association* (1944) for holding the insurance industry subject to the Sherman Antitrust Act. In *Paul* v. *Virginia* (1879) the Court had first ruled that writing an insurance policy on property in another state was not interstate commerce. Later decisions and an elaborate structure of regulation in every state were built upon that precedent. Congress had essayed no regulation of insurance. The executive branch had not previously sought to apply the Sherman Act. Justices Black, Douglas, Murphy, and Rutledge seemed not to hesitate in sustaining the Department of Justice's novel assertion of federal power, a position supportable by the literal words of the statute and the logic of the expansive view of the commerce power. Respect for precedent and a strong sense of the importance of institutional continuity led the Chief Justice and Justices Frankfurter and Jackson to protest so sharp a departure from the status quo in the absence of a specific congressional directive: "It is the part of wisdom and self-restraint and good government to leave the initiative to Congress. . . . To force the hand of Congress is no more the proper function of the judiciary than to tie the hands of Congress." Congress responded to the majority by limiting the application of the Sherman Act to the insurance business, and by confirming the states' powers of regulation and taxation.

New constitutional issues that would lead to the next major phase in the history of constitutional adjudication began to emerge as wartime restrictions and the multiplication of government activities stirred fears for personal liberties. The war against Nazi Germany reinvigorated ideals of human dignity, equality, and democracy. As more civil liberties and civil rights litigation came upon the docket, a number of Justices began to have second thoughts about the philosophy of judicial deference to legislative determinations. That philosophy had well fitted the prevailing desire for progressive social and economic reform so long as the states and the executive and legislative branches of the federal government were engaged in the redistribution of power and the protection of the disadvan-

taged and distressed. The recollection of past judicial mistakes and the need for consistency of institutional theory cautioned against activist judicial ventures even in so deserving an area as civil liberty. On the other hand, continued self-restraint would leave much civil liberty at the mercy of executive or legislative oppression. The libertarian judicial activist could achieve a measure of logical consistency by elevating civil liberties to a preferred position justifying stricter standards of judicial review than those used in judging economic measures. The older dissenting opinions by Justices Oliver Wendell Holmes and Louis D. Brandeis pleading for greater constitutional protection for freedom of speech pointed the way even though they had failed to rationalize a double standard.

Stone himself, as an Associate Justice, had suggested one rationale in a now famous footnote in *United States* v. *Carolene Products Co.* (1938). Holding that the Court should indulge a strong presumption of constitutionality whenever the political processes of representative government were open, he nonetheless suggested that stricter judicial review might be appropriate when the challenge was to a statute that interfered with the political process—for example, a law restricting freedom of speech—or that was a result of prejudice against a discrete and insular minority—for example, a law discriminating against black people.

The issue was first drawn sharply under the First and Fourteenth Amendments in the *Flag Salute Cases* (1940, 1943). The substantive question was whether the constitutional guarantees of the freedom of speech and free exercise of religion permitted a state to expel from school and treat as truants the children of Jehovah's Witnesses, who refused to salute the United States flag. In the first case, the expulsions were sustained. Speaking for the Court, Justice Frankfurter invoked the then conventional rationale of judicial self-restraint. National unity and respect for national tradition, he reasoned, were permissible legislative goals. The compulsory flag

The new Chief Justice soon came to view his brethren as "a team of wild horses."

salute could not be said to be an irrational means of seeking to secure those goals, even though the Court might be convinced that deeper patriotism would be engendered by refraining from coercing a symbolic gesture. To reject the legislative conclusion "would amount to no less than the pronouncement of pedagogical and psychological dogma in a field where courts possess no marked and certainly no controlling competence." The lone dissent came from Stone, who was still an Associate Justice.

Three years later the Court reversed itself. Justice Jackson, for the Court, summarized the core philosophy of the First Amendment: "If there is any fixed star in our constitutional constellation, it is that no official, high or petty, can prescribe what shall be orthodox in politics, nationalism, religion, or other matters of opinion or force citizens to confess by word or act their faith therein." First Amendment freedoms, the Court reasoned, rejecting Justice Frankfurter's plea for consistent application of the principle of judicial self-restraint, might not be curtailed for "such slender reasons" as would constitutionally justify restrictions upon economic liberty. Freedom of speech, of assembly, and of religion were susceptible of restriction "only to prevent grave and immediate danger to interests that the State may lawfully protect. We cannot because of modest estimates of our competence in such specialities as public education, withhold the judgment that history authenticates as the function of this Court when liberty is infringed."

Even in the 1980s, the deep and pervasive cleavage between the advocates of judicial self-restraint and the proponents of active judicial review in some categories of cases still divides both the Justices and constitutional scholars. It is now pretty clear, however, that judicial review will be stricter and there will be little deference to legislative judgments when restrictions upon freedom of expression, religion, or political association are at stake.

In later years the Court would come also to scrutinize strictly, without deference to the political process, not only some laws chal-lenged as denials of the equal protection of the laws guaranteed by the Fourteenth Amendment but even statutes claimed to infringe fundamental rights in violation of the due process clauses of the Fifth and Fourteenth Amendments. The Stone Court broke the ground for strict scrutiny of statutory classifications prejudicing an "insular minority" in a opinion in one of the *Japanese American Cases* declaring that "all legal restrictions which curtail the civil rights of a single racial group are immediately suspect . . . the courts must subject them to the most rigid scrutiny." In later years the constitutional standard thus declared became the basis for many decisions invalidating hostile racial discrimination at the hands of government, segregation laws, and other "invidious" statutory classifications.

Earlier the Stone Court opened the door to strict review in a second and still highly controversial class of cases under the equal protection clause. An Oklahoma statute mandated the sterilization of persons thrice convicted of specified crimes, including grand larceny, but not of persons convicted of other crimes of much the same order and magnitude, such as embezzlement. The somewhat obscure opinion by Justice Douglas in *Skinner* v. *Oklahoma* (1942), holding the differential treatment to violate the equal protection clause, emphasized the need for "strict scrutiny" of classifications made in a sterilization law, and referred to procreation as "a basic liberty." Later reforms by constitutional adjudication in the area of voting rights and legislative representation would be based upon the proposition that a legislative classification is subject to strict scrutiny not only when it is invidious but also when it differentiates among individuals in their access to a basic liberty. The precedent would also be invoked to support still later controversial decisions upholding claims of individual liberty in matters of sexual activity, childbirth, and abortion.

The Stone Court also sharpened the weapons for challenging crucial discrimination in the processes of representative government. In most of the states of the Old South, nomination as the candidate of the Democratic party still assured election to office. A political party was regarded as a private organization not subject to the equal protection clause of the Fourteenth Amendment or to the Fifteenth Amendment's prohibition against denial or abridgment of voting rights by reason of race or color. Even after primary elections regulated by state law became the standard method for nominating party candidates, "white primaries" remained an accepted method of excluding black citizens from participation in self government.

The first step in upsetting this neat device was taken in an opinion by Justice Stone just before he became Chief Justice. Interference with the right to cast an effective ballot in a primary held to nominate a party's candidate for election as senator or representative was held in *United States* v. *Classic* (1938) to interfere with the election itself and thus to be punishable under legislation enacted by Congress pursuant to its power to regulate the time, place, and manner of holding elections under Article I, section 4. Next, in *Smith* v. *Allwright* (1944) the Stone Court ruled that if black citizens are excluded because of race or color from a party primary prescribed and extensively regulated by state law, their "right . . . to vote" has been denied or abridged by the state in violation of the Fifteenth Amendment. Opening the polls to effective participation by racial minorities throughout the South, in accordance with the promise of the Fifteenth Amendment, would have to await the civil rights revolution and the enactment of the Voting Rights Act of 1965, but these decisions eliminating "white primaries" were the first major steps in that direction.

While marking its contributions to the mainstream of constitutional history, one should not forget that the Stone Court was a wartime court subject to wartime pressures as it faced dramatic cases posing the underlying and unanswerable question, "How much liberty and judicial protection for liberty may be sacrificed to ensure survival of the Nation?"

Economic measures were uniformly upheld, even a scheme for concentrating the review of the legality of administrative price regulations in a special Emergency Court of Appeals, thus denying a defendant charged in an ordinary court with a criminal violation the right to assert the illegality of the regulation as a defense. Extraordinary deference to military commanders under wartime pressures alone can account for the Court's shameful decision sustaining the constitutionality of a military order excluding every person of Japanese descent, even American-born United States citizens, from most of the area along the Pacific Coast.

More often, the majority resisted the pressures when individual liberty was at stake. In *Duncan* v. *Kahanamoku* (1946), an opinion with constitutional overtones, the substitution of military tribunals for civilian courts in Hawaii was held beyond the statutory authority of Army commanders. Prosecution of a naturalized citizen of German descent who had befriended a German saboteur landed by German submarine and who took his funds for safekeeping was held in *Cramer* v. *United States* (1945) not to satisfy the constitutional definition of treason because the only overt acts proved by the testimony of two witnesses—meetings with the enemy saboteur in public places—were not shown to give aid and comfort to the enemy. In *Schneiderman* v. *United States* (1943) the Court held that proof that a naturalized citizen was an avowed Marxist and longtime active member, organizer, and officer of the Communist Party of the United States, both before and after his naturalization, was insufficient to warrant stripping him of citizenship on the ground that, when naturalized, he had not been "attached to the principles of the Constitution . . . and well disposed to the good order and happiness of the United States."

The delicate balance that the Stone Court maintained between the effective prosecution of the war and the constitutional safeguards of liberty is perhaps best illustrated by the dramatic proceedings in *Ex Parte Quirin* (1942). In June 1942 eight trained Nazi saboteurs were put ashore in the United States by submarine, four on Long Island and four in Florida. They were quickly apprehended. President Roosevelt immediately appointed a military commission to try the saboteurs. The president was determined upon swift military justice. The proclamation declared the courts of the United States closed to subjects of any nation at war with the United States who might enter the United States and be charged with sabotage or attempt to commit sabotage. The trial was prosecuted with extraordinary speed and secrecy. Before the trial was complete, counsel for the saboteurs sought relief by petition for habeas corpus. By extraordinary procedure the case was rushed before the Supreme Court. The Justices broke their summer recess to hear oral argument. An order was promptly entered denying the petitions and promising a subsequent opinion. Within a few days the military tribunal passed sentence and six of the saboteurs were executed.

In the post-execution opinion the Court explained that the offense was triable by military commission; that the military commission was lawfully constituted; and that the proceedings were conducted without violation of any applicable provision of the Articles of War. The Justices were greatly troubled upon the last question. Some realized that in truth the swift and secret procedure ordained by the president left them with little ability to give meaningful protection to the saboteurs' legal rights in the military proceedings. Yet, even while recognizing that wartime pressures bent traditional legal safeguards in this as in other instances before the Stone Court, one should not conclude "inter arma silent leges." The hard core of the Court's decision was that judicial review of the saboteurs' constitutional contentions could not be barred even by the president as commander-in-chief. One may therefore hope that, if similar circumstances again arise, the Stone Court's basic defense of constitutionalism in time of war will prove more significant than its occasional yielding to the pressures of emergency.

—ARCHIBALD COX

Bibliography

Mason, Alpheus (1956). *Harlan Fiske Stone, Pillar of the Laws.* Chaps. 34–42. New York: Viking Press.

Rostow, Eugene (1945). The Japanese American Cases: A Disaster. *Yale Law Journal* 54:489–533.

Swindler, William F. (1970). *Court and Constitution in the Twentieth Century.* Vol. 2, chaps. 6–10. Indianapolis: Bobbs-Merrill.

Woodward, J. (1968). *Mr. Justice Murphy.* Chaps. 11–13. Princeton, N.J.: Princeton University Press.

STONE v. FARMERS' LOAN & TRUST CO.

116 U.S. 307 (1886)

This case marks a transition in our constitutional law from the Supreme Court's use of the contract clause as a bastion of vested rights protected by corporate charter to its use of substantive due process as a check on state regulation of business. Here, however, the Court sustained the regulation before it even as it laid the basis for the new doctrine. The facts seemingly constituted an open-and-shut case for a victory of the contract clause. A railroad company's charter explicitly authorized the railroad to set rates for carrying passengers and freight. Thirty-eight years after granting the charter, the state of Mississippi empowered a railroad commission to revise rates. The trust company, a stockholder of the railroad, sued to enjoin Stone and other members of the commission from enforcing the state rate regulations. In past rate cases, whenever the contract clause argument had lost, the reserved police power doctrine had prevailed; in this case the state had reserved no power to alter the company's charter. The inalienable police power doctrine had defeated the contract clause argument only in cases involving the public health, safety, or morals. Yet the Court, by a vote of 7–2, held that the state had not violated the company's charter.

Chief Justice Morrison R. Waite, in his opinion for the Court, reasoned that the explicit grant of rate-making powers to the railroad did not imply either a grant of exclusive powers or that the state had surrendered a power to revise rates set by the railroad. The state's power to regulate rates, Waite declared, cannot be "bargained away" except by a positive grant. Never before had the Court construed a contract so broadly in favor of the public and so strictly against a corporation.

Waite added, however, that the regulatory power was not unlimited: under pretense of regulating rates, the state could not require the railroad to carry persons or property free, and "neither can it do that which in law amounts to a taking of private property . . . without due process of law. What would have this effect we need not now say, because no tariff has yet been fixed by the commission." Waite also declared that state rate making does "not necessarily" deny due process. In effect he undercut his own proposition, asserted in *Munn* v. *Illinois* (1877), that the question of the reasonableness of rates is purely legislative in nature. In *Stone* the implied principle was that reasonableness was subject to judicial review. Moreover, the references to due process of law in effect reflected substantive due process, because a rate regulation could not violate due process except in a substantive sense. *Stone* heralded a new era in constitutional law, which the Court entered during the next decade.

—LEONARD W. LEVY

STONE v. POWELL

428 U.S. 465 (1976)

By act of Congress, a state prisoner may petition a federal court for a writ of habeas corpus on a claim that he was imprisoned in violation of his constitutional rights. In *Stone*, however, the Supreme Court ruled that federal courts should not entertain habeas corpus claims by prisoners who charge that they were convicted on unconstitutionally seized evidence, when the prisoner has had an opportunity for a full and fair hearing on the issue in the state courts.

The Court differentiated, for habeas corpus purposes, between the guarantees of the Fifth and Sixth Amendments, which are vital to the trustworthiness of the fact-finding process, and the Fourth Amendment, which is not. Exclusion of evidence is not a personal right of the defendant but a judicial remedy designed to deter the police from unlawful searches. Thus the exclusionary rule is not an "absolute" but must be balanced against competing policies. Indiscriminate application of the rule, far from fostering respect for constitutional values, might generate disrespect for the judicial system. On the other hand, denying the right to raise search and seizure claims in habeas corpus proceedings would not seriously diminish the educational effect of the rule; it was scarcely likely that police would be deterred by the possibility that the legality of the search would be challenged in habeas corpus proceedings after the state courts had upheld it.

Dissenting Justices William J. Brennan and Thurgood Marshall averred that the exclusionary rule is a right of the defendant and not a "mere utilitarian tool" which turns on its deterrent value.

—JACOB W. LANDYNSKI

STOP AND FRISK

Most courts recognize that a police officer has the authority to detain a person briefly for questioning even without probable cause to believe that the person is guilty of a crime. The Supreme Court first addressed the "stop and frisk" issue in *Terry* v. *Ohio* (1968). In *Terry*, an experienced police officer observed three unknown men conducting themselves in a manner that suggested the planning of an imminent robbery. With his suspicion aroused—but clearly without probable cause to make an arrest—the officer stopped and

Never before had the Court construed a contract so broadly in favor of the public and so strictly against a corporation.

Exclusion of evidence is not a personal right of the defendant but a judicial remedy designed to deter the police from unlawful searches.

See also
Exclusionary Rule
Search and Seizure

A frisk is authorized where an officer reaches a reasonable conclusion that the person stopped for questioning may be armed and presently dangerous.

patted the men down, finding weapons on two of them. The holders of the two guns were arrested and convicted of possession of a concealed weapon. The Supreme Court ruled that the officer's actions in stopping the suspects were constitutional.

Terry, therefore, authorized law enforcement officials, on the grounds of reasonable suspicion, to stop briefly a suspicious person in order to determine his identity or to maintain the status quo while obtaining more information. Such a "stop" is proper when: the police observe unusual conduct; the conduct raises reasonable suspicion that criminal activity may be afoot; and the police can point to specific and articulable facts that warrant that suspicion. A "frisk" is proper when the following prerequisites are met: a "frisk" cannot be justified on "inchoate and unparticularized suspicion or 'hunch,' " but must be grounded on facts which, in light of the officer's experience, support "specific reasonable inferences" that justify the intrusion; a "frisk" is proper only after "reasonable inquiries" have been made, although such inquiries need not be extensive; and a "frisk" is authorized where an officer reaches a reasonable conclusion that the person stopped for questioning may be armed and presently dangerous.

Further clarifying the test permitting a valid "stop and frisk," the Supreme Court has stated that the totality of the circumstances must be taken into account. Looking at the whole picture, the detaining officers must have a particularized and objective basis for suspecting the particular person stopped of criminal activity. The Court has emphasized that the process of assessing all the circumstances often will not involve hard certainties but rather probabilities; the evidence to justify the stop must be weighed in accordance with the understanding and experience of law enforcement personnel.

Applying that standard in *United States* v. *Cortez* (1981), the Court upheld the propri-

ety of stopping a defendant whose camper van was observed late at night near a suspected pick-up point for illegal aliens. The size of the vehicle, the lateness of the hour, and the remoteness of the spot all combined to make the stop reasonable.

Moreover, in *Adams* v. *Williams* (1972) the Supreme Court extended the *Terry* doctrine in the following ways: (1) a "stop and frisk" is authorized for such offenses as possession of illegal drugs or a concealed weapon; (2) an informant's tip may provide reasonable cause for a "stop and frisk" even where no unusual conduct has been observed by an officer; and (3) the "identification" and "reasonable inquiries" requirements of the *Terry* decision are no longer absolute prerequisites. The *Terry* doctrine was again extended in *Michigan* v. *Long* (1983) where a "frisk" for weapons was not restricted to the person but was extended to any area that might contain a weapon posing danger to the police. A search of the passenger compartment of a car was held reasonable due to the observance of a hunting knife, the intoxicated state of the defendant, and the fact that the encounter took place at night in an isolated rural area.

In *Pennsylvania* v. *Mimms* (1977) the Court held that, whenever a vehicle is lawfully detained for a traffic violation, the police officer may order the driver out of the vehicle for questioning without violating the proscriptions of the Fourth Amendment.

In *Sibron* v. *New York* (1968) a patrolman observed Sibron with a group of known drug addicts. The officer approached Sibron in a restaurant and ordered him outside. During a brief conversation with the officer, Sibron reached into his pocket. The patrolman promptly thrust his hand into the same pocket and found several glassine envelopes containing heroin.

The Supreme Court found the search to be unlawful on several grounds, including the fact that the "mere act of talking with a number of known addicts" was not enough to produce a reasonable inference that a person was armed and dangerous. The officer's motive, which was clearly to search for drugs, not for a weapon, invalidated the search as well. The *Sibron* decision is important because it made clear that *Terry* established only a narrow power to search on less than probable cause to arrest, and that the right to frisk is not an automatic concomitant to a lawful stop. *Sibron* also established proper motive as a prerequisite to a proper frisk.

In *Peters* v. *New York* (1968), *Sibron*'s companion case, an off-duty policeman saw through the peephole of his apartment door two strangers tiptoeing down the hallway. After calling the police station, dressing, and arming himself, the officer pursued the men and questioned Peters. Peters said he was visiting a married girlfriend but would not identify her. The officer then patted down Peters and felt in his pocket a hard, knife-like object. He removed the object, which turned out to be a plastic envelope containing burglar's tools. Peters was charged with unlawful possession of burglar's tools. The search was held proper as incident to a lawful arrest because the circumstantial evidence available to the officer reached the level of probable cause to arrest Peters for attempted burglary.

After *Sibron* and *Peters,* the issue arises as to the legal consequences when a police officer pats down a suspect, reaches into the suspect's pocket, and pulls out evidence of a crime but not a weapon. The questions are whether the officer could reasonably have believed the item was a weapon, and whether the item was visible even without removing it. Using *Sibron* and *Peters* as models, a box of burglar's tools would satisfy the test (*Peters*), while a soft bag of heroin would not be admissible (*Sibron*).

The lower courts have expanded the scope of a constitutionally permissible frisk beyond a limited pat-down of a suspect's outer clothing. Courts have included within the scope of a permissible frisk the area under a

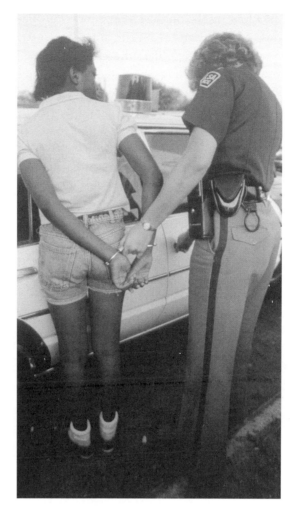

suspect's car seat, after the suspect appeared to hide something there, and a glove compartment within the reach of a suspect. In addition, the lower courts have relaxed their supervision over police judgments concerning objects that seem to be weapons when suspects are frisked, allowing officers to search after they have touched objects such as razor blades, cigarette lighters, and even lipstick containers.

The Supreme Court has declined to impose a rigid time limit for stop and frisk situations. In *United States* v. *Sharpe* (1985), where a pickup truck involved in drug trafficking was detained for twenty minutes, the Court determined that the length of the stop was reasonable by considering the purpose of the stop, the reasonableness of the time in

See also

Terry v. *Ohio*

effectuating the purpose, and the reasonableness of the means of investigation. In *United States* v. *Hensley* (1985) the Court widened the application of permissible investigative stops to include investigations of completed crimes. The Court also articulated that a police officer's reliance on a "wanted flyer" issued by another police department provided reasonable basis to conduct a stop if the flyer was based on "specific and articulable facts."

Finally, courts have handled the special case of airport "stop and frisk" situations in three ways. The first treats the problem through a straightforward application of the *Terry* test. The second method involves courts lowering the *Terry* level of "reasonable suspicion" to a less stringent standard. The third approach overtly abandons the *Terry* formula, opting for an administrative search consent rationale which does not even require reasonable suspicion. Today, the use of electronic scanning devices at most airports has diminished this area of "stop and frisk" concern.

—CHARLES H. WHITEBREAD

Bibliography

Whitebread, Charles H. (1980). *Criminal Procedure.* Mineola, N.Y.: Foundation Press.

STRADER v. GRAHAM

10 Howard (51 U.S.) 83 (1851)

In a suit under a Kentucky statute making an abettor of fugitive slaves liable to the master for their value, defendant attempted to evade liability by arguing that the slaves, who had previously been permitted by their master, the plaintiff, to sojourn in free states, became free there and retained that status upon their return to their slave-state domicile. Defendant sought a reversal of the Kentucky Court of Appeals' determination that their slave status reattached.

On the central question, Chief Justice Roger B. Taney held that a state court's determination of the status of blacks was conclusive on federal courts. But he went on to assert in dictum that every state had the right to de-

SOJOURNING SLAVES

Fugitive slave Thomas Sims is moved to the Boston docks for extradition to Georgia. Strader challenged the premise that a slave is returned to such status upon return to his master. (Corbis)

termine the status of persons within its territory "except in so far as the powers of the states in this respect are restrained, or duties and obligations imposed on them" by the federal Constitution, thus suggesting that the Constitution might somehow invalidate northern abolition statutes or statutes regulating the permissible stay of sojourning slaves. He also insisted that the Northwest Ordinance was defunct, its famous sixth article no longer a basis for the exclusion of slavery from the five states of the former Northwest Territory, thus suggesting that Congress might not be able to impose an enforceable antislavery condition on a territory's admission as a state.

Had the United States Supreme Court in 1857 wished to evade the controversial question raised in *Dred Scott* v. *Sandford* of the constitutionality of congressional prohibition of slavery in the territories, it might have used *Strader* to hold that the determination of Scott's status by the Missouri Supreme Court was binding on federal courts. Justice Samuel Nelson's concurrence in *Dred Scott*, originally intended to be the opinion for the Court, did in fact adopt this approach.

—WILLIAM M. WIECEK

STRAUDER v. WEST VIRGINIA

100 U.S. 303 (1880)

VIRGINIA v. RIVES

100 U.S. 313 (1880)

EX PARTE VIRGINIA AND J. D. COLES

100 U.S. 339 (1880)

On a day in 1880 the Supreme Court handed down three opinions that fixed the constitutional law of jury discrimination for over half a century. The effect of the three, taken collectively, barred overt state denial of the rights of blacks to serve on juries and effectively barred blacks from jury service in the South. Anything so crude as an announced and deliberate effort to exclude persons on ground of race was unconstitutional; but if official policy did not refer to race and yet blacks were systematically excluded by covert practices, the Constitution's integrity remained unimpaired. No estimate can be made of the miscarriages of justice that occurred in the South and border states where only whites sat in judgment in civil cases involving the property of blacks or in criminal cases involving their life and liberty over a period of at least fifty-five years.

Strader was a case in which official state policy was overtly discriminatory on racial grounds. West Virginia by statute declared that only whites might serve on juries. Justice William Strong, for the Court, holding the act to be a violation of the equal protection clause of the Fourteenth Amendment, declared that denying citizens the right to participate in the administration of justice solely for racial reasons "is practically a brand upon them, affixed by law; an assertion of their inferiority, and a stimulant to that race prejudice which is an impediment to securing to individuals of the race that equal justice which the law aims to secure to all others." The Court also sustained the constitutionality of a section of the Civil Rights Act of 1866 by which Congress authorized the removal of a case from a state court to a federal court in order to prevent the denial of civil rights by the state court. Justice Stephen J. Field and Nathan Clifford dissented without opinion.

In *Ex Parte Virginia and J. D. Coles*, the Court sustained the constitutionality of an act of Congress that provided that no qualified person should be disqualified because of race for service as a grand or petit juror in any court, state or federal. Coles, a county court judge of Virginia charged with selecting jurors, excluded from jury lists all black persons. He was indicted by the United States

S

STRAUDER v. WEST VIRGINIA

100 U.S. 303 (1880)

VIRGINIA v. RIVES

100 U.S. 313 (1880)

EX PARTE VIRGINIA AND J. D. COLES

100 U.S. 339 (1880)

The defendant argued that slaves permitted to sojourn in free states retained that status upon returning to their slave-state domicile.

No estimate can be made of the miscarriages of justice that occurred in the South where only whites sat in judgment in civil and criminal cases involving blacks.

See also

Dred Scott v. *Sandford*

STRAUDER v. WEST VIRGINIA

100 U.S. 303 (1880)

VIRGINIA v. RIVES

100 U.S. 313 (1880)

EX PARTE VIRGINIA AND J. D. COLES

100 U.S. 339 (1880)

♦ **declaratory judgment**
A judicial order determining the legal rights of the parties in a particular case, anticipating future controversy rather than remedying past injury.

See also
Civil Rights
Equal Protection of the Laws
Racial Discrimination

and was liable to be fined $5,000. On petition for a writ of habeas corpus, he alleged that the federal court had no jurisdiction over him and that the act of Congress was unconstitutional. Strong declared that under the Fourteenth Amendment, Congress could reach any act of a state that violated the right of black citizens to serve on juries or their right to be tried by juries impartially selected without regard to race. The act of Judge Coles was the act of the state of Virginia, for a state acts through its officers and agents, none of whom may deny the equal protection of the laws. By so ruling, the Court prepared the ground for the doctrine of state action. Field and Clifford, again dissenting, thought the act of Congress regulated purely local matters and destroyed state autonomy.

The effects of *Strauder* and *Ex Parte Virginia* were vitiated by the *Rives* decision. Two black men, indicted for the murder of a white man, sought to have their cases removed from a state court to a federal court on the ground that the grand jury that indicted them and the petit jury summoned to try them were composed entirely of whites. The prisoners claimed that the jury lists should include one third blacks, in proportion to the population, and, most important, that no

blacks had ever been allowed to serve on juries in the county where they were to be tried. In this case the record did not show, as it did in the other two, overt and direct exclusion of blacks. Strong, for the Court, this time supported by Field and Clifford concurring separately, simply stated, without further ado, that the "assertions" that no blacks ever served on juries in the county "fall short" of showing the denial of a civil right or the existence of racial discrimination. The defendants might still be tried impartially. Similarly, they had no right to a jury composed in part of members of their race. A mixed jury, said the Court, is not essential to the equal protection of the laws. There was no "unfriendly legislation" in this case. In effect the Court placed upon black prisoners the burden of proving deliberate and systematic exclusion on ground of race. As a result, blacks quickly disappeared from jury service in the South.

—LEONARD W. LEVY

Bibliography

Schmidt, Benno C. (1983). Juries, Jurisdiction, and Race Discrimination: The Lost Promise of *Strauder* v. *West Virginia*. *Texas Law Review* 61:1401–1499.

JURY DISCRIMINATION

Jury discrimination was first recognized as a constitutional problem shortly after the Civil War, when certain southern and border states excluded blacks from jury service. The Supreme Court had little difficulty in holding such blatant racial discrimination invalid as a denial of the equal protection of the laws guaranteed by the recently adopted Fourteenth Amendment. But, beyond such obvious improprieties, what should the principle of nondiscrimination forbid? Some kinds of "discrimination" in the selection of the jury are not bad but good: for example, those incompetent to serve ought to be excused from service, whether their incompetence arises from mental or physical defect, from demonstrably bad character, or from bias. No one has seriously argued that American jury service ought to be determined wholly by lot, as it was among the citizens of Athens. In addition, it has been the uniform policy of American jurisdictions to excuse from service some who are competent, but whose service would work a hardship on them or others: doctors, ministers, and parents who care for small children have been exempted from service on such grounds.

STREAM OF COMMERCE DOCTRINE

The Supreme Court introduced the "stream" or "current" metaphor in *Swift & Co.* v. *United States* (1905) to represent the movement of goods in interstate commerce. The doctrine is significant because it marks the Court's first recognition that commercial markets ignored state lines; the Justices departed from decades of constitutional interpretation in which economic reality had yielded to formal legal discrimination. The doctrine itself may be stated as follows: what appears, when out of context, to be intrastate commerce comes within the reach of the interstate commerce power if that commerce is but an incident related to an interstate continuum. Thus Congress can regulate the local aspects of commerce that are inseparably related to the current of interstate commerce, even though the flow has been temporarily interrupted by a kind of whirlpool or eddy while the product goes through some stage in the transformation of the raw material into the finished goods before being shipped again in the interstate stream to reach its final destination.

In *Swift* the government charged the nation's largest meatpackers with conspiring to monopolize interstate commerce in violation of the Sherman Antitrust Act. The packers asserted that their activities took place at the stockyards—solely within the boundaries of a single state—and thus involved only local or intrastate commerce. Justice Oliver Wendell Holmes, for a unanimous Court, rejected the packers' contentions.

> [C]ommerce among the states is not a technical legal conception, but a practical one drawn from the course of business. When cattle are sent for sale from a place in one state, with the expectation that they will end their transit, after purchase, in another, and when in effect they do so, with only the interruption necessary to find a purchaser at the stock yards, and when this is a typical, constantly recurring course, the current thus existing is a current of commerce among the states, and the purchase of cattle is a part and incident of such commerce.

The opinion struck hard at the rigid separation between production and commerce approved in *United States* v. *E. C. Knight & Co.* (1895). In recognizing that the United States no longer comprised a group of small, discrete markets, the Court began to confront the legal implications of the transportation and communications revolutions.

Although Holmes did not create the pithy metaphor, it stuck. In *Stafford* v. *Wallace* (1922) Chief Justice William Howard Taft declared that the stockyards were "a throat through which the current flows, and the transactions which occur therein are only incident to this current." The doctrine marked the "inevitable recognition of the great central fact" that such streams of commerce are interstate "in their very essence."

By the 1930s, as the circumstances that had given rise to the doctrine disappeared, the doctrine's pragmatism became increasingly well accepted. Though the stream of commerce terminology made frequent appearances, the Court began to ignore the doctrine itself. In *Schechter Poultry Corp.* v. *United States* (1935) and *Carter* v. *Carter Coal Co.* (1936) the Court refused to apply it. When a 5–4 Court sustained government regulation of interstate commerce in *NLRB* v. *Jones & Laughlin Steel Corp.* (1937), the Justices still chose not to base their opinion merely on the stream of commerce doctrine. Drawing upon both *Stafford* and *Houston, East & West Texas Railway Co.* v. *United States* (1914), Chief Justice Charles Evans Hughes declared that only those intrastate activities that had "such a close and substantial relation" to interstate commerce would be subject to congressional control.

The doctrine is significant because it marks the Court's first recognition that commercial markets ignore state lines.

The Supreme Court continued to use Holmes's language into the 1940s, but the doctrine almost disappeared. Indeed, although the phrase "stream of commerce" has enjoyed renewed use in the 1970s and 1980s, the Court almost never invokes the doctrine. Instead, the Justices have echoed Holmes's rejection of technical legal inquiries.

—DAVID GORDON

Bibliography

Gordon, David (1984). *Swift & Company* v. *United States:* The Beef Trust and the Stream of Commerce Doctrine. *American Journal of Legal History* 28:244–279.

STRICT SCRUTINY

In its modern use, "strict scrutiny" denotes judicial review that is active and intense. Although the "constitutional revolution" of the late 1930s aimed at replacing judicial activism with a more restrained review using the rational basis formula, even that revolution's strongest partisans recognized that "a more exacting judicial scrutiny" might be appropriate in some cases. Specific prohibitions of the Bill of Rights, for example, might call for active judicial defense, and legislation might be entitled to a diminished presumption of validity when it interfered with the political process itself or was directed against discrete and insular minorities. The term "strict scrutiny" appears to have been used first by Justice William O. Douglas in his opinion for the Supreme Court in *Skinner* v. *Oklahoma* (1942), in a context suggesting special judicial solicitude both for certain rights that were "basic" and for certain persons who seemed the likely victims of legislative prejudice.

Both these concerns informed the Warren Court's expansion of the reach of the equal protection clause. "Strict scrutiny" was required for legislation that discriminated against the exercise of fundamental interests or employed suspect classifications. In prac-

tice, as Gerald Gunther put it, the Court's heightened scrutiny was " 'strict' in theory and fatal in fact." The Court took a hard look at both the purposes of the legislature and the means used for achieving them. To pass the test of strict scrutiny, a legislative classification must be "necessary to achieve a compelling state interest." Thus the state's objectives must be not merely legitimate but of compelling importance, and the means used must be not merely rationally related to those purposes but necessary to their attainment.

The same demanding standard of review has emerged in other areas of constitutional law. Thus even some "indirect" regulations of the freedom of speech—that is, regulations that do not purport to regulate message content—must be strictly scrutinized. Similarly, strict scrutiny is appropriate for general legislation whose application is attacked as a violation of the right of free exercise of religion. And in those places where substantive due process has made a comeback—notably in defense of liberties having to do with marriage and family relations, abortion and contraception, and more generally the freedom of intimate association—the same strict judicial scrutiny is the order of the day.

The Court has developed intermediate standards of review falling between the rational basis and strict scrutiny standards. Not every heightening of the intensity of judicial review, in other words, implies strict scrutiny. Most critics of the Supreme Court's modern activism reject not only its employment of the strict scrutiny standard but also its use of any heightened standard of review. For these critics, there is little room in the Constitution for any judicial inquiry into the importance of governmental goals or the utility of governmental means. Some action by the state is forbidden by the Constitution, more or less explicitly. Beyond these prohibitions, say these critics, lie no principled guides to judicial behavior.

Yet strict judicial scrutiny of legislation is almost as old as the Constitution itself. From

---

To pass the test of strict scrutiny, a legislative classification must be "necessary to achieve a compelling state interest."

one season to another, the special objects of the judiciary's protection have varied, but from John Marshall's day to our own the courts have always found *some* occasions for "a more exacting judicial scrutiny" of the political branches' handiwork. It is hard to imagine what our country would be like if they had not done so.

—KENNETH L. KARST

Bibliography

Gunther, Gerald (1972). The Supreme Court, 1971 Term—Foreword: In Search of Evolving Doctrine on a Changing Court: A Model for a Newer Equal Protection. *Harvard Law Review* 86:1–48.

EMBLEM OF OPPOSITION

Stromberg *overruled a California law that prohibited the display of the Communist "workers' red flag."* (Corbis/Tim Page)

STROMBERG v. CALIFORNIA

283 U.S. 359 (1931)

A California law made it a crime to display a red flag or banner "as a sign, symbol or emblem of opposition to organized government or as an invitation or stimulus to anarchistic action or as an aid to propaganda that is of a seditious character. . . ." A member of the Young Communist League who ran a summer camp where the daily ritual included the raising of "the workers' red flag" was convicted for violating the statute, although a state appellate court noted that the prohibition contained in the first clause—"opposition to organized government"—was so vague as to be constitutionally questionable. That court nonetheless upheld the conviction on the grounds that the defendant had been found guilty of violating the entire statute and that the other two clauses relating to "anarchistic action" and "seditious character" were sufficiently definite.

Chief Justice Charles Evans Hughes and six other members of the Supreme Court reversed the conviction. In his opinion, Hughes pointed out that, the jury having rendered a

general verdict, it was impossible to know under which clause or clauses the defendant had been convicted. If any of the three clauses were invalid, the conviction could not stand. The Court found the first clause "so vague and indefinite" that it violated the due process clause of the Fourteenth Amendment because it prohibited not only violent, illegal opposition to organized government but also "peaceful and orderly opposition to government by legal means. . . ." Justices James C. McReynolds and Pierce Butler dissented.

—MICHAEL E. PARRISH

Is it a crime to display a red flag as a symbol of opposition to organized government?

STUMP v. SPARKMAN

435 U.S. 349 (1978)

This decision confirmed judges' absolute immunity from damage suits for alleged constitutional violations. At the request of a mother who was displeased with her "somewhat retarded" fifteen-year-old daughter's behavior, and *in ex parte* proceeding in which the child was not represented, Judge Stump ordered the child to be sterilized. The girl was told she was having an appendectomy, and she discovered some years later she had been sterilized. In an action brought by the

This decision confirmed judges' absolute immunity from damage suits for alleged constitutional violations.

A retail druggist sold a potentially toxic drug in a box without the mandatory warning.

sterilization victim and her husband, the Supreme Court held, 5–3, that the judge was immune from liability. Because signing the sterilization order was a judicial act, and because there was no express statement in state law that judges lacked jurisdiction to entertain sterilization requests, the judge's behavior was covered by the doctrine of judicial immunity. In the name of judicial independence, the majority immunized conduct that the three dissenters aptly called "lawless," "beyond the pale of anything that could sensibly be called a judicial act."

—THEODORE EISENBERG

SULLIVAN, UNITED STATES v.

332 U.S. 689 (1948)

In no other case has the Supreme Court more sweepingly construed the commerce clause. To protect consumers the Federal Food, Drug, and Cosmetic Act of 1938, passed under the national police power, prohibited the misbranding of drugs "held for sale after interstate shipment." Nine months after a bottle of sul-

fathiazole tablets had been shipped from Chicago to Atlanta, a retail druggist in Columbus, Georgia, who had purchased the bottle, properly labeled with a warning that the drug could be toxic, sold twelve tablets in a box without the mandatory warning. The local druggist thereby committed a federal crime. A federal court of appeals reversed his conviction on the ground that the words "held for sale after interstate shipment" extended only to the first intrastate sale and could not apply to all subsequent local sales after any lapse of time.

The Supreme Court, in an opinion by Justice Hugo L. Black for a bare majority, reversed and sustained the constitutionality of the statute. Black declared that it prohibited misbranding no matter when the drug was sold and without regard to how many local sales intervened; the statute remained in force "to the moment of . . . delivery to the ultimate consumer" in an intrastate transaction. Sullivan, the druggist, had contended that the statute so construed exceeded the commerce power and invaded powers reserved to the states under the Tenth Amendment. Black replied merely that a 1913 precedent, *McDermott* v. *Wisconsin*, which had sustained the misbranding provi-

SUBSTANTIVE DUE PROCESS OF LAW

To say that governmental action violates "substantive due process" is to say that the action, while adhering to the forms of law, unjustifiably abridges the Constitution's fundamental constraints upon the content of what government may do to people in the name of "law." As the Supreme Court put the matter most succinctly in *Hurtado* v. *California* (1884), "Law is something more than mere will exerted as an act of power. . . . [It] exclud[es], as not due process of law, acts of attainder, bills of pains and penalties, acts of confiscation . . . and other similar special,

partial and arbitrary exertions of power under the forms of legislation. Arbitrary power, enforcing its edicts to the injury of the persons and property of its subjects, is not law, whether manifested as the decree of a personal monarch or of an impersonal multitude."

Substantive due process thus restricts government power, requiring coercive actions of the state to have public as opposed to merely private ends, defining certain means that government may not employ absent the most compelling necessity, and identifying certain aspects of behavior that it may not reg-

ulate without a clear showing that no less intrusive means could achieve government's legitimate public aims.

Substantive due process was used, as in *Lochner* v. *New York* (1905), to overturn many attempts to regulate prices, wages and hours of work until the Court in the 1930s shifted to a narrower view of that concept, commencing in *Nebbia* v. *New York* (1934). In more recent decades the Court has revived substantive due process as the foundation for the fundamental right of privacy.

sion of the Pure Food and Drug Act of 1906, controlled the case. He thought that the "variants" between the two cases were "not sufficient" to distinguish *McDermott*, although he conceded that the retailer in *McDermott* had been the direct consignee of an interstate shipment. That fact should have made the precedent inapplicable. Black did not take notice that in *McDermott* the Court had reversed the state conviction of a grocer who misbranded under state law but complied with federal law. Black did not consider that under the original package doctrine the druggist sold local merchandise. Justice Wiley Rutlege concurred without reaching the constitutional issue and like the three dissenters wrote only on the construction of the statute.

After *Sullivan* the commerce power seemed to have no stable limits, though the rationale of the decision is unclear. The transaction involved in *Sullivan* was neither intrastate commerce that affected interstate commerce, nor the production of goods for interstate commerce. The reach of the national police power, which began with *Champion* v. *Ames* (1903), seems to have no end.

—LEONARD W. LEVY

SUPREME COURT

(History)

The only court whose existence is mandated by the Constitution is the Supreme Court. Article III states: "The judicial power of the United States shall be vested in one supreme court, and in such inferior courts as the Congress may from time to time ordain and establish." Besides its existence, a few attributes are constitutionally entrenched by Article III. The tenure of the judges is to be "during good behavior," and their compensation "shall not be diminished during their continuance in office." These provisions, modeled on English law and made applicable to all federal judges, were obviously intended to assure the independence of a judiciary appointed, pursuant to Article II, by the president with the advice and consent of the Senate.

Other features having a bearing on the character and independence of the Court were not addressed, presumably to be left at large or determined from time to time by Congress. Qualifications for membership on the Court were not specified; nor were the size of the Court, the period of its terms, or the level of the judges' compensation. The Court was to have both original jurisdiction and appellate jurisdiction, but the latter was subject to "such exceptions, and under such regulations, as the Congress shall make." Nothing was said concerning the relation of the Supreme Court to the courts of the states.

Thus from the outset the Court was only partially sheltered from the politics of republican government. The status of the Court was one of those creative ambiguities that have marked the Constitution as no less an organism than a mechanism, Darwinian as well as Newtonian. The position of the Court may have been in the mind of an eminent modern foreign-born mathematician who, contemplating American citizenship, regretted that he could not swear allegiance to the Constitution because "it is full of inconsistencies." In a self-governing nation, to be sure, the Court is detached but not disengaged, distant but not remote. Therein lay its potential either for popular neglect and scorn or for power and prestige.

The need for a federal judiciary, and so for an ultimate tribunal, was felt by the Framers as part of the transition from a confederation to a federal union. The Articles of Confederation supplied no such institution, except a supreme tribunal for prize and admiralty cases. A system of federal courts, parallel to those of the states, was one of the innovative conceptions of 1787. Their function was to serve as impartial tribunals, free of local bias, in suits between states, or controversies involving citizens of different states or a foreign country; to establish a uniform interpretation of federal laws; and to maintain the supremacy of federal law in cases where a state law conflicted with the Constitution, federal statutes, or treaties of the United States. In sum, the jurisdiction of the federal courts could rest on the nature of the parties or of the question presented. Only in cases where a state, or a foreign country or its diplomatic representative, was a party was the Supreme Court given original (nonappellate) jurisdiction.

These skeletal provisions of Article III were fleshed out by Congress in the Judiciary Act of 1789. That act set the number of Supreme Court Justices at five associate Justices and one Chief Justice, with salaries of $3,500 and $4,000, respectively. (The monetary differential remained at $500 until 1969, when it was increased to $2,500.) Three provisions of the act led to developments that proved to be of seminal importance for the prestige and power of the Supreme Court: a requirement that the Justices serve on regional circuit courts ("circuit riding"); a provision in section 13 that seemed to grant original jurisdiction to the Court to issue writs of mandamus; and a grant of power in section 25 to review the decisions of state supreme courts in cases turning on the Constitution, laws, or treaties of the United States. Each of these merits attention.

The circuit duties meant sitting with a federal district judge to form a circuit court, which heard appeals from district courts and had original jurisdiction in diversity of citizenship cases. In the early years circuit riding consumed the greater part of a Justice's time and surely his energy; travel by carriage or horseback over rough roads and stopovers at uncomfortable inns resulted in a weariness of flesh and spirit, against which the Justices complained bitterly, but which they forbore to resist. Yet these excursions into the local courthouses brought them into touch with lawyers, journalists, and townspeople, and gave a reality to the Supreme Court that its functioning in the capital city could not match. Moreover, the assignment of each Justice to a particular circuit affected significantly the appointments to the Court, for a vacancy on the Court would normally be filled by an appointment from the same circuit, and so at any time the practical range of nominees was limited and the influence of a small group of senators was proportionately great. Not until 1891, with the passage of the Circuit Courts of Appeals Act, were the Justices fully relieved of circuit-riding duties. Thereafter geography played a decreasing role in appointments. A striking instance was the widely acclaimed appointment by President Herbert C. Hoover in 1932 of Judge Benjamin N. Cardozo of New York to succeed Justice Oliver Wendell Holmes of Massachusetts, although two New Yorkers, Chief Justice Charles Evans Hughes and Justice Harlan Fiske Stone, were already on the Court. A comparable instance was the appointment by President Reagan in 1981 of Judge Sandra Day O'Connor of Arizona to succeed Justice Potter Stewart of Ohio even though another Arizonan, Justice William H. Rehnquist, was already serving.

As circuit riding was a cardinal factor in gaining popular recognition of the Court (at considerable cost to the Justices) and in determining appointments, so did the practice furnish an early opportunity for the Court to judge the validity of an act of Congress. In the waning days of the Federalist administration, Congress passed the Judiciary Act of 1801, compounded of partisanship and principle, which created new judgeships and abolished circuit riding. When the Jeffersonians took office, however, they countered with the Judiciary Act of 1802, which abolished the judgeships and restored circuit riding. Chief Justice

John Marshall, sensing a political crisis for the Court, solicited the opinions of his brethren on the question of complying with the law or treating it as beyond the authority of Congress. The Justices had serious doubts about the law's validity, and a strong distaste for the resumption of the burden it imposed, yet a majority counseled compliance, in accord with Marshall's own inclination. But a private litigant, defeated in a circuit court in Virginia at which Marshall himself presided, appealed to the Supreme Court, arguing the unconstitutionality of the 1802 act. The Congress, fearing a judgment voiding the act, had abolished the 1802 term of the Supreme Court. When the case, *Stuart* v. *Laird,* was decided, in February of 1803, the Court, with Marshall not participating, surprised and gratified the Jeffersonians by upholding the act, in a brief opinion which simply declared that acquiescence by the Court in circuit duty for twelve years under the Judiciary Act of 1789 had given a practical construction of the Constitution that would not now be disturbed. That the Court would at least consider the validity of an act of Congress had been resolved just six days earlier in the landmark case of *Marbury* v. *Madison* (1803).

That case, establishing the power of judicial review of acts of Congress, marked the second of the three germinal developments from the Judiciary Act of 1789. Section 13, which gave the Court power to issue mandamus and other writs, might have been read simply as conferring the power where the jurisdiction of the Court rested on one of the grounds specified in Article III. But the Court was not of a mind for so narrow a reading. When William Marbury of Maryland invoked the original jurisdiction of the Court to enforce a right to an office of justice of the peace pursuant to an appointment by President John Adams, and sought a mandamus to compel Secretary of State James Madison to deliver his commission, the Court regarded section 13 as conferring jurisdiction, and as so construed beyond the ambit of original jurisdiction defined in Article III. The suit for mandamus was therefore dismissed, again to the gratification of the Jeffersonians, but in the process the Court had declared the far more significant principle that in the decision of a case where a federal law was arguably incompatible with the Constitution, the Court, in deciding what "the law" was, must, if necessary, vindicate the higher law and treat the legislative act as ineffectual.

Despite some provocative language in Marshall's opinion (the executive branch cannot "sport away" the rights of others), the Jeffersonians focused on the immediate result and regarded it as a victory at the hands of a still-Federalist Court. Indeed, judicial review was not then the divisive party issue; the Jeffersonians would have welcomed a Supreme Court decision holding the Sedition Act of 1798 unconstitutional. Whether Marshall's doctrine of judicial review was a usurpation later became a subject of heated debate, scholarly and unscholarly. Although the Constitution contains no specific mention of the power, and although Marshall's opinion, resting on the logic of the decisional process, can be said to beg the question of who is to decide, the debates in the constitutional convention do indicate obliquely an acceptance of the power, in explaining the rejection of attempts to involve judges in an extrajudicial power of veto of legislation. But the debates were not cited in *Marbury;* Madison's Notes, the most authoritative source, pursuant to the policy of secrecy, were not published until fifty years after the Convention.

The third of the salient projections from the Judiciary Act of 1789, involving section 25, produced more immediate partisan repercussions. Section 25 empowered the Court to review decisions of state courts that denied rights claimed under the federal Constitution, statutes, or treaties. Again, no constitutional provision explicitly conferred such power on the Supreme Court, although Article VI does declare the supremacy of federal law: "the judges in every state shall be bound

thereby." By their silence, the Framers may have sought to avoid confrontations in the ratifying process, as in forbearing to be explicit about a national power to issue paper money or to establish a national bank.

The storm over the Court's power to review state court decisions was precipitated by its decision in *Martin* v. *Hunter's Lessee* (1816) sustaining the validity of section 25. The case was a contest over title to the extensive Fairfax estate in the northern neck of Virginia, turning on the intricate interrelations of Virginia land law and treaties of the United States with Great Britain concerning ownership of land by British nationals. Holding that the Virginia court had misapplied both Virginia and federal law, the Supreme Court in 1813, through Justice Joseph Story, reversed the state court's judgment and remanded the case to that court. A number of factors weakened the force of the decision. Story's opinion controverted the state court's even on points of the interpretation of state law, although section 25 itself limited review to federal questions. At a time when seven Justices constituted the Court, only four participated in the decision; the vote was 3–1, and the mandate to the Virginia court was unfortunately in the traditional form addressed to an inferior court, "you are hereby commanded, etc." The Virginia court was outraged and refused to obey the mandate. On a new writ of error to the Supreme Court, Story elaborated the justification of Supreme Court review in terms of the need for uniformity and supremacy of national law. The nature of the cause, not the court, was determinative of the Supreme Court's power to review (though critics wondered, no doubt unfairly, if the Supreme Court could then be given authority to review certain decisions of the House of Lords). John Marshall could not have uttered a pronouncement more nationalistic than that of the New England Republican appointed by President James Madison. (Marshall had excused himself because of his family's ownership of part of the land. Story, appointed in 1811 at the age of thirty-two, one of the most learned and powerful of Justices and a firm ally of Marshall, had been Madison's fourth choice to succeed William Cushing of Massachusetts: Levi Lincoln declined the nomination, Alexander Wolcott was rejected by the Senate, and John Quincy Adams also declined. Thus are the inevitabilities of history determined.)

In a sequel to the decision, the Court took the further step of sustaining its power to review even criminal judgments of state courts where a federal question, such as the interpretation of a federal law, was implicated. The opinion by Chief Justice Marshall in *Cohens* v. *Virginia* (1821) was the climactic realization of the Court's vision of a uniform federal law and a Constitution that was supreme in reality as well as in principle.

Reaction to the *Cohens* decision by Jeffersonians, particularly in Virginia, was intense. Judge Spencer Roane, who instead of Marshall would probably have become Chief Justice if Oliver Ellsworth had not resigned before Jefferson took office, published a series of bitter letters under pseudonyms, paying his respects to "a most monstrous and unexampled decision. It can only be accounted for from that love of power which all history informs us infects and corrupts all who possess it, and from which even the upright and eminent Judges are not exempt." The Court's "extravagant pretension" reached "the zenith of despotic power." In the following years a series of bills were introduced in Congress to repeal, in whole or in part, the appellate jurisdiction of the Supreme Court. Under these genial auspices was thus established a particularly sensitive and probably the most crucial power of the highest court in our federal union: the review of decisions of state courts in the interest of vindicating rights secured by the Constitution.

Conflicts between the Supreme Court, on the one hand, and the executive or legislative branches, or both, on the other, have occurred continually. The other branches have utilized the full spectrum of measures made available by the constitution. The most drastic of these, impeachment, was the first to be tried; indeed it was designed as a trial run by Jefferson to prepare the way for a similar attack on Chief Justice Marshall. The immediate target was Justice Samuel Chase, ardent Federalist, whose partisan outbursts in charges to the grand jury in Maryland furnished the occasion. The attempt misfired, however; Chase was narrowly acquitted in the Senate, owing probably to comparable overreaching by the fiery John Randolph, who managed the case for the Jeffersonians.

A milder form of resistance to the Court was the doctrine of departmental independence, whereby the President was as free to act on his view of constitutional authority as the Court was to act on its own. Despite the prospect of endless oscillation that this theory implied, it was espoused in some form by Jefferson, Andrew Jackson, and Abraham Lincoln. President Jackson's veto of the Bank Bill (1832) was based partly on grounds of unconstitutionality, although the earlier law creating the bank had been sustained by the Supreme Court. In his message justifying the veto, Jackson had the advice and aid of his attorney general, Roger B. Taney. By an irony of history, when President Lincoln in his first inaugural address dealt with Taney's opinion in *Dred Scott* v. *Sandford* (1857), he adopted something of the Jackson-Taney philosophy, maintaining that although he offered no resistance to the decision as a settlement of the lawsuit he could not regard it as binding on the political branches for the future.

The indeterminate size of the Court became a weapon in the contest between President Andrew Johnson and Congress over Reconstruction. By successive statutory changes, following the admission of new states and the creation of new circuits, the authorized membership of the Court had been increased to ten. A radical Congress, distrustful of Johnson and wishing to deprive him of the power to make new appointments to the Court, reduced the number of seats prospectively to seven. (Contributing to the move was a plan of Chief Justice Salmon P. Chase to induce a reluctant Congress to increase the Justices' salaries in return for a decrease in the number to be compensated. That plan failed, but Chase did succeed in having the title of his office changed from Chief Justice of the Supreme Court to Chief Justice of the United States.) The actual number of Justices did not fall below eight, and in 1869 the number was fixed at nine.

More famous is the action of the same Congress in withdrawing the appellate jurisdiction of the Supreme Court in cases under a habeas corpus act, giving rise to the decision in *Ex Parte McCardle* in 1869. While the immediate issue in the case was whether a military commission in Mississippi could try a newspaper editor for inflammatory writings urging citizens not to cooperate with the military government, Congress was fearful that a politically minded majority on the Court would hold the entire plan of Reconstruction unconstitutional. The Court, which had already heard argument in the case, bowed to the withdrawal of jurisdiction, but carefully pointed out that another appellate route remained unaffected by the repealing statute. Consequently the value of *McCardle* as a precedent, which is the centerpiece of constitutional argument on the extent of congressional power to limit the Court's jurisdiction, is at best doubtful.

The post-Reconstruction Court alienated labor and progressives by decisions taking a narrow view of state power to regulate and tax business; the commerce clause and freedom of contract protected by substantive due process served as shields for industry. The Progressive party platform in 1912, under the aegis of Theodore Roosevelt, advocated the recall of judges and judicial decisions by popular vote. Although this thrust was aimed at state courts rather than the Supreme Court, the latter had set a tone for judicial review in

a triad of decisions in 1895. *United States* v. *E. C. Knight Co.* held that a combination of sugar refiners controlling ninety percent of sugar production in the nation was not subject to the Sherman Antitrust Act because processing is not commerce. *In re Debs* held that a labor leader could be imprisoned for violating a federal court's injunction in a railroad labor strike, without judicial reliance on any statutorily defined offense. *Pollock* v. *Farmers Loan And Trust Co.* held the federal income tax law unconstitutional as applied to income from real property, stocks, and bonds, though valid as applied to wages, because an income tax is tantamount to a tax on its source, and where the source is property in some form the tax is a direct tax which under the constitution is forbidden to Congress unless apportioned according to population.

The most serious conflict with the Court, certainly since Marshall's time, culminated in President Franklin D. Roosevelt's Court reorganization plan in early 1937. The Court had held unconstitutional a series of major New Deal measures designed for economic recovery and reform: the National Industrial Recovery Act; Agricultural Adjustment Act; Railway Pension Act; Farm Mortgage Act; Guffey-Snyder Bituminous Coal Act; Municipal Bankruptcy Act; and a state minimum wage law for women. Still to be decided was the validity of the Wagner National Labor Relations Act, the Social Security Act, the Public Utility Holding Company Act, and the Tennessee Valley Authority Act in its full scope. The administration was persuaded that the barrier did not inhere in the Constitution but was the handiwork of Justices who were out of sympathy both with the New Deal and with the best traditions of constitutional decision. Apparently accepting the validity of this analysis, Chief Justice Hughes, appointed by President Hoover, though he greatly disliked 5–4 decisions, nevertheless joined Justices Louis D. Brandeis, Stone, and Cardozo as dissenters in the last five of the cases listed above as holding measures invalid. During his first term President Roosevelt had no opportunity to make an appointment to the Court.

The reorganization plan, which was formulated by Attorney General Homer S. Cummings, called for the appointment of an additional member of the Court for each Justice who did not retire at the age of seventy, up to a maximum membership of fifteen. Despite the president's sweeping electoral victory in 1936, and intensive political efforts by the administration for four months, the plan failed to pass the Senate. A number of factors contributed to the result. The argument based on age and inefficiency, stressed by proponents at the outset, was transparently disingenuous. A letter from Chief Justice Hughes, joined by Justices Willis Van Devanter and Brandeis, to Senator Burton K. Wheeler, at the latter's request, effectively refuted the charge that the Court needed additional members to keep abreast of its docket. The Court itself, while the bill was pending, sustained a state minimum wage law, the National Labor Relations Act, an amended Farm Bankruptcy Act, and the Social Security Act. As one senator remarked, "Why keep on running for the bus after you've caught it?" Moreover, Congress enacted a new retirement act for Supreme Court Justices, which made retirement more acceptable. Since 1869 a full pension had been provided for, but as retirement was equivalent to resignation under the statute, the pension was subject to the will of Congress and in 1932, as an economy measure, it had been reduced by half and was later restored. The act of 1937, by enabling retired Justices to serve on the lower federal courts, placed their retirement compensation under constitutional protection against diminution. Justice Van Devanter availed himself of this new law, giving the president his first opportunity to make an appointment and lessening further the need for enactment of his plan. But perhaps the most powerful factor leading to its defeat was a pervasive feeling, even among groups holding grievances against particular decisions, that the independence of the judiciary was too important a principle to be sacrificed, even under the extreme provocation furnished by a majority of the Court itself.

The appellate jurisdiction of the Court became a target of attack in 1958, as it had been in the early nineteenth century. Senator William E. Jenner of Indiana, reacting against decisions curtailing governmental actions in the field of loyalty investigations, introduced a series of bills withdrawing Supreme Court jurisdiction in this and related classes of cases. Passage was narrowly averted by the efforts of the then majority leader, Senator Lyndon B. Johnson. Comparable bills were introduced in 1982 to preclude review of decisions concerning abortion and school prayers. Such efforts, if successful, would produce chaotic results. In the name of the federal Constitution, varying decisions, for and against local laws, would stand unreconciled; the Supreme Court would have no opportunity to reconsider or modify its precedents; state and federal judges would be left to take different positions on the binding effect of prior Supreme Court decisions.

It is apparent that in the recurrent clashes of party, section, and class that have marked American history, the Court, whose role, in principle, is that of an arbiter, has not escaped the role of participant. In these judicial involvements, extraordinary force on one side has induced similar force on the other. A dramatic example is the contest over the production of the White House tapes for use as evidence in the prosecutions growing out of the Watergate break-in. President Richard M. Nixon refused to comply with a subpoena issued by the district court, on the ground of executive privilege. The tension between the rule of law and presidential immunity from suit had been resolved in part by bringing suit against a subordinate who was carrying out presidential orders, as in the steel seizure case, *Youngstown Sheet And Tube Co.* v. *Sawyer*

(1952), where the named defendant was the secretary of commerce. President Nixon, however, forced the issue by taking sole custody of the tapes. On appeal, the Supreme Court responded with the countervailing measure of holding the president amenable to the process of a court where the need of evidence in a criminal trial outweighs a generalized claim of privilege. The unanimity of the decision (with one abstention) was doubtless a factor impelling the president to yield, thus avoiding an ultimate confrontation.

That the supreme judicial tribunal, without the power of purse or sword, should have survived crises and vicissitudes and maintained its prestige can be ascribed partly to its own resourcefulness and partly to the recognition by a mature people of the Court's necessary functions in the American constitutional democracy. The Court's resourcefulness owes much to the central paradox of its work: it decides issues of great political moment, yet it does so in the context of a controversy between ordinary litigants in a conventional lawsuit. That setting provides a test of concreteness in the formulation of doctrine, allows flexibility of development, and enables the Court to adapt and refine doctrine as new factual and procedural settings may suggest.

The Supreme Court's essential functions, performed within the framework of conventional lawsuits, are fourfold: to resolve controversies between states; to assure the uniform application of national law; to maintain a common market in a continental union; and to enforce the guarantees of liberty and equality embodied in the bill of rights, the post-Civil War Amendments, and other provisions of the Constitution.

Although the Court's jurisdiction over suits between states is statistically insignificant, the function is of practical and symbolic importance, serving as a substitute for diplomacy and war in disputes over boundaries, allotment of waters, and the like. Because these cases originate in the Supreme Court, factual disputes are referred to a special master for hearings, findings, and recommendations, which are then presented to the Court for argument and decision.

The uniform interpretation and application of national law has become increasingly important with the proliferation of federal regulatory statutes and administrative rules. For almost a century, until 1938, the Supreme Court essayed a broader concept of uniformity in the common law itself, in fields such as commercial law and torts, under the doctrine of *Swift* v. *Tyson* (1842), which empowered the federal courts to pronounce a federal common law without regard to the common law of particular states. Sweeping as it was, the doctrine was truncated, for the federal common law could have no binding authority in state courts, and thus a bifurcated system of common law developed, along with a practice of forum shopping by lawyers as between federal and state courts. The doctrine was repudiated by the Court in *Erie Railway* v. *Tompkins* (1938) in an opinion by Justice Brandeis that branded as unconstitutional the course theretofore pursued by the federal courts. With the demise of *Swift* v. *Tyson* the rationale for retaining diversity of citizenship jurisdiction in the federal courts, for the decision of matters of state law, was materially weakened.

The maintenance of a common market is a modern description of a historic function of the Court, exercised since Marshall and his colleagues decided in *Gibbons* v. *Ogden* (1824) that the constitutional power of Congress over commerce among the states implied a negative on state power, even when Congress has not acted, and that the Supreme Court would enforce that implied prohibition. For a generation these commerce clause cases elicited a series of decisions upholding or setting aside state regulations—of quarantine, pilotage, intoxicating liquors, entry fees—by classifying them as either regulations of commerce, and so invalid, or regulations of local health or safety, and so valid as police power measures. This effort at classification obscured the process of judgment by treating a conclusory label as if it were a premise for reasoning. A pivotal change in methodology occurred in *Cooley* v. *Board of Wardens* (1852), a pilotage case where the opinion by Justice Benjamin Curtis recognized that commercial regulation and police power were not mutually exclusive categories, and that decision should turn on an empirical judgment, weighing the necessity of the local law, the seriousness of the impact on commerce, the need for uniformity of treatment, and the possible discriminatory impact on out-of-state enterprise. This kind of scrutiny, and comparable analysis of local taxation when challenged by multistate business, have been staples of Supreme Court adjudication and exemplars for other economic federations struggling to accommodate local interests and those of a union.

The most intensive, acclaimed, and in some quarters questioned, aspects of the Court's work has been the elaboration of fundamental human rights. While in England the great expressions of these rights are found in the writings of philosophers and poets—the secular trinity of John Milton, John Locke, and John Stuart Mill—in America the pronouncements are embodied—Jefferson apart—in the judicial opinions of Holmes, Brandeis, Hughes, Stone, Robert H. Jackson, Hugo L. Black, and other Justices. The development of a body of civil liberties guarantees, mainly under the Bill of Rights and the Fourteenth Amendment, reached its fullest flowering during the Chief Justiceship of Earl Warren (1953–69), though the seeds were planted in the Hughes Court.

During the 1930s, while public attention was focused on the Court's struggle with national power over the economy, pathbreaking advances were made in a series of decisions applying federal constitutional guarantees against the states. It is more than coincidence that this development occurred at a time of rising totalitarianism abroad. Freedom of the press and freedom of association and assembly were unmistakably put under the protection of the liberty secured by the Fourteenth Amendment in *Near* v. *Minnesota* (1931) and *DeJonge* v. *Oregon* (1937), respectively. The principle that a conviction in a state court following the use of a coerced confession is a violation of due process of law was announced for the first time *Brown* v. *Mississippi* (1936). A state's duty to afford racial equality in education was sharpened in *Missouri ex rel. Gaines* v. *Canada* (1938): it could not be satisfied by resort to a neighboring state. Mayors and governors were subjected to the reach of federal judicial process in *Hague* v. *CIO* (1939) and *Sterling* v. *Constantin* (1932), an accountability that came to be important in later contests over desegregation.

If the drama of these seminal developments was largely overlooked, the same cannot be said of the great expansion of civil liberties and civil rights by the Warren Court. The leading decisions have become familiar landmarks. *Baker* v. *Carr* (1962), requiring substantial equality of population in electoral districts within a state, asserted judicial power over what had previously been deemed a political question; Chief Justice Warren regarded it as the most important decision of his tenure, because of its potential for redistributing basic political power. *Brown* v. *Board of Education* (1954, 1955) was both the culmination and the beginning in the long drive against racial discrimination: doctrinally a climax, practically a starting point in the devising of remedies. *Miranda* v. *Arizona* (1966), limiting police interrogation of suspects in custody and giving suspects the right to counsel during interrogation, has become a symbol of the Court's intense concern for standards of criminal procedure, a concern that has sometimes been viewed as an index to a society's civilization. The equal protection guarantee, which Justice Holmes in 1927 could call the last refuge of a constitutional lawyer, was revitalized in the service not only of racial minorities but of other stereotyped groups: aliens, illegitimates, and women. Freedom of the press was extended well beyond freedom from restraint on publication: In actions for libel brought by public figures following *New York Times* v. *Sullivan* (1964), the defendant publisher would be liable only if he acted with legal malice, that is, with knowledge of the publication's falsity or with reckless disregard for its truth or falsity.

A constitutional right of privacy, of uncertain scope, extending beyond the explicit search and seizure guarantee to encompass at least certain conjugal intimacies, was established in *Griswold* v. *Connecticut* (1965). The religion clauses of the First Amendment were given new vitality in decisions rejecting organized prayer in the public schools, such as *Engel* v. *Vitale* (1962).

On any measure, it is an impressive performance. The momentum was somewhat slackened during the first decade and a half of Chief Justice Warren E. Burger's tenure, particularly in the areas of criminal procedure and nonestablishment of religion; yet during this period the Court reached the high-water mark of constitutionally protected autonomy in *Roe* v. *Wade* (1973), upholding freedom of choice respecting abortion in the first two trimesters of pregnancy.

Criticism of the modern Court has taken diverse directions. Some critics have complained that the Court has been unfaithful to the historic meaning of constitutional provisions. But the argument begs the question of "meaning." If the term signifies denotative meaning, the particular instances that the Framers envisioned as comprehended in the text, the original meaning has indeed been departed from. If, however, the purposive meaning is accepted, and the application does not contradict the language of the text, there is no infidelity. Such an analysis will not disapprove, for example, the "meaning" ascribed to the freedom of the press in the First Amendment.

Another criticism charges defenders of the Court with a double standard: the modern Court is a mirror image of the pre-1937 Court, the judicial vetoes coming now from the left instead of the right. The asserted parallel, however, is inexact. The problem is to identify the appropriate role for judicial review in a representative democracy. The older Court set aside such products of the political process as minimum wage, price control, and tax legislation. The modern Court, by and large, has given its intensive scrutiny to two areas of law that are of peculiarly legitimate concern to the judiciary. One is the field of procedure, in a large sense, civil and criminal. The other is the set of issues concerning representation of interests in the formation of public opinion and lawmaking. This category would include freedom of speech and press and association, voting rights, education, and the interests of groups underrepresented in the formulation of public policy. This approach gives a certain coherence to constitutional theory: as the commerce clause protects out-of-state enterprise against hostility, open or covert, the Bill of Rights and the Civil War amendments especially protect the political, social, or ethnic "outsider" against official neglect or ostracism.

A more qualified criticism is addressed to two tendencies of the modern Court. One is a perceived disposition to carry a constitutional safeguard to excessive lengths, as in *Buckley* v. *Valeo* (1976), which held invalid, in the name of freedom of expression, statutory limits on expenditures by or on behalf of candidates for federal offices. The other, illustrated by the abortion and police interrogation cases, is an inclination, when holding a state law or practice invalid, to prescribe only a single form of corrective that will not offend constitutional standards.

A problem faced by the Court throughout much of its history, one that has again become acute, is the burden of an expanding caseload. In the last hundred years two statutory jurisdictional revisions brought temporary relief.

The Circuit Courts of Appeals Act of 1891, by establishing a system of regional appellate courts, assured litigants of one opportunity for review without resort to the Supreme Court. The Judiciary Act of 1925, sponsored by the Justices themselves and promoted by Chief Justice William Howard Taft, made discretionary review by writ of certiorari, instead of appeal as of right, the normal mode of access to the Supreme Court.

Each solution, however, has in time become part of the problem. With thirteen courts of appeals, and the burgeoning of federal statutory law, there is a growing incidence of conflicting decisions calling for review. Moreover, the disposition of petitions for certiorari has occupied an increasing amount of the Justices' time, with more than 4,000 filed each term. Of these, approximately 175 are granted and the cases decided with full opinion after oral argument.

A study group appointed under the auspices of the Federal Judicial Center reported in 1972 that the caseload was reaching the saturation point. Certain ameliorative measures had already been taken. The normal time allowed for oral argument had been reduced from an hour to a half hour for each side. The number of law clerks had been increased in stages from one to four for each Justice. The study group expressed disquiet at what it viewed as a bureaucratic movement, and recommended the creation of a national court of appeals to review decisions that warranted review but not necessarily by the Supreme Court. Others proposed variations on this plan, notably one or more courts of appeals having specialized jurisdiction, in tax or criminal or regulatory cases. Sixty years after the 1925 act, the problem has not been resolved. And yet without adequate time for reflection, collegial discussion, critical scrutiny, mutual accommodation, and persuasive exposition, the Court cannot function at its best.

At its best, the Court can recall the legal profession and the people to an appreciation of their constitutional heritage, by translating the ideals and practices embodied in an eighteenth-century charter of the Enlightenment into the realities of a modern industrial democracy.

—PAUL A. FREUND

Bibliography

Bickel, Alexander M. (1962). *The Least Dangerous Branch*. Indianapolis: Bobbs-Merrill.

Congressional Quarterly (1981). *The Supreme Court and Its Work*. Washington, D.C.: Congressional Quarterly.

Freund, Paul A. (1961). *The Supreme Court of the United States*. Cleveland and New York: Meridian Books.

Freund, Paul A., and Katz, Stanley N. (1971–). *The Oliver Wendell Holmes Devise History of the Supreme Court of the United States*. 11 vols. New York: Macmillan. The following volumes have been published: vol. 1, Goebel, Julius, Jr. (1971), *Antecedents and Beginnings to 1801*; vol. 2, Haskins, George L., and Johnson, Herbert A. (1981), *Foundations of Power: John Marshall, 1801–1815*; vol. 5, Swisher, Carl B. (1974), *The Taney Period, 1836–1864*; vols. 6 and 7, Fairman, Charles (1971), *Reconstruction and Reunion, 1864–1888, Part One*; (1986) *Part Two*; vol. 9, Bickel, Alexander M., and Schmidt, Benno C., Jr. (1984), *The Judiciary and Responsible Government, 1910–1921*.

Friedman, Leon, and Israel, Fred L., eds. (1969–1978). *The Justices of the United States Supreme Court, 1789–1969*. 5 vols. New York: Chelsea House.

Lewis, Anthony (1964). *Gideon's Trumpet*. New York: Random House.

Pollak, Louis H., ed. (1966). *The Constitution and the Supreme Court: A Documentary History*. 2 vols. Cleveland: World Publishing Co.

Swindler, William F. (1970). *Court and Constitution in the Twentieth Century: The New Legality, 1932–1968*. Indianapolis: Bobbs-Merrill.

Warren, Charles (1926). *The Supreme Court in United States History.* 2 vols. Boston: Little, Brown.

Westin, Alan, ed. (1961). *The Supreme Court: Views from Inside.* New York: Norton.

SUPREME COURT, 1789–1801

The nation neglected the Court so much that when the United States government moved to Washington, D.C., in late 1800, the Court had no building or courtroom.

On January 8, 1801, twelve days before President John Adams appointed John Marshall as Chief Justice, a Jeffersonian newspaper reported: "John Jay, after having thru' decay of age become incompetent to discharge the duties of Governor, has been appointed to the sinecure of Chief Justice of the United States. That the Chief Justiceship is a sinecure needs no other evidence than that in one case the duties were discharged by one person who resided at the same time in England, and by another during a year's residence in France." The one in France was Oliver Ellsworth, sent there by President Adams as a special ambassador to negotiate peace. Ellsworth had recently resigned, and Jay, whose appointment as Ellsworth's successor had been confirmed by the Senate, had himself been the first Chief Justice, whom President George Washington had sent to England to negotiate a treaty that bore Jay's name. The chief justiceship was no sinecure: although the Supreme Court then met for only two short terms a year, the Justices also served as circuit court judges, and riding circuit was extremely arduous. When Jay was offered the position again, he declined it because of the circuit responsibilities and because the Court had neither "the energy, weight and dignity" necessary for it to support the national government nor "the public confidence and respect."

Jay's judgment was harsh although the Court did have problems, some of its own making. All the Justices were Federalists; their decisions en banc or on circuit seemed partisan—pro-administration, pro-English, or procreditor—and they presided at trials under the infamous Sedition Act, whose constitutionality they affirmed. But the Court was not responsible for most of its difficulties. It had no official reporter (Alexander J. Dallas's unofficial reports first appeared in 1798) and the press publicized only a few of the Court's decisions. The public knew little about the Court, and even members of its own bar were unfamiliar with its decisions. Nothing better symbolizes the nation's neglect of the Court than the fact that when the United States government moved to Washington, D.C., in late 1800, the Court had been forgotten. Not only did it lack a building; it had no courtroom. Congress hastily provided a small committee room in the basement of the Senate wing of the Capitol for the Court to meet.

The Court's beginnings were hardly more auspicious, however distinguished its membership. At its first term in February 1790 it had nothing to do except admit attorneys to its bar, and it shortly adjourned. It began as a court without a reporter, litigants, a docket, appeals, or decisions to make. It was chiefly an appellate court whose appellate jurisdiction scarcely matched the breadth of the Judicial Power of the United States stated in Article III. Congress in the Judiciary Act of 1789 had authorized the Court to review state court decisions that denied claims based on federal law, including the Constitution. Review was not authorized when the state court upheld a claim of federal right. The system of appellate jurisdiction thus permitted the Supreme Court to maintain federal law's supremacy but not its uniform interpretation. The Court's review of civil decisions of the lower federal courts was limited to cases involving more than $2,000 in controversy, and it could not review criminal cases from those courts. Congress had stingily authorized the Court to hear cases in its appellate capacity in order to keep it weak, to prevent centralization of judicial powers, to preserve the relative importance of state courts, and to insulate the Court from many matters that concerned ordinary citizens. For its first two years it heard no cases, and it made no substantive decisions until 1793. Its docket never got crowded. Dallas reported less than seventy cases for the pre-Marshall Court, and fewer than 10 percent of them involved constitutional law. The Court was then first a common law court, second a court of admiralty and maritime jurisdiction.

Although its members were able, the pre-Marshall Court had difficulty attracting and keeping them. When Marshall became Chief Justice, only William Cushing of the original six Justices appointed by Washington remained. Robert H. Harrison, one of the original six, was confirmed but declined appointment, preferring instead the chancellorship of Maryland. James Iredell accepted Harrison's place, so that the first Court consisted of Chief Justice Jay and Justices Cushing, John Blair, John Rutledge, James Wilson, and Iredell. Rutledge performed his circuit duties but had never attended a session of the Court when he resigned after two years to become chief justice of South Carolina. Charles C. Pinckney and Edward Rutledge declined appointment to John Rutledge's seat, preferring to serve in their state legislature. Thomas Johnson accepted that seat but resigned it in less than two years because circuit riding was too strenuous. William Paterson succeeded him. The February 1794 term was Jay's last. That he reentered New York politics after negotiating Jay's Treaty says something about the Court's prestige at the time. So too does the fact that Alexander Hamilton preferred private practice to the chief justiceship. At that point, John Rutledge, who had quit the Court, applied for the post vacated by Jay. Washington appointed Rutledge, who attended the August 1795 term of the Court when it decided only two cases. The Senate, having reconvened, rejected him because of his opposition to Jay's Treaty. Washington offered the chief justiceship to Patrick Henry who declined it. The president then named Justice Cushing, whom the Senate con-

firmed; but he too declined, preferring to remain Associate Justice. In 1796 Oliver Ellsworth became Chief Justice but quit after four years. John Blair retired early in 1796 and Washington again had to fill a vacancy on the Court. After Edmund Randolph refused the position, Samuel Chase accepted. In 1798 Wilson became the first Justice to die in office. Richard Peters refused to be considered for the position, and John Marshall also declined. Adams then appointed Bushrod Washington, and after Iredell died in 1798, he appointed Alfred Moore, who resigned within five years. When Ellsworth resigned and Jay declined reappointment, even though the Senate confirmed him, Adams turned to Marshall. The rapid turnover in personnel during the Court's first decade did not ease its work or enhance its reputation.

Jeffersonians grumbled about the Court's Federalist constitutional theories, but Jay kept his Court out of politics and established its independence from the other branches of the government. That achievement and the Court's identification of its task as safeguarding the supreme law of the land kept the Court a viable institution, despite its many problems during the first decade, and laid the groundwork for the achievements of the Marshall Court.

Late in 1790 Virginia's legislature denounced as unconstitutional the bill for national assumption of state debts. Washington allowed Hamilton to send a copy of the Virginia resolves to Jay and to inquire whether the various branches of the government should employ their "collective weight . . . in exploding [Virginia's strict construction] principles." Hamilton warned that Virginia had shown "the first symptom of a spirit which must either be killed or it will kill the Constitution of the United States." However, Jay, who privately advised Washington and drafted his proclamation of neutrality, recognized the difference between a judicial pronouncement and an extrajudicial one. The Court, strongly believing in the principle of separation of powers, would not express ex officio opinions except in judicial cases before it. Jay calmly declined the executive's invitation.

Similar principles motivated the Justices when confronted by Congress's Invalid Pensioners' Act of 1792, which required the circuit courts to pass on the pension applications of disabled veterans, subject to review by the secretary of war and Congress. Justices Wilson and Blair together with Judge Peters on circuit in the district of Pennsylvania, having refused to pass on an application from one Hayburn, explained their conduct in a letter to the president. They could not proceed because first, the business directed by the statute was not judicial in nature, there being no constitutional authority for it, and second, because the possible revision of the Court's judgment by the other branches of government would be "radically inconsistent with the independence" of the judiciary. In their circuits, Jay, Cushing, and Iredell similarly explained that a judicial decision must be a final decision. *Hayburn's Case* (1792), which was not really a "case" and in which nothing was judicially decided, was important because the Court, in Wilson's words, affirmed "a principle important to freedom," that the judicial branch must be independent of the other branches.

Similarly, Jay established another principle vital to the Court's independent, judicial, and nonpolitical character when he declined Washington's request for an advisory opinion. That request arose out of apparent conflicts between American treaty obligations to France and the Proclamation of Neutrality. The French commissioned privateers in American ports and established prize courts to condemn vessels captured by those privateers. Washington sought the Court's opinion on twenty-nine questions involving international law and treaty interpretation, in connection with the French practices. Jay, relying again on the principle of separation of powers, observed that the Court should not "extra-judicially" decide questions that might

come before it in litigation. Thus, by preserving its purely judicial character, the Court was free to decide some of those questions when real cases posed them. From the beginning, the Court staked its power and prestige on its special relationship to the supreme law of the land, which it safeguarded, expounded, and symbolized.

The pre-Marshall Court also exercised the power of judicial review. The Justices on circuit quickly held state acts unconstitutional for violating the supreme law of the land. Jay and Cushing on circuit in the district of Connecticut held that that state, by adversely affecting debts owed to British creditors, had violated the treaty of peace with Britain; Iredell in Georgia and Paterson in South Carolina made similar decisions. The Justices held that United States treaties were superior to state laws. The Supreme Court confronted the issue in *Ware* v. *Hylton* (1796). With Iredell alone dissenting, the Court rejected the arguments of John Marshall, making his only appearance before the Justices, as counsel for the debtor interests of Virginia. He opposed "those who wish to impair the sovereignty of Virginia" and contended first that the Constitution had not authorized the Court to question the validity of state statutes and, second, that a treaty could not annul them. Seriatim opinions by Chase, Paterson, Wilson, and Cushing held otherwise.

In *Clarke* v. *Harwood* (1797) the Court ruled that *Ware* "settled" the question before it. *Clarke* was the Court's first decision against the validity of a state act in a case arising on a writ of error to a state court under section 25 of the Judiciary Act of 1789. Section 25 authorized the Court to reverse or affirm state decisions that denied rights claimed under United States treaties. Maryland's high court, relying on a state statute sequestering debts owed to British creditors, had barred a claim based on the treaty of peace with Britain. By reversing the Maryland court, the Supreme Court in effect voided the state act. However, the Court rarely heard cases on a writ of error to a state court. Indeed, it had not decided its first such case until shortly before *Clarke*. In *Olney* v. *Arnold* (1796) the Court had reversed a Rhode Island decision that misconstrued a revenue act of Congress. The Court's power of reviewing state decisions under section 25 did not become controversial until 1814. During the Court's first decade, judicial review of state legislation was uncontested, and it was exercised.

On circuit the Justices also struck down state acts as violating the contract clause of the Constitution. The first such decision occurred in 1792 in *Champion and Dickason* v. *Casey,* which voided a Rhode Island state law. Given the hullaballoo in that state when its own judiciary was suspected of having voided a state act in *Trevett* v. *Weeden* (1787), the meek acceptance of the 1792 decision showed the legitimacy of judicial review over the states.

In *Hylton* v. *United States* (1796) the Court for the first time determined the constitutionality of an act of Congress, ruling that an excise on carriages, not being a direct tax, was valid even if not apportioned among the states. Those hoping for the Court to hold the federal excise unconstitutional were Jeffersonians; they did not then or at any time during the Court's first decade challenge the legitimacy of the Court's power to refuse to enforce an unconstitutional statute. Until the debate on the repeal of the Judiciary Act of 1801, scarcely anyone opposed judicial review, whether over state or over congressional legislation. *Hayburn's Case* in 1792 was misunderstood throughout the nation. Not only did Attorney General Randolph believe that the Court had annulled an act of Congress; so did Congress. The House established an investigating committee, "this being the first instance in which a Court of Justice had declared a law of Congress unconstitutional." Jeffersonians gleefully praised the Justices and hoped the Court would extend the precedent by holding unconstitutional other congressional legislation that promoted Hamilton's economic programs. Later, Jeffer-

sonians in Sedition Act trials sought to persuade the Justices on circuit that they should declare the statute void. Repeatedly during the first decade, bills arose in Congress that provoked members in both houses to state that the Court should and would hold them unconstitutional. The way to the doctrine of judicial review announced in *Marbury* v. *Madison* (1803) was well paved, and the opposition to the Court's opinion did not derive from its assumption of a power to void an act of Congress.

Another major theme in the work of the Court during its first decade was nationalism. Once again, the Marshall Court built on what the Jay and Ellsworth Courts had first shaped. The early Courts helped vindicate the national character of the United States government, maintain the supremacy of the nation over the states, and keep the states from undermining the new constitutional system. On circuit duty the Justices frequently lectured federal grand juries, inculcating doctrines from *The Federalist,* and these grand jury charges were well publicized in the newspapers. In one of his charges, Jay, in 1790, having declared, "We had become a Nation," explained why national tribunals became necessary for the interpretation and execution of national law, especially in a nation accustomed only to state courts and state policies. Circuit court opinions striking down state laws in violation of the contract clause or federal treaties preached nationalism and national supremacy. Many of the criminal prosecutions before the federal circuit courts during the first decade were connected with national suppression of the Whiskey Rebellion and the Fries Rebellion. Similarly, prosecutions under the Sedition Act were intended to vindicate the reputations of Congress and the president.

The development of a federal common law of crimes, expanding the jurisdiction of the national courts, fit the nationalist pattern. Whether the courts could try nonstatutory offenses was a question that first arose in *Henfield's Case* (1793). Wilson maintained that an American citizen serving on a French privateer commissioned in an American port and attacking ships of England, with whom the United States was at peace, had committed an indictable offense under the Proclamation of Neutrality, the law of nations, and the treaty with England, even though Congress had not made his act a crime.

The same nationalist pattern unified several of the Court's opinions in cases dealing with various issues. In *Chisholm* v. *Georgia* (1793) the Court's holding, that its jurisdiction extended to suits against a state by citizens of another state, was founded on nationalist principles as well as on the text of Article III. Wilson, for example, began with the principles that the people of the United States form a nation, making ridiculous the "haughty notions of state independence, state sovereignty, and state supremacy." "As to the purposes of the Union," he said, "therefore, Georgia is not a sovereign state." Jay's opinion also stressed "the national character" of the United States and the "inexpediency" of allowing state courts to decide questions that involved the performance of national treaties. The denunciation of the Court for its "consolidation of the Union" and its "annihilation of the sovereignty of the States" led to the Eleventh Amendment, which was intended to nullify *Chisholm*.

In *Glass* v. *Sloop Betsy* (1794) the Court supported the government's neutrality policy by ruling that France, after capturing a neutral ship, could not hold or award her as a prize in an American port. Only the United States courts could determine the lawfulness of prizes brought into its ports, and no foreign nation controlled its admiralty law or could subvert American rights under international law. In *Penhallow* v. *Doane* (1795) the Court resolved an old dispute over the ownership of a prize. One party's claims relied on decisions of a New Hampshire court, the other's on a decision of a prize court established by the old Congress of the Confederation. Paterson, in the Supreme Court's principal opinion, up-

held the lower federal courts, which had decided against the state court and claimed jurisdiction. No nation, he said, had recognized the states as sovereign for the purpose of awarding prizes. The old Congress had been the supreme council of the nation and center of the Union, he claimed, whose sovereignty was approved by the people of America and recognized by foreign nations. The federal courts succeeded to that sovereignty in prize matters. New Hampshire angrily remonstrated against the "destruction" of its sovereignty but the Court's ruling prevailed.

Its decision in *Hylton* v. *United States* gave life to the government's revenue powers. When the Court upheld federal treaties as paramount to state laws, in *Ware* v. *Hylton* (1796), Chase, in the principal opinion for the Court, indulged in fanciful nationalism when declaring, "There can be no limitation on the power of the people of the United States. By their authority the State Constitutions were made."

Other notable cases of the first decade were *Van Horne's Lessee* v. *Dorrance* (1794) and *Calder* v. *Bull* (1798), in which the Court laid the foundation for the judicial doctrine of vested rights, which it developed further in contract clause and higher law decisions during Marshall's chief justiceship. Although the Court was left out of the planning for the new national capital, it had been enunciating doctrines—of judicial review, national supremacy, and vested rights—that helped shape the United States and would in time make the judicial branch of government impossible to ignore.

—LEONARD W. LEVY

Bibliography

Currie, David P. (1981). The Constitution in the Supreme Court: 1789–1801. *University of Chicago Law Review* 48:819–885.

Goebel, Julius (1971). *Antecedents and Beginnings.* Vol. 1 of the *Oliver Wendell Holmes Devise History of the Supreme Court,* ed. Paul Freund. New York: Macmillan.

Haines, Charles Grove (1944). *The Role of the Supreme Court in American Government and Politics, 1789–1835*. Berkeley: University of California Press.

Henderson, Dwight F. (1971). *Courts for a New Nation*. Washington, D.C.: Public Affairs Press.

Warren, Charles (1923). *The Supreme Court in United States History*. Vol. 1. Boston: Little, Brown.

SUPREME COURT AT WORK

In its first decade, the Supreme Court had little business, frequent turnover in personnel, no chambers or staff, no fixed customs, and no institutional identity. When the Court initially convened on February 1, 1790, only Chief Justice John Jay and two other Justices arrived at the Exchange Building in New York City. They adjourned until the next day, when Justice John Blair arrived. With little to do other than admit attorneys to practice before its bar, the Court concluded its first sessions in less than two weeks. When the capital moved from New York City to Philadelphia in the winter of 1790, the Court met in Independence Hall and in the Old City Hall for ten years, until the capital again moved to Washington, D.C. Most of the first Justices' time, however, was spent riding circuit. Under the Judiciary Act of 1789, they were required twice a year to hold circuit court, in the company of district judges, to try some types of cases and to hear appeals from the federal district courts. Hence, the Justices resided primarily in their circuits rather than in Washington and often felt a greater allegiance to their circuits than to the Supreme Court.

The Supreme Court is a human institution that has adapted to changing conditions. The Justices no longer ride circuit and the caseload now keeps them in Washington most of the year. As the caseload increased, sessions became longer, and an annual term was established. Throughout the nineteenth century, Congress moved the beginning of each term back in stages to the present opening day on the first Monday in October; the term now runs through to the following June or July. These and other changes in the Court's conduct of its business have been shaped by American society and politics. The Justices' chambers have come to resemble "nine little law firms," and the Court has become a more bureaucratic institution.

When the capital moved to Washington, D.C., in 1800, no courtroom was provided. Between 1801 and 1809, the Justices convened in various rooms in the basement of the Capitol. In 1810, they shared a room in the capitol with the Orphans' Court of the District of Columbia. This room was destroyed when the British burned the Capitol on August 24, 1814, and for two years, the Court met in the Bell Tavern. In 1817 the Court moved back into the Capitol, holding sessions in a small dungeon-like room for two years. In 1819 it returned to its restored courtroom, where it met for almost half a century.

For most of the nineteenth century, the Justices resided in their circuits and stayed in boardinghouses during the Court's terms. Chief Justice Roger Brooke Taney (1836–64) was the first to reside in the Federal City, and as late as the 1880s most Justices did not maintain homes there. Lacking offices and sharing the law library of Congress, the Justices relied on a single clerk to answer correspondence, collect fees, and to locate boardinghouse rooms for them.

Coincident with the 1801 move into the Capitol, John Marshall assumed the Chief Justiceship. During his thirty-four years on the Court, Marshall established regularized procedures and a tradition of collegiality. He saw to it that the Justices roomed in the same boardinghouse and, thereby, turned the disadvantage of transiency into strategic opportunity for achieving unanimity in decision making. After a day of hearing oral arguments, the Justices would dine together, and around 7:00 P.M. they would discuss cases.

After 1860 the Court met upstairs in the old Senate Chamber, between the new chambers of the Senate and those of the House of Representatives. The Justices still had no offices or staff of their own. After the Civil War, however, the caseload steadily grew, the Court's terms lengthened, and the Justices deserted boardinghouses for fashionable hotels along Pennsylvania Avenue. Instead of dining together and discussing cases after dinner, they held conferences on Saturdays and announced decisions on Monday.

By the turn of the century, the Justices resided in the capitol and for the most part worked at home, where each had a library and employed a messenger and a secretary. The Court's collegial procedures had evolved into institutional norms based on majority rule. The Chief Justice assumed a special role in scheduling and presiding over conferences and oral arguments. But the Court's deliberative process was firmly rooted in the Justices' interaction as equals. Each Justice was considered a sovereign in his or her own right, even though the Justices decided cases together and strove for institutional opinions.

After becoming Chief Justice in 1921, William Howard Taft persuaded four Justices to support his lobbying Congress for the construction of a building for the Court. Taft envisioned a marble temple symbolizing the modern Court's prestige and independence. Yet, when the building that houses the Court was completed in 1935, none of the sitting Justices moved in, although sessions and conferences were held there in the later years of the Hughes Court (1930–41). Upon his appointment in 1937, Hugo L. Black was the first to move in, leading the way for President Franklin D. Roosevelt's other appointees. Even when Harlan Fiske Stone was elevated from Associate to Chief Justice, he still worked at home. The Vinson Court (1946–53) was the first to see all nine Justices regularly working in the Supreme Court building.

The marble temple stands for more than a symbol of the modern Court. Once again, the institutional life of the Court changed. As Taft hoped, the building buttressed the Court's prestige and reinforced the basic norms of secrecy, tradition, and collegiality that condition the Court's work. The Justices continued to function independently, but the work of the Court grew more bureaucratic. Along with the rising caseload in the decades following World War II, the number of law clerks more than tripled and the number of other employees dramatically increased as well. The Justices in turn delegated more and incorporated modern office technology and managerial practices into their work. The Warren Court (1953–69) started delivering opinions on any day of open session, and the Burger Court (1969–86) moved conferences back to Fridays.

When Potter Stewart joined the Court in 1958, he expected to find "one law firm with nine partners, if you will, the law clerks being the associates." But Justice John Marshall Harlan told him, "No, you will find here it is like nine firms, sometimes practicing law against one another." Even today, each Justice and his or her staff works in rather secluded chambers with little of the direct daily interaction that occurs in some appellate courts. Nor do recent Justices follow Felix Frankfurter's practice of sending clerks ("Felix's happy hotdogs") scurrying around the building to lobby other clerks and Justices.

A number of factors isolate the Justices, but most important is the caseload. The Justices, in Justice Byron R. White's view, "stay at arm's length" and rely on formal printed communications because the workload discourages them "from going from chamber to chamber to work things out." Each chamber averages about seven: the Justice, three to four law clerks, two secretaries, and a messenger. As managing chambers and supervising paperwork consumes more time, the Justices talk less to each other and read and write more memoranda and opinions. Each chamber now has a photocopying machine and four to five terminals for word processing and legal research.

Law clerks became central to the work of the Court. In 1882 Justice Horace Gray initiated the practice of hiring a "secretary" or law clerk. When Oliver Wendell Holmes Jr. succeeded Gray, he continued the practice, and other Justices gradually followed. By Chief Justice Stone's time it was well established for each Justice to have one clerk. During the chief justiceships of Fred M. Vinson and Earl Warren, the number increased to two. In the 1970s the number grew to three and to four. The number of secretaries likewise increased—initially, in place of adding clerks and, later, to assist the growing number of clerks. A Legal Office, staffed by two attorneys, was created in 1975 to assist with cases in the Court's original jurisdiction and with expedited appeals.

Although the duties and functions of clerks vary with each chamber, all share certain commonly assigned responsibilities. Most notably, Justices have delegated to them the task of initially screening all filings for writs of certiorari. This practice originated with the handling of indigents' petitions by Chief Justice Charles Evans Hughes and his clerks. Unlike the "paid" petitions that are filed in multiple copies, an indigent's petition is typically a handwritten statement. Except when an unpaid petition raised important legal issues or involved a capital case, Hughes neither circulated the petitions to the other Justices nor discussed them at conference. Stone, Vinson, and Warren, however, circulated to the chambers their clerks' memoranda, which summarized the facts and questions presented, and recommended whether the case should be denied, dismissed, or granted a review. But Chief Justice Warren E. Burger refused to have his clerks shoulder the entire burden of screening these petitions. And in 1972 a majority of the Justices began to pool their clerks, dividing up all paid and unpaid filings and having a single clerk's certiorari memo circulate to those Justices participating in what is called the "cert. pool." With more than a hundred filings each week, even those Justices who objected to the "cert. pool" have found it necessary to give their clerks considerable responsibility for screening petitions. Justice John Paul Stevens describes his practice: "[The clerks] examine them all and select a small minority that they believe I should read myself. As a result, I do not even look at the papers in over 80 percent of the cases that are filed."

Law clerks have also assumed responsibility for the preliminary drafting of the Justices' opinions. Chief Justice William H. Rehnquist's practice, for instance, is to have one of his clerks do a first draft, without bothering about style, in about ten days. Before beginning work on an opinion, Rehnquist goes over the conference discussion with the clerk and explains how he thinks "an opinion can be written supporting the result reached by the majority." Once the clerk finishes a draft and Rehnquist works the draft into his own opinion, it circulates three or four times among the other clerks in the chambers before it circulates to the other chambers.

In addition to law clerks, five officers and their staffs also assist the Justices. Central to the Court's work is the Office of the Clerk. For most of the Court's history, the clerk earned no salary, but this changed in 1921 when Taft lobbied for legislation making the clerk a salaried employee. The clerk's office collects filing and admission fees; receives and records all motions, petitions, briefs, and other documents; and circulates those necessary items to each chamber. The clerk also establishes the oral-argument calendar and maintains the order list of cases granted or denied review and final judgments. In 1975 the office acquired a computer system that automatically notifies counsel in over 95 percent of all cases of the disposition of their filings.

There was no official reporter of decisions during the first quarter-century of the Court, and not until 1835 were the Justices' opinions given to the clerk. Early reporters worked at their own expense and for their own profit. In 1922, Congress established the present arrangement (at Chief Justice Taft's request): the reporter's salary is fixed by the Justices and paid by the government, and the Gov-

Less than 3 percent of the more than 5,000 cases on the Court's annual docket are granted and decided by fully written opinion.

ernment Printing Office publishes the *United States Reports*. The reporter has primary responsibility for supervising the publication of the Court's opinions, writing headnotes or syllabi that accompany each opinion, and for making editorial suggestions subject to the Justices' approval.

Order in the courtroom was preserved by U.S. marshals until 1867, when Congress created the Office of Marshal of the Supreme Court. The Marshal not only maintains order in the courtroom and times oral arguments but also oversees building maintenance and serves as business manager for the more than two hundred Court employees, including messengers, carpenters, police and workmen, a nurse, physiotherapist, barber, seamstress, and cafeteria workers.

The Justices acquired their first small library in 1832. It was run by the clerk until the marshal's office took over in 1884. In 1948 Congress created the Office of the Librarian, which employs several research librarians to assist the Justice.

Unlike other members of the Court, the Chief Justice has special administrative duties. Over fifty statutes confer duties ranging from chairing the judicial conference and the Federal Judicial Center to supervising the Administrative Office of the U.S. Courts and serving as chancellor of the Smithsonian Institution. Unlike Taft and Hughes, Stone felt overwhelmed by these duties. His successor, Vinson, appointed a special assistant to deal with administrative matters, whereas Warren delegated such matters to his secretary. By contrast, Burger became preoccupied with administrative matters and pushed for judicial reforms. In historical perspective, he brought Taft's marble temple into the world of modern technology and managerial practices. Burger also lobbied Congress to create a fifth legal officer of the Court, the administrative assistant to the Chief Justice. While also employing an administrative assistant, Chief Justice Rehnquist has less interest in judicial administration, and his assistant is less occupied with liaison work with organizations outside the Court.

The caseload remains the driving force behind the Court's work; its increase has changed the Court's operations. After Taft campaigned for relief for the Court, Congress passed the Judiciary Act of 1925, which enlarged the Court's discretionary jurisdiction and enabled it to deny cases review. Subsequently, on a piecemeal basis, the Court's discretion over its jurisdiction was further expanded, and in 1988, virtually all mandatory appeals were eliminated. As a result, the Court has the power to manage its docket and set its agenda for decision making.

The cornerstone of the modern Court's operation, in Justice John Harlan's words, "is the control it possesses over the amount and character of its business." The overwhelming majority of all cases are denied review; less than 3 percent of the more than 5,000 cases on the Court's annual docket are granted and decided by fully written opinion.

When a petition is filed at the Court, the clerk's staff determines whether it satisfies the rules as to form, length, and fees. After receiving opposing papers from respondents, the clerk circulates to the chambers a list of cases ready for consideration and a set of papers for each case. For much of the Court's history, every Justice reviewed every case, but this practice no longer prevails. Since the creation of the "cert. pool" in 1972, most of the Justices have delegated to their clerks much of this initial screening task. Moreover, the Court has found it necessary to hold its initial conference in the last week of September, before the formal opening of its term. At this conference, the Justices dispose of more than 1,000 cases, discussing less than two hundred. Before the start of the term, the Court has thus disposed of approximately one-fifth of its entire docket, with more than four-fifths of those cases effectively screened out by law clerks and never collectively considered by the Justices.

In conference, attended only by the Justices, the Court decides which cases to accept and discusses the merits of argued cases. During the weeks in which the Court hears oral arguments, conferences are held on Wednesday afternoons to take up the four cases argued on Monday, and then on Fridays to discuss new filings and the eight cases argued on Tuesday and Wednesday. In May and June, when oral arguments are not heard, conferences are held on Thursdays, from 10:00 A.M. to 4:00 P.M., with a forty-five-minute lunch break around 12:30 P.M.

Summoned by a buzzer five minutes before the hour, the Justices meet in their conference room, located directly behind the courtroom itself. Two conference lists circulate to each chamber by noon on the Wednesday before a conference. On the first list are those cases deemed worth discussing; typically, the discuss list includes about fifty cases. Attached is a second list, the "Dead List," containing those cases considered unworthy of discussion. Any Justice may request that a case be discussed, but over 70 percent of the cases on the conference lists are denied review without discussion.

Since the Chief Justice presides over conferences, he has significant opportunities for structuring and influencing the Court's work. Chief Justices, however, vary widely in their skills, style, and ideological orientations. Hughes is widely considered to be the greatest Chief Justice in this century because of his photographic memory and ability to state concisely the relative importance of each case. "Warren was closer to Hughes than any others," in Justice William O. Douglas's view, and "Burger was closer to Vinson. Stone was somewhere in between." Rehnquist, by all accounts, is an effective Chief Justice because he moves conferences along quickly and has the intellectual and temperamental wherewithal to be a leader.

For a case to be heard by the Court, at least four Justices must agree that it warrants consideration. This informal Rule of Four was adopted when the Justices were trying to persuade Congress that important cases would still be decided after the Court was given discretionary control over much of its jurisdiction under the Judiciary Act of 1925. Unanimity in case selection, nevertheless, remains remarkably high because the Justices agree that only a limited number of cases may be taken. "As a rule of thumb," Justice White explains, "the Court should not be expected to produce more than 150 opinions per term in argued cases." The Rule of Four, however, also permits an ideological bloc to grant review in cases it wants to hear and, thus, to influence the Court's agenda.

Immediately after conference, the Chief Justice traditionally had the task of reporting to the clerk which cases were granted review, which were denied review, and which were ready to come down. Burger, however, delegated this task to the junior Justice. The clerk then notifies both sides in a case granted review that they have thirty days to file briefs on merits and supporting documents. Once all briefs (forty copies of each) are submitted, cases are scheduled for oral argument.

The importance of oral argument, Chief Justice Charles Evans Hughes observed, lies in the fact that often "the impression that a judge has at the close of a full oral argument accords with the conviction which controls his final vote." Because the Justices vote in conference within a day or two of hearing arguments, oral arguments come at a crucial time. Still, oral arguments were more prominent in the work of the Court in the nineteenth century. Unlimited time was allowed, until the Court began cutting back on oral argument in 1848, allowing eight hours per case. The time has been reduced periodically, and since 1970, arguments have been limited to thirty minutes per side. The argument calendar permits hearing no more than 180 cases a year. For fourteen weeks each term, from the first Monday in October until the end of April, the Court hears arguments from 10:00 to 12:00 and 1:00 to 3:00 on Monday, Tuesday, and Wednesday about every two weeks.

Justices differ in their preparation for oral arguments. Douglas insisted that "oral arguments win or lose a case," but Chief Justice

Earl Warren claimed that they were "not highly persuasive." Most Justices come prepared with "bench memos" drafted by their law clerks, identifying the central facts, issues, and possible questions. On the bench, they also vary in their style and approach toward questioning attorneys. Justices Sandra Day O'Connor and Antonin Scalia, for example, are aggressive and relentless in the questioning of attorneys, while Justices William J. Brennan and Harry A. Blackmun tend to sit back and listen.

Conference discussions following oral arguments no longer play the role they once did. When the docket was smaller, conferences were integral to the Court's work. Cases were discussed in detail, differences hammered out, and the Justices strove to reach agreement on an institutional opinion for the Court. As the caseload grew, conferences became largely symbolic of past collective deliberations. They currently serve only to discover consensus. "In fact," Justice Scalia points out, "to call our discussion of a case a conference is really something of a misnomer. It's much more a statement of the views of each of the nine Justices."

Most of the time spent in conference is consumed by the Justices deciding which cases should be granted review. Moreover, less time is spent in conference (now about 108 hours) each term. The caseload and conference schedule permits on average only about six minutes for each case on the discuss list and about twenty-nine minutes for those granted full consideration. Perhaps as a result, the Justices agree less often on the opinion announcing the Court's decision and file a greater number of separate opinions. In short, the combination of more cases and less collective deliberation discourages the compromises necessary for institutional opinions and reinforces the tendency of the Justices to function independently.

All votes at conference are tentative until the final opinion comes down. Voting thus presents each Justice with opportunities to negotiate which issues are to be decided and

how they are to be resolved. Before, during, and after conference, Justices may use their votes in strategic ways to influence the outcome of a case. At conference, a Justice may vote with others who appear to constitute a majority, even though the Justice may disagree with their reasoning. The Justice may then suggest changes in draft opinions to try to minimize the damage, from his or her perspective, of the Court's decision.

Because conference votes are tentative, the assignment, drafting, and circulation of opinions is crucial to the Court's work. Opinions justify or explain votes at conference. The opinion of the Court is the most important and most difficult to write because it represents a collective judgment. Writing the Court's opinion, as Justice Holmes put it, requires that a "judge can dance the sword dance; that is he can justify an obvious result without stepping on either blade of opposing fallacies." Because Justices remain free to switch votes and to write separate opinions, concurring in or dissenting from the Court's decision, they continue after conference to compete for influence on the final decision and opinion.

The power of opinion assignment is the Chief Justice's "single most influential function," observed Justice Tom C. Clark, and an exercise in "judicial-political discretion." By tradition, when the Chief Justice votes with the majority, he assigns the Court's opinion. If the Chief Justice is not with the majority, then the senior Associate Justice in the majority either writes the opinion or assigns it to another Justice.

Chief Justices may keep the Court's opinion for themselves, especially when a case is unanimously decided. Since Vinson, however, Chief Justices have generally sought parity in their opinion assignments. Opinions may be assigned to pivotal Justices to ensure or expand the size of the majority joining the opinion for the Court. But the Chief Justice may also take other factors into account, such as a Justice's expertise or what kind of reaction a ruling may engender.

Hughes, for example, was inclined to assign the opinions in "liberal" decisions to "conservative" Justices.

The circulation of draft opinions among the chambers has added to the Supreme Court's workload and changed its deliberative process. The practice of circulating draft opinions began around 1900 and soon became pivotal in the Court's decision-making process, especially with the Justices spending less time in conference discussing and reconciling their differences. Occasionally, proposed changes in a draft opinion will lead to a complete recasting or to having the opinion reassigned to another Justice. To accommodate the views of others, the author of an opinion for the Court must negotiate language and bargain over substance. At times, however, Justices may not feel that a case is worth fighting over; as Justice George Sutherland noted on the back of one of Stone's drafts, "probably bad—but only a small baby. Let it go."

Final published opinions for the Court are the residue of compromises among the Justices. But they also reflect changing norms in the work of the Court. Up until the 1930s, there were few concurring or dissenting opinions. But individual opinions now predominate over opinions for the Court. When the Court's practice in the 1980s is compared with that of forty years ago, there are roughly ten times the number of concurring opinions, four times more dissenting opinions, and seven times the number of separate opinions in which the Justices explain their views and why they concur and dissent from parts of the Court's opinion. Even though the business of the Court is to give institutional opinions, as Justice Stewart observed, "that view has come to be that of a minority of the Justices."

The Justices are more interested in merely the tally of votes at conference than in arriving at a consensus on an institutional decision and opinion. As a result, whereas unanimity remains high on case selection (around 80 percent), unanimous opinions for the Court count for only about 30 percent of the Court's written opinions. The number of cases decided by a bare majority also sharply grew in the 1970s and 1980s, and frequently, no majority could agree on an opinion announcing the Court's rulings.

A Justice writing separate concurring or dissenting opinions carries no burden of massing other Justices. Concurring opinions explain how the Court's decision could have been otherwise rationalized. A concurring opinion surely is defensible when a compromised opinion might be meaningless or impossible to achieve. The cost of concurring opinions is that they add to the workload and may create confusion over the Court's rulings.

A dissenting opinion, in the words of Chief Justice Hughes, appeals "to the brooding spirit of the law, to the intelligence of a future day, when a later decision may possibly correct the error into which the dissenting judge believes the Court to have been betrayed." Even the threat of a dissent may be useful in persuading the majority to narrow its holding or tone down the language of its opinion.

The struggles over the work of the Court (and among the Justices) continue after the writing of opinions and final votes. Opinion days, when the Court announces its decisions, may reveal something of these struggles and mark the beginning of larger political struggles for influence within the country.

Decisions are announced in the courtroom, typically crowded with reporters, attorneys, and spectators. Before 1857, decisions came down on any day of the week, but thereafter they were announced only on Mondays. In 1965 the Court reverted to its earlier practice, and in 1971 the Justices further broke with the tradition of "Decision Mondays." On Mondays, the Court generally releases memorandum orders and admits new attorneys to its bar. In weeks when the Justices hear oral arguments, opinions are announced on Tuesdays and Wednesdays and then on any day of the week during the rest of the term. By tradition, there is no prior announcement of the decisions to be handed down. In 1971 the practice of reading full opinions was abandoned; typically, only the ruling and the line-up of the Justices is stated.

Media coverage of the Court's work has grown since the 1930s, when fewer than a half-dozen reporters covered the Court and shared six small cubicles on the ground floor, just below the courtroom, where they received copies of opinions sent down through pneumatic tube. In 1970 the Court established a Public Information Office, which provides space for a "press room" and makes available all filings and briefs for cases on the docket, as well as the Court's conference lists and final opinions. More than fifty reporters and all major television networks currently cover the Court, although cameras are still not allowed in the courtroom.

When deciding major issues of public law and policy, Justices may consider strategies for winning public acceptance of their rulings. When holding "separate but equal" schools unconstitutional in 1954 in *Brown* v. *Board of Education,* for instance, the Court waited a year before issuing its mandate for "all deliberate speed" in ending school segregation. Some of the Justices sacrificed their preference for a more precise guideline in order to achieve a unanimous ruling, and the Court tolerated lengthy delays in the implementation of *Brown,* in recognition of the likelihood of open defiance.

Although the Justices are less concerned about public opinion than are elected public officials, they are sensitive to the attitudes of their immediate "constituents": the solicitor general, the attorney general and Department of Justice, counsel for federal agencies, states' attorneys general, and the legal profession. These professionals' responses to the Court's rulings help determine the extent of compliance. With such concerns in mind, Chief Justice Warren sought to establish an objective bright-line rule that police could not evade, when holding, in *Miranda* v. *Arizona* (1966), that police must inform criminal suspects of their Fifth Amendment right against self-incrimination and their Sixth Amendment right to counsel, which included the right to consult and have the presence of an attorney during police interrogation. The potential costs of securing compliance may also convince the Justices to limit the scope or application of their decisions.

Compliance with the Court's decisions by lower courts is uneven. They may extend or limit decisions in anticipation of later rulings. Ambiguities created by plurality opinions, or 5–4 decisions invite lower courts to pursue their own policy goals. Differences between the facts on which the Court ruled and the circumstances of a case at hand may be emphasized so as to reach a different conclusion.

Major confrontations between Congress and the Court have occurred a number of times, and Congress has tried to pressure the Court in a variety of ways. The Senate may try to influence the appointment of Supreme Court Justices, and Justices may be impeached. More frequently, Congress has tried to pressure the Court when setting its terms and size and when authorizing appropriations for salaries, law clerks, secretaries, and office technology. Only once, in 1802, when repealing the Judiciary Act of 1801 and abolishing a session for a year, did Congress actually set the Court's term in order to delay and influence a particular decision. The size of the Court is not preordained, and changes generally reflect attempts to control the Court. The Jeffersonian Republicans' quick repeal of the act passed by the Federalists in 1801, reducing the number of Justices, was the first of several attempts to influence the Court. Presidents James Madison, James Monroe, and John Adams all claimed that the country's geographical expansion warranted increasing the number of Justices. Congress, however, refused to do so until the last day of Andrew Jackson's term in 1837. During the Civil War, the number of Justices increased to ten. This was ostensibly due to the creation of a circuit in the West, but it also gave Abraham Lincoln his fourth appointment and a chance to secure a pro-Union majority on the bench. Antagonism toward Andrew Johnson's Reconstruction policies, then, led to a reduction from ten to seven Justices. After General Ulysses S. Grant's election, Congress again authorized nine Justices. In the nineteenth century at least, Congress rather successfully denied presidents additional appointments in order to preserve the Court's policies, and increased the number of Justices so as to change the ideological composition of the Court.

More direct attacks are possible. Under Article III, Congress is authorized "to make exceptions" to the Court's apellate jurisdiction. This has been viewed as a way of denying the Court review of certain kinds of cases. But Congress succeeded only once in affecting the Court's work in this way; an 1868 repeal of jurisdiction over writs of habeas corpus was upheld in *Ex Parte McCardle* (1869).

Court-curbing legislation is not a very viable weapon. Congress has greater success in reversing the Court by constitutional amendment, which three-fourths of the states must ratify. The process is cumbersome, and thousands of amendments to overrule the Court have failed. But four rulings have been overturned by constitutional amendment. *Chisholm* v. *Georgia* (1793), holding that citizens of one state could sue another state in federal courts, was reversed by the Eleventh Amendment, guaranteeing sovereign immunity for states from suits by citizens of other states. The Thirteenth Amendment and Fourteenth Amendment, abolishing slavery and making blacks citizens of the United States, technically overturned *Dred Scott* v. *Sandford* (1857). With the ratification in 1913 of the Sixteenth Amendment, Congress reversed *Pollock* v. *Farmers' Loan and Trust Company* (1895), which had invalidated a federal income tax. In 1970 an amendment to the Voting Rights Act of 1965 lowered the voting age to eighteen years for all elections. Although signing the act into law, President Richard M. Nixon had his attorney general challenge the validity of lowering the voting age in state and local elections. Within six months, in *Oregon* v. *Mitchell* (1970), a bare majority held that Congress had exceeded its power. Less than a year later, the Twenty-Sixth Amendment was rati-

fied, thereby overriding the Court's ruling and extending the franchise to eighteen-year-olds in all elections.

Even more successful are congressional enactments and rewriting of legislation in response to the Court's rulings. Congress, of course, cannot overturn the Court's interpretations of the Constitution by mere legislation. But Congress may enhance or thwart compliance with its rulings. After the landmark ruling in *Gideon* v. *Wainwright* (1963) that indigents have a right to counsel, for instance, Congress provided attorneys for indigents charged with federal offenses. By contrast, in the Crime Control and Safe Streets Act of 1968, Congress permitted federal courts to use evidence obtained from suspects who had not been read their *Miranda* rights if their testimony appeared voluntary based on the "totality of the circumstances" surrounding their interrogation.

Congress may also openly defy the Court's rulings. When holding in *Immigration and Naturalization Service* v. *Chadha* (1983) that Congress may not delegate decision-making authority to federal agencies and still retain the power of vetoing decisions with which it disagrees, the Court invalidated over two hundred provisions for congressional vetoes of administrative actions. Congress largely responded by deleting or substituting joint resolutions for one-House veto provisions. However, in the year following *Chadha*, Congress passed no less than thirty new provisions for legislative vetoes.

Congress indubitably has the power to delay and undercut implementation of the Court's rulings. On major issues of public policy, Congress is likely to prevail or at least temper the impact of the Court's rulings.

The Court has often been the focus of presidential campaigns and power struggles as well. Presidents rarely openly defy particular decisions by the Court, and in major confrontations, they have tended to yield. Still, presidential reluctance to enforce rulings may thwart implementation of the Court's rulings. In the short and long run, presidents may undercut the Court's work by issuing contradictory directives to federal agencies and assigning low priority for enforcement by the Department of Justice. Presidents may also make broad moral appeals in response to the Court's rulings, and those appeals may transcend their limited time in office. The Court put school desegregation and abortion on the national political agenda. Yet John F. Kennedy's appeal for civil rights captivated a generation and encouraged public acceptance of the Court's ruling in *Brown* v. *Board of Education.* Similarly, Ronald Reagan's opposition to abortion focused attention on "traditional family values" and served to legitimate resistance to the Court's decisions.

Presidential influence over the Court in the long run remains contingent on appointments to the Court. Vacancies occur on the average of one every twenty-two months, and there is no guarantee as to how a Justice will vote or whether that vote will prove the key to limiting or reversing past rulings with which a president disagrees. Yet through their appointments, presidents leave their mark on the Court and possibly align it and the country or precipitate later confrontations.

The Supreme Court at work is unlike any other. It has virtually complete discretion to select which cases are reviewed, to control its work load, and to set its own substantive agenda. From the thousands of cases arriving each year, less than two hundred are accepted and decided. The Court thus functions like a superlegislature. But the Justices' chambers also work like nine separate law offices, competing for influence when selecting and deciding those cases. The Justices no longer spend time collectively deliberating cases at conference. Instead, they simply tally votes and then hammer out differences, negotiating and compromising on the language of their opinions during the postconference period when drafts are circulated among the chambers. When the final opinions come down, the Court remains dependent on the cooperation of other political branches and public acceptance for compliance with its rulings. The work of the Court, in Chief Justice Edward D. White's words, "rests solely upon the approval of a free people."

—DAVID M. O'BRIEN

Bibliography

Abraham, Henry J. (1986). *The Judicial Process.* 5th ed. New York: Oxford University Press.

Choper, Jesse (1980). *Judicial Review and the National Democratic Process.* Chicago: University of Chicago Press.

Congressional Quarterly (1989). *Guide to the U.S. Supreme Court.* 2nd ed. Washington, D.C.: Congressional Quarterly Press.

Diamond, Paul (1989). *The Supreme Court & Judicial Choice: The Role of Provisional Judicial Review.* Ann Arbor: University of Michigan Press.

Fisher, Louis (1988). *Constitutional Dialogues.* Princeton, N.J.: Princeton University Press.

Johnson, Charles, and Cannon, Bradley (1984). *Judicial Policies: Implementation and Impact.* Washington, D.C.: Congressional Quarterly Press.

O'Brien, David M. (1990). *Storm Center: The Supreme Court in American Politics.* 2nd ed. New York: W. W. Norton.

Stern, Robert and Gressman, Eugene (1987). *Supreme Court Practice.* 6th ed. Washington, D.C.: Bureau of National Affairs.

SUPREME COURT BAR

The bar of the Supreme Court is not cohesive, and it is not active in any organizational sense. The number of lawyers admitted to practice before the Supreme Court is greatly in excess of the number who actually appear there.

The first rule of the Supreme Court with respect to admissions was adopted on February 5, 1790, three days after the Court opened in New York. The Court then made the provision, which continues to this day, that applicants for admission shall have been admitted "for three years past in the Supreme

Courts of the State to which they respectively belong." The formula also provided, then and throughout the nineteenth century, that the private and professional character of the applicants "shall appear to be fair." As the American language evolved, the word "fair" acquired a dual meaning, and the use of the phrase in oral motions sometimes produced a laugh in the courtroom. So the wording was changed, and for most of the twentieth century the sponsor was required to say that he "vouched" for the applicant. Under the rule as it stands now, he affirms "that the applicant is of good moral and professional character." All motions for admissions were made in open court until about 1970. Now the whole procedure can be done by mail.

Under the first rule for admission, the applicant was required to elect whether he would practice as an attorney (office lawyer) or as a counselor (appearing in court), and he could not practice as both. If this rule had remained in effect (it was eliminated in 1801), the long-established division in England between solicitors and barristers would have been perpetuated in the United States and the bar of the Supreme Court would have been drawn from a much narrower group.

There is no published list of the members of the bar of the Supreme Court. Indeed, no one knows how many members there are. The clerk of the Supreme Court maintains a list of those admitted since October 1925. In early 1990 the number of those who had been admitted was about 185,000. But there is no record of those who have died or retired from active practice (though the list does record 800 names of lawyers who have been disbarred). By an estimate there are now 75,000 lawyers in the United States who have been admitted to practice before the Supreme Court and thus are members of its bar. No more than 300 of these actually present arguments before the Supreme Court in any year, and there are probably fewer than 5,000 living lawyers in the country (out of a total of close to 700,000 lawyers altogether) who have ever made a personal appearance before the Court.

The first member of the bar of the Supreme Court was Elias Boudinot of New Jersey, who was admitted to practice in February 1790. There was, of course, no one to move his admission. No procedure had yet been established for the filing of credentials. After a short interval, the Court turned to the attorney general, Edmund Randolph. Though he was never admitted to practice before the Court, he was treated as an officer of the Court. Before long, the practice was established of admission to the bar on motions of persons already admitted.

During the first ten years of its existence, the Supreme Court heard very few cases. Alexander Hamilton made his sole appearance before the Court in the case of *Hylton* v. *United States* in 1796. John Marshall made his sole appearance before the Court in *Ware* v. *Hylton* (1796). This was the famous British debts case, and Marshall was unsuccessful.

As time passed, and the country developed, the number of cases before the Court steadily increased. Thomas A. Emmet arrived in New York from Ireland in 1804 and was soon established as a leading lawyer. He appeared before the Supreme Court for the first time in 1815. The culmination of his career was his argument in the famous steamboat case of *Gibbons* v. *Ogden* (1824). Another of the early leaders was Littleton W. Tazewell of Virginia, who specialized in criminal law and admiralty. Daniel Webster wrote of him, "He is a correct, fluent, easy & handsome speaker and a learned, ingenuous & *subtle* lawyer"—a standard to which any Supreme Court lawyer might aspire. Others who appeared during the early years of the nineteenth century were Luther Martin, William Pinkney, and Francis Scott Key of Maryland; Roger Griswold of Connecticut; Edmund J. Lee and William Wirt of Virginia; John Quincy Adams, Samuel Dexter, Levi Lincoln, and Rufus G. Amory of Massachusetts; Jared Ingersoll and Horace Binney of Pennsylvania; and Edward Livingston of New York and Louisiana.

Daniel Webster made his first appearance in 1814. Early in his career he argued *Dart-*

mouth College v. Woodward (1818). The decision of the Court in this case, announced in 1819, relied on the obligation of contracts clause in the Constitution to uphold the charter of Dartmouth College against efforts of the legislature of New Hampshire to change it. The argument in *Dartmouth College* lasted for three days and was a great social event in Washington. Webster concluded with an emotional peroration that has become part of American folklore. He is supposed to have said, "It is . . . a small college. And yet *there are those who love it.*" But there is no contemporaneous record of this passage. It first appeared in a eulogy on Webster spoken by Rufus Choate in July 1853, thirty-five years after the argument. Choate's source was a letter written to him in 1852 by Chauncey Goodrich, a professor at Yale University, who attended the March 1818 argument.

Webster (perhaps aided by geography and travel limitations of the times) was for more than thirty years the acknowledged leader of the Supreme Court bar. Indeed, he still holds the record for arguing the most cases before the Court—more than three hundred of them. The second largest total of cases argued was also achieved at this time by a little-known figure, Walter Jones, a District of Columbia lawyer. He appeared in more than two hundred cases before the Court. The next highest total of arguments, and the highest total in the twentieth century, was made by John W. Davis, who was active from about 1910 to 1954. He argued a total of 141 cases. Davis was solicitor general of the United States from 1913 to 1918 and in 1924 was the Democratic presidential candidate. Today no one makes such a high number of arguments unless he is a solicitor general or a member of the staff of the solicitor general's office.

The first black lawyer to be admitted to the bar of the Supreme Court was Dr. John S. Rock, who was born of free parents in New Jersey in 1825. He was admitted on February 1, 1865, just short of his fortieth birthday. Before then, he had been a teacher, a dentist, and a doctor. He had moved to Boston in 1853 and was one of the founders of the Republican party in Massachusetts. In 1858 he wanted to go to France for medical treatment, but he was refused a passport on the ground that he was not a citizen. The Massachusetts legislature then passed a law providing for state passports, and this was accepted in France.

A year or so later, Dr. Rock returned to Boston where he read law. He was admitted to practice in Massachusetts in September 1861 and in the Supreme Court in 1865, shortly after the appointment of Salmon P. Chase as Chief Justice. It is interesting to note that this came before the termination of the Civil War and before the adoption of the Thirteenth, Fourteenth and Fifteenth amendments—and with *Dred Scott* v. *Sandford* (1857) still on the books. As the *New York Times* reported, "By Jupiter the sight was good." Rock's admission was moved by Senator Charles Sumner. The newspaper reporter observed that the "assenting nod" of the Chief Justice "dug . . . the grave to bury the Dred Scott decision."

The next of these significant events was the admission of the first woman to the Supreme Court bar. In *Bradwell* v. *Illinois* (1873) the Supreme Court refused to interfere with the action of the supreme court of Illinois, which denied admission to Myra Bradwell, publisher of a successful legal newspaper in Chicago. Bradwell relied in the Supreme Court on the privileges and immunities clause of the recently adopted Fourteenth Amendment, but persuaded only Chief Justice Chase.

Less than seven years later, however, Belva A. Lockwood became the first woman admitted to practice before the Supreme Court. This was on March 3, 1879. So quick was the change of view that this action evoked no opinion from any member of the Court. Indeed, Myra Bradwell herself, who had been denied admission in 1872, was finally admitted when she applied again in 1892.

Despite this opening of the door, it took fifty years, or until 1929, before the number of women admitted to the bar of the Supreme Court reached a total of one hundred. Some of the early admittees had distinguished careers in the law. These included Florence Allen, who became the first woman judge of a constitutional federal court; Mabel Walker Willebrandt, who was assistant attorney general under President Herbert C. Hoover; and Helen Carloss, who had a long and distinguished career in the Tax Division of the Department of Justice. The great increase in the number of women lawyers, however, has occurred in the past fifteen years. In another fifteen years, if present trends continue, they will constitute perhaps 30 percent of the members of the bar of the Supreme Court.

There have been periods when relatively few lawyers were widely recognized as leaders of the bar practicing before the Supreme Court. There were the orators of the nineteenth century, starting with Daniel Webster and continuing through John G. Johnson of Pennsylvania. There was such a bar in the 1920s and the 1930s, when Charles Evans Hughes, Owen D. Roberts, John W. Davis, George Wharton Pepper, and William D. Mitchell made frequent appearances before the Court. By this time, oratory had become passé. The presentations were less flowery, but they were mellifluous. Davis showed great skill in persuasion, though his record of wins over losses was not especially high, reflecting the fact that the cases in which he was retained were often especially difficult. There is one case that brought together three of these giants. In *United States* v. *George Otis Smith* (1932) the question was whether the Senate could reconsider its confirmation of a presidential nomination after the president had acted on it by making the appointment. The Senate retained Davis as its counsel. Attorney General William D. Mitchell appeared for the United States, essentially representing the president, and George Wharton Pepper represented Smith, the

nominee. That argument was one of the high points of advocacy in this century.

One group has long provided the backbone of the Supreme Court bar: the solicitor general and his staff, and his associates in the Department of Justice. This office has long maintained a high standard and a great tradition. It appears, in one way or another, in nearly half the cases heard on the merits by the Court and in a high percentage of all applications for review.

A considerable number of cases are now brought to the Supreme Court by parties representing particular interests. The National Association for the Advancement of Colored People was first represented by one of the country's great lawyers, Charles H. Houston—work carried on with great ability by Thurgood Marshall. Other similar work has been done by lawyers representing groups interested in the rights of women, in other civil rights, in the environment, and in other causes.

The bar of the Supreme Court can never be assembled, nor is it possible to take a consensus of the bar. It is clear that it plays an important role in the work of the Court. Yet the demands on the Court are such that the bar has difficulty in making its full contribution. In 1935, arguments were heard five days a week for a total of about seventy-five days a year. Now the Court hears arguments on about forty-five days during the year. Fifty years ago, the time made available for oral argument was an hour on each side, and there were frequent substantial allowances of additional time. Now the time allotted is thirty minutes on a side, and additional time is rarely granted. This inevitably presents problems for oral arguments and requires a wholly different type of argument from that customary even fifty years ago. The advocate today can rarely present his case as a case. He has to pick out certain salient points and hope that with questioning by the justices he will still have time to deal with the matters he regards as vital. The printed briefs filed by counsel today appear to be much bet-

ter than they were fifty years ago, probably more greatly improved than is commonly recognized. But oral argument remains a difficult and tantalizing field.

The Supreme Court moved into its new building in 1935. According to newspaper articles, the first words spoken by Chief Justice Hughes in the new courtroom were "Are there any admissions?" Thus was the bar recognized, and thus has it been recognized at every session since.

The bar of the Supreme Court, diverse and divided as it is, plays an important part in the work of the third branch of American constitutional government. Though Alexander Hamilton called the judiciary "the least dangerous branch," its role is central to the effective operation of our federal system. If the work of the Court is central to American government, the efforts of the Supreme Court bar may well be regarded as an essential buttress to the Court.

—ERWIN N. GRISWOLD

Bibliography

Contee, Clarence G. (1976). The Supreme Court Bar's First Black Member. Pages 82–85 in *Supreme Court Historical Society Year Book, 1976.* Washington, D.C.: Supreme Court Historical Society.

Harbaugh, William H. (1973). *Lawyer's Lawyer.* New York: Oxford University Press.

O'Donnell, Alice L. (1977). Women and Other Strangers Before the Bar. Pages 59–62 in *Supreme Court Historical Society Year Book, 1977.* Washington, D.C.: Supreme Court Historical Society.

Warren, Charles ([1908] 1970). *History of the Harvard Law School and of Early Legal Conditions in America.* New York: Da Capo.

———— ([1911] 1980). *A History of the American Bar.* Boston: Longwood.

White, Edward G. (1988). *The Marshall Court and Cultural Change, 1815–34.* New York: Macmillan.

SUPREME COURT PRACTICE

The Supreme Court is the only judicial body created by the Constitution. Article III, Section 1, specifies that "The judicial Power of the United States, shall be vested in one supreme Court, and in such inferior Courts as the Congress may from time to time ordain and establish." The judges of that "one supreme Court," like the judges of the inferior courts created by Congress, are to hold their offices "during good Behaviour" and to suffer no diminution of compensation during their continuance in office. Supreme Court Justices can be impeached, however. And it is not constitutionally clear that their "good Behaviour" term of office is the equivalent of a life term, as generally thought.

In practice, this "one supreme Court" has always acted as a unitary body. That means that the Court never divides into panels or groups of Justices for purposes of resolving matters submitted to the Court. All petitions and briefs are circulated to, and considered by, all participating Justices; and all Court decisions are rendered on behalf of the Court as a unit of nine Justices.

Article III of the Constitution, in establishing the judicial institution known as the Supreme Court, vests in the Court two basic kinds of jurisdiction: original jurisdiction and appellate jurisdiction. The Court's original jurisdiction is its power to decide certain cases and controversies in the first instance. Its appellate jurisdiction is its power to review certain cases and controversies decided in the first instance by lower courts.

In *Cohens* v. *Virginia* (1821), Chief Justice John Marshall stated that the Court "must decide" a case before it that is properly within one of these two areas of jurisdiction, and that the Court has "no more right to decline the exercise of jurisdiction which is given, than to usurp that which is not given . . . [either of which] would be treason to the Con-

PRACTICE

stitution." But in the Court's judicial world, Marshall's proposition is no longer universally true, if it ever was. The modern need to control and limit the voluminous number of cases clamoring for review has forced the Court to resist demands that every facet of the Court's vested jurisdiction be exercised. Limitations of time and human energy simply do not permit the luxury of resolving every dispute that comes before the Court. Notions of judicial prudence and sound discretion, given these limitations, have thus become dominant in the Court's selection of those relatively few cases it feels it can afford to review in a plenary fashion and to resolve the merits. Such factors are evident in the Court's control of both its original docket and its appellate docket.

Section 2 of Article III specifies that the Supreme Court "shall have original jurisdiction" in all cases "affecting Ambassadors, other public Ministers and Consuls, and those in which a State shall be Party." Compared with cases on the appellate docket,

cases on the original docket are quite few in number. Indeed, cases involving ambassadors, ministers, and consuls have never been common and have virtually disappeared from the original docket. The typical original case has thus become that in which a state is the plaintiff or defendant; most frequent are suits between two or more states over boundaries and water rights, suits that cannot appropriately be handled by any other tribunal. States have also sued each other over state financial obligations, use of natural resources, multistate domiciliary and escheat problems, breaches of contracts between states, and various kinds of injuries to the public health and welfare of the complaining state.

States can also invoke the Court's original jurisdiction to sue private nonresident citizens, or aliens, for alleged injuries to the sovereign interests of the complaining state. And a state may bring such suits on behalf of all its citizens to protect the economy and natural resources of the state, as well as the health and welfare of the citizens. The Eleventh

OVERWORKED

An 1885 depiction of the Supreme Court shows the Justices deluged by a pile of cases marked "important," freshly delivered from the lower courts. (Corbis)

Amendment bars an original action against a defendant state brought by a private plaintiff who is a citizen of another state; and the sovereign immunity principle recognized by that Amendment also bars such an action by a citizen of the defendant state. Because that amendment does not apply to the federal sovereign as plaintiff, the United States can bring an original action in the Supreme Court against a defendant state. All cases brought by a state against a private party defendant, however, fall within the nonexclusive category of the Court's original jurisdiction; such suits can alternatively be brought in some other federal or state court. The Court in recent years has sought to reduce its original docket workload by rejecting some nonexclusive causes of action and requiring the parties to proceed in an available alternative forum.

Original cases often involve factual disputes. In processing such cases, the Court considers itself the equivalent of a federal trial court, though with significant differences. The Court's rules and procedures in this respect are not very specific, and practices may vary from case to case. The case starts with a motion for leave to file a complaint, a requirement that permits the Court to consider and resolve jurisdictional and prudential objections. If the Court denies the motion for leave to file, the case terminates. If the motion is granted, the complaint is ordered filed, the defendant files an answer, and in most instances a trial ensues.

The Justices themselves do not conduct trials in original cases. Instead, they appoint a member of the bar or a retired lower court judge to serve as a special master. The special master then takes evidence, hears witnesses, makes fact-findings, and recommends legal conclusions. But all rulings, findings, and conclusions of the special master are subject to review by the Court. That review occurs after parties aggrieved by the special master's actions have filed exceptions thereto; all parties then brief and orally argue the exceptions before the entire Court, which decides the case by written opinion. A complicated case may require more than one hearing before the special master and more than one opinion by the Court, prolonging the case for years.

The Court itself has admitted that it is "ill-equipped for the task of fact-finding and so forced, in original cases, awkwardly to play the role of factfinder without actually presiding over the introduction of evidence." Original cases take away valuable time and attention from the Court's main mission, the exercise of its appellate jurisdiction, where the Court serves as the prime overseer of important matters of federal constitutional and statutory law. The Court is thus increasingly disposed to construe its original jurisdiction narrowly, exercising that jurisdiction only where the parties cannot secure an initial resolution of their controversy in another tribunal. If there is such an alternative proceeding, the Court prefers to remand the parties to the lower court and to deal with any important issues in the case on review of the lower court's determination.

The Court's appellate jurisdiction is also defined and vested by Article III, section 2. That jurisdiction extends to all categories of cases and controversies, decided in the first instance by lower federal courts or state courts, that fall within the judicial power of the United States. Those categories include: cases arising under the Constitution, laws, and treaties of the United States; cases affecting ambassadors, ministers, and consuls; cases of admiralty and maritime jurisdiction; controversies to which the United States is a party; controversies between two or more states; and controversies between a state and citizens of another state, between citizens of different states, between citizens of the same state claiming lands under grants of different states, or between a state or its citizens and foreign states or citizens. The Court's appellate jurisdiction extends "both as to Law and Fact, with such Exceptions, and under such Regulations as the Congress shall make."

The exceptions clause in section 2 contains within it a constitutional enigma, as yet unsolved. The problem is the extent of Congress's power to control and limit the Supreme Court's appellate jurisdiction. The Court has never held that its appellate jurisdiction is coterminous with the section 2 categories of judicial power. Consistently since *Wiscart* v. *Dauchy* (1796) the Court has said, albeit often by way of obiter dictum, that it can exercise appellate jurisdiction only to the extent permitted by acts of Congress, and that a legislative denial of jurisdiction may be implied from a failure by Congress to make an affirmative grant of jurisdiction. The Court, in other words, assumes that its appellate jurisdiction comes from statutes, not directly from section 2 of Article III. The assumption is that Congress cannot add to the constitutional definitions of appellate jurisdiction, but that Congress can subtract from or make exceptions to those definitions.

It is clear that Congress has made broad statutory grants of jurisdiction to the Court, though not to the full extent permitted by section 2. These affirmative grants have always been sufficient to permit the Court to fulfill its essential function of interpreting and applying the Constitution and of insuring the supremacy of federal law. So far, the statutory omissions and limitations have not hobbled the performance of that function.

At the same time, periodic proposals have been made in Congress to use the exceptions clause to legislate certain exclusions from the appellate jurisdiction previously granted by Congress. Such proposals usually spring from displeasure with Court decisions dealing with specific constitutional matters. The proponents would simply excise those areas of appellate jurisdiction that permit the Court to render the objectionable decisions. Many commentators contend that the exceptions clause was not designed to authorize Congress to strip the Court of power to perform its essential function of overseeing the development of constitutional doctrines and guarantees. Objections are also raised that such legislative excisions are mere subterfuges for overruling constitutional rights established by the Court, a most serious infringement of the separation of powers doctrine. Because no jurisdictional excisions of this broad nature have been enacted, the Court has yet to speak to this constitutional conundrum.

Whatever the outer limits of the exceptions clause, Congress since 1789 has vested in the Court broad appellate power to review lower court decisions that fall within the constitutional "case or controversy" categories. Statutes permit the Court to review virtually all decisions of lower federal appellate courts, as well as a limited number of decisions of federal trial courts. And Congress has from the start given the Court jurisdiction to review decisions of the highest state courts that deal with federal constitutional, treaty, or statutory matters.

An ingredient of most jurisdictional statutes are legislative directions as to the mode by which the Court's appellate powers are to be invoked. In modern times, most lower court decisions are made reviewable by way of writ of certiorari or, in a declining number of specialized instances, by way of appeal. Congress permits the Court to issue its own extraordinary writs, such as habeas corpus or mandamus, and to review certain matters not otherwise reviewable on certiorari or appeal; and there is a rarely used authorization for lower federal appellate court certification of difficult questions to be answered by the Supreme Court.

At common law, the term "certiorari" means an original writ commanding lower court judges or officers to certify and transfer the record of the lower court proceedings in a case under review by a higher court. In the Supreme Court lexicon, the common law meaning of the term has been modified and expanded. Certiorari refers generally to the entire process of discretionary review by the Supreme Court of a lower court decision. Such review is sought by filing a petition for writ of certiorari. That document sets forth in short order the reasons why the questions presented by the decision below are so nationally important that the Court should review the case and resolve those questions on the merits. In most cases, the record in the court below is not routinely filed in the Court along with the petition.

Each Justice, after reviewing the petition for certiorari, the brief in opposition, and the opinion below, makes his or her own subjective assessment as to the appropriateness of plenary review by the entire Court. Such review is granted only if at least four Justices vote to grant the petition, a practice known as the Rule of Four. If the petition is granted, a formal order to that effect is entered; copies of the order are sent to the parties and to the court below, which is then requested to transmit a certified copy of the record. But at no time does any writ of certiorari issue from the Court. The parties proceed thereafter to brief and argue orally the questions presented in the petition.

An appeal, on the other hand, refers to a theoretically obligatory type of review by the Supreme Court. That means that once the appeal is properly filed and docketed, the Court must somehow consider and dispose of the case on its merits. There is said to be no discretion to refuse to make such a decision on the merits of the appeal, which serves to distinguish an appeal from a certiorari case.

To invoke the Court's review powers by way of appeal, the aggrieved party first files a short notice of appeal in the lower court and then dockets the appeal in the Supreme Court by filing a document entitled "jurisdictional statement." Apart from the different title, a jurisdictional statement is remarkably like a petition for writ of certiorari. Like a petition, the jurisdictional statement sets forth briefly the reasons why the issues are so substantial, or important, "as to require plenary consideration, with briefs on the merits and oral argument, for their resolution." The Rule of Four is followed in considering whether to

grant plenary consideration of an appeal. Such a grant takes the form of an order to the effect that "probable jurisdiction is noted," although if there remains any question as to whether the case complies with the technical jurisdictional requirements of an appeal, the order is changed to read: "further consideration of the question of jurisdiction is postponed to the hearing of the case on the merits." The appeal then follows the pattern of a certiorari case with respect to obtaining the record from the lower court(s), briefing the questions presented, and arguing orally before the Court.

As if to underscore the similarity between a jurisdictional statement and a petition for writ of certiorari, Congress has directed the Court, in situations where a party has "improvidently" taken an appeal "where the proper mode of review is by petition for certiorari," to consider and act on the jurisdictional statement as if it were a petition for writ of certiorari, and then either granting or denying certiorari. Thus a party cannot be prejudiced by seeking the wrong mode of Supreme Court review.

There is, however, one historical and confusing difference in the Court's summary disposition of certiorari cases and appeals, a difference springing from the notion that the Court is obliged to dispose of all appeals on their merits. When a petition for writ of certiorari is denied, the order denying the petition has no precedential value. It means only that fewer than four Justices, or perhaps none at all, want to hear and decide the merits of the questions presented. That is the end of the case.

But when fewer than four Justices wish to hear an appeal in a plenary manner, the long-held theory is that the Court is still compelled to dispose of the appeal on the merits of the questions presented. To comply with this theory, which is judge-made and not dictated by Congress, the Court has constructed a number of one-line orders, any one of which can be used to dismiss or dispose of the appeal without further briefing or oral argument. A typical order of this nature, used particularly in appeals from state court decisions, reads: "the appeal is dismissed for want of a substantial federal question." Such summary orders, which are devoid of explanation of the insubstantiality of the question involved, consistently have been held to be precedents. The Court has said that they must be understood and followed by state and lower federal courts.

In 1978 all nine Justices publicly conceded to the Congress that, while these summary dispositions of appeals are decisions on the merits, experience has shown that they "often are uncertain guides to the courts bound to follow them and not infrequently create more confusion than clarity." The Justices accordingly asked Congress to eliminate virtually all appeals, thereby recognizing formally that the Court's appellate jurisdiction is almost wholly discretionary. Congress has yet to respond.

At the start in 1789 and for a century thereafter, the Court was authorized to exercise only mandatory jurisdiction, either by way of appeal or a closely related process known as writ of error. But as the nation expanded and matured, litigation proliferated. It became evident toward the end of the nineteenth century that the Court could not keep up with its growing docket if it had to continue resolving the merits of every case that was filed. Gradually, Congress began to withdraw some of this mandatory jurisdiction from the Court, replacing it with discretionary jurisdiction by way of certiorari. But it was not until 1925 that Congress decreed a major shift toward discretionary review powers. At that time the dockets of the Court were so clogged with mandatory appeals and writs of error that litigants had to wait two and three years to have their cases decided. In the Judiciary Act of 1925, written largely at the suggestion of the Court, Congress transferred large segments of appellate jurisdiction from the obligatory to the discretionary category. Fully 80 percent of the Court's docket thereafter was of the certiorari variety.

But the 1925 transfer proved insufficient. During the 1970s Congress eliminated many of the remaining appeals that could be taken from lower federal courts, leaving only a handful within the federal sector of Supreme Court jurisdiction. The largest pocket of mandatory appeals left untouched consists of appeals from state court decisions validating state statutes in the face of federal constitutional challenges. The caseload explosions in the 1970s and 1980s, which saw the Court's annual case filings rising near the 5,000 mark, created pressure to eliminate all significant remnants of mandatory appeal jurisdiction.

Nearly one-half of these filed cases are petitions and applications filed by prisoners, petitions that are often frivolous and thus quickly disposed of. But from the overall pool of some 5,000 cases the Justices select about 150 cases each term for plenary review and resolution. The Justices feel that time limitations do not permit them to dispose of many more than 150 important and complex controversies, although they do manage to dispose of another 200 or so cases in a summary fashion, without briefs or oral arguments. In any event, the number of cases granted full review has hovered around the 150 mark for many of the last fifty years. This constancy is largely the product of the discretion and the docket control inherent in the certiorari jurisdiction. Without discretion to deny review to more than ninety-five percent of the certiorari petitions filed each year, the Court's ability to function efficiently would soon cease.

The procedures by which the Court achieves this docket control and makes this vital selection of cases for plenary review are simple but not well understood by the public. And some of the processes change as workloads increase and issues tend to become more difficult of resolution. As of the 1980s, the procedures could be summarized as follows:

*The Court's effective
performance is due
in no small part to
the procedures and
rules established for
those who practice
before it.*

By law, the Supreme Court begins its annual term, or working session, on the first Monday in October. Known as the October Term, this session officially runs for a full year, eliminating the prior practice of convening special sessions during the summer to hear urgent matters. But for most administrative purposes, each term continues for about nine months, October through June, or until all cases considered ready for disposition have been resolved. At that point, the Court normally recesses without formally adjourning until the following October.

The Court usually disposes of requests for review, hears oral arguments, and issues written opinions only during the nine-month working portion of the term. But the Court never closes for purposes of accepting new cases, as well as briefs and motions in pending cases. That means that filing time requirements are never waived during the summer recess; parties must respect those requirements in all seasons. In most civil cases, certiorari petitions and jurisdictional statements must be filed within ninety days from the entry of judgment, or from the denial of rehearing, in the court below. This filing period is only sixty days in criminal cases, federal or state.

As soon as opposing parties have filed briefs or motions in response to a certiorari petition or jurisdictional statement, these documents are circulated to all nine Justices. These circulations occur on a weekly basis all year round. The circulated cases are then scheduled by the Court's clerk for disposition by the Justices at the next appropriate conference. Cases circulated during the summer recess accumulate for consideration at a lengthy conference held just before the opening of the new October term. Cases circulated during term time are considered at a conference held about two weeks after a given weekly circulation.

The massive numbers of case filings make it impossible for every Justice personally to examine these thousands of documents, although some may try. Most are aided in this task by law clerks, each Justice being entitled to employ four. The clerks often have the task of reading these documents and reducing them to short memoranda for the convenience of their respective Justices. In recent years, a number of Justices have used a "cert. pool" system, whereby law clerk resources in several chambers are pooled to produce memoranda for the joint use of all the participating Justices. But whether a Justice reads all these matters or is assisted by law clerk memoranda, the ultimate discretionary judgments made respecting the grant or denial of review are necessarily those of each Justice. Law clerks simply do not make critical judgments or cast votes.

Law clerks are selected personally by each Justice, a practice dating back to 1882 when Justice Horace Gray first employed a top Harvard Law School graduate. In modern times, clerks are invariably selected from among recent law school graduates with superior academic records. And many Justices require that their clerks also have clerked for lower court judges. The clerks normally stay with their Justices for one term only, though some have served longer. Many law clerks have gone on to distinguished legal careers of their own. Three of them have become Supreme Court Justices: Justices Byron R. White, William H. Rehnquist, and John Paul Stevens.

An important element of each Justice's workload is to act in the capacity of Circuit Justice, a vestigial remnant of the earlier circuit-riding tasks. For this purpose, each Justice is assigned one or more federal judicial circuits, which divide the nation into twelve geographical areas. The Justice assigned to a particular circuit handles a variety of preliminary motions and applications in cases originating in the area covered by the circuit. Included are such matters as applications for stays of lower court judgments pending action on a petition for certiorari, applications in criminal cases for bail or release pending such action, and applications to extend the time for filing certiorari or appeal cases. Law clerks frequently assist in processing these applications, and on occasion an application may be disposed of by a written "in chambers" opinion of the Circuit Justice.

The Court no longer discusses every certiorari petition at conference. The excessive number of petitions makes it necessary and appropriate to curtail collegial discussion of petitions at the formal conferences of the Justices. At present, the Chief Justice circulates a "discuss list," a list of cases in a given weekly circulation deemed worthy of discussion and formal voting at conference. All appeals are discussed at conference, but rarely more than thirty percent of the certiorari cases are listed for discussion. Any Justice may add an omitted case to the list, however. Review is then automatically denied to any unlisted case, without conference consideration.

Decisions whether to grant or deny review of cases on the "discuss list" are reached at one of the periodic secret conferences. During term time, conferences are normally held each Friday during the weeks when oral arguments are heard, and on the Friday just before the commencement of each two-week oral argument period. Conferences can be held on other days as well. Only the Justices are present at these conferences; no law clerks or secretaries are permitted to attend.

Conferences are held in a well-appointed room adjacent to the Chief Justice's chambers, which are to the rear of the courtroom. The conference begins with exchanges of handshakes among the Justices, a custom originating in 1888. Coffee is available from a silver urn. The typical conference begins with discussion and disposition of the "discuss list" cases, appeals being considered first. The Chief Justice leads the discussion of each case, followed by each associate Justice in order of seniority. Any formal voting takes place in reverse order of seniority. Then, if there are argued cases to be decided, a similar order of discussion and voting is followed.

Argued cases, however, may be discussed at other conferences scheduled immediately after a day or two of oral arguments, thus making the Friday conferences less lengthy.

Using the Rule of Four at these conferences, the Court selects from the pool of "discuss list" cases those that it will review and resolve on the merits, following full briefs and oral argument. A few cases, however, may be granted review and then resolved immediately in a summary manner without briefs or oral argument, by way of a per curiam written opinion. Such summary disposition has been much criticized by those who lose their cases without being fully heard, but the practice has been codified in the Court's rules. The important point is that it is the cases that are selected at these conferences for plenary review that account for the 150 or so cases at the core of the Court's workload each term.

The cases thus selected for full review reflect issues that, in the Justices' view, are of national significance. It is not enough that the issues are important to the parties to the case; they must be generally important. But the Court rarely if ever explains why review is denied, or why the issues were not deemed important enough to warrant plenary attention. There are occasional written explanatory dissents from the denial of review, but these can only express the views of a minority. Review is granted only when four or more Justices are subjectively convinced that there are special and important reasons for reviewing the questions presented, which may or may not involve a conflict among lower courts as to how to resolve such questions. It bears emphasis that the exercise of this kind of discretionary judgment enables the Court to control its docket and to limit the extent of its plenary workload.

When a "discuss list" case is granted review, the petitioning party has forty-five days in which to file a brief on the merits, together with a printed record appendix. The opposing party then has thirty days to file a brief on the merits. Briefs of intervening parties and amici curiae, if there are any in a given case, are filed during these periods. When all briefs are in, the case is ready to be scheduled for oral argument.

Oral argument before the Justices occurs only on Monday, Tuesday, and Wednesday of a scheduled week of argument, leaving the other weekdays available for work and conferences. Usually, fourteen weeks of oral argument are scheduled, in two-week segments from October through April. One hour of argument is allowed in most cases, one-half hour for each side. Arguments start promptly at 10 A.M. and end at 3 P.M., with a lunch adjournment from noon to 1 P.M. The Justices are well prepared, having read the briefs. Some may also be aided by "bench memos" prepared by their law clerks, memoranda that outline the critical facts and the opposing arguments. Counsel arguing a case may thus expect sharp and penetrating questions from the bench; and counsel are warned by the Court's rules not to read arguments from a prepared text.

Sometime during the week in which a particular case has been argued, the Court meets in secret conference to decide the merits of that case. With the Chief Justice presiding and leading the discussion, the normal pattern of collegial discussion and voting takes place. But the vote reached at conference is necessarily tentative and subject to change as work begins on opinion writing. Shortly after the vote is taken, the case is assigned to one of the Justices to draft an opinion for the Court. The assignment is made by the senior Justice in the majority, if the vote is split. Normally, the assignment is made by the Chief Justice, unless he is in dissent.

The Justice assigned to write an opinion for the Court then begins work on a draft. This is essentially a lonely task. Following the conference discussion, there is little time for further collegial consultation among the Justices in the preparation of an opinion. Depending upon the work patterns of a particu-

lar Justice, the law clerks may engage in much of the research and analysis that underlie scholarly opinions; some clerks may be assigned the task of producing drafts of an opinion, while some Justices may do all the drafting themselves. Since 1981, drafting of opinions has been mechanically made easier by the installation of word processors in each Justice's chambers.

Once the draft of the majority opinion has been completed, it is circulated to all other members of the Court. The other Justices may suggest various changes or additions to the draft. To become an opinion of the Court, the draft opinion must attract the adherence and agreement of a majority of five Justices, which sometimes requires the author of the draft to accept modifications suggested by another Justice as the price of the latter's adherence. One or more of the Justices who cannot accept the reasoning or the result of the draft opinion then may produce their own drafts of concurring or dissenting opinions. The circulation of these separate opinion drafts may in turn cause the author of the majority draft to make further changes by way of answer to arguments made in a draft concurrence or dissent. Thus nothing is truly final until the collegial exchange of opinions is complete, the votes are set in concrete, and the result is considered ready for public announcement. Even then, there are cases in which the Court cannot reach a majority censensus, resulting in simply an announcement of the judgment of the Court accompanied by a number of plurality, concurring, and dissenting opinions. The difficulty sometimes encountered in reaching a clear-cut majority result, while distressing to the bar and the lower courts, is generally reflective of the difficulty and complexity of some of the momentous issues that reach the Court.

The opinions and judgments of the Court in argued cases are announced publicly in the courtroom. At one time, opinions were uniformly announced on what became known as Opinion Monday. But the Court found that too many opinions announced on a Monday, particularly toward the end of a term, made it difficult for the press to give adequate media coverage to important Court rulings. The Court now announces opinions on any day it sits, thereby spreading out opinion announcements. In weeks in which oral arguments are scheduled for three days, the practice is to announce opinions only on a Tuesday or Wednesday, leaving Monday for the announcement of summary orders. Opinions may still be announced on a Monday, particularly if no oral arguments are scheduled for that day. After all oral arguments have been heard, usually by the end of April, opinions can be announced on any given Monday, when the Court sits to announce summary orders, or on any other day of the week that the Court wishes to sit solely to announce opinions.

The practices regarding the announcement of opinions in open court change from time to time. At one time, many opinions were read by the authors in full or in substantial part. More recently the Justices have tended merely to give short summaries save in the most important cases; in some less important cases only the result is announced. All opinions and orders are made available to the public and the news media a few moments after the courtroom announcements. Eventually, opinions and orders appear in bound volumes known as the United States Reports.

When the Court first convened in February of 1790, one of its first actions was to prescribe qualifications for lawyers wishing to practice before the Court. The original rule, in language very like that of the present rule, established two requirements: the attorney must have been admitted to practice in a state supreme court "for three years past," and the attorney's "private and professional character" must appear to be good.

Nearly 200,000 attorneys have been admitted to the Supreme Court bar since the Court was established. In recent times, as many as 6,000 have been admitted in a year. Prior to 1970, an attorney could be admitted only on motion of a sponsor in open court, before all the Justices. But the Court found that so much time was taken in listening to these routine motions and admissions and that it was often so expensive for a lawyer to travel to Washington from afar just to engage in this briefest of ceremonies, that an alternative "mail-order" procedure should be made available. Most attorneys today are admitted by mail, although some prefer to follow the earlier practice of being admitted in open court.

The modern Supreme Court bar has no formal structure or leadership. It is largely a heterogeneous collection of individual lawyers located in all parts of the nation. Many members of the bar never practice before the Court, and even fewer ever have the opportunity to argue orally. Most private practitioners who do have occasion to argue orally do so on a "once-in-a-lifetime" basis. Those who appear with some regularity before the Court are usually connected with an organization or governmental group specializing in Supreme Court litigation, such as the office of the solicitor general of the United States. Gone are the days when private legal giants, such as Daniel Webster, were repeatedly employed specially by litigants to present oral arguments before the Court.

While a lay litigant may prepare and file petitions and briefs on the litigant's own behalf, without the aid of a member of the bar, the complexities and subtleties of modern practice make such self-help increasingly inadvisable. Only in the rarest of circumstances will the Court permit a lay litigant to present oral argument. Those imprisoned have frequently filed their own petitions for certiorari, seeking some sort of review of their criminal convictions. Indeed, about half of the nearly 5,000 case filings per year can be ascribed to prisoner petitions. The Court catalogues these petitions on its in forma pauperis docket but gives them the same careful treatment it gives petitions filed on behalf of clients who can afford to pay filing and printing costs.

The Court will, on application by an impecunious litigant or prisoner, appoint a member of the Court's bar to prepare briefs on the merits and to present oral arguments, once review has been granted in the case. But the Court will not appoint a lawyer to aid in preparing and filing a petition for certiorari or jurisdictional statement. Legal aid programs operating in most lower courts usually insure that a lawyer appointed or volunteering to represent a prisoner in the lower courts will be available to file such documents in the Supreme Court.

Such are the basic processes and procedures that enable the Court to perform its historic missions. As the Court approaches its third century, the Justices are deeply concerned with the Court's growing workload and the resulting effect upon the quality of its decision making. The Court's internal and external procedures have been streamlined and perfected about as much as possible. Some restructuring of its jurisdiction and functions seems necessary. Yet despite these perceived shortcomings, the Court has managed to maintain its prime role in the evolving history of the American legal system. The Court's effective performance of that role is due in no small part to the procedures and rules established for those who practice before it.

—EUGENE GRESSMAN

Bibliography

Stern, Robert L.; Gressman, Eugene; and Shapiro, Stephen M. (1986). *Supreme Court Practice*. 6th ed. Washington, D.C.: Bureau of National Affairs.

SUPREME COURT'S WORKLOAD

With the growth of population and the enormous expansion of federal law in the post-

New Deal period, the business of the federal courts has mushroomed. This increase is most striking in the first two tiers of the federal judicial pyramid. In the years 1960–83, cases filed in United States District Courts more than tripled, from 80,000 to 280,000, but cases docketed in the United States Courts of Appeals during the same period increased eightfold, from 3,765 to 25,580. To cope with this rise in appeals, Congress more than doubled the number of appellate judgeships. Not surprisingly, a similar growth can be found in Supreme Court filings: decade averages have increased in units of a thousand, from 1,516 per term in the 1950s to 2,639 in the 1960s, to 3,683 in the 1970s, to 4,422 in the 1981 term and 4,806 in the 1988 term.

The contrast between this explosion in federal judicial business and the fixed decisional capacity of the Supreme Court—the nine Justices sitting as a full bench hear an average of 150 argued cases per year—has led to persistent calls for enhancing the appellate capacity of the federal system. A number of proposals have emerged since 1970, none resulting in legislation. In 1971 the Study Commission on the Caseload of the Supreme Court, chaired by Paul A. Freund of the Harvard Law School, recommended creation of a National Court of Appeals (NCA) that would assume the Supreme Court's task of selecting cases for review. The Freund committee believed that the selection process consumed time and energy the Justices might better spend in deliberation and opinion writing. This proposal died at birth. In 1972 Congress created the Commission on Revision of the Federal Court Appellate System, chaired by Senator Roman Hruska. The Hruska commission envisioned a mechanism for national resolution of open intercircuit conflicts, recommending an NCA that would hear cases referred to it by the Supreme Court or the United States Courts of Appeals. This NCA was to be a permanent tribunal, with its own institutional identity and personnel. In 1983 Chief Justice Warren E.

See also

Cases and Controversies

Rule of Four

Burger publicly endorsed proposed legislation to create on an experimental basis an Intercircuit Tribunal of the United State Courts of Appeals (ICT), which would decide cases referred to it by the Supreme Court. The ICT would be comprised of judges drawn from the current courts of appeals who would sit for a specified number of years. This proposal drew faint support.

Other proposals have sought to enhance national appellate capacity without establishing new tribunals. The most recent recommendation of this type can be found in the 1990 report of the Federal Courts Study Committee, chaired by Judge Joseph F. Weis Jr. The report urges Congress to give the Supreme Court authority, for an experimental period, to refer cases presenting unresolved intercircuit conflicts to a randomly selected court of appeals for a ruling by that court's full bench. These en banc determinations would be binding on all other courts, save the Supreme Court.

Many of these proposals are conceived as measures to alleviate the Supreme Court's workload. The work load problem is, however, not one of obligatory jurisdiction; the Court's appellate jurisdiction has been largely discretionary as far back as the Judiciary Act of 1925, but even more so after 1988 legislation repealing virtually all mandatory appeals. The Justices do have to screen all of the petitions filed. It is doubtful, though, that any of the recent proposals promise much relief on this score. The Freund committee's NCA did, but received widespread criticism for suggesting delegation of the selection function. It is hard to believe referral to an NCA or a randomly selected court of appeals would reduce the Court's screening burden, for the losing party would still be free to appeal to the High Court. Moreover, the Justices will not likely tolerate nationally binding resolutions with which they disagree. Indeed, the Court's case selection process may be significantly complicated by adoption of any of these proposals.

If the Court's overload is not a function of its mandatory jurisdiction and if its selection burden cannot be alleviated (under current proposals), what function is the Court failing to perform that it ought to perform?

Critics claim that the Court is unable to ensure uniformity in federal law, because 150 appeals a year must leave unresolved an intolerable number of intercircuit conflicts. The evidence for this contention is largely anecdotal, and what little empirical work exists is sharply contested in the literature. Significant disagreement exists as to what constitutes a "conflict." Are conflicts clear disagreements over a governing issue of law or simply different approaches to a legal issue that are capable ultimately of being reconciled? Much also depends on one's view of the costs and benefits of leaving particular conflicts unresolved for a time. Does the absence of a rule of intercircuit stare decisis in the federal system reflect a deliberate policy of allowing disagreements to percolate? The continuing conflicts may aid the Court's selection process by highlighting legal issues requiring national resolution. Through the process of multicourt consideration, the conflicts may improve the final decision of the Supreme Court when it does intervene. Moreover, some conflicts do not require immediate resolution, because they involve questions of local procedure, or do not frustrate planning concerns of multicircuit actors, or are not capable of being exploited by litigant forum shopping.

A broader claim, one not dependent upon the incidence of intercircuit conflict, is also made: that the problem is fundamentally one of insufficient supervision of the panel rulings of the courts of appeals. That conflicts are appropriately left unresolved does not matter, the argument goes. Given the sheer number of appeals, the practical inability of many of the circuits to engage in en banc review, and the infinitesimal probability of Supreme Court review, the panels operate as a law unto themselves. This version of the

An explosion in federal judicial business and the fixed capacity of the Supreme Court has led to persistent calls for enhancing the appellate capacity of the federal system.

◆ **appellate jurisdiction**
The legitimate authority of a higher court to hear and decide appeals from lower courts.

Swann *set the pattern for school desegregation litigation.*

case for enhancing appellate capacity does have some force. It is undeniable that the Court can no longer engage in the kind of direct oversight of the courts of appeals that was possible in the 1920s, when it reviewed one in ten appellate rulings.

Whether this inability to supervise creates a problem requiring new institutional arrangements is, however, debatable. At present the Supreme Court appears not to have on its docket enough cases warranting plenary review to fill its argument calendar. Moreover, whether the panels operate as such wayward institutions is not clear. Many a circuit has, for example, adopted a "mini" en banc procedure to ensure uniformity of law within the circuit and to promote reconciliation of intercircuit splits. Even if one concedes that the Supreme Court has a workload problem (or that there is a need for additional appellate capacity), will the oversight benefits of an additional layer of review in, say, another 150 cases outweigh the attendant costs? Or will these otherwise nationally binding rulings be irresistible candidates for immediate plenary review by the Supreme Court—and hence a new category of practically mandatory jurisdiction?

The expansion of federal judicial business is the result of an explosion in federal law. Creating new layers of appeals creates more law, but not law enjoying the peculiar finality of a Supreme Court resolution. Improvements can be made. They are more likely to be found, however, in legislation reducing forum choice in federal statutes and imposing sanctions for unwarranted appeals; better management by the courts of appeals of panel disagreements and a greater willingness to reconsider circuit law in light of developments elsewhere; and strategic deployment by the High Court of its scarce decisional resources.

—SAMUEL ESTREICHER

Bibliography

Baker, Thomas E., and McFarland, Douglas D. (1987). The Need for a New National Court. *Harvard Law Review* 100: 1401–1416.

Estreicher, Samuel, and Sexton, John E. (1986). *Redefining the Supreme Court's Role: A Theory of Managing the Federal Judicial Process.* New Haven, Conn.: Yale University Press.

Ginsburg, Ruth Bader, and Huber, Peter W. (1987). The Intercircuit Committee. *Harvard Law Review* 100:1417–1435.

Posner, Richard (1985). *The Federal Courts: Crisis and Reform.* Cambridge, Mass.: Harvard University Press.

Strauss, Peter L. (1987). One Hundred Fifty Cases per Year: Some Implications of the Supreme Court's Limited Resources for Judicial Review of Agency Action. *Columbia Law Review* 87:1093–1136.

SWANN v. CHARLOTTE-MECKLENBURG BOARD OF EDUCATION

402 U.S. 1 (1971)

Three years before *Swann* was decided, the Supreme Court had established a school board's affirmative duty to dismantle a school system that had been racially segregated by the command of law or by the board's deliberate actions. In *Swann*, the Court was asked to apply this standard to a large metropolitan school district including the city of Charlotte, North Carolina, and its surrounding county. President Richard M. Nixon had made two appointments to the Court in the intervening years, and some observers expected the Justices' previous unanimity in school desegregation cases to be shattered in this case. In the event, no such thing happened; a unanimous Court affirmed a sweeping order by the federal district judge, James B. McMillan, calling for districtwide busing of children for the purpose of improving the schools' racial balance.

(After issuing this order, Judge McMillan received death threats and was given police protection.) The *Swann* opinion was signed by Chief Justice Warren E. Burger. However, internal evidence strongly suggests that the opinion was a negotiated patchwork of drafts, and investigative journalists have asserted plausibly that Justice Potter Stewart contributed its main substantive points.

Once a constitutional violation was found, the Court said, the school board had an obligation to take steps to remedy both present de jure segregation and the present effects of past de jure segregation. These steps must achieve "the greatest possible degree of actual desegregation, taking into account the practicalities of the situation." The Court thus approved Judge McMillan's use of districtwide racial percentages as "a starting point" in shaping a remedy and placed on the school board the very difficult burden of showing that the continued existence of one-race schools was not the result of present or past de jure segregation. Finally, the Court approved the busing of children to schools not in their own neighborhoods as one permissible remedy within a court's discretion. The matter of busing, however, was not left to lower court discretion. In a companion case from Mobile, Alabama, *Davis* v. *Board of School Commissioners,* the Court *required* busing the lower courts had not ordered.

Swann set the pattern for school desegregation litigation not only in southern cities but in the North and West as well. Once a court finds deliberate acts of segregation, *Swann*'s affirmative duties arise.

—KENNETH L. KARST

Bibliography

Fiss, Owen M. (1974). School Desegregation: The Uncertain Path of the Law. *Philosophy & Public Affairs* 4:3–39.
Woodward, Bob, and Armstrong, Scott (1979). *The Brethren: Inside the Supreme Court.* Pages 96–112. New York: Simon & Schuster.

SWEATT v. PAINTER

339 U.S. 629 (1950)

MCLAURIN v. OKLAHOMA STATE REGENTS

339 U.S. 637 (1950)

Texas had established a separate law school for blacks; the state university law school thus rejected Sweatt, a black applicant. In *McLaurin,* the state university admitted a black to graduate study in education but made him sit in segregated classroom alcoves and at separate tables in the library and cafeteria. In both cases, state courts upheld the challenged segregation. In *Sweatt* the NAACP recruited some law professors to file a brief amicus curiae urging the Supreme Court to abandon the separate but equal doctrine and hold that state-sponsored segregation was unconstitutional. Eleven states supported the Texas position.

The Court unanimously held the practices of segregation in these cases unconstitutional, but it did not reach the broader issue. Chief Justice Fred M. Vinson wrote both opinions. In *Sweatt* he emphasized the intangibles of legal education: faculty reputation, influential alumni, traditions, prestige, and—most significant for the doctrinal future—a student body including members of a race that would produce an overwhelming majority of the judges, lawyers, witnesses, and jury members Sweatt might face. Assuming the continued vitality of "separate but equal," the new law school for blacks was not equal to the state university law school, and Sweatt must be admitted to the latter.

The *McLaurin* opinion, too, avoided direct attack on the separate-but-equal principle, but it sapped that principle's foundations: segregation impaired McLaurin's ability to study and learn, to discuss questions with other students and be accepted by them on

Texas had established a separate law school for blacks; the state university law school thus rejected Sweatt, a black applicant.

See also

Brown v. *Board of Education*

Segregation

Separate but Equal Doctrine

his merits; thus the state must lift its restrictions on him.

In neither case did the Court discuss segregation's stigmatizing effects. In neither did the Court consider any asserted justifications for segregation. The only question was whether segregation produced significant inequality; affirmative answers to that question ended the Court's inquiries. Taken seriously, these decisions must lead—as they did, four years later—to the conclusion that racial segregation in public education is unconstitutional.

—KENNETH L. KARST

SWIFT & COMPANY v. UNITED STATES

196 U.S. 375 (1905)

Justice Oliver Wendell Holmes's opinion for a unanimous Supreme Court in *Swift* announced the stream of commerce doctrine, fundamental to constitutional commerce clause adjudication ever since.

In 1902 Attorney General Philander C. Knox ordered that an equity complaint be filed against the Beef Trust, the five largest meatpacking concerns in the country. The complaint alleged conspiracy and combination in restraint of interstate trade, suppression of competition, and price-fixing, all in violation of the Sherman Antitrust Act. In 1903 federal district court judge Peter S. Grosscup issued a perpetual injunction against the packers. On appeal to the Supreme Court, the packers, though admitting the truth of the government allegations, contended that they were not involved in interstate commerce. The entire transaction between the packers and those who purchased meat from them had occurred completely within the state where the packers slaughtered and prepared their meat. The sale had been consumated in-state and thus only intrastate commerce was involved. Knox's suc-

"Commerce among the states is not a technical legal conception, but a practical one, drawn from the course of the business."

See also

E. C. Knight Co., United States v.

Stream of Commerce Doctrine

cessor, William H. Moody, asserted that the restraint of trade directly affected interstate commerce even if no interstate acts were involved. Armed with the packers' admissions, Moody stressed the unity of the transactions, arguing that the operation had to be viewed as a whole.

The Court accepted Moody's view. The trust's "effect upon commerce is not accidental, secondary, remote, or merely probable," Holmes declared, as he revised the Court's view of interstate commerce, affecting decisions for decades to come: "Commerce among the states is not a technical legal conception, but a practical one, drawn from the course of the business." Livestock moving from the range to the retailer, "with the only interruption necessary to find a purchaser at the stock yards," created "a current of commerce among the states, and the purchase of cattle is a part and incident of such commerce." Thus a local activity might be seen as part of interstate commerce. This stream of commerce doctrine fundamentally redirected the Court's examination of commerce clause questions and brought the Court face to face with economic reality, modifying the doctrinal effect of *United States* v. *E.C. Knight Company* (1895).

—DAVID GORDON

Bibliography

Gordon, David (1983). *The Beef Trust: Antitrust Law and the Meat Packing Industry, 1902-1922.* Ph.D. diss., Claremont Graduate School.

SYMBOLIC SPEECH

Does communication by conduct rather than by words constitute "speech" within the First Amendment's guarantee of freedom of speech? The status of communicative conduct, as with most free speech questions, is usually presented in an emotion-laden context: Does the burning of a flag, or of a draft card, constitute a First-Amendment-protected activity? Is the act of marching in a public demonstration (as distinguished from the placards which the marchers carry) a form of protected "speech"? Are school or other governmental regulations of hair styles an abridgment of freedom of speech? Does nude dancing constitute a form of First Amendment "speech"? Although the lower federal and state courts frequently have wrestled with all of these questions, the United States Supreme Court has yet to articulate a theoretical base that explains the status of symbolic speech under the First Amendment.

At least since *Stromberg* v. *California* (1931), the Supreme Court has assumed that "speech" within the meaning of the First Amendment's guarantee of "freedom of speech" includes more than merely verbal communications. In *Stromberg* the Court declared invalid a California statute that prohibited the public display of "any flag, badge, banner or device . . . as a sign, symbol or emblem of opposition to organized government." Among other decisions applying the First Amendment to nonverbal conduct, perhaps the most striking was *Tinker* v. *Des Moines Independent Community School District* (1969). The Court there upheld the right of high school students to wear black armbands as a protest against American participation in the Vietnam War, calling their conduct "the type of symbolic act that is within the Free Speech Clause of the First Amendment."

But if conduct sometimes constitutes protected "speech," sometimes it does not. *United States* v. *O'Brien* (1968) affirmed a conviction for draft card burning. Chief Justice Earl Warren, speaking for the Court, answered the defendant's symbolic speech defense by opining, "We cannot accept the view that an apparently limitless variety of conduct can be labeled 'speech' whenever the person engaging in the conduct intends thereby to express an idea."

Any attempt to disentangle "speech" from conduct that is itself communicative will not withstand analysis. The speech element in symbolic speech is entitled to no lesser (and also no greater) degree of protection than that accorded to so-called pure speech. Indeed, in one sense all speech is symbolic. At this moment the reader is observing black markings on paper that curl and point in various directions. We call such markings letters, and in groups they are referred to as words. What is being said in this sentence is meaningful only because the reader recognizes these markings as symbols for particular ideas. The same is true of oral speech which is simply the use of symbolic sounds. Outside the science fiction realm of mind-to-mind telepathic communication, all communications necessarily involve the use of symbols.

But because all expression necessarily requires the use of symbols, it does not necessarily follow as a matter of logic that First Amendment protection is or should be available for all symbolic expressions. The "speech" protected by the First Amendment might be limited to expressions in which the symbols employed consist of conventional words. The Supreme Court has found so restrictive a reading of the First Amendment to be unacceptable. Significantly, in First Amendment cases, the Court often refers to "freedom of expression" as the equivalent of freedom of speech. Justice Oliver Wendell Holmes's "free trade in ideas" may not be reduced to mere trade in words. It is the freedom to express ideas and feelings, not merely the freedom to engage in verbal locutions, that must be protected if the First Amendment's central values are to be realized.

In *Cohen* v. *California* (1971) the Supreme Court held that the emotive form of speech is as entitled to First Amendment protection as is its cognitive content. Emotive expression can be fully as important as intellectual, or cognitive, content in the competition of ideas for acceptance in the marketplace. Of course, most communications encompass both cognitive and emotive content. But even if a communication is substantially devoid of all cognitive content, its emotive content surely

Any attempt to disentangle "speech" from conduct that is itself communicative will not withstand analysis.

S

lies within the First Amendment scope. Symphonic compositions or nonrepresentational art are protected against governmental censorship, notwithstanding their lack of verbal or cognitive content.

The Court recognized this need to safeguard actions with symbolic value, and limited *O'Brien*, in *Texas* v. *Johnson* (1989), where it held flag burning for political protest to be constitutionally protected symbolic speech. As it noted, flag burning with "communicative impact" is "expressive conduct," and may not be made criminal "simply because society finds the idea itself offensive or disagreeable."

Of course, not all conduct should be regarded as "speech" within the meaning of the First Amendment. Not even the most ardent free speech advocate would contend that all legislation regulating human conduct is subject to First Amendment restrictions. If, as the Court stated in the *O'Brien* opinion, the First Amendment is not to apply to a "limitless variety of conduct," what standards should be applied in determining whether given restrictions on conduct constitute First Amendment abridgment of symbolic speech?

If government's purpose in restricting is to suppress the message conveyed by the conduct, then the state should not be heard to deny the actor's claim that the conduct in question was intended to communicate a message. Such a message-restricting motivation by the state should also establish that the conduct in question constitutes symbolic speech. But such a conclusion does not necessarily imply that the speech is entitled to First Amendment protection. Even speech in words may in some circumstances be subordinated to a counter-speech interest. Likewise, no First Amendment absolutism will protect communicative conduct. In some contexts symbolic speech may be overbalanced by counter-speech interests. If, however, the asserted or actual counter-speech interest is simply commitment to a particular view of the world—political, ethical, aesthetic, or otherwise—this interest will not justify abridgment of the right to express a contrary view, either by words or by conduct.

Just as First Amendment principles apply equally to expression in the symbols of the English or French languages, for example, the same principles govern when the symbols are of neither of these languages, nor of any conventional language. The crucial question under the First Amendment is whether meaningful symbols are being employed by one who wishes to communicate to others.

The courts have resisted equating symbolic speech with verbal speech because of a fear of immunizing all manner of conduct from the controls of the law. This fear is unjustifiable; it stems from a false premise as to the First Amendment protection accorded to verbal speech. In fact, speech in words is not immune from regulation. For example, an interest in excluding trespassers will justify abridging the verbal speech of those who wish to speak on property from which they may properly be excluded. Similarly, words that presage an imminent and likely breach of the peace will justify regulation just as much as if the idea be conveyed by nonverbal symbols. These are but two of many instances when verbal speech is subordinated to counter-speech interests.

According full and equal status to symbolic speech under the First Amendment will not open the floodgates to abuses, immunizing *O'Brien*'s "apparently limitless variety of conduct" from legal regulation. Recognition of such equality of forms of expression would mean that no one will be penalized because he chooses to communicate—or is able to communicate—only in a language other than conventional words. We shall all be the richer for such recognition.

—MELVILLE B. NIMMER

Bibliography

Nimmer, Melville B. (1973). The Meaning of Symbolic Speech to the First Amendment. *UCLA Law Review* 21:29-62.

See also

Freedom of Speech

O'Brien, United States v.

Stromberg v. *California*

Tinker v. *Des Moines*
    Independent Community
    School District

T

TAFT, WILLIAM HOWARD

(1857–1930)

William Howard Taft's life was amazing both for length of public service (1881–1930) and for the variety of his activities: prosecuting attorney in his native state of Ohio, superior court judge in Cincinnati, solicitor general of the United States, federal circuit court judge, governor general of the Philippine Islands, cabinet member, president of the United States (1908–12), professor of law at Yale, and Chief Justice of the United States (1921–30).

Taft appeared to be almost the prototype of a Chief Justice. Large of frame and good-natured, weighing well over 350 pounds, he filled out the popular image. His gallantry was famous. "I heard recently," Justice David J. Brewer reported, "that he arose in a street car and gave his seat to three women."

Taft idolized Chief Justice John Marshall. One day, passing by the west entrance to the Capitol, he paused in front of the bronze statue of Marshall. "Would you rather have been Marshall than President?" a friend asked. "Of course," Taft answered, "I would rather have been Marshall than any other American unless it had been Washington, and I am inclined to think I would rather have been Marshall than Washington. He made this country." Taft himself became the only man in history to occupy both the White House and the Supreme Court's center chair.

During Roosevelt's administration Taft rejected two opportunities to join the Supreme Court as associate justice. As successor to Roosevelt in the White House, Taft thought longingly about the future and pined to succeed aging Chief Justice Melville W. Fuller. "If the Chief Justice would only retire," Taft lamented, "how simple everything would become!"

As president Taft signed Associate Justice Edward D. White's commission as Chief Justice, he grieved: "There is nothing I would have liked more than being Chief Justice of the United States. I can't help seeing the irony in the fact that I, who desired that office so much, should now be signing the commission of another man." Rating Supreme Court appointments as among his most important presidential functions, Taft had the opportunity to appoint five associate Justices as well as the Chief—Willis Van Devanter, Horace H. Lurton, Joseph R. Lamar, Charles Evans Hughes, and Mahlon Pitney. Each appointment was a continuing source of pride to Taft, who at every opportunity underscored the importance of the judiciary.

Taft's cordial relations with Roosevelt did not last. Differences developed during Taft's presidency over questions of policy and administration. Finally the clash led to a split in the Republican party. As a result, when Taft ran for reelection in 1912 Roosevelt ran as a Progressive. The upshot was a Democratic victory and the election of Woodrow Wilson as president.

After Justice Lamar died, rumor began to spread that the new president might, rising above party politics, follow the example of his predecessor's high-mindedness when in 1910 Taft had selected as Chief Justice a southern Democrat and Roman Catholic, Associate Justice Edward D. White. But Wilson appointed Louis D. Brandeis instead, and Taft,

Taft appeared to be almost the prototype of a Chief Justice.

outraged by that appointment, declared that Brandeis was "not a fit person to be a member of the Court."

In 1919 Taft was off the public payroll for the first time. Soon he took a position at Yale, teaching constitutional law. Meanwhile, the chief justiceship seemed a remote possibility. Prospects brightened in 1920 with the smashing Republican victory of Warren G. Harding. Shortly after Harding's election the unblushing aspirant made the pilgrimage to Marion, Ohio. Taft was "nearly struck dumb" when the president-elect broached a Supreme Court appointment. Of course, the former president was available, but he made it clear that, having appointed three of the present bench and three others and, having vigorously opposed Brandeis's appointment in 1916, he would accept only the chief justiceship.

Taft's opportunity to achieve his ambition was not altogether accidental. During his presidency, when Chief Justice Fuller died, two choices loomed as possibilities—Charles Evans Hughes and Edward D. White. The latter, seventeen years Hughes's senior, received the nod. Had Taft chosen Hughes, instead of White, his lifelong ambition would not have been realized.

The office of Chief Justice carries scant inherent power. He manages the docket, presents the cases in conference, and guides discussion. When in the majority, he assigns the writing of opinions. In 1921 Taft remarked: "The Chief Justice goes into a monastery." Yet it is difficult to think of a Chief Justice who more frequently violated the American Bar Association's canons of judicial propriety on so many fronts. During the presidency of Calvin Coolidge he was often a White House visitor. His political activities ranged widely over legislation and judicial appointments at all levels. In his choice of judges his alleged purpose was competence. But Taft even opposed selection of the eminent New York judge Benjamin N. Cardozo, fearful lest he "herd with [Oliver Wendell] Holmes and

Brandeis." At the outset, he had kind words for Harlan F. Stone, indeed claimed credit for his appointment to the Court. But when Stone began to join Holmes and Brandeis, the Chief Justice became increasingly critical.

As institutional architect, Taft ranks second only to Oliver Ellsworth, the third Chief Justice, who originally devised the judicial system. Taft's best known extrajudicial achievement, "The Judges' Bill" of 1925, giving the Supreme Court control over its docket, passed with only token opposition. Soon Congress authorized other procedural changes Taft had long advocated. To achieve these reforms Taft lobbied presidents and members of Congress and sought press support. The most striking example of his effectiveness as a lobbyist was his campaign for the marble palace in which the Court now sits. At the cornerstone ceremony, in October 1932, Chief Justice Hughes declared: "For this enterprise progressing to completion we are indebted to the late Chief Justice William Howard Taft more than anyone else. The building is the result of his intelligent persistence."

Taft's goals as Chief Justice were efficiency, prompt dispatch of the Court's business, and harmonious relations among his colleagues. His overwhelming desire was to "mass" the Court. For the ex-president, Brandeis's appointment had been "one of the deepest wounds that I have had as an American and a lover of the constitution and a believer in progressive conservatism." Naturally Taft anticipated strained relations with his new colleague. To smooth this possible difficulty he wrote Brandeis long letters on the desirability of taking prompt steps to make the Court more efficient. Such friendly appeals moved his brother Horace to predict: "I expect to see you and Brandeis hobnobbing together with the utmost good will." Taft's strategy worked. Soon he was able to write: "I've come to like Brandeis very much." The feeling was mutual. Brandeis thought of Taft as "a cultivated man" and enjoyed talking with him. The Chief Justice's brother thought

Brandeis "had been taken into camp." Justice John H. Clarke resigned because he believed that Brandeis could no longer be counted on to uphold the liberal stance.

"Things go happily in the conference room with Taft," Brandeis commented. "The judges go home less tired emotionally and less weary physically than in White's day. When we differ, we agree to differ without any ill feelings." It seems likely that certain of Brandeis's unpublished opinions reflect his high regard for the Chief Justice. In one decision in particular, the second child labor case, *Bailey* v. *Drexel Furniture Co.* (1922), Taft writing for the Court invoked the authority of *Hammer* v. *Dagenhart* (1918), a singularly conservative ruling. Yet, Brandeis went along with the majority, explaining: "I can't always dissent. I sometimes endorse an opinion with which I do not agree. I acquiesce." Brandeis's silence may have been the measure of Taft's gift for leadership.

In Alexander Bickel's volume *The Unpublished Opinions of Mr. Justice Brandeis* (1957), eight out of eleven were prepared during less than ten years of Taft's chief justiceship. Taft went to great pains to create esprit de corps. Seemingly trivial personal considerations—the sending of a salmon to Justice Willis Van Devanter, the customary ride he gave Holmes and Brandeis after the Saturday conference, the Christmas card that always went out to Justice Joseph McKenna—all such thoughtful attention to highly dissimilar human beings contributed immeasurably to judicial teamwork.

Justice Van Devanter posed a unique problem. He was indispensable in conference where Taft was not always acquainted with judicial technicalities or even facts of the cases. But Van Devanter was "opinion shy." This, however, evoked no complaint from the Chief Justice, even if he wrote no opinions at all. Taft regarded him as "the mainstay of the Court" and dubbed him "my Lord Chancellor."

Taft was determined to make the Court's promptness "a model for the courts of the

TAFT, WILLIAM HOWARD

(1857–1930)

UNIQUE DISTINCTION

Taft was the only man in history to serve both as president and as Chief Justice of the Supreme Court. (Corbis/Oscar White)

country." His colleagues, as Holmes said, approved the Chief's "way of conducting business . . . especially his disinclination to put cases over." To accelerate the Court's work, Taft urged cutting vacations from seventeen to twelve weeks and using various time-saving devices.

Taft's first major opinion, *Truax* v. *Corrigan* (1921), involved the constitutionality of an Arizona statute barring state courts from issuing injunctions in labor cases, except under special conditions. Owners of a restaurant sought an injunction against a boycott and picketing of their place of business. A majority of five Justices, concluding that the bar against injunctions denied due process of law and equal protection of the law, declared the act unconstitutional. "A law which operates to make lawful such a wrong as described in the plaintiff's complaint," the Chief Justice observed, "deprives the owner of the business and the premises of his property without due process of law and cannot be held valid under the Fourteenth Amendment. . . . The Constitution was intended, its very purpose was to prevent experimentation with the fundamental rights of the individual."

Taft's next major opinion, *Stafford* v. *Wallace* (1922), upheld broad federal power under the commerce clause, announcing that Congress had a "wide area of discretion, free from judicial second guessing." At issue was the Packers and Stockyard Act of 1929, regulating the business of packers done in interstate commerce. The "chief evil" Congress aimed at was the monopoly of packers, "enabling them unduly and arbitrarily to lower prices to the shipper who sells, and unduly and arbitrarily to increase the price to the consumer who buys." In deciding *Stafford* Taft relied mainly on Holmes's majority opinion in *Swift* v. *United States* (1905). "That case," wrote the Chief Justice, "was a milestone in the interpretation of the Commerce Clause of the Constitution. It recognized the great changes and development in the business of this vast country and drew again the dividing line between interstate and intrastate commerce where the Constitution intended it to be. It refused to permit local incidents of great interstate movements which, taken alone, were intrastate, to characterize the movement as such. The *Swift* case merely fitted the Commerce Clause to the real and practical essence of modern business growth."

Another example of Taft's effort to keep the Court "consistent with itself" was *Adkins* v. *Children's Hospital* (1923) involving an act of Congress fixing the minimum wage for women and minors. Speaking for the Court, Justice Sutherland invalidated the act, relying primarily on Justice Rufus Peckham's reactionary decision in *Lochner* v. *New York* (1905). Refusing to endorse *Lochner,* Taft and Holmes dissented: "It is impossible," the Chief Justice explained, "for me to reconcile the *Bunting* [v. *Oregon*] case of 1917 and the *Lochner* case and I have always supposed that the *Lochner* case was thus overruled *sub silentio.*" Although Sutherland and Taft disagreed in *Adkins,* Taft could not bring himself to endorse Holmes's dissent because of its irreverent treatment of the freedom of contract doctrine. And in *Wolff Packing Co.* v. *Court of Industrial Relations* (1923) Taft for the Court

approvingly cited Sutherland's *Adkins* opinion on that doctrine.

The year 1926 witnessed a significant decision in American constitutional history: the 6–3 ruling in *Myers* v. *United States* upholding the President's power to remove a postmaster without the consent of the Senate. Said Taft: "I never wrote an opinion that I felt to be so important in its effect." The Chief Justice's unqualified appraisal reflects his White House experience. There were three dissenters—Holmes, James C. McReynolds, and Brandeis. Brandeis wrote: "The separation of powers of government did not make each branch completely autonomous. It left each in some measure dependent on the other. . . . The doctrine of separation of powers was adopted by the [Constitutional] Convention of 1787, not to promote efficiency but to preclude the exercise of arbitrary power. The purpose was not to avoid friction, but by means of the inevitable friction incident to the distribution of governmental powers among the departments, to save the people from autocracy."

Taft did not live to see the Court's later qualification of the president's power to remove executive officers. In *Humphrey's Executor* v. *United States* (1935) the president was denied executive power to remove a federal trade commissioner, appointed for seven years with the advice and consent of the Senate, on the score of inefficiency or neglect of duty. Speaking for the Court in that later case, Justice Sutherland, who had enjoyed most cordial relations with Taft, went out of his way to say that the authority of the *Myers* case remained intact. The Court did not adopt the views of the *Myers* dissenters, but shifted emphasis from the "simple logic" of Article II of the Constitution—that the removal power is inherently "executive"—to the theory that a postmaster "is merely one of the units in the executive department and hence inherently subject to the exclusive and illimitable power of removal by the Chief Executive whose subordinate and aide he is."

As Taft's tenure drew to a close, dissents came more frequently and vehemently. Holmes and Brandeis, who had dissented from Taft's first major opinion in *Truax*, dissented from his last major opinion in *Olmstead* v. *United States* (1928). Justice Stone and even Justice Pierce Butler joined the dissenters. Taft, a crusader for stricter enforcement of the criminal law, narrowly construed the Fourth Amendment's ban on unreasonable searches and seizures by ruling that evidence obtained by wiretapping could be introduced at a criminal trial. In the face of hostile criticism of his *Olmstead* opinion, Taft declared privately, "If they think we are going to be frightened in our effort to stand by the law and give the public a chance to punish criminals, they are mistaken, even though we are condemned for lack of high ideals." Taft thought that Holmes's dissent was sentimental in declaring that "it is a lesser evil that some criminals should escape than that the Government should play an ignoble part."

Near the end, Taft winced nervously whenever he contemplated his probable successor. Knowing that President Herbert C. Hoover's attachment to Stone was "very great," Taft feared the worst: "I have no doubt that if I were to retire or die, the President would appoint Stone head of the Court." Once in the Chief Justice's good graces, Stone had fallen into profound disfavor. "He definitely has ranged himself with Brandeis and with Holmes in a good many of our constitutional differences." Nor was Stone's "herding" with the Court's "kickers" his only shortcoming. He was "not a great leader and would have a great deal of trouble in massing the Court." The Chief was not entirely without hope: "With Van and Mac and Sutherland and you and Sanford," he wrote to Justice Butler in 1929, "there will be five to steady the boat. So there would be a great deal of difficulty in working through reversals of present positions, even if I either had to retire or were gathered to my fathers, so that we must not give up at once."

Taft's triumphant march continued to the end, but the future was clouded with uncertainty. By 1929 the world he had known and the people on whom he relied were in eclipse. As the economy slid rapidly toward the abyss, government intervention was openly advocated. To combat these forces, Taft's determination stiffened. "As long as things continue as they are and I am able to answer in my place," he resolved to "stay on the Court in order to prevent the Bolsheviki from getting control." President Hoover, Taft thought, "would put in some rather extreme destroyers of the Constitution. . . ."

None of Taft's predecessors, with the possible exception of Marshall, entertained so expansive a view of the chief justiceship, or used it so effectively on so many fronts. Taft was a great administrator, a great judicial architect, a skillful harmonizer of human relations. Yet he is not commonly considered a great Chief Justice.

—ALPHEUS THOMAS MASON

Bibliography

Mason, Alpheus Thomas (1930). The Labor Decisions of Chief Justice Taft. *University of Pennsylvania Law Review* 78:585–625.

———— (1979). *The Supreme Court from Taft to Burger.* Baton Rouge: Louisiana State University Press.

———— (1964). *William Howard Taft: Chief Justice.* New York: Simon & Schuster.

McHale, Francis (1931). *President and Chief Justice: The Life and Public Services of William Howard Taft.* Philadelphia: Dorrance.

Murphy, W. F. (1962). Chief Justice Taft and the Lower Court Bureaucracy. *Journal of Politics* 24:453–476.

———— (1961). In His Own Image: Mr. Justice Taft and Supreme Court Appointments. *Supreme Court Review* 1961: 159–193.

Pringle, H. F. (1939). *The Life and Times of William Howard Taft.* New York: Farrar & Rinehart.

T

TAFT, WILLIAM HOWARD

(1857–1930)

TAFT COURT

(1921–1930)

William Howard Taft became Chief Justice of the United States on June 30, 1921. Never before or since has any person brought such a range of distinguished experience in public affairs and professional qualifications to the bench. Taft presided over a court that included Justices of highly varied abilities and achievements. In 1921 Oliver Wendell Holmes, already a great figure of the law, had served nineteen years on the Supreme Court. He remained on the Court throughout Taft's tenure and beyond. Holmes's only equal on the Court was Louis D. Brandeis, who had been on the Court barely five years at Taft's accession. Taft, a private citizen in 1916, had vigorously opposed the appointment of Brandeis to the High Court. Although they remained ideological opponents and although some mistrust persisted on both sides, they maintained cordial relations, carrying on their opposition in a highly civil manner.

The rest of the Court that Taft inherited lacked the stature or ability of Holmes and Brandeis. Three Justices, John J. Clarke, Mahlon Pitney, and William R. Day would retire within the first two years of Taft's tenure. Their retirements gave President Warren C. Harding a chance to reconstitute the Court. The president appointed his former Senate colleague George H. Sutherland to one of the vacancies. The other two spots were filled by men strongly recommended by Taft: Pierce Butler and Edward T. Sanford.

The other Justices on the Court in 1921 were Willis Van Devanter, James C. McReynolds, and Joseph McKenna. Van Devanter had been appointed to the bench by Taft when he was president. He, like Butler and Sanford, continued to be strongly influenced by the Chief Justice. During the Taft years, he served the Chief Justice in the performance of many important institutional tasks outside the realm of decision making and opinion writing. For example, Van De-vanter led the drive to revamp the jurisdiction of the Supreme Court in the "Judges' Bill," the Judiciary Act of 1925. McReynolds, a Wilson appointee, was an iconoclastic conservative of well-defined prejudices.

Finally, Taft inherited Joseph McKenna, whose failing health impaired his judicial performance. In 1925 Taft, after consulting the other justices, urged McKenna to retire. McKenna was succeeded by Harlan F. Stone. Though deferential to Taft at the outset, by the end of the decade Stone became increasingly identified with the dissenting positions of Holmes and Brandeis. From early 1923 through Taft's resignation only that one change took place.

Because of the substantial continuity of personnel the Taft Court can be thought of as an institution with a personality and with well-defined positions on most critical issues that came before it. Outcomes were as predictable as they ever can be, and the reasoning, persuasive or not, was consistent.

Taft was a strong Chief Justice. He lobbied powerfully for more federal judges, for a streamlined federal procedure, for reorganization of the federal judiciary, and for greater control by the Supreme Court over the cases it would decide. The most concrete of Taft's reforms was a new building for the Court itself, though the building was not completed until after his death.

A second major institutional change was completed during Taft's term. In 1925 Congress passed the "Judges' Bill." The Supreme Court's agenda is one of the most important factors in determining the evolution of constitutional law. Until 1891 that agenda had been determined largely at the initiative of litigants. In 1891 the Court received authority to review certain classes of cases by the discretionary writ of certiorari. However, many lower court decisions had continued to be reviewable as of right in the Supreme Court even after 1891. The 1925 act altered the balance by establishing the largely discretionary certiorari jurisdiction of the Supreme

Court as it has remained for six decades. The act was one of Taft's major projects. It relieved the docket pressure occasioned by the press of obligatory jurisdiction, and placed agenda control at the very center of constitutional politics.

The successful initiatives of the Court in seizing control of its own constitutional agenda and constructing a new home should not obscure the fact that the Court's institutional position was, as always, under attack during the 1920s. A spate of what were perceived as antilabor decisions in 1921–22 led to calls from the labor movement and congressional progressives to circumscribe the Court's powers. In the 1924 election Robert LaFollette, running as a third-party candidate on the Progressive ticket, called for a constitutional amendment to limit judicial review. Both the Republican incumbent, Calvin Coolidge, and the 1924 Democratic candidate, John W. Davis, defended the Court against LaFollette. The upshot of the unsuccessful LaFollette campaign was a heightened sensitivity to judicial review as an issue and a firm demonstration of the consensus as to its legitimacy and centrality in the American constitutional system.

Much of the labor movement had supported LaFollette's initiatives against judicial review, but labor specifically sought limitations on federal court labor injunctions. Labor's campaign against injunctions peaked in 1927 after the Supreme Court simultaneously declined to review a series of controversial injunctions in the West Virginia coal fields and approved an injunction in *Bedford Cut Stone Company* v. *Journeyman Stonecutters*, holding that a union's nationwide refusal to handle nonunion stone should be enjoined as an agreement in restraint of trade. Between 1928 and 1930 the shape of what was to become the Norris-LaGuardia Act of 1932 emerged in Congress. The impetus behind that law, the politics of it, indeed, the language and theory of the statute itself are rooted in the Taft years.

A description of the Court's institutional role must consider the relations between Congress and the Court in shaping constitutional law and constitutional politics. During the Taft years a dialogue between Court and Congress persisted on a variety of crucial constitutional issues. The decision of the Court striking down the first Child Labor Act in *Hammer* v. *Dagenhart* (1918) led to congressional interest in using the taxing power to circumvent apparent limitations on the direct regulatory authority of Congress under the commerce clause. The second Child Labor Act imposed an excise tax on the profits of firms employing child labor. That act was struck down as unconstitutional in 1922.

From 1922 on Congress had before it various versions of antilynching legislation—most notably the Dyer Bill, which had actually passed the House. Opponents of the antilynching legislation argued that it was an unconstitutional federal usurpation of state functions. In *Moore* v. *Dempsey* (1923), decided shortly after the Dyer Bill had nearly succeeded in passage, the Court held that a state criminal trial dominated by a mob constituted a denial of due process of law, appropriately redressed in a federal habeas corpus proceeding. *Moore* v. *Dempsey* did not establish that an antilynching law would be constitutional. Yet a conclusion that mob domination of a criminal trial did *not* deny due process surely would have been a constitutional nail in the coffin of antilynching laws. And prior to *Moore* v. *Dempsey* the relatively recent precedent of *Frank* v. *Mangum* (1915) had pointed toward just such a conclusion. Considerations concerning the response of Congress regularly influenced the constitutional decision making of the Taft Court. When Taft was appointed, three important labor cases were pending that had been argued but not decided by the White Court. The Court had reached an impasse. Two of the cases presented questions about the use of injunctions to restrain labor picketing.

Section 20 of the Clayton Act appeared to deny the federal courts the power to issue such injunctions subject to certain exceptions, most notably the power to use the injunction to protect property from damage. *American Steel Foundries* v. *Tri-City Labor Council* presented questions of construction of this section, and *Truax* v. *Corrigan*, involving a state law, presented a constitutional variant of the Clayton Act problem.

In *American Steel Foundries*, Taft's first significant opinion as Chief Justice, the Court read section 20 to encompass protection of the property interest in an ongoing business from unreasonable or intimidating picketing or from illegal boycotts or strikes. Statutory construction thus preserved the injunction as a restraint on labor.

But not all state courts saw the issue as the Taft Court did. The Arizona Supreme Court read its statute to bar injunctions in labor disputes, at least where actual destruction of physical property was not threatened. In *Truax* v. *Corrigan*, decided a week after *American Steel Foundries*, Taft wrote for a majority of five, holding that Arizona had unconstitutionally denied employers the injunction in labor disputes. *Truax* in effect created a constitutional *right* to a labor injunction. It did so on two grounds. First, it held that employers were denied the equal protection of the laws insofar as their particular type of property interest was denied the same protection afforded other property interests. Second, it held that the failure to protect the interest in the continued operation of a business deprived the business owner of property without due process of law. *Truax* v. *Corrigan* was the cornerstone of the Taft Court edifice of industrial relations. Not only did the decision suggest that Congress could not constitutionally prevent the federal courts from granting labor injunctions, but it also ushered in a decade of the most intensive use of the labor injunction the country had ever seen. A desperate battle was fought to save the unionized sector of coal from competition from the newer, largely nonunion, southern mines. That union campaign was broken by dozens of labor injunctions upheld by the Fourth Circuit in a consolidated appeal. The Supreme Court's refusal to review those decisions in 1927 attracted larger headlines than all but the most significant of Supreme Court opinions ever get. The Fourth Circuit opinion later cost Circuit Judge John J. H. Parker a seat on the Supreme Court. In fact, however, his conclusion was an all but inevitable consequence of the Supreme Court's position in *Truax* v. *Corrigan*.

The industrial order that the Taft Court sought to protect from labor insurgency was itself built upon uncertain constitutional foundations. The Taft Court was not committed, unambiguously, to a laissez-faire market. The Court distinguished sharply between legislation regulating the price (wage or rent) terms of a contract and laws regulating other terms. Thus, in the best known of its apparent inconsistencies, the Taft Court held void a District of Columbia law prescribing a minimum wage for women, although only a year later it upheld a New York law establishing maximum hours for women. The Court also struck down a state statute regulating fees or commissions for employment brokers while intimating that other reasonable regulatory measures directed at employment brokerage would be upheld.

Sutherland, in his peculiar majority opinion in the minimum wage case—*Adkins* v. *Children's Hospital* (1923)—seemed preoccupied with the redistributive aspects of the minimum wage law. There was nothing wrong with a legislative preference for a living (minimum) wage; the problem lay in imposing an obligation on the employer to pay it. One person's need, he argued, could not, in itself, justify another's obligation to satisfy it. The regulation of nonprice terms need not be redistributive in effect, for the costs of any such regulation could be recaptured by negotiated changes in price. If the Court was seeking to protect bargains against regulation with redistribution effect, then shielding price terms from governmental interference was the most visible and easily understood way to accomplish its purpose.

In general the Taft Court sought to maintain principled distinctions among three forms of economic activity. Government enterprise was subject to the usual constitutional constraints upon government. This form of economic activity was relatively unimportant in the 1920s, although in cases involving municipal utilities the Court had some opportunity to address such issues as contractual rate structure. The Court spoke more frequently to the problem of transition from private to public or from public to private enterprise. World War I had seen government control of the railroads, shipping, coal, and, to a lesser degree, labor relations generally. The Court had to develop principles of compensation to govern the takeover and return of such large-scale enterprises.

More important than the dichotomy between governmental and private economic activity was the distinction drawn between private activity affected with a public interest and the more general run of private economic endeavor. Upon this distinction turned the constitutionality of public regulation—including price regulation in some circumstances—of various forms of economic activity. Although the category of business affected with a public interest had been part of the Court's rhetorical stock in trade for almost half a century when Taft took his seat, it assumed particular significance through the decade beginning with a case from Kansas. In 1920, having survived the effects of a bitter coal strike, Kansas passed its Industrial Court Act, declaring all production and distribution of food, clothing, shelter, and fuel for human consumption or use to be business affected with a public interest. Public transportation and public utilities were also so labeled. The act forbade strikes, lockouts, and plant closings in all such industries except by order of

the Kansas Court of Industrial Relations. Moreover, that court upon its own motion or upon the petition of virtually any person could adjudicate the fitness or adequacy of wages and prices in any such business. The act contemplated a form of compulsory arbitration to replace labor bargaining against a background of strikes and lockouts.

In a series of unanimous opinions the Supreme Court struck down one after another of these innovative aspects of the Kansas act. Taft, in the leading opinion, *Wolff Packing Corporation* v. *Court of Industrial Relations* (1923) held that the state could not, by legislative fiat, declare businesses to be affected with a public interest for purposes so comprehensive as to include supervision of their wage and price structures. Taft's opinion wholly failed to state a principled distinction between those businesses traditionally subject to price regulation (such as grain elevators), on the one hand, and meatpacking, on the other. In obiter dictum he suggested that the competitive structure of the industry was not determinative of the legislature's power to regulate. But the opinion did acknowledge that long-established law permitted regulation of publicly conferred monopolies and of common carriers or inns even if not monopolies.

The Taft Court thus rejected a generalization, based on the war experience, that all basic economic activity could be defined as affected with a public interest. But the Court was not unmindful of the war's lessons. Unanimously it upheld the recapture provisions of the [Railroad] Transportation Act of 1920 despite the overt redistributive effect of the law. The act required the payment into a federal trust fund of half the profits earned by strong railroads, for redistribution to failing ones. The Chief Justice, at least, understood the recapture provisions as justified in part because the alternative to such a scheme might have to be nationalization. Furthermore, the Court had already gone to great lengths to uphold other, seemingly inevitable,

Never before or since has any Chief Justice brought such a range of distinguished experience in public affairs and professional qualifications to the job.

characteristics of rate regulation in an integrated transportation system. The Interstate Commerce Commission (ICC), if it were to be effective at all, needed power to regulate joint rates over hauls using more than one line for a single journey. It was apparent that the apportionment of joint rates could be used to redistributive effect. In the *New England Divisions Case* (1923) the Court had already upheld the ICC's explicit consideration of the need to strengthen the weaker New England lines when it apportioned revenues from joint rates. It was a short step from such use of joint rates to the recapture provisions.

The Court's willingness to accept some qualifications of vested property rights in the interest of planning was not confined to such traditional areas of regulation as transportation and public utilities. The Court decided its first cases challenging general zoning ordinances in the 1920s and, on the whole, upheld the power, though not without significant dissent and important qualifications.

Despite the Court's upholding of zoning and of regulatory initiatives such as the recapture provisions, the Taft Court has long been considered to have been ardent in imposing constitutional limits upon legislation that restricted vested property interests. That reputation is soundly based, although the extent to which the Taft Court differed from predecessor and successor Courts has been substantially exaggerated by Felix Frankfurter and his followers.

Perhaps the best known of the Taft Court pronouncements on the constitutional protection of property is Justice Holmes's opinion for the Court in *Pennsylvania Coal Company* v. *Mahon* (1923). Pennsylvania's Kohler Act required anthracite coal mining to be done so as to avoid subsidence of surface areas at or near buildings, streets, and other structures used by human beings. The Court held unconstitutional the application of the law to mining in an area where the mining company had conveyed surface rights, expressly reserving to itself and to its successors the subsurface mining rights.

Despite Brandeis's dissenting opinion, Holmes's opinion was moderate in tone and antithetical to the sort of dogmatics that characterized Sutherland's opinions in the wage and price regulation area. Indeed, Holmes's methodology was explicitly one that reduced the takings/regulation distinction to a matter of degree—as Holmes himself once recognized in a flippant reference to "the petty larceny of the police power." Moreover, the Court that decided *Pennsylvania Coal* decided the case of *Miller* v. *Schoene* (1928) five years later, upholding a Virginia law providing for the uncompensated (or less than fully compensated) destruction of cedar trees infected with cedar rust, a condition harmful only to neighboring apple trees.

The Court also had to face the implications of the constitutional protection of property in considering the methodology of public utility rate regulation. In a series of cases beginning in 1923 and proceeding throughout the Taft period, Justice Brandeis posed a major challenge to the "fair value" methodology of *Smyth* v. *Ames* (1895). Industry during the 1920s argued that the rate base—the "property" upon which the Constitution guaranteed a reasonable rate of permissible return—should be valued according to the replacement cost of capital items—despite a general inflationary trend, accelerated by World War I. Brandeis formulated a comprehensive critique both of this particular windfall calculation and of the rule that produced it. Brandeis first reformulated the problem in a characteristically daring way. The issue was not so much a vested right to a return on capital as it was the necessity for a level of profit that could attract the new capital required for effective operation of the public utility. Brandeis lost the battle for a new approach to ratemaking. Yet here, no less than in other arenas for disputes over the constitutional protection of property, doctrinal lines had been drawn that anticipated the issues of the New Deal.

Traditional, genteel conservativism is neither overtly ideological in content nor strident in manner. In most respects the Taft Court was traditionally conservative. The Court was hostile to labor and to any insurgency from the left, but the hostility usually took the form of a neutral defense of civil order. That neutrality, though it almost always worked against the left, was not explicitly one-sided and was, in fact, applied occasionally against rightist militant politics and street activity as well.

The constitutional defense of civil order entailed a strong commitment to ratify the acts of local government and of the national political branches so long as their power and authority were used to put down militant politics and especially politics of the street. Thus, the Court consistently upheld criminal syndicalism laws, even while recognizing, in *Gitlow* v. *New York* (1925), that the First Amendment limited state as well as federal legislative power. Moreover, in a theoretically interesting, though practically less significant case, the Court upheld a New York law requiring the registration and disclosure of names of members of certain secret societies—a measure directed against the Ku Klux Klan. Brandeis and Holmes repeatedly dissented in the criminal syndicalism cases, sketching an alternative version of the political process far more hospitable to insurgent initiatives for change.

A second pillar of the defense of civic order was the reliance upon independent courts as guarantors of vested property rights against street politics. To this end the injunction was elevated to a constitutional pedestal. *Truax* v. *Corrigan*, which constitutionalized capital's right to a labor injunction, must be seen not only as a part of a larger antilabor *corpus* but also as the link between that work and the principle of civic order.

For traditional conservatives the injunction had much to commend it. It was in the hands of politically independent judges, who were less susceptible than other officials to mass pressure. It was governed—or supposed to be governed—by neutral principles rather than special interests; it permitted the adaptation of principle to local needs and adjusted the level of intervention to that necessary to shore up appropriately sound local elites. No wonder, then, that the issue of the injunction pervaded the constitutional politics of the 1920s.

If Taft was committed to the courts' playing a dominant role in labor discipline and the guarantee of civic order, he was at the same time committed to an efficient, unintimidated, and uncorrupted judiciary to do the job. In *Tumey* v. *Ohio* (1927) he wrote for a unanimous Court striking down as a denial of due process an Ohio scheme through which a public official judging traffic violations was paid a percentage of the fines collected. Of greater significance was *Moore* v. *Dempsey* (1923), in which a divided Court upheld the power of a federal district court in federal habeas corpus proceedings to go behind the record of a state court murder conviction to determine whether the trial had been dominated by a mob.

Racist justice was a deeply rooted problem, not high on the conservative agenda for reform. Taft was, however, very concerned with the potential for corruption of the courts inherent in the great national experiment of the decade, prohibition. The Chief Justice realized that there were many opportunities for organized crime in the liquor business to buy friendly judges and other officials, especially in states where prohibition was unpopular. The Court refused to extend the protection of the double jeopardy principle to cases of successive prosecutions under state and federal law for substantially the same conduct. Part of the reason for this limit upon the double jeopardy principle was the potential under any contrary rule of insulating conduct from federal prosecution by securing a state conviction and paying a small fine. The Court's interpretation of federalism to tolerate structural redundancy was thus a major prophylactic against the dangers of local corruption of courts.

T

TAFT COURT

(1921–1930)

Like all its predecessors, however conservative, the Taft Court paid lip service to the idea that the people are sovereign and, consequently, that popular government is a pervasive and overriding principle in constitutional interpretation. Even though dissenters within the court (Holmes and Brandeis) and critical commentators without (Frankfurter, Edward S. Corwin, and Thomas Reed Powell) claimed that the Justices ignored the presumption of constitutionality that ought to attach to the work of the popular branches, the simple fact is that no Justice denied, as an abstract principle, either the presumption of constitutionality or the deference that ought to be paid to legislative judgments. It was the application of the principle that divided the Court.

Most of the Justices were skeptical of the capacity of the masses intelligently to exercise the rights and discharge the obligations of participatory, popular government. Taft himself welcomed a leading role for elites in suppressing, or at least damping, the demands of the rabble and in representing the "better class" of citizens. But Taft's views in these matters were not very different from those of Holmes. Holmes doubted the capacity of the masses and considered a dominant role for elites in politics to be almost a natural law. Brandeis, the only real contrast, was considerably more committed to reform and to its promise. But he, in his own way, also distrusted the masses. He saw hope for change in a shift from a propertied oligarchy to a technically trained meritocracy. At the same time Brandeis understood the limits of this vision. His support of states' rights and localism in politics and his hostility to concentration in industry had common roots: the recognition of limits to techniques of effective organization; the affirmation of political principles limiting concentrations of power; and the affirmation of the principles of maximum participation in public affairs. Chiefly in this last respect, Brandeis stood committed to a principle that the other Justices ignored or rejected.

In what ways did the general attitudes of the Justices to popular government affect the work of the Court? Perhaps the most direct effect was visible in the great, perennial debate over the power of judicial review. The Justices appear to have been unanimous in their private opposition to schemes such as that of LaFollette to limit the power of judicial review by statute or constitutional amendment. Even Brandeis, who was personally close to LaFollette and who supported the Wisconsin senator's positions on many substantive issues, opposed initiatives to curb the Court.

In at least one important area the Taft Court initiated a significant reform in the mechanics of popular government itself. The Court struck down the first version of the Texas system of white primaries, which, through official state action, denied blacks the right to vote in statewide primary elections. *Nixon* v. *Herndon* (1927) was the first in a line of cases that ultimately destroyed the white primary device.

The Court upheld the power of Congress to conduct legislative investigations and to use compulsory process to that end. The Court also appeared to uphold an enlarged vision of an exclusive presidential power to remove executive officers. A special constitutional status for government of territories was approved. Finally, the Court struggled mightily but produced no satisfactory or consistent principles in the area of state taxation of commerce and state regulation of commerce.

The 1920s saw a determined attack upon the ethnic pluralism, the cultural and ethical relativism, and the absence of traditional controls that characterized a newly emergent urban America. The prohibition movement, resurgent religious fundamentalism, virulent nativism, and racism gave rise to a reactionary program for legal reform. In the area of prohibition the Court did more than give full effect to a constitutional amendment and its implementing legislation. The Justices also decided a host of criminal procedure issues in such a way as to arm the enforcers against what was perceived as a concerted attack on law and order themselves.

But the Court was actively hostile to groups like the "new" Ku Klux Klan. It not only upheld a Klan registration statute but also, in *Pierce* v. *Society of Sisters* (1925), held invalid an Oregon statute that had effectively outlawed private schools. The law was the product of a popular initiative organized and vigorously supported by the Klan as part of its nativist and anti-Catholic crusade. The decision in *Meyer* v. *Nebraska* (1923) striking down laws forbidding the teaching of German in the schools also reflected the Justices' unwillingness to permit nativist sentiment to cut too deeply into the social fabric.

But the Court did uphold state alien land ownership laws directed principally against Asian immigrants and upheld the disgraceful national discrimination against Asian immigration in the face of constitutional attack. The Court also permitted the continuation of restrictive covenants in housing (*Corrigan* v. *Buckley*, 1926) and segregation in public schools (*Gong Lum* v. *Rice*, 1927), though in each instance it avoided an explicit articulation of constitutional approval for these practices.

The constitutional work of the Taft Court extended over the customary broad area of national life, but it was dominated by the motif of conflict between property and labor. Civil strife, policies toward insurgency, free or regulated markets, confiscation—all were issues that arose principally from the overarching conflict. It is a measure of the Taft Court's achievement that, through Brandeis on the one hand and Taft on the other, a measure of clarity was achieved in articulating the implications of this conflict for constitutional structure and doctrine over a wide range of subjects. It was Taft's vision alone, however, that dominated the Court's action—consistently hostile to labor and its interests. The traditional conservative structure of property and order was one legacy of Taft's Court to the era of the Great Depression; Brandeis's vision—as yet wholly unrealized—was the other.

—ROBERT M. COVER

Bibliography

Bernstein, Irving (1960). *The Lean Years: A History of the American Worker, 1920–1933.* Boston: Houghton Mifflin.

Bickel, Alexander M. (1957). *The Unpublished Opinions of Mr. Justice Brandeis: The Supreme Court at Work.* Cambridge, Mass.: Belknap Press of Harvard University Press.

Danelski, David J. (1964). *A Supreme Court Justice Is Appointed.* New York: Random House.

Frankfurter, Felix, and Greene, Nathan (1930). *The Labor Injunction.* New York: Macmillan.

Mason, Alpheus Thomas (1946). *Brandeis: A Free Man's Life.* New York: Viking.

——— (1956). *Harlan Fiske Stone: Pillar of the Law.* New York: Viking.

TAKAHASHI v. FISH AND GAME COMMISSION

334 U.S. 410 (1948)

Under California law, aliens ineligible for citizenship (mainly Asians) could not hold commercial fishing licenses. Citing the broad power of Congress to regulate aliens, the Supreme Court held, 7–2, that the preemption doctrine barred the law. The Civil Rights Act of 1866 was taken to protect the rights of aliens to pursue their livelihoods under nondiscriminatory state laws. The opinion also conveyed overtones of Fourteenth Amendment reasoning.

—KENNETH L. KARST

——— (1964). *William Howard Taft: Chief Justice.* New York: Simon & Schuster.

Murphy, Walter F. (1964). *Elements of Judicial Strategy.* Chicago: University of Chicago Press.

Pringle, Henry F. (1939). *The Life and Times of William Howard Taft.* New York: Farrar & Rinehart.

Rabban, David M. (1983). The Emergence of Modern First Amendment Doctrine. *University of Chicago Law Review* 50: 1205–1355.

TAKING OF PROPERTY

The authority of government to acquire private property from an involuntary owner (usually called the power of eminent domain) is recognized in the Fifth Amendment to the Constitution, which provides: "nor shall private property be taken for public use, without just compensation." The public use and compensation requirements of the Constitution apply not only to acquisitions by the federal government but—by incorporation in the Fourteenth Amendment—to acquisitions by the states as well. Similar provisions appear in the state constitutions, and the state and federal requirements are usually identically interpreted. It is, however, possible that a taking would pass muster under the federal Constitution and still be held to violate the state constitutional provision (or vice versa).

The requirement of public use has been liberally interpreted by the courts, which rarely find that a taking is not for a public use. For example, property may be taken for resale to private developers in an urban renewal project, or for the development of an industrial park. Indeed, the courts have permitted authority to take private property to be vested by legislation in privately owned public utilities, such as water companies. The test is not ultimate public ownership, or even direct public benefit, but rather the general benefit to the public from projects that are publicly sponsored or encouraged to promote the economy or the public welfare. The only clear limits on the broad interpretation of "public use" would be (1) the grant of the taking authority to a private company simply to improve its private economic position; or (2) the use of the taking power by the government if government itself were simply seeking to make money by engaging in strictly entrepreneurial activities.

The requirement of "just compensation" has been interpreted to mean the amount a willing seller would get from a willing buyer in the absence of the government's desire to acquire the property. The owner is not entitled to receive more for the property simply because the government has an urgent need for it—as for a military base. Neither may the owner receive less compensation because the government's plan for the area—to install a garbage dump, for example, has depressed neighborhood values. Nor is the owner entitled to increased compensation merely because the property has special value to him, such as sentimental or family value, or because he would not sell the property at any price. Compensation must be given in cash immediately upon the taking; government cannot oblige the owner to accept future promises of payment which may be unmarketable, or marketable only at a discount from the just compensation value.

Ordinarily there is no ambiguity about whether a property has been taken. Nor is there any ambiguity about the principle of takings law, stated at the most general level: if the public wants something, it should pay for it and not coerce private owners into contributing their property to the public. If government wants a site for a post office, for example, it is obliged to institute condemnation proceedings in court, leading to an involuntary transfer of title and possession, at which time it will pay the owner just compensation. But in many instances government legislates or behaves in a way that reduces or destroys the value of private property without formally taking title or possession and without instituting condemnation proceedings. If the owner complains, seeking just compensation for a taking, government may reply that it has simply regulated under the police power, but has not "taken" the property and thus need not compensate. The great bulk of all legal controversies over the taking of property turn on the question whether there has been a "taking" at all.

Plainly government sometimes gets the benefits of a taking without any of the formal incidents of ownership. A celebrated case, *Causby* v. *United States* (1946), involved the flight of military planes just above the surface of privately owned farmland adjacent to a military airport. As a result of noise from the overflights the farm was made virtually worthless for agricultural purposes. The farmer claimed that his farm had in practical effect been taken, that government was using it as a sort of extension of the runway, and that government should have to pay for it as it had for the rest of the airport. The Supreme Court agreed that this use of the farmland was a taking in effect, if not in form, and that the farmer was entitled to just compensation for what is called inverse condemnation.

This ruling does not mean that the neighbors of a public airport or highway subjected to noise that reduces their property values will always be compensated. In general such disadvantaged neighbors are not viewed by the courts as having had their property taken in the constitutional sense. The reason is that although a nearly total loss (such as the farmer sustained) is judicially viewed as a taking, some modest diminution of value resulting from neighboring public activities is viewed as one of the disadvantages of modern life that must be accepted by property owners.

The judicial focus on the quantum of loss as a test of a taking is called the diminution of value theory and was put forward many years ago by Justice Oliver Wendell Holmes in *Pennsylvania Coal Co.* v. *Mahon* (1922). There is no clear line, Holmes believed, between the formal taking of property by government (in which title and possession are acquired) and the various forms of government regulation (such as zoning and pollution control), which do not transfer ownership formally, but restrict private owners' uses and values for the benefit of the general public. In both cases, according to Holmes, the traditional rights of private owners are being restricted for the benefit of the public. If there were no legal limits on such restrictions, he said, private property would be worthless and wholly at the mercy of government. On the other hand, Holmes said, if every value-diminishing regulation were viewed as a compensable taking of property, government would be unable to function, for essentially all of its regulatory activities (speed limits, liquor control, safety standards, rent control) disadvantage property owners to some degree.

He thus devised a practical test. We must all accept some impairment of property values so that society can function in a civilized way, and government must be permitted to make regulations requiring such impairments. If, however, the losses from such regulations become extreme—nearing total destruction of the property's value for any owner—then the society should compensate the owner and bear the losses of the regulation commonly. Thus, under the Holmesian theory, the amount of the loss and the ability of the owner to continue to earn some return from his property after the regulation has been imposed become the critical determinants of the constitutional question: has there been a taking for which compensation must be paid?

Although Holmes's test continues to dominate taking cases, there are a number of other theories that are widely found in the literature and in judicial opinions. One theory holds that prohibitions of certain socially undesirable uses do not qualify as compensable takings despite considerable loss to the owners, because one cannot be viewed as having a property right to engage in "noxious" conduct, and losses flowing from prohibition of such conduct is not a taking away of property. The illegalization of manufacture and sale of a dangerous drug, or of polluting activity, has been so categorized.

Another theory sometimes advanced is that certain government restrictions imposed on property owners are not a taking of property from the owners by the government, but are the merely regulation by the government of activities by which it mediates between various private uses in conflict with each other. Under this theory compensation is required only when the government as an enterprise itself benefits directly from the regulation (it gets additional space for its military airport, for example). The enterprise/regulation theory has sometimes been used to justify zoning and other land use controls that restrict the amount or type of building permitted to a landowner on his land. Modern historic preservation ordinances as well as safety and environmental controls are sometimes justified on this theory.

Still another view suggests that government may, without compensation, impose much greater restrictions to prevent future additional exploitation of property, while leaving existing uses, than it may cut back on existing uses. Thus, in *Penn Central Transportation Co. v. New York* (1978), an important case, the Supreme Court upheld a historic preservation ordinance prohibiting the owners of Grand Central Terminal in New York from building a high rise office tower above the railroad station, noting that the existing station did produce some economic return to the owners. The claimed "taking" of a property right to build a bigger building was rejected.

Although no single theory wholly dominates taking law, two guidelines permit safe prediction about the great majority of cases. Courts will find a taking and require just compensation if (1) the government acquires physical possession of the property; or if (2) regulation so reduces the owner's values that virtually no net economic return is left to the proprietor.

—JOSEPH L. SAX

Bibliography

Ackerman, Bruce A. (1977). *Private Property and the Constitution.* New Haven, Conn.: Yale University Press.

Bosselman, Fred; Callies, David; and Banta, John (1973). *The Taking Issue.* Washington, D.C.: Council on Environmental Quality.

Michelman, Frank I. (1967). Property, Utility and Fairness: Comments on the Ethical Foundations of "Just Compensation" Law. *Harvard Law Review* 80:1165–1258.

Sax, Joseph L. (1971). Taking and the Police Power. *Yale Law Journal* 74:36–76.

——— (1971). Takings, Private Property and Public Rights. *Yale Law Journal* 81:149–186.

TAKING OF PROPERTY

(Update)

Recent historical scholarship indicates that the taking clause was something of an innovation. Only two of the state constitutions adopted between 1776 and 1780 required the government to pay compensation when private property was taken for a public use. The lack of constitutional protection for property rights was consistent with the republican ethos of the period. Benjamin Franklin, for example, once said that "Private Property . . . is a Creature of Society, and is subject to the Calls of that Society, whenever its Necessities shall require it, even to its last Farthing; its contributions therefore to the public Exigencies are . . . to be considered . . . the Return of an obligation previously received, or the Payment of a just Debt." The taking clause seems to represent a victory of Lockean liberalism over this earlier republican philosophy.

The Supreme Court has recently used the taking clause to strike down a variety of government regulations. In one case, the federal government claimed that the public had the right to use a marina that a private developer had connected with a public waterway. The Court held that giving the public access to the marina would be an unconstitutional taking of the developer's property. In another case, Congress was concerned because certain lands belonging to American Indians had so many owners that managing the lands had become impractical. As a way of consolidating landholdings, a federal statute mandated that some of the tiniest interests would revert to the tribe on the owners' deaths. This, too, was an unconstitutional taking. The Court also found a taking when New York required landlords to give their tenants access to cable television. The reason was that the cable box would "take" some of the space on the building's roof.

A 1987 case, *Nollan* v. *California Coastal Commission,* exemplifies the Court's revived interest in protecting property rights. The case involved a couple who wanted to build a larger beach house. As a condition for receiving a permit, the California Coastal Commission required them to allow the public to walk along the beach. The majority opinion was written by Justice Antonin Scalia, who had quickly emerged as the strongest guardian of property rights on the Rehnquist Court. Scalia was willing to concede, at least for the purposes of argument, that California could have banned the construction entirely as a means of preserving the public's right to see the ocean from the street. Alternatively, he conceded, the Nollans could have been required to allow the public to walk from the street around to the back of their house. But because the government had chosen to give the public direct access laterally along the beach, rather than from the street, Justice Scalia held the permit condition unconstitutional.

The Court's rationale in *Nollan* was that lateral access was not closely enough related to the government's right to protect the view of the ocean. Justice Scalia seemed suspicious of the government's motives in imposing the permit condition, at one point referring to similar permit conditions as a form of "extortion."

In contrast to *Nollan,* another 1987 case rather surprisingly failed to find a taking. *Keystone Bituminous Coal Association* v. *DeBenedictus* was a replay of *Pennsylvania Coal Co.* v. *Mahon* (1922), the classic decision of Justice Oliver Wendell Holmes Jr. Holmes had struck down a Pennsylvania statute that required underground coal mines to maintain adequate support for surface structures. The *DeBenedictus* Court, however, found a similar but more recently enacted Pennsylvania

statute to be constitutional. The Court distinguished *Mahon* on the ground that the newer statute had a broader public purpose. No taking was found, because the statute required mining companies to leave only a small fraction of their coal in the ground.

More recently, in a series of decisions the Court has thrown the takings concept into high gear. In *Lucas* v. *South Carolina Coastal Council* (1992) it held that a law depriving a landowner of all reasonable investment-based expectations is a compensable taking even though enacted to avoid flood and storm damage. The Court held the fact that a regulatory statute was designed to avoid harm to the community did not excuse what would otherwise be a taking, unless the state could have prevented the harm anyway through the law of public nuisance or similar common-law principles.

Later, in *Dolan* v. *City of Tigard* (1994), the Court annulled a condition of a permit to expand a store requiring the owner to dedicate a public pathway across her property. Though the city claimed the path was needed to prevent the owner from building in an area subject to flooding, the Court held that the city's requirement was not "roughly proportional" to its goal of flood control.

Most recently, in two decisions the Court has shown some willingness to extend the taking concept to control over personal property as well. In *Eastern Enterprises* v. *Apfel* (1998) four Justices viewed a federal statute requiring former coal mine operators to fund health benefits for their retired employees to be a taking, because of the law's retroactive effect. Justice Anthony M. Kennedy, concurring, rejected the taking claim but considered the law a deprivation of property without due process. And in *Phillips* v. *Washington Legal Foundation* (1998) a narrow majority ruled that the interest earned on money held by lawyers in short-term accounts payable to their clients is property within the meaning of the takings clause. Under the challenged Texas law the interest goes to the state to fund legal services for needy persons. Texas vainly argued that prior to this statute the interest was not payable to the client at all, since the bank charges exceeded the interest. The Court stopped short of finding that the interest had been unconstitutionally taken, and sent the case back to the lower court to decide that question. These cases plainly evince an increased willingness to use the law of taking to strike down legislation limiting the use of property in a variety of contexts, much as earlier courts used a now properly rejected view of the due process clause in the era of *Lochner* v. *New York* (1905).

It is often difficult to predict whether a given government regulation will be found to be a taking, but two factors seem particularly significant. First, if the regulation takes away the owner's right to control physical access to the property, it is much more likely to be found a taking—and almost sure to be found a taking if there is a permanent physical occupation of the property. Second, unless physical access is involved, the owner probably will not be able to claim a taking unless the regulation virtually destroys the value of the property.

At present, the use of the takings doctrine is expanding. Under Chief Justices Harlan F. Stone and Earl Warren, the Court took little interest in the taking clause. The Burger Court began to take a renewed interest in the area, but did not aggressively use the taking clause as a means of attacking important government regulations. The Rehnquist Court has clearly introduced a greater degree of activism.

Most of the current scholarship on the taking clause may be divided into three camps. One group argues for minimal judicial scrutiny of economic regulations, so that very few government actions would be held a taking. In contrast, a second group argues for vigorous scrutiny under the auspices of the taking clause—reminiscent of the *Lochner* era. A third group argues for renewed judicial protection, but limited to a particular category of property, that of peculiar personal significance to individuals, as opposed to ordinary business interests. The second of these groups of scholars seems to be currently succeeding in influencing a narrow majority of the Justices.

—DANIEL A. FARBER

Bibliography

Epstein, Richard A. (1985). *Takings: Private Property and the Power of Eminent Domain.* Cambridge, Mass.: Harvard University Press.

Levy, Leonard W. (1988). Property as a Human Right. *Constitutional Commentary* 5:169–184.

Note (1985). The Origins and Original Significance of the Just Compensation Clause of the Fifth Amendment. *Yale Law Journal* 94:694–716.

TANEY, ROGER BROOKE

(1777–1864)

Roger B. Taney, Chief Justice of the United States from 1836 until his death in 1864, profoundly shaped American constitutional development in cases dealing with states' regulatory powers, corporations, slavery, and the jurisdiction of federal courts. His reputation long suffered from invidious and inappropriate comparisons with his predecessor Chief Justice John Marshall and because of his disastrous opinion in *Dred Scott* v. *Sandford* (1857). But his influence has been enduring and, on balance, beneficial.

Taney was born in 1777 in Calvert County, Maryland. His father, a well-to-do planter, destined him for a career in law. After graduation from Dickinson College (Pennsylvania), he was admitted to the bar in 1799 and began a thirty-six-year career of politics and law practice in Maryland. He served intermittently in both houses of the state legislature until 1821, at first as a Federalist. But finding that affiliation intolerable because of the conduct of New England Federalists during the War of 1812, he assumed leadership of a local faction known as Coodies and then after 1825 supported Andrew

Jackson. Practicing first in Frederick, where he maintained his lifelong residence, and then in Baltimore, he became a preeminent member of the Maryland bar, state attorney general from 1827 to 1831, and then attorney general of the United States, a position he held until 1833, when he served for a year as secretary of the treasury.

Taney urged President Jackson to veto the bill to recharter the Bank of the United States and contributed that part of Jackson's veto of the Bank Bill in which the president denied that the Supreme Court's opinion on constitutional matters bound the president. As treasury secretary, Taney ordered removal of the federal deposits from the Bank and their distribution to certain "pet banks." In these bank matters, Taney was not the mere pliant tool of Jackson; rather, he acted in accord with his own deep suspicions of centralized and monopolistic economic power.

As attorney general, Taney also had occasion to explore issues involving slavery and free blacks. Upholding South Carolina's Negro Seamen's Act, which prohibited black seamen from disembarking from their vessels while in Carolina waters, Taney insisted that the state's sovereign right to control slaves and free blacks overrode any inconsistent exercise of federal treaty and commerce powers. Presaging his *Dred Scott* opinion, he maintained that blacks were "a separate and degraded people," incapable of being citizens. He also expressed doubt that a Supreme Court decision holding the statute unconstitutional would bind the states.

As Chief Justice of the United States after 1836, Taney left an enduring imprint on the American Constitution. Most of the landmark cases coming before the Court in the first decade of his tenure involved questions of the power of the states to regulate the economic behavior of persons or corporations within their jurisdictions. In *Charles River Bridge* v. *Warren Bridge* (1837) Taney employed a paradigmatic balance between investors' demands for autonomy and the states' insistence on public control of that

new legal creature, the private corporation. Refusing to read into a bridge company's charter an implicit grant of a transportation monopoly, Taney held that "in charters, . . . no rights are taken from the public, or given to the corporation, beyond those which the words of the charter, by their natural and proper construction, purport to convey."

Subsequent decisions of the Taney Court confirmed the *Charles River Bridge* doctrine: where the state had explicitly conveyed monopoly rights or otherwise conferred valuable privileges, a majority of the Court honored the grant and held the state to it under contract clause doctrines deriving from *Fletcher* v. *Peck* (1810). On the other hand, the Court refused to infer monopoly grants or other restrictions on state regulatory power if they were not explicitly conferred in a corporate charter. Thus in *Bank of Augusta* v. *Earle* (1839) Taney held that states could regulate the activities of foreign corporations within their jurisdictions, or exclude them altogether, but that such regulations would have to be explicit. Absent express declarations of state policy, the Taney Court refused to hold that banking corporations could not enter into contracts outside the state that chartered them.

Yet Taney entertained an instinctive sympathy for states' efforts to control economic activity within their jurisdictions. In another case from his maiden term, *Briscoe* v. *Bank of Kentucky* (1837), Taney supported the majority's holding that a state was not precluded from creating a bank wholly owned by it and exercising note-issuing powers, so long as the state did not pledge its credit to back the notes. Such notes would have been a subterfuge form of the state bills of credit that had been struck down in *Craig* v. *Missouri* (1830). In *Bronson* v. *Kinzie* (1843), however, Taney invalidated state statutes that restricted foreclosure sales and granted mortgagors rights to redeem foreclosed property. Even here, however, he emphasized that states could modify contractual remedies so long as they did not tamper with the substance of existing contracts.

T

TANEY, ROGER
BROOKE

(1777–1864)

Taney is second only to Marshall in the constitutional history of our country, yet no other Justices have so gravely damaged the federal system because of sectional bias.

Taney's opinions dealing with the jurisdiction of federal courts proved to be among his most significant. Some of these restricted the autonomy of the states in the interests of protecting the national market. Thus in *Swift* v. *Tyson* (1842) the Court unanimously supported an opinion by Justice Joseph Story holding that in commercial law matters, federal courts need not look to the forum state's common law for rules of decision, but instead might formulate commercial law doctrines out of "the general principles and doctrines of commercial jurisprudence," a principle that survived until *Swift* was overruled in *Erie Railroad* v. *Tompkins* (1938). In *Propeller Genesee Chief* v. *FitzHugh* (1851), Taney discarded the English tidewater rule of admiralty jurisdiction that Story had imported into American law, and held instead that the inland jurisdiction of federal courts in admiralty matters extended to all navigable waters, tidal or not, thus expanding the reach of federal admiralty jurisdiction to the Great Lakes and the interior rivers. But in *Luther* v. *Borden* (1849), he reasserted the political question doctrine, holding that a challenge to the legitimacy of Rhode Island's government after the Dorr Rebellion of 1842 was to be resolved only by the legislative and executive branches of the national government, not the judicial.

It might be expected that Taney would have been warmly sympathetic to the emerging doctrine of the police power, first fully articulated by Massachusetts Chief Justice Lemuel Shaw in *Commonwealth* v. *Alger* (1851). But Taney held unspoken reservations about the police power doctrine, fearing that if the states' regulatory powers were defined too explicitly or couched under a rubric, they might somehow be restricted by the federal Constitution. He thus preferred to avoid an explicit definition of the police power, and instead emphasized the states' inherent powers of sovereignty over persons and things within their jurisdiction, believing that if the issue were framed in terms of sovereignty rather than regulatory power, the states' autonomy from external interference might be more secure.

This issue of state regulatory power remained sensitive throughout Taney's tenure and was prominent in cases arising out of the attempt of Democratic majorities in the Ohio legislature to levy taxes on banks that had been exempted from certain forms of taxation by their charters. In *Ohio Life Insurance & Trust Co.* v. *Debolt* (1854) Taney held, in accordance with the *Charles River Bridge* paradigm, that the Court would not read into bank charters an implicit exemption from taxes. But in *Dodge* v. *Woolsey* (1856), Taney joined a majority in defending an explicit charter exemption against a state constitutional amendment empowering the state to tax exempted banks. Taney was not hostile to banks and corporations as such; he had an alert appreciation of the role that they would play in developing the national market.

Another issue—indeed, the critical one—that kept Taney and his colleagues sensitized to issues of state regulatory power was the protean matter of slavery and black people. This issue, deep in the background, skewed all but one of the Taney Court's commerce clause decisions. In his first term, the Court skirted slavery complications in a case, *Mayor of New York* v. *Miln* (1837), challenging the right of a state to impose some measure of control over the ingress of foreign passengers, by holding that the challenged authority was not a regulation of commerce but rather an exercise of the police power. But this evasion would not dispose of subsequent cases challenging the power of the state to control the importation of liquor or the immigration of persons. In the *License Cases* (1847), the Court rendered six opinions, including one by Taney who was with the majority for the result, sustaining the efforts of three New England states to prohibit the importation and sale of liquor. But in the *Passenger Cases* (1849), raising issues similar to *Miln*, the court produced eight opinions, this time with Taney in the minority, striking down state laws regulating or taxing the influx of aliens. Taney was consistent throughout, insisting that no federal constitutional restraints existed on the power of the states to control persons or objects coming into their borders. His brush with the controversy over the Negro Seamen's Act as United States attorney general had left him hostile to any constitutional restraints that might inhibit the power of the slave states to control the ingress of free blacks, slaves, abolitionists, or antislavery propaganda.

The Taney Court did manage to filter slavery complications out of one major commerce clause case, thereby producing another paradigm of state regulatory power. In *Cooley* v. *Board of Wardens of Philadelphia* (1851) the Court, with Taney in the majority, held that the commerce clause did not restrain the states from regulating matters essentially local in nature (such as, in this case, pilotage fees or harbor regulations) even if they had some impact on interstate or foreign commerce.

Curiously, the Court was more successful, in the short run, in disposing of cases where the question of slavery was overt rather than implicit. Taney, deeply dedicated to the welfare of his state and region, and anxious above all to protect the slave states from external meddling that would threaten their control of the black population, free or slave, or that would promote widespread emancipation, adopted passionate and extremist postures in slavery cases. In *Groves* v. *Slaughter* (1841), which involved the validity of a contract for sale of a slave under a state constitution that prohibited the commercial importation of slaves, Taney was provoked to a sharp reiteration of his attorney general's opinion, insisting that the power of a state to control blacks within its borders was exclusive of all federal power, including that under the commerce clause.

In *Prigg* v. *Pennsylvania* (1842) Taney was again prodded into another concurrence. Though he agreed with most of Justice Joseph Story's opinion for the majority holding unconstitutional a Pennsylvania personal liberty law, he firmly disavowed Story's dictum that states need not participate in the recapture and rendition of fugitive slaves. Taney rejected Story's assertion that states could not enact legislation supplemental to

the federal Fugitive Slave Act, and maintained that states must do so; his colleagues *Peter* v. *Daniel* and Smith Thompson merely asserted that a state could adopt such laws.

In *Strader* v. *Graham* (1851) Taney spoke for the Court in a case raising American variants of issues earlier canvassed in *Somerset's Case* (1772), a doctrinally seminal English decision that had passed into the mainstream of American constitutional thought. Appellant sought to have the Court overturn a Kentucky Court of Appeals decision that slaves permitted by their master to sojourn in a free state who then returned to their slave domicile did not become liberated because of their free-state sojourn. Taney held that the state court determination of the slaves' status was conclusive on federal courts (a point consistent with his emphasis on state control of blacks and a doctrinal opportunity for evading the issues of *Dred Scott* later). But Taney uttered obiter dicta disturbing to the free states. He suggested that the power of states over persons in their jurisdictions was unfettered "except in so far as the powers of the states in this respect are restrained . . . by the Constitution of the United States," thus hinting that there might be some federal constitutional impediment to the abolition statutes of the free states. He further insisted, needlessly, that the antislavery provisions of the Northwest Ordinance were defunct, no longer an effective prohibition of the introduction of slavery in the states that had been carved out of the Northwest Territory.

Dred Scott (1857) was Taney's definitive utterance on the slavery question. His opinion, though one of nine, was taken by contemporaries to be for the Court, and Taney himself so considered it. Taney first excluded blacks descended from slaves from the status of "Citizens" as that term was used both in the Article III diversity clause and the Article IV privileges and immunities clause. In order to support this conclusion, Taney asserted, incorrectly, that blacks in 1787 had been "considered as a subordinate and inferior class of beings, who . . . had no rights which

T

TANEY, ROGER BROOKE

(1777–1864)

T

TANEY, ROGER BROOKE

(1777–1864)

the white man was bound to respect." Taney further insisted that the meaning of the Constitution does not change over time, so that the connotations of its words in 1787 remained rigid and static, unalterable except by formal amendment.

In the second half of his long opinion, Taney held that the federal government lacked power to exclude slavery from the territories, thus holding the Missouri Compromise unconstitutional (even though it had already been declared void by the Kansas-Nebraska Act of 1854). He grounded this lack of federal power not in the territories clause of Article IV, but in its textual sibling, the new states clause, insisting that Congress could not impose conditions on the admission of new states that would put them in a position inferior to those already admitted. Taney also suggested in passing that the due process clause of the Fifth Amendment prohibited Congress from interfering with the property rights of slaveholders. But the significance of this utterance as a source of the later doctrine of substantive due process has been overrated. Taney was not a devotee of higher law doctrines, such as those enunciated by Justice Samuel Chase in *Calder* v. *Bull* (1798), by Justice Story in cases like *Terrett* v. *Taylor* (1815) and *Wilkinson* v. *Leland* (1829), and by numerous state court judges, most recently in the landmark case of *Wynehamer* v. *New York* (1856).

In his *Dred Scott* opinion Taney also adopted three points of proslavery constitutional thought previously voiced in Southern legislatures and doctrinal writings: the federal government had no power over slavery except to protect the rights of slaveholders; the federal government was the "trustee" of the states for the territories, and as such must protect the interests of all of them there; and the territorial legislature could not exclude slavery during the territorial period. His performance in the *Dred Scott* case was widely condemned. Justice Benjamin R. Curtis effectively controverted it in his scholarly dissent in *Dred Scott;* northern legislators, political leaders, attorneys, and polemicists poured forth innumerable rebut-

tals; and the Vermont legislature and the Maine Supreme Judicial Court flatly rejected its doctrines. Abraham Lincoln insisted that *Dred Scott*'s doctrine must be overruled.

Taney remained unmoved by such criticism, insisting in private correspondence that his position would be validated in time. Though aged and in intermittent ill health, he continued his judicial labors unabated. In *Ableman* v. *Booth* (1859), a magisterial treatise on the role of the federal judiciary in the American federal system, Taney held that state courts could not interfere with the judgment of a federal court through use of the writ of habeas corpus. He adumbrated the doctrine of dual sovereignty: the federal and state governments "are yet separate and distinct sovereignties, acting separately and independently of each other." But he insisted on the unfettered independence of federal courts in their execution of federal laws. In *dictum,* he asserted that the Fugitive Slave Act of 1850 was constitutional.

Taney produced significant published and unpublished opinions during the Civil War. In private communications, he supported secession and condemned Lincoln's resort to force to save the Union. In keeping with such views, he drafted opinions, probably to be incorporated into conventional judicial opinions when the opportunity arose, condemning the Emancipation Proclamation, conscription, and the Legal Tender Acts. He also extended the first half of his *Dred Scott* opinion to exclude all blacks, not just those descended from slaves, from citizenship; and he reasserted the obligation of the free states to return fugitive slaves. In an official opinion on circuit he condemned Lincoln's suspension of the writ of habeas corpus in *Ex Parte Merryman* (1861), an opinion Lincoln refused to honor. He also joined the dissenters in the *Prize Cases* (1863), who insisted that because only Congress can declare war, Lincoln's military response to secession and southern military actions was "private" and of no legal effect. His death in 1864 relieved him from the painful necessity of seeing his vision of the constitutional and social order destroyed by the victory of Union arms.

Taney's lasting contributions consisted of his reinforcement of the political question doctrine, his strong defense of the states' regulatory powers, and his vigorous aggrandizement of the jurisdiction of the federal courts. More than his colleagues, he keenly appreciated the role of technological change in American law, a sensitivity apparent in *Charles River Bridge* and *Genesee Chief*. His defense of regional autonomy and his hostility to the power of concentrated capital retain a perennial relevance. His instinct for dynamic balance in the formulation of enduring rules of law, as in the *Charles River Bridge* paradigm, evinced judicial statesmanship of the first rank.

Constitutional problems related to slavery combined with Taney's personal failings to blight his reputation and eclipse his real achievements. *Dred Scott* remains a monument to judicial hubris, and all the slavery cases that came before the Taney Court bear the impress of Taney's determination to bend the Constitution to the service of sectional interest. Though he manumitted nearly all his own slaves and was in his personal relations a kind and loving man, Taney as Chief Justice was immoderate and willful when the times called for judicial caution. His tolerance of multiple opinions permitted dissents and concurrences to proliferate, blurring the clarity of doctrine in commerce clause cases. In any case touched directly or indirectly by slavery, Taney's sure instincts for viable doctrine, as well as his nobler personal qualities, deserted him and gave way to a blind and vindictive sectionalism unworthy of the Chief Justice of the United States.

It is the tragic irony of Taney's career that his virtues were so closely linked to his faults, especially in their results. He fully merited Felix Frankfurter's warm appreciation of his role in shaping the American federal system: "the intellectual power of his opinions and their enduring contribution to a workable adjustment of the theoretical distribution of authority between two governments for a single people, place Taney second only to Marshall in the constitutional history of our country." Yet no other Justices have so gravely damaged the federal system because of sectional bias, and the real merits of Taney's defense of localist values have been obscured by his racial antipathies and sectional dogmatism.

—WILLIAM M. WIECEK

Bibliography

Fehrenbacher, Don E. (1979). *The Dred Scott Case: Its Significance in American Law and Politics.* New York: Oxford University Press.

Harris, Robert J. (1957 [1966]). Chief Justice Taney: Prophet of Reform and Reaction. Pages 93–118 in Leonard W. Levy, ed., *American Constitutional Law: Historical Essays.* New York: Harper & Row.

Lewis, Walker (1965). *Without Fear or Favor: A Biography of Chief Justice Roger Brooke Taney.* Boston: Houghton Mifflin.

Swisher, Carl B. (1935). *Roger B. Taney.* New York: Macmillan.

——— (1974). *The Taney Period, 1835–64.* Volume 5 of *The Oliver Wendell Holmes Devise History of The Supreme Court of the United States.* New York: Macmillan.

TANEY COURT

(1836–1864)

The Supreme Court under Chief Justice Roger B. Taney (1836–64) has not been a favorite among historians, perhaps because it defies easy generalization. There were few great constitutional moments and no dramatic lawmaking decisions comparable to those handed down by the Marshall Court. The fifteen Justices who served with Taney (not counting Abraham Lincoln's Civil War appointees) varied immensely in ability—from Joseph Story of Massachusetts who was the leading scholar on the bench until his death in 1845 to John McKinley of Alabama whose twenty-five years on the Court left barely a trace. Institutional unity and efficiency were often disrupted by abrasive personalities like Henry Baldwin (who became mentally unstable shortly after his appointment in 1830) and *Peter* v. *Daniel* (whose passion for states' rights drove him into chronic dissent). Division was constant and bitter as the Justices disagreed openly over corporation, banking, and slavery questions—all of which tended to be seen from a sectional point of view. Fortunately for the ongoing work of the Court, most of its members shared a respect for the Constitution and had a common commitment to economic progress and property rights that cut across ideological and sectional differences. All were Democrats, too, except Story, John McLean, and Benjamin R. Curtis. Most of the Court respected the Chief Justice—whose legal mind was of a high order—and responded well to his patient, democratic style of leadership. Still the Court under Taney did not quite cohere. There was no "leading mind," as Daniel Webster complained, and no clear-cut doctrinal unity.

Clearly the Taney Court was not the Marshall Court—but then again it was not the age of Marshall. The society that conditioned the Taney Court and defined the perimeters within which it made law was democratic in its politics, pluralistic in social composition, divided in ideology, and shaped by capitalist forces which increasingly sought freedom from traditional governmental restraints. Most threatening to judicial unity, because it was directly reflected in the opinions of the Court, was the intensification of sectional rivalry. As northern states committed themselves to commerce and manufacturing, they came to see themselves—taking their cultural cues from the abolitionists—as a section united in defense of liberty and freedom. The South found ideological conservatism an ideal umbrella for an expansive social-economic system based on cotton and organized around plantation slavery. As the sections competed for political power and control of the new West, each came to think of itself as the last best hope of mankind. And each insisted that

the Constitution accommodate its policy preferences—a demand that the Supreme Court could satisfy only by compromising doctrinal purity and finally could not satisfy at all.

In short, the political and economic problems of the new age became constitutional problems just as Alexis de Tocqueville had said they would. Whether the Supreme Court would be the primary agency to resolve those problems was, of course, a matter of debate. Andrew Jackson, armed with a mandate from the people, did not believe that the Court had a monopoly of constitutional wisdom. Newly organized political parties stood ready to dispute judicial decisions that offended their constituencies. States armed with John C. Calhoun's theory of nullification insisted that they, not the Court, had the final word on the Constitution. Accordingly, the margin of judicial error was drastically reduced. The Court was obliged to make the Constitution of 1787 work for a new age; the high nationalism of the Marshall Court, along with its Augustan style of judging, would have to be toned down. Changes would have to come. The question—and it was as yet a new one in American constitutional law—was whether they could be made without disrupting the continuity upon which the authority of the law and the prestige of the Court rested.

The moment of testing came quickly. Facing the Court in its 1837 term were three great constitutional questions dealing with state banking, the commerce clause, and corporate contracts. Each had been argued before the Marshall Court and each involved a question of federalism which pitted new historical circumstances against a precedent from the Marshall period. The Court's decisions in these cases would set the constitutional tone for the new age.

In *Briscoe* v. *Bank of Kentucky* the challenge was simple and straightforward. The issue was whether notes issued by the state-owned Commonwealth Bank were prohibited by Article I, section 10, of the Constitution, which prevented states from issuing bills of credit. The Marshall Court had ruled broadly against state bills of credit in *Craig* v. *Missouri* (1830), but the new Jacksonian majority ruled for the state bank. Justice McLean's opinion paid deference to legal continuity by distinguishing *Briscoe* from *Craig*, but political and economic expediency controlled the decision as Story's bitter dissent made clear. The fact was that, after the demise of the second Bank of the United States, state bank notes were the main currency of the country. To rule against the bank would put such notes in jeopardy, a risk the new Court refused to take.

Policy considerations of a states' rights nature also overwhelmed doctrinal consistency in commerce clause litigation, the Court's primary means of drawing the line between national and state power. Marshall's opinion in *Gibbons* v. *Ogden* (1824) had conceded vast power over interstate commerce to Congress, although the Court had not gone so far as to rule that national power automatically excluded states from passing laws touching foreign and interstate commerce. The new age needed a flexible interpretation of the commerce clause that would please states' rights forces in both the North and the South and at the same time encourage the growth of a national market.

In *Mayor of New York* v. *Miln*, the second of the trio of great cases in 1837, the Court struggled toward such a reinterpretation. A New York law required masters of all vessels arriving at the port of New York to make bond that none of their passengers should become wards of the city. The practical need for such a law seemed clear enough; the question was whether it encroached unconstitutionally on federal power over interstate commerce as laid out in the *Gibbons* decision. The Chief Justice assigned the opinion to Justice Smith Thompson who was prepared to justify the New York law as a police regulation and as a legitimate exercise of concurrent commerce power. His narrow definition of state police power displeased some of his brethren, however, and even more so his position on concurrent power. When he refused to compromise, the opinion was reassigned to Philip P.

Barbour, who upheld the state regulation as a valid exercise of state police power. Barbour's contention that police power was "unqualified and exclusive" far exceeded anything that precedent could justify, however, as Story pointed out in his dissent. Indeed, Barbour's opinion, so far as it ruled that states could regulate interstate passengers, went beyond the position agreed upon in conference and lacked the full concurrence of a majority.

The *Miln* case settled little except that the New York regulation was constitutional. The Court remained sharply divided over the basic questions: whether congressional power over foreign and interstate commerce was exclusive of the states or concurrent with them and, if it was concurrent, how much congressional action would be necessary to sustain national predominance. The doctrine of state police power had taken a tentative step toward maturity, but its relation to the commerce clause remained unsettled. That the states reserved some power to legislate for the health and welfare of their citizens seemed clear enough, but to establish an enclave of state power prior to, outside the scope of, and superior to powers delegated explicitly to Congress was to beg, not settle the crucial constitutional question.

The uncertainty regarding the questions generated by *Miln* continued throughout the 1840s in such cases as *Groves* v. *Slaughter* (1841) where the Court refused to rule on whether the provision of the Mississippi Constitution of 1832 touching the interstate slave trade was a violation of national commerce power. Confusion increased in the *License Cases* (1847) and the *Passenger Cases* (1849), which dealt with state regulation of alcohol and immigration respectively. The Justices upheld state authority in the first and denied it in the second, but in neither did they clarify the relation of state police power to federal authority over interstate commerce.

Not until *Cooley* v. *Board of Wardens* (1852), which considered the constitutionality of a Pennsylvania law regulating pilotage in the port of Philadelphia, did the Court

The Taney Court had few great constitutional moments and no dramatic lawmaking decisions.

supply guidelines for commerce clause litigation. Congress had twice legislated on pilotage, but in neither case was there any conflict with the Pennsylvania law. The issue came, therefore, precisely and unavoidably to focus on exclusive power versus concurrent power: whether the constitutional grant of commerce power to Congress automatically prohibited state regulation of commerce or whether the states could regulate commerce as long as such regulations did not actually conflict with congressional legislation.

Justice Curtis's majority opinion upheld the state law and in the process salvaged some doctrinal regularity. Starting from the undeniable premise that the commerce power granted to Congress did not expressly exclude the states from exercising authority over interstate commerce, he ruled that exclusive congressional jurisdiction obtained only when the subject matter itself required it. The subjects of commerce, however, were vast and varied and did not require blanket exclusiveness. Some matters, he said, needed a "single uniform rule, operating equally on the commerce of the United States in every port." Some just as certainly admitted of local regulation. Power, in other words, followed function: if the subject matter required uniform regulation, the power belonged to Congress; if it did not, the states might regulate it. State police power remained to be settled, but the pressure to do so was lessened because the concurrent commerce power of the states was now clearly recognized.

Selective exclusiveness, as the Court's approach in *Cooley* came to be called, was not a certain and final answer to the problem of allocating commerce power between the national government and the states, however. The rule was clear enough but how to apply it was not, which is to say that Curtis gave no guidelines for determining which aspects of commerce required uniform regulation or which permitted diversity. What was clear was that the Court had retreated from the constitutional formalism of the Marshall period. The opinion was short, only ten pages

long; it made no reference to precedent, not even *Gibbons*. The Justices now willed to do what they had previously done unwillingly: they decided cases without a definitive pronouncement of doctrine. The important difference in *Cooley* was that the Court devised a rule of thumb recognizing the judicial interest-balancing that previously had been carried on covertly in the name of formal distinctions. Ordered process, not logical categories, would be the new order of the day.

The Court's flexibility also signaled a shift of power in the direction of the states. The constitutional legacy of the Marshall Court had been altered to fit Jacksonian priorities. Still, national authority had not been destroyed. The Taney Court had refused to extend the nationalist principles of *McCulloch* v. *Maryland* (1819) and *Gibbons,* to be sure, but the principles stood. The Court's new federalism did not rest on new states' rights constitutional doctrine. Neither did the new federalism threaten economic growth, as conservatives had predicted. Agrarian capitalism, for example, fared as well under the Taney Court as it had under its predecessor. The Justices did sometimes resist the most exorbitant demands of land speculators, and occasionally a dissenting Justice spoke for the little man as did Daniel in *Arguello* v. *United States* (1855). But the majority took their cue from *Fletcher* v. *Peck* (1810), which is to say that plungers in the land market mostly got free rein, as for example in *Cervantes* v. *United States* (1854) and *Fremont* v. *United States* (1855). That slaveholding agrarian capitalists were to benefit from this judicial largess was clear from the decision in *Dred Scott* v. *Sandford* (1857).

The Court's promotion of commercial-industrial-corporate capitalism proved more difficult because of the sectional disagreements among the Justices. But there is no doubt that the Taney Court served as a catalyst for the release of American entrepreneurial energies. Its plan for a democratic, nonmonopolistic capitalism, Jacksonian style, was unveiled in *Charles River Bridge* v. *Warren Bridge*, the last of the three landmark decisions of the 1837 term. Here the question was whether the toll-free Warren Bridge, chartered and built in 1828 a few hundred feet from the Charles River Bridge, destroyed the property rights of the old bridge, in violation of its charter as protected by *Dartmouth College* v. *Woodward* (1819). The difficulty was that the charter of 1785, although granting the Charles River Bridge the right to collect tolls, had not explicitly granted a monopoly. The fate of the old bridge depended, therefore, on the willingness of the Taney Court to extend the principle of *Dartmouth College* by implication.

Taney, who spoke for the new Jacksonian majority on the Court, refused to do so. The Chief Justice agreed that "the rights of private property are sacredly guarded," but he insisted "that the community also have rights, and that the happiness and well-being of every citizen depends on their faithful preservation." The Court should not venture into the no-man's land of inference and construction when the public interest rested in the balance, Taney argued. He cleverly supported this position by citing Marshall's opinion in *Providence Bank* v. *Billings* (1830). And the public interest, as Taney saw it, lay in extending equality of economic opportunity. "Modern science," he said with an eye on new railroad corporations, "would be throttled and transportation set back to the last century if turnpike and canal companies could turn charter rights into monopoly grants.

The *Bridge* decision, like the Court's decisions in banking and commerce, revealed a distinct instrumentalist tone as well as a new tolerance for state legislative discretion. The Court also showed its preference for dynamic over static capital. Still, property rights were not generally threatened. To be sure, in *West River Bridge Company* v. *Dix* (1848) the Court recognized the power of state legislatures to take property for public purposes with just compensation, but conservatives themselves were willing to recognize that power. The Court also took a liberal view of state debtor's relief legislation, especially laws applying to mortgages for land, but even here

the Court could claim the Marshall Court's decision in *Ogden* v. *Saunders* (1827) as its guide. There was no doubt, on the other hand, as *Bronson* v. *Kinzie* (1843) showed, that state relief laws that impaired substantial contractual rights would not be tolerated.

Corporate property also remained secure under the *Bridge* ruling. Indeed, corporate expansion was strongly encouraged by the Taney Court despite the resistance of some of the southern agrarian Justices. After 1837 the Court consistently refused to extend charter rights by implication, but it also upheld corporate charters that explicitly granted monopoly rights even though in some cases such rights appeared hostile to community interest. Corporations also greatly profited from *Bank of Augusta* v. *Earle* (1839), which raised the question whether corporations chartered in one state could do business in another. Taney conceded that the legislature could prohibit foreign corporations from doing business in the state and some such laws were subsequently passed. But such prohibitions, he went on to say, had to be explicit; practically speaking, this limitation assured corporations the right to operate across state lines. Hardly less important to corporate expansion was *Louisville Railroad* v. *Letson* (1844), which held that corporations could be considered citizens of the states in which they were chartered for purposes of diversity jurisdiction—Thus removing the increasingly unworkable fiction created in *Bank of United States* v. *Deveaux* (1809) and assuring corporate access to federal courts where the bias in favor of local interests would be minimized.

The Court's promotion of capitalism showed the basic continuity between the Marshall and Taney periods and the fact that antebellum law followed the contours of economic development. Acknowledgment of this continuity, however, should not obscure the real changes in constitutional federalism as the Taney Court deferred more to state power and legislative discretion. Overall the Court spoke more modestly, too, readily acknowledging former errors and generally toning down its rhetoric. In *Luther* v. *Borden* (1849), it went so far as to promise judicial self-restraint regarding political questions, though that promise ought not to be confused with a hard-and-fast doctrine, which it clearly was not. Although the Court avoided stridency, it did not claim less power. The constitutional nationalism which the Taney Court reduced was not the same as the judicial nationalism which it actually extended. In short, the Court did things differently, but it did not surrender its power to do them. Although the *Bridge* case conceded new power to state legislatures and promised judicial restraint, the Court still monitored the federal system in corporate contract questions. The Court's commerce clause decisions worked to make the federal system more flexible. But in every case from *Miln* through *Cooley*, the Court retained the right to judge—and often, as in *Cooley*, by vague constitutional standards. This judicial authority, moreover, was used throughout the Taney period to expand the jurisdiction of the Court, often at the expense of state judiciaries which the Court claimed to respect.

Never was federal judicial expansion more striking than in *Swift* v. *Tyson* (1842), a commercial law case which arose under federal diversity jurisdiction. For a unanimous Court, Story held that, in matters of general commercial law, state "laws," which section 34 of the Judiciary Act of 1789 obliged the federal courts to follow in diversity cases, did not include state court decisions. In the absence of controlling state statutes, then, federal courts were free to apply general principles of commercial law, which they proceeded to do until *Swift* was overruled in 1938. Almost as expansive was Taney's opinion in *Propeller Genesee Chief* v. *FitzHugh* (1851), which bluntly overturned the tidewater limitation imposed by the Marshall Court and extended the admiralty jurisdiction of the federal courts over the vast network of inland lakes and rivers.

Both these decisions were part of the Court's consistent effort to establish a system of uniform commercial principles conducive to the interstate operation of business. Both paved the way for federal judicial intrusion into state judicial authority. When state courts objected to this judicial nationalism, as the Wisconsin Supreme Court did in the slave rendition case of *Ableman* v. *Booth* (1859), Jacksonian Roger Taney put them in their place with a ringing defense of federal judicial authority that was every bit as unyielding as was Federalist John Marshall's in *Cohens* v. *Virginia* (1821). *Ableman* was an assertion of power that would have astonished conservative critics in 1837 who predicted the imminent decline and fall of the Court. Instead, by 1850 the Taney Court was even more popular than the Marshall Court had been and the Chief Justice was praised by men of all political persuasions. All this would change when the Court confronted the issue of slavery.

Adjudicating the constitutional position of slavery fell mainly to the Taney Court; there was no escape. Slavery was the foundation of the southern economy, a source of property worth billions, a social institution that shaped the cultural values of an entire section and the politics of the whole nation. Moreover, it was an integral part of the Constitution, which the Court had to interpret. At the same time, it was, of all the issues facing the antebellum Court, least amenable to a rational legal solution—and in this respect, it foreshadowed social issues like abortion and affirmative action which have troubled the contemporary Court. No other single factor so much accounts for the divisions on the Taney Court or its inability to clearly demarcate power in the federal system.

Given the slavery question's explosive nature, the Justices not surprisingly tried to avoid confronting it directly. Thus the obfuscation in *Groves* v. *Slaughter* (1841), where the issue was whether a provision in the Mississippi Constitution prohibiting the importation of slaves for sale after 1833 illegally encroached upon federal power over interstate commerce. The Court circumvented this issue by ruling that the state constitutional clause in question was not self-activating—a position that, while avoiding trouble for the

Court, also guaranteed the collection of millions of dollars of outstanding debts owed slave traders and in effect put the judicial seal of approval on the interstate slave trade. The Court also dodged the substantive issue in *Strader* v. *Graham* (1851), which raised the question whether slaves who resided in Kentucky had become free by virtue of their temporary residence in the free state of Ohio. The Court refused jurisdiction on the ground that Kentucky law reasserted itself over the slaves on their return, so that no federal question was involved.

Where the substantive question could not be side-stepped, the Court aimed to decide cases on narrow grounds and in such a way as to please both North and South. Thus in *The Amistad* (1841), Justice Story ruled that Africans on their way to enslavement who escaped their Spanish captors were free by virtue of principles of international law and a close reading of the Treaty of 1794 with Spain. Extremists in neither section were pleased. Even less were they content with Story's efforts to juggle sectional differences, morality, and objective adjudication in *Prigg* v. *Pennsylvania* (1842). There the question was whether and to what extent states were allowed to pass personal liberty laws protecting the rights of free Negroes in rendition cases. The South was pleased when Story declared the Pennsylvania liberty law of 1826 to be a violation of the constitutional and statutory obligation to return fugitive slaves. He went on to say, with his eye on northern opinion (and with doubtful support from a majority on the Court), that the power over fugitives belonged exclusively to the federal government and that states were not obliged to cooperate in their return. The decision encouraged northern states to pass personal liberty laws but also necessitated the more stringent federal fugitive slave law of 1850. Both developments fueled sectional conflict.

The Court's strategy of avoidance aimed to keep slavery on the state level where the Constitution had put it, but the slavery question would not stay put. What brought it forth politically and legally as a national question was slavery in the territories, a problem which confronted the Court and the nation in *Dred Scott*. The nominal issue in that famous case was whether a Negro slave named Scott, who had resided in the free state of Illinois and the free territory of Minnesota (made free by the Missouri Compromise of 1820) and who returned to the slave state of Missouri, could sue in the federal courts. Behind this jurisdictional issue lay the explosive political question of whether Congress could prohibit slavery in the territories, or to put it another way, whether the Constitution guaranteed it there. The future of slavery itself was on the line.

The first inclination of the Justices when they confronted the case early in 1856 was to continue the strategy of avoidance by applying *Strader* v. *Graham* (1851); by that precedent Scott would have become a slave on his return to Missouri with no right to sue in the federal courts. This compromise was abandoned: in part because of pressure from President James Buchanan and Congress; in part because northern Justices McLean and Curtis planned to confront the whole issue in dissent; in part because the proslave, pro-South wing of the Court (led by Taney and Wayne) wanted to silence the abolitionists by putting the Constitution itself behind slavery in the territories; in part because the Justices pridefully believed they could put the troublesome question to rest and save the Union.

Taney's was the majority opinion so far as one could be gleaned from the cacophony of separate opinions and dissents. It was totally prosouthern and brutally racist: Scott could not sue in the federal courts because he was not a citizen of the United States. He was not a citizen because national citizenship followed state citizenship, and in 1787 the states had looked upon blacks as racially inferior (which the states in fact did) and unqualified for citizenship (which several states did not). Scott's argument that he was free by virtue of residence in a free state was wrong, said Taney, because of *Strader* (which had been relied upon by the Supreme Court of Missouri); Scott's argument that residence in a free territory made him free carried no weight because Congress had no authority to prohibit slavery in the territories—an assertion that ignored seventy years of constitutional practice and permitted Taney to set forth the substantive due process theory of the Fifth Amendment against the taking of property. Scott was still a slave. Congress could not prohibit slavery in the territories, because the Constitution guaranteed it there; neither, as the creatures of Congress, could territorial legislatures prohibit slavery as claimed by proponents of the doctrine of popular sovereignty. Taney's Constitution was for whites only.

Instead of saving the Union the decision brought it closer to civil war and put the Court itself in jeopardy. In effect, the decision outlawed the basic principle of the Republican party (opposition to the extension of slavery in the territories), forcing that party to denounce the Court. The Democratic party, the best hope for political compromise, was now split between a southern wing (which in 1860 chose the certainty of *Dred Scott* over the vagueness of popular sovereignty) and northern antislavery forces who, if they did not defect to the Republicans, went down to defeat with Stephen Douglas and popular sovereignty. Sectional hatred intensified and the machinery of political compromise was seriously undercut—along with the prestige of the Court. From its peak of popularity in 1850 the Taney Court descended to an all-time low. After secession it served only the section of the Union that ignored *Dred Scott* entirely, condemned the Court as a tool of southern expansionism, and looked upon the Chief Justice as an archtraitor to liberty and national union.

Fortunately, these disabilities were not permanent. Northern hatred focused less on the Court as an institution and more on the particular decision of *Dred Scott*, which was obliterated by the Thirteenth and Fourteenth Amendments. *Dred Scott* seemed less impor-

tant, too, after President Lincoln "Republicanized" the Court with new appointments (five, including a new Chief Justice who had been an abolitionist). More important, the Court brought itself into harmony with the northern war effort by doing what the Supreme Court has always done in wartime: deferring to the political branches of government and bending law to military necessity. Sometimes the Court deferred by acting (as in the *Prize Cases* of 1863 where it permitted the president to exercise war powers and still not recognize the belligerent status of the Confederacy) and sometimes it deferred by not acting (as when it refused to interfere with the broad use of martial law during the war).

The Taney Court not only survived but it also salvaged its essential powers—and with time even a grudging respect from historians. The memory of *Dred Scott* could not be totally exorcised, of course, but it diminished along with the idealism of the war years and with the recognition that the racism of the opinion was shared by a majority of white Americans. In any case, the reform accomplishments of the Taney Court helped to balance the reactionary ones. Its modest style of judging fit the new democratic age. Through its decisions ran a new appreciation of the democratic nature and reform potential of state action and a tacit recognition as well of the growing maturity of legislative government. The Court's pragmatic federalism, while it could support the evil of slavery, also embodied a tradition of cultural pluralism, local responsibility, and suspicion of power. This it did without destroying the foundations of constitutional nationalism established by the Marshall Court. Change is the essence of American experience. The Taney Court accepted this irresistible premise and accommodated the Constitution to it. The adjustment was often untidy, but the Court's preference for process over substance looked to the modern age and prefigured the main direction of American constitutional law.

—R. KENT NEWMYER

Bibliography

Cover, Robert M. (1975). *Justice Accused: Antislavery and the Judicial Process.* New Haven, Conn.: Yale University Press.

Fehrenbacher, Don E. (1978). *The Dred Scott Case: Its Significance in American Law and Politics.* New York: Oxford University Press.

Frankfurter, Felix (1937). *The Commerce Clause under Marshall, Taney and Waite.* Chapel Hill: University of North Carolina Press.

Harris, Robert J. (1957). Chief Justice Taney: Prophet of Reform and Reaction. *Vanderbilt Law Review* 10:227–257.

Kutler, Stanley (1971). *Privilege and Creative Destruction: The Charles River Bridge Case.* Philadelphia: J. B. Lippincott.

Swisher, Carl B. (1974). *The Taney Period, 1836–1864.* Volume 5 of *The Oliver Wendell Holmes Devise History of the Supreme Court of the United States.* New York: Macmillan.

Warren, Charles (1926). *The Supreme Court in United States History,* vol. 2. New and revised ed. Boston: Little, Brown.

TAYLOR v. LOUISIANA

419 U.S. 522 (1975)

Under Louisiana law women were selected for jury service only when they explicitly volunteered for duty; men were selected irrespective of their desires. In *Hoyt* v. *Florida* (1961), the Supreme Court had employed a rational basis standard of review to uphold a similar law against due process and equal protection attacks. In *Taylor,* however, the Court invalidated this jury selection system as a denial of the Sixth Amendment right of the accused to "a jury drawn from a fair cross section of the community." That the accused was male was irrelevant to this claim. The vote was 8–1; Justice William H. Rehnquist dissented, and Chief Justice Warren E. Burger concurred only in the result.

Writing for the other seven Justices, Justice Byron R. White declined to follow *Hoyt;*

if the fair cross section requirement ever "permitted the almost total exclusion of women, this is not the case today." Women had entered the work force in large numbers, undermining their exemption "solely on their sex and the presumed role in the home." *Taylor* is not only an important jury discrimination precedent but also a strong judicial rejection of laws resting on stereotypical assumptions about "woman's role."

—KENNETH L. KARST

TENNEY v. BRANDHOVE

341 U.S. 367 (1951)

This decision established the absolute immunity of state legislative officials from damages actions, brought under Section 1983, Title

ABSOLUTELY IMMUNE

The Court found that Senator Jack B. Tenney was not responsible for damages stemming from alleged violations of constitutional rights. (Corbis/Bettmann-UPI)

42, United States Code, alleging violations of constitutional rights. William Brandhove claimed that Senator Jack B. Tenney and other members of a California state legislative committee had violated his constitutional rights by conducting hearings to intimidate and silence him. In an opinion by Justice Felix Frankfurter, the Supreme Court noted the history of parliamentary immunity in England, and cited the speech or debate clause as a recognition of the need for a fearless and independent legislature. It held that, despite the unequivocal language of section 1983, Congress had not meant to "impinge on a tradition so well grounded in history and reason."

—THEODORE EISENBERG

TERM

(Supreme Court)

As prescribed by congressional statute, the Supreme Court holds a regular annual term of court, beginning on the first Monday in October. The term usually concludes in late June or early July of the following year. The Court is also authorized to hold special terms outside the normal October terms but does so only infrequently, in urgent circumstances (*Ex Parte Quirin*, 1942, German saboteurs convicted by military commission; *O'Brien* v. *Brown*, 1972, seating of delegates to Democratic National Convention).

Although Congress manipulated the Court's terms to postpone decision of *Marbury* v. *Madison* (1803) for nearly a year, modern times have seen no similar stratagems.

—KENNETH L. KARST

TERRY v. ADAMS

345 U.S. 461 (1953)

With confidence, we can call *Terry* the last of the series of *Texas Primary Cases* beginning with *Nixon* v. *Herndon* (1927). The decision is also a clear modern example of the "public function" strand of state action doctrine. In a Texas county, a group called the Jaybird Democratic Association conducted pre-primary elections, from which black voters were excluded. The winners of these elections consistently won both the Democratic primaries and the general elections. The Supreme Court held that black plaintiffs were entitled to a declaratory judgment that their exclusion from the Jaybird election amounted to state action in violation of the Fifteenth Amendment. There was no majority opinion. Three Justices said that the state could not constitutionally permit a racial exclusion from the only election that mattered in the county. The electoral process was inescapably public, subject to the Fifteenth Amendment's commands. Four other Justices said the Jaybirds were an auxiliary of the local Democratic party organization, and thus included within the doctrine of *Smith* v. *Allwright* (1944). Justice Felix Frankfurter found state action in the participation of state election officials as voters in the Jaybird election. Justice Sherman Minton dissented, calling the Jaybirds nothing but a "pressure group."

—KENNETH L. KARST

TEST CASE

Whenever a unit of government, or an interest in the private sector, wants a favorable constitutional decision on a point in question, a test case is often organized to gain a ruling from the Supreme Court. The Court has not defined the term, and need not, as there is no judicial criterion for "test case" under the cases and controversies clause of Article III. Scholarship on the judicial process provides the best understanding of the term as a strategy employed by different interests, for differing ends. *Fletcher* v. *Peck* (1810) showed that systematically plotting a test case, so framing it as to elicit particular answers based on prediction concerning how the Justices are likely to respond, and then using the judicial decision for political advantage is not a strategy unique

---

The Supreme Court's annual term begins in October and ends in June or July.

This case is the last of the series of Texas Primary Cases.

See also

Marbury v. *Madison*

to recent civil rights cases but a durable aspect of constitutional litigation since the early years of the Republic.

Organizers of test cases sometimes look upon victory in the Supreme Court as a secondary goal. For example, the arguments of the National Woman Suffrage Association that women, as citizens, were already enfranchised by terms of the Fourteenth Amendment breathed new life into the organization

---

TERRY v. OHIO, 392 U.S. 1 (1968)

SIBRON v. NEW YORK, 392 U.S. 40 (1968)

*T*erry v. Ohio marked the first attempt by the Supreme Court to deal with a pervasive type of police conduct known as stop and frisk. Where an individual's suspicious conduct gives rise to an apprehension of danger, but probable cause for an arrest does not exist, it is common police practice to stop the suspect for questioning and to pat down (frisk) his outer clothing in a search for concealed weapons. While this may be an effective way to deter crime it is susceptible to abuse. Though far less intrusive on privacy and security than formal arrest and thorough search, a stop and, especially, a frisk can be a frightening and humiliating experience.

It was this consideration that led the Court in *Terry* to hold that stop and frisk is subject to limitations established by the Fourth Amendment. Chief Justice Earl Warren declared that the forcible restraint of an individual, however temporary, is a "seizure," and a frisk, though limited in scope, is a "search," within the meaning of the Fourth Amendment. However, the imperative of sound law enforcement, as well as the need of the police to assure their own safety and that of the citizenry, requires that the amendment's reasonableness clause—rather than the probable cause standard of the warrant clause—should govern this type of police conduct. Balancing individual freedom against community needs, Warren concluded that if "a reasonably prudent [officer] in the circumstances [is] warranted in the belief that his safety or that of others [is] in danger," he is, under the reasonableness clause, entitled to stop and frisk the suspect in order to avoid the threatened harm. Any weapon thus seized is admissible at trial. However, in *Terry*'s companion case, *Sibron* v. *New York,* the Court held that where the motivation for the frisk is the discovery of evidence rather than the confiscation of weapons, the evidence seized is inadmissible.

The officer's apprehension of danger must be based on articulable facts rather than mere hunch; the difference between probable cause and the less strict standard authorized in *Terry* is a difference between reasonable belief and reasonable suspicion. Paradoxically, the case both significantly limited and momentously expanded the police search power: it placed "on the street" police-citizen encounters under the protection of the Fourth Amendment even as it allowed, for the first time, a standard less exacting than probable cause to meet the requirement of reasonableness for searches made in exigent circumstances.

—JACOB W. LANDYNSKI

NO PROBABLE CAUSE

The Court in Terry *concluded that under the reasonableness clause, an officer is entitled to stop and frisk a suspect in order to avoid threatened harm. (Corbis)*

Test cases are often organized to gain a ruling from the Supreme Court.

through publicity of test cases. *Minor* v. *Happersett* (1875) and two other cases failed but they produced national news.

The Department of Justice took little initiative in enforcing new legislation in the nineteenth century, largely because Congress intended enforcement to come through complaints of individuals entitled to sue violators. An example of this is the *Civil Rights Cases* (1883). Individuals challenged about a hundred violations of the Civil Rights Act of 1875. Eventually, five came to the Supreme Court as test cases, where they were unsuccessfully argued by the Solicitor General. These test cases were not managed; they simply happened as individual blacks complained.

Business interests may bring test cases to prevent enforcement of new regulatory legislation, as in 1917 when David Clark for the Southern Cotton Manufacturers sought to invalidate the Keating-Owen Act, which prohibited shipment in interstate commerce of designated products manufactured in plants employing children. Stephen Wood reports the advice of a Philadelphia lawyer to the manufacturers:

> *No legal proceeding will lie until the [Keating-Owen] bill is in operation. Some action must be taken under some provision of the bill so that a real and not a moot question is raised. A court, in order to pass upon any phase of it, must have before it an actual case, and if the measure is to be contested, the case should not only be carefully selected in order that the constitutional principle desired to be raised may be clearly presented, but I believe then that when the issue is raised, if possible, a judicial district should be selected in which the judge is a man of known courage. This is no case to try before a weak character [1968: 87–88].*

Clark proceeded to raise money, select suitable counsel, identify Judge James Edmund Boyd as courageous, and locate cotton com-

panies in the western district of North Carolina ready to cooperate. After searching for the "perfect combination of factors," Clark worked up four possible test cases to submit to the attorneys in New York. There the *Dagenhart* case was selected as the best. The Dagenharts, a father and two minor sons, and the company "were mere figureheads" whom Clark persuaded to set up the case. First, the company posted notices that under-age employees would be dismissed when the Keating-Owen law went into effect. The attorneys employed by Clark then prepared a complaint for Dagenhart asserting that this threat would deprive him of his vested rights, because he was entitled to the services of his minor sons and the compensation arising from their labors. By moving before the law became effective, the cotton manufacturers put the Department of Justice on the defensive, trapped within the confines of their test case. Judge Boyd, who ruled the Keating-Owen Act invalid under the Fifth and Tenth Amendments, was upheld by the Supreme Court in 1918 in *Hammer* v. *Dagenhart*.

Success in managing constitutional litigation requires understanding of both substantive law and litigation practice. Following enactment of the Wagner Act in 1935, lawyers for the National Labor Relations Board combined these talents in impressive fashion, gaining a stunning triumph from the Supreme Court in *NLRB* v. *Jones & Laughlin* in March 1937. Against hostile attacks by the National Lawyers' Committee of the American Liberty League, NLRB lawyers carefully developed cases running the gamut of size and type to make the first tests establishing wide congressional power to regulate labor practices in businesses affecting interstate commerce.

NLRB lawyers, even before the Wagner Act was signed, had designed a "master plan" envisioning test cases built around commerce clause issues stressing the type of industry, characteristics of individual businesses, the degree of actual or threatened obstruction of commerce, and the type of unfair labor practices charged. In Peter Irons's words, this "master plan" gave clear directions for "sifting through their massive case loads in search of ideal test cases, charting a clear path from the picket line to the Supreme Court." The NLRB staff functioned as legal craftsmen, "as much meticulous technicians as partisan advocates," who "winnowed and selected cases with care; scrutinized records with a fine-tooth comb; chose courts with a shopper's discriminating eye; wrote briefs to draw the issues narrowly and precisely."

Although numerous voluntary associations with litigation programs, such as the Anti-Saloon League of America, the National Consumers' League, and the American Jewish Congress, have sponsored test cases as a way of influencing public policy, the organizations most noted for this practice have been the National Association for the Advancement of Colored People (NAACP), formed in 1909, and the NAACP Legal Defense Fund, Inc., organized in 1939.

Modern test cases by associations, public interest law firms, or lawyers working *pro bono publico* are often cast as class actions under the Federal Rules of Civil Procedure. Although they may attack conditions that are widespread, these cases rest on particularized explorations of fact, often through discovery and expert testimony. In attacking school segregation in the five cases styled as *Brown* v. *Board of Education*, the NAACP sought to develop full factual records, building upon the experience of Thurgood Marshall and others as counsel in the earlier white primary cases and racial restrictive covenant cases. Widespread test cases will continue because both government and private counsel can approach the Supreme Court only by representing particular parties with particular concrete claims.

—CLEMENT E. VOSE

Bibliography

Cortner, Richard C. (1964). *The Wagner Act Cases.* Pages 106–141. Knoxville: University of Tennessee Press.

Freund, Paul A. (1951). *On Understanding the Supreme Court.* Pages 77–116. Boston: Little, Brown.

Irons, Peter (1982). *The New Deal Lawyers.* Pages 234–289. Princeton, N.J.: Princeton University Press.

Kluger, Richard (1975). *Simple Justice: The History of* Brown v. Board of Education *and Black America's Struggle for Equality.* Pages 256–540. New York: Vintage Books.

Vose, Clement E. (1959). *Caucasians Only: The Supreme Court, the NAACP, and the Restrictive Covenant Cases.* Pages 50–73, 151–176. Berkeley: University of California Press.

Wood, Stephen B. (1968). *Constitutional Politics in the Progressive Era.* Pages 81–110. Chicago: University of Chicago Press.

TEXAS v. BROWN

460 U.S. 730 (1983)

This case is significant for Justice William H. Rehnquist's exposition of the scope and applicability of the plain view doctrine, which had emerged in *Coolidge* v. *New Hampshire* (1971) as an exception to the warrant requirement for a search and seizure. According to Rehnquist, the answer to the question of whether property in plain view may be seized depends on the lawfulness of the intrusion that allows the police to see that property. Plain view therefore provides the basis for seizure if an officer's access to the object has a prior Fourth Amendment justification. The police may seize a suspicious object if they are engaged in a lawful activity; they do not have to know at once that the object inadvertently exposed to their sight is evidence of a crime. Reasonable suspicion on probable cause is sufficient even if the property seized was not immediately apparent as evidence of crime. No Justice dissented in this case, but Rehnquist spoke for a mere plurality, and a mere plurality had announced the plain view doctrine in *Coolidge.* Accordingly, judicial

Plain view provides the basis for seizure if an officer's access to the object has a prior Fourth Amendment justification.

See also

Search and Seizure

This case adopted a flexible approach to Article III's limitations on Congress's employment of nonjudicial tribunals.

controversy about the doctrine will continue, as will controversy about its application to particular facts.

—LEONARD W. LEVY

THOMAS v. UNION CARBIDE AGRICULTURAL PRODUCTS CO.

473 U.S. (1985)

The Supreme Court's decision in *Northern Pipeline Construction Co.* v. *Marathon Pipe Line Co.* (1982) left considerable confusion about the power of Congress to confer jurisdiction on administrators or legislative courts over cases falling within the judicial power of the United States. *Thomas* provided some useful clarification.

The Federal Insecticide, Fungicide, and Rodentcide Act (FIFRA) requires a manufacturer, as a condition on registering a pesticide, to supply research data on the pesticide's health, safety, and environmental effects to the Environmental Protection Agency (EPA). These data may be used in evaluating a second manufacturer's registration of a similar product, provided that the second manufacturer offers to compensate the first. If the two manufacturers cannot agree on the compensation, FIFRA requires binding arbitration of the dispute. An arbitrator's decision is reviewable by a court only for "fraud, misrepresentation or other misconduct."

Various pesticide manufacturers sued the EPA administrator challenging the constitutionality of the scheme of binding arbitration with limited court review. The federal district court held that the scheme violated Article III of the Constitution; on direct appeal, the Supreme Court unanimously reversed, upholding the law.

Justice Sandra Day O'Connor, writing for the Court, recognized a broad policy in Article III "that federal judicial power shall be vested in courts whose judges enjoy life tenure and fixed compensation." *Marathon* effectuated a part of that policy but was distinguishable here. Considering the origin of the claims to compensation in federal law, along with the reasons of public policy that persuaded Congress to impose binding arbitration, the manufacturers' claimed rights were properly considered "public rights," the adjudication of which Congress could place in administrative hands. Cases involving "public rights" were not limited to those in which the government itself was a party. Nor, said the Court in an important obiter dictum, is Article III's requirement of independent judges irrelevant merely because the government is a party. Here the assignment of decision to nonjudicial arbitrators was softened somewhat by FIFRA's provision of some minimal review by constitutional courts of arbitrators' decisions. (In some cases, the Court noted, due process considerations might independently require further court review.)

Thomas thus adopted a flexible approach to Article III's limitations on Congress's employment of nonjudicial tribunals—the very approach urged by the *Marathon* dissenters. Justice William J. Brennan, for three Justices, concurred separately on the basis of his plurality opinion in *Marathon*. Justice John Paul Stevens concurred, saying the manufacturers lacked standing to challenge the law's validity.

—KENNETH L. KARST

THOMAS, CLARENCE

(1948–)

Probably no Justice on the Supreme Court was ever chosen amid more furious and divisive controversy than Clarence Thomas. Thomas had been a judge on the U.S. Court of Appeals for the District of Columbia for fifteen months when he was chosen by President George Bush in July 1991 to succeed retiring Justice Thurgood Marshall, a towering figure in the civil rights movement and on the Supreme Court. Clarence Thomas's nomination was controversial, and his appointment was not guaranteed, even before allegations of sexual harassment threw his chances into doubt and the entire nominating and approval process into (at least temporary) disrepute. To be fair, any person nominated to fill Thurgood Marshall's seat on the bench would have had a hard time "measuring up" to Marshall's reputation among civil rights and civil liberties advocates.

Clarence Thomas was better known—and liked—among conservative Republicans than he was among Democrats or civil rights groups; among the latter, those who did know him were suspicious of how sympathetic a justice Thomas might be to their interests. For eight years (1982–90) Thomas had served as chairman of the Equal Employment Opportunity Commission. It was no secret that the Reagan and Bush administrations were less than eager to spend time and resources defending the EEOC regulations, and civil rights groups were distinctly unimpressed with Thomas's record as chief of the EEOC. But by his choice, Bush had put liberals in something of a bind, for it would be politically difficult to challenge the nomination of an African American, even if prominent black groups also opposed Bush's selection.

When word leaked about allegations of sexual harassment involving a former employee of Thomas's, now a professor of law in Oklahoma, an already troubled nomination was shaken and nearly derailed.

Clarence Thomas was born on June 23, 1948, in Savannah, Georgia, the second child and first son of Leola Williams and M. C. Thomas. He grew up in nearby Pin Point, a poor community of about five hundred (many of whom were descendants of slaves) on the marshy grounds of a former plantation, where most inhabitants worked for very little money, cleaning crabs and shucking oysters. Leola Williams worked as a maid and clothed her children with secondhand clothes donated to their Baptist church. M.

C. Thomas abandoned the family when Clarence was two and Leola was pregnant with a third child. Sometime later, after their wooden house burned down and Leola Thomas remarried, Clarence and his younger brother were sent to live with their grandfather, Myers Anderson.

Coming to live with his grandfather was possibly the best thing that ever happened to Clarence Thomas; it certainly set him on a path where he could make the most of his abilities and opportunities. Myers Anderson was a devout Catholic and staunch Democrat, and an active member of the NAACP. In a time when most Southern blacks had few choices in employment, and hard-set discrimination was a daily fact of life, Anderson determined that the only tolerable way to work was to be his own boss. He built up a thriving fuel delivery business, transporting wood, coal, and heating oil in his truck, and thus was able to provide his grandsons with "amenities" they had never been able to take for granted, such as indoor plumbing and three meals a day.

As hard as Myers Anderson pushed himself, so he urged his grandsons to excel in school. He enrolled them in an all-black grammar school, St. Benedict the Moor. The white nuns who taught at St. Benedict maintained strict discipline and expected excellence from their students. After school each day the Thomas boys helped their grandfather with the fuel deliveries. Clarence Thomas recalls his childhood as a time when his grandparents instilled in him a conviction that "school, discipline, hard work and 'right-from-wrong' were of the highest priority."

Thomas attended a black Catholic high school for his first two years. Then, because his grandfather wanted him to become a priest, he transferred to St. John Vianney Minor Seminary, a Catholic boarding school near Savannah. He went from being one among many to being the only black student in his class. He knew about racism in society in general, but he was astonished to find such

T

THOMAS, CLARENCE

(1948–)

bigotry in a seminary. Perhaps in part because of the treatment he endured from many of his fellow students, he excelled in his studies.

Continuing his preparation for the priesthood, in 1967 Thomas enrolled in Immaculate Conception Seminary in Missouri. Here, too, he was shocked by the racist attitudes he found in many of his fellow students, who would be going out into the world to preach brotherly love. Finally Thomas quit in disgust when a student expressed delight at hearing of the assassination of the Reverend Martin Luther King Jr.

That same year, 1968, Thomas went to Holy Cross, a Jesuit college in Worcester, Massachusetts, which was making a strong effort to recruit minority students after the riots following the King assassination. He was among the students who founded the Black Student Union at Holy Cross, but when its members decided that all black students should live together in one dormitory, Clarence Thomas dissented. He preferred, as he later wrote, to "profit from the experience

by learning to associate [with] and understand the white majority." He did eventually live in the black student dorm, but brought his white former roommate to live with him.

He graduated ninth in his class with an English honors (B.A.) degree in 1971. The day after graduation, Thomas married Kathy Grace Ambush, whom he had met at a nearby Catholic women's college. Their son, Jamal Adeen, would be born two years later.

Thomas was accepted into Yale Law School, thanks in part to an affirmative action program to recruit minority students. Naturally he was proud to be at Yale, but the fact that he was the beneficiary of affirmative action troubled him. He explained later, "You had to prove yourself every day because the presumption was that you were dumb and didn't deserve to be there on merit." As would become customary for him, Thomas deliberately concentrated not on "black" subjects like civil rights and constitutional law, but on tax and antitrust law. Indeed, after law school, it was in tax law that Thomas requested to work under Missouri attorney general John C. Danforth.

After graduating from Yale in 1974, he returned to Missouri to take a position as assistant attorney general under Danforth, where he concentrated on tax and environmental cases. Danforth was elected to the U.S. Senate in 1977, and Thomas moved to work in corporate law at Monsanto, where he supervised the government registration and regulation of its pesticides. After several years at Monsanto, Thomas rejoined Senator Danforth as a legislative assistant in charge of energy and environmental issues. Again, he deliberately steered clear of civil rights legislation.

It was around this time, in the late 1970s, that Thomas began to be active in black conservative circles, forging ties with other professionals like himself who believed that welfare, busing, affirmative action, and government "set-asides" harmed African Americans more than they helped by inducing dependence on government assistance. What black Americans needed instead, Thomas contended, was education, self-reliance, and work. Thomas made speeches and wrote articles espousing the view that quotas and racial preferences had the insidious effect of reinforcing the idea that blacks cannot compete with whites without artificial assistance. In a 1987 article for the *Yale Law and Policy Review*, Thomas described affirmative action as "social engineering."

The Reagan administration saw much to admire in this young conservative, and chose him to serve as assistant secretary for civil rights in the U.S. Department of Education (1981–82), even though Thomas had resolutely steered clear of civil rights from law school onward. In a 1987 speech he said, "I had, initially, resisted and declined taking the position of assistant secretary for civil rights simply because my career was not in civil rights and I had no intention of moving into this area. . . . I always found it curious that even though my background was in energy, taxation, and general corporate regulatory matters, that I was not seriously sought after to move into one of these areas." In May 1982, after Thomas had been in the Education Department for ten months, Reagan promoted him to chairman of the Equal Employment Opportunity Commission, where he stayed until 1990.

At the EEOC, Thomas's responsibility was to oversee the enforcement of federal laws against discrimination in the workplace. The Reagan administration was opposed to numerical goals and timetables, traditional tools for fighting discrimination, and Thomas's obedience (albeit independent-minded) to the administration's view brought him into disfavor with Democrats and civil rights advocates. Under Thomas's watch, the Commission also for the most part abandoned the use of class action suits in cases of widespread discrimination by corporations, relying instead on individual cases. He was criticized for letting some 9,000 age discrimination complaints languish, an oversight (or neglect) Thomas has admitted was the "single most devastating event" of his time at EEOC. During the 1990 Senate Judiciary Committee hearings before his confirmation to the U.S. Court of Appeals, Senator Howard M. Metzenbaum (D-Ohio) charged Thomas with having allowed 1,700 complaints filed with state antidiscrimination agencies to lapse without investigation. Thomas denied the allegation.

President Bush appointed him as judge of the U.S. Court of Appeals for the District of Columbia Circuit, and he was sworn in on March 12, 1990. It was from this position that Bush pulled Thomas fifteen months later to sit as a successor to Thurgood Marshall when that justice announced his retirement.

While on the D.C. Circuit Justice Thomas showed instances of the judicial conservatism he would soon bring to the Supreme Court. He believed courts should defer greatly to the expertise of government agencies, and in two controversial decisions made plain his view that factual issues are for the agency, not the reviewing court, to decide. In rebuffing objections to a Federal Aviation Administration decision approving an airport expansion, he rejected claims that the agency's environmental impact statement under the National Environmental Policy Act (NEPA) was inadequate, noting: "Just as NEPA is not a green Magna Carta, federal judges are not the barons at Runnymede." He also, concurring in another decision, disagreed with the majority and concluded a competitor of a ferry service lacked standing to question the company's exemption from federal regulation of its service. As one pair of writers described his views: "Agencies have followed the proper procedures, the federal courts have no role in judging the judgments made by the agencies."

On July 1, 1991, in Kennebunkport, Maine, President Bush appeared with Thomas before reporters to announce his nomination of the judge as "the best man" to replace retiring Justice Thurgood Marshall.

T

Thomas believed that welfare, busing, affirmative action, and racial quotas harmed African Americans more than they helped by inducing dependence on government assistance.

Bush was at pains to insist that race had nothing to do with his selection. "I don't feel he's a quota. . . . I expressed my respect for the ground that Mr. Justice Marshall plowed, but I don't feel there should be a black seat on the Court or an ethnic seat on the Court."

After the president spoke, Thomas said, "As a child, I could not dare dream that I would ever see the Supreme Court, not to mention be nominated to it. . . . Indeed my most vivid childhood memory of a Supreme Court was the 'Impeach Earl Warren' signs which lined Highway 17 near Savannah. I didn't quite understand who this Earl Warren fellow was, but I knew he was in some kind of trouble."

Because Thomas had already made quite public his opposition to quotas and racial preferences, as well as his position that government affirmative action programs are unconstitutional, Democrats and civil rights advocates quickly protested his nomination. It had not been forgotten that in a 1984 interview with the *Washington Post* Thomas remarked that all the traditional civil rights leaders do is "bitch, bitch, bitch, moan and whine." It had also not gone unnoticed when Thomas publicly criticized some aspects of the Supreme Court's 1954 landmark *Brown* v. *Board of Education* decision; the ruling, he said, had been based too much on sentiment and had assumed that black schools were automatically inferior to white schools. (In striking down the *Plessy v. Ferguson* doctrine of "separate but equal," that is precisely what *Brown* did, on the ground that segregation conveyed a clear message of black inferiority.) The NAACP and the Congressional Black Caucus announced that they would not support the nomination of Clarence Thomas.

The Democrats on the Judiciary Committee, who regarded acceptance of privacy rights a requirement for any nominee to the high court, pressed Thomas repeatedly to say whether he thought the Supreme Court had made the right decision in extending the right to privacy to include a woman's right to abortion. They wanted to know why, when speaking to a conservative audience, he had praised an article advocating that all abortions be declared unconstitutional; he dismissed it as a "throwaway line." The committee gave him an opportunity to disavow a 1987 speech in which he had called the Senate's rejection of Judge Robert H. Bork as a "tragedy," but he would not. Thomas was tight-lipped when questioned about his opinions on matters of policy or approaches to constitutional interpretation. Members of the Judiciary Committee could not conceal their incredulity when Thomas insisted he had never formed an opinion on the *Roe* v. *Wade* decision and that he had never even discussed the matter with anyone.

In October 1991, just before the Senate was to vote on Thomas's confirmation, information was leaked to the press concerning an FBI report, which the Judiciary Committee had seen, containing allegations that Thomas had sexually harassed a former employee at the EEOC. Anita Hill, an African-American professor of law at the University of Oklahoma, was also a graduate of Yale Law School and had worked for Thomas at the EEOC. Although she was clearly reluctant to speak in public about a private matter that had happened ten years before, Hill was brought to Washington to testify before the Judiciary Committee. The hearings were nationally televised, and gripped the public as no spectacle had done in years. Many found the specific details of Hill's testimony, and her calm, composed demeanor, too convincing to be anything other than accurate. Thomas categorically denied the allegations, insisted he had not watched her testimony, and charged, in a heated self-defense, that the entire proceedings were a "high-tech lynching for uppity blacks." (It should be pointed out that although Thomas's refutation of the allegations was forceful and bitter, at no time did he speak ill of Professor Hill; some of his defenders, however, were not so gentle in casting doubt upon her veracity.)

On October 15, 1991, after a week of testimony and deliberations, and 107 days after his nomination, the Senate voted to confirm Thomas by a vote of 52–48, the closest confirmation vote in a hundred years.

The Thomas-Hill hearings were a landmark in American jurisprudence, not only because of the unforgettable spectacle of two attractive and polished black professionals vying in a highly charged debate on the most prominent stage in the nation, but also because the controversy introduced much of the nation—men in particular—to the phenomenon of sexual harassment. Though the hearings disgusted many, the event had the positive effect of opening a dialogue and beginning a process of educating the public about a very real form of workplace harassment, and, some say, predation and oppression.

Since taking his seat on the Court, Thomas has often been described as quiet, little given to questioning of attorneys arguing before the bar, and quite at home in the conservative wing. He often votes with Justice Antonin Scalia, of whose opinions he had spoken with admiration before his confirmation. In the Senate Judiciary Committee hearings, Thomas spoke repeatedly of his belief in "judicial restraint," and claimed that he would not bring any particular agenda to the Court.

As he indicated in his confirmation testimony, Thomas tends to view as a strict constructionist any constitutional guarantees, or absence of guarantees. Early in his tenure, in the case of *Hudson* v. *McMillian* (1992), the Court ruled that a prison's guard's use of excessive force may violate the Constitution even if it does not result in serious injury to a prisoner. Thomas alone dissented. The Eighth Amendment's prohibition against cruel and unusual punishment, he wrote in his dissent, "should not be turned into a national code of prison regulation," and he observed that the majority ruling was "yet another manifestation of the pervasive view that the federal constitution must address all ills in our society."

That same term Justice Thomas again demonstrated this view. In *Nordlinger* v. *Hahn* (1992) the Court upheld a California law that required local tax assessors to value property based on its purchase price when acquired, as opposed to its current worth. This worked to the advantage of longtime property owners, and was challenged as a violation of the Equal Protection Clause. The Court had earlier unanimously found a West Virginia assessment based on purchase price to be unconstitutional in *Allegheny Pittsburgh Coal Co.* v. *County Commission* (1989), where the state law required assessments to reflect current market value. Though Thomas, who was not on the Court in 1989, concurred with the result in *Nordlinger*, he alone would have overruled *Allegheny*, arguing that a "violation of state law does not by itself constitute a violation of the Federal Constitution."

When the Court, in *United States* v. *Fordice* (1992), ruled Mississippi had to end dual admission standards for its historically white and historically black state colleges, Justice Thomas once more concurred separately. He argued that the Court did "not foreclose the possibility that there exists 'sound educational justification' for maintaining historically black colleges as such," though there seems scant evidence of that possibility in the majority opinion of Justice Byron R. White.

In *Holder* v. *Hall*, a 1994 case that unsuccessfully challenged a Georgia county's at-large voting for its county commission as violation of the Voting Rights Act of 1965 and the Constitution, Justice Thomas, concurring, joined by Justice Scalia, wrote that the Voting Rights Act had been too broadly construed and had led to a "misadventure in judicial policymaking," "a device for . . . apportioning political power among racial and ethnic groups." He disputed the idea that race defines political interest and the expectation that people of a given skin color will have a common view on political matters. He believed attempts to create single-member districts would "deepen racial divisions by destroying any need for voters or candidates to build bridges between racial groups."

Indeed, the right to think his own thoughts has been a consistent theme—and struggle—of Clarence Thomas's career, from the time he broke with the Black Student Union at Holy Cross on the matter of an all-black dormitory to more recent times when he has been criticized as a traitor to his race. Almost every time Thomas is invited to speak to a predominantly black group, a faction within the group protests; sometimes the inviting group will hold firm in its welcome of the justice, and other times they will cave in to the protestors. In a flap in the summer of 1998, when Thomas was invited to speak to the National Bar Association, he told the group that he would not "follow the prescription assigned to blacks." He asserted that those who expect him to think a certain way simply because he is black are denying his humanity and want him to be "an intellectual slave." His use of charged language in defense of his views is not limited to the Senate Judiciary Committee hearings.

Justice Thomas once more showed his individualistic approach in his view of the protection the Constitution accords commercial speech, such as advertising. Although the Court has held since its 1973 ruling in *Virginia State Board of Pharmacy* v. *Virginia Citizens Consumer Council* that advertising enjoys some First Amendment protection, it has consistently given regulations of commercial speech less scrutiny than attempts to control political, educational, or other fully protected speech. This stems from recognition of the government's need to safeguard the public from false and fraudulent advertising. Yet Thomas's concurring opinion in *44 Liquormart* v. *Rhode Island* (1996), where the Court set aside a law that banned advertising the prices of alcoholic beverages, argued that the courts should treat commercial and noncommercial speech identically in cases where gov-

ernment has suppressed speech so as to limit knowledge.

Justice Thomas dissented, joined by Justice Scalia and Chief Justice William H. Rehnquist, in *M.L.B.* v. *S.L.J.* (1996), where the majority held an indigent mother found unfit to be a parent was entitled to a free trial transcript in order to appeal. Though the decision was firmly grounded in cases so holding with regard to criminal appeals, Justice Thomas wrote that this entire line of decisions would "have startled the Fourteenth Amendment's framers" and that states have no duty to provide transcripts (or presumably legal assistance) for appeals from criminal convictions.

In *Kansas* v. *Hendricks* (1997), writing for the Court, Justice Thomas upheld a law requiring violent sex offenders to be committed civilly after their prison sentence ended. Prior decisions had ruled that civil commitment must be based on a finding of mental illness and the availability of treatment. Justice Thomas nonetheless concluded the state's declaration that the prisoner was diagnosed with "pedophilia" and that this was a "mental disorder" satisfied the Due Process Clause. He finessed the treatment requirement by ruling that no treatment for pedophilia was available. Justice Stephen G. Breyer and three others dissented on that point.

In *Camps Newfound/Owatonna* v. *Town of Harrison* (1997) Justice Thomas dissented from a decision holding Maine could not condition its exemption from real property tax for charitable institutions on the institution primarily serving residents of the state. The Court ruled a camp run by a religious group could not, consistent with the Commerce Clause, lose its exemption simply because most of its campers were nonresidents. This decision was based on a series of cases decided over the past several decades holding states may not discriminate against commerce to or from other states—the doctrine known as the Dormant Commerce Clause. The *Camps Newfound* decision was noteworthy only for applying this well-established rule to services provided by a not-for-profit organization. In his dissent, however, Justice Thomas urged the Court to abandon the entire rule as "virtually unworkable" and "policy-laden decisionmaking" by the Court, with, in his view, no support in the Constitution itself. As in *44 Liquormart* and some of his other concurrences and dissents, Thomas showed a willingness to discard rules followed for decades. As one scholar has described it, Justice Thomas is not "one to eschew provocative arguments or avoid engaging in wholesale reconceptualizations."

At the end of the 1997–98 term, three decisions on sexual harassment in the workplace provided clearer guidelines for employers and employees and the Court's opinions were received with unusual approval across the political spectrum. In *Faragher* v. *City of Boca Raton*, whose majority opinion was written by Justice David H. Souter, the Court held that employers are legally responsible for harassing behavior of a supervisory employee even when the company has in place a clear policy against sexual harassment and top management is unaware that an employee is violating the policy. If a harassed employee suffers harm, the employer is liable. Justice Anthony M. Kennedy wrote the majority opinion in a related case, *Burlington Industries, Inc.* v. *Ellerth*, ruling that an employer can be held liable for a supervisor's acts, even though unaware of those acts, and even when the harassed employee has resisted and has suffered no adverse effects on the job; the employer can, however, defend itself by showing that it had an effective antiharassment policy in place and that the employee did not make adequate use of it.

The *Faragher* and *Burlington* decisions were 7–2; in each, Justice Thomas dissented, joined by Justice Scalia. Taking a narrow view of the law of sexual harassment, he argued in *Faragher* that employers ought not be liable for supervisors' sexual harassment unless the victim proved he or she suffered specific adverse employment consequences like dis-

missal or demotion. Dissenting in *Burlington*, Thomas asserted that employers ought not be liable for a hostile work environment created by supervisors unless the employer was itself negligent in allowing the supervisor's conduct.

Justice Thomas continues to be an exponent of narrow judicial review of Constitutional questions and a believer in adhering to the original intent of the Founders.

—PHILIP WEINBERG AND MARK LAFLAUR

Bibliography

Cushman, Clare, ed. Clarence Thomas, (1991–). *The Supreme Court Justices: Illustrated Biographies, 1789–1995*. 2nd ed. Washington, D.C.: Congressional Quarterly and the Supreme Court Historical Society.

Kass, Stephen L., and Michael B. Gerrard (1991). Judge Thomas and the Environment. *New York Law Journal*.

Denning, Brandon P. (1999). Justice Thomas, the Export-Import Clause, and *Camps Newfound/Owatonna* v. *Harrison*. *University of Colorado Law Review* 70: 155.

THOMPSON v. OKLAHOMA

487 U.S. 815 (1988)

The Court held that the cruel and unusual punishment clause of the Eighth Amendment, applicable to the states by the incorporation doctrine, prohibited the death sentence against a first-degree murderer who committed the offense at the age of fifteen. Justice John Paul Stevens spoke for a four-member plurality in whose judgment Justice Sandra Day O'Connor joined. Stevens asserted that the execution of the juvenile would "offend civilized standards of decency" and be "abhorrent to the conscience of the community."

Justice John Paul Stevens asserted that the execution of the juvenile would "offend civilized standards of decency."

See also

Capital Punishment

O'Connor discerned no such consensus from the evidence adduced by the plurality. Indeed, the Court divided 4–4 on the question as to whether such a consensus existed. O'Connor believed that the sentence must be set aside because of the risk that the state did not realize that its capital punishment statute might apply to fifteen-year-olds.

Stevens had a second string to his bow. He declared that the execution of the minor did not contribute to the purposes underlying the death penalty. O'Connor and the dissenters believed that the plurality Justices failed to understand that some fifteen-year-olds were as blameworthy as adults.

Justice Antonin Scalia, for the three dissenters (Justice Anthony M. Kennedy did not participate), believed that a consensus ex-isted showing that the execution of juveniles under fifteen years of age did not offend community standards and therefore did not violate the Eighth Amendment. In *Standford v. Penry* (1988) the Court ruled that the execution of juveniles who murdered at sixteen years of age was constitutional.

—LEONARD W. LEVY

THORNTON v. CALDOR, INC.

105 S. Ct. 2914 (1985)

The Supreme Court held unconstitutional, on establishment clause grounds, a state act authorizing employees to designate a sabbath

THORNHILL v. ALABAMA

310 U.S. 88 (1940)

This case involved a First Amendment challenge to convictions under an Alabama antipicketing statute. Normally one has standing only to plead one's own constitutional rights. In *Thornhill,* however, the Supreme Court did not ask whether the particular activity in which the pickets had engaged was constitutionally protected. Instead it asked whether the statute itself, rather than its application to these particular persons, violated the First Amendment. Because the statute was invalid on its face, it could be challenged, even by a union that itself might have engaged in violent picketing not protected by the First Amendment. The theory was that the statute's general ban on all labor dispute picketing would threaten peaceful picketers as well, even though no peaceful picketers had even been prosecuted.

Justice Frank Murphy acknowledged that the state legislature legitimately might have written a narrowly drawn statute that condemned only violent or mass picketing. Instead it wrote a general ban on all picketing in labor-management disputes. "The existence of such a statute . . . which does not aim specifically at evils within the allowable area of state control but, on the contrary, sweeps within its ambit other activities that in ordinary circumstances constitute an exercise of freedom of speech . . . readily lends itself to . . . discriminatory enforcement by local prosecuting officials [and] results in a continuous and pervasive unconstitutional restraint on all freedom of discussion." Subsequently the Court was to speak of the unconstitutional chilling effect of such "facially overbroad" statutes.

—MARTIN SHAPIRO

PROTECTED SPEECH

Peaceful picketing in labor-management disputes constitutes an exercise of freedom of speech. (Corbis/Bettmann)

day and not work that day. Applying the three-part test of *Lemon* v. *Kurtzman* (1971), Chief Justice Warren E. Burger found that by vesting in employees an "absolute and unqualified" right not to work on the sabbath of one's choice, and by forcing employers to adjust work schedules to the religious practices of employees, the act constituted a law respecting an establishment of religion. In purpose and effect it advanced religion, preferring those who believe in not working on the sabbath to those who hold no such belief. By implication, a statute giving employers some leeway would be constitutional. Only Justice William H. Rehnquist dissented, without opinion. No member of the Court defended the statute as a state effort to prevent discrimination against sabbath believers by preventing the imposition of employment penalties on those acting in obedience to conscience by refusing to work.

—LEONARD W. LEVY

TINKER v. DES MOINES INDEPENDENT COMMUNITY SCHOOL DISTRICT

393 U.S. 503 (1969)

Tinker is a leading modern decision on the subjects of symbolic speech and children's rights. A group of adults and students in Des Moines planned to protest the Vietnam War by wearing black armbands during the 1965 holiday season. On learning of this plan, the public school principals adopted a policy to forbid the wearing of armbands. Two high school students and one junior high school student wore armbands to school, refused to remove them, and were suspended until they might return without armbands. They sued in federal court to enjoin enforcement of the principals' policy and for nominal damages.

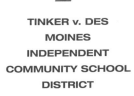

Student expression could be forbidden if it disrupts school work but here the principals lacked justification for imposing any limitations.

"PURE SPEECH"

Tinker *allowed a "silent, passive expression of opinion" among students who wore black armbands in protest of the Vietnam War. (Corbis/Bettmann)*

See also

Symbolic Speech

867

A unanimous Supreme Court held that a federal court in a habeas corpus proceeding always has the power to try the facts anew.

The district court dismissed the complaint, and the court of appeals affirmed by an equally divided court. The Supreme Court reversed, 7–2, in an opinion by Justice Abe Fortas.

The wearing of these armbands was "closely akin to 'pure speech' and protected by the First Amendment. The school environment did imply limitations on the freedom of expression, but here the principals lacked justification for imposing any such limitations. The authorities' "undifferentiated fear" of disturbance was insufficient. While student expression could be forbidden when it materially disrupted school work or school discipline, these students had undertaken "a silent, passive expression of opinion, unaccompanied by any disorder or disturbance." Furthermore, only this "particular symbol . . . was singled out for prohibition"; political campaign buttons had been allowed, and even "the Iron Cross, traditionally a symbol of Nazism." (Justice Fortas may have been unaware of the vogue among surfers and their inland imitators.)

Justice Hugo L. Black dissented, accusing the majority of encouraging students to defy their teachers and arguing that the wearing of the armbands had, in fact, diverted other students' minds from their schoolwork. He did not ask how much the principals' reaction to the planned protest might have contributed to that diversion.

—KENNETH L. KARST

TOWNSEND v. SAIN

372 U.S. 29 (1963)

When a state prisoner seeks federal habeas corpus review of a constitutional error in his or her case, the federal court must decide what weight to give the state court fact findings that are relevant to the prisoner's claim. The fairness and accuracy of such findings are crucial to the proper adjudication of federal constitutional rights, because most

habeas corpus petitions raise mixed questions of law and fact, such as the voluntariness of a waiver of constitutional rights, or the suggestiveness of a line-up identification. In *Townsend*, a unanimous Supreme Court held that a federal court in a habeas corpus proceeding always has the power to try the facts anew, and that it must do so if the defendant did not receive a full and fair evidentiary hearing in any state court proceeding. The Court split 5–4 over the need for more specific directives concerning mandatory hearings, with Chief Justice Earl Warren setting forth the majority's view that a hearing is required in six particular circumstances.

In 1966 Congress enacted a modified form of the *Townsend* criteria in an amendment to the Judicial Code, specifying eight circumstances when the validity of state court findings may not be presumed. In other circumstances, the habeas corpus petitioner bears the burden of proving that the state fact findings were erroneous.

—CATHERINE HANCOCK

TREVETT v. WEEDEN

(Rhode Island, 1786)

A Rhode Island case of 1786, this is the best known of the alleged state precedents for judicial review. The Superior Court of Judicature, the state's highest tribunal, did not hold a state act unconstitutional but it did construe it in a manner that left it inoperative. The case arose under a force act passed by the legislature to compel observance of the state paper-money laws; anyone refusing to accept paper money at par with specie was triable without a jury or right of appeal "according to the laws of the land" and on conviction was subject to a 100 pound fine and costs or be committed "till sentence be performed." Trevett filed an information before the state chief justice charging that Weeden refused tender of paper money at face value. James Varnum, representing Weeden, argued that the force act violated the right to trial by jury, guaranteed by the unwritten state constitution, which was fundamental law that limited legislative powers; the legislature could make law "not repugnant to the constitution" and the judiciary had "the sole power of judging those laws . . . but cannot admit any act of the legislative as law, which is against the constitution."

The court refused to decide the issue, ruling that it lacked jurisdiction. Its judgment was simply that Trevett's complaint "does not come under the cognizance of the Justices . . . and it is hereby dismissed." Orally, however, some of the judges, according to the newspaper accounts, declared the force act "to be repugnant and unconstitutional," and one of them pointed out that its phrase, "without trial by jury, according to the laws of the land," was self-contradictory and thus unenforceable.

The governor called the legislature into special session, and the legislature summoned the high court judges to explain their reasons, the legislature said, for holding an act "unconstitutional, and so absolutely void," an "unprecedented" judgment that tended "to abolish the legislative authority." Judge David Howell, the court's main spokesman, defended judicial review and judicial independence. Although he summarized Varnum's argument that the act was unconstitutional, Howell insisted that the legislature had confused the argument, for the judgment was just that the complaint was "cognizable."

The legislature, unconvinced by the court's technical distinction, recognized that the judgment made the paper money laws unenforceable; in effect the court had exercised judicial review, which the legislature deemed subversive of its supremacy. Howell, by contrast, had claimed that if the legislature could pass on the court's judgment, "the Legislature would become the supreme judiciary—a perversion of power totally subversive of civil liberty." Anticipating a motion to unseat them, the judges presented a memorial demanding

due process of law. Varnum and the attorney general supported them, arguing that they could not be removed except on a criminal charge. The motion to remove the judges failed, and the legislature even repealed the force act, but it revenged itself on the judges by failing to reelect four of the five members when their annual terms expired, and by ousting Congressman Varnum and the state attorney general. Varnum published a one-sided pamphlet on the case, giving it publicity even in Philadelphia while the Constitution Convention of 1787 met. Although the pamphlet popularized the doctrine of judicial review, in Rhode Island no judge endorsed it for seventy years after.

—LEONARD W. LEVY

TRUAX v. CORRIGAN

257 U.S. 312 (1921)

A 1913 Arizona law, similar to the labor provisions of the Clayton Antitrust Act, prohibited state court injunctions against peaceful picketing. Following a dispute with restaurant proprietor William Truax, a local union peacefully picketed and distributed handbills calling for a boycott. Truax's business receipts dropped dramatically, and after the Arizona courts denied him relief, he appealed to the Supreme Court, contending that the state law deprived him of his property without due process of law and violated the equal protection clause of the Fourteenth Amendment.

Chief Justice William Howard Taft, speaking for a 5–4 majority, held the state statute unconstitutional. He reasoned that Truax held a property right in his business; free access to it by employees and customers was incidental to that right. Concerted action that intentionally injured that right was a conspiracy and a tort. In this case, the union's activities constituted an "unlawful annoyance and hurtful nuisance." Such wrongs, Taft concluded, could not be remediless, and he declared that the anti-injunction law deprived Truax of due

This is the best known of the alleged state precedents for judicial review.

An Arizona law prohibiting injunctions against peaceful picketing was deemed unconstitutional.

process. He also ruled that the law violated equal protection by limiting the application of an injunction to a particular class.

Justice Louis D. Brandeis, dissenting, maintained that even if the employer had a constitutional right to be free from boycotting and picketing, the state was not compelled to protect that right with an injunction, as states were free to expand or control their equity jurisdiction. In a separate dissent, Justice Oliver Wendell Holmes argued that the state law was a valid "social experiment," however "futile or even noxious." Beyond that, he challenged the assumption equating "business" with a property right. Business, he asserted, was "a course of conduct," and like any other was subject to modification regarding what would justify doing it a harm.

—STANLEY I. KUTLER

U

ULLMANN v. UNITED STATES

350 U.S. 422 (1956)

Ullmann, relying on his right not to be a witness against himself, refused to testify before a federal grand jury concerning his alleged communist activities. Though he received immunity against prosecution for any criminal transaction concerning which he was compelled to testify, he continued pertinacious. Ullmann argued against the constitutionality of the congressional Immunity Act of 1954 on the grounds that it did not immunize him from such disabilities as loss of job, expulsion from labor unions, compulsory registration as a subversive, passport ineligibility, and general public opprobrium. Thus he distinguished his case from *Brown* v. *Walker* (1896) on the theory that he had not received full transactional immunity. The Court rejected Ullmann's argument, 7–2. Justice Felix Frankfurter for the majority reasoned that the Fifth Amendment's right to silence operated only to prevent the compulsion of testimony that might expose one to a criminal charge. The disabilities to which Ullmann claimed exposure were not criminal penalties. Justices William O. Douglas and Hugo L. Black, dissenting, would have held the immunity act unconstitutional on the ground that the right of silence created by the Fifth Amendment is beyond the reach of Congress. Douglas contended that the amendment was designed to protect against infamy, as well as prosecution, and against forfeitures—those disabilities of which Ullmann spoke—as well as criminal fines and imprisonment.

—LEONARD W. LEVY

"ULYSSES," ONE BOOK ENTITLED, UNITED STATES v.

5F. Supp. 182 (1933); 72 F.2d 705 (1934)

Although it was not a decision of the Supreme Court, *Ulysses* was not merely a case involving a famous book and prominent judges but also a harbinger of modern decisions on obscenity. Its standards for construing the common law terms embodied in federal customs regulations were transmuted in *United States* v. *Roth* (1957) into constitutional principles for testing both federal and state legislation on the subject.

The handful of early obscenity cases that reached the Supreme Court mainly presented claims of technical error in the trials below. *Ulysses* presented clear questions of substantive standards for adjudging obscenity and lewdness. The established reputation of the book insured careful attention; Judge John M. Woolsey's lower court opinion was unmistakably written for the anthologies it ultimately graced. Judge Augustus N. Hand's appellate majority opinion was straightforward, but Judge Martin T. Manton's dissent was somewhat verbose.

Woolsey declared that the book successfully showed "how the screen [*sic*] of consciousness with its ever-shifting kaleidoscopic impression carries, as it were on a plastic palimpsest, . . . a penumbral zone residual of past impressions . . . not unlike the result of a double or, if that is possible, a multiple exposure on a cinema film. . . ."

The relevant statute on importation of books prohibited not pandering but obscenity.

The Fifth Admendment's right to silence operated only to prevent the compulsion of testimony that might expose one to a criminal charge.

Ulysses *presented clear questions of substantive standards for adjudging obscenity and lewdness.*

See also
Obscenity

UNITED JEWISH ORGANIZATIONS v. CAREY

430 U.S. 144 (1977)

AN APHRODISIAC?

The Shakespeare and Company bookstore in Paris published James Joyce's Ulysses *when no publishers in England would take it. (Corbis/Owen Franken)*

The Court upheld a race-conscious reapportionment of voters in state legislative districts in Greater New York City.

See also

Voting Rights

Woolsey announced without discussion that the test for obscenity required examination of the whole work. The standard was the effect on "what the French would call *l'homme moyen sensuel*—who plays, in this branch of legal inquiry . . . the same role . . . as does the 'reasonable man in the law of torts. . . .' With this standard he found the book "somewhat emetic, nowhere . . . an aphrodisiac." He also found Joyce to have been sincere and lacking pornographic intent or the "leer of the sensualist."

At the appellate level Augustus Hand for himself and Learned Hand managed to come to grips with the central legal issue—whether isolated passages could render a work of art obscene. This was the test derived from *Regina* v. *Hicklin* (1868), the classic British case, and, they conceded, followed in *United States* v. *Bennett* (1879), a circuit court decision by Justice Samuel Blatchford. They discounted other alleged precedents and argued that the isolated passages concept was not followed for works of science or medicine and should not be followed for literature either. They cited state decisions embracing the "dominant effect" notion, and read that test (together with their definition of the relevant

audience) into the statute, concluding that other readings would be impractical and overrestrictive.

Manton, dissenting, insisted that federal decisions in the past had accepted the "isolated passages" test. As literature was for amusement only, the community could reasonably demand that it meet moral standards—those of average, not exceptional, individuals.

—SAMUEL KRISLOV

Bibliography

Lockhart, William B., and McClure, Robert C. (1954). Literature, the Law of Obscenity, and the Constitution. *Minnesota Law Review* 38:295–395.

UNITED JEWISH ORGANIZATIONS v. CAREY

430 U.S. 144 (1977)

Under the Voting Rights Act of 1965 New York sought approval of the United States attorney general for its reapportionment of voters in state legislative districts in Greater New York City. To increase the nonwhite majorities in certain districts, and thus secure approval, the legislature divided a Hasidic Jewish community into two districts, each with a nonwhite majority. Petitioners claimed that assignment of voters solely on the basis of race violated the Fourteenth and Fifteenth Amendments.

By a 7–1 vote, the Supreme Court upheld the race-conscious reapportionment. There was no majority opinion but a series of overlapping alignments. Four Justices, noting that the percentage of nonwhite-majority districts was less than the percentage of nonwhites in the county in question, said that the use of racial criteria to comply with the act was not limited to compensating for past discrimination. Other Justices emphasized the lack of stigma or legislative purpose to disadvantage the Hasidim. Justice William J. Brennan, in a comprehensive opinion on race-conscious remedies, appeared to look ahead to *Regents of University of California* v. *Bakke* (1978). Chief Justice Warren E. Burger dissented.

—KENNETH L. KARST

UNITED MINE WORKERS v. CORONADO COAL COMPANY

259 U.S. 344 (1922)

CORONADO COAL COMPANY v. UNITED MINE WORKERS

268 U.S. 295 (1925)

In two nearly identical cases, the Supreme Court provided opposite answers to the same question: Does the Sherman Antitrust Act apply to local strikes that indirectly restrain commerce? The United Mine Workers (UMW) struck to prevent an employer from closing its mines despite valid union contracts; violence and property damage resulted. The company sued the union claiming a Sherman Act conspiracy to restrain interstate commerce. In its defense, the UMW claimed that it was exempt from suit because it was unincorporated and, because mining was local, that there had been no Sherman Act violation. On appeal to the Supreme Court, Chief Justice William Howard Taft declared for a unanimous bench that, although unions (even though unincorporated) could clearly be sued, the union had not violated the Sherman Act here. Mining was merely local; any interference concerned the production rather than the distribution of goods. Taft said no restraint of trade existed, absent an explicit showing of intent to restrain trade, unless the obstruction had "such a direct, material and substantial effect to restrain [commerce] that intent reasonably may be inferred." Taft thus introduced new tests of reasonableness and intent.

The company soon appealed with new evidence. Again unanimous, the Supreme Court now said that when intent to restrain trade attended a decrease in production, a previously "indirect and remote obstruction" became a direct interference in violation of the law. The Court asserted that the evidence at the second trial demonstrated such intent. The Court's near reversal, a finding of intent where none had previously existed, probably resulted from a fear of the implications of the first decision. The effect of the later opinion was to hamper union organizing efforts and cast doubt on the legality of strikes generally; certainly intent could be found by Justices who were looking for it.

—DAVID GORDON

U

UNITED MINE WORKERS v. CORONADO COAL COMPANY

259 U.S. 344 (1922)

CORONADO COAL COMPANY v. UNITED MINE WORKERS

268 U.S. 295 (1925)

In nearly identical cases, the Court provided opposite answers to the same question about the Sherman Antitrust Act.

See also

Rule of Reason

UNITED STEELWORKERS OF AMERICA v. WEBER

443 U.S. 193 (1979)

This was one of an important series of decisions upholding the legality of affirmative action. In *Weber,* the Court held, 5-2, in an opinion by Justice William J. Brennan, that a private affirmative action plan reserving for blacks fifty percent of the openings in a training program leading to plant employment did not violate Title VII of the Civil Rights Act of 1964. *Weber* left open important questions about the permissible scope of affirmative action, including whether governments might resort to affirmative action without violating the Fifth or Fourteenth Amendment, and the extent to which private affirmative action programs may "trammel the interests" of white employees.

—THEODORE EISENBERG

VALLEY FORGE CHRISTIAN COLLEGE v. AMERICANS UNITED FOR SEPARATION OF CHURCH AND STATE

454 U.S. 464 (1982)

Severely limiting the precedent of *Flast* v. *Cohen* (1968), the Supreme Court here tightened the requirements for standing in a taxpayer's suit against the federal government.

Under a general power from Congress to dispose of surplus federal property, the Department of Health, Education and Welfare (HEW) transferred land and buildings worth over $500,000 to a religious college that trained students for the ministry. Because HEW calculated that the government benefited from the transfer at a rate of 100 percent, the college paid nothing.

Federal taxpayers sued to set aside the transfer, contending that it amounted to an establishment of religion. The Supreme Court held, 5–4, that the taxpayers lacked standing. The majority distinguished *Flast*, which had upheld taxpayer standing to challenge federal subsidies to church schools: *Flast* challenged an act of Congress; here plaintiffs challenged a decision by HEW. Furthermore, *Flast* involved injury to the plaintiffs as taxpayers: tax money was to be spent unconstitutionally. Here the Court dealt not with Congress's spending power but with the power to dispose of property.

The dissenters emphasized what everyone knew: absent taxpayer standing, no one has standing to challenge government donations of property to churches. In such cases the establishment clause is enforceable in the consciences of government officials, but not in court.

—KENNETH L. KARST

VINSON, FRED M.

(1890–1953)

Fred M. Vinson was appointed thirteenth Chief Justice of the United States by President Harry S Truman in 1946 and served in that office until his death. His appointment followed a distinguished career in all three branches of the federal government. That career profoundly influenced his performance as Chief Justice.

Born and raised in the jail of Louisa, Kentucky—his father was the town jailer—he devoted almost his entire professional career to the public sector. Shortly after his admission to the bar, he served as city attorney and as Commonwealth attorney. Elected to Congress in 1928, he was an influential member of that legislative body during the New Deal years. His judicial experience commenced with appointment as judge of the United States Court of Appeals for the District of Columbia in 1937, and was broadened in 1942 when Chief Justice Harlan Fiske Stone named him Chief Judge of the Emergency Court of Appeals. His executive branch experience began with his 1943 appointment as director of Economic Stabilization, followed in 1945 by three posts in rapid succession: Federal Loan administrator, director of War Mobilization and Reconversion, and secretary of the treasury.

He was appointed Chief Justice in 1946 to a Court widely regarded as ridden not only

The dissenters emphasized what everyone knew: absent taxpayer standing, no one has standing to challenge government donations of property to churches.

See also

Establishment of Religion

Flast v. *Cohen*

Separation of Church and State

Standing

His philosophy reflected his experience during the New Deal and World War II years when a strong national government was deemed a sine qua non.

with the usual ideological disagreements but also with severe personal animosities. One successful aspect of his tenure as Chief Justice was the substantial reduction of public exposure of these conflicts.

In 1949 the deaths of Justices Frank Murphy and Wiley B. Rutledge were followed by the appointments of Tom C. Clark and Sherman Minton. These changes, which occurred just short of the midpoint of his tenure, shifted the balance of the Court to a more conservative position, one more consonant with his own judicial and political philosophy.

That philosophy must be ascertained more by inference than through direct revelation. During his seven years as Chief Justice, the number of cases heard by the Court declined; as Chief Justice he assigned comparatively few opinions to himself. The evidence makes clear, however, that his philosophy reflected his public and political experience, acquired during the New Deal and World War II years, when a strong na-

tional government was deemed a *sine qua non* and loyalty to one's party and political confreres was a necessary condition of the success of the political process.

For him, the governmental institutions were democratically based, sound, and trustworthy; they were entitled to the loyalty of those whom they served and to protection from those who would destroy them. The judgments of the president and Congress that communism threatened both from without and from within were entitled to respect. The nation and its people fared better with a stable regime than with one of disruption; government was entitled at least to have time to respond to conflicts. The lowest person could rise to the highest office. Concomitantly—although the enactments of legislatures were normally to be respected—legal restrictions based upon race, disabling handicaps to the realization of the American dream, were disfavored. Even as his extensive federal governmental experience made him sympathetic to a strong central government, so his executive branch experience rendered him unafraid of strong executive power.

His tenure as Chief Justice spanned the Cold War era in which pro-Soviet attitudes that had developed during World War II became suspect. The rise of McCarthyism, the trial of Alger Hiss, the Korean War, the theft of atomic secrets, and like events dominated public discussion and government reaction.

These events pervaded the atmosphere in which major constitutional issues were presented. Thus, his views about loyalty are perhaps best represented in those cases that sustained noncriminal deprivations addressed to communists and those considered disloyal, for example, his opinion for the Court in *American Communications Association* v. *Douds* (1950); denial of Taft-Hartley collective bargaining benefits); and his votes in *Bailey* v. *Richardson* (1951; denial of federal employment) and *Joint Anti-Fascist Refugee Committee* v. *Mcgrath* (1951; blacklisting of suspected organizations).

His lack of sympathy for those whose purpose he viewed as destructive of the governmental institutions is evidenced in his plurality opinion in *Dennis* v. *United States* (1951), which sustained against a First Amendment claim the criminal convictions of communist leaders under the Smith Act, and his majority opinion in *Feiner* v. *New York* (1951), affirming the conviction of an antigovernment speaker who refused to stop speaking when ordered to do so by a police officer after members of the audience threatened to assault him.

His concern for institutional stability is reflected in his opinion in *United States* v. *United Mine Workers* (1947), sustaining the judiciary's use of the contempt power to halt a disruptive strike, and his dissenting opinion in *Youngstown Sheet & Tube Co.* v. *Sawyer* (1951), where he would have sustained the power of the president to seize steel mills to maintain steel production interrupted by a strike.

Overtaken by later cases, several of Vinson's most significant opinions advanced the elimination of racial discrimination and in theoretical terms expanded the interpretation of the equal protection clause. Although the unanimous opinions he authored in *Sweatt* v. *Painter* (1950) and *McLaurin* v. *Board of Regents* (1950) did not in terms overrule the separate but equal doctrine of *Plessy* v. *Ferguson* (1896), the rejection of the separate Texas law school in *Sweatt* and of the special treatment of *McLaurin* made the demise of that doctrine inevitable. His most interesting and venturesome equal protection opinion was *Shelley* v. *Kraemer* (1948), the restrictive covenant case, whose doctrinal implications have yet to be satisfactorily delineated.

Vinson accorded the federal government expansive legislative power under the commerce clause. Perceived conflicts between the federal government and the states were resolved in favor of a strong central government. Where the federal government had not spoken, his concern focused on discrimination against interstate commerce and the out-of-stater, a position most clearly seen in the state taxation of commerce cases and *Toomer* v. *Witsell* (1948), the path-breaking interpretation of the privileges and immunities clause of Article IV, which in effect extended his commerce clause philosophy to areas he thought the clause did not reach.

His general judicial approach inclined Vinson to focus on the particular facts of the case and to eschew promulgation of sweeping legal principles. He was slow to overrule earlier opinions and doctrines. The power of the Court to invalidate federal executive and legislative actions on constitutional grounds was to be used sparingly; he never voted to invalidate an act of Congress or a presidential action. He was as apt as any member of his Court, save perhaps Justice Felix Frankfurter, to avoid constitutional questions and, when those issues were faced, to take an intermediate rather than ultimate constitutional position. Clearly, Fred M. Vinson belonged to the "judicial restraint" school of Supreme Court Justices.

—MURRAY L. SCHWARTZ

Bibliography

Kirkendall, K. (1969). Fred M. Vinson. In Leon Friedman and Fred L. Isracl, *The Justices of the United States Supreme Court.* Vol. 4:2639–2649. New York: Chelsea House.

Pritchett, C. Herman (1954). *Civil Liberties and the Vinson Court.* Chicago: University of Chicago Press.

Symposium (1954). *Northwestern University Law Review* 49:1–76.

VINSON COURT

(1946–1953)

Fred M. Vinson was Chief Justice of the United States from June 24, 1946, until his death on September 8, 1953. During his seven-year period of service the Supreme Court was considerably less interesting, colorful, or originative of significant constitutional doctrine than its predecessor, the Stone Court, or its successor, the Warren Court. However, the Vinson Court did deal with serious and important issues, particularly Cold War challenges to civil liberties and awakening concerns about racial discrimination.

Vinson was a close friend of President Harry S Truman and an active Democrat who had had the unique experience of serving in all three branches of the federal government. Immediately preceding his appointment to the Court he had been secretary of the treasury. President Truman had made one previous appointment, naming Harold Burton, a Republican and former Senate colleague of Truman, to replace Owen Roberts in 1945. The other seven justices were of course all holdovers from the Stone Court, which guaranteed a continuation of the judicial dialogue that had pitted the liberal activism of Hugo L. Black, William O. Douglas, Frank Murphy, and Wiley B. Rutledge against the brilliant critiques of Felix Frankfurter and Robert H. Jackson, with the moderate Stanley F. Reed somewhere in the center.

The four-judge liberal bloc had within itself the votes required to grant certiorari petitions, which ensured that civil liberties issues would continue to appear on the Court's agenda. When the liberals agreed, they needed only one additional vote to constitute a majority. But in the summer of 1949 Justices Murphy and Rutledge died, cutting the liberal bloc in half. President Truman filled these two vacancies by the appointment of Tom C. Clark, his attorney general, and Sherman Minton, who had been a New Deal senator from Indiana. The two new justices joined with Vinson, Reed, and Burton in a moderately conservative bloc that dominated the remaining four terms of the Vinson Court. An indication of the balance of power on the Court is provided by the number of dissents registered by each of the Justices during this four-year period: Clark 15, Vinson 40, Burton 44, Minton 47, Reed 59, Jackson 80, Frankfurter 101, Douglas 130, Black 148.

The most famous decision of the Vinson Court in terms of public reaction, and probably the most noteworthy as a contribution to constitutional theory, was *Youngstown Sheet & Tube Co.* v. *Sawyer* (1952), generally known as the *Steel Seizure Case.* Here the Court by a vote of 6–3 held unconstitutional President Truman's seizure of the nation's steel mills in 1952, an action he justified as necessary to avert a nationwide strike that might have affected the flow of munitions to American troops in Korea. The president had no statutory authority for the seizure, which consequently had to be justified on a theory of inherent presidential power to meet emergencies.

Justice Black, supported by Douglas, flatly denied the existence of any inherent presidential powers. Justices Jackson and Frankfurter were less dogmatic, and the doctrine of the case is generally drawn from their opinions. As they saw it, the controlling factor was that Congress had considered granting the president seizure power to deal with nationwide strikes when adopting the Taft-Hartley Act in 1947 but had decided against it. In addition, Jackson contributed a situational scale for ruling on claims of executive emergency power. Vinson, in his most famous dissent, upheld the president as having moved in an emergency to maintain the status quo until Congress could act, and he rejected the majority's "messenger boy" concept of the presidential office.

The fact that the Court could have avoided the constitutional issue in the *Steel Seizure Case* by various alternatives suggested that most of the justices believed it important to announce a check on presidential power. The decision was enormously popular with the press and public and has subsequently been accepted as an authoritative statement on the separation of powers, establishing that actions of the president are subject to judicial review. There had been some doubt on this point since the failure of the post-Civil War suit against the president in *Mississippi* v. *Johnson* (1867). It established also that executive claims of power for which statutory authority is lacking, and which must consequently rely on the president's general Article II authority, are subject to strict judicial scrutiny.

Less significant in its doctrine than the *Steel Seizure Case* but almost as controversial was the Court's contempt ruling against John L. Lewis, leader of the coal miners, in 1947 (*United States* v. *United Mine Workers*). The government had seized the nation's bituminous coal mines in 1946 to end a crippling strike and had entered into a contract with Lewis on wages and working conditions. When Lewis subsequently terminated the contract unilaterally and resumed the strike, the government secured a contempt judgment and heavy fine against Lewis and the union. In his first major opinion Vinson upheld the conviction for contempt, ruling that the Norris-LaGuardia Act limiting the issuance of labor injunctions was not binding on the government as an employer.

A significant difference between the Stone and Vinson Courts was that World War II had ended and the Cold War against communism had begun. The hunt for subversives in which the nation was caught up soon after the shooting war was over tainted the entire period of the Vinson Court and created difficult civil liberties issues. The government's principal weapon against suspected subversion was the Smith Act of 1940, which made it unlawful to teach and advocate the overthrow of the United States government by force and violence, or to organize a group for such a purpose.

Convictions of eleven leaders of the American Communist party under the Smith Act were upheld by the Supreme Court in *Dennis* v. *United States* (1951). In the most memorable event of his judicial career, Chief Justice Vinson wrote the Court's majority opinion defending the Smith Act against contentions that it violated the First Amendment. The defendants admittedly had taken no action with the immediate intention of initiating a revolution. But Vinson held that the clear and present danger test, developed by Justice Oliver Wendell Holmes and Louis D. Brandeis, did not require the government to wait until a "putsch" was about to be executed before acting against a conspiracy. Vinson accepted the reformulation of the test developed by Judge Learned Hand: "Whether the gravity of the 'evil,' discounted by its improbability, justifies such invasion of free speech as is necessary to avoid the danger." He considered the communist "evil" to be that grave. Justices Black and Douglas dissented; Douglas pointed out that the prosecution had introduced no evidence of Communist party action aimed at overthrow of the government.

Vinson also wrote the Court's opinion in *American Communications Association* v. *Douds* (1950), upholding the Taft-Hartley Act noncommunist oath. This statute denied the protections and services of the Wagner (National

The Vinson Court dealt with Cold War challenges to civil liberties and awakening concerns about racial discrimination.

Labor Relations) Act to any labor organization whose officers failed to file affidavits that they were not members of the Communist party. The Chief Justice held that Congress in adopting this statute was acting to prevent the obstruction of commerce by "political strikes." The law was not aimed at speech but rather at harmful conduct carried on by persons who could be identified by their political affiliations and beliefs.

The Vinson Court was caught up in the final moments of the Cold War's most spectacular event, the execution of Julius and Ethel Rosenberg, who were charged with passing atomic "secrets" to the Russians. Review of the lower court conviction and subsequent appeals was routinely denied by the Supreme Court in 1952 and early 1953, as were also the initial petitions for stay of execution. But Justice Douglas thought that one final petition filed the day before execution was scheduled raised a new legal issue deserving consideration. He consequently granted a stay which the full Court set aside the next day, and the executions were then carried out. Douglas's action caused a brief furor and a congressman demanded his impeachment. In the last opinion before his death Vinson defended Douglas's action as a proper response to protect the Court's jurisdiction over the case pending a consideration of the legal issue raised. Black and Frankfurter joined Douglas in asserting that the stay should have been granted.

During the era of the Vinson Court, congressional committee investigations of communism developed into major political and media events. Senator Joseph McCarthy's pursuit of "Fifth Amendment Communists" got under way in 1950, too late to create issues for the Vinson Court. But the House Committee on Un-American Activities had begun operations in 1938, and by 1947 petitions for review of contempt citations against witnesses who had refused to reply to committee interrogation began to reach the Supreme Court. However, it declined review of all the cases that would have required a ruling on the constitutionality of the use of investigatory power, and it dealt only with certain less controversial issues of committee procedure and use of the Fifth Amendment privilege by witnesses.

A prominent feature of the Cold War period was concern about the loyalty of government employees. A loyalty oath fad developed in nearly every state, which the Vinson Court legitimated in *Gerende* v. *Board of Supervisors of Elections* (1951) by upholding a Maryland law that required candidates for public office to file affidavits that they were not "subversive persons."

A loyalty program covering federal employees was set up by President Truman in 1947 and was continued by President Dwight D. Eisenhower. It required checking the loyalty of all incumbent employees and all applicants for federal employment. A complex administrative organization of loyalty review boards was created, and to assist the boards the attorney general issued a list of organizations he found to be "totalitarian, fascist, communist, or subversive." Consideration of the constitutionality of this program split the Court 4–4 in *Bailey* v. *Richardson* (1951). But in *Joint Anti-Fascist Refugee Committee* v. *McGrath* (1951), decided the same day, the Court by a vote of 5–3 challenged the attorney general's list as having been drawn up without appropriate investigation or due process. The dissenters were Reed, Vinson, and Minton. In spite of this opinion the list continued to be used for a number of years in government hiring and investigation.

At the state level a New York law providing for the removal of public school teachers on grounds of membership in listed subversive organizations was upheld in *Adler* v. *Board of Education of City of New York* (1952), Justice Minton reasoning that the purpose was constitutional and that procedural protections provided by the statute were adequate. Justices Black and Douglas dissented, and Frankfurter would have denied the appeal on technical grounds of standing and ripeness.

Apart from Cold War cases, freedom of speech and freedom of the press did not suffer seriously at the hands of the Vinson Court. *Burstyn* v. *Wilson* (1952) was in fact an advance in its holding that a motion picture could not be censored on the ground that it was "sacrilegious." A law censoring magazines featuring bloodshed and lust was struck down in *Winters* v. *New York* (1948) as void for vagueness. *Poulos* v. *New Hampshire* (1953) upheld licensing of meetings in public parks and streets, but only if the licenses were granted without discrimination, and the use of licensing ordinances to prevent unpopular religious groups or preachers from holding meetings in public parks was rebuffed in *Niemotko* v. *Maryland* (1951) and *Kunz* v. *New York* (1951).

In *Terminiello* v. *Chicago* (1949) a divided Court reversed on rather technical grounds the conviction of a rabble-rouser for breach of the peace resulting from an incendiary speech. But *Feiner* v. *New York* (1951) upheld the conviction of a soap-box orator even though the situation was much less inflammatory than in *Terminiello*. Moreover, *Beauharnais* v. *Illinois* (1952) approved a state law treating critical comments about racial groups as criminal and subjecting their authors to prosecution for group libel.

The Vinson Court dealt with a number of conflicts between freedom of expression and privacy but without producing any theories justifying or limiting privacy claims such as those subsequently developed in *Griswold* v. *Connecticut* (1965) by the Warren Court. Use of sound trucks in streets and parks was initially upheld in *Saia* v. *New York* (1948) against contentions of infringement on privacy, but in the following year the Court conceded that "loud and raucous" sound trucks could be forbidden (*Kovacs* v. *Cooper*). Radio broadcasts including commercial messages in District of Columbia streetcars were permit-

ted to continue by *Public Utilities Commission* v. *Pollak* (1952), even though captive audiences might suffer, but *Breard* v. *City of Alexandria* (1951) protected householders by approving an ordinance forbidding door-to-door selling of magazine subscriptions. Justice Black charged that the latter decision violated the "preferred position" for First Amendment freedoms originated by the Roosevelt Court. The severest blow to that philosophy was *United Public Workers* v. *Mitchell* (1947) which upheld by a vote of 4–3 the Hatch Act limits on political activity by public employees.

In a 1940 case, *Thornhill* v. *Alabama,* the Court had strongly asserted that picketing in labor disputes was protected by the First Amendment. Almost immediately, however, the Court found it necessary to announce limits on this holding, a process the Vinson Court continued. The most significant case was *Giboney* v. *Empire Storage & Ice Co.* (1949), where the Court ruled unanimously against a union that was picketing to force an employer to enter into an illegal restrictive contract.

The issue of public financial aid to religious schools required the Vinson Court to make the first significant effort to interpret and apply the First Amendment ban on establishment of religion. *Everson* v. *Board of Education* (1947) involved a state arrangement under which parents could be reimbursed from public moneys for their children's bus fare to parochial schools. An unusual five-judge majority composed of three liberals (Black, Douglas, and Murphy) and two conservatives (Vinson and Reed) held that the subsidy was simply a social welfare measure and that the First Amendment did not require exclusion of persons of any faith from the benefits of "public welfare legislation." Rutledge's vigorous dissent regarded payment for transportation to church schools as a direct aid to religious education and so unconstitutional.

The following year *McCollum* v. *Board of Education* presented another church-state issue. The case involved a released time program of religious education under which public school children attended classes in Protestant, Roman Catholic, or Jewish religious instruction during school hours and in the school building. The Court's almost unanimous verdict of unconstitutionality aroused a storm of criticism in church circles, and within four years the Court substantially reversed this ruling, upholding a New York City released time program that differed from *McCollum* only in that the classes were held off the school grounds (*Zorach* v. *Clausen*, 1952.) A similar reluctance to disturb the religious community was seen as the Court avoided on technical grounds of standing a ruling on the constitutionality of Bible-reading in the public schools (*Doremus* v. *Board of Education*).

The Vinson Court's civil liberties record was distinctly better than that of its predecessors in one area, protection of minorities from discrimination. The prevailing constitutional rule was that established by *Plessy* v. *Ferguson* in 1896—that segregation of the races was constitutional provided treatment or facilities were equal. In practice, they were never equal, but over the years the Court had consistently avoided the difficult task of enforcing the *Plessy* rule. In the field of education, none of the few efforts to challenge unequal facilities had been successful. But in 1938 the Hughes Court made a small beginning, ruling in *Missouri ex rel. Gaines* v. *Canada* that Missouri, which denied blacks admission to state law schools, must do so or set up a separate law school for blacks. *Morgan* v. *Virginia* (1946) invalidated a state Jim Crow law requiring racial segregation of passengers on public motor carriers, but the constitutional ground given was burden on interstate commerce rather than denial of equal protection.

The Vinson Court undertook cautiously to build on these beginnings. The commerce clause justification used in the Virginia bus case was likewise employed in *Bob-Lo Excursion Co.* v. *Michigan* (1948). But the Vinson Court's boldest action against segregation came shortly thereafter in *Shelley* v. *Kraemer* (1948). With Vinson writing the opinion, the Court declared that restrictive covenants binding property owners not to sell to minorities, although within the legal rights of property owners, were unenforceable. For a court to give effect to such a discriminatory contract, Vinson held, would amount to state action in violation of the Fourteenth Amendment.

The separate law school for blacks that Texas had established was declared unequal in *Sweatt* v. *Painter* (1950). The University of Oklahoma, forced to admit a black graduate student, required him to sit in a separate row in class, at a separate desk in the library, and at a separate table in the cafeteria. *McLaurin* v. *Oklahoma State Regents* (1950), with Vinson again writing the opinion, held these practices to be an unconstitutional impairment of the student's ability to learn his profession.

Vinson's opinion, however, rejected the opportunity to consider the broader issue of the *Plessy* separate but equal rule. So attacks on the segregation principle continued, and the test cases moved from the universities and graduate schools to the primary and secondary schools. In December 1952 *Brown* v. *Board of Education of Topeka* and four other school segregation cases were argued for three days before the Court. But instead of a decision in June, the Court set the cases for reargument in October. The Chief Justice died in September, and so the Vinson Court's most momentous issue was passed on to the Warren Court.

Although the Stone Court had broken some new ground in criminal procedure, its record was mixed, particularly in guaranteeing the right to counsel and protection against unreasonable searches and seizures. This latter issue surfaced in the Vinson Court's first term. One of the oldest problems in American constitutional law is whether the due process clause of the Fourteenth Amendment "incorporated" and made effective in state criminal proceedings the protections of the Fourth through the Eighth Amendments. As recently as 1937 in *Palko* v. *Connecticut* the Court had reiterated the principle that all state procedures consistent with ordered liberty are acceptable.

In *Adamson* v. *California* (1947) the *Palko* doctrine survived on the Vinson Court, but by only a 5–4 vote. Justice Black led the minority. He relied on legislative history to establish his version of the intention of the framers of the Fourteenth Amendment and attacked the ordered liberty test as substituting natural law and the notions of individual Justices for the precise and protective language of the Bill of Rights.

Although Black lost in *Adamson*, "ordered liberty" was a standard powerful enough to bring state criminal processes within the ambit of the Fourth Amendment in *Wolf* v. *Colorado* (1949). However, Justice Frankfurter for the six-judge majority held only that searches and seizures by state law officers are bound by the standard of reasonableness; he declined to go further and impose on state prosecutions the exclusionary rule that prevents evidence secured by unconstitutional means from being offered in federal prosecutions. Justices Murphy, Douglas, and Rutledge, dissenting, contended that the exclusionary rule provided the only effective protection against police violation of the Fourth Amendment, and their view was finally adopted on the Warren Court in *Mapp* v. *Ohio* (1961).

With respect to right to counsel, the Vinson Court accepted the rule announced by the Stone Court in *Betts* v. *Brady* (1942) that the necessity for counsel depended upon the circumstances, such as the seriousness of the crime, the age and mental capacity of the defendant, and the ability of the judge. Applying the "special circumstances" rule in twelve cases, the Vinson Court concluded that in six the absence of counsel had resulted in denial of a fair trial. In only one of the twelve was the Court unanimous. This experience was a factor in the Warren Court's decision in *Gideon* v. *Wainwright* (1963) to abolish the confusing special circumstances rule and make counsel mandatory in all state felony prosecutions.

What was potentially one of the Vinson Court's most significant decisions for the federal system was nullified by Congress. In 1947 the Court ruled that subsurface land and mineral rights in California's three-mile coastal area belonged to the federal government (*United States* v. *California*), and in 1950 the Court applied the same rule to Texas. Congress retaliated in 1953 by ceding to the states ownership of land and resources under adjoining seas up to a distance of three miles from shore or to the states' historic boundaries.

In summary, the tendency of the Vinson Court was to follow a policy of judicial restraint, rejecting innovation or activism. The number of cases decided by full opinion fell below one hundred during three of the last four years, far less than the number typically decided by earlier Courts. The five justices who dominated the Court in its latter period were capable but lacking in style or originality. The four Justices of intellectual distinction—Black, Douglas, Frankfurter, and Jackson—generally paired off and pulled in opposite directions.

The pall of the Cold War hung over the Court. Confronted with the scandal of McCarthyism, it was quiescent. Facing Smith Act prosecutions, the loyalty inquisition of federal employees, lists of subversive organizations, scrutiny of school teachers' associates, loyalty oaths, and deportation of ex-communists, the Court's response was usually to legitimate the government's action.

But in one field, significantly, there was a different kind of response. The Vinson Court did not evade the issue of racial discrimination. Although moving cautiously, as was appropriate considering the enormity of the problem, the Court nevertheless proceeded

The Court's opinion indicated that false or misleading commercial advertising might be regulated—a rule the Court would never apply to political speech.

See also

Central Hudson Gas & Electric v. Public Service Commission

Freedom of Speech

to bring denial of equal protection out of the limbo of neglect and unconcern into the focus of national consciousness and thereby prepared the way for its successor's historic decision on May 17, 1954.

—C. HERMAN PRITCHETT

Bibliography

Frank, John P. (1954). Fred Vinson and the Chief Justiceship. *University of Chicago Law Review* 21:212–246.

Murphy, Paul L. (1972). *The Constitution in Crisis Times, 1919–1969.* New York: Harper & Row.

Pritchett, C. Herman ([1954] 1966). *Civil Liberties and the Vinson Court.* Chicago: University of Chicago Press.

Swindler, William F. (1970). *Court and Constitution in the Twentieth Century: The New Legality, 1932–1968.* Indianapolis: Bobbs-Merrill.

VIRGINIA STATE BOARD OF PHARMACY v. VIRGINIA CITIZENS CONSUMER COUNCIL

425 U.S. 748 (1976)

Traditionally commercial speech was assumed to lie outside the First Amendment's protection. This decision made clear that this assumption was obsolete. Virginia's rules governing professional pharmacists forbade the advertising of prices of prescription drugs. The Supreme Court, 7–1, held this rule invalid at the behest of a consumers' group, thus promoting the notion of a "right to receive" in the freedom of speech. The Court's opinion indicated that false or misleading commercial advertising might be regulated—a rule the Court would never apply to political speech. For a few years, this decision stood as the Court's principal commercial speech precedent, only to be assimilated in the compre-

hensive opinion in *Central Hudson Gas v. Public Service Commission* (1980).

—MARTIN SHAPIRO

VOTING RIGHTS

"The right to vote freely for the candidate of one's choice is of the essence of a democratic society, and any restrictions on that right strike at the heart of representative government." So spoke Chief Justice Earl Warren, on behalf of the Supreme Court, in *Reynolds v. Sims* (1964).

The Chief Justice's words were in direct philosophic succession to principles of the primacy of representative political institutions announced by the First Continental Congress 190 years before, in the Declaration and Resolves of October 14, 1774:

[T]he foundation of English liberty, and of all free government, is a right in the people to participate in their legislative council: and as the English colonists are not represented, and from their local and other circumstances, cannot properly be represented in the British parliament, they are entitled to a free and exclusive power of legislation in their several provincial legislatures, where their right of representation can alone be preserved, in all cases of taxation and internal policy, subject only to the negative of their sovereign, in such manner as has been heretofore used and accustomed.

The failure of King George III, through his ministers, to recognize the urgency of the colonists' demand for true representative institutions was one of the chief causes of revolution set forth in the Declaration of Independence: "He has dissolved Representative Houses repeatedly, for opposing with manly firmness his invasions in the rights of the people. He has refused for a long time, after such dissolutions, to cause others to be elected; whereby the Legislative Powers, incapable of Annihilation, have returned to the People at large for their exercise."

The severing of the ties with Britain required the establishment, at the state level and at the national level, of new and more representative institutions of government. American constitutional history is characterized in part by the continuing enlargement of the right to vote, the mechanism that, in the American political tradition, has become the *sine qua non* of a valid system of representation. An anomaly presents itself: the Constitution, as amended, addresses aspects of the right to vote with far greater frequency than any other topic. Nonetheless, it has never been the function of the Constitution affirmatively to define the universe of voters. The Constitution's function has been narrower—progressively to limit the permissible grounds of disenfranchisement.

Prior to the American Revolution, eligibility to vote was not uniform among the colonies, but the variations were relatively minor. Broadly speaking, voting for colonial (as distinct from township or borough) officials was reserved to adult (generally meaning twenty-one or older) "freeholders." In equating property ownership and suffrage, the colonies were following a familiar English model. But landowning was far more widely dispersed in the colonies than in the mother country, so the proportion of colonists eligible to vote was larger.

There were not more than a few black or women freeholders in any of the colonies, and pursuant either to convention or to formal legal specification those few did not vote. Religious restrictions were also commonplace but varied somewhat among the colonies and at different times. In general, the franchise was the prerogative of the propertied, Protestant, white male.

With the coming of independence, all of the newly sovereign states except Connecticut and Rhode Island adopted new charters of government—"constitutions." Impelled by the rhetoric of revolution and the eagerness

of thousands of militiamen to participate in the processes of governance, the drafters of the new state constitutions relaxed but did not abandon the property and religious qualifications for voting for state officials (and the correlative, and generally more stringent, qualifications for holding state office). As Max Farrand observed, Americans

> might declare that "all men are created equal," and bills of rights might assert that government rested upon the consent of the governed; but these constitutions carefully provided that such consent should come from property owners, and, in many of the States, from religious believers and even followers of the Christian faith. "The man of small means might vote, but none save well-to-do Christians could legislate, and in many states none but a rich Christian could be a governor." In South Carolina, for example, a freehold of 10,000 currency was required of the Governor, Lieutenant Governor, and members of the council; 2,000 of the members of the Senate; and, while every elector was eligible to the House of Representatives, he had to acknowledge the being of a God and to believe in a future state of rewards and punishments, as well as to hold "a freehold at least of fifty acres of land, or a town lot."

Under the Articles of Confederation, the state delegates in Congress constituted the nation's government. The Articles limited the numbers of delegates (no fewer than two and no more than seven per state) but left each state legislature free to determine the qualifications of those selected and the mode of their annual selection. The Articles did not preclude popular election of delegates, but the word "appointed," in the phrase "appointed in such manner as the legislature of each State shall direct," suggests that it was not anticipated that legislatures would remit to their constituents the power to choose those who would speak and vote for the states in Congress.

At the Constitutional Convention of 1787, the Framers divided on how the lower house was to be selected. James Madison told his fellow delegates that he "considered an election of one branch at least of the legislature by the people immediately, as a clear principle of true government." Madison's view carried the day. But then the Convention faced the question whether the Constitution should set the qualifications of those who were to elect representatives. Gouverneur Morris of Pennsylvania proposed that only freeholders should vote. Colonel George Mason of Virginia found this proposal regressive: "Eight of nine States have extended the right of suffrage beyond the freeholders. What will the people there say, if they should be disfranchised." Oliver Ellsworth of Connecticut also challenged Morris's proposal: "How shall the freehold be defined? Ought not every man who pays a tax to vote for the representative who is to levy and dispose of his money?" Morris was unpersuaded: "He had long learned not to be the dupe of words. . . . Give the votes to people who have no property, and they will sell them to the rich who will be able to buy them." But Benjamin Franklin took decisive issue with his fellow Pennsylvanian: "It is of great consequence that we should not depress the virtue and public spirit of our common people; of which they displayed a great deal during the war, and which contributed principally to the favorable issue of it." Morris's proposal was decisively defeated. The Convention instead approved the provision that has endured ever since, under which eligibility to vote for representatives is keyed, in each state, to that state's rules of eligibility to vote for members of the most numerous house of the state legislature.

When it came to designing the method of selecting the president and vice president, the Convention devised the indirect election system of the Electoral College. The expectation was that the electors—themselves chosen from among the leading citizens of their respective states—would, through disinterested deliberation, select as the nation's chief executive officials the two persons of highest civic virtue, wholly without regard for the vulgar demands of "politics." According to Alexander Hamilton in *The Federalist* #68, "[T]he mode of appointment of the Chief Magistrate of the United States is almost the only part of the system, of any consequence, which has escaped without severe censure, or which has received the slightest mark of approbation from its opponents." But measured against its intended purpose, no other structural aspect of the Constitution has wound up wider of the mark. The Framers of the Constitution wholly failed to anticipate the development of national political parties whose chief political goal would be the election of the party leader as president. That development has meant that since the fourth presidential election—that of 1800, in which Thomas Jefferson defeated John Adams—the electors in each state have themselves been selected as adherents of the political party prevailing in that state and thus have, with the rarest of exceptions, cast their electoral votes for the party's presidential and vice-presidential candidates. The system of electors remains to this day, but it has been entirely drained of its intended function.

Those who drafted the Constitution in 1787, and who saw it through ratification to the launching of the new ship of state in 1789, were America's aristocracy. The transformation of American politics from 1789 to the Civil War can be measured in the marked shift in class status of those who occupied the presidency. The presidents from George Washington to John Quincy Adams were all patricians. Most of the Presidents from Andrew Jackson to Abraham Lincoln were not. The growth of national parties, beginning with Jefferson and accelerating with Jackson, democratized politics by putting politicians in the business of seeking to enlarge their voting constituencies. Property qualifications gave way, for the most part, to taxpayer qualifications. And, in many states, these in turn were soon largely abandoned.

The erosion of property tests for voting did not mean that anything approximating universal suffrage was at hand. As one political scientist has summarized the situation:

Apart from a few midwestern states, hungry for settlers, no one was very warm to the prospect of aliens and immigrants at the polls; all the states but Maine, Massachusetts, Vermont, New Hampshire, Rhode Island, and New York explicitly barred free blacks from voting, and New York imposed special property requirements on blacks which, while repeatedly challenged, were repeatedly upheld in popular referenda. Even in the tiny handful of northern states that did not exclude blacks by law, social pressures tended to accomplish the same end. New Hampshire and Vermont in 1857 and 1858 had to pass special laws against excluding blacks from voting. Chancellor James Kent concluded that only in Maine could the black man participate equally with the white man in civil and political rights. Women were universally denied the vote [Elliott 1974, p. 40].

In 1848, a year of revolution in Europe, 300 people gathered in a church in the little upstate New York town of Seneca Falls to consider the status of women. The most revolutionary item on the agenda was voting. Half a century before there had been a small outcropping of female voting in New Jersey, whose 1776 constitution had, perhaps inadvertently, used the word "inhabitants" to describe those who, if they met the property qualifications, could vote. It appears that by 1807, respectable New Jersey opinion had reached the consensus that laxity was slipping into license (at a local election in Trenton even slaves and Philadelphians were said to have cast ballots). At this point, "reform" was clearly called for: the legislature promptly altered the electoral code to bring New Jersey's

voting qualifications back into conformity with the white maleness that characterized the electorate in the rest of the country and remained the accepted order of things until Seneca Falls.

The chief driving energies behind the Seneca Falls Convention were Elizabeth Cady Stanton and Lucretia Mott. Stanton drafted the "Declaration of Principles" and the several resolutions which the convention was asked to adopt. The only resolution to receive less-than-unanimous endorsement was the ninth: "Resolved, that it is the duty of the women of this country to secure to themselves their sacred right to the elective franchise." That the franchise was a far more chimerical goal than other concerns (for example, property rights for married women) was recognized by Mott. She had asked Stanton not to submit the ninth resolution for the reason that "Thou will make us ridiculous." The factor that may have tipped the balance in Stanton's decision not to subordinate her principle to Mott's pragmatism was the strong encouragement of Frederick Douglass. The great black leader supported the ninth resolution. He joined the cause of equal rights for women to the cause of abolition.

The women's movement maintained its close association with abolitionism through the Civil War. After the freeing of the slaves, the country's attention focused on the terms on which American blacks were to be brought into the mainstream of American life. The leaders of the women's movement hoped that the drive for women's suffrage would complement and be reinforced by the drive for black suffrage. But that was not to be. As the war neared its end, a number of Republican leaders began to recognize a strong partisan interest in creating black voters to counter the feared resurgence of the Democratic party; there were no comparable reasons for creating women voters. Many of the women leaders, recognizing the political realities, accepted—albeit with no enthusiasm—the priority given to the rights of blacks. But not Elizabeth Cady Stanton and Susan B. Anthony. Said Anthony: "I will cut off this right arm before I will ever work for or demand the ballot for the Negro and not the woman." (Anthony and Stanton then formed the National Woman Suffrage Association, while the other leaders worked through the American Woman Suffrage Association; the split was not to be healed for twenty-five years.)

In 1864 Abraham Lincoln appointed Salmon P. Chase—Lincoln's former secretary of the treasure and one of his chief rivals for the Republican presidential nomination in 1860—to succeed Roger B. Taney as Chief Justice of the United States. Chase's elevation to the Court did not abate his presidential ambitions and his attendant interest in promoting a favorable political environment. The new Chief Justice wrote to Lincoln, as he subsequently wrote to President Andrew Johnson, urging that black suffrage be made a condition of the reconstruction of the rebel states. And by 1867 Chase had taken the position that Congress had constitutional authority to enfranchise blacks as a mode of enforcing the Thirteenth Amendment: "Can anything be clearer than that the National Legislature charged with the duty of 'enforcing by appropriate legislation' the condition of universal freedom, is authorized and bound to provide for universal suffrage? Is not *suffrage* the best security against *slavery* and *involuntary servitude*? Is not the legislation which provides the *best* security the most *appropriate*?" Chase lost interest in active promotion of black voting when it became apparent that his modest chances of being nominated for the presidency were more likely to be realized in the Democratic party than in the Republican party. In any event, the question whether the Thirteenth Amendment could have been a platform for enlarging the franchise became moot upon the adoption of the two other post-Civil War Amendments, both of which expressly addressed the franchise—for blacks, not for women.

The Fourteenth Amendment, ratified in 1868, dealt with black voting by indirection. By declaring that "[a]ll persons born or naturalized in the United States, and subject to the jurisdiction thereof, are citizens of the United States and of the State wherein they reside," the first sentence of the first section of the amendment overruled Roger B. Taney's pronouncement in *Dred Scott* v. *Sandford* (1857), that blacks, whether slave or free, could not be citizens within the contemplation of the Constitution. The second sentence of the first section sought to protect the civil rights of blacks: first, it guaranteed "the privileges and immunities of citizens of the United States" against state abridgment and, second, it prohibited state denial to any person, whether citizen or not, of "life, liberty or property without due process of law," or deprivation of the "equal protection of the laws." The second section of the amendment spoke to the political rights of blacks. It provided that any state that denied participation in federal or state elections to "any of the male inhabitants of such State, being twenty-one years of age, and citizens of the United States . . . except for participation in rebellion, or other crime," should have its allocation of representatives and of presidential electors proportionately reduced. The framers of the amendment thus preserved the states' entitlement to discriminate but proposed a substantial penalty as the price of discrimination.

By 1869, after General Ulysses S. Grant's narrow victory in the 1868 presidential election, the Republican party recognized that black votes were essential to its survival. So the Republican leadership in Congress fashioned the Fifteenth Amendment. That amendment, ratified in 1870, addressed the question of black voting directly. A citizen's entitlement to vote could not be "abridged by the United States or by any State on account of race, color, or previous condition of servitude."

Notwithstanding that the express language of the Fourteenth Amendment addressed male voting, and that the express language of the Fifteenth Amendment addressed discriminations rooted in "race, color or previous condition of servitude," some leaders of the women's movement contended that women were constitutionally entitled to vote. Arguing that the right to vote in a federal election was a privilege of national citizenship protected by section 1 of the Fourteenth Amendment, Susan B. Anthony actually persuaded election officials in Rochester, New York, to let her vote in 1872 notwithstanding that the New York constitution limited the franchise to men. Anthony was promptly charged with the crime of casting a ballot in a federal election in which she was not an eligible voter. The presiding judge was Justice Ward Hunt of the Supreme Court. Justice Hunt rejected Anthony's constitutional claim in the following words:

The right of voting, or the privilege of voting, is a right or privilege arising under the constitution of the state, and not under the Constitution of the United States. The qualifications are different in the different states. Citizenship, age, sex, residence, are variously required in the different states, or may be so. If the right belongs to any particular person, it is because such person is entitled to it by the laws of the state where he offers to exercise it, and not because of citizenship of the United States. If the state of New York should provide that no person should vote until he had reached the age of thirty years, or after he had reached the age of thirty years, or after he had reached the age of fifty, or that no person having grey hair, or who had not the use of all his limbs, should be entitled to vote, I do not see how it could be held to be a violation of any right derived or held under the Constitution of the United States. We might say that such regulations were unjust, tyrannical, unfit for the regulation of an intelligent state; but, if rights of a citizen are thereby violated they are of that funda-

mental class, derived from his position as a citizen of the state, and not those limited rights belonging to him as a citizen of the United States.

Read through the prism of a century of doctrinal hindsight, Justice Hunt's words seem—at least at first blush—somewhat surprising. The surprise is not occasioned by the fact that the Justice gave such short shrift to arguments based on the Fourteenth Amendment's privileges and immunities clause, for we are accustomed to the fact that, ever since the *Slaughterhouse Cases* (1873), the Supreme Court has read the grant of privileges and immunities flowing from national citizenship very restrictively. The surprise stems from Hunt's failure—which may also have been counsel's failure—to approach sex-based denial of the franchise (not to mention the assertedly analogous hypothetical denials based on age, physical handicap, or color of hair) in equal protection terms. The likely explanation is that in *Slaughterhouse* the Court doubted that "any action of a State not directed by way of discrimination against the negroes as a class, or on account of their race, will ever be held to come within the" equal protection clause.

Justice Hunt directed the jury to return a verdict of guilty and imposed a fine of $100.

Justice Hunt's rejection of Anthony's privileges and immunities claim was vindicated two years later by Chief Justice Morrison R. Waite's opinion for the unanimous Court in *Minor* v. *Happersett* (1875). This was a civil suit brought in a Missouri state court by Virginia L. Minor, and her lawyer husband, Francis Minor, to challenge the refusal of a Missouri election official to register her as a voter. The Minors contended that the provision of the Missouri constitution limiting the electorate to male citizens transgressed the privileges and immunities clause. In rejecting the Minors' contention, Chief Justice Waite demonstrated that limitation of the franchise to males had been the norm, despite the fact that women were citizens. Voting had not been a privilege of national citizenship prior to the Fourteenth Amendment. As the amendment "did not add to the privileges and immunities of a citizen," but merely "furnished an additional guaranty for the protection of such as he already had," Missouri's refusal to let Minor vote was not unconstitutional. *Minor* v. *Happersett* ended attempts to win the campaign for woman's suffrage by litigation. The road to the ballot box was to be political—persuading male legislators to pass laws giving women the vote.

It was to be a long road. In 1870 Wyoming's territorial legislature enacted a law entitling women to vote. Utah followed suit, but the victory there was temporary. An 1887 congressional statute forbidding Utah's Mormons from practicing polygamy also overrode the territorial legislature's grant of the franchise to women. Three years later Wyoming's first state constitution called for women's suffrage. Thereafter progress was slow. Many state campaigns were fought and most were lost. In the South, votes for women were seen as a harbinger of votes for blacks, and the states resisted accordingly; in the East, many industrialists mistrusted the links between some women's suffragists and trade union and other reform groups; in the Midwest, the women's suffrage movement was seen by the brewing interests as the advance guard of prohibition. By 1913 women could vote in only nine states; in that year Illinois admitted women to participation in presidential elections.

In 1912 Theodore Roosevelt's Progressive party endorsed women's suffrage. This endorsement served as a reminder that Susan B. Anthony and her associates had sought to achieve women's suffrage not state-by-state but by amending the Constitution. Pressure for a women's suffrage amendment mounted during World War I when women entered the work force in record numbers. In 1918 Woodrow Wilson announced support for the proposed amendment, notwithstanding that

women's suffrage was anathema to the white Democratic South. In 1919, with Democrats divided and Republicans strongly in favor, Congress submitted to the states a proposed amendment barring denial or abridgment of the right to vote in any election on grounds of sex. In 1920 the Nineteenth Amendment was ratified. In the 1920 elections one of the voters was Charlotte Woodward Pierce who, as a nineteen-year-old farm girl, had attended the Seneca Falls Convention in 1848.

Following the Civil War, the military occupation of the South ushered in a period in which blacks not only voted but were elected to office. With the adoption of the Fifteenth Amendment, there appeared to be some ground for supposing that black voting had achieved a legal infrastructure which might suffice even after the army departed. However, although the amendment bars race, color, and previous condition of servitude as criteria of eligibility to vote, it does not proscribe other criteria—such as literacy or taxpayer status—susceptible of adaptation as surrogates for racism. The lesson was that most blacks might be prevented from voting by educational or property qualifications.

Following the Compromise of 1877, which led to the withdrawal from the South of the last military units, the twilight of black participation in the southern political process began. Through the 1880s some black voting continued—frequently in Populist alliance with poor whites. But in the 1890s, as a corollary of the spreading gospel of Jim Crow, the southern white political leadership forged a consensus to exclude blacks from the ballot box. Some of this was achieved by force, and some by skulduggery, but in large measure the forms of law were utilized. Literacy tests and poll taxes were common exclusionary devices, as was closing Democratic primaries—the only real elections in most of the South—to blacks. The underlying rationale was that offered by Senator James Vardaman of Mississippi: "I am just as much opposed to Booker Washington as a voter, with all his Anglo-Saxon reinforcements, as I am to the cocoanut-headed, chocolate-covered, typical little coon, Andy Dottson, who blacks my shoes every morning. Neither is fit to perform the supreme function of citizenship."

By and large, the legal stratagems employed by the southern states to disenfranchise blacks succeeded. Poll taxes and literacy tests which did not on their face show a discriminatory purpose easily passed constitutional muster from *Breedlove* v. *Suttles* (1937) to *Lassiter* v. *Northampton Election Board* (1959). To be sure, the Supreme Court did intervene in those rare instances in which the purpose to discriminate was evident on the face of the challenged restraint. A flagrant example was the so-called grandfather clause in Oklahoma's 1910 constitution, which exempted from the literacy requirement any would-be voter "who was, on January 1, 1866, or at any time prior thereto, entitled to vote under any form of government, or who at that time resided in some foreign nation, and [any] lineal descendant thereof." In *Guinn* v. *United States* (1915) the Supreme Court held this literacy test invalid.

Because during the first half of the twentieth century the decisive voting in the South took place in Democratic primaries, not in the general elections, the cases of greatest practical as well as doctrinal consequence were those that challenged devices to maintain the whiteness of the "white primary."

In *Nixon* v. *Herndon* (1927) a unanimous Court, speaking through Justice Oliver Wendell Holmes, sustained the complaint of L. A. Nixon, who contended that he had been unconstitutionally barred from voting in a Texas Democratic primary through enforcement of a Texas statute that recited that "in no event shall a negro be eligible to participate in a Democratic party primary election held in the state of Texas." The Court held that this statutory racial exclusion contravened the Fourteenth Amendment.

The consequence of this ruling was described by Justice Benjamin N. Cardozo in his opinion in *Nixon* v. *Condon* (1932): "Promptly after the announcement of [the Herndon] decision, the legislature of Texas enacted a new statute . . . repealing the article condemned by this court; declaring that the effect of the decision was to create an emergency with a need for immediate action; and substituting for the article so repealed another bearing the same number. By the article thus substituted, 'every political party in this State through its State Executive Committee shall have the power to prescribe the qualifications of its own members and shall in its own way determine who shall be qualified to vote or otherwise participate in such political party. . . .'" Thereupon the executive committee of the Texas Democratic party voted to limit party membership and participation to whites, and L. A. Nixon was once again barred from voting in the Democratic primary. Once again Nixon brought a lawsuit, and once again he prevailed in the Supreme Court. Justice Cardozo, speaking for a majority of five, concluded that the new Texas statute delegated exercise of the state's power over primaries to party executive committees, with the result that the racial exclusion decided on by the executive committee was in effect the racially discriminatory act of the State of Texas and hence prohibited by the Fourteenth Amendment. Justice James C. McReynolds, joined by three other Justices, dissented.

Three years later, in *Grovey* v. *Townsend* (1935), the Court considered the next refinement in the Texas Democratic primary—exclusion of blacks by vote of the party convention. Speaking through Justice Owen J. Roberts, the Court this time unanimously concluded that the action taken by the Texas Democratic party was an entirely private decision for which the State of Texas was not accountable; accordingly, neither the Fourteenth nor the Fifteenth Amendment was transgressed.

Nine years later, toward the end of World War II, the Court, in *Smith* v. *Allwright*

In the course of two centuries law and conscience have combined to make the American suffrage almost truly universal.

(1944), again considered the *Grovey* v. *Townsend* question. In the interval, seven of the Justices who had participated in *Grovey* v. *Townsend* had died or retired. Approaching the matter in a common sense way, the Court, with Justice Roberts dissenting, concluded that the role of the primary as a formal and vital predicate of the election made it an integral part of the state's voting processes and hence subject to the requirement of the Fifteenth Amendment. Accordingly, the Court in *Smith* v. *Allwright* overruled *Grovey* v. *Townsend*.

The resumption, after three-quarters of a century, of significant black participation in the southern political process dates from the decision in *Smith* v. *Allwright*. But the elimination of the most egregious legal barriers did not mean that all blacks were automatically free to vote. Hundreds of thousands of would-be black voters were still kept from the polls by fraud or force or both. In 1957, three years after the Court, in *Brown* v. *Board of Education* (1954), held that legally mandated racial segregation contravened the Fourteenth Amendment, Congress passed the first federal civil rights law enacted since the 1870s: a voting rights law that authorized modest federal supervision of the southern voting process. And the year 1964 witnessed ratification of the Twenty-fourth Amendment, barring exclusion of American citizens from voting in any federal election on grounds of failure to pay any poll tax or other tax. But as black demands for equal treatment multiplied, responsive abuses escalated.

In the spring of 1965 a Boston minister, one of scores of clergymen who had gone to Selma, Alabama, to help Martin Luther King Jr. launch a voter registration drive, was murdered. A few days later, on March 15, 1965, President Lyndon B. Johnson addressed Congress:

Many of the issues of civil rights are very complex and most difficult. But about this there can and should be no argument.

Every American citizen must have an equal right to vote. There is no reason which can excuse the denial of that right. There is no duty which weighs more heavily on us than the duty we have to ensure that right.

Yet the harsh fact is that in many places in this country men and women are kept from voting simply because they are Negroes.

Every device of which human ingenuity is capable has been used to deny this right. The Negro citizen may go to register only to be told that the day is wrong, or the hour is late, or the official in charge is absent. And if he persists and if he manages to present himself to the registrar, he may be disqualified because he did not spell out his middle name or because he abbreviated a word on the application. And if he manages to fill out an application, he is given a test. The registrar is the sole judge of whether he passes this test. He may be asked to recite the entire constitution, or explain the most complex provisions of state laws. And even a college degree cannot be used to prove that he can read and write.

For the fact is that the only way to pass these barriers is to show a white skin.

Experience has clearly shown that the existing process of law cannot overcome systematic and ingenious discrimination. No law that we now have on the books—and I have helped to put three of them there—can ensure the right to vote when local officials are determined to deny it. . . .

This time, on this issue, there must be no delay, or no hesitation or no compromise with our purpose.

We cannot, we must not refuse to protect the right of every American to vote in every election that he may desire to participate in. And we ought not, we must not wait another eight months before we get a bill. We have already waited a hundred years and more and the time for waiting is gone. . . .

But even if we pass this bill, the battle will not be over. What happened in Selma is part of a far larger movement which reaches into every section and state of America. It is the effort of American Negroes to secure for themselves the full blessings of American life.

Their cause must be our cause too. Because it is not just Negroes, but really it is all of us, who must overcome the crippling legacy of bigotry and injustice. And we shall overcome.

As a man whose roots go deeply into Southern soil I know how agonizing racial feelings are. I know how difficult it is to reshape the attitudes and the structure of our society.

But a century has passed, more than a hundred years, since the Negro was freed. And he is not fully free tonight.

It was more than a hundred years ago that Abraham Lincoln, the great President of the Northern party, signed the Emancipation Proclamation, but emancipation is a proclamation and not a fact.

A century has passed, more than a hundred years since equality was promised. And yet the Negro is not equal.

A century has passed since the day of promise. And the promise is unkept.

The time of justice has now come. I tell you that I believe sincerely that no force can hold it back. It is right in the eyes of man and God that it should come. And when it does, I think that day will brighten the lives of every American.

Congress enacted the Voting Rights Act of 1965. The act provided, among other things, for the suspension of literacy tests for five years in states or political subdivisions thereof in which fewer than "50 per cent of its voting-age residents were registered on November 1, 1964, or voted in the presidential election of November, 1964." This and other major provisions of the 1965 act were thereafter sustained in *South Carolina* v. *Katzen-*

bach (1966), *Rome* v. *United States* (1980), and *Katzenbach* v. *Morgan* (1966), as appropriate ways of enforcing the Fifteenth and Fourteenth Amendments. Subsequent amendments to the 1965 act have broadened its coverage.

The 1944 decision in *Smith* v. *Allwright* was more than a new and hospitable judicial approach to the right of blacks to participate in the American political process. It was a major advance (as, four years later, was *Shelley* v. *Kraemer*, 1948) toward the day—May 17, 1954—when a unanimous Court, speaking through Chief Justice Warren, was to hold, in *Brown* v. *Board of Education*, that the equal protection clause barred the legally mandated racial segregation of school children. Subsequent decisions, building on *Brown* v. *Board of Education*, soon made it plain that the equal protection clause barred all the legal trappings of Jim Crow. *Brown* v. *Board of Education* worked a fundamental change in the Court's and the nation's perception of the scope of judicial responsibility to vindicate those values.

In 1962, eight years after *Brown* v. *Board of Education*, the Court, in *Baker* v. *Carr*, held that allegations that a state legislature suffered from systematic malapportionment, under which districts of widely different populations were each represented by one legislator, stated a claim cognizable under the equal protection clause. The importance of *Baker* v. *Carr* cannot be overestimated. Chief Justice Warren thought it the most significant decision handed down by the Court during his sixteen years in the center chair. Even those who rank *Brown* v. *Board of Education* ahead of *Baker* v. *Carr* must nonetheless acknowledge that the latter decision set in motion a process that resulted in the redesign of numerous state legislatures and a myriad of local governing bodies, and, indeed, of the House of Representatives. That redesign has been required to meet the Court's pronouncement, in *Gray* v. *Sanders* (1963), that "[t]he conception of political equality from the Declaration of Independence, to Lincoln's Gettysburg

Address, to the Fifteenth, Seventeenth, and Nineteenth Amendments can mean only one thing—one person, one vote." Long-standing patterns of malapportionment in which rural districts with relatively few inhabitants were represented on equal terms with heavily populated urban districts have become a thing of the past.

Guaranteeing the voting rights of women and blacks and overcoming rampant malapportionment have cured the major inexcusable deficiencies of the American political process. In recent decades, certain lesser inequalities have also begun to be addressed.

From the beginning of the republic, Americans residing in the continental United States but not within any state—for example, those who lived in federal territories—had no way of voting in national elections. In the most egregious of anomalies, residents of the nation's capital were voiceless in the selection of the president who dwelt and governed in their own home town. So matters stood until 1964, when the Twenty-third Amendment was added to the Constitution, giving the District of Columbia a minimum of three electoral votes in presidential elections.

In the late 1960s profound divisions in American opinion about America's military involvement in the Vietnam War forced recognition of another anomaly—that tens of thousands of young men were being drafted to fight in an unpopular foreign war although they were not old enough to vote in national elections choosing the officials responsible for making decisions for war or for peace. In 1970, Congress, in amending the Voting Rights Act, included a provision forbidding abridgment of the right of any citizen to vote "on account of age if such citizen is eighteen years or older." The statute was promptly challenged in *Oregon* v. *Mitchell* (1970). Four Justices concluded that Congress had the power to lower the voting age to eighteen. Four Justices concluded that Congress had no such power. The casting vote was that of Justice Hugo L. Black, who held that Congress could regulate the voting age in national elections but not in state elections. Because Americans vote every two years for state and national officials at the same time, *Oregon* v. *Mitchell* was an invitation to chaos. Within six months, Congress proposed and the requisite three-fourths of the states ratified, the Twenty-sixth Amendment, which accomplished by constitutional mandate what Congress had been unable to achieve by statute.

In the course of two centuries law and conscience have combined to make the American suffrage almost truly universal. One massive obstacle remains: apathy. In recent national elections in the European democracies, 72 percent of the eligible electorate voted in Great Britain, 79 percent in Spain, 85 percent in France, and 89 percent in Italy and West Germany. By contrast, in the American presidential election of 1980, only 53 percent of those eligible voted. In America's 1984 presidential election, after both major parties had made massive efforts to register new voters, not more than 55 percent of those who could have voted made their way to the ballot box. A fateful question confronting American democracy is whether tens of millions of self-disenfranchised Americans will in the years to come find the energy and good sense to exercise the precious right won at such great labor at the Constitutional Convention, in Congress and state legislatures and the Supreme Court, and at Selma and Seneca Falls.

—LOUIS H. POLLAK

Bibliography

Chute, Marchette G. (1969). *First Liberty: A History of the Right to Vote in America, 1619–1850.* New York: Dutton.

Dubois, Ellen Carol, ed. (1981). *Elizabeth Cady Stanton, Susan B. Anthony: Correspondence, Writings, Speeches.* New York: Shocken.

Elliott, Ward E. Y. (1974). *The Rise of Guardian Democracy: The Supreme Court's*

See also

Role in Voting Rights Disputes, 1845–1969. Cambridge, Mass.: Harvard University Press.

Fairman, Charles (1971). *Reconstruction and Reunion, 1864–1888.* New York: Macmillan.

Farrand, Max, ed. (1921). *The Fathers of the Constitution.* New Haven, Conn.: Yale University Press.

———, ed. (1911). *The Records of the Federal Convention of 1787.* New Haven, Conn.: Yale University Press.

Flexner, Eleanor (1975). *Century of Struggle: The Woman's Right to Vote Movement in the United States.* Rev. ed. Cambridge, Mass.: Harvard University Press.

Higginbotham, A. L., Jr. (1984). "States' 'Rights' and States' 'Wrongs': Apartheid, Virginia and South African Style." Du Bois Lecture, Harvard University.

McKay, Robert B. (1965). *Reapportionment: The Law and Politics of Equal Representation.* New York: Twentieth Century Fund.

Williamson, Chilton (1960). *American Suffrage from Property to Democracy, 1760–1860.* Princeton, N.J.: Princeton University Press.

Woodward, C. Vann (1951). *Origins of the New South, 1877–1913.* Baton Rouge: Louisiana State University Press.

——— (1957). *The Strange Career of Jim Crow.* New York: Oxford University Press.

WABASH, ST. LOUIS & PACIFIC RAILWAY v. ILLINOIS

118 U.S. 557 (1886)

Tremendous growth in a national railroad network after the Civil War led to increasingly scandalous and harmful abuses. State efforts to control the problems were generally ineffective until *Munn* v. *Illinois* (1877). In that case, Chief Justice Morrison R. Waite allowed state regulation of railroads where Congress had not yet acted, "even though it may indirectly affect" those outside the state. Illinois had attempted to curb one area of abuse by forbidding long haul-short haul discrimination. So pervasive was this evil that it would be outlawed later in the Interstate Commerce and Mann-Elkins Acts. The state sued the Wabash company to prevent it from charging more for shorter hauls; because significant portions of most long hauls lay outside Illinois, the issue lay in the constitutionality of a state regulation of interstate commerce.

A 6–3 Supreme Court struck down the Illinois statute, undercutting the decisions in the *Granger Cases* (1877) without impairing the doctrine of affectation with a public interest. Justice Samuel F. Miller looked to the commerce clause as securing a "freedom of commerce" across the country. The imposition, by individual states, of varying patterns of rates and regulations on interstate commerce was "oppressive" and rendered the commerce clause a "very feeble and almost useless provision." Miller then relied on the decision in *Cooley* v. *Board of Wardens of Philadelphia* (1851) to declare that such regulation was clearly national, not local, in character even though Congress had not yet acted. In so doing, he altered the thrust of the *Cooley* test by examining the impact of state regulation on the nation instead of on the subjects involved. Miller concluded that "it is not, and never has been, the deliberate opinion of a majority of this court that a statute of a state which attempts to regulate the fare and charges by railroad companies [affecting interstate commerce] is a valid law."

Justices Horace Gray, Joseph P. Bradley, and Chief Justice Waite dissented, contending that the *Granger Cases* should have ruled the decision here. Citing *Willson* v. *Black Bird Creek Marsh Company* (1829), Gray and his colleagues argued that "in the absence of congressional legislation to the contrary, [the railroads] are not only susceptible of state regulation, but properly amenable to it." They recited the litany of rights and powers granted the railroads by the state: "its being, its franchises, its powers, its road, its right to charge" all confirmed the state's right to regulate the road. The dissenters asserted that the Illinois statute affected interstate commerce only "incidentally" and not adversely. Subject to future congressional action, they would have affirmed the state action.

This decision effectively created a vacuum—Congress had not acted and the states were forbidden to act or even to control intrastate abuses. Together with an increasingly powerful reform movement, *Wabash* helped contribute to the passage of the Interstate Commerce Act in 1887, creating the first national regulatory body.

—DAVID GORDON

This decision created a vacuum.

See also

Cooley v. *Board of Wardens*

Witness identification is treacherously subject to mistake.

WADE, UNITED STATES v.

388 U.S. 218 (1967)

Wade's conviction of bank robbery depended heavily on the identification of him as the robber by two bank employees. After he was indicted and counsel appointed for him, the Federal Bureau of Investigation arranged a lineup, which included Wade and five or six other people. Wade's counsel was not notified of the procedure; neither he nor anyone else representing Wade's interests was present.

The Supreme Court held that the lineup was a "critical stage" of the proceedings; thus, the Sixth Amendment guarantees a right to the presence of counsel at the pretrial identification if evidence of the lineup were to be used at the trial. The Court reasoned that counsel was necessary at this early stage in order to assure the fairness of the trial itself. The two premises were that eyewitness identification is treacherously subject to mistake, and that police methods in obtaining identifications are often and easily unduly suggestive. If a lawyer has been present at the lineup, later, at the trial, by his questioning of the eyewitnesses he will be able to show how any irregularities have tainted the in-court identification of the defendant.

Wade established a per se rule: if counsel is absent at the pretrial confrontation, the government may not use evidence that such an event happened. Whether the witness can nevertheless make an in-court identification depends on whether the unfair procedure tainted his present ability to identify: If he had not seen the uncounseled lineup, would he still be able to pick out the defendant?

Finally, the Court suggested that the pretrial confrontation might not be a "critical

"CRITICAL STAGE"

In Wade, *the Court ruled that the Sixth Amendment guarantees a right to have counsel present at a lineup if the results of the lineup are to be used at the trial. (Corbis/Bettmann)*

See also

Kirby v. *Illinois*

stage" if other methods were developed to assure against the risk of irreparable mistaken identification. In *Kirby* v. *Illinois* (1972) the Court restricted the holding in *Wade* to line-ups held after defendants have been formally charged with crime.

—BARBARA ALLEN BABCOCK

WAGNER ACT CASES

NLRB v. Jones & Laughlin Steel Corp.
301 U.S. 1 (1937)

NLRB v. Fruehauf Trailer Co.
301 U.S. 49 (1937)

NLRB v. Friedman-Harry Marks Clothing Co.
301 U.S. 58 (1937)

Associated Press Co. v. NLRB
301 U.S. 103 (1937)

The reinvigoration of the commerce clause as a source of congressional power began with the first cases to reach the Supreme Court under the Wagner (National Labor Relations) Act. That statute had been passed in 1935 in an effort to preserve the rights of employees in interstate industries to choose their own representatives and to bargain collectively with their employers. In 1930 the Supreme Court had held that the Railway Labor Act gave such rights to railroad employees. The National Industrial Recovery Act (NIRA) of 1933 sought to extend such rights to other employees by requiring all codes of fair competition for other industries to contain similar provisions. The code system collapsed when the NIRA was invalidated in *Schechter Poultry Corp.* v. *United States* in May 1935. The president and Congress believed that the denial of collective bargaining rights would lead to industrial unrest and strikes, which would necessarily obstruct interstate commerce, and would also aggravate the Great Depression by depressing wage rates and the purchasing power of

wage earners. As a result the National Labor Relations Act became law less than six weeks after the *Schechter* decision.

The act authorized the newly created National Labor Relations Board (NLRB), which succeeded similar boards created under the NIRA, to prevent employers from engaging in unfair labor practices "affecting [interstate] commerce," which was defined to mean "in commerce, or burdening or obstructing commerce," or which had led or might lead to a labor dispute burdening or obstructing commerce. These definitions were designed to embody the decisional law upholding the authority of Congress to regulate acts that "directly" obstructed interstate commerce. Congress assumed, correctly as it turned out, that the courts would construe the statute as "contemplating the exercise of control within constitutional bounds."

The NLRB's first cases were brought against employers engaged in interstate transportation and communication (bus lines and the Associated Press) and manufacturers who purchased their supplies and sold their products across state lines. Before these cases were decided, the Supreme Court, in *Carter* v. *Carter Coal Co.* (1936), held that the substantially identical provisions of the Guffey-Snyder (Bituminous Coal Conservation) Act, enacted shortly after the Labor Relations Act, did not fall within the commerce power of Congress. In the *Carter* case the government had proved that coal strikes would burden not merely the interstate commerce of the immediate employers but also the interstate rail system and many other industries dependent upon coal. No stronger showing could be made under the Wagner Act for employers engaged in mining or manufacturing. As was to be expected, the courts of appeals, though sustaining the act as to companies engaged in interstate transportation and communication, deemed themselves bound by *Carter,* as well as *Schechter* and *United States* v. *Butler* (1936) to hold that the act did not extend to manufacturers.

W

WAGNER ACT CASES

NLRB *v.* Jones &
Laughlin Steel Corp.
301 U.S. 1 (1937)

NLRB *v.* Fruehauf
Trailer Co.
301 U.S. 49 (1937)

NLRB *v.*
Friedman-Harry Marks
Clothing Co.
301 U.S. 58 (1937)

Associated Press Co.
v. NLRB
301 U.S. 103 (1937)

*The act authorized
the NLRB to prevent
employers from
engaging in unfair
labor practices
affecting commerce.*

The first five NLRB cases to reach the Supreme Court involved a bus line, the Associated Press, and three manufacturers. The cases were argued together, beginning on February 8, 1937. Three days before, President Franklin D. Roosevelt had announced his plan to appoint up to six new Supreme Court Justices, one for each justice over 70 years of age. On April 12 the Court affirmed the NLRB's rulings in all five cases. The opinions on the commerce clause issue in the bus and press cases were unanimous, although in the press case, four Justices dissented on First Amendment grounds. The cases against manufacturers—the Jones & Laughlin Steel Corporation, the Fruehauf Trailer Co., and a medium-size men's clothing manufacturer—were decided by a 5–4 vote. The membership of the Court had not changed since *Schechter* and *Carter.* But Chief Justice Charles Evans Hughes and Justice Owen Roberts, who had been part of the majority of six who had rejected the labor relations provisions of the Guffey Act in *Carter,* now joined with Justices Louis D. Brandeis, Harlan Fiske Stone, and Benjamin N. Cardozo. The Chief Justice wrote the opinions in the manufacturers' cases.

In the *Carter* case, the majority opinion of Justice George Sutherland had not denied the magnitude of the effect of coal strikes upon interstate commerce. The question, he held, was whether the effect was "direct," and that did not turn upon the "extent of the effect" or its "magnitude," but "entirely upon the manner in which the effect has been brought about"; "it connotes the absence of an efficient intervening agency or condition." The effect must "operate proximately—not mediately, remotely, or collaterally." Why "direct" should be so defined was not otherwise explained, except by the need for preserving the power of the states over production, even in interstate industries in which interstate competition would preclude state regulation.

The opinion of Chief Justice Hughes in the *Jones & Laughlin* case flatly rejected the *Butler* approach.

Giving full weight to respondent's contention with respect to a break in the complete continuity of the "stream of commerce" by reason of respondent's manufacturing operations, the fact remains that the stoppage of those operations by industrial strife would have a most serious effect upon interstate commerce. In view of respondent's far-flung activities, it is idle to say that the effect would be indirect or remote. It is obvious that it would be immediate and might be catastrophic. We are asked to shut our eyes to the plainest facts of our national life and to deal with the question of direct and indirect effects in an intellectual vacuum. . . . When industries organize themselves on a national scale, making their relation to interstate commerce the dominant factor in their activities, how can it be maintained that their industrial labor relations constitute a forbidden field into which Congress may not enter when it is necessary to protect interstate commerce from the paralyzing consequences of industrial war? We have often said that interstate commerce itself is a practical conception. It is equally true that interferences with that commerce must be appraised by a judgment that does not ignore actual experience.

The Chief Justice also met head on the argument that the federal power did not extend to activities in the course of production or manufacturing. Citing many antitrust cases, he declared: "The close and intimate effect which brings the subject within the reach of Federal power may be due to activities in relation to productive industry although the industry when separately viewed is local. . . . It is thus apparent that the fact that the employees here concerned were engaged in production is not determinative."

"The fundamental principle," Hughes stated, "is that the power to regulate commerce is the power to enact 'all appropriate legislation' for 'its protection and advancement'; to adopt measures 'to promote its growth and insure its safety'; 'to foster, protect, control and restrain.' That power is plenary and may be exerted to protect interstate commerce 'no matter what the source of the dangers which threatened it.' " Hughes also invoked the Shreveport Doctrine he had announced in *Houston East and West Texas Railway* v. *United States* (1914): "Although activities may be intrastate in character when separately considered, if they have such a close and substantial relation to interstate commerce that their control is essential or appropriate to protect that commerce from burdens and obstructions, Congress cannot be denied the power to exercise that control."

In deference to his own opinion in *Schechter*, the Chief Justice declared that "undoubtedly the scope of this power must be considered in the light of our dual system of government" so as not to "obliterate the distinction between what is national and what is local." In *Schechter* the effect upon commerce had been too "remote"; "to find 'immediacy or directness' there was to find it 'almost everywhere', a result inconsistent with the maintenance of our Federal system." With little explanation Hughes added that *Carter* was "not controlling."

Within a few weeks the Court sustained the constitutionality of the Social Security Act. Soon after Justices Willis Van Devanter and Sutherland retired. And President Roosevelt's court-packing plan, not very surprisingly, got nowhere.

Subsequent Labor Board cases extended the application of the Labor Act far beyond the three manufacturers in the center of the interstate movement; it was sufficient that a strike would interfere with interstate movement of products (for example, *Santa Cruz Fruit Packing Co.* v. *NLRB*, 1938; *NLRB* v. *Fainblatt*, 1939; *Consolidated Edison Co.* v. *NLRB*, 1938). The unanimous opinion of the Court speaking through Justice Stone, with Hughes and Roberts still on the bench, in *United States* v. *Darby* (1941) explicitly re-

jected the concept that the Tenth Amendment limited the powers granted Congress by the Constitution. And other cases by now have extended the commerce power "almost everywhere." Nevertheless, the opinion in *Jones & Laughlin* remains a landmark in the interpretation of the commerce clause, as the definitive acceptance of the modern theories which recognize the power of Congress to control all aspects of the nation's integrated economic system.

—ROBERT L. STERN

Bibliography

Cortner, Richard C. (1970). *The Jones & Laughlin Case.* New York: Knopf.
——— (1964). *The Wagner Act Cases.* Knoxville: University of Tennessee Press.
Dodd, E. Merrick (1945). The Supreme Court and Organized Labor, 1941–1945. *Harvard Law Review* 58:1018–1071.
Gross, James A. (1974). *The Making of the National Labor Relations Board: A Study in Economics, Politics, and the Law,* vol. 1 (1933–1937). Albany: State University of New York Press.
Stern, Robert L. (1946). The Commerce Clause and the National Economy, 1933–1946. *Harvard Law Review* 59:645–693, 888–947.

WAITE, MORRISON R.

(1816–1888)

WAITE, MORRISON R.

(1816–1888)

Morrison Remick Waite, sixth Chief Justice of the United States, successfully led the Supreme Court in dealing with major constitutional problems concerning Reconstruction and business-government relations between 1874 and 1888.

Son of Henry Matson Waite, Chief Justice of the Connecticut Supreme Court of Errors, Morrison Waite read law after graduating from Yale College in 1837. In 1838 he removed to Ohio, where he built a flourishing

See also

Butler, United States v.

Carter v. Carter Coal Company

Houston, East and West Texas Railway v. United States

Labor and Employment Law

Schechter Poultry Corp. v. United States

legal practice specializing in commercial law, acquired substantial property interests, and joined the Whig party. Although prominent in the legal profession, Waite was virtually unknown in national affairs prior to his appointment as Chief Justice. He served one term in the Ohio legislature and a term on the Toledo city council, was appointed counsel to the Geneva Tribunal to negotiate the *Alabama* claims in 1872, and was elected president of the Ohio Constitutional Convention of 1873.

The circumstances of Waite's appointment to the Court were remarkable, not so much because he lacked national political recognition as because he was the fifth person whom President Ulysses S. Grant nominated or asked to serve as Chief Justice. Yet Waite had early been touted for the position by leading Ohio politicians, and Grant had considered him a possibility from the beginning. His effective service at the Geneva Arbitration, professional reputation, and unwavering Republican party loyalty recommended him, and in January 1874 the Senate confirmed him by a 63–0 vote.

Waite's significance in American constitutional history is threefold. He wrote the first Supreme Court opinions interpreting the Fourteenth and Fifteenth Amendments in cases involving Negroes' civil rights. Second, his 1877 opinions in *Munn* v. *Illinois* and the other *Granger Cases* established the basic principles of constitutional law governing state governments as they attempted to deal with economic changes caused by the industrial revolution. Third, Waite expressed a conception of judicial review that summarized dominant nineteenth-century ideas about constitutional adjudication and provided a model for twentieth-century theorists of judicial restraint.

The northern retreat from Reconstruction was well underway when Waite became Chief Justice, and the Waite Court did not attempt to reverse this political development. Under the circumstances, and given the cir-

cumscribed role of the judiciary in nineteenth-century constitutional politics, it had little choice but to acquiesce. In determining the meaning of the Fourteenth and Fifteenth Amendments and in applying federal civil rights laws, however, the Court could choose among several possible conceptions of national legislative power and federal-state relations. Waite guided the Court toward a moderate position of states' rights nationalism which upheld national power to protect civil rights within the framework of traditional federalism.

To understand this development it is necessary to advert to the *Slaughterhouse Cases* (1873) and to Justice Joseph P. Bradley's circuit court opinion in *United States* v. *Cruikshank* (1874). In the former, the Supreme Court confirmed the theory of dual American citizenship, stated that the Fourteenth Amendment did not add to the rights of national citizenship, and concluded that ordinary civil rights were attributes of state citizenship, regulation of which was beyond the authority of the United States. In the *Cruikshank* case, involving prosecution of whites in Colfax, Louisiana, for violating the civil rights of Negro citizens, Justice Bradley held that although the Fourteenth Amendment prohibited state rather than private denial of civil rights, under certain conditions the federal government was authorized to guarantee civil rights against interference by private individuals. The relevant circumstance, according to Bradley, was state failure to fulfill its affirmative duty to protect citizens' rights.

Chief Justice Waite wrote the majority opinion when *United States* v. *Cruikshank* (1876) was decided in the Supreme Court. Defendants were indicted under a section of the Force Act of 1870 that declared it a federal crime for two or more persons to deprive any citizen of rights secured by the Constitution or laws of the United States. Like Bradley in the circuit court, Waite found numerous flaws in the indictments and on that ground ordered the defendants to be discharged, thus frustrating the federal civil rights enforcement effort. Nevertheless, Waite asserted national authority to enforce civil rights.

The Chief Justice followed the *Slaughterhouse* opinion in positing separate federal and state citizenships and in stating that the federal government could protect only those rights placed within its jurisdiction. He held further that the freedom of assembly, which the defendants were charged with violating, was a right of state rather than federal citizenship. The indictment, however, had incorrectly stated that denial of freedom of assembly by private persons was a federal crime within the meaning of the Force Act; therefore the indictment was invalid. Yet federal authority was not nugatory in civil rights matters. Waite pointed out that if the indictment had charged a violation of the right to assemble in order to petition the national government, it would have been proper under the act. Thus in protecting a federal right national authority was putatively effective against private individuals as well as states. Waite furthermore asserted an indirect federal power to protect rights of state citizenship against both state and private interference. The ordinary right of assembly was a state right, said Waite, over which "no direct power" was granted to Congress. This appeared to mean that if states failed to uphold civil rights within their jurisdiction, the federal government could provide the needed protection. Finally Waite noted that the indictments did not allege that the full and equal benefit of laws for the protection of whites was denied to blacks on account of race; accordingly the Civil Rights Act of 1866 was not in point. The implication was that if a racially discriminatory purpose had been alleged, federal authority under the 1866 law could have been employed against private as well as against state denial of rights.

Waite also gave the opinion in *United States* v. *Reese* (1876), the first Supreme Court

WAITE, MORRISON R.

(1816–1888)

ABLE GUIDANCE

Morrison Waite successfully led the Supreme Court in dealing with major constitutional problems concerning Reconstruction. (Corbis/Bettmann)

case involving Fifteenth Amendment voting rights. State officials in Kentucky were indicted for refusing to accept the vote of a Negro citizen. Again the Court ruled against the federal government. Waite declared two provisions of the Force Act of 1870 unconstitutional because they did not in express terms limit the offense of state officials to denial of the right to vote on account of color. Insisting on the need for strict construction of criminal statutes, he interpreted the act in a strained and technical manner as preventing any wrongful interference with voting rights, rather than simply interferences that were racially motivated. The Fifteenth Amendment authorized the federal government to deal only with the latter. It did not, said Waite, secure the right to vote, but only the right not to be discriminated against in voting on racial grounds. Observing that "Congress has not as yet provided by 'appropriate legislation' for the punishment of the offense charged in the indictment," Waite in effect invited Republican lawmakers to enact a more tightly drawn enforcement act.

Waite's personal sympathies were enlisted in efforts to assist Negroes. As a trustee of the Peabody Fund in 1874 he signed a report endorsing a constitutional argument for federal aid to education, thus breaking the rule against extra-Court political involvement to which he scrupulously adhered throughout his judicial career. Although Waite accepted the abandonment of Reconstruction and held that Congress had no power "to do mere police duty in the States," his opinions nevertheless authorized federal interference against state and in some circumstances private denial of rights when racially motivated. In subsequent cases, most notably *United States* v. *Harris* (1883), the *Civil Rights Cases* (1883), and *Ex Parte Yarbrough* (1884), the Waite Court amplified the principles set forth in the *Cruikshank* and *Reese* cases.

In the sphere of government-business relations, Waite was sympathetic to regulatory legislation within a political and legal framework that encouraged industrial expansion and a national free trade area. In the early 1870s, in response to farmers' and merchants' demands for relief from high shipping costs, several midwestern states adopted legislation setting maximum railroad rates. These laws appeared to discourage further railroad construction, and within a few years most of them were repealed or modified. Nevertheless, in the landmark *Granger Cases* the Supreme Court ruled on the constitutionality of these regulatory measures.

Munn v. *Illinois* (1877), Waite's most famous opinion, sustained an 1871 Illinois law that established maximum rates for grain elevators. Waite based his approval of the legislation on a broad conception of the state police power, which he said authorized states to regulate the use of private property "when such regulation becomes necessary for the public good." He rejected the contention that state regulation of the rates charged by ferries, common carriers, or bakers was a deprivation of property without due process of law in violation of the Fourteenth Amendment.

Support for Waite's conclusion lay in numerous state common law precedents asserting a public interest in certain kinds of property, such as lands bordering on watercourses, which were subject to government regulation. Like other judges in similar cases, and influenced by a memorandum prepared by Justice Bradley dealing with the instant case, Waite relied on a treatise of the seventeenth-century English judge Lord Chief Justice Sir Matthew Hale in asserting: "When property is 'affected with a public interest, it ceases to be juris privati only.'" The grain elevator companies, Waite explained, exercised a virtual monopoly in the regional market structure; thus, they were affected with a public interest and subject to regulation by the state legislature. In the other *Granger Cases* Waite employed this principle to uphold state regulation of railroad rates.

Waite also approved state regulation of corporations in a series of decisions that carried to a logical conclusion the principle by which the contract clause of the Constitution did not prevent state legislatures from reserving the power to alter charter grants. These cases included *Stone* v. *Mississippi* (1880), *Ruggles* v. *Illinois* (1883), and *Spring Valley Water Works* v. *Schotteler* (1883). This trend culminated in *Stone* v. *Farmers Loan and Trust Co.* (1886), known as the *Railroad Commission Cases,* in which Waite held that a state charter authorizing railroads to set reasonable rates did not divest a state of the power ultimately to determine what was a reasonable rate.

While generally approving regulatory legislation, Waite placed limitations on the police power with a view toward protecting private property. In the *Railroad Commission Cases* he admonished: "This power to regulate is not a power to destroy; and limitation is not the equivalent of confiscation. Under pretence of regulating fares and freights the state cannot require a railroad corporation to carry persons or property without reward; neither can it do that which in law amounts to a taking of private property without due process of law."

Rather than suggesting an irresistible tendency to accept the argument for substantive due process that was later adopted by the Supreme Court, these and similar dicta indicate that Waite, like Justice Stephen J. Field who dissented in *Munn* and the other *Granger* cases, believed the essential constitutional problem in cases involving government-business relations was to determine the extent of the police power. Shortly after the *Munn* decision Waite wrote: "The great difficulty in the future will be to establish the boundary between that which is private, and that in which the public has an interest."

Waite epitomized nineteenth-century thinking about the nature of the judicial function and the power of judicial review. He believed the judiciary should play a subordinate role in public-policy making, and should especially defer to the political branches in questions concerning the reasonableness of legislation. His clearest and most forceful expression of this view appeared in *Munn* v. *Illinois* when he stated: "For us the question is one of power, not of expediency. If no state of circumstances could justify such a statute, then we may declare this one void, because in excess of the legislative power of the States. But if it could we must presume it did. Of the propriety of legislative interference within the scope of legislative power, the legislature is the exclusive judge." Waite acknowledged that legislative power might be abused. But "[f]or protection against abuses by legislatures," he observed, "the people must resort to the polls, not to the courts."

Waite effectively balanced the competing demands of state and federal authority as constitutional equilibrium was restored after the end of Reconstruction. In addition to the decisions already noted, he wrote the opinions in *Louisiana* v. *Jumel* (1882) and *New Hampshire* v. *Louisiana* (1882), both of which held that the Eleventh Amendment prevented suits by bondholders attempting to force a state government to redeem its bonds. These decisions expressed the political logic of the Compromise of 1877 and marked a significant broadening of states' sovereign immunity under the Eleventh Amendment. In another notable case involving state power and women's rights, *Minor* v. *Happersett* (1875), Waite adhered to a narrow interpretation of the Fourteenth Amendment in deciding that the right to vote was not an attribute of federal citizenship and that states could regulate the suffrage as they saw fit.

On the other hand, Waite upheld federal authority in the controversial *Sinking Fund Cases* (1879) and in *Pensacola Telegraph Co.* v. *Western Union Telegraph Co.* (1878). In the former, the Court confirmed the constitutionality of an act of Congress requiring the Union Pacific and Central Pacific railroads to set aside money from current income for the subsequent payment of its mortgage debts. In the latter case the Court upheld the rights of an interstate telegraph company operating under authority of an act of Congress against the rights of a company acting under a state charter. Waite also voted to strike down state tax legislation when it interfered with interstate commerce, although he was less inclined than his colleagues to regard state taxation of commerce in this light.

Overcoming the resentment of several Justices who had aspired to the Chief Justiceship, Waite performed the administrative and other tasks of his position with great skill. In a larger political sense he was also a successful judicial statesman. During his tenure, as at few times in American constitutional history, the Supreme Court was remarkably free of congressional criticism. Waite achieved this success by confining judicial policymaking within limits approved by the nation's representative political institutions and public opinion.

—HERMAN BELZ

Bibliography

Benedict, Michael Les (1979). Preserving Federalism: Reconstruction and the Waite Court. *Supreme Court Review* 1978:39–79.

See also

Frantz, Lauren B. (1964). Congressional Power to Enforce the Fourteenth Amendment Against Private Acts. *Yale Law Journal* 73:1352–1384.

Magrath, Peter C. (1963). *Morrison R. Waite: The Triumph of Character.* New York: Macmillan.

Scheiber, Harry N. (1971). The Road to *Munn:* Eminent Domain and the Concept of Public Purpose in the State Courts. *Perspectives in American History* 5:329–402.

Trimble, Bruce R. (1938). *Chief Justice Waite: Defender of the Public Interest.* Princeton, N.J.: Princeton University Press.

WAITE COURT

(1874–1888)

A new age of American constitutional law was at hand when Morrison R. Waite became Chief Justice of the United States in 1874. Not only had the Civil War discredited many antebellum glosses on the "old" Constitution, consisting of the venerable document framed in 1787 and the twelve amendments adopted during the early republic, but it had also generated a "new" Constitution consisting of the Thirteenth Amendment, the Fourteenth Amendment, and the Fifteenth Amendment. The range of choices at the Court's disposal was virtually unlimited as it reconstituted the old organic law and integrated the new. Charles Sumner said it best just four years before Waite took the Court's helm. The tumultuous events of 1861–69, he exclaimed, had transformed the Constitution into "molten wax" ready for new impression. An extraordinarily homogeneous group of men made this impression. Of the fourteen associate Justices who sat with Waite between 1874 and his death in 1888, only Nathan Clifford had been appointed by a Democrat and all but two—Samuel F. Miller and John Marshall Harlan, both of Kentucky—had been born in the free states. All of them were Protestants. Thus the Republi-

can party, which had subdued the South and created the "new" Constitution, had also reconstructed the federal judiciary. As the Waite Court proceeded to refashion the structure of American constitutional law, its work ineluctably reflected the values, aspirations, and fears that had animated the Republican party's northern Protestant constituency since the 1850s.

Fierce opposition to state sovereignty concepts was a core element of Republican belief from the party's very inception. Republicans asociated state sovereignty with proslavery constitutionalism in the 1850s, with secession in 1861, and ultimately with the tragic war both engendered. Waite and his colleagues shared this aversion to state sovereignty dogma and repeatedly expressed it in controversies involving the implied powers of Congress under the "old" Constitution. In case after case the Court resisted limitations on federal power derived from state sovereignty premises and held, in effect, that Congress's authority to enact statutes deemed necessary and proper for the enumerated powers had the same scope under the Constitution as it would if the states did not exist. On several occasions the Court even revived the idea that Congress might exercise any power inherent in national sovereignty as long as it was not specifically prohibited by the Constitution. This doctrine, first expounded by Federalist congressmen during debate on the Sedition Act of 1798, had been regarded as "exploded" by most antebellum statesmen. But its revival after the Civil War did have a certain logic. If there was one impulse that every member of the Waite Court had in common, it was the urge to extirpate every corollary of "southern rights" theory from American constitutional law and to confirm the national government's authority to exercise every power necessary to maintain its existence.

The revival of the implied powers doctrine began in the often overlooked case of *Kohl* v. *United States* (1876). There counsel challenged Congress's authority to take private property in Cincinnati as a site for public buildings on the ground that the Constitution sanctioned federal exercise of the eminent domain power only in the District of Columbia. Article I, section 8, vested Congress with authority to acquire land elsewhere "for the erection of forts . . . and other needful buildings" only "by the consent of the legislature of the State in which the same shall be." This was by no means a novel argument. James Madison and James Monroe had pointed to the national government's lack of a general eminent domain power when vetoing internal improvement bills, and proslavery theorists had invoked the same principle as a bar to compensated emancipation and colonization schemes. In *Pollard's Lessee* v. *Hagan* (1845), moreover, the Taney Court had said that "the United States have no constitutional capacity to excrcise municipal jurisdiction, sovereignty, or eminent domain within the limits of a State or elsewhere, except in the cases in which it is expressly granted." But William Strong, speaking for the Court in *Kohl,* refused to take this doctrine "seriously." Congress's war, commerce, and postal powers necessarily included the right to acquire property for forts, lighthouses, and the like. "If the right to acquire property for such uses be made a barren right by the unwillingness of property holders to sell, or by the action of a State prohibiting a sale to the Federal Government," Strong explained, "the constitutional grants of power may be rendered nugatory. . . . This cannot be." Congress's eminent domain power must be implied, Strong concluded, for commentators on the law of nations had always regarded it as "the offspring of political necessity, and . . . inseparable from sovereignty."

Horace Gray sounded the same theme in the *Legal Tender Cases* (*Juilliard* v. *Greenman,* 1884), where the Court sustained Congress's authority to emit legal tender notes even in peacetime. With only Stephen J. Field dissenting, Gray asserted that because the power to make government paper a legal tender was "one of the powers belonging to sovereignty in other civilized nations, and not expressly withheld from Congress by the Constitution," it was unquestionably "an appropriate means, conducive and plainly adapted" to the execution of Congress's power to borrow money. In *Ex Parte Yarbrough* (1884), decided the same day, the Court spoke the language of national sovereignty in an especially significant case. At issue there was the criminal liability of a Georgia man who had savagely beaten a black voter en route to cast his ballot in a federal election. The Court unanimously sustained the petitioner's conviction under the 1870 Civil Rights Act, which made it a federal crime to "injure, oppress, threaten, or intimidate any citizen in the free exercise or enjoyment of any right or privilege secured to him by the Constitution or laws of the United States." It did so on the ground that Congress's duty "to provide in an election held under its authority, for security of life and limb to the voter" arose not from its interest in the victim's rights so much as "from the necessity of the government itself." Samuel F. Miller explained that Congress's power to regulate the time, place, and manner of holding federal elections, conferred in Article I, section 4, implied a "power to pass laws for the free, pure, and safe exercise" of the suffrage. "But it is a waste of time," he added, "to seek for specific sources to pass these laws. . . . If this government is anything more than a mere aggregation of delegated agents of other States and governments, each of which is superior to the general government, it must have the power to protect the elections on which its existence depends from violence and corruption."

The Court's decisions in *Kohl, Juilliard,* and *Yarbrough* merely jettisoned antebellum canons of strict construction. They did not impair the autonomy of state governments. The eminent domain power of the several states was not threatened by *Kohl,* the Constitution expressly prohibited the states from making anything but gold and silver a legal tender, and *Yarbrough* did not jeopardize Georgia's power to prosecute political assassins for assault or murder. Yet the Waite Court was as quick to defend exercises of Congress's powers in situations where counsel claimed that the states' autonomy was in jeopardy as in cases where their reserved powers remained unimpaired. *Ex Parte Siebold* (1880) was the leading case in point. There the Court sustained a conviction for ballot stuffing under the 1871 Enforcement Act, which made it a federal crime for any state official at a congressional election to neglect duties required of him by either state or federal law. Counsel for the petitioner argued that in *Prigg* v. *Pennsylvania* (1842) and *Kentucky* v. *Dennison* (1861) the Taney Court had held that the principle of divided sovereignty precluded acts of Congress compelling the cooperation of state officials in the execution of national law. "We cannot yield to such a transcendental view of State sovereignty," Joseph Bradley proclaimed for the Court in *Siebold.* "As a general rule," he said, "it is no doubt expedient and wise that the operations of the State and National Governments should, as far as practicable, be conducted separately, in order to avoid undue jealousies and jars." But the Constitution neither mandated an immutable boundary between spheres of federal and state power nor restricted Congress's choice of means in implementing its enumerated authority to regulate federal elections.

The Court's constitutional nationalism did have limits. Like most Republicans of the age, Waite and his colleagues resisted the idea of centralization with as much ardor as the concept of state sovereignty. They regarded the national government's competence as deriving from the powers specified in the Constitution or fairly implied from it; the residual powers of government, usually called "internal police," belonged exclusively to the several states. Thus decisions like *Kohl* and *Siebold,* as Waite and his associates understood them, did not contract the ambit of

state jurisdiction. Rather the court simply refused to recognize implied limitations on the powers of Congress derived from state sovereignty premises. The *Trade-Mark Cases* (1879) underscored the Waite Court's allegiance to this view of the federal system. There a unanimous Court, speaking through Miller, held that Congress had no authority to enact a "universal system of trade-mark registration." Miller's method of analysis was more revealing than the result. His first impulse was to determine which sphere of government ordinarily had responsibility for such matters in the constitutional scheme. "As the property in trade-marks and the right to their exclusive use rest on the laws of the States, and like the great body of the rights of persons and of property, depend on them for security and protection," he explained, "the power of Congress to legislate on the subject . . . must be found in the Constitution of the United States, which is the source of all the powers the Congress can lawfully exercise." This two-tier method not only reified dual federalism but also put the burden of demonstrating Congress's authority to act on the government. In the *Trade-Mark Cases* it could not do so. Trade-marks lacked "the essential characteristics" of creative work in the arts and sciences, consequently the statute could not be sustained under the copyright or patent powers. And the commerce power, though admittedly "broad," could not be construed as to permit federal regulation of commercial relations between persons residing in the same state.

When the Waite Court turned to cases involving the "new" Constitution, the instinct to conceptualize rights and powers in terms of dual federalism had fateful consequences. Beginning in *United States* v. *Cruikshank* (1876), the Court emasculated Congress's power "to enforce, by appropriate legislation," the rights guaranteed by the Fourteenth and Fifteenth Amendments. At issue was the validity of conspiracy convictions under the 1870 Civil Rights Act against a band of whites who had attacked a conclave of blacks in Grants Parish, Louisiana, killing from sixty to one hundred of them. The government claimed that the defendants had deprived the black citizens of their constitutional rights to hold a peaceful assembly, to bear arms, to vote, and to equal protection of the laws safeguarding persons and property. The Court unanimously overturned the convictions. The conspiracy law was not voided; indeed, the Court sustained a conviction under that very statute in *Yarbrough*. But Waite and his associates were determined to confine Congress's power to enact "appropriate legislation" in such a way to preserve what Miller called "the main features of the federal system." The Court had no choice in the matter, Joseph Bradley remarked on circuit in 1874, unless it was prepared "to clothe Congress with power to pass laws for the general preservation of social order in every State," or, in short, with a plenary power of "internal police."

Waite's opinion for the Court in *Cruikshank* contained two separate lines of argument. He began the first foray by pointing out that every American citizen "owes allegiance to two sovereigns, and claims protection from both." Because the two levels of government could protect the rights of citizens only "within their respective spheres," federal authorities could assert jurisdiction over perpetrators of violence only if the rights denied to victims were derived from the Constitution and laws of the United States. But in the *Slaughterhouse Cases* (1873), decided ten months before Waite came to the Court, a majority of five had concluded that there were very few privileges or immunities of national citizenship and that the Fourteenth Amendment had not created any new ones. Fundamental rights of life, liberty, and property still rested upon the laws of the states, and citizens had to rely upon the states for the protection of those rights. Among the privileges of state citizenship, Waite explained in *Cruikshank,* were the rights to assemble, to bear arms, and to vote. Although

guaranteed against infringement by Congress in the Bill of Rights, the rights to assemble and bear arms were not "granted by the Constitution" or "in any manner dependent upon that instrument for existence." The right to vote in state and local elections stood on the same footing because "the right to vote in the States comes from the States." The Fifteenth Amendment did give citizens a new right under the Constitution—exemption from racial discrimination when attempting to vote. Because the Grants Parish indictments did not aver that the defendants had prevented their victims "from exercising the right to vote on account of race," however, that count was as defective as the rest.

Waite's second line of argument in *Cruikshank* was designed to hold the votes of Joseph Bradley, Stephen J. Field, and Noah Swayne. They had dissented in the *Slaughterhouse Cases,* claiming that the Fourteenth Amendment had been designed to reconstruct the federal system by creating a third sphere in the constitutional scheme—that of the individual whose fundamental rights were now protected against unequal and discriminatory state laws. Waite satisfied them by stating what came to be known as the state action doctrine. He not only conceded that "[t]he equality of the rights of citizens is a principle of republicanism" but strongly implied that the Fourteenth Amendment had nationalized this principle under the equal protection clause, if not the privileges or immunities clause. But the amendment, he added, "does not . . . add any thing to the rights which one citizen had under the Constitution against another." The very language of the amendment's first section—"No state shall . . ."—suggested that it must be read not as a grant of power to Congress but as a limitation on the states. It followed that the exercise of fundamental rights did not come under the Constitution's protection until jeopardized by the enactment or enforcement of a state law. "This the amendment guarantees, but no more," Waite declared. "The

The tumultuous events of 1861–69 transformed the Constitution into "molten wax" ready for new impression.

power of the national government is limited to the enforcement of this guaranty."

The principles announced in *Cruikshank* doomed the rest of Congress's civil rights program, all of which had been based on the assumption that the "new" Constitution might be employed as a sword to protect any interference with fundamental rights. A voting rights statute went down in *United States* v. *Reese* (1876) because Congress had failed to limit federal jurisdiction over state elections to the prevention of racially motivated fraud or dereliction; the antilynching provisions of the 1871 Civil Rights Act were invalidated for want of state action in *United States* v. *Harris* (1883). One latent function of *Cruikshank,* however, was to draw renewed attention to the equal protection clause as a shield for blacks and other racial minorities whose civil rights were imperiled by discriminatory state laws. Soon the docket was crowded with such cases, and the Court was compelled to wrestle with longstanding ambiguities in the Republican party's commitment to racial equality.

Republicans had always been quick to defend equal rights in the market, for it was the rights to make contracts and own property that distinguished free people from slaves. But many Republicans regarded the idea of equality before the law as wholly compatible with legalized race prejudice in the social realm. Words like "nation" and "race" were not merely descriptive terms in the nineteenth century; they were widely understood as objective manifestations of natural communities, the integrity of which government had a duty to maintain. Thus most Republicans never accepted the proposition that blacks ought to be free to marry whites and many denied the right of blacks to associate with whites even in public places. The framers of the "new" Constitution had neither abjured this qualified view of equality not incorporated it into the Fourteenth Amendment. The discretion of Waite and his colleagues was virtually unfettered. They could weave prevailing prejudices into equal protection jurisprudence or they could interpret the equality concept broadly, declare that the "new" Constitution was color-blind, and put the Court's enormous prestige squarely behind the struggle for racial justice.

Exponents of racial equality were greatly encouraged by *Strauder* v. *West Virginia* (1880), the case of first impression. There a divided Court reversed the murder conviction of a black defendant who had been tried under a statute that limited jury service to "white male persons." The Fourteenth Amendment, William Strong explained for the majority, "was designed to secure the colored race the enjoyment of all the civil rights that under the law are enjoyed by white persons." This formulation was acceptable even to the two dissenters. According to Stephen J. Field and Nathan Clifford, however, jury service was not a "civil right." It was a "political right." The only rights Congress intended to protect with the Fourteenth Amendment, they contended, were those enumerated in the Civil Rights Act of 1866—to own property, to make and enforce contracts, to sue and give evidence. The equal protection clause, Field said, "secures to all persons their civil rights upon the same terms; but it leaves political rights . . . and social rights . . . as they stood previous to its adoption." But the *Strauder* majority was unimpressed by Field's version of the "original understanding" and it set a face of flint against his typology of rights. "The Fourteenth Amendment makes no attempt to enumerate the rights it designed to protect," Strong declared. "It speaks in general terms, and those are as comprehensive as possible." The very term equal protection, he added, implied "that no discrimination shall be made against [blacks] by the law because of their color."

Strauder seemed to open the door for judicial proscription of all racial classifications in state laws. John R. Tompkins, counsel for an interracial couple that had been sentenced to two years in prison for violating Alabama's

antimiscegenation law, certainly read the case that way. But the idea of distinct spheres of rights—"civil" and "social" if no longer "political"—furtively reentered the Waite Court's jurisprudence in *Pace* v. *Alabama* (1883). Field, speaking for a unanimous Court, held that antimiscegenation laws were not barred by the Fourteenth Amendment as long as both parties received the same punishment for the crime. Equal protection mandated equal treatment, not freedom of choice; antimiscegenation laws restricted the liberty of blacks and whites alike. Underlying this disingenuous view was an unarticulated premise of enormous importance. In settings involving the exercise of "social rights" the equal protection clause did not prohibit state legislatures from enacting statutes that used race as a basis for regulating the rights of persons. The legal category "Negro" was not suspect per se.

The concept of "social rights" also figured prominently in the *Civil Rights Cases* (1883), decided ten months after *Pace*. There the Court struck down the Civil Rights Act of 1875, which forbade the owners of theaters, inns, and public conveyances to deny any citizen "the full and equal benefit" of their facilities. Joseph Bradley, speaking for the majority, rejected the claim that the businesses covered by the act were quasi-public agencies; consequently the state action doctrine barred federal intervention under the Fourteenth Amendment. But Bradley conceded that the state action doctrine was not applicable in Thirteenth Amendment contexts. It not only "nullif[ies] all state laws which establish or uphold slavery," he said, but also "clothes Congress with power to pass all laws necessary and proper for abolishing all badges and incidents of slavery in the United States." With the exception of John Marshall Harlan, however, every member of the Waite Court equated the "badges and incidents of slavery" with the denial of "civil rights" and concluded that Congress had nearly exhausted its authority to enact appropriate legislation under the Thirteenth Amendment with the Civil Rights Act of 1866. "[A]t that time," Bradley explained, "Congress did not assume, under the authority given by the Thirteenth Amendment, to adjust what may be called the social rights of man and races in the community; but only to declare and vindicate those fundamental rights which appertain to the essence of citizenship, and the enjoyment or deprivation of which constitutes the essential distinction between freedom and slavery." Bradley's opinion was circumspect in only one respect. Whether denial of equal accommodation "might be a denial of a right which, if sanctioned by the state law, would be obnoxious to the [equal protection] prohibitions of the Fourteenth Amendment," he said, "is another question." But that was true only in the most formal sense. Once the Court had identified two distinct spheres of rights under the Thirteenth Amendment, one "civil" and another "social," it was difficult to resist the impulse to link that standard with the doctrine expounded in *Pace* when deciding equal protection cases. Stephen J. Field and Horace Gray, the only members of the *Civil Rights Cases* majority still alive when *Plessy* v. *Ferguson* (1896) was decided, had no qualms about state laws that required separate but equal accommodations for blacks on public conveyances. Harlan was the sole dissenter on both occasions.

Equal opportunity in the market was one civil right that every member of the Waite Court assumed was guaranteed by the equal protection clause. Thus in *Yick Wo* v. *Hopkins* (1886) the Court invalidated the racially discriminatory application of a San Francisco ordinance that required all laundries, except those specifically exempted by the board of supervisors, to be built of brick or stone with walls one foot thick and metal roofs. No existing San Francisco laundry could meet such stringent building regulations, but the ordinance had the desired effect. The authorities promptly exempted the city's white operators and denied the petitions of their 240 Chinese competitors. "[T]he conclusion cannot be resisted," Stanley Matthews asserted for a unanimous Court, "that no reason for [this discrimination] exists except hostility to the race and nationality to which the petitioners belong, and which in the eye of the law is not justified." Yet the type of right divested was at least as important in *Yick Wo* as the fact of discrimination. The Court described laws that arbitrarily impaired entrepreneurial freedom as "the essence of slavery" while laws that denied racial minorities free choice in the selection of marriage partners and theater seats were not. But that was not all. The court invoked the absence of standards for administering the laundry ordinance as an independent ground for its unconstitutionality. The boundless discretion, or, as Matthews put it, "the naked and arbitrary power" delegated to the authorities was as decisive for the Court as the fact that the ordinance had been applied with "an evil eye and an unequal hand." In the Waite Court's view, however, the same kind of concern about official discretion was neither possible nor desirable in jury-service cases. In *Strauder* Strong conceded that jury selection officials might constitutionally employ facially neutral yet impossibly vague tests of good character, sound judgment, and the like. The Court had no choice but to presume that the jury commissioners had acted properly, Harlan explained in *Bush* v. *Kentucky* (1883), in the absence of state laws expressly restricting participation to whites. As blacks began to disappear from jury boxes throughout the South, it became clear that although *Strauder* put jury service in the "civil rights" category, in practical application it stood on a far lower plane than the rights enumerated in the Civil Rights Act of 1866. When Booker T. Washington counseled blacks to place economic opportunities ahead of all others in 1895, he expressed priorities that the Waite Court had long since embroidered into equal protection jurisprudence.

The path of due process was at once more tortuous and less decisive than the develop-ment of equal protection doctrine. In *Dent* v. *West Virginia* (1888), decided at the close of the Waite era, the Court conceded, as it had in the beginning, that "it may be difficult, if not impossible, to give to the terms 'due process of law' a definition which will embrace every permissible exertion of power affecting private rights and exclude such as are forbidden." Yet two generalizations about the Waite Court's understanding of due process can be advanced with confidence. First, the modern distinction between procedural and substantive due process had no meaning for Waite and his colleagues. In their view, the Fifth and Fourteenth Amendments furnished protection for fundamental rights against arbitrary action, regardless of the legal form in which the arbitrary act had been clothed. In *Hurtado* v. *California* (1884), where the majority rejected counsel's claim that the Fourteenth Amendment incorporated the Bill of Rights, Stanley Matthews explained that because the due process concept embraced "broad and general maxims of liberty and justice," it "must be held to guaranty not particular forms of procedure, but the very substance of individual rights to life, liberty, and property." Even Miller, the most circumspect member of the Court, agreed in 1878 that a law declaring the property of A to be vested in B, "without more," would "deprive A of his property without due process of law." It is equally clear that the Court assumed that corporations were persons within the meaning of the Fifth and Fourteenth Amendments long before Waite acknowledged as much during oral argument in *Santa Clara County* v. *Southern Pacific Railroad Co.* (1886). As early as the *Granger Cases* (1877) the Court decided controversies in which railroad corporations challenged state regulation on due process grounds, and neither the defendant states nor the Justices breathed a doubt about the Court's jurisdiction. In the *Sinking Fund Cases* (1879), moreover, Waite stated emphatically in obiter dictum that the Fifth Amendment had always barred Congress "from depriving persons or corporations of property without due process of law."

Although every member of the Court accepted the essential premises of substantive due process, no statute was voided on due process grounds during the Waite era. Conventional assumptions about the boundary between the legislative and judicial spheres were largely responsible for the Court's reticence. In due process cases, at least, most of the period's Justices meant it when they stated, as Waite did in the *Sinking Fund Cases,* that "[e]very possible presumption is in favor of the validity of a statute, and this continues until the contrary is shown beyond a reasonable doubt." The most disarming demonstration of that Court's adherence to this principle came in *Powell* v. *Pennsylvania* (1888). At issue was an act that prohibited the manufacture and sale of oleomargarine. The legislature had labeled the statute as a public health measure, but it was no secret that the law really had been designed to protect the dairy industry against a new competitor. Harlan, speaking for everyone but Field, conceded that counsel for the oleomargarine manufacturer had stated "a sound principle of constitutional law" when he argued that the Fourteenth Amendment guaranteed every person's right to pursue "an ordinary calling or trade" and to acquire and possess property. Indeed, the Court had furnished protection for those very rights in *Yick Wo.* "But we cannot adjudge that the defendant's rights of liberty and property, as thus defined, have been infringed," Harlan added, "without holding that, although it may have been enacted in good faith for the objects expressed in its title . . . it has, in fact, no real or substantial relation to those objects." And this the Court was not prepared to do. Defendant's offer of proof as to the wholesomeness of his product was insufficient, for it was the legislature's duty, not the judiciary's, "to conduct investigations of facts entering into questions of public policy." Nor could the Court consider the reasonableness of the means selected by the legislature: "Whether the manufacture of oleomargarine . . . is, or may be, conducted in such a way . . . as to baffle ordinary inspection, or whether it involves such danger to the public health as to require . . . the entire suppression of the business, rather than its regulation . . . are questions of fact and of public policy which belong to the legislative department to determine." Field, dissenting, claimed that the majority had not simply deferred to the legislature but had recognized it as "practically omnipotent."

Field overstated the predisposition of his colleagues, and he knew it. The Court seldom spoke with a luminous, confident voice in due process cases; majority opinions almost invariably revealed lingering second thoughts. Each time the Court said yes to legislatures, it reminded them that someday the Court might use the due process clause to say no. In *Powell,* for example, Harlan warned lawmakers that the Court was ready to intercede "if the state legislatures, under the pretence of guarding the public health, the public morals, or the public safety, should invade the rights of life, liberty, and property." Harlan did not explain how the Court might identify an act that had been passed "under the pretence" of exercising the police power, but he seemed to be confident that the Justices would be able to identify a tainted statute once they saw one. Waite's opinion in *Munn* v. *Illinois* (1877) was equally ambiguous. In one series of paragraphs he stated that the power to regulate prices was inherent in the police power; in another he suggested that price fixing was legitimate only if the regulated concern was a "business affected with a public interest." It followed from the latter proposition, though not from the former, that "under some circumstances" the Court might disallow regulation of prices charged by firms that were "purely and exclusively private." In *Munn* Waite was more certain about the reasonableness of rates lawfully fixed. "We know that it is a power which may be abused," he said; "but . . . [f]or protection

against abuses by the legislatures the people must resort to the polls, not the courts." By 1886, however, Waite and some of his colleagues were not so sure. "[U]nder the pretense of regulating fares and freights," Waite declared in the *Railroad Commission Cases* (1886), "the State cannot require a railroad corporation to carry persons or property without reward; neither can it do that which in law amounts to a taking of private property for public use without just compensation, or without due process of law." This statement, like Harlan's similar remark in *Powell,* warranted many conflicting inferences. At the close of the Waite era, then, the scope of the judicial power under the due process clause was as unsettled as the clause's meaning.

When Waite died in 1888, a St. Louis law journal observed that he had been "modest, conscientious, careful, conservative, and safe." It was a shrewd appraisal not only of the man but of his Court's work in constitutional law. The Court's unwillingness to use judicial power as an instrument of moral leadership evoked scattered protests from racial egalitarians, who accused Waite and his colleagues of energizing bigotry, and from exponents of laissez-faire who complained that the Court had failed to curb overweening regulatory impulses in the state legislatures. But no criticism was heard from the Republican party's moderate center, where the Court had looked for bearings as it reconstructed the "old" Constitution and integrated the "new." In retrospect, it was Thomas M. Cooley, not Charles Sumner, who supplied the Waite Court with an agenda and suggested an appropriate style for its jurisprudence. The Republican party had resorted to "desperate remedies" and had treated the Constitution as if it were "wax" during the Civil War, he said in 1867. Now it was time for the bench and bar to ensure that postwar institutions were "not mere heaps of materials from which to build something new, but the same good old ship of state, with some progress toward justice and freedom."

—CHARLES W. MCCURDY

Bibliography

Benedict, Michael Les (1979). Preserving Federalism: Reconstruction and the Waite Court. *Supreme Court Review* 1978:39–79.

Corwin, Edward S. (1913). *National Supremacy: Treaty Power versus State Power.* New York: Henry Holt.

——— (1948). *Liberty against Government.* Baton Rouge: Louisiana State University Press.

Magrath, C. Peter (1963). *Morrison R. Waite: The Triumph of Character.* New York: Macmillan.

McCurdy, Charles W. (1975). Justice Field and the Jurisprudence of Government-Business Relations. *Journal of American History* 61:970–1005.

Schmidt, Benno C. (1983). Juries, Jurisdiction, and Race Discrimination: The Lost Promise of Strauder v. West Virginia. *Texas Law Review* 61:1401–1499.

WAIVER OF CONSTITUTIONAL RIGHTS

A potential beneficiary may waive almost any constitutional claim. Rights not of constitutional dimension also may be waived. The Supreme Court has struggled with the questions of whether any special doctrine governs waivers of constitutional rights and, if so, whether the special doctrine applies to all constitutional rights. These waiver issues, like much of the rest of constitutional law, took on massive new proportions with the rapid expansion of constitutional rights in the 1960s and 1970s. Prior to that era, there were relatively few rights eligible for waiver.

Distinctions between waivers of constitutional rights and waivers of other rights do not appear in very early cases. The most frequent waiver issue probably was whether a civil litigant had waived the Seventh Amendment right to trial by jury. *Hodges* v. *Easton*

(1882), a case raising this issue, was the setting for one of the Supreme Court's important statements concerning waiver. In *Hodges* the Court acknowledged that litigants may waive the right but cautioned, in an oft-quoted statement that seemed to contemplate special treatment for waivers of constitutional rights, that "every reasonable presumption should be indulged against . . . waiver."

Then, as later would be true, there seemed to be a gap between the Court's statement of the waiver standard and its application of the standard in deciding cases. The Court's casual attitude toward waiver emerged in *Pierce* v. *Somerset Railway* (1898) and *Eustis* v. *Bolles* (1893), in which the Court found waivers of claims that state laws unconstitutionally impaired the obligation of contract. In each case not only was "every reasonable presumption" against waiver not indulged; the Court went so far as to indicate that a state court's finding of waiver of constitutional rights did not even raise a federal issue reviewable by the Supreme Court. It may be, however, that the Court was insufficiently attentive to differences between the waiver issue and the existence of an independent and adequate state ground for decision, which would preclude Supreme Court review of the state court's judgment.

Although the Court had not become deeply involved in waiver issues, the legal community knew that waiver doctrine might have to be attuned to differences among constitutional rights. Through eight editions from 1868 to 1927, Thomas M. Cooley's treatise on constitutional law acknowledged that litigants may waive constitutional rights but it stated that in criminal cases this "must be true to a very limited extent only." Subsequent Supreme Court waiver doctrine at first would adhere to, and later partially undermine, Cooley's suggested distinction. But in his time, Cooley, himself a state supreme court justice, was on safe ground. As long as there were few constitutional rights regulating criminal procedure, one easily could limit their waivability.

The Court became more involved with waivers of constitutional rights in the 1930s. In *Aetna Insurance Co.* v. *Kennedy* (1937) and *Johnson* v. *Zerbst* (1938), cases raising civil and criminal procedure waiver issues, the Court seemed to indulge presumptions against waiver. And *Johnson* v. *Zerbst* supplied a new guiding rhetoric. Waiver required "an intentional relinquishment or abandonment of a known right or privilege." Again, though, the Court's articulated waiver standard sometimes was difficult to reconcile with the standard it applied. In *Rogers* v. *United States* (1951) a grand jury witness who answered many questions was held to have waived her Fifth Amendment right against self-incrimination with respect to additional information.

The 1930s doctrinal seeds restricting waiver flowered in the 1960s. The most significant waiver developments concerned the question of a state criminal defendant's waiver of the right to assert a federal constitutional claim in a federal habeas corpus proceeding. A habeas corpus case, *Fay* v. *Noia* (1963), became the touchstone for analysis of waiver of constitutional rights. *Fay* reaffirmed *Johnson* v. *Zerbst*'s waiver standard and required a conscious decision to forgo the privilege of seeking to vindicate federal rights. On the language of *Fay*, accidental waivers seemed impossible. The Court's reluctance to allow waivers of constitutional rights reached a high point in *Miranda* v. *Arizona* (1966), when the Court required that police inform suspects of their constitutional rights to assure that any waiver would be knowing.

The late Warren Court's reluctance to allow waivers of constitutional rights contrasts with the Burger Court's attitude. In one respect, a retreat from the 1960s standard seemed inevitable. For *Fay* and *Johnson* soon collided with the realities of the American criminal justice system. Through the plea bargaining process, the entire system depends upon widespread waivers of constitutional

*Waiver issues took
on massive new
proportions with the
rapid expansion of
constitutional rights
in the 1960s and
1970s.*

rights. In the trilogy of *McMann* v. *Richardson* (1970), *Parker* v. *North Carolina* (1970), and *Brady* v. *United States* (1970), holdings difficult to reconcile with the *Fay-Johnson* standard, this reality took hold. The trilogy effectively made a plea of guilty a waiver of nearly all constitutional procedure rights, known or unknown.

Another waiver issue, one with perhaps less of a foregone conclusion, further signaled the Court's shift in attitude. The Fourth Amendment guarantees the right to be free of unreasonable searches and seizures and often requires police to obtain a warrant before conducting a search. For many years there was doubt about the relationship between searches conducted with consent, which need not comply with the Fourth Amendment's warrant requirement, and the concept of waiver. If consent were equated with a waiver of Fourth Amendment rights, then the *Johnson* standard seemed applicable. But since few who consent to searches are informed of their Fourth Amendment rights, it was difficult to characterize any waiver as knowing. The widespread practice of consent searches seemed to hang in the balance.

A Court reluctant to allow waivers of constitutional rights might have adopted the *Miranda*-like solution of generally requiring the police to inform suspects of their Fourth Amendment rights before obtaining consent to a search. In *Schneckloth* v. *Bustamonte* (1973) the Court, opting for a different extreme, preempted most Fourth Amendment waiver problems. It found that the *Johnson* standard had, almost without exception, "been applied only to those rights which the Constitution guarantees to a criminal defendant in order to preserve a fair trial." Fourth Amendment claims were held not to be subject to the knowing and intelligent waiver requirement.

Schneckloth's reasoning may have implications for other constitutional rights. It suggests that rights other than those relating to a fair trial are subject to a waiver standard more

lenient than the *Johnson* test. But it did not signal a wholesale retreat from *Johnson*. After *Schneckloth*, in cases such as *Edwards* v. *Arizona* (1981), the Court reaffirmed that the *Johnson* standard governs waivers of the right to counsel.

In *Wainwright* v. *Sykes* (1977), where the Court squarely confronted *Fay*, it further limited 1960s waiver doctrine. Under *Wainwright*, failure to comply with state procedural rules effectively waives the right to raise a constitutional claim on federal habeas corpus. A habeas applicant must both explain his failure to comply with state procedures and show that his case was prejudiced by the constitutional flaw. The Court rejected *Fay's* requirement of a knowing and deliberate waiver. In effect, the burden of proving nonwaiver had been placed on the defendant.

The waiver question also continued to arise in contexts not involving criminal procedure. In *D. H. Overmyer Co.* v. *Frick Company* (1972) and *Swarb* v. *Lennox* (1972) the Court reconfirmed earlier holdings that at least some civil litigants may contractually waive due process rights to notice and hearing prior to a judgment and thereby effectively waive the opportunity to contest the validity of a debt. In *Parden* v. *Terminal Railway* (1964) states may have been surprised to learn that certain activities effectively waived their constitutional immunity from suit in federal court. For many years prior to *Parden*, it appeared that only an express waiver by states would be effective. But the Court found that by operating a railroad in interstate commerce, a state effectively waived its immunity from employees' suits in federal court under the federal Employers Liability Act. *Parden's* reach was limited by *Employees* v. *Department of Public Health and Welfare* (1973), which refused to rely on the Fair Labor Standards Act to subject states to federal damage suits by employees. More important, *Edelman* v. *Jordan* (1974) held that state participation in a federal program did not amount to consent to suit in federal court on claims relating to the program.

—THEODORE EISENBERG

Bibliography

Cover, Robert M. and Aleinikoff, T. Alexander (1977). Dialectical Federalism: Habeas Corpus and the Court. *Yale Law Journal* 86:1035–1102.

LaFave, Wayne R. (1978). *Search and Seizure: A Treatise on the Fourth Amendment* §8.1, 8.2, 11.1, 11.7 (f). St. Paul, Minn.: West Publishing Co.

Tigar, Michael E. (1970). Foreword: Waiver of Constitutional Rights: A Disquiet in the Citadel. *Harvard Law Review* 84:1–28.

Tribe, Laurence H. (1978). *American Constitutional Law.* Pages 133–138. Mineola, N.Y.: Foundation Press.

WALKER v. BIRMINGHAM

388 U.S. 307 (1967)

The Supreme Court, 5–4, upheld criminal contempt convictions of eight black ministers, including Martin Luther King Jr., for holding a civil rights protest parade in violation of an injunction issued by an Alabama state court. The injunction, which forbade them from engaging in street parades without a permit, was issued *ex parte,* two days before the intended march. The order was based on a city ordinance that the Court later held unconstitutional for vagueness in *Shuttlesworth* v. *Birmingham* (1969), a case arising out of the same events.

For the majority, Justice Potter Stewart concluded that the ministers, once enjoined by a court order, were not entitled to disregard the injunction even if it had been granted unconstitutionally. Rather, they were obliged to ask the court to modify the order, or to seek relief from the injunction in another court.

Justice William J. Brennan, for the four dissenters, pointed out that, in the absence of a court order, the First Amendment would have entitled the marchers to disregard the ordinance, which was invalid on its face. It was incongruous, he argued, to let the state alter this result simply by obtaining "the *ex parte* stamp of a judicial officer on a copy of the invalid ordinance." These views were echoed in separate dissents by Chief Justice Earl Warren and Justice William O. Douglas. The *Walker* principle, though much criticized, remains the doctrine of the Court.

—KENNETH L. KARST

WALLACE v. JAFFREE

472 U.S. (1985)

A 6–3 Supreme Court, in an opinion by Justice John Paul Stevens, held unconstitutional an Alabama statute that required public school children to observe a period of silence "for meditation or voluntary prayer." No member of the Court contested the constitutionality of the period of silence for meditation. As Justice Sandra Day O'Connor said in her concurring opinion, no threat to religious liberty could be discerned from a room of "silent, thoughtful school children." Chief Justice Warren E. Burger added that there was no threat "even if they chose to pray." Burger willfully misunderstood or missed the point. Any student in any public school may pray voluntarily and silently at almost any time of the school day, if so moved. The state, in this case, sought to orchestrate group prayer by capitalizing on the impressionability of youngsters. Compulsory attendance laws and the coercive setting of the school provided a captive audience for the state to promote religion. Justice John Paul Stevens emphasized the fact that the state act was "entirely motivated by a purpose to advance

The majority concluded that the eight Black ministers, once enjoined by a court order, were not entitled to disregard the injunction even if it had been granted unconstitutionally.

See also

Civil Rights

*Compulsory
attendance laws
and the coercive
setting of the school
provided a captive
audience for the
state to promote
religion.*

See also

Establishment of Religion

Lemon v. *Kurtzman*

Religious Liberty

religion" and had "*no* secular purpose." The evidence irrefutably showed that. Accordingly, the Alabama act failed to pass the test of *Lemon* v. *Kurtzman* (1971) used by the Court to determine whether a state violated the First Amendment's prohibition against an establishment of religion.

Justice O'Connor, observing that Alabama already had a moment of silence law on its books, noted that during the silence, no one need be religious, no one's religious beliefs could be compromised, and no state encouragement of religion existed. "The crucial question," she wrote, "is whether the State has conveyed or attempted to convey the message that children should use the moment of silence for prayer." The only possible answer was that the state, by endorsing the decision to pray during the moment of silence, sponsored a religious exercise, thereby breaching the First Amendment's principle of separation of church and state.

—LEONARD W. LEVY

WARDEN v. HAYDEN

387 U.S. 294 (1976)

In *Gouled* v. *United States* (1921) the Court announced a rule that rings strange to the modern ear; when conducting an otherwise lawful search, police are authorized to search for contraband, fruits of crime, means and instrumentalities of crime, or weapons of escape, but they are not authorized to search for "mere evidence." The rationale for the mere evidence rule was never clear, but its main theme was that police could not take objects from an accused without asserting a superior property interest in the object seized. This requirement spurred judicial creativity in recognizing property interests and in broadly defining their scope.

In *Warden* v. *Hayden* the Supreme Court rejected this property-centered conception of Fourth Amendment jurisprudence. Police could seize evidence after all. Questions remained concerning the scope of searches for items previously regarded as mere evidence (such as diaries) and concerning the applicable standards for searches and seizures of "mere evidence" belonging to innocent parties.

—STEVEN SHIFFRIN

WARE v. HYLTON

3 Dallas 199 (1796)

Ware established the fundamental principle of constitutional law that a state act may not violate a national treaty. An act of Virginia during the Revolution sequestered sterling debts owed by Virginians to British subjects and provided that such debts be discharged on payment (in depreciated currency) to the state. The Treaty of Paris of 1783 provided that creditors should meet with no lawful impediments to the recovery of full value in sterling, and Article VI of the Constitution made treaties of the United States the supreme law of the land. Ware, a British subject, brought an action in a federal court seeking such a recovery from Hylton, a Virginian. The prewar debts of Virginians to British creditors exceeded $2,000,000. Justice James Iredell, on circuit, ruled that the treaty did not revive any debt that had been discharged, and on the writ of error from the circuit court, John Marshall, for Hylton, argued that a United States treaty could not annul a statute passed when the state was sovereign. He also denied the authority of the Supreme Court to question the validity of a state law, arguing that the Constitution had not expressly granted such an authority.

Iredell persisted in his opinion expressed below, but Justice Samuel Chase, supported by the concurring opinions of the remainder of the Justices, declared that the supremacy clause (Article VI), operating retroactively, nullified the state act, thereby reviving the sterling debt. Chase cloaked his opinion in sweeping nationalist doctrine that twisted history: "There can be no limitations on the power of the people to change or abolish the state constitutions, or to make them yield to the general government, and to treaties made by their authority." A treaty, he ruled, could not be supreme law if any state act could stand in its way; state laws contrary to the treaty were prostrated before it and the Constitution, which was the "creator" of the states. The *Ware* decision intensified Jeffersonian hostility to the consolidating and procreditor opinions of the federal courts. The decision's imperishable principle of the supremacy of national treaties survived its origins—no doubt in part because Jay's Treaty of 1794 had provided that the United States should assume the payment of the controversial debts.

—LEONARD W. LEVY

WARREN, EARL

(1891–1974)

The fourteenth Chief Justice of the United States, Earl Warren presided over the most sweeping judicial reinterpretation of the Constitution in generations. He served from October 1953 to June 1969. In that time the Supreme Court, overruling the doctrine that separate but equal facilities for black persons satisfied the requirement of equal protection, outlawed official racial segregation in every area of life. The Court ended the long-established rural bias of legislative representation by opening the question to judicial scrutiny and then ruling that citizens must be represented equally in state legislatures and the national House of Representatives. It imposed constitutional restraints for the first time on the law of libel, hitherto a matter entirely of state concern. It applied to the states the standards set by the Bill of Rights for federal criminal procedure: the right of all poor defendants to free counsel, for example, and the prohibition of unreasonable searches and seizures, enforced by the exclusionary rule. It limited government power to

WARREN, EARL

(1891–1974)

"There can be no limitations on the power of the people to change or abolish the state constitutions."

See also

Mere Evidence Rule

Search and Seizure

919

punish unorthodox beliefs and enlarged the individual's freedom to express herself or himself in unconventional, even shocking ways.

The Warren Court, as it was generally called, had as profound an impact on American life as any Supreme Court since the time of John Marshall. It was extraordinary not only in the scale but in the direction of its exercise of power. From Marshall's day to the Court's clash with President Franklin D. Roosevelt in the 1930s judges had exercised a conservative influence in the American system. Shortly before his appointment to the Court in 1941 Robert H. Jackson wrote that "never in its entire history can the Supreme Court be said to have for a single hour been representative of anything except the relatively conservative forces of its day." But the Warren Court in its time was perhaps *the* principal engine of American liberal reform.

Earl Warren seemed an unlikely figure to lead such a judicial revolution. He was a Republican politician, the elected attorney general of California and for three terms its phenomenally popular governor. In 1948 he was the Republican candidate for vice president, on the ticket headed by Thomas E. Dewey. On naming him Chief Justice, President Dwight D. Eisenhower emphasized his "middle-of-the-road philosophy." Yet within a few years billboards in the South demanded Warren's impeachment, and the paranoid right charged that he was doing the work of communism. Putting aside the rantings of extremists, there was no doubt that as Chief Justice Warren consistently favored liberal values and unembarrassedly translated them into constitutional doctrine. Where did that commitment come from in a man whose appearance was that of a bland, hearty political figure?

There were in fact clues in his life and earlier career. He was born in Los Angeles in 1891, the son of a Norwegian immigrant who worked for the Southern Pacific Railroad. He knew poverty and personal tragedy. As a young man he was a railroad callboy,

waking up the gangs, and he saw men with their legs cut off in accidents carried in on planks. His father was murdered, the murderer never found: a traumatic event that must have helped to point Warren in the direction of justice, legal and social. He put himself through college and law school at the University of California. After a brief try at private practice he spent all his life in public office, as a local prosecutor and crusading district attorney before winning statewide office.

In California politics he at first had the support of conservatives. As attorney general he blocked the nomination of Max Radin, a law professor known as a legal realist, to the state supreme court because Radin was a "radical." As attorney general and governor Warren was a leading proponent of the World War II federal order removing all persons of Japanese ancestry from the West Coast and putting them in desolate camps; opposing their return in 1943, he said, "If the Japs are released, no one will be able to tell a saboteur from any other Jap." (In a memoir published after his death, Warren wrote: "I have since deeply regretted the removal order and my own testimony advocating it, because it was not in keeping with our American concept of freedom and the rights of citizens. . . .")

But in 1945 Warren astounded political California by proposing a state program of prepaid medical insurance. Characteristically, he did so not for ideological but for human, practical reasons: he had fallen ill and realized how catastrophic serious illness would be for a person without resources. Then, in his last two terms as governor, he became an apostle of liberal Republicanism. A later Democratic governor, Edmund G. Brown, said Warren "was the best governor California ever had. . . . He felt the people of California were in his care, and he cared for them."

Many Americans and other people around the world saw that same paternal image in Earl Warren the Chief Justice, for he became an international symbol. He represented the hope of authority bringing justice to the downtrodden, an American vision of change by law rather than by rebellion. A single case gave Warren that status: *Brown* v. *Board of Education,* the 1954 school segregation decision. In recent years the Supreme Court had chipped away at *Plessy* v. *Ferguson,* the 1896 decision allowing what were termed "separate but equal" facilities but what were almost always in fact grossly inferior schools and other public institutions for blacks. Yet in 1953 seventeen southern and border states, with 40 percent of the national enrollment, still confined black children to separate public schools; moreover, there was involved here, unlike higher education, the compulsory daily association of children. The emotional content of the legal question was high. The Court had given the most gingerly handling to the question, restoring the issue to the calendar for reargument.

Warren became Chief Justice before the second argument. The following May he delivered the opinion for a unanimous Court holding public school segregation unconstitutional. The unanimity was itself a striking feature of the result, and a surprising one. Expected southern resistance made unanimity politically essential, but the known attitudes of some members of the Court had suggested the likelihood of dissents. Richard Kluger's exhaustive study has demonstrated that the new Chief Justice played a crucial part in his management of the process inside the Court. After argument he delayed formal discussion of the cases in conference to avoid the development of rigid positions among the nine Justices. Then he stated as his view that the separate-but-equal doctrine could not be maintained unless one thought blacks inherently inferior: an approach likely to induce shame in any judge prepared to argue for that outcome. He persuaded his colleagues even then to avoid a formal vote but to continue discussing the cases, in tight secrecy, among themselves. He wrote an opinion in simple terms. Finally, he persuaded reluctant mem-

WARREN, EARL

(1891–1974)

THE END OF "SEPARATE BUT EQUAL"

Earl Warren presided over the most sweeping judicial reinterpretation of the Constitution in generations. (Corbis)

bers of the Court to join for the sake of unanimity. A law clerk present at a late meeting between the Chief Justice and the most reluctant, Stanley F. Reed, remembers him saying, "Stan, you're all by yourself in this now. You've got to decide whether it's really the best thing for the country."

What is known about the process of decision in the school cases throws lights on one question asked during his lifetime: Did Chief Justice Warren exercise leadership or have influence in the Court beyond his own vote in conference? He shared that bench with men of strong personality and conviction: in particular Hugo L. Black, who said the judicial duty was to follow the literal language of the Constitution and found in it absolutes, and Felix Frankfurter, who scorned absolutes and said the Court should defer to the political branches of government in applying the uncertain commands of the Constitution. Warren came to the Court utterly inexperienced in its work; how could he have effective influence? The school cases show that he did.

Many regarded Warren as a heroic figure because he put aside philosophical concerns and technical legal issues and dealt squarely with what he considered outrageous situations.

No Chief Justice can command his associates' beliefs. If Warren had served with different, more conservative colleagues, many of the views that made history might have been expressed by him in dissent. Changes while he was on the Court greatly affected the trend of doctrine, in particular the retirement of Justice Frankfurter in 1962 and his replacement by Arthur J. Goldberg, who was much readier to join Warren in intervening on behalf of liberal values. But the identification of that Court with its Chief Justice, for all its logical imperfection, has substantial basis in reality.

Warren wrote the opinions of the Court not only in *Brown* but in later cases that dramatically overturned expectations. The most important of these—Warren himself thought them the weightiest decisions of his years on the Court—were the reapportionment cases. A divided Supreme Court in *Colegrove* v. *Green* (1946) had refused to entertain an attack on numerical inequality in political districts, an opinion by Justice Frankfurter saying that courts must stay out of the "political thicket." In 1962 the Warren Court, in an opinion by Justice William J. Brennan, overthrew that doctrine of reluctance and said that federal courts could consider issues of fairness in districting. The decision in *Baker* v. *Carr* left open the substantive questions: Must the population be the test of equality, or may states weigh geography or other factors in districting? Does the same standard apply to both houses of legislatures? The answers were given by Chief Justice Warren in 1964, in terms so firm that some who listened in the courtroom felt as if they were at a second American constitutional convention. In *Reynolds* v. *Sims* Warren said for a 6–3 majority that every house of every state legislature must be apportioned on the basis of population alone, with the districts as nearly equal as practicable. Few cases in any court ever had so direct and immediate an impact on a nation's politics; reapportionment was required in most of the fifty states, ancient legislative expectations were upset, new suburban power

vindicated. Justice John Marshall Harlan predicted in dissent, as had Justice Frankfurter in *Baker* v. *Carr,* that the courts would not be able to manage the apportionment litigation—or to enforce their decisions against political resistance. But the gloomy prediction was wrong. Resistance from political incumbents quickly collapsed; nothing like the emotional public opposition to the school segregation cases developed in any region.

Emotions were aroused by Warren's opinion in *Miranda* v. *Arizona* (1966), holding that before questioning an arrested person the police must warn him that he has a right to remain silent and a right to see a lawyer first—one provided by the state if he cannot afford one—and that a confession obtained in violation of that rule is inadmissible at trial. The decision touched a nerve among police, prosecutors, and others convinced that judges were impeding the fight against crime. *Miranda* climaxed a series of cases holding local police to the standards of the Bill of Rights: for example, *Mapp* v. *Ohio* (1961), exclusion of illegally obtained evidence; *Gideon* v. *Wainwright* (1963), right to counsel; *Griffin* v. *California* (1965), right against self-incrimination;, each overruling an earlier decision. In *Spano* v. *New York* (1959) Warren commented: "The abhorrence of society to the use of involuntary confessions does not turn alone on their inherent untrustworthiness. It also turns on the deep-rooted feeling that the police must obey the law while enforcing the law; that in the end life and liberty can be as much endangered from illegal methods used to convict those thought to be criminals as from the actual criminals themselves." Impatient with reviewing the facts in case after case of claimed coercion, the Court under Warren sought a general prophylactic rule—and wrote it in *Miranda*.

Objection to the *Miranda* decision came not only from the law enforcement community. More dispassionate critics saw it as an example of overreaching by the Warren Court. The opinion seemed more legislative in character than judicial, laying out what amounted to a code of police procedure with little basis in precedent. Moreover, the Court did not confront a situation in which reform by other means was blocked, as it had with school segregation and malapportioned legislatures; various reformers were working on the confession problem.

Freedom of expression was another subject of fundamental constitutional development during the Warren years. The most important single decision was probably *New York Times* v. *Sullivan* (1964), holding that a public official may not recover libel damages unless the statement was published with knowledge of its falsity or in reckless disregard of truth or falsity. That opinion was by Justice Brennan. Justice William O. Douglas wrote for the Court in *Lamont* v. *Postmaster General* (1965), holding that a statute requiring the post office to detain "Communist political propaganda" from abroad unless the addressee requested its delivery violated the First Amendment—the first federal statute that the Supreme Court ever held invalid under that amendment. Warren joined in these and other expansive decisions. He wrote for a 5–4 majority in *United States* v. *Robel* (1967), striking down a law that forbade the employment in defense plants of any member of an organization required to register under the Subversive Activities Control Act. Warren's opinion for a unanimous Court in *Bond* v. *Floyd* (1966) held that the Georgia legislature could not exclude a duly elected member because he had expressed admiration for draft resisters.

The one area of expression in which Warren departed from the majority of his colleagues was obscenity. He thought that local and national authorities should have a relatively free hand to combat what he evidently regarded as a social evil. Thus, while in *Miranda* imposing a national standard for fair pretrial procedures in criminal cases, he argued in dissent in *Jacobellis* v. *Ohio* (1964) that each local community should be allowed to fix its own standard of obscenity, a view

that became the law under Chief Justice Warren E. Burger in *Miller* v. *California* (1973). Another example of a departure from Warren's usual approach came when gambling was involved. He generally favored broad application of the right against self-incrimination; but when the rule was applied for the benefit of a gambler in *Marchetti* v. *United States* (1968), he alone dissented. Once again he saw a social evil.

Scholarly critics of Chief Justice Warren saw the obscenity and gambling cases as illustrating a fundamental shortcoming in a judge: a concern to reach particular results rather than to work out principles applicable whoever the parties in a case might be. In Warren's view, it seemed, justice consisted not in providing a philosophically satisfactory process and basis of decision but in seeing that the right side, the good side, won in each case. Many of the commentators regretted the lack of a consistent doctrinal thread in his opinions. There was nothing like Justice Black's exaltation of the constitutional text, or Justice Frankfurter's institutional concern for self-restraint.

G. Edward White, in a full-length study of Warren's work, rejected the general scholarly view that Warren had no rudder as a judge and lacked craftsmanship. He was an ethicist, White concluded, who saw his craft as "discovering ethical imperatives in a maze of confusion"—and in the Constitution. Thus the prosecutor so hard on corruption that he was called a boy scout, the Californian politician who stood aloof from party machines lest he be sullied, became a judicial enforcer of ethical imperatives. In general his sympathy lay with the little person, with victims, with people excluded from the benefits of our democracy. But he also was in the tradition of the American Progressives, who thought that government could be made to work for the people. Those two themes came together in the reapportionment cases, decisions designed to make democracy work better by making the electoral process fairer. John Hart

Ely, in an analysis of judicial review as practiced in the Warren years, suggested that many of the pathbreaking decisions had a democratic structural purpose: to assure access for the powerless and thus make the system work.

There was a directness, a simplicity in Warren's opinions on the largest issues. "Legislators represent people," he wrote in the reapportionment cases, "not acres or trees. Legislators are elected by voters, not farms or cities or economic interests. . . . The weight of a citizen's vote cannot be made to depend on where he lives." When the Court held unconstitutional a statute depriving a native-born American of his citizenship for deserting the armed forces in time of war, *Trop* v. *Dulles* (1958), Warren for a plurality argued that expatriation was a cruel and unusual punishment in violation of the Eighth Amendment. The death penalty would not have been "cruel," he conceded, but the deprivation of citizenship was, for it caused "the total destruction of the individual's status in organized society" and cost him "the right to have rights."

Warren's whole career suggests that he was a person born not to muse but to act—and to govern. That view provides a connecting thread through all the offices he held. In each he exerted his powerful abilities in the ways open to him. As a prosecutor he fought crime. As wartime attorney general and governor he was a patriot, worrying about spies. In the postwar years, he turned to the social problems of an expanding California. As Chief Justice, too, he was committed to action, to using the opportunities available to make an impression on American life: to break the pattern of malapportionment, to attack local police abuses, to condemn racial discrimination. The instinct to govern did not leave Earl Warren when he put on a robe.

Many regarded him as a heroic figure because he put aside philosophical concerns and technical legal issues and dealt squarely with what he considered outrageous situations. And there were outrages in American life: of-ficial racism, political discrimination, abuse of police authority, suppression of free expression. Warren as Chief Justice had the conviction, the humanity, and the capacity for growth to deal effectively with those issues inside that prickly institution, the Supreme Court. But there were those who shared Justice Learned Hand's doubts about rule by judges, however beneficent. "For myself," Hand wrote in 1958, with the contemporary Supreme Court in mind, "it would be most irksome to be ruled by a bevy of Platonic Guardians, even if I knew how to choose them, which I assuredly do not." Earl Warren may have been the closest thing the United States has had to a constitutional Platonic Guardian, dispensing law without any sensed limit of authority except what he saw as the good of society. He was a decent, kindly lawgiver. But the exercise of such power by other judges—before and after Warren—has not always had kindly or rational results. The questions about judicial power remain after its extraordinary uses in the Warren years.

—ANTHONY LEWIS

Bibliography

Ely, John Hart (1980). *Democracy and Distrust: A Theory of Judicial Review.* Cambridge, Mass.: Harvard University Press.

Kluger, Richard (1975). *Simple Justice: The History of Brown* v. *Board of Education and Black America's Struggle for Equality.* New York: Knopf.

Schwartz, Bernard (1983). *Superchief.* Garden City, N.Y.: Doubleday.

White, G. Edward (1982). *Earl Warren: A Public Life.* New York: Oxford University Press.

WARREN COURT

(1953-1969)

It was surely the best known Supreme Court in history, and probably the most controversial. Its grand themes—racial equality, reapportionment, the separation of religion and education, due process—became matters of public consciousness. Its leading judges—Hugo L. Black, William O. Douglas, Felix Frankfurter, John Marshall Harlan, and Earl Warren—became personages in whom the general public took an interest. When the Warren Court came into being in October 1953, the Supreme Court was the least known and least active of the major branches of government; by the retirement of Chief Justice Warren in June 1969, nearly everyone in American life had been affected by a Warren Court decision, and a great many Americans had firm opinions about the Supreme Court. When Warren was appointed Chief Justice, few commentators took note of the fact that he had had no previous judicial experience and had spent the last twelve years as a state politician. By the time Warren E. Burger succeeded Warren as Chief Justice the process of nominating a Justice to the Supreme Court had become an elaborate search for the "experienced," uncontroversial, and predictable nominee, and the Court was to lower its profile again.

The Warren Court years, then, were years in which the Supreme Court of the United States made itself a vital force in American culture. A striking pattern of interchange between the Court and the general public emerged in these years. As public issues, such as civil rights or legislative malapportionment surfaced, these issues became translated into constitutional law cases. The Court, expanding the conventional ambit of its jurisdiction, reached out to decide those cases, thereby making an authoritative contribution to the public debate. As the Court continued to reach out, the public came to rely on its presence, and the American judicial system came to be perceived as a forum for the resolution of contemporary social problems. The use of the Supreme Court as an institution for redressing grievances ignored by Congress or state legislatures became common with the Warren Court.

The origins of the Warren Court can officially be traced to September 8, 1953, when Chief Justice Fred M. Vinson died of a heart attack. By September 30, President Dwight D. Eisenhower had named Warren, the governor of California who had been a rival candidate for the Republican presidential nomination in 1952, as Vinson's successor. This nominal creation of the Warren Court did not, however, hint at its character. Indeed that character was not immediately apparent. Even the Court's first momentous decision, *Brown* v. *Board of Education* (1954), announced in May of its first term, was in some respects a holdover from the Vinson Court. *Brown* had been argued before the Vinson Court, was based in part on Vinson Court precedents chipping away at racial discrimination in education, and was decided by a Court whose only new member was its Chief Justice. It was a cautious decision, apparently assuming that desegregation would be a long and slow process.

But *Brown* was also the Warren Court's baptism of fire. All the elements that were to mark subsequent major Warren Court decisions were present in *Brown. Brown* involved a major social problem, racial discrimination, translated into a legal question, the constitutionality of separate but equal public schools. It posed an issue that no other branch of government was anxious to address. It raised questions that had distinctively moral implications: in invalidating racial segregation the Court was condemning the idea of racial supremacy. And it affected the lives of ordinary citizens, not merely in the South, not merely in public education, for the Court's series of per curiam decisions after *Brown* revealed that it did not consider racial segregation any more valid in other public facilities than it had in schools. The Warren Court had significantly altered race relations in America.

The context of the Warren Court's first momentous decision was decisive in shaping the Court's character as a branch of government that was not disinclined to resolve

difficult social issues, not hesitant to foster social change, not reluctant to involve itself in controversy. By contrast, the legislative and executive branches appeared as equivocators and fainthearts. The Warren Court was deluged with criticism for its decision in *Brown*, both from persons who resisted having to change habits of prejudice and from scholars who faulted the reasoning of the Court's opinion. This response only seemed to make the Court more resolute.

The deliberations of *Brown* also served to identify some of the Justices whose presence was to help shape the character of the Warren Court. Earl Warren transformed a closely divided Court, which had postponed a decision on *Brown* because it was uncertain and fragmented on the case's resolution, into a unanimous voice. That transformation was a testament to Warren's remarkable ability to relate to other people and to convince them of the rightness of his views. In *Brown* he had argued that those who would support the separate but equal doctrine should recognize that it was based on claims of racial superiority. That argument struck home to at least two Justices, Tom C. Clark and Stanley F. Reed, who had grown up in the South. When Warren had finished his round of office visits and discussions, he had secured nine votes for his majority opinion and had suppressed the writing of separate concurrences. Robert H. Jackson, a long holdout in *Brown* who was dubious about the possibility of finding a doctrinal rationale to invalidate the separate but equal principle, joined Warren's opinion and left a hospital bed to appear in court the day the decision was announced.

A silent partner in the *Brown* decision had been Felix Frankfurter. By the late 1950s Frankfurter's jurisprudence, which stressed a limited role for judges in reviewing the constitutionality of legislative decisions, had rigidified, isolating Frankfurter from many other justices and identifying him as one of the guardians of a theory of judicial self-restraint. Judicial self-restraint in *Brown* would

have supported the separate but equal doctrine, since that doctrine itself signified a judicial reluctance to disturb legislative enactments forcibly separating persons on the basis of race. Frankfurter, however, could not abide the consequences of continued deference to the separate but equal doctrine, but he did not want to expose the lack of "restraint" that his position assumed. He accordingly confided his views on *Brown* only to Warren and worked toward fashioning a decree—containing the controversial phrase all deliberate speed as a guideline for implementing desegregation—that would temper the shock of the *Brown* mandate. At the appropriate moment he joined Warren's opinion.

The partnership of Warren and Frankfurter in the segregation cases contrasted with the usual posture of both Justices on the Warren Court. Warren's approach to judging, with its relative indifference to doctrinal reasoning and to institutional considerations, its emphasis on the morally or ethically appropriate result, and its expansive interpretation of the Court's review powers, was the antithesis of Frankfurter's. For the most part the two men sharply disagreed over the results or the reasoning of major Warren Court decisions, with Frankfurter enlisting a stable of academic supporters in his behalf and Warren seeking to bypass doctrinal or institutional objections to make broad ethical appeals to the public at large.

The presence of two other significant Warren Court Justices, Hugo Black and William O. Douglas, was also felt in *Brown*. Black, a native of Clay County, Alabama, and fleetingly a member of the Ku Klux Klan, had been an opponent of racial discrimination since being elected to the Senate in 1926. He had supported the Vinson Court precedents crippling "separate but equal," for which he had received outspoken criticism in his home state. His position in *Brown* was well known early on: an uncompromising opposition to discriminatory practices. Such positions were

characteristic of Black on the Warren Court. He staked out positions decisively, held them with tenacity, and constantly sought to convert others to his views. His theory of constitutional adjudication, which placed great emphasis on a "literal" but "liberal" construction of Bill of Rights protections, was a major contribution to Warren Court jurisprudence.

Equally outspoken and tenacious, and even more activist than Black, was William O. Douglas, whose academic experience, which paralleled Frankfurter's, had generated a strikingly different conception of judicial behavior. Douglas did not agonize over issues of institutional deference and doctrinal principle; he took his power to make law as a given and sought to use it to promote values in which he believed. The values were principally those associated with twentieth-century libertarianism and egalitarianism. Douglas spoke out for small business, organized labor, disadvantaged minorities, consumers, the poor, dissidents, and those who valued their privacy and their freedom from governmental restraint. Douglas's role on the Warren Court was that of an ideologue, anxious to secure results and confident that he could find doctrinal justifications. Together, Black and Douglas prodded the Court to vindicate even the most unpopular forms of free expression and minority rights.

While the Warren Court was generally regarded as an activist Court and a liberal Court, it was not exclusively so, and not all its members could be characterized as either activists or liberals. Until his retirement in 1962, at the midway point of Warren's tenure, Frankfurter had vociferously protested against an excessively broad interpretation of the Court's review powers, a position that resulted in his supporting the constitutionality of a number of "conservative" legislative policies. Other Justices on the Warren Court were either disinclined to exercise sweeping review powers or less enthusiastic than Warren, Black, or Douglas about the policies of twentieth-century liberalism. Most influen-

tial among those Justices was John Harlan, an Eisenhower appointee who joined the Court in 1955 and remained until 1971.

Harlan frequently and adroitly rejected the assumptions of Warren Court majorities that "every major social ill in this country can find its cure in some constitutional 'principle' and that the Court could be "a general haven for reform movements." Moreover, in a group of Justices who were often impatient to reach results and not inclined to linger over the niceties of doctrinal analysis, Harlan distinguished himself by producing painstakingly crafted opinions. Often Harlan's quarrels with a majority would be over the method by which results were reached; his concurrences and dissents regularly demonstrated the complexities of constitutional adjudication.

The Warren Court will be best known for its identification with three themes: egalitarianism, liberalism, and activism. From *Brown* through *Powell* v. *McCormack* (1969), Earl Warren's last major opinion, the Court demonstrated a dedication to the principle of equality, a principle that, in Archibald Cox's felicitous phrase, "once loosed . . . is not easily cabined." Race relations were the initial context in which the Court attempted to refine the meaning of equal justice in America. Once the ordeal of *Brown* was concluded, that meaning seemed comparatively straightforward. In a series of *per curiam* opinions, the Court extended *Brown* to public beaches, parks, recreational facilities, housing developments, public buildings, eating facilities, and hospitals. The conception of equality embodied by these decisions was that of equality of opportunity: blacks could not be denied the opportunity of access to public places.

Brown had been rationalized by the Court on similar grounds: the gravamen of the injustice in a segregated school system was a denial of equal educational opportunities to blacks. But equality of opportunity became difficult to distinguish, in the race cases, from the conception of equality of condition. The

Court presumed that classifications based on race were constitutionally suspect and seemed to suggest that equal justice in the race relations area required something like color blindness. Classifications based on race or skin color not only denied black Americans equal opportunities, they also were not based on any rational judgment, since the human condition transcended superficial differences of race. After the *per curiams,* the massive resistance to *Brown,* and the civil rights movement of the 1960s, the Court gradually perceived that equality in race relations necessitated the eradication of stigmas based on skin color. This momentum of egalitarianism culminated in *Loving* v. *Virginia* (1967), in which the Court invalidated state prohibitions of miscegenous marriages, thereby affirming the absence of fundamental differences between blacks and whites.

Between the *per curiams* and *Loving* had come skirmishes between the Court and groups resisting its mandates for change in race relations. *Cooper* v. *Aaron* (1963) involved a challenge by the governor of Arkansas to compulsory integration in the Little Rock school system. The Court, in an unprecedented opinion signed individually by all nine Justices, reaffirmed the obligations of Southern schools to integrate. *Goss* v. *Board of Education* (1963) invalidated minority-to-majority transfer plans whose purpose was to allow students to attend schools outside their districts in which their race was in the majority. *Heart of Atlanta Motel* v. *United States* (1964) and *Katzenbach* v. *McClung* (1964) used the Constitution's commerce clause and the Civil Rights Act of 1964 to prevent hotels and restaurants from refusing service to blacks. *Burton* v. *Wilmington Parking Authority* (1961) and *Evans* v. *Newton* (1966) showed the Court's willingness to use the doctrine of "state action" to compel ostensibly private establishments (restaurants and parks) to admit blacks.

After *Loving* the Court grew impatient with resistance to the implementation of its decrees in *Brown.* In *Green* v. *New Kent County School Board* (1968) the Court scrutinized the actual effect of "freedom of choice" plans, where students attended schools of their own choice. The Court found that the system perpetuated segregation when 85 percent of the black children in a school district had remained in a previously all-black school and no white child had chosen to attend that school, and advised that "delays are no longer tolerable." Finally, in *Alexander* v. *Holmes County Board of Education* (1969) the Court declared that the time for racial integration of previously segregated school systems was "at once." *Green* and *Alexander* compelled integration of schools and other public facilities. Equality of condition had become the dominant means to achieve the goal of equality.

One can see a similar trend in the area of reapportionment. For the first half of the twentieth century, including the early years of the Warren Court, state legislatures were not apportioned solely on the basis of population. Upper houses of legislatures had a variety of means for electing their members, some deliberately unresponsive to demographic concerns, and few states apportioned legislative seats on the basis of one person, one vote. In *Baker* v. *Carr* (1962), however, the Court announced that it would scrutinize Tennessee's system of electing state legislators to see if it conformed to the population of districts in the state. Justice William J. Brennan, a former student of Frankfurter's, rejected the political question doctrine Frankfurter had consistently imposed as a barrier to Court determination of reapportionment cases. Frankfurter wrote an impassioned dissent in *Baker,* but the way was clear for constitutional challenges to malapportioned legislatures. By 1964 suits challenging legislative apportionment schemes had been filed in more than thirty states.

Chief Justice Warren's opinion for the Court in *Reynolds* v. *Sims* (1964), a case testing Alabama's reapportionment system, demonstrated how the idea of equality had infused the reapportionment cases. "We are cautioned," he wrote, "about the dangers of entering into political thickets and mathematical quagmires. Our answer to this: a denial of constitutionally protected rights demands judicial protection; our oath and our office require no less of us. . . . To the extent that a citizen's right to vote is debased, he is that much less a citizen." Equality did not mean merely an equal opportunity to have representatives from one's district in a state legislature, but that all votes of all citizens were to be treated equally: voting, like race relations, was to be an area in which equality of condition was to prevail.

The Court provided for such equality even where the state's citizens had indicated a preference for another scheme. In *Lucas* v. *Forty-fourth General Assembly* (1964), the Court invalidated Colorado's districting plan apportioning only one house of the legislature on a population basis. This plan had been adopted after a statewide referendum in which a majority rejected population-based apportionment for both houses. Warren found that the scheme did not satisfy the equal protection clause because it was not harmonious with the principle of one person, one vote. Voting was a condition of citizenship, not just an opportunity to participate in government.

In free speech cases, the Warren Court struggled to move beyond a "marketplace" approach, in which majorities could perhaps suppress speech with distasteful content, to an approach where all speakers were presumed to have an equal right to express their thoughts. The approach was first developed in "communist sympathizer" cases, where a minority of the Court objected to laws making it a crime to be a member of the Communist party or to advocate Communist party doctrine. Eventually, in *Brandenburg* v. *Ohio* (1969), a unanimous Court distinguished between "mere advocacy" of views and "incitement to imminent lawless action."

That case involved statements made by a member of the Ku Klux Klan at a rally that were derogatory of blacks and Jews. The fact that the speaker was known to belong to an organization historically linked to racism and violence was not enough to hinder expression of his views.

Brandenburg united, without entirely clarifying, a number of strands of Warren Court First Amendment doctrine. In the overbreadth cases, such as *NAACP* v. *Alabama ex rel. Flowers* (1964), *Aptheker* v. *Secretary of State* (1964), *Keyishian* v. *Board of Regents* (1967), and *United States* v. *Robel* (1967), the Court found that legitimate governmental prohibitions on speech that employed "means which sweep unnecessarily broadly" violated the First Amendment, because they might deter the behavior of others who could not legitimately be prohibited from speaking. In the symbolic speech cases, the Court considered the permissibility of wearing black arm bands (*Tinker* v. *Des Moines Community School District,* 1969) or burning draft cards (*United States* v. *O'Brien,* 1968) or mutilating flags (*Street* v. *New York,* 1969) as a means of protesting the Vietnam War. Finally, in the "sit-in" and "picketing" cases, such as *Cox* v. *Louisiana* (1964), *Brown* v. *Louisiana* (1966), and *Adderley* v. *Florida* (1966), the Court sought to distinguish protected "expression" from unprotected but related "conduct." In none of these areas was the Court's doctrinal position clear—draft card burners and picketers were denied constitutional protection, although flag mutilators and "sit-in" demonstrators were granted it—but the decisions revealed the Warren Court's interest in carving out an area of First Amendment protection that was not dependent on public support for the speaker or his actions.

The Warren Court also attempted to extend the First Amendment's reach into other doctrinal areas, notably defamation and obscenity. In *New York Times* v. *Sullivan* (1964) the Court concluded that common law libel actions could raise First Amendment issues.

It was the best known Supreme Court in history and probably the most controversial.

The Court's opinion, which found that the First Amendment gave rise to a constitutional privilege to make false and defamatory statements about public officials if the statements were not made with recklessness or malice, expressed concern that libel law could be used as a means of punishing "unpopular" speech. Justice Brennan's majority opinion referred to "a profound national commitment to the principle that debate on public issues should be uninhibited, robust, and wide-open," and spoke of the "inhibiting" effects of civil damages on "those who would give voice to public criticism."

Once the First Amendment was seen as relevant to defamation cases, the future of common law principles in the area of libel and slander seemed precarious. *New York Times* v. *Sullivan* had established a constitutional privilege to publish information about "public officials." *Rosenblatt* v. *Baer* (1966) widened the meaning of "public official" to include a supervisor of a county-owned ski resort; *Curtis Publishing Co.* v. *Butts* (1967) and *Associated Press* v. *Walker* (1967) included "public figures" as well as public officials in the category of those in whose affairs the general public had a special interest; *Time, Inc.* v. *Hill* (1967) found a privilege to disclose "private" but newsworthy information.

The defamation cases showed the tendency of the equality principle to expand once set in motion: it seemed hard to distinguish different rules for public officials, public figures, and matters of public interest. Such was also true in the area of obscenity. Once the Court recognized, as it did in *Roth* v. *United States* (1957), that First Amendment concerns were relevant in obscenity cases, and yet a core of unprotected expression remained, it was forced to define obscenity. Thirteen obscenity cases between 1957 and 1968 produced fifty-five separate opinions from the Justices, but the meaning of "obscene" for constitutional purposes was not made much clearer. Some Justices, such as Black and Douglas, decided that obscene

speech was entitled to as much constitutional protection as any other speech, but a shifting majority of the Court continued to deny protection for expressions that, by one standard or another, could be deemed "obscene." Among the criteria announced by Court majorities for labeling a work "obscene" was that it appeal to a "prurient interest," and that it be "patently offensive" and "utterly without redeeming social value." Justice Stewart, in *Jacobellis* v. *Ohio* (1964), announced a different criterion: "I know [obscenity] when I see it." Eventually, after *Redrup* v. *New York* (1967), the Court began to reverse summarily all obscenity convictions whenever five Justices, for whatever reason, adjudged a work not to be obscene.

A final area of unprotected expression involved the fighting words doctrine of *Chaplinsky* v. *New Hampshire* (1942). A series of Warren Court cases, including *Edwards* v. *South Carolina* (1963), *Gregory* v. *Chicago* (1969) and even *New York Times* v. *Sullivan*, with its language about "vehement, caustic, and sometimes unpleasantly sharp attacks on government and public officials," may have reduced *Chaplinsky* to insignificance.

The pattern of First Amendment decisions, taken with its opinions on race relations and reapportionment, not only demonstrated the Warren Court's shifting conceptions of equality but stamped it in the popular mind as a "liberal" Court. Liberalism has been identified, in the years after World War II, with support for affirmative government and protection of civil rights; the Warren Court was notable for its efforts to insure that interventionist government and civil libertarianism could coexist. But in so doing the Warren Court redefined the locus of interventionist government in America. *Brown* v. *Board of Education* was a classic example. Congress and the state legislatures were not taking sufficient action to preserve the rights of blacks, so the Court intervened to scrutinize their conduct and, where necessary, to compel them to act. This role for the Court was a major change from that performed by its predecessors. "Liberal" judging in the early twentieth century, according to such defenders of interventionist government as Felix Frankfurter and Louis D. Brandeis, meant judicial self-restraint: the Supreme Court was to *avoid* scrutiny of state and federal legislation whose purpose was to aid disadvantaged persons. The Warren Court eschewed that role to become the principal interventionist branch of government in the 1950s and 1960s.

In addition to its decisions in race relations and reapportionment, two other areas of Warren Court activity helped augment its public reputation as a "liberal" Court. The first area was criminal procedure: here the Court virtually rewrote the laws of the states to conform them to its understanding of the Constitution's requirements. The most important series of its criminal procedure decisions, from a doctrinal perspective, were the incorporation doctrine cases, where the Court struggled with the question of whether, and to what extent, the due process clause of the Fourteenth Amendment incorporates procedural protections in the Bill of Rights, making those protections applicable against the states. The Warren Court began a process of "selective incorporation" of Bill of Rights safeguards, applying particular protections in given cases but refusing to endorse the incorporation doctrine in its entirety. This process produced some landmark decisions, notably *Mapp* v. *Ohio* (1961), which applied Fourth Amendment protections against illegal searches and seizures to state trials, and *Benton* v. *Maryland* (1969), which held that the Fifth Amendment's double jeopardy guarantee applied to the states. Other important "incorporation" cases were *Griffin* v. *California* (1965), maintaining a right against self-incrimination; *Malloy* v. *Hogan* (1964), applying the Fifth Amendment's self-incrimination privilege to state proceedings; and *Duncan* v. *Louisiana* (1968), incorporating the Sixth Amendment's right to trial by jury in criminal cases.

A major consequence of selective incorporation was that fewer criminal convictions were obtained in state trials. Particularly damaging to state prosecutors were the decisions in *Mapp* and *Mallory*, which eliminated from state court trials illegally secured evidence and coerced statements of incrimination. The Court also tightened the requirements for police conduct during the incarceration of criminal suspects. *Mallory* v. *United States* (1957) insisted that criminal defendants be brought before a magistrate prior to being interrogated. *Miranda* v. *Arizona* (1966) announced a series of constitutional "warnings" that the police were required to give persons whom they had taken into custody. *Miranda* had been preceded by another significant case, *Escobedo* v. *Illinois* (1964), which had required that a lawyer be present during police investigations if a suspect requested one. Further, the landmark case of *Gideon* v. *Wainwright* (1963) had insured that all persons suspected of crimes could secure the services of a lawyer if they desired such, whether they could afford them or not.

The result of this activity by the Warren Court in the area of criminal procedure was that nearly every stage of a police interrogation was fraught with constitutional complexities. The decisions, taken as a whole, seemed to be an effort to buttress the position of persons suspected of crimes by checking the power of the police: some opinions, such as *Miranda*, were explicit in stating that goal. By intervening in law enforcement proceedings to protect the rights of allegedly disadvantaged persons—a high percentage of criminals in the 1960s were poor and black—the Warren Court Justices were acting as liberal policymakers.

Church and state cases were another area in which the Court demonstrated its liberal sensibility, to the concern of many observers. Affirmative state action to promote religious values in the public schools—heretofore an aspect of America's educational heritage—was likely to be struck down as a violation of the establishment clause. In *Engel* v. *Vitale* (1962) the Court struck down nondenominational prayer readings in New York public schools. A year after *Engel* the Court also invalidated a Pennsylvania law that required reading from the Bible in *Abington Township School District* v. *Schempp* (1963) and a Maryland law that required recitation of the Lord's Prayer in *Murrary* v. *Curlett* (1963). In *Mc-Gowan* v. *Maryland* (1961), however, the Court permitted the state to impose Sunday closing laws. Chief Justice Warren, for the Court, distinguished between laws with a religious purpose and laws "whose present purpose and effect" was secular, even though they were originally "motivated by religious forces." The Court invoked *McGowan* in a subsequent case, *Board of Education* v. *Allen* (1968), which sustained a New York law providing for the loaning of textbooks from public to parochial schools.

Liberalism, as practiced by the Warren Court, produced a different institutional posture from earlier "reformist" judicial perspectives. As noted, liberalism required that the Court be both an activist governmental institution and a defender of minority rights. This meant that unlike previously "activist" Courts, such as the Courts of the late nineteenth and early twentieth century, its beneficiaries would be nonelites, and unlike previously "reformist" Courts, such as the Court of the late 1930s and 1940s, it would assume a scrutinizing rather than a passive stance toward the actions of other branches of government. Had the Warren Court retained either of these former roles, *Brown, Baker* v. *Carr,* and *Miranda* would likely not have been decided as they were. These decisions all offended entrenched elites and required modifications of existing governmental practices. In so deciding these cases the Warren Court was assuming that activism by the judiciary was required in order to produce liberal results. With this assumption came a mid-twentieth-century fusion of affirmative governmental action and protection for civil liberties.

Maintaining a commitment to liberal theory while at the same time modifying its precepts required some analytical refinements in order to reconcile the protection of civil liberties with claims based on affirmative governmental action. In *Brown* the desires of some whites and some blacks to have a racially integrated educational experience conflicted with the desires of some whites and some blacks to limit their educational experiences to persons of their own race. The Court chose to prefer the former desire, basing its judgment on a theory of the educational process that minimized the relevance of race. That theory then became a guiding assumption for the Court's subsequent decisions in the race relations area.

Similar sets of intermediate distinctions between goals of liberal theory were made in other major cases. In the reapportionment cases the distinction was between representation based on population, a claim put forth by a disadvantaged minority, and other forms of proportional representation that had been endorsed by legislative majorities. The Court decided to prefer the former claim as more democratic and then made the one-person, one-vote principle the basis of its subsequent decisions. In the school prayer cases the distinction was between the choice of a majority to ritualize the recognition of a public deity in the public school and the choice of a minority to deny that recognition as out of place. The Court decided to prefer the latter choice as more libertarian. In the criminal procedure cases the distinction was between a majoritarian decision to protect the public against crime by advantaging law enforcement personnel in their encounters with persons suspected of committing crimes, and the claims of such persons that they were being unfairly disadvantaged. The Court chose to prefer the latter claims as being more consistent with principles of equal justice.

When the Warren Court reached the end of its tenure, liberalism clearly did not merely mean deference toward the decisions of democratic and representative bodies of government. It meant deference toward these decisions only if they promoted the goals of liberal policy: equality, fairness, protection of civil rights, support for disadvantaged persons. Under this model of liberal policymaking, the Supreme Court was more concerned with achieving enlightened results than it was with the constitutional process by which these results were reached. Liberalism and judicial activism went hand in hand.

As it became clear that the Court's activism was designed to promote a modified version of liberalism, the Court became vulnerable to public dissatisfaction with liberal policies. Such dissatisfaction emerged in the 1970s. The internal contradictions of liberalism became exposed in such areas as affirmative action in higher education and forced busing in primary education, and the saving distinctions made by the Court in earlier cases appeared as naked policy choices whose legitimacy was debatable. If affirmative preference, based on race, for one class of applicants to an institution of higher learning results in disadvantage to other classes, equality of condition has not been achieved and equality of educational opportunity has been undermined. If some families are compelled to send their children to schools where they are racial minorities in order to achieve "racial balance" throughout the school system, the resulting "balance" may well disadvantage more people than it advantages. Equality and social justice have turned out to be more complicated concepts than mid-twentieth-century liberalism assumed.

The egalitarianism and the liberalism of the Warren Court paled in significance when compared to its activism. If contemporary America has become a "litigious society," as it is commonly portrayed, the Warren Court helped set in motion such trends. Social issues have habitually been transformed into legal questions in America, but the Warren Court seemed to welcome such a transformation, finding constitutional issues raised in

contexts as diverse as reapportionment and prayers in the public schools. As the Court created new sources of constitutional protection, numerous persons sought to make themselves the beneficiaries. Sometimes the Court went out of its way to help the organizations litigating a case, as in the civil rights area. The result was that the lower courts and the Supreme Court became "activist" institutions—repositories of grievances, scrutinizers of the conduct of other branches of government, havens for the disadvantaged.

In the academic community, Warren Court activism was from the first regarded as more controversial than Warren Court egalitarianism. The reason was the prominence in academic circles of a two-pronged theory of judicial review, one prong of which stressed the necessity of grounding judicial decisions, in the area of constitutional law, in textually supportable principles of general applicability, and the other prong of which resurrected Frankfurter's conception of a limited, deferential role for the Court as a lawmaking institution. The Warren Court, according to academic critics, repeatedly violated the theory's dual standards. Decisions like *Brown* v. *Board, Baker* v. *Carr, Griswold* v. *Connecticut* (1965), a case discovering a right of privacy in the Constitution that was violated by statutes forbidding the use of birth control pills, and *Harper* v. *Virginia Board of Elections* (1966), a case invalidating poll tax requirements on voting as violating the equal protection clause because such requirements conditioned voting rights on wealth, had not been sufficiently grounded in constitutional doctrine. There was no evidence that the Fourteenth Amendment was intended to reach segregated schools and there were no judicial decisions supporting that position. The Constitution did not single out for protection a right to vote, let alone a right to have one's vote weighed equally with the votes of others. "Privacy" was nowhere mentioned in the constitutional text. The framers of the Constitution had assumed a variety of suffrage restrictions, including ones based on wealth. In short, leading Warren Court decisions were not based on "neutral principles" of constitutional law.

Nor had the Court been mindful, critics felt, of its proper lawmaking posture in a democratic society where it was a conspicuously nondemocratic institution. In *Brown* it had ostensibly substituted its wisdom for that of Congress and several Southern states. In *Baker* it had forced legislatures to reapportion themselves even when a majority of a state's voters had signified their intention to staff one house of the legislature on grounds other than one person, one vote. In *Engel* v. *Vitale* it had told the public schools that they could not have government-formulated compulsory prayers, even though the vast majority of school officials and parents desired them. It had fashioned codes of criminal procedure for the police, ignoring Congress's abortive efforts in that direction. It had decided, after more than 200 years of defamation law, that the entire area needed to be reconsidered in light of the First Amendment.

A role for the Court as a deferential, principled decision maker was, however, not sacrosanct. Few Supreme Courts had assumed such a role in the past. All of the "great cases" in American constitutional history could be said to have produced activist decisions: *Marbury* v. *Madison* (1803), establishing the power of judicial review; *McCulloch* v. *Maryland* (1819) and *Gibbons* v. *Ogden* (1824), delineating the scope of the federal commerce power; *Dred Scott* v. *Sandford* (1857), legitimizing slavery in the territories; the *Legal Tender Cases*, deciding the constitutionality of legal tender notes; *Pollock* v. *Farmers Loan and Trust* (1895), declaring an income tax unconstitutional; *Lochner* v. *New York* (1905), scuttling state hours and wages legislation; *United States* v. *Butler* (1936), invalidating a major portion of the New Deal's administrative structure. Activism was an ancient judicial art.

The Warren Court's activism differed from other Courts' versions principally not because its reasoning was more specious or its grasp of power more presumptuous but because its beneficiaries were different. Previous activist decisions had largely benefited entrenched elites, whether slaveowners, entrepreneurs, "combinations of capital," or businesses that sought to avoid government regulation. The activist decisions of the Warren Court benefited blacks, disadvantaged suburban voters, atheists, criminals, pornographers, and the poor. The Warren Court's activism facilitated social change rather than preserving the status quo. The critics of the Court had forgotten that the role they espoused for the judiciary had been created in order to facilitate change and promote the interests of the disadvantaged. In the 1950s and 1960s the "democratic" institutions charged with that responsibility had become unresponsive, so the Warren Court had acted in their stead. It was ironic that the same critics who were shocked at the Court of the 1930s' resistance to the New Deal should protest against a Court that was reaching the results they had then sought.

Activism was the principal basis of the Court's controversiality; egalitarianism its dominant instinctual reaction; liberalism its guiding political philosophy. The combination of these ingredients, plus the presence of some judicial giants, gave the Warren Court a prominence and a visibility that are not likely to be surpassed for some time. But even though countless persons in the American legal profession today were shaped by Warren Court decisions, one can see the Warren Court receding into history. That Court seemed to have been led, in the final analysis, by a conception of American life that appeared vindicated by the first fifty years of twentieth-century experience. That conception held that American society was continually progressing toward a nobler and brighter and more enlightened future. As Earl Warren wrote in a passage that appears on his tomb-stone:

Where there is injustice, we should correct it;
where there is poverty, we should eliminate it;
where there is corruption, we should stamp it
out;
where there is violence, we should punish it;
where there is neglect, we should provide
care;
where there is war, we should restore peace;
and wherever corrections are achieved we
should add them permanently to our store-
house of treasures.

In that passage appears the Warren Court sensibility: a sensibility dedicated to the active pursuit of ideals that have seemed less tangible and achievable with the years.

—G. EDWARD WHITE

Bibliography

Bickel, Alexander (1970). *The Supreme Court and the Idea of Progress.* New York: Harper & Row.

Black, Charles (1970). The Unfinished Business of the Warren Court. *University of Washington Law Review* 46:3–45.

Cox, Archibald (1968). *The Warren Court.* Cambridge, Mass.: Harvard University Press.

Kurland, Philip (1970). *Politics, the Constitution, and the Warren Court.* Chicago: University of Chicago Press.

Levy, Leonard W., ed. (1972). *The Supreme Court under Earl Warren.* New York: Quadrangle Books.

McCloskey, Robert (1960). *The American Supreme Court.* Chicago: University of Chicago Press.

Wechsler, Herbert (1959). Toward Neutral Principles of Constitutional Law. *Harvard Law Review* 73:1–23.

White, G. Edward (1976). *The American Judicial Tradition.* New York: Oxford University Press.

——— (1982). *Earl Warren: A Public Life.* New York: Oxford University Press.

WASHINGTON v. DAVIS

426 U.S. 229 (1976)

This landmark decision concerns the relevance of a decision maker's motives in equal protection cases. Black candidates for the Washington, D.C., police force alleged that the District's selection criteria had an adverse discriminatory effect upon the employment prospects of minorities and that the effect violated the Fourteenth Amendment's equal protection clause and antidiscrimination legislation. In an opinion by Justice Byron R. White, the Supreme Court held that discriminatory effects, standing alone, are insufficient to establish an equal protection violation. Proof of purposeful discrimination is necessary. The Court also rejected the candidates' statutory claim. In an opinion that did not address the constitutional question, Justice William J. Brennan, joined by Justice Thurgood Marshall, dissented from the Court's disposition of the statutory issue. In a concurring opinion, Justice John Paul Stevens discussed the relationship between discriminatory effects and proof of discriminatory intent and articulated his reasons for rejecting the statutory claim.

In settling a long-standing controversy over whether a decision maker's motives may constitute the basis for an equal protection claim, the Court climbed two interesting doctrinal hills. Prior to *Davis*, cases such as *Whitcomb* v. *Chavis* (1971) and *White* v. *Regester* (1973) expressly had suggested that unintentional disproportionate effects on a minority may constitute the basis for an equal protection claim. Justice White's opinion ignores these precedents but warns against the broad consequences of such a holding. Such a rule "would raise serious questions about, and perhaps invalidate, a whole range of tax, welfare,

The Court held that discriminatory effects, standing alone, are insufficient to establish an equal protection violation.

public service, regulatory, and licensing statutes that may be more burdensome to the poor and to the average black than to the more affluent white."

In addition, contrary to *Davis's* holding, a line of opinions dating back to *Fletcher* v. *Peck* (1810) and reaffirmed in *United States* v. *O'Brien* (1968) and *Palmer* v. *Thompson* (1971), clearly had stated that legislators' motives may not form the basis of constitutional attacks on statutes. Without alluding to all of the relevant precedents, the Court reinterpreted *Palmer* and suggested that some of its language had constituted mere obiter dicta.

As a practical matter, *Davis,* when combined with subsequent similar cases such as *Arlington Heights* v. *Metropolitan Housing Development Corp.* (1977) and *Mobile* v. *Bolden* (1980), curtailed litigants' ability to bring successful equal protection claims. Proof of intentional discrimination is difficult to obtain and judges are reluctant to deem officials intentional wrongdoers. Indeed, it was six years after *Davis* before the Court, in *Rogers* v. *Lodge* (1982), sustained a finding of intentional discrimination in a racial equal protection case.

—THEODORE EISENBERG

WASHINGTON v. GLUCKSBERG

521 U.S. 702 (1997)

The Supreme Court unanimously held in this case that the constitutionally protected right to die does not encompass a right to physician-assisted suicide. It therefore sustained a Washington statute criminalizing either causing or aiding a suicide. The suit was brought by physicians seeking to assist the suicide of their terminally ill patients, together with a group of such patients.

Earlier litigation in the highest courts of several states had established a patient's right to withhold life-sustaining equipment such as feeding tubes and artificial life support. These decisions were grounded either in state constitutional due process provisions or in common-law principles allowing patients to refuse unwanted medical treatment. Then in *Cruzan* v. *Director, Missouri Department of Health* (1990), the Supreme Court strongly suggested that this right was encompassed in the fundamental liberty protected by the due process clause of the Fourteenth Amendment. In *Cruzan* the Court upheld the Missouri courts' insistence that a patient show by clear and convincing proof his or her desire to be free of artificial life support. However, a majority of the Justices found the right to refuse such treatment to be fundamental under due process liberty. The even more difficult question in *Glucksberg* was whether this right ought to be extended to physician-assisted suicide.

The Court's opinion by Chief Justice William H. Rehnquist sharply differentiated the right to decline medical treatment from the plaintiffs' claimed right to assisted suicide. The Chief Justice began by noting that in nearly every state it is a crime to assist a suicide. Indeed suicide, as well as assisting suicide, was regarded as a crime under common law. Only Oregon broke ranks in 1994 by adopting, through a ballot initiative approved by its voters, a law legalizing physician-assisted suicide on the part of mentally competent but terminally ill adults.

Against this backdrop of state laws all but universally barring assisted suicide, the plaintiffs' claim that it was a fundamental right within the due process clause was, in the Court's view, difficult to sustain, since the contours of due process are measured by what has historically been part of "the concept of ordered liberty," as the Court held in the landmark *Palko* v. *Connecticut.* The plaintiffs contended the right to refrain from unwanted treatment recognized in *Cruzan,* as well as the right to an abortion free of undue state interference established in *Roe* v. *Wade,* implied a constitutional right to assisted suicide as well. However, the Court rebuffed those analogies. The right in *Cruzan*, it noted, was based on "the long legal tradition protecting the decision to refuse unwanted medical treatment," and was recognized by every state as totally distinct from any right to assisted suicide—an affirmative act intended to end life. As for abortion, the Court held not every decision relating to personal autonomy is a fundamental part of due process liberty. The Court marshaled a series of powerful state interests weighing in heavily against any right to assisted suicide.

First, the Court noted, the states have a strong interest in preserving human life—the basis for universal laws against homicide. More specifically, it pointed out, patients contemplating assisted suicide are apt to be especially vulnerable: terminally ill, depressed, often in pain. In addition, the states have a concern over "the integrity and ethics of the medical profession," and legalizing physician-assisted suicide could well "undermine the trust that is essential to the doctor-patient relationship by blurring the time-honored line between healing and harming." In addition, as the Court noted, the states have an independent interest in protecting the elderly, the poor, the disabled, and other particularly vulnerable groups from "abuse, neglect and mistakes"—and especially from "the risk of subtle coercion and undue influence in end-of-life situations."

The concerning opinions of Justices Sandra Day O'Connor, John Paul Stevens, David H. Souter, Ruth Bader Ginsburg, and Stephen G. Breyer all emphasized the fact that the Court was ruling on a facial challenge to the Washington statute, requiring the plaintiffs to prove the law invalid under all circumstances. They believed, in varying degree, that there might be a limited constitutional right to assisted suicide in certain situations, but agreed that this would not warrant overturning the statute entirely. However, it might, in their view, justify a court holding

the law could not constitutionally be applied in a particular case not now before the Court.

In a related case, *Vacco* v. *Quill*, decided together with *Glucksberg*, the Court rejected a claim that a New York law against assisted suicide denied physicians and terminal patients the equal protection of the laws. The plaintiffs there unsuccessfully contended that since New York allows competent patients to decline life-sustaining treatment, its ban on assisted suicide violated the equal protection clause. However, the Court held the statute was rationally based on the state's concerns for preserving life, the integrity of the medical profession, and protecting the vulnerable that were enumerated in *Glucksberg*.

As noted earlier, Oregon has in fact repealed its ban on assisted suicide. The Court's upholding the constitutionality of laws prohibiting assisted-suicide does not likely jeopardize the validity of Oregon's repeal. Indeed, the Court emphasized that the debate over this controversial issue should continue at the legislative level.

—PHILIP WEINBERG

WASHINGTON v. HARPER

110 S.Ct. 1028 (1990)

A Washington state prison policy authorized the treatment of a prisoner with antipsychotic drugs against his or her will, provided that the prisoner be (1) mentally ill, and (2) either gravely disabled or likely to do serious harm to others. These two findings were to be made by a committee consisting of a psychiatrist, a psychologist, and an official of the institution in which mentally ill prisoners were held. The state supreme court held that this procedure, which lacked fully adversarial procedural guarantees such as those available in a court proceeding, denied a mentally ill prisoner procedural due process of law. The Supreme Court reversed, 6–3.

WASHINGTON v. HARPER

110 S.Ct. 1028 (1990)

The Court pointed out that patients contemplating assisted suicide are apt to be especially vulnerable: terminally ill, depressed, often in pain.

See also

Equal Protection of the Laws

Palko v. *Connecticut*

Right to Die

W

**WATKINS v.
UNITED STATES**

354 U.S. 178 (1957)

**SWEEZY v.
NEW HAMPSHIRE**

354 U.S. 234 (1957)

*This decision
overturned a
Washington state
ruling that prisoners
could not be treated
with antipsychotic
drugs against
their will.*

*The Court reversed
Watkins's conviction
of contempt of
Congress.*

Justice Anthony M. Kennedy wrote for the Court. The prisoner had a "liberty interest" in being free from arbitrary administration of a psychotropic drug; however, the procedure provided by the state was sufficient to satisfy the demands of due process. A court in a single proceeding cannot adequately evaluate the intentions or likely behavior of a medically ill person; such an evaluation requires ongoing observation of the kind available to the members of the committee given responsibility for the decisions here. The risks of an antipsychotic drug are mainly medical risks, which can best be evaluated by professionals. Although the state's policy does not allow representation by counsel, it does provide for a lay adviser who understands the psychiatric issues; this assistance is sufficient to satisfy due process.

Justice John Paul Stevens wrote for the dissenters. In his view, the state policy violated both substantive due process and procedural due process. In support of the first objection, he argued that the policy authorized invasion of the prisoner's liberty not only for his own medical interests but also to maintain order in the institution. The second objection was that, considering the seriousness of the invasion of the prisoner's liberty interest, the committee was insufficiently independent of the institution's administration to satisfy the requirements of a fair hearing.

—KENNETH L. KARST

WATKINS v. UNITED STATES

354 U.S. 178 (1957)

SWEEZY v. NEW HAMPSHIRE

354 U.S. 234 (1957)

Watkins, a labor leader called to testify before the House Committee on Un-American Ac-

tivities, had been told by the union president that he would lose his position if he claimed his right against self-incrimination. He thus claimed a First Amendment privilege when he declined to answer the committee's questions about the membership of other people in the Communist party. He also objected that these questions were beyond the scope of the committee's activities. For his refusal to answer, Watkins was convicted of contempt of Congress. The Supreme Court reversed his conviction, 8-1.

Writing for the Court, Chief Justice Earl Warren rested decision on a narrow point: Watkins had been denied procedural due process, for he had not been given a sufficient explanation of the subject of inquiry, and thus could not know whether the committee's questions were "pertinent to the questions under inquiry," as the contempt statute specified. Warren's opinion, however, strongly suggested that the Court would be prepared to confront the whole issue of legislative investigations into political association. He remarked on the use of such investigations to subject people to public stigma, and the absence in such proceedings of effective protection of procedural fairness. "We have no doubt that there is no congressional power to expose for the sake of exposure," Warren wrote. "Who can define the meaning of 'un-American'?" Justice Tom C. Clark, the sole dissenter, appeared to object as much to these broad obiter dicta as to the actual decision. He complained of the Court's "mischievous curbing of the informing function of Congress."

In *Sweezy*, a companion case to *Watkins*, the Court held, 6-2, that a state legislative investigation could not constitutionally compel Sweezy to answer questions about the Progressive party and about a lecture he had given at the University of New Hampshire. Chief Justice Warren wrote a plurality opinion for four Justices, concluding that Sweezy's contempt conviction violated procedural due process because the state legislature had not clearly authorized the attorney general, who conducted the investigation, to inquire into those subjects. Justice Felix Frankfurter, joined by Justice John Marshall Harlan, concurred, arguing that the state had unconstitutionally invaded Sweezy's Fourteenth Amendment liberty—here, his "political autonomy," a plain reference to the First Amendment. Justice Frankfurter used a (for him) familiar balancing test, but articulated a compelling state interest standard for cases of invasions of political privacy. The Frankfurter opinion is notable for its early articulation of the constitutional dimension of academic freedom. It also led, the following year, to the Court's explicit recognition of the freedom of association in *NAACP* v. *Alabama* (1958). Justice Clark again dissented, now joined by Justice Harold H. Burton.

A number of members of Congress reacted angrily to these opinions and others decided the same year, such as *Yates* v. *United States* (1957) and *Jencks* v. *United States* (1957). Bills were proposed in Congress to limit the Supreme Court's jurisdiction over cases involving controls of subversive activities. In the event, not much "curbing" was done, and in retrospect *Watkins* and *Sweezy* appeared to be no more than trial balloons. Two years later, in *Barenblatt* v. *United States* (1959), a majority of the Court backed away from the expected confrontation with Congress.

—KENNETH L. KARST

WAYTE v. UNITED STATES

471 U.S. (1985)

After a presidential proclamation directing young men to register for a possible draft, David Wayte did not register, but wrote let-

ters to government officials stating that he did not intend to do so. These letters went into a Selective Service file of men who had given similar notices or who had been reported by others for failing to register. The government adopted a policy of "passive enforcement" of registration: it would prosecute only men named in this file. Government officials wrote letters warning the men to register or face prosecution, and Federal Bureau of Investigation agents urged Wayte in person to register during a grace period. He refused and was indicted for failure to register. The federal district court dismissed Wayte's indictment, holding that the government had not rebutted his preliminary showing of selective prosecution. The court of appeals reversed, holding that Wayte had not shown that the government had prosecuted him because of his protest. The Supreme Court affirmed, 7-2.

Justice Lewis F. Powell wrote the opinion of the court. Claims of selective prosecution, he said, must be judged under ordinary equal protection standards, which, as the Court held in *Washington* v. *Davis* (1976), require a showing of intentional discrimination. Here, the government's awareness that "passive enforcement" would fall disproportionately on protesters was an insufficient showing of intent to punish protest. Given the government's policy of urging compliance after receiving notice of failure to register, Wayte was not prosecuted for protesting, but for persisting in refusing registration.

Wayte's First Amendment challenge also focused on the enforcement system's disparate impact on protesters. Applying the formula of *United States* v. *O'Brien* (1968), Justice Powell concluded that "passive enforcement" passed the test. The government interest in national security was important, and unrelated to the suppression of expression; and the enforcement system burdened speech no more than was necessary to secure registration.

The government adopted a policy of "passive enforcement" of draft registration: it would prosecute only those men who had written their intention not to register or who had been reported as failing to register.

Justice Thurgood Marshall dissented, joined by Justice William J. Brennan, arguing that Wayte had been denied effective opportunity for discovery of information concerning the motivations of high government officials for prosecuting him. Thus, he could not fully support his claim that the prosecution was designed to punish his protest. The majority dismissed this argument, saying—contrary to the dissenters' view—that Wayte had not presented the issue to the Supreme Court.

—KENNETH L. KARST

DRAFT DODGER

Wayte was not prosecuted for protesting, but for his persistence in refusing to register for the draft. (Corbis/Ted Streshinsky)

WEBSTER v. REPRODUCTIVE HEALTH SERVICES

492 U.S. (1989)

The *Webster* case had been advertised as the one in which the Supreme Court might overrule *Roe* v. *Wade* (1973), but in the event the decision offered only minor adjustments at the margins of the constitutional doctrine governing a woman's right to have an abortion. The decision's political consequences, however, were anything but minor.

From the time of the *Roe* decision, Missouri has produced a steady stream of legislation designed to restrict women who seek abortions and the doctors who attend them. In this case the Court considered several provisions of a 1986 Missouri law: (1) the preamble, containing the legislature's "findings" that human life begins at conception and that "unborn children have protectable interests in life, health, and well-being"; (2) a prohibition on the use of public facilities or employees to perform abortions; (3) a prohibition against public funding of abortion counseling; and (4) a requirement that a doctor conduct a fetal viability test before performing an abortion. Chief Justice William H. Rehnquist wrote for the Court.

The Court refused to pass on the preamble, saying that, for all the Justices knew, the "findings" had no effect beyond the expression of the legislature's value judgment. The Court upheld the prohibition on using public facilities or public employees in performing abortions, reaffirming the holdings of *Maher* v. *Roe* (1977) and *Harris* v. *McRae* (1980) that the state has no constitutional duty to provide assistance to women who cannot afford abortions. The controversy over the prohibition on using public money for abortion counseling was dismissed for mootness because the plaintiffs agreed that this part of law did not affect them.

***ROE* REAFFIRMED**

Norma McCorvey, the "Roe" in
Roe v. Wade, *is the center of
media attention following
arguments in* Webster.
Webster *helped mobilize
nationwide support for reproductive freedom.
(Corbis/Bettmann)*

On the validity of the viability-testing provision there was no opinion of the Court.
Chief Justice Rehnquist, for three Justices, interpreted this requirement to conflict with the
analysis in *Roe* v. *Wade* and concluded that, to
the extent of the conflict, *Roe* must give way.
The testing requirement might make abortions more costly, but it "permissibly further[ed] the State's interest in protecting potential human life" and was constitutional.
Justice Sandra Day O'Connor agreed that the
testing requirement was valid, but thought it
was consistent with the Court's prior decisions. She thus resisted the invitation to address the question of *Roe*'s continuing force
and reaffirmed her earlier position that a law
should not be invalidated unless it "unduly
burdens" the right to seek an abortion. Justice
Antonin Scalia, concurring in upholding the
testing requirement, agreed with the dissenters that the Chief Justice's opinion on this
issue would effectively overrule *Roe.* He
thought, however, that the Court should perform its overruling of *Roe* more explicitly and

criticized the majority for failing to do so. In
an especially scornful footnote, he rejected
Justice O'Connor's position and lectured her
on the vocabulary of "viability."

Justice Harry A. Blackmun, for three Justices, dissented, strongly reaffirming the correctness of *Roe* v. *Wade* and its successor decisions. He saw the Chief Justice's opinion on
Missouri's requirement of viability testing as,
in effect, calling for *Roe* to be overruled and
added his gloomy prediction of a piecemeal
process of overruling "until sometime, a new
regime of old dissenters and new appointees
will declare what the plurality intends: that
Roe is no longer good law."

The most important result of *Webster* was
political: the mobilization of nationwide support for reproductive freedom. In the year following *Webster,* forty-four legislatures met, and
about two-thirds of them considered proposals to restrict abortions; only four adopted restrictions. If *Roe* was a catalyst for the "pro-life"
movement, *Webster* was a catalyst for the "pro-
choice" movement. Governors, legislators, and

If Roe *was a
catalyst for the "pro-
life" movement,*
Webster *was a
catalyst for the "pro-
choice" movement.*

even the president seemed to recognize that two strong views now demanded a hearing.

Three years later, the Court in *Planned Parenthood of Southeastern Pennsylvania* v. *Casey* (1992) in fact upheld the "essential holding" of *Roe*, explaining at length why in the majority's view overruling *Roe* would be inappropriate.

—KENNETH L. KARST

WEEKS v.
UNITED STATES

232 U.S. 383 (1914)

Weeks v. *United States* was the Court's single most creative decision under the Fourth Amendment. To save the amendment as a living constitutional guarantee, the Court endowed it with an enforcement feature, ordering the exclusion from federal trials of evidence obtained through unlawful seizure. Without this exclusionary rule, seized evidence, regardless of its origin, would always be admissible. The rule thus has provided the occasion for judicial articulation of Fourth Amendment reasonableness in later cases.

Under common law, and for the first century of the Constitution's existence, evidence unlawfully seized by government officers was nonetheless admissible in evidence. In *Boyd* v. *United States* (1886) the Court implicitly discarded this common law principle, but the exclusionary rule, as it has come to be called, was not explicitly enthroned until the *Weeks* decision. The reason for admitting unlawfully seized evidence, a standard still followed in nearly all other countries, is readily understood. Unlike coerced confessions, which are excluded from trial in all civilized countries because of their untrustworthiness, the fruit of an illegal search is just as reliable when taken without a shadow of authority as when taken under warrant. To exclude the evidence allows a criminal to go free. Absent the exclusionary rule, however, the Fourth Amendment might become a mere paper guarantee of freedom from unreasonable searches with-

out an effective enforcement process. Unlike other guarantees in the Bill of Rights (for example, right to counsel), the Fourth Amendment affects the pretrial stage of the case and is—apart from the exclusionary rule—not within the power of the trial court to enforce. The secrecy in which searches are planned and executed makes it impossible to seek the advance protection of an injunction, a regular practice when First Amendment freedoms are threatened.

The unanimous *Weeks* opinion said that if unconstitutionally seized evidence were admitted, the Fourth Amendment "might as well be stricken from the Constitution." Furthermore, if the evidence were admitted, courts become parties to the misdeeds of the police, thus compromising the integrity of the judicial process.

The opinion did not, however, make clear whether the exclusionary rule was required by the Constitution or merely was the product of the Court's supervisory power over the lower federal courts and thus subject to negation by Congress. Even if the rule is rooted in the Fourth Amendment, the question remains whether it is a personal right of the defendant or just a deterrent against unlawful searches, discardable if other deterrents can be found. The *Weeks* opinion appeared to endorse the first position; use of the evidence, said the Court, would constitute "a denial of the constitutional rights of the accused." More recent decisions, however, favor the deterrent theory. Nonetheless, one who is not himself the victim of an unlawful search but is implicated in crime by the seizure does not have standing to challenge admission of the evidence.

—JACOB W. LANDYNSKI

WEST COAST HOTEL
COMPANY v. PARRISH

300 U.S. 379 (1937)

This decision sustaining a Washington state minimum wage statute in March 1937 sig-

The unanimous Weeks *opinion said that if unconstitutionally seized evidence were admitted, the Fourth Amendment "might as well be stricken from the Constitution."*

See also

Boyd v. *United States*
Exclusionary Rule
Right to Counsel
Search and Seizure

naled a seismic shift in judicial philosophy toward acceptance of the validity of social and economic legislation. Together with the *Wagner Act Cases,* the decision reflected a new, favorable judicial attitude toward the New Deal, thus defusing Franklin D. Roosevelt's court-packing proposal.

The constitutionality of minimum wage legislation had a peculiar history. In *Muller* v. *Oregon* (1908) and *Bunting* v. *Oregon* (1917) the Justices had approved state laws regulating maximum working hours, including provisions for overtime wages. In 1917, the Court divided evenly on an Oregon minimum wage law. William Howard Taft, among others, confidently presumed that *Lochner* v. *New York*'s (1905) rigorous freedom of contract doctrines no longer applied. Yet in 1923, a 5–3 majority of the Court reaffirmed the *Lochner* ruling, and in *Adkins* v. *Children's Hospital* (1923) the Court invalidated a District of Columbia minimum wage statute. New Chief Justice Taft sharply attacked the majority's reasoning. He found no distinction between maximum hour and minimum wage laws: one was the "multiplier and the other the multiplicand." Although Taft reiterated his belief that *Lochner* had been tacitly overruled, *Lochner* nevertheless persisted until the *Parrish* decision in 1937.

After *Adkins,* the Court invalidated other state minimum wage laws. The Great Depression, however, stimulated new state laws, perhaps encouraged by Justice George Sutherland's obiter dictum that "exceptional circumstances" might justify such legislation. But in *Morehead* v. *New York ex rel. Tipaldo* (1936), a 5–4 majority held to the *Adkins* precedent and invalidated a recent New York law. The Court's opinion masked Justice Owen J. Roberts's uneasiness. Roberts had supported Pierce Butler, James C. McReynolds, George Sutherland, and Willis Van Devanter in *Tipaldo,* but he later revealed that the state counsel's argument that *Adkins* merely be distinguished, and not overthrown, had obliged him to follow the prece-

dent. Six months later, Roberts provided the key vote to consider the Washington law. On the surface, the procedure was justified on the ground that the state court had upheld the statute, but the combination of the *Tipaldo* dissenters' strongly held views on constitutionality and Roberts's skepticism toward *Adkins* dictated a full-scale review of the issue.

Roberts later stated that he had decided in favor of the statutes after arguments in December 1936 and that he had successfully urged delaying the decision pending Harlan Fiske Stone's recovery from illness in order to mass a majority. Stone returned shortly after Roosevelt submitted his court-packing proposal in early February. Chief Justice Charles Evans Hughes then withheld the announcement until March 29, perhaps to avoid appearances of political submission.

Hughes's majority opinion decisively repudiated *Lochner* and *Adkins.* He argued that the Constitution nowhere enshrined freedom of contract and that "regulation which is reasonable in relation to its subject and is adopted in the interests of the community is due process." Seeking to deflect the outraged protests of his more conservative brethren, Hughes invoked Taft's *Adkins* dissent: "That challenge persists and is without any satisfactory answer."

Invoking the public interest doctrine of *Nebbia* v. *New York* (1934), Hughes asked what could be "closer to the public interest than the health of women and their protection from unscrupulous and overreaching employers?" Accordingly, Hughes held that the minimum wage statute was reasonable and not "arbitrary or capricious." That, he concluded, "is all we have to decide."

Sutherland, speaking for the dissenters, passionately reiterated his *Adkins* doctrine. More broadly, Sutherland also implicitly addressed Stone's scathing dissent in *United States* v. *Butler* (1936), which had pleaded for judicial self-restraint and an end to judges' imposition of their own social and economic predilections. The notion of self-restraint,

W

WEST COAST HOTEL COMPANY v. PARRISH

300 U.S. 379 (1937)

This decision reflected a new, favorable judicial attitude toward the New Deal.

See also

Adkins v. *Children's Hospital*

Lochner v. *New York*

Morehead v. *New York ex rel. Tipaldo*

Muller v. *Oregon*

Nebbia v. *New York*

United States v. *Butler*

The Court ruled valid a New York law requiring storage of the names and addresses of persons who obtain by doctors' prescription drugs such as opium, cocaine, and amphetamines.

See also

Right to Privacy

Sutherland retorted, was "ill considered and mischievous"; it belonged "in the domain of will and not of judgment." Judges were bound to enforce the Constitution, he said, according to their own "conscientious and informed convictions." Sutherland concluded that freedom of contract remained the rule. The intervening economic conditions altered nothing, for "the meaning of the Constitution," he said, "does not change with the ebb and flow of economic events." Sutherland's dissent was both an apologia and an obituary for a judicial philosophy eclipsed by new realities.

—STANLEY I. KUTLER

Bibliography

Mason, Alpheus T. (1956). *Harlan Fiske Stone.* New York: Viking Press.

WHALEN v. ROE

429 U.S. 589 (1977)

Rejecting a claim based on the constitutional right of privacy, a unanimous Supreme Court upheld a New York law requiring storage in a computer file of the names and addresses of persons who obtain, by doctors' prescriptions, such drugs as opium, methadone, cocaine, and amphetamines. Justice John Paul Stevens, writing for the Court, noted that previous decisions recognizing a right of privacy had involved two different kinds of interests: (1) "avoiding disclosure of personal matters"; and (2) "independence in making certain kinds of important decisions." Both interests were arguably implicated here; there was some risk of disclosure of a drug user's name, and that risk could have deterred the prescription or use of such drugs even when they were medically advisable. Nonetheless, and despite a district court finding that the state had not proved the necessity of storing this personal information, the Court concluded that the law was valid. The state's

interest in drug regulation was vital; the legislature was entitled to experiment with reasonable means for achieving that end. Balanced against this objective, the invasions of privacy were too slight to constitute invasions of either patients' or doctors' constitutional liberties.

—KENNETH L. KARST

WHITE, BYRON R.

(1917–)

When he was appointed to the Supreme Court in 1962, Byron White, at the age of forty-four, was a symbol of the vigor, youth, and intellectual power of the John F. Kennedy administration. From a poor rural background, he had ranked first in the class of 1938 at the University of Colorado, becoming a football All-American and winning a Rhodes Scholarship. By the time he graduated from Yale Law School in 1946, he had briefly studied at Oxford, played two seasons of professional football, served as a naval intelligence officer in the Pacific, and twice encountered John Kennedy (once at Oxford, once in the Pacific). After clerking for Chief Justice Fred M. Vinson, White joined a law practice in Denver where he remained for fourteen years. When Kennedy won the Democratic nomination for president in 1960, White chaired the nationwide volunteer group Citizens for Kennedy. His service as deputy attorney general under Robert Kennedy included screening candidates for judicial appointments and supervising federal marshals protecting workers in the civil rights movement in the South. He had been at the job only fourteen months when the president nominated him to fill the vacancy created by the resignation of Charles Whittaker.

During his years on the Court, White generally reflected the commitments of the president who appointed him: to equal opportunity, to effective law enforcement, and to enablement of government as it responds to new challenges—with less concern for individual rights, group rights, and states' rights. To the distress of those who would prefer greater elaboration of a philosophical vision, he approached the judicial task in a lawyerly and pragmatic fashion, although sometimes in excessively cryptic opinions. His independence and analytic bent of mind often isolated him from more ideological colleagues. As he served with twenty other Justices during times of great ferment on the Court, his role changed considerably. He was in the majority in fewer than half of the 5–4 decisions during the 1960s, in more than 60 percent of the 5–4 decisions during the 1970s, and in nearly three-fourths of the 5–4 decisions during the 1980s—more frequently than any other Justice during that decade. Although profound changes in American society (often shaped by the Court itself) significantly affected the issues before him and, to a lesser extent, his resolution of particular issues, a review of his work on the Court reveals significant consistency in perspective, method, and conviction.

White knew that judges make law. His time at Yale Law School was the heyday of that school's celebration of legal realism. As he explained in dissent in *Miranda* v. *Arizona* (1966), "[T]he Court has not discovered or found the law in making today's decision; what it has done is to make new law and new public policy in much the same way that it has in the course of interpreting other great clauses of the Constitution. . . . [I]t is wholly legitimate . . . to inquire into the advisability of its end product in terms of the long-range interest of the country."

White also understood that the triumph of the administrative state, marked especially by an affirmative and vigorous federal government, had forever altered the shape of American political institutions, including the Court. For White, however, neither legal

W

WHITE, BYRON R.

(1917–)

ALL-AMERICAN

White was a symbol of the vigor, youth, and intellectual power of the Kennedy Administration.

realism nor expanding concepts of national political authority and responsibility justified the exercise of "raw judicial power." A recurring theme of his opinions was that the judiciary undermines its own legitimacy when it seeks to achieve political objectives not sanctioned by the other branches of government or when it promotes social transformation resisted by the democratic institutions of society.

White's confidence in the good faith and capabilities of democratic institutions—Congress especially, but also the executive, state legislatures, and juries—exceeded that of other justices of the "left" or of the "right." For White, the powers of government were limited neither by abstract conceptions of individual autonomy, nor by any extrademocratic mandate for perfection in human affairs. Rather, government power is limited by the very forces that legitimate it: the people acting through fair and free elections and a Constitution that both authorizes and specifically checks government actors.

In the spirit of the New Deal and of President Kennedy, White gave great weight to securing and preserving federal authority, especially Congress's authority. Where Congress legislated (or federal agencies have acted pursuant to delegated power), he was disposed to find federal preemption of state law. Where Congress has not legislated, he gave wide berth to the dormant commerce clause. Where states sought to regulate federal entities, he was disposed to place limits on state power. He did not view the Tenth Amendment as a limitation on Congress's regulatory power; he would permit Congress to abrogate state sovereign immunity under the Eleventh Amendment; and he recognized significant legislative power to implement the Fourteenth Amendment. Where Congress had delegated interpretative authority to administrative agencies, he was strongly disposed to defer to agency interpretations of statutes. In many ways, he was the preeminent nationalist on the Court in the modern era. For instance, White was the only dissenter to the Court's 1978 decision upholding the multistate tax compact, which had not been approved by Congress, because of its "*potential* encroachment on federal supremacy."

White's understanding of the separation of powers in our national government, as set forth in a series of powerful dissents, was similarly rooted in his recognition that Congress needs latitude to solve economic problems and to reallocate governance authorities in response to the growing demands on national institutions in the post-New Deal era. Thus, he urged in *Buckley* v. *Valeo* (1976) that "Congress was entitled to determine that personal wealth ought to play a less important role in political campaigns than it has in the past." He lamented in *Northern Pipeline Co.* v. *Marathon Pipe Line Co.* (1982) that "at this point in the history of constitutional law" the Court should not have "looked[ed] only to the constitutional text" to determine Congress's power "to create adjudicatory institutions designed to carry out federal policy." He explained in *Immigration and Naturalization Service* v. *Chadha* (1983) that the legislative veto "is an indispensable political invention that . . . assures the accountability of independent regulatory agencies and preserves Congress' control on lawmaking." And the budget-balancing legislation of *Bowsher* v. *Synar* (1986) was "one of the most novel and far reaching legislative responses to a national crisis since the New Deal."

White conceived of a more limited role for the federal courts, not to supplement or second-guess Congress's policies, but to ensure their implementation by state and federal actors. His concurrence in *Chapman* v. *Houston Welfare Rights Organization* (1979)—urging that in the civil rights legislation of the Reconstruction Congress had provided a remedy for denial not only of constitutional rights but also of rights created by federal statutes—was subsequently adopted by a majority of the Court. White also more narrowly construed executive immunity than did a majority of his colleagues. He was less willing than many others on the Court, however, to infer a private cause of action to enforce federal rights where Congress has lodged responsibility for enforcement with a federal agency or has provided for administrative remedies. Nor was he uniformly activist on issues of political question, standing, and other prudential limitations on judicial review. Although he sometimes resisted efforts to restrict habeas corpus jurisdiction, he joined in limiting the bases on which habeas review may upset a criminal conviction.

To achieve consistency in constitutional interpretation, White took an expansive view of the Supreme Court's jurisdiction over state court decisions. Moreover, often dissenting from denial of certiorari, he regularly urged the Court to use its discretionary jurisdiction to review apparent inconsistencies in the lower courts. His longstanding extrajudicial campaign for creation of a national court of appeals or similar structure to ensure uniformity in federal law finally ran its course when Supreme Court's workload was reduced.

White's clear sense of the primacy of democratic institutions was reflected in his commitment to the protection of rights to participate in the electoral process. From *Avery* v. *Midland County* (1968) to *Board of Estimate of the City of New York* v. *Morris* (1989), he led the Court in expansively interpreting the principle of one person, one vote to subject varieties of political apportionment and gerrymandering to judicial review, even as he took a relatively permissive and pragmatic approach to apportionment disparities. His dissent in *Mobile* v. *Bolden* (1980) effectively became the majority position two terms later in *Rogers* v. *Lodge* (1982), which eased the burden of minority challenges to electoral districting schemes that perpetuate purposeful racial discrimination. As indicated in *Buckley* and subsequent cases, White would go further than other Justices in permitting Congress to regulate the electoral processes to root out potential corruption and inequality, even at the cost of some inhibition of free speech.

More generally, his First Amendment jurisprudence permitted significant intrusions on the media, whether in the form of the fairness doctrine as in *Red Lion Broadcasting Co.* v. *F.C.C.* (1969); search warrants, as in *Zurcher* v. *Stanford Daily* (1978); subpoenas, as in *Branzburg* v. *Hayes* (1972); or libel law, as in *Herbert* v. *Lando* (1979) and his dissent in *Gertz* v. *Robert Welch, Inc.* (1974). White was likewise deferential toward regulation and prosecution of obscenity, child pornography, and subversive advocacy. He was a leading opponent of a strict, separatist conception of the establishment of religion and would have, for instance, permitted state aid for secular activities in parochial schools.

Although White gave broad scope to legislative power, he usually subjected the legislative product to close scrutiny for invidious purpose or for insufficient relationship to a legitimate purpose. For a time, White's purpose analysis produced a more activist Fourteenth Amendment jurisprudence than the majority of the Court was willing to embrace; for example, he argued in dissent in *Palmer* v. *Thompson* (1971) that a Mississippi town should not be permitted to close its swimming pool where its purpose was to prevent implementation of a desegregation order. White's scrutiny of purpose was decidedly nonactivist, however, in the face of minority challenges to government programs that had disparate racial impact without discriminatory intent. In the seminal case of *Washington* v. *Davis* (1976), he held for a 7–2 majority that disparate impact alone does not constitute the kind of racial discrimination that presumptively violates the constitutional principle of equal protection of the laws. White did not adopt the view that the Constitution prohibits all "reverse discrimination" to counteract diffuse societal discrimination. His joint opinion in *Regents of University of California* v. *Bakke* (1978), permitting government to take race into account in university admissions, reflected his oft-demonstrated concern for equal educational opportunity. His votes, in *Fullilove* v. *Klutznick* (1980) and *Metro Broadcasting, Inc.* v. *Federal Communications Commission* (1990), to uphold federal minority "set-aside" and race-preference requirements, underscored his deference to Congress even as he voted, in *Richmond (City of)* v. *J. A. Croson Co.* (1989), to strike down a local government's "set-aside" scheme.

For a decade after he joined the majority opinion in *Griggs* v. *Duke Power Co.* (1971), White appeared content with permitting disparate impact alone to be sufficient for broad race-conscious remedies in employment discrimination cases brought under Title VII of the Civil Rights Act of 1964. In 1979 he even joined in endorsing a private employer's use of racial quotas intended to eliminate the ef-

White's individualism produced a powerful egalitarian ethic that took two different forms.

fects of societal discrimination. White began to express significant dissatisfaction with aspects of the prevailing Title VII jurisprudence in a series of opinions, mostly dissenting, in the mid-1980s. By the end of the decade, amid indications that the disparate-impact test invited use of racial quotas, White commanded a majority in *Wards Cove Packing Co.* v. *Antonio* (1989) to shift the burden of proof in disparate-impact cases.

In school desegregation cases, however, White has been as ready as any member of the Court to find evidence of past purposeful discrimination and to approve broad remedies. His majority opinion in *Columbus Board of Education* v. *Penick* (1979) permitted inference of purposeful discrimination from evidence of long-past misconduct and a continued discriminatory effect, and placed the burden on the defendant school system to prove that it had not caused any current racial segregation in its schools. In addition, he held the state, not the defendant school district, ultimately responsible for removing the effects of purposeful discrimination; in this view, neither the happenstance of school-district boundaries nor state laws impeding school funding may stand in the way of remedial decrees. Thus he was in a minority in *Milliken* v. *Bradley* (1974) in arguing and a remedy of interdistrict school busing, and he wrote the 5–4 decision in *Jenkins* v. *Missouri* (1990) upholding the power of the federal district court to order a defendant school board to impose tax increases in violation of fiscally restrictive state law.

One may infer several reasons for White's different stances in school desegregation cases and employment discrimination cases. Even outside the race-discrimination context, White adopted an ethic of group equality in education, as demonstrated in his dissent in *San Antonio Independent School District* v. *Rodriguez* (1973), where he would have struck down school-financing schemes that leave the poorest school districts with

the most impoverished schools. Moreover, the proof of purposeful racial discrimination by school districts is often palpable, but it is difficult to trace disparate racial impact in the job market to purposeful discrimination by a defendant employer. In addition, although busing does not deny schooling to any child, White expressed particular unhappiness with quota systems that take jobs away from nondiscriminating white workers. Finally, judicial imposition of systems of racial preference in employment would cause upheavals in collective bargaining, seniority systems, and other underpinnings of industrial society.

White's belief in the legitimacy of the law in ordering our social life, along with his confidence in the institutions of government, made him reluctant to impose "decriminalization," either directly (by limiting legislative power to punish) or indirectly (by insisting on perfection from police, prosecutors, and others charged with achieving criminal justice). Even as he joined the holding in *Furman* v. *Georgia* (1972), striking down a scheme of capital punishment that provided no guidance for the sentencing authority, White noted the good faith of Georgia in granting discretion to sentencing juries out of a "desire to mitigate the harshness" of capital punishment laws. Subsequently, he voted to uphold carefully structured death penalty laws, rejecting the arguments that juries "disobey or nullify their instructions" and that others who retain discretion, such as prosecutors, inevitably wield it arbitrarily. Invoking the Court's ill-famed journey earlier in this century into the realm of substantive due process, he refused to make the judgment that the death penalty cannot comport with the Constitution. White, however, recognized substantive limitations on the types of crimes for which this penalty may be imposed; he wrote the Court's opinion in *Coker* v. *Georgia* (1977), holding the death penalty disproportionate for the rape of an adult, and the Court's opinion in *Enmund* v. *Florida*

(1982), holding capital punishment improper where a murder conviction was based solely on a theory of felony murder.

The criteria of "reasonableness" and "good faith," at the core of much of White's jurisprudence, were especially prominent in his approach to the Fourth Amendment—which has largely become the law of the land. He was the leading proponent of clear and simple rules governing police search and seizure. He understood the Constitution's requirement that searches and seizures be "reasonable" to have broad applicability, if shallow in depth; he wrote the opinion in *Camara* v. *Municipal Court* (1967), which spawned a new jurisprudence upholding an array of regulatory searches on less than probable cause, but he also wrote *Tennessee* v. *Garner* (1985), which prohibited use of deadly force against fleeing felons, and he recognized the Fourth Amendment's applicability to subpoenas issued by grand juries. His oft-stated antipathy to the exclusionary rule as a remedy for Fourth Amendment violations finally led to adoption of the good faith exception to this rule in *United States* v. *Leon* (1984). White likewise took a functional and pragmatic approach to the Sixth Amendment's right to trial by jury. He resisted efforts to limit criminal investigations and forfeitures through broad application of the right to counsel; he dissented from interpretations of the Fifth Amendment right against self-incrimination that depart from historical practice and impede reliable administration of justice; and he was at the forefront of the Court in permitting great leeway in plea bargaining, as in *Brady* v. *United States* (1970).

White's opinions on criminal procedure revealed not only his perspective on issues of criminal justice but also his unusual commitment to the rule of *stare decisis* in constitutional adjudication, which sometimes led to the perception that he was "unpredictable." Like many Justices, White was ready to overrule previous decisions that prove unworkable or ill-advised. For instance, he joined *Batson* v. *Kentucky* (1986), which, overruling his own *Swain* v. *Alabama* (1965), subjected preemptory jury challenges to judicial review for racial discrimination; *Batson* acknowledged that *Swain*'s confidence in state prosecutors had not been vindicated. Yet White, more than other Justices and regardless of ideological inclination, on most issues sought to adhere to constitutional precedent not yet overruled. Thus, although he dissented forcefully in *Miranda*, he clearly accepted the major contours of that decision. Indeed, he wrote *Edwards* v. *Arizona* (1981), which went beyond the core of *Miranda* in prohibiting all questioning once the suspect in custody has requested an attorney. Similarly, despite his long, carefully composed dissent in *Payton* v. *New York* (1980), which required an arrest warrant to arrest persons in their homes, White ten years later wrote the majority opinion applying *Payton* to the arrest of someone hiding out overnight in a friend's home. Even where he would vote to overrule a precedent, White sometimes exasperated observers by refusing to cast the fifth vote for simply narrowing the reach of the precedent, insisting he was bound until it was expressly overruled.

The most controversial decision by White upholding government power to invoke the criminal process is *Bowers* v. *Hardwick* (1986), which refused to strike down a Georgia law forbidding consensual sodomy between men. White conceived the issue much as he had the issue in the death penalty cases: whether the Supreme Court should bypass political institutions to establish a new social order. White had long objected to the Court's discovery of new constitutional rights deriving from the concept of "privacy." His concurrence in *Griswold* v. *Connecticut* (1965) declined to find a general right of privacy, emphasizing instead the lack of a rational relationship between the statute's ban on distributing birth control information to married persons and the pur-

W

ported purpose of the statute. *Roe* v. *Wade* (1973), the decision establishing a broad right to abortion throughout pregnancy, evoked a response reminiscent of his *Miranda* dissent: "The Court simply fashions and announces a new constitutional right . . . with scarcely any reason or authority." In dissents in subsequent privacy rights cases during the 1970s and early 1980s, including *Moore* v. *City of East Cleveland* (1977), which struck down a zoning ordinance that narrowly defined "single family," White even more explicitly compared the Court's "new" substantive due process with the efforts of the Court in *Lochner* v. *New York* (1905) to impose its will on a divided polity. By 1986, in *Thornburgh* v. *American College of Obstetricians and Gynecologists*, he advocated overruling *Roe*, urging that the right it recognized was neither "implicit in the concept of ordered liberty," nor "deeply rooted in the nation's history and traditions." For White, *Bowers* was a replay of *Thornburgh*, with the important difference that he was writing the majority opinion. As White must have anticipated, once the majority had adopted his approach to enunciation of a fundamental right, it was only a matter of time before *Roe* itself would begin to collapse, as indeed it did in *Webster* v. *Reproductive Health Services* (1989).

Yet White himself had recognized certain fundamental liberty interests that may be subsumed under the label substantive due process—including, in *Griswold*, "the right to be free of regulation of the intimacies of the marriage relationship" and, in a long series of cases (continuing even after *Bowers*) dealing with illegitimacy, the rights of natural parents "in the companionship . . . of their children." White's purpose-based jurisprudence might have considered proscriptions of sodomy as different from antiabortion laws. In the latter, the organized community may have the purpose of protecting human life, whereas in the former, its motivation may simply be antipathy toward homosexuals—a purpose that could be recognized (but that White in 1986 declined to recognize) as invidious. Here as elsewhere, White's jurisprudence seldom put the Court ahead of the country. For him, the Court's primary role in constitutional lawmaking was not to pioneer or even to lead, but rather to secure for the whole nation the democratic consensus that has already been reached.

—KATE SMITH

Bibliography

Hutton, Mary Christine (1986). The Unique Perspective of Justice White: Separation of Powers, Standing and Section 1983 Cases. *Administrative Law Review* 40:377–414.

Liebman, Lance (1987). Justice White and Affirmative Action. *University of Colorado Law Review* 58:471–496.

Nelson, William E. (1987). Deference and the Limits to Deference in the Constitutional Jurisprudence of Justice Byron R. White. *University of Colorado Law Review* 58:347–364.

O'Donnell, Pierce (1987). Common Sense and the Constitution: Justice White and the Egalitarian Ideal. *University of Colorado Law Review* 58:433–470.

Student Note (1987). The Intercircuit Tribunal and Perceived Conflicts: An Analysis of Justice White's Dissents from Denial of Certiorari During the 1985 Term. *New York University Law Review* 62:610–650.

Varat, Jonathan D. (1987). Justice White and the Breadth and Allocation of Federal Authority. *University of Colorado Law Review* 58:371–428

WHITE, EDWARD D.

(1845-1921)

Born and raised in Louisiana, the son of a slaveholding sugar planter and a Confederate veteran, Edward Douglass White was an archetype of the "New South" political leader.

The masters of the region's economic and social development from the 1880s until World War I combined the interests of antebellum planters with those of northern and local capitalists eager to build railroads and tap the area's coal, iron, and timber. The South's new ruling class "redeemed" Dixie from the egalitarian schemes of Radical Republicans and carpetbaggers by supporting Rutherford B. Hayes for president and accepting the national hegemony of the GOP's conservative wing. In return, these leaders of the "New South" received from the Republicans a promise to remove federal troops from the region, a free hand with respect to the Negro, and a junior partnership in the management of the nation's economic affairs.

While tending his family's plantation and building a prosperous legal practice in New Orleans, White became a chief political confidant and ally of Governor Francis Nicholls, the leader of the state's conservative Democrats, who rewarded him with an appointment to the Louisiana Supreme Court and then a seat in the United States Senate in 1891. While in Washington, the portly, florid, long-haired junior senator from Louisiana adopted a rigid states' rights and laissez-faire posture on most issues. However, he fervently supported high duties on foreign sugar and lavish federal bounties to the planters in his home state. White led the Senate's successful revolt against President Grover Cleveland's efforts to lower the protective tariff in 1893. Nevertheless, the beleaguered head of the Democratic party nominated him to the Supreme Court a year later, following the death of Samuel Blatchford and the Senate's rejection of two earlier nominees.

White took his seat as the junior member of the Fuller Court at one of the important turning points in the history of the federal judiciary. The country seethed with unrest generated by the worst depression of the nineteenth century. Violent confrontations between workers and employers erupted on the nation's major railroads as well as in coal mines, steel mills, and other factories. Debt-ridden farmers formed the radical Populist party, which demanded government control of the money supply and banking system and nationalization of the major trunk rail lines. Insurgent Democrats nominated the youthful William Jennings Bryan, who ran on a platform promising inflation of the money supply, higher taxes on the wealthy, and a curb on trusts and other monopolies. In this atmosphere of class strife and regional polarization, men of property and standing looked to the Supreme Court to defend the constitutional ark against dangerous innovations. Fuller and most of his colleagues were equal to the task of repelling the radical hordes.

Even before the economic collapse, a majority of the Justices had served warning that they would not tolerate legislative attacks on corporate property and profits. Legislative power to fix railroad rates, they warned, was not without limits; corporations were persons, entitled to the judicial protection of the Fourteenth Amendment's due process clause; and no rate imposed by legislative fiat could be deemed "reasonable" without final judicial review. Then, in a series of cases that reached the Court together during the depths of the depression in 1895, the Justices quashed federal efforts to prosecute the sugar trust under the Sherman Antitrust Act in *United States* v. *E. C. Knight Co.* (1895); upheld the contempt conviction of the labor leader Eugene V. Debs for his role in the Pullman boycott in *In re Debs* (1895); and declared unconstitutional the first federal income tax levied since the Civil War in *Pollock* v. *Farmer's Loan & Trust Co.* (1895). These three decisions displayed the Fuller Court's conservative colors and represented a major victory for big business, the wealthy, and the enemies of organized labor.

Like the majority of his brethren, Justice White showed no sympathy for Debs and the militant working class movement he represented. White also endorsed Fuller's reasoning

About White, Oliver Wendell Holmes wrote, "His writing leaves much to be desired, but his thinking is profound."

in the sugar trust case, which limited the scope of the Sherman Act to monopolies of interstate trade or commerce and left to the individual states all authority to curb monopolies over production. But he joined Justice John Marshall Harlan, the outspoken champion of nationalism and federal power, in denouncing the majority's assault on the income tax statute. White had been a member of the Senate that passed the income tax measure as part of the tariff package in 1892, and, although he did not endorse the levy, neither did he doubt the constitutional power of Congress to adopt it. In order to invalidate the law, the majority had to ignore two weighty precedents, one dating from 1796. This was too much for White, who argued eloquently that "the conservation and orderly development of our institutions rests on our acceptance of the results of the past, and their use as lights to guide our steps in the future. Teach the lesson that settled principles may be overthrown at any time, and confusion and turmoil must ultimately result."

The income tax dissent revealed an important aspect of White's jurisprudence which remained constant during his years as an associate Justice and later as Chief Justice after 1911. Although deeply conservative and devoted to the judicial protection of private property, White was also a pragmatist capable of endorsing moderate reforms that had clear constitutional sanction and that served to cap the pressures for more radical change. Though not adverse to overturning a few precedents himself, White usually did so in the pursuit of policies that strengthened rather than weakened the dominant economic forces of corporate capitalism.

In this spirit, he endorsed the judicial imperialism inherent in Justice Harlan's opinion in *Smyth* v. *Ames* (1898), which made the federal judiciary the final arbiter of utility rates, but he also enforced the progressive reforms of the Theodore Roosevelt-William Howard Taft era, which revitalized the regulatory authority of the Interstate Commerce Com-

mission (ICC) over the nation's major railroads. In a series of decisions, culminating in White's opinion in *Interstate Commerce Commission* v. *Illinois Central Railroad Co.* (1910), the majority sustained the ICC's fact-finding and rate-fixing powers as mandated by Congress. White's views were compatible with the interests of the railroads, which looked to the ICC to prevent financially ruinous rate wars, and with those of reformers like Roosevelt, who believed that such regulation would curb the appetite for government ownership of the carriers.

White rendered his greatest service to the conservative cause in the area of antitrust law by promoting the view that the Sherman Act prohibited only "unreasonable" restraints of trade, a perspective pregnant with possibilities for enlarged judicial control over the country's economic structure, yet wholly compatible with the desires of big business. But it took White over a decade to defeat the contrary views of other Justices, who remained more wedded to the old Jacksonian belief in competition and the dangers of monopoly.

In the wake of the *E. C. Knight* decision restricting federal antitrust efforts to interstate commerce, the Department of Justice began a campaign to stamp out railroad cartels and pools designed to divide up traffic and fix rates. A majority of the Justices, led by Harlan and Rufus W. Peckham, a passionate spokesman for laissez-faire economics, sustained the government's efforts in this area on the theory that the Sherman Act outlawed *all* restraints of trade, even those that might be deemed "reasonable" in view of particular business conditions such as rate wars and destructive competition. In the first of these cases, *United States* v. *Trans-Missouri Freight Association* (1897), White wrote a long, rambling dissent which accused the majority of misreading the antitrust law, defying the traditions of the common law with respect to restraints of trade, and jeopardizing the economic progress brought to the nation by business combinations and consolidations.

White continued to dissent in the *Joint Traffic Association Case* (1898) and in *Northern Securities Co. v. United States* (1904), where a five-Justice majority upheld the government's suit against the Morgan-Harriman rail monopoly between Chicago and the Pacific Northwest. In each case, White argued that the antitrust law, incorporating the ancient doctrines of the common law, prohibiting only "unreasonable" restraints of trade. Technically, White was correct, but all of the methods condemned in *Trans-Missouri, Joint Traffic Association,* and *Northern Securities* would have been indictable at common law as well, because their fundamental objective had been to fix prices contrary to the public interest. This fact seems to have eluded White, who believed that the Harlan-Peckham approach threatened the demise of valuable business enterprises by virtue of judicial abdication to the prosecutorial zeal of misguided reformers in the executive branch. In this perception, he enjoyed the support of three other justices, including Oliver Wendell Holmes, who also looked upon the Rockefellers, Morgans, and Harrimans as agents of social and economic progress.

Four changes in the personnel of the Court between 1909 and 1911 gave White a new majority for his doctrine a year later when the government's suits against Standard Oil and American Tobacco finally reached the Justices after years of litigation. Speaking now as Chief Justice of the United States, having been appointed to the center chair by President Taft, White sustained the government's case against the monopolists but cast aside the Harlan-Peckham interpretation of the Sherman Act. Henceforth, the majority decreed, only "unreasonable" trade restraints would be indictable under the Sherman Act and the Justices on the Supreme Court would determine where the line should be drawn between legal and illegal competitive behavior. Harlan wrote a melancholy dissent against this sharp reversal of doctrine, which seemed to teach that "settled principles may be overthrown at any time, and confusion and turmoil must ultimately result."

White's rule of reason doctrine provoked a storm of protest from progressives in the Congress, who denounced the Justices for mutilating the antitrust law, arrogating to themselves too much power over the economic system, and giving big business a hunting license to continue its predatory ways. Although Congress added the Clayton Act amendments to the antitrust law in 1914, specifically outlawing a substantial list of business practices, White's rule of reason carried the day. The Court quashed the government's efforts to break up the shoe machinery monopoly in 1913 and also threw out the case against United States Steel in 1920, a year before White died. There was extraordinary historical irony in the fact that it was a Southerner and a veteran of the Rebel army who advanced antitrust doctrines that sealed the triumph of industrial capitalism and big business in American life.

For a Southerner, a Democrat, and a spokesman for states' rights in the Senate, White displayed considerable toleration for the expansion of federal economic controls by means of the commerce clause and the taxing and spending power. In the Senate he had taken an active role in fighting a federal law to regulate the trade in agricultural "futures," noting that it would invade the jurisdiction of the states and create "the most unlimited and arbitrary government on the face of God's earth." As a Justice, however, he joined Harlan's path-breaking opinion in the Lottery Case, *Champion v. Ames* (1903), which greatly expanded the national police power via the interstate commerce clause. A year later he wrote the Court's opinion in *McCray v. United States* (1904), which affirmed the power of Congress to impose a prohibitive levy upon oleomargarine and thus employ its tax powers for regulatory purposes.

White drew back, however, from the logical implications of the national police power when Congress sought to apply it to other areas of social and economic life. He was willing to permit the extension of the commerce power to federal regulation of adulterated foods and interstate traffic in prostitution, but he joined Justice William R. Day's opinion in *Hammer* v. *Dagenhart* (1918), which declared unconstitutional Congress's attempt to eradicate child labor. He also rejected federal efforts to tax and regulate narcotics traffic in *United States* v. *Doremus* (1919), although the majority found this use of the federal taxing power compatible with White's own views in *McCray*. He sanctioned Congress's adoption of an eight-hour day for interstate train crews which brought an end to the disastrous nationwide rail strike, but he joined three other dissenters in *Block* v. *Hirsh* (1921) when Holmes and the majority upheld the national legislature's power to impose rent controls upon property in the District of Columbia during the emergency of World War I.

White displayed equal inconsistency in cases where state economic regulations came under due process challenge. The one thread of coherence seemed to be his growing conservatism and abiding dislike for organized labor. He dissented in *Lochner* v. *New York* (1905) along with Harlan and Day, noting that "no evils arising from such legislation could be more far-reaching than those that might come to our system of government if the judiciary . . . should enter the domain of legislation, and upon grounds merely of justice or reason or wisdom, annul statutes that had received the sanction of the people's representatives." He also voted to sustain the Oregon and California maximum hours laws for women in *Muller* v. *Oregon* (1908) and *Miller* v. *Wilson* (1915). But he balked at the overtime pay provisions and general maximum hours limitation in *Bunting* v. *Oregon* (1917) and sided with the majority in the three leading cases of the period which protected employers' use of yellow dog contracts against both state and federal efforts to eliminate this notorious antiunion de-

vice: *Adair* v. *United States* (1908), *Coppage* v. *Kansas* (1915), and *Hitchman* v. *Hitchman Coal & Coke Co.* (1917).

In 1919, White joined Joseph McKenna, Willis Van Devanter, and James C. McReynolds in dissent against the Court's opinion in the *Arizona Employers' Liability Cases* (1919), which upheld that state's law shifting the cost of industrial accidents to employers. And during his final term on the Court, he joined the majority in scuttling the anti-injunction provisions of the Clayton Antitrust Act and affirming the illegality of secondary boycotts. If not the most reactionary member of the Supreme Court with respect to organized labor, White certainly ran a close race for that honor with Justices Day, Mahlon Pitney, and McReynolds.

White had been elevated to the chief justiceship by William Howard Taft, who coveted the position for himself and feared that a younger nominee might forever prevent that happy development. Taft realized his lifelong ambition in 1921, when White died. Predictably, White's eulogizers compared his career to that of John Marshall and other immortals of the bench, but a more accurate assessment is that constitutional law showed his imprint until 1937.

—MICHAEL E. PARRISH

Bibliography

Dishman, Robert (1951). Mr. Justice White and the Rule of Reason. *The Review of Politics* 13:229–248.

Highsaw, Robert B. (1981). *Edward Douglass White: Defender of the Conservative Faith.* Baton Rouge: Louisiana State University Press.

Klinkhamer, Marie Carolyn (1943). *Edward Douglass White, Chief Justice of the United States.* Washington, D.C.: Catholic University Press.

Semonche, John E. (1978). *Charting the Future: The Supreme Court Responds to a Changing Society, 1890–1920.* Westport, Conn.: Greenwood Press.

WHITE COURT

(1910–1921)

"The condition of the Supreme Court is pitiable, and yet those old fools hold on with a tenacity that is most discouraging," President William Howard Taft wrote in May 1909 to his old friend Horace H. Lurton. Taft would have his day. One year later, Chief Justice Melville W. Fuller spoke at the Court's memorial service for Justice David J. Brewer: "As our brother Brewer joins the great procession, there pass before me the forms of Mathews and Miller, of Field and Bradley and Lamar and Blatchford, of Jackson and Gray and of Peckham, whose works follow them now that they rest from their labors." These were virtually Fuller's last words from the bench, for he died on Independence Day, 1910, in his native Maine. Rufus W. Peckham had died less than a year earlier. William H. Moody, tragically and prematurely ill, would within a few months have to cut short by retirement one of the few notable short tenures on the Court. John Marshall Harlan had but one year left in his remarkable thirty-four-year tenure. By 1912 five new Justices had come to the Court who were not there in 1909: a new majority under a new Chief Justice.

The year 1910 was a significant divide in the history of the country as well. The population was nearly half urban, and immigration was large and growing. The country stood on the verge of enacting humane and extensive labor regulation. A year of Republican unrest in Congress and Theodore Roosevelt's decisive turn to progressive agitation, 1910 was the first time in eight elections that the Democrats took control of the House. In the same year, the National Association for the Advancement of Colored People was founded. It was a year of progressive tremors that would eventually shake the Supreme Court to its foundations with the appointment of Louis D. Brandeis in 1916. But the five appointments with which President Taft rehabili-

tated his beloved Court between 1909 and 1912 had no such dramatic impact. There was a significant strengthening of a mild progressive tendency earlier evident within the Court, but the new appointments brought neither a hardening nor a decisive break with the doctrines of laissez-faire constitutionalism and luxuriant individualism embodied in such decisions as *Lochner* v. *New York* (1905) and *Adair* v. *United States* (1908). Taft's aim was to strengthen the Court with active men of sound, if somewhat progressive, conservative principles. Neither Taft nor the nation saw the Court, as both increasingly would a decade later, as the storm center of pressures for fundamental constitutional change.

Taft's first choice when Peckham died in 1909 was his friend Lurton, then on the Sixth Circuit, and a former member of the Tennessee Supreme Court. Lurton, a Democrat, had been a fiery secessionist in his youth, and in his short and uneventful four-year tenure he combined conservationism on economic regulation, race, and labor relations. Taft's second choice was not so modest. When Taft went to Governor Charles Evans Hughes of New York to replace Brewer, he brought to the Court for the first of his two tenures a Justice who would emerge as one of the greatest figures in the history of American law, and a principal architect of modern civil liberties and civil rights jurisprudence. As governor of New York, Hughes was already one of the formidable reform figures of the Progressive era, and his later career as a presidential candidate who came within a whisper of success in 1916, secretary of state during the 1920s, and Chief Justice during the tumultuous years of the New Deal, mark him as one of the most versatile and important public figures to sit on the Court since John Marshall.

Taft's choice of the Chief Justice to fill the center seat left vacant by Fuller was something of a surprise, although reasons are obvious in retrospect. Edward D. White was a Confederate veteran from Louisiana, who

White took his seat as the junior member of the Fuller Court at one of the important turning points in the history of the federal judiciary.

had played a central role in the Democratic reaction against Reconstruction in that state and had emerged as a Democratic senator in 1891. He had been appointed Associate Justice in 1894 by President Grover Cleveland and had compiled a respectable but unobtrusive record in sixteen years in the side seat. He had dissented with able force from the self-inflicted wound of *Pollock* v. *Farmers' Loan & Trust Co.* (1895), holding unconstitutional the federal income tax, and his antitrust dissents in *Trans-Missouri Freight Association* (1897) and *Northern Securities Company* v. *United States* (1904) embodied sound good sense. He had done "pioneer work," as Taft later called it, in administrative law. White had a genius for friendship and, despite a habit of constant worrying, extraordinary personal warmth. Oliver Wendell Holmes summed him up in these words in 1910: "His writing leaves much to be desired, but his thinking is profound, especially in the legislative direction which we don't recognize as a judicial requirement but which is so, especially in our Court, nevertheless." White was sixty-five, a Democrat, a Confederate veteran, and a Roman Catholic, and his selection by Taft was seen as adventurous. But given Taft's desire to bind up sectional wounds, to spread his political advantage, to put someone in the center seat who might not occupy Taft's own ultimate ambition for too long, to exemplify bipartisanship in the choice of Chief Justice, and on its own sturdy merits, the selection of White seems easy to understand.

Along with White's nomination, Taft sent to the Senate nominations of Willis Van Devanter of Wyoming and Joseph R. Lamar of Georgia. Van Devanter would sit for twenty-seven years, and would become one of the Court's most able, if increasingly conservative, legal craftsmen. Lamar would last only five years, and his death in 1915, along with Lurton's death in 1914 and Hughes's resignation to run for president, opened up the second important cycle of appointments to the White Court.

The Taft appointees joined two of the most remarkable characters ever to sit on the Supreme Court. John Marshall Harlan, then seventy-eight, had been on the Court since his appointment by President Rutherford B. Hayes in 1877. He was a Justice of passionate strength and certitude, a man who, in the fond words of Justice Brewer, "goes to bed every night with one hand on the Constitution and the other on the Bible, and so sleeps the sleep of justice and righteousness." He had issued an apocalyptic dissent in *Pollock*, the income tax case, and his dissent in *Plessy* v. *Ferguson* (1986), the notorious decision upholding racial segregation on railroads, was an appeal to the conscience of the Constitution without equal in our history. The other, even more awesome, giant on the Court in 1910 was Holmes, then seventy, but still not quite recognized as the jurist whom Benjamin N. Cardozo would later call "probably the greatest legal intellect in the history of the English-speaking judiciary." The other two members of the Court were Joseph McKenna, appointed by President William McKinley in 1898, and William R. Day, appointed by President Theodore Roosevelt in 1903.

The Supreme Court in 1910 remained in "truly republican simplicity," as Dean Acheson would recall, in the old Senate chamber, where the Justices operated in the midst of popular government, and in the sight of visitors to the Capitol. No office space was available, and the Justices worked in their homes. Their staff allowance provided for a messenger and one clerk, and their salaries were raised in 1911 to $14,500 for the Associate Justices and $15,000 for the Chief Justice. The Court was badly overworked and the docket was falling further and further behind, not to be rescued until the Judiciary Act of 1925 gave the Court discretion to choose the cases it would review.

In the public's contemporaneous view, if not in retrospect, the most important cases before the White Court between 1910 and

1921 did not involve the Constitution at all, but rather the impact of the Sherman Antitrust Act on the great trusts. *Standard Oil Company* v. *United States* (1911) and *American Tobacco Company* v. *United States* (1911) had been initiated by the Roosevelt administration to seek dissolution of the huge combinations, and when the cases were argued together before the Supreme Court in 1911, the *Harvard Law Review* thought public attention was concentrated on the Supreme Court "to a greater extent than ever before in its history."

The problem for the Court was to determine the meaning of restraint of trade amounting to monopoly. The answer offered by Chief Justice White for the Court was the famous rule of reason, under which not all restraints of trade restrictive of competition were deemed to violate the Sherman Act, but rather only those "undue restraints" which suggested an "intent to do wrong to the general public . . . thus restraining the free flow of commerce and tending to bring about the evils, such as enhancement of riches, which were considered to be against public policy." Under this test, the Court deemed Standard Oil to have engaged in practices designed to dominate the oil industry, exclude others from trade, and create a monopoly. It was ordered to divest itself of its subsidiaries, and to make no agreements with them that would unreasonably restrain trade. The court ruled that the American Tobacco Company was also an illegal combination and forced it into dissolution.

Antitrust was perhaps the dominant political issue of the 1912 presidential campaign, and the rule of reason helped to fuel a heated political debate that produced the great Clayton Act and Federal Trade Commission Act of 1914. Further great antitrust cases came to the White Court, notably *United States* v. *United States Steel Company*, begun in 1911, postponed during the crisis of World War I, and eventually decided in 1920. A divided Court held that United States Steel had not violated the Sherman Act, mere size alone not constituting an offense.

The tremendous public interest generated by the antitrust cases before the White Court was a sign of the temper of the political times, in which the regulation of business and labor relations was the chief focus of progressive attention. In this arena of constitutional litigation, the White Court's record was mixed, with perhaps a slight progressive tinge. On the great questions of legislative power to regulate business practices and working arrangements, the White Court maintained two parallel but opposing lines of doctrines, the one protective of laissez-faire constitutionalism and freedom from national regulation, the other receptive to the progressive reforms of the day.

In the first four years after its reconstitution by Taft, the Supreme Court handed down a number of important decisions upholding national power to regulate commerce for a variety of ends. The most expansive involved federal power to regulate railroads—and to override competing state regulation when necessary. *Atlantic Coast Line Railroad* v. *Riverside Mills* (1911) upheld Congress's amendment of the Hepburn Act imposing on the initial carrier of goods liability for any loss occasioned by a connecting carrier, notwithstanding anything to the contrary in the bill of lading. Freedom of contract gave way to the needs of shippers for easy and prompt recovery. More significantly, in the second of the *Employers' Liability Cases* (1912), the Court upheld congressional legislation imposing liability for any injury negligently caused to any employee of a carrier engaged in interstate commerce. This legislation did away with the fellow-servant rule and the defense of contributory negligence, again notwithstanding contracts to the contrary. In 1914, in the famous *Shreveport Case* (*Houston, East & West Texas Railway Company* v. *United States*), the Court upheld the power of the Interstate Commerce Commission to set the rates of railroad hauls entirely within Texas, because those rates competed against traffic between Texas and Louisiana. The Court overrode the rates set by the Texas Railroad Commission in the process. And in the most important commerce clause decision of the early years of the White Court, the *Minnesota Rate Cases* (1913), the Court upheld the power of the states to regulate railroad rates for intrastate hauls, even when that regulation would force down interstate rates, so long as there had been no federal regulation of those rates. Thus, state power over rates was not invalidated because of the possibility of prospective federal regulation, and a large loophole between state and federal power was closed.

Outside the area of carrier regulation, the White Court was also friendly to national regulation by expanding the national police power doctrine. *Hipolite Egg Co.* v. *United States* (1911) upheld the Pure Food and Drug Act of 1906 in regulating adulterated food and drugs shipped in interstate commerce, whether or not the material had come to rest in the states. "Illicit articles" that traveled in interstate commerce were subject to federal control, the Court said, although with a doctrinal vagueness and confusion that would come back to haunt the Court in *Hammer* v. *Dagenhart* (1918). In *Hoke* v. *United States* (1913) the Court upheld the Mann Act, which punished the transportation in interstate commerce of women "for the purpose of prostitution or debauchery, or for any other immoral purpose."

Taft got his opportunity for a sixth appointment—more appointments in one term than any president in our history since George Washington—when Harlan died in 1911. He filled the vacancy with Mahlon Pitney, chancellor of New Jersey. The reasons for this appointment are obscure, but like other Taft appointments Pitney was a sound, middle-of-the-road, good lawyer with little flair or imagination. As if to prepare for the coming flap over Brandeis, the Pitney appointment ran into trouble because of the nomi-

nee's alleged antilabor positions. But Pitney prevailed, and he would serve on the Court until 1922.

If ever in the history of the Supreme Court successive appointments by one president have seemed to embrace dialectical opposites, Woodrow Wilson's appointments of James C. McReynolds in 1914 and Louis D. Brandeis in 1916 are the ones. McReynolds would become an embittered and crude anti-Semite; Brandeis was the first Jew to sit on the Supreme Court. McReynolds would become the most rigid and doctrinaire apostle of laissez-faire conservatism in constitutional history, the most recalcitrant of the "Four Horsemen of Reaction" who helped to scuttle New Deal legislation in the early 1930s. Brandeis was the greatest progressive of his day, on or off the Court. McReynolds was an almost invariable foe of civil liberties and civil rights for black people; Brandeis was perhaps the driving force of his time for the development of civil liberties, especially freedom of expression and rights of personal privacy. What brought these opposites together in Wilson's esteem, although he came to regret the McReynolds appointment, was antitrust fervor. McReynolds's aggressive individualism and Brandeis's progressive concern for personal dignity and industrial democracy coalesced around antitrust law, and this was the litmus test of the day for Wilson. Thus, possibly the most difficult and divisive person ever to sit on the Supreme Court and possibly the most intellectually gifted and broadly influential Justice in the Court's history took their seats in spurious, rather Wilsonian, juxtaposition.

Wilson's third appointment was handed him by the resignation of his rival in the presidential election of 1916. As it became plain that Hughes was the only person who could unite the Republican party, he came under increasing pressure from Taft and others to make himself available. He did. Wilson nominated John J. Clark of Ohio to replace Hughes. One of the most pregnant speculations about the history of the Supreme Court is what might have happened had Hughes remained on the bench. He might well have become a Chief Justice in 1921 instead of Taft, and under his statesmanlike influence, the hardening of doctrine that led to the confrontation over the New Deal and the Court-packing plan might not have happened.

Although two of Wilson's three appointments were staunch progressives, the Supreme Court seemed to adopt a somewhat conservative stance as it moved toward the decade of erratic resistance to reform that would follow in the 1920s. Federal reform legislation generally continued to pass muster, but there was the staggering exception of the *Child Labor Case* in 1918. And the Court seemed to strike out at labor unions, in both constitutional and antitrust decisions.

In *Hammer* v. *Dagenhart* (1918) the Supreme Court stunned Congress and most of the country when it invalidated the first federal Child Labor Act. The extent of child labor in the United States during the Progressive era was an affront to humanitarian sensibilities. One child out of six between the ages of ten and fifteen was a wage earner. Prohibition and regulation of child labor became the central reform initiatives of the progressive impulse. In 1916, overcoming constitutional doubts, Wilson signed the Keating-Owen Act, which forbade the shipment in interstate or foreign commerce of the products of mines where children sixteen and under had been employed, or of factories where children younger than fourteen worked, or where children fourteen to sixteen had worked more than eight hours a day, six days a week. Child labor was not directly forbidden, but was severely discouraged by closing the channels of interstate commerce.

A narrow majority of the Court, in an opinion by Justice Day, held that this law exceeded the federal commerce power. Day reasoned that the goods produced by child labor were in themselves harmless, and that the interstate transportation did not in itself accomplish any harm. This reasoning was entirely question-begging, because it was the possibility of interstate commerce that imposed a competitive disadvantage in states that outlawed child labor in comparison with less humanitarian states. Moreover, the reasoning was flatly inconsistent with the opinion in *Hipolite Egg* and *Hoke*. But the majority plainly regarded the federal child labor legislation as an invasion of the domestic preserves of the states. Holmes, joined by McKenna, Brandeis, and Clarke, issued a classic dissent.

With the preparations for an advent of American involvement in World War I, the Supreme Court recognized broad federal power to put the economy on a wartime footing. The burden of constitutional resistance to reform legislation shifted to cases involving state laws. Here the main hardening in doctrinal terms came in cases involving labor unions. Otherwise, a reasonable progressivism prevailed. Thus, in *Bunting* v. *Oregon* (1917) the Court upheld the maximum ten-hour day for all workers in mills and factories, whether men or women. However, two minimum wage cases from Oregon were upheld only by the fortuity of an equally divided Supreme Court, Brandeis having recused himself.

The most chilling warning to progressives that laissez-faire constitutionalism was not dead came in *Coppage* v. *Kansas* (1915). The issue was the power of a state to prohibit by legislation the so-called yellow dog contract, under which workers had to promise their employers not to join a union. The Court in *Coppage* held such laws unconstitutional: to limit an employer's freedom to offer employment on its own terms was a violation of freedom of contract.

The Supreme Court's race relations decisions between 1910 and 1921 constitute one of the Progressive era's most notable, and in some ways surprising, constitutional developments. Each of the Civil War amendments was given unprecedented application. For the

W

WHITE COURT
(1910–1921)

first time, in the *Grandfather Clause Cases* (1915), the Supreme Court applied the Fifteenth Amendment and what was left of the federal civil rights statutes to strike down state laws calculated to deny blacks the right to vote. For the first time, in *Bailey* v. *Alabama* (1911) and *United States* v. *Reynolds* (1914), the Court used the Thirteenth Amendment to strike down state laws that supported peonage by treating breach of labor contracts as criminal fraud and by encouraging indigent defendants to avoid the chain gang by having employers pay their fines in return for commitments to involuntary servitude. For the first time, in *Buchanan* v. *Warley* (1917), it found in the Fourteenth Amendment constitutional limits on the spread of laws requiring racial separation in residential areas of cities and towns, and also for the first time, in *McCabe* v. *Atchison, Topeka & Santa Fe Railway* (1914), it put some teeth in the equality side of the separate but equal doctrine by striking down an Oklahoma law that said that railroads need not provide luxury car accommodations for blacks on account of low demand.

To be sure, only with respect to peonage could the White Court be said to have dismantled the legal structure of racism in any fundamental way. After the White Court passed into history in 1921, blacks in the South remained segregated and stigmatized by Jim Crow laws, disfranchised by invidiously administered literacy tests, white primary elections, and poll taxes; and victimized by a criminal process from whose juries and other positions of power they were wholly excluded. But if the White Court did not stem the newly aggressive and self-confident ideology of racism inundating America in the Progressive era, neither did it put its power and prestige behind the flood, as had the Waite Court and Fuller Court that preceded it—and, at critical points, it resisted. The White Court's principled countercurrents were more symbols of hope than effective bulwarks against the racial prejudice that permeated American law. But the decisions

taken together mark the first time in American history that the Supreme Court opened itself in more than a passing way to the promises of the Civil War amendments.

World War I generated the first set of cases that provoked the Supreme Court for the first time since the First Amendment was ratified in 1791 to consider the meaning of freedom of expression. The cases, not surprisingly, involved dissent and agitation against the war policies of the United States. The war set off a major period of political repression against critics of American policy.

In the first three cases, *Schenck* v. *United States, Frohwerk* v. *United States,* and *In re Debs* (1919), following the lead of Justice Holmes, the Supreme Court looked not to the law of seditious libel for justification in punishing speech but rather to traditional principles of legal responsibility for attempted crimes. In English and American common law, an unsuccessful attempt to commit a crime could be punished if the attempt came dangerously close to success, while preparations for crime—in themselves harmless—could not be punished. With his gift of great utterance, Holmes distilled these doctrinal nuances into the rule that expression could be punished only if it created a clear and present danger of bringing about illegal action, such as draft resistance or curtailment of weapons production. Given his corrosive skepticism and his Darwinian sense of flux, the clear and present danger rule later became in Holmes's hands a fair protection for expression. But in the hands of judges and juries more passionate or anxious, measuring protection for expression by the likelihood of illegal action proved evanescent and unpredictable.

There were other problems with the clear and present danger rule. It took no account of the value of a particular expression, but considered only its tendency to cause harmful acts. Because the test was circumstantial, legislative declarations that certain types of speech were dangerous put the courts in the awkward position of having to second-guess the legislature's factual assessments of risk in order to protect the expression. This problem became clear to Holmes in *Abrams* v. *United States* (1919), in which a statute punishing speech that urged curtailment of war production was used to impose draconian sanctions on a group of radical Russian immigrants who had inveighed against manufacture of war material that was to be used in Russia. In this case, Holmes and Brandeis joined in one of the greatest statements of political tolerance ever uttered.

In 1921, the year Edward Douglass White died and Taft became Chief Justice, Benjamin Cardozo delivered his immortal lectures, "The Nature of the Judicial Process." Cardozo pleaded for judges to "search for light among the social elements of every kind that are the living forces behind the facts they deal with." The judge must be "the interpreter for the community of its sense of law and order . . . and harmonize results with justice through a method of free decision." Turning to the Supreme Court, Cardozo stated: "Above all in the field of constitutional law, the method of free decision has become, I think, the dominant one today."

In this view, we can see that Cardozo was too hopeful, although his statement may have been offered more as an admonition than a description. The method of "free decision," exemplified for Cardozo by the opinions of Holmes and Brandeis, remained in doubt notwithstanding the inconsistent progressivism of the White Court, and would become increasingly embattled in the decades to come.

—BENNO C. SCHMIDT, JR.

Bibliography

Bickel, Alexander M., and Schmidt, Benno C., Jr. (1984). *The Judiciary and Responsible Government 1910–1921*. Vol. 9 of *The Holmes Devise History of the Supreme Court.* New York: Macmillan.

Cardozo, Benjamin N. (1921). *The Nature of the Judicial Process*. New Haven, Conn.: Yale University Press.

Chafee, Zechariah (1949). *Free Speech in the United States.* Cambridge, Mass.: Harvard University Press.

Highsaw, Robert B. (1981). *Edward Douglass White*. Baton Rouge: Louisiana State University Press.

Semonche, John E. (1978). *Charting the Future: The Supreme Court Responds to a Changing Society 1890–1920*. Westport, Conn.: Greenwood Press.

Swindler, William F. (1969). *Court and Constitution in the 20th Century: The Old Legality 1889–1932*. Indianapolis: Bobbs-Merrill.

WHITNEY v. CALIFORNIA

274 U.S. 357 (1927)

Schenck v. *United States* (1919), *Abrams* v. *United States* (1919), *Gitlow* v. *New York* (1925), and *Whitney* are the four leading freedom of speech cases of the 1920s in which the clear and present danger rule was announced but then rejected by the majority in favor of the bad tendency test announced in *Gitlow*. In *Whitney*, Justice Edward Sanford repeated his *Gitlow* argument that a state law does not violate First Amendment rights by employing the "bad tendency" test as the standard of reasonableness in speech cases. The state may reasonably proscribe "utterances . . . tending to . . . endanger the foundations of organized government." Here Justice Sanford added that "united and joint action involves even greater danger to the public peace and security than the isolated utterances . . . of individuals." Miss Whitney had been convicted of organizing and becoming a member of an organization that advocated and taught criminal syndicalism in violation of the California Criminal Syndicalism Act of 1919. The Court upheld the act's constitutionality.

After *Schenck*, the clear and present danger position had been reiterated in dissenting opinions by Oliver Wendell Holmes and

Whitney is often cited for an addition by Brandeis to the original clear and present danger formula.

Louis D. Brandeis in *Abrams* and *Gitlow*. Brandeis, joined by Holmes, concurred in *Whitney*. Brandeis's reason for concurring rather than dissenting was that Whitney had not properly argued to the California courts that their failure to invoke the danger test was error, and that the Supreme Court might not correct errors by state courts unless those errors were properly raised below.

Brandeis's concurrence was a forceful reiteration of the value to a democracy of freedom of speech for even the most dissident speakers. The framers knew that "fear breeds repression; that repression breeds hate; that hate menaces stable government; that the path of safety lies in the opportunity to discuss freely supposed grievances . . . and that the fitting remedy for evil counsels is good ones." Brandeis reemphasized the imminence requirement of the danger rule. "To courageous, self-reliant men, with confidence in the power of free and fearless reasoning applied through the processes of popular government, no danger flowing from speech can be deemed clear and present, unless the incidence of the evil apprehended is so imminent that it may befall before there is opportunity for full discussion. If there be time . . . to avert the evil by the process of education, the remedy to be applied is more speech, not enforced silence."

Whitney is often cited for an addition by Brandeis to the original clear and present danger formula. The evil anticipated must be not only substantive but also serious. "The fact that speech is likely to result in some violence or in destruction of property is not enough to justify its suppression. There must be the probability of serious injury to the state. . . ."

The Court overruled *Whitney* in *Brandenburg* v. *Ohio* (1969).

—MARTIN SHAPIRO

WICKARD v. FILBURN

317 U.S. 111 (1942)

In 1941, by an amendment to the Agricultural Adjustment Act of 1938, Congress brought the national power to regulate the economy to a new extreme, yet the Supreme Court unanimously sustained the regulation in a far-reaching expansion of the commerce power. The price of wheat, despite marketing controls, had fallen. A bushel on the world market in 1941 sold for only forty cents as a result of a worldwide glut, and the wheat in American storage bins had reached record levels. To enable American growers to benefit from government fixed prices of $1.16 per bushel, Congress authorized the secretary of agriculture to fix production quotas for all wheat, even that consumed by individual growers. Filburn sowed twenty-three acres of wheat, despite his quota of only eleven, and produced an excess of 239 bushels for which the government imposed a penalty of forty-nine cents a bushel. Filburn challenged the constitutionality of the statute, arguing that it regulated production and consumption, both local in character; their effects upon interstate commerce, he maintained, were "indirect."

Justice Robert H. Jackson for the Court wrote that the question would scarcely merit consideration, given *United States* v. *Darby* (1941), "except for the fact that this Act extends federal regulation to production not intended in any part for commerce but wholly for consumption on the farm." The Court had never before decided whether such activities could be regulated "where no part of the product is intended for interstate commerce intermingled with the subjects thereof." Taking its law on the scope of the commerce power from *Gibbons* v. *Ogden* (1824) and the Shreveport Doctrine, the Court repudiated the use of mechanical legal formulas that ignored the reality of a national economic market; no longer would the reach of the commerce clause be limited by a finding that the regulated activity was "production" or its economic effects were "indirect." The rule laid down by Jackson, which still controls, is that even if an activity is local and not regarded as commerce, "it may still, whatever its nature, be reached by Congress if it exerts a substantial economic effect on interstate commerce, and this irrespective of whether such effect is what might at some earlier time have been defined as 'direct' or 'indirect.'"

How could the wheat grown by Filburn, which he fed to his own animals, used for his own food, and kept for next year's seed, be regarded as having a "substantial economic effect" on interstate commerce? Wheat consumed on the farm by its growers, the government had proved, amounted to over twenty percent of national production. Filburn consumed a "trivial" amount, but if he had not produced what he needed for his own use in excess of his allotted quota, he would have had to buy it. By not buying wheat, such producer-consumers depressed the price by cutting the demand. His own contribution to the demand for wheat was trivial, but "when taken with that of others similarly situated," it was significant. Congress had authorized quotas to increase the price of the commodity; wheat consumed on the farm where grown could burden a legitimate congressional purpose to stimulate demand and force up the price. Thus, even if a single bushel of Filburn's infinitesimal production never left

his farm, Congress could reach and regulate his activity, because all the Filburns, taken collectively, substantially affected commerce.

—LEONARD W. LEVY

Bibliography

Stern, Robert L. (1946). The Commerce Clause and the National Economy, 1933–1946. *Harvard Law Review* 59: 901–909.

WIDMAR v. VINCENT

454 U.S. 263 (1981)

In order to avoid activity that might constitute an establishment of religion, the University of Missouri at Kansas City barred a student religious group from meeting on the campus for religious teaching or worship. The Supreme Court, 8–1, held that the University, having "created a forum generally open for use by student groups," was forbidden by the First Amendment's guarantee of the freedom of speech to exclude the religious group. Because the exclusion was based on the content of the group's speech, it was

Congress authorized the secretary of agriculture to fix production quotas for all wheat, even that consumed by individual growers.

See also

Gibbons v. *Ogden*

WILLIAMS v. FLORIDA

399 U.S. 78 (1970)

The rule of *Williams* is that trial by a jury of six in a noncapital felony case does not violate the constitutional right to trial by jury in a state prosecution. Trial by jury had historically meant trial by a jury of twelve, neither more nor less. Justice Byron R. White for the Supreme Court found no rationale for the figure of twelve, which he called "accidental" and "superstitious." If Congress enacted a statute providing for juries of less than twelve in federal prosecutions, the Sixth Amendment would be no bar, according to this case. A jury of six is practical: it can be selected in half the time, costs only half as much, and may reach its verdict more quickly. According to White, "There is no discernible difference between the results reached by the two different-sized juries," but in fact a jury of six hangs less frequently, significantly changes the probability of conviction, and convicts different persons. White claimed that the size of the jury should be large enough to promote group deliberation and allow for a representative cross-section of the community, and he claimed that a jury of six serves those functions as well as a jury of twelve. In fact the Court was wrong. Only Justice Thurgood Marshall dissented on the question of jury size, in an opinion that rested strictly on precedent. *Williams* also contended that Florida violated his right against self-incrimination by its notice-of-alibi rule, but he convinced only Justices Hugo L. Black and William O. Douglas.

LEONARD W. LEVY

*In Mississippi at
that time, a black
graduate of
Harvard Law School
could not satisfy
white officials'
standards for voting
registration.*

See also

Racial Discrimination

unconstitutional unless necessary to serve a compelling state interest. The exclusion was not necessary to avoid establishment clause problems, for no state sponsorship of religion was implied when the university provided a forum generally open to all student groups.

Justice John Paul Stevens, concurring, said that any university necessarily makes many distinctions based on speech content. Here, however, the university discriminated on the basis of the viewpoint of particular speakers, and that was forbidden by the First Amendment.

Justice Byron R. White dissented, arguing that the state could constitutionally "attempt to disentangle itself from religious worship."

—KENNETH L. KARST

WILLIAMS v. MISSISSIPPI

170 U.S. 213 (1898)

Williams is a realistic snapshot of our constitutional law on race at the turn of the century. A black man was tried in Mississippi for the murder of a white, convicted by an all-white jury, and sentenced to death. He alleged that he had been denied the equal protection of the laws guaranteed by the Fourteenth Amendment, because the laws of the state were rigged in such a way as to exclude members of his race from jury service. In Mississippi, to be eligible for jury service one must be qualified to vote. To be a voter one must have paid his poll tax and have satisfied registration officials that he could not only pass a literacy test but also could understand or reasonably interpret any clause of the state constitution; registration officials had sole discretion to decide whether an applicant had the requisite understanding. In Mississippi at that time, a black graduate of Harvard Law School could not satisfy white officials. The state convention of 1890 clearly adopted new qualifications on the right to vote in order to insure white supremacy by disfranchising black voters. Under prior laws there were

190,000 black voters; by 1892 only 8,600 remained, and these were soon eliminated. Blacks disappeared from jury lists after 1892.

A unanimous Supreme Court, speaking through Justice Joseph McKenna, held that the state constitution and laws passed under it, prescribing the qualifications of voters and jurors, did not on their face discriminate racially. McKenna also declared that the discretion vested in state and local officials who managed elections and selected juries, while affording the opportunity for unconstitutional racial discrimination, was not constitutionally excessive. Yet McKenna said, "We gather . . . that this discretion can be and has been exercised against the colored race, and from these lists jurors are selected." The Court recognized that a law on its face might be impartial and be administered "with an evil eye and an unequal hand," but it held that "it has not been shown that their actual administration was evil; only that evil was possible under them."

LEONARD W. LEVY

WIRETAPPING

Telephone tapping is probably the best known form of electronic surveillance. The Supreme Court originally ruled in *Olmstead* v. *United States* (1928) that neither the Fifth nor the Fourth Amendment could be used to control wiretapping. In *Katz* v. *United States* (1967), however, the Supreme Court declared that what people reasonably expect to keep private is entitled to constitutional protection under the Fourth Amendment.

Both before and after the *Katz* decision, wiretapping was regulated by statute. Between 1934 and 1968, Section 605 of the Communications Act prohibited virtually all wiretapping except for national security purposes. The Justice Department construed the statute so narrowly, however, that it had little effect: federal and state officials tapped extensively, as did private parties, and there were few prosecutions.

In 1968 Congress enacted Title III of the Omnibus Crime Control and Safe Streets Act, which prohibits telephone tapping except by federal and state officials who obtain prior judicial approval. Before issuing such approval, the court must have probable cause to believe that evidence of a specific crime listed in the statute, and relating to a particular person, will be found by tapping a specific phone. Interceptions must be minimized, and notice of the interception must ultimately be given to the target of the surveillance.

Critics claim that the minimization and judicial supervision requirements are ineffective, that wiretapping is inherently indiscriminate, and that it is of little value for major crimes. Proponents assert that the technique is useful, and that the procedural protections are effective.

Wiretapping within the United States to obtain foreign national security intelligence is governed by the Foreign Intelligence Surveillance Act (1978), which creates a special warrant procedure for judicial issuance of permission to wiretap. Both wiretap statutes have been held constitutional.

— HERMAN SCHWARTZ

Bibliography

Schwartz, Herman (1977). *Taps, Bugs, and Fooling the People.* New York: Field Foundation.

WISCONSIN v. YODER

406 U.S. 205 (1972)

Wisconsin's school-leaving age was sixteen. Members of the Old Order Amish religion declined, on religious grounds, to send their children to school beyond the eighth grade. Wisconsin chose to force the issue, and counsel for the Amish defendants replied that while the requirement might be valid as to others, the free exercise clause of the First Amendment required exemption in the case of the Amish.

Chief Justice Warren E. Burger, speaking for the Supreme Court, was much impressed by the Amish way of life. He rejected Wisconsin's argument that belief but not action was protected by the free exercise clause, and cited *Sherbert* v. *Verner* (1963). Nor was the Chief Justice convinced by the state's assertion of a compelling state interest. Nothing indicated that Amish children would suffer from the lack of high school education. Burger stressed that the Amish would have lost had they based their claim on "subjective evaluations and rejections of the contemporary social values accepted by the majority."

Justice Byron R. White filed a concurring opinion in which Justices William J. Brennan and Potter Stewart joined. White found the issue in *Yoder* much closer than Burger. White pointed out that many Amish children left the religious fold upon attaining their majority and had to make their way in the larger world like everyone else.

Justice William O. Douglas dissented in part. He saw the issue as one of children's rights in which Frieda Yoder's personal feelings and desires should be determinative. Justice Stewart, joined by Justice Brennan, filed a brief concurrence which took issue with Douglas on this point, and noted that there was nothing in the record that indicated that the religious beliefs of the children in the case differed in any way from those of the parents.

—RICHARD E. MORGAN

WITTERS v. WASHINGTON DEPARTMENT OF SERVICES FOR THE BLIND

474 U.S. 481 (1986)

Suffering from a progressive eye condition, Witters sought state financial assistance to

Chief Justice Burger rejected Wisconsin's argument that belief but not action was protected by the free exercise clause.

See also

Sherbert v. *Verner*

W

WOLF v. COLORADO

338 U.S. 25 (1949)

In this case it would be inappropriate to view the funds ultimately flowing to the Bible college as the result of state action to aid religion.

attend a Bible college to prepare himself for a career as a minister. Washington State generally provided aid to visually handicapped persons seeking education or training for careers so they could be self-supporting. Nevertheless, the state denied Witters aid, citing the Washington State constitution's prohibition of public aid to religion. The state supreme court upheld the denial, but on establishment clause grounds, holding that aid to Witters would advance religion as its primary effect and thus violate the second prong of the *Lemon* test. The U.S. Supreme Court unanimously reversed.

Writing the opinion of the Court, Justice Thurgood Marshall said it would be inappropriate to view the funds ultimately flowing to the Bible college in this case as the result of state action to aid religion. Marshall noted that the financial assistance "is paid directly to the student, who transmits it to the educational institution of his or her choice. Any aid provided under Washington's program that ultimately flows to religious institutions does so only as a result of the genuinely independent and private choices of aid recipients." Marshall further emphasized that the program "is in no way skewed toward religion" and "creates no financial incentive for students to undertake sectarian education." Finally, Marshall stressed that nothing indicated any significant proportion of state money provided under the program would flow to religious institutions if Witters's claim was granted.

That last reason was not dispositive for a majority of Justices, five of whom joined concurring opinions that noted the applicability of *Mueller* v. *Allen* (1983) to *Witters*. In *Mueller* the Court had upheld general tax deductions for certain school expenses, despite the fact that over 90 percent of these tax benefits went to those who sent their children to religious schools.

—JOHN G. WEST, JR.

WOLF v. COLORADO

338 U.S. 25 (1949)

In *Wolf* the Supreme Court held that "the core" of the Fourth Amendment's freedom from unreasonable searches was "basic" and thus incorporated in the Fourteenth Amendment as a restriction on searches by state officers, but that its enforcement feature, the exclusionary rule (in effect for federal trials since 1914), was not. The refusal to require the exclusionary rule for state trials was largely based on considerations of federalism. The Court reasoned, first, that the exclusionary rule could scarcely be considered "basic" when the common law rule of admissibility was still followed both in the English-speaking world outside the United States and in most of the American states, and second, that suits in tort against offending officers could be "equally effective" in deterring unlawful searches. The experience of the following twelve years proved the suit in tort to be a paper remedy rather than an effective sanction, leading the Court to overrule *Wolf* and impose the exclusionary rule on the states in *Mapp* v. *Ohio* (1961).

—JACOB W. LANDYNSKI

WYGANT v. JACKSON BOARD OF EDUCATION

476 U.S. 267 (1986)

Although the *Wygant* decision did not produce a majority opinion, it advanced the growth of constitutional doctrine governing affirmative action. A school board and a teachers' union had approved an affirmative action plan as a response to complaints of past racial discrimination in the hiring of teachers. To maintain minority-hiring gains in the event of a contraction in teacher employment, the plan protected some minority teachers against layoffs. When some minor-

See also

Establishment Clause

Mueller v. *Allen*

PUBLIC INTEREST

A snaking line to the Supreme Court forms as interested spectators hope to hear arguments in an affirmative action case. (Corbis/Bettmann)

ity teachers were retained while some nonminority teachers with greater seniority were laid off, the laid-off teachers challenged the layoff provision in federal court. By a 5–4 vote, the Supreme Court held the provision a violation of the equal protection of the laws.

Justice Lewis F. Powell, for four Justices, concluded that the appropriate standard of review was strict scrutiny. Using this standard, he rejected the lower courts' two justifications for the layoff provision: as a means of keeping minority teachers to serve as role

967

Wygant *was a way
station on the road
to* Richmond
(City of) *v.*
J. A. Croson Co.

models for students and as a remedy for past societal discrimination. He agreed that past discrimination by the school board itself was a compelling state interest that would justify some race-conscious remedies, assuming that the board had evidentiary support for determining that remedial action was warranted. Here no such determination had been made, but Justice Powell was unwilling to remand the case for exploration of this issue. Even if the purpose were remedial, he concluded, the layoff provision was an impermissible remedy because it was too burdensome on innocent nonminority teachers. Preferential hiring, he intimated, would be acceptable; layoffs, however, placed the whole burden on particular individuals.

Justice Sandra Day O'Connor concurred separately to emphasize that a public employer that wished to adopt an affirmative action plan need not make a contemporaneous finding of past wrongdoing. Such a requirement would undermine the employer's incentive to meet its civil rights obligations. Rather, the employer could show "a disparity between the percentage of qualified blacks on a school's teaching staff and the percentage of qualified minorities in the relevant labor pool" that would support a prima facie case of employment discrimination under Title VII of the Civil Rights Act of 1964. Justice Byron R. White added a brief concurrence emphasizing the difference between a hiring preference and a preference in avoiding layoffs.

Justice Thurgood Marshall dissented, joined by Justices William J. Brennan, Jr. and Harry A. Blackmun. Marshall argued that the case should be remanded to the trial court for further findings about the board's past discrimination, but also disagreed with the majority Justices' disposition on the merits. The board's interest in preserving a valid policy for affirmative action in hiring, he argued, was a sufficient state purpose, and the layoff provision was sufficiently narrowly tailored to pass the test of constitutionality. Justice John Paul Stevens also dissented, arguing that the

board's interest in educating children justified measures to assure a racially integrated faculty, irrespective of any showing of past discrimination.

Wygant was a way station on the road to *Richmond* v. *J. A. Croson Co.* (1989), in which a majority of the Supreme Court explicitly adopted the rhetoric of strict scrutiny for reviewing state-sponsored affirmative action programs. Justice Powell's and Justice O'Connor's opinions, taken together, also provided a "how to do it" manual for public employers that want to adopt affirmative-action plans for achieving integrated work forces.

—KENNETH L. KARST

Bibliography

Karst, Kenneth L. (1989). *Belonging to America: Equal Citizenship and the Constitution,* pages 158–167. New Haven, Conn.: Yale University Press.

Sullivan, Kathleen (1986). Sins of Discrimination: Last Term's Affirmative Action Cases. *Harvard Law Review* 100:78–98.

WYNEHAMER v. PEOPLE OF NEW YORK

13 N.Y. 378 (1856)

Although out of joint with its times, *Wynehamer* became a classic case of pre-1937 American constitutional history, exemplifying our constitutional law as a law of judicially implied limitations on legislative powers, drawn from the due process clause for the benefit of vested rights. The case involved the constitutionality of a state prohibition act. More than a dozen states had such legislation before the Civil War. The New York law involved in *Wynehamer* prohibited the sale of intoxicating liquor and the possession of liquors for sale, and it ordered the forfeiture and destruction of existing supplies as public nuisances. The fundamental issue raised by such legislation was whether property that had not been taken for a public use could be destroyed in the name of the public health and morals, without any compensation to the owner. Everywhere, except in New York, the state courts held that a mere license to sell liquor was not a contract in the meaning of the contract clause, and that a charter to make and sell liquor was subject to the reserved police power to alter, amend, or repeal it. Moreover, liquor, like explosives or narcotics, was a peculiar kind of property, dangerous to the public safety, morals, and health. Legislatures could never relinquish their control over such matters, not even by a contract in the form of a charter. As Chief Justice Roger B. Taney had said in the 1847 *License Cases,* nothing in the United States Constitution prevented a state from regulating the liquor traffic "or from prohibiting it altogether."

The New York Court of Appeals, however, held the state prohibition statute unconstitutional on the grounds that it violated the due process clause of the state constitution. The various opinions of the state judges used the novel concept of substantive due process about half a century before the Supreme Court of the United States accepted that concept. The conventional and previously sole understanding of due process had been that it referred to regularized and settled procedures insuring mainly a fair accusation, hearing, and conviction. And, the doctrine of vested rights notwithstanding, the orthodox view of the police power authorized the legislature, as Chief Justice Lemuel Shaw of Massachusetts had said, "to declare the possession of certain articles of property . . . unlawful because they would be injurious, dangerous, and noxious; and by due process of law, by proceeding in rem, to provide both for the abatement of the nuisance and for the punishment of the offender, by the seizure and confiscation of the property, by the removal, sale or destruction of the noxious article" (*Fisher v. McGirr,* 1854). Accordingly the opinion of the New York court was startling

when it said, "All property is alike in the characteristic of inviolability. If the legislature has no power to confiscate and destroy property in general, it has no such power over any particular species." The court showed that the prohibition statute simply annihilated existing property right in liquors. The crucial lines of the opinion declared that the right not to be deprived of life, liberty, or property without due process of law "necessarily imports that the legislature cannot make the mere existence of the rights secured the occasion of depriving a person of any of them, even by the forms which belong to 'due process of law.' For if it does not necessarily import this, then the legislative power is absolute."

Thus even if the legislature provided all the forms of due process by laying down proper procedures for prosecuting violators of the statute, as in this case, due process had still been denied. The court, in effect, looked at the substance of the statute, found it denied persons of their property, and then held it unconstitutional for denying "due process," even if it did not deny due process. One can make sense out of this by realizing that the court had rewritten the due process clause to mean that property cannot be deprived with or without due process. The Court in effect red-penciled the due process clause out of the constitution, or as Edward S. Corwin said, *Wynehamer* stands for "nothing less than the elimination of the very phrase under construction from the constitutional clause in which it occurs." The difficulty, however, is that the court had to its own mind kept and relied on the due process clause. It added a new meaning to supplement the old one. It constitutionally changed process into substance by holding that the statute's infirmity lay in what it did, not how it did it. Due process as a substantive limitation on legislative powers was then an absurd concept. Substantive process was oxymoronic, like thunderous silence.

Another way of understanding *Wynehamer*'s substantive due process is to realize that the court believed that due process had

Wynehamer, *an aberration at the time, was everywhere repudiated yet destined for ultimate acceptance by the highest court of the land.*

**WYNEHAMER
v. PEOPLE
OF NEW YORK**

13 N.Y. 378 (1856)

substance. The court in effect accused the legislature of retaining the forms of due process without its substance, that is, of providing mere empty formalities and labeling them due process, because the effective deprivation of property was not by judicial process but by legislative fiat.

Wynehamer, an aberration at the time, was everywhere repudiated yet destined for ultimate acceptance by the highest court of the land and destined, too, to become the source of a major doctrine in American constitutional history.

—LEONARD W. LEVY

Bibliography

Corwin, Edward S. (1948). *Liberty against Government.* Chap. 3. Baton Rouge: Louisiana State University Press.

Mott, Rodney L. (1926). *Due Process of Law.* Pages 311–326. Indianapolis: Bobbs-Merrill.

Y

YARBROUGH, EX PARTE

110 U.S. 651 (1884)

This is the only nineteenth-century case in which the Supreme Court sustained the power of the United States to punish private persons for interfering with voting rights. Yarbrough and other members of the Ku Klux Klan assaulted a black citizen who voted in a congressional election. The United States convicted the Klansmen under a federal statute making it a crime to conspire to injure or intimidate any citizen in the free exercise of any right secured to him by the laws of the United States. The Court, in a unanimous opinion by Justice Samuel F. Miller, held that the United States "must have the power to protect the elections on which its existence depends, from violence and corruption." Miller's reasoning is confused. Congress had passed the statute in contemplation of its power to enforce the Fourteenth Amendment. In *United States* v. *Cruikshank* (1876) the Court had ruled that

ELECTION INTERFERENCE

In Yarbrough, *members of the Ku Klux Klan were convicted for assaulting a black citizen who voted in a congressional election. (Corbis/Hutlon-Deutsch Collection)*

This is the only nineteenth-century case in which the Supreme Court sustained the power of the United States to punish private persons for interfering with voting rights.

Without formally repudiating the "sliding scale" set forth in the Dennis *opinion, the Court erected a stern new standard for evaluating convictions under the Smith Act.*

See also

Clear and Present Danger

Dennis v. United States

the same statute could not reach private, rather than state, actions. Miller thought the situation different when Congress sought to protect rights constitutionally conferred, and he stressed Article I, section 4, which empowered Congress to alter state regulations for the election of members of Congress. But that provision did not apply here. In *United States* v. *Reese* (1876) the Court had ruled that the Fifteenth Amendment did not confer the right to vote on anyone, but only a right to be free from racial discrimination in voting. Here, however, Miller ruled that "under some circumstances," the Fifteenth Amendment, which was not the basis of the statute, may operate as the source of a right to vote. In the end Miller declared, "But it is a waste of time to seek for specific sources of the power to pass these laws." In *James* v. *Bowman* (1903), involving the right to vote in a federal election, the Court held unconstitutional an act of Congress without reference to *Yarbrough.*

—LEONARD W. LEVY

YATES v.
UNITED STATES

354 U.S. 298 (1957)

Following *Dennis* v. *United States* (1951), Smith Act conspiracy prosecutions were brought against all second-rank United States Communist party officials, and convictions were secured in every case brought to trial between 1951 and 1956. In June 1957, however, the Supreme Court, in *Yates,* reversed the convictions of fourteen West Coast party leaders charged with Smith Act violations. The Court, speaking through Justice John Marshall Harlan, declared that the *Dennis* decision had been misunderstood. The Smith Act did not outlaw advocacy of the abstract doctrine of violent overthrow, because such advocacy was too remote from concrete action to be regarded as the kind of

indoctrination preparatory to action condemned in *Dennis.* The essential distinction, Harlan argued, was that those to whom the advocacy was addressed had to be urged to *do* something, now or in the future, rather than merely *believe* in something. Without formally repudiating the "sliding scale" reformulation of clear and present danger set forth in the *Dennis* opinion, the Court erected a stern new standard for evaluating convictions under the Smith Act, making conviction under the measure difficult. As to indictments for involvement in organizing the Communist party in the United States, the Court also took a narrow view. Organizing, Harlan maintained, was only the original act of creating such a group, not any continuing process of proselytizing and recruiting. Since the indictments had been made some years following the postwar organizing of their party, the federal three-year statute of limitations had run out. The Court cleared five of the defendants, remanding the case of nine others for retrial. The ruling brought an abrupt end to the main body of Smith Act prosecutions then under way.

—PAUL L. MURPHY

YICK WO v. HOPKINS

118 U.S. 356 (1886)

This is one of the basic decisions interpreting the equal protection of the laws clause of the Fourteenth Amendment. A San Francisco ordinance made criminal the conduct of a laundry business in any building not made of stone or brick, with such exceptions for wooden structures as administrative officials might make. Officials used their discretion in a grossly discriminatory manner, licensing about eighty wooden laundries run by Caucasians and denying licenses to about two hundred applicants of Chinese extraction. The Supreme Court unanimously held, in an opinion by Justice Stanley Matthews, that the ordinance, though racially neutral on its face, was applied so unequally and oppressively by public authorities as to deny equal protection. Thus the Court looked beyond the law's terms to its racially discriminatory administration and applied the benefits of the Fourteenth Amendment to Oriental aliens, that is, "to all persons . . . without regard to any difference of race, of color, or of nationality."

—LEONARD W. LEVY

YOUNG, EX PARTE

209 U.S. 123 (1908)

The question in this case—one of the most important of the present century—was whether a citizen might resort to a federal court to vindicate a constitutional right against state infringement and, pending a final judgment, obtain freedom from civil or criminal suits by a temporary injunction directed to an officer of the state. The Supreme Court held that, the Eleventh Amendment notwithstanding, a federal court might issue such an injunction.

A Minnesota statute fixed railroad rates and (to deter institution of a test case) made the officers and employees of the railroads personally liable to heavy fines and imprisonment if those rates were exceeded. A stockholder's suit in equity was filed in federal Circuit Court to prevent enforcement of or compliance with the statute, on the ground that it violated the Fourteenth Amendment by depriving the railroads of property without due process of law. The federal court issued a temporary injunction restraining the state attorney general, Edward T. Young, from taking steps to enforce the statute. When Young defied the injunction the court found him in contempt and committed him to the custody of the United States marshal.

Young petitioned the Supreme Court for a writ of habeas corpus, contending that the suit for injunction was really against the state and that, under the Eleventh Amendment, the state could not be sued in federal court without its consent. The Court denied Young's petition, Justice John Marshall Harlan alone dissenting.

Justice Rufus Peckham, for the Court, argued that if the Minnesota law was unconstitutional, then Young, attempting to enforce it, was stripped of his official character and became merely a private individual using the state's name to further his own illegitimate end. Incongruously, the end Young was furthering was unconstitutional only because it involved state action. The "private wrong" was a fiction adopted by the Court to circumvent the Eleventh Amendment.

Congress reacted to the *Young* decision by passing a law (substantially repealed in 1976)

The question in this case was one of the most important of the century.

YOUNG v. AMERICAN MINI THEATRES, INC.

427 U.S. 50 (1976)

In *Young* v. *American Mini Theatres, Inc.* the Supreme Court upheld a Detroit zoning ordinance requiring adult theaters to be located certain distances from residential areas and specified businesses. Four Justices led by Justice John Paul Stevens argued that adult movies ranked low in the hierarchy of First Amendment values. Four dissenting Justices led by Justice Potter Stewart argued that the First Amendment recognized no hierarchy for types of protected speech. Justice Lewis F. Powell agreed with the dissent, but voted to uphold the ordinance, arguing that the theater owners had asserted no First Amendment interest of their own and that the First Amendment interests of others, including moviemakers and potential audiences, were not endangered.

—STEVEN SHIFFRIN

Four Justices led by Justice John Paul Stevens argued that adult movies ranked low in the hierarchy of First Amendment values.

One of the two reasons for this decision was that the national government should avoid intruding into "the legitimate activities of the state."

requiring that federal court injunctions against enforcement of state laws alleged to be unconstitutional issue only from special three-judge courts and providing, in such cases, for direct appeal to the Supreme Court.

The doctrine of *Young* remains valid law today. Although it originally arose in connection with due process protection of economic liberty, the doctrine provides a remedy for state action infringing civil rights or civil liberties. But the doctrine of *Young* applies only to equitable relief, and the Eleventh Amendment remains bar to actions for monetary damages that will be paid out of the state treasury.

—DENNIS J. MAHONEY

YOUNGER v. HARRIS

401 U.S. 37 (1971)

Harris, indicted under California's criminal syndicalism law, sought a federal court injunction to compel the district attorney to cease prosecution in the state court. The district court held the law unconstitutional and issued the injunction. The Supreme Court reversed, 8–1, severely limiting *Dombrowski v. Pfister* (1965).

Justice Hugo L. Black, for the Court, rested decision on two interlocking grounds. First, a state prosecution was pending; because any claim that the underlying state law was unconstitutional could be made in the state proceeding, there was no "irreparable injury" to justify an injunction. Second, the national government should avoid intruding into "the legitimate activities of the state." Although a federal court might enjoin a state prosecution commenced in bad faith to harass the exercise of First Amendment rights, the claim that the law was unconstitutional on its face did not satisfy this bad-faith harassment requirement.

After *Younger,* the California courts held the syndicalism law invalid.

—KENNETH L. KARST

YOUNGSTOWN SHEET & TUBE CO. v. SAWYER

343 U.S. 579 (1952)

In a landmark restriction on presidential power, the Supreme Court in 1952 held invalid President Harry S Truman's seizure of the steel mills. Justice Hugo L. Black, joined by five other Justices, delivered the opinion of the Court. Chief Justice Fred M. Vinson, dissenting with Justices Stanley F. Reed and Sherman Minton, believed that military and economic emergencies justified Truman's action.

Each of the five concurring Justices wrote separate opinions, advancing different views of the president's emergency power. Only Justices Black and William O. Douglas insisted on specific constitutional or statutory authority to support presidential seizure of private property. Assigning the lawmaking function exclusively to Congress, they allowed the president a role only in recommending or vetoing laws. On existing precedent, this concept of the separation of powers doctrine was far too rigid. Previous presidents had engaged directly in the lawmaking function without express constitutional or statutory authority, often with the acquiescence and even blessing of Congress and the courts.

The other four concurring Justices (Felix Frankfurter, Robert H. Jackson, Harold Burton, and Tom C. Clark) did not draw such a strict line between the executive and legislative branches, nor did they try to delimit the president's authority to act in future emergencies. Frankfurter thought it inadvisable to attempt a comprehensive definition of presidential power, based on abstract principles, without admitting powers that had evolved by custom: a "systematic, unbroken, executive practice, long pursued to the knowledge of the Congress and never before questioned . . . may be treated as a gloss on 'executive Power.'" Burton withheld opinion on the president's constitutional power when facing an "imminent invasion or threatened attack," while Clark agreed that the Constitution gave the president extensive authority in time of grave and imperative national emergency.

Jackson identified three categories of presidential power, ranging from actions based on express or implied congressional authorization (putting executive authority at its maximum) to executive measures that were incompatible with congressional policy (reducing presidential power to its lowest ebb). In between lay a "zone of twilight" in which president and Congress shared authority. Jackson said that congressional inertia, indifference, or acquiescence might enable, if not invite, independent presidential action. He further argued that the enumerated powers of the president required "scope and elasticity" and said he would "indulge the widest latitude of interpretation" when presidential powers were turned against the outside world for the security of the United States.

Considering the four concurrences and three dissents, the *Steel Seizure Case* was far from a repudiation of the inherent power doctrine. Nevertheless, a majority of the Court did reach agreement on important principles: presidential actions, including those of an "emergency" nature, are subject to judicial review; the courts may enjoin executive officers from carrying out presidential orders that conflict with statutory policy or the Constitution; and independent presidential powers in domestic affairs are especially vulnerable to judicial scrutiny when Congress has adopted a contrary statutory policy. The *Steel Seizure Case* has supplied the Supreme Court with an important precedent for curbing subsequent exercises of presidential power in areas such as the *Pentagon Papers Case* (*New York Times* v. *United States,* 1971), electronic surveillance, impoundment, and executive privilege.

—LOUIS FISHER

Bibliography

Marcus, Maeva (1977). *Truman and the Steel Seizure Case: The Limits of Presidential Power.* New York: Columbia University Press.

Westin, Alan F. (1958). *The Anatomy of a Constitutional Law Case.* New York: Macmillan.

Y

YOUNGSTOWN SHEET & TUBE CO. v. SAWYER

343 U.S. 579 (1952)

This landmark restriction on presidential power disallowed President Harry S Truman's seizure of the steel mills.

See also

New York Times v. *United States*

ENUMERATED POWERS

Instead of establishing a national government with a general power to do whatever it might deem in the public interest, the Constitution lists the authorized powers of Congress. The chief source of these "enumerated powers" is Article I, section 8, which authorizes Congress to regulate commerce among the several states, tax and spend, raise and support military forces, and so on. This enumeration has been supplemented by other grants, including authority to enforce the Civil War Amendments.

The enumeration of powers has both a negative and a positive implication. Enumerating or specifying powers implies that some of government's ordinary concerns are beyond the constitutional competence of the national government. This implication is made explicit by the Tenth Amendment. Nevertheless, the founding generation wanted to solve such specific problems as commercial hostility among the states and an unpaid war debt. When *The Federalist* defended the proposed national powers it cited the desiderata that might be achieved through their successful exercise. The enumeration of powers thus implies affirmative responsibilities as well as limited concerns. These competing implications are associated with competing approaches to constitutional interpretation and different conceptions of the normative character of the Constitution as a whole. As a reminder of a line between national and state powers, the enumeration of powers suggests Thomas Jefferson's view of the Constitution as a contract between sovereign states to be construed with an eye to preserving state prerogatives. As a reminder of affirmative responsibilities the enumeration suggests John Marshall's view of the Constitution as a charter of government to be construed in ways that permit achievement of the social objectives it envisions. History has not favored the Jeffersonian view.

ZABLOCKI v. REDHAIL

434 U.S. 374 (1978)

In *Loving* v. *Virginia* (1967) the Supreme Court had struck down a miscegenation statute flatly forbidding interracial marriage, resting decision on both equal protection and substantive due process grounds. In *Zablocki* the Court protected the "right to marry" in a setting where race was irrelevant. Wisconsin required a court's permission for the marriage of a resident parent who had been ordered to support a child not in his or her custody. Permission would be granted only when the candidate proved compliance with the support obligation and showed that the children were not likely to become public charges. Because he could not comply with the law, Redhail was denied a marriage license. The Supreme Court held, 8–1, that this denial was unconstitutional.

The case produced six opinions. Justice Thurgood Marshall, for the majority, rested on equal protection grounds. Marriage was a fundamental interest, protected by the constitutional right of privacy. The Wisconsin law interfered "directly and substantially" with the right to marry and was not necessary to effectuate important state interests. Justice Potter Stewart concurred on due process grounds. Justice Lewis F. Powell, also concurring, objected to the Court's strict scrutiny test; such an inquiry would cast doubt on such limits on marriage as "bans on incest, bigamy, and homosexuality, as well as various preconditions to marriage, such as blood tests." Using a more relaxed standard of review, he nonetheless found the statute wanting on both due process and equal protection grounds. Justice John Paul Stevens con-

curred, calling the law a "clumsy and deliberate legislative discrimination between the rich and poor" whose irrationality violated equal protection. Justice William H. Rehnquist, in lone dissent, rejected the notion that marriage was a "fundamental" right and argued for the strict judicial nonscrutiny that had become his trademark.

For all the diversity of the Justices' views, little turns on the choice between equal protection and due process grounds, or on conclusory assertions about the proper standard of review. *Zablocki* makes clear that significant state interference with the freedom to marry demands correspondingly weighty justification.

—KENNETH L. KARST

> *Zablocki makes clear that significant state interference with the freedom to marry demands weighty justification.*

ZORACH v. CLAUSEN

343 U.S. 306 (1952)

This was the Supreme Court's second encounter with a released time program. In *McCollum* v. *Board of Education* (1948), the Court had invalidated an arrangement by which teachers entered public schools to provide religious instruction. *Zorach* involved New York City's released time program in which instruction was offered off school premises. According to the requests of their parents, public school children were allowed to leave school for specific periods of time to go to church facilities. Nonparticipating students remained in their regular classrooms.

Justice William O. Douglas delivered the opinion of the Court sustaining the constitutionality of New York's program. Douglas emphasized that, as opposed to *McCollum*, no public facilities were used. The schools,

> *The Court ruled a New York program allowing children to leave school to go to church facilities to be constitutional.*

See also
Loving v. *Virginia*
Right of Privacy
Strict Scrutiny

Douglas said, were merely rearranging their schedules to accommodate the needs of religious people.

Justices Hugo L. Black, Robert H. Jackson, and Felix Frankfurter dissented. Black and Jackson argued that children were compelled by law to attend public schools and that to release them for religious instruction used governmental compulsion to promote religion. In a slap at Douglas's presumed presidential ambitions, Jackson said, "Today's judgment will be more interesting to students of psychology and of the judicial process than to students of constitutional law."

—RICHARD E. MORGAN

ZURCHER v. STANFORD DAILY

436 U.S. 547 (1978)

In *Zurcher* v. *Stanford Daily* the police chief of Palo Alto, California, appealed from a federal district court decision declaring that a search of a college newspaper's office conducted pursuant to a duly authorized search warrant had infringed upon Fourth Amendment and First Amendment rights. There was no contention that the newspaper or any of its staff was reasonably suspected of the commission of a crime, nor was it contended that weapons, contraband, or fruits of a crime were likely to be found on the premises. Rather, the police secured a warrant on a showing of probable cause for the conclusion that photographic evidence of a crime was to be found somewhere on the premises. The Supreme Court thus addressed the general question of the standards that should govern the issuance of warrants to search the premises of persons not themselves suspected of criminal activity and the specific question whether any different standards should apply to press searches.

The Court ruled that the innocence of the party to be searched was of no constitutional importance. So long as there was probable cause to believe that evidence of a crime was

The Court addressed the standards that should govern the issuance of warrants to search the premises of persons not themselves suspected.

See also

Mere Evidence Rule

Search and Seizure

to be found on premises particularly described, no further showing was needed. Specifically, the Court declined to "reconstrue the Fourth Amendment" to require a showing that it would be impracticable to secure a subpoena *duces tecum* before a warrant could be issued.

That the party to be searched was a newspaper the Court regarded as of some moment but not enough to prefer subpoenas over warrants. Instead, the Court observed that warrant requirements should be applied with "particular exactitude when First Amendment interests would be endangered by the search."

The Court expressed confidence that magistrates would safeguard the interests of the press. Magistrates could guard against the type of intrusions that might interfere with the timely publication of a newspaper or otherwise deter normal editorial and publication decisions. Nor, said the Court, "will there be any occasion or opportunity for officers to rummage at large in newspaper files." The Court asserted that "the warrant in this case authorized nothing of this sort." Yet, as the *Zurcher* opinion discloses, the police searched "the Daily's photographic laboratories, filing cabinets, desks, and wastepaper baskets." The Court's application of the particular exactitude standard seems neither particular nor exact.

Zurcher is the first case squarely to authorize the search and seizure of mere evidence from an innocent party; it has raised difficult questions of Fourth Amendment reasonableness as applied to searches of other innocent third parties such as lawyers and judges. By suggesting that press values be considered in an assessment of reasonableness, it opens the door for further distinctions between searches of media and nonmedia persons. By suggesting that the reasonableness of a search is a requirement that may go beyond probable cause and specificity, it reopens discussion about the relationship between the two clauses of the Fourth Amendment.

—STEVEN SHIFFRIN

Justices of the Supreme Court: 1789–1999

John Jay (Chief: 1789–1795)
John Rutledge (Associate: 1790–1791; Chief: 1795)
William Cushing (Associate: 1790–1810)
James Wilson (Associate: 1789–1798)
John Blair (Associate: 1790–1795)
James Iredell (Associate: 1790–1799)
Thomas Johnson (Associate: 1792–1793)
William Paterson (Associate: 1793–1806)
Samuel Chase (Associate: 1796–1811)
Oliver Ellsworth (Chief: 1796–1800)
Bushrod Washington (Associate: 1799–1829)
Alfred Moore (Associate: 1800–1804)
John Marshall (Chief: 1801–1835)
William Johnson (Associate: 1804–1834)
Brockholst Livingston (Associate: 1807–1823)
Thomas Todd (Associate: 1807–1826)
Gabriel Duvall (Associate: 1811–1835)
Joseph Story (Associate: 1812–1845)
Smith Thompson (Associate: 1823–1843)
Robert Trimble (Associate: 1826–1828)
John McLean (Associate: 1830–1861)
Henry Baldwin (Associate: 1830–1844)
James M. Wayne (Associate: 1835–1867)
Roger B. Taney (Chief: 1836–1864)
Philip P. Barbour (Associate: 1836–1841)
John Catron (Associate: 1837–1865)
John McKinley (Associate: 1838–1852)
Peter V. Daniel (Associate: 1842–1860)
Samuel Nelson (Associate: 1845–1872)
Levi Woodbury (Associate: 1845–1851)
Robert C. Grier (Associate: 1846–1870)
Benjamin R. Curtis (Associate: 1851–1857)
John A. Campbell (Associate: 1853–1861)
Nathan Clifford (Associate: 1858–1881)
Noah Swayne (Associate: 1862–1881)
Samuel F. Miller (Associate: 1862–1890)
David Davis (Associate: 1862–1877)
Stephen J. Field (Associate: 1863–1897)
Salmon P. Chase (Chief: 1864–1873)
William Strong (Associate: 1870–1880)
Joseph P. Bradley (Associate: 1870–1892)
Ward Hunt (Associate: 1873–1882)
Morrison R. Waite (Chief: 1874–1888)
John M. Harlan (Associate: 1877–1911)
William B. Woods (Associate: 1881–1887)
Stanley Matthews (Associate: 1881–1889)
Horace Gray (Associate: 1882–1902)

Samuel Blatchford (Associate: 1882–1893)
Lucius Q. C. Lamar (Associate: 1888–1893)
Melville W. Fuller (Chief: 1888–1910)
David J. Brewer (Associate: 1890–1910)
Henry B. Brown (Associate: 1891–1906)
George Shiras, Jr. (Associate: 1892–1903)
Howell E. Jackson (Associate: 1893–1895)
Edward D. White (Associate: 1894–1910; Chief: 1910–1921)
Rufus Peckham (Associate: 1896–1909)
Joseph McKenna (Associate: 1898–1925)
Oliver Wendell Holmes (Associate: 1902–1932)
William R. Day (Associate: 1903–1922)
William H. Moody (Associate: 1906–1910)
Horace R. Lurton (Associate: 1910–1914)
Charles Evans Hughes (Associate: 1910–1916; Chief: 1930–1941)
Willis Van Devanter (Associate: 1911–1937)
Joseph R. Lamar (Associate: 1911–1916)
Mahlon Pitney (Associate: 1912–1922)
James C. McReynolds (Associate: 1914–1941)
Louis D. Brandeis (Associate: 1916–1939)
John H. Clarke (Associate: 1916–1922)
William Howard Taft (Chief: 1921–1930)
George Sutherland (Associate: 1922–1938)
Pierce Butler (Associate: 1923–1939)
Edward T. Sanford (Associate: 1923–1930)
Harlan Fiske Stone (Associate: 1925–1941; Chief: 1941–1946)
Owen J. Roberts (Associate: 1930–1945)
Benjamin N. Cardozo (Associate: 1932–1938)
Hugo L. Black (Associate: 1937–1971)
Stanley Reed (Associate: 1938–1957)
Felix Frankfurter (Associate: 1939–1962)
William O. Douglas (Associate: 1939–1975)
Frank Murphy (Associate: 1940–1949)
James F. Byrnes (Associate: 1941–1942)
Robert H. Jackson (Associate: 1941–1954)
Wiley B. Rutledge (Associate: 1943–1949)
Harold Burton (Associate: 1945–1958)
Fred M. Vinson (Chief: 1946–1953)
Tom C. Clark (Associate: 1949–1967)
Sherman Minton (Associate: 1949–1956)
Earl Warren (Chief: 1953–1969)
John M. Harlan (Associate: 1955–1971)
William J. Brennan, Jr. (Associate: 1956–1990)
Charles E. Whittaker (Associate: 1957–1962)
Potter Stewart (Associate: 1959–1981)
Byron R. White (Associate: 1962–1993)
Arthur J. Goldberg (Associate: 1962–1965)

Abe Fortas (Associate: 1965–1969)
Thurgood Marshall (Associate: 1967–1991)
Warren E. Burger (Chief: 1969–1986)
Harry A. Blackmun (Associate: 1970–1994)
Lewis F. Powell, Jr. (Associate: 1972–1987)
William H. Rehnquist (Associate: 1972–1986; Chief: 1986–)
John Paul Stevens (Associate: 1975–)

Sandra Day O'Connor (Associate: 1981–)
Antonin Scalia (Associate: 1986–)
Anthony M. Kennedy (Associate: 1988–)
David H. Souter (Associate: 1990–)
Clarence Thomas (Associate: 1991–)
Ruth Bader Ginsburg (Associate: 1993–)
Stephen G. Breyer (Associate: 1994–)

Chief Justices of the Supreme Court: 1789–1999

Chief Justice	Date of Birth	Year Appointed*	Appointed by	Age When Appointed
John Jay	12/12/1745	1789	Washington	43
John Rutledge	09/ ?/1739	1795	Washington	55
Oliver Ellsworth	04/29/1745	1796	Washington	50
John Marshall	09/24/1755	1801	J. Adams	45
Roger B. Taney	03/17/1777	1836	Jackson	59
Salmon P. Chase	01/13/1808	1864	Lincoln	56
Morrison R. Waite	11/29/1816	1874	Grant	57
Melville W. Fuller	02/11/1833	1888	Cleveland	55
Edward D. White	11/03/1845	1910	Taft	65
William Howard Taft	09/15/1857	1921	Harding	63
Charles Evans Hughes	04/11/1862	1930	Hoover	67
Harlan Fiske Stone	10/11/1872	1941	F. Roosevelt	68
Fred M. Vinson	01/22/1890	1946	Truman	56
Earl Warren	03/19/1891	1953	Eisenhower	62
Warren E. Burger	09/17/1907	1969	Nixon	61
William H. Rehnquist	10/01/1924	1986	Reagan	61

*The Year Appointed is the year named Chief Justice. John Rutledge, Edward D. White, Charles Evans Hughes, Harlan Fiske Stone, and William H. Rehnquist served before that year as Associate Justices.

Supreme Court Facts

The Justices

- The first Justice was John Jay, appointed in 1789.
- The first Roman Catholic Justice was Roger B. Taney, appointed in 1836.
- Louis Brandeis was the first Jewish Justice, appointed in 1916.
- The first African-American Justice was Thurgood Marshall, who served from 1967 to 1991.
- Sandra Day O'Connor was the first female Justice, appointed in 1981.
- William Howard Taft was the only person to serve as both a president (1901–13) and as a Justice. Taft was Chief Justice of the Court from 1921 to1930.
- Samuel Chase (1796–1811) was the only Justice impeached by the House of Representatives. He was accused of judicial misconduct for his partisan opposition to the Jeffersonian government of his time. Proving to be a formidable opponent, Chase denied that his actions were indictable offenses, and he was later acquitted by the Senate.
- In 1998 an associate Justice of the Supreme Court earned an annual salary of $164,100. The Chief Justice earned $171,500.

Appointments to the Court

- According to the Constitution, the president should make Supreme Court appointments with the advice and consent of only the Senate. This time-honored practice is known as "Senatorial courtesy."
- Although most presidents choose Supreme Court Justices whose political philosophies align with their own, presidents often find themselves unable to predict the ultimate voting patterns of their appointees. President Harry Truman once said, "Whenever you put a man on the Supreme Court he ceases to be your friend."
- Of the current Justices on the Court, Ronald Reagan appointed the most: Sandra Day O'Connor (1981), Antonin Scalia (1986), and Anthony M. Kennedy (1988). Reagan also appointed William H. Rehnquist, originally appointed as an associate by Richard Nixon, to Chief Justice in 1986. George Bush appointed David H. Souter (1990) and Clarence Thomas (1991), and Bill Clinton appointed Ruth Bader Ginsburg (1993) and Stephen Breyer (1994).

- Jimmy Carter is the only president to serve a full term and never appoint a Supreme Court Justice.

Workings of the Court

- Lawyers presenting a case before the Supreme Court are allotted only thirty minutes in which to make their arguments, often under tough, rapid-fire questioning from the Justices.
- During John Marshall's tenure (1801–35), the Court began the practice of issuing single majority opinions, enabling it to speak with a more definitive, unified voice.
- The Court receives more than 5,000 petitions each year. Of these, only about 3 percent are granted and decided by fully written opinion.
- For a case to be heard by the Court, at least four Justices must agree that it warrants consideration. This informal agreement is known as the Rule of Four.
- The Supreme Court has virtually complete discretion to select which cases warrant consideration, to control its workload, and to set its own substantive agenda.

Did You Know . . .

- That the solicitor general is known as the "Tenth Justice"? A member of the Justice Department, the solicitor general represents federal agencies. One well-known former solicitor general is Independent Counsel Kenneth Starr, who conducted the investigation into President Clinton, leading to the president's impeachment by the House of Representatives in 1998.
- That Justice Felix Frankfurter used to send his law clerks, known as "Felix's Happy Hotdogs," to lobby other clerks and Justices when deciding an important case?
- That when the Supreme Court initially convened on February 1, 1790, only Chief Justice John Jay and two other Justices showed up at the Court's first home, the Exchange Building in New York City?
- That the Supreme Court met in Independence Hall in Philadelphia from 1790 to 1800, before the capital moved to Washington, D.C.?
- That the words "oyez, oyez, oyez" are used to announce the opening of a Supreme Court session? The word "oyez" is Anglo-Norman for "hear ye."

Case Index

Subject Index